RENAISSANCE ENGLAND

Renaissance England

Poetry and Prose FROM THE *Reformation to the Restoration*

SELECTED AND EDITED BY

ROY LAMSON, 1908-
Williams College
AND
HALLETT SMITH
California Institute of Technology

W · W · NORTON & COMPANY · INC · *New York*

Renaissance England
is an expanded edition of the editors'
anthology of Elizabethan poetry and prose
entitled *The Golden Hind.*

PRINTED IN THE UNITED STATES OF AMERICA
FOR THE PUBLISHERS BY THE VAIL-BALLOU PRESS
2 3 4 5 6 7 8 9

Contents

Preface

THIS VOLUME is a collection of the nondramatic prose and poetry of the period called generally the English Renaissance and Reformation. It extends from the reign of Henry VIII to the restoration of Charles II, from just before the middle of the sixteenth century to just after the middle of the seventeenth. The first part of the book is a reprint of the revised edition of *The Golden Hind,* an Elizabethan anthology which ends with the work of Ben Jonson and John Donne.

These two poets, in revolt against the prevailing tendencies of Elizabethan poetry, dominated the scene for the first half of the seventeenth century. Classical or metaphysical, profane or sacred, musical or meditative—these are the general alternatives between which practicing poets had, or felt they had, to choose. But just as Jonson and Donne were friends and fellow craftsmen, so some of their followers did not allow themselves to be bound by the dichotomy which, according to the literary histories, characterized the period.

In the Elizabethan age there was a pervading restlessness and exuberance working in many fields of human activity—economic, geographical, literary, historical, social. But the period was far from a carefree one; Hamlet, a representative figure, can be gay only by fits and starts.

The Stuart epoch likewise was an age of change and innovation. In science, the microscope and telescope opened new worlds; in medicine, Harvey demonstrated the circulation of the blood; in religion occurred the great conflict between traditionalists and reformers; in politics, the English dethroned and executed a king, trying for some years the experiment of a military dictatorship called a Commonwealth. The energy of the Tudor-Stuart period is expressed in its literature as well as in its science and politics. Poetry found its liberation among the Elizabethans; foreign forms and classical meters merged with native folk song and ballad to create a style both new and native, elaborately contrived yet rooted in English soil. Prose won its freedom later; in the first half of the seventeenth century we can see Senecan brevity and pithiness striving to supplant Ciceronian oratorical rhetoric. There are achievements, and great ones, in both styles, but it is the prose fit for ordinary discourse, suitable as the instrument for science and reason, that wins out eventually over the beautiful and sonorous periods of Sir Thomas Browne.

The selections in this volume were chosen to represent the great tendencies in the nondramatic literature of England from the intellectual awakening under the early Tudors to the restoration of the Stuarts to the throne. But this, like all anthologies, tends to slight the major figures; Shakespeare, Spenser, and Milton should be read in the easily available editions of their collected works. They shared in the tendencies represented here, and sometimes they helped create them, but in any event, no author of the stature of these three should be studied primarily for tendencies. Such a writer deserves attention to the whole world of values that he creates.

This book does not present, even within its limits, all of the best writing of the period; however, room has been found for some pieces of little artistic merit when they illustrate extravagances of taste or exaggerations of manner peculiarly characteristic of the time.

Many scholars, teachers and readers have helped in the revision of *The Golden Hind* which forms the first part of this book. Others have made useful suggestions about the added seventeenth-century material. The editor offers thanks to all of them, and he must also mention his abiding gratitude to two great institutions of learning which foster his studies, the Henry E. Huntington Library and the California Institute of Technology.

RENAISSANCE ENGLAND

Elizabethan England

England, when Elizabeth Tudor came to the throne in 1558, was a country small in population, backward in industrial techniques and in exploration and discovery, and poor in the production of wealth and the consumption of goods. She was relatively isolated and provincial. During the previous century and a half her social fabric had been torn by the civil wars of the Roses in the fifteenth century and by the dispossession of the monastic orders under Henry VIII. The two short reigns of Edward VI and Mary had sharply focused the struggle, which was both religious and political, between Catholics and Protestants. There was little reason to suppose that the next half century would be one of the most glorious periods in English history.

How it came about is one of the complexes of history, and no narrative does real justice to the facts. Probably the most important development is the growth of the population, from the two and a half to three millions for England and Wales at the beginning of the reign, to a point at which the need for new markets, new sources of raw materials, new country for settlers caused the expansion and energy we think of as typical of the age. Since the feudal aristocracy and the vested interests of Rome had been destroyed, the men who felt the new spirit and who profited from it were new people, the middle class.

Chief among these was the Queen herself. Her royal line went back only two generations before her, and she was still able to feel and see like the new men who were her most gifted statesmen and her most enterprising adventurers. To be sure, she had more political talent than any of them, and this ability, coupled with a set of fortunate circumstances, brought about the unification of England and the growth of a real feeling of nationality. It was painfully evident to Englishmen that any alternative to Elizabeth, such as Mary Queen of Scots, would mean civil war. And the Papal bull excommunicating Elizabeth, issued in 1570, made it a pious act for any Catholic to assassinate her. The response of Englishmen was fervent and typical: they did not like civil war and they did not like political interference by a foreign power. So national spirit and loyalty to the crown rose to a great pitch, climaxed by the glorious defeat of the Spanish Armada in 1588. After that there was a certain disillusionment. The Queen had not married and the succession to the crown was in some doubt; the two extremist parties were not fundamentally reconciled; and even though England had successfully challenged the might of Spain and established herself as a sea power, one felt that domestic peace and security were only temporary. Elizabeth's middle ground in religion was to insist upon outward conformity, order, and discipline, without prying too much into men's private opinions. Naturally, the religious compromise, or Settlement as it was called, was attacked by the Catholics on one side and the Puritans on the other. Although no compromise would work permanently, Elizabeth's position was probably closer than either of its alternatives to the hearts of the majority of Englishmen.

In spite of the prominence of the religio-political controversy, English civilization became markedly more secular during the second half of the sixteenth century. England was not ready for the influences of the Italian Renaissance when they were first offered in the fourteenth and fifteenth centuries. Chaucer was an early but false spring. And when these influences, for the glorification of life on this earth, for the realization of the tremendous possibilities inherent in man, began to be really felt in England, they coincided with a great economic and social change. The enclosure of fields for pasture altered the whole agricultural character of the country and carried with it profound social disruption. The decrease in the supply of wood for fuel led to the exploitation of coal and laid a foundation for the industrial revolution. The one great English export trade, wool and woolen cloth, was supplemented by others, and these new businesses offered to any enterprising English yeoman the opportunity to become a capitalist, as many of them did. The difficulties of trade with Europe and the East forced Englishmen to turn to the Western Hemisphere. Strange as it may seem, the Atlantic was a safer highway for English ships than the Mediterranean. Enterprise in America meant, of course, rivalry with the Spaniard; but conveniently enough, Spain was also the enemy on political and religious grounds. So Francis Drake, in harassing the ships of King Philip, was a kind of pirate-patriot. (Besides, his ventures sometimes returned a profit on the investment of as high as 5,000 per cent!)

The influx of American mineral wealth, the argosies that yearly stuffed old Philip's treasury and sometimes the coffers of English stockholders, naturally produced in Europe in the latter half of the century an ever-increasing rise in prices. This phenomenon meant great hardship for the poor, and the literature of the time is full of pictures of beggars, rogues, and vagabonds. At the other extreme, those who had money spent it lavishly. The English were conscious of their lack of splendor in comparison with continental countries, and they indiscriminately aped the fashions of the continent. Dress was expensive, luxurious, and sometimes fantastic.

Houses were no longer built of timber and clay, but of oak (formerly reserved for churches, noblemen's houses, and ships) or even of stone, lath, and plaster. And as usual in such periods, there were many complaints that the accumulation of wealth meant the decay of men.

Intellectually the movement known as Humanism, with its return to the classics, its critical approach to the philosophy of the medieval schoolmen, had reached England in the reign of Henry VIII, when More and Erasmus, Grocyn and Colet were the lights of Europe. Their successors in the reign of Elizabeth were lesser men but not unworthy to carry on the tradition. The second generation of humanists, however, saw a very grave moral danger in the influence of Italy, mother of the Renaissance. The free secular spirit had gone so far there, they thought, that even human values had been undermined; and the English imitator of the Italians was the subject of a proverb: *The Italianate Englishman is a devil incarnate.*

The new scientific thought of the century received welcome and attention in England. Peter Ramus, the notorious opponent of Aristotelian authority, had considerable influence at Cambridge, and Englishmen like Robert Recorde, Thomas Digges, John Dee, and Sir Walter Ralegh's man Harriot were alive to new developments in mathematics and astronomy and made contributions of their own. The liberalizing effect of scientific thought went hand in hand with the intellectual emancipation provided by the classics.

LITERATURE AND SOCIETY

First among the sources of literary production in the Elizabethan age was of course the court, as it was first in everything which had to do with fashion. The courtier was not a professional writer, that is, he did not depend for a living on his writing. He wrote either because he wished to show his wit and ability, or because he had an irresistible itch to write, or because he was genuinely devoted to his subject. But the courtier, if he were a poet, did not publish his compositions. That would have been unseemly for one of his social position. He merely handed them around to his friends in manuscript, and they finally reached print by way of the anthologies which may reproduce commonplace books of some lover of verse, or else some greedy printer came by a copy of the poems and published them without the author's consent. Sir John Harington, the Queen's godson, amused the court ladies with a translation of some indecent sections of Ariosto; the Queen, when she heard of it, imposed on him the penance of translating the whole romantic epic from which the lines had come. This sort of thing, the translation of a standard or classical author, the poet himself could publish, without losing social caste. But the ordinary lyric would not be sent to the press by the courtier-poet.

In the court the greatest opportunities existed, but there also were the greatest disappointments to be found. "It was over-run with place-seekers," says Miss Byrne's account of it, "but it was also undeniably the focus of the national life. It drew to it the clever mountebanks, but also the real vigour and talent. It captured and stimulated men's imaginations, even if, eventually, it disheartened them." Men like Sir Christopher Hatton and Sir Walter Ralegh leaped from obscurity to great power and prominence as a result of their success as courtiers, but it must not be forgotten that they had abilities other than those of the gallantry and dancing which have made them famous in anecdote. The security of the courtier was always precarious, and there was scarcely one of Queen Elizabeth's courtiers who did not know, at some time or other, the harshness of the sovereign's disapproval. The great guide and conduct book for the courtier was of course Castiglione's *Il Cortegiano* (1528, translated into English in 1561), and according to its theses the function of the courtier was to give good and honest advice to the prince. But Sidney found out, when he tried to advise the Queen against a French marriage, that advice is not always relished by a monarch whose powers over any individual subject are almost absolute. As a result there is a long tradition of literature against court life, comparing it unfavorably to the country life of the retired and obscure man. Wyatt's epistles to Bryan and Poins are early examples of this attitude, and it runs all through the period. Of course the fact that there was a tradition means that everything said about the court should not be taken at its face value. But enough evidence exists to show that there was a definite feeling that court life was too precarious, too superficial, too corrupt, too hypocritical. From the time of Wyatt to the time of Ralegh the tone is consistent.

For literary men like Spenser and Lyly, men who by birth were not in a position to be real courtiers, the court offered a faint hope of livelihood, notice, and encouragement. But for these two, at any rate, it was a source of bitter disappointment. Lyly's long wait for the office of the Revels, and Spenser's disillusionment which is reflected in *Mother Hubberd's Tale* and *Colin Clouts Come Home Againe* tell the story. Much of the satire of the period is directed against the superficiality and treachery of the court atmosphere. "A thousand hopes, but all nothing," wailed Lyly, "a hundred promises, but yet nothing."

Though most of the literature which is still considered worth reading shows the predominant influence of the court, it would be a mistake to underestimate the influence of the city of London on the literary taste and production of the period. London had grown tremendously since the time of Chaucer. Instead of a population of about 50,000, it had 93,276 in 1563; 123,034 in 1580; 152,478 in 1593–1595; and 224,275 in 1605. It was by far the most important city in the realm, and the political history of the seventeenth century is understandable only if one recognizes the great power the city had, even as against the crown. The printing press was located in London, the publishers were located in London, and the mass of the middle-class population which set the style for the literature written for the ordinary man lived in London. The middle class found among the university men some writers who catered to them: Thomas Heywood is a good example. And although Nashe scornfully rejects the claim of the bourgeois to have any literary taste at all or to have any ability at producing literature, still the class had its own writers, like Thomas Deloney, and it knew what it liked. Whether the aristocrats admitted it or not, the standards and tastes of the middle class affected all writing, all publishing, and all literary success. For finally the writer saw his work exhibited on the stalls of St. Paul's churchyard, and the customers who frequented that center of the book trade were more often members of the middle class than of the court circle. Louis B. Wright has shown in his *Middle Class Culture in Elizabethan England* how extensive and profound was the influence of the citizenry upon the writing and publication of books, and how bourgeois standards of edification and utility dictated to most of the authors of the time.

Next to the court and the city, the most important source of literature was of course the two universities. In Elizabeth's reign they were old-fashioned in their curriculum, poor in discipline, and undistinguished in learning, in comparison with what they had been a generation before. There was a great shortage of ministers in the country, partly because of the poor living standard provided for members of the clergy and partly because of the loss of ministers through the religious changes of the middle of the century. So the universities were trying to train ministers to the exclusion of almost everything else.

The university graduate who came to London to make a literary career for himself faced a very difficult situation. It is best pictured, perhaps, in the Cambridge trilogy of *Parnassus* plays, performed at the end of the century but fairly faithfully reflecting conditions which held good during the whole period. It was the university wits, to be sure, who gave to the drama some of the classical form which it needed, and who inaugurated the great literary vogue of the nineties. But the lives of Nashe and Greene and Peele and Marlowe do not suggest that the path was easy. The diary of Philip Henslowe has entry after entry showing university graduates in prison or in debt or even at best miserably eking out an existence patching plays.

The university man had either to get a fellowship and remain in academic life (which almost always meant taking holy orders) or to enter the church and get a poor living, or to go into law or medicine. No literary career as such was open to him. It must be secondary to something else.

Financial rewards for writing and publishing prose or poetry came mostly in the form of gifts from patrons—in reality the old system of master and servant which had come down from the Middle Ages and had not changed much with the invention of printing. The writer by a dedication hoped for a suitable reward, and in an age when honor and vanity were motives much more sharply defined or observed than they are today, this procedure sometimes worked. Yet the patron whose vanity was amply satisfied by his own conceit remained a constant irritation to the writers of the time, and we hear many complaints about the degeneration of the age because patrons are not more munificent. There were some generous and literary-minded patrons, notably Sir Philip Sidney and his sister Mary, the Countess of Pembroke. Shakespeare's relations with his patron, the Earl of Southampton, little as we know about them, seem to have been satisfactory, as the second dedication is much warmer and more personal than the first. But the experience of Robert Greene is perhaps more typical than that of Shakespeare in this respect. He had sixteen different patrons for seventeen books; this suggests that he was not fortunate in finding favor or support from any one. The satirists attacked the niggardliness of men of wealth and position in this age. A fraudulent practice grew up of printing the book and then printing off separate dedications, so that an impecunious author could deceive several patrons each into thinking that he was the one to be honored by the volume. Two or three pounds seems to have been the usual reward for the dedication of a pamphlet or small volume of verse. Of course it might be more, but it is difficult to believe that Shakespeare once received a thousand pounds from the Earl of Southampton, as the legend has it; if he did, the relationship between them was surely not that of a patron and a poet. Ben Jonson, who fared much better than most of his contemporaries, sums up the matter, for poets at least, when he says:

> Poetry in this latter age hath proved but a mean mistress to such as have wholly addicted themselves to her, or given their names up to her family. Those who have but saluted her on the way, and now and then tendered their visits, she hath done much for, and advanced in the way of their own professions (both the law and the gospel) beyond all they could have hoped or done for themselves without her favour.

The other possible source of reward, besides the patron, was the publisher. And rewards from the publisher in the sixteenth century were nothing at all like the rewards from that source now. In the first place there was no such thing as copyright, and no such thing, in the ordinary way, as royalties paid according to the sale of the book. An author sold his manuscript to the publisher once and for all, for what seems now like a ridiculously low price. The author would get, for a pamphlet or small book of poetry, usually forty shillings. One would have to turn them out very fast to make even a bare subsistence at that rate.

Some men, to be sure, raised themselves by their literary efforts to positions of comfort and responsibility, claiming the rank of gentlemen and living as if they were successful merchants or lawyers. Shakespeare is the most familiar example of this class. But rewards on this scale were not the result of writing alone. They were the result of business shrewdness, of being a shareholder in a profitable theatrical property, or something of the sort. The theater did after all attract the talents of a large number of the literary men of the time, and when they could combine the functions of acting and managing and owning a share of the company with that of writing they came out well.

The writer's troubles were not over when he had written his book, gone through the difficulty of finding a publisher, and finally come to terms with him for the sale of it. He still had to face the many and stringent regulations of the press by political and ecclesiastical authorities, and the fact that he had sold the manuscript did not exempt him from responsibility for what was in it. The authorities were, first, the Privy Council and the Court of Star Chamber, the highest political authority in the realm below the Queen; then the Court of High Commission, the supreme ecclesiastical authority, which sometimes supervised matters which had only the slightest connection with religion; then the Stationers' Company, with whom a book had to be registered but who supervised and protected the publisher and printer rather than the author.

The principal rules governing the publication of books were that the number of printers (not publishers) was strictly limited; that nothing could be printed except in the city of London and the Universities of Oxford and Cambridge; that everything printed must receive the *imprimatur* of the Archbishop of Canterbury and the Bishop of London or their designees; and that everything published in London must be entered in the registers of the Stationers' Company, if any kind of property protection were desired for it.

An example of the regulation which reached back of the publisher to the author himself can be seen in the history of John Stubbs, who protested against the French marriage scheme in a pamphlet called *The Discovery of a Gaping Gulf* (1579). For writing this pamphlet, Stubbs was condemned to have his right hand cut off with one stroke of a butcher's cleaver. When the execution had taken place, Stubbs took off his hat with his left hand and cried "God save the Queen!"

Regulation could not only punish for what was already written and published; it could forbid the publication of works of a certain sort. For example, on June 1, 1599, Archbishop Whitgift ordered the suppression and burning of several works of satire and specified that no more satires were to be published. Included in this interdict were works by Nashe and Harvey.

Almost every writer of the period got into some sort of trouble for publishing a book. It might be prison, it might be merely a reprimand, it might be an investigation by the Star Chamber. It was dangerous to put pen to paper, and it was so unprofitable that it is a wonder that any original writing was published at all. Yet the Elizabethan age is an extremely prolific one in writing and publishing. The *Short Title Catalogue* of the Bibliographical Society, which lists works and editions published between 1475 and 1640, includes over 26,000 items, and this is not all.

TASTE AND FASHION

Elizabethan taste had some very definite and particular characteristics of its own, and the student who wishes to read Elizabethan literature in the spirit of its own time must adjust his mind to the differences between the esthetic principles of the sixteenth century and those of our own day. In the sixteenth century there still remained much of the medieval awareness of the arts as *crafts,* and every writer of the period shows an amazing knowledge of the techniques of many crafts or "mysteries" now unfamiliar. Shakespeare is not an isolated example, and it has been often noticed by students of his works that he seems to have an intimate knowledge of such matters as gardening, hawking, dressmaking, archery, building, and so on. Managing the great horse in the tournament was an art. Sailing was an art. Planting a kitchen garden was an art. What they have in common is that they all use the materials of nature but exploit the ingenuity of man's mind. The same fundamental characteristic was thought to apply to the art or craft of writing.

We have been taught by the romantic movement to glorify nature and to regard the works of art as attempts, usually unsuccessful, to emulate nature. This conception would have seemed strange indeed to the Elizabethans. They recognized, of course, that nature was the cause and basis of all; but that seemed to them no reason why the ingenuity of man should not be used in enabling nature to outdo herself. In *The Winter's Tale* Polixenes is amused at the naïveté of Perdita, who protests that she will have no streaked carnations or gillyflowers in her garden because

> I have heard it said
> There is an art which in their piedness shares
> With great creating nature.

"Say there be," replies Polixenes,

> Yet nature is made better by no mean,
> But nature makes that mean: so, over that art
> Which you say adds to nature, is an art

That nature makes. You see, sweet maid, we marry
A gentler scion to the wildest stock,
And make conceive a bark of baser kind
By bud of nobler race: this is an art
Which does mend nature, change it rather, but
The art itself is nature.

There was no uneasiness in the Elizabethan mind about a possible conflict between art and nature, for the reason that Polixenes gives. And the improvement by device, by arrangement, by art, of something naturally beautiful extended to all aspects of life, so that there was felt to be no great gulf between literature and the sports of the field or the arts of the kitchen in this respect. Puttenham, in discussing ornament in his *Arte of English Poesie,* compares poetry to dress and to jewelry:

And as we see in these great Madames of honour, be they for personage or otherwise neuer so comely and bewtifull, yet if they want their courtly habiliments or at leastwise such other apparell as custome and ciuilitie haue ordained to couer their naked bodies, would be halfe ashamed or greatly out of countenaunce to be seen in that sort, and perchance do then thinke themselues more amiable in euery mans eye, when they be in their richest attire, suppose of silkes or tyssewes & costly embroderies, then when they go in cloth or in any other plaine and simple apparell. Euen so cannot our vulgar Poesie shew it selfe either gallant or gorgious, if any lymme be left naked and bare and not clad in his kindly clothes and coulours, such as may conuey them somwhat out of sight, that is from the common course of ordinary speach and capacitie of the vulgar iudgement, and yet being artificially handled must needes yeld it much more bewtie and commendation. This ornament we speake of is giuen to it by figures and figuratiue speaches, which be the flowers as it were and coulours that a Poet setteth vpon his language by arte, as the embroderer doth his stone and perle, or passements of gold vpon the stuffe of a Princely garment, or as th' excellent painter bestoweth the rich Orient coulours vpon his table of pourtraite. . . .

"Artificially" is used by Puttenham, and by the other Elizabethans, as a word of praise. It means "done with artifice, with skill, with art." And the word "curious" meant to the Elizabethans "skillfully, elaborately or beautifully wrought" or, in a more general sense, "excellent or fine."

The Elizabethan garden was designed as a square, filled with elaborate and intricate, but perfectly regular, design. Bacon protests at gardens which include plots of different colored earths, so arranged as to form a design even without the flowers planted in them; he says he sees enough of this kind of thing in confections and tarts. Yet the very protest shows that his taste was perhaps not typical, and a contemporary might well have asked him why a garden should not look like a confection from the baker's—they were both samples of the art of design. Some Elizabethans had their houses built in the shape of an E, out of honor to the Queen, and one man, John Thorpe, designed his house in the form of his own initials. These instances were extreme, of course, but they show the tendency.

The contrapuntal music of the Elizabethans, which they sang in an accomplished amateur manner, was an intricate kind of music, with elaborate patterns and complex harmonies. Thomas Morley says of the madrigal:

> As for the musick it is next vnto the Motet, the most artificiall and to men of vnderstanding most delightful. If therefore you will compose in this kind you must possesse yourselfe with an amorous humour . . . so that you must in your musicke be wauering like the wind, sometime wanton, sometime graue and staide, otherwhile effeminat, you may maintaine points and reuert them, vse triplaes and shew the verie vttermost of your varietie, and the more varietie you shew the better shal you please.

But a rigid form was to control all of this extravagance, just as the square border of a garden and the regularity of the pattern controlled the exuberance of the curves in the "knot" or design.

All of this has its counterpart in poetry. The geometrical design is present in such poems as the one of Gorges' which begins

Your face	Your tongue	Your wit
So faire	So sweet	So sharpe
First bent	Then drew	So hit
Mine eye	Mine ear	My heart . . .

(It can be read both ways, across and down.) The balance and antithesis in Lyly's prose style is an example of the same kind of literary interest. The sestina, a poem in which the last words of each line in the first stanza are repeated in a different order in each of the following stanzas, was a favorite form of Sidney and other craftsmen in poetry.

Decoration was not always geometrical; it was sometimes too rich, luxurious and profuse to submit tamely to the straitness of the pattern. It is still decoration, though the taste for it may not seem as foreign to us as the taste for knot gardens or sestinas. Spenser in many places, Marlowe and Shakespeare in their love poems, have this kind of decoration. We are prepared for it if our romantic predilections have been centered on Keats, a poet with whom young Shakespeare and Marlowe have much in common. At its best, Elizabethan poetry utilized these two kinds of decoration. The strictness of the one and the luxuriance of the other combined to make a unified impression which is hard to describe but is unmistakably Elizabethan.

Toward the end of the century highly decorated style became unfashionable, and if we trace through the revisions of poets like Daniel and Drayton who wrote early and then continued to issue their works, revised, in a later age, we can see a kind of plainness and restraint taking the place of the rich and fanciful and ornate poetry of the earlier period.

The criticism produced by the age does not give much idea of the esthetic doctrines which supported Elizabethan creative writing. It is for this reason: that the literary critic had as his first concern the defense of literary art against the stern attacks of those who saw in the whole worldly and beautiful energy of the Renaissance a source of evil. The Puritan attackers were merely repeating the exordia of the fathers of the church or the complaints of classical philosophers. Yet they dictated the grounds on which men of letters discussed their art. More specific treatises, like those of Puttenham, Webbe, and Gascoigne, tended to treat merely the technical aspects of the subject, following the tradition of the old textbooks of rhetoric which were made for orators, not poets. Therefore one must abstract from the poetry itself if one is to discover what the primary qualities of excellence in poetry were thought to be.

For the modern reader a negative approach is perhaps necessary. He must dismiss from his mind certain assumptions about poetry which still remain from the strong influence of the romantic movement. He must see that, however magnificent the creations of Romanticism may be, its doctrine of poetry was a special one, and that the creations of another, earlier, period are not to be judged by its rules or assumptions.

The first of these assumptions has to do with the relationship between the poetry and the poet. Romanticism assumes that the poetry is a quite direct reflection of the personality of the poet, that the works are really a biography of the man. But this is certainly not true of Marlowe or Ralegh or Spenser or Shakespeare in the sense in which it is true of Byron or Shelley or Browning or Hardy. In fact, the Elizabethan mind was interested in the poet behind the poetry hardly at all; the poetry was a *thing,* an object created, like a cathedral or a bridge. The poem had its own merits or faults as if it were independent of its maker. A modern reader who is still influenced by the romantic point of view (and who is not?) is often, when he reads a poem, responding to the personality of the poet rather than to the poem itself.

Of course Elizabethan poems did not happen in a vacuum. They were written by poets, by men who were conscious of, and humble before, a tradition. The modern reader must therefore rid himself of lurking tendencies, whether romantic or naïve, to attribute too great value to "originality." This applies not only to subject matter but to style. The finest lyric in this collection may well be written on the most commonplace, platitudinous theme, and the brilliant new burst of poetry that revitalizes everything may be a return to the style of old, antique Chaucer. Any reader of Elizabethan poetry will finally come to appreciate the characterization of it by Ralegh's editor, Miss Agnes Latham:

> In so many ways typical of his age, in poetry Ralegh stands curiously, if not incomprehensibly, apart from the ruck. He is thoughtful and melancholy, personal and passionate, and these last two qualities, which to some of us *are* poetry, were not common in the sixteenth-century lyric. The typical Elizabethan poem contains no jot of personal emotion: as often as not it is translated from a Frenchman, who had it from an Italian, who found it in Plato, and the author is perhaps a literary hack, like Robert Greene, living squalidly—and for all that the poem is as fresh as a flower. It is baffling and beautiful: baffling because it is beautiful and nothing else. Thought is not permitted to distort it nor feeling to betray it into incoherencies.

Elizabethan prose, too, has its modes and conventions which are different from ours. It was closer to medieval rhetoric, with its schemes and tropes, and the organization of its sentences is not so logical in syntax as the modern reader would wish. But if he remembers the richness of the old style which was attained in the King James Bible, he may be more patient with its dark and cumbersome periods. The comprehension of art and artifice in the Elizabethan sense will finally enable him to enjoy the jeweled and ornamented style of John Lyly—not a prose for every day, of course, and easily open to parody by Shakespeare and others after the vogue had declined, but an art work, nevertheless, of great delicacy and beauty.

To the Englishman of the sixteenth century the question of whether to write in English or in Latin was a question of great seriousness. The vernaculars seemed relatively new and unstable to learned men of that time, and with their great desire for eternal fame it was natural that they should concern themselves about the durability of their medium. Furthermore, the preceding age, that of the humanists, had emphasized the value of the classical languages; Cicero and the other masters of rhetoric were imitated in their own tongues. But in Italy, France, and England alike, there was a revolt against this sterile and slavish imitation of the classics. It is the contention of Du Bellay's *Défense et Illustration de la Langue Française* (1549) that the value of a language is not inherent in the language itself, but depends upon what great and fine works are written in that language; furthermore, and this is even more important, the feeling of nationality itself dictates that the vernacular should be used. If the tongue of the people is not so refined and polished as the Greek or Latin, all the more reason why men of learning should improve it by studying it and writing their most ambitious works in it. Roger Ascham included in his *Toxophilus* (1545) a defense of writing in English, although it would have been easier for him, he said, to write in Latin or Greek. And Richard Mulcaster, principal of the Merchant Taylors' School and teacher of Edmund Spenser, said:

I do write in my naturall English tungue, bycause though I make the learned my judges, which understand Latin, yet I meane good to the unlearned, which understand but English. . . . For is it not in dede a marvellous bondage, to becom servants to one tung for learning sake, the most of our time, with losse of most time, whereas we maie have the verie same treasur in our own tung, with the gain of most time? our own bearing the joyfull title of our libertie and freedom, the Latin tung remembering us, of our thraldom and bondage? I love Rome, but London better, I favor Italie, but England more, I honor the Latin, but I worship the English.

The patriotic motive went far beyond the choice of language. It stimulated the translator to turn the most distinguished works of foreign literature into his own tongue; it prompted the epic poet to try to match or "overgo" Tasso and Ariosto; it even playfully spurred on the love poet so to praise his mistress that Petrarch's Laura, famous over Europe, would seem but a kitchen wench to her.

The Tudor sovereigns of England were themselves highly literate, and Henry VIII and Elizabeth, at least, had definite ambitions as authors. What more natural, therefore, than that the writers should see in the glorification of their ruler a service which was both humanistic and political? Much of the praise of the Queen which is so prominent in Elizabethan literature seems to modern taste fulsome and fawning, and no doubt the possibility of personal reward was present in the mind of most authors. But there was also a social service performed by this propaganda; it was the concentration of the feeling of many inarticulate Englishmen, and it was a great builder of what we would now call public morale.

The Elizabethans, having a very different view of history from the one we now hold, were extremely conscious of posterity. They did not consider that future ages would look down on them with contempt, because they thought the world was not getting better, but worse. Rather they felt that it was the duty of their generation to give posterity something worthy of the veneration the future would feel for them. Hamlet, in many ways a representative of the English Renaissance, makes his last concern in this life a concern for the fame that will outlive him. Every sixteenth-century gentleman would have understood and sympathized. From the time of Homer's celebration of Achilles it had been notorious that the poet had more to do with the fame of a great man than anyone else. The social utility of poetry was that it preserved and recorded for the admiration and guidance of the future the heroism of the past. Poetry could do this more effectively than history, and it could preserve the memory of greatness far longer than material monuments or inscriptions. "Not marble nor the gilded monuments of princes shall outlive this powerful rhyme," promised Shakespeare, and other poets with less justification felt equal assurance.

QUEEN ELIZABETH AND HER RELATIONS

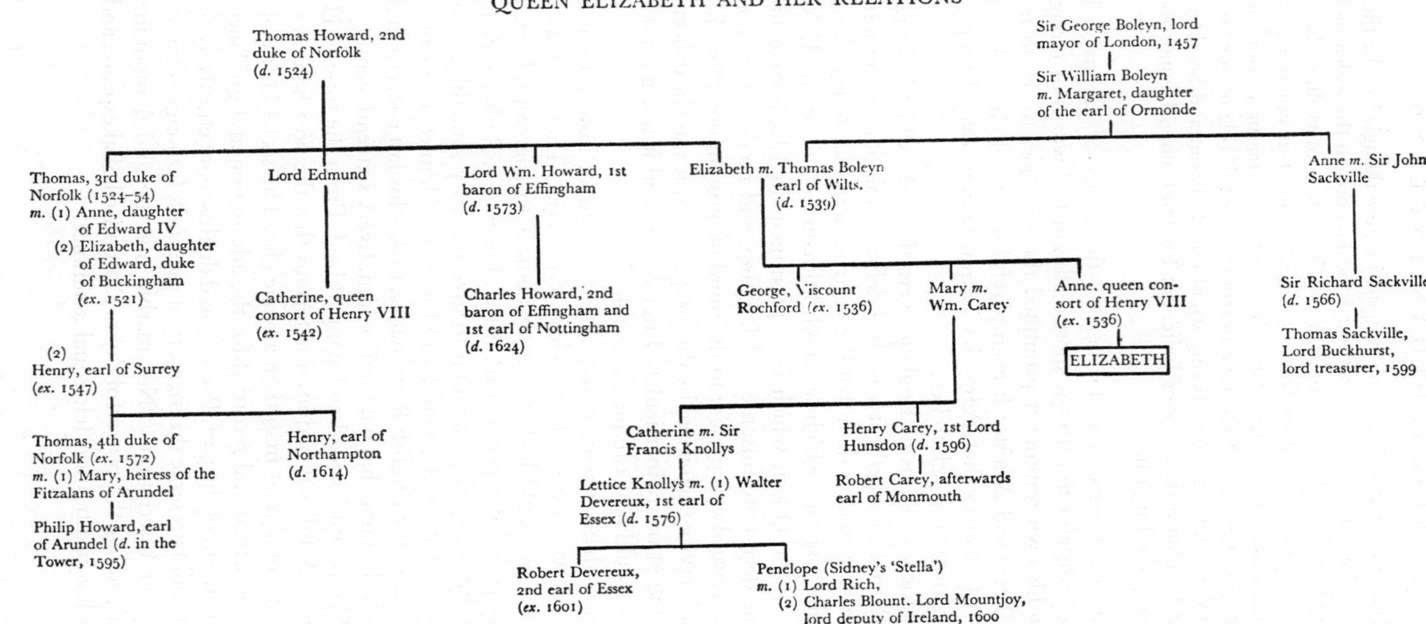

Courtesy of J. B. Black, The Reign of Elizabeth.

John Skelton

1460?–1529

NOT MANY beneficed clergymen become the heroes of jest-books or anthologies of merry tales. John Skelton was one who did. According to one of the tales, Skelton was preaching in his parish church at Diss in Norfolk, when he suddenly called his congregation knaves, and worse than knaves, because they had complained to the Bishop that Skelton kept a fair wench in the rectory. To be sure, said the preacher, he did keep a fair wench, fairer than his parishioners' wives, and he had a son by her. At that he called to her not to be afraid but to bring the baby to him, which she did. Holding the child up naked before the congregation, he exclaimed, "How say you, neighbors all? Is not this child as fair as is the best of all yours? It hath nose, eyes, hands and feet, as well as any of yours. It is not like a pig, nor a calf, nor like no foul nor no monstrous beast. If I had brought forth this child without arms or legs, or that it were deformed being a monstrous thing, I would never have blamed you to have complained to the Bishop of me, but to complain without a cause! I say as I said before, in my antetheme, *vos estis,* you be, and have been, and will and shall be knaves to complain of me without a cause reasonable."

Such a mad wag is not easy to visualize as tutor to a prince (the future Henry VIII), a rhetorician of such note and accomplishment that he was given the title of Poet Laureate by both Oxford and Cambridge universities, and the chief serious poet of his time, but Skelton was all of these. In 1490 he was addressed by Caxton, in the preface to his *Eneydos,* as a master of polished and ornate terms and a translator.

In style Skelton's work is mediaeval, though his arrogant, boastful, self-conscious spirit seems at times very modern. He approved of scholastic logic, and to that degree was no humanist. The chief principle upon which his poetry is constructed is that of amplification, on which the mediaeval rhetoricians had so much to offer of both precept and example. But a very fresh breeze blows through Skelton's poems, and sometimes he seems closer to us than more modern writers do.

His *Philip Sparrow* profanely intermingles phrases from the services for the dead with a eulogy for a pet sparrow killed by a cat; the first part of the poem is supposedly spoken by Jane Scroop, an actual girl and the owner of the bird. The conclusion consists of an equally ambiguous, and somehow haunting, praise of Jane herself. Skelton's tribute to Margaret Hussy in his late work, *Garland of Laurel,* and the tavern ballad of "Mannerly Margery Milk and Ale" show Skelton's versatility as a poet celebrating the charms of women. But in his own time Skelton was known chiefly as a satirist. His *Bouge of Court, Speak, Parrot, Why Come Ye Not to Court,* and, perhaps most effectively of all, *Colin*

Clout, show Skelton's tough, astringent satirical style. He directed his satires most often at Cardinal Wolsey, the easiest and most obvious, though probably the most dangerous, target; but he was willing to take on lesser antagonists when the occasion offered.

Skelton's roughness, his vulgarity, and his mediaeval prolixity stood between him and appreciative readers for several centuries, but in our own time he is again valued.

Bibliography: H. L. R. Edwards, *Skelton*, London, 1949; Ian A. Gordon, *John Skelton*, Melbourne and London, 1943; L. J. Lloyd, *John Skelton*, Oxford, 1938; William Nelson, *John Skelton, Laureate*, New York, 1939. *The Complete Poems of John Skelton*, ed. Philip Henderson, London, 1931; Alan Swallow, "John Skelton: Structure of the Poem," *P.Q.* XXXII (1953) 29–42; "The Pentameter Line in Skelton and Wyatt," *M.P.* XLVIII (1950) 1–11; R. S. Kinsman, "*Phyllyp Sparowe:* Titulus" *S.P.* XLVII (1950) 473–484; W. H. Auden, "John Skelton" in *The Great Tudors*, ed. K. Garvin, London, 1935; J. M. Berdan, *Early Tudor Poetry*, New York, 1920.

FROM

PHILIP SPARROW

Pla ce bo! [1]
Who is there, who?
Di le xi! [2]
Dame Margery.
Fa, re, mi, mi.
Wherefore and why, why?
For the soul of Philip Sparrow,
That was late slain at Carrow,
Among the Nuns Black.[3]
For that sweet soul's sake,
And for all sparrows' souls
Set in our bead-rolls,
Pater noster qui,
With an *Ave Marie,*
And with the corner of a Creed
The more shall be your meed.
  When I remember again
How my Philip was slain,
Never half the pain
Was between you twain,
Pyramus and Thisbe,
As then befell to me;
I wept and I wailed
THE teares down hailed,
But nothing it availed
To call Philip again
Whom Gib, our cat, hath slain.
  Gib, I say, our cat
Worrowed [4] her on that
Which I loved best.
It cannot be expressed
My sorrowful heaviness,
But without all redress,
For within that stound,[5]
Half slumbering in a swound,[6]
I fell down to the ground.
  Uneath [7] I cast mine eyes
Toward the cloudy skies,
But when I did behold
My sparrow dead and cold,
No creature but that wold
Have rued upon me,
To behold and see
What heaviness did me pang,
Wherewith my hands I wrang,
That my sinews cracked,
As though I had been racked,
So pained and so strained
That no life well nigh remained.
I sighed and I sobbed,
For that I was robbed
Of my sparrow's life.
Oh maiden, widow, and wife,
Of what estate ye be,
Of high or low degree,
Great sorrow then ye might see,
And learn to weep at me!
Such pains did me freat [8]
That mine heart did beat,
My visage pale and dead,

[1] The antiphon in the Office for the Dead. From Vulgate Psalm 114:9: "I will walk [before the Lord in the land of the living]."

[2] From Vulgate Psalm 114:1: "I love [the Lord because he hath heard my voice]."

[3] Jane Scroop, the owner of the sparrow, was living in a Benedictine nunnery at Carrow, near Norwich; she was not a nun.

[4] *worrowed:* choked.

[5] *stound:* moment.

[6] *swound:* swoon.

[7] *uneath:* scarcely.

[8] *freat:* fret.

Wan, and blue as lead,
The pangs of hateful death
Wellnigh had stopped my breath.

. . . .

For, as I tofore have said,
I am but a young maid,
And cannot in effect
My style as yet direct
With English words elect.
Our natural tongue is rude,
And hard to be ennued[9]
With polished terms lusty;
Our language is so rusty,
So cankered and so full
Of frowards,[10] and so dull,
That if I would apply
To write ordinately,
I wot not where to find
Terms to serve my mind.
Gower's English is old,
And of no value is told;
His matter is worth gold,
And worthy to be enrolled.
In Chaucer I am sped,
His *Tales* I have read;
His matter is delectable,
Solacious[11] and commendable,
His English well allowed,
So as it is enprowed,[12]
For as it is employed,
There is no English void,
At those days much commended.
And now men would have amended
His English, whereat they bark,
And mar all they wark.[13]
Chaucer, that famous clerk,
His terms were not dark,
But pleasant, easy and plain.
No word he wrote in vain.
Also John Lydgate
Writeth after an higher rate;
It is diffuse to find
The sentence of his mind,
Yet writeth he in his kind.
No man that can amend
Those matters that he hath penned,
Yet some men find a fault,
And say he writeth too haut.[14]
Wherefore hold me excused
If I have not well perused
Mine English half-abused.
Though it be refused,
In worth I shall it take
And fewer wordes make.
But for my sparrow's sake,
Yet, as a woman may,
My wit I shall assay
An epitaph to write
In Latin plain and light,
Whereof the elegy
Followeth by and by:
Flos volucrum formose, vale!
Philippe, sub isto
Marmore iam recubas
Qui mihi carus eras.
Semper erunt nitido
Radiantia sidera coelo;
Impressusque meo
Pectore semper eris.[15]

. . . .

[The Commendations]

. . . .

Now Phoebus me ken
To sharp my pen,
And lead my fist
As him best list,

[9] *ennued:* restored.
[10] *frowards:* awkwardnesses.
[11] *solacious:* pleasant.
[12] *enprowed:* improved.
[13] *wark:* work, do.
[14] *haut:* elevated, dignified.

[15] "Fair flower of fowls, farewell! Philip, under that marble now you lie who were so dear to me. Always will there be stars shining in the bright sky, and always will you be engraved on my heart."

That I may say
Honor alway
Of womankind!
Truth doth me bind
And loyalty
Ever to be
Their true bedell [16]
To write and tell
How women excell
In nobleness;
As my mistress
Of whom I think
With pen and ink
For to compile
Some goodly style;
For this most goodly flower,
This blossom of fresh colour,
So Jupiter me succour,
She flourisheth new and new
In beauty and virtue;
Hac claritate gemina,
O gloriosa femina,[17]
Legem pone mihi, domina, in viam
justificationum tuarum! [18]
Quemadmodum desiderat cervus ad
fontes aquarum.[19]

How shall I report
All the goodly sort
Of her features clear,
That hath none earthly peer?
The favour of her face
Ennewed all with grace,
Comfort, pleasure and solace.
Mine heart doth so embrace,
And so hath ravished me
Her to behold and see,
That in wordes plain
I cannot me refrain
To look on her again:
Alas, what should I feign?
It were a pleasant pain
With her aye to remain.

Her eyen gray and steep [20]
Causeth mine heart to leap;
With her brows bent
She may well represent
Fair Lucres, as I ween,
Or else fair Polexene,
Or else Calliope,
Or else Penelope:
For this most goodly flower,
This blossom of fresh colour,
So Jupiter me succour,
She flourisheth new and new
In beauty and virtue;
Hac claritate gemina,
O gloriosa femina,
Memor esto verbi tui servo tuo! [21]
Servus tuus sum ego.[22]

The Indy sapphire blue
Her veins doth ennew;
The orient pearl so clear,
The whiteness of her leer; [23]
Her lusty ruby ruddes [24]
Resemble the rose buddes;
Her lips soft and merry
Enbloomed like the cherry;
It were an heavenly bliss
Her sugared mouth to kiss.
Her beauty to augment,
Dame Nature hath her lent
A wart upon her cheek.
Who so list to seek

[16] *bedell:* messenger, servant.

[17] This pearl of beauty, oh glorious lady!

[18] "Teach me, oh Lady, the way of thy statutes!"—a parody of Vulgate Psalm 118:33.

[19] "As the hart panteth after the water brooks [so panteth my soul after thee, Oh God]." Vulgate Psalm 41:1.

[20] *steep:* bright.

[21] "Remember the word unto thy servant," Vulgate Psalm 118:49.

[22] "I am thy servant," Vulgate Psalm 118:125.

[23] *leer:* complexion.

[24] *ruddes:* blushes.

In her visage a scar,
That seemeth from afar
Like to the radiant star,
All with favour fret,
So properly it is set.
She is the violet,
The daisy delectable,
The columbine commendable.
The jillyflower amiable;
For this most goodly flower,
This blossom of fresh colour,
So Jupiter me succour,
She flourisheth new and new
In beauty and virtue;
Hac claritate gemina,
O gloriosa femina
Bonitatem fecisti cum servo tuo, domina,[25]
Et ex praecordiis sonant praeconia! [26]

And when I perceived
Her wart and conceived,
It cannot be denayed
But it was well conveyed
And set so womanly,
And nothing wantonly,
But right conveniently,
And full congruently,
As Nature could devise,
In most goodly wise.
Who so list behold,
It maketh lovers bold
To her to sue for grace,
Her favor to purchase;
The scar upon her chin,
Enhatched on her fair skin,
Whiter than the swan,
It would make any man
To forget deadly sin
Her favour to win.
For this most goodly flower,
This blossom of fresh colour,
So Jupiter me succour,
She flourisheth new and new
In beauty and virtue;
Hac claritate gemina,
O gloriosa femina,
Defecit in salutatione tua anima mea: [27]
Quid petis filio, mater dulcissima? [28]

Soft, and make no din,
For now I will begin
To have in remembrance
Her goodly dalliance,
Her goodly pastance;
So sad and so demure,
Behaving her so sure,
With words of pleasure
She would make to the lure
And any man convert
To give her his whole heart.
She made me sore amazed
Upon her when I gazed,
Methought mine heart was crazed,
My eyen were so dazed.
For this most goodly flower,
This blossom of fresh colour,
So Jupiter me succour,
She flourisheth new and new
In beauty and virtue;
Hac claritate gemina,
O gloriosa femina,
Quomodo dilexi legem tuam, domina! [29]
Recedant vetera, nova sunt omnia.[30]

---

[25] "Thou hast dealt well with thy servant, oh Lady," parody of Vulgate Psalm 118:65.

[26] "And praises sound from the heart," from the Hymn of St. Thomas Aquinas sung at Matins on the Feast of Corpus Christi.

[27] "My soul fainteth in greeting Thee," a parody of Vulgate Psalm 118:81: *Defecit in salutare tuum anima mea,"* My soul fainteth for thy salvation."

[28] "What do you ask from your son, sweetest mother?"

[29] "Oh how I love thy law, lady!" A parody of Vulgate Psalm 118:97.

[30] "Old things fade and all is new."

And to amend her tale,
When she list to avail,
And with her fingers smale,
And handes soft as silk,
Whiter than the milk,
That are so quickly veined,
Wherewith my hand she stained,
Lord, how I was pained!
Unneth I me refrained!
How she me had reclaimed,
And me to her retained,
Embracing therewithal
Her goodly middle small
With sides long and strait.
To tell you what conceit
I had then in a trice,
The matter were too nice—
And yet there was no vice,
Nor yet no villainy,
But only fantasy.
For this most goodly flower,
This blossom of fresh colour,
So Jupiter me succour,
She flourisheth new and new
In beauty and virtue;
Hac claritate gemina,
O gloriosa femina,
Iniquos odio habui! [31]
Non calumnientur me superbi.[32]

But whereto should I note
How often did I toot [33]
Upon her pretty foot?
It rased [34] mine heart-root
To see her tread the ground
With heeles short and round!
She is plainly express
Egeria, the goddess,
And like to her image,
Emportured with corage,
A lovers' pilgrimage;
There is no beast savage,
Ne no tiger so wood,[35]
But she would change his mood,
Such relucent [36] grace
Is formed in her face.
For this most goodly flower,
This blossom of fresh colour,
So Jupiter me succour,
She flourisheth new and new
In beauty and virtue;
Hac claritate gemina,
O gloriosa femina,
Mirabilia testimonia tua! [37]
Sicut novellae plantationes in juventate sua.[38]

So goodly as she dresses,
So properly she presses
The bright golden tresses
Of her hair so fine,
Like Phoebus' beames shine.
Whereto should I disclose
The gartering of her hose?
It is for to suppose
How that she can wear
Gorgeously her gear;
Her fresh habiliments
With other implements
To serve for all intents,
Like Dame Flora, queen
Of lusty summer green;
For this most goodly flower,
This blossom of fresh colour,
So Jupiter me succour,
She flourisheth new and new
In beauty and virtue;
Hac claritate gemina

[31] "I hate vain thoughts" Vulgate Psalm 118:113.

[32] "Let not the proud oppress me," Vulgate Psalm 118:122.

[33] *toot:* peep, look at.

[34] *rased:* penetrated.

[35] *wood:* mad.

[36] *relucent:* shining, bright.

[37] "Wonderful are thy testimonies," Vulgate Psalm 118:129.

[38] "[That our sons may be] as plants grown up in their youth," Vulgate Psalm 143:12.

O gloriosa femina,
Clamavi in toto corde, exaudi me! [39]
Misericordia tua magna est super me.[40]

Her kirtle so goodly laced,
And under that is braced [41]
Such pleasures that I may
Neither write nor say!
Yet though I write with ink,
No man can let me think,
For thought hath liberty,
Thought is frank and free;
To think a merry thought
It cost me little or naught.
Would God mine homely style
Were polished with the file
Of Cicero's eloquence
To praise her excellence.
For this most goodly flower,
This blossom of fresh colour,
So Jupiter me succour,
She flourisheth new and new
In beauty and virtue;
Hac claritate gemina,
O gloriosa femina,
Principes persecuti sunt me gratis! [42]
Omnibus consideratis,
Paradisus voluptatis
Haec virgo est dulcissima.[43]

My pen it is unable,
My hand it is unstable,
My reason rude and dull
To praise her at the full;
Goodly Mistress Jane,
Sober, demure Diane;
Jane this mistress hight,
The lode-star of delight,
Dame Venus of all pleasure,
The well of worldly treasure.
She doth exceed and pass
In prudence Dame Pallas;
For this most goodly flower,
This blossom of fresh colour,
So Jupiter me succour,
She flourisheth new and new
In beauty and virtue;
Hac claritate gemina,
O gloriosa femina!

. . . .

FROM

THE GARLAND OF LAUREL

To Mistress Margaret Hussey

Merry Margaret,
As midsummer flower,
Gentle as falcon
Or hawk of the tower:
With solace and gladness,
Much mirth and no madness,
All good and no badness;
So joyously,
So maidenly,
So womanly

[39] "I cried with my whole heart, hear me!" Vulgate Psalm 118:145.

[40] "Great is thy mercy toward me" Vulgate Psalm 85:13.

[41] *braced:* embraced, encircled.

[42] "Princes have persecuted me without a cause," Vulgate Psalm 118:161.

[43] "All things considered, this girl is the sweetest among the pleasures of paradise."

Her demeaning
In every thing,
Far, far passing
That I can indite,
Or suffice to write
Of Merry Margaret
As midsummer flower,
Gentle as falcon
Or hawk of the tower.
As patient and still
And as full of good will
As fair Isaphill,
Coliander,
Sweet pomander,
Good Cassander,
Steadfast of thought,
Well made, well wrought,
Far may be sought
Ere that he can find
So courteous, so kind
As Merry Margaret,
This midsummer flower,
Gentle as falcon
Or hawk of the tower.

MANNERLY MARGERY MILK AND ALE

Ay, beshrew you, by my fay,
These wanton clerks be nice alway,
Avaunt, avaunt, my popinjay!
What, will you do nothing but play?
Tilly vally straw, let be I say!
Gup,[44] Christian Clout, gup, Jack of the Vale!
With Mannerly Margery milk and ale.

By God, ye be a pretty pode,[45]
And I love you an whole cart-load.
Straw, James Foder, ye play the fode,[46]
I am no hackney for your rode:[47]
Go watch a bull, your back is broad!
Gup, Christian Clout, gup, Jack of the Vale!
With Mannerly Margery milk and ale.

Ywis ye deal uncourteously;
What, would ye frumple[48] me? now fie!
What, and ye shall not be my pigsny?[49]
By Christ, ye shall not, no hardily:
I will not be japed[50] bodily!
Gup, Christian Clout, gup, Jack of the Vale!
With Mannerly Margery milk and ale.

Walk forth your way, ye cost me naught;
Now have I found that I have sought:
The best cheap flesh that ever I bought.
Yet, for his love that hath all wrought,
Wed me, or else I die for thought.

[44] *gup:* contracted from "go up," an ejaculation to arouse somebody.
[45] *pode:* toad.
[46] *fode:* deceiver, seducer.
[47] *rode:* riding.
[48] *frumple:* rumple, tumble.
[49] *pigsny:* darling.
[50] *japed:* tricked, deceived.

Gup, Christian Clout, your breath is stale!
Go, Mannerly Margery milk and ale!

Gup, Christian Clout, gup, Jack of the Vale!
With Mannerly Margery milk and ale.

FROM

COLIN CLOUT

And if ye stand in doubt
Who brought this rhyme about,
My name is Colin Clout.
I purpose to shake out
All my conning [51] bag,
Like a clerkly hag.
For though my rhyme be ragged,
Tattered and jagged,
Rudely rain-beaten,
Rusty and moth-eaten,
If ye take well therewith,
It hath in it some pith.
For, as far as I can see,
It is wrong with each degree:
For the temporality
Accuseth the spirituality;
The spiritual again
Doth grudge and complain
Upon the temporal men;
Thus each of other blother [52]
The one against the other;
Alas, they make me shudder!
For in hugger-mugger
The Church is put in fault;
The prelates be so haut,
They say, and look so high,
As though they would fly
Above the starry sky.

. . . .

With language thus polluted
Holy Church is bruted [53]
And shamefully confuted.
My pen now will I sharp,
And wrest up my harp
With sharp twinking trebles,
Against all such rebels
That labour to confound
And bring the Church to the ground;
As ye may daily see
How the laity
Of one affinity
Consent and agree
Against the Church to be
And the dignity
Of the bishop's see.
And either ye be too bad,
Or else they are mad
Of this to report.
But, under your support,
Till my dying day
I shall both write and say,
And ye shall do the same,
How they are to blame
You thus to defame:
For it maketh me sad
How that the people are glad
The Church to deprave;
And some there are that rave,
Presuming on their wit,
When there is never a whit
To maintain arguments
Against the sacraments.

[51] *conning:* studying, learning.
[52] *blother:* blether, talk nonsense.
[53] *bruted:* noised abroad.

Some make epilogation
Of high predestination;
And of recidivation [54]
They make interpretation
Of an awkward fashion;
And of the prescience
Of divine essence;
And what hypostasis
Of Christ's manhood is.
Such logic men will chop,
And in their fury hop,
When the good ale sop
Doth chance in their foretop.
Both women and men,
Such ye may well know and ken,
That against priesthood
Their malice spread abroad,
Railing heinously
And disdainously
Of priestly dignities,
And their malignities.
And some have a smack
Of Luther's sack
And a burning spark
Of Luther's wark,
And are somewhat suspect
In Luther's sect;
And some of them bark,
Clatter and carp
Of that heresiarch
Called Wicliffista,
The devilish dogmatista;
And some be Hussians,
And some be Arians,
And some be Pelagians,
And make much variance
Between the clergy
And the temporality,
How the Church hath too
mickle,
And they have too little,
And bring in materialities
And qualified qualities
Of pluralities,
Of trialities,[55]
And of *tot quots* [56]
They commune like sots,
As cometh to their lots;
Of prebendaries and deans,
How some of them gleans
And gathereth up the store
For to catch more and more;
Of parsons and vicaries
They make many outcries;
They cannot keep their wives
From them for their lives.
And thus the losels [57] strives
And lewdly says by Christ
Against the silly [58] priest.
Alas and weylaway,
What ails them thus to say?
They might be better advised
Than to be so disguised.
But they have enterprised,
And shamefully surmised
How prelacy is sold and bought
And come up of naught,
And where the prelates be
Come of low degree,
And set in majesty
And spiritual dignity,
Farewell benignity,
Farewell simplicity,
Farewell humility,
Farewell good charity!

. . . .

Shall I tell you more? yea,
shall.
I am loth to tell all;
But the commonalty you call
Idols of Babylon,
De Terra Zabulon,
De Terra Neptalim;

[54] *recidivation:* relapse into sin.

[55] *trialities:* holding of three benefices simultaneously.

[56] *tot quots:* holding of an unlimited number of benefices.

[57] *losels:* worthless persons, scoundrels.

[58] *silly:* innocent.

For ye love to go trim,
Brought up of poor estate,
With pride inordinate,
Suddenly upstart
From the dung-cart,
The mattock and the shule,[59]
To reign and to rule;
And have no grace to think
How ye were wont to drink
Of a leather bottle
With a knavish stopple,
When mannocks [60] was your meat,
With mouldy bread to eat;
Ye could none other get
To chew and to gnaw,
To fill therewith your maw;
Lodging in fair straw,
Couching your drowsy heads
Sometime in lousy beds.
Alas, this is out of mind!
Ye grow now out of kind;
Many one ye have untwined,
And make the commons blind.
But *qui se existimat stare,*[61]
Let him well beware
Lest that his foot slip,
And have such a trip,
And fall in such decay,
That all the world may say,
"Come down, in the Devil way!"

59 *shule:* shovel.

60 *mannocks:* leavings.

61 "Let him that thinketh he standeth [take heed lest he fall]," I. Corinthians 10:12.

Sir Thomas More

1477 or 1478–1535

THE GREAT luminary of English humanism, Thomas More was at once a lawyer, statesman, controversialist, masterly writer of English prose, and saint. He was born in London, the son of a prominent lawyer; as a boy he served in Archbishop Morton's household, then proceeded to Oxford and to the Inns of Court. In 1499 he first met Erasmus and took him to see the royal children when the future Henry VIII was eight years old. Mingling a successful legal career with humanistic studies in Greek, More was a defender of the new classical learning and of the Roman church. He wrote the *History of King Richard III* in English about 1513; a few years later he composed his famous *Utopia* in Latin. By 1516 his great gifts as an advocate made it apparent that he could not long resist becoming the King's servant or minister; in 1517 he quelled the Evil May Day riot and in the next year was made Master of Requests and Privy Councillor. He was knighted in 1521, became Speaker of the House of Commons in 1523 and succeeded Wolsey as Lord Chancellor in 1529. He resigned in 1532, declined to attend Anne Boleyn's coronation in 1533, and, upon refusing to take the oath for the Act of Succession and Supremacy, was sent to the Tower. The next year he was indicted for high treason and on July 6 executed.

"He gets pleasure out of everything that life brings him," said Erasmus of his friend More, "even matters of the greatest gravity. Among sober men of learning he admires their intelligence; among the stupid and ignorant he amuses himself with their absurdity. He can accommodate himself even to fools, so skilfull is he in hitting off the tastes of others. With most women and even with his own wife his talk is all of jesting and of fun . . . No one is less swayed by public opinion; but again no one shows more common sense in his judgments."

More's *Utopia,* though more famous, is not so characteristic a work of English humanism as the *History of Richard III.* More's sources probably included members of Morton's household who were prejudiced against Richard; indeed it was difficult for any partisan of the Tudors to see the hunchback Yorkist as anything but a monster. More's history, at any rate, set the pattern which lasted down to Shakespeare; it became the staple account in Grafton's (1543) and Halle's (1548) chronicles, so of course it influenced Holinshed and Shakepeare. True or not, More's history is vivid, not to say theatrical, and it appreciates all of the ironies.

BIBLIOGRAPHY: *Utopia,* tr. Ralph Robinson, many editions; J. H. Hexter, *More's Utopia. The Biography of an Idea,* Princeton, 1954; Russell Ames, *Citizen Thomas More and his Utopia,* Princeton, 1949; P. S. and H. M. Allen, *Sir Thomas More: Selections from his English Works,* Oxford, 1924; *More's English Works,* ed. W. E. Campbell and others, 2 vols., London, 1927,

1931. An important book on More's circle is A. W. Reed, *Early Tudor Drama,* London, 1926. Students of More's *Richard III* should consult James Gairdner, *Richard III* (Cambridge, 1898), and, for the heretical view that Richard was innocent of the murder of the princes, Horace Walpole's *Historic Doubts* (1768) and a modern detective story, Josephine Tey's *Daughter of Time* (1951); A. F. Pollard, "The Making of Sir Thomas More's *Richard III,*" *Historical Essays in Honor of James Tait,* Manchester, 1933, pp. 223–238; L. F. Dean, "Literary Problems in More's *Richard III*" *PMLA,* LVIII (1943), pp. 22–36. There are many biographies of More; among the early ones those by William Roper (ed. E. V. Hitchcock, E. E. T. S., 1935) and by Nicholas Harpsfield (ed. E. V. Hitchcock, E. E. T. S., 1932) are the most important; the standard modern life is by R. W. Chambers, London and New York, 1935.

FROM

THE HISTORY OF KING RICHARD III

A King's Mistress

Now then, bye and bye, as it were for anger not for covetise, the Protector [1] sent into the house of Shore's wife [2] (for her husband dwelled not with her) and spoiled her of all that ever she had, above the value of two or three thousand marks, and sent her body to prison. And when he had a while laid unto her for the manner' sake,[3] that she went about to bewitch him, and that she was of counsel with the Lord Chamberlain to destroy him; in conclusion when that no color could fasten upon these matters, then he laid heinously to her charge that thing that herself could not deny, that all the world wist was true, and that natheles [4] every man laughed at to hear it then so suddenly so highly taken, that she was naught of her body. And for this cause (as a goodly continent prince clean and faultless of himself, sent out of heaven into this vicious world for the amendment of men's manners) he caused the Bishop of London to put her to open penance, going before the cross in procession upon a Sunday with a taper in her hand. In which she went in countenance and pace demure, so womanly, and albeit she were out of all array save her kirtle only, yet went she so fair and lovely, namely while the wondering of the people cast a comely rud [5] in her checks (of which she before had most miss) that her great shame won her much praise among those that were more amorous of her body than curious of her soul. And many good folk also that hated her living and glad were to see sin corrected, yet pitied they more her penance than rejoiced therein when they considered that the Protector procured it, more of a corrupt intent than any virtuous affection.

This woman was born in London, worshipfully friended, honestly brought up, and very well married, saving somewhat too soon, her husband an honest citizen, young and goodly and of good substance. But forasmuch as they were coupled ere she were well ripe, she not very fervently loved for whom she never longed. Which was haply the thing that the more easily made her incline unto the King's appetite when he re-

[1] *the Protector:* the future Richard III.

[2] *Shore's wife:* Jane Shore, the wife of a London merchant and mistress of the late king, Edward IV.

[3] *the manner' sake:* for the sake of appearances.

[4] *natheles:* nevertheless.

[5] *rud:* blush.

quired her. Howbeit that respect of his royalty, the hope of gay apparel, ease, pleasure and other wanton wealth was able soon to pierce a soft tender heart. But when the king had abused her, anon her husband (as he was an honest man and one that could his good,[6] not presuming to touch a King's concubine) left her up to him altogether. When the king died, the Lord Chamberlain took her, which in the King's days, albeit he was sore enamored upon her, yet he forbare her, either for reverence or for a certain friendly faithfulness. Proper she was, and fair: nothing in her body that you would have changed, but if you would have wished her somewhat higher. Thus say they that knew her in her youth. Albeit some that now see her (for yet she liveth) deem her never to have been well visaged. Whose judgment seemeth me somewhat like as though men should guess the beauty of one long before departed by her scalp taken out of the charnel house; for now she is old, lean, withered and dried up, nothing left but rivelled skin and hard bone. And yet being even such, whoso well advise her visage might guess and devise which parts how filled might make it a fair face. Yet delighted men not so much in her beauty as in her pleasant behavior. For a proper wit had she, and could both read well and write, merry in company, ready and quick of answer, neither mute nor full of babble, sometime taunting without displeasure and not without disport. The King would say that he had three concubines, which in three divers properties diversly excelled: one the merriest, one the wiliest, and one the holiest harlot in his realm, as one whom no man could get out of the church lightly to any place but it were to his bed. The other two were somewhat greater personages, and natheles of their humility content to be nameless and to forbear the praise of those properties. But the merriest was this Shore's wife, in whom the King therefore took special pleasure. For many he had, but her he loved, whose favor, to say the truth, (for sin it were to belie the devil) she never abused to any man's hurt, but to many a man's comfort and relief. Where the King took displeasure, she would mitigate and appease his mind. Where men were out of favor, she would bring them in his grace. For many that had highly offended, she attained pardon. Of great forfeitures she gat men remission. And finally in many weighty suits, she stood many men in great stead, either for none or very small rewards, and those rather gay than rich, either for that she was content with the deed' self well done, or for that she delighted to be sued unto and to show what she was able to do with the king, or for that wanton women and wealthy be not always covetous.

I doubt not some shall think this woman so slight a thing to be written of and set among the remembrances of great matters, which they shall specially think that haply shall esteem her only by that they now see her. But me seemeth the chance so much the more worthy to be remembered, in how much she is now in the more beggarly condition, unfriended and worn out of acquaintance, after good substance, after as great favor with the prince,

[6] *could his good:* knew his own best interests.

after as great suit and seeking to with all those that those days had business to speed, as many other men were in their times, which be now famous only by the infancy of their ill deeds. Her doings were not much less, albeit they be much less remembered, because they were not so evil. For men use if they have an evil turn to write it in marble; and whoso doth us a good turn, we write it in dust, which is not worst proved by her; for at this day she beggeth of many at this day living, that at this day had begged if she had not been.

Death of the Princes

But in the mean time for this present matter I shall rehearse you the dolorous end of those babes, not after every way that I have heard, but after the way that I have so heard by such men and by such means as methinketh it were hard but it should be true. King Richard after his coronation, taking his way to Gloucester to visit in his new honor the town of which he bare the name of his old,[7] devised as he rode, to fulfill that thing which he before had intended. And forasmuch as his mind gave him that his nephews living, men would not reckon that he could have right to the realm, he thought therefore without delay to rid them, as though the killing of his kinsmen could amend his cause and make him a kindly king. Whereupon he sent one John Green, whom he specially trusted, unto Sir Robert Brackenbury, constable of the Tower, with a letter and credence also, that the same Sir Robert should in any wise put the two children to death. This John Green did his errand unto Brackenbury, kneeling before Our Lady in The Tower, who plainly answered that he would never put them to death to die therefor, with which answer John Green returning recounted the same to King Richard at Warwick yet in his way. Wherewith he took such displeasure and thought, that the same night he said unto a secret page of his, "Ah, whom shall a man trust? Those that I have brought up myself, those that I had went [8] would most surely serve me, even those fail me, and at my commandment will do nothing for me," "Sir," quod [9] his page, "there lieth one on your pallet without, that I dare well say to do your grace pleasure, the thing were right hard that he would refuse," meaning this by Sir James Tyrell, which was a man of right goodly personage, and for nature's gifts worthy to have served a much better prince, if he had well served God and by grace obtained as much truth and good will as he had strength and wit. The man had as high heart and sore longed upward, not rising yet so fast as he had hoped, being hindered and kept under by the means of Sir Richard Ratcliff and Sir William Catesby, which longing for no more partners of the prince's favor, and namely [10] not for him whose pride they wist would bear no peer, kept him by secret

[7] *i.e.* Richard, now King, had formerly been Duke of Gloucester.

[8] *went:* weened, supposed.

[9] *quod:* said.

[10] *namely:* especially.

drifts out of all secret trust. Which thing this page well had marked and known. Wherefore, this occasion offered, of very special friendship he took his time to put him forward and by such wise do him good, that all the enemies he had except the devil could never had done him so much hurt. For upon this page's words King Richard arose. For this communication had he sitting at the draught,[11] a convenient carpet for such a counsel, and came out into the pallet chamber, on which he found in bed Sir James and Sir Thomas Tyrell, of person like and brethren of blood, but nothing of kin in conditions. Then said the King merely to them, "What, sirs, be ye in bed so soon?" and calling up Sir James, brake to him secretly his mind in this mischievous matter. In which he found him nothing strange. Wherefore on the morrow he sent him to Brackenbury with a letter by which he was commanded to deliver Sir James all the keys of the Tower for one night, to the end he might there accomplish the King's pleasure in such thing as he had given him commandment. After which letter delivered and the keys received, Sir James appointed the night next ensuing to destroy them, devising before and preparing the means. The prince as soon as the Protector left that name and took himself as King, had it showed unto him that he could not reign but his uncle should have the crown. At which word the prince, sore abashed, began to sigh and said "Alas, I would my uncle would let me have my life yet, though I lose my kingdom." Then he that told him the tale used him with good words and put him in the best comfort he could. But forthwith was the prince and his brother both shut up, and all other removed from them, only one called Black Will or William Slaughter except, set to serve them and sure. After which time the prince never tied his points nor aught wrought of himself, but with that young babe his brother lingered in thought and heaviness till this traitorous death delivered them of that wretchedness. For Sir James Tyrell devised that they should be murdered in their beds, to the execution whereof he appointed Miles Forest, one of the four that kept them, a fellow fleshed in murder beforetime. To him he joined one John Dighton, his own horse-keeper, a big, broad, square, strong knave. Then all the other being removed from them, this Miles Forest and John Dighton about midnight (the silly [12] children lying in their beds) came into the chamber and suddenly lapped them up among the clothes, so bewrapped them and entangled them, keeping down by force the featherbed and pillows hard unto their mouths, that within a while smored [13] and stifled, their breath failing, they gave up to God their innocent souls into the joys of heaven, leaving to the tormentors their bodies dead in the bed. Which after that the wretches perceived, first by the struggling with the pains of death and after long lying still to be thoroughly dead, they laid their bodies naked out upon the bed, and fetched Sir James to see them. Which upon the sight of them caused those murderers to bury them at the stair foot meetly deep in

[11] *draught:* toilet.

[12] *silly:* innocent.

[13] *smored:* smothered.

the ground under a great heap of stones. Then rode Sir James in great haste to King Richard, and showed [14] him all the manner of the murder, who gave him great thanks and as some say there made him knight. But he allowed not, as I have heard, that burying in so vile a corner, saying that he would have them buried in a better place, because they were a King's sons. Lo the honorable courage of a King! Whereupon they say that a priest of Sir Robert Brackenbury took up the bodies again and secretly entered them in such place as by the occasion of his death which only knew it, could never since come to light. Very truth is it and well known that at such time as Sir James Tyrell was in the Tower for treason committed against the most famous prince King Henry the Seventh, both Dighton and he were examined and confessed the murder in manner above written, but whither the bodies were removed they could nothing tell. And thus as I have learned of them that much knew and little cause had to lie, were these two noble princes, these innocent tender children, born of most royal blood, brought up in great wealth, likely long to live to reign and rule in the realm, by traitorous tyranny taken, deprived of their estate, shortly shut up in prison and privately slain and murdered, their bodies cast God wot where by the cruel ambition of their unnatural uncle and his dispiteous tormentors. Which things on every part well pondered, God never gave this world a more notable example, neither in what unsurety standeth this worldly weal, or what mischief worketh the proud enterprise of an high heart, or finally what wretched end ensueth such dispiteous cruelty. For first to begin with the ministers, Miles Forest at St. Martin's piecemeal rotted away. Dighton indeed yet walketh on alive in good possibility to be hanged ere he die. But Sir James Tyrell died at Tower Hill, beheaded for treason. King Richard himself, as ye shall hereafter hear, slain in the field, hacked and hewed of his enemies' hands, harried on horseback dead, his hair in despite torn and togged [15] like a cur dog. And the mischief that he took, within less than three years of the mischief that he did. And yet all the mean time spent in much pain and trouble outward, much fear, anguish and sorrow within. For I have heard by credible report of such as were secret with his chamberers that after this abominable deed done, he never had quiet in his mind, he never thought himself sure. Where he went abroad, his eyen [16] whirled about, his body privily fenced,[17] his hand ever on his dagger, his countenance and manner like one alway ready to strike again, he took ill rest arights, lay long waking and musing, sore wearied with care and watch, rather slumbered than slept, troubled with fearful dreams, suddenly sometime start up, leap out of his bed and run about the chamber, so was his restless heart continually tossed and tumbled with the tedious impression and stormy remembrance of his abominable deed.

---

[14] *showed:* told.

[15] *togged:* dishevelled.

[16] *eyen:* eyes.

[17] *privily fenced:* wearing armor under his clothes.

Sir Thomas Elyot

1490?–1546

As an English nationalist and a secularist, Sir Thomas Elyot provides a contrast with his friend Sir Thomas More. Elyot, like More, was the son of a lawyer; his father, Sir Richard Elyot, had been a sergeant-at-law and Attorney General to the Queen Consort of Henry VII, and in the next reign was a Justice of Assize for the western circuit. Thomas Elyot was educated at home, became a clerk of assize in his father's circuit, and assiduously pursued humanistic studies in literature and moral philosophy as well as the professional subjects of law and medicine. He was on friendly terms with the leading humanists of the period, More, Erasmus, Linacre, Colet, Fisher and Grocyn, and it is said that both Elyot and his wife pursued literary studies in the group who frequented the house of More.

Elyot's public employments were not fortunate. He was made Clerk of the Council by Wolsey in 1523, but because of legal and political technicalities he was never able to draw his salary and was dismissed in 1530, in his own words "discharged without any recompense, rewarded only with the order of Knighthood, honorable and onorous, having much less to live on than before." In the next year he was appointed ambassador to the court of the Emperor Charles V, in an attempt to persuade the emperor to favor the King's side in his divorce proceedings. Though Elyot was at this time in the service of Anne Boleyn, he seems to have sympathized with the deposed Queen Catherine. In the long run, Elyot was bound by his political philosophy to be on the King's side, so we find him accepting the Oath of Supremacy which More rejected, and in 1535 Elyot was one of the commissioners for the visitation of the religious houses. For his share in the expropriation of the monasteries he was finally rewarded with a manor formerly belonging to one of them.

The assertion by Roper that Elyot heard of More's execution from the Emperor Charles has been shown to be an error, but there is no doubt that Elyot's friendship with More caused him to be suspect, for there is a letter from Elyot to Cromwell protesting that his friendship with More did not cause him to be disloyal to the King.

Elyot was a very prolific writer. His *Boke Named the Governour,* published in 1531 and dedicated to the King, was followed by other works of political philosophy, *Of the Knowledge Which Maketh a Wise Man* in 1533 and *The Image of Governaunce* in 1540; by translations from Plutarch, Isocrates and various classical moralists; by a medical work called *The Castel of Helth* (1534) and by a Latin-English dictionary (1538).

Elyot is an important English humanist. In his secular, moral and political emphasis he foreshadows the Elizabethan temper. His style is vigorous and readable, and his contributions to the English vocabulary are many and interesting.

Bibliography: *The Boke Named The Governour,* ed. H. H. S. Croft, 2 vols., London, 1883, with an important biographical introduction; A. F. Pollard, "More and Elyot," *TLS* July 17, 1930, p. 592; L. C. Warren, *Humanistic Doctrines of The Prince from Petrarch to Sir Thomas Elyot,* Chicago, 1939; James Wortham, "Sir Thomas Elyot and the Translation of Prose," *H.L.Q.* XI (1948), 219–240.

THE GOVERNOR

From Book I

What order should be in learning and which authors should be first read.

Now let us return to the order of learning apt for a gentleman. Wherein I am of the opinion of Quintilian that I would have him learn Greek and Latin authors both at one time, or else to begin with Greek, for as much as that it is hardest to come by, by reason of the diversity of tongues which be five in number, and all must be known or else uneth [1] any poet can be well understand.[2] And if a child do begin therein at seven years of age he may continually learn Greek authors three years and in the mean time use the Latin tongue as a familiar language. Which in a noble man's son may well come to pass, having none other persons to serve him or keeping him company but such as can speak Latin elegantly. And what doubt is there but so may he as soon speak good Latin as he may do pure French which now is brought into as many rules and figures and as long a grammar as is Latin or Greek? I will not contend who among them that do write grammars of Greek (which now almost be innumerable) is the best, but that I refer to the discretion of a wise master. Always I would advise him not to detain the child too long in that tedious labors, either in the Greek or Latin grammar. For a gentle wit is therewith soon fatigate.

Grammar being but an introduction to the understanding of authors, if it be made too long or exquisite to the learner it in a manner mortifieth his courage. And by that time he cometh to the most sweet and pleasant reading of old authors, the sparks of fervent desire of learning is extinct with the burden of grammar, like as a little fire is soon quenched with a great heap of small sticks, so that it can never come to the principal logs where it should long burn in a great pleasant fire. Now to follow my purpose: after a few and quick rules of grammar, immediately or interlacing it therewith would be read to the child Aesop's fables in Greek, in which argument children much do delight. And surely it is a much pleasant lesson, and also profitable, as well for that it is elegant and brief (and notwithstanding it hath much variety in words and therewith much helpeth to the understanding of Greek) as also in those fables is included much moral and politic wisdom. Wherefore in the teaching of them the master diligently must gather together those fables which may be most accommodate to the advancement of some virtue whereto he perceiveth the child inclined, or to the rebuke of some vice whereto he findeth his nature disposed. And therein the master ought to exercise his wit as well to make the child

[1] *uneth:* scarcely.

[2] *understand:* understood.

plainly to understand the fable as also declaring the signification thereof compendiously and to the purpose. Fore seen alway that as well this lesson as all other authors which the child shall learn, either Greek or Latin, verse or prose, be perfectly had without the book, whereby he shall not only attain plenty of the tongues called Copy, but also increase and nourish remembrance wonderfully. The next lesson would be some quick and merry dialogs elect out of Lucian which be without ribaldry or too much scorning, for either of them is exactly to be eschewed, specially for a noble man, the one annoying the soul the other his estimation concerning his gravity. The comedies of Aristophanes may be taken in place of Lucian, and by reason that they be in meter they be the sooner learned by heart. I dare make none other comparison between them for offending the friends of them both; but thus much dare I say, that it were better that a child should never read any part of Lucian than all Lucian.

I could rehearse divers other poets which for matter and eloquence be very necessary, but I fear me to be too long from noble Homer, from whom as from a fountain proceeded all eloquence and learning. For in his books be contained and more perfectly expressed not only the documents martial and discipline of arms but also incomparable wisdoms and instructions for politic governance of people, with the worthy commendation and laud of noble princes, wherewith the readers shall be so all inflamed that they most fervently shall desire and covet by the imitation of their virtues to acquire semblable glory. For the which occasion Aristotle, most sharpest witted and excellent learned philosopher, as soon as he had received Alexander from King Philip his father, he before anything taught him the works of Homer. Wherein Alexander found such sweetness and fruit that ever after he had Homer not only with him in all his journeys but also laid him under his pillow when he went to rest, and often times would purposely wake some hours of the night to take as it were his pastime with that most noble poet. For by the reading of his work called Iliados where the assembly of the most noble Greeks again Troy is recited with their affairs, he gathered courage and strength again his enemies, wisdom and eloquence for consultations and persuasions to his people and army. And by the other work called Odyssea which recounteth the sundry adventures of the wise Ulysses, he by the example of Ulysses apprehended many noble virtues, and also learned to escape the fraud and deceitful imaginations of sundry and subtle crafty wits. Also there shall he learn to ensearch and perceive the manners and conditions of them that be his familiars, sifting out (as I mought say) the best from the worst, whereby he may surely commit his affairs and trust to every person after his virtues.

Therefore I now conclude that there is no lesson for a young gentle man to be compared with Homer if he be plainly and substantially expounded and declared by the master.

Notwithstanding forasmuch as the said works be very long and do require therefore a great time to be all learned and kenned, some Latin author would be therewith mixed, and especially Virgil, which in his work called Eneidos is most like to Homer and almost the same Homer in Latin. Also by the joining together of those authors, the one shall be the better understand by the other. And verily (as I before said) none one author serveth to so divers wits as doth Virgil. For there is not that effect or desire whereto any child's fantasy is disposed but in some of Virgil's works may be founden matter thereto apt and propice.[3] For what thing can be more familiar than his Bucolics? Nor no work so nigh approacheth to the common dalliance and manners of children and the pretty controversies of the simple shepherds therein contained wonderfully rejoiceth the child that heareth it well declared, as I know by mine own experience. In his Georgics Lord what pleasant variety there is! The divers grains, herbs and flowers that be there described that reading therein it seemeth to a man to be in a delectable garden or paradise. What plowman knoweth so much of husbandry as there is expressed? Who delighting in good horses shall not be thereto more enflamed, reading there of the breeding choosing and keeping of them? In the declaration whereof Virgil leaveth far behind him all breeders, hackney-men and scoursers.[4] Is there any astronomer that more exactly setteth out the order and course of the celestial bodies or that more truly doth divine in his pronostications of the times of the year in their qualities with the future estate of all things provided by husbandry than Virgil doth recite in that work?

If the child have a delight in hunting, what pleasure shall he take of Aristeus? Semblably in the hunting of Dido and Aeneas which is described most elegantly in his book of Eneidos. If he have pleasure in wrestling, running or other like exercise where shall he see any more pleasant esbatements[5] than that which was done by Eurealus and other Trojans which accompanied Aeneas? If he take solace in hearing minstrels what minstrel may be compared to Iopas which sang before Dido and Aeneas? Or to blind Demodocus that played and sang most sweetly at the dinner that the King Alcinous made to Ulysses, whose ditties and melody excelled as far the songs of our minstrels as Homer and Virgil excel all other poets.

* * *

I would set next unto him two books of Ovid, the one called Metamorphosios which is as much to say as changing men into other figure or form. The other is entitled *De Fastis* where the ceremonies of the gentiles and especially the Romans be expressed, both right necessary for the understanding of the poets. But by cause there is little other learning in them concerning either virtuous manners or policy, I suppose it were better that as fables and ceremonies happen to come in a lesson it were declared abundantly by the master than that in the said two books a long time should be spent and almost lost, which mought[6] be better employed on such authors

[3] *propice:* propitious.
[4] *scoursers:* horse traders.
[5] *esbatements:* amusements.
[6] *mought:* might.

that do minister both eloquence, civil policy and exhortation to virtue.

Wherefore in his place let us bring in Horace in whom is contained much variety of learning and quickness of sentence. This poet may be interlaced with the lesson of Odyssea of Homer wherein is declared the wonderful prudence and fortitude of Ulysses in his passage from Troy.

And if the child were induced to make verses by the imitation of Virgil and Homer it should minister to him much delectation and courage to study. Ne the making of verses is not discommended in a noble man, since the noble Augustus and almost all the old emperors made books in verses.

The two noble poets Silius and Lucan be very expedient to be learned, for the one setteth out the emulation in qualities and prowess of two noble and valiant captains, one enemy to the other, that is to say Silius writeth of Scipio the Roman and Hannibal, Duke of Cartaginensis. Lucan declareth a semblable matter but much more lamentable. For as much as the wars were civil and as it were in the bowels of the Romans, that is to say under the standards of Julius Caesar and Pompey. Hesiodus in Greek is more brief than Virgil, where he writeth of husbandry, and doth not rise so high in philosophy, but is fuller of fables, and therefore is more illecebrous.[7]

And here I conclude to speak any more of poets necessary for the childhood of a gentleman, for as much as these I doubt not will suffice until he pass the age of thirteen years. In which time childhood declineth and reason waxeth ripe and deprehendeth[8] things with a more constant judgment. Here I would should be remembered that I require not that all these works should be thoroughly read of a child in this time, which were almost impossible. But I only desire that they have in every of the said books so much instruction that they may take thereby some profit. Then the child's courage, inflamed by the frequent reading of noble poets daily more and more desireth to have experience in those things that they so vehemently do commend in them that they write of.

ON DANCING[9]

It is diligently to be noted that the associating of man and woman in dancing, they both observing one number and time in their movings, was not begun without a special consideration, as well for the necessary conjunction of those two persons as for the intimation of sundry virtues which be by them represented. And for as much as by the association of a man and a woman in dancing may be signified matrimony, I could, in declaring the dignity and commodity of that sacrament, make entire volumes, if it were not so commonly known to all men that almost every friar limitor[10] carrieth it written in his bosom. Wherefore lest in repeating a thing

[7] *illecebrous:* alluring, attractive.

[8] *deprehendeth:* notices, discovers.

[9] For a modern use of this passage, see T. S. Eliot's "East Coker" in *Four Quartets.*

[10] *friar limitor:* a friar licensed to beg within a limited area.

so frequent and common my book should be as fastidious or fulsome to the readers as such merchant preachers be now to their customers, I will reverently take my leave of divines. And for my part I will endeavor myself to assemble out of the books of ancient poets and philosophers matter as well apt to my purpose as also new or at the least ways infrequent or seldom heard of them that have not read very many authors in Greek and Latin.

But now to my purpose. In every dance of a most ancient custom there danceth together a man and a woman holding each other by the hand or the arm, which betokeneth concord. Now it behoveth the dancers and also the beholders of them to know all qualities incident to a man and also qualities to a woman likewise appertaining.

A man in his natural perfection is fierce, hardy, strong in opinion, covetous of glory, desirous of knowledge, appetiting by generation to bring forth his semblable.[11] The good nature of a woman is to be mild, timorous, tractable, benign, of sure remembrance, and shamefast; divers other qualities of each of them mought be found out but these be most apparent and for this time sufficient.

Wherefore when we behold a man and a woman dancing together let us suppose there to be a concord of all the said qualities being joined together as I have set them in order. And the moving of the man would be more vehement, of the woman more delicate, and with less advancing of the body, signifying the courage and strength that ought to be in a man and the pleasant soberness that should be in a woman. And in this wise *fierceness* joined with *mildness* maketh *severity; audacity* with *timorosity* maketh *magnanimity; willful opinion* and *tractability* (which is to be shortly persuaded and moved) maketh *constancy* a virtue; *covetise of glory* adorned with *benignity* causeth honor; *desire of knowledge* with *sure remembrance* procureth *sapience; shamefastness* joined to *appetite of generation* maketh *continence,* which is a mean between *chastity* and *inordinate lust.* These qualities in this wise being knit together and signified in the personages of man and woman dancing do express or set out the figure of very nobility, which in the higher estate it is contained the more excellent is the virtue in estimation.

From Book II

THE THREE PRINCIPAL PARTS OF HUMANITY

The nature and condition of man, wherein he is less than God Almighty and excelling notwithstanding all other creatures in earth, is called humanity, which is a general name to those virtues in whom seemeth to be

[11] *appetiting . . . semblable:* desiring by sexual instinct to reproduce his kind.

a mutual concord and love in the nature of man. And although there be many of the said virtues yet there be three principal by whom humanity is chiefly compact: benevolence, beneficence and liberality, which maketh up the said principal virtue called benignity or gentleness.

Benevolence if it do extend to a whole country or city is properly called charity, and sometime zeal, and if it concern one person then is it called benevolence. And if it be very fervent and to one singular person then may it be named love or amity. Of that virtuous disposition proceedeth an act whereby something is employed which is profitable and good to him that receiveth it. And that virtue if it be in operation or (as I mought say) endeavor, it is called then beneficence and the deed (vulgarly named a good turn) may be called a benefit. If it be in money or other thing that hath substance it is then called liberality, which is not alway a virtue as beneficence is: for in well doing, which is the right interpretation of beneficence, can be no vice included. But liberality, though it proceed of a free and gentle heart willing to do something thankful, yet it may transgress the bonds of virtue either in excessive rewards or expenses, or else employing treasure, promotion or other substance on persons unworthy, or on things inconvenient and of small importance. Albeit some think such manner of erogation [12] not to be worthy the name of liberality. For Aristotle defineth a liberal man to be he which doth erogate according to the rate of his substance and as opportunity happeneth. He saith also in the same place that liberality is not in the multitude or quantity of that which is given but in the habit or faction of the giver, for he giveth according to his ability. Neither Tully approveth it to be liberality wherein is any mixture of avarice or rapine; for it is not properly liberality to exact injustly, or by violence or craft to take goods from particular persons and distribute them in a multitude, or to take from many unjustly and enrich therewith one person or few. For as the same author saith, the last precept concerning benefits or rewards is to take good heed that he contend not again [13] equity ne that he uphold none injury.

Now will I proceed seriously and in a due form to speak more particularly of these three virtues. Notwithstanding there is such affinity between beneficence and liberality, being always a virtue, that they tend to one conclusion or purpose, that is to say, with a free and glad will to give to a nother that thing which he before lacked.

---

[12] *erogation:* spending.

[13] *again:* against.

William Tyndale

1494–1536

WILLIAM TYNDALE or Hutchins, the protestant martyr and creator of the English Bible, came from a yeoman-farmer family long settled in western Gloucestershire, on the border of Wales. By some means Tyndale went to Oxford, and later to Cambridge. In 1522 he returned to Gloucestershire as a tutor in the household of Sir John Walsh. At his employer's table he would meet eminent divines, abbots, deans and learned doctors with whom he would argue on points of religion. When Sir John and Lady Walsh asked him why he so stubbornly held to his opinions in the face of authority, he answered by translating for them Erasmus' *Enchiridion*. This satisfied his employers, but his clerical opponents had him summoned before the clergy of the diocese and threatened with removal. Tyndale is said to have replied that he cared not; let him have ten pounds a year and freedom to teach and preach anywhere in England and he would be content.

It must have been about this time that Tyndale decided to translate the New Testament. Erasmus had published the first Greek text in 1516 and Luther's German translation had appeared in 1522. According to a famous story, Tyndale was engaged in argument with a cleric who said, "We were better without God's law than the Pope's." "I defy the Pope and all his laws," replied Tyndale; "if God spare my life, ere many years I will cause that a boy that driveth the plow shall know more of scripture than thou dost."

Knowing that he would be allowed to translate and publish the scriptures only if properly authorized, Tyndale tried to enlist the support of Cuthbert Tunstall, Bishop of London, but failed. Instead his backing came from English merchants; his work would have to be done abroad and the English Bible smuggled into England. In 1524 Tyndale went to Hamburg, then to Wittenberg where Luther was, then to Cologne where the printing of the New Testament in English was begun. Before it was finished the church and the government were aroused and Tyndale had to flee with his manuscript and some printed sheets to Worms, where the publication was completed. By 1526 copies were circulating in England; in that year a baker was charged with heresy for owning one.

Tyndale became almost immediately the foremost English protestant. Recognizing the strength of the man who had asked for his patronage only a few years before, Bishop Tunstall secured the services of his friend Sir Thomas More, most eminent man of learning and Chancellor of the realm, to write against Tyndale. In sanctuary in the free city of Antwerp, Tyndale defended himself and his translation against the onslaughts of the opposition.

Despite More's charges of venality, Tyndale's motives seem to have been single-heartedly devoted to promotion of the knowledge of the Bible by every man who could read. When, in 1531, attempts were made by high government authorities to get Tyndale to return to England, he answered,

"If it would stand with the King's most gracious pleasure to grant only a bare text of the scriptures to be put forth among his people, be it of the translation of what person soever shall please his majesty, I shall immediately make faithful promise never to write more, ne abide two days in these parts after the same, but immediately to repair into his realm, and there most humbly submit myself at the feet of his royal majesty, offering my body to suffer what pain and torture, yea, what death, his grace will, so this be obtained."

But the triumph of Tyndale's English scriptures was to be in the face of official opposition, not with royal support. According to the chronicler Halle, Bishop Tunstall was once in Antwerp and told an English merchant, Anthony Packington, that he would gladly buy up any English Testaments to prevent their being smuggled into England. Packington reported this offer to his friend Tyndale. "Who is the merchant?" asked the translator. "The Bishop of London," replied Packington. "Oh, that is because he will burn them," said Tyndale. "Yes, marry," said Packington. Then the chronicle continues:

"I am the gladder, said Tyndale, for these two benefits shall come thereof: I shall get money for these books, to bring myself out of debt (and the whole world shall cry out upon the burning of God's word) and the overplus of the money that shall remain to me shall make me more studious to correct the New Testament and so newly to imprint the same once again and I trust the second will much better like you than did ever the first. And so forward went the bargain: the bishop had the books, Packington had the thanks and Tyndale had the money."

The pursuit of Tyndale continued; in 1535 he was enticed into a trap outside the walls of Antwerp and was taken to Vilvorde, where he was burned at the stake the next year. His last words, according to Foxe, were "Lord, open the King of England's eyes." Within seven years of Tyndale's martyrdom, The Great Bible in English (a slightly revised version of Tyndale's translation) was set up, by order, in every parish church in England. And when, in 1611, the Authorized King James Version was adopted, its language was very largely the language of Tyndale. So it must be said of Tyndale that he, more than any other man, created the greatest monument of English prose.

Bibliography: *The Beginning of the New Testament Translated by William Tyndale,* ed. A. W. Pollard, Oxford, 1926, with parallel versions of Matthew V from all the early English Bibles, J. F. Mosley, *William Tyndale,* London, 1937; A. W. Pollard, *Records of the English Bible,* Oxford, 1911.

TYNDALE'S PROLOGUE TO THE READER

HERE thou hast, most dear reader, the New Testament or covenant made with us of God in Christ's blood, which I have looked over again, now at the last, with all diligence, and compared it unto the Greek, and have weeded out of it many faults which lack of help at the beginning and oversight did sow therein. If aught seemed changed or not altogether agreeing with the Greek, let the finder of fault consider the Hebrew phrase or the manner of speech left in the Greek words, whose preterperfect tense and present tense is oft both one, and the future tense is the optative mode also and the future tense is oft the imperative mode in the active voice and in the passive ever. Likewise person for person, number for number, and an interrogation for a conditional and such like is with the Hebrews a common usage.

I have also in many places set light in the margin to understand the text by. If any man find faults either with the translation or aught beside (which is easier for many to do than so well to have translated it themselves of their own pregnant wits at the beginning without for ensample,[1] to the same it shall be lawful to translate it themselves and to put what they lust thereto. If I shall perceive either by my self or by the information of other that aught be escaped me or might be more plainly translated I will shortly after cause it to be amended. Howbeit in many places me thinketh it better to put a declaration in the margin than to run too far from the text. And in many places where the text seemeth at the first chop[2] hard to be understand, yet the circumstances before and after and often reading together make it plain enough.

Moreover because the Kingdom of Heaven which is the scripture and word of God may be so locked up that he which readeth or heareth it cannot understand it, as Christ testifieth how that the scribes and pharisees had so shut it up, (Math. xxiii) and had taken away the key of knowledge (Luke xi) that the Jews which thought themselves within were yet so locked out, and are to this day, that they can understand no sentence of the scripture unto their salvation, though they can rehearse the texts everywhere and dispute thereof as subtly as the Popish Doctors of Dunce's Dark Learning which with their sophistry served us as the pharisees did the Jews; therefore, that I might be found faithful to my Father and Lord in distributing unto my brethren and fellows of one faith their due and necessary food, so dressing it and seasoning it that the weak stomachs may re-

[1] *ensample:* example, model.

[2] *first chop:* immediately.

ceive it also and be better for it, I thought it my duty, most dear reader, to warn thee before and to show thee the right way in, and to give thee the true key to open it withal, and to arm thee against false prophets and malicious hypocrites, whose perpetual study is to leaven the scripture with glozes [3] and there to lock it up where it should save thy soul and to make us shoot at a wrong mark to put our trust in those things that profit their bellies only and slay our souls.

The right way, yea and the only way, to understand the scripture unto salvation is that we earnestly and above all thing search for the profession of our baptism or covenants made between God and us. As for an ensample, Christ saith (Mat. V) "Happy are the merciful, for they shall obtain mercy." Lo here God hath made a covenant with us to be merciful unto us if we will be merciful one to another . . .

Also ye see that two things are required to begin a Christian man. The first is a steadfast faith and trust in almighty God to obtain all the mercy that he hath promised us through the deserving and merits of Christ's blood only, without respect to our own works. And the other is that we forsake evil and turn to God to keep his laws and fight against ourselves and our corrupt nature perpetually, that we may do the will of God every day better and better.

This I have said, most dear reader, to warn thee lest thou shouldst be deceived, and shouldst not only read the scriptures in vain and to no profit but also unto thy greater damnation. For the natures of God's word is that whosoever read it or hear it reasoned and disputed before him it will begin immediately to make him every day better and better, till he be grown into a perfect man in the knowledge of Christ and love of the law of God, or else make him worse and worse till he be hardened that he openly resist the spirit of God and then blaspheme after the ensample of Pharaoh, Korah, Abiram, Balaam, Judas, Simon Magus and such other.

Moreover I take God, which alone seeth the heart to record to my conscience, beseeching him that my part be not in the blood of Christ if I wrote of all that I have written throughout all my book aught of an evil purpose, of envy or malice to any man, or to stir up any false doctrine or opinion in the church of Christ, or to be the author of any sect, or to draw disciples after me, or that I would be esteemed or had in price above the least child that is born, save only of pity and compassion I had and yet have on the blindness of my brethren, and to bring them unto the knowledge of Christ and to make every one of them, if it were possible, as perfect as an angel of heaven; and to weed out all that is not planted of our heavenly Father, and to bring down all that lifteth up itself against the knowledge of the salvation that is in the blood of Christ. Also my part be not in Christ if mine heart be not to follow and live according as I teach; and also if mine heart weep not night and day for mine own sin and other men's indifferently, beseeching God to convert us all and to take his

[3] *glozes:* marginal comments, with a connotation of lying.

wrath from us, and to be merciful as well to all other men as to mine own soul, caring for the wealth of the realm I was born in, for the king and all that are thereof as a tender-hearted mother would do for her only son.

As concerning all I have translated or otherwise written, I beseech all men to read it for that purpose I wrote it: even to bring them to the knowledge of the scripture. And as far as the scripture approveth it, so far to allow it, and if in any place the word of God disallow it, there to refuse it, as I do before Our Saviour Christ and his congregation. And where they find faults, let them show it me if they be nigh, or write to me if they be far off, or write openly against it and improve it; and I promise them, if I shall perceive that their reasons conclude, I will confess mine ignorance openly.

Sir Thomas Wyatt the Elder

1503–1542

WYATT was born at Allington Castle, in Kent, and educated at St. John's College, Cambridge. Most of his life he devoted to the service of the crown, in posts ranging from clerk of the king's jewels to ambassador to Spain and to the Emperor Charles V. He was also a member of missions to France and to Italy, so that much of his mature life was spent on the continent. Twice he was arrested and imprisoned by Henry VIII: first in May, 1536, in connection with the charges of adultery against Queen Anne Boleyn, the poet's first cousin, and again in January, 1541, when he was charged with treason, lodged in the Tower of London, and stripped of his property. On both occasions, however, Wyatt regained the king's favor and was pardoned. It remained for his son, Sir Thomas Wyatt the Younger, to be executed for treason when the southern rebellion which he led was suppressed in the reign of Queen Mary.

Wyatt's personality is described by Surrey, who was a contemporary of his son, in an elegy in this volume. His appearance is preserved in the well-known portrait by Holbein, which shows a heavy, square face, typical of Henry's courtiers, thoughtful eyes, and a dignified beard. His poems, even when they are translations, show something of his personal tastes and opinions; he is always manly and independent and English.

None of Wyatt's poetry was published in his lifetime, although it was circulated in manuscripts which are still extant, and the author's corrections in one of these (Egerton 2711 in the British Museum) suggest that publication may have been contemplated. But in general, poets of the social class of Wyatt did not write for publication in the sixteenth century; they were interested only in the acclaim of the cultivated ladies and gentlemen of the court circle, and these readers could be reached by manuscript.

The general public saw courtiers' poems only when some enterprising publisher acquired manuscripts (sometimes in the form of a commonplace book or manuscript anthology) and issued a miscellany. By far the most important of the dozen miscellanies of the second half of the century was one published by the printer Richard Tottel in 1557 under the title *Songes and Sonettes, written by the ryght honourable Lorde Henry Haward late Earle of Surrey, and other*. To the Elizabethans it was known as *Songs and Sonnets* ("I had rather than forty shillings I had my book of Songs and Sonnets here," says Master Slender in Shakespeare's *Merry Wives*); but since 1870 it has been called *Tottel's Miscellany*. The first edition contained 271 poems, 40 attributed to Surrey, 97 to Wyatt, 40 to Nicholas Grimald, and 94 to "Uncertain Authors." This is surely one of the most important volumes in the history of English literature, for it made the main currents of European Renaissance poetry flow into the British Isles. The sonnet, blank verse, *terza rima, ottava rima,* rondeau, and other forms were naturalized into English. And a "crew of courtly makers," gentleman poets and singers, set the style for a great half-century of English verse.

Even before Tottel, though, some of Wyatt's poems had appeared in a collection. It was called *The Court of Venus* or *The Book of Ballets,* and two editions of it appeared near the middle of the century. There were attacks upon it as a "book of lecherous ballads," and a pious group tried, without much success, to get the courtiers to sing translated psalms and spiritual hymns instead of these gay lyrics of love.

Wyatt's verse is vigorous and virile. The obvious violation of accent in some of his lines raises the still unsettled question as to whether he knew what he was doing or not. Some scholars have suggested that his system of versification is based on the bad editions of Chaucer available in his time; if this is so, a modernized text of Wyatt cannot do him justice. But it is just as likely that Wyatt had an attitude toward accent like that of Donne half a century later, for which Ben Jonson declared that Donne deserved hanging.

Wyatt's greatest achievement is in the native ballet or song, not in the French or Italian forms he used. His gaiety, his manly independence in love, his quiet English resignation have lost nothing of their power in four centuries.

Bibliography: *Tottel's Miscellany,* ed. Hyder E. Rollins, Harvard, 1928–1929; *The Poems of Sir Thomas Wiat,* ed. A. K. Foxwell, London, 1913; A. K. Foxwell, *A Study of Sir Thomas Wyatt's Poems,* London, 1909; E. M. W. Tillyard, *The Poetry of Sir Thomas Wyatt,* Oxford, 1929; Sir E. K. Chambers, *Sir Thomas Wyatt and Some Collected Studies,* London, 1933; J. M. Berdan, *Early Tudor Poetry,* New York, 1920; Ruth Hughey, "The Harington MS at Arundel Castle and Related Documents," *4 Library,* XV (1934–1935), 388–444; Hallett Smith, "The Art of Sir Thomas Wyatt," *H.L.Q.,* IX (1946), 323–355; D. W. Harding, "The Rhythmical Intention in Wyatt's Poetry," *Scrutiny,* XIV (1947), 90–102; *Collected Poems of Sir Thomas Wyatt,* ed. Kenneth Muir, London, 1949.

THE long love that in my thought doth harbor,[1]
And in my heart doth keep his residence,
Into my face presseth with bold pretense
And there encampeth, spreading his banner.
She that me learns to love and suffer
And wills that my trust and lust's negligence
Be reined by reason, shame and reverence
With his hardiness takes displeasure.
Wherewithal unto the heart's forest he flieth,
Leaving his enterprise with pain and cry,
And there him hideth, and not appeareth.
What may I do, when my master feareth,
But in the field with him to live and die?
For good is the life ending faithfully.

FAREWELL, Love, and all thy laws forever,
Thy baited hooks shall tangle me no more;
Senec and Plato call me from thy lore,
To perfect wealth my wit for to endeavor.
In blind error when I did persever,
Thy sharp repulse, that pricketh aye so sore,
Hath taught me to set in trifles no store
And scape forth since liberty is lever.[2]
Therefore farewell, go trouble younger hearts,
And in me claim no more authority;
With idle youth go use thy property,
And thereon spend thy many brittle darts.
For hitherto though I have lost all my time,
Me lusteth no longer rotten boughs to climb.

[1] A translation of Petrarch, *Sonnetto in Vita* 91. See the note on Surrey's "Love, that doth reign." The text is based on the recently discovered Harington MS as given by Ruth Hughey in *4 Library,* XV, 442–443.

[2] *lever:* more pleasing, dearer.

I FIND no peace and all my war is done,[3]
I fear and hope, I burn and freeze like ice,
I fly above the wind, yet can I not arise,
And naught I have and all the world I seize on;
That [4] looseth nor locketh holdeth me in prison,
And holdeth me not; yet can I 'scape nowise;
Nor letteth me live nor die at my devise,[5]
And yet of death it giveth none occasion.
Without eyen [6] I see; and without tongue I plain;
I desire to perish, and yet I ask health;
I love another, and thus I hate myself;
I feed me in sorrow, and laugh in all my pain.
Likewise displeaseth me both death and life,
And my delight is causer of this strife.

MY galley charged with forgetfulness [7]
Thorough sharp seas, in winter nights doth pass
'Tween rock and rock; and eke mine enemy, alas,
That is my lord, steereth with cruelness.
And every oar a thought in readiness,
As though that death were light in such a case.
An endless wind doth tear the sail apace
Of forced sighs and trusty fearfulness.
A rain of tears, a cloud of dark disdain,
Hath done the wearied cords great hinderance,
Wreathed with error and eke with ignorance.
The stars be hid that led me to this pain,
Drowned is reason that should me consort,
And I remain despairing of the port.

[3] Translated from Petrarch, *Sonnetto in Vita* 90. The opening lines of this sonnet exemplify the early sixteenth-century preference for one-syllable words in poetry. As Gascoigne put it, "the more monasyllables that you use, the truer Englishman you shall seeme."

[4] Supply *Love* as the first word in the line.

[5] *devise:* wish.

[6] *eyen:* eyes.

[7] Translated from Petrarch, *Sonnetto in Vita* 137. This sonnet, an elaboration of a favorite conceit, is perhaps Wyatt's most famous.

LIKE to these unmeasurable mountains,[8]
Is my painful life the burden of ire;
For of great height be they, and high is my desire;
And I of tears, and they be full of fountains;
Under craggy rocks they have full barren plains,
Hard thoughts in me my woeful mind doth tire;
Small fruit and many leaves their tops do attire,
Small effect with great trust in me remains.
The boisterous winds oft their high boughs do blast,
Hot sighs from me continually be shed;
Cattle in them, and in me love is fed;
Immovable am I, and they are full steadfast;
Of the restless birds they have the tune and note,
And I always plaints that pass thorough my throat.

DIVERS doth use, as I have heard and know,
(When that to change their ladies do begin),
To moan and wail, and never for to lin,[9]
Hoping thereby to pease their painful woe.
And some there be, that when it chanceth so
That women change, and hate where love hath been,
They call them false, and think with words to win
The hearts of them which otherwhere doth go.
But as for me, though that by chance indeed
Change hath outworn the favor that I had,
I will not wail, lament, nor yet be sad,
Nor call her false that falsely did me feed;
But let it pass, and think it is of kind,[10]
That often change doth please a woman's mind.

[8] Translated from Sannazaro, *Rime*, Part 3, Sonnetto 3. Tottel calls this poem "The Lover's Life Compared to the Alps."

[9] *lin:* cease.

[10] *kind:* nature.

WHOSO list to hunt, I know where is an hind,[11]
But as for me—alas, I may no more.
The vain travail hath wearied me so sore,
I am of them that farthest cometh behind.
Yet may I, by no means, my wearied mind
Draw from the deer; but as she fleeth afore,
Fainting I follow. I leave off therefore,
Since in a net I seek to hold the wind.
Who list her hunt, I put him out of doubt,
As well as I, may spend his time in vain.
And graven with diamonds in letters plain
There is written, her fair neck round about:
Noli me tangere,[12] for Caesar's I am,
And wild for to hold, though I seem tame.

MINE own John Poins, since ye delight to know[13]
The cause why that homeward I me draw,
And flee the press of courts, whereso they go,
Rather than to live thrall, under the awe
Of lordly looks, wrapped within my cloak,
To will and lust learning to set a law;
It is not for because I scorn and mock
The power of them to whom Fortune hath lent
Charge over us, of right to strike the stroke.
But true it is that I have always meant
Less to esteem them than the common sort,
Of outward things that judge in their intent[14]
Without regard what doth inward resort.
I grant sometime that of glory the fire
Doth touch my heart; me list not to report
Blame by honor, and honor to desire.

[11] An adaptation of Petrarch, *Rime,* 190, perhaps influenced by Romanello, Sonnetto 3, another adaptation. Wyatt's sonnet is conventionally supposed to refer to Anne Boleyn, in whom Henry VIII became interested in 1526.

[12] *Noli me tangere:* Touch me not.

[13] Based on the tenth satire of Luigi Alamanni (1495–1556), but personalized and Anglicized in detail by Wyatt. Apparently written during Wyatt's banishment from court to his father's place in Kent in 1536.

[14] *But true . . . intent:* He values rank less than the mob does; the mob judges by externals only.

But how may I this honor now attain
That cannot dye the color black a liar?
My Poins, I cannot frame me tune to feign,
To cloak the truth, for praise without desert,
Of them that list all vice for to retain.
I cannot honor them that sets their part
With Venus and Bacchus all their life long;
Nor hold my peace of them, although I smart.
I cannot crouch nor kneel to do so great a wrong,
To worship them like God on earth alone,
That are as wolves these sely [15] lambs among.
I cannot with my words complain and moan
Nor suffer naught, nor smart without complaint,
Nor turn the word that from my mouth is gone;
I cannot speak and look like a saint,
Use wiles for wit, or make deceit a pleasure;
And call craft counsel, for profit still to paint;
I cannot wrest the law to fill the coffer,
With innocent blood to feed myself fat,
And do most hurt where most help I offer.
I am not he that can allow the state
Of high Caesar, and damn Cato to die,
That with his death did scape out of the gate
From Caesar's hands, if Livy do not lie,
And would not live where liberty was lost,
So did his heart the common weal apply.
I am not he, such eloquence to boast
To make the crow in singing as the swan,
Nor call the lion of coward beasts the most,
That cannot take a mouse as the cat can;
And he that dieth of hunger of the gold,
Call him Alexander, and say that Pan
Passeth Apollo in music manifold;
Praise Sir Thopas [16] for a noble tale,
And scorn the story that the Knight told;
Praise him for counsel that is drunk of ale;
Grin when he laugheth that beareth all the sway,
Frown when he frowneth, and groan when he is pale;
On others' lust to hang both night and day,—
None of these points would ever frame in me;
My wit is naught: I cannot learn the way;
And much the less of things that greater be

[15] *sely:* innocent.

[16] *Sir Thopas:* The silly tale of Sir Thopas, in Chaucer's *Canterbury Tales,* is told by Chaucer himself, until the Host forces him to stop. The *Knight's Tale* is the most courtly and dignified of the tales.

That asken help of colors of device
To join the mean with each extremity.
With nearest virtue to cloak alway the vice,
And as to purpose, likewise it shall fall
To press the virtue that it may not rise;
As drunkenness, good fellowship to call;
The friendly foe, with his double face,
Say he is gentle and courteous therewithal;
And say that favel[17] hath a goodly grace
In eloquence; and cruelty to name
Zeal of justice, and change in time and place;
And he that suff'reth offense without blame,
Call him pitiful, and him true and plain
That raileth reckless to every man's shame,
Say he is rude that cannot lie and feign,
The lecher a lover, and tyranny
To be the right of a prince's reign.
I cannot, I: no, no, it will not be.
This is the cause that I could never yet
Hang on their sleeves, that weigh, as thou mayst see,
A chip of chance more than a pound of wit.
This maketh me at home to hunt and hawk,
And in foul weather at my book to sit,
In frost and snow then with my bow to stalk.
No man doth mark whereso I ride or go.
In lusty leas at liberty I walk,
And of these news I feel nor weal nor woe,
Save that a clog[18] doth hang yet at my heel.
No force for that, for it is ordered so
That I may leap both hedge and dike full well;
I am not now in France, to judge the wine,
With sav'ry sauce those delicates to feel;
Nor yet in Spain, where one must him incline,
Rather than to be, outwardly to seem.
I meddle not with wits that be so fine;
Nor Flanders' cheer letteth[19] not my sight to deem
Of black and white, nor taketh my wit away
With beastliness, they beasts do so esteem.
Nor am I not where Christ is given in prey
For money, poison and treason—at Rome[20]
A common practice, used night and day.

---

[17] *favel:* flattery.

[18] *clog:* Wyatt was paroled in his father's custody.

[19] *letteth:* hinders, prevents.

[20] *Nor am . . . Rome* In *Tottel's Miscellany,* published in the reign of the Catholic Mary, these lines were altered as follows: "where *truth* is given in prey / For money, poison, and treason; *of some* / A common practice."

But here I am in Kent and Christendom,
Among the Muses, where I read and rhyme;
Where, if thou list, my Poins, for to come,
Thou shalt be judge how I do spend my time.

Madame, withouten many words,[21]
Once, I am sure, ye will or no.
And if ye will, then leave your bords,[22]
And use your wit, and show it so;
And with a beck ye shall me call;
And if of one that burneth alway
Ye have any pity at all,
Answer him fair with yea or nay.
If it be yea, I shall be fain;
If it be nay, friends as before.
Ye shall another man obtain
And I mine own, and yours no more.

My lute, awake! Perform the last [23]
Labor that thou and I shall waste,
And end that I have now begun;
For when this song is sung and past,
My lute, be still, for I have done.

As to be heard where ear is none,
As lead to grave in marble stone,[24]
My song may pierce her heart as soon.
Should we then sigh or sing or moan?
No, no, my lute, for I have done.

---

[21] A court poem, to which an answer, supposedly written by a lady, is extant.

[22] *bords:* jests.

[23] Usually considered the best of Wyatt's songs.

[24] *As to . . stone:* When sound may be heard with no ear to hear it, or when soft lead is able to carve hard marble . . .

The rocks do not so cruelly
Repulse the waves continually
As she my suit and affection.
So that I am past remedy,
Whereby my lute and I have done.

Proud of the spoil that thou hast got
Of simple hearts, thorough love's shot;
By whom, unkind, thou hast them won,
Think not he hath his bow forgot,
Although my lute and I have done.

Vengeance shall fall on thy disdain
That makest but game on earnest pain.
Think not alone under the sun
Unquit to cause thy lovers plain,
Although my lute and I have done.

Perchance thee lie withered and old[25]
The winter nights that are so cold,
Plaining in vain unto the moon.
Thy wishes then dare not be told.
Care then who list, for I have done.

And then may chance thee to repent
The time that thou hast lost and spent
To cause thy lovers sigh and swoon.
Then shalt thou know beauty but lent,
And wish and want as I have done.

Now cease, my lute. This is the last
Labor that thou and I shall waste,
And ended is that we begun.
Now is this song both sung and past;
My lute, be still, for I have done.

---

[25] Ronsard's most famous sonnet is on this theme: "Quand vous serez bien vielle au soir à la chandelle."

Blame not my lute, for he must sound
Of this or that as liketh me,
For lack of wit the lute is bound
To give such tunes as pleaseth me.
Though my songs be somewhat strange,
And speaks such words as touch thy change,
Blame not my lute.

My lute, alas, doth not offend,
Though that perforce he must agree
To sound such tunes as I intend,
To sing to them that heareth me.
Then, though my songs be somewhat plain,
And toucheth some that use to feign,
Blame not my lute.

My lute and strings may not deny
But as I strike they must obey.
Break not them then so wrongfully,
But wreak thyself some wiser way;
And though the songs which I indite
Do quit thy change with rightful spite,
Blame not my lute.

Spite asketh spite and changing change,
And falsed faith must needs be known.
The fault so great, the case so strange,
Of right it must abroad be blown.
Then since that by thine own desert
My songs do tell how true thou art,
Blame not my lute.

Blame but thyself that hast misdone
And well deserved to have blame.
Change thou thy way so evil begun
And then my lute shall sound that same.
But if till then my fingers play,
By thy desert, their wonted way,
Blame not my lute.

Farewell, unknown, for though thou brake
My strings in spite, with great disdain,
Yet have I found out for thy sake
Strings for to string my lute again.
And if perchance this foolish rhyme
Do make thee blush at any time,
Blame not my lute.

Forget not yet the tried intent
Of such a truth as I have meant;
My great travail so gladly spent
Forget not yet!

Forget not yet when first began
The weary life ye know, since whan
The suit, the service none tell can:
Forget not yet!

Forget not yet the great assays,
The cruel wrong, the scornful ways,
The painful patience in denays:[26]
Forget not yet!

Forget not yet, forget not this,
How long ago hath been and is
The mind that never meant amiss:
Forget not yet!

Forget not, then, thine own approved,
The which so long hath thee so loved,
Whose steadfast faith yet never moved:
Forget not this!

A face that should content me wondrous well
Should not be fair, but lovely to behold,
With gladsome cheer, all grief for to expel;
With sober looks, so would I that it should
Speak without words such words as none can tell;
The tress also should be of crisped gold.
With wit, and these, might chance I might be tied,
And knit again the knot that should not slide.

[26] *denays:* denials, frustrations.

AND wilt thou leave me thus?
(Say nay, say nay, for shame!)
To save thee from the blame
Of all my grief and grame?[27]
And wilt thou leave me thus?
Say nay, say nay.

And wilt thou leave me thus,
That hath loved thee so long,
In wealth and woe among?
And is thy heart so strong
As for to leave me thus?
Say nay, say nay.

And wilt thou leave me thus
That hath given thee my heart,
Never for to depart,
Nother for pain nor smart?
And wilt thou leave me thus?
Say nay, say nay.

And wilt thou leave me thus,
And have no more pity
Of him that loveth thee?
Alas, thy cruelty!
And wilt thou leave me thus?
Say nay, say nay!

WHAT should I say,
Since faith is dead,
And truth away
From you is fled,
Should I be led
With doubleness?
Nay, nay, mistress!

---

[27] *grame*: sorrow

I promised you,
And you promised me,
To be as true
As I would be.
But since I see
Your double heart,
Farewell my part!

Though for to take
It is not my mind,
But to forsake,
I am not blind,
And as I find
So will I trust.
Farewell, unjust!

Can ye say nay?
But you said
That I alway
Should be obeyed.
And thus betrayed
Or that I wist,
Farewell, unkissed!

TAGUS,[28] farewell, that westward with thy streams
Turns up the grains of gold already tried;
With spur and sail for I go seek the Thames,
Gainward the sun, that showeth her wealthy pride;
And to the town which Brutus [29] sought by dreams,
Like bended moon [30] doth lend her lusty side,
My king, my country, alone for whom I live—
Of mighty love the wings for this me give!

[28] Written at the poet's departure from Spain in 1539. *Tagus:* The River Tagus flows through Spain and Portugal.

[29] *Brutus:* the legendary Trojan founder of London.

[30] *bended moon:* crescent moon.

THEY flee from me, that sometime did me seek,
With naked foot stalking [31] in my chamber.
I have seen them, gentle, tame, and meek,
That now are wild, and do not remember
That sometime they put themselves in danger
To take bread at my hand; and now they range,
Busily seeking with a continual change.

Thanked be Fortune it hath been otherwise,
Twenty times better; but once in special,
In thin array, after a pleasant guise,
When her loose gown from her shoulders did fall,
And she me caught in her arms long and small,
And therewith all sweetly did me kiss
And softly said, "Dear heart, how like you this?"

It was no dream, I lay broad waking.
But all is turned, thorough my gentleness,
Into a strange fashion of forsaking;
And I have leave to go, of her goodness,
And she also to use newfangleness.[32]
But since that I so kindely [33] am served,
I fain would know what she hath deserved.

TANGLED I was in love's snare,
Oppressed with pain, torment with care,
Of grief right sure, of joy full bare,
Clean in despair by cruelty,—
But ha! ha! ha! full well is me,
For I am now at liberty.

The woeful day so full of pain,
The weary night all spent in vain,
The labor lost for so small gain,
To write them all it will not be.
But ha! ha! ha! full well is me,
For I am now at liberty.

---

[31] *stalking:* walking softly.
[32] *newfangleness:* fickleness.
[33] *kindely:* naturally.

Everything that fair doth show,
When proof is made it proveth not so,
But turneth mirth to bitter woe;
Which in this case full well I see.
But ha! ha! ha! full well is me,
For I am now at liberty.

Too great desire was my guide
And wanton will went by my side;
Hope ruled still, and made me bide
Of love's craft th' extremity.
But ha! ha! ha! full well is me,
For I am now at liberty.

With feigned words which were but wind
To long delays I was assigned;
Her wily looks my wits did blind;
Thus as she would I did agree.
But ha! ha! ha! full well is me,
For I am now at liberty.

Was never bird tangled in lime[34]
That brake away in better time
Than I, that rotten boughs did climb,
And had no hurt, but scaped free.
Now ha! ha! ha! full well is me,
For I am now at liberty.

34 *lime:* a sticky substance made from holly bark, used to catch small birds.

Henry Howard, Earl of Surrey

1517–1547

SURREY was the eldest son of Thomas Howard, third Duke of Norfolk, and the grandson of the victor of Flodden Field. On both sides of his family he was descended from kings; in fact, his family tree was more aristocratic than that of his master, Henry VIII. He was considered as a possible husband for the Princess Mary; he was trained at Windsor and at the French court as the companion of the King's illegitimate son, the Duke of Richmond, who later married his sister. In his veins ran the blood of Hotspur, and he was called by one of his sober elders "the most foolish, proud boy that is in England."

He saw military service in the north against the rebels, and in France as commander of the garrison at Boulogne. But his fortunes at the court of Henry depended not so much upon his own abilities, military or other, as upon the position of the Howard family as opposed to rival families, and this position in turn depended upon the identity of Henry's current queen. When his cousin, Catherine Howard, was queen, 1540–1542, Surrey was made a Knight of the Garter, seneschal of the King's domain in Norfolk, and steward of Cambridge University. After Catherine's execution he was the victim of the growing power and jealousy of the Seymour family. Toward the end of 1546, when the King's death was near, Surrey's enemies were able to arrest him and his father on a trumped-up charge of treason, with the excuse that the poet had used the royal arms on his scutcheon and was preparing to interfere with the succession of Prince Edward to the throne. He was convicted and executed on Tower Hill on January 19, 1547, before he had reached his thirtieth birthday. Only the death of the king a few days later saved his father from the same fate. The most brilliant of courtiers, the finest poet in English since Chaucer, he immediately became a figure of romantic legend.

Surrey is represented in *Tottel's Miscellany* by forty poems. In addition to these, his translation of two books of Virgil's *Aeneid,* II and IV, has an important place in the history of English poetry, for it was here that unrhymed iambic pentameter or "blank verse" was introduced into English. Many of his poems in Tottel are also extant in manuscript. He established the so-called English or Shakespearean form of the sonnet, consisting of three quatrains and a couplet. His versification seems more modern than that of his master Wyatt, because he kept the accent of the line on the natural accent of the word, and he is less "rough" and often more eloquent than Wyatt. This means usually that he has learned something about pauses within the line, and about the smooth flow obtained by running one line over into the next without a pause. His debt to Wyatt he freely and gladly acknowledged; but his own contribution in making

English verse modern and mellifluous had a greater influence than Wyatt's on the poets of the Elizabethan age.

Bibliography: *Tottel's Miscellany*, ed. Hyder E. Rollins, Harvard, 1928–1929; *The Poems of Henry Howard, Earl of Surrey*, ed. F. M. Padelford, Revised edition, Seattle, 1928; *Surrey's Fourth Boke of Virgill*, ed. H. Hartman, Purchase, N.Y., 1933; E. Bapst, *Deux gentilshommes-poètes de la cour de Henry VIII*, Paris, 1891; E. Casady, *Henry Howard, Earl of Surrey*, New York, 1938; J. M. Berdan, *Early Tudor Poetry*, New York, 1920; "Surrey's Triumphs," *TLS*, Jan. 18, 1947, p. 37; A. Oras, "Surrey's Technique of Phonetic Echoes," *JEGP*, L (1951) 289–308.

The soote season, that bud and bloom forth brings,[1]
With green hath clad the hill and eke [2] the vale;
The nightingale with feathers new she sings;
The turtle to her make [3] hath told her tale.
Summer is come, for every spray now springs;
The hart hath hung his old head on the pale;
The buck in brake his winter coat he flings,
The fishes float with new repaired scale;
The adder all her slough away she slings,
The swift swallow pursueth the flies small;
The busy bee her honey now she mings.[4]
Winter is worn, that was the flowers' bale.
And thus I see among these pleasant things,
Each care decays, and yet my sorrow springs.

Love, that doth reign and live within my thought,[5]
And built his seat within my captive breast,
Clad in the arms wherein with me he fought,
Oft in my face he doth his banner rest.
But she that taught me love and suffer pain,
My doubtful hope and eke my hot desire
With shamefast [6] look to shadow and refrain,
Her smiling grace converteth straight to ire.
And coward Love, then, to the heart apace
Taketh his flight, where he doth lurk and plain,[7]
His purpose lost, and dare not show his face.
For my lord's guilt thus faultless bide I pain,
Yet from my lord shall not my foot remove:
Sweet is the death that taketh end by love.

1 Adapted from Petrarch, *Sonnetto in Morte* 42. Surrey has changed the details of nature from Italian to English. Notice that the sonnet has only two rhymes. *soote:* sweet.

2 *eke:* also.

3 *turtle:* turtle dove; *make:* mate.

4 *mings:* remembers.

5 Translated from Petrarch, *Sonnetto in Vita* 91. Compare this poem with Wyatt's translation of the same original, "The long love that in my thought doth harbor." Surrey's version is usually considered superior in melody and strength not only to Wyatt's but to Petrarch's. The last line became a commonplace in Renaissance poetry.

6 *shamefast:* modest.

7 *plain:* complain.

FROM Tuscan came my lady's worthy race; [8]
Fair Florence was sometime her ancient seat;
The western isle, whose pleasant shore doth face
Wild Chambar's [9] cliffs, did give her lively heat;
Fostered she was with milk of Irish breast;
Her sire an earl, her dame of princes' blood;
From tender years in Britain she doth rest,
With a king's child, where she tastes ghostly [10] food;
Hunsdon [11] did first present her to mine eyen;
Bright is her hue, and Geraldine she hight;
Hampton [12] me taught to wish her first for mine;
And Windsor,[13] alas! doth chase me from her sight.
Beauty of kind, her virtues from above,
Happy is he that may obtain her love.

ALAS! so all things now do hold their peace,[14]
Heaven and earth disturbed in no thing;
The beasts, the air, the birds their song do cease,
The nightes chare [15] the stars about doth bring.
Calm is the sea, the waves work less and less;
So am not I, whom love, alas, doth wring,
Bringing before my face the great increase
Of my desires, whereat I weep and sing,
In joy and woe, as in a doubtful ease.
For my sweet thoughts sometime do pleasure bring,
But by and by the cause of my disease [16]
Gives me a pang that inwardly doth sting,
When that I think what grief it is again
To live and lack the thing should rid my pain.

[8] On this sonnet was constructed one of the most elaborate legends in English literary history, of the love of Surrey for "the fair Geraldine," Elizabeth Fitzgerald, ninth daughter of the Earl of Kildare. Nashe's *The Unfortunate Traveller, or the Life of Jack Wilton* and Drayton's "Henry Howard, Earl of Surrey, to the Lady Geraldine" elaborate the legend. Actually the lady was nine years old when Surrey wrote this poem; he was nineteen, married, and a father.

[9] *Chambar's:* of Cambria, or Wales.

[10] *ghostly:* spiritual.

[11] *Hunsdon:* The girl entered the household of Princess Mary at Hunsdon in 1537.

[12] *Hampton:* Hampton Court, a royal palace.

[13] *Windsor:* For Surrey's imprisonment at Windsor, see the poem, "So cruel prison how could betide, alas," p. 70, and note 24.

[14] Adapted from Petrarch, *Sonnetto in Vita* 113.

[15] *chare:* Italian *carro,* the Great Bear.

[16] *disease:* dis-ease, discomfort.

Set me whereas the sun doth parch the green,[17]
Or where his beams may not dissolve the ice,
In temperate heat, where he is felt and seen;
With proud people, in presence sad and wise,
Set me in base, or yet in high degree;
In the long night, or in the shortest day;
In clear weather, or where mists thickest be;
In lusty youth, or when my hairs be gray;
Set me in earth, in heaven, or yet in hell;
In hill, in dale, or in the foaming flood;
Thrall, or at large,—alive whereso I dwell;
Sick or in health, in ill fame or in good;
Yours I will be, and with that only thought
Comfort myself when that my hap is naught.

Wyatt resteth here, that quick could never rest;[18]
Whose heavenly gifts increased by disdain,[19]
And virtue sank the deeper in his breast;
Such profit he of envy could obtain.
A head where wisdom mysteries did frame;
Whose hammers beat still in that lively brain
As on a stithy,[20] where some work of fame
Was daily wrought, to turn to Britain's gain.
A visage stern and mild; where both did grow,
Vice to contemn, in virtues to rejoice;
Amid great storms, whom grace assured so,
To live upright, and smile at fortune's choice.
A hand that taught what might be said in rhyme;
That reft Chaucer the glory of his wit;
A mark, the which—unperfited, for time—
Some may approach, but never none shall hit.

---

[17] Translated from Petrarch, *Sonnetto in Vita* 95, which is in turn based on Horace.

[18] Apparently Surrey's first published poem. Wyatt, who was fourteen years older than Surrey, died in 1542. There can have been little personal relationship between them; this is a tribute from one poet to another. Lines 34–36 may refer to Wyatt's translation of the Seven Penitential Psalms.

[19] *disdain:* lack of pride.

[20] *stithy:* forge.

A tongue that served in foreign realms his king;
Whose courteous talk to virtue did enflame
Each noble heart; a worthy guide to bring
Our English youth, by travail, unto fame.
An eye whose judgment no affect could blind,
Friends to allure, and foes to reconcile;
Whose piercing look did represent a mind
With virtue fraught, reposed, void of guile.
A heart where dread yet never so impressed
To hide the thought that might the truth avance;
In neither fortune lift,[21] nor so repressed,
To swell in wealth, nor yield unto mischance.
A valiant corpse,[22] where force and beauty met,
Happy, alas! too happy, but for foes,
Lived, and ran the race that nature set;
Of manhood's shape, where she the mold did lose.
But to the heavens that simple soul is fled;
Which left with such as covet Christ to know
Witness of faith that never shall be dead;
Sent for our health, but not received so.
Thus, for our guilt, this jewel have we lost;
The earth his bones, the heavens possess his ghost.

MARTIAL, the things for to attain [23]
The happy life be these, I find:
The riches left, not got with pain;
The fruitful ground; the quiet mind;
The equal friend; no grudge, nor strife;
No charge of rule nor governance;
Without disease, the healthful life;
The household of continuance;
The mean diet, no delicate fare;
Wisdom joined with simplicity;
The night discharged of all care,
Where wine may bear no sovereignty;
The chaste wife, wise, without debate;
Such sleeps as may beguile the night;
Contented with thine own estate,
Neither wish death, nor fear his might.

---

21 *lift:* raised aloft.

22 *corpse:* body (not dead).

23 A translation of Martial's epigram X, 47, a favorite with English and continental poets. The theme, a glorification of "the mean estate," is very common in Elizabethan literature, especially of the pastoral sort.

Give place, ye lovers, here before
That spent your boasts and brags in vain;
My lady's beauty passeth more
The best of yours, I dare well sayn,
Than doth the sun the candlelight,
Or brightest day the darkest night:

And thereto hath a troth as just
As had Penelope the fair.
For what she saith, ye may it trust
As it by writing sealed were;
And virtues hath she many mo
Than I with pen have skill to show.

I could rehearse, if that I wold,
The whole effect of Nature's plaint
When she had lost the perfit mold,
The like to whom she could not paint;
With wringing hands how she did cry,
And what she said, I know it, I.

I know she swore with raging mind,
Her kingdom only set apart,
There was no loss, by law of kind,
That could have gone so near her heart.
And this was chiefly all her pain:
She could not make the like again.

Sith Nature thus gave her the praise
To be the chiefest work she wrought,
In faith, me think some better ways
On your behalf might well be sought
Than to compare, as ye have done,
To match the candle with the sun.

So CRUEL prison how could betide, alas,[24]
As proud Windsor? Where I in lust [25] and joy
With a king's son my childish years did pass
In greater feast than Priam's sons of Troy;
Where each sweet place returns a taste full sour:
The large green courts where we were wont to hove [26]
With eyes cast up unto the maidens' tower,
And easy sighs, such as folk draw in love;
The stately sales,[27] the ladies bright of hue,
The dances short, long tales of great delight;
With words and looks that tigers could but rue,
Where each of us did plead the other's right;
The palm play,[28] where, despoiled for the game,
With dazed eyes oft we by gleams of love
Have missed the ball and got sight of our dame,
To bait her eyes, which kept the leads above;
The graveled ground, with sleeves tied on the helm,
On foaming horse, with swords and friendly hearts,
With cheer, as though the one should overwhelm;
Where we have fought, and chased oft with darts,
With silver drops the meads yet spread for ruth,
In active games of nimbleness and strength,
Where we did strain, trailed by swarms of youth,
Our tender limbs that yet shot up in length;
The secret groves which oft we made resound
Of pleasant plaint and of our ladies' praise,
Recording soft what grace each one had found,
What hope of speed, what dread of long delays;
The wild forest, the clothed holt with green,
With reins avaled,[29] and swift ybreathed horse,
With cry of hounds and merry blasts between,
Where we did chase the fearful hart aforce; [30]
The void walls eke that harbored us each night,
Wherewith, alas, revive within my breast
The sweet accord; such sleeps as yet delight,
The pleasant dreams, the quiet bed of rest;
The secret thoughts imparted with such trust,
The wanton talk, the divers change of play,
The friendship sworn, each promise kept so just,

---

[24] In the summer of 1537 Surrey was imprisoned at Windsor for striking a courtier. In the poem he recalls his boyhood there with Henry Fitzroy, Duke of Richmond, who had died in the previous year, aged seventeen.

[25] *lust:* pleasure.

[26] *hove:* linger.

[27] *sales:* halls.

[28] *palm play:* handball.

[29] *avaled:* slackened.

[30] *aforce:* in the open.

Wherewith we passed the winter nights away.
And with this thought the blood forsakes my face,
The tears berain my cheeks of deadly hue,
The which as soon as sobbing sighs, alas,
Upsupped have, thus I my plaint renew:
O place of bliss, renewer of my woes,
Give me accompt—where is my noble fere? [31]
Whom in thy walls thou didst each night enclose,
To other lief,[32] but unto me most dear!
Echo, alas, that doth my sorrow rue,
Returns thereto a hollow sound of plaint.
Thus I, alone, where all my freedom grew,
In prison pine with bondage and restraint;
And with remembrance of the greater grief
To banish the less, I find my chief relief.

LONDON, hast thou accused me [33]
Of breach of laws, the root of strife?
Within whose breast did boil to see,
So fervent hot, thy dissolute life,
That even the hate of sins that grow
Within thy wicked walls so rife,
For to break forth did convert so
That terror could it not repress.
The which, by words, since preachers know
What hope is left for to redress,
By unknown means, it liked me
My hidden burden to express,
Whereby it might appear to thee
That secret sin hath secret spite;

[31] *fere:* companion.

[32] *lief:* dear.

[33] Surrey was arrested with some companions, including Thomas Wyatt the younger, son of the poet, in April, 1543, and committed to Fleet Prison for eating meat in Lent and for "a lewde and unsemely manner of walking in the night abowght the stretes and breaking with stonebowes off certeyne wyndowes." He admitted his guilt when charged with the latter misdemeanor, but in prison he seems to have amused himself by writing this mock-serious poem, pretending that he was a crusader against the sins of London. The idea that the gay young aristocrat roaring about the streets at night was an appropriate moral censor of the sober and respectable citizens asleep in their beds is of course preposterous.

From justice' rod no fault is free;
But that all such as work unright
In most quiet are next ill rest.
In secret silence of the night
This made me, with a reckless breast,
To wake thy sluggards with my bow—
A figure of the Lord's behest,
Whose scourge for sin the Scriptures show.
That, as the fearful thunderclap
By sudden flame at hand we know,
Of pebble-stones the soundless rap
The dreadful plague might make thee see
Of God's wrath that doth thee enwrap;
That pride might know, from conscience free
How lofty works may her defend;
And envy find, as he hath sought
How other seek him to offend;
And wrath taste of each cruel thought,
The just shapp [34] higher in the end;
And idle sloth, that never wrought,
To heaven his spirit lift may begin;
And greedy lucre live in dread
To see what hate ill-got goods win;
The lechers, ye that lusts do feed,
Perceive what secrecy is in sin;
And gluttons' hearts for sorrow bleed,
Awaked, when their fault they find:
In loathsome vice each drunken wight
To stir to God, this was my mind.
Thy windows had done me no spite,
But proud people that dread no fall,
Clothed with falsehead and unright,
Bred in the closures of thy wall;
But wrested to wrath in fervent zeal,
Thou haste to strife, my secret call.
Endured hearts no warning feel;
O shameless whore, is dread then gone
By such thy foes as meant thy weal?
O member of false Babylon!
The shop of craft, the den of ire!
Thy dreadful doom draws fast upon;
Thy martyrs' blood, by sword and fire,

---

[34] *shapp:* imagine, conceive.

In heaven and earth for justice call.
The Lord shall hear their just desire,
The flame of wrath shall on thee fall,
With famine and pest lamentably
Stricken shall be thy lechers all;
Thy proud towers and turrets high,
En'mies to God, beat stone from stone,
Thine idols burnt that wrought iniquity;
When none thy ruin shall bemoan,
But render unto the right wise Lord
That so hath judged Babylon,
Immortal praise with one accord.

O HAPPY dames, that may embrace [35]
The fruit of your delight,
Help to bewail the woeful case
And eke the heavy plight
Of me, that wonted to rejoice
The fortune of my pleasant choice.
Good ladies, help to fill my mourning voice.

In ship, freight with rememberance
Of thoughts and pleasures past,
He sails, that hath in governance
My life, while it will last;
With scalding sighs, for lack of gale,
Furthering his hope, that is his sail,
Toward me, the sweet port of his avail.

[35] This is a poem written for a lady; an extant MS copy is in the handwriting of Mary Shelton, the sweetheart of Sir Thomas Clere, Surrey's companion on a trip to France. The poem is an adaptation of Serafino's fifth epistle.

Alas! how oft in dreams I see
Those eyes that were my food,
Which sometime so delighted me
That yet they do me good;
Wherewith I wake with his return
Whose absent flame did make me burn;
But when I find the lack, Lord, how I mourn!

When other lovers, in arms across
Rejoice their chief delight,
Drowned in tears, to mourn my loss,
I stand the bitter night
In my window, where I may see
Before the winds how the clouds flee.
Lo, what a mariner Love hath made me!

And in green waves, when the salt flood
Doth rise by rage of wind,
A thousand fancies in that mood
Assail my restless mind.
Alas! now drencheth my sweet foe,
That with the spoil of my heart did go,
And left me; but, alas, why did he so?

And when the seas wax calm again,
To chase from me annoy,
My doubtful hope doth cause me plain,
So dread cuts off my joy.
Thus is my wealth mingled with woe,
And of each thought a doubt doth grow:
Now he comes! Will he come? Alas, no, no!

FROM

THE FOURTH BOOK OF VIRGIL,

entreating of the love between Aeneas and Dido, translated into English and drawn into a strange meter by Henry late Earl of Surrey, worthy to be embraced.[36]

THEN from the seas the dawning gan arise.
The sun once up, the chosen youth gan throng
Unto the gates; the hayes[37] so rarely knit,
The hunting staves with their broad heads of steel,
And of Massile[38] the horsemen, forth they brake;
Of scenting hounds a kennel huge likewise.
And at the threshold of her chamber door
The Carthage lords did there the queen await;
The trampling steed, with gold and purple decked,
Chawing the foamy bit, there fiercely stood.
Then issued she, backed with a great rout,
Clad in a cloak of Tyre embroidered rich.
Her quiver hung behind her back, her tresses
Wound up with gold, her purple vestures eke
Buttoned with gold. The Troyans of her train
Before her go, with gladsome Iulus.[39]
Aeneas eke, the goodliest of the rout,[40]
Makes one of them and joineth close the throngs;
Like when Apollo leaveth Lycia,[41]
His wintering place, and Xanthus'[42] floods likewise,
To visit Delos,[43] his mother's mansion,
[For to repair and furnish new her choir,][44]
The Candians and folk of Driopis,
And painted Agathyrsies shout and cry,
[Environing the altars round about,]
When he walks upon Mount Cynthus' top,

[36] Surrey's translation of *Aeneid* IV was first published by William Owen in 1554; three years later Tottel brought out an edition of Books II and IV. This is of great importance as the first English blank verse. The question of Surrey's possible indebtedness to the Scottish translation of Gavin Douglas (1513) is still in dispute.

[37] *hayes:* nets.

[38] *Massile:* Massilia (Marseilles).

[39] *Iulus:* son of Aeneas.

[40] *rout:* band, troop.

[41] *Lycia:* a country on the south coast of Asia Minor.

[42] *Xanthus:* chief river of Lycia.

[43] *Delos:* an island, birthplace of Apollo.

[44] The bracketed lines, missing in Owen's text, are supplied from the Hargrave MS 205.

His sparkled tresses he pressed with garlands soft
Of tender leaves, and trussed up in gold,
His quivering darts clattering behind his back,—
So fresh and lusty did Aeneas seem,
Such lordly port in countenance present.
But to the hills and wild holts when they came,
From the rock's top then driven, savage roes
Avail the hill, above to the other side,
Through the wide lands, whereas their course,
The harts likewise, in troops taking their flight,
Raising the dust, the mountains fast forsake.
The child Iulus, blithe of his swift steed,
Amidst the plain now pricks by them, now these,
And to encounter wisheth oft in mind
The foaming boar, instead of timorous beasts,
Or lion brown might from the hill descend.
In the mean while the heavens gan rumble sore;
In tail thereof, a mingled shower with hail.
The Tyrian folk and eke the Troyan youth
And Venus' nephew the cottages for fear
Sought round about; the floods fell from the hills.
Dido, a den, the Troyan prince likewise
Chanced upon. Our mother then, the Earth,
And Juno that hath charge of marriage,
First tokens gave with burning gledes[45] of flame,
And, privy to the wedlock, lightning skies,
And the nymphs wailed from the mountain's top.

[45] *gledes:* coals, embers.

Roger Ascham

1515–1568

ROGER ASCHAM belongs to the second generation of English humanists along with Sir Thomas Elyot, Sir John Cheke, and Sir Thomas Wilson. Before him an enterprising group of Englishmen, eager to learn Greek, had gone to Italy and had brought back both knowledge of the classics and inspiration from great scholars. Among them, Thomas Linacre (1460–1524) and William Grocyn (1446–1519) had established the study of Greek at Oxford in the 1490's. John Colet (1467–1519) in founding St. Paul's school had given new vigor and meaning to the secondary school based on the teaching of Latin and Greek.

Of the scholars who inherited the learning of these early teachers, Erasmus and Sir Thomas More contributed most in a literary way to the furtherance of humanism. More's *Utopia* written in Latin in 1516 is England's foremost literary document of pure humanism. Removed from the influence of pictorial and plastic art, English humanism tended early to be concerned with the moral aspects of the humanistic philosophy. The humanists wished to set up classical living as the model for a happy life.

The broader aims of the first generation of humanists, much nearer in time, imagination, and thought to the humanism of Italy, became rather specialized in the educational and critical treatises of Elyot, Wilson, and Ascham. Elyot's *Boke of the Governour* and Ascham's *Scholemaster* emphasized the dual development of body and mind of the student toward moral ends through a classical discipline. Ascham in particular attacked the vices of Italy, a country in which the moral force of the humanistic ideal had in his opinion been lost. Both writers differ from the earlier More in that their work is practical advice and hard-headed theory. The *Utopia* was the work of the imagination, fired by the wonder and squalor of the contemporary world.

Ascham's career began about 1530 with his entrance into St. John's College, Cambridge, one of the largest and most learned of English colleges. He studied under Cheke and Smith, and made friends with Haddon and Watson. Upon taking his B.A. in 1534, he became a fellow of St. John's, and lectured on classics, mathematics, and music.

His life from 1543 to his death was taken up with writing his English works and his Latin letters, his official duties at St. John's, and a continental tour as secretary to Sir Richard Moryson, ambassador to Charles V. From 1548 on throughout his life he served Elizabeth first as tutor and later as reader.

In his first important English work, *Toxophilus* (1545), Ascham had argued for the wakening of the spirit in youth through the manly exercise of archery. In *The Scholemaster,* published posthumously by Ascham's wife in 1570, he proposed to show how Latin should be taught and studied. The system of "double translation," based ultimately on a passage in Cicero's *De Oratore* (Bk. I, Ch. 34), was probably suggested to Ascham by his friend John Sturm, who had edited a selection of Cicero for the classroom. But *The Scholemaster* was not merely an educational treatise on linguistics. It was in many ways a kind of conduct book for youth in which the ideals of the Renaissance and Reformation were combined to develop a dignified and well-ordered character, based on "truth in religion, honesty of living, and right order in learning."

Besides being a personal record of a morally earnest Renaissance teacher and an attack on the Italianate Englishman, *The Scholemaster* is one of the best early examples in the sixteenth century of the practicability of English prose, which was in its infancy as a literary medium.

BIBLIOGRAPHY: *The Whole Works of Roger Ascham,* ed. J. A. Giles, 3 vols. in 4, London, 1864–1865; *English Works of Roger Ascham,* ed. W. Aldis Wright, Cambridge, 1904; *The Scholemaster,* ed. J. E. B. Mayor, London, 1863; L. B. Radford, "Roger Ascham," *The Quarterly Review,* CCLVI (Jan. 1931), 96–111; G. P. Krapp, *The Rise of English Literary Prose,* Oxford, 1915; G. B. Parks, "The First Draft of Ascham's *Scholemaster,*" *Huntington Library Quarterly,* I (1937–1938), 318–327.

THE SCHOOLMASTER

A PREFACE TO THE READER

WHEN the great plague [1] was at London, the year 1563, the Queen's Majesty, Queen Elizabeth, lay at her castle of Windsor; where, upon the tenth day of December, it fortuned that in Sir William Cecil's chamber, her highness's principal secretary, there dined together these personages: Mr. Secretary himself, Sir William Peter, Sir J. Mason, D. Wotton, Sir Richard Sackville, treasurer of the exchequer, Sir Walter Mildmay, chancellor of the exchequer, Mr. Haddon, master of requests, Mr. John Astley, master of the jewel house, Mr. Bernard Hampton, Mr. Nicasius,[2] and I. Of which number the most part were of her Majesty's most honorable Privy Council, and the rest serving her in very good place. I was glad then, and do rejoice yet to remember, that my chance was so happy to be there that day in the company of so many wise and good men together as hardly then could have been picked out again out of all England beside.

Mr. Secretary hath his accustomed manner; though his head be never so full of most weighty affairs of the realm, yet at dinnertime he doth seem to lay them always aside; and findeth ever fit occasion to talk pleasantly of other matters, but most gladly of some matter of learning, wherein he will courteously hear the mind of the meanest at his table.

Not long after our sitting down, "I have strange news brought me," saith Mr. Secretary, "this morning, that divers scholars of Eton be run away from the school for fear of beating." Whereupon, Mr. Secretary took occasion to wish that some more discretion were in many schoolmasters, in using correction, than commonly there is; who many times punish rather the weakness of nature than the fault of the scholar; whereby many scholars, that might else prove well, be driven to hate learning before they know what learning meaneth; and so are made willing to forsake their book, and be glad to be put to any other kind of living.

---

[1] *the great plague:* For a discussion of plagues in sixteenth and seventeenth century London see F. P. Wilson, *The Plague in Shakespeare's London* (Oxford: Clarendon Press, 1927).

[2] *Cecil . . . Nicasius:* Most of these distinguished men were Ascham's friends. William Cecil, Lord Burghley (1520–1598) had been at St. John's College, Cambridge, with Ascham. Sir William Peter, Sir John Mason, and Dean Nicholas Wotton had served under Henry VIII, Edward VI, and Mary as well as under Elizabeth in important capacities. Sir Richard Sackville (d. 1566), undertreasurer of the exchequer and first cousin of Anne Boleyn, was the father of Thomas Sackville (see pp. 149–166). Ascham's *Report and Discourse of the Affairs and State of Germany* was written ostensibly in answer to a request of John Astley.

Mr. Peter, as one somewhat severe of nature, said plainly that the rod only was the sword that must keep the school in obedience and the scholar in good order. Mr. Wotton, a man mild of nature, with soft voice and few words, inclined to Mr. Secretary's judgment, and said, "In mine opinion, the schoolhouse should be in deed, as it is called by name, the house of play and pleasure and not of fear and bondage; and, as I do remember, so saith Socrates in one place of Plato.[3] And therefore, if a rod carry the fear of a sword, it is no marvel if those that be fearful of nature choose rather to forsake the play than to stand always within the fear of a sword in a fond[4] man's handling."

Mr. Mason, after his manner, was very merry with both parties, pleasantly playing both with the shrewd touches of many curst[5] boys and with the small discretion of many lewd[6] schoolmasters. Mr. Haddon was fully of Mr. Peter's opinion, and said, that the best schoolmaster of our time[7] was the greatest beater, and named the person. "Though," quoth I, "it was his good fortune to send from his school unto the university one of the best scholars indeed of all our time, yet wise men do think that that came so to pass rather by the great towardness of the scholar than by the great beating of the master; and whether this be true or no, you yourself are best witness." I said somewhat farther in the matter, how and why young children were sooner allured by love than driven by beating to attain good learning; wherein I was the bolder to say my mind because Mr. Secretary courteously provoked me thereunto; or else in such a company, and namely in his presence, my wont is to be more willing to use mine ears than to occupy my tongue.

Sir Walter Mildmay, Mr. Astley, and the rest, said very little; only Sir Richard Sackville said nothing at all. After dinner I went up to read with the Queen's Majesty. We read then together in the Greek tongue, as I well remember, that noble oration of Demosthenes against Aeschines, for his false dealing in his embassage to King Philip of Macedonia. Sir Richard Sackville came up soon after, and finding me in her Majesty's privy chamber he took me by the hand and carrying me to a window said: "Mr. Ascham, I would not for a good deal of money have been this day absent from dinner. Where, though I said nothing, yet I gave as good ear, and do consider as well the talk that passed, as any one did there. Mr. Secretary said very wisely, and most truly, that many young wits be driven to hate learning before they know what learning is. I can be good witness to this myself; for a fond schoolmaster, before I was fully fourteen years old, drave me so with fear of beating from all love of learning, as now, when I know what difference it is to have learning and to have little or none at all, I feel

[3] *Plato:* in the *Republic,* Book VII.

[4] *fond:* foolish, bungling.

[5] *curst:* vicious.

[6] *lewd:* ignorant.

[7] *the best schoolmaster of our time:* Nicholas Udall (1505–1556), master of Eton, author of *Ralph Roister Doister,* was well known for his severity.

it my greatest grief and find it my greatest hurt that ever came to me that it was my so ill chance to light upon so lewd a schoolmaster. But seeing it is but in vain to lament things past, and also wisdom to look to things to come, surely, God willing, if God lend me life, I will make this my mishap some occasion of good hap to little Robert Sackville,[8] my son's son. For whose bringing up I would gladly, if it so please you, use specially your good advice. I hear say you have a son much of his age; [9] we will thus deal together: point you out a schoolmaster who by your order shall teach my son and yours, and for all the rest I will provide, yea though they three do cost me a couple of hundred pounds by year; and beside, you shall find me as fast a friend to you and yours as perchance any you have." Which promise the worthy gentleman surely kept with me until his dying day.

We had then farther talk together of bringing up of children, of the nature of quick and hard wits, of the right choice of a good wit, of fear and love in teaching children. We passed from children and came to young men, namely gentlemen; we talked of their too much liberty to live as they lust; of their letting loose too soon to overmuch experience of ill, contrary to the good order of many good old commonwealths of the Persians and Greeks; of wit gathered, and good fortune gotten by some, only by experience without learning. And, lastly, he required of me very earnestly to show what I thought of the common going of Englishmen into Italy. "But," saith he, "because this place and this time will not suffer so long talk as these good matters require, therefore I pray you, at my request, and at your leisure, put in some order of writing the chief points of this our talk, concerning the right order of teaching, and honesty of living, for the good bringing up of children and young men; and surely, beside contenting me, you shall both please and profit very many others." I made some excuse by lack of ability and weakness of body. "Well," saith he, "I am not now to learn what you can do; our dear friend, good Mr. Goodricke, whose judgment I could well believe, did once for all satisfy me fully therein. Again, I heard you say, not long ago, that you may thank Sir John Cheke [10] for all the learning you have; and I know very well myself that you did teach the Queen.[11] And therefore, seeing God did so bless you, to make you the scholar of the best master, and also the schoolmaster of the best scholar, that ever were in our time, surely you should please God, benefit your country, and honest your own name, if you would take the pains to impart to others what you learned of such a master, and how ye taught such a scholar. And in uttering the

[8] *Robert Sackville,* second earl of Dorset (1561–1609), eldest son of Thomas Sackville.

[9] *a son much of his age:* Sturm Ascham, one of Ascham's three sons, born in 1562 and named after John Sturm, the humanist, his father's friend. Sturm Ascham died in 1568.

[10] *Sir John Cheke* (1514–1557), tutor to Edward VI, secretary of state, a leader in the revival of Greek in England, reputedly one of the most learned men of his age.

[11] *did teach the Queen:* Ascham was Elizabeth's tutor from 1548 to 1550 and from her accession to his death in 1568.

stuff ye received of the one, in declaring the order ye took with the other, ye shall never lack neither matter nor manner, what to write nor how to write, in this kind of argument."

I beginning some farther excuse suddenly was called to come to the Queen. The night following I slept little, my head was so full of this our former talk and I so mindful somewhat to satisfy the honest request of so dear a friend. I thought to prepare some little treatise for a New Year's gift [12] that Christmas; but, as it chanceth to busy builders, so, in building this my poor schoolhouse (the rather because the form of it is somewhat new, and differing from others), the work rose daily higher and wider than I thought it would at the beginning.

And though it appear now, and be in very deed, but a small cottage, poor for the stuff and rude for the workmanship; yet in going forward I found the site so good as I was loath to give it over; but the making so costly, outreaching my ability, as many times I wished that some one of those three, my dear friends, with full purses, Sir Thomas Smith,[13] Mr. Haddon, or Mr. Watson,[14] had had the doing of it. Yet, nevertheless, I myself spending gladly that little that I got at home by good Sir John Cheke, and that that I borrowed abroad of my friend Sturmius,[15] beside somewhat that was left me in reversion by my old masters, Plato, Aristotle, and Cicero, I have at last patched it up, as I could, and as you see. If the matter be mean, and meanly handled, I pray you bear both with me and it; for never work went up in worse weather, with more lets [16] and stops, than this poor schoolhouse of mine. Westminster Hall can bear some witness,[17] beside much weakness of body, but more trouble of mind, by some such sores as grieve me to touch them myself and therefore I purpose not to open them to others. And in the midst of outward injuries and inward cares, to increase them withal, good Sir Richard Sackville dieth, that worthy gentleman; that earnest favorer and furtherer of God's true religion; that faithful servitor to his prince and country; a lover of learning and all learned men; wise in all doings; courteous to all persons, showing spite to none, doing good to many; and, as I well found, to me so fast a friend as I never lost the like before. When he was gone, my heart was dead. There was not one that wore a black gown for him who carried a heavier heart for him than I;

---

[12] In the sixteenth century gifts were exchanged at New Year's rather than at Christmas.

[13] *Sir Thomas Smith* (1513–1577), statesman, Greek scholar, political writer, friend of the chief scholars of his time in England and on the Continent.

[14] *Mr. Watson:* Thomas Watson (1513–1584), bishop of Lincoln, friend of Ascham, Cheke, Redman, and Sir Thomas Smith, who led the revival of Greek learning at Cambridge.

[15] *Sturmius:* John Sturm (1507–1589), famous humanist of Strasbourg and friend of Ascham.

[16] *lets:* hindrances.

[17] *Westminster Hall can bear some witness:* Ascham is probably alluding to the financial troubles that had come upon him from mortgaging his farm at Walthomstow in behalf of his wife's mother. Westminster Hall, a common name in Elizabethan times for the law, was the seat of the Court of the King's Bench and the Court of Chancery. Perhaps Ascham's business or litigation over the mortgage may have taken place there.

when he was gone, I cast this book away; I could not look upon it but with weeping eyes, in remembering him who was the only setter-on to do it; and would have been not only a glad commender of it, but also a sure and certain comfort to me and mine for it.

Almost two years together this book lay scattered and neglected, and had been quite given over of me, if the goodness of one[18] had not given me some life and spirit again. God, the mover of goodness, prosper always him and his, as he hath many times comforted me and mine, and, I trust to God, shall comfort more and more. Of whom most justly I may say, and very oft, and always gladly I am wont to say, that sweet verse of Sophocles, spoken by Oedipus to worthy Theseus: ἔχω [γὰρ] ἅχω διὰ σὲ, κοὐκ ἄλλον βροτῶν.[19]

This hope hath helped me to end this book; which, if he allow, I shall think my labors well employed, and shall not much esteem the misliking of any others. And I trust he shall think the better of it, because he shall find the best part thereof to come out of his school whom he of all men loved and liked best.

Yet some men, friendly enough of nature, but of small judgment in learning, do think I take too much pains and spend too much time in setting forth these children's affairs. But those good men were never brought up in Socrates's school, who saith plainly that no man goeth about a more godly purpose, than he that is mindful of the good bringing up both of his own and other men's children.

Therefore, I trust, good and wise men will think well of this my doing. And of other, that think otherwise, I will think myself they are but men to be pardoned for their folly and pitied for their ignorance.

In writing this book, I have had earnest respect to three special points: truth of religion, honesty in living, right order in learning. In which three ways, I pray God my poor children may diligently walk; for whose sake, as nature moved, and reason required, and necessity also somewhat compelled, I was the willinger to take these pains.

For, seeing at my death I am not like to leave them any great store of living, therefore in my lifetime I thought good to bequeath unto them, in this little book, as in my will and testament, the right way to good learning; which if they follow, with the fear of God, they shall very well come to sufficiency of living.

I wish also, with all my heart, that young Mr. Robert Sackville may take that fruct of this labor that his worthy grandfather purposed he should have done; and if any other do take either profit or pleasure hereby, they have cause to thank Mr. Robert Sackville, for whom specially this my Schoolmaster was provided.

And one thing I would have the reader consider in reading this book, that, because no schoolmaster hath charge of any child before he enter into

---

18 *one:* Sir William Cecil.

19 ἔχω . . . βροτῶν: "For all I have I owe to thee alone," *Oedipus at Colonus,* 1129.

his school, therefore, I, leaving all former care of their good bringing up to wise and good parents, as a matter not belonging to the schoolmaster, I do appoint this my Schoolmaster then and there to begin, where his office and charge beginneth. Which charge lasteth not long, but until the scholar be made able to go to the university, to proceed in logic, rhetoric, and other kinds of learning.

Yet if my Schoolmaster, for love he beareth to his scholar, shall teach him somewhat for his furtherance and better judgment in learning that may serve him seven year after in the university, he doth his scholar no more wrong, nor deserveth no worse name thereby, than he doth in London who, selling silk or cloth unto his friend, doth give him better measure than either his promise or bargain was.

Farewell in Christ.

THE FIRST BOOK FOR THE YOUTH

After the child hath learned perfitly the eight parts of speech, let him then learn the right joining together of substantives with adjectives, the noun with the verb, the relative with the antecedent. And in learning farther his syntaxis, by mine advice, he shall not use the common order in common schools, for making of Latins: whereby the child commonly learneth, first, an evil choice of words (and "right choice of words," saith Caesar, "is the foundation of eloquence"); then, a wrong placing of words; and lastly, an ill framing of the sentence, with a perverse judgment, both of words and sentences. These faults, taking once root in youth, be never or hardly plucked away in age. Moreover, there is no one thing that hath more either dulled the wits or taken away the will of children from learning, than the care they have to satisfy their masters in making of Latins.

For the scholar is commonly beat for the making, when the master were more worthy to be beat for the mending, or rather marring of the same; the master many times being as ignorant as the child, what to say properly and fitly to the matter.

Two schoolmasters have set forth in print, either of them a book of such kind of Latins, Horman and Whittington. A child shall learn of the better of them that which another day, if he be wise and come to judgment, he must be fain to unlearn again.

There is a way, touched in the first book of *Cicero de Oratore,* which, wisely brought into schools, truly taught, and constantly used, would not only take wholly away this butcherly fear in making of Latins, but would also with ease and pleasure, and in short time, as I know by good experience, work a true choice and placing of words, a right ordering of sentences, an easy understanding of the tongue, a readiness to speak, a facility to write, a true judgment both of his own and other men's doings, what tongue soever he doth use.

The way is this. After the three concordances[20] learned, as I touched before, let the master read unto him the Epistles of Cicero, gathered together and chosen out by Sturmius, for the capacity of children. First let him teach the child cheerfully and plainly the cause and matter of the letter; then let him construe it into English so oft, as the child may easily carry away the understanding of it; lastly, parse it over perfitly. This done thus, let the child, by and by,[21] both construe and parse it over again; so that it may appear that the child doubteth in nothing that his master taught him before. After this, the child must take a paper book, and sitting in some place, where no man shall prompt him, by himself, let him translate into English his former lesson. Then showing it to his master, let the master take from him his Latin book, and pausing an hour at the least, then let the child translate his own English into Latin again in another paper book. When the child bringeth it turned into Latin, the master must compare it with Tully's[22] book, and lay them both together; and where the child doth well, either in choosing or true placing of Tully's words, let the master praise him, and say, "Here ye do well." For I assure you, there is no such whetstone to sharpen a good wit, and encourage a will to learning, as is praise.

But if the child miss, either in forgetting a word, or in changing a good with a worse, or misordering the sentence, I would not have the master either frown or chide with him, if the child have done his diligence, and used no truantship therein. For I know by good experience that a child shall take more profit of two faults gently warned of, than of four things rightly hit; for then the master shall have good occasion to say unto him, "*N.*,[23] Tully would have used such a word, not this; Tully would have placed this word here, not there; would have used this case, this number, this person, this degree, this gender: he would have used this mood, this tense, this simple, rather than this compound; this adverb here, not there: he would have ended the sentence with this verb, not with that noun or participle," etc.

In these few lines I have wrapped up the most tedious part of grammar; and also the ground of almost all the rules that are so busily taught by the master, and so hardly learned by the scholar, in all common schools; which, after this sort, the master shall teach without all error, and the scholar shall learn without great pain; the master being led by so sure a guide, and the scholar being brought into so plain and easy a way. And therefore we do not contemn rules, but we gladly teach rules; and teach them more plainly, sensibly, and orderly, than they be commonly taught in common schools. For when the master shall compare Tully's book with his scholar's transla-

[20] *three concordances:* formal grammatical agreements, number, gender, and person.

[21] *by and by:* immediately.

[22] *Tully's:* I.e., Cicero's, Marcus Tullius Cicero (106–43 B.C.).

[23] *N.:* an abbreviation for Latin *nomen.* The schoolmaster should here insert the name of the scholar whom he is correcting.

tion, let the master, at the first, lead and teach his scholar to join the rules of his grammar book with the examples of his present lesson, until the scholar by himself be able to fetch out of his grammar every rule for every example; so as the grammar book be ever in the scholar's hand, and also used of him as a dictionary for every present use. This is a lively and perfit way of teaching of rules; where the common way used in common schools, to read the grammar alone by itself, is tedious for the master, hard for the scholar, cold and uncomfortable for them both.

Let your scholar be never afraid to ask you any doubt, but use discreetly the best allurements ye can to encourage him to the same; lest his overmuch fearing of you drive him to seek some misorderly shift; as to seek to be helped by some other book, or to be prompted by some other scholar; and so go about to beguile you much and himself more.

With this way of good understanding the matter, plain construing, diligent parsing, daily translating, cheerful admonishing, and heedful amending of faults, never leaving behind just praise for well doing, I would have the scholar brought up withal, till he had read and translated over the first book of Epistles chosen out by Sturmius, with a good piece of a comedy of Terence also.

All this while, by mine advice, the child shall use to speak no Latin; for as Cicero saith in like matter, with like words, "Loquendo, male loqui discunt"; and that excellent learned man G. Budaeus,[24] in his Greek commentaries, sore complaineth that when he began to learn the Latin tongue, use of speaking Latin at the table and elsewhere unadvisedly did bring him to such an evil choice of words, to such a crooked framing of sentences, that no one thing did hurt or hinder him more all the days of his life afterward, both for readiness in speaking and also good judgment in writing.

In very deed, if children were brought up in such a house, or such a school, where the Latin tongue were properly and perfitly spoken, as Tiberius and Caius Gracchi were brought up in their mother Cornelia's house; surely then the daily use of speaking were the best and readiest way to learn the Latin tongue. But now commonly in the best schools in England, for words, right choice is smally regarded, true propriety wholly neglected, confusion is brought in, barbariousness is bred up so in young wits, as afterward they be not only marred for speaking, but also corrupted in judgment, as with much ado, or never at all, they be brought to the right frame again.

Yet all men covet to have their children speak Latin; and so do I very earnestly too. We both have one purpose; we agree in desire, we wish one end; but we differ somewhat in order and way, that leadeth rightly to that end. Other would have them speak at all adventures; and, so they be speaking, to speak the master careth not, the scholar knoweth not, what. This is to seem, and not to be; except it be, to be bold without shame, rash without skill, full of words without wit. I wish to have them speak so as it may well appear that the brain doth govern the tongue, and that reason leadeth forth

24 *G. Budaeus:* Guillaume Budé (1467–1540), famous French scholar and humanist.

the talk. Socrates's doctrine is true in Plato, and well marked and truly uttered by Horace in *Arte Poetica,* that, wheresoever knowledge doth accompany the wit, there best utterance doth always await upon the tongue. For good understanding must first be bred in the child, which being nourished with skill and use of writing (as I will teach more largely hereafter) is the only way to bring him to judgment and readiness in speaking; and that in far shorter time (if he follow constantly the trade of this little lesson) than he shall do by common teaching of the common schools in England.

But to go forward. As you perceive your scholar to go better and better on away, first, with understanding his lesson more quickly, with parsing more readily, with translating more speedily and perfitly than he was wont; after, give him longer lessons to translate; and withal, begin to teach him both in nouns and verbs, what is *Proprium,* and what is *Translatum;* what *Synonymum,* what *Diversum;* which be *Contraria,* and which be most notable *Phrases,* in all his lecture; as:

Proprium.[25]	Rex sepultus est magnifice.
Translatum.[26]	Cum illo principe, sepulta est et gloria, et salus reipublicae.
Synonyma.[27]	Ensis, gladius; Laudare, praedicare.
Diversa.[28]	Diligere, amare; Calere, exardescere; Inimicus, hostis
Contraria.[29]	Acerbum et luctuosum bellum. Dulcis et laeta pax.
Phrases.	Dare verba; Abjicere obedientiam.

Your scholar then must have the third paper book; in the which, after he hath done his double translation, let him write, after this sort, four of these fore-named six, diligently marked out of every lesson.

Quatuor.	Propria. Translata. Synonyma. Diversa. Contraria. Phrases.

[25] *Proprium:* literal statement.

[26] *Translatum:* figurative statement.

[27] *Synonyma:* synonyms

[28] *Diversa:* distinctions.

[29] *Contraria:* contraries or antonyms, words or phrases of opposite meanings.

Or else three, or two, if there be no more; and if there be none of these at all in some lecture, yet not omit the order, but write these:

Diversa nulla,
Contraria nulla, etc.

This diligent translating, joined with this heedful marking in the foresaid Epistles, and afterward in some plain oration of Tully, as *pro Lege Manilia, pro Archia Poeta,* or in those three *ad C. Caesarem,* shall work such a right choice of words, so straight a framing of sentences, such a true judgment, both to write skillfully and speak wittily, as wise men shall both praise and marvel at.

If your scholar do miss sometimes, in marking rightly these foresaid six things, chide not hastily; for that shall both dull his wit and discourage his diligence; but monish him gently; which shall make him both willing to amend and glad to go forward in love and hope of learning.

I have now wished twice or thrice this gentle nature to be in a schoolmaster. And that I have done so neither by chance nor without some reason, I will now declare at large, why in mine opinion love is better than fear, gentleness better than beating, to bring up a child rightly in learning.

With the common use of teaching and beating in common schools of England I will not greatly contend; which, if I did, it were but a small grammatical controversy, neither belonging to heresy nor treason, nor greatly touching God nor the prince; although in very deed, in the end, the good or ill bringing up of children doth as much serve to the good or ill service of God, our prince, and our whole country as any one thing doth beside.

I do gladly agree with all good schoolmasters in these points: to have children brought to good perfitness in learning, to all honesty in manners, to have all faults rightly amended, to have every vice severely corrected; but for the order and way that leadeth rightly to these points, we somewhat differ. For commonly many schoolmasters, some as I have seen, more as I have heard tell, be of so crooked a nature as, when they meet with a hard-witted scholar, they rather break him than bow him, rather mar him than mend him. For when the schoolmaster is angry with some other matter, then will he soonest fall to beat his scholar; and though he himself should be punished for his folly, yet must he beat some scholar for his pleasure, though there be no cause for him to do so, nor yet fault in the scholar to deserve so. These ye will say be fond schoolmasters, and few they be that be found to be such.

They be fond indeed, but surely over-many such be found everywhere. But this will I say, that even the wisest of your great beaters do as oft punish nature as they do correct faults. Yea, many times the better nature is sorer punished. For, if one by quickness of wit take his lesson readily, another by hardness of wit taketh it not so speedily, the first is always commended, the other is commonly punished: when a wise schoolmaster should rather discreetly consider the right disposition of both their natures, and not so much weigh what either of them is able to do now, as what either of them is likely to do hereafter. For this I know, not only by reading of books in my study, but also by experience of life abroad in the world, that those which be commonly the wisest, the best learned, and best men also, when they be old, were never commonly the quickest of wit when they were young. The causes why, amongst other, which be many, that move me thus to think, be these few, which I will reckon.

Quick wits commonly be apt to take, unapt to keep; soon hot, and desirous of this and that; as cold, and soon weary of the same again; more quick to enter speedily than able to pierce far; even like over-sharp tools, whose edges be very soon turned. Such wits delight themselves in easy and pleasant studies, and never pass far forward in high and hard sciences. And therefore the quickest wits commonly may prove the best poets, but not the wisest orators; ready of tongue to speak boldly, not deep of judgment, either for good counsel or wise writing. Also for manners and life quick wits commonly be, in desire, newfangled; in purpose, unconstant; light to promise anything, ready to forget everything, both benefit and injury, and thereby neither fast to friend nor fearful to foe; inquisitive of every trifle, not secret in the greatest affairs; bold with any person; busy in every matter; soothing such as be present, nipping any that is absent; of nature, also, always flattering their betters, envying their equals, despising their inferiors; and by quickness of wit, very quick and ready to like none so well as themselves.

Moreover, commonly, men very quick of wit be also very light of conditions; and thereby very ready of disposition to be carried over quickly, by any light company, to any riot and unthriftiness when they be young; and therefore seldom either honest of life or rich in living when they be old. For quick in wit and light in manners be either seldom troubled or very soon weary, in carrying a very heavy purse. Quick wits also be, in most part of all their doings, over-quick, hasty, rash, heady, and brainsick. These two last words, "heady" and "brainsick," be fit and proper words, rising naturally of the matter, and termed aptly by the condition of overmuch quickness of wit. In youth also they be ready scoffers, privy mockers, and ever over-light and merry: in age, soon testy, very waspish, and always overmiserable. And yet few of them come to any great age, by reason of their misordered life when they were young; but a great deal fewer of them come to show any great countenance, or bear any great authority abroad in the world, but either live obscurely, men know not how, or die obscurely, men mark not when. They be like trees, that show forth fair blossoms and broad leaves in springtime, but bring out small and not long lasting fruit in harvesttime; and that only such as fall and rot before they be ripe, and so never, or seldom, come to any good at all. For this ye shall find most true by experience, that amongst a number of quick wits in youth few be found in the end either very fortunate for themselves or very profitable to serve the commonwealth, but decay and vanish, men know not which way; except a very few, to whom peradventure blood and happy parentage may perchance purchase a long standing upon the stage. The which felicity, because it cometh by others' procuring, not by their own deserving, and stand by other men's feet, and not by their own, what outward brag soever is borne by them is indeed of itself, and in wise men's eyes, of no great estimation.

Some wits, moderate enough by nature, be many times marred by overmuch study and use of some sciences, namely, music, arithmetic, and geometry. These sciences, as they sharpen men's wits overmuch, so they change men's manners over-sore, if they be not moderately mingled and wisely applied to some good use of life. Mark all mathematical heads, which be only and wholly bent to those sciences, how solitary they be themselves, how unfit to live with others, and how unapt to serve in the world. This is not only known now by common experience, but uttered long before by wise men's judgment and sentence. Galen saith, "Much music marreth men's manners"; and Plato hath a notable place of the same thing in his books *de Repub.,* well marked also and excellently translated by Tully himself. Of this matter I wrote once more at large, twenty year ago, in my book of Shooting.[30] Now I thought but to touch it, to prove that overmuch quickness of wit, either given by nature or sharpened by study, doth not commonly bring forth either greatest learning, best manners, or happiest life in the end.

Contrariwise, a wit in youth that is not over-dull, heavy, knotty, and lumpish; but hard, rough, and though somewhat staffish,[31] as Tully wisheth, "otium quietum non languidum,"[32] and "negotium cum labore, non cum periculo,"[33] such a wit, I say, if it be at the first well handled by the mother, and rightly smoothed and wrought as it should, not over-thwartly and against the wood, by the schoolmaster, both for learning and whole course of living proveth always the best. In wood and stone not the softest, but hardest, be always aptest for portraiture, both fairest for pleasure and most durable for profit. Hard wits be hard to receive, but sure to keep; painful without weariness, heedful without wavering, constant without newfangleness; bearing heavy things, though not lightly, yet willingly; entering hard things, though not easily, yet deeply; and so come to that perfitness of learning in the end, that quick wits seem in hope, but do not indeed, or else very seldom, ever attain unto. Also for manners and life, hard wits commonly are hardly carried either to desire every new thing or else to marvel at every strange thing; and therefore they be careful and diligent in their own matters, not curious and busy in other men's affairs; and so they become wise themselves, and also are counted honest by others. They be grave, steadfast, silent of tongue, secret of heart; not hasty in making, but wary in considering every matter; and thereby not quick in speak-

---

30 *my book of Shooting: Toxophilus,* published in 1545.

31 *staffish:* stubborn, unmanageable.

32 *otium . . . languidum:* "calm but by no means indolent leisure."

33 *negotium . . . periculo:* "one's time taken up with hard work, but with no risk involved."

ing, but deep of judgment, whether they write or give counsel in all weighty affairs. And these be the men that become in the end both most happy for themselves, and also always best esteemed abroad in the world.

I have been longer in describing the nature, the good or ill success, of the quick and hard wits than perchance some will think this place and matter doth require. But my purpose was hereby plainly to utter what injury is offered to all learning, and to the commonwealth also, first by the fond father in choosing, but chiefly by the lewd schoolmaster in beating, and driving away the best natures from learning. A child that is still, silent, constant, and somewhat hard of wit, is either never chosen by the father to be made a scholar, or else when he cometh to the school he is smally regarded, little looked unto; he lacketh teaching, he lacketh couraging, he lacketh all things, only he never lacketh beating, nor any word that may move him to hate learning, nor any deed that may drive him from learning to any other kind of living.

And when this sad-natured and hard-witted child is beat from his book, and becometh after either student of the common law, or page in the court, or servingman, or bound prentice to a merchant or to some handicraft, he proveth, in the end, wiser, happier, and many times honester too, than many of these quick wits do by their learning.

Learning is both hindered and injured too by the ill choice of them that send young scholars to the universities; of whom must needs come all our divines, lawyers, and physicians.

These young scholars be chosen commonly, as young apples be chosen by children in a fair garden about St. James's tide.[34] A child will choose a sweeting,[35] because it is presently fair and pleasant, and refuse a runnet,[36] because it is then green, hard, and sour; when the one, if it be eaten, doth breed both worms and ill humours; the other, if it stand his time, be ordered and kept as it should, is wholesome of itself, and helpeth to the good digestion of other meats. Sweetings will receive worms, rot, and die on the tree, and never or seldom come to the gathering for good and lasting store.

For very grief of heart I will not apply the similitude; but hereby is plainly seen how learning is robbed of her best wits, first by the great beating, and after by the ill choosing of scholars to go to the universities; whereof cometh partly that lewd and spiteful proverb, sounding to the great hurt of learning and shame of learned men, that "the greatest clerks be not the wisest men."

And though I, in all this discourse, seem plainly to prefer hard and rough wits before quick and light wits, both for learning and manners; yet am I not ignorant that some quickness of wit is a singular gift of God, and so most rare amongst men; and, namely, such a wit as is quick without lightness, sharp without brittleness, desirous of good things without newfangle-

---

[34] *St. James's tide:* May 1.

[35] *sweeting:* a sweet-flavored variety of apple.

[36] *runnet:* often "rennet," one of a large class of dessert apples of French origin, good for keeping.

ness, diligent in painful things without wearisomeness, and constant in good will to do all things well; as I know was in Sir John Cheke, and is in some that yet live, in whom all these fair qualities of wit are fully met together.

But it is notable and true, that Socrates saith in Plato to his friend Crito; that that number of men is fewest which far exceed, either in good or ill, in wisdom or folly; but the mean betwixt both be the greatest number. Which he proveth true in divers other things; as in greyhounds, amongst which few are found exceeding great or exceeding little, exceeding swift or exceeding slow. And therefore I speaking of quick and hard wits, I meant the common number of quick and hard wits; amongst the which, for the most part, the hard wit proveth many times the better learned, wiser, and honester man. And therefore do I the more lament that such wits commonly be either kept from learning by fond fathers, or beat from learning by lewd schoolmasters.

And speaking thus much of the wits of children for learning, the opportunity of the place and goodness of the matter might require to have here declared the most special notes of a good wit for learning in a child; after the manner and custom of a good horseman, who is skillful to know, and able to tell others, how by certain sure signs a man may choose a colt that is like to prove another day excellent for the saddle. And it is pity that commonly more care is had, yea, and that amongst very wise men, to find out rather a cunning man for their horse than a cunning man for their children. They say nay in word, but they do so in deed; for to the one they will gladly give a stipend of two hundred crowns by year, and loath to offer to the other two hundred shillings. God that sitteth in heaven laugheth their choice to scorn, and rewardeth their liberality as it should; for he suffereth them to have tame and well-ordered horse, but wild and unfortunate children; and therefore in the end they find more pleasure in their horse than comfort in their children.

But concerning the true notes of the best wits for learning in a child, I will report not mine own opinion but the very judgment of him that was counted the best teacher and wisest man that learning maketh mention of; and that is Socrates in Plato, who expresseth orderly these seven plain notes,[37] to choose a good wit in a child for learning.

1. Εὐφυής.
2. Μνήμων.
3. Φιλομαθής.
4. Φιλόπονος.
5. Φιλήκοος.
6. Ζητητικός.
7. Φιλέπαινος.

[37] *these seven plain notes:* These requirements were suggested by a passage in Plato's *Republic,* Book VII.

And because I write English, and to Englishmen, I will plainly declare in English both what these words of Plato mean, and how aptly they be linked, and how orderly they follow one another.

1. Εὐφυής.

Is he that is apt by goodness of wit, and appliable by readiness of will, to learning, having all other qualities of the mind and parts of the body that must another day serve learning; not troubled, mangled, and halved, but sound, whole, full, and able to do their office; as, a tongue not stammering, or over-hardly drawing forth words, but plain and ready to deliver the meaning of the mind; a voice not soft, weak, piping, womanish, but audible, strong, and manlike; a countenance not wearish[38] and crabbed, but fair and comely; a personage not wretched and deformed, but tall and goodly; for surely a comely countenance with a goodly stature giveth credit to learning, and authority to the person; otherwise, commonly, either open contempt or privy disfavor doth hurt or hinder both person and learning. And even as a fair stone requireth to be set in the finest gold, with the best workmanship, or else it leeseth much of the grace and price; even so excellence in learning, and namely divinity, joined with a comely personage, is a marvelous jewel in the world. And how can a comely body be better employed than to serve the fairest exercise of God's greatest gift? And that is learning. But commonly the fairest bodies are bestowed on the foulest purposes. I would it were not so; and with examples herein I will not meddle; yet I wish that those should both mind it and meddle with it, which have most occasion to look to it, as good and wise fathers should do; and greatest authority to amend it, as good and wise magistrates ought to do. And yet I will not let openly to lament the unfortunate case of learning herein.

For if a father have four sons, three fair and well formed both mind and body, the fourth wretched, lame, and deformed, his choice shall be to put the worst to learning, as one good enough to become a scholar. I have spent the most part of my life in the university, and therefore I can bear good witness that many fathers commonly do thus; whereof I have heard many wise, learned, and as good men as ever I knew make great and oft complaint. A good horseman will choose no such colt, neither for his own nor yet for his master's saddle. And thus much of the first note.

* * *

[At this point Ascham takes up the rest of the "seven plain notes." The child should be good of memory, given to love learning, should have a desire to work and a will to take pains, should be glad to hear and learn of another, be bold to ask any question, and should love to be praised by his father or master.]

---

[38] *wearish:* sickly-looking.

Yet some men will say that children, of nature, love pastime, and mislike learning; because, in their kind, the one is easy and pleasant, the other hard and wearisome. Which is an opinion not so true as some men ween. For the matter lieth not so much in the disposition of them that be young, as in the order and manner of bringing up by them that be old; nor yet in the difference of learning and pastime. For beat a child if he dance not well, and cherish him though he learn not well, you shall have him unwilling to go to dance, and glad to go to his book; knock him always when he draweth his shaft ill, and favor him again though he fault at his book, you shall have him very loath to be in the field, and very willing to be in the school. Yea, I say more, and not of myself, but by the judgment of those from whom few wise men will gladly dissent; that if ever the nature of man be given at any time more than other to receive goodness, it is in innocency of young years, before that experience of evil have taken root in him. For the pure clean wit of a sweet young babe is, like the newest wax, most able to receive the best and fairest printing; and, like a new bright silver dish never occupied, to receive, and keep clean, any good thing that is put into it.

And thus, will in children, wisely wrought withal, may easily be won to be very well willing to learn. And wit in children, by nature, namely memory, the only key and keeper of all learning, is readiest to receive and surest to keep any manner of thing that is learned in youth. This, lewd and learned, by common experience, know to be most true. For we remember nothing so well when we be old as those things which we learned when we were young. And this is not strange, but common in all nature's works. Every man sees (as I said before) new wax is best for printing, new clay fittest for working, new-shorn wool aptest for soon and surest dyeing, new-fresh flesh for good and durable salting. And this similitude is not rude, nor borrowed of the larder-house, but out of his schoolhouse of whom the wisest of England need not be ashamed to learn. Young grafts grow not only soonest but also fairest, and bring always forth the best and sweetest fruit; young whelps learn easily to carry; young popinjays learn quickly to speak. And so, to be short, if in all other things, though they lack reason, sense, and life, the similitude of youth is fittest to all goodness, surely nature in mankind is most beneficial and effectual in this behalf.

Therefore, if to the goodness of nature be joined the wisdom of the teacher, in leading young wits into a right and plain way of learning, surely children kept up in God's fear and governed by his grace may most easily be brought well to serve God and their country, both by virtue and wisdom.

But if will and wit, by farther age, be once allured from innocency, delighted in vain sights, filled with foul talk, crooked with willfulness, hardened with stubbornness, and let loose to disobedience, surely it is hard with gentleness, but unpossible with severe cruelty, to call them back to good frame again. For where the one perchance may bend it, the other shall surely break it; and so, instead of some hope, leave an assured desperation, and shameless contempt of all goodness; the farthest point in all mischief, as Xenophon doth most truly and most wittily mark.

Therefore, to love or to hate, to like or contemn, to ply this way or that way to good or to bad, ye shall have as ye use a child in his youth.

And one example, whether love or fear doth work more in a child for virtue and learning, I will gladly report; which may be heard with some pleasure, and followed with more profit.

Before I went into Germany, I came to Broadgate in Leicestershire, to take my leave of that noble lady, Jane Grey,[39] to whom I was exceeding much beholding. Her parents, the duke and duchess, with all the household, gentlemen and gentlewomen, were hunting in the park. I found her in her chamber, reading *Phaedon Platonis* in Greek, and that with as much delight as some gentleman would read a merry tale in Boccace.[40] After salutation and duty done, with some other talk, I asked her why she would leese such pastime in the park. Smiling, she answered me, "I wiss, all their sport in the park is but a shadow to that pleasure that I find in Plato. Alas! good folk, they never felt what true pleasure meant." "And how came you, madam," quoth I, "to this deep knowledge of pleasure, and what did chiefly allure you unto it, seeing not many women, but very few men, have attained thereunto?" "I will tell you," quoth she, "and tell you a truth, which perchance ye will marvel at. One of the greatest benefits that ever God gave me is that he sent me so sharp and severe parents, and so gentle a schoolmaster. For when I am in presence either of father or mother, whether I speak, keep silence, sit, stand, or go, eat, drink, be merry, or sad, be sewing, playing, dancing, or doing any thing else, I must do it, as it were, in such weight, measure, and number, even so perfectly, as God made the world; or else I am so sharply taunted, so cruelly threatened, yea presently sometimes with pinches, nips, and bobs, and other ways, which I will not name for the honor I bear them, so without measure misordered, that I think myself in hell, till time come that I must go to Mr. Elmer; [41] who teacheth me so gently, so pleasantly, with such fair allurements to learning, that I think all the time nothing whiles I am with him. And when I am called from him I fall on weeping, because whatsoever I do else but learning is full of grief, trouble, fear, and whole misliking unto me. And thus my book hath been so much my pleasure, and bringeth daily to me more pleasure and more, that in respect of it all other pleasures, in very deed, be but trifles and troubles unto me."

---

[39] *Jane Grey* (1537–1554), cousin to Edward VI, and actually queen for a short time after his death until the claims of Mary were acknowledged. By fifteen she was accomplished in Greek, Latin, Italian, and French and was taking up the study of Hebrew. Ascham's visit here mentioned was in the summer of 1550. In a letter to his friend John Sturm, December 15, 1550, he wrote: "Inveni nobilem puellam, Dii boni! legentem Graecae Phaedonem Platonis." All contemporary records emphasize her beauty in person, mind, and character.

[40] *Boccace:* Giovanni Boccaccio (1313–1375), author of the *Decameron.*

[41] *Mr. Elmer:* John Aylmer (1521–1594), who was educated at Cambridge by the Marquis of Dorset, father of Lady Jane Grey. He became Bishop of London in 1577. He is, according to some scholars, supposed to be designated by Spenser in *The Shepheardes Calender* (July) as Morrell, "the proude and ambitious pastour."

I remember this talk gladly, both because it is so worthy of memory and because also it was the last talk that ever I had, and the last time that ever I saw that noble and worthy lady.

* * *

Learning teacheth more in one year than experience in twenty; and learning teacheth safely, when experience maketh more miserable than wise. He hazardeth sore that waxeth wise by experience. An unhappy master he is that is made cunning by many shipwrecks; a miserable merchant, that is neither rich nor wise but after some bankrouts.[42] It is costly wisdom that is bought by experience. We know by experience itself that it is a marvelous pain to find out but a short way by long wandering. And, surely, he that would prove wise by experience, he may be witty indeed, but even like a swift runner, that runneth fast out of his way, and upon the night, he knoweth not whither. And verily they be fewest of number that be happy or wise by unlearned experience. And look well upon the former life of those few, whether your example be old or young, who without learning have gathered by long experience a little wisdom and some happiness; and when you do consider what mischief they have committed, what dangers they have escaped (and yet twenty for one do perish in the adventure), then think well with yourself whether you would that your own son should come to wisdom and happiness by the way of such experience or no.

It is a notable tale, that old Sir Roger Chamloe, sometime chief justice, would tell of himself. When he was ancient in inn of court,[43] certain young gentlemen were brought before him to be corrected for certain misorders: and one of the lustiest said, "Sir, we be young gentlemen; and wise men before us have proved all fashions, and yet those have done full well." This they said because it was well known that Sir Roger had been a good fellow in his youth. But he answered them very wisely: "Indeed," saith he, "in youth I was as you are now; and I had twelve fellows like unto myself, but not one of them came to a good end. And therefore follow not my example in youth, but follow my counsel in age, if ever ye think to come to this place, or to these years that I am come unto; lest ye meet either with poverty or Tyburn [44] in the way."

This experience of all fashions in youth, being in proof always dangerous, in issue seldom lucky, is a way indeed to overmuch knowledge, yet used commonly of such men which be either carried by some curious affection of mind, or driven by some hard necessity of life, to hazard the trial of over-many perilous adventures.

Erasmus,[45] the honor of learning of all our time, said wisely that experi-

---

[42] *bankrouts:* bankruptcies.

[43] *ancient in inn of court:* one of the senior barristers in the Inns of Court.

[44] *Tyburn:* the principal place of execution of criminals until 1783. The gallows was often called "Tyburn tree."

[45] *Erasmus:* Desiderius Erasmus (1466–1536), great Dutch humanist, often resident in England and friend of the leading English scholars.

ence is the common schoolhouse of fools and ill men. Men of wit and honesty be otherwise instructed. For there be, that keep them out of fire, and yet was never burned; that be ware of water, and yet was never nigh drowning; that hate harlots, and was never at the stews; that abhor falsehood, and never brake promise themselves.

But will ye see a fit similitude of this adventured experience? A father that doth let loose his son to all experiences is most like a fond hunter that letteth slip a whelp to the whole herd; twenty to one he shall fall upon a rascal, and let go the fair game. Men that hunt so be either ignorant persons, privy stealers, or nightwalkers.

Learning therefore, ye wise fathers, and good bringing up, and not blind and dangerous experience, is the next and readiest way that must lead your children, first to wisdom, and then to worthiness, if ever ye purpose they shall come there.

And to say all in short, though I lack authority to give counsel, yet I lack not goodwill to wish, that the youth in England, especially gentlemen, and namely nobility, should be by good bringing up so grounded in judgment of learning, so founded in love of honesty, as, when they should be called forth to the execution of great affairs, in service of their prince and country, they might be able to use and to order all experiences, were they good, were they bad, and that according to the square, rule, and line of wisdom, learning, and virtue.

And I do not mean, by all this my talk, that young gentlemen should always be poring on a book, and by using good studies should leese honest pleasure and haunt no good pastime; I mean nothing less. For it is well known that I both like and love, and have always, and do yet still use, all exercises and pastimes that be fit for my nature and ability; and beside natural disposition, in judgment also I was never either Stoic in doctrine or Anabaptist in religion, to mislike a merry, pleasant, and playful nature, if no outrage be committed against law, measure, and good order.

Therefore I would wish that beside some good time fitly appointed and constantly kept, to increase by reading the knowledge of the tongues and learning, young gentlemen should use and delight in all courtly exercises and gentlemanlike pastimes. And good cause why; for the selfsame noble city of Athens, justly commended of me before, did wisely, and upon great consideration, appoint the Muses, Apollo, and Pallas, to be patrons of learning to their youth. For the Muses, besides learning, were also ladies of dancing, mirth, and minstrelsy; Apollo was god of shooting, and author of cunning playing upon instruments; Pallas also was lady mistress in wars. Whereby was nothing else meant but that learning should be always mingled with honest mirth and comely exercises; and that war also should be governed by learning and moderated by wisdom; as did well appear in those captains of Athens named by me before, and also in Scipio and Caesar, the two diamonds of Rome. And Pallas was no more feared in wearing *aegida*[46] than she was praised for choosing *oliva;*[47] whereby shineth the glory of learning, which thus was governor and mistress in the noble city of Athens, both of war and peace.

Therefore to ride comely, to run fair at the tilt or ring; to play at all weapons, to shoot fair in bow, or surely in gun; to vault lustily, to run, to leap, to wrestle, to swim; to dance comely, to sing, and play of instruments cunningly; to hawk, to hunt; to play at tennis, and all pastimes generally, which be joined with labor, used in open place, and on the daylight, containing either some fit exercise for war, or some pleasant pastime for peace, be not only comely and decent, but also very necessary for a courtly gentleman to use.

But of all kind of pastimes fit for a gentleman, I will, God willing, in fitter place more at large declare fully, in my book of the cockpit;[48] which I do write to satisfy some, I trust with some reason, that be more curious in marking other men's doings than careful in mending their own faults. And some also will needs busy themselves in marveling, and adding thereunto unfriendly talk, why I, a man of good years, and of no ill place, I thank God and my prince, do make choice to spend such time in writing of trifles, as the School of Shooting, the Cockpit, and this book of the First Principles of Grammar, rather than to take some weighty matter in hand, either of religion or civil discipline.

Wise men, I know, will well allow of my choice herein; and as for such who have not wit of themselves but must learn of others to judge right of men's doings, let them read that wise poet Horace in his *Arte Poetica,* who willeth wise men to beware of high and lofty titles. For great ships require costly tackling, and also afterward dangerous government: small boats be neither very chargeable in making, nor very oft in great jeopardy; and yet they carry many times as good and costly ware as greater vessels do. A mean argument may easily bear the light burden of a small fault, and have always at hand a ready excuse for ill handling; and some praise it is, if it so chance to be better indeed than a man dare venture to seem. A high title doth charge a man with the heavy burden of too great a promise; and therefore saith Horace, very wittily, that that poet was a very fool that began his book with a goodly verse indeed but overproud a promise:

Fortunam Priami cantabo, et nobile bellum.[49]

And after as wisely:

Quanto rectius hic, qui nil molitur inepte![50] etc.;

---

[46] *aegida:* the shield of Jupiter.

[47] *oliva:* the olive branch.

[48] *my book of the cockpit:* If Ascham ever wrote such a book, it has not survived.

[49] *Fortunam . . . bellum:* "Of Priam's fate and famous war I'll sing," *Ars poetica,* 137.

[50] *Quanto . . . inepte:* "How much better he who makes no foolish effort," *Ars poetica,* 140.

meaning Homer; who, within the compass of a small argument of one harlot and of one good wife, did utter so much learning in all kind of sciences as, by the judgment of Quintilian,[51] he deserveth so high a praise, that no man yet deserved to sit in the second degree beneath him. And thus much out of my way, concerning my purpose in spending pen and paper and time upon trifles; and namely, to answer some that have neither wit nor learning to do anything themselves, neither will nor honesty to say well of other.

To join learning with comely exercises, Conto Baldesar Castiglione, in his book *Cortegiano,*[52] doth trimly teach; which book advisedly read and diligently followed but one year at home in England would do a young gentleman more good, I wiss, than three years' travel abroad spent in Italy. And I marvel this book is no more read in the court than it is, seeing it is so well translated into English by a worthy gentleman, Sir Thomas Hoby,[53] who was many ways furnished with learning, and very expert in knowledge of divers tongues.

And beside good precepts in books, in all kind of tongues, this court also never lacked many fair examples for young gentlemen to follow; and surely one example is more valuable, both to good and ill, than twenty precepts written in books; and so Plato, not in one or two, but divers places, doth plainly teach.

If King Edward[54] had lived a little longer, his only example had bred such a race of worthy learned gentlemen as this realm never yet did afford.

And in the second degree two noble primroses of nobility, the young Duke of Suffolk and Lord Henry Matrevers, were two such examples to the court for learning as our time may rather wish than look for again. At Cambridge, also, in St. John's College, in my time, I do know that not so much the good statutes as two gentlemen of worthy memory, Sir John Cheke and Dr. Redman, by their only example of excellency in learning, of godliness in living, of diligency in studying, of counsel in exhorting, of good order in all things, did breed up so many learned men in that one college of St. John's at one time, as I believe the whole university of Louvain in many years was never able to afford.

Present examples of this present time I list[55] not to touch; yet there is one example for all the gentlemen of this court to follow, that may well satisfy them, or nothing will serve them, nor no example move them to goodness and learning.

It is your shame (I speak to you all, you young gentlemen of England) that one maid should go beyond you all in excellency of learning and knowledge of divers tongues. Point forth six of the best given gentlemen of this court, and all they together show not so much good will, spend not so

---

[51] *Quintilian:* Roman rhetorician (35–94 A.D.).

[52] *Cortegiano:* On this book and on Castiglione, see pp. 115–134.

[53] *Sir Thomas Hoby:* See pp. 113–134.

[54] *King Edward:* Edward VI (*reg.* 1547–1553).

[55] *list:* desire.

much time, bestow not so many hours daily, orderly, and constantly, for the increase of learning and knowledge, as doth the Queen's Majesty herself. Yea, I believe that beside her perfit readiness in Latin, Italian, French, and Spanish, she readeth here now at Windsor more Greek every day than some prebendary of this church doth read Latin in a whole week. And that which is most praiseworthy of all, within the walls of her privy chamber she hath obtained that excellency of learning to understand, speak, and write both wittily with head and fair with hand, as scarce one or two rare wits in both the universities have in many years reached unto. Amongst all the benefits that God hath blessed me withal, next the knowledge of Christ's true religion, I count this the greatest, that it pleased God to call me to be one poor minister in setting forward these excellent gifts of learning in this most excellent prince; whose only example if the rest of our nobility would follow, then might England be for learning and wisdom in nobility a spectacle to all the world beside. But see the mishap of men: the best examples have never such force to move to any goodness, as the bad, vain, light, and fond have to all illness.

And one example, though out of the compass of learning, yet not out of the order of good manners, was notable in this court not fully twenty-four years ago; when all the acts of Parliament, many good proclamations, divers strait commandments, sore punishment openly, special regard privately, could not do so much to take away one misorder as the example of one big one of this court did, still to keep up the same; the memory whereof doth yet remain in a common proverb of Birching-lane.[56]

Take heed, therefore, ye great ones in the court, yea though ye be the greatest of all, take heed what ye do; take heed how ye live; for as you great ones use to do, so all mean men love to do. You be indeed makers or marrers of all men's manners within the realm. For though God hath placed you to be chief in making of laws, to bear greatest authority, to command all others; yet God doth order that all your laws, all your authority, all your commandments, do not half so much with mean men as doth your example and manner of living. And for example, even in the greatest matter, if you yourselves do serve God gladly and orderly for conscience sake, not coldly and sometime for manner sake, you carry all the court with you, and the whole realm beside, earnest and orderly to do the same. If you do otherwise, you be the only authors of all misorders in religion, not only to the court, but to all England beside. Infinite shall be made cold in religion by your example, that never were hurt by reading of books.

And in meaner matters, if three or four great ones in court will needs outrage in apparel, in huge hose, in monstrous hats, in garish colors, let the prince proclaim, make laws, order, punish, command every gate in London daily to be watched, let all good men beside do everywhere what they can;

[56] *a common proverb of Birching-lane:* There is no satisfactory explanation of Ascham's allusion here, for the proverb mentioned is lost. Birchen lane was well known for its drapers' shops.

surely the misorder of apparel in mean men abroad shall never be amended, except the greatest in court will order and mend themselves first. I know some great and good ones in court were authors that honest citizens of London should watch at every gate to take misordered persons in apparel; I know that honest Londoners did so; and I saw, which I saw then, and report now with some grief, that some courtly men were offended with these good men of London; and, that which grieved me most of all, I saw the very same time, for all these good orders commanded from the court and executed in London—I saw, I say, come out of London even unto the presence of the prince a great rabble of mean and light persons in apparel, for matter against law, for making against order, for fashion, namely hose, so without all order as he thought himself most brave that durst do most in breaking order, and was most monstrous in misorder. And for all the great commandments that came out of the court, yet this bold misorder was winked at and borne withal in the court. I thought it was not well that some great ones of the court durst declare themselves offended with good men of London for doing their duty, and the good ones of the court would not show themselves offended with ill men of London for breaking good order. I found thereby a saying of Socrates to be most true, that ill men be more hasty than good men be forward to prosecute their purposes; even as Christ himself saith of the children of light and darkness.

Beside apparel, in all other things too, not so much good laws and strait commandments as the example and manner of living of great men doth carry all mean men everywhere to like, and love, and do, as they do. For if but two or three noblemen in the court would but begin to shoot, all young gentlemen, the whole court, all London, the whole realm, would straightway exercise shooting.

What praise should they win to themselves? What commodity should they bring to their country, that would thus deserve to be pointed at, "Behold, there goeth the author of good order, the guide of good men"? I could say more, and yet not overmuch. But perchance some will say I have stepped too far out of my school into the commonwealth, from teaching a young scholar to monish great and noble men; yet I trust good and wise men will think and judge of me that my mind was not so much to be busy and bold with them that be great now, as to give true advice to them that may be great hereafter; who, if they do as I wish them to do, how great soever they be now by blood and other men's means, they shall become a great deal greater hereafter by learning, virtue, and their own deserts; which is true praise, right worthiness, and very nobility indeed. Yet, if some will needs press me that I am too bold with great men, and stray too far from my matter, I will answer them with St. Paul, "Sive per contentionem, sive quocunque modo, Christus praedicetur,"[57] etc. Even so whether in place or out of place, with my matter, or beside my matter, if I

---

[57] *Sive . . . praedicetur:* "Whether in contention or in any way whatever, Christ is proclaimed," a paraphrase of St. Paul to the Philippians, 1: 18.

can hereby either provoke the good or stay the ill I shall think my writing herein well employed.

But to come down from great men and higher matters to my little children and poor schoolhouse again; I will, God willing, go forward orderly, as I purposed, to instruct children and young men both for learning and manners.

Hitherto I have showed what harm overmuch fear bringeth to children; and what hurt ill company and overmuch liberty breedeth in youth; meaning thereby, that from seven year old to seventeen love is the best allurement to learning; from seventeen to seven-and-twenty, that wise men should carefully see the steps of youth surely stayed by good order, in that most slippery time, and especially in the court, a place most dangerous for youth to live in without great grace, good regard, and diligent looking to.

Sir Richard Sackville, that worthy gentleman of worthy memory, as I said in the beginning, in the Queen's privy chamber at Windsor, after he had talked with me for the right choice of a good wit in a child for learning, and of the true difference betwixt quick and hard wits, of alluring young children by gentleness to love learning, and of the special care that was to be had to keep young men from licentious living; he was most earnest with me to have me say my mind also, what I thought concerning the fancy that many young gentlemen of England have to travel abroad, and namely to lead a long life in Italy. His request, both for his authority and good will toward me, was a sufficient commandment unto me to satisfy his pleasure with uttering plainly my opinion in that matter. "Sir," quoth I, "I take going thither, and living there, for a young gentleman that doth not go under the keep and guard of such a man as both by wisdom can and authority dare rule him, to be marvelous dangerous."

And why I said so then I will declare at large now, which I said then privately and write now openly; not because I do contemn either the knowledge of strange and divers tongues, and namely the Italian tongue, which, next the Greek and Latin tongue, I like and love above all other, or else because I do despise the learning that is gotten or the experience that is gathered in strange countries; or for any private malice that I bear to Italy; which country, and in it namely Rome, I have always specially honored; because time was when Italy and Rome have been to the great good of us that now live, the best breeders and bringers up of the worthiest men, not only for wise speaking, but also for well doing, in all civil affairs, that ever was in the world. But now that time is gone; and though the place remain, yet the old and present manners do differ as far as black and white, as virtue and vice. Virtue once made that country mistress over all the world; vice now maketh that country slave to them that before were glad to serve it. All men seeth it; they themselves confess it, namely such as be best and wisest amongst them. For sin, by lust and vanity, hath and doth breed up everywhere common contempt of God's word, private contention in many families, open factions in every city; and so, making themselves bond to vanity and vice at home, they are content to bear the yoke of serving strangers abroad. Italy now is not that Italy that it was wont to be; and therefore now not so fit a place as some do count it, for young men to fetch either wisdom or honesty from thence. For surely they will make others but bad scholars that be so ill masters to themselves. Yet, if a gentleman will needs travel into Italy, he shall do well to look on the life of the wisest traveler that ever traveled thither, set out by the wisest writer that ever spake with tongue, God's doctrine only excepted; and that is Ulysses in Homer.

Ulysses and his travel I wish our travelers to look upon, not so much to fear them with the great dangers that he many times suffered, as to instruct them with his excellent wisdom, which he always and everywhere used. Yea, even those that be learned and witty travelers, when they be disposed to praise traveling, as a great commendation, and the best scripture they have for it, they gladly recite the third verse of Homer, in his first book of the Odyssey, containing a great praise of Ulysses for the wit he gathered and wisdom he used in his traveling.

Which verse, because in mine opinion it was not made at the first more naturally in Greek by Homer, nor after turned more aptly into Latin by Horace, than it was a good while ago in Cambridge translated into English, both plainly for the sense and roundly for the verse, by one of the best scholars that ever St. John's College bred, Mr. Watson, mine old friend, sometime Bishop of Lincoln; therefore for their sake that have lust to see how our English tongue in avoiding barbarous rhyming may as well receive right quantity of syllables and true order of versifying (of which matter more at large hereafter) as either Greek or Latin, if a cunning man have it in handling; I will set forth that one verse in all three tongues, for an example to good wits that shall delight in like learned exercise.

Homerus.—πολλῶν δ' ἀνθρώπων ἴδεν ἄστεα καὶ νόον ἔγνω.

Horatius.—Qui mores hominum multorum vidit, et urbes.

Mr. Watson:

All travelers do gladly report great praise of Ulysses,
For that he knew many men's manners, and saw many cities.

And yet is not Ulysses commended so much, nor so oft in Homer, because he was πολύτροπος, this is, skillful in many men's manners and fashions; as because he was πολύμητις, that is, wise in all purposes, and ware in all places. Which wisdom and wareness will not serve neither a traveler, except Pallas be always at his elbow, that is, God's special grace from heaven, to keep him in God's fear in all his doings, in all his journey. For he shall not always, in his absence out of England, light upon a gentle Alcinous, and walk in his fair gardens full of all harmless pleasures; but he shall sometimes fall either into the hands of some cruel Cyclops, or into the lap of some wanton and dallying dame Calypso; and so suffer the danger of many a deadly den, not so full of perils to destroy the body as full of vain pleasures to poison the mind. Some Siren shall sing him a song, sweet in tune, but sounding in the end to his utter destruction. If Scylla drown him not, Charybdis may fortune to swallow him. Some Circe shall make him of a plain Englishman a right Italian. And at length to hell, or to some hellish place, is he likely to go, from whence is hard returning, although one Ulysses, and that by Pallas's aid, and good counsel of Tiresias, once escaped that horrible den of deadly darkness.

Therefore, if wise men will needs send their sons into Italy, let them do it wisely, under the keep and guard of him who, by his wisdom and honesty, by his example and authority, may be able to keep them safe and sound in the fear of God, in Christ's true religion, in good order, and honesty of living; except they will have them run headlong into over-many jeopardies, as Ulysses had done many times if Pallas had not always governed him; if he had not used to stop his ears with wax, to bind himself to the mast of his ship, to feed daily upon that sweet herb Moly, with the black root and white flower, given unto him by Mercury to avoid all the enchantments of Circe. Whereby the divine poet Homer meant covertly (as wise and godly men do judge) that love of honesty and hatred of ill which David more plainly doth call the fear of God, the only remedy against all enchantments of sin.

I know divers noble personages, and many worthy gentlemen of England, whom all the siren songs of Italy could never untwine from the mast of God's Word, nor no enchantment of vanity overturn them from the fear of God and love of honesty.

But I know as many, or more, and some sometime my dear friends, for whose sake I hate going into that country the more, who parting out of England fervent in the love of Christ's doctrine, and well furnished with the fear of God, returned out of Italy worse transformed than ever was any in Circe's court. I know divers, that went out of England men of innocent life, men of excellent learning, who returned out of Italy not only with worse manners but also with less learning; neither so willing to live orderly, nor yet so able to speak learnedly, as they were at home, before they went abroad. And why? Plato, that wise writer, and worthy traveler himself, telleth the cause why. He went into Sicilia, a country no nigher Italy by site of place than Italy that is now is like Sicilia that was then, in all corrupt manners and licentiousness of life. Plato found in Sicilia every city full of vanity, full of factions, even as Italy is now. And as Homer, like a learned poet, doth feign that Circe by pleasant enchantments did turn men into beasts, some into swine, some into asses, some into foxes, some into wolves, etc., even so Plato, like a wise philosopher, doth plainly declare that pleasure by licentious vanity, that sweet and perilous poison of all youth, doth engender, in all those that yield themselves to her, four notorious properties,

1. λήθην.
2. δυσμαθίαν.
3. ἀφροσύνην.
4. ὕβριν.

The first, forgetfulness of all good things learned before; the second, dullness to receive either learning or honesty ever after; the third, a mind embracing lightly the worse opinion, and barren of discretion to make true difference betwixt good and ill, betwixt truth and vanity; the fourth, a proud disdainfulness of other good men in all honest matters.

Homer and Plato have both one meaning, look both to one end. For if a man inglut himself with vanity, or welter in filthiness like a swine, all learning, all goodness, is soon forgotten. Then quickly shall he become a dull ass to understand either learning or honesty; and yet shall he be as subtle as a fox in breeding of mischief, in bringing in misorder, with a busy head, a discoursing tongue, and a factious heart, in every private affair, in all matters of state; with this pretty property, always glad to commend the worse party, and ever ready to defend the falser opinion. And why? For where will is given from goodness to vanity, the mind is soon carried from right judgment to any fond opinion in religion, in philosophy, or any other kind of learning. The fourth fruit of vain pleasure, by Homer and Plato's judgment, is pride in themselves, contempt of others, the very badge of all those that serve in Circe's court. The true meaning of both Homer and Plato is plainly declared in one short sentence of the holy prophet of God, Hieremy, crying out of the vain and vicious life of the Israelites: "This people," saith he, "be fools and dull-heads to all goodness, but subtle, cunning, and bold in any mischief,"[58] etc.

The true medicine against the enchantments of Circe, the vanity of licentious pleasure, the enticements of all sin, is in Homer the herb Moly, with the black root and white flower, sour at the first, but sweet in the end; which Hesiodus termeth the study of virtue, hard and irksome in the beginning, but in the end easy and pleasant. And that which is most to be marveled at, the divine poet Homer saith plainly that this medicine against sin and vanity is not found out by man, but given and taught by God. And for some one's sake that will have delight to read that sweet and godly verse, I will recite the very words of Homer, and also turn them into rude English meter:

χαλεπὸν δέ τ' ὀρύσσειν
ἀνδράσι γε θνητοῖσι θεοὶ δέ τε πάντα δύνανται.

In English thus:

No mortal man, with sweat of brow or toil of mind,
But only God, who can do all, that herb doth find.

Plato also, that divine philosopher, hath many godly medicines against the poison of vain pleasure, in many places, but specially in his epistles to Dionysius, the tyrant of Sicily. Yet against those that will needs become beasts with serving of Circe, the prophet David crieth most loud: "Nolite fieri sicut equus et mulus"; and by and by giveth the right medicine, the

[58] *This . . . mischief:* Jeremiah, 4: 22.

true herb Moly, "In camo et freno maxillas eorum constringe"; that is to say, let God's grace be the bit, let God's fear be the bridle, to stay them from running headlong into vice, and to turn them into the right way again. David, in the second psalm after, giveth the same medicine, but in these plainer words, "Diverte a malo, et fac bonum." [59]

But I am afraid that over-many of our travelers into Italy do not eschew the way to Circe's court, but go, and ride, and run, and fly thither; they make great haste to come to her; they make great suit to serve her; yea, I could point out some with my finger that never had gone out of England but only to serve Circe in Italy. Vanity and vice, and any license to ill living in England, was counted stale and rude unto them. And so, being mules and horses before they went, returned very swine and asses home again; yet everywhere very foxes with subtle and busy heads; and where they may, very wolves, with cruel malicious hearts. A marvelous monster, which for filthiness of living, for dullness to learning himself, for wiliness in dealing with others, for malice in hurting without cause, should carry at once in one body the belly of a swine, the head of an ass, the brain of a fox, the womb of a wolf. If you think we judge amiss, and write too sore against you, hear what the Italian saith of the Englishman; what the master reporteth of the scholar; who uttereth plainly what is taught by him and what is learned by you, saying, "Inglese Italianato è un diabolo incarnato"; [60] that is to say, "You remain men in shape and fashion, but become devils in life and condition."

This is not the opinion of one for some private spite, but the judgment of all in a common proverb, which riseth of that learning, and those manners, which you gather in Italy; a good schoolhouse of wholesome doctrine, and worthy masters of commendable scholars; where the master had rather defame himself for his teaching than not shame his scholar for his learning. A good nature of the master, and fair conditions of the scholars. And now choose you, you Italian Englishmen, whether you will be angry with us for calling you monsters, or with the Italians for calling you devils, or else with your own selves, that take so much pains, and go so far, to make yourselves both. If some yet do not well understand what is an Englishman Italianated, I will plainly tell him: he that by living and traveling in Italy bringeth home into England out of Italy the religion, the learning, the policy, the experience, the manners of Italy. That is to say, for religion, papistry, or worse; for learning, less commonly than they carried out with them; for policy, a factious heart, a discoursing head, a mind to meddle in all men's matters; for experience, plenty of new mischiefs never known in England before; for manners, variety of vanities, and change of filthy living.

These be the enchantments of Circe, brought out of Italy, to mar men's manners in England; much by example of ill life, but more by precepts of fond books, of late translated out of Italian into English, sold in every shop

59 *Diverte . . . bonum:* "Turn away from evil, and do good."

60 *Inglese . . . incarnato:* "An Italianate Englishman is a devil incarnate."

in London; commended by honest titles, the sooner to corrupt honest manners; dedicated over-boldly to virtuous and honorable personages, the easilier to beguile simple and innocent wits. It is pity, that those which have authority and charge to allow and disallow books to be printed be no more circumspect herein than they are. Ten sermons at Paul's Cross do not so much good for moving men to true doctrine as one of those books do harm with enticing men to ill living. Yea, I say farther, those books tend not so much to corrupt honest living as they do to subvert true religion. More papists be made by your merry books of Italy than by your earnest books of Louvain. And because our great physicians do wink at the matter, and make no count of this sore, I, though not admitted one of their fellowship, yet having been many years a prentice to God's true religion, and trust to continue a poor journeyman therein all days of my life, for the duty I owe and love I bear both to true doctrine and honest living, though I have no authority to amend the sore myself, yet I will declare my good will to discover the sore to others.

St. Paul saith [61] that sects and ill opinions be the works of the flesh and fruits of sin. This is spoken no more truly for the doctrine than sensible for the reason. And why? For ill doings breed ill thinkings; and of corrupted manners spring perverted judgments. And how? There be in man two special things: man's will, man's mind. Where will inclineth to goodness, the mind is bent to truth. Where will is carried from goodness to vanity, the mind is soon drawn from truth to false opinion. And so the readiest way to entangle the mind with false doctrine is first to entice the will to wanton living. Therefore, when the busy and open papists abroad could not by their contentious books turn men in England fast enough from truth and right judgment in doctrine, then the subtle and secret papists at home procured bawdy books to be translated out of the Italian tongue, whereby over-many young wills and wits allured to wantonness do now boldly contemn all severe books that sound to honesty and godliness.

In our forefathers' time, when papistry, as a standing pool, covered and overflowed all England, few books were read in our tongue, saving certain books of chivalry, as they said for pastime and pleasure; which, as some say, were made in monasteries by idle monks or wanton canons. As one for example, *Morte Arthur;* the whole pleasure of which book standeth in two special points, in open manslaughter and bold bawdry. In which book those be counted the noblest knights that do kill most men without any quarrel, and commit foulest adulteries by subtlest shifts: as Sir Launcelot, with the wife of King Arthur his master; Sir Tristram, with the wife of King Mark his uncle; Sir Lamerock, with the wife of King Lote, that was his own aunt. This is good stuff for wise men to laugh at, or honest men to take pleasure at; yet I know when God's Bible was banished the court and *Morte Arthur* received into the prince's chamber.

What toys the daily reading of such a book may work in the will of a

---

[61] *St. Paul saith:* in Galatians 5:19.

young gentleman, or a young maid, that liveth wealthily and idly, wise men can judge and honest men do pity. And yet ten *Morte Arthurs* do not the tenth part so much harm as one of these books made in Italy and translated in England. They open, not fond and common ways to vice, but such subtle, cunning, new, and divers shifts, to carry young wills to vanity and young wits to mischief, to teach old bawds new school points, as the simple head of an Englishman is not able to invent, nor never was heard of in England before, yea, when papistry overflowed all. Suffer these books to be read, and they shall soon displace all books of godly learning. For they, carrying the will to vanity, and marring good manners, shall easily corrupt the mind with ill opinions and false judgment in doctrine; first to think ill of all true religion, and at last to think nothing of God himself, one special point that is to be learned in Italy and Italian books. And that which is most to be lamented, and therefore more needful to be looked to, there be more of these ungracious books set out in print within these few months than have been seen in England many score year before. And because our Englishmen made Italians cannot hurt but certain persons, and in certain places, therefore these Italian books are made English, to bring mischief enough openly and boldly to all states, great and mean, young and old, everywhere.

And thus you see how will enticed to wantonness doth easily allure the mind to false opinions; and how corrupt manners in living breed false judgment in doctrine; how sin and fleshliness bring forth sects and heresies; and therefore suffer not vain books to breed vanity in men's wills, if you would have God's truth take root in men's minds.

That Italian that first invented the Italian proverb against our Englishmen Italianated meant no more their vanity in living than their lewd opinion in religion; for in calling them devils he carrieth them clean from God; and yet he carrieth them no farther than they willingly go themselves; that is, where they may freely say their minds to the open contempt of God, and all godliness, both in living and doctrine.

And how? I will express how; not by a fable of Homer, nor by the philosophy of Plato, but by a plain truth of God's word, sensibly uttered by David thus: these men, "abominabiles facti in studiis suis," think verily and sing gladly the verse before, "Dixit insipiens in corde suo, non est Deus":[62] that is to say, they giving themselves up to vanity, shaking off the motions of Grace, driving from them the fear of God, and running headlong into all sin, first lustily contemn God, then scornfully mock his word, and also spitefully hate and hurt all well-willers thereof. Then they have in more reverence the *Triumphs* of Petrarch[63] than the *Genesis* of Moses; they make more account of Tully's *Offices*[64] than St. Paul's *Epis-*

---

[62] *Dixit . . . Deus:* "The fool hath said in his heart, there is no God."

[63] *Triumphs of Petrarch:* I.e., The *Trionfi* of Petrarch (1304–1374), semi-epical or allegorical poems written in *terza rima.* The poems include "Triumphs of Love, Chastity, Death, Fame, Time, and Divinity," with elaborate prose commentaries.

[64] *Tully's Offices:* I.e., Cicero's *De officiis,* his last work, a treatise in three books on moral duties.

tles; of a tale in Boccace[65] than a story of the Bible. Then they count as fables the holy mysteries of Christian religion. They make Christ and his gospel only serve civil policy. Then neither religion cometh amiss to them; in time they be promoters of both openly; in place again mockers of both privily; as I wrote once in a rude rhyme:

Now new, now old, now both, now neither;
To serve the world's course, they care not with whether.

For where they dare, in company where they like, they boldly laugh to scorn both protestant and papist. They care for no Scripture; they make no count of general councils; they contemn the consent of the church; they pass for no doctors; they mock the pope, they rail on Luther; they allow neither side; they like none, but only themselves. The mark they shoot at, the end they look for, the heaven they desire, is only their own present pleasure and private profit; whereby they plainly declare of whose school, of what religion they be; that is, Epicures in living, and *ἄθεοι*[66] in doctrine. This last word is no more unknown now to plain Englishmen than the person was unknown sometime in England, until some Englishman took pains to fetch that devilish opinion out of Italy. These men thus Italianated abroad cannot abide our godly Italian church at home; they be not of that parish; they be not of that fellowship; they like not the preacher; they hear not his sermons; except sometimes for company they come thither to hear the Italian tongue naturally spoken, not to hear God's doctrine truly preached.

And yet these men in matters of divinity openly pretend a great knowledge, and have privately to themselves a very compendious understanding of all; which nevertheless they will utter when and where they list. And that is this: all the mysteries of Moses, the whole law and ceremonies, the psalms and prophets, Christ and his gospel, God and the devil, heaven and hell, faith, conscience, sin, death, and all, they shortly wrap up, they quickly expound with this one half verse of Horace, "Credat Judaeus Apella."[67]

Yet though in Italy they may freely be of no religion, as they are in England in very deed too; nevertheless returning home into England they must countenance the profession of the one or the other, howsoever inwardly they laugh to scorn both. And though for their private matters they can follow, fawn, and flatter noble personages contrary to them in all respects; yet commonly they ally themselves with the worst papists, to whom they be wedded, and do well agree together in three proper opinions: in open contempt of God's word, in a secret security of sin, and in a bloody

---

[65] *a tale in Boccace:* Ascham may here have in mind some stories of Boccaccio which appeared in English versions in William Painter's *Palace of Pleasure* (see pp. 144–147). The *Decameron* in any complete form in English was not published until 1620.

[66] *ἄθεοι*: atheists.

[67] *Credat Judaeus Apella:* The whole phrase from Horace (*Satires,* I, 5, 100) is "Credat Judaeus Apella, non ego," "Apella, the Jew, may believe it, not I." Jews in Rome under Augustus were regarded by the Romans as being very superstitious.

desire to have all taken away by sword or burning that be not of their faction. They that do read with indifferent judgment Pighius[68] and Machiavel,[69] two indifferent patriarchs of these two religions, do know full well that I say true.

Ye see what manners and doctrine our English men fetch out of Italy; for finding no other there, they can bring no other hither. And therefore many godly and excellent learned Englishmen, not many years ago, did make a better choice; when open cruelty drave them out of this country, to place themselves there where[70] Christ's doctrine, the fear of God, punishment of sin, and discipline of honesty were had in special regard.

I was once in Italy myself; but I thank God my abode there was but nine days; and yet I saw in that little time, in one city,[71] more liberty to sin than ever I heard tell of in our noble city of London in nine year. I saw it was there as free to sin, not only without all punishment, but also without any man's marking, as it is free in the city of London to choose without all blame whether a man lust to wear shoe or pantocle.[72] And good cause why; for being unlike in truth of religion, they must needs be unlike in honesty of living. For, blessed be Christ, in our city of London commonly the commandments of God be more diligently taught and the service of God more reverently used, and that daily in many private men's houses, than they be in Italy once a week in their common churches; where masking ceremonies to delight the eye, and vain sounds to please the ear, do quite thrust out of the churches all service of God in spirit and truth. Yea, the lord mayor of London, being but a civil officer, is commonly for his time more diligent in punishing sin, the bent enemy against God and good order, than all the bloody inquisitors in Italy be in seven year. For their care and charge is, not to punish sin, not to amend manners, not to purge doctrine, but only to watch and oversee that Christ's true religion set no sure footing where the pope hath any jurisdiction.

I learned, when I was at Venice, that there it is counted good policy, when there be four or five brethren of one family, one only to marry, and all the rest to welter with as little shame in open lechery as swine do here in the common mire. Yea, there be as fair houses of religion, as great provision, as diligent officers to keep up this misorder, as Bridewell[73] is, and all the masters there, to keep down misorder. And therefore, if the pope himself do not only grant pardons to further these wicked purposes abroad in Italy,

---

[68] *Pighius:* Albertus Pighius (1490–1542), theologian, mathematician, astronomer, one of the champions of Catholicism against Luther. His most important rejoinder was against Henry VIII in 1538.

[69] *Machiavel:* Niccolo Machiavelli (1469–1527), Florentine statesman, political philosopher, and author of *The Prince,* considered by the Elizabethans an assistant to Satan.

[70] *to place themselves there where, etc.:* Germany.

[71] *one city:* Venice. Ascham had probably visited Italy in 1551.

[72] *pantocle:* slipper, commonly called pantofle.

[73] *Bridewell:* originally a royal palace, later a hospital, but in Ascham's time a house of correction.

but also (although this present pope [74] in the beginning made some show of misliking thereof) assign both meed and merit to the maintenance of stews [75] and brothel houses at home in Rome; then let wise men think Italy a safe place for wholesome doctrine and godly manners, and a fit school for young gentlemen of England to be brought up in.

Our Italians bring home with them other faults from Italy, though not so great as this of religion, yet a great deal greater than many good men can well bear. For commonly they come home common contemners of marriage, and ready persuaders of all others to the same; not because they love virginity, nor yet because they hate pretty young virgins, but being free in Italy to go whithersoever lust will carry them, they do not like that law and honesty should be such a bar to their like liberty at home in England. And yet they be the greatest makers of love, the daily dalliers with such pleasant words, with such smiling and secret countenances, with such signs, tokens, wagers purposed to be lost before they were purposed to be made, with bargains of wearing colors, flowers, and herbs, to breed occasion of ofter meeting of him and her, and bolder talking of this and that, etc. And although I have seen some innocent of all ill, and staid in all honesty, that have used these things without all harm, without all suspicion of harm; yet these knacks were brought first into England by them that learned them before in Italy in Circe's court; and how courtly courtesies soever they be counted now, yet if the meaning and manners of some that do use them were somewhat amended, it were no great hurt neither to themselves nor to others.

Another property of this our English Italians is to be marvelous singular in all their matters; singular in knowledge, ignorant of nothing; so singular in wisdom (in their own opinion) as scarce they count the best counselor the prince hath comparable with them; common discoursers of all matters; busy searchers of most secret affairs; open flatterers of great men; privy mislikers of good men; fair speakers with smiling countenances and much courtesy openly to all men; ready backbiters, sore nippers, and spiteful reporters privily of good men. And being brought up in Italy, in some free city, as all cities be there; where a man may freely discourse against what he will, against whom he lust, against any prince, against any government, yea, against God himself and his whole religion; where he must be either Guelf or Ghibelline,[76] either French or Spanish; and always compelled to be of some party, of some faction, he shall never be compelled to be of any religion; and if he meddle not overmuch with Christ's true religion, he shall have free liberty to embrace all religions, and become if he lust, at once, without any let or punishment, Jewish, Turkish, papish, and devilish.

A young gentleman, thus bred up in this goodly school to learn the next

[74] *this present pope:* probably Pius V (1566–1572) who excommunicated Elizabeth in 1570.

[75] *stews:* originally public hot-air rooms for vapor baths which were later used for immoral purposes.

[76] *Guelf or Ghibelline:* the two leading political parties in medieval Italy.

and ready way to sin, to have a busy head, a factious heart, a talkative tongue, fed with discoursing of factions, led to contemn God and his religion, shall come home into England but very ill taught, either to be an honest man himself, a quiet subject to his prince, or willing to serve God, under the obedience of true doctrine, or within the order of honest living.

I know none will be offended with this my general writing, but only such as find themselves guilty privately therein; who shall have good leave to be offended with me, until they begin to amend themselves. I touch not them that be good, and I say too little of them that be naught. And so, though not enough for their deserving, yet sufficiently for this time, and more elsewhen, if occasion require.

And thus far have I wandered from my first purpose of teaching a child, yet not altogether out of the way, because this whole talk hath tended to the only advancement of truth in religion and honesty of living; and hath been wholly within the compass of learning and good manners, the special points belonging to the right bringing up of youth.

But to my matter: as I began plainly and simply with my young scholar, so will I not leave him, God willing, until I have brought him a perfect scholar out of the school, and placed him in the university, to become a fit student for logic and rhetoric; and so after to physic, law, or divinity, as aptness of nature, advice of friends, and God's disposition shall lead him.

Sir Thomas Hoby

1530–1566

ONE of the most famous books of the Italian Renaissance was *Il Cortegiano* of Count Baldassare Castiglione, first published in 1528. It is primarily a "courtesy book," portraying the qualities of an ideal courtier, but it also affords, through its dialogue form, witty conversation and repartee which resemble high comedy, and in the fourth book a great and serious exposition of Platonic love, which is put into the mouth of Peter Bembo. Castiglione is reflecting the personalities and atmosphere of the court of the Duke of Urbino, where he spent the years 1504–1508. The contents of the book, as briefly summarized by Gabriel Harvey in his copy of the English translation, are:

> Above all things it importeth a courtier to be graceful and lovely in countenance and behavior; fine and discreet in discourse and entertainment; skillful and expert in letters and arms; active and gallant in every courtly exercise; nimble and speedy of body and mind; resolute, industrious and valorous in action; as profound and invincible in execution as is possible; and withal ever generously bold, wittily pleasant, and full of life in all his sayings and doings. His apparel must be like himself, comely and handsome, fine and cleanly to avoid contempt but not gorgeous or stately to incur envy or suspicion of pride, vanity, self-love or other imperfection. Both inside and outside, [he] must be a fair pattern of worthy, fine and lovely virtue.

The principal speakers in the dialogue are:

1. "Lord Gaspar," Gasparo Pallavicino (1486–1511), the woman-hater.
2. "Lord Octavian," Ottaviano Fregoso (d. 1524), soldier, Doge of Genoa 1513–1515, who wonders why lovers delight in their torments.
3. Peter Bembo (1470–1547), poet, Platonist, grammarian, and historian; later a Cardinal.
4. The Duchess, Elizabetta Gonzaga (b. 1471), daughter of Frederick, Marquis of Mantua and wife of Duke Guidobaldo of Urbino.
5. Morello da Ortona, a courtier and musician.
6. "Count Lewis," Lodovico Canossa, later Bishop of Bayeux.
7. "Frederick," Federico Fregoso, later Archbishop of Salerno.
8. "Julian," Giuliano de Medici (1479–1516), youngest son of Lorenzo the Magnificent and commander-in-chief of the Papal armies.
9. Lady Emilia Pio, friend and confidante of the Duchess.
10. Lord Cesar Gonzaga, cousin of Castiglione.
11. "The Lord general," Francesco Maria della Rovere (b. 1490), nephew and successor of the Duke.

These refined and cultivated speakers carry on the game of discussion of the qualities of the ideal courtier, of his obligations to the prince he is to guide, to the public for whom he is to be an example, and to the lady whom he loves.

Thomas Hoby, the translator, was born in 1530, attended St. John's College, Cambridge, for two years, where he came under the influence of Sir John Cheke and Roger Ascham, and then set out on his travels. From 1547, when he first went abroad, to 1564, two years before his death, he kept a diary which gives a picture of the earnest traveler-student of those days. His object was a diplomatic career, and during the reign of Edward VI he served in several diplomatic missions. The accession of Mary, however, sent him abroad as an exile, and during this period he seems to have completed his translation of Castiglione. But the old-fashioned Catholic jests at the clergy in his original were too strong for the times, and he had to wait for the reign of Elizabeth to publish. The first edition appeared in 1561 with a commendatory sonnet by Sackville and a letter to the author from Sir John Cheke. "I am of this opinion," wrote the great humanist, "that our own tung shold be written cleane and pure, unmixt and unmangeled with borowing of other tunges, wherein if we take not heed by tijm, ever borowing and never payeing, she shall be fain to keep her house as bankrupt."

Hoby was a good scholar of his master: his chief dependence is on the vigorous native Saxon element in the language, not foreign and borrowed words. He is not so extreme as Cheke, however, and his prose is natural, not fantastically English. He shows the Elizabethan love for the vivid, material, concrete word as against the more elegant abstraction, and he so thoroughly Anglicizes his speakers that the reader would do well to visualize *Master Peter Bembo* rather than *Messer Pietro.*

Italy meant many things to Englishmen of the sixteenth century. It was the country of Iago and such Machiavellian villains, the country of *The Unfortunate Traveller,* of *The Duchess of Malfi* and *The Merchant of Venice.* But however dark and violent and unnatural it seemed, it was also the country of Castiglione's *Courtier,* that mirror in which such men as Hamlet and Sir Philip Sidney might see themselves.

Bembo's discourse on love in the Fourth Book is a central document in Renaissance Platonism. Its relationship to Spenser's *Hymne* (p. 351, below) is close, and no complete understanding of Elizabethan sonnets is possible without taking into account the physiological explanation of the effect of beauty on the lover, the justification of the kiss, and the whole philosophy of the passage. In its point of view, the claims of esthetic sensitiveness, love, and courtliness are reconciled with religion, morality, and that proper decency which Ascham and the others so earnestly sought.

Bibliography: *The Book of the Courtier,* with an introduction by Walter Raleigh, Tudor Translations, London, 1900; *Il Cortegiano,* ed. V. Cian, Firenze, 1929; T. F. Crane, *Italian Social Customs of the Sixteenth Century,* New Haven, 1920; F. O. Matthiessen, *Translation, An Elizabethan Art,* Harvard, 1931; Thomas Hoby, *A Booke of the Travaile and Lief of Me,* ed. E. Powell, Camden Miscellany, X, 1902; R. Roeder, *The Man of the Renaissance,* New York, 1933; C. Ruutz-Rees, "Harvey's Notes on Castiglione's *Courtier,*" *PMLA,* XXV (1910), 608–639.

THE COURTIER

(1561)

[From Book First]

BOUND am I not (quoth the Count) to teach you to have a good grace, nor anything else, saving only to show you what a perfect courtier ought to be. Neither will I take upon me to teach you this perfection, since a while ago I said that the courtier ought to have the feat of wrestling and vaulting, and such other things, the which how I should be able to teach them, not having learned them myself, I am sure ye know it all. It sufficeth that as a good soldier can speak his mind to an armorer, of what fashion, of what temper and goodness he will have his harness, and for all that cannot teach him to make it, nor to hammer or temper it, so perhaps I am able to tell you what a perfect courtier ought to be, but not to teach you how ye should do to be one. Notwithstanding, to fulfill your request in what I am able, although it be (in manner) in a proverb that *Grace is not to be learned,* I say unto you, whoso mindeth to be gracious or to have a good grace in the exercises of the body (presupposing first that he be not of nature unapt) ought to begin betimes, and to learn his principles of cunning men. The which thing how necessary a matter Philip, king of Macedonia, thought it, a man may gather in that his will was that Aristotle, so famous a philosopher, and perhaps the greatest that ever hath been in the world, should be the man that should instruct Alexander, his son, in the first principles of letters. And of men whom we know nowadays, mark how well and with what a good grace Sir Galeazzo Sanseverino, master of the horse to the French king, doth all exercises of the body; and that because, beside the natural disposition of person that is in him, he hath applied all his study to learn of cunning men, and to have continually excellent men about him, and, of every one, to choose the best of that they have skill in. For as in wrestling, in vaulting, and in learning to handle sundry kind of weapons he hath taken for his guide our Master Peter Mount, who (as you know) is the true and only master of all artificial force and sleight, so in riding, in jousting, and in every other feat, he hath always had before his eyes the most perfectest that hath been known to be in those professions.

He therefore that will be a good scholar, beside the practising of good things, must evermore set all his diligence to be like his master, and, if it were possible, change himself into him. And when he hath had some entry, it profiteth him much to behold sundry men of that profession; and, governing himself with that good judgment that must always be his guide, go about to pick out, sometime of one and sometime of another, sundry matters. And even as the bee in the green meadows flieth always about the grass choosing out flowers, so shall our courtier steal this grace from them that to his seeming have it, and from each one that parcel that shall be most worthy praise. And not do as a friend of ours whom you all know, that thought he resembled much King Ferdinand the younger, of Aragon, and regarded not to resemble him in any other point but in the often lifting up his head, wrying therewithal a part of his mouth, the which custom the king had gotten by infirmity. And many such there are that think they do much, so they resemble a great man in somewhat and take many times the thing in him that worst becometh him.

But I, imagining with my self often times how this grace cometh, leaving apart such as have it from above, find one rule that is most general which in this part (me think) taketh place in all things belonging to a man in word or deed above all other. And that is to eschew as much as a man may, and as a sharp and dangerous rock, *Affectation* or curiosity, and, to speak a new word, to use in everything a certain *Recklessness,*[1] to cover art withal, and seem whatsoever he doth and sayeth to do it without pain, and, as it were, not minding it. And of this do I believe grace is much derived, for in rare matters and well brought to pass every man knoweth the hardness of them, so that a readiness therein maketh great wonder. And contrariwise to use force, and, as they say, to hale by the hair, giveth a great disgrace and maketh everything, how great soever it be, to be little esteemed. Therefore that may be said to be a very art that appeareth not to be art; neither ought a man to put more diligence in anything than in covering it, for in case it be open, it loseth credit clean, and maketh a man little set by. And I remember that I have read in my days that there were some most excellent orators which among other their cares enforced themselves to make every man believe that they had no sight in letters, and dissembling their cunning, made semblant their orations to be made very simply, and rather as nature and truth made them, than study and art, the which if it had been openly known would have put a doubt in the people's mind, for fear lest he beguiled them. You may see then how to show art and such bent study taketh away the grace of everything.

1 *Recklessness:* a rather unfortunate and misleading translation of the Italian *sprezzatura,* which means a natural, easy grace.

[From Book Fourth]

THEN the Lord Gaspar: "I remember," quoth he, "that these lords yesternight, reasoning of the Courtier's qualities, did allow him to be a lover; and in making rehearsal of as much as hitherto hath been spoken, a man may pick out a conclusion that the Courtier which with his worthiness and credit must incline his prince to virtue must in manner of necessity be aged, for knowledge cometh very seldom time before years, and specially in matters that be learned with experience. I cannot see, when he is well drawn in years, how it will stand well with him to be a lover, considering, as it hath been said the other night, love frameth not with old men, and the tricks that in young men be gallantness, courtesy, and preciseness so acceptable to women, in them are mere follies and fondness [1] to be laughed at, and purchase him that useth them hatred of women and mocks of others. Therefore, in case this your Aristotle, an old Courtier, were a lover and practised the feats that young lovers do, as some that we have seen in our days, I fear me he would forget to teach his prince; and peradventure boys would mock him behind his back, and women would have none other delight in him but to make him a jesting-stock."

Then said the Lord Octavian: "Since all the other qualities appointed to the Courtier are meet for him, although he be old, methink we should not then bar him from this happiness to love."

"Nay rather," quoth the Lord Gaspar, "to take this love from him is a perfection over and above, and a making him to live happily out of misery and wretchedness."

M. Peter Bembo said: "Remember you not, my Lord Gaspar, that the Lord Octavian declared the other night in his device of pastimes, although he be not skillful in love, to know yet that there be some lovers which reckon the disdains, the angers, the debates and torments which they receive of their ladies, sweet? Whereupon he required to be taught the cause of this sweetness. Therefore, in case our Courtier, though he be old, were kindled with those loves that be sweet without any bitter smack, he should feel no misery nor wretchedness at all. And being wise, as we set case [2] he is, he should not be deceived in thinking to be meet for him whatsoever were meet for young men, but in loving should perhaps love after a sort that might not only not bring him in slander, but to much praise and

[1] *fondness:* foolishness.

[2] *set case:* assume.

great happiness, without any loathsomeness at all, the which very seldom or in manner never happeneth to young men; and so should he neither lay aside the teaching of his prince, not yet commit anything that should deserve the mocking of boys."

Then spake the Duchess: "I am glad, M. Peter, that you have not been much troubled in our reasonings this night, for now we may be the bolder to give you in charge to speak, and to teach the Courtier this so happy a love, which bringeth with it neither slander nor any inconvenience; for perhaps it shall be one of the necessariest and profitablest qualities that hitherto hath been given him; therefore speak, of good fellowship, as much as you know therein."

M. Peter laughed and said: "I would be loath, madam, where I say it is lawful for old men to love, it should be an occasion for these ladies to think me old; therefore hardily [3] give ye this enterprise to another."

The Duchess answered: "You ought not to refuse to be counted old in knowledge, though ye be young in years. Therefore say on, and excuse yourself no more."

M. Peter said: "Surely, madam, if I must entreat upon this matter, I must first go ask counsel of my hermit Lavinello."

The Lady Emilia said then half in anger: "There is never a one in all the company so disobedient as you be, M. Peter, therefore should the Duchess do well to chastise you somewhat for it."

M. Peter said smiling: "For love of God, madam, be not angry with me, for I will say whatever you will have me."

"Go to, say on then," answered the Lady Emilia.

Then M. Peter after a while's silence, somewhat settling himself as though he should entreat upon a weighty matter, said thus: "My Lords, to show that old men may love not only without slander, but otherwhile more happily than young men, I must be enforced to make a little discourse to declare what love is, and wherein consisteth the happiness that lovers may have. Therefore I beseech you give the hearing with heedfulness, for I hope to make you understand that it were not unfitting for any man here to be a lover, in case he were fifteen or twenty years elder than M. Morello."

And here, after they had laughed awhile, M. Peter proceeded: "I say, therefore, that according as it is defined of the wise men of old time, love is nothing else but a certain coveting to enjoy beauty; and forsomuch as coveting longeth for nothing but for things known, it is requisite that knowledge go evermore before coveting, which of his own nature willeth the good, but of himself is blind and knoweth it not. Therefore hath nature so ordained that to every virtue of knowledge there is annexed a virtue of longing. And because in our soul there be three manner [4] ways to know, namely, by sense, reason, and understanding: of sense ariseth appetite or longing, which is common to us with brute beasts; of reason ariseth election or choice, which is proper to man; of understanding, by the which man

[3] *hardily:* by all means.

[4] *manner:* kinds of.

may be partner with angels, ariseth will. Even as therefore the sense knoweth not but sensible matters and that which may be felt, so the appetite or coveting only desireth the same; and even as the understanding is bent but to behold things that may be understood, so is that will only fed with spiritual goods. Man of nature endowed with reason, placed, as it were, in the middle between these two extremities, may, through his choice inclining to sense or reaching to understanding, come nigh to the coveting, sometime of the one, sometime of the other part. In these sorts therefore may beauty be coveted, the general name whereof may be applied to all things, either natural or artificial, that are framed in good proportion and due temper, as their nature beareth. But speaking of the beauty that we mean, which is only it that appeareth in bodies, and especially in the face of man, and moveth this fervent coveting which we call love, we will term it an influence of the heavenly bountifulness, the which for all it stretcheth over all things that be created (like the light of the sun), yet when it findeth out a face well proportioned, and framed with a certain lively agreement of several colors, and set forth with lights and shadows, and with an orderly distance and limits of lines, thereinto it distilleth itself and appeareth most well favored, and decketh out and lighteneth the subject where it shineth with a marvelous grace and glistering, like the sunbeams that strike against beautiful plate of fine gold wrought and set with precious jewels, so that it draweth unto it men's eyes with pleasure, and piercing through them imprinteth himself in the soul, and with an unwonted sweetness all to-stirreth[5] her and delighteth, and setting her on fire maketh her to covet him. When the soul then is taken with coveting to enjoy this beauty as a good thing, in case she suffer herself to be guided with the judgment of sense, she falleth into most deep errors, and judgeth the body in which beauty is discerned to be the principal cause thereof; whereupon to enjoy it she reckoneth it necessary to join as inwardly as she can with that body, which is false; and therefore whoso thinketh in possessing the body to enjoy beauty, he is far deceived, and is moved to it, not with true knowledge by the choice of reason, but with false opinion by the longing of sense. Whereupon the pleasure that followeth it is also false and of necessity full of errors. And therefore into one of the two vices run all those lovers that satisfy their unhonest lusts with the women whom they love; for either as soon as they come to the coveted end, they not only feel a fullness and loathsomeness, but also conceive a hatred against the right beloved, as though longing repented him of his offense and acknowledged the deceit wrought him by the false judgment of sense, that made him believe the ill to be good, or else they continue in the very same coveting and greediness, as though they were not indeed come to the end which they sought for. And albeit through the blind opinion that hath made them drunken (to their seeming) in that instant they feel a contentation, as the diseased otherwhile, that dream they drink of some clear spring, yet they are not satisfied, nor leave off so. And

[5] *to-stirreth:* moves violently.

because of possessing coveted goodness there arises always quietness and satisfaction in the possessor's mind, in case this were the true and right end of their coveting, when they possess it they would be at quietness and throughly satisfied, which they be not: but rather deceived through that likeness, they forthwith return again to unbridled coveting, and with the very same trouble which they felt at the first, they fall again into the raging and most burning thirst of the thing, that they hope in vain to possess perfectly. These kind of lovers therefore love most unluckily for either they never come by their covetings, which is a great unluckiness, or else if they do come by them, they find they come by their hurt and end their misery with other greater miseries, for both in the beginning and middle of this love, there is never other thing felt but afflictions, torments, griefs, pining travail, so that to be wan, vexed with continual tears and sighs, to live with a discontented mind, to be always dumb, or to lament, to covet death, in conclusion to be most unlucky are the properties which, they say, belong to lovers. The cause therefore of this wretchedness in men's minds, is principally sense, which in youthful age beareth most sway, because the lustiness of the flesh and of the blood in that season adds unto him even so much force as it withdraweth from reason. Therefore doth it easily train the soul to follow appetite or longing, for when she seeth herself drowned in the earthly prison, because she is set in the office to govern the body, she cannot of herself understand plainly at the first the truth of spiritual beholding. Wherefore to compass the understanding of things, she must go beg the beginning at the senses, and therefore she believeth them and giveth ear to them, and is contented to be led by them, especially when they have so much courage, that (in a manner) they enforce her, and because they are deceitful they fill her with errors and false opinions. Whereupon most commonly it happeneth that young men be wrapped in this sensual love, which is a very rebel against reason, and therefore they make themselves unworthy to enjoy the favors and benefits which love bestows upon his true subjects, neither in love feel they any other pleasures, than what beasts without reason do, but much more grievous afflictions. Setting case therefore this to be so, which is most true, I say that the contrary chanceth to them of a more ripe age. For in case they, when the soul is not now so much weighed down with the bodily burden, and when the natural burning assuageth and draweth to a warmth, if they be inflamed with beauty, and to it bend their coveting guided by reasonable choice, they be not deceived, and possess beauty perfectly, and therefore through the possessing of it, always goodness ensueth to them. Because beauty is good and consequently the true love of it is most good and holy, and evermore bringeth forth good fruits in the souls of them that with the bridle of reason restrain the ill disposition of sense, the which old men can much sooner do than young. It is not therefore out of reason to say that old men may also love without slander and more happily, than young men, taking notwithstanding this name old, not for the age at the pit's brink, nor when the canals of the body be so feeble, that the soul cannot through them work her feats, but when knowledge in us is in his right strength. And I will not also hide this from you: namely, that I suppose where sensual love in every age is naught, yet in young men it deserveth excuse, and perhaps in some case lawful; for although it puts them in afflictions, dangers, travails, and the unfortunateness that is said, yet are there many that to win them the goodwill of their ladies practise virtuous things, which for all they be not bent to a good end, yet are they good of themselves; and so of that much bitterness they pick out a little sweetness, and through the adversities which they sustain, in the end they acknowledge their error. As I judge therefore those young men that bridle their appetites, and love with reason, to be godly; so do I hold excused such as yield to sensual love, whereunto they be so inclined through the weakness and frailties of man—so they show therein meekness, courtesy, and prowess, and the other worthy conditions that these Lords have spoken of; and when those youthful years be gone and past, leave it off clean, keeping aloof from this sensual coveting as from the lowermost step of the stairs, by which a man may ascend to true love. But in case after they draw in years once, they reserve in their cold heart the fire of appetites, and bring stout reason in subjection to feeble sense, it cannot be said how much they are to be blamed: for like men without sense they deserve with an everlasting shame to be put in the number of unreasonable living creatures, because the thoughts and ways of sensual love be far unfitting for ripe age."

Here Bembo paused awhile, and when all things were whist [6] M. Morello, of Ortona, said: "And in case there were some old man more fresh and lusty and of a better complexion than many young men, why would you not have it lawful for him to love with the love that young men love?"

The Duchess laughed, and said: "If the love of young men be so unlucky, why would you, M. Morello, that old men should also love with this unluckiness? But in case you were old, as these men say you be, you would not thus procure the hurt of old men."

M. Morello answered: "The hurt of old men, meseemeth, M. Peter Bembo procureth, who will have them to love after a sort that I for my part understand not; and, methink, the possessing of this beauty which he praiseth so much, without the body, is a dream."

"Do you believe, M. Morello," quoth then Count Lewis, "that beauty is always so good a thing as M. Peter Bembo speaketh of?"

"Not I, in good sooth," answered M. Morello. "But I remember rather that I have seen many beautiful women of a most ill inclination, cruel and spiteful, and it seemeth that, in a manner, it happeneth always so, for beauty maketh them proud, and pride, cruel."

Count Lewis said, smiling: "To you perhaps they seem cruel, because they content you not with it that you would have. But cause M. Peter Bembo to teach you in what sort old men ought to covet beauty, and what

[6] *whist:* quiet.

to seek at their ladies' hands, and what to content themselves withal; and in not passing out of these bounds you shall see that they shall be neither proud nor cruel, and will satisfy you with what you shall require."

M. Morello seemed then somewhat out of patience, and said: "I will not know the thing that toucheth[7] me not. But cause you to be taught how the young men ought to covet this beauty that are not so fresh and lusty as old men be."

Here Sir Frederick, to pacify M. Morello and to break their talk, would not suffer Count Lewis to make answer, but interrupting him said: "Perhaps M. Morello is not altogether out of the way in saying that beauty is not always good, for the beauty of women is many times cause of infinite evils in the world—hatred, war, mortality, and destruction, whereof the razing of Troy can be a good witness; and beautiful women for the most part be either proud and cruel, as is said, or unchaste; but M. Morello would find no fault with that. There be also many wicked men that have the comeliness of a beautiful countenance, and it seemeth that nature hath so shaped them because they may be the readier to deceive, and that this amiable look were like a bait that covereth the hook."

Then M. Peter Bembo: "Believe not," quoth he, "but beauty is always good."

Here Count Lewis, because he would return again to his former purpose, interrupted him and said: "Since M. Morello passeth not to understand that which is so necessary for him, teach it me, and show me how old men may come by this happiness of love, for I will not care to be counted old, so it may profit me."

M. Peter Bembo laughed, and said: "First will I take the error out of these gentlemen's mind, and afterward will I satisfy you also." So beginning afresh: "My Lords," quoth he, "I would not that with speaking ill of beauty, which is a holy thing, any of us as profane and wicked should purchase him the wrath of God. Therefore, to give M. Morello and Sir Frederick warning, that they lose not their sight, as Stesichorus[8] did—a pain most meet for whoso dispraiseth beauty—I say that beauty cometh of God and is like a circle, the goodness whereof is the center. And therefore, as there can be no circle without a center, no more can beauty be without goodness. Whereupon doth very seldom an ill soul dwell in a beautiful body. And therefore is the outward beauty a true sign of the inward goodness, and in bodies this comeliness is imprinted, more and less, as it were, for a mark of the soul, whereby she is outwardly known; as in trees, in which the beauty of the buds giveth a testimony of the goodness of the fruit. And the very same happeneth in bodies, as it is seen that palmisters by the visage know many times the conditions and otherwhile the thoughts of men. And, which is more, in beasts also a man may discern by the face

[7] *toucheth:* concerns.

[8] *Stesichorus:* "A notable poet which lost his sight for writing against Helena and recanting had his sight restored him again."—Hoby's note.

the quality of the courage, which in the body declareth itself as much as it can. Judge you how plainly in the face of a lion, a horse, and an eagle, a man shall discern anger, fierceness, and stoutness; in lambs and doves, simpleness and very innocency; the crafty subtlety in foxes and wolves; and the like, in a manner, in all other living creatures. The foul, therefore, for the most part be also evil, and the beautiful good. Therefore it may be said that beauty is a face pleasant, merry, comely, and to be desired for goodness; and foulness a face dark, uglesome, unpleasant, and to be shunned for ill. And in case you will consider all things, you shall find that whatsoever is good and profitable hath also evermore the comeliness of beauty. Behold[9] the state of this great engine of the world, which God created for the health and preservation of everything that was made: the heaven round beset with so many heavenly lights; and in the middle the earth environed with the elements and upheld with the very weight of itself; the sun, that compassing about giveth light to the whole, and in winter season draweth to the lowermost sign, afterward by little and little climbeth again to the other part; the moon, that of him taketh her light, according as she draweth nigh or goeth farther from him; and the other five stars that diversely keep the very same course. These things among themselves have such force by the knitting together of an order so necessarily framed that, with altering them any one jot, they should all be loosed and the world would decay. They have also such beauty and comeliness that all the wits men have cannot imagine a more beautiful matter.

"Think now of the shape of man, which may be called a little world, in whom every parcel of his body is seen to be necessarily framed by art and not by hap, and then the form altogether most beautiful, so that it were a hard matter to judge whether the members (as the eyes, the nose, the mouth, the ears, the arms, the breast, and in like manner the other parts) give either more profit to the countenance and the rest of the body, or comeliness. The like may be said of all other living creatures. Behold the feathers of fowls, the leaves and boughs of trees, which be given them of nature to keep them in their being, and yet have they withal a very great sightliness. Leave nature, and come to art. What thing is so necessary in sailing vessels as the forepart, the sides, the main yards, the mast, the sails, the stern, oars, anchors, and tacklings? All these things notwithstanding are so well-favored in the eye that unto whoso beholdeth them they seem to have been found out as well for pleasure as for profit. Pillars and great beams uphold high buildings and palaces, and yet are they no less pleasureful unto the eyes of the beholders than profitable to the buildings. When men began to build, in the middle of temples and houses they reared the ridge of the roof, not to make the works to have a better show, but because the water might the more commodiously avoid on both sides; yet unto profit there was forthwith adjoined a fair sightliness, so that if, under the sky where there

---

[9] Compare Ulysses' speech on degree in Shakespeare's *Troilus and Cressida,* I, iii, 85 ff.

falleth neither hail nor rain, a man should build a temple without a reared ridge, it is to be thought that it could have neither a sightly show nor any beauty. Beside other things, therefore, it giveth a great praise to the world in saying that it is beautiful. It is praised in saying the beautiful heaven, beautiful earth, beautiful sea, beautiful rivers, beautiful woods, trees, gardens, beautiful cities, beautiful churches, houses, armies. In conclusion, this comely and holy beauty is a wondrous setting out of everything. And it may be said that good and beautiful be after a sort one self thing, especially in the bodies of men; of the beauty whereof the nighest cause, I suppose, is the beauty of the soul; the which, as a partner of the right and heavenly beauty, maketh sightly and beautiful whatever she toucheth, and most of all, if the body, where she dwelleth, be not of so vile a matter that she cannot imprint in it her property. Therefore beauty is the true monument and spoil of the victory of the soul, when she with heavenly influence beareth rule over material and gross nature, and with her light overcometh the darkness of the body. It is not, then, to be spoken that beauty maketh women proud or cruel, although it seem so to M. Morello. Neither yet ought beautiful women to bear the blame of that hatred, mortality, and destruction which the unbridled appetites of men are the cause of. I will not now deny but it is possible also to find in the world beautiful women unchaste; yet not because beauty inclineth them to unchaste living, for it rather plucketh them from it, and leadeth them into the way of virtuous conditions, through the affinity that beauty hath with goodness; but otherwhile [10] ill bringing up, the continual provocations of lovers' tokens, poverty, hope, deceits, fear, and a thousand other matters, overcome the steadfastness, yea, of beautiful and good women; and for these and like causes may also beautiful men become wicked."

Then said the Lord Cesar: "In case the Lord Gaspar's saying be true of yesternight, there is no doubt but the fair women be more chaste than the foul."

"And what was my saying?" quoth the Lord Gaspar.

The Lord Cesar answered: "If I do well bear in mind, your saying was that the women that are sued to, always refuse to satisfy him that sueth to them, but those that are not sued to, sue to others. There is no doubt but the beautiful women have always more suitors, and be more instantly laid at in love, than the foul. Therefore the beautiful always deny, and consequently be more chaste than the foul, which, not being sued to, sue unto others."

M. Peter Bembo laughed, and said: "This argument cannot be answered to."

Afterward he proceeded: "It chanceth also, oftentimes, that as the other senses, so the sight is deceived and judgeth a face beautiful which indeed is not beautiful. And because in the eyes and in the whole countenance of some woman a man beholdeth otherwhile a certain lavish wantonness

[10] *otherwhile:* occasionally.

painted, with dishonest flickerings, many, whom that manner delighteth because it promiseth them an easiness to come by the thing that they covet, call it beauty; but indeed it is a cloaked unshamefastness,[11] unworthy of so honorable and holy a name."

M. Peter Bembo held his peace, but those lords still were earnest upon him to speak somewhat more of this love and of the way to enjoy beauty aright, and at the last: "Methink," quoth he, "I have showed plainly enough that old men may love more happily than young, which was my drift; therefore it belongeth not to me to enter any farther."

Count Lewis answered: "You have better declared the unluckiness of young men than the happiness of old men, whom you have not as yet taught what way they must follow in this love of theirs; only you have said that they must suffer themselves to be guided by reason, and the opinion of many is that it is unpossible for love to stand with reason."

Bembo notwithstanding sought to make an end of reasoning, but the Duchess desired him to say on, and he began thus afresh: "Too unlucky were the nature of man, if our soul, in which this so fervent coveting may lightly arise, should be driven to nourish it with that only which is common to her with beasts, and could not turn it to the other noble part, which is proper to her. Therefore, since it is so your pleasure, I will not refuse to reason upon this noble matter. And because I know myself unworthy to talk of the most holy mysteries of Love, I beseech him to lead my thought and my tongue so that I may show this excellent Courtier how to love contrary to the wonted manner of the common ignorant sort. And even as from my childhood I have dedicated all my whole life unto him, so also now that my words may be answerable to the same intent, and to the praise of him: I say, therefore, that since the nature of man in youthful age is so much inclined to sense, it may be granted the Courtier, while he is young, to love sensually; but in case afterward also, in his riper years, he chance to be set on fire with this coveting of love, he ought to be good and circumspect, and heedful that he beguile not himself to be led willfully into the wretchedness that in young men deserveth more to be pitied than blamed and contrariwise in old men, more to be blamed than pitied. Therefore when an amiable countenance of a beautiful woman cometh in his sight, that is accompanied with noble conditions and honest behaviors, so that, as one practised in love, he wotteth well that his hue hath an agreement with hers, as soon as he is aware that his eyes snatch that image and carry it to the heart, and that the soul beginneth to behold it with pleasure, and feeleth within herself the influence that stirreth her and by little and little setteth her in heat, and that those lively spirits that twinkle out through the eyes put continually fresh nourishment to the fire, he ought in this beginning to seek a speedy remedy and to raise up reason, and with her to fence the fortress of his heart, and to shut in such wise the passages against sense and appetites that they may enter neither with force nor subtle practise. Thus, if the flame be

[11] *unshamefastness:* immodesty.

quenched, the jeopardy is also quenched. But in case it continue or increase, then must the Courtier determine, when he perceiveth he is taken, to shun throughly all filthiness of common love, and so enter into the holy way of love with the guide of reason, and first consider that the body where that beauty shineth is not the fountain from whence beauty springeth, but rather because beauty is bodiless and, as we have said, an heavenly shining beam, she loseth much of her honor when she is coupled with that vile subject and full of corruption, because the less she is partner thereof, the more perfect she is, and, clean sundered from it, is most perfect. And as a man heareth not with his mouth, nor smelleth with his ears, no more can he also in any manner wise enjoy beauty, nor satisfy the desire that she stirreth up in our minds, with feeling, but with the sense unto whom beauty is the very butt to level at, namely, the virtue of seeing. Let him lay aside, therefore, the blind judgment of the sense, and enjoy with his eyes the brightness, the comeliness, the loving sparkles, laughters, gestures, and all the other pleasant furnitures of beauty, especially with hearing the sweetness of her voice, the tunableness of her words, the melody of her singing and playing on instruments (in case the woman beloved be a musician), and so shall he with most dainty food feed the soul through the means of these two senses which have little bodily substance in them and be the ministers of reason, without entering farther toward the body with coveting unto any longing otherwise than honest. Afterward let him obey, please, and honor with all reverence his woman, and reckon her more dear to him than his own life, and prefer all her commodities and pleasures before his own, and love no less in her the beauty of the mind than of the body. Therefore let him have a care not to suffer her to run into any error, but with lessons and good exhortations seek always to frame her to modesty, to temperance, to true honesty, and so to work that there may never take place in her other than pure thoughts and far wide from all filthiness of vices. And thus in sowing of virtue in the garden of that mind, he shall also gather the fruits of most beautiful conditions, and savor them with a marvelous good relish. And this shall be the right engendering and imprinting of beauty in beauty, the which some hold opinion to be the end of love. In this manner shall our Courtier be most acceptable to his lady, and she will always show herself toward him tractable, lowly, and sweet in language, and as willing to please him as to be beloved of him; and the wills of them both shall be most honest and agreeable, and they consequently shall be most happy."

Here M. Morello: "The engendering," quoth he, "of beauty in beauty aright were the engendering of a beautiful child in a beautiful woman; and I would think it a more manifest token a great deal that she loved her lover, if she pleased him with this than with the sweetness of language that you speak of."

M. Peter Bembo laughed, and said: "You must not, M. Morello, pass your bounds. I may tell you it is not a small token that a woman loveth when she giveth unto her lover her beauty, which is so precious a matter; and by the ways that be a passage to the soul (that is to say, the sight and the hearing) sendeth the looks of her eyes, the image of her countenance, and the voice of her words, that pierce into the lover's heart and give a witness of her love."

M. Morello said: "Looks and words may be, and oftentimes are, false witnesses. Therefore whoso hath not a better pledge of love, in my judgment he is in an ill assurance. And surely I looked still that you would have made this woman of yours somewhat more courteous and free toward the Courtier than my Lord Julian hath made his; but meseemeth ye be both of the property of those judges that, to appear wise, give sentence against their own."

Bembo said: "I am well pleased to have this woman much more courteous toward my Courtier not young than the Lord Julian's is to the young; and that with good reason, because mine coveteth but honest matters, and therefore may the woman grant him them all without blame. But my Lord Julian's woman, that is not so assured of the modesty of the young man, ought to grant him the honest matters only, and deny him the dishonest. Therefore more happy is mine, that hath granted him whatsoever he requireth, than the other, that hath part granted and part denied. And because you may moreover the better understand that reasonable love is more happy than sensual, I say unto you that selfsame things in sensual ought to be denied otherwhile, and in reasonable granted; because in the one they be honest, and in the other dishonest. Therefore the woman, to please her good lover, besides the granting him merry countenances, familiar and secret talk, jesting, dallying, hand-in-hand, may also lawfully and without blame come to kissing, which in sensual love, according to the Lord Julian's rules, is not lawful. For since a kiss is a knitting together both of body and soul, it is to be feared lest the sensual lover will be more inclined to the part of the body than of the soul; but the reasonable lover wotteth well that although the mouth be a parcel [12] of the body, yet is it an issue for the words that be the interpreters of the soul, and for the inward breath, which is also called the soul; and therefore hath a delight to join his mouth with the woman's beloved with a kiss—not to stir him to any unhonest desire, but because he feeleth that that bond is the opening of an entry to the souls, which, drawn with a coveting the one of the other, pour themselves by turn the one into the other's body, and be so mingled together that each of them hath two souls, and one alone so framed of them both ruleth, in a manner, two bodies. Whereupon a kiss may be said to be rather a coupling together of the soul than of the body, because it hath such force in her that it draweth her unto it, and, as it were, separateth her from the body. For this do all chaste lovers covet a kiss as a coupling of souls together. And therefore Plato, the divine lover, saith that in kissing his soul came as far as his lips to depart out of the body. And because the separating of the soul from the matters of the sense, and the thorough coupling of her with matters of understanding, may be betokened by a kiss, Solomon saith [13] in his

[12] *parcel:* part.

[13] *Solomon saith:* Song of Solomon 1: 2.

heavenly book of ballads, 'Oh that he would kiss me with a kiss of his mouth,' to express the desire he had that his soul might be ravished through heavenly love to the beholding of heavenly beauty in such manner that, coupling herself inwardly with it, she might forsake the body."

They stood all hearkening heedfully to Bembo's reasoning, and after he had stayed a while and saw that none spake, he said: "Since you have made me to begin to show our not young Courtier this happy love, I will lead him yet somewhat farther forwards, because to stand still at this stay were somewhat perilous for him, considering, as we have oftentimes said, the soul is most inclined to the senses, and for all reason with discourse chooseth well, and knoweth that beauty not to spring of the body, and therefore setteth a bridle to the unhonest desires, yet to behold it always in that body doth oftentimes corrupt the right judgment. And where no other inconvenience ensueth upon it, one's absence from the wight beloved carrieth a great passion with it; because the influence of that beauty when it is present giveth a wondrous delight to the lover, and, setting his heart on fire, quickeneth and melteth certain virtues in a trance and congealed in the soul, the which, nourished with the heat of love, flow about and go bubbling nigh the heart, and thrust out through the eyes those spirits which be most fine vapors made of the purest and clearest part of the blood, which receive the image of beauty and deck it with a thousand sundry furnitures. Whereupon the soul taketh a delight, and with a certain wonder is aghast, and yet enjoyeth she it, and, as it were, astonied together with the pleasure, feeleth the fear and reverence that men accustomably have toward holy matters, and thinketh herself to be in paradise. The lover, therefore, that considereth only the beauty in the body, loseth this treasure and happiness as soon as the woman beloved with her departure leaveth the eyes without their brightness, and consequently the soul as a widow without her joy. For since beauty is far off, that influence of love setteth not the heart on fire, as it did in presence. Whereupon the pores be dried up and withered, and yet doth the remembrance of beauty somewhat stir those virtues of the soul in such wise that they seek to scatter abroad the spirits, and they, finding the ways closed up, have no issue, and still they seek to get out, and so with those shootings enclosed prick the soul and torment her bitterly, as young children when in their tender gums they begin to breed teeth. And hence come the tears, sighs, vexations, and torments of lovers; because the soul is always in affliction and travail and, in a manner, waxeth wood,[14] until the beloved beauty cometh before her once again, and then she is immediately pacified and taketh breath, and, throughly bent to it, is nourished with most dainty food, and by her will would never depart from so sweet a sight. To avoid, therefore, the torment of this absence, and to enjoy beauty without passion, the Courtier by the help of reason must full and wholly call back again the coveting of the body to beauty alone, and, in what he can, behold it in itself simple and pure, and frame it within his imagination sundered from all

[14] *wood:* mad.

matter, and so make it friendly and loving to his soul, and there enjoy it, and have it with him day and night, in every time and place, without mistrust ever to lose it; keeping always fast in mind that the body is a most diverse thing from beauty, and not only not increaseth but diminisheth the perfection of it. In this wise shall our not young Courtier be out of all bitterness and wretchedness that young men feel, in a manner continually, as jealousies, suspicions, disdains, angers, desperations, and certain rages full of madness, whereby many times they be led into so great error that some do not only beat the women whom they love, but rid themselves out of their life. He shall do no wrong to the husband, father, brethren, or kinsfolk of the woman beloved. He shall not bring her in slander. He shall not be in case with much ado otherwhile to refrain his eyes and tongue from discovering his desires to others. He shall not take thought at departure or in absence, because he shall evermore carry his precious treasure about with him shut fast within his heart. And besides, through the virtue of imagination, he shall fashion within himself that beauty much more fair than it is indeed. But among these commodities the lover shall find another yet far greater, in case he will take this love for a stair, as it were, to climb up to another far higher than it. The which he shall bring to pass, if he will go and consider with himself what a strait bond it is to be always in the trouble to behold the beauty of one body alone. And therefore, to come out of this so narrow a room, he shall gather in his thought by little and little so many ornaments that meddling all beauties together he shall make a universal concept, and bring the multitude of them to the unity of one alone, that is generally spread over all the nature of man. And thus shall he behold no more the particular beauty of one woman, but an universal, that decketh out all bodies. Whereupon, being made dim with this greater light, he shall not pass upon the lesser, and, burning in a more excellent flame, he shall little esteem it that he set great store by at the first. This stair of love, though it be very noble and such as few arrive at it, yet is it not in this sort to be called perfect, forsomuch as where the imagination is of force to make conveyance and hath no knowledge but through those beginnings that the senses help her withal, she is not clean purged from gross darkness; and therefore, though she do consider that universal beauty in sunder and in itself alone, yet doth she not well and clearly discern it, nor without some doubtfulness, by reason of the agreement that the fancies have with the body. Wherefore such as come to this love are like young birds almost flush,[15] which for all they flutter a little their tender wings, yet dare they not stray far from the nest, nor commit themselves to the wind and open weather. When our Courtier, therefore, shall be come to this point, although he may be called a good and happy lover, in respect of them that be drowned in the misery of sensual love, yet will I not have him to set his heart at rest, but boldly proceed farther, following the highway after his guide, that leadeth him to the point of true happiness. And thus, instead of going out

[15] *flush:* fledged.

of his wit with thought, as he must do that will consider the bodily beauty, he may come into his wit to behold the beauty that is seen with the eyes of the mind, which then begin to be sharp and through-seeing, when the eyes of the body lose the flower of their sightliness.

"Therefore the soul, rid of vices, purged with the studies of true philosophy, occupied in spiritual, and exercised in matters of understanding, turning her to the beholding of her own substance, as it were raised out of a most deep sleep, openeth the eyes that all men have and few occupy,[16] and seeth in herself a shining beam of that light which is the true image of the angel-like beauty partened with her, whereof she also partneth[17] with the body a feeble shadow; therefore, waxed blind about earthly matters, is made most quick of sight about heavenly. And otherwhile when the stirring virtues of the body are withdrawn alone through earnest beholding, either fast bound through sleep, when she is not hindered by them, she feeleth a certain privy smell of the right angel-like beauty, and, ravished with the shining of that light, beginneth to be inflamed, and so greedily followeth after, that in a manner she waxeth drunken and beside herself, for coveting to couple herself with it, having found, to her weening,[18] the footsteps of God, in the beholding of whom, as in her happy end, she seeketh to settle herself. And therefore, burning in this most happy flame, she ariseth to the noblest part of her, which is the understanding, and there, no more shadowed with the dark night of earthly matters, seeth the heavenly beauty; but yet doth she not for all that enjoy it altogether perfectly, because she beholdeth it only in her particular understanding, which cannot conceive the passing great universal beauty; whereupon, not throughly satisfied with this benefit, love giveth unto the soul a greater happiness. For like as through the particular beauty of one body he guideth her to the universal beauty of all bodies, even so in the last degree of perfection through particular understanding he guideth her to the universal understanding. Thus the soul kindled in the most holy fire of heavenly love fleeth to couple herself with the nature of angels, and not only clean forsaketh sense, but hath no more need of the discourse of reason, for, being changed into an angel, she understandeth all things that may be understood; and without any veil or cloud she seeth the main sea of the pure heavenly beauty, and receiveth it into her, and enjoyeth that sovereign happiness that cannot be comprehended of the senses. Since, therefore, the beauties which we daily see with these our dim eyes in bodies subject to corruption, that nevertheless be nothing else but dreams and most thin shadows of beauty, seem unto us so well-favored and comely that oftentimes they kindle in us a most burning fire, and with such delight that we reckon no happiness may be compared to it that we feel otherwhile through the only look which the beloved countenance of a woman casteth at us; what happy wonder, what blessed abashment, may we reckon that to be that taketh the souls which come to

---

[16] *occupy:* use.

[17] *partneth:* shares.

[18] *weening:* opinion, thought.

have a sight of the heavenly beauty? What sweet flame, what sweet incense, may a man believe that to be which ariseth of the fountain of the sovereign and right beauty? Which is the origin of all other beauty, which never increaseth nor diminisheth, always beautiful, and of itself, as well on the one part as on the other, most simple, only like itself, and partner of none other, but in such wise beautiful that all other beautiful things be beautiful because they be partners of the beauty of it.

"This is the beauty unseparable from the high bounty which with her voice calleth and draweth to her all things; and not only to the endowed with understanding giveth understanding, to the reasonable reason, to the sensual sense and appetite to live, but also partaketh with plants and stones, as a print of herself, stirring, and the natural provocation of their properties. So much, therefore, is this love greater and happier than others as the cause that stirreth it is more excellent. And therefore, as common fire trieth gold and maketh it fine, so this most holy fire in souls destroyeth and consumeth whatsoever is mortal in them, and relieveth and maketh beautiful the heavenly part, which at the first by reason of the sense was dead and buried in them. This is the great fire in the which, the poets write, that Hercules was burned on the top of the mountain Oeta,[19] and, through that consuming with fire, after his death was holy and immortal. This is the fiery bush of Moses; the divided tongues of fire; the inflamed chariot of Elias; which doubleth grace and happiness in their souls that be worthy to see it, when they forsake this earthly baseness and flee up into heaven. Let us, therefore, bend all our force and thoughts of soul to this most holy light, which showeth us the way which leadeth to heaven; and after it, putting off the affections we were clad withal at our coming down, let us climb up the stairs which at the lowermost step have the shadow of sensual beauty, to the high mansion place where the heavenly, amiable, and right beauty dwelleth, which lieth hid in the innermost secrets of God, lest unhallowed eyes should come to the sight of it; and there shall we find a most happy end for our desires, true rest for our travails, certain remedy for miseries, a most healthful medicine for sickness, a most sure haven in the troublesome storms of the tempestuous sea of this life.

"What tongue mortal is there then, Oh most holy love, that can sufficiently praise thy worthiness? Thou most beautiful, most good, most wise, art derived of the unity of heavenly beauty, goodness, and wisdom, and therein dost thou abide, and unto it through it, as in a circle, turnest about. Thou the most sweet bond of the world, a mean betwixt heavenly and earthly things, with a bountiful temper bendest the high virtues to the government of the lower, and turning back the minds of mortal men to their beginning, couplest them with it. Thou with agreement bringest the elements in one, and stirrest nature to bring forth that which ariseth and is born for the succession of the life. Thou bringest severed matters into one, to the unperfect

[19] *Oeta:* "A mountain between Thessalia and Macedonia where is the sepulchre of Hercules."—Hoby's note.

givest perfection, to the unlike likeness, to enmity amity, to the earth fruits, to the sea calmness, to the heaven lively light. Thou art the father of true pleasures, of grace, peace, lowliness, and goodwill, enemy to rude wildness and sluggishness—to be short, the beginning and end of all goodness. And forsomuch as thou delightest to dwell in the flower of beautiful bodies and beautiful souls, I suppose that thy abiding-place is now here among us, and from above otherwhile showest thyself a little to the eyes and minds of them that be worthy to see thee. Therefore vouchsafe, Lord, to hearken to our prayers, pour thyself into our hearts, and with the brightness of thy most holy fire lighten our darkness, and, like a trusty guide in this blind maze, show us the right way; reform the falsehood of the senses, and after long wandering in vanity give us the right and sound joy. Make us to smell those spiritual savors that relieve the virtues of the understanding, and to hear the heavenly harmony so tunable that no discord of passion take place any more in us. Make us drunken with the bottomless fountain of contentation that always doth delight and never giveth fill, and that giveth a smack of the right bliss unto whoso drinketh of the running and clear water thereof. Purge with the shining beams of thy light our eyes from misty ignorance, that they may no more set by mortal beauty, and well perceive that the things which at the first they thought themselves to see be not indeed, and those that they saw not to be in effect. Accept our souls that be offered unto thee for a sacrifice. Burn them in the lively flame that wasteth all gross filthiness, that after they be clean sundered from the body they may be coupled with an everlasting and most sweet bond to the heavenly beauty. And we, severed from ourselves, may be changed like right lovers into the beloved, and, after we be drawn from the earth, admitted to the feast of the angels, where, fed with immortal ambrosia and nectar, in the end we may die a most happy and lively death, as in times past died the fathers of old time, whose souls with most fervent zeal of beholding thou didst hale from the body and coupledst them with God."

When Bembo had hitherto spoken with such vehemency that a man would have thought him, as it were, ravished and beside himself, he stood still without once moving, holding his eyes toward heaven as astonied, when the Lady Emilia, which together with the rest gave most diligent ear to this talk, took him by the plait of his garment and plucking him a little, said: "Take heed, M. Peter, that these thoughts make not your soul also to forsake the body."

"Madam," answered M. Peter, "it should not be the first miracle that love hath wrought in me."

Then the Duchess and all the rest began afresh to be instant upon M. Bembo that he would proceed once more in his talk, and every one thought he felt in his mind, as it were, a certain sparkle of that godly love that pricked him, and they all coveted to hear farther; but M. Bembo: "My Lords," quoth he, "I have spoken what the holy fury of love hath, unsought for, indited to me; now that, it seemeth, he inspireth me no more, I wot not what to say. And I think verily that love will not have his secrets discovered any farther, nor that the Courtier should pass the degree that his pleasure is I should show him, and therefore it is not perhaps lawful to speak any more in this matter."

"Surely," quoth the Duchess, "if the not young Courtier be such a one that he can follow this way which you have showed him, of right he ought to be satisfied with so great a happiness, and not to envy the younger."

Then the Lord Cesar Gonzaga: "The way," quoth he, "that leadeth to this happiness is so steep, in my mind, that I believe it will be much ado to get to it."

The Lord Gaspar said: "I believe it be hard to get up for men, but unpossible for women."

The Lady Emilia laughed, and said: "If you fall so often to offend us, I promise you you shall be no more forgiven."

The Lord Gaspar answered: "It is no offense to you in saying that women's souls be not so purged from passions as men's be, nor accustomed in beholdings, as M. Peter hath said is necessary for them to be that will taste of the heavenly love. Therefore it is not read that ever woman hath had this grace; but many men have had it, as Plato, Socrates, Plotinus, and many other, and a number of our holy fathers, as Saint Francis, in whom a fervent spirit of love imprinted the most holy seal of the five wounds. And nothing but the virtue of love could hale up Saint Paul the Apostle to the sight of those secrets which is not lawful for man to speak of; nor show Saint Stephen the heavens open."

Here answered the Lord Julian: "In this point men shall nothing pass women, for Socrates himself doth confess that all the mysteries of love which he knew were oped unto him by a woman, which was Diotima. And the angel that with the fire of love imprinted the five wounds in Saint Francis hath also made some women worthy of the same print in our age. You must remember, moreover, that Saint Mary Magdalen had many faults forgiven her, because she loved much; and perhaps with no less grace than Saint Paul was she many times through angelic love haled up to the third heaven. And many other, as I showed you yesterday more at large, that for love of the name of Christ have not passed upon life, nor feared torments, nor any other kind of death how terrible and cruel ever it were. And they were not, as M. Peter will have his Courtier to be, aged, but soft and tender maidens, and in the age when he saith that sensual love ought to be borne withal in men."

The Lord Gaspar began to prepare himself to speak, but the Duchess: "Of this," quoth she, "let M. Peter be judge, and the matter shall stand to his verdict, whether women be not as meet for heavenly love as men. But because the plead between you may happen be too long, it shall not be amiss to defer it until tomorrow."

"Nay, tonight," quoth the Lord Cesar Gonzaga.

"And how can it be tonight?" quoth the Duchess.

The Lord Cesar answered: "Because it is day already," and showed her the light that began to enter in at the clefts of the windows. Then every man arose upon his feet with much wonder, because they had not thought that the reasonings had lasted longer than the accustomed wont, saving only that they were begun much later, and with their pleasantness had deceived so the lords' minds that they wist not of the going away of the hours. And not one of them felt any heaviness of sleep in his eyes, the which often happeneth when a man is up after his accustomed hour to go to bed. When the windows then were opened on the side of the palace that hath his prospect toward the high top of Mount Catri, they saw already risen in the east a fair morning like unto the color of roses, and all stars voided, saving only the sweet governess of the heaven, Venus, which keepeth the bounds of the night and the day, from which appeared to blow a sweet blast that, filling the air with a biting cold, began to quicken the tunable notes of the pretty birds among the hushing woods of the hills at hand. Whereupon they all, taking their leave with reverence of the Duchess, departed toward their lodgings without torch, the light of the day sufficing.

And as they were now passing out at the great chamber door, the Lord General turned him to the Duchess and said: "Madam, to take up the variance between the Lord Gaspar and the Lord Julian, we will assemble this night with the judge sooner than we did yesterday."

The Lady Emilia answered: "Upon condition that in case my Lord Gaspar will accuse women, and give them, as his wont is, some false report, he will also put us in surety to stand to trial, for I reckon him a wavering starter."

John Foxe

1517–1587

JOHN FOXE, the great martyrologist of the English church, was born in Lincolnshire in 1517 and educated at Brasenose College, Oxford. He was a fellow of Magdalen from 1538 to 1545, finally resigning because his extreme Protestant opinions conflicted with the rules of the college. He became a tutor in the family of the Duke of Norfolk, began publishing theological tracts, and in 1550 was ordained deacon by Bishop Ridley, whose martyrdom he later described in a passage given below. From 1554 to 1559 he was an exile on the continent; he published at Strasbourg in 1554 a first draft, in Latin, of what was to become his great history of the martyrs. A considerably enlarged version appeared at Basel in 1559. Returning to England in that year, Foxe prepared a still longer version in his mother tongue; it appeared in 1563 under the title *Actes and Monuments of These Latter and Perilous Dayes.* Seven years later he issued a still further enlarged version, in two volumes, containing 2300 double-column folio pages.

Foxe was moved to undertake his gigantic task by the profound conviction, shared by many of his contemporaries, that God had especially chosen England as the scene of the triumph of Christ over Antichrist in the struggle for the soul of man. This triumph was of course the Reformation, and it began in England, with John Wycliffe. As one of Foxe's contemporaries put it, Wycliffe begat Huss, who begat Luther, who begat truth.

Just as the prime event of the Reformation, the raising up of Wycliffe, took place in England, so did the strongest assaults of Antichrist: the persecution of Protestants in the reign of Queen Mary. Foxe's most vivid and energetic narratives are those of the martyrdoms in "these latter and perilous days" preceding the accession of Elizabeth. But as a Protestant, Foxe was also concerned to show that his church was no modern novelty. As he expanded the book, he included martyrs from early times, like St. Laurence, to show that emperors and Catholic bishops alike were tools of Antichrist, and that the significance of the English Reformation was universal in history.

Few writers have had the enormous influence of Foxe. His *Acts and Monuments* became a standard companion to the Bible. A copy was, by order of convocation, to be kept in all cathedral churches and in the houses of bishops, deans and archdeacons; in practice almost every parish church owned a copy as well. The effect of the book upon the Protestant mind could hardly be exaggerated, and it was of no little power in preparing the way for the English revolutions of the seventeenth century.

BIBLIOGRAPHY: J. F. Mozley, *John Foxe and his Book*, London, 1940; W. Haller, "John Foxe and the Puritan Revolution," in R. F. Jones *et. al., The Seventeenth Century,* Stanford, 1951, 209–224.

FROM

THE ACTS AND MONUMENTS OF THE CHURCH

("FOXE'S BOOK OF MARTYRS")

[ST. LAURENCE] [1]

NOW let us draw near to the fire of martyred Laurence, that our cold hearts may be warmed thereby. The merciless tyrant, understanding this virtuous Levite not only to be a minister of the sacraments but a distributor also of the church riches (whereof mention is made before in the words of Xistus) promised himself a double prey, by the oppression of one silly soul. First with the rake of avarice to scrape to himself the treasure of poor Christians, then with the fiery fork of tyranny so to toss and turmoil them that they should wax weary of their Christian profession; with furious face and cruel countenance the greedy wolf demanded where this Deacon Laurence had bestowed the substance of the church. Who, craving three days' respite, promised to declare where the treasure might be had. In the meantime he caused a good number of poor Christians to be congregated. So when the day of his answer was come, the prosecutor straightly charged him to stand to his promise. Then valiant Laurence, stretching out his arms over the poor, said, "These are the precious treasure of the church; these are the treasure indeed, in whom the faith of Christ reigneth, in whom Jesus Christ hath his mansion place. What more precious jewels can Christ have than those in whom he hath promised to dwell? For it is so written: 'I was hungry and ye gave me to eat; I was thirsty and ye gave me to drink; I was harborless and ye lodged me.' And again: 'Look what ye have done to the least of these, the same have ye done to me.' What greater riches can Christ our master possess than the poor people in whom he loveth to be seen?"

Oh, what tongue is able to express the fury and madness of the tyrant's heart? Now he stamped, he stared, he ramped, he fared as one out of his wit; his eyes like fire glowed, his mouth like a boar foamed, his teeth like an hellhound grinded. Now not a reasonable man but a roaring lion he might be called. "Kindle the fire!" he cried. "Of wood make no spare! Hath this villain deluded the emperor? Away with him, away with him! Whip him with scourges, jerk him with rods, buffet him with fists, brain him with clubs! Jesteth the traitor with the emperor? Pinch him with fiery

[1] *St. Laurence:* Roman deacon and martyr, died 258.

tongs, gird him with burning plates, bring out the strongest chains and the fireforks and the grated bed of iron. On the fire with it! Bind the rebel hand and foot, and when the bed is fire hot, on with him. Roast him, broil him, toss him, turn him! On pain of our high displeasure do every man his office, Oh ye tormentors!"

The word was no sooner spoken, but all was done. After many cruel handlings, this meek lamb was laid I will not say on his fiery bed of iron but on his soft bed of down. So mightily God wrought with his martyr Laurence, so miraculously God tempered his element the fire, not a bed of consuming pain, but a pallet of nourishing rest was it to Laurence. Not Laurence, but the emperor, might seem to be tormented—the one broiling in the flesh, the other burning in the heart. When this triumphant martyr had been pressed down with firepikes for a great space, in the mighty spirit of God he spake to the vanquished tyrant,

> This side is now roasted enough: turn up, Oh tyrant great,
> Assay whether roasted or raw, thou thinkest the better meat.

Oh rare and unaccustomed patience! Oh faith invincible, that not only not burnest, but by means unspeakable dost recreate, refresh, stablish, and strengthen those that are burned, afflicted, and troubled. And why so mightily comfortest thou the persecuted? Because through thee they believe in God's promises infallible. By thee this glorious martyr overcometh his torments, vanquisheth this tyrant, confoundeth his enemies, confirmeth the Christians, sleepeth in peace, reigneth in glory. The God of might and mercy grant us grace, by the life of Laurence to learn in Christ to live, and by his death to learn for Christ to die. Amen.

The Words and Behavior of the Lady Jane [Grey] upon the Scaffold

These are the words that the Lady Jane spake upon the scaffold, at the hour of her death. First, when she mounted upon the scaffold, she said to the people standing thereabout, "Good people, I am come hither to die, and by a law I am condemned to the same. The fact against the queen's highness was unlawful, and the consenting thereunto by me; but, touching the procurement and desire thereof by me, or on my behalf, I do wash my hands thereof in innocency before God and the face of you, good Christian people, this day." And therewith she wrung her hands, wherein she had her book. Then said she, "I pray you all, good Christian people, to bear me witness that I die a true Christian woman, and that I do look to be saved by no other mean, but only by the mercy of God, in the blood of his only Son Jesus Christ; and I confess that when I did know the word of God I neglected the same, loved myself and the world; and therefore this plague and punishment is happily and worthily happened unto me for my sins; and yet I thank God of his goodness that he hath thus given me a time and respite to repent.

And now, good people, while I am alive, I pray you assist me with your prayers." And then, kneeling down, she turned her to Fecknam,[2] saying, "Shall I say this psalm?" And he said, "Yea." Then said she the psalm of *Miserere mei Deus* in English, in the most devout manner, throughout to the end; and then she stood up, and gave her maiden, Mistress Ellen, her gloves and handkerchief, and her book to Master Bruges. And then she untied her gown, and the hangman pressed upon her to help her off with it; but she, desiring him to let her alone, turned towards her two gentlewomen, who helped her off therewith, and also with her frows, paste, and neckerchief, giving her a fair handkerchief to knit about her eyes.

Then the hangman kneeled down and asked her forgiveness, whom she forgave most willingly. Then he willed her to stand upon the straw; which doing, she saw the block. Then she said, "I pray you, despatch me quickly." Then she kneeled down, saying, "Will you take it off before I lay me down?" And the hangman said, "No, madam." Then tied she the kerchief about her eyes, and feeling for the block she said, "What shall I do? Where is it? Where is it?" One of the standers-by guiding her thereunto she laid her head down upon the block, and then stretched forth her body, and said, "Lord, into thy hands I commend my spirit"; and so finished her life, in the year of our Lord God 1553, the twelfth day of February.

The Behavior of Dr. Ridley and Master Latimer, at the Time of Their Death, which was the Sixteenth of October, an. 1555

Upon the north side of the town, in the ditch over against Baliol College, the place of execution was appointed; and for fear of any tumult that might arise, to let the burning of them, the Lord Williams was commanded by the queen's letters, (and the householders of the city,) to be there assistant, sufficiently appointed. And when everything was in a readiness, the prisoners were brought forth by the mayor and the bailiffs.

Master Ridley had a fair black gown furred, and faced with foins,[3] such as he was wont to wear being bishop, and a tippet of velvet furred likewise about his neck, a velvet nightcap upon his head, and a corner cap upon the same, going in a pair of slippers to the stake, and going between the mayor and an alderman, etc. After him came Master Latimer in a poor Bristol frieze frock all worn, with his buttoned cap, and a kerchief on his head all ready to the fire, a new long shroud hanging over his hose down to the feet; which at the first sight stirred men's hearts to rue upon them, beholding on the one side the honor they sometime had, and on the other, the calamity whereunto they were fallen.

---

[2] *Fecknam:* John de Feckenham, last abbot of Westminster, employed by Mary to convert obdurate heretics. He had tried in vain to convert Lady Jane to Catholicism and failed also with Latimer and Ridley (see below).

[3] *foins:* fur trimmings.

Master Doctor Ridley, as he passed towards Bocardo,[4] looking up where Master Cranmer did lie, hoping belike to have seen him at the glass window and to have spoken unto him. But then Master Cranmer was busy with Friar Soto and his fellows, disputing together, so that he could not see him through that occasion. Then Master Ridley, looking back, espied Master Latimer coming after, unto whom he said, "Oh, be ye there?" "Yea," said Master Latimer, "have after as fast as I can follow." So he following a pretty way off, at length they came both to the stake, one after the other, where first Dr. Ridley entering the place, marvelous earnestly holding up both his hands, looked towards heaven. Then shortly after espying Master Latimer, with a wondrous cheerful look, ran to him, embraced, and kissed him; and, as they that stood near reported, comforted him saying, "Be of good heart, brother, for God will either assuage the fury of the flame, or else strengthen us to abide it." With that went he to the stake, kneeled down by it, kissed it, and most effectuously prayed, and behind him Master Latimer kneeled, as earnestly calling upon God as he. After they arose, the one talked with the other a little while, till they which were appointed to see the execution removed themselves out of the sun. What they said I can learn of no man.

Then Dr. Smith,[5] of whose recantation in King Edward's time ye heard before, began his sermon to them upon this text of St. Paul in the 13 chap. of the first epistle to the Corinthians: "Si corpus meum tradam igni, charitatem autem non habeam, nihil inde utilitatis capio," that is, "If I yield my body to the fire to be burned and have not charity, I shall gain nothing thereby." Wherein he alleged that the goodness of the cause, and not the order of death, maketh the holiness of the person; which he confirmed by the examples of Judas, and of a woman in Oxford that of late hanged herself, for that they, and such like as he recited, might then be adjudged righteous, which desperately sundered their lives from their bodies, as he feared that those men that stood before him would do. But he cried still to the people to beware of them, for they were heretics, and died out of the church. And on the other side, he declared their diversities in opinions, as Lutherans, Oecolampadians,[6] Zwinglians, of which sect they were, he said, and that was the worst; but the old church of Christ and the catholic faith believed far otherwise. At which place they lifted up both their hands and eyes to heaven, as it were calling God to witness of the truth; the which countenance they made in many other places of his sermon, whereas they thought he spake amiss. He ended with a very short exhortation to them to recant, and come home again to the church, and save their lives and souls, which else were condemned. His sermon was scant in all a quarter of an hour.

---

[4] *Bocardo:* the prison in Oxford.

[5] *Dr. Smith:* Richard Smith, D.D. (1500–1563). He had recanted in 1547 but later repudiated his recantation.

[6] *Oecolampadians:* followers of Johann Oecolampadius (1482–1531), organizer of Protestantism at Basle.

Doctor Ridley said to Master Latimer, "Will you begin to answer the sermon, or shall I?" Master Latimer said: "Begin you first, I pray you." "I will," said Master Ridley.

Then the wicked sermon being ended, Dr. Ridley and Master Latimer kneeled down upon their knees towards my Lord Williams of Tame, the vice-chancellor of Oxford, and divers other commissioners appointed for that purpose, which sat upon a form thereby. Unto whom Master Ridley said: "I beseech you, my lord, even for Christ's sake, that I may speak but two or three words." And whilst my lord bent his head to the mayor and vice-chancellor, to know (as it appeared) whether he might give him leave to speak, the bailiffs and Dr. Marshall, vice-chancellor, ran hastily unto him, and with their hands stopped his mouth, and said: "Master Ridley, if you will revoke your erroneous opinions, and recant the same, you shall not only have liberty so to do, but also the benefit of a subject; that is, have your life." "Not otherwise?" said Master Ridley. "No," quoth Dr. Marshall. "Therefore if you will not so do, then there is no remedy but you must suffer for your deserts." "Well," quoth Master Ridley, "so long as the breath is in my body, I will never deny my Lord Christ, and his known truth; God's will be done in me!" And with that he rose up and said with a loud voice: "Well then, I commit our cause to almighty God, which shall indifferently judge all." To whose saying, Master Latimer added his old posy,[7] "Well! There is nothing hid but it shall be opened." And he said he could answer Smith well enough, if he might be suffered.

Incontinently they were commanded to make them ready, which they with all meekness obeyed. Master Ridley took his gown and his tippet,[8] and gave it to his brother-in-law Master Shipside, who all his time of imprisonment, although he might not be suffered to come to him, lay there at his own charges to provide him necessaries, which from time to time he sent him by the sergeant that kept him. Some other of his apparel that was little worth, he gave away; other the bailiffs took. He gave away besides divers other small things to gentlemen standing by, and divers of them pitifully weeping, as to Sir Henry Lea he gave a new groat; and to divers of my Lord Williams' gentlemen some napkins, some nutmegs, and races of ginger; his dial, and such other things as he had about him, to everyone that stood next him. Some plucked the points of his hose. Happy was he that might get any rag of him. Master Latimer gave nothing, but very quickly suffered his keeper to pull off his hose and his other array, which to look unto was very simple; and being stripped into his shroud, he seemed as comely a person to them that were there present as one should lightly see; and whereas in his clothes he appeared a withered and crooked silly old man, he now stood bolt upright, as comely a father as one might lightly behold.

Then Master Ridley, standing as yet in his truss, said to his brother: "It

---

[7] *posy:* motto.

[8] *tippet:* "This was no Popish tippet, but made only to keep his neck warm."—Foxe.

were best for me to go in my truss still." "No," quoth his brother, "it will put you to more pain; and the truss will do a poor man good." Whereunto Master Ridley said: "Be it, in the name of God"; and so unlaced himself. Then being in his shirt, he stood upon the foresaid stone, and held up his hand and said: "Oh heavenly Father, I give unto thee most hearty thanks, for that thou hast called me to be a professor of thee, even unto death. I beseech thee, Lord God, take mercy upon this realm of England, and deliver the same from all her enemies."

Then the smith took a chain of iron, and brought the same about both Dr. Ridley's and Master Latimer's middles; and as he was knocking in a staple, Dr. Ridley took the chain in his hand, and shaked the same, for it did gird in his belly, and looking aside to the smith, said: "Good fellow, knock it in hard, for the flesh will have his course." Then his brother did bring him gunpowder in a bag, and would have tied the same about his neck. Master Ridley asked what it was. His brother said, "Gunpowder." "Then," said he, "I take it to be sent of God; therefore I will receive it as sent of him. And have you any," said he, "for my brother?" meaning Master Latimer. "Yea, sir, that I have," quoth his brother. "Then give it unto him," said he, "betime; lest ye come too late." So his brother went, and carried of the same gunpowder unto Master Latimer.

In the meantime Dr. Ridley spake unto my Lord Williams, and said: "My lord, I must be a suitor unto your lordship in the behalf of divers poor men, and specially in the cause of my poor sister; I have made a supplication to the Queen's Majesty in their behalfs. I beseech your lordship for Christ's sake, to be a mean to her Grace for them. My brother here hath the supplication, and will resort to your lordship to certify you hereof. There is nothing in all the world that troubleth my conscience, I praise God, this only excepted. Whiles I was in the see of London divers poor men took leases of me, and agreed with me for the same. Now I hear say the bishop [9] that now occupieth the same room will not allow my grants unto them made, but contrary unto all law and conscience hath taken from them their livings, and will not suffer them to enjoy the same. I beseech you, my lord, be a mean for them; you shall do a good deed, and God will reward you."

Then they brought a faggot, kindled with fire, and laid the same down at Dr. Ridley's feet. To whom Master Latimer spake in this manner: "Be of good comfort, Master Ridley, and play the man. We shall this day light such a candle, by God's grace, in England, as I trust shall never be put out."

And so the fire being given unto them, when Dr. Ridley saw the fire flaming up toward him, he cried with a wonderful loud voice: "In manus tuas, Domine, commendo spiritum meum; Domine, recipe spiritum meum." And after, repeated this latter part often in English, "Lord, Lord, receive my spirit"; Master Latimer crying as vehemently on the other side,

---

[9] *the bishop:* Edmund Bonner (1500?–1569). He had preceded Ridley as bishop of London during the reign of Edward VI, and regained the see upon the accession of Mary.

"Oh Father of heaven, receive my soul!" who received the flame as it were embracing of it. After, as he had stroked his face with his hands, and as it were bathed them a little in the fire, he soon died (as it appeared) with very little pain or none. And thus much concerning the end of this old and blessed servant of God, Master Latimer, for whose laborious travails, fruitful life, and constant death the whole realm hath cause to give great thanks to almighty God.

But Master Ridley, by reason of the evil making of the fire unto him, because the wooden faggots were laid about the gosse[10] and over-high built, the fire burned first beneath, being kept down by the wood; which when he felt, he desired them for Christ's sake to let the fire come unto him. Which when his brother-in-law heard, but not well understood, intending to rid him out of his pain (for the which cause he gave attendance), as one in such sorrow not well advised what he did, heaped faggots upon him, so that he clean covered him, which made the fire more vehement beneath, that it burned clean all his nether parts, before it once touched the upper; and that made him leap up and down under the faggots, and often desire them to let the fire come unto him, saying, "I cannot burn." Which indeed appeared well; for, after his legs were consumed by reason of his struggling through the pain (whereof he had no release, but only his contentation[11] in God), he showed that side toward us clean, shirt and all untouched with flame. Yet in all this torment he forgat not to call unto God still, having in his mouth, "Lord have mercy upon me," intermingling this cry, "Let the fire come unto me, I cannot burn." In which pains he labored till one of the standers-by with his bill pulled off the faggots above, and where he saw the fire flame up, he wrested himself unto that side. And when the flame touched the gunpowder, he was seen stir no more, but burned on the other side, falling down at Master Latimer's feet. Which some said happened by reason that the chain loosed; other said that he fell over the chain by reason of the poise of his body and the weakness of the nether limbs.

Some said that before he was like to fall from the stake, he desired them to hold him to it with their bills. Howsoever it was, surely it moved hundreds to tears, in beholding the horrible sight; for I think there was none that had not clean exiled all humanity and mercy which would not have lamented to behold the fury of the fire so to rage upon their bodies. Signs there were of sorrow on every side. Some took it grievously to see their deaths, whose lives they held full dear; some pitied their persons, that thought their souls had no need thereof. His brother moved many men, seeing his miserable case, seeing (I say) him compelled to such infelicity, that he thought then to do him best service when he hastened his end. Some cried out of the luck, to see his endeavor (who most dearly loved him, and sought his release) turn to his greater vexation and increase of pain. But whoso considered their preferments in time past, the places of honor that

[10] *gosse:* gorse, used as kindling.

[11] *contentation:* satisfaction.

they sometime occupied in this commonwealth, the favor they were in with their princes, and the opinion of learning they had, could not choose but sorrow with tears to see so great dignity, honor, and estimation, so necessary members sometime accounted, so many godly virtues, the study of so many years, such excellent learning, to be put into the fire and consumed in one moment. Well! dead they are, and the reward of this world they have already. What reward remaineth for them in heaven, the day of the Lord's glory, when he cometh with his saints, shall shortly, I trust, declare.

William Painter • George Pettie

ca. 1540–1594 *ca.* 1548–1589

IN 1566 appeared the first volume of a book that must rank with Holinshed's *Chronicle* and Plutarch's *Lives* as a source for the Elizabethan drama. It was called *The Palace of Pleasure,* and was the compilation of William Painter, the Clerk of Her Majesty's Ordnance in the Tower of London. Painter came from a Kentish family, had been to Cambridge, and had served a brief term as a schoolmaster at Sevenoaks. His venture was popular, and at the end of the next year he brought out a second volume. Altogether he presented 101 tales, about a third collected from classical sources and the rest from Italian, French, and English. He offered the reader "varietie of hystories," so he said, "which as they be for diversitie of matter pleasaunt and plausible, even so for example and imitation good and commendable." They were lively enough, but to stern moralists like Ascham this spreading abroad of Italian *novelle* in English for the innocent to read was a social evil (see above, p. 106). To Painter the tales seemed profitable, "profitable I say, in that they do reveale the miseries of rapes and fleshly actions, the overthrow of noble men and princes by disordered government, the tragical ends of them that unhappely do attempt practises vicious and horrible." To the reading public and the dramatists they offered sensational stories, told with energy and economy, which fed and developed a taste for fiction rather than for morality. Shakespeare's *Romeo and Juliet* depends upon Arthur Brooke's poem *Romeus and Juliet,* which antedates Painter's story by five years; but both Painter and Brooke used as their source a French version of an Italian tale by Matteo Bandello, and Painter's story is typical of his book.

Many other compilers and translators offered volumes of tales to the public in the next two decades. Geoffrey Fenton's *Certaine Tragicall Discourses* (1567), Thomas Fortescue's *The Forest* (1571), Henry Wotton's *A Courtlie Controversie of Cupid's Cautels* (1578), Barnaby Rich's *Farewell to Militarie Profession* (1581), and George Whetstone's *An Heptameron of Civill Discourses* (1582) are all miscellanies of this sort. The only one that ranks with Painter in importance, however, is a volume by George Pettie called *A Petite Pallace of Pettie His Pleasure* (1576). As the title indicates, it is imitated from Painter, but Pettie included only twelve stories, eleven of which are on classical subjects.

George Pettie was an Oxfordshire man who attended Christ Church, Oxford, and then became a soldier. Apparently he wrote the stories without thought of publication, for the amusement of friends who were themselves "darkly figured forth" in the characters. A friend named R. B. (if we can believe the story) let a private copy slip into the hands of a printer. Pettie wrote for women: he expanded the courtship element in all his stories and he revealed his characters in long soliloquies or dialogues discussing the various questions raised by love. His style is refined and elaborate, with the rhetorical devices popularized by Lyly under the name of Euphuism (see p. 209) and saturated with proverbs, but not so heavily laden with "unnatural natural history." He is the strongest possible contrast to Painter, who usually told a melodramatic story baldly and plainly. He sacrificed plot for any opportunity to display his style, and he looked for situations in which love could be analyzed, rather than for violent catastrophes to thrill and instruct. He is important not only as a predecessor of Lyly in Euphuism, but as a link between the lighter parts of Castiglione's *Courtier* and the amatory analyses of *Euphues* and the romances.

BIBLIOGRAPHY: Painter, *The Palace of Pleasure,* ed. Hamish Miles, London, 1929; D. Bush, "The Classical Tales in Painter's *P. of P.*", *JEGP,* XXIII (1924), 331–341; *A Petite Pallace of Pettie His Pleasure,* ed. H. Hartman, New York, 1938; D. Bush, *"A Petite Pallace," JEGP,* XXVII (1928), 162–169; M. P. Tilley, *Elizabethan Proverb Lore in Lyly's Euphues and in Pettie's Petite Pallace,* New York, 1926.

WILLIAM PAINTER

THE PALACE OF PLEASURE

From The Ninety-first Novel, "The Goodly History of the True and Constant Love Between Romeo and Julietta . . ."

JULIETTA, perceiving her time to approach, dissembled the matter so well as she could; and when time forced her to retire to her chamber, her woman would have waited upon her and have lain in her chamber as her custom was. But Julietta said unto her, "Good and faithful mother, you know that tomorrow is my marriage day, and for that [1] I would spend the most part of the night in prayer, I pray you for this time to let me alone, and tomorrow in the morning about six of the clock come to me again to help make me ready." The good old woman, willing to follow her mind, suffered her alone and doubted nothing of that which she did mean to do. Julietta being within her chamber having an ewer full of water standing upon the table, filled the vial which the friar gave her; and after she had made the mixture, she set it by her bedside and went to bed. And being laid, new thoughts began to assail her with a conceit [2] of grievous death, which brought her into such case as she could not tell what to do, but plaining incessantly, said, "Am I not the most unhappy and desperate creature that ever was born of woman? For me there is nothing left in this wretched world but mishap, misery, and mortal woe; my distress hath brought me to such extremity as, to save mine honor and conscience, I am forced to devour the drink whereof I know not the virtue. But what know I," said she, "whether the operation of this powder will be too soon or too late, or not correspondent to the due time, and that my fault being discovered, I shall remain a fable to the people? What know I, moreover, if the serpents and other venomous and crawling worms which commonly frequent the graves and pits of the earth will hurt me, thinking that I am dead? But how shall I endure the stynche [3] of so many carrions and bones of mine ancestors which rest in the grave, if by fortune I do awake before Romeo and Friar Laurence do come to help me?"

And as she was thus plunged in the deep contemplation of things, she thought that she saw a certain vision or fancy of her cousin Thibault in the very same sort as she saw him wounded and imbrued with blood, and,

1 *for that:* because.
2 *conceit:* mental picture.
3 *stynche:* stench, stink.

musing how that she must be buried quick[4] amongst so many dead carcasses and deadly naked bones, her tender and delicate body began to shake and tremble, and her yellow locks to stare[5] for fear, in such wise as, frightened with terror, a cold sweat began to pierce her heart and bedew the rest of all her members, in such wise as she thought that an hundred thousand deaths did stand about her, haling her on every side and plucking her in pieces, and, feeling that her forces diminished little by little, fearing that through too great debility she was not able to do her enterprise, like a furious and insensate woman, without further care, gulped up the water within the vial; then crossing her arms upon her stomach, she lost at that instant all the powers of her body, resting in a trance.

And when the morning light began to thrust his head out of his orient, her chamberwoman which had locked her in with the key did open the door, and, thinking to awake her, called her many times, and said unto her, "Mistress, you sleep too long; the Count Paris will come to raise you." The poor old woman spake unto the wall and sang a song unto the deaf. For if all the horrible and tempestuous sounds of the world had been cannoned forth out of the greatest bombards[6] and sounded through her delicate ears, her spirits of life were so fast-bound and stopped, as she by no means could awake; wherewith the poor old woman, amazed, began to shake her by the arms and hands, which she found so cold as marble stone.

GEORGE PETTIE

A PETITE PALACE OF PETTIE HIS PLEASURE

FROM "PYGMALION'S FRIEND, AND HIS IMAGE."

IN the country of Piedmont had his being one Pygmalion, a gentleman descended of noble birth, indued with perfection of person, and perfectly portrayed forth with the lineaments of learning, so that it was doubtful whether he were more indebted to fortune for his birth, to nature for his beauty, or to his parents for his learning. But as beauty, birth, riches, and the rest must needs give place to learning, so no doubt but his parents deserved the preeminence of praise. For the others are but dim stars, where learning giveth light. And as when the sun shineth, the light of the stars is not seen, so where learning appeareth, all other gifts are nothing to be accounted of. Besides that, beside his learning, he was indued with a great dexterity in all things, insomuch as nothing came amiss unto him which was meet for a gentleman: in feats of arms no man more courageous, in exercises of the

[4] *quick:* alive.

[5] *stare:* stand on end.

[6] *bombards:* earliest kind of cannon.

body none more active, in game or play none more politic; amongst the ancient, who more grave? amongst the youthful, who more merry? so that there was no time, no person, no place, whereto he aptly applied not himself. By reason whereof, he was acceptable to all good companies, and well was he that might entertain him in his house. But most of all he frequented the house of one Luciano, a noble gentleman of the same country, and in continuance of time grew so far in familiarity with his wife, that he reposed his only pleasure in her presence. Yea, she had made such a stealth of his heart that neither father nor mother, sister nor brother, nor all the friends he had in the country beside, could keep him one week together out of her company. Yea, this faithful love he bare her seemed in a manner to extinguish all natural love towards his allies and kinsfolk, who, being, as they were wont, desirous of his company at hawking, hunting, and suchlike pastimes, could not by any craving or importunity obtain it; but, being ignorant of the cause, they thought it had proceeded of this, that his mind upon some occasion had been alienated from them, which caused them on the contrary, somewhat to withdraw their goodwills from him. But he forced [1] little thereof; he cared not whom he displeased, so he might work her contentation; [2] she was the star by whose aspect he did direct his doings; she was the haven wherein he sought to harborough; she was the heaven whither he coveted to come; she was the saint to whom he did lend such devotion that he could find in his heart to bend no liking to any other whatsoever. Insomuch that, having the proffer of many rich marriages, he alway refused them, as having his heart so replenished with the love of her that there was no roomth for the love of any other to remain within him. Now she, on the other side, whose name was Penthea, being a courteous, courtly wench, gave him such friendly entertainment and used him so well in all respects that, her husband excepted, she seemed to hold him most dear unto her of any wight in the whole world. She never made feast, but he must be her guest; she never rode journey, but he must be her companion; she never danced, but he must direct her; she never diced, but he must be her partner; she, in a manner, did nothing, wherein he did not something. Her husband all this while being fully assured of her virtue and very well persuaded of the honesty of the gentleman, suspected no evil between them, but liked very well of their love and familiarity together, neither indeed had he any cause to the contrary.

---

1 *forced:* cared. 2 *contentation:* satisfaction.

Thomas Sackville, Earl of Dorset

1536–1608

THOMAS SACKVILLE, Earl of Dorset, was first of all a distinguished statesman, who began his career as a Member of Parliament and rose to important ambassadorships and a seat in the Privy Council. He was also Chancellor of the University of Oxford and served Elizabeth with distinction as Lord High Treasurer. To the huge estates his father, Sir Richard Sackville, left him, he devoted his energy and good taste, and Knole House in Sevenoaks, Kent, stands as evidence of his labors.

His interests were not confined solely to architecture and politics: he was a patron of music and had his own band of musicians. Like many Elizabethan men of affairs—Ralegh and Sidney, for example—Sackville was a poet. His literary fame rests on a small but important production in a period of rather mediocre versifying. Although his contemporaries speak of his many works, only his contribution to *The Mirror for Magistrates,* his part in *Gorboduc,* and a few scattered lyrics remain. He seems to have given up poetry, "his first love," as Bacon called it, at the age of twenty-five. Yet he remains a pioneer in English Renaissance literature.

It is a commonplace of literary history not only to regard Sackville's "Induction" as by far the best poetry in the *Mirror,* but to speak of it, as Pope did, as the best poem written between Chaucer and Spenser. Sackville's "Induction" appeared in the 1563 edition of the *Mirror,* but the plan and bibliographical history of the *Mirror* date from 1554 or 1555. At the end of Mary's reign, seven scholars under the leadership of William Baldwin collaborated to write an appendage to a new edition of Lydgate's *Falls of Princes* "to have the storye contynewed from where as Bochas [*i.e.,* Boccaccio, whose *De Casibus Virorum Illustrium* Lydgate adapted in the *Falls of Princes*] lefte, vnto this presente time, chiefly of suche as Fortune had dalyed with here in this ylande." The reprint of Lydgate was published, but the appendage was suppressed, obviously because some of its tragedies furnished sympathetic historical parallels to dangerous political and religious conditions in Mary's reign. Furthermore, the proclamation of June 13, 1555, had banned mirrors of history, especially Hall's chronicle, one of the sources of the appendage. Only a few title pages and fragments remain.

In 1559, however, Thomas Marshe was granted a license "to prynte *The myrroure of maiestrates.*" William Baldwin's preface to the reader contains the main facts and purpose of the work. To Baldwin as interlocutor, the unfortunate English princes were to make their complaints, which were to be written by the several collaborators. The work was to begin with the reign of Richard II and draw its material from the English chronicles. Four authors in the 1559 edition have been identified: William Baldwin, George Ferrers,

Thomas Chaloner, and Thomas Phaer. The nineteen tragedies include the falls of Owen Glendower, Henry Percy, Jack Cade, King Henry VI, and King Edward IV. In addition to Sackville's "Induction" and his "Buckingham," the 1563 edition printed eight new tragedies, among them "Richard Plantagenet Duke of Gloucester," "Shore's Wife," and "Edmund Duke of Somerset."

Though its form obviously follows a medieval *De Casibus* model, the philosophy of the *Mirror* represents a transition from the medieval to the Renaissance conception of man. The tragedies deal in medieval fashion with the fall from high estate of noble persons who suffer "the slyppery deceytes of the waveryng lady," Fortune, but they also seek to display in the characters some moral flaw or tragic fault which makes plausible the fall. In other words, not blind Fortune alone at her wheel, but man's own acts fashion his life. Man pays for his sin. Let princes study tragical stories and avoid tragedy. The tragedies are sample truths, not dogma.

The success of the *Mirror* in its various editions and expansions from 1559 to 1610 did not depend on its art. It was not the work of artists who were exploring the poetical and dramatic possibilities of tragic stories in real life but the labor of a group of responsible and thoughtful men of affairs, under the leadership of a moralist, who were trying to present, in the most effective way they knew, warnings to princes and public alike. The tragedies, says Miss Campbell, "were chosen for their usefulness in teaching political truth, rather than for their historical importance." Yet in this versified history and biography with its emphasis on morality and tragedy are many dramatic passages which reach their ultimate expression in the Elizabethan historical tragic plays.

Sackville's "Induction" was unique not only in its literary quality but in its conception. In a prose link "To the Reader," Baldwin gives an explanation of the "Induction":

"Hath he made a preface (quoth one) what meaneth he thereby, seeing none other hath vsed the like order? I wyl tell you the cause thereof (quoth I) which is thys: After that he understoode that some of the counsayle would not suffer the booke to be printed in such order as we had agreed and determined, he purposed with him selfe to have gotten at my handes, all the tragedies that were before the duke of Buckinghams, which he would have preserued in one volume. And from that time backward euen to the time of William the conqueror, he determined to continue and perfect all the story him selfe, in such order as Lydgate (folowing Bochas) had already used. And therefore to make a meete induction into the matter, he devised this poesye: which in my iudgement is so wel penned, that I woulde not have any verse thereof left out of our volume. . . ."

But whether Sackville planned the "Induction" for the purpose Baldwin says or whether the verses are simply an introduction to his own contribution, "Buckingham's Complaint," is in dispute. From the evidence of the *Mirror* itself and of the St. John's manuscript, the "Induction" seems to serve the latter purpose only. It is certain that, though Sackville knew of the suppressed edition, the original design for the *Mirror* is not his.

The function of the "Induction" is taken up in the rest of the *Mirror* by prose links of brief, usually bloody, descriptions of the tragic character, ending "he may lament after this maner," or "may make his mone to Baldwin as foloweth."

The "Induction," then, may be viewed, apart from its introduction of Buckingham in the last stanzas, as a separate poem—a description of a descent into hell after the manner of Virgil and Dante. The medieval elements are obvious: pseudo-Chaucerian language, verse form (rhyme royal), and the idea of the overthrow of men by fortune, which occurs often. But its gloomy imaginative verse is a product of the Renaissance. The pictures of Dread, Revenge, Death, and Old Age are exceeded in pictorial power only by Spenser's portraits in *The Faerie Queene*. What distinguishes the "Induction" as a work of art comes not from medieval inspiration or technique but largely from Renaissance imagination.

BIBLIOGRAPHY: *The Mirror for Magistrates,* ed. Lily B. Campbell, Cambridge University Press, 1938; ed. Joseph Haslewood, 3 vols., London, 1815; Thomas Sackville, *The Complaint of Henry Duke of Buckingham,* ed. Marguerite Hearsey, New Haven, 1936; Willard Farnham, *The Medieval Heritage of Elizabethan Tragedy,* Berkeley, 1936; J. Swart, *Thomas Sackville, A Study in Sixteenth Century Poetry,* Groningen, 1949.

FROM

THE MIRROR FOR MAGISTRATES (1563)

The Induction

The wrathful winter, 'proaching on apace,
With blustering blasts had all ybared the treen,
And old Saturnus, with his frosty face,
With chilling cold had pierced the tender green;
The mantles rent, wherein enwrapped been
The gladsome groves that now lay overthrown,
The tapets torn, and every bloom [1] down blown.

The soil, that erst so seemly was to seen,
Was all despoiled of her beauty's hue;
And soote [2] fresh flowers, wherewith the summer's queen
Had clad the earth, now Boreas' blasts down blew;
And small fowls flocking, in their song did rue
The winter's wrath, wherewith each thing defaced
In woeful wise bewailed the summer past.

Hawthorn had lost his motley livery,
The naked twigs were shivering all for cold,
And dropping down the tears abundantly;
Each thing, methought, with weeping eye me told
The cruel season, bidding me withhold
Myself within, for I was gotten out
Into the fields, whereas I walked about.

When lo, the night with misty mantles spread,
Gan dark the day and dim the azure skies;
And Venus in her message Hermes sped
To bloody Mars, to will him not to rise,
Which she herself approached in speedy wise;
And Virgo, hiding her disdainful breast,
With Thetis now had laid her down to rest.

---

[1] *tapets:* tapestries, here figuratively as foliage: *bloom:* tree.

[2] *soote:* sweet.

Whiles Scorpio, dreading Sagittarius' dart,
Whose bow prest bent in fight, the string had slipped,
Down slid into the ocean flood apart;
The Bear, that in the Irish seas had dipped
His grisly feet, with speed from thence he whipped;
For Thetis, hasting from the Virgin's bed,
Pursued the Bear, that ere she came was fled.

And Phaethon [3] now, near reaching to his race
With glistering beams, gold streaming where they bent,
Was prest [4] to enter in his resting place;
Erythius, that in the cart first went,
Had even now attained his journey's stent;
And, fast declining, hid away his head,
While Titan couched him in his purple bed.

And pale Cynthia, with her borrowed light,
Beginning to supply her brother's place,
Was past the noonstead six degrees in sight,
When sparkling stars amid the heaven's face
With twinkling light shone on the earth apace,
That, while they brought about the nighte's chare,[5]
The dark had dimmed the day ere I was ware.

And sorrowing I to see the summer flowers,
The lively green, the lusty leas forlorn,
The sturdy trees so shattered with the showers,
The fields so fade that flourished so beforn,
It taught me well all earthly things be born
To die the death, for naught long time may last;
The summer's beauty yields to winter's blast.

Then looking upward to the heaven's leams,[6]
With nighte's stars thick powdered everywhere,
Which erst so glistened with the golden streams
That cheerful Phoebus spread down from his sphere,
Beholding dark oppressing day so near;
The sudden sight reduced to my mind
The sundry changes that in earth we find.

That musing on this worldly wealth in thought,
Which comes and goes more faster than we see
The flickering flame that with the fire is wrought,
My busy mind presented unto me

---

[3] *Phaethon:* here used as in Homer and Virgil as an epithet or surname for Helios, the sun.

[4] *prest:* ready. Cf. French *prêt.*

[5] *chare:* the Big Dipper.

[6] *leams:* rays of light.

Such fall of peers as in this realm had be,
That oft I wished some would their woes descrive,
To warn the rest whom fortune left alive.

And straight forth stalking with redoubled pace,
For that I saw the night drew on so fast,
In black all clad there fell before my face
A piteous wight, whom woe had all forwaste;
Forth from her eyne the crystal tears out brast,[7]
And sighing sore, her hands she wrung and fold,
Tare all her hair, that ruth was to behold.

Her body small, forwithered and forspent,
As is the stalk that summer's drought oppressed;
Her welked [8] face with woeful tears besprent,
Her color pale, and, as it seemed her best,
In woe and plaint reposed was her rest;
And as the stone that drops of water wears,
So dented were her cheeks with fall of tears.

Her eyes swollen with flowing streams afloat,
Wherewith, her looks thrown up full piteously,
Her forceless hands together oft she smote,
With doleful shrieks that echoed in the sky;
Whose plaint such sighs did straight accompany,
That, in my doom, was never man did see
A wight but half so woebegone as she.

I stood aghast, beholding all her plight,
'Tween dread and dolor, so distrained [9] in heart
That, while my hairs upstarted with the sight,
The tears outstreamed for sorrow of her smart;
But when I saw no end that could apart
The deadly deule [10] which she so sore did make,
With doleful voice then thus to her I spake:

Unwrap thy woes, whatever wight thou be,
And stint betime to spill thyself with plaint;
Tell what thou art, and whence, for well I see
Thou canst not dure,[11] with sorrow thus attaint.
And with that word of sorrow, all forfaint
She looked up, and prostrate as she lay,
With piteous sound, lo, thus she gan to say:

[7] *brast:* burst.
[8] *welked:* withered, faded, dried up.
[9] *distrained:* torn asunder.
[10] *deule:* lamentation, sorrow.
[11] *dure:* endure.

Alas, I, wretch whom thus thou seest distrained
With wasting woes that never shall aslake,
Sorrow I am, in endless torments pained
Among the Furies in the infernal lake
Where Pluto, god of Hell, so grisly black,
Doth hold his throne, and Lethe's deadly taste
Doth reave [12] remembrance of each thing forepast.

Whence come I am, the dreary destiny
And luckless lot for to bemoan of those
Whom Fortune, in this maze of misery,
Of wretched chance, most woeful mirrors chose;
That when thou seest how lightly they did lose
Their pomp, their power, and that they thought most sure,
Thou mayst soon deem no earthly joy may dure.

Whose rueful voice no sooner had out brayed
Those woeful words wherewith she sorrowed so,
But Out, alas! she shright [13] and never stayed,
Fell down, and all to-dashed [14] herself for woe;
The cold pale dread my limbs gan overgo,
And I so sorrowed at her sorrows eft [15]
That, what with grief and fear, my wits were reft.

I stretched myself and straight my heart revives,
That dread and dolor erst did so appall;
Like him that with the fervent fever strives,
When sickness seeks his castle health to scale,
With gathered spirits so forced I fear to avale; [16]
And rearing her with anguish all fordone,
My spirits returned and then I thus begun:

O Sorrow, alas, sith Sorrow is thy name,
And that to thee this drear doth well pertain,
In vain it were to seek to cease the same;
But as a man himself with sorrow slain,
So I, alas, do comfort thee in pain,
That here in sorrow art forsunk so deep
That at thy sight I can but sigh and weep.

I had no sooner spoken of a sike,[17]
But that the storm so rumbled in her breast
As Aeolus could never roar the like;

---

[12] *reave:* steal away.
[13] *shright:* shrieked.
[14] *to-dashed:* dashed to pieces.
[15] *eft:* in turn.
[16] *avale:* yield.
[17] *sike:* sigh.

And showers down rained from her eyne so fast
That all bedrent [18] the place, till at the last
Well eased they the dolor of her mind,
As rage of rain doth swage the stormy wind.

For forth she paced in her fearful tale:
Come, come [19] (quod she) and see what I shall show;
Come hear the plaining and the bitter bale
Of worthy men by Fortune overthrow;
Come thou and see them rueing all in row;
They were but shades that erst in mind thou rolled;
Come, come with me, thine eyes shall them behold.

What could these words but make me more aghast,
To hear her tell whereon I mused whilere?
So was I mazed therewith, till at the last,
Musing upon her words, and what they were,
All suddenly well-lessoned was my fear;
For to my mind returned how she telled
Both what she was and where her wone [20] she held.

Whereby I knew that she a goddess was,
And therewithal resorted to my mind
My thought, that late presented me the glass
Of brittle state, of cares that here we find,
Of thousand woes to silly men assigned;
And how she now bid me come and behold,
To see with eye that erst in thought I rolled.

Flat down I fell, and with all reverence
Adored her, perceiving now that she,
A goddess sent by godly providence,
In earthy shape thus showed herself to me,
To wail and rue this world's uncertainty;
And while I honored thus her godhead's might,
With plaining voice these words to me she shright:

I shall guide thee first to the grisly lake
And thence unto the blissful place of rest
Where thou shalt see and hear the plaint they make
That whilom here bare swing [21] among the best;
This shalt thou see, but great is the unrest
That thou must bide before thou canst attain

[18] *bedrent:* drenched.

[19] *Come, come,* etc.: Sorrow is to be the poet's guide through the lower world like the Cumean Sibyl who guided Aeneas and like Virgil who led Dante.

[20] *wone:* dwelling place.

[21] *swing:* full sway.

Unto the dreadful place where these remain.

And with these words, as I upraised stood,
And gan to follow her that straight forth paced,
Ere I was ware, into a desert wood
We now were come, where, hand in hand embraced,
She led the way and through the thick so traced
As, but I had been guided by her might,
It was no way for any mortal wight.

But lo, while thus amid the desert dark
We passed on with steps and pace unmeet,
A rumbling roar, confused with howl and bark
Of dogs, shook all the ground under our feet,
And struck the din within our ears so deep
As, half distraught, unto the ground I fell,
Besought return, and not to visit hell.

But she, forthwith, uplifting me apace,
Removed my dread, and with a steadfast mind
Bade me come on; for here was now the place,
The place where we our travail end should find;
Wherewith I arose, and to the place assigned
Astoined [22] I stalk, when straight we approached near
The dreadful place that you will dread to hear.

An hideous hole all vast, withouten shape,[23]
Of endless depth, o'erwhelmed with ragged stone,
With ugly mouth and grisly jaws doth gape,
And to our sight confounds itself in one;
Here entered we, and yeding [24] forth, anon
An horrible loathly lake we might discern,
As black as pitch, that cleped is Avern.

A deadly gulf where naught but rubbish grows,
With foul black swelth [25] in thickened lumps that lies,
Which up in the air such stinking vapors throws
That over there may fly no fowl but dies,
Choked with the pestilent savors that arise;
Hither we come, whence forth we still did pace,
In dreadful fear amid the dreadful place.

And first, within the porch and jaws of hell,
Sat deep Remorse of Conscience, all besprent

---

[22] *Astoined:* stunned or confounded.

[23] Sackville's description of Hell is modeled on Virgil (*Aeneid,* VI, 237 ff.). Cf. Spenser's *The Faerie Queene,* I, v, 31–35.

[24] *yeding:* a pseudo-archaic form based on the obsolete past tense of "go," which is "yode" or "yede."

[25] *swelth:* foul water.

With tears, and to herself oft would she tell
Her wretchedness, and cursing never stent[26]
To sob and sigh, but ever thus lament
With thoughtful care as she that, all in vain,
Would wear and waste continually in pain.

Her eyes unsteadfast, rolling here and there,
Whirled on each place, as place that vengeance brought,
So was her mind continually in fear,
Tossed and tormented with the tedious thought
Of those detested crimes which she had wrought;
With dreadful cheer[27] and looks thrown to the sky,
Wishing for death, and yet she could not die.

Next saw we Dread, all trembling how he shook,
With foot uncertain, proffered here and there,
Benumbed of speech, and with a ghastly look,
Searched every place, all pale and dead for fear,
His cap borne up with staring of his hair,[28]
'Stoined and amazed at his own shade for dread,
And fearing greater dangers than was need.

And next, within the entry of this lake,
Sat fell Revenge, gnashing her teeth for ire,
Devising means how she may vengeance take,
Never in rest till she have her desire;
But frets within so far forth with the fire
Of wreaking[29] flames, that now determines she
To die by death, or venged by death to be.

When fell Revenge, with bloody foul pretense
Had showed herself as next in order set,
With trembling limbs we softly parted thence,
Till in our eyes another sight we met,
When from my heart a sigh forthwith I fet,
Rueing, alas, upon the woeful plight
Of Misery, that next appeared in sight.

His face was lean and somedeal pined away,
And eke his hands consumed to the bone,
But what his body was I cannot say,
For on his carcass raiment had he none,
Save clouts and patches, pieced one by one;

26 *stent:* cease.
27 *cheer:* countenance.
28 *staring of his hair:* his hair's standing on end.
29 *wreaking:* avenging.

With staff in hand and scrip on shoulders cast,
His chief defense against the winter's blast.

His food, for most, was wild fruits of the tree,
Unless sometime some crumbs fell to his share,
Which in his wallet long, God wot, kept he,
As on the which full daint'ly would he fare;
His drink, the running stream; his cup, the bare
Of his palm closed; his bed, the hard cold ground;
To this poor life was Misery ybound.

Whose wretched state when we had well beheld,
With tender ruth on him and on his feres,[30]
In thoughtful cares forth then our pace we held;
And by and by another shape appears,
Of greedy Care, still brushing up the breres,[31]
His knuckles knobbed, his flesh deep dented in,
With tawed [32] hands and hard ytanned skin.

The morrow gray no sooner had begun
To spread his light, even peeping in our eyes,
When he is up and to his work yrun;
But let the night's black misty mantles rise,
And with foul dark never so much disguise
The fair bright day, yet ceaseth he no while,
But hath his candles to prolong his toil.

By him lay heavy Sleep, the cousin of Death,
Flat on the ground and still as any stone,
A very corpse, save yielding forth a breath;
Small keep took he whom Fortune frowned on
Or whom she lifted up into the throne
Of high renown; but as a living death,
So, dead alive, of life he drew the breath.

The body's rest, the quiet of the heart,
The travail's ease, the still night's fere was he,
And of our life in earth the better part;
Reaver [33] of sight, and yet in whom we see
Things oft that tide, and oft that never be;
Without respect, esteeming equally
King Croesus' pomp, and Irus' poverty.[34]

[30] *feres:* companions.

[31] *breres:* briars.

[32] *tawed:* lacerated.

[33] *reaver:* thief, robber.

[34] *Irus' poverty:* Irus, the beggar of Ithaca in the *Odyssey,* who was slain by Odysseus.

And next in order sad Old Age we found,
His beard all hoar, his eyes hollow and blind,
With drooping cheer still poring on the ground,
As on the place where nature him assigned
To rest, when that the sisters had untwined
His vital thread and ended with their knife
The fleeting course of fast declining life.

There heard we him with broken and hollow plaint
Rue with himself his end approaching fast,
And all for naught his wretched mind torment
With sweet remembrance of his pleasures past,
And fresh delights of lusty youth forewaste;
Recounting which, how would he sob and shriek,
And to be young again of Jove beseek!

But, and the cruel fates so fixed be
That time forepast cannot return again,
This one request of Jove yet prayed he,
That in such withered plight and wretched pain
As eld,[35] accompanied with his loathsome train,
Had brought on him, all were it woe and grief,
He might a while yet linger forth his life,

And not so soon descend into the pit
Where Death, when he the mortal corpse hath slain,
With retchless[36] hand in grave doth cover it,
Thereafter never to enjoy again
The gladsome light, but in the ground ylain,
In depth of darkness waste and wear to naught,
As he had never into the world been brought.

But who had seen him sobbing, how he stood
Unto himself and how he would bemoan
His youth forepast, as though it wrought him good
To talk of youth, all were his youth foregone,
He would have mused and marveled much, whereon
This wretched Age should life desire so fain,
And knows full well life doth but length his pain.

Crookbacked he was, tooth-shaken, and blear-eyed,
Went on three feet, and sometime crept on four,
With old lame bones that rattled by his side,
His scalp all pilled[37] and he with eld forlore;

[35] *eld:* old age.

[36] *retchless:* an obsolete variant of "reck-less," meaning "careless."

[37] *pilled:* bald.

His withered fist still knocking at Death's door,
Fumbling and driveling as he draws his breath;
For brief, the shape and messenger of Death.

And fast by him pale Malady was placed,
Sore sick in bed, her color all foregone,
Bereft of stomach, savor, and of taste,
Ne could she brook no meat, but broths alone;
Her breath corrupt, her keepers every one
Abhorring her, her sickness past recure,
Detesting physic and all physic's cure.

But oh, the doleful sight that then we see!
We turned our look and on the other side
A grisly shape of Famine mought we see,
With greedy looks and gaping mouth that cried
And roared for meat, as she should there have died;
Her body thin and bare as any bone,
Whereto was left naught but the case alone.

And that, alas, was gnawn on everywhere,
All full of holes that I ne mought refrain
From tears to see how she her arms could tear,
And with her teeth gnash on the bones in vain,
When all for naught, she fain would so sustain
Her starven corpse, that rather seemed a shade
Than any substance of a creature made.

Great was her force, whom stone wall could not stay,
Her tearing nails snatching at all she saw;
With gaping jaws that by no means ymay
Be satisfied from hunger of her maw,
But eats herself as she that hath no law;
Gnawing, alas, her carcass all in vain,
Where you may count each sinew, bone, and vein.

On her while we thus firmly fixed our eyes,
That bled for ruth of such a dreary sight,
Lo, suddenly she shright in so huge wise
As made hell gates to shiver with the might;
Wherewith a dart we saw, how it did light
Right on her breast, and therewithal, pale Death
Enthrilling it, to reave her of her breath.

And by and by a dumb dead corpse we saw,
Heavy and cold, the shape of Death aright,
That daunts all earthly creatures to his law;
Against whose force in vain it is to fight;

Ne peers, ne princes, nor no mortal wight,
No towns, ne realms, cities, ne strongest tower,
But all, perforce, must yield unto his power.

His dart, anon, out of the corpse he took,
And in his hand (a dreadful sight to see)
With great triumph eftsoons the same he shook,
That most of all my fears affrayed me;
His body dight with naught but bones, perdy,
The naked shape of man there saw I plain,
All save the flesh, the sinew, and the vein.

Lastly, stood War, in glittering arms yclad,
With visage grim, stern looks, and blackly hued;
In his right hand a naked sword he had,
That to the hilts was all with blood imbrued;
And in his left, that kings and kingdoms rued,
Famine and fire he held, and therewithal
He razed towns and threw down towers and all.

Cities he sacked and realms that whilom flowered
In honor, glory, and rule above the best,
He overwhelmed and all their fame devoured,
Consumed, destroyed, wasted, and never ceased
Till he their wealth, their name, and all oppressed;
His face forhewed with wounds, and by his side
There hung his targe, with gashes deep and wide.

In midst of which, depainted there, we found
Deadly Debate, all full of snaky hair,
That with a bloody fillet was ybound,
Out-breathing naught but discord everywhere,
And round about were portrayed, here and there,
The hugy hosts, Darius [38] and his power,
His kings, princes, his peers, and all his flower.

Whom great Macedo vanquished there in sight
With deep slaughter, despoiling all his pride,
Pierced through his realms and daunted all his might;
Duke Hannibal beheld I there beside,
In Canna's field victor how he did ride,
And woeful Romans that in vain withstood,
And consul Paulus [39] covered all in blood.

---

[38] *Darius:* King of Persia, overthrown by Alexander of Macedon (*Macedo* of line 407).

[39] *consul Paulus:* Lucius Paulus, who after advising against the battle of Cannae died in it.

Yet saw I more: the fight at Thrasimene,
And Treby [40] field, and eke when Hannibal
And worthy Scipio last in arms were seen
Before Carthago gate, to try for all
The world's empire, to whom it should befall;
There saw I Pompey and Caesar clad in arms,
Their hosts allied and all their civil harms.

With conquerors' hands, forbathed in their own blood,
And Caesar weeping over Pompey's head;
Yet saw I Sulla and Marius where they stood,
Their great cruelty and the deep bloodshed
Of friends; Cyrus I saw and his host dead,
And how the queen with great despite hath flung
His head in blood of them she overcome.

Xerxes, the Persian king, yet saw I there
With his huge host that drank the rivers dry,
Dismounted hills, and made the vales uprear,
His host and all yet saw I plain, perdy;
Thebes I saw, all razed how it did lie
In heaps of stones, and Tyrus put to spoil,
With walls and towers flat evened with the soil.

But Troy, alas, methought above them all
It made mine eyes in very tears consume,
When I beheld the woeful word befall,
That by the wrathful will of gods was come;
And Jove's unmoved sentence and foredoom
On Priam king, and on his town so bent,
I could not lin,[41] but I must there lament.

And that the more, sith destiny was so stern
As, force perforce, there might no force avail,
But she must fall, and by her fall we learn
That cities, towers, wealth, world, and all shall quail;
No manhood, might, nor nothing mought prevail;
All were there prest, full many a prince and peer,
And many a knight that sold his death full dear.

Not worthy Hector, worthiest of them all,
Her hope, her joy, his force is now for naught;
O Troy, Troy, there is no boot but bale,
The hugy horse within thy walls is brought;
Thy turrets fall, thy knights, that whilom fought

---

[40] *Treby:* Trebia, a river in upper Italy, where Hannibal defeated the Romans.

[41] *lin:* cease.

In arms amid the field, are slain in bed,
Thy gods defiled and all thy honor dead.

The flames upspring and cruelly they creep
From wall to roof till all to cinders waste;
Some fire the houses where the wretches sleep,
Some rush in here, some run in there as fast;
In everywhere or sword or fire they taste;
The walls are torn, the towers whirled to the ground;
There is no mischief but may there be found.

Cassandra yet there saw I how they haled
From Pallas' house, with spercled [42] tress undone,
Her wrists fast bound and with Greeks' rout empaled;
And Priam eke, in vain how did he run
To arms, whom Pyrrhus with despite hath done
To cruel death, and bathed him in the baign
Of his son's blood, before the altar slain.

But how can I descrive the doleful sight
That in the shield so livelike fair did shine?
Sith in this world I think was never wight
Could have set forth the half, not half so fine;
I can no more but tell how there is seen
Fair Ilium fall in burning red gledes down,
And from the soil great Troy, Neptunus' town.

Herefrom when scarce I could mine eyes withdraw,
That filled with tears as doth the springing well,
We passed on so far forth till we saw
Rude Acheron, a loathsome lake to tell,
That boils and bubs up swelth as black as hell;
Where grisly Charon, at their fixed tide,
Still ferries ghosts unto the farther side.

The aged god no sooner Sorrow spied,
But hasting straight unto the bank apace,
With hollow call unto the rout he cried
To swerve apart and give the goddess place;
Straight it was done, when to the shore we pace,
Where, hand in hand as we then linked fast,
Within the boat we are together placed.

And forth we launch full fraughted to the brink,
When with the unwonted weight, the rusty keel
Began to crack as if the same should sink;

[42] *spercled:* disheveled.

We hoise up mast and sail, that in a while
We fetched the shore, where scarcely we had while
For to arrive, but that we heard anon
A three-sound bark confounded all in one.

We had not long forth passed but that we saw
Black Cerberus, the hideous hound of hell,
With bristles reared and with a three-mouthed jaw
Fordinning the air [43] with his horrible yell,
Out of the deep dark cave where he did dwell;
The goddess straight he knew, and by and by,
He peased [44] and couched while that we passed by.

Thence come we to the horror and the hell,
The large great kingdoms and the dreadful reign
Of Pluto in his throne where he did dwell,
The wide waste places and the hugy plain,
The wailings, shrieks, and sundry sorts of pain,
The sighs, the sobs, the deep and deadly groan,
Earth, air, and all, resounding plaint and moan.

Here puled the babes, and here the maids unwed
With folded hands their sorry chance bewailed,
Here wept the guiltless slain, and lovers dead,
That slew themselves when nothing else availed;
A thousand sorts of sorrows here, that wailed
With sighs and tears, sobs, shrieks, and all yfere,[45]
That oh, alas, it was a hell to hear.

We stayed us straight, and with a rueful fear,
Beheld this heavy sight, while from mine eyes
The vapored tears down stilled here and there,
And Sorrow eke, in far more woeful wise,
Took on with plaint, upheaving to the skies
Her wretched hands, that with her cry the rout
Gan all in heaps to swarm us round about.

Lo here, quoth Sorrow, princes of renown,
That whilom [46] sat on top of Fortune's wheel,
Now laid full low, like wretches whirled down,
Even with one frown, that stayed but with a smile;
And now behold the thing that thou, erewhile,
Saw only in thought, and what thou now shalt hear,
Recount the same to kesar, king, and peer.

---

[43] *Fordinning the air:* making a complete din in the air.

[44] *peased:* became still.

[45] *yfere:* together.

[46] *whilom:* formerly, at one time.

Then first came Henry, Duke of Buckingham,
His cloak of black all pilled[47] and quite forworn,
Wringing his hands, and Fortune oft doth blame,
Which of a duke hath made him now her scorn;
With ghastly looks, as one in manner lorn,
Oft spread his arms, stretched hands he joins as fast
With rueful cheer and vapored eyes upcast.

His cloak he rent, his manly breast he beat,
His hair all torn, about the place it lay;
My heart so molt to see his grief so great,
As feelingly methought it dropped away;
His eyes they whirled about withouten stay,
With stormy sighs the place did so complain,
As if his heart at each had burst in twain.

Thrice he began to tell his doleful tale,
And thrice with sighs did swallow up his voice,
At each of which he shrieked so withal,
As though the heavens rived with the noise;
Till at the last, recovering his voice,
Supping the tears that all his breast berained,
On cruel fortune, weeping, thus he plained.

[47] *pilled:* torn.

Sir Thomas North

ca. 1535–1603

THE *Parallel Lives* of Plutarch, one of the greatest and most widely read works handed down from classical antiquity, had a special charm and significance for men of the Renaissance. Montaigne, for instance, expressed his appreciation of it several times; to him Plutarch, more than any other author, mingled art with nature and judgment with learning. Plutarch's method was to describe at length a great leader of Greece and a great leader of Rome, then to compare them. His primary interest was in character, and he chose for subjects men in public life. His twenty-three pairs extend from Theseus and Romulus, fabled founders of cities, and Lycurgus and Numa, lawgivers and religious leaders, down to Alexander and Caesar the conquerors, and Demosthenes and Cicero the orators. Plutarch was a moralist, and he dwelt with fascinated interest on those episodes in the lives of men when they encounter ideals and issues greater than any personal concerns. At such times his subjects become models for him or examples to avoid; they are not historical figures being revived, but the most significant and present characters one could imagine.

Montaigne owed his knowledge of Plutarch to the translation of Jacques Amyot (1559), the earliest French work to be accepted by the French Academy as a classic of the language. English readers owed a debt to Amyot too, for it was Amyot's French version which Thomas North translated into English (1579). So great was the style of this retranslation that North's book has been placed with Malory's *Morte d' Arthur* and *The Book of Common Prayer* as the foundation of modern English prose.

North was the second son of Edward, first Baron North. He was born about 1535 and followed his father's course of Peterhouse, Cambridge, and Lincoln's Inn, but instead of law he produced from the latter address a translation of Guevara's *Dial of Princes,* from a French version of the Spanish original. In 1570 he published a translation from the Italian, *The Moral Philosophy of Doni,* and nine years later his Plutarch. He settled in Cambridge, commanded a company of men from Ely in 1588 at the time of the Armada, was knighted in 1591, and died before 1603.

North's version is great because the book he was translating was intensely alive for him. Accordingly he used natural and vivid English. Colloquialisms, the figurative speech Elizabethans loved so well, proverbs, the concrete and homely native word in place of the abstract or formal phrase of the French—all made North's translation an English book.

The best testimony to the quality of North's style is that Shakespeare used more of the actual words and phrases from it than he did from any other of his sources. *Julius Caesar, Antony and Cleopatra,* and *Coriolanus* can be rightly appreciated only by one who sees in them the magnificent collaboration between the genius of North and the genius of Shakespeare, both being enriched by the wisdom and perception of the mind of Plutarch.

The Elizabethans were constantly comparing their great with the heroes of antiquity; Jonson thought about the classical writers when he was evaluating Shakespeare in the poem in the First Folio, and Chapman thought of Achilles and the ill-fated Essex as comparable. Plutarch was the great source for knowledge of what men might rise to, and how they might fall, as exemplified in the heroes of classical ages toward which Elizabethans looked back with wonder and envy.

BIBLIOGRAPHY: *North's Plutarch,* with an introduction by George Wyndham, Tudor Translations VII, London, 1895; F. O. Matthiessen, *Translation, an Elizabethan Art,* Harvard, 1931; A. de Guevara, *The Dial of Princes,* tr. North, ed. K. N. Colville, 1919; translations of other works of Plutarch are the *Quyete of Mynde* by Wyatt, ed. Baskervill, Harvard, 1931; *De Curiositate* by Queen Elizabeth, ed. C. Pemberton, E. E. T. S., original series, no. 113, 1899; and *The Philosophie, commonlie called the Morals,* tr. Ph. Holland, ed. F. B. Jevons, 1892.

FROM

THE LIFE OF JULIUS CAESAR

AND for the war he made in Alexandria, some say he needed not have done it, but that he willingly did it for the love of Cleopatra, wherein he won little honor and besides did put his person in great danger. Others do lay the fault upon the king of Egypt's ministers, but specially on Pothinus the Eunuch, who, bearing the greatest sway of all the king's servants, after he had caused Pompey to be slain and driven Cleopatra from the court, secretly laid wait all the ways he could, how he might likewise kill Caesar. Wherefore Caesar, hearing an inkling of it, began thenceforth to spend all the night long in feasting and banqueting, that his person might be in the better safety. And besides all this, Pothinus the Eunuch spoke many things openly not to be borne, only to shame Caesar, and to stir up the people to envy him. For he made his soldiers have the worst and oldest wheat that could be gotten; then if they did complain of it, he told them they must be contented, seeing they eat at another man's cost. And he would serve them also at the table in treen [1] and earthen dishes, saying that Caesar had away all their gold and silver, for a debt that the king's father (that then reigned) did owe unto him, which was a thousand seven hundred and fifty myriads,[2] whereof Caesar had before forgiven seven hundred and fifty thousand unto his children. However, then he asked a million to pay his soldiers withal. Thereto Pothinus answered him, that at that time he should do better to follow his other causes of greater importance, and afterwards that he should at more leisure recover his debt, with the king's good will and favor. Caesar replied unto him and said that he would not ask counsel of the Egyptians for his affairs, but would be paid, and thereupon secretly sent for Cleopatra which was in the country to come unto him. She only taking Apollodorus Sicilian of all her friends, took a little boat and went away with him in it in the night and came and landed hard by the foot of the castle. Then, having no other means to come in to the court without being known, she laid herself down upon a mattress or flockbed,[3] which Apollodorus her friend tied and bound up together like a bundle with a great leather thong, and so took her up on his back and brought her thus hampered in this fardel unto Caesar, in at the castle gate. This was the first occasion (as it is reported) that made Caesar to love her, but afterwards, when he saw her sweet conversation and pleasant entertainment, he fell then in further lik-

---

1 *treen:* wooden.

2 *myriads:* 10,000 of an understood coin.

3 *flockbed:* a covering filled with tufts of wool.

ing with her, and did reconcile her again unto her brother the king, with condition that they two jointly should reign together. Upon this new reconciliation, a great feast being prepared, a slave of Caesar's that was his barber, the fearfulest wretch that lived, still busily prying and listening abroad in every corner, being mistrustful by nature, found that Pothinus and Achillas did lie in wait to kill his master Caesar. This being proved unto Caesar, he did set such sure watch about the hall where the feast was made, that in fine, he slew the eunuch Pothinus himself. Achillas, on the other side, saved himself, and fled unto the king's camp where he raised a marvelous dangerous and difficult war for Caesar, because he having then but a few men about him as he had, he was to fight against a great and strong city. The first danger he fell into, was for the lack of water he had, for that his enemies had stopped the mouth of the pipes which conveyed the water unto the castle. The second danger he had was, that seeing his enemies came to take his ships from him, he was driven to repulse that danger with fire, the which burnt the arsenal where the ships lay, and that notable library of Alexandria withal. The third danger was in the battle by sea, that was fought by the tower of Phar, where meaning to help his men that fought by sea, he leapt from the pier into a boat. Then the Egyptians made toward him with their oars on every side, but he leaping into the sea, with great hazard saved himself by swimming. It is said that, then holding divers books in his hand, he did never let them go, but kept them always upon his head above water and swam with the other hand, notwithstanding that they shot marvelously at him, and was driven some time to duck into the water. Howbeit, the boat was drowned presently. In fine, the king coming to his men that made war with Caesar, he went against him and gave him battle and won it with great slaughter and effusion of blood. But for the king, no man could ever tell what became of him after. Thereupon Caesar made Cleopatra, his sister, Queen of Egypt, who being great with child by him, was shortly brought to bed of a son whom the Alexandrians named Caesarion.

* * *

Caesar also had Cassius in great jealousy and suspected him much. Whereupon he said on a time to his friends, "What will Cassius do, think ye? I like not his pale looks." Another time when Caesar's friends complained unto him of Antonius and Dolabella, that they pretended some mischief towards him, he answered them again, "As for those fat men and smooth-combed heads," quoth he, "I never reckon of them, but these pale visaged and carrion lean people, I fear them most" (meaning Brutus and Cassius). Certainly destiny may easier be foreseen than avoided, considering the strange and wonderful signs that were said to be seen before Caesar's death. For, touching the fires in the element and spirits running up and down in the night, and also these solitary birds to be seen at noondays sitting in the great market place; are not all these signs perhaps worth the noting, in such a wonderful chance as happened? But Strabo the philosopher writeth that divers men were seen going up and down in fire, and furthermore, that there was a slave of the soldiers that did cast a marvelous burning flame out of his hand, insomuch as they that saw it, thought he had been burnt, but when the fire was out, it was found he had no hurt. Caesar self, also doing sacrifice unto the gods, found that one of the beasts which was sacrificed had no heart, and that was a strange thing in nature, how a beast could live without a heart. Furthermore, there was a certain soothsayer that had given Caesar warning long time before to take heed of the day of the Ides of March (which is the fifteenth of the month), for on that day he should be in great danger. That day being come, Caesar going unto the Senate house, and speaking merrily to the soothsayer, told him, "The Ides of March be come." "So be they," softly answered the soothsayer, "but yet are they not past." And the very day before, Caesar supping with Marcus Lepidus, sealed certain letters as he was wont to do at the board. So talk falling out amongst them, reasoning what death was best, he preventing their opinions, cried out aloud, "Death unlooked for." Then going to bed the same night as his manner was and lying with his wife Calpurnia, all the windows and doors of his chamber flying open, the noise awoke him and made him afraid when he saw such light, but more, when he heard his wife Calpurnia, being fast asleep, weep and sigh and put forth many fumbling lamentable speeches. For she dreamed that Caesar was slain and that she had him in her arms. Others also do deny that she had any such dream, as amongst other, Titus Livius writeth that it was in this sort: The Senate having set upon the top of Caesar's house, for an ornament and setting forth of the same, a certain pinnacle, Calpurnia dreamed that she saw it broken down and that she thought she lamented and wept for it. Insomuch that Caesar rising in the morning, she prayed him if it were possible, not to go out of doors that day, but to adjourn the session of the Senate until another day. And if that he made no reckoning of her dream, yet that he would search further of the soothsayers by their sacrifices, to know what should happen him that day. Thereby it seemed that Caesar likewise did fear and suspect somewhat, because his wife Calpurnia until that time was never given to any fears or superstition, and then for that he saw her so troubled in mind with this dream she had. But much more afterwards, when the soothsayers having sacrificed many beasts one after another, told him that none did like them. Then he determined to send Antonius to adjourn the session of the Senate. But in the meantime came Decius Brutus, surnamed Albinus, in whom Caesar put such confidence that in his last will and testament he had appointed him to be his next heir, and yet was of the conspiracy with Cassius and Brutus, he fearing that if Caesar did adjourn the session that day, the conspiracy would out, laughed the soothsayers to scorn, and reproved Caesar, saying that he gave the Senate occasion to mislike with him and that they might think he mocked them, considering that by his commandment they were assembled and that they were ready, willingly, to grant him all things, and to proclaim him king of all the provinces of the Empire of Rome out of Italy, and that he should wear his diadem in all other places, both by sea and land. And furthermore, that if any man should tell them from him, they should depart for that present time and return again when Calpurnia should have better dreams, what would his enemies and ill-willers say, and how could they like of his friends' words? And who could persuade them otherwise, but that they would think his dominion a slavery unto them, and tyrannical in himself? "And yet if it be so," said he, "that you utterly mislike of this day, it is better that you go yourself in person, and saluting the Senate, to dismiss them till another time." Therewithal he took Caesar by the hand, and brought him out of his house. Caesar was not gone far from his house, but a bondman, a stranger, did what he could to speak with him, and when he saw he was put back by the great prease [4] and multitude of people that followed him, he went straight unto his house, and put himself into Calpurnia's hands to be kept, till Caesar came back again, telling her that he had great matters to impart unto him.

FROM

THE LIFE OF MARCUS ANTONIUS

FOR he understood not many of the thefts and robberies his officers committed by his authority in his treasury and affairs, not so much because he was careless, as for that he over-simply trusted his men in all things. For he was a plain man, without subtlety, and therefore over-late found out the foul faults they committed against him; but when he heard of them, he was much offended and would plainly confess it unto them whom his officers had done injury unto by countenance of his authority. He had a noble mind, as well to punish offenders, as to reward well-doers, and yet he did exceed more in giving than in punishing. Now for his outrageous manner of railing he commonly used, mocking and flouting of every man—that was remedied by itself. For a man might as boldly exchange a mock with him, and he was as well contented to be mocked, as to mock others. But yet it oftentimes marred all. For he thought that those which told him so plainly and truly in mirth would never flatter him in good earnest, in any matter of weight. But thus he was easily abused by the praises they gave him, not finding how these flatterers mingled their flattery, under this familiar and plain manner of speech unto him, as a fine device to make difference of meats with sharp and tart sauce, and also to keep him, by this frank jesting and bourding [5] with him at the table, that their common flattery should not be troublesome unto him, as men do easily mislike to have too much of one thing; and that they handled him finely thereby, when they would give him place in any matter of weight, and follow his counsel, that it might not appear to him that they did it so much to please him, but because they were ignorant and understood not so much as he did.

---

[4] *prease:* crowd.

[5] *bourding:* joking.

Antonius being thus inclined, the last and extremest mischief of all other (to wit, the love of Cleopatra) lighted on him, who did waken and stir up many vices yet hidden in him, and were never seen to any; and if any spark of goodness or hope of rising were left him, Cleopatra quenched it straight and made it worse than before. The manner how he fell in love with her was this. Antonius going to make war with the Parthians, sent to command Cleopatra to appear personally before him when he came into Silicia, to answer unto such accusations as were laid against her, being this: that she had aided Cassius and Brutus in their war against him. The messenger sent unto Cleopatra to make this summons unto her was called Dellius, who when he had thoroughly considered her beauty, the excellent grace and sweetness of her tongue, he nothing mistrusted that Antonius would do any hurt to so noble a lady, but rather assured himself that within few days she should be in great favor with him. Thereupon he did her great honor and persuaded her to come into Silicia, as honorably furnished as she could possible,[6] and bade her not to be afraid at all of Antonius, for he was a more courteous lord than any that she had ever seen. Cleopatra, on the other side, believing Dellius' words, and guessing by the former access and credit she had with Julius Caesar and Cneius Pompey, the son of Pompey the Great, only for her beauty; she began to have good hope that she might more easily win Antonius. For Caesar and Pompey knew her when she was but a young thing, and knew not then what the world meant; but now she went to Antonius at the age when a woman's beauty is at the prime, and she also of best judgment. So, she furnished herself with a world of gifts, store of gold and silver, and of riches and other sumptuous ornaments, as is credible enough she might bring from so great a house, and from so wealthy and rich a realm as Egypt was. But yet she carried nothing with her wherein she trusted more than in herself, and in the charms and enchantment of her passing beauty and grace. Therefore,[7] when she was sent unto by divers letters, both from Antonius himself, and also from his friends, she made so light of it, and mocked Antonius so much, that she disdained to set forward otherwise, but to take her barge in the river of Cydnus, the poop whereof was of gold, the sails of purple, and the oars of silver, which kept stroke in rowing after the sound of the music of flutes, hautboys, citherns, viols, and such other instruments as they played upon in the barge. And now for the person of herself: she was laid under a pavilion of cloth of gold of tissue, appareled and attired like the goddess Venus commonly drawn in picture, and hard by her, on either hand of her, pretty fair boys appareled as painters do set forth god Cupid, with little fans in their hands, with the which they fanned wind upon her. Her ladies and gentlewomen also, the fairest of them were appareled like the nymphs Nereides (which are the mermaids of the waters) and like the Graces, some steering the helm, others tending the tackle and ropes of

---

[6] *possible:* possibly.

[7] Shakespeare's treatment of this passage is very remarkable. (*Antony and Cleopatra,* II, ii, 198–226.)

the barge, out of which there came a wonderful passing sweet savor of perfumes, that perfumed the wharf's side, pestered with innumerable multitudes of people. Some of them followed the barge all alongst the river's side; others also ran out of the city to see her coming in. So that in the end there ran such multitudes of people, one after another to see her, that Antonius was left post alone in the market place, in his imperial seat to give audience, and there went a rumor in the people's mouths that the goddess Venus was come to play with the god Bacchus, for the general good of all Asia. When Cleopatra landed, Antonius sent to invite her to supper to him. But she sent him word again, he should do better rather to come and sup with her. Antonius, therefore, to show himself courteous unto her at her arrival, was contented to obey her, and went to supper to her, where he found such passing sumptuous fare that no tongue can express it. But amongst all other things, he wondered at the infinite number of lights and torches hanging on the top of the house, giving light in every place, so artificially set and ordered by devices, some round, some square, that it was the rarest thing to behold that eye could discern, or that ever books could mention. The next night, Antonius feasting her, contended to pass her in magnificence and fineness, but she overcame him in both. So that he himself began to scorn the gross service of his house in respect of Cleopatra's sumptuousness and fineness. And when Cleopatra found Antonius' jests and slents [8] to be but gross and soldierlike, in plain manner, she gave it him finely, and without fear taunted him thoroughly. Now her beauty (as it is reported) was not so passing, as unmatchable of other women, nor yet such, as upon present view did enamor men with her, but so sweet was her company and conversation that a man could not possibly but be taken. And besides her beauty, the good grace she had to talk and discourse, her courteous nature that tempered her words and deeds, was a spur that pricked to the quick. Furthermore, besides all these, her voice and words were marvelous pleasant, for her tongue was an instrument of music to divers sports and pastimes, the which she easily turned to any language that pleased her. She spake unto few barbarous people by interpreter, but made them answer herself, or at the least the most part of them: [9] as the Aethiopians, the Arabians, the Troglodytes,[10] the Hebrews, the Syrians, the Medes, and the Parthians, and to many others also, whose languages she had learned. Whereas divers of her progenitors, the kings of Egypt, could scarce learn the Egyptian tongue only, and many of them forgot to speak the Macedonian. Now Antonius was so ravished with the love of Cleopatra, that though his wife Fulvia had great wars and much ado with Caesar for his affairs and that the army of the Parthians (the which the king's lieutenants had given to the only leading of Labienus) was now

[8] *slents:* sly digs, sarcasms.

[9] Gabriel Harvey, in his notes on the *Courtier,* grouped Cleopatra and Queen Elizabeth together as linguists.

[10] *Troglodytes:* cave dwellers of the west coast of the Red Sea.

assembled in Mesopotamia ready to invade Syria; yet, as though all this had nothing touched him, he yielded himself to go with Cleopatra into Alexandria, where he spent and lost in childish sports (as a man might say) and idle pastimes, the most precious thing a man can spend, as Antiphon saith—and that is time. For they made an order between them, which they called *Amimetobion* (as much to say, no life comparable and matchable with it) one feasting each other by turns, and in cost exceeding all measure and reason. And for proof hereof, I have heard my grandfather Lampryas report that one Philotas, a physician, born in the city of Amphissa, told him that he was at that present time in Alexandria, and studied physic, and that having acquaintance with one of Antonius' cooks, he took him with him to Antonius' house (being a young man desirous to see things) to show him the wonderful sumptuous charge and preparation of one only supper. When he was in the kitchen and saw a world of diversities of meats, and amongst others, eight wild boars roasted whole, he began to wonder at it, and said, "Sure you have a great number of guests to supper." The cook fell a-laughing and answered him. "No," quoth he, "not many guests, nor above twelve in all, but yet all that is boiled or roasted must be served in whole, or else it would be marred straight. For Antonius peradventure will sup presently, or it may be a pretty while hence, or likely enough he will defer it longer, for that he hath drunk well today, or else hath had some other great matters in hand; and therefore we do not dress one supper only, but many suppers, because we are uncertain of the hour he will sup in."

* * *

But now again to Cleopatra. Plato writeth that there are four kinds of flattery, but Cleopatra divided it into many kinds. For she, were it in sport, or in matter of earnest, still devised sundry new delights to have Antonius at commandment, never leaving him night nor day, nor once letting him go out of her sight. For she would play at dice with him, drink with him, and hunt commonly with him, and also be with him when he went to any exercise or activity of body. And sometime also, when he would go up and down the city disguised like a slave in the night, and would peer into poor men's windows and their shops, and scold and brawl with them within the house, Cleopatra would be also in a chambermaid's array and amble up and down the streets with him, so that oftentimes Antonius bare away both mocks and blows. Now, though most men misliked this manner, yet the Alexandrians were commonly glad of this jollity and liked it well, saying very gallantly and wisely, that Antonius showed them a comical face, to wit, a merry countenance, and the Romans a tragical face, to say, a grim look. But to reckon up all the foolish sports they made, reveling in this sort, it were too fond a part of me, and therefore I will only tell you one among the rest. On a time he went to angle for fish, and when he could take none, he was as angry as could be, because Cleopatra stood by. Wherefore, he secretly commanded the fishermen that when he cast in his line, they should straight dive under the water and put a fish on his hook which they had taken before, and so snatched up his angling rod, and brought up fish twice or thrice. Cleopatra found it straight,[11] yet she seemed not to see it, but wondered at his excellent fishing; but when she was alone by herself among her own people, she told them how it was, and bade them the next morning to be on the water to see the fishing. A number of people came to the haven, and got into the fisher boats to see this fishing. Antonius then threw in his line and Cleopatra straight commanded one of her men to dive under water before Antonius' men and to put some old salt fish upon his bait, like unto those that are brought out of the country of Pont. When he had hung the fish on his hook, Antonius thinking he had taken a fish indeed, snatched up his line presently. Then they all fell a-laughing. Cleopatra laughing also, said unto him, "Leave us, my Lord, Egyptians, which dwell in the country of Pharus and Canobus, your angling rod; this is not thy profession, thou must hunt after conquering of realms and countries." Now Antonius delighting in these fond and childish pastimes, very ill news were brought him from two places. The first from Rome, that his brother Lucius, and Fulvia his wife, fell out first between themselves, and afterwards fell to open war with Caesar, and had brought all to naught, that they were both driven to fly out of Italy. The second news, as bad as the first, that Labienus conquered all Asia with the army of the Parthians, from the river of Euphrates, and from Syria, unto the countries of Lydia and Ionia. Then began Antonius with much ado a little to rouse himself as if he had been wakened out of a deep sleep, and as a man may say, coming out of a great drunkenness. So first of all, he bent himself against the Parthians, and went as far as the country of Phoenicia, but there he received lamentable letters from his wife Fulvia. Whereupon he straight returned towards Italy with two hundred sail, and as he went, took up his friends by the way that fled out of Italy, to come to him. By them he was informed that his wife Fulvia was the only cause of this war, who being of a peevish, crooked, and troublesome nature, had purposely raised this uproar in Italy, in hope thereby to withdraw him from Cleopatra. But by good fortune, his wife Fulvia going to meet with Antonius, sickened by the way, and died in the city of Sicyon; and therefore, Octavius Caesar and he were the easier made friends together. For when Antonius landed in Italy, and that men saw Caesar asked nothing of him, and that Antonius on the other side laid all the fault and burden on his wife Fulvia, the friends of both parties would not suffer them to unrip any old matters and to prove or defend who had the wrong or right and who was the first procurer of this war, fearing to make matters worse between them; but they made them friends together and divided the Empire of Rome between them, making the sea Ionium the bounds of their division. For they gave all the provinces eastward unto Antonius, and the countries westward unto Caesar, and left Africa unto Lepidus, and made a law that they three, one after another, should make

[11] *found it straight:* saw through it immediately.

their friends Consuls, when they would not be themselves. This seemed to be a sound counsel, but yet it was to be confirmed with a straiter bond, which fortune offered thus. There was Octavia, the eldest sister of Caesar, not by one mother, for she came of Ancharia, and Caesar himself afterwards of Accia. It is reported that he dearly loved his sister Octavia, for indeed she was a noble lady and left the widow of her first husband Caius Marcellus, who died not long before; and it seemed also that Antonius had been widower ever since the death of his wife Fulvia. For he denied not that he kept Cleopatra, but so did he not confess that he had her as his wife, and so with reason he did defend the love he bare unto this Egyptian Cleopatra. Thereupon, every man did set forward this marriage, hoping thereby that this lady Octavia, having an excellent grace, wisdom, and honesty, joined unto so rare a beauty, that when she were with Antonius (he loving her as so worthy a lady deserveth) she should be a good means to keep good love and amity betwixt her brother and him. So when Caesar and he had made the match between them, they both went to Rome about this marriage, although it was against the law that a widow should be married within ten months after her husband's death. Howbeit, the Senate dispensed with the law, and so the marriage proceeded accordingly.

* * *

Antonius also leaving his wife Octavia and little children begotten of her, with Caesar, and his other children which he had by Fulvia, he went directly into Asia. Then began this pestilent plague and mischief of Cleopatra's love (which had slept a long time, and seemed to have been utterly forgotten, and that Antonius had given place to better counsel) again to kindle, and to be in force, so soon as Antonius came near unto Syria. And in the end, the horse of the mind, as Plato termed it, that is so hard of rein (I mean the unreined lust of concupiscence) did put out of Antonius' head all honest and commendable thoughts, for he sent Fonteius Capito to bring Cleopatra into Syria. Unto whom, to welcome her, he gave no trifling things, but unto that she had already, he added the provinces of Phoenicia, those of the nethermost Syria, the Isle of Cyprus, and a great part of Silicia, and that country of Jewry where the true balm is, and that part of Arabia where the Nabatheians do dwell, which stretcheth out towards the ocean. These great gifts much misliked the Romans. But now, though Antonius did easily give away great seigniories, realms, and mighty nations unto some private men, and that also he took from other kings their lawful realms (as from Antigonus, King of the Jews, whom he openly beheaded, where never king before had suffered like death) yet all this did not so much offend the Romans, as the unmeasurable honors which he did unto Cleopatra. But yet he did much more aggravate their malice and ill will towards him because that Cleopatra, having brought him two twins, a son and a daughter, he named his son Alexander, and his daughter Cleopatra, and gave them to their surnames, the Sun to the one and the Moon to the other. This notwithstanding, he that could finely cloak his shameful deeds with fine words, said that the greatness and magnificence of the Empire of Rome appeared most, not where the Romans took, but where they gave much; and nobility was multiplied amongst men by the posterity of kings when they left of their seed in divers places, and that by this means his first ancestor was begotten of Hercules, who had not left the hope and continuance of his line and posterity in the womb of one only woman, fearing Solon's laws or regarding the ordinances of men touching the procreation of children, but that he gave it unto nature and established the foundation of many noble races and families in divers places.

* * *

Now whilst Antonius was busy in this preparation, Octavia, his wife, whom he had left at Rome, would needs take sea to come unto him. Her brother, Octavius Caesar, was willing unto it, not for his respect at all (as most authors do report) as for that he might have an honest color[12] to make war with Antonius if he did misuse her and not esteem her as she ought to be. But when she was come to Athens, she received letters from Antonius, willing her to stay there until his coming, and did advertise her of his journey and determination. The which though it grieved her much, and that she knew it was but an excuse, yet by her letters to him of answer, she asked him whether he would have those things sent unto him which she had brought him, being great store of apparel for soldiers, a great number of horse, sum of money and gifts to bestow on his friends and captains he had about him, and besides all those, she had two thousand soldiers, chosen men, all well armed, like unto the Praetor's bands. When Niger, one of Antonius' friends whom he had sent unto Athens, had brought these news from his wife Octavia, and withal did greatly praise her, as she was worthy and well deserved, Cleopatra, knowing that Octavia would have Antonius from her, and fearing also that if with her virtue and honest behavior (besides the great power of her brother Caesar) she did add thereunto her modest kind love to please her husband, that she would then be too strong for her, and in the end win him away, she subtly seemed to languish for the love of Antonius, pining her body for lack of meat. Furthermore, she every way so framed her countenance that when Antonius came to see her, she cast her eyes upon him like a woman ravished for joy. Straight again when he went from her, she fell a-weeping and blubbering, looked ruefully of the matter, and still found the means that Antonius should oftentimes find her weeping, and then when he came suddenly upon her, she made as though she dried her eyes and turned her face away, as if she were unwilling that he should see her weep. All these tricks she used, Antonius being in readiness to go into Syria, to speak with the king of Medes. Then the flatterers that furthered Cleopatra's mind blamed Antonius, and told him that he was a hard-natured man, and that he had small love in him, that would see a poor lady in such torment for his sake, whose

[12] *color:* pretext.

life depended only upon him alone. "For Octavia," said they, "that was married unto him as it were of necessity, because her brother Caesar's affairs so required it, hath the honor to be called Antonius' lawful spouse and wife; and Cleopatra, being born a queen of so many thousands of men, is only named Antonius' leman,[13] and yet that she disdained not so to be called, if it might please him she might enjoy his company, and live with him, but if he once leave her, that then it is impossible she should live." To be short, by these their flatteries and enticements, they so wrought Antonius' effeminate mind, that fearing lest she would make herself away, he returned again unto Alexandria, and referred the king of Medes to the next year following, although he received news that the Parthians at that time were at civil wars among themselves.

* * *

About noon there rose a little gale of wind from the sea, and then Antonius' men waxing angry with tarrying so long, and trusting to the greatness and height of their ships, as if they had been invincible, they began to march forward with their left wing. Caesar, seeing that, was a glad man and began a little to give back from the right wing, to allure them to come further out of the strait and gulf: to the end that he might with his light ships well manned with watermen, turn and environ the galleys of the enemies, the which were heavy of yarage,[14] both for their bigness, as also for lack of watermen to row them. When the skirmish began, and that they came to join, there was no great hurt at the first meeting, neither did the ships vehemently hit one against the other, as they do commonly in fight by sea. For on the one side, Antonius' ships for their heaviness could not have the strength and swiftness to make their blows of any force, and Caesar's ships, on the other side, took great heed not to rush and shock with the forecastles of Antonius' ships, whose prows were armed with great brazen spurs. Furthermore, they durst not flank them, because their points were easily broken, whichsoever way they came to set upon his ships, that were made of great main square pieces of timber bound together with great iron pins, so that the battle was much like to a battle by land, or to speak more properly, to the assault of a city. For there were always three or four of Caesar's ships about one of Antonius' ships, and the soldiers fought with their pikes, halberds, and darts, and threw pots and darts with fire. Antonius' ships on the other side bestowed among them, with their crossbows and engines of battery, great store of shot from their high towers of wood that were upon their ships. Now Publicola, seeing Agrippa put forth his left wing of Caesar's army to encompass Antonius' ships that fought, he was driven also to loose off to have more room, and going a little at one side, to put those further off that were afraid and in the midst of the battle. For they were sore distressed by Aruntius. However, the

[13] *leman:* lover.

[14] *heavy of yarage:* difficult to move or manage.

battle was yet of even hand, and the victory doubtful, being indifferent to both, when suddenly they saw the threescore ships of Cleopatra busy about their yard masts, and hoisting sail to fly. So they fled through the midst of them that were in fight, for they had been placed behind the great ships, and did marvelously disorder the other ships. For the enemies themselves wondered much to see them sail in that sort with full sail towards Peloponnesus. There Antonius showed plainly that he had not only lost the courage and heart of an emperor, but also of a valiant man, and that he was not his own man (proving that true which an old man spake in mirth, that the soul of a lover lived in another body, and not in his own) he was so carried away with the vain love of this woman, as if he had been glued unto her, and that she could not have removed without moving of him also. For when he saw Cleopatra's ship under sail, he forgot, forsook, and betrayed them that fought for him and embarked upon a galley with five banks of oars, to follow her that had already begun to overthrow him and would in the end be his utter destruction.

* * *

He was no sooner comen thither, but he straight set all the city of rioting and banqueting again and himself to liberality and gifts. He caused the son of Julius Caesar and Cleopatra to be enrolled (according to the manner of the Romans) amongst the number of young men and gave Antillus his eldest son he had by Fulvia, the man's gown, which was a plain gown without guard or embroidery of purple. For these things, there was kept great feasting, banqueting, and dancing in Alexandria many days together. Indeed they did break their first order they had set down, which they called *Amimetobion* (as much to say, no life comparable) and did set up another which they called *Synapothanumenon* (signifying the order and agreement of those that will die together) the which in exceeding sumptuousness and cost was not inferior to the first. For their friends made themselves to be enrolled in this order of those that would die together, and so made great feasts one to another, for every man when it came to his turn, feasted their whole company and fraternity. Cleopatra in the meantime was very careful in gathering all sorts of poisons together to destroy men. Now to make proof of those poisons which made men die with least pain, she tried it upon condemned men in prison. For when she saw the poisons that were sudden and vehement and brought speedy death with grievous torments, and in contrary manner, that such as were more mild and gentle, had not that quick speed and force to make one die suddenly, she afterwards went about to prove the stinging of snakes and adders and made some to be applied unto men in her sight, some in one sort, and some in another. So when she had daily made divers and sundry proofs she found none of all them she had proved so fit, as the biting of an aspic, the which only causeth a heaviness of the head without swooning or complaining and bringeth a great desire also to sleep, with a little sweat in the face, and so by little and little taketh away the senses and vital powers, no living creature perceiving that the patients feel any pain. For they are so sorry when anybody waketh them and taketh them up as those that being taken out of a sound sleep are very heavy and desirous to sleep. This notwithstanding, they sent ambassadors unto Octavius Caesar in Asia, Cleopatra requesting the realm of Egypt for her children, and Antonius praying that he might be suffered to live at Athens like a private man, if Caesar would not let him remain in Egypt.

* * *

So Caesar came and pitched his camp hard by the city, in the place where they run and manage their horses. Antonius made a sally upon him and fought very valiantly, so that he drave Caesar's horsemen back, fighting with his men even into their camp. Then he came again to the palace, greatly boasting of this victory, and sweetly kissed Cleopatra, armed as he was when he came from the fight, recommending one of his men of arms unto her, that had valiantly fought in this skirmish. Cleopatra, to reward his manliness, gave him an armor and headpiece of clean gold. However, the man-at-arms when he had received this rich gift, stale away by night and went to Caesar. Antonius sent again to challenge Caesar to fight with him hand to hand. Caesar answered him that he had many other ways to die than so. Then Antonius, seeing there was no way more honorable for him to die than fighting valiantly, he determined to set up his rest, both by sea and land. So being at supper (as it is reported) he commanded his officers and household servants that waited on him at his board, that they should fill his cups full and make as much of him as they could. "For," said he, "you know not whether you shall do so much for me tomorrow or not, or whether you shall serve another master, and it may be you shall see me no more, but a dead body." This notwithstanding, perceiving that his friends and men fell a-weeping to hear him say so, to salve that he had spoken, he added this more unto it, that he would not lead them to battle where he thought not rather safely to return with victory than valiantly to die with honor. Furthermore, the selfsame night within little of midnight, when all the city was quiet, full of fear and sorrow, thinking what would be the issue and end of this war, it is said that suddenly they heard a marvelous sweet harmony of sundry sorts of instruments of music, with the cry of a multitude of people, as they had been dancing and had sung as they use in Bacchus' feasts, with movings and turnings after the manner of the satyrs, and it seemed that this dance went through the city unto the gate that opened to the enemies, and that all the troop that made this noise they heard went out of the city at that gate. Now, such as in reason sought the depth of the interpretation of this wonder, thought that it was the god unto whom Antonius bare singular devotion to counterfeit and resemble him, that did forsake them. The next morning by break of day, he went to set those few footmen he had in order upon the hills adjoining unto the city, and there he stood to behold his galleys which departed from the haven and rowed against the galleys of his enemies, and so stood still, looking what exploits his soldiers in them would do. But when by force of rowing they were come near unto them, they first saluted Caesar's men, and then Caesar's men resaluted them also and of two armies made but one, and then did all together row toward the city. When Antonius saw that his men did forsake him and yielded unto Caesar, and that his footmen were broken and overthrown, he then fled into the city, crying out that Cleopatra had betrayed him unto them with whom he had made war for her sake. Then she, being afraid of his fury, fled into the tomb which she had caused to be made, and there locked the doors unto her and shut all the springs of the locks with great bolts and in the meantime sent unto Antonius to tell him that she was dead. Antonius believing it, said unto himself, "What dost thou look for further, Antonius, sith spiteful fortune hath taken from thee the only joy thou hadst for whom thou yet reservedst thy life?" When he had said these words, he went into a chamber and unarmed himself, and being naked said thus, "O Cleopatra, it grieveth me not that I have lost thy company, for I will not be long from thee; but I am sorry that having been so great a captain and emperor, I am indeed condemned to be judged of less courage and noble mind than a woman." Now he had a man of his called Eros, whom he loved and trusted much, and whom he had long before caused to swear unto him that he should kill him when he did command him, and then he willed him to keep his promise. His man drawing his sword, lift it up as though he had meant to have stricken his master, but turning his head at one side, he thrust his sword into himself and fell down dead at his master's foot. Then said Antonius, "O noble Eros, I thank thee for this, and it is valiantly done of thee, to show me what I should do to myself, which thou couldst not do for me." Therewithal he took his sword and thrust it into his belly and so fell down upon a little bed. The wound he had killed him not presently, for the blood stinted a little when he was laid, and when he came somewhat to himself again he prayed them that were about him to dispatch him. But they all fled out of the chamber and left him crying out and tormenting himself, until at last there came a secretary unto him called Diomedes, who was commanded to bring him into the tomb or monument where Cleopatra was. When he heard that she was alive, he very earnestly prayed his men to carry his body thither, and so he was carried in his men's arms into the entry of the monument. Notwithstanding, Cleopatra would not open the gates, but came to the high windows and cast out certain chains and ropes in the which Antonius was trussed; and Cleopatra her own self, with two women only, which she had suffered to come with her into these monuments, triced[15] Antonius up. They that were present to behold it, said they never saw so pitiful a sight. For they plucked up poor Antonius all bloody as he was, and drawing on with pangs of death, who holding up his hands to Cleopatra, raised up himself as well as he could. It was a hard thing for these women to do, to lift him up, but Cleopatra stooping down with her head, putting to all her

[15] *triced:* pulled.

strength to her uttermost power, did lift him up with much ado, and never let go her hold, with the help of the women beneath that bade her be of good courage and were as sorry to see her labor so as she herself. So when she had gotten him in after that sort, and laid him on a bed, she rent her garments upon him, clapping her breast and scratching her face and stomach. Then she dried up his blood that had berayed [16] his face, and called him her lord, her husband, and emperor, forgetting her own misery and calamity, for the pity and compassion she took of him. Antonius made her cease her lamenting and called for wine, either because he was athirst or else that he thought thereby to hasten his death. When he had drunk, he earnestly prayed her, and persuaded her, that she would seek to save her life, if she could possible without reproach and dishonor, and that chiefly she should trust Proculeius above any man else about Caesar. And as for himself, that she should not lament nor sorrow for the miserable change of his fortune at the end of his days, but rather, that she should think him the more fortunate, for the former triumphs and honors he had received, considering that while he lived he was the noblest and greatest prince of the world, and that now he was overcome, not cowardly, but valiantly, a Roman by another Roman. As Antonius gave the last gasp, Proculeius came that was sent from Caesar. For after Antonius had thrust his sword in himself, as they carried him into the tombs and monuments of Cleopatra, one of his guard, called Dercetaeus, took his sword with the which he had stricken himself and hid it. Then he secretly stale away and brought Octavius Caesar the first news of his death and showed him his sword that was bloodied. Caesar hearing these news, straight withdrew himself into a secret place of his tent and there burst out with tears, lamenting his hard and miserable fortune that had been his friend and brother-in-law, his equal in the Empire, and companion with him in sundry great exploits and battles.

---

[16] *berayed:* soiled.

George Gascoigne

1539–1578

GASCOIGNE was the son of Sir John Gascoigne of Cardington, Bedfordshire, and was educated at Cambridge, the Middle Temple, and Gray's Inn. It was at these latter institutions, supposedly residences for law students but as often as not clubs for young wits and literary men, that Gascoigne began his extensive and versatile literary production. His translations, with a collaborator, of *Jocasta* and *The Supposes* are important as examples of early tragedy and comedy for amateur production. He also competed with his fellows in poetical compositions on set themes, some of which he later published. His life was turbulent in what has come to be thought of as typically Elizabethan fashion; he married Elizabeth Bacon Breton, the mother of Nicholas Breton the poet, while she was still the wife of another man, and became involved in a street brawl over the affair. In 1572 a petition was circulated which prevented him from taking a seat in Parliament, where he had already served twice, on the ground that he was a common rhymer, a spy, atheist, and godless person, as well as a notorious ruffian. In the same year he embarked for military service in the Low Countries; he sent back to Lord Grey of Wilton a versified account of his trip, filled with charges of the treachery and drunkenness and immorality of the Dutch. He remained abroad for about three years, returning to England to find that a collection of his youthful poems, and his two plays, had been published anonymously under the title *A Hundreth Sundrie Flowres*. "I find that some of them," he says, "have not only been offensive for sundry wanton speeches and lascivious phrases, but further I hear that the same have been doubtfully construed, and therefore scandalous." He proceeded to reissue his poems, revised and classified into groups called "Flowers," "Herbs," and "Weeds," under the title of *The Posies of George Gascoigne*. He advertised his double career as soldier and poet by using the motto *Tam Marti quam Mercurio* in addition to the mottoes or "posies" which had been appended to the *Sundrie Flowres*. He also made successful attempts to reach the Queen's ear for favor; he helped to write and produce the famous entertainment at Kenilworth in July, 1575 and a similar royal festivity at Woodstock in the same year. In 1576 he published seven new compositions in prose and verse and was sent by Burleigh on a diplomatic mission to France. He died in 1577 or 1578, still in his thirties, and still trying to live down his wild youth and achieve a position of dignity at the court.

Gascoigne is the most representative writer of the seventies, and aside from Sackville, the most important poet between Surrey and Spenser. His importance lies in his versatility: he was a pioneer in the drama, his *Adventures of Master F.I.* has been called the first English novel, his *Steel Glass* is important early satire, and his *Certain Notes of Instruction* is a major contribution to Elizabethan literary criticism. The selections given here illustrate his use of varied verse forms: fourteeners, poulter's measure, rhyme royal, and blank verse. Gascoigne's style is usually conversational and journalistic rather than "poetic"; he likes homely images and seldom preserves a sustained level of emotion; but the resemblance to Byron which has been often observed is perhaps not entirely fanciful.

BIBLIOGRAPHY: *The Complete Works of George Gascoigne,* ed. J. W. Cunliffe, Cambridge, 1907–1910; *A Hundreth Sundrie Flowers,* ed. C. T. Prouty, *Univ. of Missouri Studies,* XVII, 2 (1942); S. A. Tannenbaum, *George Gascoigne, A Concise Bibliography,* New York, 1942; D. T. Starnes, "Gascoigne's *Complaint of Philomene,*" *Texas Studies in English* (1947), 26–41.

AMID my bale I bathe in bliss,[1]
I swim in heaven, I sink in hell;
I find amends for every miss,
And yet my moan no tongue can tell.
I live and love—what would you more?
As never lover lived before.

I laugh sometimes with little lust,
So jest I oft and feel no joy;
My ease is builded all on trust,
And yet mistrust breeds mine annoy.
I live and lack, I lack and have:
I have and miss the thing I crave.

These things seem strange, yet are they true,
Believe me, sweet, my state is such;
One pleasure which I would eschew
Both slakes my grief and breeds my grutch;[2]
So doth one pain which I would shun
Renew my joys where grief begun.

Then, like the lark that passed the night
In heavy sleep with cares oppressed,
Yet when she spies the pleasant light,
She sends sweet notes from out her breast,
So sing I now because I think
How joys approach, when sorrows shrink.

And as fair Philomene again
Can watch and sing when others sleep,
And taketh pleasure in her pain
To wray[3] the woe that makes her weep,
So sing I now for to bewray
The loathsome life I lead alway.

The which to thee, dear wench, I write,
That know'st my mirth but not my moan;
I pray God grant thee deep delight
To live in joys when I am gone.

---

[1] The first five poems are selected from *A Hundreth Sundrie Flowres,* but the text is that corrected by the poet himself in *The Posies. bale:* torment.

[2] *grutch:* grudge.

[3] *wray:* bewray, expose.

I cannot live: it will not be.
I die to think to part from thee.

Ferenda Natura.[4]

GASCOIGNE'S ARRAIGNMENT

At Beauty's bar as I did stand,
When False Suspect accused me,
"George," quod[5] the judge, "hold up thy hand;
Thou art arraigned of flattery.
Tell therefore how thou wilt be tried.
Whose judgment here wilt thou abide?"

"My lord," quod I, "this lady here,
Whom I esteem above the rest,
Doth know my guilt, if any were,
Wherefore her doom[6] shall please me best;
Let her be judge and juror both,
To try me, guiltless by mine oath."

Quod Beauty, "No, it fitteth not,
A Prince herself to judge the cause;
Will is our Justice, well you wot,
Appointed to discuss our laws;
If you will guiltless seem to go,
God and your country quit you so."

Then Craft, the crier, called a quest,[7]
Of whom was Falsehood foremost fere;[8]
A pack of pickthanks[9] were the rest,
Which came false witness for to bear;
The jury such, the judge unjust,
Sentence was said I should be trussed.

Jealous, the jailer, bound me fast,
To hear the verdict of the bill;

---

[4] *Ferenda Natura:* This and the other mottoes or "posies" appended to the poems are explained by Gascoigne himself as follows: "If ever I wrote lyne for myselfe in causes of love, I have written tenne for other men in layes of lust. . . . And by that it proceedeth, that I have so often chaunged my Posie or worde."

[5] *quod:* quoth, said.

[6] *doom:* judgment.

[7] *quest:* inquest.

[8] *fere:* companion, fellow.

[9] *pickthanks:* flatterers.

"George," quod the judge, "now thou art cast,[10]
Thou must go hence to Heavy Hill,
And there be hanged, all but the head;
God rest thy soul when thou art dead."

Down fell I then upon my knee,
All flat before Dame Beauty's face,
And cried, "Good Lady, pardon me,
Which here appeal unto your Grace;
You know if I have been untrue,
It was in too much praising you.

"And though this judge do make such haste
To shed with shame my guiltless blood,
Yet let your pity first be placed,
To save the man that meant you good;
So shall you show yourself a queen,
And I may be your servant seen."

Quod Beauty, "Well; because I guess
What thou dost mean henceforth to be,
Although thy faults deserve no less
Than Justice here hath judged thee,
Wilt thou be bound to stint [11] all strife,
And be true prisoner all thy life?"

"Yea, madam," quod I, "that I shall;
Lo, Faith and Truth, my sureties."
"Why, then," quod she, "come when I call,
I ask no better warrantise."
Thus am I Beauty's bounden thrall,
At her command when she doth call.

Ever or never.

GASCOIGNE'S GOOD-NIGHT

WHEN thou hast spent the lingering day in pleasure and delight,
Or after toil and weary way, dost seek to rest at night,
Unto thy pains or pleasures past, add this one labor yet:
Ere sleep close up thine eye too fast, do not thy God forget,
But search within thy secret thoughts, what deeds did thee befall;
And if thou find amiss in aught, to God for mercy call.

---

[10] *cast:* convicted.

[11] *stint:* cease.

Yea, though thou find nothing amiss which thou canst call to mind,
Yet evermore remember this: there is the more behind;
And think how well so ever it be that thou hast spent the day,
It came of God, and not of thee, so to direct thy way.
Thus, if thou try thy daily deeds and pleasure in this pain,
Thy life shall cleanse thy corn from weeds, and thine shall be the gain;
But if thy sinful, sluggish eye will venture for to wink,
Before thy wading will may try how far thy soul may sink,
Beware and wake; for else, thy bed, which soft and smooth is made,
May heap more harm upon thy head than blows of en'my's blade.
Thus if this pain procure thine ease, in bed as thou dost lie,
Perhaps it shall not God displease to sing thus, soberly:
"I see that sleep is lent me here to ease my weary bones,
As death at last shall eke appear, to ease my grievous groans.
My daily sports, my paunch full fed, have caused my drowsy eye,
As careless life, in quiet led, might cause my soul to die.
The stretching arms, the yawning breath, which I to bedward use,
Are patterns of the pangs of death, when life will me refuse.
And of my bed each sundry part in shadows doth resemble
The sundry shapes of death, whose dart shall make my flesh to tremble.
My bed itself is like the grave, my sheets the winding sheet,
My clothes the mold which I must have to cover me most meet;
The hungry fleas, which frisk so fresh, to worms I can compare,
Which greedily shall gnaw my flesh and leave the bones full bare.
The waking cock, that early crows to wear the night away
Puts in my mind the trump that blows before the Latter Day.
And as I rise up lustily when sluggish sleep is past,
So hope I to rise joyfully to Judgment at the last.
Thus will I wake, thus will I sleep, thus will I hope to rise,
Thus will I neither wail nor weep, but sing in godly wise;
My bones shall in this bed remain, my soul in God shall trust,
By whom I hope to rise again from death and earthly dust."

Haud ictus sapio.

GASCOIGNE'S LULLABY

Sing lullaby, as women do,
Wherewith they bring their babes to rest,
And lullaby can I sing too,
As womanly as can the best.
With lullaby they still the child,
And if I be not much beguiled,

Full many wanton babes have I,
Which must be stilled with lullaby.

First, lullaby, my youthful years,
It is now time to go to bed,
For crooked age and hoary hairs
Have won the haven within my head.
With lullaby then, youth, be still,
With lullaby content thy will,
Since courage quails and comes behind,
Go sleep, and so beguile thy mind.

Next, lullaby, my gazing eyes,
Which wonted were to glance apace.
For every glass may now suffice
To show the furrows in my face.
With lullaby then wink awhile,
With lullaby your looks beguile.
Let no fair face nor beauty bright
Entice you eft with vain delight.

And lullaby, my wanton will,
Let reason's rule now rein thy thought,
Since all too late I find by skill
How dear I have thy fancies bought.
With lullaby now take thine ease,
With lullaby thy doubts appease.
For trust to this, if thou be still,
My body shall obey thy will.

Eke lullaby, my loving boy,
My little Robin, take thy rest.
Since age is cold and nothing coy,
Keep close thy coin, for so is best.
With lullaby be thou content,
With lullaby thy lusts relent.
Let others pay which hath mo pence;
Thou art too poor for such expense.

Thus, lullaby, my youth, mine eyes,
My will, my ware, and all that was.
I can no mo delays devise,
But welcome pain, let pleasure pass.
With lullaby now take your leave,
With lullaby your dreams deceive,
And when you rise with waking eye,
Remember Gascoigne's lullaby.

Ever or never.

A LIBEL[12] OF DIVORCE

Divorce me now, good Death, from Love and ling'ring Life;
That one hath been my concubine, that other was my wife.
In youth I lived with Love, she had my lusty days;
In age I thought with lingering Life to stay my wandering ways;
But now, abused by both, I come for to complain
To thee, good Death, in whom my help doth wholly now remain.
My libel lo, behold, wherein I do protest,
The process of my plaint is true, in which my grief doth rest.
First, Love, my concubine, whom I have kept so trim,
Even she, for whom I seemed of yore in seas of joy to swim;
To whom I dare avow that I have served as well
And played my part as gallantly as he that bears the bell;[13]
She cast me off long since, and holds me in disdain;
I cannot prank to please her now, my vaunting is but vain.
My writhled[14] cheeks bewray that pride of heat is past,
My stagg'ring steps eke tell the truth that Nature fadeth fast,
My quaking crooked joints are cumbered with the cramp,
The box of oil is wasted well which once did feed my lamp.
The greenness of my years doth wither now so sore
That lusty love leaps quite away and liketh me no more.
And Love, my leman, gone, what liking can I take
In loathsome Life, that crooked crone, although she be my make?
She cloys me with the cough, her comfort is but cold;
She bids me give mine age for alms where first my youth was sold.
No day can pass my head, but she begins to brawl,
No merry thoughts conceived so fast but she confounds them all.
When I pretend to please, she overthwarts me still;
When I would fainest part with her, she overweighs my will.
Be judge, then, gentle Death, and take my cause in hand,
Consider every circumstance, mark how the case doth stand.
Percase thou wilt allege that cause thou canst none see
But that I like not of that one, that other likes not me?
Yes, gentle judge, give ear, and thou shalt see me prove
My concubine incontinent, a common whore is Love.
And in my wife I find such discord and debate,
As no man living can endure the torments of my state.
Wherefore thy sentence say; divorce me from them both;
Since only thou may'st right my wrongs; good Death, now be not loath,

[12] *Libel:* a writing by which a plaintiff starts suit.

[13] *bears the bell:* is preeminent.

[14] *writhled:* wrinkled, withered.

But cast thy piercing dart into my panting breast,
That I may leave both Love and Life, and thereby purchase rest.

Haud ictus sapio.

FROM

THE STEEL GLASS[15]

I

BUT that my lord may plainly understand
The mysteries of all that I do mean,
I am not he whom slanderous tongues have told,
(False tongues indeed, and crafty subtle brains)
To be the man which meant a common spoil
Of loving dames whose ears would hear my words
Or trust the tales devised by my pen.
I n' am a man, as some do think I am;
(Laugh not, good lord) I am indeed a dame,
Or at the least, a right hermaphrodite;
And who desires at large to know my name,
My birth, my line, and every circumstance,
Lo, read it here: Plain Dealing was my sire,
And he begat me by Simplicity;
A pair of twins at one self burden born,
My sister and I into this world were sent:
My sister's name was pleasant Poesy,
And I myself had Satyra to name,
Whose hap was such that, in the prime of youth,
A lusty lad, a stately man to see,
Brought up in place where pleasures did abound—
(I dare not say "—in court," for both mine ears)
Began to woo my sister, not for wealth,
But for her face was lovely to behold,
And therewithal her speech was pleasant still.
This noble's name was called Vain Delight,
And in his train he had a comely crew
Of guileful wights: False Semblant was the first,

[15] The first section is an introductory passage from the poem, an apology for satire. It adapts the myth of Philomela, sister to Procne, who was ravished by Tereus and changed into a nightingale. The second section is the description of the plowman, in imitation of the great medieval poem *The Vision of Piers Plowman*

The second man was Fleering[16] Flattery,
(Brethren belike, or very near of kin).
Then followed them, Detraction and Deceit.
Sym Swash did bear a buckler for the first,
False Witness was the second's seemly page,
And thus well armed, and in good equipage,
This gallant came unto my father's court
And wooed my sister, for she elder was,
And fairer eke, but out of doubt, at least
Her pleasant speech surpassed mine so much
That Vain Delight to her addressed his suit.
Short tale to make, she gave a free consent,
And forth she goeth to be his wedded make,
Enticed percase with gloss of gorgeous show,
Or else, perhaps, persuaded by his peers
That constant love had harbored in his breast;
Such errors grow where such false prophets preach.
How so it were, my sister liked him well,
And forth she goeth, in court with him to dwell,
Where, when she had some years ysojourned
And saw the world, and marked each man's mind,
A deep desire her loving heart enflamed
To see me sit by her in seemly wise,
That company might comfort her sometimes
And sound advice might ease her weary thoughts.
And forth with speed, even at her first request,
Doth Vain Delight his hasty course direct;
To seek me out his sails are fully bent,
And wind was good, to bring me to the bower
Whereas she lay, that mourned days and nights
To see herself so matched and so deceived.
And when the wretch—I cannot term him bet—[17]
Had me on seas full far from friendly help,
A spark of lust did kindle in his breast
And bade him hark to songs of Satyra.
I, sely soul, which thought nobody harm,
Gan clear my throat, and strave to sing my best,
Which pleased him so, and so enflamed his heart,
That he forgot my sister Poesy
And ravished me, to please his wanton mind.
Not so content, when this foul fact was done,
Yfraught with fear, lest that I should disclose
His incest and his doting, dark desire,

[16] *Fleering:* smiling in a fawning fashion. [17] *bet:* better.

He caused straightway the foremost of his crew,
With his compeer, to try me with their tongues;
And when their guiles could not prevail to win
My simple mind from track of trusty truth,
Nor yet Deceit could blear mine eyes through fraud,
Came Slander then, accusing me, and said
That I enticed Delight to love and lust.
Thus was I caught, poor wretch, that thought none ill.
And furthermore, to cloak their own offense,
They clapt me fast in cage of misery,
And there I dwelt, full many a doleful day,
Until this thief, this traitor, Vain Delight,
Cut out my tongue with razor of restraint
Lest I should wray this bloody deed of his.
And thus, my lord, I live a weary life,
Not as I seemed, a man sometimes of might,
But womanlike, whose tears must venge her harms.
And yet, even as the mighty gods did deign
For Philomel, that though her tongue were cut,
Yet should she sing a pleasant note sometimes;
So have they deigned, by their divine decrees,
That with the stumps of my reproved tongue,
I may sometimes reprovers' tongues reprove,
And sing a verse to make them see themselves.

2

Behold him, priests, and though he stink of sweat
Disdain him not; for shall I tell you what?
Such climb to heaven before the shaven crowns.[18]
But how? Forsooth, with true humility.
Not that they hoard their grain when it is cheap,
Nor that they kill the calf to have the milk,
Nor that they set debate between their lords
By earing up the balks that part their bounds;[19]
Nor for because they can both crouch and creep
(The guileful'st men that ever God yet made)
Whenas they mean most mischief and deceit,
Nor that they can cry out on landlords loud
And say they rack their rents an ace too high,
When they themselves do sell their landlord's lamb
For greater price than ewe was wont be worth;

[18] *shaven crowns:* monks' tonsures.

[19] *By . . . bounds:* by plowing up the strips which should stand as boundaries.

(I see you, Piers,[20] my glass was lately scoured.)
But for they feed, with fruits of their great pains,
Both king and knight, and priests in cloister pent;
Therefore I say that sooner some of them
Shall scale the walls which lead us up to heaven,
Than corn-fed beasts, whose belly is their god,
Although they preach of more perfection.

. . . .

But here methinks my priests begin to frown,
And say that thus they shall be overcharged,
To pray for all which seem to do amiss;
And one I hear, more saucy than the rest,
Which asketh me, "When shall our prayers end?"
I tell thee, priest, when shoemakers make shoes
That are well sewed, with never a stitch amiss,
And use no craft in utt'ring of the same;[21]
When tailors steal no stuff from gentlemen;
When tanners are with curriers well agreed,
And both so dress their hides that we go dry;
When cutlers leave to sell old rusty blades,
And hide no cracks with solder nor deceit;
When tinkers make no more holes than they found;
When thatchers think their wages worth their work;
When colliers put no dust into their sacks;
When maltmen make us drink no fermenty;[22]
When Davie Diker digs and dallies not;
When smiths shoe horses as they would be shod;
When millers toll not with a golden thumb;
When bakers make not barm[23] bear price of wheat;
When brewers put no baggage in their beer;
When butchers blow not over all their flesh;
When horse-coursers beguile no friends with jades;
When weaver's weight is found in huswives' web;
(But why dwell I so long among these louts?)
When mercers make more bones to swear and lie;
When vintners mix no water with their wine;
When printers pass none errors in their books;
When hatters use to buy none old cast robes;
When goldsmiths get no gains by soldered crowns;
When upholsters sell feathers without dust;

[20] *Piers:* conventional name for a peasant, from *Piers Plowman.*

[21] *use . . . same:* use no deceit in selling them.

[22] *fermenty:* unfermented mash.

[23] *barm:* froth, yeast.

When pewterers infect no tin with lead;
When drapers draw no gains by giving day;
When parchmentiers put in no ferret silk;
When surgeons heal all wounds without delay.
Tush! these are toys; but yet my glass showeth all.

FROM

THE GRIEF OF JOY

THE grief of joy in worthy wise to write,
That by the vice the virtue might be found,
Requireth skill and cunning to endite:
First, skill to judge of every grief the ground,
Then art, to tell wherein men's joys abound.
My muse, therefore, not causeless dreadeth blame,
Whose art and skill, God knows, long since were lame.

The wandering ways of reckless ranging youth
Made Will forget the little skill I had,
And wanton rhymes, whereof no fruit ensu'th,
Have made my style, which never good was, bad;
Well may I then accompted be but mad
To take in hand a work so great and grave
With those few tools, which yet untoucht I have.

But, as the man which serves his prenticehood
With artisans whose cunning doth excel,
Although his skill be never half so good
As theirs hath been, whose bruit [24] did bear the bell;
Yet will the world expect he should do well,
And partly grant that he deserveth fame
Because his masters were of worthy name;

Even so myself, who sometime bare the books
Of such as were great clerks and men of skill,
Presume to think that everybody looks [25]
I should be like unto my teachers still.
And thereupon I venture my good will

[24] *bruit:* noise, fame.

[25] *looks:* expects.

In barren verse to do the best I can,
Like Chaucer's boy, and Petrarch's journeyman.[26]

You, then, who read and rifle in my rhymes
To seek the rose, where nothing grows but thorns,
Of courtesy yet pardon him which climbs
To purchase praise, although he find but scorns.
Full well wot you that Corinth shoeing-horns [27]
May not be made like everybody's nose;
No buckler serves to bear all kind of blows.

But if some English word herein seem sweet,
Let Chaucer's name exalted be therefor;
If any verse do pass on pleasant feet,
The praise thereof redound to Petrarch's lore.
(Few words to use! If either less or more
Be found herein which seem to merit fame,
The laud thereof be to my Sovereign's name.)

Reproof, mine own, for all that is amiss;
And faults must swarm where little skill doth reign.
Yet for myself, I can allege but this:
The 'mazed man, whom Beauty's blaze hath slain,
Doth go in grief, and yet perceives no pain;
And they whom love hath daunted with delight
Find seldom fault, but think that all goeth right.

My seasick brains are giddy with the gaze
Which Fancy cast at lovely looks long since;
And forward still I wander in the maze
Where sweet Deceit my reason doth convince;
Yet as I may, you see, my Muse must mince
Such nice conceits as tumble in my head
To please her mind who knows what life I lead.

Such potherbs grow where Fancy digs the soil
And hot Desire bestows the willing seed.
But what for that? More fruitless were his toil
Whom any grief could make repent the deed

---

[26] *Petrarch's journeyman:* Gascoigne confessed in his dedication to Queen Elizabeth that *The Grief of Joy* was an attempt to make the subject matter of Petrarch's *De remediis utriusque fortunae* into English songs, in "the Interims and vacant howres of those daies which I spent this sommer in your service."

[27] *Corinth shoeing-horns:* a Greek and Latin proverb, *non cuivis homini contingit adire Corinthum* (Horace, *Epistles,* I, xvii, 36). The idea of the proverb is that not everybody gets to Corinth, because its harbor is a dangerous and difficult one for ships, or perhaps because the luxurious life there is so expensive. Gascoigne, in making the figure homely, has partly obscured the meaning.

Which once with joy his jolly thoughts did feed.
One sight of Heaven might make my mind to dwell
Seven years, content, in depth of darksome hell.

There is a grief in every kind of joy.
That is my theme, and that I mean to prove.
And who were he which would not drink annoy
To taste thereby the lightest dram of love?
But whilst I dream, it better shall behoove
To wake a braid [28] and take my work in hand,
Lest Will be shent,[29] when toys by truth are scanned.

Then let me say that life to man is lent
To dwell on earth in jollity and joy;
But therewithal, it seems that God was bent
To visit man, in mirth, with much annoy.
These contraries are truth, and like no toy.
For look who list, and doubtless he shall find
Some grudge of grief in every joyful mind.

[28] *wake a braid:* awake with a start.

[29] *shent:* hindered.

Raphael Holinshed

died *ca.* 1580

THE writing of history in the reign of Elizabeth was an occupation that seized upon men's imaginations just as voyages of exploration and discovery did. The earlier Tudor monarchs had encouraged the writing of history which would justify their dynasty and their right to the throne, and there had been history written from the Protestant point of view (see Foxe, pp. 135–143) and from the Catholic point of view, as propaganda. But the motive of the real historian is not to serve the political purposes of monarch or church, but to satisfy the curiosity of men, and the scope of Elizabethan curiosity is nowhere better illustrated than by the projects for writing world history which were conceived and in part carried out in the latter half of the sixteenth century.

Raphael Holinshed explains, in his dedication to Lord Burleigh, how the great history published under his name in 1577 came to be written. The printer Reginald Wolfe, printer to the Queen, "meant in his life time to publish an vniuersall Cosmographie of the whole worlde, and therewith also certaine perticular Histories of euery knowen nation" and for the purpose employed learned men, of whom Holinshed was one. Wolfe had in his possession the notes of "that learned and painful antiquary" (as Holinshed calls him), John Leland, and Holinshed was to use these and all other available sources for compiling his narrative. After twenty-five years of labor in this great scheme, Reginald Wolfe died without seeing it completed. His heirs wished the work to continue, but when they saw what a huge book would result, their courage faltered, and they resolved to publish first the histories of England, Scotland, and Ireland. But the descriptions of those countries were not as advanced as the descriptions of foreign countries, so two more experts were employed, William Harrison to write the description of England and Richard Stanihurst to finish the account of Ireland. Holinshed's own narrative of the history of these countries formed the bulk of the work, however; it appeared in 1577, and in an expanded version in 1587. Burleigh, Leicester, and Sir Henry Sidney were the patrons of the English, Scottish, and Irish histories respectively. The book was illustrated with woodcuts of executions and coronations, battle scenes and progresses, and a large double-page illustration of the siege of Edinburgh castle.

Holinshed drew upon earlier published chronicles as well as on manuscript material; he expresses gratitude in his list of authorities to John Stow, "by whose diligent collected summarie, I haue ben not only ayded, but also by diuers rare monuments, ancient wryters, and necessarie register Bookes of his, which he hath lente me out of his owne Librarie." In his marginal notes and in the text itself Holinshed took the opportunity offered by historical episodes to moralize, teach, and draw lessons of patriotism and religion. There is of course prejudice in his sources, too, but when Holinshed could find disagreement among reputable authorities, he was cautious: "for my parte, I haue in things doubtfull rather chosen to shewe the diuersitie of their writings, than by ouer ruling them, and vsing a peremptory censure, to frame them to agree to my liking, leauing it neuerthelesse to eche mans iudgement to controlle them as he seeth cause. If some where I shew my fancie what I thinke, and that the same dislike them, I craue pardon, specially if by probable reasons or playner matter to be produced, they can shew mine errour, vpon knowledge whereof I shalbe ready to reforme it accordingly."

The great fame of Holinshed's *Chronicle* in modern times derives mostly from the fact that Shakespeare learned his English history from it. The selections given below parallel his dramatic treatment of the same events in the two parts of *Henry IV* and *Henry V*. But it should be remembered that an earlier play on the subject, *The Famous Victories of Henry V,* was also known to Shakespeare, so this is not as simple a relationship between the prose source and the play as exists, say, between Lodge's *Rosalynde* and *As You Like It.* The text given here is based upon the first edition, 1577; Shakespeare used a somewhat revised second edition of a decade later.

BIBLIOGRAPHY: W. G. Boswell-Stone, *Shakespeare's Holinshed: The Chronicle and the Historical Plays Compared,* London, 1896; C. L. Kingsford, "Fifteenth-century History in Shakespeare's Plays" in *Prejudice and Promise in XVth Century England,* Oxford, 1925; C. L. Kingsford, ed., *The First English Life of King Henry V,* Oxford, 1911.

[THE BATTLE OF SHREWSBURY]

BUT now to return where we left, King Henry, advertised of the proceedings of the Percies, forthwith gathered about him such power as he might make, and being earnestly called upon by the Scot, the Earl of March, to make haste and give battle to his enemies, before their power by delaying of time should still too much increase, he passed forward with such speed that he was in sight of his enemies lying in camp near to Shrewsbury before they were in doubt [1] of any such thing, for the Percies thought that he would have stayed at Burton-upon-Trent till his Council had come thither to him to give their advice what he were best to do. By reason of the King's sudden coming in this sort, they stayed from assaulting the town of Shrewsbury, which enterprise they were ready at that instant to have taken in hand, and forthwith the Lord Percy,[2] as a captain of high courage, began to exhort the captains and soldiers to prepare themselves to battle, sith the matter was grown to that point that by no means it could be avoided, so that, said he, "this day shall either bring us all to advancement and honor, or else if it shall chance us to be overcome, shall deliver us from the King's spiteful malice and cruel disdain, for playing the men as we ought to do; better it is to die in battle for the commonwealth's cause than through coward-like fear to prolong life which after shall be taken from us by sentence of the enemy."

Hereupon, the whole army, being in number about a fourteen thousand chosen men, promised to stand with him so long as life lasted.

There were with the Percies as chieftains of this army the Earl of Douglas, a Scottish man, the Baron of Kinderton, Sir Hugh Browne and Sir Richard Vernon, Knights, with divers other stout and right valiant captains.

Now when the two armies were encamped the one against the other, the Earl of Worcester and the Lord Percy with their complices sent the articles (whereof I spake before) by Thomas Cayton and Thomas Salvain Esquires, to King Henry under their hands and seals, which articles in effect charged him with manifest perjury, in that, contrary to his oath received upon the Evangelists at Doncaster when he first entered the realm after his exile, he had taken upon him the crown and royal dignity, imprisoned King Richard, caused him to resign his title and finally to be murthered. Divers other matters they laid to his charge, as levying of taxes and tallages [3] contrary to his promise, infringing laws and customs of the realm and suffering

[1] *in doubt:* aware.

[2] *Lord Percy:* Hotspur. For Shakespeare's version of his speech see *I Henry IV*, V, ii, 82–89.

[3] *tallages:* feudal taxes.

the Earl of March to remain in prison without travailing to have him delivered—all which things they as proctors and protectors of the commonwealth took upon them to prove against him, as they protested to the whole world.

King Henry, after he had read their articles, with the defiance which they annexed to the same, answered the esquires that he was ready with dint of sword and fierce battle to prove their quarrel false and nothing else than forged matter, not doubting but that God would aid and assist him in his righteous cause against the disloyal and false forsworn traitors.

The next day in the morning early, being the even of Mary Magdalene,[4] they set their battles in order on both sides, and now whilst the warriors looked when the token of battle should be given, the Abbot of Shrewsbury and one of the Clerks of the Privy Seal were sent from the King unto the Percies to offer them pardon if they would come to any reasonable agreement.

By their persuasions, the Lord Henry Percy began to give ear unto the King's offers, and so sent with them his uncle the Earl of Worcester to declare unto the King the causes of those troubles and to require some effectual reformation in the same.

It was reported for a truth that now when the King had condescended unto all that was reasonable at his hands to be required and seemed to humble himself more than was meet for his estate, the Earl of Worcester upon his return to his nephew made relation clean contrary to that the King had said, in such sort that he set his nephew's heart more in displeasure towards the King than ever it was before, driving him by that means to fight whether he would or not. Then suddenly blew the trumpets, the King's part cried "St. George! Upon them!", the adversaries cried "Esperance! Percy!", and so the two armies furiously joined. The archers on both sides shot for the best game, laying on such load with arrows that many died, and were driven down, that never rose again.

* * *

The Prince that day holp his father like a lusty young gentleman, for although he was hurt in the face with an arrow so that divers noblemen that were about him would have conveyed him forth of the field, yet he would in no wise suffer them so to do, lest his departure from among his men might haply have stricken some fear into their hearts; and so, without regard of his hurt, he continued with his men and never ceased either to fight where the battle was most hottest or to encourage his men where it seemed most need. This battle lasted three long hours, with indifferent fortune on both parts, till at length the King, crying "St. George! Victory!", brake the array of his enemies and adventured so far that, as some write, the Earl Douglas strake him down, and at that instant slew Sir Walter Blunt and three other appareled in the King's suit and clothing, saying,

---

[4] *even of Mary Magdalene:* July 21.

"I marvel to see so many kings thus suddenly to arise, one in the neck of another." The King indeed was raised, and did that day many a noble feat of arms, for as it is written, he slew that day with his own hands six-and-thirty persons of his enemies. The other on his part [5] encouraged by his doings, fought valiantly and slew the Lord Percy, called Sir Henry Hotspur. To conclude, the King's enemies were vanquished and put to flight, in which flight the Earl of Douglas, for haste, falling from the crag of a mountain, brake one of his genitals, and was taken, and for his valiantness, of the King frankly and freely delivered.

* * *

[THE DEATH OF KING HENRY IV] [6]

During this his last sickness,[7] he caused his crown, as some write, to be set on a pillow at his bed's head, and suddenly his pangs so sore troubled him that he lay as though all his vital spirits had been from him departed. Such as were about him, thinking verily that he had been departed, covered his face with a linen cloth.

The Prince his son, being hereof advertised, entered into the chamber, took away the crown, and departed. The father being suddenly revived out of that trance, quickly perceived the lack of his crown, and having knowledge that the Prince his son had taken it away, caused him to come before his presence, requiring of him what he meant so to misuse himself. The Prince, with a good audacity, answered, "Sir, to mine and all men's judgments you seemed dead in this world, wherefore I as your next heir apparent took that as mine own, and not as yours." "Well, fair son," said the King, with a great sigh, "what right [8] I had to it, God knoweth." "Well," quoth the Prince, "if you die King, I will have the garland and trust to keep it with the sword against all mine enemies as you have done." "Then," said the King, "I commit all to God, and remember you to do well," and with that turned himself in his bed and shortly after departed to God in a chamber of the Abbot's of Westminster called Jerusalem, the twentieth day of March in the year 1413, and in the year of his age forty-six, when he had reigned thirteen years five months and odd days in great perplexity and little pleasure.

We find that he was taken with his last sickness while he was making his prayers at Saint Edward's shrine, there as it were to take his leave [9] and so to proceed forth on his journey; he was so suddenly and grievously taken that such as were about him feared lest he would have died pres-

---

[5] *The other on his part:* I.e., the King's soldiers (plural), not Prince Hal, as in Shakespeare.

[6] For this episode, see *II Henry IV*, IV, v.

[7] *sickness:* "An apoplexie," according to Holinshed's marginal note.

[8] *what right:* Holinshed's note: "A guilty conscience in extremity of sickness pincheth sore."

[9] *take his leave:* Holinshed's note: "I can not think he was so near ready to set forward, whatsoever Fabyan writeth hereof."

ently;[10] wherefore to relieve him if it were possible, they bare him into a chamber that was next at hand, belonging to the Abbot of Westminster, where they laid him on a pallet before the fire and used all remedies to revive him. At length he recovered his speech, and, understanding and perceiving himself in a strange place which he knew not, he willed to know if the chamber had any particular name, whereunto answer was made that it was called Jerusalem. Then said the King, "Lauds be given to the Father of Heaven, for now I know that I shall die here in this chamber, according to the prophecy of me declared, that I should depart this life in Jerusalem." Whether this was true that so he spake, as one that too much gave credit to foolish prophecies and vain tales, or whether it was feigned, as in such cases it commonly happeneth, we leave it to the advised reader to judge.

[THE REFORMATION OF HENRY V]

But whatsoever men's fancies hereof might conjecture, this king was the man that, according to the old proverb, declared and showed in what sort honors ought to change manners, for immediately after that he was invested king and had received the crown, he determined with himself to put upon him the shape of a new man, turning insolency and wildness into gravity and soberness. And whereas he had passed his youth in wanton pastime and riotous misorder, with a sort of misgoverned mates and unthrifty playferes,[11] he now banished them from his presence (not unrewarded, nor yet unpreferred), inhibiting them upon a great pain not once to approach, lodge, or sojourn within ten miles of his court or mansion. And in their places he elected and chose men of gravity, wit, and high policy, by whose wise counsel and prudent advertisement he might at all times rule to his honor and govern to his profit, whereas if he should have retained the other lusty companions about him, he doubted lest they might have allured him unto such lewd and light parts as with them beforetime he had youthfully used, not always to his own commendation, nor yet to the contentation of his father, insomuch that where on a time he struck the Chief Justice on the face with his fist for imprisoning one of his mates, he was not only committed to strait prison himself by the said Chief Justice, but also of his father put out of the Privy Council and banished the Court, and his brother Thomas, Duke of Clarence, elected President of the Council, to his great displeasure and open reproach; but now that he was once placed in the royal throne and regal seat of the realm, he considering with himself what charge he had in hand and what appertained to his duty and office, trusted not too much to the readiness of his own wit, nor to the judgment of his own wavering will, and therefore, as I said, called to his Council such prudent and politic persons as might help to ease his charge and instruct him with such good reasons and fruitful persuasions as he might show him-

---

10 *presently:* immediately.

11 *playferes:* companions.

self to his subjects a mirror of virtue and an example of upright dealing. After he had laid this politic foundation, he, virtuously considering in his mind that all goodness cometh of God, determined to begin with something acceptable to His Divine Majesty, and therefore first commanded the clergy sincerely and truly to preach the word of God, and to live accordingly, that they might be the lanterns of light to the temporalty, as their profession required. The laymen he willed to serve God and obey their Prince, prohibiting them above all things breach of matrimony, use of swearing, and namely willful perjury. Beside this, he elected the best learned men in the laws of the realm to the offices of justice, and men of good living he preferred to high degrees and authority.

John Lyly

1554–1606

JOHN LYLY was born in Kent, the son of the Registrar of Canterbury and the grandson of William Lyly, the humanist and author of a standard Latin grammar. He was educated at Magdalen College, Oxford; he received the B.A. degree in 1573 and the next year wrote to Burleigh asking for political pressure on Magdalen College to elect him a fellow. He took his M.A. in 1575 and soon after moved to London, where he took up residence in the Savoy, apparently making his career one of service to Burleigh and more especially to his son-in-law, the Earl of Oxford. In December, 1578, his book *Euphues: the Anatomy of Wit* was licensed, and the publication of it made him famous. The sequel, *Euphues and his England,* appeared in 1580. His literary activities during the next decade were almost entirely dramatic: he wrote, principally for the children's company of "Paul's Boys," a group of brilliant court comedies, refined, witty, and topical in their cleverly developed allegory. He remained a follower of the Earl of Oxford, pointing out to that glittering nobleman that the hexameters called *Speculum Tuscanismi* in one of Harvey's letters to Spenser, 1580, were a hit at him. Lyly married in 1583, received a grant of £30 a year from his patron in 1584, and in 1589 served the first of his four terms as a Member of Parliament. When the extreme Puritans began to attack the bishops with tracts signed "Martin Marprelate," Lyly was engaged, along with other literary men like Nashe and Greene, to answer them, and Lyly contributed a pamphlet called *Pappe with an Hatchet.* During all this time Lyly was waiting hopefully for a reversion to the office of Master of the Revels, but he suffered the common disappointment of courtiers and never got it. He died in 1606.

"He is but a little fellow," Lyly's friend Nashe wrote of him, "but he hath one of the best wits in England." His wit was of the kind, moreover, that appealed most strongly to the ladies and gentlemen of the court, and what the court took up with enthusiasm became later the vogue of the city and the populace. The first part of *Euphues* went through thirteen editions before 1614; the sequel appeared in twelve editions before 1610; and four more editions of the two parts together appeared between 1617 and 1636. His comedies, too, so far surpassed anything of the kind written in English up to that time that he virtually had the field to himself.

"Our nation are in his debt for a new English which he first taught them," wrote the publisher Blount in his edition of *Six Court Comedies* in 1632; "*Euphues and his England* began first that language. [He should have said *Euphues: the Anatomy of Wit.*] All our ladies were then his scholars, and that beauty in court which could not parley Euphuism was as little regarded as she which now there speaks not French." This "new English" had a long tradition behind it, and it was new only in the combination of traits Lyly gave to it and the high polish and conscious artistry of its presentation. Euphuism is a prose style which has two aspects: an especially elaborate sentence structure and a wealth of ornament of various kinds. Sentence structure is based on the classical and medieval schemata of *isocolon* (succeeding clauses or phrases equal in length), *parison* (succeeding clauses or phrases identical in structure), and *paromoion* (succeeding clauses or phrases, or corresponding syllables, alike in sound). These schemes are used in combination, and the additional effects of repetition, antithesis, rhetorical questions, and exclamations are also combined with them. The ornament is of three kinds: *exempla* or incidents from history or poetry used to illustrate a point; *sententiae* or proverbs; and *similia* or similes drawn from science or pseudo-science, the famous "unnatural natural history" which comes from Erasmus or Pliny or the medieval encyclopedists or the author's own imagination.

It is of course a highly artificial kind of prose, delicate and extremely graceful, suitable only for formal use and so difficult to construct well that we may suspect Blount of exaggeration when he says the court ladies all "parleyed" it. There were a good many Euphuists before Euphues in England, of varying degrees of similarity to Lyly, and the student who is interested in tracing the predecessors would include in his study George Pettie (see p. 144), John Grange's novel *The Golden Aphroditis* (1577), Queen Elizabeth's letters, some sermons, translations by Geoffrey Fenton, and the lectures in Latin of John Rainolds at Oxford between 1572 and 1578, which may have been Lyly's most immediate inspiration. The vogue of Euphuism flourished in sophisticated circles for only a few years. By 1590 it was felt to be démodé, and Shakespeare ridicules it in Falstaff's mock speech to Prince Hal, *I Henry IV,* II, iv. Euphuism is after all only a special instance of the dominating Elizabethan passion for language—that fascination with words and what can be done with them that marks all classes of society, from the nobles in *Love's Labour's Lost* down to Dogberry the watchman in *Much Ado.* "It is a world to see," Lyly wrote, "how Englishmen desire to hear finer speech than the language will allow, to eat finer bread than is made of wheat, to wear finer cloth than is wrought of wool."

It would be a mistake to consider Lyly only from the point of view of prose style. He is one of the very important teachers of Elizabethan England. His first book bears the sub-title *The Anatomy of Wit.* It analyses wit and wisdom by means of a story; it presents an ideal of conduct in love; it treats that favorite Elizabethan theme of the rivalry between love and friendship, just as *Two Gentlemen of Verona* and Lyly's *Endimion* do. It even contains an attack upon the shortcomings of University education, which everybody took to refer to Oxford, though Lyly denied it. In short, *The Anatomy of Wit* should be read along with Castiglione's *The Courtier* (see Hoby, pp. 113–134), Ascham's *The Scholemaster* (see pp. 77–112), Sidney's *Arcadia,* and Spenser's *The Faerie Queene* as a projection of Renaissance ideals for the conduct of a gentleman. *Euphues and his England* also has a love story and it exhibits Lyly's skill in plotting, but its main interest derives from the picture it gives of England and the English court. Central in this picture is of course the portrait of Elizabeth. Even with all its fulsome flattery of the Queen, perfectly characteristic of the age, this part of the book is serious and important historical analysis. It would be difficult to find a better explanation of the nature of English loyalty to Elizabeth. One who understands this document of 1580 will be able to see why the triumph over Spain eight years later produced the fervent patriotism and self-confident unity of spirit that inspires the glorious literature of the last fifteen years of the reign.

Bibliography: *The Complete Works of John Lyly,* ed. R. W. Bond, 3 vols., Oxford, 1902; *Euphues,* ed. Croll and Clemons, London, 1916; A. Feuillerat, *John Lyly: Contribution à l'Histoire de la Renaissance en Angleterre,* Cambridge, 1910; M. W. Tilley, *Elizabethan Proverb-Lore in Lyly's Euphues,* New York, 1926; P. W. Long, "From *Troilus* to *Euphues*" in *Kittredge Anniversary Papers,* Boston, 1913; Deborah Jones, "John Lyly at St. Bartholomew's" in *Thomas Lodge and Other Elizabethans,* ed. C. J. Sisson, Harvard, 1933; W. Ringler, "The Immediate Source of Euphuism," *PMLA,* LIII (1938), 678–686; V. M. Jeffery, *John Lyly and the Italian Renaissance,* Paris, 1928. G. B. Parks, "Before *Euphues,*" *Adams Memorial Studies,* Washington, 1948, 475–494.

EUPHUES: THE ANATOMY OF WIT[1]

Very pleasant for all Gentlemen to read and most necessary to remember; wherein are contained the delights that wit followeth in his youth by the pleasantness of love, and the happiness he reapeth in age by the perfectness of wisdom . . . 1578

THERE dwelt in Athens a young gentleman of great patrimony, and of so comely a personage that it was doubted[2] whether he were more bound to nature for the lineaments of his person or to fortune for the increase of his possessions. But nature, impatient of comparisons, and as it were disdaining a companion or co-partner in her working, added to this comeliness of his body such a sharp capacity of mind that not only she proved fortune counterfeit, but was half of that opinion that she herself was only current. This young gallant, of more wit than wealth, and yet of more wealth than wisdom, seeing himself inferior to none in pleasant conceits, thought himself superior to all in honest conditions, insomuch that he deemed himself so apt to all things that he gave himself almost to nothing but practicing of those things commonly which are incident to these sharp wits, fine phrases, smooth quipping, merry taunting, using jesting without mean, and abusing mirth without measure. As therefore the sweetest rose hath his prickle, the finest velvet his brack,[3] the fairest flour his bran, so the sharpest wit hath his wanton will, and the holiest head his wicked way. And true it is that some men write and most men believe that in all perfect shapes a blemish bringeth rather a liking every way to the eyes than a loathing any way to the mind. Venus had her mole in her cheek which made her more amiable; Helen her scar on her chin which Paris called *Cos amoris,* the whetstone of love, Aristippus his wart, Lycurgus his wen. So likewise in the disposition of the mind, either virtue is overshadowed with some vice, or vice overcast with some virtue. Alexander valiant in war, yet given to wine. Tully eloquent in his gloses,[4] yet vainglorious. Solomon wise, yet too too wanton. David holy but yet an homicide. None more witty than Euphues, yet at the first none more wicked. The freshest colors soonest fade, the teenest[5] razor soonest turneth his edge, the finest cloth is soonest eaten with moths, and the cambric sooner stained than the coarse canvas; which appeared well in this Euphues, whose wit being like wax apt to receive any impression, and having the bridle in his own hands either to use the rein or the spur,

[1] For the meaning of "Euphues," see Ascham's *Scholemaster*, p. 93, above. *Anatomy:* dissection, or as we would say, analysis.

[2] *doubted:* wondered.

[3] *brack:* break, flaw.

[4] *gloses:* panegyrics.

[5] *teenest:* keenest.

disdaining counsel, leaving his country, loathing his old acquaintance, thought either by wit to obtain some conquest or by shame to abide some conflict, and leaving the rule of reason, rashly ran unto destruction, who, preferring fancy before friends and his present humor before honor to come, laid reason in water, being too salt for his taste, and followed unbridled affection, most pleasant for his tooth. When parents have more care how to leave their children wealthy than wise, and are more desirous to have them maintain the name than the nature of a gentleman; when they put gold into the hands of youth where they should put a rod under their girdle; when instead of awe they make them past grace, and leave them rich executors of goods and poor executors of godliness; then it is no marvel that the son, being left rich by his father's will, become retchless [6] by his own will.

But it hath been an old said saw, and not of less truth than antiquity, that wit is the better if it be the dearer bought; as in the sequel of this history shall most manifestly appear. It happened this young imp to arrive at Naples, a place of more pleasure than profit, and yet of more profit than piety, the very walls and windows whereof showed it rather to be the tabernacle of Venus than the temple of Vesta.

There was all things necessary and in readiness that might either allure the mind to lust or entice the heart to folly, a court more meet for an atheist than for one of Athens, for Ovid than for Aristotle, for a graceless lover than for a godly liver; more fitter for Paris than Hector, and meeter for Flora than Diana.

Here my youth (whether for weariness he could not, or for wantonness would not go any further) determined to make his abode; whereby it is evidently seen that the fleetest fish swalloweth the delicatest bait, that the highest soaring hawk traineth to the lure, and that the wittest sconce is inveigled with the sudden view of alluring vanities.

Here he wanted no companions which courted him continually with sundry kinds of devices, whereby they might either soak [7] his purse to reap commodity or soothe his person to win credit, for he had guests and companions of all sorts.

There frequented to his lodging and mansion house as well the spider to suck poison of his fine wit, as the bee to gather honey, as well the drone as the dove, the fox as the lamb, as well Damocles [8] to betray him as Damon to be true to him. Yet he behaved himself so warily that he singled his game wisely. He could easily discern Apollo's music from Pan his pipe, and Venus' beauty from Juno's bravery, and the faith of Laelius [9] from the flattery of Aristippus.[10] He welcomed all but trusted none; he was merry, but yet so wary that neither the flatterer could take advantage to entrap

---

[6] *retchless:* reckless.

[7] *soak:* drain dry, exhaust.

[8] *Damocles:* a flatterer of Dionysius the tyrant.

[9] *Laelius:* the friend of Scipio Africanus.

[10] *Aristippus:* philosopher and courtier of Dionysius the tyrant.

him in his talk, nor the wisest any assurance of his friendship. Who, being demanded of one what countryman he was, he answered, "What countryman am I not? If I be in Crete I can lie, if in Greece I can shift, if in Italy I can court it. If thou ask whose son I am also, I ask thee whose son I am not. I can carouse with Alexander, abstain with Romulus, eat with the Epicure, fast with the Stoic, sleep with Endymion, watch with Chrisippus"—using these speeches and other like.

An old gentleman in Naples seeing his pregnant wit, his eloquent tongue somewhat taunting, yet with delight, his mirth without measure, yet not without wit, his sayings vainglorious, yet pithy, began to bewail his nurture and to muse at his nature, being incensed against the one as most pernicious, and enflamed with the other as most precious; for he well knew that so rare a wit would in time either breed an intolerable trouble, or bring an incomparable treasure to the commonweal; at the one he greatly pitied, at the other he rejoiced.

Having therefore gotten opportunity to communicate with him his mind, with watery eyes, as one lamenting his wantonness, and smiling face, as one loving his wittiness, encountered him on this manner:

"Young gentleman, although my acquaintance be small to intreat you, and my authority less to command you, yet my good will in giving you good counsel should induce you to believe me, and my hoary hairs, ambassadors of experience, enforce you to follow me; for by how much the more I am a stranger to you, by so much the more you are beholding to me; having therefore opportunity to utter my mind, I mean to be importunate with you to follow my meaning. As thy birth doth show the express and lively image of gentle blood, so thy bringing up seemeth to me to be a great blot to the lineage of so noble a brute,[11] so that I am enforced to think that either thou didest want one to give thee good instructions, or that thy parents made thee a wanton with too much cockering; [12] either they were too foolish in using no discipline, or thou too froward in rejecting their doctrine; either they willing to have thee idle, or thou willful to be ill employed. Did they not remember that which no man ought to forget, that the tender youth of a child is like the tempering of new wax, apt to receive any form? He that will carry a bull with Milo [13] must use to carry him a calf also; he that coveteth to have a straight tree must not bow him being a twig. The potter fashioneth his clay when it is soft, and the sparrow is taught to come when he is young. As therefore the iron being hot receiveth any form with the stroke of the hammer, and keepeth it, being cold, forever, so the tender wit of a child, if with diligence it be instructed in youth, will with industry use those qualities in his age.

"They might also have taken example of the wise husbandmen, who in their fattest and most fertile ground sow hemp before wheat, a grain that

[11] *brute:* hero, from Brutus, the legendary founder of Britain.

[12] *cockering:* pampering.

[13] *Milo:* the famous athlete, who was able to carry a bull because he had carried it every day as it grew up from a calf.

drieth up the superfluous moisture and maketh the soil more apt for corn. Or of good gardeners who in their curious knots[14] mix hyssop with thyme as aiders the one to the growth of the other, the one being dry, the other moist; or of cunning painters who for the whitest work cast the blackest ground, to make the picture more amiable. If therefore thy father had been as wise an husbandman as he was a fortunate husband, or thy mother as good a housewife as she was a happy wife, if they had been both as good gardeners to keep their knot as they were grafters to bring forth such fruit, or as cunning painters as they were happy parents, no doubt they had sowed hemp before wheat, that is, discipline before affection, they had set hyssop with thyme, that is, manners with wit, the one to aid the other; and to make thy dexterity more, they had cast a black ground for their white work, that is, they had mixed threats with fair looks.

"But things past are past calling again; it is too late to shut the stable door when the steed is stolen. The Troyans repented too late when their town was spoiled. Yet the remembrance of thy former follies might breed in thee a remorse of conscience, and be a remedy against further concupiscence. But now to thy present time: the Lacedemonians were wont to show their children drunken men and other wicked men, that by seeing their filth they might shun the like fault and avoid such vices when they were at the like state. The Persians to make their youth abhor gluttony would paint an epicure sleeping with meat in his mouth and most horribly overladen with wine, that by the view of such monstrous sights they might eschew the means of the like excess.

"The Parthians, to cause their youth to loathe the alluring trains of women's wiles and deceitful enticements, had most curiously carved in their houses a young man blind, besides whom was adjoined a woman so exquisite that in some men's judgment Pygmalion's image[15] was not half so excellent, having one hand in his pocket, as noting their theft, and holding a knife in the other hand to cut his throat. If the sight of such ugly shapes caused a loathing of the like sins, then, my good Euphues, consider their plight and beware of thine own peril. Thou art here in Naples a young sojourner, I an old senior; thou a stranger, I a citizen; thou secure, doubting no mishap, I sorrowful dreading thy misfortune. Here mayst thou see that which I sigh to see, drunken sots wallowing in every house, in every chamber, yea, in every channel;[16] here mayst thou behold that which I cannot without blushing behold nor without blubbering utter, those whose bellies be their gods, who offer their goods as sacrifice to their guts; who sleep with meat in their mouths, with sin in their hearts, and with shame in their houses.

"Here, yea, here, Euphues, mayst thou see not the carved visard of a lewd woman, but the incarnate visage of a lascivious wanton, not the shadow of

---

14 *knots:* gardens of intricate design.

15 *Pygmalion's image:* Cf. Shakespeare, *Measure for Measure,* III, ii, 49.

16 *channel:* gutter.

love, but the substance of lust. My heart melteth in drops of blood, to see a harlot with the one hand rob so many coffers, and with the other to rip so many corses.

"Thou art here amidst the pikes [17] between Scylla and Charybdis,[18] ready if thou shun Syrtes to sink into Symplegades.[19] Let the Lacedemonian, the Persian, the Parthian, yea, the Neapolitan, cause thee rather to detest such villainy, at the sight and view of their vanity.

"Is it not far better to abhor sins by the remembrance of others' faults than by repentance of thine own follies? Is not he accompted most wise whom other men's harms do make most wary? But thou wilt haply say, that although there be many things in Naples to be justly condemned, yet there are some things of necessity to be commended, and as thy will doth lean unto the one, so thy wit would also embrace the other.

"Alas, Euphues, by how much the more I love the high climbing of thy capacity, by so much the more I fear thy fall. The fine crystal is sooner crased [20] than the hard marble, the greenest beech burneth faster than the driest oak, the fairest silk is soonest soiled, and the sweetest wine turneth to the sharpest vinegar, the pestilence doth most rifest [21] infect the clearest complexion, and the caterpillar cleaveth unto the ripest fruit, the most delicate wit is allured with small enticement unto vice, and most subject to yield unto vanity; if therefore thou do but hearken to the Sirens, thou wilt be enamored; if thou haunt their houses and places, thou shalt be enchanted.

"One drop of poison infecteth the whole tun of wine, one leaf of coloquintida [22] marreth and spoileth the whole pot of porridge, one iron mold defaceth the whole piece of lawn. Descend into thine own conscience, and consider with thyself the great difference between staring and stark blind, wit and wisdom, love and lust. Be merry but with modesty, be sober but not too sullen, be valiant but not too venturous. Let thy attire be comely but not costly, thy diet wholesome but not excessive, use pastime as the word importeth, to pass the time in honest recreation. Mistrust no man without cause, neither be thou credulous without proof; be not light to follow every man's opinion, nor obstinate to stand in thine own conceit. Serve God, love God, fear God, and God will so bless thee as either heart can wish or thy friends desire. And so I end my counsel, beseeching thee to begin to follow it."

This old gentleman having finished his discourse, Euphues began to shape him an answer in this sort:

"Father and friend (your age showeth the one, your honesty the other), I am neither so suspicious to mistrust your good will, nor so sottish to mis-

---

[17] *pikes:* rocks.

[18] *Scylla and Charybdis:* the rock and whirlpool of proverbial difficulty to mariners.

[19] *Syrtes, Symplegades:* dangerous gulfs on the north shore of Africa, and the two islands off the mouth of the Bosporus. Lyly uses the latter word for its sound, or else he mistakenly thought the Symplegades were quicksands.

[20] *crased:* cracked.

[21] *rifest:* most readily.

[22] *coloquintida:* colocynth or bitter-apple.

like your good counsel; as I am therefore to thank you for the first, so it stands me upon [23] to think better on the latter. I mean not to cavil with you as one loving sophistry, neither to control [24] you as one having superiority; the one would bring my talk into the suspicion of fraud, the other convince me of folly. Whereas you argue I know not upon what probabilities, but sure I am upon no proof, that my bringing up should be a blemish to my birth; I answer, and swear too, that you were not therein a little overshot; either you gave too much credit to the report of others, or too much liberty to your own judgment; you convince my parents of peevishness,[25] in making me a wanton, and me of lewdness, in rejecting correction. But so many men, so many minds; that may seem in your eye odious which in another's eye may be gracious. Aristippus,[26] a philosopher, yet who more courtly? Diogenes, a philosopher, yet who more carterly? [27] Who more popular than Plato, retaining always good company? Who more envious than Timon, denouncing all human society? Who so severe as the Stoics, which like stocks were moved with no melody? Who so secure as the Epicures, which wallowed in all kind of licentiousness? Though all men be made of one metal, yet they be not cast all in one mold; there is framed of the selfsame clay as well the tile to keep out water as the pot to contain liquor, the sun doth harden the dirt and melt the wax, fire maketh the gold to shine and the straw to smother,[28] perfumes doth refresh the dove and kill the beetle, and the nature of the man disposeth that consent of the manners. Now whereas you seem to love my nature and loathe my nurture, you bewray your own weakness, in thinking that nature may any ways be altered by education, and as you have ensamples to confirm your pretense, so I have most evident and infallible arguments to serve for my purpose. It is natural for the vine to spread; the more you seek by art to alter it, the more in the end you shall augment it. It is proper for the palm tree to mount; the heavier you load it the higher it sprouteth. Though iron be made soft with fire it returneth to his hardness; though the falcon be reclaimed to the fist she retireth to her haggardness; [29] the whelp of a mastiff will never be taught to retrieve the partridge; education can have no show, where the excellency of nature doth bear sway. The silly mouse will by no manner of means be tamed; the subtle fox may well be beaten, but never broken from stealing his prey; if you pound spices they smell the sweeter; season the wood never so well, the wine will taste of the cask; plant and translate the crab tree where and whensoever it please you and it will never bear sweet apple, unless you graft by art, which nothing toucheth nature.

"Infinite and innumerable were the examples I could allege and declare to confirm the force of Nature, and confute these your vain and false for-

---

[23] *stands me upon:* behooves me.

[24] *control:* rebuke.

[25] *convince . . . peevishness:* convict my parents of folly.

[26] *Aristippus:* founder of Cyrenaic school; a Hedonist.

[27] *carterly:* boorish.

[28] *smother:* smolder.

[29] *haggardness:* wildness.

geries, were not the repetition of them needless, having showed sufficient, or bootless, seeing those alleged will not persuade you. And can you be so unnatural, whom dame Nature hath nourished and brought up so many years, to repine as it were against Nature?

"The similitude you rehearse of the wax argueth your waxing and melting brain, and your example of the hot and hard iron showeth in you but cold and weak disposition. Do you not know that which all men do affirm and know, that black will take no other color? that the stone Abeston[30] being once made hot will never be made cold? that fire cannot be forced downward? that Nature will have course after kind? that everything will dispose itself according to Nature? Can the Ethiop change or alter his skin? or the leopard[31] his hue? Is it possible to gather grapes of thorns, or figs of thistles?[32] or to cause any thing to strive against Nature?

"But why go I about to praise Nature, the which as yet was never any imp so wicked and barbarous, any Turk so vile and brutish, any beast so dull and senseless, that could or would or durst dispraise or contemn? Doth not Cicero conclude and allow that if we follow and obey Nature, we shall never err? Doth not Aristotle allege and confirm that Nature frameth or maketh nothing in any point rude, vain, and unperfect?

"Nature was had in such estimation and admiration among the heathen people that she was reputed for the only goddess in heaven. If Nature, then, have largely and bountifully endued me with her gifts, why deem you me so untoward and graceless? If she have dealt hardly with me, why extol you so much my birth? If Nature bear no sway, why use you this adulation? If Nature work the effect, what booteth any education? If Nature be of strength or force, what availeth discipline or nurture? If of none, what helpeth Nature? But let these sayings pass, as known evidently and granted to be true, which none can or may deny unless he be false, or that he be an enemy to humanity.

"As touching my residence and abiding here in Naples, my youthly and lusty affections, my sports and pleasures, my pastimes, my common dalliance, my delights, my resort and company, and companions, which daily use to visit me; although to you they breed more sorrow and care than solace and comfort, because of your crabbed age; yet to me they bring more comfort and joy than care and grief, more bliss than bale, more happiness than heaviness, because of my youthful gentleness. Either you would have all men old as you are, or else you have quite forgotten that you yourself were young, or ever knew young days; either in your youth you were a very vicious and ungodly man, or now being aged very superstitious and devout above measure.

"Put you no difference between the young flourishing bay tree and the

[30] *Abeston:* asbestos. The erroneous statement about its retention of heat is found in medieval authorities like Bartholomaeus Anglicus and Isidore of Seville.

[31] *Ethiop . . . leopard:* Jeremiah 13:23.

[32] *grapes . . . thistles:* Matthew 7:16.

old withered beech? no kind of distinction between the waxing and the waning of the moon? and between the rising and the setting of the sun? Do you measure the hot assaults of youth by the cold skirmishes of age? whose years are subject to more infirmities than our youth, we merry, you melancholy, we zealous in affection, you jealous in all your doings, you testy without cause, we hasty for no quarrel. You careful, we careless, we bold, you fearful, we in all points contrary unto you, and ye in all points unlike unto us.

"Seeing therefore we be repugnant each to the other in nature, would you have us alike in qualities? Would you have one potion ministered to the burning fever and to the cold palsy? one plaster to an old issue and a fresh wound? one salve for all sores? one sauce for all meats? No, no, Eubulus, but I will yield to more than either I am bound to grant, either thou able to prove: suppose that which I never will believe, that Naples is a cankered storehouse of all strife, a common stews for all strumpets, the sink of shame and the very nurse of all sin. Shall it therefore follow of necessity that all that are wooed of love should be wedded to lust? Will you conclude as it were *ex consequenti* that whosoever arriveth here shall be enticed to folly, and being enticed, of force shall be entangled? No, no, it is the disposition of the thought that altereth the nature of the thing. The sun shineth upon the dunghill and is not corrupted; the diamond lieth in the fire and is not consumed; the crystal toucheth the toad and is not poisoned; [33] the bird Trochilus [34] liveth by the mouth of the crocodile and is not spoiled; a perfect wit is never bewitched with lewdness, neither enticed with lasciviousness.

"Is it not common that the holm [35] tree springeth amidst the beach? that the ivy spreadeth upon the hard stones? that the soft feather-bed breaketh the hard blade? If experience have not taught you this, you have lived long and learned little, or if your moist brain have forgot it, you have learned much and profited nothing. But it may be that you measure my affections by your own fancies, and knowing yourself either too simple to raise the siege of policy, or too weak to resist the assault by prowess, you deem me of as little wit as yourself, or of less force, either of small capacity, or of no courage. In my judgment, Eubulus, you shall as soon catch a hare with a tabor,[36] as you shall persuade youth, with your aged and overworn eloquence, to such severity of life, which as yet there was never Stoic so strict, nor Jesuit so superstitious, neither votary so devout, but would rather allow it in words than follow it in works, rather talk of it than try it. Neither were you such a saint in your youth, that abandoning all pleasures, all pastimes, and delights, you would choose rather to sacrifice the first fruits of your life

---

[33] *crystal . . . poisoned:* Pliny, *Natural History,* XXXVII, xv.

[34] *Trochilus:* Pliny, *Natural History,* VIII, xxxvii. This bird, which was supposed to live in the mouth of the crocodile and clean its host's teeth, is a favorite of Lyly's, and of the Elizabethans generally.

[35] *holm:* holly.

[36] *tabor:* a small drum.

to vain holiness than to youthly affections. But as to the stomach quatted [37] with dainties all delicates seem queasy, and as he that surfeiteth with wine useth afterward to allay with water; so these old huddles,[38] having overcharged their gorges with fancy, accompt all honest recreation mere folly, and having taken a surfeit of delight seem now to savor it with despite. Seeing therefore it is labor lost for me to persuade you, and wind vainly wasted for you to exhort me, here I found you, and here I leave you, having neither bought nor sold with you, but changed ware for ware; if you have taken little pleasure in my reply, sure I am that by your counsel I have reaped less profit. They that use to steal honey burn hemlock to smoke the bees from their hives, and it may be that to get some advantage of me you have used these smoky arguments, thinking thereby to smother me with the conceit of strong imagination. But as the chameleon though he have most guts draweth least breath,[39] or as the elder tree though he be fullest of pith is farthest from strength, so though your reasons seem inwardly to yourself somewhat substantial, and your persuasions pithy in your own conceit, yet being well weighed without, they be shadows without substance, and weak without force. The bird Taurus [40] hath a great voice but a small body, the thunder [41] a great clap yet but a little stone, the empty vessel giveth a greater sound than the full barrel. I mean not to apply it, but look into yourself and you shall certainly find it; and thus I leave you seeking it, but were it not that my company stay my coming I would surely help you to look [42] it, but I am called hence by my acquaintance."

Euphues having thus ended his talk departed, leaving this old gentleman in a great quandary; who, perceiving that he was more inclined to wantonness than to wisdom, with a deep sigh, the tears trickling down his cheeks, said: "Seeing thou wilt not buy counsel at the first hand good cheap, thou shalt buy repentance at the second hand, at such an unreasonable rate that thou wilt curse thy hard pennyworth, and ban thy hard heart. Ah, Euphues, little dost thou know that if thy wealth waste, thy wit will give but small warmth, and if thy wit incline to willfulness, that thy wealth will do thee no great good. If the one had been employed to thrift, the other to learning, it had been hard to conjecture whether thou shouldst have been more fortunate by riches or happy by wisdom, whether more esteemed in the commonweal for wealth to maintain war or for counsel to conclude peace. But alas! why do I pity that in thee which thou seemest to praise in thyself?" And immediately he went to his own house, heavily bewailing the young man's unhappiness.

Here ye may behold, gentlemen, how lewdly wit standeth in his own

---

[37] *quatted:* surfeited.

[38] *huddles:* old men bent double.

[39] Most authorities in animal lore said the chameleon lived on air. See *Hamlet,* III, ii, 93.

[40] *Taurus:* Eramus, *Similia,* 614 F. The bird was so called because his voice was supposed to be like the roaring of a bull.

[41] *thunder:* Meteorites and belemnites were formerly supposed to fall with the sound of thunder.

[42] *look:* seek.

light, how he deemeth no penny good silver but his own, preferring the blossom before the fruit, the bud before the flower, the green blade before the ripe ear of corn, his own wit before all men's wisdoms. Neither is that geason,[43] seeing for the most part it is proper to all those of sharp capacity to esteem of themselves as most proper; if one be hard in conceiving, they pronounce him a dolt; if given to study, they proclaim him a dunce; if merry, a jester; if sad, a saint; if full of words, a sot; if without speech, a cipher. If one argue with them boldly, then is he impudent; if coldly, an innocent; if there be reasoning of divinity, they cry, *Quae supra nos nihil ad nos;*[44] if of humanity, *Sententias loquitur carnifex.*[45] Hereof cometh such great familiarity between the ripest wits, when they shall see the disposition the one of the other, the *sympathia* of affections and as it were but a pair of shears to go between their natures, one flattereth another in his own folly, and layeth cushions under the elbow of his fellow when he seeth him take a nap with fancy, and as their wit wresteth them to vice, so it forgeth them some feat[46] excuse to cloak their vanity.

Too much study doth intoxicate their brains, for (say they) although iron the more it is used the brighter it is, yet silver with much wearing doth waste to nothing; though the cammock[47] the more it is bowed the better it serveth, yet the bow the more it is bent and occupied[48] the weaker it waxeth; though the camomile,[49] the more it is trodden and pressed down the more it spreadeth, yet the violet the oftener it is handled and touched, the sooner it withereth and decayeth. Besides this, a fine wit, a sharp sense, a quick understanding, is able to attain to more in a moment or a very little space than a dull and blockish head in a month; the scythe cutteth far better and smoother than the saw; the wax yieldeth better and sooner to the seal than the steel to the stamp or hammer; the smooth and plain beech is easier to be carved and occupied than the knotty box. For neither is there any thing, but that hath his contraries. Such is the nature of these novices that think to have learning without labor, and treasure without travail, either not understanding or else not remembering that the finest edge is made with the blunt whetstone, and the fairest jewel fashioned with the hard hammer. I go not about, gentlemen, to inveigh against wit, for then I were witless; but frankly to confess mine own little wit, I have ever thought so superstitiously of wit that I fear I have committed idolatry against wisdom, and if Nature had dealt so beneficially with me to have given me any wit, I should have been readier in the defense of it to have made an apology than any way to turn to apostasy. But this I note, that for the most part they stand so on their pantofles[50] that they be secure[51] of perils, obstinate in

---

[43] *geason:* rare.

[44] *Quae . . . nos:* "What is above us is nothing to us," Erasmus, *Adagia,* I, vi, 69.

[45] *Sententias . . . carnifex:* "Even a murderer utters moral sayings."

[46] *feat:* apt.

[47] *cammock:* the shepherd's crook.

[48] *occupied:* used.

[49] *camomile:* Falstaff uses this simile in *I Henry IV,* II, iv, 441.

[50] *pantofles:* slippers with thick cork soles. The phrase here means to show pride.

[51] *secure:* free from fear (not "danger").

their own opinions, impatient of labor, apt to conceive wrong, credulous to believe the worst, ready to shake off their old acquaintance without cause and to condemn them without color. All which humors are by so much the more easier to be purged, by how much the less they have festered the sinews. But return we again to Euphues.

Euphues having sojourned by the space of two months in Naples, whether he were moved by the courtesy of a young gentleman named Philautus,[52] or enforced by destiny; whether his pregnant wit, or his pleasant conceits wrought the greater liking in the mind of Euphues, I know not for certainty; but Euphues showed such entire love towards him that he seemed to make small accompt of any others, determining to enter into such an inviolable league of friendship with him as neither time by piecemeal should impair, neither fancy utterly dissolve, nor any suspicion infringe. "I have read," [53] saith he, "and well I believe it, that a friend is in prosperity a pleasure, a solace in adversity, in grief a comfort, in joy a merry companion, at all times another I, in all places the express image of mine own person; insomuch that I cannot tell whether the immortal gods have bestowed any gift upon mortal men either more noble or more necessary than friendship. Is there anything in the world to be reputed (I will not say compared) to friendship? Can any treasure in this transitory pilgrimage be of more value than a friend? In whose bosom thou mayst sleep secure without fear, whom thou mayst make partner of all thy secrets without suspicion of fraud, and partaker of all thy misfortune without mistrust of fleeting, who will accompt thy bale his bane, thy mishap his misery, the pricking of thy finger the piercing of his heart. But whither am I carried? Have I not also learned that one should eat a bushel of salt with him whom he meaneth to make his friend? that trial maketh trust? that there is falsehood in fellowship? And what then? Doth not the sympathy of manners make the conjunction of minds? Is it not a byword, like will to like? Not so common as commendable it is, to see young gentlemen choose them such friends with whom they may seem being absent to be present, being asunder to be conversant, being dead to be alive. I will therefore have Philautus for my fere, and by so much the more I make myself sure to have Philautus, by how much the more I view in him the lively image of Euphues."

Although there be none so ignorant that doth not know, neither any so impudent that will not confess, friendship to be the jewel of human joy; yet whosoever shall see this amity grounded upon a little affection will soon conjecture that it shall be dissolved upon a light occasion; as in the sequel of Euphues and Philautus you shall see, whose hot loved waxed soon cold. For as the best wine doth make the sharpest vinegar, so the deepest love turneth to the deadliest hate. Who deserved the most blame, in mine opinion it is doubtful, and so difficult that I dare not presume to give verdict. For love being the cause for which so many mischiefs have been attempted,

---

52 *Philautus:* The name means "the selfish man."

53 *I have read:* in Cicero, *De amicitia,* XX–XXII.

I am not yet persuaded whether of them was most to be blamed, but certainly neither of them was blameless. I appeal to your judgment, gentlemen, not that I think any of you of the like disposition able to decide the question, but being of deeper discretion than I am, are more fit to debate the quarrel. Though the discourse of their friendship and falling out be somewhat long, yet being somewhat strange, I hope the delightfulness of the one will attenuate the tediousness of the other.

Euphues had continual access to the place of Philautus, and no little familiarity with him, and finding him at convenient leisure, in these short terms unfolded his mind unto him:

"Gentleman and friend, the trial I have had of thy manners cutteth off divers terms which to another I would have used in the like matter. And sithens a long discourse argueth folly, and delicate words incur the suspicion of flattery, I am determined to use neither of them, knowing either of them to breed offense. Weighing with myself the force of friendship by the effects, I studied ever since my first coming to Naples to enter league with such a one as might direct my steps being a stranger, and resemble my manners being a scholar, the which two qualities as I find in you able to satisfy my desire, so I hope I shall find a heart in you willing to accomplish my request. Which if I may obtain, assure yourself that Damon to his Pythias,[54] Pylades to his Orestes,[55] Titus to his Gysippus,[56] Theseus to his Peirithous,[57] Scipio to his Laelius, was never found more faithful than Euphues will be to his Philautus."

Philautus, by how much the less he looked for this discourse, by so much the more he liked it, for he saw all qualities both of body and mind in Euphues, unto whom he replied as followeth:

"Friend Euphues (for so your talk warranteth me to term you), I dare neither use a long process, neither loving speech, lest unwittingly I should cause you to convince me of those things which you have already condemned. And verily I am bold to presume upon your courtesy, since you yourself have used so little curiosity,[58] persuading myself that my short answer will work as great an effect in you as your few words did in me. And seeing we resemble (as you say) each other in qualities, it cannot be that the one should differ from the other in courtesy; seeing the sincere affection of the mind cannot be expressed by the mouth, and that no art can unfold the entire love of the heart, I am earnestly to beseech you not to measure the firmness of my faith by the fewness of my words, but rather

---

[54] *Damon, Pythias:* Greeks who proved their friendship by contending, before Dionysius tyrant of Syracuse, which should be put to death to save the other. There is an English play on the subject by R. Edwards, *ca.* 1564.

[55] *Pylades, Orestes:* cousins and close friends who accomplished revenge for the death of Orestes' father, Agamemnon.

[56] *Titus, Gysippus:* friends in Boccaccio's *Decameron,* 10th day, novel 8.

[57] *Theseus, Peirithous:* the great Attic hero and his friend the king of the Lapiths. They fought the Centaurs together and went to hell to rescue Proserpine.

[58] *curiosity:* ceremony.

think that the overflowing waves of good will leave no passage for many words. Trial shall prove trust; here is my hand, my heart, my lands, and my life at thy commandment. Thou mayst well perceive that I did believe thee, that so soon I did love thee, and I hope thou wilt the rather love me, in that I did believe thee." Either Euphues and Philautus stood in need of friendship or were ordained to be friends. Upon so short warning to make so soon a conclusion might seem in mine opinion, if it continued, miraculous, if shaken off, ridiculous.

But after many embracings and protestations one to another, they walked to dinner, where they wanted neither meat, neither music, neither any other pastime, and having banqueted, to digest their sweet confections they danced all that afternoon; they used not only one board but one bed, one book (if so be it they thought not one too many). Their friendship augmented every day, insomuch that the one could not refrain the company of the other one minute; all things went in common between them, which all men accompted commendable. Philautus being a town-born child, both for his own continuance and the great countenance which his father had while he lived, crept into credit with Don Ferardo,[59] one of the chief governors of the city, who although he had a courtly crew of gentlewomen sojourning in his palace, yet his daughter, heir to his whole revenues, stained[60] the beauty of them all, whose modest bashfulness caused the other to look wan for envy, whose lily cheeks dyed with a vermilion red made the rest to blush at her beauty. For as the finest ruby staineth the color of the rest that be in place, or as the sun dimmeth the moon that she cannot be discerned, so this gallant girl more fair than fortunate, and yet more fortunate than faithful, eclipsed the beauty of them all, and changed their colors. Unto her had Philautus access, who won her by right of love, and should have worn her by right of law, had not Euphues by strange destiny broken the bonds of marriage and forbidden the banns of matrimony.

It happened that Don Ferardo had occasion to go to Venice about certain his own affairs, leaving his daughter the only steward of his household, who spared not to feast Philautus, her friend, with all kinds of delights and delicates, reserving only her honesty as the chief stay of her honor. Her father being gone she sent for her friend to supper, who came not as he was accustomed, solitarily alone, but accompanied with his friend Euphues. The gentlewoman, whether it were for niceness or for niggardness of courtesy, gave him such a cold welcome that he repented that he was come.

Euphues, though he knew himself worthy every way to have a good countenance, yet could he not perceive her willing any way to lend him a friendly look. Yet lest he should seem to want gestures, or to be dashed out

[59] *Don Ferardo:* possibly the Mayor of Brackley, in England; Philautus would then represent Lyly's fellow student at Magdalen, John Thornborough, and Euphues would be Lyly himself. The identification rests on the Diary of Dr. Simon Forman, and was first made by Feuillerat.

[60] *stained:* surpassed.

of conceit with her coy countenance, he addressed him to a gentlewoman called Livia, unto whom he uttered this speech: "Fair lady, if it be the guise of Italy to welcome strangers with strangeness, I must needs say the custom is strange and the country barbarous; if the manner of ladies to salute gentlemen with coyness, then I am enforced to think the women without courtesy to use such welcome, and the men past shame that will come. But hereafter I will either bring a stool on mine arm, for an unbidden guest, or a vizard [61] on my face, for a shameless gossip." Livia replied:

"Sir, our country is civil, and our gentlewomen are courteous, but in Naples it is compted a jest, at every word to say, 'In faith you are welcome.'" As she was yet talking, supper was set on the board; then Philautus spake thus unto Lucilla: "Gentlewoman, I was the bolder to bring my shadow with me (meaning Euphues), knowing that he should be the better welcome for my sake." Unto whom the gentlewoman replied: "Sir, as I never when I saw you thought that you came without your shadow, so now I cannot a little marvel to see you so overshot in bringing a new shadow with you." Euphues, though he perceived her coy nip, seemed not to care for it, but taking her by the hand said:

"Fair lady, seeing the shade doth often shield your beauty from the parching sun, I hope you will the better esteem of the shadow, and by so much the less it ought to be offensive, by how much the less it is able to offend you, and by so much the more you ought to like it, by how much the more you use to lie in it."

"Well, gentlemen," answered Lucilla, "in arguing of the shadow, we forego the substance. Pleaseth you therefore to sit down to supper." And so they all sat down; but Euphues fed of one dish which ever stood before him, the beauty of Lucilla.

Here Euphues at the first sight was so kindled with desire, that almost he was like to burn to coals. Supper being ended, the order was in Naples that the gentlewomen would desire to hear some discourse, either concerning love or learning. And although Philautus was requested, yet he posted it over to Euphues, whom he knew most fit for that purpose. Euphues being thus tied to the stake by their importunate entreaty, began as followeth:

"He that worst may is always enforced to hold the candle; the weakest must still to the wall; where none will, the devil himself must bear the cross. But were it not, gentlewomen, that your list [62] stands for law, I would borrow so much leave as to resign mine office to one of you, whose experience in love hath made you learned, and whose learning hath made you so lovely; for me to entreat of the one, being a novice, or to discourse of the other, being a truant, I may well make you weary but never the wiser, and give you occasion rather to laugh at my rashness than to like my reasons. Yet I care the less to excuse my boldness to you, who were the cause of my blindness. And since I am at mine own choice either to talk of love or of

[61] *vizard:* mask.

[62] *list:* pleasure.

learning, I had rather for this time be deemed an unthrift in rejecting profit, than a Stoic in renouncing pleasure.

"It hath been a question often disputed but never determined, whether the qualities of the mind, or the composition of the man, cause women most to like, or whether beauty or wit move men most to love. Certes, by how much the more the mind is to be preferred before the body, by so much the more the graces of the one are to be preferred before the gifts of the other, which if it be so, that the contemplation of the inward quality ought to be respected more than the view of the outward beauty, then doubtless women either do or should love those best whose virtue is best, not measuring the deformed man with the reformed mind. The foul toad [63] hath a fair stone in his head, the fine gold is found in the filthy earth, the sweet kernel lieth in the hard shell. Virtue is harbored in the heart of him that most men esteem misshapen. Contrariwise, if we respect more the outward shape than the inward habit, good God, into how many mischiefs do we fall? Into what blindness are we led? Do we not commonly see that in painted pots is hidden the deadliest poison? that in the greenest grass is the greatest serpent? in the clearest water the ugliest toad? Doth not experience teach us that in the most curious sepulcher are enclosed rotten bones? that the cypress tree beareth a fair leaf but no fruit? [64] that the estridge carrieth fair feathers, but rank flesh? How frantic are those lovers which are carried away with the gay glistering of the fine face! the beauty whereof is parched with the summer's blaze and chipped [65] with the winter's blast, which is of so short continuance that it fadeth before one perceive it flourish, of so small profit that it poisoneth those that possess it, of so little value with the wise, that they accompt it a delicate bait with a deadly hook, a sweet panther [66] with a devouring paunch, a sour poison in a silver pot. Here I could enter into discourse of such fine dames as being in love with their own looks make such coarse accompt of their passionate lovers; for commonly if they be adorned with beauty, they be so strait-laced, and made so high in the instep, that they disdain them most that most desire them. It is a world to see the doting of their lovers, and their dealing with them, the revealing of whose subtle trains would cause me to shed tears, and you gentlewomen to shut your modest ears. Pardon me, gentlewomen, if I unfold every wile, and show every wrinkle of women's disposition. Two things do they cause their servants to vow unto them, secrecy, and sovereignty, the one to conceal their enticing sleights, by the other to assure themselves of their only service. Again—but ho there! If I should have waded any further and sounded the depth of their deceit, I should either have procured your displeasure, or incurred

[63] *foul toad:* This famous myth did not originate with Pliny, but with medieval "scientists." Shakespeare uses it in *As You Like It,* I, ii, 12 ff. For a refutation, see Sir Thomas Browne, *Vulgar Errors,* III, 13.

[64] *cypress . . . fruit:* from a picture in Alciati's *Emblemata* (London, 1566, sig. P_8).

[65] *chipped:* chapped.

[66] *sweet panther:* Pliny, *Natural History,* VIII, xxiii, and many other sources.

the suspicion of fraud, either armed you to practice the like subtlety, or accused myself of perjury. But I mean not to offend your chaste minds with the rehearsal of their unchaste manners, whose ears I perceive to glow, and hearts to be grieved at that which I have already uttered, not that amongst you there be any such, but that in your sex there should be any such. Let not gentlewomen therefore make too much of their painted sheath, let them not be so curious in their own conceit or so currish to their loyal lovers. When the black crow's foot shall appear in their eye, or the black ox tread on their foot, when their beauty shall be like the blasted rose, their wealth wasted, their bodies worn, their faces wrinkled, their fingers crooked, who will like of them in their age, who loved none in their youth? If you will be cherished when you be old, be courteous while you be young; if you look for comfort in your hoary hairs, be not coy when you have your golden locks; if you would be embraced in the waning of your bravery, be not squeamish in the waxing of your beauty; if you desire to be kept like the roses when they have lost their color, smell sweet as the rose doth in the bud; if you would be tasted for old wine, be in the mouth a pleasant grape; so shall you be cherished for your courtesy, comforted for your honesty, embraced for your amity, so shall you be preserved with the sweet rose, and drunk with the pleasant wine. Thus far I am bold, gentlewomen, to counsel those that be coy that they weave not the web of their own woe nor spin the thread of their own thralldom by their own overthwartness. And seeing we are even in the bowels of love, it shall not be amiss to examine whether man or woman be soonest allured, whether be most constant the male or the female. And in this point I mean not to be mine own carver, lest I should seem either to pick a thank with men, or a quarrel with women. If, therefore, it might stand with your pleasure, Mistress Lucilla, to give your censure, I would take the contrary, for sure I am though your judgment be sound yet affection will shadow it."

Lucilla, seeing his pretense, thought to take advantage of his large proffer, unto whom she said: "Gentleman, in mine opinion women are to be won with every wind, in whose sex there is neither force to withstand the assaults of love, neither constancy to remain faithful. And because your discourse hath hitherto bred delight, I am loath to hinder you in the sequel of your devices."

Euphues, perceiving himself to be taken napping, answered as followeth: "Mistress Lucilla, if you speak as you think, these gentlewomen present have little cause to thank you; if you cause me to commend women, my tale will be accompted a mere trifle, and your words the plain truth. Yet knowing promise to be debt, I will pay it with performance. And I would the gentlemen here present were as ready to credit my proof as the gentlewomen are willing to hear their own praises, or I as able to overcome as Mistress Lucilla would be content to be overthrown. Howsoever the matter shall fall out, I am of the surer side, for if my reasons be weak, then is our sex strong, if forcible, then your judgment feeble; if I find truth on my side, I hope I shall for my wages win the good will of women; if I want proof, then, gentlewomen, of necessity you must yield to men. But to the matter.

"Touching the yielding to love, albeit their hearts seem tender, yet they harden them like the stone of Sicilia, the which the more it is beaten the harder it is. For being framed as it were of the perfection of men, they be free from all such cogitations as may any way provoke them to uncleanness, insomuch as they abhor the light love of youth which is grounded upon lust and dissolved upon every light occasion. When they see the folly of men turn to fury, their delight to doting, their affection to frenzy; when they see them as it were pine in pleasure, and to wax pale through their own peevishness, their suits, their service, their letters, their labors, their loves, their lives, seem to them so odious that they harden their hearts against such concupiscence, to the end they might convert them from rashness to reason, from such lewd disposition to honest discretion. Hereof it cometh that men accuse women of cruelty; because they themselves want civility, they accompt them full of wiles in not yielding to their wickedness, faithless for resisting their filthiness. But I had almost forgot myself; you shall pardon me, Mistress Lucilla, for this time, if thus abruptly I finish my discourse; it is neither for want of good will, or lack of proof, but that I feel in myself such alteration that I can scarcely utter one word. Ah, Euphues! Euphues!"

The gentlewomen were struck into such a quandary with this sudden change that they all changed color. But Euphues, taking Philautus by the hand and giving the gentlewomen thanks for their patience and his repast, bade them all farewell and went immediately to his chamber.

* * *

FROM

SIX COURT COMEDIES[67]

(1632)

Cupid and my Campaspe played
At cards for kisses; Cupid paid.
He stakes his quiver, bow, and arrows,

[67] In editions of Lyly's plays published in his lifetime no songs were printed, but in *Six Court Comedies* (1632), published by the printer, Edward Blount, twenty-one songs appeared of which the authorship is in dispute. Some scholars argue that Dekker wrote the songs; others defend Lyly's authorship. See *PMLA,* XLII (1927), 623; *MLR,* I (1905) 43; *TLS,* December 20, 1923, p. 894.

His mother's doves and team of sparrows,
Loses them too; then down he throws
The coral of his lip, the rose
Growing on 's cheek (but none knows how),
With these the crystal of his brow,
And then the dimple of his chin:
All these did my Campaspe win.
At last he set her both his eyes;
She won, and Cupid blind did rise.
  Oh Love! has she done this to thee?
  What shall, alas, become of me?

From *Alexander and Campaspe* (1584)

SONG BY FAIRIES

Omnes. PINCH him, pinch him, black and blue,
Saucy mortals must not view
What the queen of stars is doing,
Nor pry into our fairy wooing.
1 *Fairy.* Pinch him blue.
2 *Fairy.* And pinch him black.
3 *Fairy.* Let him not lack
Sharp nails to pinch him blue and red,
Till sleep has rocked his addlehead.
4 *Fairy.* For the trespass he hath done,
Spots o'er all his flesh shall run.
Kiss Endymion, kiss his eyes,
Then to our midnight haydegyes.[68]

From *Endymion* (*ca.* 1588)

[68] *haydegyes:* frolics, revels. Cf. the "fairy" song in *The Merry Wives of Windsor,* V, v, 97–107.

Stephen Gosson

1554–1624

GOSSON was a Kentishman who graduated at Oxford in 1576 and came to London and wrote plays. His association with the stage was accordingly in the period just after the building of the first public theaters. In 1579 he had a change of heart and published an attack on poetry and plays which he dedicated to Master Philip Sidney. Soon after the book appeared Spenser wrote to his friend Harvey, "Newe Bookes I heare of none, but only of one that writing a certain Booke called *The Schoole of Abuse* and dedicating it to Maister Sidney was for hys labor scorned: if at leaste it be in the goodnesse of that nature to scorne." There were several answers to it, one called *Strange News out of Africk*, now lost, and one by Thomas Lodge of Lincoln's Inn, which the authorities would not allow to be published but which was privately printed anyway. The players also replied to Gosson by a dramatic effort called *The Play of Plays* and by reviving Gosson's own trifles to embarrass him. He continued his campaign with an apology appended to *The Ephemerides of Phialo* (1579) and by *Playes Confuted in Five Actions* (1582), in which he attacked Lodge.

Gosson's position and his arguments were not new; Puritanical preachers had been inveighing against the theaters for many years past. And he had many successors: John Rainolds of Oxford, who carried on a long dispute with William Grager in the nineties, William Stubbes and William Prynne in the reign of Charles I, and Jeremy Collier at the end of the century.

The distance between moral English Humanism and strict Puritanism was sometimes not very great. Gosson, for example, does not go far beyond Ascham in the following passage: "First hee [the Devil] sente ouer many wanton Italian bookes, which being translated into english, have poysoned the olde maners of our Country with foreine delights, they have so hardned the readers harts, y[t] seuerer writers are trode under foote, none are so pleasannte or plausible as they, that sound some kinde of libertie in our eares. . . . Therefore the Devill not contented with the number he hath corrupted with reading Italian baudery, because all cannot reade, presenteth vs Comedies cut by the same paterne, which drag such a monstrous taile after them, as is able to sweep whole Cities into his lap." (*Playes Confuted*, pp. 172–173.)

By 1584 Gosson was a preacher, and he was later rector of parishes in the country and in London until his death in 1624. He is of interest because he may well have stimulated Sidney to write his *Apology* (see pp. 271–309), because he is a precursor of Euphuism (see pp. 206–226), and because he gives a lively, if biased, picture of how Elizabethans behaved at the playhouse.

BIBLIOGRAPHY: *The Schoole of Abuse* and *A Short Apologie of the School of Abuse*, ed. E. Arber, English Reprints, London, 1868; *Plays Confuted in Five Actions*, in W. C. Hazlitt, *The English Drama and Stage*, Roxburghe Library, 1869; E. K. Chambers, *The Elizabethan Stage*, I, 256–259 and IV, 203–207, Oxford, 1923; E. N. S. Thompson, *The Controversy Between the Puritans and the Stage*, New York, 1903; W. Ringler, *Stephen Gosson, A Biographical and Critical Study*, Princeton, 1941.

FROM

THE SCHOOL OF ABUSE

(1579)

CONSIDER with thyself, gentle reader, the old discipline of England; mark what we were before and what we are now. Leave Rome awhile, and cast thine eye back to thy predecessors and tell me how wonderfully we have been changed since we were schooled with these abuses. Dion [1] saith that Englishmen could suffer watching and labor, hunger and thirst, and bear of all storms with head and shoulders. They used slender weapons, went naked, and were good soldiers. They fed upon roots and barks of trees, they would stand up to the chin many days in marshes without victuals, and they had a kind of sustenance in time of need, of which if they had taken but the quantity of a bean or the weight of a pease, they did neither gape after meat nor long for the cup a great while after, the men in valor not yielding to Scythia, the women in courage passing the Amazons. The exercise of both was shooting and darting, running and wrestling and trying such masteries as either consisted in swiftness of feet, agility of body, strength of arms, or martial discipline. But the exercise that is now among us is banqueting, playing, piping, and dancing and all such delights as may win us to pleasure or rock us asleep.

Oh, what a wonderful change is this! Our wrestling at arms is turned to wallowing in ladies' laps, our courage to cowardice, our running to riot, our bows into bowls, and our darts to dishes. We have robbed Greece of gluttony, Italy of wantonness, Spain of pride, France of deceit, and Dutchland of quaffing. Compare London to Rome, and England to Italy; you shall find the theaters of the one, the abuses of the other, to be rife among us. *Experto crede;* [2] I have seen somewhat and therefore I think may say more. In Rome, when plays or pageants are shown, Ovid [3] chargeth his pilgrims to creep close to the saints whom they serve, and show their double diligence to lift the gentlewomen's robes from the ground, for soiling in the dust; to sweep motes from their kirtles, to keep their fingers in ure, to lay their hands at their backs for an easy stay, to look upon those whom they behold, to praise that which they commend, to like everything that pleaseth them, to present them pomegranates, to pick as they sit; and when all is done, to wait on them mannerly to their houses. In our assemblies at plays in London, you shall see such heaving, and shoving, such itching

[1] *Dion:* Dio Cassius, Roman historian (b. 155 A.D.).

[2] *Experto crede:* "believe the experienced."

[3] *Ovid: Ars amatoria,* I, 135–162.

and shouldering, to sit by women. Such care for their garments, that they be not trod on! Such eyes to their laps that no chips light in them! Such pillows to their backs, that they take no hurt! Such masking in their ears—I know not what! Such giving them pippins to pass the time! Such playing at foot-cent [4] without cards! Such ticking, such toying, such smiling, such winking, and such manning them home, when the sports are ended, that it is right comedy to mark their behavior, to watch their conceits, as the cat for the mouse, and as good as a course at the game itself to dog them a little, or follow aloof by the print of their feet and so discover by slot [5] where the dear [6] taketh soil.[7] If this were as well noted as ill seen, or as openly punished, as secretly practiced, I have no doubt but the cause would be seared to dry up the effect and these pretty rabbits very cunningly ferreted from their burrows. For they that lack customers all the week, either because their haunt is unknown, or the constables and officers of their parish watch them so narrowly, that they dare not quetch,[8] to celebrate the Sabbath, flock to theaters, and there keep a general market of bawdry. Not that any filthiness, indeed, is committed within the compass of that ground, as was done in Rome, but that every wanton and his paramour, every man and his mistress, every John and his Joan, every knave and his queen are there first acquainted and cheapen [9] the merchandise in that place, which they pay for elsewhere as they can agree. These worms when they dare not nestle in the peascod at home, find refuge abroad and are hid in the ears of other men's corn. Every vawter [10] in one blind tavern or other is tenant at will, to which she tolleth resort [11] and plays the stale [12] to utter [13] their victuals, and help them to empty their musty casks. There is she so intreated with words and received with courtesy that every back room in the house is at her commandment. Some that have neither land to maintain them, nor good occupation to get their bread, desirous to strut it with the best, yet disdaining to live by the sweat of their brows, have found out this cast of legerdemain, to play fast and loose among their neighbors. If any part of music have suffered shipwreck and arrived by fortune at their fingers' ends, with show of gentility they take up fair houses, receive lusty lasses at a price for boarders, and pipe from morning to evening for wood and coal. By the brothers, cousins, uncles, great-grandsires, and such like acquaintance of their guests, they drink of the best, they sit rent free, they have their own table spread to their hands without wearing the strings of their purse, or anything else but household and honesty. When resort so increaseth that they grow in suspicion, and the pots which are sent so often to the tavern get such a knock before they come home, that

[4] *foot-cent:* cent-foot, a card game in which the language was that of love.

[5] *slot:* track.

[6] *dear:* pun on "deer."

[7] *soil:* water used as refuge by a hunted animal.

[8] *quetch:* move from one place to another.

[9] *cheapen:* bargain for.

[10] *vawter:* votary (?); cf. "Venus' nuns," below, p. 230.

[11] *tolleth resort:* entices customers.

[12] *stale:* thief's accomplice.

[13] *utter:* sell.

they return their master a crack to his credit. Though he be called in question of his life, he hath shifts enough to avoid the blank. If their houses be searched, some instrument of music is laid in sight to dazzle the eyes of every officer, and all that are lodged in the house by night, or frequent it by day, come thither as pupils to be well schooled. Other there are which being so known that they are the byword of every man's mouth, and pointed at commonly as they pass the streets, either couch themselves in alleys or blind lanes, or take sanctuary in friaries, or live a mile from the city like Venus' nuns in a cloister at Newington, Ratliff, Islington, Hogsdon,[14] or some such place, where like penitents they deny the world and spend their days in double devotion. And when they are weary of contemplation to comfort themselves and renew their acquaintance, they visit theaters, where they make full account of a prey before they depart. Solon made no law for parricides, because he feared that he should rather put men in mind to commit such offenses, than by any strange punishment, give them a bit to keep them under. And I intend not to show you all that I see, nor half that I hear of these abuses, lest you judge me more willful to teach them, than willing to forbid them.

I look still when players should cast me their gauntlets and challenge a combat for entering so far into their possessions, as though I made them Lords of this misrule,[15] or the very schoolmasters of these abuses. Though the best clerks be of that opinion, they hear not me say so. There are more houses than parish churches, more maids than Maulkin, more ways to the wood than one, and more causes in nature than efficients.[16] The carpenter raiseth not his frame without tools, nor the Devil his work without instruments; were not the players the mean to make these assemblies, such multitudes would hardly be drawn in so narrow room. They seek not to hurt, but desire to please; they have purged their comedies of wanton speeches, yet the corn which they sell is full of cockle, and the drink that they draw overcharged with dregs. There is more in them than we perceive; the Devil stands at our elbows when we see not, speaks when we hear him not, strikes when we feel not, and woundeth sore when he razeth no skin, nor rents the flesh. In those things that we least mistrust, the greatest danger doth often lurk. The countryman is more afraid of the serpent that is hid in the grass than the wild beast that openly feeds upon the mountains. The mariner is more endangered by privy shelves than known rocks. The soldier is sooner killed with a little bullet than a long sword. There is more peril in close fistoles[17] than outward sores, in secret ambush than main battles, in undermining than plain assaulting, in friends than foes, in civil discord than foreign wars. Small are the abuses, and slight are the faults,

14 *Newington . . . Hogsdon:* suburbs of London.

15 *Lords of this misrule:* The Lord of Misrule was the master of ceremonies at a rowdy party or celebration.

16 *efficients:* causes which make effects what they are.

17 *fistoles:* fistulas.

that now in theaters escape the poet's pen. But tall cedars from little grains shoot high; great oaks from slender roots spread wide. Large streams from narrow springs run far. One little spark fires a whole city. One dram of *Eleborus* [18] ransacks every vein. The fish *Remora* [19] hath a small body and great force to stay ships against wind and tide. *Ichneumon,*[20] a little worm, overcomes the elephant. The viper slays the bull, the weasel the cockatrice. And the weakest wasp stingeth the stoutest man of war. The height of heaven is taken by the staff; the bottom of the sea, sounded with lead; the farthest coast, discovered by compass; the secrets of nature, searched by wit; the anatomy of man, set out by experience. But the abuses of plays cannot be shown because they pass the degrees of the instrument, reach the plummet, sight of the mind, and for trial are never brought to the touchstone. Therefore, he that will avoid the open shame of privy sin, the common plague of private offenses, the great wracks of little rocks, the sure decease of uncertain causes, must set hand to the stern and eye to his steps to shun the occasion as near as he can, neither running to bushes for renting his clothes, nor rent his clothes for impairing his thrift, nor walk upon ice for taking a fall, nor take a fall for bruising himself, nor go to theaters for being allured, nor once be allured for fear of abuse.

---

[18] *Eleborus:* "It is a full violent herb . . . for it grieveth sore and slayeth soon." *Batman upon Bartholome,* XVII, 55.

[19] *Remora:* "As touching this strange fish, whose smallness, with his virtue of staying ships, doth pass man's reason; the Grecians call *Ethneis,* of the Latins *Remora.*" *Batman upon Bartholome,* XIII, 29.

[20] *Ichneumon:* the Egyptian mongoose. The old authorities say it attacks serpents but not elephants. Gosson may be thinking of the chameleon.

Sir Philip Sidney

1554–1586

THOUGH to the popular mind Sir Walter Ralegh is the typical Elizabethan gentleman, numerous biographers have accorded Sir Philip Sidney first place as the ideal Elizabethan courtier, soldier, humanist, and man of letters. Sidney's background was that of the intelligent aristocracy. He was the son of Sir Henry Sidney, thrice lord deputy of Ireland, and the Earl of Leicester's sister. At nine he entered Shrewsbury school with his life-long friend and biographer, Fulke Greville. He later went to Christ Church, Oxford, but left in 1571, during the time of the plague, without a degree.

The following year he traveled in the Earl of Lincoln's suite to Paris, where in his stay of three months he became acquainted with the chief French writers and Protestant leaders. His zeal for Protestantism was undoubtedly heightened on St. Bartholomew's day, August 23, when Huguenots throughout France were massacred. Leaving Paris he visited Frankfort-on-the-Main, meeting the scholar and controversialist Hubert Languet, who influenced him strongly in literary and religious matters. He pushed on to Vienna, then to Venice, where he became a friend of Tintoretto and Paolo Veronese. It is possible that the crowded canvases of Veronese (to whom Sidney sat for a portrait) may have given Sidney models for the many tumultuous scenes of action in the *Arcadia*.

After a further visit to Vienna and Poland, he was summoned home to begin the life of a courtier and servant of the Queen on official and diplomatic missions. He followed the Queen on one of her progresses to Chartley Castle, home of the Earl of Essex, and there he is supposed to have seen for the first time Essex' daughter, Penelope Devereux, a young girl of thirteen, later the "Stella" of the sonnets. In 1577 he was sent abroad to congratulate the new Elector Palatine and Emperor and to further the Protestant cause.

During his life at court Sidney was gaining prominence among artists and literary men. He shared with his friends Spenser, Dyer, and Greville a genuine interest in the problems confronting the new English poetry and considered seriously with them (some scholars say in a group called the Areopagus) the introduction of classical meters in English verse. He wrote a masque, *The Lady of May,* for Leicester's entertainment of the Queen at Wanstead in 1578.

Within two years, however, Sidney's life at court was interrupted for a time, because he incurred the disfavor of the Queen for opposing her proposal to marry the Duke of Anjou and, perhaps, for his refusal to apologize at the Queen's command to the Earl of Oxford after a quarrel on the tennis court. In 1580 Sidney left the court and went to Wilton to stay with his sister, the Countess of Pembroke.

At Wilton he began to write the early draft of the *Arcadia,* because, as he says in a letter to his sister, "you desired me to do it, and your desire to my heart is an absolute commandment." Before 1583 or 1584 he also wrote *An Apologie for Poetrie,* a reply to the Puritan Stephen Gosson's *Schoole of Abuse* (see above, p. 228). He was knighted in 1583, and in the autumn married Frances, a daughter of Sir Francis Walsingham.

Though prominent and renowned at court, Sidney shared the desire of many Elizabethan gentlemen to see the New World. He had followed with interest the voyages of Frobisher, Gilbert, and Ralegh. In 1585 he was actually planning to sail with Drake on an expedition to America when the Queen recalled him to do service for the Protestant cause in the Netherlands, where he was appointed governor of Flushing.

In September of 1586 with the forces of Sir John Norris, he took part in an attack on a convoy of provisions near Zutphen. Just before the attack he had removed his leg-armor because his friend Sir William Pelham was starting without any. Unfortunately a bullet hit him in the left thigh, and though he succeeded in riding back to camp, he died twenty-six days later, braving without protest the painful treatment of his surgeons. He even composed a song about his own wound, entitled *La cuisse rompue.* The well-known story, told by Greville, that the wounded Sidney gave his own bottle of water to a dying foot soldier with the words, "Thy necessity is greater than mine," is typical of the man, even though it may be apocryphal.

All England and Protestant Europe mourned his death. Of the two hundred elegies on his death Spenser's *Astrophel* is best known. After several months of delay, seven hundred mourners walked in procession to St. Paul's Cathedral to see the ideal English courtier of the age laid to rest.

Sidney did display, perhaps more than any Englishman of his time, the characteristics of the true Renaissance courtier, as that ideal was pictured in Castiglione's *Courtier* (see below, pp. 113–134). He was a man of action, a soldier, and a courtier, but with action he combined grace, dignity, and learning. A recent student of Sidney (K. O. Myrick, *Sir Philip Sidney as a Literary Craftsman,* p. 298) characterized Sidney both as a man and as a literary artist, as one who possessed *sprezzatura,* "courtly grace which conceals a sober purpose and is, indeed, the mark of consummate artistry." Such a quality underlies all Sidney's literary work and conditioned his own judgment of it.

Except for two poems, none of Sidney's literary work was printed in his lifetime. In 1590 William Ponsonby printed a quarto edition of *The Countesse of Pembrokes Arcadia,* an incomplete version of the romance, which was Sidney's own revision of the first draft or "old Arcadia" he had written at Wilton in 1580. In 1593 appeared a folio edition made up of slight modifications of the 1590 quarto and additions from Sidney's rejected first draft to complete the story. The first draft itself, inferior to the 1590 version, had been circulated among Sidney's friends, but the manuscripts dropped out of sight for over three hundred years, when in 1907, the late Bertram Dobell turned up two copies. Others have since come to light: three at Oxford, two in the British Museum, and two in the United States. The 1590 edition represents Sidney's careful reworking of the early version. The *Arcadia* is a story highly complicated in plot, very conscious in style, containing pastoral, chivalric, and heroic elements. It follows the pattern of Renaissance romances in being interspersed with songs and eclogues, about eighty in all, many of them ingenious metrical experiments. Although it is an original work reflecting much of Sidney's own experience, it has many literary models: the Greek prose romances, Renaissance pastoral romances, and the medieval chivalric romances. Sidney's contemporary, Gabriel Harvey, advised the reading of the *Arcadia* as a "gallant Legendary, full of pleasurable accidents, and profitable discourses; for three thinges especially, very notable, for amorous Courting, (he was young in yeeres;) for sage counselling, (he was ripe in judgment;) and valorous fighting, (his soueraine profession was Armes:) and delightfull pastime by way of Pastoral exercises, may passe for the fourth." Harvey's farewell to the *Arcadia* was in an aureate vein, typical of tasteless Elizabethan extravagance: "Live ever sweete Booke:" "the siluer Image of his [Sidney's] gentle witt, and the golden Pillar of his noble courage: and ever notify vnto the worlde, that thy writer, was the Secretary of Eloquence; the breath of the Muses; the hooney-bee of the dayntiest flowers of Witt, and Arte; the Pith of morall, and intellectual Vertues; the arme of Bellona in the field; the toung of Suada in the chamber; the spirite of Practise in esse; and the Paragon of Excellency in Print." Its "excellency," or rather its popularity, was to carry it through fourteen editions within a century. From the episode of the Paphlagonian king in Book II, Shakespeare took suggestion for the story of Gloucester and his two sons in *Lear*.

The seriousness of Sidney's intention in writing the *Arcadia* (it is not mere playful pastime in the pastoral mood) is evident not only in his praise of courage and the active, heroic life but in the conscious artistry of the style itself, which differs widely from the sheer ornament of Lyly. Present-day criticism of the *Arcadia* sees in the work a thoughtful, carefully executed, elaborate piece of art, and not what Hazlitt called "one of the greatest monuments of the abuse of intellectual power upon record."

Astrophel and Stella was published in 1591, about nine years after it was written. Next to Spenser's *Shepheardes Calender,* which was dedicated to Sidney, it is the most influential and important pioneer of the "new poetry" which was to make glorious the last two decades of Elizabeth's reign. It created a fad for sonnet cycles in England and revived an interest in Petrarchan love poetry which had been almost dormant since the time of Surrey. In spite of his protestations of originality and sincerity (Sonnets I, III, XV, LXXIV, XC), Sidney utilizes most of the conventions and themes of Petrarch and his followers. Yet the greatness of the sonnets comes from their grave and simple eloquence, their freshness of expression, even when the theme is trite, and their vivid impression of the poet's vigorous and speculative mind. Sidney preferred the Italian to the English form of the sonnet, but he shows great versatility in structure and is fond of a final strong couplet, which is not typically Italian. The dialogues between reason and sensuality (a heritage from the Middle Ages) and the Cupid sonnets (of Anacreontic inspiration) have less interest for the modern reader than they had for Sidney's contemporaries, but the philosophical ones, the "autobiographical" ones, and the best of those on standard themes (e.g., XXXIX, on sleep) have lost nothing in the passage of time.

In 1595 two editions of Sidney's important critical work appeared. The first bore the title, *The Defense of Poesy;* the second, *An Apologie for Poetrie.* The treatise had probably been begun in 1579 or 1581, shortly after Gosson's attack, but had not been completed until 1583 or later. Framed in the form of a classical oration, it is, according to Professor Spingarn, "a veritable epitome of the literary criticism of the Renaissance." Its basis is the Aristotelianism of the Renaissance critics such as Minturno and Scaliger. Sidney, taking a wide view of poetry as any work of the imagination, defends poetry against its detractors, and adds his critical appreciation of English poetry and drama. Its style is clear, simple, vigorous; its temper noble and idealistic. In upholding the dignity and value of poetry in society, it was a useful bulwark for the "new poetry" against Puritan and narrow-minded critics. For Sidney it was a statement of faith which is illustrated in all his works.

BIBLIOGRAPHY: *The Complete Works of Sir Philip Sidney,* ed. A. Feuillerat, 4 vols., Cambridge, 1912–1926; R. W. Zandvoort, *Sidney's Arcadia: a Comparison of the Two Versions,* Amsterdam, 1929; M. S. Goldman, *Sir Philip Sidney and the Arcadia,* Urbana, 1934; K. O. Myrick, *Sir Philip Sidney as a Literary Craftsman,* Harvard University Press, 1935; Mona Wilson, *Sir Philip Sidney,* London, 1931; M. Poirier, *Sir Philip Sidney,* Lille, 1948; L. C. John, *The Elizabethan Sonnet Sequences,* New York, 1938; J. G. Scott, *Les Sonnets Elisabéthains,* Paris, 1929; Theodore Spencer, "The Poetry of Sir Philip Sidney," *ELH,* XII (1945), 251–278; Hallett Smith, *Elizabethan Poetry* (1952), 142–158; W. Ringler, "Master Drant's Rules," *PQ,* XXIX (1950), 70–74; "Poems Attributed to Sir Philip Sidney," *SP,* XLVII (1950), 126–151; John Buxton, *Sir Philip Sidney and the English Renaissance,* London, 1954.

ASTROPHEL AND STELLA

I[1]

Loving in truth, and fain in verse my love to show,
That she, dear she, might take some pleasure of my pain,
Pleasure might cause her read, reading might make her know,
Knowledge might pity win, and pity grace obtain,
I sought fit words to paint the blackest face of woe:
Studying inventions fine, her wits to entertain,
Oft turning others' leaves, to see if thence would flow
Some fresh and fruitful showers upon my sunburnt brain.
But words came halting forth, wanting Invention's stay;
Invention, Nature's child, fled stepdame Study's blows;
And others' feet still seemed but strangers in my way.
Thus, great with child to speak, and helpless in my throes,
Biting my truant pen, beating myself for spite:
"Fool," said my Muse to me, "look in thy heart, and write!"

II

Not at the first sight, nor with a dribbed shot,[2]
Love gave the wound which, while I breathe, will bleed;
But known worth did in mine [3] of time proceed,
Till, by degrees, it had full conquest got.
I saw, and liked; I liked, but loved not;
I loved, but straight did not what Love decreed;
At length to Love's decrees I, forced, agreed,
Yet with repining at so partial lot.
Now even that footstep of lost liberty
Is gone; and now, like slave-born Muscovite,
I call it praise to suffer tyranny;
And now employ the remnant of my wit
To make myself believe that all is well,
While, with a feeling [4] skill, I paint my hell.

---

[1] This and five other sonnets of the original sequence are in hexameter.

[2] *dribbed shot:* one wide or short of the mark.

[3] *mine:* tunnel, dug under a fortress in a siege.

[4] *feeling:* perceptive, understanding.

III

Let dainty wits cry on the Sisters nine,
That bravely masked, their fancies may be told;
Or, Pindar's apes,[5] flaunt they in phrases fine,
Enameling with pied flowers their thoughts of gold;
Or else let them in statelier glory shine,
Ennobling new-found tropes with problems old;
Or with strange similes enrich each line,
Of herbs or beasts which Ind or Afric hold.[6]
For me, in sooth, no Muse but one I know;
Phrases and problems from my reach do grow,
And strange things cost too dear for my poor sprites.[7]
How then? Even thus—in Stella's face I read
What love and beauty be; then all my deed
But copying is, what, in her, Nature writes.

IV

Virtue, alas, now let me take some rest;
Thou set'st a bate [8] between my will and wit;
If vain love have my simple soul oppressed,
Leave what thou lik'st not, deal not thou with it.
Thy scepter use in some old Cato's [9] breast,
Churches or schools are for thy seat more fit;
I do confess—pardon a fault confessed—
My mouth too tender is for thy hard bit.
But if that needs thou wilt usurping be
The little reason that is left in me,
And still the effect of thy persuasions prove,
I swear, my heart such one shall show to thee
That shrines in flesh so true a deity
That, Virtue, thou thyself shalt be in love.

---

5 *Pindar's apes:* lyric poets, after the Greek Pindar (522–448 B.C.).

6 *Ennobling . . . hold,* a part of what was called in prose Euphuism. See p. 514, below.

7 *sprites:* spirits.

8 *bate:* strife.

9 *Cato:* the Censor (234–149 B.C.), famous for his moral severity.

V

It is most true that eyes are formed to serve
The inward light, and that the heavenly part
Ought to be king,[10] from whose rules who do swerve,
Rebels to nature, strive for their own smart.
It is most true, what we call Cupid's dart
An image is, which for ourselves we carve,
And, fools, adore in temple of our heart,
Till that good god make church and churchmen starve.
True, that true beauty virtue is indeed,
Whereof this beauty can be but a shade,
Which elements with mortal mixture breed.
True, that on earth we are but pilgrims made,
And should in soul up to our country move.
True, and yet true that I must Stella love.

VI

Some lovers speak, when they their Muses entertain,
Of hopes begot by fear, of wot not what desires,
Of force of heavenly beams infusing hellish pain,
Of living deaths, dear wounds, fair storms, and freezing fires;
Someone his song in Jove and Jove's strange tales attires,
Bordered with bulls and swans, powdered with golden rain;
Another humbler wit to shepherd's pipe retires,
Yet hiding royal blood full oft in rural vein.
To some a sweetest plaint a sweetest style affords,
While tears pour out his ink, and sighs breathe out his words,
His paper pale despair, and pain his pen doth move.
I can speak what I feel, and feel as much as they,
But think that all the map of my state I display
When trembling voice brings forth, that I do Stella love.

---

[10] *It . . . king:* an idea very common in Elizabethan literature.

VII

WHEN Nature made her chief work, Stella's eyes,
In color black why wrapt she beams so bright?
Would she, in beamy black, like painter wise,
Frame daintiest luster, mixed of shades and light?
Or did she else that sober hue devise
In object best to knit and strength our sight;
Lest, if no veil these brave gleams did disguise,
They, sun-like, should more dazzle than delight?
Or would she her miraculous power show,
That, whereas black [11] seems beauty's contrary,
She, even in black, doth make all beauties flow?
Both so, and thus—she, minding Love should be
Placed ever there, gave him this mourning weed
To honor all their deaths who for her bleed.

X

REASON, in faith thou art well served, that still
Wouldst brabbling [12] be with Sense and Love in me;
I rather wished thee climb the Muses' hill;
Or reach the fruit of Nature's choicest tree;
Or seek heaven's course or heaven's inside to see.
Why shouldst thou toil our thorny soil to till?
Leave Sense and those which Sense's objects be;
Deal thou with powers of thoughts, leave Love to Will.
But thou wouldst needs fight both with Love and Sense,
With sword of wit giving wounds of dispraise,
Till downright blows did foil thy cunning fence;
For, soon as they strake thee with Stella's rays,
Reason, thou kneel'dst, and offer'dst straight to prove,
By reason good, good reason her to love.

---

[11] *black:* The word often means "ugly."   [12] *brabbling:* quarreling.

XI

In truth, O Love, with what a boyish kind[13]
Thou dost proceed in thy most serious ways,
That when the heaven to thee his best displays,
Yet of that best thou leav'st the best behind!
For, like a child that some fair book doth find,
With gilded leaves or colored vellum plays,
Or, at the most, on some fine picture stays,
But never heeds the fruit of writer's mind;
So when thou saw'st, in Nature's cabinet,
Stella, thou straight look'st babies[14] in her eyes,
In her cheeks' pit thou didst thy pitfold set,
And in her breast bo-peep or couching lies,
Playing and shining in each outward part;
But, fool, seek'st not to get into her heart.

XII

Cupid, because thou shin'st in Stella's eyes,
That from her locks, thy day-nets,[15] none 'scapes free,
That those lips swelled so full of thee they be,
That her sweet breath makes oft thy flames to rise,
That in her breast thy pap well sugared lies,
That her grace gracious makes thy wrongs, that she,
What words soe'er she speak, persuades for thee,
That her clear voice lifts thy fame to the skies—
Thou countest Stella thine, like those whose powers
Having got up a breach by fighting well,
Cry, "Victory, this fair day all is ours!"
Oh no! Her heart is such a citadel,
So fortified with wit, stored with disdain,
That to win it is all the skill and pain.

---

[13] *kind:* nature.

[14] *look'st babies:* saw tiny reflections of yourself.

[15] *day-nets:* nets for catching small birds.

XIV

ALAS, have I not pain enough, my friend,
Upon whose breast a fiercer gripe doth tire
Than did on him [16] who first stole down the fire,
While Love on me doth all his quiver spend—
But with your rhubarb [17] words ye must contend,
To grieve me worse, in saying that Desire
Doth plunge my well-formed soul even in the mire
Of sinful thoughts, which do in ruin end?
If that be sin which doth the manners frame,
Well stayed with truth in word and faith of deed,
Ready of wit, and fearing naught but shame;
If that be sin, which in fixed hearts doth breed
A loathing of all loose unchastity,
Then love is sin, and let me sinful be.

XV

You that do search for every purling spring
Which from the ribs of old Parnassus flows,
And every flower, not sweet perhaps, which grows
Near thereabouts, into your poesy wring;
You that do dictionary's method bring
Into your rhymes, running in rattling rows;
You that poor Petrarch's long deceased woes
With newborn sighs and denizened wit do sing:
You take wrong ways; those far-fet [18] helps be such
As do bewray [19] a want of inward touch,
And sure at length stolen goods do come to light;
But if, both for your love and skill, your name
You seek to nurse at fullest breasts of Fame,
Stella behold, and then begin to indite.

---

[16] *him:* Prometheus.
[17] *rhubarb:* sharp, sour.
[18] *far-fet:* farfetched.
[19] *bewray:* reveal.

XVIII

WITH what sharp checks I in myself am shent [20]
When into Reason's audit I do go,
And by just counts myself a bankrupt know
Of all those goods which heaven to me hath lent;
Unable quite to pay even Nature's rent,
Which unto it by birthright I do owe;
And, which is worse, no good excuse can show,
But that my wealth I have most idly spent!
My youth doth waste, my knowledge brings forth toys; [21]
My wit doth strive those passions to defend,
Which, for reward, spoil it with vain annoys.
I see my course to lose myself doth bend;
I see—and yet no greater sorrow take
Than that I lose no more for Stella's sake.

XXI

YOUR words, my friend, right healthful caustics, blame
My young mind marred, whom Love doth windlass [22] so;
That mine own writings, like bad servants, show
My wits quick in vain thoughts, in virtue lame;
That Plato [23] I read for naught but if he tame
Such coltish years; that to my birth I owe
Nobler desires, lest else that friendly foe,
Great expectation, wear a train of shame;
For since mad March great promise made of me,
If now the May of my years much decline
What can be hoped my harvest-time will be?
Sure, you say well. Your wisdom's golden mine
Dig deep with learning's spade. Now tell me this—
Hath this world aught so fair as Stella is? [24]

[20] *shent:* punished.
[21] *toys:* trifles.
[22] *windlass:* decoy, ensnare.
[23] *Plato: The Symposium* especially.
[24] Lines 3–11 are a digest of the friend's words. The last three lines are the poet's reply.

XXIII

THE curious wits, seeing dull pensiveness
Bewray itself in my long-settled eyes,
When those same fumes of melancholy rise,
With idle pains and missing aim do guess.
Some, that know how my spring I did address,
Deem that my Muse some fruit of knowledge plies;
Others, because the prince my service tries,
Think that I think state errors to redress.
But harder judges judge ambition's rage,
Scourge of itself, still climbing slippery place,
Holds my young brain captived in golden cage.
Oh fools, or over-wise: alas, the race
Of all my thoughts hath neither stop nor start
But only Stella's eyes and Stella's heart.

XXIV

RICH [25] fools there be whose base and filthy heart
Lies hatching still the goods wherein they flow,
And damning their own selves to Tantal's [26] smart,
Wealth breeding want, more rich, more wretched grow.
Yet to those fools heaven doth such wit impart
As what their hands do hold, their heads do know,
And knowing, love, and loving, lay apart
As sacred things, far from all danger's show.
But that rich fool who by blind fortune's lot
The richest gem of love and life enjoys,
And can with foul abuse such beauties blot,
Let him, deprived of sweet but unfelt joys,
Exiled for aye from those high treasures which
He knows not, grow in only folly rich!

[25] *Rich:* This sonnet and others (cf. XXXVII) pun on the name of Stella's husband, Lord Rich.

[26] *Tantal:* Tantalus; his "smart" was to suffer in hell from thirst and hunger, but the water and fruit near him always retreated as he approached.

XXV

THE wisest scholar of the wight most wise [27]
By Phoebus' doom, with sugared sentence says
That Virtue, if it once met with our eyes,
Strange flames of love it in our souls would raise;
But, for that [28] man with pain this truth descries,
While he each thing in sense's balance weighs,
And so nor will nor can behold those skies
Which inward sun to heroic mind displays,
Virtue of late, with virtuous care to stir
Love of herself, took Stella's shape, that she
To mortal eyes might sweetly shine in her.
It is most true; for since I her did see,
Virtue's great beauty in that face I prove,
And find the effect, for I do burn in love.

XXVI

THOUGH dusty wits dare scorn astrology,
And fools can think those lamps of purest light,
Whose numbers, ways, greatness, eternity,
Promising wonders, wonder do invite,
To have for no cause birthright in the sky
But for to spangle the black weeds [29] of night;
Or for some brawl which in that chamber high
They should still dance to please a gazer's sight.
For me, I do nature unidle know,
And know great causes great effects procure;
And know those bodies high reign on the low.
And if these rules did fail, proof makes me sure,
Who oft forejudge my after-following race
By only those two stars in Stella's face.

[27] *scholar:* Plato; *the wight most wise by Phoebus' doom:* Socrates, declared to be the wisest by an oracle.

[28] *for that:* because.

[29] *weeds:* clothes.

XXVII

BECAUSE I oft in dark abstracted guise
Seem most alone in greatest company,
With dearth of words, or answers quite awry,
To them that would make speech of speech arise,
They deem, and of their doom the rumor flies,
That poison foul of bubbling pride doth lie
So in my swelling breast that only I
Fawn on myself, and others do despise.
Yet pride, I think, doth not my soul possess,
Which looks too oft in his unflattering glass;
But one worse fault, ambition, I confess,
That makes me oft my best friends overpass,
Unseen, unheard, while thought to highest place
Bends all his powers, even unto Stella's grace.

XXVIII

YOU that with allegory's curious frame
Of others' children changelings use to make,[30]
With me those pains, for God's sake, do not take;
I list not dig so deep for brazen fame.
When I say Stella, I do mean the same
Princess of beauty, for whose only sake
The reins of Love I love, though never slack,
And joy therein, though nations count it shame.
I beg no subject to use eloquence,
Nor in hid ways do guide philosophy;
Look at my hands for no such quintessence;[31]
But know that I in pure simplicity
Breathe out the flames which burn within my heart,
Love only reading unto me this art.

---

[30] *You . . . make:* you who interpret all poetry as if it were allegory.

[31] *quintessence:* mystery, the "fifth essence" for which alchemists ("philosophers") searched.

XXX

WHETHER the Turkish new moon minded be
To fill her horns this year on Christian coast;
How Poles' right king means without leave of host
To warm with ill-made fire cold Muscovy;
If French can yet three parts in one agree;
What now the Dutch in their full diets boast;
How Holland hearts, now so good towns be lost,
Trust in the shade of pleasant Orange-tree;
How Ulster likes of that same golden bit
Wherewith my father [32] once made it half tame;
If in the Scotch court be no weltering [33] yet—
These questions [34] busy wits to me do frame.
I, cumbered with good manners, answer do,
But know not how; for still I think of you.

XXXI

WITH how sad steps, Oh Moon, thou climb'st the skies!
How silently, and with how wan a face!
What, may it be that even in heavenly place
That busy archer his sharp arrows tries?
Sure, if that long-with-love-acquainted eyes
Can judge of love, thou feel'st a lover's case,
I read it in thy looks; thy languished grace,
To me, that feel the like, thy state descries.
Then, even of fellowship, Oh Moon, tell me,
Is constant love deemed there but want of wit?
Are beauties there as proud as here they be?
Do they above love to be loved, and yet
Those lovers scorn whom that love doth possess?
Do they call virtue there ungratefulness? [35]

---

[32] *my father:* Sir Henry Sidney, formerly Lord Deputy of Ireland.

[33] *weltering:* writhing, unrest.

[34] *These questions:* matters of news, gossip, or speculation about 1580–1581.

[35] *Do . . . ungratefulness:* Do they call ungratefulness there a virtue?

XXXII

Morpheus, the lively son of deadly sleep,
Witness of life to them that living die,
A prophet oft, and oft an history,
A poet eke, as humors fly or creep:[36]
Since thou in me so sure a power dost keep
That never I with closed-up sense do lie
But by thy work my Stella I descry,
Teaching blind eyes both how to smile and weep,
Vouchsafe, of all acquaintance, this to tell,
Whence hast thou ivory, rubies, pearl, and gold,
To show her skin, lips, teeth, and head so well?
"Fool!" answers he. "No Indes such treasures hold;
But from thy heart, while my sire charmeth thee,
Sweet Stella's image I do steal to me."

XXXIII

I might—unhappy word—oh me, I might,
And then would not, or could not, see my bliss;
Till now wrapped in a most infernal night,
I find how heavenly day (wretch) I did miss.
Heart, rent[37] thyself, thou dost thyself but right;
No lovely Paris made thy Helen his;
No force, no fraud robbed thee of thy delight,
Nor Fortune of thy fortune author is;
But to myself myself did give the blow,
While too much wit, forsooth, so troubled me
That I respects for both our sakes must show;
And yet could not, by rising morn, foresee
How fair a day was near. Oh punished eyes,
That I had been more foolish, or more wise!

---

[36] *Morpheus . . . creep:* Morpheus, god of dreams, presents prophecy, history, or poetry, according to the action of the "humors" in the sleeper's body. For arguments on the veracity of dreams, see Chaucer's *Nun's Priest's Tale.*

[37] *rent:* rend, tear.

XXXVII[38]

My mouth doth water, and my breast doth swell,
My tongue doth itch, my thoughts in labor be.
Listen then, lordings, with good ear to me,
For of my life I must a riddle tell.
Toward Aurora's court a nymph doth dwell,
Rich in all beauties which man's eyes can see;
Beauties so far from reach of words, that we
Abase her praise saying she doth excel;
Rich in the treasure of deserved renown,
Rich in the riches of a royal heart,
Rich in those gifts which give the eternal crown;
Who, though most rich in these and every part
Which make the patents of true worldly bliss,
Hath no misfortune but that Rich she is.

XXXIX

Come sleep! Oh sleep, the certain knot of peace,
The baiting place[39] of wit, the balm of woe,
The poor man's wealth, the prisoner's release,
The indifferent judge between the high and low;
With shield of proof shield me from out the prease[40]
Of those fierce darts Despair at me doth throw;
Oh make in me those civil wars to cease;
I will good tribute pay, if thou do so.
Take thou of me smooth pillows, sweetest bed,
A chamber deaf to noise and blind to light,
A rosy garland and a weary head;
And if these things, as being thine by right,
Move not thy heavy grace, thou shalt in me,
Livelier than elsewhere, Stella's image see.

---

[38] This sonnet, which like XXIV puns on the name of Lord Rich, Stella's husband, first appeared in the 1598 folio *Arcadia*.

[39] *baiting place:* the place at which, or occasion when, a halt is made for refreshment on a journey.

[40] *proof:* proven strength; *prease:* press, crowd.

XLI

Having this day [41] my horse, my hand, my lance
Guided so well that I obtained the prize,
Both by the judgment of the English eyes
And of some sent from that sweet enemy, France,
Horsemen my skill in horsemanship advance,
Town-folks my strength; a daintier judge applies
His praise to sleight which from good use [42] doth rise;
Some lucky wits impute it but to chance;
Others, because of both sides I do take
My blood from them who did excel in this,
Think nature me a man-at-arms did make.
How far they shoot awry! The true cause is,
Stella looked on, and from her heavenly face
Sent forth the beams which made so fair my race.

XLV

Stella oft sees the very face of woe
Painted in my beclouded stormy face,
But cannot skill to pity my disgrace,
Not though thereof the cause herself she know.
Yet hearing late a fable which did show
Of lovers never known a grievous case,
Pity thereof gat in her breast such place
That, from that sea derived, tears' spring did flow.
Alas, if fancy, drawn by imaged things
Though false, yet with free scope, more grace doth breed
Than servant's wreck, where new doubts honor brings;
Then think, my dear, that you in me do read
Of lovers' ruin some sad tragedy.
I am not I; pity the tale of me.

---

[41] *this day:* a tournament in the summer of 1581.

[42] *sleight which from good use:* cleverness from experience.

XLVII

WHAT, have I thus betrayed my liberty?
Can those black beams such burning marks engrave
In my free side; or am I born a slave,
Whose neck becomes such yoke of tyranny?
Or want I sense to feel my misery,
Or sprite, disdain of such disdain to have,
Who for long faith, though daily help I crave,
May get no alms, but scorn of beggary?
Virtue, awake! Beauty but beauty is;
I may, I must, I can, I will, I do
Leave following that which it is gain to miss.
Let her go! Soft, but here she comes! Go to,
Unkind, I love you not. Oh me, that eye
Doth make my heart give to my tongue the lie!

XLIX

I ON my horse, and Love on me, doth try
Our horsemanships, while by strange work I prove
A horseman to my horse, a horse to Love,
And now man's wrongs in me, poor beast, descry.
The reins wherewith my rider doth me tie
Are humbled thoughts, which bit of reverence move,
Curbed in with fear, but with gilt boss above
Of hope, which makes it seem fair to the eye.
The wand is will; thou, fancy, saddle art,
Girt fast by memory; and while I spur
My horse, he spurs with sharp desire my heart;
He sits me fast, however I do stir;
And now hath made me to his hand so right
That in the manege [43] myself takes delight.

---

[43] *manege:* horsemanship.

L

Stella, the fullness of my thoughts of thee
Cannot be stayed within my panting breast,
But they do swell and struggle forth of me
Till that in words thy figure be expressed;
And yet, as soon as they so formed be,
According to my lord Love's own behest,
With sad eyes I their weak proportion see
To portrait that which in this world is best.
So that I cannot choose but write my mind,
And cannot choose but put out what I write,
While these poor babes their death in birth do find;
And now my pen these lines had dashed quite
But that they stopped his fury from the same
Because their forefront bare sweet Stella's name.

LII

A strife is grown between Virtue and Love,
While each pretends that Stella must be his.
Her eyes, her lips, her all, saith Love, do this,
Since they do wear his badge, most firmly prove.
But Virtue thus that title doth disprove,
That Stella (oh dear name!) that Stella is
That virtuous soul, sure heir of heavenly bliss,
Not this fair outside which our hearts doth move.
And therefore, though her beauty and her grace
Be Love's indeed, in Stella's self he may
By no pretense claim any manner [44] place.
Well, Love, since this demur [45] our suit doth stay,
Let Virtue have that Stella's self; yet thus,[46]
That Virtue but that body grant to us.

[44] *manner:* kind of.
[45] *demur:* demurrer.
[46] *yet thus:* provided only.

LIII

In martial sports I had my cunning tried,
And yet to break more staves did me address,
While with the people's shouts, I must confess,
Youth, luck, and praise even filled my veins with pride;
When Cupid, having me, his slave, descried
In Mars's livery prancing in the press:
"What now, Sir Fool!" said he—I would no less—
"Look here, I say!" I looked, and Stella spied,
Who, hard by, made a window send forth light.
My heart then quaked, then dazzled were mine eyes,
One hand forgot to rule, the other to fight,
Nor trumpets' sound I heard, nor friendly cries.
My foe came on, and beat the air for me,
Till that her blush taught me my shame to see.

LIV

Because I breathe not love to everyone,
Nor do not use set colors for to wear,
Nor nourish special locks of vowed hair,[47]
Nor give each speech a full point[48] of a groan,
The courtly nymphs, acquainted with the moan
Of them who in their lips Love's standard bear,
"What, he!" say they of me, "now I dare swear
He cannot love; no, no, let him alone."
And think so still, so Stella know my mind;
Profess indeed I do not Cupid's art;
But you, fair maids, at length this true shall find,
That his right badge is but worn in the heart.
Dumb swans, not chattering pies,[49] do lovers prove;
They love indeed who quake to say they love.

---

47 *vowed hair:* locks of hair given with a pledge.

48 *full point:* period.

49 *dumb swans:* Swans were supposed to sing only once, just before dying; *pies:* magpies.

LVI

Fie, school of Patience, fie! Your lesson is
Far, far too long to learn it without book.
What, a whole week without one piece of look,
And think I should not your large precepts miss?
When I might read those letters fair of bliss
Which in her face teach virtue, I could brook
Somewhat thy leaden counsels, which I took
As of a friend that meant not much amiss.
But now that I, alas, do want her sight,
What, dost thou think that I can ever take
In thy cold stuff a phlegmatic delight?
No, Patience; if thou wilt my good, then make
Her come and hear with patience my desire,
And then with patience bid me bear my fire.

LVII

Woe having made, with many fights, his own
Each sense of mine, each gift, each power of mind;
Grown now his slaves, he forced them out to find
The throughest [50] words fit for Woe's self to groan,
Hoping that when they might find Stella alone,
Before she could prepare to be unkind,
Her soul, armed but with such a dainty rind,
Should soon be pierced with sharpness of the moan.
She heard my plaints, and did not only hear,
But them, so sweet is she, most sweetly sing,
With that fair breast making woe's darkness clear.
A pretty case! I hoped her to bring
To feel my griefs; and she, with face and voice,
So sweets my pains that my pains me rejoice.

[50] *throughest:* most satisfactory.

LVIII

Doubt [51] there hath been, when with his golden chain
The orator so far men's hearts doth bind
That no pace else their guided steps can find
But as he them more short or slack doth rein,
Whether with words this sovereignty he gain,
Clothed with fine tropes, with strongest reasons lined,
Or else pronouncing grace, wherewith his mind
Prints his own lively form in rudest brain.
Now judge by this: in piercing phrases late
The anatomy of all my woes I wrate; [52]
Stella's sweet breath the same to me did read.
Oh voice, oh face! Mauger [53] my speech's might
Which wooed woe, most ravishing delight
Even those sad words even in sad me did breed.

LXII

Late tired with woe, even ready for to pine
With rage of love, I called my love unkind;
She in whose eyes love, though unfelt, doth shine,
Sweet said that I true love in her should find.
I joyed; but straight thus watered was my wine—
That love she did, but loved a love not blind;
Which would not let me, whom she loved, decline
From nobler course, fit for my birth and mind;
And therefore, by her love's authority,
Willed me these tempests of vain love to fly,
And anchor fast myself on Virtue's shore.
Alas, if this the only metal be
Of love new coined to help my beggary,
Dear, love me not, that you may love me more.

---

[51] *Doubt:* a question or problem.
[52] *wrate:* wrote.
[53] *Mauger:* in spite of.

LXIV

No more, my dear, no more these counsels try;
Oh give my passions leave to run their race;
Let Fortune lay on me her worst disgrace;
Let folk o'ercharged with brain against me cry;
Let clouds bedim my face, break in mine eye;
Let me no steps but of lost labor trace;
Let all the earth with scorn recount my case;—
But do not will me from my love to fly.
I do not envy Aristotle's wit,
Nor do aspire to Caesar's bleeding fame;
Nor aught do care though some above me sit;
Nor hope nor wish another course to frame
But that which once may win thy cruel heart.
Thou art my wit, and thou my virtue art.

LXVI

And do I see some cause a hope to feed,
Or doth the tedious burden of long woe
In weakened minds quick apprehending breed
Of every image which may comfort show?
I cannot brag of word, much less of deed,
Fortune's wheel's still with me in one sort slow;
My wealth no more, and no whit less my need;
Desire still on the stilts of fear doth go.
And yet amid all fears a hope there is,
Stolen to my heart since, last fair night, nay day,
Stella's eyes sent to me the beams of bliss,
Looking on me while I looked other way.
But when mine eyes back to their heaven did move,
They fled with blush which guilty seemed of love.

LXVII

Hope, art thou true, or dost thou flatter me?
Doth Stella now begin with piteous eye
The ruins of her conquest to espy?
Will she take time before all wracked be?
Her eyes-speech is translated thus by thee,
But fail'st thou not in phrase so heavenly high?
Look on again, the fair text better try;
What blushing notes dost thou in margin see?
What sighs stol'n out, or killed before full-born?
Hast thou found such and such-like arguments,
Or art thou else to comfort me forsworn?
Well, how so thou interpret the contents,
I am resolved thy error to maintain,
Rather than by more truth to get more pain.

LXVIII

Stella, the only planet of my light,
Light of my life, and life of my desire,
Chief good whereto my hope doth only aspire,
World of my wealth, and heaven of my delight,
Why dost thou spend the treasures of thy sprite
With force more fit to wed Amphion's lyre,[54]
Seeking to quench in me the noble fire
Fed by thy worth and kindled by thy sight?
And all in vain; for while thy breath most sweet
With choicest words, thy words with reasons rare,
Thy reasons firmly set on Virtue's feet,
Labor to kill in me this killing care,
Oh think I then, what paradise of joy
It is, so fair a virtue to enjoy!

---

[54] *Amphion's lyre:* Its music was so powerful that it caused a wall to erect itself around Thebes.

LXIX

Oh joy too high for my low style to show!
Oh bliss fit for a nobler state than me!
Envy, put out thine eyes, lest thou do see
What oceans of delight in me do flow!
My friend, that oft saw through all masks my woe,
Come, come, and let me pour myself on thee.
Gone is the winter of my misery!
My spring appears; oh see what here doth grow.
For Stella hath, with words where faith doth shine,
Of her high heart given me the monarchy.
I, I, oh I, may say that she is mine!
And though she give but thus conditionly
This realm of bliss, while virtuous course I take,
No kings be crowned but they some covenants make.

LXX

My Muse may well grudge at my heavenly joy
If still I force her in sad rhymes to creep.
She oft hath drunk my tears, now hopes to enjoy
Nectar of mirth, since I Jove's cup do keep.
Sonnets be not bound prentice to annoy;
Trebles sing high, as well as basses deep;
Grief but Love's winter livery is; the boy
Hath cheeks to smile as well as eyes to weep.
Come then, my Muse, show thou height of delight
In well-raised notes; my pen, the best it may,
Shall paint out joy, though but in black and white.
Cease, eager Muse; peace, pen, for my sake stay,
I give you here my hand for truth of this:
Wise silence is best music unto bliss.

LXXI

Who will in fairest book of Nature know
How virtue may best lodged in beauty be,
Let him but learn of love to read in thee,
Stella, those fair lines which true goodness show.
There shall he find all vices' overthrow,
Not by rude force, but sweetest sovereignty
Of reason, from whose light those night birds fly,
That inward sun in thine eyes shineth so.
And, not content to be perfection's heir
Thyself, dost strive all minds that way to move,
Who mark in thee what is in thee most fair.
So while thy beauty draws the heart to love,
As fast thy virtue bends that love to good.
But, ah, Desire still cries, "Give me some food."

LXXII

Desire, though thou my old companion art,
And oft so clings to my pure love that I
One from the other scarcely can descry,
While each doth blow the fire of my heart,
Now from thy fellowship I needs must part;
Venus is taught with Dian's wings to fly;
I must no more in thy sweet passions lie;
Virtue's gold now must head my Cupid's dart.
Service and honor, wonder with delight,
Fear to offend, will worthy to appear,
Care shining in mine eyes, faith in my sprite—
These things are left me by my only dear.
But thou, Desire, because thou wouldst have all,
Now banished art; but yet, alas, how shall?

LXXIII

Love still a boy, and oft a wanton, is,
Schooled only by his mother's tender eye.
What wonder then if he his lesson miss,
When for so soft a rod dear play he try?
And yet my Star, because a sugared kiss
In sport I sucked while she asleep did lie,
Doth lour, nay chide, nay threat for only this.
Sweet, it was saucy Love, not humble I.
But no 'scuse serves; she makes her wrath appear
In Beauty's throne. See now, who dares come near
Those scarlet judges, threatening bloody pain?
Oh heavenly fool, thy most kiss-worthy face
Anger invests with such a lovely grace
That anger's self I needs must kiss again.

LXXIV [55]

I never drank of Aganippe [56] well,
Nor ever did in shade of Tempe [57] sit,
And Muses scorn with vulgar brains to dwell;
Poor layman I, for sacred rites unfit.
Some do I hear of poets' fury tell,
But, God wot, wot not what they mean by it;
And this I swear by blackest brook of hell,
I am no pick-purse of another's wit.
How falls it then that with so smooth an ease
My thoughts I speak; and what I speak doth flow
In verse, and that my verse best wits doth please?
Guess we the cause. What, is it thus? Fie, no.
Or so? Much less. How then? Sure thus it is:
My lips are sweet, inspired with Stella's kiss.

---

[55] Sidney's sonnets, in spite of his protestations, often borrow from foreign originals.

[56] *Aganippe:* a well at the foot of Mt. Helicon, sacred to the Muses.

[57] *Tempe:* a gorge between Mts. Olympus and Ossa, famous for its beauty and as a place sacred to Apollo.

LXXIX

Sweet kiss, thy sweets I fain would sweetly indite,
Which even of sweetness sweetest sweetener art;
Pleasing'st consort,[58] where each sense holds a part;
Which, coupling doves, guides Venus' chariot right.
Best charge and bravest retreat in Cupid's fight;
A double key, which opens to the heart,
Most rich when most his riches it impart;
Nest of young joys, schoolmaster of delight,
Teaching the mean at once to take and give;
The friendly fray, where blows both wound and heal,
The pretty death, while each in other live.
Poor hope's first wealth, hostage of promised weal;
Breakfast of love. But lo, lo, where she is!
Cease we to praise; now pray we for a kiss.

LXXXIV

Highway, since you my chief Parnassus be,
And that my Muse, to some ears not unsweet,
Tempers her words to trampling horses' feet
More oft than to a chamber melody,
Now blessed you bear onward blessed me
To her, where I my heart, safe left, shall meet;
My Muse and I must you of duty greet
With thanks and wishes, wishing thankfully.
Be you still fair, honored by public heed,
By no encroachment wronged, nor time forgot,
Nor blamed for blood, nor shamed for sinful deed;
And that you know I envy you no lot
Of highest wish, I wish you so much bliss:
Hundreds of years you Stella's feet may kiss.

---

[58] *consort:* an ensemble performance by musical instruments.

XC

Stella, think not that I by verse seek fame
Who seek, who hope, who love, who live but thee;
Thine eyes my pride, thy lips mine history.
If thou praise not, all other praise is shame.
Nor so ambitious am I as to frame
A nest for my young praise in laurel tree.
In truth, I swear I wish not there should be
Graved in mine epitaph a poet's name.
Ne, if I would, I could just title make
That any laud to me thereof should grow,
Without my plumes from others' wings I take.
For nothing from my wit or will doth flow,
Since all my words thy beauty doth indite
And Love doth hold my hand, and makes me write.

XCII

Be your words made, good Sir, of Indian ware,[59]
That you allow me them by so small rate?
Or do you cutted [60] Spartans imitate?
Or do you mean my tender ears to spare,
That to my questions you so total are?
When I demand of Phoenix-Stella's [61] state
You say, forsooth, you left her well of late.
Oh God, think you that satisfies my care?
I would know whether she did sit or walk;
How clothed; how waited on; sighed she, or smiled;
Whereof, with whom, how often did she talk;
With what pastime Time's journey she beguiled;
If her lips deigned to sweeten my poor name.
Say all; and all well said, still say the same.

---

59 *Indian ware:* jewels from India.
60 *cutted:* short, curt.
61 *Phoenix-Stella:* the unique; the phoenix was a mythical bird, of which only one was alive at one time.

XCIV

Grief, find the words; for thou hast made my brain
So dark with misty vapors which arise
From out thy heavy mold, that inbent eyes
Can scarce discern the shape of mine own pain.
Do thou, then—for thou canst—do thou complain
For my poor soul, which now that sickness tries
Which even to sense, sense of itself denies,
Though harbingers of death lodge there his train.
Or if thy love of plaint yet mine forbears,
As of a caitiff worthy so to die,
Yet wail thyself, and wail with causeful tears,
That though in wretchedness thy life doth lie
Yet grow'st more wretched than thy nature bears
By being placed in such a wretch as I.

XCVI

Thought, with good cause thou likest so well the night,
Since kind or chance gives both one livery,
Both sadly black, both blackly darkened be;
Night barred from sun, thou from thy own sunlight;
Silence in both displays his sullen might;
Slow heaviness in both holds one degree,
That full of doubts, thou of perplexity;
Thy tears express Night's native moisture right;
In both amazeful solitariness;
In night, of sprites the ghastly powers do stir,
In thee, or sprites or sprited ghastliness.
But, but, alas, Night's side the odds hath furr,[62]
For that, at length, yet doth invite some rest;
Thou, though still tired, yet still [63] dost it detest.

---

[62] *furr:* (old comparative of "far") by a great deal.

[63] *still:* always.

XCVII

Dian, that fain would cheer her friend the Night,
Shows her oft, at the full, her fairest face,
Bringing with her those starry nymphs, whose chase
From heavenly standing hits each mortal wight.
But ah, poor Night, in love with Phoebus' light
And endlessly despairing of his grace,
Herself, to show no other joy hath place,
Silent and sad, in mourning weeds doth dight.[64]
Even so, alas, a lady, Dian's peer,
With choice delights and rarest company
Would fain drive clouds from out my heavy cheer.
But, woe is me, though Joy herself were she,
She could not show my blind brain ways of joy,
While I despair my sun's sight to enjoy.

XCVIII

Ah, bed! the field where joy's peace some do see,
The field where all my thoughts to war be trained,
How is thy grace by my strange fortune stained!
How thy lee shores by my sighs stormed be!
With sweet soft shades thou oft invitest me
To steal some rest; but, wretch, I am constrained—
Spurred with Love's spur, though gold, and shortly reined
With Care's hard hand—to turn and toss in thee,
While the black horrors of the silent night
Paint Woe's black face so lively to my sight
That tedious leisure marks each wrinkled line.
But when Aurora leads out Phoebus' dance
Mine eyes then only wink;[65] for spite, perchance,
That worms should have their sun, and I want mine.

---

[64] *dight:* dress.

[65] *wink:* close.

XCIX

When far-spent Night persuades each mortal eye,
To whom nor Art nor Nature granteth light,
To lay his then mark-wanting shafts of sight,
Closed with their quivers, in Sleep's armory;
With windows ope then most my mind doth lie,
Viewing the shape of darkness, and delight
Takes in that sad hue which with the inward night
Of his mazed [66] powers keeps perfect harmony.
But when birds charm and that sweet air which is
Morn's messenger, with rose-enameled skies
Calls each wight to salute the flower of bliss,
In tomb of lids then buried are mine eyes,
Forced by their lord, who is ashamed to find
Such light in sense, with such a darkened mind.

CIII

Oh happy Thames, that didst my Stella bear!
I saw thyself with many a smiling line
Upon thy cheerful face, Joy's livery wear,
While those fair planets on thy streams did shine.
The boat for joy could not to dance forbear,
While wanton winds, with beauties so divine
Ravished, stayed not, till in her golden hair
They did themselves—Oh sweetest prison!—twine.
And fain those Aeol's youth [67] there would their stay
Have made, but forced by Nature still to fly,
First did, with puffing kiss, those locks display.
She, so disheveled, blushed. From window I
With sight thereof cried out, "O fair disgrace!
Let Honor's self to thee grant highest place!"

[66] *mazed:* confused.

[67] *Aeol's youth:* breezes (from Aeolus, god of winds).

CVII

Stella, since thou so right a princess art
Of all the powers which life bestows on me,
That ere by them aught undertaken be
They first resort unto that sovereign part—
Sweet, for a while give respite to my heart,
Which pants as though it still should leap to thee,
And on my thoughts give thy lieutenancy
To this great cause, which needs both use and art.
And as a queen, who from her presence sends
Whom she employs, dismiss from thee my wit
Till it have wrought what thy own will attends.
On servants' shame oft master's blame doth sit.
Oh let not fools in me thy works reprove,
And scorning say, "See what it is to love!"

FOURTH SONG[68]

Only joy, now here you are,
Fit to hear and ease my care;
Let my whispering voice obtain
Sweet reward for sharpest pain;
Take me to thee, and thee to me—
No, no, no, no, my dear, let be.

Night hath closed all in her cloak,
Twinkling stars love-thoughts provoke,
Danger hence, good care doth keep,
Jealousy itself doth sleep;
Take me to thee, and thee to me—
No, no, no, no, my dear, let be.

Better place no wit can find,
Cupid's yoke to loose or bind;
These sweet flowers on fine bed too,
Us in their best language woo;
Take me to thee, and thee to me—
No, no, no, no, my dear, let be.

This small light the moon bestows
Serves thy beams but to disclose;
So to raise my hap more high,
Fear not else, none can us spy;
Take me to thee, and thee to me—
No, no, no, no, my dear, let be.

That you heard was but a mouse,
Dumb sleep holdeth all the house;
Yet asleep, methinks they say,
Young folks, take time while you may;
Take me to thee, and thee to me—
No, no, no, no, my dear, let be.

[68] Also published in *England's Helicon* (1600), and the first stanza set to music by Henry Youll, *Canzonets* (1608), VI. In the Folio of 1598, prepared under the direction of Sidney's sister, this song comes between Sonnets LXXXV and LXXXVI of *Astrophel and Stella*.

Niggard time threats, if we miss
This large offer of our bliss,
Long stay ere he grant the same;
Sweet, then, while each thing doth frame,
Take me to thee, and thee to me—
No, no, no, no, my dear, let be.

Your fair mother is abed,
Candles out and curtains spread;
She thinks you do letters write;
Write, but let me first endite;
Take me to thee, and thee to me—
No, no, no, no, my dear, let be.

Sweet, alas, why strive you thus?
Concord better fitteth us;
Leave to Mars the force of hands,
Your power in your beauty stands;
Take thee to me, and me to thee—
No, no, no, no, my dear, let be.

Woe to me, and do you swear
Me to hate? but I forbear;
Cursed be my destines all,
That brought me so high to fall;
Soon with my death I will please thee—
No, no, no, no, my dear, let be.

ELEVENTH SONG[69]

Who is it that this dark night
Underneath my window plaineth?
It is one who from thy sight
Being, ah, exiled, disdaineth
Every other vulgar light.

Why, alas, and are you he?
Be not yet those fancies changed?
Dear, when you find change in me,
Though from me you be estranged,
Let my change to ruin be.

Well, in absence this will die;
Leave to see and leave to wonder.
Absence sure will help, if I
Can learn how myself to sunder
From what in my heart doth lie.

But time will these thoughts remove;
Time doth work what no man knoweth.
Time doth as the subject prove;
With time still the affection groweth
In the faithful turtle dove.

What if you new beauties see,
Will not they stir new affection?
I will think they pictures be,
Image-like, of saint's perfection,
Poorly counterfeiting thee.

But your reason's purest light
Bids you leave such minds to nourish.
Dear, do reason no such spite;
Never doth thy beauty flourish
More than in my reason's sight.

But the wrongs love bears will make
Love at length leave undertaking.
No, the more fools it do shake,
In a ground of so firm making
Deeper still they drive the stake.

[69] This comes between Sonnets CIV and CV in the 1598 Folio, where it was first published.

Peace, I think that some give ear;
Come no more lest I get anger.
Bliss, I will my bliss forbear;
Fearing, sweet, you to endanger;
But my soul shall harbor there.

Well, begone, begone, I say,
Lest that Argus' eyes perceive you.
Oh, unjust Fortune's sway,
Which can make me thus to leave you,
And from louts to run away.

The nightingale, as soon as April bringeth[70]
Unto her rested sense a perfect waking,
While late bare earth, proud of new clothing, springeth,
Sings out her woes, a thorn her song-book making,
And mournfully bewailing,
Her throat in tunes expresseth
What grief her breast oppresseth
For Tereus'[71] force on her chaste will prevailing.
Oh Philomela fair, Oh take some gladness,
That here is juster cause of plaintful sadness:
Thine earth now springs, mine fadeth;
Thy thorn without, my thorn my heart invadeth.

Alas, she hath no other cause of anguish
But Tereus' love, on her by strong hand wroken,[72]
Wherein she suffering, all her spirits languish;
Full womanlike complains her will was broken.
But I, who daily craving,
Cannot have to content me,
Have more cause to lament me,
Since wanting is more woe than too much having.
O Philomela fair, O take some gladness,
That here is juster cause of plaintful sadness:
Thine earth now springs, mine fadeth;
Thy thorn without, my thorn my heart invadeth.

---

[70] Composed to the tune of *Non credo gia che piu infelice amante.*

[71] *Tereus:* See note 15 on Gascoigne, *Steel Glass.*

[72] *wroken:* imposed.

Ring out your bells, let mourning shows be spread;
For Love is dead—
All Love is dead, infected
With plague of deep disdain;
Worth, as naught worth, rejected,
And Faith fair scorn doth gain.
From so ungrateful fancy,
From such a female franzy,
From them that use men thus,
Good Lord, deliver us!

Weep, neighbors, weep; do you not hear it said
That Love is dead?
His deathbed, peacock's folly;
His winding sheet is shame;
His will, false-seeming holy;
His sole exec'tor, blame.
From so ungrateful, &c.

Let dirge be sung and trentals [73] rightly read,
For Love is dead;
Sir Wrong his tomb ordaineth
My mistress Marble-heart,
Which epitaph containeth,
Her eyes were once his dart.
From so ungrateful, &c.

Alas, I lie, rage hath this error bred;
Love is not dead;
Love is not dead, but sleepeth
In her unmatched mind,
Where she his counsel keepeth,
Till due desert she find.
Therefore from so vile fancy,
To call such wit a franzy,
Who Love can temper thus,
Good Lord, deliver us!

[73] *trentals:* service of thirty masses for the dead.

THOU blind man's mark, thou fool's self-chosen snare,[74]
Fond fancy's scum, and dregs of scattered thought;
Band of all evils, cradle of causeless care;
Thou web of will, whose end is never wrought;
Desire, desire! I have too dearly bought,
With price of mangled mind, thy worthless ware;
Too long, too long, asleep thou hast me brought,
Who should my mind to higher things prepare.
But yet in vain thou hast my ruin sought;
In vain thou madest me to vain things aspire;
In vain thou kindlest all thy smoky fire;
For virtue hath this better lesson taught,—
Within myself to seek my only hire,
Desiring naught but how to kill desire.

LEAVE me, O love which reachest but to dust;
And thou, my mind, aspire to higher things;
Grow rich in that which never taketh rust,
Whatever fades but fading pleasure brings.
Draw in thy beams, and humble all thy might
To that sweet yoke where lasting freedoms be;
Which breaks the clouds and opens forth the light,
That doth both shine and give us sight to see.
O take fast hold; let that light be thy guide
In this small course which birth draws out to death,
And think how evil becometh him to slide,
Who seeketh heav'n, and comes of heav'nly breath.
Then farewell, world; thy uttermost I see;
Eternal Love, maintain thy life in me.

Splendidis longum valedico nugis.

[74] This and the following eloquent sonnet of renunciation belong to an old convention, but it is unwarranted to make them the concluding sonnets of *Astrophel and Stella*, as some modern editions do.

My true love hath my heart and I have his,[75]
By just exchange, one for the other given;
I hold his dear, and mine he cannot miss;
There never was a better bargain driven.
His heart in me keeps me and him in one,
My heart in him his thoughts and senses guides;
He loves my heart, for once it was his own;
I cherish his, because in me it bides.
His heart his wound received from my sight;
My heart was wounded with his wounded heart, 
For as from me on him his hurt did light,
So still methought in me his hurt did smart;
Both equal hurt, in this change sought our bliss:
My true love hath my heart and I have his.

[75] Preserved in *The Arte of English Poesie* (1589) as a song, the first two quatrains each a stanza, and the first line repeated as a refrain.

AN APOLOGY FOR POETRY[1]

(1595)

WHEN the right virtuous Edward Wotton [2] and I were at the Emperor's court [3] together, we gave ourselves to learn horsemanship of John Pietro Pugliano,[4] one that with great commendation had the place of an esquire in his stable. And he, according to the fertileness of the Italian wit, did not only afford us the demonstration of his practice, but sought to enrich our minds with the contemplations therein which he thought most precious. But with none I remember mine ears were at any time more loaden, than when (either angered with slow payment, or moved with our learner-like admiration) he exercised his speech in the praise of his faculty. He said, soldiers were the noblest estate of mankind, and horsemen the noblest of soldiers. He said they were the masters of war and ornaments of peace; speedy goers and strong abiders; triumphers both in camps and courts. Nay, to so unbelieved a point he proceeded, as that no earthly thing bred such wonder to a prince as to be a good horseman. Skill of government was but a *pedanteria* [5] in comparison. Then would he add certain praises, by telling what a peerless beast a horse was, the only serviceable courtier without flattery, the beast of most beauty, faithfulness, courage, and such more, that, if I had not been a piece of a logician before I came to him, I think he would have persuaded me to have wished myself a horse. But thus much at least with his no few words he drove into me, that self-love is better than any gilding to make that seem gorgeous wherein ourselves are parties.

Wherein, if Pugliano's strong affection and weak arguments will not satisfy you, I will give you a nearer example of myself, who (I know not by what mischance) in these my not old years and idlest times having slipped into the title of a poet, am provoked to say something unto you in the

---

[1] Also called, in early editions, *The Defense of Poesy.*

[2] *Edward Wotton* (1548–1626): elder half-brother of Sir Henry Wotton.

[3] *Emperor's court:* in 1573 at the court of Maximilian II (*reg.* 1564–1576).

[4] *John Pietro Pugliano:* an Italian equerry of the Emperor's. For Sidney's own interest in horsemanship see *Astrophel and Stella,* Sonnets XLI and XLIX, pp. 95, 96.

[5] *pedanteria:* Italian for "school learning."

defense of that my unelected vocation, which if I handle with more good will than good reasons, bear with me, since the scholar is to be pardoned that followeth the steps of his master. And yet I must say that, as I have just cause to make a pitiful defense of poor poetry, which from almost the highest estimation of learning is fallen to be the laughingstock of children, so have I need to bring some more available proofs, since the former is by no man barred of his deserved credit, the silly latter hath had even the names of philosophers used to the defacing of it, with great danger of civil war among the Muses.

And first, truly, to all them that professing learning inveigh against poetry may justly be objected, that they go very near to ungratefulness, to seek to deface that which, in the noblest nations and languages that are known, hath been the first light-giver to ignorance, and first nurse, whose milk by little and little enabled them to feed afterwards of tougher knowledges. And will they now play the hedgehog that, being received into the den, drove out his host, or rather the vipers, that with their birth kill their parents? Let learned Greece in any of her manifold sciences be able to show me one book before Musaeus, Homer, and Hesiod, all three nothing else but poets. Nay, let any history be brought that can say any writers were there before them, if they were not men of the same skill, as Orpheus, Linus, and some other are named, who, having been the first of that country that made pens deliverers of their knowledge to their posterity, may justly challenge to be called their fathers in learning, for not only in time they had this priority (although in itself antiquity be venerable) but went before them, as causes to draw with their charming sweetness the wild untamed wits to an admiration of knowledge, so, as Amphion was said to move stones with his poetry to build Thebes, and Orpheus to be listened to by beasts—indeed stony and beastly people. So among the Romans were Livius Andronicus, and Ennius. So in the Italian language the first that made it aspire to be a treasure-house of science were the poets Dante, Boccaccio, and Petrarch. So in our English were Gower and Chaucer, after whom, encouraged and delighted with their excellent foregoing, others have followed, to beautify our mother tongue, as well in the same kind as in other arts.

This did so notably show itself, that the philosophers of Greece durst not a long time appear to the world but under the masks of poets. So Thales, Empedocles, and Parmenides sang their natural philosophy in verses; so did Pythagoras and Phocylides their moral counsels; so did Tyrtaeus in war matters, and Solon in matters of policy: or rather, they, being poets, did exercise their delightful vein in those points of highest knowledge, which before them lay hid to the world. For that wise Solon was directly a poet it is manifest, having written in verse the notable fable of the Atlantic Island, which was continued by Plato. And truly, even Plato, whosoever well considereth shall find that in the body of his work, though the inside and strength were philosophy, the skin as it were and beauty depended most of poetry: for all standeth upon dialogues, wherein he feigneth many honest burgesses of Athens to speak of such matters, that, if they had been set on the rack, they would never have confessed them, besides his poetical describing the circumstances of their meetings, as the well ordering of a banquet, the delicacy of a walk, with interlacing mere tales, as Gyges' Ring,[6] and others, which who knoweth not to be flowers of poetry did never walk into Apollo's garden.

And even historiographers [7] (although their lips sound of things done, and verity be written in their foreheads) have been glad to borrow both fashion and perchance weight of poets. So Herodotus entitled his history by the name of the nine Muses; and both he and all the rest that followed him either stole or usurped of poetry their passionate describing of passions, the many particularities of battles, which no man could affirm, or, if that be denied me, long orations put in the mouths of great kings and captains, which it is certain they never pronounced. So that, truly, neither philosopher nor historiographer could at the first have entered into the gates of popular judgments, if they had not taken a great passport of poetry, which in all nations at this day, where learning flourisheth not, is plain to be seen, in all which they have some feeling of poetry.

In Turkey, besides their law-giving divines, they have no other writers but poets. In our neighbor country Ireland, where truly learning goeth very bare, yet are their poets held in a devout reverence. Even among the most barbarous and simple Indians where no writing is, yet have they their poets, who make and sing songs, which they call *Areytos,*[8] both of their ancestors' deeds and praises of their gods—a sufficient probability that, if ever learning come among them, it must be by having their hard dull wits softened and sharpened with the sweet delights of poetry. For until they find a pleasure in the exercises of the mind, great promises of much knowledge will little persuade them that know not the fruits of knowledge. In Wales, the true remnant of the ancient Britons, as there are good authorities to show the long time they had poets, which they called bards, so through all the conquests of Romans, Saxons, Danes, and Normans, some of whom did seek to ruin all memory of learning from among them, yet do their poets, even to this day, last; so as it is not more notable in soon beginning than in long continuing. But since the authors of most of our sciences were the Romans, and before them the Greeks, let us a little stand upon their authorities, but even so far as to see what names they have given unto this now scorned skill.

Among the Romans a poet was called *Vates,* which is as much as a diviner, foreseer, or prophet, as by his conjoined words *vaticinium* and *vaticinari* is manifest: so heavenly a title did that excellent people bestow upon this heart-ravishing knowledge. And so far were they carried into the admira-

---

[6] *Gyges' Ring:* story of a Lydian shepherd who had a ring which could make him invisible. (Plato, *Republic,* II, 359–360.)

[7] *historiographers:* historians.

[8] *Areytos:* Spanish *aréito,* used by the West Indians to describe dance-songs. See *MLN,* XXIX (1924), 121–123.

tion thereof, that they thought in the chanceable hitting upon any such verses great foretokens of their following fortunes were placed. Whereupon grew the word of *Sortes Virgilianae,* when, by sudden opening Virgil's book, they lighted upon any verse of his making: whereof the histories of the emperors' lives are full, as of Albinus,[9] the governor of our island, who in his childhood met with this verse,

Arma amens capio nec sat rationis in armis; [10]

and in his age performed it: which, although it were a very vain and godless superstition, as also it was to think that spirits were commanded by such verses—whereupon this word charms, derived of *carmina,*[11] cometh—so yet serveth it to show the great reverence those wits were held in. And altogether not without ground, since both the Oracles of Delphos and Sibylla's prophecies were wholly delivered in verses. For that same exquisite observing of number and measure in words, and that high-flying liberty of conceit proper to the poet, did seem to have some divine force in it.

And may not I presume a little further, to show the reasonableness of this word *Vates,* and say that the holy David's Psalms are a divine poem? If I do, I shall not do it without the testimony of great learned men, both ancient and modern. But even the name Psalms will speak for me, which, being interpreted, is nothing but songs; then that it is fully written in meter, as all learned Hebricians agree, although the rules be not yet fully found; lastly and principally, his handling his prophecy, which is merely poetical. For what else is the awaking his musical instruments, the often and free changing of persons, his notable *prosopopeias,*[12] when he maketh you, as it were, see God coming in his majesty, his telling of the beasts' joyfulness, and hills' leaping, but a heavenly poesy, wherein almost he showeth himself a passionate lover of that unspeakable and everlasting beauty to be seen by the eyes of the mind, only cleared by faith? But truly now having named him, I fear me I seem to profane that holy name, applying it to poetry, which is among us thrown down to so ridiculous an estimation. But they that with quiet judgments will look a little deeper into it, shall find the end and working of it such, as, being rightly applied, deserveth not to be scourged out of the Church of God.

But now, let us see how the Greeks named it, and how they deemed of it. The Greeks called him "a poet," which name hath, as the most excellent, gone through other languages. It cometh of this word *Poiein,* which is "to make": wherein, I know not whether by luck or wisdom, we Englishmen have met with the Greeks in calling him "a maker": which name, how high and incomparable a title it is, I had rather were known by marking the scope of other sciences than by my partial allegation.

[9] *Albinus:* a Roman commander in Britain (192–197 A.D.).

[10] *Arma . . . armis:* "madly I take up arms, though arms are senseless now." *Aeneid,* II, 314.

[11] *carmina:* verses.

[12] *prosopopeias:* personifications.

There is no art delivered to mankind that hath not the works of nature for his principal object, without which they could not consist, and on which they so depend, as they become actors and players, as it were, of what nature will have set forth. So doth the astronomer look upon the stars, and, by that he seeth, setteth down what order nature hath taken therein. So do the geometrician and arithmetician in their diverse sorts of quantities. So doth the musician in times tell you which by nature agree, which not. The natural philosopher thereon hath his name, and the moral philosopher standeth upon the natural virtues, vices, and passions of man; and "follow nature" (saith he) "therein, and thou shalt not err." The lawyer saith what men have determined; the historian what men have done. The grammarian speaketh only of the rules of speech; and the rhetorician and logician, considering what in nature will soonest prove and persuade, thereon give artificial rules, which still are compassed within the circle of a question according to the proposed matter. The physician weigheth the nature of a man's body, and the nature of things helpful or hurtful unto it. And the metaphysic, though it be in the second and abstract notions, and therefore be counted supernatural, yet doth he indeed build upon the depth of nature. Only the poet, disdaining to be tied to any such subjection, lifted up with the vigor of his own invention, doth grow in effect another nature, in making things either better than nature bringeth forth, or, quite anew, forms such as never were in nature, as the Heroes, Demigods, Cyclops, Chimeras, Furies, and such like: so as he goeth hand in hand with nature, not enclosed within the narrow warrant of her gifts, but freely ranging only within the zodiac of his own wit.

Nature never set forth the earth in so rich tapestry as divers poets have done—neither with pleasant rivers, fruitful trees, sweet-smelling flowers, nor whatsoever else may make the too much loved earth more lovely. Her world is brazen, the poets only deliver a golden. But let those things alone, and go to man—for whom as the other things are, so it seemeth in him her uttermost cunning is employed—and know whether she have brought forth so true a lover as Theagenes,[13] so constant a friend as Pylades,[14] so valiant a man as Orlando,[15] so right a prince as Xenophon's Cyrus,[16] so excellent a man every way as Virgil's Aeneas. Neither let this be jestingly conceived, because the works of the one be essential, the other in imitation or fiction; for any understanding knoweth the skill of the artificer standeth in that idea or foreconceit of the work, and not in the work itself. And that the poet hath that idea is manifest, by delivering them forth in such excellency as he hath imagined them. Which delivering forth also is not wholly imaginative, as we are wont to say by them that build castles in the air: but so far substantially it worketh, not only to make a Cyrus, which

[13] *Theagenes:* hero of the Greek prose romance, *Aethiopica,* written by Heliodorus about 400 A.D., which influenced Sidney's *Arcadia.*

[14] *Pylades:* the constant friend of Orestes.

[15] *Orlando:* the Roland of the Charlemagne legend, hero of Ariosto's *Orlando Furioso.*

[16] *Xenophon's Cyrus:* in the *Cyropedia.*

had been but a particular excellency, as nature might have done, but to bestow a Cyrus upon the world, to make many Cyruses, if they will learn aright why and how that maker made him.

Neither let it be deemed too saucy a comparison to balance the highest point of man's wit with the efficacy of nature; but rather give right honor to the heavenly Maker of that maker, who, having made man to his own likeness, set him beyond and over all the works of that second nature: which in nothing he showeth so much as in poetry, when with the force of a divine breath he bringeth things forth far surpassing her doings, with no small argument to the incredulous of that first accursed fall of Adam, since our erected wit maketh us know what perfection is, and yet our infected will keepeth us from reaching unto it. But these arguments will by few be understood, and by fewer granted. Thus much (I hope) will be given me, that the Greeks with some probability of reason gave him the name above all names of learning. Now let us go to a more ordinary opening of him, that the truth may be more palpable: and so I hope, though we get not so unmatched a praise as the etymology of his names will grant, yet his very description, which no man will deny, shall not justly be barred from a principal commendation.

Poesy therefore is an art of imitation, for so Aristotle termeth it [17] in his word *Mimesis,* that is to say, a representing, counterfeiting, or figuring forth —to speak metaphorically, a speaking picture; with this end, to teach and delight. Of this have been three several kinds.

The chief, both in antiquity and excellency, were they that did imitate the inconceivable excellencies of God. Such were David in his Psalms; Solomon in his Song of Songs, in his Ecclesiastes, and Proverbs; Moses and Deborah in their Hymns; and the writer of Job, which, beside other, the learned Emanuel Tremellius and Franciscus Junius [18] do entitle the poetical part of the Scripture. Against these none will speak that hath the Holy Ghost in due holy reverence. In this kind, though in a full wrong divinity, were Orpheus, Amphion, Homer in his Hymns, and many other, both Greeks and Romans, and this poesy must be used by whosoever will follow St. James's counsel in singing psalms when they are merry, and I know is used with the fruit of comfort by some, when, in sorrowful pangs of their death-bringing sins, they find the consolation of the never-leaving goodness.

The second kind is of them that deal with matters philosophical: either moral, as Tyrtaeus, Phocylides, and Cato; [19] or natural, as Lucretius and Virgil's *Georgics;* or astronomical, as Manilius and Pontanus; or historical,

---

[17] *Aristotle termeth it:* in the *Poetics,* i, 2, but Sidney is probably drawing here on Scaliger's *Poetice,* I, i.

[18] *Emanuel Tremellius and Franciscus Junius:* two sixteenth-century Protestant scholars who published a widely used Latin translation of the Bible in 1575–1580.

[19] *Cato:* Dionysius Cato, reputed author of *Disticha de moribus,* four books of epigrammatic moral precepts in Latin hexameters, popular in the Middle Ages, and later used as a textbook in Elizabethan schools.

as Lucan; which who mislike, the fault is in their judgments quite out of taste, and not in the sweet food of sweetly uttered knowledge.

But because this second sort is wrapped within the fold of the proposed subject, and takes not the course of his own invention, whether they properly be poets or no let grammarians dispute; and go to the third, indeed right poets, of whom chiefly this question ariseth, betwixt whom and these second is such a kind of difference as betwixt the meaner sort of painters, who counterfeit only such faces as are set before them, and the more excellent, who, having no law but wit, bestow that in colors upon you which is fittest for the eye to see, as the constant though lamenting look of Lucretia,[20] when she punished in herself another's fault (wherein he painteth not Lucretia whom he never saw, but painteth the outward beauty of such a virtue). For these third be they which most properly do imitate to teach and delight, and to imitate borrow nothing of what is, hath been, or shall be; but range, only reined with learned discretion, into the divine consideration of what may be, and should be. These be they that, as the first and most noble sort may justly be termed *Vates,* so these are waited on in the excellentest languages and best understandings, with the foredescribed name of poets; for these indeed do merely make to imitate, and imitate both to delight and teach, and delight to move men to take that goodness in hand, which without delight they would fly as from a stranger, and teach, to make them know that goodness whereunto they are moved: which being the noblest scope to which ever any learning was directed, yet want there not idle tongues to bark at them.

These be subdivided into sundry more special denominations. The most notable be the heroic, lyric, tragic, comic, satiric, iambic, elegiac, pastoral, and certain others, some of these being termed according to the matter they deal with, some by the sorts of verses they liked best to write in; for indeed the greatest part of poets have appareled their poetical inventions in that numbrous kind of writing which is called verse—indeed but appareled, verse being but an ornament and no cause to poetry, since there have been many most excellent poets that never versified, and now swarm many versifiers that need never answer to the name of poets. For Xenophon, who did imitate so excellently as to give us *effigiem iusti imperii,* "the portraiture of a just Empire," under name of Cyrus (as Cicero saith of him), made therein an absolute heroical poem. So did Heliodorus in his sugared invention of that picture of love in Theagenes and Chariclea;[21] and yet both these writ in prose: which I speak to show that it is not rhyming and versing that maketh a poet—no more than a long gown maketh an advocate, who

[20] *Lucretia:* wife of L. Tarquinius Colatinus, outraged by Sextus, son of Tarquinius Superbus.

[21] *Heliodorus . . . Chariclea:* See note 13, above.

though he pleaded in armor should be an advocate and no soldier. But it is that feigning notable images of virtues, vices, or what else, with that delightful teaching, which must be the right describing note to know a poet by, although indeed the Senate of Poets hath chosen verse as their fittest raiment, meaning, as in matter they passed all in all, so in manner to go beyond them—not speaking (table-talk fashion or like men in a dream) words as they chanceably fall from the mouth, but peizing each syllable of each word by just proportion according to the dignity of the subject.

Now therefore it shall not be amiss first to weigh this latter sort of poetry by his works, and then by his parts, and, if in neither of these anatomies [22] he be condemnable, I hope we shall obtain a more favorable sentence. This purifying of wit, this enriching of memory, enabling of judgment, and enlarging of conceit, which commonly we call learning, under what name soever it come forth, or to what immediate end soever it be directed, the final end is to lead and draw us to as high a perfection as our degenerate souls, made worse by their clayey lodgings, can be capable of. This, according to the inclination of the man, bred many formed impressions. For some that thought this felicity principally to be gotten by knowledge and no knowledge to be so high and heavenly as acquaintance with the stars, gave themselves to astronomy; others, persuading themselves to be demigods if they knew the causes of things, became natural and supernatural philosophers; some an admirable delight drew to music; and some the certainty of demonstration to the mathematics. But all, one and other, having this scope—to know, and by knowledge to lift up the mind from the dungeon of the body to the enjoying his own divine essence. But when by the balance of experience it was found that the astronomer looking to the stars might fall into a ditch, that the inquiring philosopher might be blind in himself, and the mathematician might draw forth a straight line with a crooked heart; then, lo, did proof, the overruler of opinions, make manifest that all these are but serving sciences, which, as they have each a private end in themselves, so yet are they all directed to the highest end of the mistress-knowledge, by the Greeks called *Architectonike,* which stands (as I think) in the knowledge of a man's self, in the ethic and politic consideration, with the end of well doing and not of well knowing only:—even as the saddler's next end is to make a good saddle, but his farther end to serve a nobler faculty, which is horsemanship; so the horseman's to soldiery, and the soldier not only to have the skill, but to perform the practice of a soldier. So that, the ending end of all earthly learning being virtuous action, those skills, that most serve to bring forth that, have a most just title to be princes over all the rest. Wherein we can show the poet's nobleness, by setting him before his other competitors, among whom as principal challengers step forth the moral philosophers, whom, methinketh, I see coming towards me with a sullen gravity, as though they

---

22 *anatomies:* analyses.

could not abide vice by daylight, rudely clothed for to witness outwardly their contempt of outward things, with books in their hands against glory, whereto they set their names, sophistically speaking against subtlety, and angry with any man in whom they see the foul fault of anger. These men casting largesse as they go of definitions, divisions, and distinctions, with a scornful interrogative do soberly ask whether it be possible to find any path so ready to lead a man to virtue as that which teacheth what virtue is—and teacheth it not only by delivering forth his very being, his causes, and effects, but also by making known his enemy, vice (which must be destroyed), and his cumbersome servant, passion (which must be mastered), by showing the generalities that containeth it, and the specialities that are derived from it; lastly, by plain setting down, how it extendeth itself out of the limits of a man's own little world to the government of families, and maintaining of public societies.

The historian scarcely giveth leisure to the moralist to say so much, but that he, laden with old mouse-eaten records, authorizing himself (for the most part) upon other histories, whose greatest authorities are built upon the notable foundation of hearsay; having much ado to accord differing writers and to pick truth out of partiality; better acquainted with a thousand years ago than with the present age, and yet better knowing how this world goeth than how his own wit runneth; curious for antiquities and inquisitive of novelties; a wonder to young folks and a tyrant in table talk, denieth, in a great chafe, that any man for teaching of virtue, and virtuous actions, is comparable to him. "I am *Lux vitae, Temporum magistra, Vita memoriae, Nuncia vetustatis,*" [23] etc. The philosopher (saith he) "teacheth a disputative virtue, but I do an active. His virtue is excellent in the dangerless Academy of Plato, but mine showeth forth her honorable face in the battles of Marathon, Pharsalia, Poitiers, and Agincourt.[24] He teacheth virtue by certain abstract considerations, but I only bid you follow the footing of them that have gone before you. Old-aged experience goeth beyond the fine-witted philosopher, but I give the experience of many ages. Lastly, if he make the song book, I put the learner's hand to the lute; and if he be the guide, I am the light."

Then would he allege you innumerable examples, conferring story by story, how much the wisest senators and princes have been directed by the credit of history, as Brutus, Alphonsus of Aragon, and who not, if need be? At length the long line of their disputation maketh a point in this, that the one giveth the precept, and the other the example.

Now, whom shall we find (since the question standeth for the highest

---

[23] *Lux . . . vetustatis:* A free paraphrase from Cicero's *De oratore,* II, 9, 36: *Historia vero testis temporum, lux veritatis, vita memoriae, magistra vitae, nuntia vetustatis.* ("History is in fact the witness of the times, the light of truth, the life of memory, the mistress of life, messenger of antiquity.")

[24] *battles of . . . Agincourt:* Marathon, B.C. 490; Pharsalia, B.C. 48; Poitiers, 1356; Agincourt, 1415. For Agincourt see Drayton's *Ode to the Cambro-Britons,* p. 711, below.

form in the school of learning) to be moderator? Truly, as meseemeth, the poet; and if not a moderator, even the man that ought to carry the title from them both, and much more from all other serving sciences. Therefore compare we the poet with the historian, and with the moral philosopher; and, if he go beyond them both, no other human skill can match him. For as for the Divine, with all reverence it is ever to be excepted, not only for having his scope as far beyond any of these as eternity exceedeth a moment, but even for passing each of these in themselves. And for the lawyer, though Jus be the daughter of justice, and justice the chief of virtues, yet because he seeketh to make men good rather *formidine poenae* than *virtutis amore,*[25] or, to say righter, doth not endeavor to make men good, but that their evil hurt not others, having no care, so he be a good citizen, how bad a man he be: therefore, as our wickedness maketh him necessary, and necessity maketh him honorable, so is he not in the deepest truth to stand in rank with these who all endeavor to take naughtiness away, and plant goodness even in the secretest cabinet of our souls. And these four are all that any way deal in that consideration of men's manners, which being the supreme knowledge, they that best breed it deserve the best commendation.

The philosopher therefore and the historian are they which would win the goal, the one by precept, the other by example. But both, not having both, do both halt. For the philosopher, setting down with thorny argument the bare rule, is so hard of utterance, and so misty to be conceived, that one that hath no other guide but him shall wade in him till he be old before he shall find sufficient cause to be honest. For his knowledge standeth so upon the abstract and general, that happy is that man who may understand him, and more happy that can apply what he doth understand. On the other side, the historian, wanting the precept, is so tied, not to what should be but to what is, to the particular truth of things and not to the general reason of things, that his example draweth no necessary consequence, and therefore a less fruitful doctrine.

Now doth the peerless poet perform both: for whatsoever the philosopher saith should be done, he giveth a perfect picture of it in someone by whom he presupposeth it was done; so as he coupleth the general notion with the particular example. A perfect picture I say, for he yieldeth to the powers of the mind an image of that whereof the philosopher bestoweth but a wordish description: which doth neither strike, pierce, nor possess the sight of the soul so much as that other doth.

For as in outward things, to a man that had never seen an elephant or a rhinoceros, who should tell him most exquisitely all their shapes, color, bigness, and particular marks, or of a gorgeous palace the architecture, with declaring the full beauties might well make the hearer able to repeat, as it were by rote, all he had heard, yet should never satisfy his inward conceits with being witness to itself of a true lively knowledge: but the

---

[25] *formidine . . . amore:* "rather from fear of punishment than from love of virtue," Horace, *Epistles,* I, xvi, 52–53.

same man, as soon as he might see those beasts well painted, or the house well in model, should straightways grow, without need of any description, to a judicial comprehending of them: so no doubt the philosopher with his learned definition—be it of virtue, vices, matters of public policy or private government—replenisheth the memory with many infallible grounds of wisdom, which, notwithstanding, lie dark before the imaginative and judging power, if they be not illuminated or figured forth by the speaking picture of poesy.

Tully taketh much pains, and many times not without poetical helps, to make us know the force love of our country hath in us. Let us but hear old Anchises speaking in the middest of Troy's flames, or see Ulysses in the fullness of all Calypso's delights bewail his absence from barren and beggarly Ithaca. Anger, the Stoics say, was a short madness: let but Sophocles bring you Ajax on a stage, killing and whipping sheep and oxen, thinking them the army of Greeks, with their chieftains Agamemnon and Menelaus, and tell me if you have not a more familiar insight into anger than finding in the Schoolmen his genus and difference.[26] See whether wisdom and temperance in Ulysses and Diomedes, valor in Achilles, friendship in Nisus and Euryalus,[27] even to an ignorant man carry not an apparent shining, and, contrarily, the remorse of conscience in Oedipus, the soon repenting pride of Agamemnon, the self-devouring cruelty in his father Atreus, the violence of ambition in the two Theban brothers, the sour-sweetness of revenge in Medea, and, to fall lower, the Terentian Gnatho [28] and our Chaucer's Pandar [29] so expressed that we now use their names to signify their trades; and finally, all virtues, vices, and passions so in their own natural seats laid to the view, that we seem not to hear of them, but clearly to see through them. But even in the most excellent determination of goodness, what philosopher's counsel can so readily direct a prince, as the feigned Cyrus in Xenophon; or a virtuous man in all fortunes, as Aeneas in Virgil; or a whole Commonwealth, as the way of Sir Thomas More's *Utopia?* [30] I say the way, because where Sir Thomas More erred, it was the fault of the man and not of the poet, for that way of patterning a Commonwealth was most absolute, though he perchance hath not so absolutely performed it. For the question is, whether the feigned image of poesy or the regular instruction of philosophy hath the more force in teaching: wherein if the philosophers have more rightly showed themselves philosophers than the poets have attained to the high top of their profession, as in truth,

---

[26] *genus and difference:* definition.

[27] *Nisus and Euryalus:* In the *Aeneid,* IX, Nisus died avenging his friend Euryalus.

[28] *Terentian Gnatho:* the parasite in the *Eunuchus* of Terence.

[29] *Chaucer's Pandar:* in *Troilus and Criseyde.*

[30] *Sir Thomas More's Utopia:* The *Utopia* was first printed in 1516; the first English version was made in 1551 by Ralph Robinson.

Mediocribus esse poetis,
Non Di, non homines, non concessere Columnae;[31]

it is, I say again, not the fault of the art, but that by few men that art can be accomplished. Certainly, even our Savior Christ could as well have given the moral commonplaces[32] of uncharitableness and humbleness as the divine narration of Dives and Lazarus;[33] or of disobedience and mercy, as that heavenly discourse of the lost child and the gracious father; but that his through-searching wisdom knew the estate of Dives burning in hell, and of Lazarus being in Abraham's bosom, would more constantly (as it were) inhabit both the memory and judgment. Truly, for myself, meseems I see before my eyes the lost child's disdainful prodigality, turned to envy a swine's dinner: which by the learned divines are thought not historical acts, but instructing parables. For conclusion, I say the Philosopher teacheth, but he teacheth obscurely, so as the learned only can understand him; that is to say, he teacheth them that are already taught. But the poet is the food for the tenderest stomachs, the poet is indeed the right popular philosopher, whereof Aesop's tales give good proof: whose pretty allegories, stealing under the formal tales of beasts, make many, more beastly than beasts, begin to hear the sound of virtue from these dumb speakers.

But now may it be alleged that, if this imagining of matters be so fit for the imagination, then must the historian needs surpass, who bringeth you images of true matters, such as indeed were done, and not such as fantastically or falsely may be suggested to have been done. Truly, Aristotle[34] himself, in his discourse of poesy, plainly determineth this question, saying that poetry is *Philosophoteron* and *Spoudaioteron,* that is to say, it is more philosophical and more studiously serious than history. His reason is, because poesy dealeth with *Katholou,* that is to say, with the universal consideration, and the history with *Kathekaston,* the particular: "now," saith he, "the universal weighs what is fit to be said or done, either in likelihood or necessity (which the poesy considereth in his imposed names), and the particular only marks whether Alcibiades did, or suffered, this or that." Thus far Aristotle: which reason of his (as all his) is most full of reason. For indeed, if the question were whether it were better to have a particular act truly or falsely set down, there is no doubt which is to be chosen, no more than whether you had rather have Vespasian's picture right as he was, or at the painter's pleasure nothing resembling. But if the question be for your own use and learning, whether it be better to have it set down as it should be, or as it was, then certainly is more doctrinable the feigned Cyrus in Xenophon than the true Cyrus in Justin, and the feigned Aeneas

---

[31] *Mediocribus . . . Columnae:* "neither gods, nor men, nor book-stalls have admitted mediocrity in poets," Horace, *Ars poetica,* 372–373.

[32] *commonplaces:* sentences or longer passages from literary or philosophical works; in Elizabethan and later times kept in commonplace books.

[33] *Dives and Lazarus:* Luke 16:19–31.

[34] *Aristotle:* in the *Poetics,* ix, 3.

in Virgil than the right Aeneas in Dares Phrygius:[35] as to a lady that desired to fashion her countenance to the best grace, a painter should more benefit her to portrait a most sweet face, writing Canidia upon it, than to paint Canidia as she was, who, Horace sweareth, was foul and ill favored.

If the poet do his part aright, he will show you in Tantalus, Atreus, and such like, nothing that is not to be shunned; in Cyrus, Aeneas, Ulysses, each thing to be followed; where the historian, bound to tell things as things were, cannot be liberal (without he will be poetical) of a perfect pattern, but, as in Alexander or Scipio himself, show doings, some to be liked, some to be misliked. And then how will you discern what to follow but by your own discretion, which you had without reading Quintus Curtius?[36] And whereas a man may say, though in universal consideration of doctrine the poet prevaileth, yet that the history, in his saying such a thing was done, doth warrant a man more in that he shall follow; the answer is manifest: that if he stand upon that *was*—as if he should argue, because it rained yesterday, therefore it should rain today—then indeed it hath some advantage to a gross conceit; but if he know an example only informs a conjectured likelihood, and so go by reason, the poet doth so far exceed him, as he is to frame his example to that which is most reasonable, be it in warlike, politic, or private matters; where the historian in his bare *was* hath many times that which we call fortune to overrule the best wisdom. Many times he must tell events whereof he can yield no cause: or, if he do, it must be poetical.

For that a feigned example hath as much force to teach as a true example (for as for to move, it is clear, since the feigned may be tuned to the highest key of passion), let us take one example wherein a poet and a historian do concur. Herodotus and Justin do both testify that Zopyrus, King Darius's faithful servant, seeing his master long resisted by the rebellious Babylonians, feigned himself in extreme disgrace of his king: for verifying of which, he caused his own nose and ears to be cut off, and so flying to the Babylonians, was received, and for his known valor so far credited, that he did find means to deliver them over to Darius. Much like matter doth Livy[37] record of Tarquinius and his son. Xenophon excellently feigneth such another stratagem performed by Abradates[38] in Cyrus's behalf. Now would I fain know, if occasion be presented unto you to serve your prince by such an honest dissimulation, why you do not as well learn it of Xenophon's fiction as of the other's verity—and truly so much the better, as you shall save your nose by the bargain; for Abradates did not counterfeit so far. So then the best of the historian is subject to the

[35] Dares Phrygius was in the belief of medieval and Renaissance authors an eyewitness of the fall of Troy, but a purported fifth-century Latin translation of his work, *De excidio Troiae historia*, has been proved to be a forgery. See Chapman, p. 664, below.

[36] *Quintus Curtius:* Roman author of a history of Alexander.

[37] *Livy:* I, 53–54.

[38] *Abradates:* actually Araspes in the *Cyropedia*, VI, i, 31.

poet; for whatsoever action, or faction, whatsoever counsel, policy, or war stratagem the historian is bound to recite, that may the poet (if he list) with his imitation make his own, beautifying it both for further teaching, and more delighting, as it pleaseth him, having all, from Dante's heaven to his hell, under the authority of his pen. Which if I be asked what poets have done so, as I might well name some, yet say I, and say again, I speak of the art, and not of the artificer.

Now, to that which commonly is attributed to the praise of histories, in respect of the notable learning is gotten by marking the success, as though therein a man should see virtue exalted and vice punished—truly that commendation is peculiar to poetry, and far off from history. For indeed poetry ever setteth Virtue so out in her best colors, making Fortune her well-waiting handmaid, that one must needs be enamored of her. Well may you see Ulysses in a storm, and in other hard plights; but they are but exercises of patience and magnanimity, to make them shine the more in the near-following prosperity. And of the contrary part, if evil men come to the stage, they ever go out (as the tragedy-writer answered to one that misliked the show of such persons) so manacled as they little animate folks to follow them. But the historian, being captived to the truth of a foolish world, is many times a terror from welldoing, and an encouragement to unbridled wickedness.

For see we not valiant Miltiades [39] rot in his fetters; the just Phocion and the accomplished Socrates put to death like traitors; the cruel Severus live prosperously; the excellent Severus miserably murdered; Sylla and Marius dying in their beds; Pompey and Cicero slain then when they would have thought exile a happiness? See we not virtuous Cato driven to kill himself, and rebel Caesar so advanced that his name yet, after 1,600 years, lasteth in the highest honor? And mark but even Caesar's own words of the forenamed Sylla (who in that only did honestly, to put down his dishonest tyranny), *Literas nescivit,* as if want of learning caused him to do well. He meant it not by poetry, which, not content with earthly plagues, deviseth new punishments in hell for tyrants, nor yet by philosophy, which teacheth *Occidendos esse;* but no doubt by skill in history, for that indeed can afford your Cypselus, Periander, Phalaris, Dionysius, and I know not how many more of the same kennel, that speed well enough in their abominable injustice or usurpation. I conclude, therefore, that he excelleth History, not only in furnishing the mind with knowledge, but in setting it forward to that which deserveth to be called and accounted good: which setting forward, and moving to welldoing, indeed setteth the laurel crown upon the poet as victorious, not only of the historian, but over the philosopher, howsoever in teaching it may be questionable.

For suppose it be granted (that which I suppose with great reason may be denied) that the philosopher, in respect of his methodical proceeding,

---

[39] *Miltiades:* In this paragraph Sidney draws on his general knowledge of Greek and Roman history for examples.

doth teach more perfectly than the poet, yet do I think that no man is so much *Philophilosophos*[40] as to compare the philosopher, in moving, with the poet.

And that moving is of a higher degree than teaching, it may by this appear, that it is well-nigh the cause and the effect of teaching. For who will be taught, if he be not moved with desire to be taught, and what so much good doth that teaching bring forth (I speak still of moral doctrine) as that it moveth one to do that which it doth teach? For, as Aristotle saith,[41] it is not *Gnosis* but *Praxis* must be the fruit. And how *Praxis* cannot be, without being moved to practice, it is no hard matter to consider.

The philosopher showeth you the way, he informeth you of the particularities, as well of the tediousness of the way, as of the pleasant lodging you shall have when your journey is ended, as of the many by-turnings that may divert you from your way. But this is to no man but to him that will read him, and read him with attentive studious painfulness; which constant desire whosoever hath in him, hath already passed half the hardness of the way, and therefore is beholding to the philosopher but for the other half. Nay truly, learned men have learnedly thought that where once reason hath so much overmastered passion as that the mind hath a free desire to do well, the inward light each mind hath in itself is as good as a philosopher's book; seeing in nature we know it is well to do well, and what is well and what is evil, although not in the words of art which philosophers bestow upon us. For out of natural conceit the philosophers drew it; but to be moved to do that which we know, or to be moved with desire to know, *Hoc opus, hic labor est.*[42]

Now therein of all sciences (I speak still of human, and according to the humane conceits) is our poet the monarch. For he doth not only show the way, but giveth so sweet a prospect into the way, as will entice any man to enter into it. Nay, he doth, as if your journey should lie through a fair vineyard, at the first give you a cluster of grapes, that, full of that taste, you may long to pass further. He beginneth not with obscure definitions, which must blur the margent with interpretations, and load the memory with doubtfulness; but he cometh to you with words set in delightful proportion, either accompanied with, or prepared for, the well-enchanting skill of music; and with a tale forsooth he cometh unto you, with a tale which holdeth children from play, and old men from the chimney corner. And, pretending no more, doth intend the winning of the mind from wickedness to virtue: even as the child is often brought to take most wholesome things by hiding them in such other as have a pleasant taste: which, if one should begin to tell them the nature of aloes[43] or rhubarb

[40] *Philophilosophos:* fond of philosophers.

[41] *as Aristotle saith:* In his *Ethics,* I, i: "since the ultimate object is not knowing but acting."

[42] *Hoc . . . est:* "This is a task, this is labor," *Aeneid,* VI, 129.

[43] *aloes:* a bitter drug with purgative qualities from the juice of plants of the genus *Aloe.*

they should receive, would sooner take their physic at their ears than at their mouth. So is it in men (most of which are childish in the best things, till they be cradled in their graves): glad they will be to hear the tales of Hercules, Achilles, Cyrus, and Aeneas; and, hearing them, must needs hear the right description of wisdom, valor, and justice; which, if they had been barely, that is to say philosophically, set out, they would swear they be brought to school again.

That imitation whereof poetry is, hath the most conveniency to nature of all other, insomuch that, as Aristotle saith, those things which in themselves are horrible, as cruel battles, unnatural monsters, are made in poetical imitation delightful. Truly, I have known men, that even with reading *Amadis de Gaule*[44] (which God knoweth wanteth much of a perfect poesy) have found their hearts moved to the exercise of courtesy, liberality, and especially courage. Who readeth Aeneas carrying old Anchises on his back, that wisheth not it were his fortune to perform so excellent an act? Whom do not the words of Turnus move, the tale of Turnus having planted his image in the imagination?—

Fugientem haec terra videbit?
Usque adeone mori miserum est?[45]

Where the philosophers, as they scorn to delight, so must they be content little to move, saving wrangling whether Virtue be the chief or the only good, whether the contemplative or the active life do excel: which Plato and Boethius[46] well knew, and therefore made Mistress Philosophy very often borrow the masking raiment of Poesy. For even those hard-hearted evil men who think virtue a school name, and know no other good but *indulgere genio,*[47] and therefore despise the austere admonitions of the philosopher, and feel not the inward reason they stand upon, yet will be content to be delighted—which is all the good fellow poet seemeth to promise—and so steal to see the form of goodness, which seen they cannot but love ere themselves be aware, as if they took a medicine of cherries.

Infinite proofs of the strange effects of this poetical invention might be alleged; only two shall serve, which are so often remembered as I think all men know them; the one of Menenius Agrippa,[48] who, when the whole people of Rome had resolutely divided themselves from the Senate, with apparent show of utter ruin, though he were (for that time) an excellent orator, came not among them upon trust of figurative speeches or cunning insinuations, and much less with farfetched maxims of philosophy, which

---

[44] *Amadis de Gaule:* a Spanish or Portuguese romance of chivalry. The Spanish version is by Garcia de Montalvo, dating from the second half of the fifteenth century.

[45] *Fugientem . . . est:* "Shall this ground see [Turnus] fleeing? Is it so hard to die?" *Aeneid,* XII, 645–646.

[46] *Boethius:* philosopher, author of *De consolatione philosophiae,* died 524 A.D.

[47] *indulgere genio:* "to indulge one's own inclinations," Persius, *Satires,* V, 151.

[48] *the one of Menenius Agrippa:* See Shakespeare's *Coriolanus.*

(especially if they were Platonic) they must have learned geometry before they could well have conceived; but forsooth he behaves himself like a homely and familiar poet. He telleth them a tale, that there was a time when all the parts of the body made a mutinous conspiracy against the belly, which they thought devoured the fruits of each other's labor: they concluded they would let so unprofitable a spender starve. In the end, to be short (for the tale is notorious, and as notorious that it was a tale), with punishing the belly they plagued themselves. This applied by him wrought such effect in the people, as I never read that ever words brought forth but then so sudden and so good an alteration; for upon reasonable conditions a perfect reconcilement ensued. The other is of Nathan [49] the Prophet, who, when the holy David had so far forsaken God as to confirm adultery with murder, when he was to do the tenderest office of a friend, in laying his own shame before his eyes, sent by God to call again so chosen a servant, how doth he it but by telling of a man whose beloved lamb was ungratefully taken from his bosom?—the application most divinely true, but the discourse itself feigned. Which made David (I speak of the second and instrumental cause) as in a glass to see his own filthiness, as that heavenly psalm of mercy well testifieth.

By these, therefore, examples and reasons, I think it may be manifest that the poet, with that same hand of delight, doth draw the mind more effectually than any other art doth: and so a conclusion not unfitly ensueth, that, as virtue is the most excellent resting place for all worldly learning to make his end of, so poetry, being the most familiar to teach it, and most princely to move towards it, in the most excellent work is the most excellent workman. But I am content not only to decipher him by his works (although works in commendation or dispraise must ever hold an high authority), but more narrowly will examine his parts: so that, as in a man, though all together may carry a presence full of majesty and beauty, perchance in some one defectious piece we may find a blemish. Now in his parts, kinds, or species (as you list to term them), it is to be noted that some poesies have coupled together two or three kinds, as tragical and comical, whereupon is risen the tragicomical. Some, in the like manner, have mingled prose and verse, as Sannazaro [50] and Boethius. Some have mingled matters heroical and pastoral. But that cometh all to one in this question, for, if severed they be good, the conjunction cannot be hurtful. Therefore, perchance forgetting some, and leaving some as needless to be remembered, it shall not be amiss in a word to cite the special kinds, to see what faults may be found in the right use of them.

Is it then the pastoral poem which is misliked? For perchance where the hedge is lowest they will soonest leap over. Is the poor pipe disdained, which sometime out of Melibaeus' mouth can show the misery of people

---

[49] *Nathan:* II Samuel 12:1–7.

[50] *Sannazaro:* Italian poet (1458–1530), author of the *Arcadia,* a pastoral romance of mixed prose and verse which influenced Sidney's own *Arcadia.*

under hard lords or ravening soldiers, and again, by Tityrus,[51] what blessedness is derived to them that lie lowest from the goodness of them that sit highest? sometimes, under the pretty tales of wolves and sheep, can include the whole considerations of wrongdoing and patience; sometimes show that contention for trifles can get but a trifling victory; where perchance a man may see that even Alexander and Darius, when they strave who should be cock of this world's dunghill, the benefit they got was that the after-livers may say,

Haec memini et victum frustra contendere Thirsin:
Ex illo Coridon, Coridon est tempore nobis.[52]

Or is it the lamenting elegiac, which in a kind heart would move rather pity than blame, who bewails with the great philosopher Heraclitus the weakness of mankind and the wretchedness of the world; who surely is to be praised, either for compassionate accompanying just causes of lamentation, or for rightly pointing out how weak be the passions of woefulness? Is it the bitter but wholesome iambic, which rubs the galled mind, in making shame the trumpet of villainy with bold and open crying out against naughtiness? Or the satiric, who

Omne vafer vitium ridenti tangit amico;[53]

who sportingly never leaveth until he make a man laugh at folly, and, at length ashamed, to laugh at himself, which he cannot avoid, without avoiding the folly; who, while

circum praecordia ludit,[54]

giveth us to feel how many headaches a passionate life bringeth us to; how, when all is done,

Est Ulubris, animus si nos non deficit aequus?[55]

No, perchance it is the comic, whom naughty play-makers and stage-keepers have justly made odious. To the argument of abuse I will answer after. Only thus much now is to be said, that the comedy is an imitation of the common errors of our life, which he representeth in the most ridiculous and scornful sort that may be, so as it is impossible that any beholder can be content to be such a one.

Now, as in geometry the oblique must be known as well as the right, and in arithmetic the odd as well as the even, so in the actions of our life

---

[51] *Melibaeus, Tityrus:* names for shepherds in pastoral works.

[52] *Haec . . . nobis:* "These things I remember, how the vanquished Thyrsis struggled in vain. From that day on it has been Corydon, only Corydon with us," Virgil, *Eclogues,* VII, 69–70.

[53] *Omne . . . amico:* "manages to probe every fault while making his friend laugh." Shortened from Persius, *Satires,* I, 116.

[54] *circum . . . ludit:* "he plays about the innermost feelings," Persius, *Satires,* I, 117.

[55] *Est . . . aequus:* The whole phrase is: "What you seek is here; it is at Ulubrae, if a well-balanced mind does not fail you there," Horace, *Epistles,* I, xi, 30.

who seeth not the filthiness of evil wanteth a great foil to perceive the beauty of virtue. This doth the comedy handle so in our private and domestical matters, as with hearing it we get as it were an experience, what is to be looked for of a niggardly Demea, of a crafty Davus, of a flattering Gnatho, of a vainglorious Thraso; [56] and not only to know what effects are to be expected, but to know who be such, by the signifying badge given them by the comedian. And little reason hath any man to say that men learn evil by seeing it so set out; since, as I said before, there is no man living but, by the force truth hath in nature, no sooner seeth these men play their parts, but wisheth them in *pistrinum:* [57] although perchance the sack of his own faults lie so behind his back that he seeth not himself dance the same measure; whereto yet nothing can more open his eyes than to find his own actions contemptibly set forth.

So that the right use of comedy will (I think) by nobody be blamed, and much less of the high and excellent tragedy, that openeth the greatest wounds, and showeth forth the ulcers that are covered with tissue; that maketh kings fear to be tyrants, and tyrants manifest their tyrannical humors; that, with stirring the affects of admiration and commiseration, teacheth the uncertainty of this world, and upon how weak foundations gilden roofs are builded; that maketh us know,

> *Qui sceptra saevus duro imperio regit,*
> *Timet timentes, metus in auctorem redit.*[58]

But how much it can move, Plutarch yieldeth a notable testimony [59] of the abominable tyrant Alexander Pheraeus, from whose eyes a tragedy, well made and represented, drew abundance of tears, who, without all pity, had murdered infinite numbers, and some of his own blood, so as he, that was not ashamed to make matters for tragedies, yet could not resist the sweet violence of a tragedy. And if it wrought no further good in him, it was that he, in despite of himself, withdrew himself from hearkening to that which might mollify his hardened heart.

But it is not the tragedy they do mislike; for it were too absurd to cast out so excellent a representation of whatsoever is most worthy to be learned. Is it the lyric that most displeaseth, who with his tuned lyre, and well-accorded voice, giveth praise, the reward of virtue, to virtuous acts, who gives moral precepts, and natural problems, who sometimes raiseth up his voice to the height of the heavens, in singing the lauds of the immortal God? Certainly, I must confess my own barbarousness, I never

[56] *Demea . . . Thraso:* stock characters (heavy father, clever servant, parasite, and braggart) of Terence's Latin comedies.

[57] *pistrinum:* a pounding mill, used as punishment for slaves.

[58] *Qui . . . redit:* "He who rules his people with a harsh government fears those who fear him; the fear returns upon its author," Seneca, *Oedipus,* 705.

[59] *Plutarch yieldeth . . . testimony:* Plutarch (see below, p. 615) describes Alexander, tyrant of Pherae in Thessaly (*reg.* B.C. 369–357) in the *Life of Pelopidas,* 29.

heard the old song of Percy and Douglas[60] that I found not my heart moved more than with a trumpet; and yet is it sung but by some blind crowder,[61] with no rougher voice than rude style; which, being so evil appareled in the dust and cobwebs of that uncivil age, what would it work, trimmed in the gorgeous eloquence of Pindar? In Hungary[62] I have seen it the manner at all feasts, and other such meetings, to have songs of their ancestors' valor; which that right soldierlike nation think the chiefest kindlers of brave courage. The incomparable Lacedemonians did not only carry that kind of music ever with them to the field, but even at home, as such songs were made, so were they all content to be the singers of them, when the lusty men were to tell what they did, the old men what they had done, and the young men what they would do. And where a man may say that Pindar many times praiseth highly victories of small moment, matters rather of sport than virtue; as it may be answered, it was the fault of the poet, and not of the poetry, so indeed the chief fault was in the time and custom of the Greeks, who set those toys at so high a price that Philip of Macedon reckoned a horse race won at Olympus among his three fearful felicities. But as the inimitable Pindar often did, so is that kind most capable and most fit to awake the thoughts from the sleep of idleness, to embrace honorable enterprises.

There rests the heroical, whose very name (I think) should daunt all backbiters; for by what conceit can a tongue be directed to speak evil of that which draweth with it no less champions than Achilles, Cyrus, Aeneas, Turnus, Tydeus, and Rinaldo?[63] who doth not only teach and move to a truth, but teacheth and moveth to the most high and excellent truth; who maketh magnanimity and justice shine throughout all misty fearfulness and foggy desires; who, if the saying of Plato and Tully be true, that who could see Virtue would be wonderfully ravished with the love of her beauty—this man sets her out to make her more lovely in her holiday apparel, to the eye of any that will deign not to disdain until they understand. But if anything be already said in the defense of sweet poetry, all concurreth to the maintaining the heroical, which is not only a kind, but the best and most accomplished kind of poetry. For as the image of each action stirreth and instructeth the mind, so the lofty image of such worthies most inflameth the mind with desire to be worthy, and informs with counsel how to be worthy. Only let Aeneas be worn in the tablet of your memory, how he governeth himself in the ruin of his country, in the preserving his old father, and carrying away his religious ceremonies, in obeying the gods' commandment to leave Dido, though not

---

[60] *the old song of Percy and Douglas:* either an early version of *Chevy Chase* (*The Hunting of the Cheviot;* Child no. 162) or, as Child suggests, *The Battle of Otterburn* (Child no. 161), both old Scottish ballads.

[61] *blind crowder:* blind fiddler (Welsh *crwth,* "fiddle").

[62] *Hungary:* In 1572–1573 Sidney was in Hungary with Languet.

[63] *Tydeus:* in the *Iliad; Rinaldo* in Tasso's *Gerusalemme Liberata.*

only all passionate kindness, but even the human consideration of virtuous gratefulness, would have craved other of him; how in storms, how in sports, how in war, how in peace, how a fugitive, how victorious, how besieged, how besieging, how to strangers, how to allies, how to enemies, how to his own; lastly, how in his inward self, and how in his outward government, and I think, in a mind not prejudiced with a prejudicating humor, he will be found in excellency fruitful, yea, even as Horace saith,

Melius Chrysippo et Crantore.[64]

But truly I imagine it falleth out with these poet-whippers, as with some good women, who often are sick, but in faith they cannot tell where. So the name of Poetry is odious to them, but neither his cause nor effects, neither the sum that contains him nor the particularities descending from him, give any fast handle to their carping dispraise.

Since then poetry is of all human learning the most ancient and of most fatherly antiquity, as from whence other learnings have taken their beginnings; since it is so universal that no learned nation doth despise it, nor no barbarous nation is without it; since both Roman and Greek gave divine names unto it, the one of "prophesying," the other of "making," and that indeed that name of "making" is fit for him, considering that whereas other arts retain themselves within their subject, and receive, as it were, their being from it, the poet only bringeth his own stuff, and doth not learn a conceit out of a matter, but maketh matter for a conceit; since neither his description nor his end containeth any evil, the thing described cannot be evil; since his effects be so good as to teach goodness and to delight the learners; since therein (namely in moral doctrine, the chief of all knowledges) he doth not only far pass the historian, but, for instructing, is well-nigh comparable to the philosopher, and, for moving, leaves him behind him; since the Holy Scripture (wherein there is no uncleanness) hath whole parts in it poetical, and that even our Savior Christ vouchsafed to use the flowers of it; since all his kinds are not only in their united forms but in their severed dissections fully commendable; I think (and think I think rightly) the laurel crown appointed for triumphing captains doth worthily (of all other learnings) honor the poet's triumph. But because we have ears as well as tongues, and that the lightest reasons that may be will seem to weigh greatly, if nothing be put in the counterbalance, let us hear, and, as well as we can, ponder, what objections may be made against this art, which may be worthy either of yielding or answering.

First, truly I note not only in these *Mysomousoi,* poet-haters, but in all that kind of people who seek a praise by dispraising others, that they do prodigally spend a great many wandering words in quips and scoffs, carping and taunting at each thing, which, by stirring the spleen, may stay

---

[64] *Melius . . . Crantore:* "Better than Chrysippus and Crantor," Horace, *Epistles,* I, ii, 4.

the brain from a thorough beholding the worthiness of the subject. Those kind of objections, as they are full of very idle easiness, since there is nothing of so sacred a majesty but that an itching tongue may rub itself upon it, so deserve they no other answer, but, instead of laughing at the jest, to laugh at the jester. We know a playing wit can praise the discretion of an ass, the comfortableness of being in debt, and the jolly commodity of being sick of the plague. So of the contrary side, if we will turn Ovid's verse,[65]

Ut lateat virtus proximitate mali,

that "good lie hid in nearness of the evil," Agrippa[66] will be as merry in showing the vanity of science as Erasmus[67] was in commending of folly. Neither shall any man or matter escape some touch of these smiling railers. But for Erasmus and Agrippa, they had another foundation than the superficial part would promise. Marry, these other pleasant faultfinders, who will correct the verb before they understand the noun, and confute others' knowledge before they confirm their own, I would have them only remember that scoffing cometh not of wisdom; so as the best title in true English they get with their merriments is to be called good fools, for so have our grave forefathers ever termed that humorous kind of jesters.

But that which giveth greatest scope to their scorning humors is rhyming and versing. It is already said (and, as I think, truly said) it is not rhyming and versing that maketh poesy. One may be a poet without versing, and a versifier without poetry. But yet presuppose it were inseparable (as indeed it seemeth Scaliger[68] judgeth) truly it were an inseparable commendation. For if *Oratio* next to *Ratio,* speech next to reason, be the greatest gift bestowed upon mortality, that cannot be praiseless which doth most polish that blessing of speech; which considers each word, not only (as a man may say) by his forcible quality, but by his best measured quantity, carrying even in themselves a harmony (without, perchance, number, measure, order, proportion be in our time grown odious). But lay aside the just praise it hath, by being the only fit speech for music (music, I say, the most divine striker of the senses), thus much is undoubtedly true, that if reading be foolish without remembering, memory being the only treasurer of knowledge, those words which are fittest for memory are likewise most convenient for knowledge.

Now, that verse far exceedeth prose in the knitting up of the memory, the reason is manifest—the words (besides their delight, which hath a

[65] *Ovid's verse:* in *Ars amatoria,* II, 662; altered by Sidney.

[66] *Agrippa:* Henricus Cornelius Agrippa (1486–1535), German humanist, author of *De incertitudine et vanitate scientiarum* (1531), an attack upon the methods of instruction in his day.

[67] *Erasmus:* Desiderius Erasmus (1466–1536). Published *Moriae encomium* (*The Praise of Folly*) in 1510.

[68] *Scaliger:* Julius Caesar Scaliger (1484–1558), whose *Poetice* Sidney draws on frequently.

great affinity to memory) being so set as one word cannot be lost but the whole work fails; which accuseth itself, calleth the remembrance back to itself, and so most strongly confirmeth it. Besides, one word so, as it were, begetting another, as, be it in rhyme or measured verse, by the former a man shall have a near guess to the follower: lastly, even they that have taught the art of memory have showed nothing so apt for it as a certain room divided into many places well and thoroughly known. Now, that hath the verse in effect perfectly, every word having his natural seat, which seat must needs make the words remembered. But what needeth more in a thing so known to all men? Who is it that ever was a scholar that doth not carry away some verses of Virgil, Horace, or Cato, which in his youth he learned, and even to his old age serve him for hourly lessons? But the fitness it hath for memory is notably proved by all delivery of arts: wherein for the most part, from grammar to logic, mathematic, physic, and the rest, the rules chiefly necessary to be borne away are compiled in verses. So that, verse being in itself sweet and orderly, and being best for memory, the only handle of knowledge, it must be in jest that any man can speak against it.

Now then go we [69] to the most important imputations laid to the poor poets. For aught I can yet learn, they are these. First, that there being many other more fruitful knowledges, a man might better spend his time in them than in this. Secondly, that it is the mother of lies. Thirdly, that it is the nurse of abuse, infecting us with many pestilent desires, with a siren's sweetness drawing the mind to the serpent's tale of sinful fancy —and herein, especially, comedies give the largest field to ear [70] (as Chaucer saith)—how both in other nations and in ours, before poets did soften us, we were full of courage, given to martial exercises, the pillars of manlike liberty, and not lulled asleep in shady idleness with poets' pastimes. And lastly, and chiefly, they cry out with an open mouth, as if they outshot Robin Hood, that Plato banished them out of his Commonwealth.[71] Truly, this is much, if there be much truth in it. First, to the first, that a man might better spend his time is a reason indeed: but it doth (as they say) but *petere principium:* [72] for if it be, as I affirm, that no learning is so good as that which teacheth and moveth to virtue, and that none can both teach and move thereto so much as poetry, then is the conclusion manifest that ink and paper cannot be to a more profitable purpose employed. And certainly, though a man should grant their first assumption, it should follow (methinks) very unwillingly, that good is not good because better is better. But I still and utterly deny that there is sprung out of earth a more fruitful knowledge. To the second there-

[69] *Now then go we:* Here Sidney may be beginning his direct answer to Gosson.

[70] *To ear:* to plow. The reference is purely verbal to Chaucer's *Knight's Tale,* 28: "I have, God wot, a large field to ere."

[71] *that Plato . . . Commonwealth:* one of Gosson's arguments.

[72] *petere principium:* to beg the question.

fore, that they should be the principal liars, I answer paradoxically, but truly, I think truly, that of all writers under the sun the poet is the least liar, and, though he would, as a poet can scarcely be a liar. The astronomer, with his cousin the geometrician, can hardly escape, when they take upon them to measure the height of the stars. How often, think you, do the physicians lie, when they aver things good for sicknesses, which afterwards send Charon a great number of souls drowned in a potion before they come to his ferry? And no less of the rest, which take upon them to affirm. Now, for the poet, he nothing affirms, and therefore never lieth. For, as I take it, to lie is to affirm that to be true which is false; so as the other artists, and especially the historian, affirming many things, can, in the cloudy knowledge of mankind, hardly escape from many lies. But the poet (as I said before) never affirmeth. The poet never maketh any circles about your imagination, to conjure you to believe for true what he writes. He citeth not authorities of other histories, but even for his entry calleth the sweet Muses to inspire into him a good invention; in truth, not laboring to tell you what is, or is not, but what should or should not be. And therefore, though he recount things not true, yet because he telleth them not for true, he lieth not—without we will say that Nathan lied in his speech, before alleged, to David; which as a wicked man durst scarce say, so think I none so simple would say that Aesop lied in the tales of his beasts: for who thinks that Aesop writ it for actually true were well worthy to have his name chronicled among the beasts he writeth of. What child is there that, coming to a play, and seeing *Thebes* written in great letters upon an old door, doth believe that it is Thebes? If then a man can arrive, at that child's age, to know that the poets' persons and doings are but pictures what should be, and not stories what have been, they will never give the lie to things not affirmatively but allegorically and figuratively written. And therefore, as in history, looking for truth, they go away full fraught with falsehood, so in poesy, looking for fiction, they shall use the narration but as an imaginative groundplot of a profitable invention.

But hereto is replied, that the poets give names to men they write of, which argueth a conceit of an actual truth, and so, not being true, proves a falsehood. And doth the lawyer lie then, when under the names of "John a Stile" and "John a Noakes" [73] he puts his case? But that is easily answered. Their naming of men is but to make their picture the more lively, and not to build any history; painting men, they cannot leave men nameless. We see we cannot play at chess but that we must give names to our chessmen; and yet, methinks, he were a very partial champion of truth that would say we lied for giving a piece of wood the reverend title of a bishop. The poet nameth Cyrus or Aeneas no other way than to show what men of their fames, fortunes, and estates should do.

---

[73] *John a Stile, John a Noakes:* fictitious names in a legal action; the John Doe and Richard Roe of old English law courts.

Their third is, how much it abuseth men's wit, training it to wanton sinfulness and lustful love: for indeed that is the principal, if not the only, abuse I can hear alleged. They say the comedies rather teach than reprehend amorous conceits. They say the lyric is larded with passionate sonnets, the elegiac weeps the want of his mistress, and that even to the heroical Cupid hath ambitiously climbed. Alas, Love, I would thou couldst as well defend thyself as thou canst offend others. I would those on whom thou dost attend could either put thee away, or yield good reason why they keep thee. But grant love of beauty to be a beastly fault (although it be very hard, since only man, and no beast, hath that gift to discern beauty); grant that lovely name of Love to deserve all hateful reproaches (although even some of my masters the philosophers spent a good deal of their lamp-oil in setting forth the excellency of it); grant, I say, whatsoever they will have granted; that not only love, but lust, but vanity, but (if they list) scurrility, possesseth many leaves of the poets' books: yet think I, when this is granted, they will find their sentence may with good manners put the last words foremost, and not say that poetry abuseth man's wit, but that man's wit abuseth poetry.

For I will not deny but that man's wit may make poesy, which should be *Eikastike,* which some learned have defined, "figuring forth good things," to be *Phantastike,* which doth, contrariwise, infect the fancy with unworthy objects, as the painter, that should give to the eye either some excellent perspective, or some fine picture, fit for building or fortification, or containing in it some notable example, as Abraham sacrificing his son Isaac, Judith killing Holofernes,[74] David fighting with Goliath, may leave those, and please an ill-pleased eye with wanton shows of better hidden matters. But what, shall the abuse of a thing make the right use odious? Nay truly, though I yield that poesy may not only be abused, but that being abused, by the reason of his sweet charming force, it can do more hurt than any other army of words, yet shall it be so far from concluding that the abuse should give reproach to the abused, that contrariwise it is a good reason, that whatsoever, being abused, doth most harm, being rightly used (and upon the right use each thing conceiveth his title), doth most good.

Do we not see the skill of physic (the best rampire[75] to our often-assaulted bodies), being abused, teach poison, the most violent destroyer? Doth not knowledge of law, whose end is to even and right all things, being abused, grow the crooked fosterer of horrible injuries? Doth not (to go to the highest) God's word abused breed heresy, and his Name abused become blasphemy? Truly, a needle cannot do much hurt, and as truly (with leave of ladies be it spoken) it cannot do much good. With a sword thou mayest kill thy father, and with a sword thou mayest defend thy prince and country. So that, as in their calling poets the fathers

---

[74] *Judith killing Holofernes: Apocrypha,* Book of Judith.

[75] *rampire:* rampart.

of lies they say nothing, so in this their argument of abuse they prove the commendation.

They allege herewith, that before poets began to be in price our nation hath set their hearts' delight upon action, and not upon imagination, rather doing things worthy to be written, than writing things fit to be done. What that before-time was, I think scarcely Sphinx can tell, since no memory is so ancient that hath the precedence of poetry. And certain it is that, in our plainest homeliness, yet never was the Albion nation without poetry. Marry, this argument, though it be leveled against poetry, yet is it indeed a chain shot against all learning, or bookishness, as they commonly term it. Of such mind were certain Goths, of whom it is written that, having in the spoil of a famous city taken a fair library, one hangman, belike, fit to execute the fruits of their wits, who had murdered a great number of bodies, would have set fire on it. "No," said another very gravely, "take heed what you do, for while they are busy about these toys, we shall with more leisure conquer their countries."

This indeed is the ordinary doctrine of ignorance, and many words sometimes I have heard spent in it: but because this reason is generally against all learning, as well as poetry, or rather, all learning but poetry; because it were too large a digression to handle, or at least too superfluous (since it is manifest that all government of action is to be gotten by knowledge, and knowledge best by gathering many knowledges, which is reading), I only, with Horace, to him that is of that opinion,

Iubeo stultum esse libenter; [76]

for as for poetry itself, it is the freest from this objection. For poetry is the companion of the camps.

I dare undertake, Orlando Furioso, or honest King Arthur, will never displease a soldier: but the quiddity of *Ens* and *Prima materia* [77] will hardly agree with a corslet. And therefore, as I said in the beginning, even Turks and Tartars are delighted with poets. Homer, a Greek, flourished before Greece flourished. And if to a slight conjecture a conjecture may be opposed, truly it may seem, that, as by him their learned men took almost their first light of knowledge, so their active men received their first motions of courage. Only Alexander's example may serve, who by Plutarch is accounted of such virtue, that Fortune was not his guide but his footstool; whose acts speak for him, though Plutarch did not—indeed the Phoenix of warlike princes. This Alexander left his schoolmaster, living Aristotle, behind him, but took dead Homer with him. He put the philosopher Callisthenes to death for his seeming philosophical, indeed mutinous, stubbornness, but the chief thing he ever was heard to wish for was that Homer had been alive. He well found he received more

[76] *Iubeo . . . libenter:* "I bid him be a fool to his heart's content." Altered from Horace, *Satires,* I, i, 63.

[77] *quiddity of Ens, Prima materia:* terms used in philosophy. The latter is the original substance or matter of the universe.

bravery of mind by the pattern of Achilles than by hearing the definition of fortitude: and therefore, if Cato misliked Fulvius for carrying Ennius with him to the field, it may be answered that, if Cato misliked it, the noble Fulvius liked it, or else he had not done it: for it was not the excellent Cato Uticensis (whose authority I would much more have reverenced), but it was the former, in truth a bitter punisher of faults, but else a man that had never well sacrificed to the Graces. He misliked and cried out upon all Greek learning, and yet, being eighty years old, began to learn it, belike fearing that Pluto understood not Latin. Indeed, the Roman laws allowed no person to be carried to the wars but he that was in the soldier's roll, and therefore, though Cato misliked his unmustered person, he misliked not his work. And if he had, Scipio Nasica, judged by common consent the best Roman, loved him. Both the other Scipio brothers, who had by their virtues no less surnames than of Asia and Afric, so loved him that they caused his body to be buried in their sepulcher. So as Cato's authority being but against his person, and that answered with so far greater than himself, is herein of no validity.

But now indeed my burden is great; now Plato's name is laid upon me, whom, I must confess, of all philosophers I have ever esteemed most worthy of reverence, and with great reason, since of all philosophers he is the most poetical. Yet if he will defile the fountain out of which his flowing streams have proceeded, let us boldly examine with what reasons he did it. First truly, a man might maliciously object that Plato, being a philosopher, was a natural enemy of poets. For indeed, after the philosophers had picked out of the sweet mysteries of poetry the right discerning true points of knowledge, they forthwith, putting it in method, and making a school art of that which the poets did only teach by a divine delightfulness, beginning to spurn at their guides, like ungrateful prentices, were not content to set up shops for themselves, but sought by all means to discredit their masters; which by the force of delight being barred them, the less they could overthrow them, the more they hated them. For indeed, they found for Homer seven cities strove who should have him for their citizen; where many cities banished philosophers as not fit members to live among them. For only repeating certain of Euripides' verses, many Athenians had their lives saved of the Syracusians, when the Athenians themselves thought many philosophers unworthy to live. Certain poets, as Simonides and Pindarus, had so prevailed with Hiero the First, that of a tyrant they made him a just king; where Plato could do so little with Dionysius, that he himself of a philosopher was made a slave. But who should do thus, I confess, should requite the objections made against poets with like cavilation against philosophers; as likewise one should do that should bid one read *Phaedrus* or *Symposium* in Plato, or the discourse of love in Plutarch, and see whether any poet do authorize abominable filthiness, as they do. Again, a man might ask out of what commonwealth Plato did banish them. In sooth, thence where he himself alloweth community of women. So as belike this banishment grew not for effeminate wantonness, since little should poetical sonnets be hurtful when a man might have what woman he listed. But I honor philosophical instructions, and bless the wits which bred them: so as they be not abused, which is likewise stretched to poetry.

St. Paul himself, who yet, for the credit of poets, allegeth [78] twice two poets, and one of them by the name of a prophet, setteth a watchword upon philosophy—indeed upon the abuse. So doth Plato upon the abuse, not upon poetry. Plato found fault that the poets of his time filled the world with wrong opinions of the gods, making light tales of that unspotted essence, and therefore would not have the youth depraved with such opinions. Herein may much be said; let this suffice: the poets did not induce such opinions, but did imitate those opinions already induced. For all the Greek stories can well testify that the very religion of that time stood upon many and many-fashioned gods, not taught so by the poets, but followed according to their nature of imitation. Who list may read in Plutarch the discourses of Isis and Osiris, of the cause why oracles ceased, of the divine providence, and see whether the theology of that nation stood not upon such dreams which the poets indeed superstitiously observed, and truly (since they had not the light of Christ) did much better in it than the philosophers, who, shaking off superstition, brought in atheism. Plato therefore (whose authority I had much rather justly construe than unjustly resist) meant not in general of poets, in those words of which Julius Scaliger saith, *Qua authoritate barbari quidam atque hispidi abuti velint ad poetas e republica exigendos;* [79] but only meant to drive out those wrong opinions of the Deity (whereof now, without further law, Christianity hath taken away all the hurtful belief), perchance (as he thought) nourished by the then esteemed poets. And a man need go no further than to Plato himself to know his meaning: who, in his dialogue called *Ion,* giveth high and rightly divine commendation to poetry. So as Plato, banishing the abuse, not the thing, not banishing it, but giving due honor unto it, shall be our patron and not our adversary. For indeed I had much rather (since truly I may do it) show their mistaking of Plato (under whose lion's skin they would make an ass-like braying against poesy) than go about to overthrow his authority; whom, the wiser a man is, the more just cause he shall find to have in admiration; especially since he attributeth unto poesy more than myself do, namely, to be a very inspiring of a divine force, far above man's wit, as in the afore-named dialogue is apparent.

Of the other side, who would show the honors have been by the best sort of judgments granted them, a whole sea of examples would present themselves: Alexanders, Caesars, Scipios, all favorers of poets; Laelius, called the Roman Socrates, himself a poet, so as part of *Heautontimoru-*

---

[78] *St. Paul . . . allegeth:* in Colossians 2:8.

[79] *Qua . . . exigendos:* "which authority certain barbarous and uncultivated persons would use for expelling poets from the state," *Poetice,* I, ii.

menos in Terence was supposed to be made by him, and even the Greek Socrates, whom Apollo confirmed to be the only wise man, is said to have spent part of his old time in putting Aesop's fables into verses. And therefore, full evil should it become his scholar Plato to put such words in his master's mouth against poets. But what need more? Aristotle writes the Art of Poesy: and why, if it should not be written? Plutarch teacheth the use to be gathered of them, and how, if they should not be read? And who reads Plutarch's either history or philosophy, shall find he trimmeth both their garments with guards of poesy. But I list not to defend poesy with the help of her underling historiography. Let it suffice that it is a fit soil for praise to dwell upon; and what dispraise may set upon it, is either easily overcome, or transformed into just commendation. So that, since the excellencies of it may be so easily and so justly confirmed, and the low-creeping objections so soon trodden down; it not being an art of lies, but of true doctrine; not of effeminateness, but of notable stirring of courage; not of abusing man's wit, but of strengthening man's wit; not banished, but honored by Plato; let us rather plant more laurels for to engarland our poets' heads (which honor of being laureate, as besides them only triumphant captains wear, is a sufficient authority to show the price they ought to be had in) than suffer the ill-favoring breath of such wrong-speakers once to blow upon the clear springs of poesy.

But since I have run so long a career in this matter, methinks, before I give my pen a full stop, it shall be but a little more lost time to inquire why England (the mother of excellent minds) should be grown so hard a stepmother to poets, who certainly in wit ought to pass all other, since all only proceedeth from their wit, being indeed makers of themselves, not takers of others. How can I but exclaim,

Musa, mihi causas memora, quo numine laeso! [80]

Sweet poesy, that hath anciently had kings, emperors, senators, great captains, such as, besides a thousand others, David, Adrian,[81] Sophocles, Germanicus, not only to favor poets, but to be poets; and of our nearer times can present for her patrons a Robert, King of Sicily,[82] the great King Francis of France,[83] King James of Scotland; [84] such cardinals as Bembus [85] and Bibiena; [86] such famous preachers and teachers as Beza [87]

[80] *Musa . . . laeso:* "O Muse, call to mind the causes: what divinity was injured," *Aeneid*, I, 8.

[81] *Adrian:* the Emperor Hadrian (*reg.* 117–138).

[82] *Robert, King of Sicily:* Robert d'Anjou, King of Naples (*reg.* 1309–1343), friend of Petrarch and Boccaccio.

[83] *Francis of France:* Francis I (*reg.* 1515–1547), a great patron of arts and letters.

[84] *James of Scotland:* probably James I of Scotland (*reg.* 1406–1437), author of the *King's Quair* (see note in Gregory Smith's *Elizabethan Critical Essays*, I, 396).

[85] *Bembus:* Pietro Bembo (1470–1547), scholar and man of letters, who figures in Castiglione's *Courtier*. See pp. 113–134.

[86] *Bibiena:* Bernardo da Bibbiena (1470–1520), writer of comedy and private secretary to Lorenzo de Medici.

[87] *Beza:* Theodore Beza (1519–1605), successor to Calvin at Geneva; most eminent Protestant divine in Europe.

and Melancthon;[88] so learned philosophers as Fracastorius[89] and Scaliger; so great orators as Pontanus[90] and Muretus;[91] so piercing wits as George Buchanan;[92] so grave counselors as, besides many, but before all, that Hospital of France,[93] than whom (I think) that realm never brought forth a more accomplished judgment, more firmly builded upon virtue—I say these, with numbers of others, not only to read others' poesies, but to poetize for others' reading—that poesy, thus embraced in all other places, should only find in our time a hard welcome in England, I think the very earth lamenteth it, and therefore decketh our soil with fewer laurels than it was accustomed. For heretofore poets have in England also flourished, and, which is to be noted, even in those times when the trumpet of Mars did sound loudest. And now that an overfaint quietness should seem to strew the house for poets, they are almost in as good reputation as the mountebanks[94] at Venice. Truly even that, as of the one side it giveth great praise to poesy, which like Venus (but to better purpose) hath rather be troubled in the net with Mars than enjoy the homely quiet of Vulcan; so serves it for a piece of a reason why they are less grateful to idle England, which now can scarce endure the pain of a pen. Upon this necessarily followeth, that base men with servile wits undertake it, who think it enough if they can be rewarded of the printer. And so as Epaminondas is said, with the honor of his virtue, to have made an office, by his exercising it, which before was contemptible, to become highly respected, so these, no more but setting their names to it, by their own disgracefulness disgrace the most graceful poesy. For now, as if all the Muses were got with child, to bring forth bastard poets, without any commission they do post over the banks of Helicon, till they make the readers more weary than posthorses, while, in the meantime, they,

Queis meliore uto finxit praecordia Titan,[95]

are better content to suppress the outflowing of their wit, than, by publishing them, to be accounted knights of the same order. But I that, before ever I durst aspire unto the dignity, am admitted into the company of the paper-blurrers, do find the very true cause of our wanting estimation is want of desert, taking upon us to be poets in despite of Pallas. Now, wherein we want desert were a thankworthy labor to express: but if

[88] *Melancthon:* Philip Melancthon (1497–1560), intimate friend of Martin Luther.

[89] *Fracastorius:* (1483–1553), a Veronese poet, philosopher, astronomer, and physician.

[90] *Pontanus:* John Jovius Pontanus (1420–1503), Italian medieval poet.

[91] *Muretus:* Marc Antoine Muret (1526–1585), French scholar and writer.

[92] *George Buchanan:* (1506–1582), one of the foremost Scotch writers in the sixteenth century.

[93] *that Hospital of France:* Michel de l'Hospital (1504–1573), one time Chancellor of France, who worked for the toleration of the Huguenots.

[94] *mountebanks:* (one who mounts a bench) glib vendors of quack medicines (cf. Volpone's disguise as Doctor Scoto Mantuano in Jonson's *Volpone,* II, ii).

[95] *Queis . . . Titan:* "whose hearts Titan had formed of better clay." Altered from Juvenal, *Satires,* XIV, 34–35.

I knew, I should have mended myself. But I, as I never desired the title, so have I neglected the means to come by it. Only, overmastered by some thoughts, I yielded an inky tribute unto them. Marry, they that delight in poesy itself should seek to know what they do, and how they do, and, especially, look themselves in an unflattering glass of reason, if they be inclinable unto it. For poesy must not be drawn by the ears; it must be gently led, or rather it must lead; which was partly the cause that made the ancient-learned affirm it was a divine gift, and no human skill: since all other knowledges lie ready for any that hath strength of wit; a poet no industry can make, if his own genius be not carried unto it; and therefore is it an old proverb, *Orator fit, Poeta nascitur.*[96] Yet confess I always that as the fertilest ground must be manured, so must the highest-flying wit have a Daedalus to guide him.[97] That Daedalus, they say, both in this and in other, hath three wings to bear itself up into the air of due commendation: that is, Art, Imitation, and Exercise. But these, neither artificial rules nor imitative patterns, we much cumber ourselves withal. Exercise indeed we do, but that very fore-backwardly: for where we should exercise to know, we exercise as having known: and so is our brain delivered of much matter which never was begotten by knowledge. For, there being two principal parts—matter to be expressed by words and words to express the matter—in neither we use Art or Imitation rightly. Our matter is *Quodlibet*[98] indeed, though wrongly performing Ovid's verse,

Quicquid conabar dicere, versus erit:[99]

never marshaling it into an assured rank, that almost the readers cannot tell where to find themselves.

Chaucer, undoubtedly, did excellently in his *Troilus and Cressida;* of whom, truly, I know not whether to marvel more, either that he in that misty time could see so clearly, or that we in this clear age walk so stumblingly after him. Yet had he great wants, fit to be forgiven in so reverent antiquity. I account the *Mirror of Magistrates* meetly furnished of beautiful parts, and in the Earl of Surrey's *Lyrics* many things tasting of a noble birth, and worthy of a noble mind. The *Shepherd's Calendar* hath much poetry in his Eclogues, indeed worthy the reading, if I be not deceived. That same framing of his style to an old rustic language I dare not allow, since neither Theocritus in Greek, Virgil in Latin, nor Sannazaro in Italian did affect it. Besides these, do I not remember to have

---

96 *Orator . . . nascitur:* "The orator is made, the poet is born."

97 *a Daedalus to guide him:* Daedalus invented wings for himself and his son Icarus. Disregarding his father's instructions, Icarus flew too high. The sun melted the wax in his wings, and he fell into the sea. The tale is told in Ovid, *Metamorphoses,* VIII, 261 ff.

98 *Quodlibet:* indifferent, anything you please.

99 *Quicquid . . . erit:* "Whatever I shall try to write shall become verse." An echo of Ovid's *Tristia,* IV, x, 26.

seen but few (to speak boldly) printed, that have poetical sinews in them: for proof whereof, let but most of the verses be put in prose, and then ask the meaning; and it will be found that one verse did but beget another, without ordering at the first what should be at the last; which becomes a confused mass of words, with a tingling sound of rhyme, barely accompanied with reason.

Our tragedies and comedies (not without cause cried out against), observing rules neither of honest civility nor of skillful poetry, excepting *Gorboduc*[100] (again, I say, of those that I have seen), which notwithstanding, as it is full of stately speeches and well-sounding phrases, climbing to the height of Seneca's style, and as full of notable morality, which it doth most delightfully teach, and so obtain the very end of poesy, yet in truth it is very defectious in the circumstances, which grieveth me, because it might not remain as an exact model of all tragedies. For it is faulty both in place and time, the two necessary companions of all corporal actions. For where the stage should always represent but one place, and the uttermost time presupposed in it should be, both by Aristotle's precept and common reason, but one day, there is both many days, and many places, inartificially imagined. But if it be so in *Gorboduc,* how much more in all the rest, where you shall have Asia of the one side, and Afric of the other, and so many other under-kingdoms, that the player, when he cometh in, must ever begin with telling where he is, or else the tale will not be conceived? Now ye shall have three ladies walk to gather flowers, and then we must believe the stage to be a garden. By and by we hear news of shipwreck in the same place, and then we are to blame if we accept it not for a rock. Upon the back of that comes out a hideous monster, with fire and smoke, and then the miserable beholders are bound to take it for a cave. While in the meantime two armies fly in, represented with four swords and bucklers, and then what hard heart will not receive it for a pitched field? Now, of time they are much more liberal, for ordinary it is that two young princes fall in love. After many traverses,[101] she is got with child, delivered of a fair boy; he is lost, groweth a man, falls in love, and is ready to get another child; and all this in two hours' space: which, how absurd it is in sense, even sense may imagine, and art hath taught, and all ancient examples justified, and, at this day, the ordinary players in Italy will not err in. Yet will some bring in an example of *Eunuchus* in Terence, that containeth matter of two days, yet far short of twenty years. True it is, and so was it to be played in two days, and so fitted to the time it set forth. And though Plautus hath in one place done amiss, let us hit with him, and not miss with him. But they will say, How then shall we set forth a story, which containeth both

[100] *Gorboduc:* a play on Senecan models by Thomas Sackville and Thomas Norton, in blank verse. Published in 1565, it is called the first regular English tragedy.

[101] *traverses:* difficulties, mishaps.

many places and many times? And do they not know that a tragedy is tied to the laws of poesy, and not of history; not bound to follow the story, but, having liberty, either to feign a quite new matter, or to frame the history to the most tragical conveniency? Again, many things may be told which cannot be showed, if they know the difference betwixt reporting and representing. As, for example, I may speak (though I am here) of Peru, and in speech digress from that to the description of Calicut; but in action I cannot represent it without Pacolet's horse.[102] And so was the manner the ancients took, by some Nuncius to recount things done in former time or other place. Lastly, if they will represent an history, they must not (as Horace saith) begin *ab ovo,*[103] but they must come to the principal point of that one action which they will represent. By example this will be best expressed. I have a story of young Polydorus,[104] delivered for safety's sake, with great riches, by his father Priam to Polymnestor, king of Thrace, in the Trojan war time. He, after some years, hearing the overthrow of Priam, for to make the treasure his own, murdereth the child. The body of the child is taken up by Hecuba. She, the same day, findeth a slight to be revenged most cruelly of the tyrant. Where now would one of our tragedy writers begin, but with the delivery of the child? Then should he sail over into Thrace, and so spend I know not how many years, and travel numbers of places. But where doth Euripides? Even with the finding of the body, leaving the rest to be told by the spirit of Polydorus. This need no further to be enlarged; the dullest wit may conceive it.

But besides these gross absurdities, how all their plays be neither right tragedies, nor right comedies, mingling kings and clowns, not because the matter so carrieth it, but thrust in clowns by head and shoulders, to play a part in majestical matters, with neither decency nor discretion, so as neither the admiration and commiseration, nor the right sportfulness, is by their mongrel tragicomedy obtained. I know Apuleius [105] did somewhat so, but that is a thing recounted with space of time, not represented in one moment: and I know the ancients have one or two examples of tragicomedies, as Plautus hath *Amphitruo*.[106] But, if we mark them well, we shall find, that they never, or very daintily, match hornpipes [107] and funerals. So falleth it out that, having indeed no right comedy, in that comical part of our tragedy we have nothing but scurrility, unworthy of any chaste ears, or some extreme show of doltishness, indeed fit to lift up a loud laughter, and nothing else: where the whole tract of a comedy

[102] *Pacolet's horse:* a magic horse made by the dwarf, Pacolet, in the old French romance *Valentine and Orson.*

[103] *ab ovo:* from the egg. Horace, *Ars poetica,* 147.

[104] *Polydorus:* in the *Hecuba* of Euripides.

[105] *Apuleius:* not a dramatist, but a writer of the second century, chiefly known for his satirical romance popularly called "The Golden Ass."

[106] The *Amphitruo* is tragicomic only because of the introduction of gods and heroes. Otherwise it is pure comedy.

[107] *hornpipes:* merry tunes usually for country dances.

should be full of delight, as the tragedy should be still maintained in a well-raised admiration. But our comedians think there is no delight without laughter; which is very wrong, for though laughter may come with delight, yet cometh it not of delight, as though delight should be the cause of laughter; but well may one thing breed both together. Nay, rather in themselves they have, as it were, a kind of contrariety: for delight we scarcely do but in things that have a conveniency to ourselves or to the general nature: laughter almost ever cometh of things most disproportioned to ourselves and nature. Delight hath a joy in it, either permanent or present. Laughter hath only a scornful tickling. For example, we are ravished with delight to see a fair woman, and yet are far from being moved to laughter. We laugh at deformed creatures, wherein certainly we cannot delight. We delight in good chances, we laugh at mischances; we delight to hear the happiness of our friends, or country, at which he were worthy to be laughed at that would laugh. We shall, contrarily, laugh sometimes to find a matter quite mistaken and go down the hill against the bias, in the mouth of some such men, as for the respect of them one shall be heartily sorry, yet he cannot choose but laugh; and so is rather pained than delighted with laughter. Yet deny I not but that they may go well together. For as in Alexander's picture well set out we delight without laughter, and in twenty mad antics we laugh without delight, so in Hercules, painted with his great beard and furious countenance, in woman's attire, spinning at Omphale's commandment,[108] it breedeth both delight and laughter. For the representing of so strange a power in love procureth delight: and the scornfulness of the action stirreth laughter. But I speak to this purpose, that all the end of the comical part be not upon such scornful matters as stirreth laughter only, but, mixed with it, that delightful teaching which is the end of poesy. And the great fault even in that point of laughter, and forbidden plainly by Aristotle, is that they stir laughter in sinful things, which are rather execrable than ridiculous; or in miserable, which are rather to be pitied than scorned. For what is it to make folks gape at a wretched beggar, or a beggarly clown; or, against law of hospitality, to jest at strangers, because they speak not English so well as we do? What do we learn? Since it is certain

Nil habet infelix paupertas durius in se,
Quam quod ridiculos homines facit.[109]

But rather a busy loving courtier, a heartless threatening Thraso, a self-wise-seeming schoolmaster, an awry-transformed traveler—these if we

[108] *spinning at Omphale's commandment:* Hercules, infatuated by Omphale, Queen of Lydia, submitted to being dressed as a female slave and to spin wool. The story is told in Ovid's *Heroides,* IX, 75.

[109] *Nil . . . facit:* "Unfortunate poverty has nothing in itself harder to bear than that it makes men ridiculous," Juvenal, *Satires,* III, 152–153.

saw walk in stage names, which we play naturally, therein were delightful laughter, and teaching delightfulness: as in the other, the tragedies of Buchanan do justly bring forth a divine admiration. But I have lavished out too many words of this play matter. I do it because, as they are excelling parts of poesy, so is there none so much used in England, and none can be more pitifully abused; which, like an unmannerly daughter showing a bad education, causeth her mother poesy's honesty to be called in question.

Other sorts of poetry almost have we none, but that lyrical kind of songs and sonnets: which, Lord, if he gave us so good minds, how well it might be employed, and with how heavenly fruit, both private and public, in singing the praises of the immortal beauty, the immortal goodness of that God who giveth us hands to write and wits to conceive; of which we might well want words, but never matter; of which we could turn our eyes to nothing, but we should ever have new budding occasions. But truly many of such writings as come under the banner of unresistible love, if I were a mistress, would never persuade me they were in love; so coldly they apply fiery speeches, as men that had rather read lovers' writings, and so caught up certain swelling phrases (which hang together like a man which once told me the wind was at northwest, and by south, because he would be sure to name winds enough), than that in truth they feel those passions, which easily (as I think) may be betrayed by that same forcibleness, or *Energia* (as the Greeks call it) of the writer. But let this be a sufficient though short note, that we miss the right use of the material point of poesy.

Now, for the outside of it, which is words, or (as I may term it) diction, it is even well worse. So is that honey-flowing matron Eloquence appareled, or rather disguised, in a courtesan-like painted affectation: one time with so farfetched words, they may seem monsters, but must seem strangers, to any poor Englishman; another time, with coursing of a letter,[110] as if they were bound to follow the method of a dictionary; another time, with figures and flowers,[111] extremely winter-starved. But I would this fault were only peculiar to versifiers, and had not as large possession among prose-printers, and (which is to be marveled) among many scholars, and (which is to be pitied) among some preachers. Truly I could wish, if at least I might be so bold to wish in a thing beyond the reach of my capacity, the diligent imitators of Tully and Demosthenes (most worthy to be imitated) did not so much keep Nizolian paper-books[112] of their figures and phrases, as by attentive translation (as it were) devour

[110] *with coursing of a letter:* alliteration.

[111] *with figures and flowers:* of rhetoric.

[112] *Nizolian paper-books:* Marius Nizolius or Nizzoli (1498?–1576), Italian rhetorician and lexicographer, published a thesaurus or collection of Ciceronian phrases in 1535. Ascham mentions the keeping of similar books in *The Scholemaster*. See above, p. 79.

them whole, and make them wholly theirs. For now they cast sugar and spice upon every dish that is served to the table, like those Indians, not content to wear earrings at the fit and natural place of the ears, but they will thrust jewels through their nose and lips, because they will be sure to be fine. Tully, when he was to drive out Catiline, as it were with a thunderbolt of eloquence, often used that figure of repetition, *Vivit. Vivit? Immo in Senatum venit,*[113] etc. Indeed, inflamed with a well-grounded rage, he would have his words (as it were) double out of his mouth, and so do that artificially which we see men do in choler naturally. And we, having noted the grace of those words, hale them in sometime to a familiar epistle, when it were too much choler to be choleric.

Now for similitudes in certain printed discourses, I think all Herbarists,[114] all stories of beasts, fowls, and fishes are rifled up, that they come in multitudes to wait upon any of our conceits; which certainly is as absurd a surfeit to the ears as is possible: for the force of a similitude not being to prove anything to a contrary disputer, but only to explain to a willing hearer; when that is done, the rest is a most tedious prattling, rather over-swaying the memory from the purpose whereto they were applied, than any whit informing the judgment, already either satisfied, or by similitudes not to be satisfied. For my part, I do not doubt, when Antonius and Crassus, the great forefathers of Cicero in eloquence, the one (as Cicero testifieth of them) pretended not to know art, the other not to set by it, because with a plain sensibleness they might win credit of popular ears; which credit is the nearest step to persuasion; which persuasion is the chief mark of oratory—I do not doubt (I say) but that they used these knacks very sparingly; which, who doth generally use, any man may see doth dance to his own music; and so be noted by the audience more careful to speak curiously than to speak truly.

Undoubtedly (at least to my opinion undoubtedly) I have found in divers small-learned courtiers a more sound style than in some professors of learning: of which I can guess no other cause, but that the courtier, following that which by practice he findeth fittest to nature, therein (though he know it not) doth according to art, though not by art: where the other, using art to show art, and not to hide art (as in these cases he should do), flieth from nature, and indeed abuseth art.

But what? Methinks I deserve to be pounded for straying from poetry to oratory: but both have such an affinity in this wordish consideration, that I think this digression will make my meaning receive the fuller understanding—which is not to take upon me to teach poets how they should do, but only, finding myself sick among the rest, to show some one or two spots of the common infection grown among the most part of

---

[113] *Vivit . . . venit:* Sidney quotes rather freely from memory a line from Cicero (*Catiline,* I, 2): "He lives, nay more, he comes into the Senate."

[114] *all Herbarists, etc.:* Schuckburgh points out that this passage is a gibe at the excesses of Euphuism (see *Euphues* above, p. 209) and more directly, at Gosson's own style.

writers: that, acknowledging ourselves somewhat awry, we may bend to the right use both of matter and manner; whereto our language giveth us great occasion, being indeed capable of any excellent exercising of it. I know some will say it is a mingled language. And why not so much the better, taking the best of both the other? Another will say it wanteth grammar. Nay truly, it hath that praise, that it wanteth not grammar: for grammar it might have, but it needs it not; being so easy of itself, and so void of those cumbersome differences of cases, genders, moods, and tenses, which I think was a piece of the Tower of Babylon's curse, that a man should be put to school to learn his mother tongue. But for the uttering sweetly and properly the conceits of the mind, which is the end of speech, that hath it equally with any other tongue in the world: and is particularly happy in compositions of two or three words together, near the Greek, far beyond the Latin: which is one of the greatest beauties can be in a language.

Now, of versifying there are two sorts, the one ancient, the other modern: the ancient marked the quantity of each syllable, and according to that framed his verse; the modern observing only number (with some regard of the accent), the chief life of it standeth in that like sounding of the words, which we call rhyme. Whether of these be the most excellent, would bear many speeches. The ancient, no doubt, more fit for music, both words and tune observing quantity, and more fit lively to express divers passions, by the low and lofty sound of the well-weighed syllable. The latter likewise, with his rhyme, striketh a certain music to the ear: and, in fine, since it doth delight, though by another way, it obtains the same purpose: there being in either sweetness, and wanting in neither majesty. Truly the English, before any other vulgar language I know, is fit for both sorts: for, for the ancient, the Italian is so full of vowels that it must ever be cumbered with elisions; the Dutch so, of the other side, with consonants, that they cannot yield the sweet sliding fit for a verse; the French, in his whole language, hath not one word that hath his accent in the last syllable saving two, called *Antepenultima;* and little more hath the Spanish: and, therefore, very gracelessly may they use dactyls. The English is subject to none of these defects.

Now, for the rhyme, though we do not observe quantity, yet we observe the accent very precisely: which other languages either cannot do, or will not do so absolutely. That *caesura,* or breathing place in the midst of the verse, neither Italian nor Spanish have, the French, and we, never almost fail of. Lastly, even the very rhyme itself the Italian cannot put in the last syllable, by the French named the "masculine rhyme," but still in the next to the last, which the French call the "female," or the next before that, which the Italians term *sdrucciola.* The example of the former is *buono: suono,* of the *sdrucciola, femina: semina.* The French, of the other side, hath both the male, as *bon: son,* and the female, as *plaise: taise,* but the *sdrucciola* he hath not: where the English hath all three, as *due: true, father: rather, motion: potion,* with much more which might be said, but that I find already the triflingness of this discourse is much too much enlarged.

So that since the ever-praiseworthy poesy is full of virtue-breeding delightfulness, and void of no gift that ought to be in the noble name of learning; since the blames laid against it are either false or feeble; since the cause why it is not esteemed in England is the fault of poet-apes, not poets; since, lastly, our tongue is most fit to honor poesy, and to be honored by poesy; I conjure you all that have had the evil luck to read this ink-wasting toy of mine, even in the name of the Nine Muses, no more to scorn the sacred mysteries of poesy, no more to laugh at the name of "poets," as though they were next inheritors to fools, no more to jest at the reverent title of a "rhymer"; but to believe, with Aristotle, that they were the ancient treasurers of the Grecians' divinity; to believe, with Bembus, that they were first bringers-in of all civility; to believe, with Scaliger, that no philosopher's precepts can sooner make you an honest man than the reading of Virgil; to believe, with Clauserus,[115] the translator of Cornutus, that it pleased the heavenly Deity, by Hesiod and Homer, under the veil of fables, to give us all knowledge, logic, rhetoric, philosophy, natural and moral, and *Quid non?;* to believe, with me, that there are many mysteries contained in poetry, which of purpose were written darkly, lest by profane wits it should be abused; to believe, with Landin,[116] that they are so beloved of the gods that whatsoever they write proceeds of a divine fury; lastly, to believe themselves, when they tell you they will make you immortal by their verses.

Thus doing, your name shall flourish in the printers' shops; thus doing, you shall be of kin to many a poetical preface; thus doing, you shall be most fair, most rich, most wise, most all; you shall dwell upon superlatives. Thus doing, though you be *libertino patre natus,*[117] you shall suddenly grow *Herculea proles,*[118]

Si quid mea carmina possunt.[119]

Thus doing, your soul shall be placed with Dante's Beatrix, or Virgil's Anchises. But if (fie of such a but) you be born so near the dull-making cataract of Nilus[120] that you cannot hear the planet-like music[121] of poetry, if you have so earth-creeping a mind that it cannot lift itself up to

---

115 *Clauserus:* Conrad Clauser (1520?–1611), German scholar. Sidney alludes to the preface of Clauser's Latin translation of a Greek treatise by Cornutus, who flourished in the reign of Nero.

116 *Landin:* Cristofero Landino (1424?–1504), Italian scholar, at one time tutor to Lorenzo de Medici.

117 *libertino patre natus:* "born of a freed slave father." Altered from Horace, *Satires,* I, vi, 45.

118 *Herculea proles:* "a descendant of Hercules."

119 *si . . . possunt:* "If my songs are of any avail," *Aeneid,* IX, 446.

120 *the dull-making cataract of Nilus:* Cicero (in *Somnium Scipionis*) mentions that people living near the cataracts of the Nile become deaf from the noise.

121 *planet-like music:* the music of the spheres.

look to the sky of poetry, or rather, by a certain rustical disdain, will become such a mome [122] as to be a Momus [123] of poetry; then, though I will not wish unto you the ass's ears of Midas,[124] nor to be driven by a poet's verses (as Bubonax [125] was) to hang himself, nor to be rhymed to death, as is said to be done in Ireland; [126] yet thus much curse I must send you, in the behalf of all poets, that while you live, you live in love, and never get favor for lacking skill of a sonnet, and, when you die, your memory die from the earth for want of an epitaph.

[122] *mome:* a stupid person.

[123] *Momus* in Greek mythology is the son of night; here Momus is the critical spirit.

[124] *ass's ears of Midas:* Midas, wealthy King of Phrygia, whose ears were changed into ass's ears, because he preferred Pan's playing to Apollo's. The story is told in Ovid, *Metamorphoses,* XI, 146–179.

[125] *Bubonax:* Schuckburgh thinks Bubonax is Sidney's confusion for Hipponax and Bupalus. Hipponax, a poet of Ephesus, about 500 B.C. satirized the statuary of Bupalus so bitterly that he hanged himself.

[126] *rhymed to death . . . Ireland:* Sidney here probably alludes to the belief that Irish bards had the power to cause death by their poetic incantations.

Edmund Spenser

1552–1599

EDMUND SPENSER, "the prince of poets in his time," exemplified to the Elizabethans what a poet should be. He was learned, musical, idealistic, serious and profoundly patriotic. Futhermore his genius was extensive and ample; he was preeminent in pastoral, satire, sonnet, complaint, and that kind of heroic poetry which some ages call romance and some call epic. He was, moreover, in Elizabethan eyes a philosophical poet of the first importance; it was no odd or eccentric view which Milton expressed when he referred to him as "our sage and serious poet Spenser, whom I dare be known to think a better teacher than Scotus or Aquinas." Even Ben Jonson, who could not abide Spenser's antique style, conceded that he should be read for his "matter."

Spenser was born, probably in 1552, in London, which he calls "mery London, my most kyndly Nurse." He was related, somehow, to the noble family of Spencer of Althorp, and several of his works are dedicated to lovely ladies of that house whom he could claim, however humbly and distantly, as cousins. He was entered at the Merchant Taylors' School as a "poor boy" under that school's first and most famous headmaster, Richard Mulcaster.

In 1569 he proceeded as a sizar or poor scholar to Pembroke Hall, Cambridge, and in that same year made his first appearance in print as the anonymous translator of twenty-two short poems in a crude volume of anti-Catholic propaganda by the Dutch Calvinist refugee Jan Van der Noot, called *A Theatre wherein be represented as wel the miseries and calamities that follow the voluptuous Worldlings, As also the greate ioyes and plesures which the faithfull do enioy*. At Cambridge he must have been interested in the sensationally popular new Puritan preacher, Thomas Cartwright, whose appeal to the young undergraduates was so great (and so dangerous, in official Anglican eyes) that he was silenced by the authorities in 1570.

Spenser's friendship with Gabriel Harvey may have begun about this time. It led, eventually, to the publication of *Three Proper and wittie familiar Letters* (1580), correspondence between the two, including, besides much academic jesting, a serious discussion of poetry, versification, and Spenser's literary plans. Spenser proceeded B.A. in 1573, M.A. in 1576. He then entered upon a series of positions in the retinues of eminent men, including Dr. John Young, Bishop of Rochester; Leicester, the Queen's favorite; and finally Lord Grey of Wilton, Lord Deputy of Ireland.

During his employment in Leicester's household Spenser came to know Sidney and Dyer, and to be affected by their interest in reforming English poetry. His own contribution to the new poetry was its chief monument, *The Shep-*

heardes Calender, published in 1579 and dedicated to Sidney, "to him that is the president Of noblesse and of chevalree."

In 1580 Spenser went to Ireland to serve Lord Grey; nine years later he was living in Kilcolman Castle, County Cork, where Sir Walter Ralegh visited him and took him to London to arrange for the publication of the first three books of *The Faerie Queene.* The first half of Spenser's romantic epic appeared in 1590; the next year saw the publication of his *Complaints,* a volume which included *The Tears of the Muses,* a lament for poetry, and *Mother Hubberds Tale,* a satire. His autobiographical pastoral, *Colin Clouts Come Home Againe* (1595) is a sequel to some of the eclogues in *The Shepheardes Calender* and gives Spenser's views of the court and of his fellow poets. His sonnet cycle *Amoretti,* the two marriage poems *Epithalamion* and *Prothalamion,* and his *Fowre Hymnes* all embody Spenser's Christian-Platonic philosophy of love and beauty.

Spenser returned to London in the winter of 1595–96 to arrange for the reprinting of the first three books of *The Faerie Queene* and the publication of the second three books. He returned to an Ireland soon to be ravaged by the violence of Tyrone's rebellion; Spenser's own Castle Kilcolman was destroyed and the poet found refuge in Cork. Late in 1598 Spenser was sent to England with messages from the besieged garrison in Ireland, and on January 13, 1599, he died in Westminster, a poor and no doubt discouraged man, though modern scholarship discounts Ben Jonson's story that he died "for lack of bread in King Street."

The two cantos and two stanzas on Mutability were apparently designed for some unfinished book of *The Faerie Queene.* (According to his prefatory epistle to Sir Walter Ralegh, twelve books were planned, one for each of the so-called Aristotelian virtues, but of these only six were completed.) The Mutability cantos were not really representative of the narrative, allegorical, and descriptive qualities of *The Faerie Queene;* but they form a self-contained whole in relatively small compass, and their intrinsic interest is so great that they deserve attention.

Spenser's poetry, unlike Shakespeare's, is always reprinted in Elizabethan spelling. The reasons are that Spenser was writing a deliberately quaint and antique language, and that he used many stylistic tricks, such as eye-rhymes and spelling puns, which would be obliterated by modernization.

BIBLIOGRAPHY: *The Works of Edmund Spenser: A Variorum Edition,* edited by Edwin Greenlaw, C. G. Osgood, F. M. Padelford and Ray Heffner, 10 vols., Baltimore, 1932–1949; F. I. Carpenter, *A Reference Guide to Edmund Spenser,* Chicago, 1923; Dorothy Atkinson, *Edmund Spenser, A Bibliographical Supplement,* Baltimore, 1937; H. S. V. Jones, *A Spenser Handbook,* New York, 1930; W. L. Renwick, *Edmund Spenser, An Essay on Renaissance Poetry,* London, 1925; B. E. C. Davis, *Edmund Spenser, A Critical Study,* Cambridge, 1933; C. S. Lewis, *The Allegory of Love,* Oxford, 1936; *English Literature in the Sixteenth Century,* Oxford, 1954; J. W. Bennett, *The Evolution of 'The Faerie Queene,'* Chicago, 1942; L. Bradner, *Edmund Spenser and 'The Faerie Queene,'* Chicago, 1948; Hallett Smith, *Elizabethan Poetry,* Harvard, 1952; W. R. Mueller and D. C. Allen, eds., *That Soveraine Light,* Baltimore, 1952.

THE SHEPHEARDES CALENDER

Aprill.[1]

Ægloga Quarta.[2]

ARGVMENT.

THis Æglogue is purposely intended to the honor and prayse of our most gracious soueraigne, Queene Elizabeth. The speakers herein be Hobbinoll and Thenott, two shepheardes: the which Hobbinoll being before mentioned, greatly to haue loued Colin, is here set forth more largely, complayning him of that boyes great misaduenture in Loue, whereby his mynd was alienate and with drawen not onely from him, who moste loued him, but also from all former delightes and studies, aswell in pleasaunt pyping, as conning ryming and singing, and other his laudable exercises. Whereby he taketh occasion, for proofe of his more excellencie and skill in poetrie, to recorde a songe, which the sayd Colin sometime made in honor of her Maiestie, whom abruptely he termeth Elysa.

---

[1] *Aprill:* The date of the eclogue is 1578, when Spenser (Colin, "the Southerne shepheardes boye") was secretary to the Bishop of Rochester. Eliza is Elizabeth; Hobbinoll may be Gabriel Harvey (see below, p. 414). No positive identification of Rosalind has been made.

[2] For each eclogue a gloss was provided. As a sample, the gloss of the August eclogue is printed. (See pp. 324–325.)

THENOT. HOBBINOLL.

TEll me good Hobbinoll, what garres thee greete?[3]
What? hath some Wolfe thy tender Lambes ytorne?
Or is thy Bagpype broke, that soundes so sweete?
Or art thou of thy loued lasse forlorne?

Or bene thine eyes attempred to the yeare,
Quenching the gasping furrowes thirst with rayne?
Like April shoure, so stremes the trickling teares
Adowne thy cheeke, to quenche thy thristye payne.

HOBBINOLL.

Nor thys, nor that, so muche doeth make me mourne,
But for the ladde, whome long I lovd so deare,
Nowe loues a lasse, that all his loue doth scorne:
He plongd in payne, his tressed locks dooth teare.

Shepheards delights he dooth them all forsweare,
Hys pleasaunt Pipe, whych made vs meriment,
He wylfully hath broke, and doth forbeare
His wonted songs, wherein he all outwent.

THENOT.

What is he for a Ladde, you so lament?
Ys loue such pinching payne to them, that proue?[4]
And hath he skill to make[5] so excellent,
Yet hath so little skill to brydle loue?

HOBBINOLL.

Colin thou kenst, the Southerne shepheardes boye:
Him Loue hath wounded with a deadly darte.
Whilome[6] on him was all my care and ioye,
Forcing with gyfts to winne his wanton heart.

But now from me hys madding mynd is starte,
And woes the Widdowes daughter of the glenne:
So nowe fayre *Rosalind* hath bredde hys smart,
So now his frend is chaunged for a frenne.[7]

---

[3] *garres thee greete:* makes you weep.
[4] *proue:* experience.
[5] *make:* write verse.
[6] *Whilome:* once.
[7] *frenne:* stranger.

THENOT.

But if hys ditties bene so trimly dight,[8]
I pray thee *Hobbinoll,* recorde some one:
The whiles our flockes doe graze about in sight,
And we close shrowded in thys shade alone.

HOBBINOLL.

Contented I: then will I singe his laye
Of fayre *Eliza,* Queene of shepheardes all:
Which once he made, as by a spring he laye,
And tuned it vnto the Waters fall.

YE dayntye Nymphs, that in this blessed Brooke
doe bathe your brest,
Forsake your watry bowres, and hether looke,
at my request:
And eke you Virgins,[9] that on *Parnasse* dwell,
Whence floweth *Helicon* the learned well,
Helpe me to blaze
Her worthy praise,
Which in her sexe doth all excell.

Of fayre *Elisa* be your siluer song,
that blessed wight:
The flowre of Virgins, may shee florish long,
In princely plight.
For shee is *Syrinx* [10] daughter without spotte,
Which *Pan* [11] the shepheards God of her begot:
So sprong her grace
Of heauenly race,
No mortall blemishe may her blotte.

See, where she sits vpon the grassie greene,
(O seemely sight)
Yclad in Scarlot like a mayden Queene,
And Ermines white.
Vpon her head a Cremosin [12] coronet,
With Damaske roses and Daffadillies set:
Bayleaues betweene,
And Primroses greene
Embellish the sweete Violet.

8 *dight:* adorned.
9 *Virgins:* Muses.
10 *Syrinx:* Anne Boleyn.
11 *Pan:* Henry VIII.
12 *Cremosin:* crimson.

Tell me, haue ye seene her angelick face,
    Like *Phœbe* fayre?
Her heauenly haueour, her princely grace
    can you well compare?
The Redde rose medled with the White yfere,[13]
In either cheeke depeincten liuely chere.
    Her modest eye,
    Her Maiestie,
Where haue you seene the like, but there?

I sawe *Phœbus* thrust out his golden hedde,
    vpon her to gaze:
But when he sawe, how broade her beames did spredde,
    it did him amaze.
He blusht to see another Sunne belowe,
Ne durst againe his fyrye face out showe:
    Let him, if he dare,
    His brightnesse compare
With hers, to haue the ouerthrowe.

Shewe thy selfe *Cynthia* with thy siluer rayes,
    and be not abasht:
When shee the beames of her beauty displayes,
    O how art thou dasht?
But I will not match her with *Latonaes* seede,[14]
Such follie great sorow to *Niobe* did breede.
    Now she is a stone,
    And makes dayly mone,
Warning all other to take heede.

Pan may be proud, that euer he begot
    such a Bellibone,[15]
And *Syrinx* reioyse, that euer was her lot
    to beare such an one.
Soone as my younglings cryen for the dam,
To her will I offer a milkwhite Lamb:
    Shee is my goddesse plaine,
    And I her shepherds swayne,
Albee forswonck and forswatt [16] I am.

---

[13] *medled:* mingled; *yfere:* together; *Redde . . . White:* the houses of Lancaster and York.

[14] *Latonaes seede:* Apollo and Diana. Niobe boasted of her seven sons and seven daughters.

[15] *Bellibone:* The gloss is: "Homely spoken for a fayre mayde or Bonilasse."

[16] *forswonck and forswatt:* exhausted and sweaty from work.

I see *Calliope* speede her to the place,
    where my Goddesse shines:
And after her the other Muses trace,
    with their Violines.
Bene they not Bay braunches, which they doe beare,
All for *Elisa* in her hand to weare?
    So sweetely they play,
    And sing all the way,
That it a heauen is to heare.

Lo how finely the graces can it foote
    to the Instrument:
They dauncen deffly, and singen soote,[17]
    in their meriment.
Wants not a fourth grace, to make the daunce euen?
Let that rowme to my Lady be yeuen:
    She shalbe a grace,
    To fyll the fourth place,
And reigne with the rest in heauen.

And whither rennes this beuie of Ladies bright,
    raunged in a rowe?
They bene all Ladyes of the lake behight,[18]
    that vnto her goe.
Chloris, that is the chiefest Nymph of al,
Of Oliue braunches beares a Coronall:
    Oliues bene for peace,
    When wars doe surcease:
Such for a Princesse bene principall.

Ye shepheards daughters, that dwell on the greene,
    hye you there apace:
Let none come there, but that Virgins bene,
    to adorne her grace.
And when you come, whereas shee is in place,
See, that your rudenesse doe not you disgrace:
    Binde your fillets faste,
    And gird in your waste,
For more finesse, with a tawdrie lace.

Bring hether the Pincke and purple Cullambine,
    With Gelliflowres:
Bring Coronations, and Sops in wine,
    worne of Paramoures.

---

[17] *soote:* sweet.

[18] *behight:* called.

Strowe me the ground with Daffadowndillies,
And Cowslips, and Kingcups, and loued Lillies:
The pretie Pawnce,[19]
And the Cheuisaunce,
Shall match with the fayre flowre Delice.

Now ryse vp *Elisa,* decked as thou art,
in royall aray:
And now ye daintie Damsells may depart
echeone her way,
I feare, I haue troubled your troupes to longe:
Let dame *Eliza* thanke you for her song.
And if you come hether,
When Damsines I gether,
I will part them all you among.

THENOT.

And was thilk same song of *Colins* owne making?
Ah foolish boy, that is with loue yblent:[20]
Great pittie is, he be in such taking,
For naught caren, that bene so lewdly[21] bent.

HOBBINOL.

Sicker I hold him, for a greater fon,[22]
That loues the thing, he cannot purchase.[23]
But let vs homeward: for night draweth on,
And twincling starres the daylight hence chase.

Thenots Embleme.[24]

O quam te memorem virgo?

Hobbinols Embleme.[25]

O dea certe.

---

[19] *Pawnce:* pansy.
[20] *yblent:* blinded.
[21] *lewdly:* vulgarly.
[22] *Sicker:* surely; *fon:* fool.
[23] *purchase:* get.
[24] *Thenots Embleme:* "O whatever you're called maiden," *Aeneid,* I, 327.
[25] *Hobbinols Embleme:* "O goddess indeed," *Aeneid,* I, 328. The emblems, which together constitute a tribute to the Queen, are explained in the gloss.

August.

Ægloga octaua.

ARGVMENT.

IN this Æglogue is set forth a delectable controuersie, made in imitation of that in Theocritus: whereto also Virgile fashioned his third and seuenth Æglogue. They choose for vmpere of their strife, Cuddie a neatheards boye, who hauing ended their cause, reciteth also himselfe a proper song, whereof Colin he sayth was Authour.

WILLYE. PERIGOT. CVDDIE.

TEll me *Perigot,* what shalbe the game,
  Wherefore with myne thou dare thy musick matche?
Or bene thy Bagpypes renne farre out of frame?
Or hath the Crampe thy ioynts benomd with ache?

PERIGOT.

Ah *Willye,* when the hart is ill assayde,
How can Bagpipe, or ioynts be well apayd? [26]

WILLYE.

What the foule euill hath thee so bestadde?
Whilom thou was peregall to the best,
And wont to make the iolly shepeheards gladde
With pyping and dauncing, didst passe the rest.

---

[26] *apayd:* contented.

PERIGOT.

Ah *Willye* now I haue learnd a newe daunce:
My old musick mard by a newe mischaunce.

WILLYE.

Mischiefe mought to that newe mischaunce befall,
That so hath raft vs of our meriment.
But reede me, what payne doth thee so appall?
Or louest thou, or bene thy younglings miswent?

PERIGOT.

Loue hath misled both my younglings, and mee:
I pyne for payne, and they my payne to see.

WILLYE.

Perdie and wellawaye: ill may they thriue:
Neuer knewe I louers sheepe in good plight.
But and if in rymes with me thou dare striue,
Such fond fantsies shall soone be put to flight.

PERIGOT.

That shall I doe, though mochell worse I fared:
Neuer shall be sayde that *Perigot* was dared.

WILLYE.

Then loe *Perigot* the Pledge, which I plight:
A mazer ywrought of the Maple warre:[27]
Wherein is enchased many a fayre sight
Of Beres and Tygres, that maken fiers warre:
And ouer them spred a goodly wild vine,
Entrailed with a wanton Yuie twine.

Thereby is a Lambe in the Wolues iawes:
But see, how fast renneth the shepheard swayne,
To saue the innocent from the beastes pawes:
And here with his shepehooke hath him slayne.
Tell me, such a cup hast thou euer sene?
Well mought it beseme any haruest Queene.

PERIGOT.

Thereto will I pawne yonder spotted Lambe,
Of all my flocke there nis sike[28] another:
For I brought him vp without the Dambe.
But *Colin Clout* rafte me of his brother,

[27] *Maple warre:* a knot in maple wood. [28] *sike:* such.

That he purchast of me in the playne field:
Sore against my will was I forst to yield.

WILLYE.

Sicker make like account of his brother.
But who shall iudge the wager wonne or lost?

PERIGOT.

That shall yonder heardgrome, and none other,
Which ouer the pousse hetherward doth post.

WILLYE.

But for the Sunnebeame so sore doth vs beate,
Were not better, to shunne the scortching heate?

PERIGOT.

Well agreed *Willy:* then sitte thee downe swayne:
Sike a song neuer heardest thou, but *Colin* sing.

CVDDIE.

Gynne, when ye lyst, ye iolly shepheards twayne:
Sike a iudge, as *Cuddie,* were for a king.

Perigot. It fell vpon a holly eue,[29]
Willye. hey ho hollidaye,
Per. When holly fathers wont to shrieue:[30]
Wil. now gynneth this roundelay.
Per. Sitting vpon a hill so hye
Wil. hey ho the high hyll,
Per. The while my flocke did feede thereby,
Wil. the while the shepheard selfe did spill:[31]
Per. I saw the bouncing Bellibone,
Wil. hey ho Bonibell,
Per. Tripping ouer the dale alone,
Wil. she can trippe it very well:
Per. Well decked in a frocke of gray,
Wil. hey ho gray is greete,
Per. And in a Kirtle of greene saye,

---

[29] This roundelay (ll. 53–124) may have been written to an existing tune, "Heigh ho holiday." (See *RES,* IX [1933], 54–55.) It may also have been the model for Corydon's song in Thomas Lodge's *Rosalynde,* beginning "A blithe and bonny country lass."

[30] *shrieue:* shrive.

[31] *spill:* perish.

Wil. the greene is for maydens meete:
Per. A chapelet on her head she wore,
Wil. hey ho chapelet,
Per. Of sweete Violets therein was store,
Wil. she sweeter then the Violet.
Per. My sheepe did leaue theyr wonted foode,
Wil. hey ho seely [32] sheepe,
Per. And gazd on her, as they were wood,[33]
Wil. woode as he, that did them keepe.
Per. As the bonilasse passed bye,
Wil. hey ho bonilasse,
Per. She roude [34] at me with glauncing eye,
Wil. as cleare as the christall glasse:
Per. All as the Sunnye beame so bright,
Wil. hey ho the Sunne beame,
Per. Glaunceth from *Phœbus* face forthright,
Wil. so loue into thy hart did streame:
Per. Or as the thonder cleaues the cloudes,
Wil. hey ho the Thonder,
Per. Wherein the lightsome leuin shroudes,
Wil. so cleaues thy soule a sonder:
Per. Or as Dame *Cynthias* siluer raye
Wil. hey ho the Moonelight,
Per. Vpon the glyttering waue doth playe:
Wil. such play is a pitteous plight.
Per. The glaunce into my heart did glide,
Wil. hey ho the glyder,
Per. Therewith my soule was sharply gryde,
Wil. such woundes soone wexen wider.
Per. Hasting to raunch the arrow out,
Wil. hey ho Perigot.
Per. I left the head in my hart roote:
Wil. it was a desperate shot.
Per. There it ranckleth ay more and more,
Wil. hey ho the arrowe,
Per. Ne can I find salue for my sore:
Wil. loue is a curelesse sorrowe.
Per. And though my bale with death I bought,
Wil. hey ho heauie cheere,
Per. Yet should thilk lasse not from my thought:
Wil. so you may buye gold to deare.
Per. But whether in paynefull loue I pyne,
Wil. hey ho pinching payne,

[32] *seely:* unfortunate.
[33] *wood:* mad.
[34] *roude:* looked; rove means "to shoot an arrow." See line 97.

Per. Or thriue in welth, she shalbe mine.
Wil. but if thou can her obteine.
Per. And if for gracelesse greefe I dye,
Wil. hey ho gracelesse griefe,
Per. Witnesse, shee slewe me with her eye:
Wil. let thy follye be the priefe.
Per. And you, that sawe it, simple shepe,
Wil. hey ho the fayre flocke,
Per. For priefe thereof, my death shall weepe,
Wil. and mone with many a mocke.
Per. So learnd I loue on a hollye eue,
Wil. hey ho holidaye,
Per. That euer since my hart did greue.
Wil. now endeth our roundelay.

CVDDYE.

Sicker sike a roundle neuer heard I none.
Little lacketh *Perigot* of the best.
And *Willye* is not greatly ouergone,
So weren his vndersongs well addrest.

WILLYE.

Herdgrome, I feare me, thou haue a squint eye:
Areede vprightly, who has the victorye?

CVDDIE.

Fayth of my soule, I deeme ech haue gayned.
For thy let the Lambe be *Willye* his owne:
And for *Perigot* so well hath hym payned,
To him be the wroughten mazer alone.

PERIGOT.

Perigot is well pleased with the doome:
Ne can *Willye* wite the witelesse herdgroome.

WILLYE.

Neuer dempt more right of beautye I weene,
The shepheard of *Ida,* that iudged beauties Queene.

CVDDIE.

But tell me shepherds, should it not yshend
Your roundels fresh, to heare a doolefull verse
Of Rosalend (who knowes not Rosalend?)
That Colin made, ylke can I you rehearse.

PERIGOT.

Now say it *Cuddie,* as thou art a ladde:
With mery thing its good to medle sadde.

WILLY.

Fayth of my soule, thou shalt ycrouned be
In *Colins* stede, if thou this song areede:
For neuer thing on earth so pleaseth me,
As him to heare, or matter of his deede.[35]

CVDDIE.

Then listneth ech vnto my heauy laye,
And tune your pypes as ruthful, as ye may.

YE wastefull woodes beare witnesse of my woe,
Wherein my plaints did oftentimes resound:
Ye carelesse byrds are priuie to my cryes,
  Which in your songs were wont to make a part:
  Thou pleasaunt spring hast luld me oft a sleepe,
  Whose streames my tricklinge teares did ofte augment.
Resort of people doth my greefs augment,
  The walled townes do worke my greater woe:
  The forest wide is fitter to resound
  The hollow Echo of my carefull cryes,
  I hate the house, since thence my loue did part,
  Whose waylefull want debarres myne eyes from sleepe.
Let stremes of teares supply the place of sleepe:
  Let all that sweete is, voyd: and all that may augment
  My doole, drawe neare. More meete to wayle my woe,
  Bene the wild woddes my sorrowes to resound,
  Then bedde, or bowre, both which I fill with cryes,
  When I them see so waist, and fynd no part
Of pleasure past. Here will I dwell apart
  In gastfull[36] groue therefore, till my last sleepe
  Doe close mine eyes: so shall I not augment
  With sight of such a chaunge my restlesse woe:
  Helpe me, ye banefull byrds, whose shrieking sound
  Ys signe of dreery death, my deadly cryes
Most ruthfully to tune. And as my cryes
  (Which of my woe cannot bewray least part)
  You heare all night, when nature craueth sleepe,
  Increase, so let your yrksome yells augment.
  Thus all the night in plaints, the daye in woe

[35] *matter . . . deede:* verse of his making. [36] *gastfull:* fearful.

I vowed haue to wayst, till safe and sound
She home returne, whose voyces siluer sound
To cheerefull songs can chaunge my cherelesse cryes.
Hence with the Nightingale will I take part,
That blessed byrd, that spends her time of sleepe
In songs and plaintiue pleas, the more taugment
The memory of hys misdeede, that bred her woe:
And you that feele no woe, | when as the sound
Of these my nightly cryes | ye heare apart,
Let breake your sounder sleepe | and pitie augment.

PERIGOT.

O *Colin, Colin,* the shepheards ioye,
How I admire ech turning of thy verse:
And *Cuddie,* fresh *Cuddie* the liefest boye,
How dolefully his doole thou didst rehearse.

CUDDIE.

Then blowe your pypes shepheards, til you be at home:
The night nigheth fast, yts time to be gone.

Perigot his Embleme.[37]
Vincenti gloria victi.

Willyes Embleme.[38]
Vinto non vitto.

Cuddies Embleme.[39]
Felice chi può.

GLOSSE.

Bestadde) disposed, ordered.
Peregall) equall.
Whilome) once.
Rafte) bereft, depriued.
Miswent) gon a straye.
Ill may) according to Virgile.
Infelix o semper ouis pecus.
A mazer) So also do Theocritus and Virgile feigne pledges of their strife.
Enchased) engrauen. Such pretie descriptions euery where vseth Theocritus, to bring in his Idyllia. For which speciall cause indede he by that name termeth his Æglogues: for Idyllion in Greke signifieth the shape or picture of any thyng, wherof his booke is ful. And not, as I haue heard some fondly guesse, that they be called not Idyllia, but Hædilia, of the Goteheards in them.
Entrailed) wrought betwene.
Haruest Queene) The manner of country folke in haruest tyme.
Pousse.) Pease.
It fell vpon) Perigot maketh hys song in prayse of his loue, to whom Willy answer-

[37] *Perigot his Embleme:* "To the conqueror goes the right to glory over the conquered."

[38] *Willyes Embleme:* "Vanquished, not subdued."

[39] *Cuddies Embleme:* "He is happy who can."

eth euery vnder verse. By Perigot who is meant, I can not vprightly say: but if it be, who is supposed, his love deserueth no lesse prayse, then he giueth her.

Greete) weeping and complaint.

Chaplet) a kind of Garlond lyke a crowne.

Leuen) Lightning.

Cynthia) was sayd to be the Moone.

Gryde) perced.

But if) not vnlesse.

Squint eye) partiall iudgement.

Ech haue) so saith Virgile.

Et vitula tu dignus, et hic &c.

So by enterchaunge of gyfts Cuddie pleaseth both partes.

Doome) iudgement.

Dempt) for deemed, iudged.

Wite the witelesse) blame the blamelesse.

The shepherd of Ida) was sayd to be Paris.

Beauties Queene) Venus, to whome Paris adiudged the golden Apple, as the pryce of her beautie.

Embleme.

The meaning hereof is very ambiguous: for Perigot by his poesie claming the conquest, and Willye not yeelding, Cuddie the arbiter of theyr cause, and Patron of his own, semeth to chalenge it, as his dew, saying, that he, is happy which can,—so abruptly ending; but hee meaneth eyther him, that can win the beste, or moderate him selfe being best, and leaue of with the best.

October.

Ægloga decima.

ARGVMENT.

IN Cuddie is set out the perfecte paterne of a Poete, whiche finding no maintenaunce of his state and studies, complayneth of the contempte of Poetrie, and the causes thereof: Specially hauing bene in all ages, and euen amongst the most barbarous alwayes of singular accounpt and honor, and being indede so worthy and commendable an arte: or rather no arte, but a diuine gift and heauenly instinct not to bee gotten by laboure and learning, but adorned with both: and poured into the witte by a certaine ἐνθουσιασμὸς and celestiall inspiration, as the Author hereof els where at large discourseth, in his booke called the English Poete,[40] *which booke being lately come to my hands, I mynde also by Gods grace vpon further aduisement to publish.*

PIERCE. CVDDIE.

Cvddie, for shame hold vp thy heauye head,
And let vs cast with what delight to chace,
And weary thys long lingring *Phœbus* race.
Whilome thou wont the shepheards laddes to leade,
In rymes, in ridles, and in bydding base:[41]
Now they in thee, and thou in sleepe art dead.

CVDDYE.

Piers, I haue pyped erst so long with payne,
That all mine Oten reedes bene rent and wore:
And my poore Muse hath spent her spared store,
Yet little good hath got, and much lesse gayne.
Such pleasaunce makes the Grashopper so poore,
And ligge so layd,[42] when Winter doth her straine:

The dapper ditties, that I wont deuise,
To feede youthes fancie, and the flocking fry,
Delighten much: what I the bett forthy?[43]
They han the pleasure, I a sclender prise.
I beate the bush, the byrds to them doe flye:
What good thereof to Cuddie can arise?

PIRES.

Cuddie, the prayse is better, then the price,
The glory eke much greater then the gayne:
O what an honor is it, to restraine
The lust of lawlesse youth with good aduice:
Or pricke them forth with pleasaunce of thy vaine,
Whereto thou list their trayned willes entice.

Soone as thou gynst to sette thy notes in frame,
O how the rurall routes to thee doe cleaue:
Seemeth thou dost their soule of sence bereaue,
All as the shepheard, that did fetch his dame

---

[40] *the English Poete:* a lost work of Spenser's.

[41] *bydding base:* prisoner's base.

[42] *ligge so layd:* Gloss reads: "lye so faynt and unlustye."

[43] *what I the bett forthy?:* what better am I for this reason?

From *Plutoes* balefull bowre withouten leaue:[44]
His musicks might the hellish hound did tame.

CVDDIE.

So praysen babes the Peacoks spotted traine,
And wondren at bright *Argus* blazing eye:[45]
But who rewards him ere the more forthy?
Or feedes him once the fuller by a graine?
Sike prayse is smoke, that sheddeth in the skye,
Sike words bene wynd, and wasten soone in vayne.

PIERS.

Abandon then the base and viler clowne,
Lyft vp thy selfe out of the lowly dust:
And sing of bloody Mars, of wars, of giusts,
Turne thee to those, that weld the awful crowne.
To doubted Knights, whose woundlesse armour rusts,
And helmes vnbruzed wexen dayly browne.

There may thy Muse display her fluttryng wing,
And stretch herselfe at large from East to West:[46]
Whither thou list in fayre *Elisa* rest,
Or if thee please in bigger notes to sing,
Aduaunce the worthy whome shee loueth best,
That first the white beare to the stake did bring.[47]

And when the stubborne stroke of stronger stounds,
Has somewhat slackt the tenor of thy string:
Of loue and lustihead tho mayst thou sing,
And carrol lowde, and leade the Myllers rownde,[48]
All were *Elisa*[49] one of thilke same ring.
So mought our *Cuddies* name to Heauen sownde.

CVDDYE.

Indeede the Romish *Tityrus,*[50] I heare,
Through his *Mecœnas* left his Oaten reede,

---

[44] *withouten leaue:* Orpheus and Eurydice.

[45] *Argus blazing eye:* Argus the herdsman, who guarded Io, loved by Zeus, had eyes all over his body at the request of jealous Hera. When Hermes killed Argus, he placed his eyes in the peacock's tail.

[46] *from East to West:* perhaps from the *Phaedrus* of Plato. Spenser liked this image of flight. Lines 44–45 may allude to Spenser's plans for *The Faerie Queene.*

[47] *That . . . bring:* Earl of Leicester, whose device was the bear and the ragged staff.

[48] *Myllers rownde:* an old dance.

[49] *all were Elisa:* though Elisa were.

[50] *Romish Tityrus:* Virgil, whose patrons were Augustus and Maecenas, his adviser.

Whereon he earst had taught his flocks to feede,
And laboured lands to yield the timely eare,
And eft did sing of warres and deadly drede,
So as the Heauens did quake his verse to here.

But ah *Mecœnas* is yclad in claye,
And great *Augustus* long ygoe is dead:
And all the worthies liggen wrapt in leade,
That matter made for Poets on to play:
For euer, who in derring doe [51] were dreade,
The loftie verse of hem was loued aye.

But after vertue gan for age to stoupe,
And mighty manhode brought a bedde of ease:
The vaunting Poets found nought worth a pease,
To put in preace [52] emong the learned troupe.
Tho gan the streames of flowing wittes to cease,
And sonnebright honour pend in shamefull coupe.[53]

And if that any buddes of Poesie,
Yet of the old stocke gan to shoote agayne:
Or it mens follies mote be forst to fayne,
And rolle with rest in rymes of rybaudrye:
Or as it sprong, it wither must agayne:
Tom Piper makes vs better melodie.

PIERS.

O pierlesse Poesye, where is then thy place?
If nor in Princes pallace thou doe sitt:
(And yet is Princes pallace the most fitt)
Ne brest of baser birth doth thee embrace.
Then make thee winges of thine aspyring wit,
And, whence thou camst, flye backe to heauen apace.

CVDDIE.

Ah *Percy* it is all to weake and wanne,
So high to sore, and make so large a flight:
Her peeced pyneons bene not so in plight,
For *Colin* fittes such famous flight to scanne:
He, were he not with loue so ill bedight,
Would mount as high, and sing as soote [54] as Swanne.

[51] *derring doe:* a pseudo-archaism, coined from a misunderstanding of a phrase in Chaucer and Lydgate, means "daring deeds." See *N. E. D.* for its history.

[52] *To put in preace:* to exercise, put in practice; "preace" means "multitude," "crowd."

[53] *coupe:* prison.

[54] *soote:* sweet.

PIRES.

Ah fon,[55] for loue does teach him climbe so hie,
And lyftes him vp out of the loathsome myre:
Such immortall mirrhor, as he doth admire,
Would rayse ones mynd aboue the starry skie.
And cause a caytiue [56] corage to aspire,
For lofty loue doth loath a lowly eye.

CVDDIE.

All otherwise the state of Poet stands,
For lordly loue is such a Tyranne fell:
That where he rules, all power he doth expell.
The vaunted verse a vacant head demaundes,
Ne wont with crabbed care the Muses dwell.
Vnwisely weaues, that takes two webbes in hand.

Who euer casts to compasse weightye prise,
And thinks to throwe out thondring words of threate:
Let powre in lauish cups and thriftie bitts of meate,
For *Bacchus* fruite is frend to *Phœbus* wise.
And when with Wine the braine begins to sweate,
The nombers flowe as fast as spring doth ryse.

Thou kenst not *Percie* howe the ryme should rage.
O if my temples were distaind with wine,
And girt in girlonds of wild Yuie twine,
How I could reare the Muse on stately stage,
And teache her tread aloft in bus-kin [57] fine,
With queint *Bellona* [58] in her equipage.

But ah my corage cooles ere it be warme,
For thy, content vs in thys humble shade:
Where no such troublous tydes han vs assayde,
Here we our slender pipes may safely charme.[59]

PIRES.

And when my Gates shall han their bellies layd: [60]
Cuddie shall haue a Kidde to store his farme.

Cuddies Embleme.[61]
Agitante calescimus illo &c.

---

[55] *fon:* fool.
[56] *caytiue:* wretched, base.
[57] *bus-kin:* the high thick-soled boot worn by actors in ancient Greek tragedy.
[58] *queint:* strange; *Bellona:* goddess of war.
[59] *charme:* play.
[60] *Gates:* northern form for "goats"; *bellies layd:* be delivered of their young.
[61] *Cuddies Embleme:* From Ovid, *Fasti*, VI, 5. Lines 5–6 translated are, "There is a god within us. It is when he stirs us that our bosom warms. It is his impulse that sows the seeds of inspiration."

FROM

AMORETTI[62]

SONNET. I.[63]

HAPPY ye leaues when as those lilly hands,
Which hold my life in their dead doing might,
Shall handle you and hold in loues soft bands,
Lyke captiues trembling at the victors sight.
And happy lines, on which with starry light,
Those lamping eyes will deigne sometimes to look
And reade the sorrowes of my dying spright,
Written with teares in harts close bleeding book.
And happy rymes bath'd in the sacred brooke,
Of *Helicon* whence she deriued is,
When ye behold that Angels blessed looke,
My soules long lacked foode, my heauens blis.
Leaues, lines, and rymes, seeke her to please alone,
Whom if ye please, I care for other none.

SONNET. IIII.[64]

NEW yeare forth looking out of Ianus gate,
Doth seeme to promise hope of new delight:
And bidding th'old Adieu, his passed date
Bids all old thoughts to die in dumpish spright.
And calling forth out of sad Winters night,
Fresh loue, that long hath slept in cheerlesse bower:
Wils him awake, and soone about him dight
His wanton wings and darts of deadly power.
For lusty spring now in his timely howre,
Is ready to come forth him to receiue:
And warnes the Earth with diuers colord flowre,
To decke hir selfe, and her faire mantle weaue.
Then you faire flowre, in whom fresh youth doth raine,
Prepare your selfe new loue to entertaine.

---

62 The *Amoretti* was published with the *Epithalamion* in 1595. Spenser does not follow the usual Petrarchan form, but the Elizabethan form of three quatrains and a couplet with the original Spenserian touch of linking the quatrains by a common rhyme (ab ab bc bc cd cd ee).

63 This sonnet may have been written for a presentation copy of *The Faerie Queene.* The "lilly hands" may be Lady Carey's.

64 Echoes Du Bellay and Tasso.

SONNET. XV.[65]

Ye tradefull Merchants, that with weary toyle,
Do seeke most pretious things to make your gain;
And both the Indias of their treasures spoile,
What needeth you to seeke so farre in vaine?
For loe my loue doth in her selfe containe
All this worlds riches that may farre be found,
If Saphyres, loe her eies be Saphyres plaine,
If Rubies, loe hir lips be Rubies sound:
If Pearles, hir teeth be pearles both pure and round;
If Yuorie, her forhead yuory weene;
If Gold, her locks are finest gold on ground;
If siluer, her faire hands are siluer sheene.
But that which fairest is, but few behold,
Her mind adornd with vertues manifold.

SONNET. XVI.

One day as I vnwarily did gaze
On those fayre eyes my loues immortall light:
The whiles my stonisht hart stood in amaze,
Through sweet illusion of her lookes delight.
I mote perceiue how in her glauncing sight,
Legions of loues with little wings did fly:
Darting their deadly arrowes fyry bright,
At euery rash beholder passing by.
One of those archers closely I did spy,
Ayming his arrow at my very hart:
When suddenly with twincle of her eye,
The Damzell broke his misintended dart.
Had she not so doon, sure I had bene slayne,
Yet as it was, I hardly scap't with paine.

[65] In the manner of Desportes. *Diane*, I, xxxii. See note to *Epithalamion*, ll. 167–183, below.

SONNET. XIX.

THE merry Cuckow, messenger of Spring,
His trompet shrill hath thrise already sounded:
That warnes al louers wayt vpon their king,
Who now is comming forth with girland crouned.
With noyse whereof the quyre of Byrds resounded
Their anthemes sweet devized of loues prayse,
That all the woods theyr ecchoes back rebounded,
As if they knew the meaning of their layes.
But mongst them all, which did Loues honor rayse
No word was heard of her that most it ought,
But she his precept proudly disobayes,
And doth his ydle message set at nought.
Therefore O loue, vnlesse she turne to thee
Ere Cuckow end, let her a rebell be.

SONNET. XXII.[66]

THIS holy season fit to fast and pray,
Men to deuotion ought to be inclynd:
Therefore, I lykewise on so holy day,
For my sweet Saynt some seruice fit will find.
Her temple fayre is built within my mind,
In which her glorious ymage placed is,
On which my thoughts doo day and night attend
Lyke sacred priests that neuer thinke amisse.
There I to her as th'author of my blisse,
Will builde an altar to appease her yre:
And on the same my hart will sacrifise,
Burning in flames of pure and chast desyre:
The which vouchsafe O goddesse to accept,
Amongst thy deerest relicks to be kept.

[66] Reminiscent of Tasso and Desportes. The "holy season" was probably not Lent but a saint's day.

SONNET. XXIII.

PENELOPE for her *Vlisses* sake,
Deuiz'd a Web her wooers to deceaue:
In which the worke that she all day did make
The same at night she did againe vnreaue.
Such subtile craft my Damzell doth conceaue,
Th'importune suit of my desire to shonne:
For all that I in many dayes doo weaue,
In one short houre I find by her vndonne.
So when I thinke to end that I begonne,
I must begin and neuer bring to end:
For with one looke she spils that long I sponne,
And with one word my whole yeares work doth rend.
Such labour like the Spyders web I fynd,
Whose fruitlesse worke is broken with least wynd.

SONNET. XXVI.

SWEET is the Rose, but growes vpon a brere;
Sweet is the Iunipere, but sharpe his bough;
Sweet is the Eglantine, but pricketh nere;
Sweet is the firbloome, but his braunches rough.
Sweet is the Cypresse, but his rynd is tough,
Sweet is the nut, but bitter is his pill;
Sweet is the broome-flowre, but yet sowre enough;
And sweet is Moly,[67] but his root is ill.
So euery sweet with soure is tempred still,
That maketh it be coueted the more:
For easie things that may be got at will,
Most sorts of men doe set but little store.
Why then should I accoumpt of [68] little paine,
That endlesse pleasure shall vnto me gaine.

---

[67] *Moly:* Hermes gave Odysseus the herb moly, to counteract the spells of Circe. It is said to have a white flower but a black root.

[68] *accoumpt of:* take into account.

SONNET. XXXIII.[69]

Great wrong I doe, I can it not deny,
To that most sacred Empresse my dear dred,
Not finishing her Queene of faëry,
That mote enlarge her liuing prayses dead:
But lodwick, this of grace to me aread:
Doe ye not thinck th'accomplishment of it,
Sufficient worke for one mans simple head,
All were it as the rest but rudely writ.
How then should I without another wit,
Thinck euer to endure so tædious toyle,
Sins that this one is tost with troublous fit,
Of a proud loue, that doth my spirite spoyle.
Ceasse then, till she vouchsafe to grawnt me rest,
Or lend you me another liuing brest.

SONNET. XXXIIII.

Lyke as a ship that through the Ocean wyde,
By conduct of some star doth make her way,
Whenas a storme hath dimd her trusty guyde,
Out of her course doth wander far astray.
So I whose star, that wont with her bright ray,
Me to direct, with cloudes is ouercast,
Doe wander now in darknesse and dismay,
Through hidden perils round about me plast.
Yet hope I well, that when this storme is past
My *Helice*[70] the lodestar of my lyfe
Will shine again, and looke on me at last,
With louely light to cleare my cloudy grief.
Till then I wander carefull comfortlesse,
In secret sorow and sad pensiuenesse.

[69] Addressed to Lodowick Bryskett (lodwick of line 5), Spenser's close friend in Dublin.

[70] *Helice:* the Great Bear. R. E. N. Dodge (Cambridge edition of Spenser) suggests Spenser may mean the Lesser Bear or Cynosure, in which the polestar is.

SONNET. XXXVII.

What guyle is this, that those her golden tresses,
She doth attyre vnder a net of gold:
And with sly[71] skill so cunningly them dresses,
That which is gold or heare, may scarse be told?
Is it that mens frayle eyes, which gaze too bold,
She may entangle in that golden snare:
And being caught may craftily enfold,
Theyr weaker harts, which are not wel aware?
Take heed therefore, myne eyes, how ye doe stare
Henceforth too rashly on that guilefull net,
In which if euer ye entrapped are,
Out of her bands ye by no meanes shall get.
Fondnesse it were for any being free,
To couet fetters, though they golden bee.

SONNET. LIIII.

Of this worlds Theatre in which we stay,
My loue lyke the Spectator ydly sits
Beholding me that all the pageants play,
Disguysing diuersly my troubled wits.
Sometimes I ioy when glad occasion fits,
And mask in myrth lyke to a Comedy:
Soone after when my ioy to sorrow flits,
I waile and make my woes a Tragedy.
Yet she beholding me with constant eye,
Delights not in my merth nor rues my smart:
But when I laugh she mocks, and when I cry
She laughes, and hardens euermore her hart.
What then can moue her? if nor merth nor mone,
She is no woman, but a sencelesse stone.

[71] *sly:* clever.

SONNET. LXVII.[72]

Lyke as a huntsman after weary chace,
Seeing the game from him escapt away,
Sits downe to rest him in some shady place,
With panting hounds beguiled of their pray:
So after long pursuit and vaine assay,
When I all weary had the chace forsooke,
The gentle deare returnd the selfe-same way,
Thinking to quench her thirst at the next brooke.
There she beholding me with mylder looke,
Sought not to fly, but fearelesse still did bide:
Till I in hand her yet halfe trembling tooke,
And with her owne goodwill hir fyrmely tyde.
Strange thing me seemd to see a beast so wyld,
So goodly wonne with her owne will beguyld.

SONNET. LXVIII.[73]

Most glorious Lord of lyfe, that on this day,
Didst make thy triumph ouer death and sin:
And hauing harrowd hell, didst bring away
Captiuity thence captiue vs to win:
This ioyous day, deare Lord, with ioy begin,
And grant that we for whom thou diddest dye
Being with thy deare blood clene washt from sin,
May liue for euer in felicity.
And that thy loue we weighing worthily,
May likewise loue thee for the same againe:
And for thy sake that all lyke deare didst buy,
With loue may one another entertayne.
So let vs loue, deare loue, lyke as we ought,
Loue is the lesson which the Lord vs taught.

---

[72] Like a sonnet of Tasso's.

[73] Like a sonnet of Desportes, but with Biblical echoes: Judges 5:12; Ephesians 4:8; 5:2; Revelation 1:5; John 15:12; I John 4:19.

SONNET. LXIX.

The famous warriors of the anticke world,
Vsed Trophees to erect in stately wize:
In which they would the records haue enrold,
Of theyr great deeds and valarous emprize.[74]
What trophee then shall I most fit deuize,
In which I may record the memory
Of my loues conquest, peerelesse beauties prise,
Adorn'd with honour, loue, and chastity.
Euen this verse vowd to eternity,
Shall be thereof immortall moniment:
And tell her prayse to all posterity,
That may admire such worlds rare wonderment.
The happy purchase of my glorious spoile,
Gotten at last with labour and long toyle.

SONNET. LXX.

Fresh spring the herald of loues mighty king,
In whose cote armour [75] richly are displayd
All sorts of flowers the which on earth do spring
In goodly colours gloriously arrayd.
Goe to my loue, where she is carelesse layd,
Yet in her winters bowre not well awake:
Tell her the ioyous time wil not be staid
Vnlesse she doe him by the forelock take.
Bid her therefore her selfe soone ready make,
To wayt on loue amongst his louely crew:
Where euery one that misseth then her make,
Shall be by him amearst [76] with penance dew.
Make hast therefore sweet loue, whilest it is prime,
For none can call againe the passed time.

[74] *emprize:* undertakings.
[75] *cote armour:* a herald's official garment.
[76] *amearst:* punished.

SONNET. LXXV.

ONE day I wrote her name vpon the strand,[77]
But came the waues and washed it away:
Agayne I wrote it with a second hand,
But came the tyde, and made my paynes his pray.
Vayne man, sayd she, that doest in vaine assay,
A mortall thing so to immortalize,
For I my selue shall lyke to this decay,
And eek my name bee wyped out lykewize.
Not so, (quod I) let baser things deuize
To dy in dust, but you shall liue by fame:
My verse your vertues rare shall eternize,
And in the heuens wryte your glorious name.
Where whenas death shall all the world subdew,
Our loue shall liue, and later life renew.

SONNET. LXXX.[78]

AFTER so long a race as I haue run
Through Faery land, which those six books compile,
Giue leaue to rest me being halfe fordonne,
And gather to my selfe new breath awhile.
Then as a steed refreshed after toyle,
Out of my prison I will breake anew:
And stoutly will that second worke assoyle,
With strong endeuour and attention dew.
Till then giue leaue to me in pleasant mew,[79]
To sport my muse and sing my loues sweet praise:
The contemplation of whose heauenly hew,
My spirit to an higher pitch will rayse.
But let her prayses yet be low and meane,
Fit for the handmayd of the Faery Queene.

77 *strand:* R. E. N. Dodge suggests the beach at Youghal.

78 Probably written in 1594 just before Spenser's marriage.

79 *in pleasant mew:* in pleasant hiding or confinement. "Mew" is originally a cage for hawks while they were "mewing" or moulting.

SONNET. LXXXV.

THE world that cannot deeme of worthy things,
When I doe praise her, say I doe but flatter:
So does the Cuckow, when the Mauis sings,
Begin his witlesse note apace to clatter.
But they that skill not of so heauenly matter,
All that they know not, enuy or admyre,
Rather then enuy let them wonder at her,
But not to deeme of her desert aspyre.
Deepe in the closet of my parts entyre,
Her worth is written with a golden quill:
That me with heauenly fury doth inspire,
And my glad mouth with her sweet prayses fill.
Which when as fame in her shrill trump shal thunder
Let the world chose to enuy or to wonder.

SONNET. LXXXVI.

VENEMOUS toung, tipt with vile adders sting,
Of that selfe kynd with which the Furies fell [80]
Theyr snaky heads doe combe, from which a spring
Of poysoned words and spitefull speeches well.
Let all the plagues and horrid paines of hell,
Vpon thee fall for thine accursed hyre:
That with false forged lyes, which thou didst tel,
In my true loue did stirre vp coles of yre,
The sparkes whereof let kindle thine own fyre,
And catching hold on thine owne wicked hed
Consume thee quite, that didst with guile conspire
In my sweet peace such breaches to haue bred.
Shame be thy meed, and mischiefe thy reward,
Dew to thy selfe that it for me prepard.

---

[80] *fell:* fierce, savage.

SONNET. LXXXVII.

Since I did leaue the presence of my loue,
Many long weary dayes I haue outworne:
And many nights, that slowly seemd to moue
Theyr sad protract from euening vntill morne.
For when as day the heauen doth adorne,
I wish that night the noyous [81] day would end:
And when as night hath vs of light forlorne,
I wish that day would shortly reascend.
Thus I the time with expectation spend,
And faine my griefe with chaunges to beguile,
That further seemes his terme still to extend,
And maketh euery minute seeme a myle.
So sorrow still doth seeme too long to last,
But ioyous houres doo fly away too fast.

EPITHALAMION

Ye learned sisters which haue oftentimes
Beene to me ayding, others to adorne:
Whom ye thought worthy of your gracefull rymes,
That euen the greatest did not greatly scorne
To heare theyr names sung in your simple layes,
But ioyed in theyr prayse.
And when ye list your owne mishaps to mourne,
Which death, or loue, or fortunes wreck did rayse,
Your string could soone to sadder tenor turne,
And teach the woods and waters to lament
Your dolefull dreriment.
Now lay those sorrowfull complaints aside,
And hauing all your heads with girland crownd,
Helpe me mine owne loues prayses to resound,
Ne let the same of any be enuide:
So Orpheus did for his owne bride,
So I vnto my selfe alone will sing,
The woods shall to me answer and my Eccho ring.

Early before the worlds light giuing lampe,
His golden beame vpon the hils doth spred,
Hauing disperst the nights vnchearefull dampe,

[81] *noyous:* troublesome.

Doe ye awake, and with fresh lustyhed[82]
Go to the bowre[83] of my beloued loue,
My truest turtle doue,
Bid her awake; for Hymen is awake,
And long since ready forth his maske to moue,
With his bright Tead that flames with many a flake,[84]
And many a bachelor to waite on him,
In theyr fresh garments trim.
Bid her awake therefore and soone her dight,
For lo the wished day is come at last,
That shall for al the paynes and sorrowes past,
Pay to her vsury of long delight:
And whylest she doth her dight,
Doe ye to her of ioy and solace sing,
That all the woods may answer and your eccho ring.

Bring with you all the Nymphes that you can heare
Both of the riuers and the forrests greene:
And of the sea that neighbours to her neare,
Al with gay girlands goodly wel beseene.
And let them also with them bring in hand,
Another gay girland
For my fayre loue of lillyes and of roses,
Bound trueloue wize with a blew silke riband.
And let them make great store of bridale poses,
And let them eeke bring store of other flowers
To deck the bridale bowers.
And let the ground whereas her foot shall tread,
For feare the stones her tender foot should wrong
Be strewed with fragrant flowers all along,
And diapred[85] lyke the discolored mead.
Which done, doe at her chamber dore awayt,
For she will waken strayt,
The whiles doe ye this song vnto her sing,
The woods shall to you answer and your Eccho ring.

Ye Nymphes of Mulla[86] which with carefull heed,
The siluer scaly trouts doe tend full well,
And greedy pikes which vse therein to feed,
(Those trouts and pikes all others doo excell)
And ye likewise which keepe the rushy lake,

[82] *lustyhed:* vigor, energy, activity.

[83] *bowre:* bedchamber.

[84] *Tead:* torch; *flake:* spark.

[85] *diapred:* variegated (with flowers). Diaper is an all-over surface ornamentation made of stonework or fabrics of small squares, usually with repeated conventional design.

[86] *Mulla:* the stream now called the Abweg, which brought water to Spenser's house in Ireland.

Where none doo fishes take,
Bynd vp the locks the which hang scatterd light,
And in his waters which your mirror make,
Behold your faces as the christall bright,
That when you come whereas my loue doth lie,
No blemish she may spie.
And eke ye lightfoot mayds which keepe the deere,
That on the hoary mountayne vse to towre,
And the wylde wolues which seeke them to deuoure,
With your steele darts doo chace from comming neer
Be also present heere,
To helpe to decke her and to help to sing,
That all the woods may answer and your eccho ring.

Wake, now my loue, awake; for it is time,
The Rosy Morne long since left Tithones bed,
All ready to her siluer coche to clyme,
And Phœbus gins to shew his glorious hed.
Hark how the cheerefull birds do chaunt theyr laies
And carroll of loues praise.
The merry Larke hir mattins sings aloft,
The thrush replyes, the Mauis descant [87] playes,
The Ouzell shrills, the Ruddock [88] warbles soft,
So goodly all agree with sweet consent,[89]
To this dayes merriment.
Ah my deere loue why doe ye sleepe thus long,
When meeter were that ye should now awake,
T'awayt the comming of your ioyous make,[90]
And hearken to the birds louelearned song,
The deawy leaues among.
For they of ioy and pleasance to you sing,
That all the woods them answer and theyr eccho ring.

My loue is now awake out of her dreame,
And her fayre eyes like stars that dimmed were
With darksome cloud, now shew theyr goodly beams
More bright then Hesperus his head doth rere.
Come now ye damzels, daughters of delight,
Helpe quickly her to dight,
But first come ye fayre houres which were begot
In Ioues sweet paradice, of Day and Night,
Which doe the seasons of the yeare allot,

[87] *Mauis:* thrush; *descant:* the counterpart sung extempore with plain song; here, as often, it means the top voice or melody.

[88] *Ouzell:* blackbird; *Ruddock:* redbreast.

[89] *agree:* are in accord; *consent:* harmony.

[90] *make:* mate.

And al that euer in this world is fayre
Doe make and still repayre.
And ye three handmayds of the Cyprian Queene,[91]
The which doe still adorne her beauties pride,
Helpe to addorne my beautifullest bride:
And as ye her array, still throw betweene
Some graces to be seene,
And as ye vse to Venus, to her sing,
The whiles the woods shal answer and your eccho ring.

Now is my loue all ready forth to come,
Let all the virgins therefore well awayt,
And ye fresh boyes that tend vpon her groome
Prepare your selues; for he is comming strayt.
Set all your things in seemely good aray
Fit for so ioyfull day,
The ioyfulst day that euer sunne did see.
Faire Sun, shew forth thy fauourable ray,
And let thy lifull heat not feruent be
For feare of burning her sunshyny face,
Her beauty to disgrace.
O fayrest Phœbus, father of the Muse,
If euer I did honour thee aright,
Or sing the thing, that mote thy mind delight,
Doe not thy seruants simple boone refuse,
But let this day let this one day be myne,
Let all the rest be thine.
Then I thy souerayne prayses loud wil sing,
That all the woods shal answer and theyr eccho ring.

Harke how the Minstrels gin to shrill aloud
Their merry Musick that resounds from far,
The pipe, the tabor, and the trembling Croud,[92]
That well agree withouten breach or iar.
But most of all the Damzels doe delite,
When they their tymbrels smyte,
And thereunto doe daunce and carrol sweet,
That all the sences they doe rauish quite,
The whyles the boyes run vp and downe the street,
Crying aloud with strong confused noyce,
As if it were one voyce.
Hymen io Hymen, Hymen they do shout,
That euen to the heauens theyr shouting shrill

[91] *handmayds of the Cyprian Queene:* Graces, attending Venus.

[92] *Croud:* The crwth or crowd was a primitive fiddle. Spenser in this stanza designates Irish, not classical instruments and music, for the classical masque or ballet.

Doth reach, and all the firmament doth fill,
To which the people standing all about,
As in approuance doe thereto applaud
And loud aduaunce her laud,
And euermore they Hymen Hymen sing,
That al the woods them answer and theyr eccho ring.

Loe where she comes along with portly[93] pace
Lyke Phœbe from her chamber of the East,
Arysing forth to run her mighty race,
Clad all in white, that seemes a virgin best.
So well it her beseemes that ye would weene
Some angell she had beene.
Her long loose yellow locks lyke golden wyre,
Sprinckled with perle, and perling flowres a tweene,
Doe lyke a golden mantle her attyre,
And being crowned with a girland greene,
Seeme lyke some mayden Queene.
Her modest eyes abashed to behold
So many gazers, as on her do stare,
Vpon the lowly ground affixed are.
Ne dare lift vp her countenance too bold,
But blush to heare her prayses sung so loud,
So farre from being proud.
Nathlesse doe ye still loud her prayses sing.
That all the woods may answer and your eccho ring.

Tell me ye merchants daughters did ye see
So fayre a creature in your towne before,
So sweet, so louely, and so mild as she,
Adornd with beautyes grace and vertues store,
Her goodly eyes lyke Saphyres shining bright,
Her forehead yuory white,
Her cheekes lyke apples which the sun hath rudded,
Her lips lyke cherryes charming men to byte,
Her brest like to a bowle of creame vncrudded,
Her paps lyke lyllies budded,
Her snowie necke lyke to a marble towre,
And all her body like a pallace fayre,
Ascending vppe with many a stately stayre,
To honors seat and chastities sweet bowre.
Why stand ye still ye virgins in amaze,
Vpon her so to gaze,

[93] *portly:* stately.

Whiles ye forget your former lay to sing,
To which the woods did answer and your eccho ring.[94]

Bvt if ye saw that which no eyes can see,
The inward beauty of her liuely spright,[95]
Garnisht with heauenly guifts of high degree,
Much more then would ye wonder at that sight,
And stand astonisht lyke to those which red [96]
Medusaes mazeful hed.[97]
There dwels sweet loue and constant chastity,
Vnspotted fayth and comely womanhood,
Regard of honour and mild modesty,
There vertue raynes as Queene in royal throne,
And giueth lawes alone.
The which the base affections doe obay,
And yeeld theyr seruices vnto her will,
Ne thought of thing vncomely euer may
Thereto approch to tempt her mind to ill.
Had ye once seene these her celestial threasures,
And vnreuealed pleasures,
Then would ye wonder and her prayses sing,
That al the woods should answer and your echo ring.[98]

Open the temple gates vnto my loue,
Open them wide that she may enter in,
And all the postes adorne as doth behoue,
And all the pillours deck with girlands trim,
For to recyue this Saynt with honour dew,
That commeth in to you.
With trembling steps and humble reuerence,
She commeth in, before th'almighties vew,
Of her ye virgins learne obedience,
When so ye come into those holy places,
To humble your proud faces:
Bring her vp to th'high altar, that she may
The sacred ceremonies there partake,
The which do endlesse matrimony make,
And let the roring Organs loudly play
The praises of the Lord in liuely notes,

[94] *Tell me . . . eccho ring:* Spenser describes the beauties of his lady as do Ronsard, Desportes, and the Italian sonneteers. See also *Amoretti* XV. The ultimate origin of these descriptive conventions may be the *Song of Solomon* 4–7.

[95] *spright:* soul.

[96] *red:* discern, in Spenser only.

[97] *Medusaes mazeful hed:* which turned them to stone.

[98] *Bvt if . . . echo ring:* The idea of inward beauty comes from Plato's *Parmenides* and *Phaedrus.* See Spenser's *Hymne,* pp. 351–354, below.

The whiles with hollow throates
The Choristers the ioyous Antheme sing,
That al the woods may answere and their eccho ring.

Behold whiles she before the altar stands
Hearing the holy priest that to her speakes
And blesseth her with his two happy hands,
How the red roses flush vp in her cheekes,
And the pure snow with goodly vermill stayne,
Like crimsin dyde in grayne,[99]
That euen th'Angels which continually,
About the sacred Altare doe remaine,
Forget their seruice and about her fly,
Ofte peeping in her face that seemes more fayre,
The more they on it stare.
But her sad eyes still fastened on the ground,
Are gouerned with goodly modesty,
That suffers not one looke to glaunce awry,
Which may let in a little thought vnsownd.
Why blush ye loue to giue to me your hand,
The pledge of all our band? [100]
Sing ye sweet Angels, Alleluya sing,
That all the woods may answere and your eccho ring.

Now al is done; bring home the bride againe,
Bring home the triumph of our victory,
Bring home with you the glory of her gaine,
With ioyance bring her and with iollity.
Neuer had man more ioyfull day then this,
Whom heauen would heape with blis.
Make feast therefore now all this liue long day,
This day for euer to me holy is,
Poure out the wine without restraint or stay,
Poure not by cups, but by the belly [101] full,
Poure out to all that wull,
And sprinkle all the postes and wals with wine,
That they may sweat, and drunken be withall.
Crowne ye God Bacchus with a coronall,[102]
And Hymen also crowne with wreathes of vine,
And let the Graces daunce vnto the rest;
For they can doo it best:
The whiles the maydens doe theyr carroll sing,
To which the woods shal answer and theyr eccho ring.

---

[99] *in grayne:* in durable red dye.

[100] *band:* bond or tie.

[101] *belly:* Perhaps Spenser here means bag or skin (OE *bælig*) for holding wines.

[102] *coronall:* garland of flowers.

Ring ye the bels, ye yong men of the towne,
And leaue your wonted labors for this day:
This day is holy; doe ye write it downe,
That ye for euer it remember may.
This day the sunne is in his chiefest hight,
With Barnaby [103] the bright,
From whence declining daily by degrees,
He somewhat loseth of his heat and light,
When once the Crab [104] behind his back he sees.
But for this time it ill ordained was,
To chose the longest day in all the yeare,
And shortest night, when longest fitter weare:
Yet neuer day so long, but late would passe.
Ring ye the bels, to make it weare away,
And bonefiers make all day,
And daunce about them, and about them sing:
That all the woods may answer, and your eccho ring.

Ah when will this long weary day haue end,
And lende me leaue to come vnto my loue?
How slowly do the houres theyr numbers spend?
How slowly does sad Time his feathers moue?
Hast thee O fayrest Planet to thy home
Within the Westerne fome:
Thy tyred steedes long since haue need of rest.
Long though it be, at last I see it gloome,
And the bright euening star with golden creast
Appeare out of the East.
Fayre childe of beauty, glorious lampe of loue
That all the host of heauen in rankes doost lead,
And guydest louers through the nightes dread,
How chearefully thou lookest from aboue,
And seemst to laugh atweene thy twinkling light
As ioying in the sight
Of these glad many which for ioy doe sing,
That all the woods them answer and their echo ring.

Now ceasse ye damsels your delights forepast;
Enough is it, that all the day was youres:
Now day is doen, and night is nighing fast:
Now bring the Bryde into the brydall boures.
Now night is come, now soone her disaray,

[103] *This day . . . Barnaby:* The summer solstice, old style, July 11, was also St. Barnabas's day.

[104] *the Crab:* the constellation Cancer between Gemini and Leo. The sun, passing through the zodiac, leaves the Crab behind toward the end of July.

And in her bed her lay;
Lay her in lillies and in violets,
And silken courteins ouer her display,
And odourd sheetes, and Arras couerlets.
Behold how goodly my faire loue does ly
In proud humility;
Like vnto Maia, when as Ioue her tooke,
In Tempe, lying on the flowry gras,
Twixt sleepe and wake, after she weary was,
With bathing in the Acidalian brooke.
Now it is night, ye damsels may be gon,
And leaue my loue alone,
And leaue likewise your former lay to sing:
The woods no more shal answere, nor your echo ring.

Now welcome night, thou night so long expected,
That long daies labour doest at last defray,
And all my cares, which cruell loue collected,
Hast sumd in one, and cancelled for aye:
Spread thy broad wing ouer my loue and me,
That no man may vs see,
And in thy sable mantle vs enwrap,
From feare of perrill and foule horror free.
Let no false treason seeke vs to entrap,
Nor any dread disquiet once annoy
The safety of our ioy:
But let the night be calme and quietsome,
Without tempestuous storms or sad afray:
Lyke as when Ioue with fayre Alcmena lay,
When he begot the great Tirynthian groome:[105]
Or lyke as when he with thy selfe[106] did lie,
And begot Maiesty.
And let the mayds and yongmen cease to sing:
Ne let the woods them answer, nor theyr eccho ring.

Let no lamenting cryes, nor dolefull teares,
Be heard all night within nor yet without:
Ne let false whispers, breeding hidden feares,
Breake gentle sleepe with misconceiued dout.
Let no deluding dreames, nor dreadful sights
Make sudden sad affrights;
Ne let housefyres, nor lightnings helpelesse harmes,
Ne let the Pouke,[107] nor other euill sprights,

[105] *Tirynthian groome:* Hercules.
[106] *thy selfe:* I.e., night.
[107] *Pouke:* Puck, Robin Goodfellow. He seems a more mischievous goblin than Shakespeare's Puck in *Midsummer Night's Dream.*

Ne let mischiuous witches with theyr charmes,
Ne let hob Goblins, names whose sence we see not,
Fray vs with things that be not.
Let not the shriech Oule, nor the Storke be heard:
Nor the night Rauen that still deadly yels,
Nor damned ghosts cald vp with mighty spels,
Nor griesly vultures make vs once affeard:
Ne let th'unpleasant Quyre of Frogs still croking
Make vs to wish theyr choking.
Let none of these theyr drery accents sing;
Ne let the woods them answer, nor theyr eccho ring.

Bvt let stil Silence trew night watches keepe,
That sacred peace may in assurance rayne,
And tymely sleep, when it is tyme to sleepe,
May poure his limbs forth on your pleasant playne,
The whiles an hundred little winged loues,
Like diuers fethered doues,
Shall fly and flutter round about your bed,
And in the secret darke, that none reproues,
Their prety stealthes shal worke, and snares shal spread
To filch away sweet snatches of delight,
Conceald through couert night.
Ye sonnes of Venus, play your sports at will,
For greedy pleasure, carelesse of your toyes,
Thinks more vpon her paradise of ioyes,
Then what ye do, albe it good or ill.
All night therefore attend your merry play,
For it will soone be day:
Now none doth hinder you, that say or sing,
Ne will the woods now answer, nor your Eccho ring.

Who is the same, which at my window peepes?
Or whose is that faire face, that shines so bright,
Is it not Cinthia, she that neuer sleepes,
But walkes about high heauen al the night?
O fayrest goddesse, do thou not enuy
My loue with me to spy:
For thou likewise didst loue, though now vnthought,
And for a fleece of woll, which priuily,
The Latmian shephard [108] once vnto thee brought,
His pleasures with thee wrought.
Therefore to vs be fauorable now;
And sith of wemens labours thou hast charge,

[108] *Latmian shephard:* Endymion.

And generation goodly dost enlarge,
Encline thy will t'effect our wishfull vow,
And the chast wombe informe with timely seed,
That may our comfort breed:
Till which we cease our hopefull hap to sing,
Ne let the woods vs answere, nor our Eccho ring.

And thou great Iuno, which with awful might
The lawes of wedlock still dost patronize,
And the religion of the faith first plight
With sacred rites hast taught to solemnize:
And eeke for comfort often called art
Of women in their smart,
Eternally bind thou this louely band,
And all thy blessings vnto vs impart.
And thou glad Genius, in whose gentle hand,
The bridale bowre and geniall bed remaine,
Without blemish or staine,
And the sweet pleasures of theyr loues delight
With secret ayde doest succour and supply,
Till they bring forth the fruitfull progeny,
Send vs the timely fruit of this same night.
And thou fayre Hebe,[109] and thou Hymen free,
Grant that it may so be.
Til which we cease your further prayse to sing,
Ne any woods shal answer, nor your Eccho ring.

And ye high heauens, the temple of the gods,
In which a thousand torches flaming bright
Doe burne, that to vs wretched earthly clods,
In dreadful darknesse lend desired light;
And all ye powers which in the same remayne,
More then we men can fayne,
Poure out your blessing on vs plentiously,
And happy influence vpon vs raine,
That we may raise a large posterity,
Which from the earth, which they may long possesse,
With lasting happinesse,
Vp to your haughty pallaces may mount,
And for the guerdon of theyr glorious merit
May heauenly tabernacles there inherit,
Of blessed Saints for to increase the count.
So let vs rest, sweet loue, in hope of this,
And cease till then our tymely ioyes to sing,
The woods no more vs answer, nor our eccho ring.

---

[109] *Hebe:* here as Youth.

Song made in lieu of many ornaments,
With which my loue should duly haue bene dect,
Which cutting off through hasty accidents,
Ye would not stay your dew time to expect,
But promist both to recompens,
Be vnto her a goodly ornament,
And for short time an endlesse moniment.

FROM

AN HYMNE IN HONOVR OF BEAVTIE.[110]

Ah whither, Loue, wilt thou now carrie mee?
What wontlesse fury dost thou now inspire
Into my feeble breast, too full of thee?
Whylest seeking to aslake thy raging fyre,
Thou in me kindlest much more great desyre,
And vp aloft aboue my strength doest rayse
The wondrous matter of my fyre to prayse.

That as I earst in praise of thine owne name,
So now in honour of thy Mother deare,
An honourable Hymne I eke should frame;
And with the brightnesse of her beautie cleare,
The rauisht harts of gazefull men might reare,
To admiration of that heauenly light,
From whence proceeds such soule enchaunting might.

Therto do thou great Goddesse, queene of Beauty,
Mother of loue, and of all worlds delight,
Without whose souerayne grace and kindly dewty,
Nothing on earth seemes fayre to fleshly sight,
Doe thou vouchsafe with thy loue-kindling light,
T'illuminate my dim and dulled eyne,
And beautifie this sacred hymne of thyne.

That both to thee, to whom I meane it most,
And eke to her, whose faire immortall beame,
Hath darted fyre into my feeble ghost,[111]
That now it wasted is with woes extreame,
It may so please that she at length will streame
Some deaw of grace, into my withered hart,
After long sorrow and consuming smart.

---

[110] Lines 1–140 are given.

[111] *ghost:* spirit, soul.

What time this worlds great workmaister did cast
To make al things, such as we now behold,
It seemes that he before his eyes had plast
A goodly Paterne,[112] to whose perfect mould
He fashiond them as comely as he could;
That now so faire and seemely they appeare,
As nought may be amended any wheare.

That wondrous Paterne wheresoere it bee,
Whether in earth layd vp in secret store,
Or else in heauen, that no man may it see
With sinfull eyes, for feare it to deflore,
Is perfect Beautie which all men adore,
Whose face and feature doth so much excell
All mortal sence, that none the same may tell.

Thereof as euery earthly thing partakes,
Or more or lesse by influence diuine,
So it more faire accordingly it makes,
And the grosse matter of this earthly myne,
Which clotheth it, thereafter doth refyne,
Doing away the drosse which dims the light
Of that faire beame, which therein is empight.

For through infusion of celestiall powre,
The duller earth it quickneth with delight,
And life-full spirits priuily doth powre
Through all the parts, that to the lookers sight
They seeme to please. That is thy soueraine might,
O *Cyprian* Queene,[113] which flowing from the beame
Of thy bright starre, thou into them doest streame.

That is the thing which giueth pleasant grace
To all things faire, that kindleth liuely fyre,
Light of thy lampe, which shyning in the face,
Thence to the soule darts amorous desyre,
And robs the harts of those which it admyre,
Therewith thou pointest thy Sons poysned arrow,
That wounds the life, and wastes the inmost marrow.

How vainely then doe ydle wits inuent,
That beautie is nought else, but mixture made
Of colours faire, and goodly temp'rament

[112] *A goodly Paterne:* in Platonic philosophy, the Idea of Perfection, of which the world or reality is an imperfect copy. Lines 29–35 derive from Plato's *Timaeus,* 28–29.

[113] *O Cyprian Queene:* Venus, whose favorite dwelling was in Cyprus.

Of pure complexions,[114] that shall quickly fade
And passe away, like to a sommers shade,
Or that it is but comely composition
Of parts well measurd, with meet disposition.

Hath white and red in it such wondrous powre,
That it can pierce through th'eyes vnto the hart,
And therein stirre such rage and restlesse stowre,
As nought but death can stint his dolours smart?
Or can proportion of the outward part,
Moue such affection in the inward mynd,
That it can rob both sense and reason blynd?

Why doe not then the blossomes of the field,
Which are arayd with much more orient hew,
And to the sense most daintie odours yield,
Worke like impression in the lookers vew?
Or why doe not faire pictures like powre shew,
In which oftimes, we Nature see of Art
Exceld, in perfect limming [115] euery part.

But ah, beleeue me, there is more then so
That workes such wonders in the minds of men.
I that have often prou'd, too well it know;
And who so list the like assayes to ken,[116]
Shall find by tryall, and confesse it then,
That Beautie is not, as fond men misdeeme,
An outward shew of things, that onely seeme.

For that same goodly hew of white and red,
With which the cheekes are sprinckled, shal decay,
And those sweete rosy leaues so fairely spred
Vpon the lips, shall fade and fall away
To that they were, euen to corrupted clay.
That golden wyre, those sparckling stars so bright
Shall turne to dust, and loose their goodly light.

But that faire lampe, from whose celestiall ray
That light proceedes, which kindleth louers fire,
Shall neuer be extinguisht nor decay,
But when the vitall spirits doe expyre,
Vnto her natiue planet shall retyre,
For it is heauenly borne and can not die,
Being a parcell of the purest skie.

---

[114] *goodly temp'rament of pure complexions:* perfect combination in the body of the four elements or "humors."

[115] *limming:* painting.

[116] *the like assayes to ken:* to make the same tests.

For when the soule, the which deriued was
At first, out of that great immortall Spright,
By whom all liue to loue, whilome [117] did pas
Downe from the top of purest heauens hight,
To be embodied here, it then tooke light
And liuely [118] spirits from that fayrest starre,
Which lights the world forth from his firie carre.

Which powre retayning still or more or lesse,
When she in fleshly seede is eft enraced,[119]
Through euery part she doth the same impresse,
According as the heauens haue her graced,
And frames her house, in which she will be placed,
Fit for her selfe, adorning it with spoyle
Of th'heauenly riches, which she robd erewhyle.

Therof it comes, that these faire soules, which haue
The most resemblance of that heauenly light,
Frame to themselues most beautifull and braue
Their fleshly bowre, most fit for their delight,
And the grosse matter by a soueraine might
Tempers so trim, that it may well be seene,
A pallace fit for such a virgin Queene.

So euery spirit, as it is most pure,
And hath in it the more of heauenly light,
So it the fairer bodie doth procure
To habit in, and it more fairely dight [120]
With chearefull grace and amiable sight.
For of the soule the bodie forme doth take:
For soule is forme, and doth the bodie make.

Therefore where euer that thou doest behold
A comely corpse,[121] with beautie faire endewed,
Know this for certaine, that the same doth hold
A beauteous soule, with faire conditions thewed,
Fit to receiue the seede of vertue strewed.
For all that faire is, is by nature good;
That is a signe to know the gentle blood.[122]

---

[117] *whilome:* once, formerly.

[118] *liuely:* living.

[119] *eft enraced:* again implanted.

[120] *dight:* adorn.

[121] *corpse:* living body.

[122] Most of the remainder of the *Hymne* is a plea to women who would know true love to be ever mindful of their inward spiritual beauty rather than the beauty of outward form. "Love," says Spenser, "is a celestial harmony" which binds together those whom Heaven has ordained.

Prothalamion

Or

A Spousall Verse made by
Edm. Spenser.

IN HONOVR OF THE DOV-
ble mariage of the two Honorable & vertuous
Ladies, the Ladie Elizabeth *and the Ladie* Katherine
Somerset, Daughters to the Right Honourable the
Earle of *Worcester* and espoused to the two
worthie Gentlemen M. *Henry Gilford,*
and M. *William Peter* Esquyers.

CALME was the day, and through the trembling ayre,
Sweete breathing *Zephyrus* did softly play
A gentle spirit, that lightly did delay
Hot *Titans* beames, which then did glyster fayre:
When I whom sullein care,
Through discontent of my long fruitlesse stay
In Princes Court, and expectation vayne
Of idle hopes, which still doe fly away,
Like empty shaddowes, did aflict my brayne,
Walkt forth to ease my payne
Along the shoare of siluer streaming *Themmes,*
Whose rutty [123] Bancke, the which his Riuer hemmes,
Was paynted all with variable [124] flowers,
And all the meades adornd with daintie gemmes,
Fit to decke maydens bowres,
And crowne their Paramours,
Against the Brydale day, which is not long:
  Sweete *Themmes* runne softly, till I end my Song.

There, in a Meadow, by the Riuers side,
A flocke of *Nymphes* I chaunced to espy,
All louely Daughters of the Flood thereby,
With goodly greenish locks all loose vntyde,
As each had bene a Bryde,
And each one had a little wicker basket,
Made of fine twigs entrayled curiously,
In which they gathered flowers to fill their flasket: [125]
And with fine Fingers, cropt full feateously [126]

[123] *rutty:* rooty.
[124] *variable:* various.
[125] *flasket:* a shallow flower-basket.
[126] *feateously:* neatly.

The tender stalkes on hye.
Of euery sort, which in that Meadow grew,
They gathered some; the Violet pallid blew,
The little Dazie, that at euening closes,
The virgin Lillie, and the Primrose trew,
With store of vermeil Roses,
To decke their Bridegromes posies,
Against the Brydale day, which was not long:
  Sweete *Themmes* runne softly, till I end my Song.

With that, I saw two Swannes [127] of goodly hewe,
Come softly swimming downe along the Lee;
Two fairer Birds I yet did neuer see:
The snow which doth the top of *Pindus* [128] strew,
Did neuer whiter shew,
Nor *Ioue* himselfe when he a Swan would be
For loue of *Leda,* whiter did appeare:
Yet *Leda* was they say as white as he,
Yet not so white as these, nor nothing neare;
So purely white they were,
That euen the gentle streame, the which them bare,
Seem'd foule to them, and bad his billowes spare
To wet their silken feathers, least they might
Soyle their fayre plumes with water not so fayre,
And marre their beauties bright,
That shone as heauens light,
Against their Brydale day, which was not long:
  Sweete *Themmes* runne softly, till I end my Song.

Eftsoones the *Nymphes,* which now had Flowers their fill,
Ran all in haste, to see that siluer brood,
As they came floating on the Christal Flood.
Whom when they sawe, they stood amazed still,
Their wondring eyes to fill,
Them seem'd they neuer saw a sight so fayre,
Of Fowles so louely, that they sure did deeme
Them heauenly borne, or to be that same payre
Which through the Skie draw *Venus* siluer Teeme,
For sure they did not seeme
To be begot of any earthly Seede,
But rather Angels or of Angels breede:
Yet were they bred of *Somers-heat* [129] they say,

[127] *two Swannes:* Elizabeth and Katherine Somerset, daughters of the Earl of Worcester (see title).

[128] *Pindus:* a lofty range of mountains in northern Greece.

[129] *Somers-heat:* a pun, not intended to be humorous, on "summer's heat," "Somerset."

In sweetest Season, when each Flower and weede
The earth did fresh aray,
So fresh they seem'd as day,
Euen as their Brydale day, which was not long:
  Sweete *Themmes* runne softly, till I end my Song.

Then forth they all out of their baskets drew,
Great store of Flowers, the honour of the field,
That to the sense did fragrant odours yeild,
All which vpon those goodly Birds they threw,
And all the Waues did strew,
That like old *Peneus* Waters [130] they did seeme,
When downe along by pleasant *Tempes* shore
Scattred with Flowres, through *Thessaly* they streeme,
That they appeare through Lillies plenteous store,
Like a Brydes Chamber flore:
Two of those *Nymphes,* meane while, two Garlands bound,
Of freshest Flowres which in that Mead they found,
The which presenting all in trim Array,
Their snowie Foreheads therewithall they crownd,
Whil'st one did sing this Lay,
Prepar'd against that Day,
Against their Brydale day, which was not long:
  Sweete *Themmes* runne softly, till I end my Song.

Ye gentle Birdes, the worlds faire ornament,
And heauens glorie, whom this happie hower
Doth leade vnto your louers blisfull bower,
Ioy may you haue and gentle hearts content
Of your loues couplement:
And let faire *Venus,* that is Queene of loue,
With her heart-quelling Sonne vpon you smile,
Whose smile they say, hath vertue to remoue
All Loues dislike, and friendships faultie guile
For euer to assoile.[131]
Let endlesse Peace your steadfast hearts accord,
And blessed Plentie wait vpon your bord,
And let your bed with pleasures chast abound,
That fruitfull issue may to you afford,
Which may your foes confound,
And make your ioyes redound,
Vpon your Brydale day, which is not long:
  Sweete *Themmes* run softlie, till I end my Song.

---

[130] *old Peneus Waters:* Peneus, chief river of Thessaly, flows through the Vale of Tempe.

[131] *assoile:* absolve.

So ended she; and all the rest around
To her redoubled that her vndersong,[132]
Which said, their bridale daye should not be long.
And gentle Eccho from the neighbour ground,
Their accents did resound.
So forth those ioyous Birdes did passe along,
Adowne the Lee,[133] that to them murmurde low,
As he would speake, but that he lackt a tong
Yeat did by signes his glad affection show,
Making his streame run slow.
And all the foule which in his flood did dwell
Gan flock about these twaine, that did excell
The rest, so far, as *Cynthia* doth shend [134]
The lesser starres. So they enranged well,
Did on those two attend,
And their best seruice lend,
Against their wedding day, which was not long:
Sweete *Themmes* run softly, till I end my Song.

At length they all to mery *London* came,
To mery London, my most kyndly Nurse,
That to me gaue this Lifes first natiue sourse:
Though from another place I take my name,
An house of auncient fame.[135]
There when they came, whereas those bricky towres,[136]
The which on *Themmes* brode aged backe doe ryde,
Where now the studious Lawyers haue their bowers
There whylome wont the Templer Knights to byde,
Till they decayd through pride:
Next whereunto there standes a stately place,[137]
Where oft I gayned giftes and goodly grace
Of that great Lord, which therein wont to dwell,
Whose want too well now feeles my freendles case:
But Ah here fits not well
Olde woes but ioyes to tell
Against the bridale daye, which is not long:
Sweete *Themmes* runne softly, till I end my Song.

---

[132] *redoubled that her vndersong:* re-echoed her refrain.

[133] *Lee:* perhaps the river Lea which in the sixteenth century flowed into the Thames.

[134] *shend:* surpass.

[135] *another place . . . fame:* Spenser alludes to the Spencers of Althorpe, near Northampton.

[136] *those bricky towres:* The Temple. The quarters were first occupied by the Knights Templar; in Spenser's time and now, the residence of students of the common law.

[137] *a stately place:* in 1578–1580, Leicester House, house of Spenser's chief patron, the Earl of Leicester; occupied in 1596 by the Earl of Essex, and called Essex House.

Yet therein now doth lodge a noble Peer,[138]
Great *Englands* glory and the Worlds wide wonder,
Whose dreadfull name, late through all *Spaine* did thunder,
And *Hercules* two pillors standing neere,
Did make to quake and feare:
Faire branch of Honor, flower of Cheualrie,
That fillest *England* with thy triumphs fame,
Ioy haue thou of thy noble victorie,
And endlesse happinesse of thine owne name
That promiseth the same:
That through thy prowesse and victorious armes,
Thy country may be freed from forraine harmes:
And great *Elisaes* glorious name may ring
Through al the world, fil'd with thy wide Alarmes,
Which some braue muse may sing
To ages following,
Vpon the Brydale day, which is not long:
  Sweete *Themmes* runne softly, till I end my Song.

From those high Towers, this noble Lord issuing,
Like Radiant *Hesper* when his golden hayre
In th'*Ocean* billowes he hath Bathed fayre,
Descended to the Riuers open vewing,
With a great traine ensuing.
Aboue the rest were goodly to bee seene
Two gentle Knights [139] of louely face and feature
Beseeming well the bower of anie Queene,
With gifts of wit and ornaments of nature,
Fit for so goodly stature:
That like the twins of *Ioue* [140] they seem'd in sight,
Which decke the Bauldricke of the Heauens [141] bright.
They two forth pacing to the Riuers side,
Receiued those two faire Brides, their Loues delight,
Which at th'appointed tyde,
Each one did make his Bryde,
Against their Brydale day, which is not long:
  Sweete *Themmes* runne softly, till I end my Song.

---

[138] *a noble Peer:* the Earl of Essex (see l. 137), who on his return from the sack of Cadiz in August, 1596, was at the height of his popularity.

[139] *Two gentle Knights:* Henry Gilford and William Peter.

[140] *twins of Ioue:* Castor and Pollux.

[141] *Bauldricke of the Heauens:* the zodiac, like a gem-studded girdle.

TWO CANTOS OF MUTABILITIE:

Which, both for Forme and Matter, appeare to be parcell of some following Booke of the FAERIE QUEENE UNDER THE LEGEND OF CONSTANCIE

Neuer before imprinted.

CANTO VI[1]

Proud Change (not pleasd in mortall things
Beneath the moone to raigne)
Pretends, as well of gods as men,
To be the soveraine.

I

WHAT man that sees the ever-whirling wheele
Of Change, the which all mortall things doth sway,
But that therby doth find, and plainly feele,
How Mutability in them doth play
Her cruell sports, to many mens decay?
Which that to all may better yet appeare,
I will rehearse that whylome I heard say,
How she at first her selfe began to reare
Gainst all the gods, and th' empire sought from them to beare.

[1] The two cantos and two stanzas on Mutability were first published in 1609, and they are now generally held to be a fragment intended for some unwritten book of *The Faerie Queene*.

II

But first, here falleth fittest to unfold
Her antique race and linage ancient,
As I have found it registred of old
In Faery Land mongst records permanent.
She was, to weet, a daughter by descent
Of those old Titans that did whylome strive
With Saturnes sonne for heavens regiment;
Whom though high Jove of kingdome did deprive,
Yet many of their stemme long after did survive.

III

And many of them afterwards obtain'd
Great power of Jove, and high authority:
As Hecate, in whose almighty hand
He plac't all rule and principality,
To be by her disposed diversly,
To gods and men, as she them list divide;
And drad[2] Bellona, that doth sound on hie
Warres and allarums unto nations wide,
That makes both heaven and earth to tremble at her pride.

IV

So likewise did this Titanesse aspire,
Rule and dominion to her selfe to gaine;
That as a goddesse men might her admire,
And heavenly honours yield, as to them twaine.
And first, on earth she sought it to obtaine;
Where she such proofe and sad examples shewed
Of her great power, to many ones great paine,
That not men onely (whom she soone subdewed),
But eke all other creatures, her bad dooings rewed.

V

For she the face of earthly things so changed,
That all which Nature had establisht first
In good estate, and in meet order ranged,
She did pervert, and all their statutes burst:
And all the worlds faire frame (which none yet durst
Of gods or men to alter or misguide)
She alter'd quite, and made them all accurst
That God had blest, and did at first provide
In that still happy state for ever to abide.

[2] *drad:* dreadful.

VI

Ne shee the lawes of Nature onely brake,
But eke of Justice, and of Policie;
And wrong of right, and bad of good did make,
And death for life exchanged foolishlie:
Since which, all living wights have learn'd to die,
And all this world is woxen daily worse.
O pittious worke of Mutabilitie!
By which we all are subject to that curse,
And death in stead of life have sucked from our nurse.

VII

And now, when all the earth she thus had brought
To her behest, and thralled to her might,
She gan to cast in her ambitious thought
T' attempt the empire of the heavens hight,
And Jove himselfe to shoulder from his right.
And first, she past the region of the ayre,
And of the fire, whose substance thin and slight
Made no resistance, ne could her contraire,
But ready passage to her pleasure did prepaire.

VIII

Thence to the circle of the Moone she clambe,
Where Cynthia raignes in everlasting glory,
To whose bright shining palace straight she came,
All fairely deckt with heavens goodly story:
Whose silver gates (by which there sate an hory
Old aged sire, with hower-glasse in hand,
Hight Tyme) she entred, were he liefe[3] or sory:
Ne staide till she the highest stage had scand,
Where Cynthia did sit, that never still did stand.

IX

Her sitting on an ivory throne shee found,
Drawne of two steeds, th' one black, the other white,
Environd with tenne thousand starres around,
That duly her attended day and night;
And by her side there ran her page, that hight
Vesper, whom we the evening-starre intend:[4]
That with his torche, still twinkling like twylight,
Her lightened all the way where she should wend,
And joy to weary wandring travailers did lend:

3 *liefe:* willing

4 *intend:* designate, call.

X

That when the hardy Titanesse beheld
The goodly building of her palace bright,
Made of the heavens substance, and up-held
With thousand crystall pillors of huge hight,
Shee gan to burne in her ambitious spright,
And t' envie her that in such glorie raigned.
Eftsoones she cast by force and tortious[5] might
Her to displace, and to her selfe to have gained
The kingdome of the night, and waters by her wained.[6]

XI

Boldly she bid the goddesse downe descend,
And let her selfe into that ivory throne;
For shee her selfe more worthy thereof wend,[7]
And better able it to guide alone:
Whether to men, whose fall she did bemone,
Or unto gods, whose state she did maligne,
Or to th' infernall powers, her need give lone
Of her faire light and bounty most benigne,
Her selfe of all that rule shee deemed most condigne.

XII

But shee that had to her that soveraigne seat
By highest Jove assign'd, therein to beare
Nights burning lamp, regarded not her threat,
Ne yielded ought for favour or for feare;
But with sterne countenaunce and disdainfull cheare,
Bending her horned browes, did put her back:
And boldly blaming her for comming there,
Bade her attonce from heavens coast to pack,
Or at her perill bide the wrathfull thunders wrack.

XIII

Yet nathemore[8] the Giantesse forbare:
But boldly preacing-on, raught forth her hand
To pluck her downe perforce from off her chaire;
And there-with lifting up her golden wand,
Threatned to strike her if she did withstand.
Where-at the starres, which round about her blazed,
And eke the Moones bright wagon, still did stand.
All beeing with so bold attempt amazed,
And on her uncouth habit and sterne looke still gazed.

[5] *tortious:* injurious, hurtful.
[6] *wained:* conveyed, carried.
[7] *wend:* weened, thought.
[8] *nathemore:* never the more.

XIV

Meane-while the lower world, which nothing knew
Of all that chaunced here, was darkned quite;
And eke the heavens, and all the heavenly crew
Of happy wights, now unpurvaide of light,
Were much afraid, and wondred at that sight;
Fearing least Chaos broken had his chaine,
And brought againe on them eternall night:
But chiefely Mercury, that next doth raigne,
Ran forth in haste, unto the king of gods to plaine.

XV

All ran together with a great out-cry
To Joves faire palace, fixt in heavens hight;
And beating at his gates full earnestly,
Gan call to him aloud with all their might,
To know what meant that suddaine lack of light.
The father of the gods, when this he heard,
Was troubled much at their so strange affright,
Doubting least Typhon were againe up rear'd,
Or other his old foes, that once him sorely fear'd.

XVI

Eftsoones the sonne of Maia[9] forth he sent
Downe to the circle of the Moone, to knowe
The cause of this so strange astonishment,
And why shee did her wonted course for slowe;
And if that any were on earth belowe
That did with charmes or magick her molest,
Him to attache, and downe to hell to throwe:
But, if from heaven it were, then to arrest
The author, and him bring before his presence prest.

XVII

The wingd-foot god so fast his plumes did beat,
That soone he came where-as the Titanesse
Was striving with faire Cynthia for her seat:
At whose strange sight and haughty hardinesse
He wondred much, and feared her no lesse.
Yet laying feare aside to doe his charge,
At last he bade her (with bold stedfastnesse)
Ceasse to molest the Moone to walke at large,
Or come before high Jove, her dooings to discharge.

---

[9] *son of Maia:* Mercury.

XVIII

And there-with-all, he on her shoulder laid
His snaky-wreathed mace, whose awfull power
Doth make both gods and hellish fiends affraid:
Where-at the Titanesse did sternely lower,
And stoutly answer'd, that in evill hower
He from his Jove such message to her brought,
To bid her leave faire Cynthias silver bower;
Sith shee his Jove and him esteemed nought,
No more then Cynthia's selfe; but all their kingdoms sought.

XIX

The heavens herald staid not to reply,
But past away, his doings to relate
Unto his lord; who now, in th' highest sky,
Was placed in his principall estate,
With all the gods about him congregate:
To whom when Hermes had his message told,
It did them all exceedingly amate,[10]
Save Jove; who, changing nought his count'nance bold,
Did unto them at length these speeches wise unfold:

XX

"Harken to mee awhile, yee heavenly powers:
Ye may remember since th' Earths cursed seed
Sought to assaile the heavens eternall towers,
And to us all exceeding feare did breed:
But how we then defeated all their deed,
Yee all doe knowe, and them destroied quite;
Yet not so quite, but that there did succeed
An off-spring of their bloud, which did alite
Upon the fruitfull earth, which doth us yet despite.

XXI

"Of that bad seed is this bold woman bred,
That now with bold presumption doth aspire
To thrust faire Phœbe from her silver bed,
And eke our selves from heavens high empire,
If that her might were match to her desire:
Wherefore, it now behoves us to advise
What way is best to drive her to retire;
Whether by open force or counsell wise,
Areed,[11] ye sonnes of God, as best ye can devise."

---

[10] *amate:* dismay.

[11] *areed:* declare, make known.

XXII

So having said, he ceast; and with his brow
(His black eye-brow, whose doomefull dreaded beck
Is wont to wield the world unto his vow,
And even the highest powers of heaven to check)
Made signe to them in their degrees to speake:
Who straight gan cast their counsell grave and wise.
Meane-while th' Earths daughter, thogh she nought did reck
Of Hermes message, yet gan now advise,
What course were best to take in this hot bold emprize.

XXIII

Eftsoones she thus resolv'd; that whil'st the gods
(After returne of Hermes embassie)
Were troubled, and amongst themselves at ods,
Before they could new counsels re-allie,
To set upon them in that extasie;
And take what fortune time and place would lend:
So forth she rose, and through the purest sky
To Joves high palace straight cast to ascend,
To prosecute her plot: good on-set boads good end.

XXIV

Shee there arriving, boldly in did pass;
Where all the gods she found in counsell close,
All quite unarm'd, as then their manner was.
At sight of her they suddaine all arose,
In great amaze, ne wist what way to chose.
But Jove, all fearelesse, forc't them to aby; [12]
And in his soveraine throne, gan straight dispose
Himselfe more full of grace and majestie,
That mote [13] encheare his friends, and foes mote terrifie.

XXV

That when the haughty Titanesse beheld,
All were she fraught with pride and impudence,
Yet with the sight thereof was almost queld;
And inly quaking, seem'd as reft of sense,
And voyd of speech in that drad audience;
Untill that Jove himselfe her selfe bespake:
"Speake, thou fraile woman, speake with confidence;
Whence art thou, and what doost thou here now make?
What idle errand hast thou, earths mansion to forsake?"

12 *aby:* abide, remain.

13 *mote:* might.

XXVI

Shee, halfe confused with his great commaund,
Yet gathering spirit of her natures pride,
Him boldly answer'd thus to his demaund:
"I am a daughter, by the mothers side,
Of her that is grand-mother magnifide
Of all the gods, great Earth, great Chaos child:
But by the fathers (be it not envide)
I greater am in bloud (whereon I build)
Then all the gods, though wrongfully from heaven exil'd.

XXVII

"For Titan (as ye all acknowledge must)
Was Saturnes elder brother by birth-right;
Both, sonnes of Uranus: but by unjust
And guilefull meanes, through Corybantes slight,
The younger thrust the elder from his right:
Since which thou, Jove, injuriously hast held
The heavens rule from Titans sonnes by might;
And them to hellish dungeons downe hast feld:
Witnesse, ye heavens, the truth of all that I have teld."

XXVIII

Whil'st she thus spake, the gods that gave good eare
To her bold words, and marked well her grace,
Beeing of stature tall as any there
Of all the gods, and beautifull of face
As any of the goddesses in place,
Stood all astonied; like a sort of steeres,
Mongst whom some beast of strange and forraine race
Unwares is chaunc't, far straying from his peeres:
So did their ghastly gaze bewray their hidden feares.

XXIX

Till, having pauz'd awhile, Jove thus bespake:
"Will never mortall thoughts ceasse to aspire,
In this bold sort, to heaven claime to make,
And touch celestiall seates with earthly mire?
I would have thought that bold Procrustes hire,
Or Typhons fall, or proud Ixions paine,
Or great Prometheus tasting of our ire,
Would have suffiz'd the rest for to restraine,
And warn'd all men, by their example, to refraine:

XXX

"But now this off-scum of that cursed fry
Dare to renew the like bold enterprize,
And chalenge th' heritage of this our skie;
Whom what should hinder, but that we likewise
Should handle as the rest of her allies,
And thunder-drive to hell?" With that, he shooke
His nectar-deawed locks, with which the skyes
And all the world beneath for terror quooke,
And eft his burning levin-brond [14] in hand he tooke.

XXXI

But, when he looked on her lovely face,
In which faire beames of beauty did appeare,
That could the greatest wrath soone turne to grace
(Such sway doth beauty even in heaven beare)
He staide his hand: and having chang'd his cheare,
He thus againe in milder wise began:
"But ah! if gods should strive with flesh yfere,
Then shortly should the progeny of man
Be rooted out, if Jove should doe still what he can.

XXXII

"But thee, faire Titans child, I rather weene,
Through some vaine errour, or inducement light,
To see that mortall eyes have never seene;
Or through ensample of thy sisters might,
Bellona, whose great glory thou doost spight,
Since thou hast seene her dreadfull power belowe,
Mongst wretched men, dismaide with her affright,
To bandie crownes, and kingdomes to bestowe:
And sure thy worth no lesse then hers doth seem to showe.

XXXIII

"But wote thou this, thou hardy Titanesse,
That not the worth of any living wight
May challenge ought in heavens interesse;
Much lesse the title of old Titans right:
For we by conquest of our soveraine might,
And by eternall doome of Fates decree,
Have wonne the empire of the heavens bright;
Which to ourselves we hold, and to whom wee
Shall worthy deeme partakers of our blisse to bee.

[14] *levin-brond:* lightning bolt.

XXXIV

"Then ceasse thy idle claime, thou foolish gerle,
And seeke by grace and goodnesse to obtaine
That place from which by folly Titan fell;
There-to thou maist perhaps, if so thou faine,
Have Jove thy gratious lord and soveraigne."
So having said, she thus to him replide:
"Ceasse, Saturnes sonne, to seeke by proffers vaine
Of idle hopes t' allure mee to thy side,
For to betray my right, before I have it tride.

XXXV

"But thee, O Jove, no equall judge I deeme
Of my desert, or of my dewfull right;
That in thine owne behalfe maist partiall seeme:
But to the highest him, that is behight
Father of gods and men by equall might,
To weet, the god of Nature, I appeale."
There-at Jove wexed wroth, and in his spright
Did inly grudge, yet did it well conceale;
And bade Dan Phœbus scribe her appellation seale.

XXXVI

Eftsoones the time and place appointed were,
Where all, both heavenly powers and earthly wights,
Before great Natures presence should appeare,
For triall of their titles and best rights:
That was, to weet, upon the highest hights
Of Arlo-hill [15] (Who knowes not Arlo-hill?)
That is the highest head (in all mens sights)
Of my old father Mole, whom shepheards quill
Renowmed hath with hymnes fit for a rurall skill.

XXXVII

And, were it not ill fitting for this file,[16]
To sing of hilles and woods, mongst warres and knights,
I would abate the sternenesse of my stile,
Mongst these sterne stounds to mingle soft delights;
And tell how Arlo through Dianaes spights
(Beeing of old the best and fairest hill
That was in all this holy-islands hights)
Was made the most unpleasant and most ill.
Meane while, O Clio, lend Calliope thy quill.

---

[15] *Arlo-hill:* Galteemore in southern Ireland, the highest peak in the range Spenser calls Mole; it overlooks the vale of Aherlow or Arlo. Spenser's home, Kilcolman Castle, lay at the foot of Mole.

[16] *file:* the thread of the narrative.

XXXVIII

Whylome, when Ireland florished in fame
Of wealths and goodnesse, far above the rest
Of all that beare the British Islands name,
The gods then us'd (for pleasure and for rest)
Oft to resort there-to, when seem'd them best:
But none of all there-in more pleasure found
Then Cynthia, that is soveraine queene profest
Of woods and forrests, which therein abound,
Sprinkled with wholsom waters more then most on ground.

XXXIX

But mongst them all, as fittest for her game,
Either for chace of beasts with hound or boawe,
Or for to shroude in shade from Phœbus flame,
Or bathe in fountaines that doe freshly flowe,
Or from high hilles, or from the dales belowe,
She chose this Arlo; where shee did resort
With all her nymphes enranged on a rowe,
With whom the woody gods did oft consort:
For with the nymphes the satyres love to play and sport.

XL

Amongst the which there was a nymph that hight
Molanna,[17] daughter of old Father Mole,
And sister unto Mulla, faire and bright,
Unto whose bed false Bregog whylome stole,
That Shepheard Colin dearely did condole,
And made her lucklesse loves well knowne to be.
But this Molanna, were she not so shole,[18]
Were no lesse faire and beautifull then shee:
Yet as she is, a fairer flood may no man see.

XLI

For, first, she springs out of two marble rocks,
On which a grove of oakes high-mounted growes,
That as a girlond seemes to deck the locks
Of som faire bride, brought forth with pompous showes
Out of her bowre, that many flowers strowes:
So, through the flowry dales she tumbling downe,
Through many woods and shady coverts flowes
(That on each side her silver channell crowne)
Till to the plaine she come, whose valleyes shee doth drowne.

[17] *Molanna . . . Mulla:* The river Behanagh. The story of Mulla (the river Awbeg) is told by Spenser in *Colin Clouts Come Home Againe,* lines 104 ff.

[18] *shole:* shallow.

XLII

In her sweet streames Diana used oft
(After her sweatie chace and toilesome play)
To bathe her selfe; and after, on the soft
And downy grasse, her dainty limbes to lay
In covert shade, where none behold her may:
For much she hated sight of living eye.
Foolish god Faunus, though full many a day
He saw her clad, yet longed foolishly
To see her naked mongst her nymphes in privity.

XLIII

No way he found to compasse his desire,
But to corrupt Molanna, this her maid,
Her to discover for some secret hire:
So her with flattering words he first assaid;
And after, pleasing gifts for her purvaid,
Queene-apples,[19] and red cherries from the tree,
With which he her allured and betraid,
To tell what time he might her lady see
When she her selfe did bathe, that he might secret bee.

XLIV

There-to hee promist, if shee would him pleasure
With this small boone, to quit her with a better;
To weet, that where-as shee had out of measure
Long lov'd the Fanchin,[20] who by nought did set her,
That he would undertake for this to get her
To be his love, and of him liked well:
Besides all which, he vow'd to be her debter
For many moe good turnes then he would tell;
The least of which this little pleasure should excell.

XLV

The simple maid did yield to him anone;
And eft him placed where he close might view
That never any saw, save onely one,
Who, for his hire to so foole-hardy dew,
Was of his hounds devour'd in hunters hew.
Tho, as her manner was on sunny day,
Diana, with her nymphes about her, drew
To this sweet spring; where, doffing her array,
She bath'd her lovely limbes, for Jove a likely pray.

---

[19] *Queene-apples:* a variety of early apple.

[20] *Fanchin:* the river Funsheon; it is joined by the Molanna (Behanagh) at the hamlet of Kilbeheny.

XLVI

There Faunus saw that pleased much his eye,
And made his hart to tickle in his brest,
That, for great joy of some-what he did spy,
He could him not containe in silent rest;
But breaking forth in laughter, loud profest
His foolish thought. A foolish Faune indeed,
That couldst not hold thy selfe so hidden blest,
But wouldest needs thine owne conceit areed!
Babblers unworthy been of so divine a meed.

XLVII

The goddesse, all abashed with that noise,
In haste forth started from the guilty brooke;
And running straight where-as she heard his voice,
Enclos'd the bush about, and there him tooke,
Like darred [21] larke, not daring up to looke
On her whose sight before so much he sought.
Thence forth they drew him by the hornes, and shooke
Nigh all to peeces, that they left him nought;
And then into the open light they forth him brought.

XLVIII

Like as an huswife, that with busie care
Thinks of her dairie to make wondrous gaine,
Finding where-as some wicked beast unware
That breakes into her dayr' house, there doth draine
Her creaming pannes, and frustrate all her paine,
Hath, in some snare or gin set close behind,
Entrapped him, and caught into her traine,
Then thinkes what punishment were best assign'd,
And thousand deathes deviseth in her vengefull mind:

XLIX

So did Diana and her maydens all
Use silly Faunus, now within their baile: [22]
They mocke and scorne him, and him foule miscall;
Some by the nose him pluckt, some by the taile,
And by his goatish beard some did him haile:
Yet he (poore soule!) with patience all did beare;
For nought against their wils might countervaile:
Ne ought he said, what ever he did heare;
But hanging downe his head, did like a mome [23] appeare.

---

[21] *darred:* trapped by fright.
[22] *baile:* custody.
[23] *mome:* blockhead, fool.

L

At length, when they had flouted him their fill,
They gan to cast what penaunce him to give.
Some would have gelt him, but that same would spill
The wood-gods breed, which must for ever live:
Others would through the river him have drive,
And ducked deepe; but that seem'd penaunce light:
But most agreed, and did this sentence give,
Him in deares skin to clad, and in that plight
To hunt him with their hounds, him selfe save how hee might.

LI

But Cynthia's selfe, more angry then the rest,
Thought not enough to punish him in sport,
And of her shame to make a gamesome jest;
But gan examine him in straighter sort,
Which of her nymphes, or other close consort,
Him thither brought, and her to him betraid.
He, much affeard, to her confessed short
That 't was Molanna which her so bewraid.
Then all attonce their hands upon Molanna laid.

LII

But him (according as they had decreed)
With a deeres-skin they covered, and then chast
With all their hounds, that after him did speed;
But he, more speedy, from them fled more fast
Then any deere: so sore him dread aghast.
They after follow'd all with shrill outcry,
Shouting as they the heavens would have brast:
That all the woods and dales, where he did flie,
Did ring againe, and loud reeccho to the skie.

LIII

So they him follow'd till they weary were;
When, back returning to Molann' againe,
They, by commaund'ment of Diana, there
Her whelm'd with stones. Yet Faunus (for her paine)
Of her beloved Fanchin did obtaine,
That her he would receive unto his bed.
So now her waves passe through a pleasant plaine,
Till with the Fanchin she her selfe doe wed,
And (both combin'd) themselves in one faire river spred.

LIV

Nath'lesse, Diana, full of indignation,
Thence-forth abandond her delicious brooke;
In whose sweet streame, before that bad occasion,
So much delight to bathe her limbes she tooke:
Ne onely her, but also quite forsooke
All those faire forrests about Arlo hid,
And all that mountaine, which doth overlooke
The richest champian [24] that may else be rid,[25]
And the faire Shure,[26] in which are thousand salmons bred.

LV

Them all, and all that she so deare did way,
Thence-forth she left; and parting from the place,
There-on an heavy haplesse curse did lay,
To weet, that wolves, where she was wont to space,
Should harbour'd be, and all those woods deface,
And thieves should rob and spoile that coast around.
Since which, those woods, and all that goodly chase,
Doth to this day with wolves and thieves abound:
Which too-too true that lands in-dwellers since have found.

CANTO VII

Pealing from Jove to Natur's bar,
Bold Alteration pleades
Large evidence: but Nature soone
Her righteous doome areads.

I

Ah! whither doost thou now, thou greater Muse,[27]
Me from these woods and pleasing forrests bring?
And my fraile spirit (that dooth oft refuse
This too high flight, unfit for her weake wing)
Lift up aloft, to tell of heavens king
(Thy soveraine sire) his fortunate successe,
And victory in bigger noates to sing,
Which he obtain'd against that Titanesse,
That him of heavens empire sought to dispossesse?

---

[24] *champian:* plain.
[25] *else be rid:* seen anywhere else.
[26] *Shure:* the river Suir, in Tipperary.
[27] *greater muse:* Clio. See stanza XXXVII of Canto VI.

II

Yet sith I needs must follow thy behest,
Doe thou my weaker wit with skill inspire,
Fit for this turne; and in my feeble brest
Kindle fresh sparks of that immortall fire
Which learned minds inflameth with desire
Of heavenly things: for who but thou alone,
That art yborne of heaven and heavenly sire,
Can tell things doen in heaven so long ygone,
So farre past memory of man that may be knowne?

III

Now, at the time that was before agreed,
The gods assembled all on Arlo hill;
As well those that are sprung of heavenly seed,
As those that all the other world doe fill,
And rule both sea and land unto their will:
Onely th' infernall powers might not appeare;
Aswell for horror of their count'naunce ill,
As for th' unruly fiends which they did feare;
Yet Pluto and Proserpina were present there.

IV

And thither also came all other creatures,
What-ever life or motion doe retaine,
According to their sundry kinds of features;
That Arlo scarsly could them all containe;
So full they filled every hill and plaine:
And had not Natures sergeant (that is Order)
Them well disposed by his busie paine,
And raunged farre abroad in every border,
They would have caused much confusion and disorder.

V

Then forth issewed (great goddesse) great Dame Nature,
With goodly port and gracious majesty,
Being far greater and more tall of stature
Then any of the gods or powers on hie:
Yet certes by her face and physnomy,
Whether she man or woman inly were,
That could not any creature well descry:
For, with a veile that wimpled every where,
Her head and face was hid, that mote to none appeare.

VI

That, some doe say, was so by skill devized,
To hide the terror of her uncouth hew
From mortall eyes, that should be sore agrized;[28]
For that her face did like a lion shew,
That eye of wight could not indure to view:
But others tell that it so beautious was,
And round about such beames of splendor threw,
That it the sunne a thousand times did pass,
Ne could be seene, but like an image in a glass.

VII

That well may seemen true: for well I weene
That this same day, when she on Arlo sat,
Her garment was so bright and wondrous sheene,
That my fraile wit cannot devize to what
It to compare, nor finde like stuffe to that:
As those three sacred saints, though else most wise,
Yet on Mount Thabor quite their wits forgat,
When they their glorious Lord in strange disguise
Transfigur'd sawe; his garments so did daze their eyes.

VIII

In a fayre plaine upon an equall hill
She placed was in a pavilion;
Not such as craftes-men by their idle skill
Are wont for princes states to fashion:
But th' Earth her self, of her owne motion,
Out of her fruitfull bosome made to growe
Most dainty trees, that, shooting up anon,
Did seeme to bow their bloosming heads full lowe,
For homage unto her, and like a throne did shew.

IX

So hard it is for any living wight
All her array and vestiments to tell,
That old Dan Geffrey[29] (in whose gentle spright,
The pure well head of poesie did dwell)
In his *Foules Parley* durst not with it mel,
But it transferd to Alane, who he thought
Had in his *Plaint of kindes* describ'd it well:
Which who will read set forth so as it ought,
Go seek he out that Alane where he may be sought.

---

[28] *agrized:* horrified.

[29] *Dan Geffrey:* Master Geoffrey (Chaucer). See his *Parlement of Foules* 316–318, where Chaucer refers to Alanus de Insulis *De Planctu Naturae* as Aleyn's "Pleynt of Kinde."

X

And all the earth far underneath her feete
Was dight with flowres, that voluntary grew
Out of the ground, and sent forth odours sweet;
Tenne thousand mores[30] of sundry sent and hew,
That might delight the smell, or please the view;
The which the nymphes from all the brooks thereby
Had gathered, which they at her foot-stoole threw;
That richer seem'd then any tapestry,
That princes bowres adorne with painted imagery.

XI

And Mole himselfe, to honour her the more,
Did deck himself in freshest faire attire,
And his high head, that seemeth alwaies hore
With hardned frosts of former winters ire,
He with an oaken girlond now did tire,
As if the love of some new nymph late seene
Had in him kindled youthfull fresh desire,
And made him change his gray attire to greene:
Ah, gentle Mole! such joyance hath thee well beseene.

XII

Was never so great joyance since the day
That all the gods whylome assembled were
On Hæmus hill in their divine array,
To celebrate the solemne bridall cheare
Twixt Peleus and Dame Thetis pointed there;
Where Phœbus self, that god of poets hight,
They say did sing the spousall hymne full cleere,
That all the gods were ravisht with delight
Of his celestiall song, and musicks wondrous might.

XIII

This great grandmother of all creatures bred,
Great Nature, ever young yet full of eld,
Still mooving, yet unmoved from her sted,[31]
Unseene of any, yet of all beheld,
Thus sitting in her throne, as I have teld,
Before her came Dame Mutabilitie;
And being lowe before her presence feld,
With meek obaysance and humilitie,
Thus gan her plaintif plea, with words to amplifie:

[30] *mores:* plants.

[31] *sted:* place.

XIV

"To thee, O greatest goddesse, onely great,
An humble suppliant loe! I lowely fly,
Seeking for right, which I of thee entreat,
Who right to all dost deale indifferently,
Damning all wrong and tortious injurie,
Which any of thy creatures doe to other
(Oppressing them with power, unequally)
Sith of them all thou art the equall mother,
And knittest each to each, as brother unto brother.

XV

"To thee therefore of this same Jove I plaine,
And of his fellow gods that faine to be,
That challenge to themselves the whole worlds raign;
Of which the greatest part is due to me,
And heaven it selfe by heritage in fee:
For heaven and earth I both alike do deeme,
Sith heaven and earth are both alike to thee;
And gods no more then men thou doest esteeme:
For even the gods to thee, as men to gods, do seeme.

XVI

"Then weigh, O soveraigne goddesse, by what right
These gods do claime the worlds whole soverainty,
And that is onely dew unto thy might
Arrogate to themselves ambitiously:
As for the gods owne principality,
Which Jove usurpes unjustly, that to be
My heritage, Jove's self cannot deny,
From my great grandsire Titan unto mee
Deriv'd by dew descent; as is well knowen to thee.

XVII

"Yet mauger Jove, and all his gods beside,
I doe possesse the worlds most regiment;
As, if ye please it into parts divide,
And every parts inholders to convent,
Shall to your eyes appeare incontinent.
And first, the Earth (great mother of us all)
That only seems unmov'd and permanent,
And unto Mutability not thrall,
Yet is she chang'd in part, and eeke in generall.

XVIII

"For all that from her springs, and is ybredde,
How-ever fayre it flourish for a time,
Yet see we soone decay; and, being dead,
To turne again unto their earthly slime:
Yet, out of their decay and mortall crime,
We daily see new creatures to arize,
And of their winter spring another prime,
Unlike in forme, and chang'd by strange disguise;
So turne they still about, and change in restlesse wise.

XIX

"As for her tenants, that is, man and beasts,
The beasts we daily see massacred dy,
As thralls and vassals unto mens beheasts:
And men themselves doe change continually,
From youth to eld, from wealth to poverty,
From good to bad, from bad to worst of all:
Ne doe their bodies only flit and fly;
But eeke their minds (which they immortall call)
Still change and vary thoughts, as new occasions fall.

XX

"Ne is the water in more constant case;
Whether those same on high, or these belowe.
For th' ocean moveth stil from place to place;
And every river still doth ebbe and flowe:
Ne any lake, that seems most still and slowe,
Ne poole so small, that can his smoothnesse holde,
When any winde doth under heaven blowe;
With which the clouds are also tost and roll'd;
Now like great hills; and streight, like sluces, them unfold.

XXI

"So likewise are all watry living wights
Still tost and turned with continuall change,
Never abyding in their stedfast plights.
The fish, still floting, doe at randon range,
And never rest, but evermore exchange
Their dwelling places, as the streames them carrie:
Ne have the watry foules a certaine grange
Wherein to rest, ne in one stead do tarry;
But flitting still doe flie, and still their places vary.

XXII

"Next is the ayre: which who feeles not by sense
(For of all sense it is the middle meane)
To flit still? and, with subtill influence
Of his thin spirit, all creatures to maintaine
In state of life? O weake life! that does leane
On thing so tickle as th' unsteady ayre;
Which every howre is chang'd, and altred cleane
With every blast that bloweth fowle or faire:
The faire doth it prolong; the fowle doth it impaire.

XXIII

"Therein the changes infinite beholde,
Which to her creatures every minute chaunce:
Now, boyling hot: streight, friezing deadly cold:
Now, faire sun-shine, that makes all skip and daunce:
Streight, bitter storms and balefull countenance,
That makes them all to shiver and to shake:
Rayne, hayle, and snowe do pay them sad penance,
And dreadfull thunder-claps (that make them quake)
With flames and flashing lights that thousand changes make.

XXIV

"Last is the fire: which, though it live for ever,
Ne can be quenched quite, yet, every day,
Wee see his parts, so soone as they do sever,
To lose their heat, and shortly to decay;
So makes himself his owne consuming pray.
Ne any living creatures doth he breed:
But all that are of others bredd doth slay,
And with their death his cruell life dooth feed;
Nought leaving, but their barren ashes, without seed.

XXV

"Thus all these fower (the which the ground-work bee
Of all the world, and of all living wights)
To thousand sorts of change we subject see:
Yet are they chang'd (by other wondrous slights)
Into themselves, and lose their native mights:
The fire to aire, and th' ayre to water sheere,
And water into earth: yet water fights
With fire, and aire with earth, approaching neere:
Yet all are in one body, and as one appeare.

XXVI

"So in them all raignes Mutabilitie;
How-ever these, that gods themselves do call,
Of them doe claime the rule and soverainty:
As Vesta, of the fire æthereall;
Vulcan, of this, with us so usuall;
Ops, of the earth; and Juno, of the ayre;
Neptune, of seas; and nymphes, of rivers all:
For all those rivers to me subject are;
And all the rest, which they usurp, be all my share.

XXVII

"Which to approven true, as I have told,
Vouchsafe, O goddesse, to thy presence call
The rest which doe the world in being hold:
As times and seasons of the yeare that fall:
Of all the which demand in generall,
Or judge thy selfe, by verdit of thine eye,
Whether to me they are not subject all."
Nature did yeeld thereto; and by-and-by,
Bade Order call them all before her majesty.

XXVIII

So forth issew'd the seasons of the yeare:
First, lusty Spring, all dight in leaves of flowres
That freshly budded and new bloosmes did beare
(In which a thousand birds had built their bowres,
That sweetly sung, to call forth paramours):
And in his hand a javelin he did beare,
And on his head (as fit for warlike stoures [32])
A guilt engraven morion [33] he did weare;
That, as some did him love, so others did him feare.

XXIX

Then came the jolly Sommer, being dight
In a thin silken cassock coloured greene,
That was unlyned all, to be more light:
And on his head a girlond well beseene
He wore, from which, as he had chauffed [34] been,
The sweat did drop; and in his hand he bore
A boawe and shaftes, as he in forrest greene
Had hunted late the libbard or the bore,
And now would bathe his limbes, with labor heated sore.

---

[32] *stoures:* combats.

[33] *morion:* a kind of helmet.

[34] *chauffed:* heated.

XXX

Then came the Autumne, all in yellow clad,
As though he joyed in his plentious store,
Laden with fruits that made him laugh, full glad
That he had banisht hunger, which to-fore
Had by the belly oft him pinched sore.
Upon his head a wreath, that was enrold
With eares of corne of every sort, he bore:
And in his hand a sickle he did holde,
To reape the ripened fruits the which the earth had yold.

XXXI

Lastly came Winter, cloathed all in frize,
Chattering his teeth for cold that did him chill,
Whil'st on his hoary beard his breath did freese,
And the dull drops, that from his purpled bill
As from a limbeck did adown distill.
In his right hand a tipped staffe he held,
With which his feeble steps he stayed still:
For he was faint with cold, and weak with eld;
That scarse his loosed limbes he hable was to weld.

XXXII

These, marching softly, thus in order went,
And after them the monthes all riding came:
First, sturdy March, with brows full sternly bent,
And armed strongly, rode upon a ram,
The same which over Hellespontus swam:
Yet in his hand a spade he also hent,
And in a bag all sorts of seeds ysame,
Which on the earth he strowed as he went,
And fild her womb with fruitfull hope of nourishment.

XXXIII

Next came fresh Aprill, full of lustyhed,
And wanton as a kid whose horne new buds:
Upon a bull he rode, the same which led
Europa floting through th' Argolick fluds:
His hornes were gilden all with golden studs,
And garnished with garlonds goodly dight
Of all the fairest flowres and freshest buds
Which th' earth brings forth, and wet he seem'd in sight
With waves, through which he waded for his loves delight.

XXXIV

Then came faire May, the fayrest mayd on ground,
Deckt all with dainties of her seasons pryde,
And throwing flowres out of her lap around:
Upon two brethrens shoulders she did ride,
The twinnes of Leda; [35] which on eyther side
Supported her like to their soveraine queene.
Lord! how all creatures laught, when her they spide,
And leapt and daunc't as they had ravisht beene!
And Cupid selfe about her fluttred all in greene.

XXXV

And after her came jolly June, arrayd
All in greene leaves, as he a player were;
Yet in his time he wrought as well as playd,
That by his plough-yrons mote right well appeare:
Upon a crab he rode, that him did beare
With crooked crawling steps an uncouth pase,
And backward yode, as bargemen wont to fare
Bending their force contrary to their face,
Like that ungracious crew which faines demurest grace.

XXXVI

Then came hot July boyling like to fire,
That all his garments he had cast away:
Upon a lyon raging yet with ire
He boldly rode, and made him to obay:
It was the beast that whylome did forray
The Nemæan forrest, till th' Amphytrionide [36]
Him slew, and with his hide did him array:
Behinde his back a sithe, and by his side
Under his belt he bore a sickle circling wide.

XXXVII

The sixt was August, being rich arrayd
In garment all of gold downe to the ground:
Yet rode he not, but led a lovely mayd
Forth by the lilly hand, the which was cround
With eares of corne, and full her hand was found:
That was the righteous virgin which of old
Liv'd here on earth, and plenty made abound;
But, after wrong was lov'd and justice solde,
She left th' unrighteous world and was to heaven extold.

[35] *twins of Leda:* Castor and Pollux. [36] *Amphytrionide:* Hercules.

XXXVIII

Next him September marched eeke on foote;
Yet was he heavy laden with the spoyle
Of harvests riches, which he made his boot,
And him enricht with bounty of the soyle:
In his one hand, as fit for harvests toyle,
He held a knife-hook; and in th' other hand
A paire of waights, with which he did assoyle
Both more and lesse, where it in doubt did stand,
And equall gave to each as justice duly scann'd.

XXXIX

Then came October full of merry glee:
For yet his noule was totty of the must,[37]
Which he was treading in the wine-fats see,
And of the joyous oyle, whose gentle gust
Made him so frollick and so full of lust:
Upon a dreadfull scorpion he did ride,
The same which by Dianaes doom unjust
Slew great Orion: and eeke by his side
He had his ploughing-share and coulter ready tyde.

XL

Next was November; he full grosse and fat,
As fed with lard, and that right well might seeme;
For he had been a fatting hogs of late,
That yet his browes with sweat did reek and steem,
And yet the season was full sharp and breem; [38]
In planting eeke he took no small delight.
Whereon he rode, not easie was to deeme;
For it a dreadfull centaure was in sight,
The seed of Saturne and faire Nais, Chiron hight.

XLI

And after him came next the chill December:
Yet he, through merry feasting which he made,
And great bonfires, did not the cold remember;
His Saviours birth his mind so much did glad:
Upon a shaggy-bearded goat he rade,
The same wherewith Dan Jove in tender yeares,
They say, was nourisht by th' Idæan mayd; [39]
And in his hand a broad deepe boawle he beares,
Of which he freely drinks an health to all his peeres.

---

[37] *noule . . . must:* head unsteady from the mash.

[38] *breem:* sharp, bitter.

[39] *Idaean mayd:* Amalthea.

XLII

Then came old January, wrapped well
In many weeds to keep the cold away;
Yet did he quake and quiver like to quell,[40]
And blowe his nayles to warme them if he may:
For they were numbd with holding all the day
An hatchet keene, with which he felled wood,
And from the trees did lop the needlesse spray:
Upon an huge great earth-pot steane [41] he stood,
From whose wide mouth there flowed forth the Romane floud.

XLIII

And lastly came cold February, sitting
In an old wagon, for he could not ride;
Drawne of two fishes for the season fitting,
Which through the flood before did softly slyde
And swim away: yet had he by his side
His plough and harnesse fit to till the ground,
And tooles to prune the trees, before the pride
Of hasting Prime did make them burgein round.
So past the twelve months forth, and their dew places found.

XLIV

And after these there came the Day and Night,
Riding together both with equall pase,
Th' one on a palfrey blacke, the other white:
But Night had covered her uncomely face
With a blacke veile, and held in hand a mace,
On top whereof the moon and stars were pight,
And Sleep and Darknesse round about did trace:
But Day did beare, upon his scepters hight,
The goodly sun, encompast all with beames bright.

XLV

Then came the Howres, faire daughters of high Jove
And timely Night, the which were all endewed
With wondrous beauty fit to kindle love;
But they were virgins all, and love eschewed,
That might forslack the charge to them fore-shewed
By mighty Jove; who did them porters make
Of heavens gate (whence all the gods issued)
Which they did dayly watch, and nightly wake
By even turnes, ne ever did their charge forsake.

40 *quell:* perish.

41 *earth-pot steane:* large earthen jar, here the constellation Aquarius.

XLVI

And after all came Life, and lastly Death:
Death with most grim and griesly visage seene,
Yet is he nought but parting of the breath;
Ne ought to see, but like a shade to weene,
Unbodied, unsoul'd, unheard, unseene:
But Life was like a faire young lusty boy,
Such as they faine Dan Cupid to have beene,
Full of delightfull health and lively joy,
Deckt all with flowres, and wings of gold fit to employ.

XLVII

When these were past, thus gan the Titanesse:
"Lo! mighty mother, now be judge, and say
Whether in all thy creatures more or lesse
Change doth not raign and beare the greatest sway:
For who sees not that Time on all doth pray?
But times do change and move continually:
So nothing here long standeth in one stay:
Wherefore, this lower world who can deny
But to be subject still to Mutabilitie?"

XLVIII

Then thus gan Jove: "Right true it is, that these,
And all things else that under heaven dwell,
Are chaung'd of Time, who doth them all disseise [42]
Of being: but who is it (to me tell)
That Time himselfe doth move and still compell
To keepe his course? Is not that namely wee,
Which poure that vertue from our heavenly cell
That moves them all, and makes them changed be?
So them we gods doe rule, and in them also thee."

XLIX

To whom thus Mutability: "The things
Which we see not how they are mov'd and swayd
Ye may attribute to your selves as kings,
And say they by your secret powre are made:
But what we see not, who shall us perswade?
But were they so, as ye them faine to be,
Mov'd by your might, and ordred by your ayde;
Yet what if I can prove, that even yee
Your selves are likewise chang'd, and subject unto mee?

[42] *disseise:* deprive.

L

"And first, concerning her that is the first,
Even you, faire Cynthia, whom so much ye make
Joves dearest darling; she was bred and nurst
On Cynthus hill, whence she her name did take:
Then is she mortall borne, how-so ye crake;[43]
Besides, her face and countenance every day
We changed see, and sundry forms partake,
Now hornd, now round, now bright, now brown and gray;
So that *as changefull as the moone* men use to say.

LI

"Next Mercury, who though he lesse appeare
To change his hew, and alwayes seeme as one,
Yet he his course doth altar every yeare,
And is of late far out of order gone:
So Venus eeke, that goodly paragone,
Though faire all night, yet is she darke all day;
And Phœbus self, who lightsome is alone,
Yet is he oft eclipsed by the way,
And fills the darkned world with terror and dismay.

LII

"Now Mars, that valiant man, is changed most:
For he some times so far runs out of square,
That he his way doth seem quite to have lost,
And cleane without his usuall sphere to fare;
That even these star-gazers stonisht are
At sight thereof, and damne their lying bookes:
So likewise grim Sir Saturne oft doth spare
His sterne aspect, and calme his crabbed lookes:
So many turning cranks these have, so many crookes.

LIII

"But you, Dan Jove, that only constant are,
And king of all the rest, as ye do clame,
Are you not subject eeke to this misfare?
Then let me aske you this withouten blame:
Where were ye borne? Some say in Crete by name,
Others in Thebes, and others other-where;
But wheresoever they comment the same,
They all consent that ye begotten were
And borne here in this world, ne other can appeare.

[43] *crake:* boast.

LIV

"Then are ye mortall borne, and thrall to me,
Unlesse the kingdome of the sky yee make
Immortall and unchangeable to be:
Besides, that power and vertue which ye spake,
That ye here worke, doth many changes take,
And your owne natures change: for each of you,
That vertue have, or this or that to make,
Is checkt and changed from his nature trew,
By others opposition or obliquid view.

LV

"Besides, the sundry motions of your spheares,
So sundry waies and fashions as clerkes faine,
Some in short space, and some in longer yeares;
What is the same but alteration plaine?
Onely the starrie skie doth still remaine:
Yet do the starres and signes therein still move,
And even it self is mov'd, as wizards saine.
But all that moveth doth mutation love:
Therefore both you and them to me I subject prove.

LVI

"Then since within this wide great universe
Nothing doth firme and permanent appeare,
But all things tost and turned by transverse:
What then should let, but I aloft should reare
My trophee, and from all the triumph beare?
Now judge then (O thou greatest goddesse trew!)
According as thy selfe doest see and heare,
And unto me addoom that is my dew;
That is the rule of all, all being rul'd by you."

LVII

So having ended, silence long ensewed;
Ne Nature to or fro spake for a space,
But, with firme eyes affixt, the ground still viewed.
Meane while, all creatures, looking in her face,
Expecting th' end of this so doubtfull case,
Did hang in long suspence what would ensew,
To whether side should fall the soveraigne place:
At length, she, looking up with chearefull view,
The silence brake, and gave her doome in speeches few:

LVIII

"I well consider all that ye have sayd,
And find that all things stedfastnes doe hate
And changed be: yet being rightly wayd,
They are not changed from their first estate;
But by their change their being doe dilate:
And turning to themselves at length againe,
Doe worke their owne perfection so by fate:
Then over them Change doth not rule and raigne;
But they raigne over Change, and doe their states maintaine.

LIX

"Cease therefore, daughter, further to aspire,
And thee content thus to be rul'd by me:
For thy decay thou seekst by thy desire:
But time shall come that all shall changed bee,
And from thenceforth none no more change shall see."
So was the Titaness put downe and whist,[44]
And Jove confirm'd in his imperiall see.
Then was that whole assembly quite dismist,
And Natur's selfe did vanish, whither no man wist.

THE VIII. CANTO, UNPERFITE

I

WHEN I bethinke me on that speech whyleare
Of Mutability, and well it way,
Me seemes, that though she all unworthy were
Of the heav'ns rule, yet, very sooth to say,
In all things else she beares the greatest sway:
Which makes me loath this state of life so tickle,
And love of things so vaine to cast away;
Whose flowring pride, so fading and so fickle,
Short Time shall soon cut down with his consuming sickle.

---

[44] *whist:* silenced.

II

Then gin I thinke on that which Nature sayd,
Of that same time when no more change shall be,
But stedfast rest of all things, firmely stayd
Upon the pillours of eternity,
That is contrayr to Mutabilitie:
For all that moveth doth in change delight:
But thence-forth all shall rest eternally
With Him that is the God of Sabbaoth hight:
O that great Sabbaoth God graunt me that Sabaoths sight!

Christopher Marlowe

1564–1593

CHRISTOPHER MARLOWE was born in 1564, the son of a Canterbury shoemaker. He attended the King's School and Corpus Christi College, Cambridge; the Parker scholarship he held at the University for six years presumed an intention of taking holy orders. Nothing is known of what changed Marlowe's mind, except that in June, 1587, just before he was to take his Master's degree, the Queen's Privy Council wrote to the University saying that rumors to the effect that he was going abroad to Rheims (a center for Catholics) were unfounded—that in fact he had been employed "in matters touching the benefit of his country" and that "he had done her Majesty good service." The University proceeded to grant him his degree.

For the rest of his life, somewhat less than six years, Marlowe lived in or near London. He wrote his plays, *Tamburlaine* I and II, *Dido, The Massacre at Paris, The Jew of Malta, Dr. Faustus,* and *Edward II* in this period, and translated the *Amores* of Ovid, the first book of Lucan's *Pharsalia,* and the *Hero and Leander* of Musaeus (though this last is much too free and too original to be called a translation).

He lived dangerously. In 1589 he was involved in a brawl with one William Bradley, when Thomas Watson, the poet, intervened and killed Bradley. Both poets were jailed, but Watson got off on a plea of self-defense. In 1591 he was living and writing in the same room with another poet, Thomas Kyd, but in June, 1592 the theaters were closed by order of the Privy Council because of riots, and in August of that year a great plague began which kept them closed and which probably sent Marlowe out of town to visit his friend Thomas Walsingham, cousin of Sir Francis Walsingham, at Scadbury, Kent. There he was in May, 1593, when Thomas Kyd, under examination by the authorities, alleged that some "atheistical" papers found in his lodgings belonged to his former roommate Marlowe. The Council had Marlowe brought to them, and he appeared on May 20; he was not held, but was required to give daily attendance. For the next ten days nothing was done about him, but Kyd was released, and in an attempt to ingratiate himself with the authorities, gave further information against Marlowe, charging him with atheism and treason, and linking him with some followers of Sir Walter Ralegh (see p. 490). Additional voluntary information against him was given by one Richard Baines. On May 30, Marlowe in company with another protégé of Thomas Walsingham's, Ingram Frizer, and two other men of rather shady reputation spent the day at the inn of the Widow Bull in Deptford. In the evening a quarrel arose over the reckoning, and Frizer, in defending himself, killed Marlowe.

Dying at the age of twenty-nine, Marlowe left an almost immeasurable legacy to English drama and poetry. He was an artist of great genius; his "mighty line" of blank verse made Shakespeare's possible. He was like Shakespeare, too, in being a disciple of Ovid, witty and sensual favorite of the Elizabethans, and his classical learning would receive no scoffs from Ben Jonson, for in the dreamy world of classic myth and story he was at home. His fancy was exuberant and exotic; maps and strange place names and strange creatures excited him as they did the poet who told of Othello's travels. His spirit is that of youth, of the tremendous assertion of human power and glory against the inevitable answer of time and death and God. It is the spirit of renaissance, if not of the Renaissance.

BIBLIOGRAPHY: *The Works and Life of Christopher Marlowe,* gen. ed. R. H. Case, 6 vols., London, 1931; F. S. Boas, *Christopher Marlowe,* Oxford, 1940; John Bakeless, *Christopher Marlowe,* New York, 1937; U. M. Ellis-Fermor, *Christopher Marlowe,* London, 1927; Tucker Brooke, "Marlowe's Versification and Style," *SP,* XIX (1922), 186–205; Douglas Bush, *Mythology and the Renaissance Tradition,* Minneapolis, 1932; Leslie Hotson, *The Death of Christopher Marlowe,* London, 1925; Mark Eccles, *Christopher Marlowe in London,* Harvard, 1934; Harry Levin, *The Overreacher,* Harvard, 1952; Hallett Smith, *Elizabethan Poetry* (1952), 77–89; F. P. Wilson, *Marlowe and the Early Shakespeare,* Oxford, 1953; W. W. Greg, "The Copyright of Hero and Leander," *4 Library,* XXIV (1943–44), 165–74; P. W. Miller, "The Function of Myth in Marlowe's *Hero and Leander,*" *SP,* L (1953), 158–167; L. Zocca, *Elizabethan Narrative Poetry,* New Brunswick (1950), 232–248.

THE PASSIONATE SHEPHERD TO HIS LOVE[1]

Come live with me and be my love,
And we will all the pleasures prove
That valleys, groves, hills, and fields,
Woods, or steepy mountain yields.

And we will sit upon the rocks,
Seeing the shepherds feed their flocks,
By shallow rivers to whose falls
Melodious birds sings madrigals.

And I will make thee beds of roses
And a thousand fragrant posies,
A cap of flowers, and a kirtle
Embroidered all with leaves of myrtle;

A gown made of the finest wool
Which from our pretty lambs we pull;
Fair lined slippers for the cold,
With buckles of the purest gold;

A belt of straw and ivy buds,
With coral clasps and amber studs:
And if these pleasures may thee move,
Come live with me, and be my love.

The shepherds' swains shall dance and sing
For thy delight each May morning:
If these delights thy mind may move,
Then live with me and be my love.

HERO AND LEANDER

First Sestiad[2]

On Hellespont, guilty of true love's blood,
In view and opposite, two cities stood,
Sea-borderers, disjoined by Neptune's might;
The one Abydos, the other Sestos hight.[3]

---

[1] This version of the famous poem appeared in *England's Helicon* (1600). In 1599 four verses of it had appeared in the "Sonnets to sundry notes of Musicke" appended to *The Passionate Pilgrime*. The authorship of this poem and of the answer to it (see p. 193) is referred to in a passage in Izaak Walton's *The Compleat Angler* (1653): " 'Twas that smooth song which was made by Kit Marlow, now at least fifty years ago; and the milkmaid's mother sung an answer to it, which was made by Sir Walter Raleigh in his younger dayes." More musical settings for this poem have been composed from the sixteenth century to the present than for any other Elizabethan lyric except a few of Shakespeare's. Sir Hugh Evans sings part of the song in *Merry Wives*, III, i, 17–29.

[2] *Sestiad:* a book (named from Sestos).

[3] *hight:* called.

At Sestos Hero dwelt; Hero the fair,
Whom young Apollo courted for her hair,
And offered as a dower his burning throne,
Where she should sit for men to gaze upon.
The outside of her garments were of lawn,
The lining purple silk, with gilt stars drawn;
Her wide sleeves green, and bordered with a grove
Where Venus in her naked glory strove
To please the careless and disdainful eyes
Of proud Adonis, that before her lies;
Her kirtle blue, whereon was many a stain,
Made with the blood of wretched lovers slain.
Upon her head she ware a myrtle wreath,
From whence her veil reached to the ground beneath.
Her veil was artificial flowers and leaves,
Whose workmanship both man and beast deceives;
Many would praise the sweet smell as she passed,
When 'twas the odor which her breath forth cast;
And there for honey, bees have sought in vain,
And, beat from thence, have lighted there again.
About her neck hung chains of pebble-stone,
Which, lightened by her neck, like diamonds shone.
She ware no gloves, for neither sun nor wind
Would burn or parch her hands, but to her mind [4]
Or warm or cool them, for they took delight
To play upon those hands, they were so white.
Buskins of shells all silvered, used she,
And branched with blushing coral to the knee,
Where sparrows perched, of hollow pearl and gold.
Such as the world would wonder to behold;
Those with sweet water oft her handmaid fills,
Which, as she went, would chirrup through the bills.
Some say, for her the fairest Cupid pined,
And looking in her face, was strooken blind.
But this is true: so like was one the other,
As he imagined Hero was his mother;
And oftentimes into her bosom flew,
About her naked neck his bare arms threw,
And laid his childish head upon her breast,
And with still panting rocked, there took his rest.
So lovely fair was Hero, Venus' nun,
As Nature wept, thinking she was undone,
Because she took more from her than she left
And of such wondrous beauty her bereft;

[4] *to her mind:* as she wished.

Therefore, in sign her treasure suffered wrack,
Since Hero's time hath half the world been black.
Amorous Leander, beautiful and young,
(Whose tragedy divine Musaeus [5] sung)
Dwelt at Abydos; since him dwelt there none
For whom succeeding times make greater moan.
His dangling tresses that were never shorn,
Had they been cut and unto Colchos [6] borne,
Would have allured the vent'rous youth of Greece
To hazard more than for the Golden Fleece.
Fair Cynthia wished his arms might be her sphere; [7]
Grief makes her pale, because she moves not there.
His body was as straight as Circe's wand;
Jove might have sipped out nectar from his hand.
Even as delicious meat is to the taste,
So was his neck in touching, and surpassed
The white of Pelops' shoulder.[8] I could tell ye
How smooth his breast was, and how white his belly,
And whose immortal fingers did imprint
That heavenly path, with many a curious [9] dint,
That runs along his back; but my rude pen
Can hardly blazon forth the loves of men,
Much less of powerful gods; let it suffice
That my slack [10] muse sings of Leander's eyes,
Those orient [11] cheeks and lips, exceeding his
That leapt [12] into the water for a kiss
Of his own shadow, and despising many,
Died ere he could enjoy the love of any.
Had wild Hippolytus [13] Leander seen,
Enamored of his beauty had he been;
His presence made the rudest peasant melt,
That in the vast uplandish country dwelt;
The barbarous Thracian soldier, moved with naught,
Was moved with him, and for his favor sought.
Some swore he was a maid in man's attire,
For in his looks were all that men desire:
A pleasant smiling cheek, a speaking [14] eye,

---

[5] *Musaeus:* an Alexandrian grammarian of the fifth century A.D., sometimes confused with a legendary early Musaeus—hence "divine."

[6] *Colchos:* country in Asia where the Argonauts found the Golden Fleece.

[7] *Cynthia:* the moon; *sphere:* orbit.

[8] *white of Pelops' shoulder:* Pelops had a shoulder of ivory. See Ovid, *Metamorphoses,* VI, 403–411.

[9] *curious:* exquisite.

[10] *slack:* feeble, dull.

[11] *orient:* shining, like an Eastern gem.

[12] *that leapt:* Narcissus.

[13] *Hippolytus* offended Aphrodite by preferring hunting to love. Phaedra died of unrequited love for him.

[14] *speaking:* expressive.

A brow for love to banquet royally;
And such as knew he was a man, would say,
"Leander, thou art made for amorous play;
Why art thou not in love, and loved of all?
Though thou be fair, yet be not thine own thrall."
The men of wealthy Sestos every year,
For his sake whom their goddess held so dear,
Rose-cheeked Adonis, kept a solemn feast.
Thither resorted many a wandering guest
To meet their loves; such as had none at all
Came lovers home from this great festival;
For every street, like to a firmament,
Glistered with breathing stars, who, where they went,
Frighted the melancholy earth, which deemed
Eternal heaven to burn, for so it seemed
As if another Phaeton had got
The guidance of the sun's rich chariot.
But, far above the loveliest, Hero shined,
And stole away the enchanted gazer's mind;
For like sea nymphs' inveigling harmony,
So was her beauty to the standers by.
Nor that night-wandering pale and watery star [15]
(When yawning dragons draw her thirling [16] car
From Latmus' [17] mount up to the gloomy sky,
Where, crowned with blazing light and majesty,
She proudly sits) more over-rules [18] the flood,
Than she the hearts of those that near her stood.
Even as when gaudy nymphs pursue the chase,
Wretched Ixion's shaggy-footed race,[19]
Incensed with savage heat, gallop amain
From steep pine-bearing mountains to the plain,
So ran the people forth to gaze upon her,
And all that viewed her were enamored on her.
And as in fury of a dreadful fight,
Their fellows being slain or put to flight,
Poor soldiers stand with fear of death dead-strooken,
So at her presence all, surprised and tooken,
Await the sentence of her scornful eyes;
He whom she favors lives, the other dies.
There might you see one sigh, another rage,
And some, their violent passions to assuage,

---

[15] *star:* the moon.

[16] *thirling:* flying like a spear.

[17] *Latmus:* the mountain where the moon visited Endymion.

[18] *over-rules:* rules over.

[19] *Wretched . . . race:* Ixion begot upon a cloud the shaggy-footed centaurs. For his presumption in loving Juno, he was chained to a wheel—hence "wretched."

Compile sharp satires; but alas, too late,
For faithful love will never turn to hate.
And many, seeing great princes were denied,
Pined as they went, and thinking on her, died.
On this feast day, oh, cursed day and hour!
Went Hero thorough [20] Sestos, from her tower
To Venus' temple, where unhappily,
As after chanced, they did each other spy.
So fair a church as this had Venus none;
The walls were of discolored [21] jasper stone,
Wherein was Proteus carved, and o'erhead
A lively [22] vine of green sea-agate spread,
Where, by one hand, light-headed Bacchus hung,
And with the other, wine from grapes out-wrung.
Of crystal shining fair the pavement was;
The town of Sestos called it Venus' glass;
There might you see the gods in sundry shapes,
Committing heady [23] riots, incest, rapes;
For know that underneath this radiant floor
Was Danae's statue in a brazen tower;
Jove slyly stealing from his sister's bed
To dally with Idalian [24] Ganymed,
And for his love Europa bellowing [25] loud,
And tumbling with the rainbow in a cloud;
Blood-quaffing Mars heaving the iron net [26]
Which limping Vulcan and his Cyclops set;
Love kindling fire to burn such towns as Troy;
Silvanus weeping for the lovely boy [27]
That now is turned into a cypress tree,
Under whose shade the wood gods love to be.
And in the midst a silver altar stood;
There Hero sacrificing turtles' [28] blood,
Veiled to the ground, veiling her eyelids close,
And modestly they opened as she rose;
Thence flew love's arrow with the golden head,[29]
And thus Leander was enamored.
Stone still he stood, and evermore he gazed,

[20] *thorough:* through.

[21] *discolored:* of various colors.

[22] *lively:* lifelike.

[23] *heady:* passionate, violent.

[24] *Idalian:* Ganymede was kidnaped by Jove from Mt. Ida. *Idalian* really means of Idalium, a town sacred to Venus.

[25] *bellowing:* To seduce Europa Jupiter took the form of a bull.

[26] *net:* in which Vulcan trapped his wife Venus with Mars.

[27] *boy:* Cyparissus, whom Silvanus loved and who was turned into a cypress tree. Ovid, *Metamorphoses,* X, 120.

[28] *turtles:* turtle dove, as a type of constancy in love.

[29] *golden head:* Cupid had other arrows, blunt, which produced dislike. Ovid, *Metamorphoses,* I, 468.

Till with the fire that from his countenance blazed,
Relenting Hero's gentle heart was strook;
Such force and virtue hath an amorous look.
  It lies not in our power to love or hate,
For will in us is over-ruled by fate.
When two are stripped, long ere the course begin
We wish that one should lose, the other win;
And one especially do we affect
Of two gold ingots, like in each respect.
The reason no man knows, let it suffice,
What we behold is censured by our eyes.
Where both deliberate, the love is slight;
Who ever loved, that loved not at first sight? [30]
  He kneeled, but unto her devoutly prayed;
Chaste Hero to herself thus softly said:
"Were I the saint he worships, I would hear him";
And as she spake these words, came somewhat near him.
He started up; she blushed as one ashamed;
Wherewith Leander much more was inflamed.
He touched her hand; in touching it she trembled;
Love deeply grounded hardly is dissembled.
These lovers parled [31] by the touch of hands;
True love is mute, and oft amazed stands.
Thus while dumb signs their yielding hearts entangled,
The air with sparks of living fire was spangled,
And night, deep drenched in misty Acheron,
Heaved up her head, and half the world upon
Breathed darkness forth (dark night is Cupid's day).
And now begins Leander to display
Love's holy fire with words, with sighs, and tears,
Which like sweet music entered Hero's ears;
And yet at every word she turned aside,
And always cut him off as he replied.
At last, like to a bold sharp sophister,[32]
With cheerful hope thus he accosted her:
  "Fair creature, let me speak without offense;
I would my rude words had the influence
To lead thy thoughts as thy fair looks do mine!
Then shouldst thou be his prisoner who is thine.
Be not unkind and fair; misshapen stuff [33]
Are of behavior boisterous and rough.
Oh, shun me not, but hear me ere you go,

[30] *Who . . . sight:* quoted by Phoebe in *As You Like It,* III, v, 82.

[31] *parled:* spoke.

[32] *sophister:* specious reasoner.

[33] *stuff:* persons.

God knows I cannot force love, as you do.
My words shall be as spotless as my youth,
Full of simplicity and naked truth.
This sacrifice, whose sweet perfume descending
From Venus' altar to your footsteps bending,
Doth testify that you exceed her far,
To whom you offer, and whose nun you are.
Why should you worship her? her you surpass
As much as sparkling diamonds flaring[34] glass.
A diamond set in lead his worth retains;
A heavenly nymph, beloved of human swains,
Receives no blemish, but ofttimes more grace;
Which makes me hope, although I am but base,
Base in respect of thee, divine and pure,
Dutiful service may thy love procure,
And I in duty will excel all other,
As thou in beauty dost exceed Love's mother.
Nor heaven, nor thou, were made to gaze upon;
As heaven preserves all things, so save thou one.
A stately builded ship, well rigged and tall,
The ocean maketh more majestical;
Why vowest thou then to live in Sestos here,
Who on love's seas more glorious wouldst appear?
Like untuned golden strings all women are,
Which long time lie untouched, will harshly jar.
Vessels of brass, oft handled, brightly shine;
What difference betwixt the richest mine
And basest mold, but use? for both, not used,
Are of like worth. Then treasure is abused,
When misers keep it; being put to loan,
In time it will return us two for one.
Rich robes themselves and others do adorn;
Neither themselves nor others, if not worn.
Who builds a palace, and rams up the gate,
Shall see it ruinous and desolate.
Ah, simple Hero, learn thyself to cherish!
Lone women, like to empty houses, perish.
Less sins the poor rich man that starves himself
In heaping up a mass of drossy pelf,
Than such as you; his golden earth remains,
Which, after his decease, some other gains;
But this fair gem, sweet in the loss alone,
When you fleet hence, can be bequeathed to none.
Or if it could, down from th' enameled sky

[34] *flaring:* glaring.

All heaven would come to claim this legacy,
And with intestine[35] broils the world destroy,
And quite confound nature's sweet harmony.
Well therefore by the gods decreed it is
We human creatures should enjoy that bliss.
One is no number;[36] maids are nothing, then,
Without the sweet society of men.
Wilt thou live single still? one shalt thou be
Though never-singling Hymen couple thee.
Wild savages, that drink of running springs,
Think water far excels all earthly things,
But they that daily taste neat wine, despise it;
Virginity, albeit some highly prize it,
Compared with marriage, had you tried them both,
Differs as much as wine and water doth.
Base bullion for the stamp's[37] sake we allow;
Even so for men's impression do we you,
By which alone, our reverend fathers say,
Women receive perfection every way.
This idol which you term virginity
Is neither essence[38] subject to the eye,
No, nor to any one exterior sense,
Nor hath it any place of residence,
Nor is 't of earth or mold[39] celestial,
Or capable of any form at all.
Of that which hath no being, do not boast;
Things that are not at all, are never lost.
Men foolishly do call it virtuous;
What virtue is it, that is born with us?
Much less can honor be ascribed thereto;
Honor is purchased by the deeds we do.
Believe me, Hero, honor is not won
Until some honorable deed be done.
Seek you, for chastity, immortal fame,
And know that some have wronged Diana's name?[40]
Whose name is it, if she be false or not,
So she be fair, but some vile tongues will blot?
But you are fair, ay me, so wondrous fair,
So young, so gentle, and so debonair,
As Greece will think, if thus you live alone,
Some one or other keeps you as his own.
Then, Hero, hate me not, nor from me fly

---

[35] *intestine:* civil.

[36] *one is no number:* Aristotle, *Metaphysics,* XIV, i.

[37] *stamp:* I.e., of coinage.

[38] *essence:* something that exists.

[39] *mold:* form, shape.

[40] *And . . . name:* knowing that even Diana does not have a spotless reputation.

To follow swiftly blasting [41] infamy.
Perhaps thy sacred priesthood makes thee loath;
Tell me, to whom mad'st thou that heedless oath?"
"To Venus," answered she, and as she spake,
Forth from those two tralucent cisterns [42] brake
A stream of liquid pearl, which down her face
Made milk-white paths, whereon the gods might trace [43]
To Jove's high court. He thus replied: "The rites
In which love's beauteous empress most delights
Are banquets, Doric music,[44] midnight revel,
Plays, masques, and all that stern age counteth evil.
Thee as a holy idiot [45] doth she scorn,
For thou, in vowing chastity, hast sworn
To rob her name and honor, and thereby
Commit'st a sin far worse than perjury,
Even sacrilege against her deity,
Through regular and formal purity.
To expiate which sin, kiss and shake hands;
Such sacrifice as this Venus demands."
Thereat she smiled, and did deny him so
As, put thereby, yet might he hope for mo.[46]
Which makes him quickly reinforce his speech,
And her in humble manner thus beseech:
"Though neither gods nor men may thee deserve,
Yet for her sake whom you have vowed to serve,
Abandon fruitless cold virginity,
The gentle queen of love's sole enemy.
Then shall you most resemble Venus' nun,
When Venus' sweet rites are performed and done.
Flint-breasted Pallas joys in single life,
But Pallas and your mistress are at strife.
Love, Hero, then, and be not tyrannous,
But heal the heart that thou hast wounded thus;
Nor stain thy youthful years with avarice;
Fair fools delight to be accounted nice.[47]
The richest corn dies if it be not reaped;
Beauty alone is lost, too warily kept."
These arguments he used, and many more,
Wherewith she yielded, that was won before.
Hero's looks yielded, but her words made war;

[41] *blasting:* withering.

[42] *tralucent:* translucent; *cisterns:* a conceit for her eyes.

[43] *trace:* proceed.

[44] *Doric music:* A mistake. Doric music was severe and martial. Marlowe meant Lydian, presumably.

[45] *idiot:* ignorant, uninstructed person.

[46] *put:* repelled; *mo:* more.

[47] *nice:* coy, reserved.

Women are won when they begin to jar.[48]
Thus having swallowed Cupid's golden hook,
The more she strived, the deeper was she strook;
Yet, evilly feigning anger, strove she still,
And would be thought to grant against her will.
So having paused awhile, at last she said:
"Who taught thee rhetoric to deceive a maid?
Ay me! such words as these should I abhor,
And yet I like them for the orator."
  With that Leander stooped to have embraced her,
But from his spreading arms away she cast her,
And thus bespake him: "Gentle youth, forbear
To touch the sacred garments which I wear.
Upon a rock, and underneath a hill,
Far from the town, where all is whist [49] and still
Save that the sea playing on yellow sand
Sends forth a rattling murmur to the land,
Whose sound allures the golden Morpheus
In silence of the night to visit us,
My turret stands; and there, God knows, I play
With Venus' swans and sparrows all the day.
A dwarfish beldame bears me company,
That hops about the chamber where I lie,
And spends the night, that might be better spent,
In vain discourse and apish merriment.
Come thither." As she spake this, her tongue tripped,
For unawares, "Come thither," from her slipped;
And suddenly her former color changed,
And here and there her eyes, through anger, ranged.
And like a planet moving several ways
At one self instant, she, poor soul, assays,
Loving, not to love at all, and every part
Strove to resist the motions of her heart;
And hands so pure, so innocent, nay such
As might have made heaven stoop to have a touch,
Did she uphold to Venus, and again
Vowed spotless chastity, but all in vain.
Cupid beats down her prayers with his wings;
Her vows above the empty air he flings;
All deep enraged, his sinewy bow he bent,
And shot a shaft that burning from him went;
Wherewith she, strooken, looked so dolefully,
As made Love sigh to see his tyranny.

---

[48] *jar:* dispute.

[49] *whist:* silent.

And as she wept, her tears to pearl he turned,
And wound them on his arm, and for her mourned.
Then towards the palace of the Destinies,
Laden with languishment and grief, he flies,
And to those stern nymphs humbly made request,
Both might enjoy each other, and be blest.
But with a ghastly dreadful countenance,
Threat'ning a thousand deaths at every glance,
They answered Love, nor would vouchsafe so much
As one poor word, their hate to him was such.
Hearken awhile, and I will tell you why:
Heaven's winged herald, Jove-born Mercury,
The selfsame day that he asleep had laid
Enchanted Argus,[50] spied a country maid,
Whose careless hair, instead of pearl t' adorn it,
Glistered with dew, as one that seemed to scorn it;
Her breath as fragrant as the morning rose,
Her mind pure, and her tongue untaught to gloze;[51]
Yet proud she was, for lofty pride that dwells
In towered courts is oft in shepherds' cells,
And too too well the fair vermilion knew,
And silver tincture of her cheeks, that drew
The love of every swain. On her this god
Enamored was, and with his snaky rod[52]
Did charm her nimble feet, and made her stay,
The while upon a hillock down he lay,
And sweetly on his pipe began to play,
And with smooth speech her fancy to assay;[53]
Till in his twining arms he locked her fast,
And then he wooed with kisses, and at last,
As shepherds do, her on the ground he laid,
And tumbling in the grass, he often strayed
Beyond the bounds of shame, in being bold
To eye those parts which no eye should behold.
And like an insolent commanding lover,
Boasting his parentage, would needs discover
The way to new Elysium; but she,
Whose only dower was her chastity,
Having striv'n in vain, was now about to cry,
And crave the help of shepherds that were nigh.
Herewith he stayed his fury, and began
To give her leave to rise; away she ran;

[50] *Argus:* Mercury put the hundred-eyed Argus to sleep with music and then cut off his head. Juno had his eyes transferred to the tail of the peacock.

[51] *gloze:* insinuate, flatter.

[52] *snaky rod:* the Caduceus of Mercury, now the symbol of medicine.

[53] *assay:* assail, try.

After went Mercury, who used such cunning,
As she, to hear his tale, left off her running;
Maids are not won by brutish force and might,
But speeches full of pleasure and delight;
And knowing Hermes courted her, was glad
That she such loveliness and beauty had
As could provoke his liking, yet was mute,
And neither would deny nor grant his suit.
Still vowed he love, she wanting no excuse
To feed him with delays, as women use,
Or thirsting after immortality—
All women are ambitious naturally—
Imposed upon her lover such a task
As he ought not perform, nor yet she ask.
A draught of flowing nectar she requested,
Wherewith the king of gods and men is feasted.
He, ready to accomplish what she willed,
Stole some from Hebe (Hebe Jove's cup filled)
And gave it to his simple rustic love;
Which being known (as [54] what is hid from Jove?)
He inly [55] stormed, and waxed more furious
Than for the fire filched by Prometheus,
And thrusts him down from heaven; he wand'ring here
In mournful terms, with sad and heavy cheer,
Complained to Cupid. Cupid, for his sake,
To be revenged on Jove did undertake;
And those on whom heaven, earth, and hell relies,
I mean the adamantine Destinies,
He wounds with love, and forced them equally
To dote upon deceitful Mercury.
They offered him the deadly fatal knife
That shears the slender threads of human life;
At his fair-feathered feet the engines [56] laid
Which th' earth from ugly Chaos' den upweighed;
These he regarded not, but did entreat
That Jove, usurper of his father's seat,
Might presently be banished into hell,
And aged Saturn in Olympus dwell.
They granted what he craved, and once again
Saturn and Ops began their golden reign.
Murder, rape, war, lust, and treachery
Were with Jove closed in Stygian empery.[57]
But long this blessed time continued not;

[54] *as:* for.
[55] *inly:* inwardly, deeply.
[56] *engines:* instruments.
[57] *empery:* dominion.

As soon as he his wished purpose got,
He, reckless of his promise, did despise
The love of th' everlasting Destinies.
They seeing it, both Love and him abhorred,
And Jupiter unto his place restored.
And but that Learning,[58] in despite of Fate,
Will mount aloft, and enter heaven gate,
And to the seat of Jove itself advance,
Hermes had slept in hell with Ignorance;
Yet as a punishment they added this,
That he and Poverty should always kiss.
And to this day is every scholar poor;
Gross gold from them runs headlong to the boor.[59]
Likewise, the angry sisters thus deluded,
To venge themselves on Hermes, have concluded
That Midas' brood shall sit in Honor's chair,
To which the Muses' sons are only heir;
And fruitful wits that inaspiring are
Shall, discontent, run into regions far;
And few great lords in virtuous deeds shall joy,
But be surprised with every garish toy;[60]
And still enrich the lofty servile clown,
Who with encroaching guile keeps learning down.
Then muse not Cupid's suit no better sped,[61]
Seeing in their loves the Fates were injured.

Second Sestiad

By this, sad Hero, with love unacquainted,
Viewing Leander's face, fell down and fainted.
He kissed her and breathed life into her lips,
Wherewith, as one displeased, away she trips.
Yet as she went, full often looked behind,
And many poor excuses did she find
To linger by the way, and once she stayed
And would have turned again, but was afraid,
In off'ring parley, to be counted light.[62]
So on she goes, and in her idle flight,
Her painted fan of curled plumes let fall,
Thinking to train[63] Leander therewithal.
He, being a novice, knew not what she meant,
But stayed, and after her a letter sent,

[58] *Learning:* Which Mercury (Hermes) represented.
[59] *boor:* an unlettered person.
[60] *toy:* trifle.
[61] *muse:* wonder; *sped:* succeeded.
[62] *light:* immodest.
[63] *train:* entice.

Which joyful Hero answered in such sort
As he had hoped to scale the beauteous fort
Wherein the liberal graces locked their wealth,
And therefore to her tower he got by stealth.
Wide open stood the door, he need not climb;
And she herself, before the 'pointed time,
Had spread the board, with roses strewed the room,
And oft looked out, and mused he did not come.
At last he came; Oh, who can tell the greeting
These greedy lovers had at their first meeting?
He asked, she gave, and nothing was denied;
Both to each other quickly were affied.[64]
Look how their hands, so were their hearts united,
And what he did she willingly requited.
Sweet are the kisses, the embracements sweet,
When like desires and affections meet;
For from the earth to heaven is Cupid raised,
Where fancy is in equal balance peised.[65]
Yet she this rashness suddenly repented,
And turned aside, and to herself lamented,
As if her name and honor had been wronged
By being possessed of him for whom she longed;
Aye, and she wished, albeit not from her heart,
That he would leave her turret and depart.
The mirthful god of amorous pleasure smiled
To see how he this captive nymph beguiled;
For hitherto he did but fan the fire,
And kept it down that it might mount the higher.
Now waxed she jealous lest his love abated,
Fearing her own thoughts made her to be hated.
Therefore unto him hastily she goes,
And like light Salmacis,[66] her body throws
Upon his bosom, where with yielding eyes
She offers up herself, a sacrifice
To slake his anger if he were displeased.
Oh, what god would not therewith be appeased?
Like Aesop's cock,[67] this jewel he enjoyed,
And as a brother with his sister toyed,
Supposing nothing else was to be done,
Now he her favor and good will had won.
But know you not that creatures wanting sense [68]

---

[64] *affied:* affianced, engaged.

[65] *peised:* weighed.

[66] *Salmacis:* the nymph of a fountain, who fell in love with Hermaphroditus when he bathed there. Ovid, *Metamorphoses,* IV. 285.

[67] *Aesop's cock:* In a pseudo-Aesop fable a cock did not know what to do with a jewel, but would gladly trade it for a grain of corn.

[68] *creatures wanting sense:* inanimate objects. The reference is to magnetism.

By nature have a mutual appetence,
And wanting organs to advance a step,
Moved by love's force, unto each other leap?
Much more in subjects having intellect,
Some hidden influence breeds like effect.
Albeit Leander, rude [69] in love and raw,
Long dallying with Hero, nothing saw
That might delight him more, yet he suspected
Some amorous rites or other were neglected.
Therefore unto his body hers he clung;
She, fearing on the rushes to be flung,
Strived with redoubled strength; the more she strived,
The more a gentle pleasing heat revived,
Which taught him all that elder lovers know;
And now the same gan so to scorch and glow,
As in plain terms, yet cunningly, he craved it;
Love always makes those eloquent that have it.
She, with a kind of granting, put him by it,[70]
And ever as he thought himself most nigh it,
Like to the tree of Tantalus [71] she fled,
And, seeming lavish, saved her maidenhead.
Ne'er king more sought to keep his diadem,
Than Hero this inestimable gem.
Above our life we love a steadfast friend,
Yet when a token of great worth we send,
We often kiss it, often look thereon,
And stay the messenger that would be gone;
No marvel then though Hero would not yield
So soon to part from that she dearly held;
Jewels being lost are found again, this never;
'Tis lost but once, and once lost, lost forever.
  Now had the morn espied her lover's steeds,
Whereat she starts, puts on her purple weeds,
And, red for anger that he stayed so long,
All headlong throws herself the clouds among.
And now Leander, fearing to be missed,
Embraced her suddenly, took leave, and kissed.
Long was he taking leave, and loath to go,
And kissed again, as lovers use to do.
Sad Hero wrung him by the hand and wept,
Saying, "Let your vows and promises be kept."
Then, standing at the door, she turned about,

[69] *rude:* ignorant, untaught.

[70] *put him by it:* refused it to him.

[71] *tree of Tantalus:* Tantalus was punished in the lower world by being kept in a lake, but whenever he tried to drink, the waters receded, and whenever he tried to eat fruit from the tree overhead the tree drew away.

As loath to see Leander going out.
And now the sun that through th' horizon peeps,
As pitying these lovers, downward creeps,
So that in silence of the cloudy night,
Though it was morning, did he take his flight.
But what the secret trusty night concealed,
Leander's amorous habit [72] soon revealed;
With Cupid's myrtle was his bonnet crowned,
About his arms the purple riband wound
Wherewith she wreathed her largely spreading hair;
Nor could the youth abstain, but he must wear
The sacred ring wherewith she was endowed,
When first religious chastity she vowed;
Which made his love through Sestos to be known,
And thence unto Abydos sooner blown
Than he could sail; for incorporeal Fame,
Whose weight consists in nothing but her name,
Is swifter than the wind, whose tardy plumes
Are reeking [73] water and dull earthly fumes.
Home, when he came, he seemed not to be there,
But like exiled heir thrust from his sphere,
Set in a foreign place; and straight from thence,
Alcides [74] like, by mighty violence
He would have chased away the swelling main
That him from her unjustly did detain.
Like as the sun in a diameter
Fires and inflames objects removed far,
And heateth kindly, shining laterally,
So beauty sweetly quickens when 'tis nigh,
But being separated and removed,
Burns where it cherished, murders where it loved.
Therefore even as an index to a book,
So to his mind was young Leander's look.
Oh, none but gods have power their love to hide;
Affection by the countenance is descried.
The light of hidden fire itself discovers,
And love that is concealed betrays poor lovers.
His secret flame apparently [75] was seen;
Leander's father knew where he had been,
And for the same mildly rebuked his son,
Thinking to quench the sparkles new begun.
But love, resisted once, grows passionate,
And nothing more than counsel lovers hate;

72 *amorous habit:* lover's clothing.
73 *reeking:* fuming, vaporous.
74 *Alcides:* Hercules.
75 *apparently:* clearly.

For as a hot proud horse highly disdains
To have his head controlled, but breaks the reins,
Spits forth the ringled [76] bit, and with his hooves
Checks [77] the submissive ground, so he that loves,
The more he is restrained, the worse he fares.
What is it now but mad Leander dares?
"Oh Hero, Hero!" thus he cried full oft,
And then he got him to a rock aloft,
Where having spied her tower, long stared he on 't,
And prayed the narrow toiling Hellespont
To part in twain, that he might come and go;
But still the rising billows answered "No."
With that he stripped him to the ivory skin,
And crying, "Love, I come!" leaped lively [78] in.
Whereat the sapphire-visaged god [79] grew proud,
And made his capering Triton sound aloud,
Imagining that Ganymede, displeased,
Had left the heavens; therefore on him he seized.
Leander strived; the waves about him wound,
And pulled him to the bottom, where the ground
Was strewed with pearl, and in low coral groves
Sweet singing mermaids sported with their loves
On heaps of heavy gold, and took great pleasure
To spurn in careless sort the shipwreck treasure.
For here the stately azure palace stood,
Where kingly Neptune and his train abode.
The lusty god embraced him, called him love,
And swore he never should return to Jove.
But when he knew it was not Ganymede,
For under water he was almost dead,
He heaved him up, and looking on his face,
Beat down the bold waves with his triple mace,
Which mounted up, intending to have kissed him,
And fell in drops like tears, because they missed him.
Leander, being up, began to swim,
And looking back, saw Neptune follow him;
Whereat aghast, the poor soul gan to cry:
"Oh, let me visit Hero ere I die!"
The god put Helle's [80] bracelet on his arm,
And swore the sea should never do him harm.
He clapped his plump cheeks, with his tresses played,
And smiling wantonly, his love bewrayed.[81]

---

[76] *ringled:* fitted with metal rings.

[77] *checks:* stamps.

[78] *lively:* briskly.

[79] *sapphire-visaged god:* Neptune.

[80] *Helle:* While riding on the golden ram with her brother Phrixus, she fell into the sea, whence the name Hellespont.

[81] *bewrayed:* revealed.

He watched his arms, and as they opened wide,
At every stroke betwixt them would he slide,
And steal a kiss, and then run out and dance,
And as he turned, cast many a lustful glance,
And threw him gaudy toys to please his eye,
And dive into the water, and there pry
Upon his breast, his thighs, and every limb,
And up again, and close beside him swim,
And talk of love. Leander made reply:
"You are deceived, I am no woman, I."
Thereat smiled Neptune, and then told a tale
How that a shepherd, sitting in a vale,
Played with a boy so lovely, fair, and kind,
As for his love both earth and heaven pined;
That of the cooling river durst not drink
Lest water nymphs should pull him from the brink;
And when he sported in the fragrant lawns,
Goat-footed satyrs and up-staring fauns
Would steal him thence. Ere half this tale was done,
"Ay me," Leander cried, "th' enamored sun,
That now should shine on Thetis' glassy bower,
Descends upon my radiant Hero's tower.
Oh, that these tardy arms of mine were wings!"
And as he spake, upon the waves he springs.
Neptune was angry that he gave no ear,
And in his heart revenging malice bare;
He flung at him his mace, but as it went
He called it in, for love made him repent.
The mace returning back, his own hand hit,
As meaning to be venged for darting it.
When this fresh bleeding wound Leander viewed,
His color went and came, as if he rued
The grief which Neptune felt. In gentle breasts
Relenting thoughts, remorse, and pity rests;
And who have hard hearts and obdurate minds
But vicious, harebrained, and illiterate hinds?
The god, seeing him with pity to be moved,
Thereon concluded that he was beloved.
(Love is too full of faith, too credulous,
With folly and false hope deluding us.)
Wherefore, Leander's fancy to surprise,
To the rich ocean for gifts he flies.
'Tis wisdom to give much; a gift prevails
When deep persuading oratory fails.
  By this, Leander, being near the land,
Cast down his weary feet and felt the sand.

Breathless albeit he were, he rested not
Till to the solitary tower he got,
And knocked and called, at which celestial noise
The longing heart of Hero much more joys
Than nymphs or shepherds when the timbrel rings,
Or crooked dolphin when the sailor sings;
She stayed not for her robes, but straight arose,
And drunk with gladness, to the door she goes;
Where seeing a naked man, she screeched for fear,
(Such sights as this to tender maids are rare)
And ran into the dark herself to hide.
Rich jewels in the dark are soonest spied;
Unto her was he led, or rather drawn,
By those white limbs which sparkled through the lawn.[82]
The nearer that he came, the more she fled,
And seeking refuge, slipped into her bed.
Whereon Leander sitting, thus began,
Through numbing cold all feeble, faint, and wan:
"If not for love, yet, love, for pity sake,
Me in thy bed and maiden bosom take;
At least vouchsafe these arms some little room,
Who, hoping to embrace thee, cheerly [83] swum;
This head was beat with many a churlish billow,
And therefore let it rest upon thy pillow."
Herewith affrighted Hero shrunk away,
And in her lukewarm place Leander lay,
Whose lively heat like fire from heaven fet,[84]
Would animate gross clay, and higher set
The drooping thoughts of base declining souls,
Than dreary [85] Mars carousing nectar bowls.
His hands he cast upon her like a snare;
She, overcome with shame and sallow fear,
Like chaste Diana, when Actaeon spied her,
Being suddenly betrayed, dived down to hide her;
And as her silver body downward went,
With both her hands she made the bed a tent,
And in her own mind thought herself secure,
O'ercast with dim and darksome coverture.
And now she lets him whisper in her ear,
Flatter, entreat, promise, protest, and swear;
Yet ever as he greedily assayed
To touch those dainties, she the harpy played,
And every limb did, as a soldier stout,

[82] *lawn:* thin fine cloth.
[83] *cheerly:* gladly.
[84] *fet:* brought.
[85] *dreary:* bloody.

Defend the fort and keep the foeman out;
For though the rising ivory mount he scaled,
Which is with azure circling lines empaled,
Much like a globe (a globe may I term this,
By which love sails to regions full of bliss)
Yet there with Sisyphus [86] he toiled in vain,
Till gentle parley did the truce obtain.
Wherein Leander on her quivering breast,
Breathless spoke something, and sighed out the rest;
Which so prevailed, as he with small ado
Enclosed her in his arms and kissed her too.
And every kiss to her was as a charm,
And to Leander as a fresh alarm,[87]
So that the truce was broke, and she, alas,
Poor silly maiden, at his mercy was.
Love is not full of pity, as men say,
But deaf and cruel where he means to prey.
Even as a bird, which in our hands we wring,
Forth plungeth and oft flutters with her wing,
She trembling strove; this strife of hers, like that
Which made the world, another world begat
Of unknown joy. Treason was in her thought,
And cunningly to yield herself she sought.
Seeming not won, yet won she was at length;
In such wars women use but half their strength.
Leander now, like Theban Hercules,
Entered the orchard of th' Hesperides,
Whose fruit none rightly can describe but he
That pulls or shakes it from the golden tree.
And now she wished this night were never done,
And sighed to think upon th' approaching sun;
For much it grieved her that the bright daylight
Should know the pleasure of this blessed night,
And them like Mars and Erycine [88] display,
Both in each other's arms chained as they lay.
Again she knew not how to frame her look,
Or speak to him who in a moment took
That which so long, so charily she kept;
And fain by stealth away she would have crept,
And to some corner secretly have gone,
Leaving Leander in the bed alone.
But as her naked feet were whipping out,
He on the sudden clinged her so about,

[86] *Sisyphus* was condemned to roll a stone continually up hill.

[87] *alarm:* a call to action.

[88] *Erycine:* Venus.

That mermaid-like unto the floor she slid,
One half appeared, the other half was hid.
Thus near the bed she blushing stood upright,
And from her countenance behold ye might
A kind of twilight break, which through the hair,
As from an orient cloud, glimpse here and there;
And round about the chamber this false morn
Brought forth the day before the day was born.
So Hero's ruddy cheek Hero betrayed,
And her all naked to his sight displayed;
Whence his admiring eyes more pleasure took
Than Dis [89] on heaps of gold fixing his look.
By this, Apollo's golden harp began
To sound forth music to the ocean;
Which watchful Hesperus no sooner heard,
But he the day-bright-bearing car prepared,
And ran before, as harbinger of light,
And with his flaring beams mocked ugly night
Till she, o'ercome with anguish, shame, and rage,
Danged [90] down to hell her loathsome carriage.

Desunt nonnulla.[91]

[89] *Dis:* Pluto, god of wealth.
[90] *Danged:* threw.
[91] *Desunt nonnulla:* "Some verses are missing" [i.e., the remaining four Sestiads]. They were later supplied by George Chapman.

Robert Greene Gabriel Harvey Thomas Nashe

1560?–1592 1550?–1630 1567–1601

ROBERT GREENE was the most prolific of Elizabethan pamphleteers. He wrote plays and romances, autobiographical prodigal-son stories, repentance pieces, and also a series of exposés of the tricks of cheats and criminals. He lived only thirty-four years; he was a Master of Arts of both Oxford and Cambridge; he died in poverty and misery, abandoned by his friends.

He was originally from Norwich, and there is in his plays and poems the memory of an idealized English countryside of his boyhood. But in his realistic prose pamphlets he shows both the underworld of London—thieves, pickpockets, cardsharpers, whores, and blackmailers—and the hardships of a literary hack at the end of the sixteenth century. "In a night and a day would he have yarkt up a pamphlet as well as in seven yeare," Nashe said of him, and Greene himself confessed, "Many things I have wrote to get money." Accordingly, his professed motives of patriotism for writing the cony-catching pamphlets and his over-urged piety behind the repentance pieces need not be accepted at face value.

In midsummer of 1592 Greene attended, together with Nashe and others, a fatal banquet of pickled herring and Rhenish wine. It left him ill for the whole month of August—not so ill that he was unable to write two or three books, but ill enough so that on September 3rd he died. The shoemaker's wife who was his landlady crowned him with a garland of bays. His sordid life was at an end, but his unquiet spirit walked abroad to stir up the quarrelsome tempers of Nashe and Harvey and to call to the attention of the world an upstart actor-playwright named Shakespeare.

Henry Chettle, the editor of Greene's *Groatsworth of Wit,* apologized for the slur at Shakespeare, and remarked incidentally that Greene's pamphlet was originally so libelous that he had suppressed part of it. From the happy pastoralism of his earlier Euphuistic romances (e.g., *Pandosto,* which gave Shakespeare material for *The Winter's Tale*) to the morbid groans of the repentance pamphlets is a far cry: it illuminates the scope of experience and literature in the sixteenth century.

Some of the most vivid details about the last days of Greene are preserved for us by Gabriel Harvey, a Cambridge don, and well known as a friend of Spenser since the publication of some of their correspondence (*Three Proper Letters,* 1580). Harvey is the "Hobbinol" of the *Shepheardes Calender.* (See p. 312 above.)

Greene had been one of a group of writers engaged by the bishops to answer some Puritan attacks on the clergy issued under the name of Martin Marprelate. Greene and his group were attacked by Harvey's brother Richard in *Plaine Percevall the Peace-maker of England* (1590), and Richard commented in another work published the same year, *The Lamb of God,* on the insufferable presumption of one Thomas Nashe in setting up as a critic of all his literary elders as he had done in the preface to Greene's *Menaphon.* (This in spite of the fact that Nashe had praised Gabriel Harvey in that preface.) Greene's reply was to insert in *A Quip for an Upstart Courtier* (1592) an attack on the three Harvey boys who came to Cambridge from Saffron Walden, and on their father, who was a rope-maker. The war was on. Gabriel, the oldest of the three, was the leader. His younger brother, John, the physician and almanac-maker, died about the time Greene's attack occurred, and Gabriel came to London in a fury to have the law of Greene. (Harvey was a D.C.L. of Oxford.) But Gabriel found, to his surprise, that Greene himself had just died, and he went to the scene of his death to gather details. He made his attack on the dead Greene in *Foure Letters, and Certaine Sonnets, especially touching R. Greene,* but during the composition of it there appeared from the press *Pierce Penilesse,* a book by Nashe, in which, as a sample of railing, the author had given his retort to Richard Harvey's *Lamb of God.* So in his third letter, Gabriel included Nashe, whom he had hitherto "wished well in some respects," in his attack. Nashe and Gabriel Harvey, the two champions, were now engaged. Nashe replied immediately with *Strange Newes of the Intercepting Certaine Letters and a convoy of verses as they were going privily to the Low Countries.* (Also called *Four Letters Confuted* and *The Apology of Pierce Penilesse.*) Harvey countered with *Pierce's Supererogation,* which included as one of its three parts an attack on Lyly, written some years earlier but never published. Nashe was now willing to abandon the silly quarrel and apologize to Harvey, which he did in the preface to *Christs Teares Over Jerusalem* (1593). "All acknowledgements of abundant scholarship," he wrote, "courteous well governed behaviour and ripe experienced judgment, do I attribute unto him. Only with his mild, gentle moderation hereunto hath he won me." Nashe, however, did not know that a letter from Harvey to his publisher, Wolfe, containing further denunciations of Nashe, was going to be published as *A New Letter of Notable Contents,* and probably Harvey did not know when he wrote *A New Letter* of Nashe's handsome gesture in the preface to *Christs Teares.* At any rate, in the second edition of *Christs Teares* (1594), Nashe canceled the original preface and substituted one in which he told how that Machiavel, that vain braggadocio, that Gabriel Gravedigger had betrayed the peace, and promised vengeance for it. This vengeance was delayed, and apparently Harvey tried unsuccessfully to patch up the quarrel again with a personal conference, at a time when the two enemies happened to take adjoining rooms at a Cambridge inn. Nashe reached the height of his powers as a railer in *Have With You to Saffron-Walden* (1596), an elaborate survey of Harvey's character, life, and works. It was dedicated to Richard Lichfield, the barber of Trinity College, and the reply to it, appearing in 1597, called *The Trimming of T. Nashe,* purported to be written by the barber. This ended the quarrel, for no further contributions to it appeared before June 1, 1599, when the ecclesiastical authorities ordered that "all Nashe's books and Doctor Harvey's books be taken wheresoever they may be found and that none of their books be ever printed hereafter." By 1601 Nashe is referred to as dead. Harvey lived until about 1630, in retirement at Saffron Walden.

Thomas Nashe is one of the masters of invective in English. He shows youth, spirit, a hatred of stuffiness and dullness, and his wild impatient temper breaks through the usual ornate periods of Elizabethan prose. In Harvey he had an ideal antagonist. Harvey was older, more learned, more sober; he was also pompous and affected. He was trying to compensate for his lowly origin, perhaps, when he asserted himself so pompously. Yet he was certain to come off the loser in a battle with Nashe, who was no pedant but a clever journalist. Nashe was not the artist that Lyly was, and he was not so versatile as Greene. But his *Unfortunate Traveller* or *Jack Wilton* is one of the best pieces of Elizabethan prose fiction. It has been called "the best specimen of the picaresque tale in English literature anterior to Defoe," but Jack Wilton is not really the Spanish *picaro* or rogue; he is a jester and player of pranks like the English Scogan and Tarlton and George Peele. There is much realistic journalism in the descriptions in the book; there is a generous portion of horror melodrama; and there is a skillful blending of just enough historical and geographical detail to give the narrative a feeling of authenticity.

Nashe was about 33 when he died; his life was similar to that of his fellow university wits—Marlowe (who died at 29), Peele (who died at 30), and Greene (who died at 32). He was really more conservative in his opinions than old Harvey; his view of history and of art, like Spenser's and Shakespeare's, looked back instead of forward. *Christs Teares* and *Pierce Penilesse* are medieval in content. But Nashe's extraordinary vigor, his originality of manner, and his breezy and amusing way with trifles (his *Lenten Stuffe* is a praise of red herring, all in honor of Yarmouth, which was hospitable to him when he fled London after one of his many scrapes)—all these make him one of the liveliest of dead authors. The best justification of him is a remark of his own: "No wind that blows strong but is boisterous."

Bibliography: *The Life and Complete Works in Prose and Verse of Robert Greene*, ed. A. B. Grosart, 1881–1883; *The Bodley Head Quartos*, ed. G. B. Harrison (editions of the separate tracts); J. C. Jordan, *Robert Greene*, New York, 1915; D. C. Allen, "Science and Invention in Greene's Prose," *PMLA*, LIII (1938), 1007; H. Jenkins, "Greene's *Groatsworth* and *Repentance*," *RES*, *XI* (1935), 28; C. E. Sanders, "Robert Greene and his 'Editors,'" *PMLA*, XLVIII (1933), 392–417; Gwyn Jones, *Garland of Bays*, New York, 1938 (an interesting novel about Greene). For rogue literature see F. W. Chandler, *The Literature of Roguery*, Boston, 1907; F. Aydelotte, *Elizabethan Rogues and Vagabonds*, Oxford, 1913; A. V. Judges, *The Elizabethan Underworld*, New York, 1930; E. A. Baker, *History of the English Novel*, vol. II, London, 1929.

The Works of Thomas Nashe, ed. R. B. McKerrow, 5 vols., London, 1904–1910. (A great work of scholarship. Volume 5 contains the best account yet written of Nashe's life, the Martin Marprelate Controversy and the Nashe-Harvey quarrel.) *The Works of Gabriel Harvey, D.C.L.*, ed. A. B. Grosart, 3 vols., The Huth Library, 1884; F. R. Johnson, "The First Edition of Gabriel Harvey's *Foure Letters*," *4 Library*, XV (1934), 212–223; Henry Morley, "Gabriel Harvey," in *Clement Marot and other Studies*, London, 1871; Virginia Woolf, "The Strange Elizabethans," in *The Second Common Reader*, New York, 1932; *Letter-Book of Gabriel Harvey*, ed. E. J. L. Scott, Camden Society Publ. vol. 33, 1884; *Gabriel Harvey's Marginalia*, ed. G. C. Moore-Smith, Stratford, 1913, and additions by S. Tannenbaum in *MLR*, XXV (1930), 327–331 and by C. Camden in *PQ*, XIII (1934), 214–218; G. M. Young, "In Defense of Gabriel Harvey," *Life and Letters*, June, 1930, reprinted in *Modern English Essays*, Oxford World's Classics; J. C. Maxwell, "Gabriel Harvey, A Reply to Mr. G. M. Young," *Essays in Criticism* I (1951), 185–8; H. S. Wilson, "The Humanism of Gabriel Harvey," *Adams Memorial Studies*, Washington, 1948, 707–722; "Gabriel Harvey's Method of Annotating his Books," *Harvard Library Bulletin*, II (1948), 344–361.

Robert Greene

1560?–1592

FROM

A NOTABLE DISCOVERY OF COZENAGE[1]

(1591)

THE ART OF CONY-CATCHING

THERE be requisite effectually to act the art of cony-catching three several parties: the setter, the verser, and the barnacle. The nature of the setter is to draw any person familiarly to drink with him, which person they call the cony, and their method is according to the man they aim at; if a gentleman, merchant, or apprentice, the cony[2] is the more easily caught, in that they are soon induced to play, and therefore I omit the circumstance which they use in catching of them. And for because the poor country farmer or yeoman is the mark which they most of all shoot at, who they know comes not empty to the term,[3] I will discover the means they put in practice to bring in some honest, simple, and ignorant men to their purpose.

The cony-catchers, appareled like honest civil gentlemen, or good fellows, with a smooth face, as if butter would not melt in their mouths, after dinner when the clients are come from Westminster Hall[4] and are at leisure to walk up and down Paul's,[5] Fleetstreet, Holborn, the Strand, and such common haunted places, where these cozening companions attend only to spy out a prey; who as soon as they see a plain country fellow well and cleanly appareled, either in a coat of homespun russet, or of frieze,[6] as the time requires, and a side pouch at his side, "There is a cony," saith one.

At that word out flies the setter, and overtaking the man, begins to salute him thus: "Sir, God save you, you are welcome to London, how doth all our good friends in the country, I hope they be all in health?"

The countryman seeing a man so courteous he knows not, half in a brown study at this strange salutation, perhaps makes him this answer:

---

1 *Discovery of Cozenage:* Revelation of Cheating.

2 *cony:* literally, a rabbit.

3 *not empty to the term:* not without cash when he comes to a sitting of the courts.

4 *Westminster Hall:* seat of the chief law court of England.

5 *Paul's:* the aisle of St. Paul's Cathedral.

6 *russet, frieze:* coarse cloth, used in the country for clothing.

"Sir, all our friends in the country are well, thanks be to God, but truly I know you not, you must pardon me."

"Why, sir," saith the setter, guessing by his tongue what country man he is, "are you not such a country man?" [7]

If he say yes, then he creeps upon him closely. If he say no, then straight the setter comes over him thus: "In good sooth, sir, I know you by your face and have been in your company before; I pray you, if without offense, let me crave your name, and the place of your abode."

The simple man straight tells him where he dwells, his name, and who be his next neighbors, and what gentlemen dwell about him.

After he hath learned all of him, then he comes over his fallows [8] kindly: "Sir, though I have been somewhat bold to be inquisitive of your name, yet hold me excused, for I took you for a friend of mine; but since by mistaking I have made you slack your business, we'll drink a quart of wine, or a pot of ale, together."

If the fool be so ready as to go, then the cony is caught; but if he smack the setter, and smells a rat by his clawing, and will not drink with him, then away goes the setter, and discourseth to the verser the name of the man, the parish he dwells in, and what gentlemen are his near neighbors. With that away goes he,[9] and crossing the man at some turning, meets him full in the face, and greets him thus:

"What, goodman Barton, how fare all our friends about you? You are well met. I have the wine for you. You are welcome to town."

The poor countryman, hearing himself named by a man he knows not, marvels, and answers that he knows him not, and craves pardon.

"Not me, goodman Barton, have you forgot me? Why, I am such a man's kinsman, your neighbor not far off; how doth this or that good gentleman my friend? Good Lord, that I should be out of your remembrance! I have been at your house divers times."

"Indeed sir," saith the farmer, "are you such a man's kinsman? Surely, sir, if you had not challenged acquaintance of me, I should never have known you. I have clean forgot you, but I know the good gentleman your cousin well, he is my very good neighbor."

"And for his sake," saith the verser, "we'll drink afore we part."

Haply the man thanks him, and to the wine or ale they go. Then ere they part, they make him a cony, and so ferret-claw him at cards that they leave him as bare of money as an ape of a tail.

Thus have the filthy fellows their subtle fetches to draw on poor men to fall into their cozening practices. Thus like consuming moths of the commonwealth they prey upon the ignorance of such plain souls as measure all by their own honesty, not regarding either conscience or the fatal revenge that's threatened for such idle and licentious persons, but do employ all their wits to overthrow such as with their handythrift satisfy their hearty

---

[7] *are you not such a country man:* don't you come from such-and-such county?

[8] *comes over his fallows:* approaches him.

[9] *he:* I.e., the verser.

thirst, they preferring cozenage before labor, and choosing an idle practice before any honest form of good living.

Well, to the method again of taking up their conies. If the poor countryman smoke [10] them still, and will not stoop unto either of their lures, then one, either the verser, or the setter, or some of their crew, for there is a general fraternity betwixt them, steppeth before the cony as he goeth, and letteth drop twelve pence in the highway, that of force the cony must see it. The countryman, spying the shilling, maketh not dainty, for *Quis nisi mentis inops oblatum respuit aurum,*[11] but stoopeth very mannerly and taketh it up. Then one of the cony-catchers behind crieth, "Half part!" and so challengeth half of his finding. The countryman, content, offereth to change the money. "Nay faith, friend," saith the verser, " 'tis ill luck to keep found money; we'll go spend it in a pottle [12] of wine"—or in a breakfast, dinner, or supper, as the time of day requires.

If the cony say he will not, then answers the verser, "Spend my part." If still the cony refuse, he taketh half and away.

If they spy the countryman to be of a having and covetous mind, then have they a further policy to draw him on; another that knoweth the place of his abode meeteth him and saith, "Sir, well met! I have run hastily to overtake you. I pray you, dwell you not in Derbyshire, in such a village?"

"Yes, marry, do I, friend," saith the cony.

Then replies the verser, "Truly, sir, I have a suit to you; I am going out of town, and must send a letter to the parson of your parish. You shall not refuse to do a stranger such a favor as to carry it him. Haply, as men may in time meet, it may lie in my lot to do you as good a turn; and for your pains I will give you twelve pence."

The poor cony in mere simplicity saith, "Sir, I'll do so much for you with all my heart; where is your letter?"

"I have it not, good sir, ready written, but may I entreat you to step into some tavern or alehouse? We'll drink the while, and I will write but a line or two."

At this the cony stoops, and for greediness of the money, and upon courtesy, goes with the setter into the tavern. As they walk, they meet the verser, and then they all three go into the tavern together.

See, gentlemen, what great logicians these cony-catchers be, that have such rhetorical persuasions to induce the poor countryman to his confusion, and what variety of villainy they have to strip the poor farmer of his money.

Well, imagine the cony is in the tavern. Then sits down the verser and saith to the setter, "What, sirrah! Wilt thou give me a quart of wine, or shall I give thee one?" "We'll drink a pint," saith the setter, "and play a game of cards for it, respecting more the sport than the loss." "Content," quoth the verser, "go call for a pair." And while he is gone to fetch them,

---

[10] *smoke:* detect.

[11] *Quis . . . aurum:* "who in his senses refuses offered money?"

[12] *pottle:* two quarts.

he saith to the cony, "You shall see me fetch over my young master for a quart of wine finely. But this you must do for me; when I cut the cards, as I will not cut above five off, mark then, of all the greatest pack, which is undermost, and when I bid you call a card for me, name that, and you shall see we'll make him pay for a quart of wine straight."

"Truly," saith the cony, "I am no great player at cards, and I do not well understand your meaning."

"Why," saith he, "it is thus: I will play at mum-chance, or decoy,[13] that he shall shuffle the cards and I will cut. Now either of us must call a card; you shall cut for me, and he for himself, and whose card comes first wins. Therefore, when I have cut the cards, then mark the nethermost of the greatest heap, that I set upon the cards which I cut off, and always call that for me."

"Oh, now," saith the cony, "I understand you. Let me alone, I warrant I'll fit your turn."

With that in comes the setter with his cards, and asketh at what game they shall play. "Why," saith the verser, "at a new game called mum-chance, that hath no policy nor knavery, but plain as a pike-staff. You shall shuffle and I'll cut. You shall call a card, and this honest man, a stranger almost to us both, shall call another for me, and which of our cards comes first shall win." "Content," saith the setter, "for that's but mere hazard." And so he shuffles the cards, and the verser cuts off some four cards, and then taking up the heap to set upon them giveth the cony a glance of the bottom card of that heap, and saith, "Now, sir, call for me."

The cony, to blind the setter's eyes, asketh as though he were not made privy to the game, "What shall I call?"

"What card?" saith the verser. "Why, what you will, either heart, spade, club, or diamond, coat-card[14] or other."

"Oh, is it so?" saith the cony. "Why, then, you shall have the four of hearts"—which was the card he had a glance of.

"And," saith the setter (holding the cards in his hand and turning up the uppermost card, as if he knew not well the game), "I'll have the knave of trumps." "Nay," saith the verser, "there is no trump, you may call what card you will." Then saith he, "I'll have the ten of spades." With that he draws, and the four of hearts comes first. "Well," saith the setter, " 'tis but hazard, mine might have come as well as yours, five is up, I fear not the set." So they shuffle and cut, but the verser wins.

"Well," saith the setter, "no butter will cleave on my bread. What, not one draught among five? Drawer, a fresh pint! I'll have another bout with you.—But, sir, I believe," saith he to the cony, "you see some card, that it goes so cross on my side."

"I?" saith the cony. "Nay, I hope you think not so of me; 'tis but hazard

[13] *mum-chance, or decoy:* the game described below.

[14] *coat-card:* face card.

and chance, for I am but a mere [15] stranger unto the game. As I am an honest man, I never saw it before."

Thus this simple cony closeth up smoothly to take the verser's part, only for greediness to have him win the wine. "Well," answers the setter, "then I'll have one cast more." And to it they go, but he loseth all, and beginneth to chafe in this manner: "Were it not," quoth he, "that I care not for a quart of wine, I could swear as many oaths for anger as there be hairs on my head. Why should not my luck be as good as yours, and fortune favor me as well as you? What, not one called card in ten cuts? I'll forswear the game forever."

"What, chafe not, man," saith the verser. "Seeing we have your quart of wine, I'll show you the game." And with that discourseth all to him, as if he knew it not. The setter, as simply as if the knave were ignorant, saith, "Aye, marry, I think so! You must needs win, when he knows what card to call. I might have played long enough before I had got a set."

"Truly," says the cony, "'tis a pretty game, for 'tis not possible for him to lose that cuts the cards. I warrant the other that shuffles may lose Saint Peter's cope if he had it. Well, I'll carry this home with me into the country, and win many a pot of ale with it."

"A fresh pint!" saith the verser. "And then we'll away. But seeing, sir, you are going homeward, I'll learn you a trick worth the noting, that you shall win many a pot with in the winter nights."

With that he culls out the four knaves, and pricks [16] one in the top, one in the midst, and one in the bottom. "Now, sir," saith he, "you see these three knaves apparently; thrust them down with your hand, and cut where you will, and though they be so far asunder I'll make them all come together."

"I pray you, let's see that trick," saith the cony. "Methinks it should be impossible."

So the verser draws, and all the three knaves comes in one heap. This he doth once or twice; then the cony wonders at it and offers him a pint of wine to teach it him. "Nay," saith the verser. "I'll do it for thanks; and therefore mark me where you have taken out the four knaves, lay two together above and draw up one of them that it may be seen, then prick the other in the midst and the third in the bottom, so when any cuts, cut he never so warily, three knaves must of force come together, for the bottom knave is cut to lie upon both the upper knaves."

"Aye, marry," saith the setter, "but then the three knaves you showed come not together."

"Truth," saith the verser. "But one among a thousand mark not it; it requires a quick eye, a sharp wit, and a reaching head to spy at the first."

"Now gramercy, sir, for this trick," saith the cony. "I'll domineer with this amongst my neighbors."

[15] *mere:* complete.

[16] *pricks:* inserts.

Thus doth the verser and the setter feign friendship to the cony, offering him no show of cozenage, nor once to draw him in for a pint of wine, the more to shadow [17] their villainy.

But now begins the sport. As thus they sit tippling, comes the barnacle and thrusts open the door, looking into the room where they are, and as one bashful, steppeth back again and saith, "I cry you mercy, gentlemen, I thought a friend of mine had been here. Pardon my boldness." "No harm," saith the verser. "I pray you drink a cup of wine with us, and welcome." So in comes the barnacle, and taking the cup drinks to the cony, and then saith, "What, at cards, gentlemen? Were it not I should be offensive to the company, I would play for a pint till my friend come that I look for." "Why, sir," saith the verser, "if you will sit down you shall be taken up for a quart of wine." "With all my heart," saith the barnacle. "What will you play at, primero, prima vista, cent, one-and-thirty, new cut, or what shall be the game?" "Sir," saith the verser, "I am but an ignorant man at cards, and I see you have them at your fingers' end. I will play with you at a game wherein can be no deceit; it is called mum-chance at cards, and it is thus: you shall shuffle the cards, and I will cut, you shall call one, and this honest country yeoman shall call a card for me, and which of our cards comes first shall win. Here you see is no deceit, and this I'll play."

"No, truly," saith the cony, "methinks there can be no great craft in this."

"Well," saith the barnacle, "for a pint of wine have at you." So they play as before, five up, and the verser wins.

"This is hard luck," saith the barnacle, "and I believe the honest man spies some card in the bottom; and therefore I'll make this, always to prick the bottom card." "Content," saith the verser, and the cony to cloak the matter saith, "Sir, you offer me injury to think that I can call a card, when I neither touch them, shuffle, cut, nor draw them." "Ah, sir," saith the barnacle, "give losers leave to speak."

Well, to it they go again, and then the barnacle, knowing the game best, by chopping [18] a card wins two of the five, but lets the verser win the set; then in a chafe he sweareth 'tis but his ill luck, and he can see no deceit in it, and therefore he will play twelve pence a cut.

The verser is content, and wins twos or threes of the barnacle, whereat he chafes, and saith, "I came hither in an ill hour; but I will win my money again, or lose all in my purse."

With that he draws out a purse with some three or four pounds and claps it on the board. The verser asketh the cony secretly by signs if he will be his half; he says, "Aye," and straight seeks for his purse. Well, the barnacle shuffles the cards thoroughly, and the verser cuts as before. The barnacle when he hath drawn one card saith, "I'll either win something or lose something, therefore I'll vie and revie [19] every card at my pleasure, till either yours or mine come out, and therefore twelve pence upon this card, my

---

[17] *shadow:* disguise.

[18] *chopping:* changing.

[19] *vie and revie:* bet and raise.

card comes first for twelve pence." "No," saith the verser. "Aye," saith the cony, "and I durst hold twelve pence more." "Why, I hold you," saith the barnacle, and so they vie and revie till some ten shillings be on the stake; and then next comes forth the verser's card, that the cony called, and so the barnacle loseth.

Well, this flesheth [20] the cony; the sweetness of gain maketh him frolic, and no man is more ready to vie and revie than he. Thus for three or four times the barnacle loseth; at last, to whet on the cony, he striketh his chopped card, and winneth a goodly stake. "Away with the witch!" cries the barnacle. "I hope the cards will turn at last."

"Aye, much!" thinketh the cony. " 'Twas but a chance that you asked so right, to ask one of the five that was cut off. I am sure there was forty to one on my side, and I'll have you on the lurch anon." So still they vie and revie, and for once that the barnacle wins, the cony gets five.

At last when they mean to shave the cony clean of all his coin, the barnacle chafeth, and upon a pawn borroweth some money of the tapster and swears he will vie it to the uttermost. Then thus he chops his card to cross-bite [21] the cony. He first looks on the bottom card, and shuffles often, but still keeping that bottom card which he knows to be uppermost; then sets he down the cards, and the verser to encourage the cony, cuts off but three cards, whereof the barnacle's card must needs be the uppermost. Then shows he the bottom card of the other heap cut off, to the cony, and sets it upon the barnacle's card which he knows, so that of force [22] the card that was laid uppermost must come first; and then the barnacle calls that card. They draw a card, and then the barnacle vies and the countryman vies upon him; for this is the law, as often as one vies or revies, the other must see it, else he loseth the stake. Well, at last the barnacle plies it so that perhaps he vies more money than the cony hath in his purse. The cony upon this, knowing his card is the third or fourth card, and that he hath forty to one against the barnacle, pawns his rings if he have any, his sword, his cloak, or else what he hath about him, to maintain the vie, and when he laughs in his sleeve, thinking he hath fleeced the barnacle of all, then the barnacle's card comes forth, and strikes such a cold humor unto his heart that he sits as a man in a trance, not knowing what to do, and sighing while his heart is ready to break, thinking on the money that he hath lost.

Perhaps the man is very simple and patient, and, whatsoever he thinks, for fear goes his way quiet with his loss, while the cony-catchers laugh and divide the spoil, and being out of the doors, poor man, goes to his lodging with a heavy heart, pensive and sorrowful, but too late, for perhaps his state [23] did depend on that money, and so he, his wife, his children, and his family are brought to extreme misery.

Another, perhaps more hardy and subtle, smokes the cony-catchers, and

---

[20] *flesheth:* (from hunting and hawking) makes him eager for game by tasting blood.

[21] *cross-bite:* swindle.

[22] *of force:* necessarily.

[23] *state:* prosperity.

smelleth cozenage, and saith they shall not have his money so; but they answer him with braves, and though he bring them before an officer, yet the knaves are so favored that the man never recovers his money, and yet he is let slip unpunished.

Thus are the poor conies robbed by these base-minded caterpillars; thus are serving men oft enticed to play and lose all; thus are prentices induced to be conies, and so are cozened of their masters' money; yea, young gentlemen, merchants, and others, are fetched in by these damnable rakehells, a plague as ill as hell, which is, present loss of money, and ensuing misery. A lamentable case in England, when such vipers are suffered to breed and are not cut off with the sword of justice!

FROM

GREENE'S GROATSWORTH OF WIT

(1592)

O horrenda fames,[24] how terrible are thy assaults! But *vermis conscientiae,*[25] more wounding are thy stings. Ah, gentlemen, that live to read my broken and confused lines, look not I should, as I was wont, delight you with vain fantasies; but gather my follies all together, and as ye would deal with so many parricides, cast them into the fire. Call them *Telegones,*[26] for now they kill their father, and every lewd line in them written is a deep piercing wound to my heart; every idle hour spent by any in reading them brings a million of sorrows to my soul. Oh that the tears of a miserable man —for never any man was yet more miserable—might wash their memory out with my death, and that those works with me together might be interred! But sith they cannot, let this my last work witness against them with me, how I detest them. Black is the remembrance of my black works, blacker than night, blacker than death, blacker than hell.

Learn wit by my repentance, gentlemen, and let these few rules following be regarded in your lives:

1. First, in all your actions, set God before your eyes, for the fear of the Lord is the beginning of wisdom. Let his word be a lantern to your feet and a light unto your paths; then shall you stand as firm rocks and not be mocked.

2. Beware of looking back, for God will not be mocked; and of him that hath received much, much shall be demanded.

---

[24] *O horrenda fames:* "Oh dreadful poverty!"

[25] *vermis conscientiae:* "worms of conscience."

[26] *Telegones:* The amatory poems of Ovid were called *Telegoni* because they supposedly caused all the poet's troubles. Telegonus was a son of Ulysses and Circe who unwittingly killed his father.

3. If thou be single, and canst abstain, turn thy eyes from vanity; for there is a kind of women bearing the faces of angels but the hearts of devils, able to entrap the elect if it were possible.

4. If thou be married, forsake not the wife of thy youth to follow strange flesh, for whoremongerers and adulterers the Lord will judge. The door of a harlot leadeth down to death, and in her lips there dwells destruction; her face is decked with odors, but she bringeth a man to a morsel of bread and nakedness, of which myself am instance.

5. If thou be left rich, remember those that want, and so deal that by thy willfulness thyself want not. Let not taverners and victualers be thy executors, for they will bring thee to a dishonorable grave.

6. Oppress no man, for the cry of the wronged ascendeth to the ears of the Lord; neither delight to increase by usury, lest thou lose thy habitation in the everlasting tabernacle.

7. Beware of building thy house to thy neighbor's hurt, for the stones will cry to the timber, "We were laid together in blood"; and those that so erect houses, calling them by their names, shall lie in the grave like sheep, and death shall gnaw upon their souls.

8. If thou be poor, be also patient, and strive not to grow rich by indirect means, for goods so gotten shall vanish like smoke.

9. If thou be a father, master, or teacher, join good example with good counsel, else little avail precepts, where life is different.

10. If thou be a son or servant, despise not reproof; for though correction be bitter at the first, it bringeth pleasure in the end.

Had I regarded the first of these rules, or been obedient to the last, I had not now at my last end been left thus desolate. But now though to myself I give *consilium post facta*,[27] yet to others they may serve for timely precepts. And therefore, while life gives leave, I will send warning to my old consorts, which have lived as loosely as myself; albeit weakness will scarce suffer me to write, yet to my fellow scholars about this city will I direct these few ensuing lines:

To those Gentlemen his quondam [28] acquaintance, that spend their wits in making plays, R. G. wisheth a better exercise, and wisdom to prevent his extremities.

If woeful experience may move you, gentlemen, to beware, or unheard-of wretchedness entreat you to take heed, I doubt not but you will look back with sorrow on your time past, and endeavor with repentance to spend that which is to come. Wonder not (for with thee will I first begin), thou famous gracer of tragedians,[29] that Greene, who hath said with thee, like the fool in his heart, "There is no God," should now give glory unto his greatness; for penetrating is his power, his hand lies heavy upon me, he

[27] *consilium post facta:* "good advice too late."

[28] *quondam:* former, sometime.

[29] *gracer of tragedians:* Marlowe.

hath spoken unto me with a voice of thunder, and I have felt he is a God that can punish enemies. Why should thy excellent wit, his gift, be so blinded, that thou shouldst give no glory to the giver? Is it pestilent Machiavellian policy [30] that thou hast studied? Oh, peevish folly! What are his rules but mere confused mockeries, able to extirpate in small time the generation of mankind? For if *Sic volo, sic jubeo,*[31] hold in those that are able to command, and if it be lawful *Fas et nefas* [32] to do anything that is beneficial, only tyrants should possess the earth, and they striving to exceed in tyranny should each to other be a slaughter-man; till the mightiest outliving all, one stroke were left for Death, that in one age [33] man's life should end. The broacher [34] of this diabolical atheism is dead, and in his life had never the felicity he aimed at; but as he began in craft, lived in fear and ended in despair. *Quam inscrutabilia sunt Dei judicia?* [35] This murderer of many brethren had his conscience seared like Cain; this betrayer of him that gave his life for him inherited the portion of Judas; this apostata perished as ill as Julian; [36] and wilt thou, my friend, be his disciple? Look but to me, by him persuaded to that liberty, and thou shalt find it an infernal bondage. I know the least of my demerits merit this miserable death, but willful striving against known truth exceedeth all the terrors of my soul. Defer not, with me, till this last point of extremity; for little knowest thou how in the end thou shalt be visited.

With thee I join young Juvenal,[37] that biting satirist, that lastly with me together writ a comedy. Sweet boy, might I advise thee, be advised, and get not many enemies by bitter words; inveigh against vain men, for thou canst do it, no man better, no man so well; thou hast a liberty to reprove all, and name none; for, one being spoken to, all are offended; none being blamed, no man is injured. Stop shallow water still running, it will rage, or tread on a worm and it will turn; then blame not scholars vexed with sharp lines, if they reprove thy too much liberty of reproof.

And thou no less [38] deserving than the other two, in some things rarer, in nothing inferior; driven, as myself, to extreme shifts, a little have I to say to thee; and were it not an idolatrous oath, I would swear by sweet St. George, thou art unworthy better hap, sith thou dependest on so mean a stay. Base-minded men all three of you, if by my misery ye be not warned; for unto none of you, like me, sought those burrs to cleave; those puppets,[39] I mean, that speak from our mouths, those antics [40] garnished in our colors.

---

[30] *Machiavellian policy:* the ideas of the Italian political philosopher, Niccolo Machiavelli (1469–1527).

[31] *Sic volo, sic jubeo:* "I command just as I wish."

[32] *Fas et nefas:* Supply *per omne.* "By any means, good or bad."

[33] *age:* generation.

[34] *broacher:* Machiavelli.

[35] *Quam . . . judicia:* "How inscrutable are God's judgments."

[36] *apostata . . . Julian:* a Roman emperor (332–363), who renounced Christianity and is supposed to have exclaimed at his death in a battle against the Persians, "Thou hast conquered, Oh Galilean!"

[37] *young Juvenal:* probably Nashe.

[38] *thou no less:* George Peele.

[39] *those puppets:* I.e., the actors.

[40] *antics:* clowns, mountebanks.

Is it not strange that I, to whom they all have been beholding; is it not like that you, to whom they all have been beholding, shall, were ye in that case that I am now, be both at once of [41] them forsaken? Yes, trust them not; for there is an upstart crow, beautified with our feathers, that with his *tiger's heart wrapped in a player's hide* supposes he is as well able to bombast out a blank verse as the best of you; and being an absolute *Johannes fac totum,*[42] is in his own conceit the only Shake-scene in a country.[43] Oh that I might entreat your rare wits to be employed in more profitable courses; and let those apes imitate your past excellence, and never more acquaint them with your admired inventions. I know the best husband [44] of you all will never prove an usurer, and the kindest of them all will never prove a kind nurse; yet whilst you may, seek you better masters; for it is pity men of such rare wits should be subject to the pleasure of such rude grooms.

In this I might insert two more, that both have writ against these buckram gentlemen; but let their own works serve to witness against their own wickedness, if they persevere to maintain any more such peasants. For other newcomers, I leave them to the mercy of these painted monsters, who, I doubt not, will drive the best minded to despise them; for the rest, it skills[45] not though they make a jest at them.

But now return I again to you three, knowing my misery is to you no news; and let me heartily entreat you to be warned by my harms. Delight not, as I have done, in irreligious oaths; for from the blasphemer's house a curse shall not depart. Despise drunkenness, which wasteth the wit, and maketh men all equal unto beasts. Fly lust, as the deathsman of the soul, and defile not the temple of the Holy Ghost. Abhor those epicures, whose loose life hath made religion loathsome to your ears; and when they soothe you with terms of mastership, remember Robert Greene, whom they have so often flattered, perishes now for want of comfort. Remember, gentlemen, your lives are like so many lighted tapers, that are with care delivered to all of you to maintain; these with wind-puffed wrath may be extinguished, which drunkenness put out, which negligence let fall; for man's time is not of itself so short but it is more shortened by sin. The fire of my light is now at the last snuff, and for want of wherewith to sustain it, there is no substance left for life to feed on. Trust not then, I beseech ye, to such weak stays; for they are as changeable in mind as in many attires. Well, my hand is tired, and I am forced to leave where I would begin; for a whole book cannot contain these wrongs, which I am forced to knit up in some few lines of words.

Desirous that you should live, though
himself be dying,
Robert Greene.

---

[41] *of:* by.

[42] *Johannes fac totum:* jack of all trades.

[43] *upstart . . . country:* The reference is to Shakespeare. He is an "upstart crow" because he is a non-University man, "beautified in our feathers" because as an actor he has spoken their lines on the stage. *tiger's . . . hide* is a parody of *III Henry VI,* I, iv, 137.

[44] *husband:* saver.

[45] *skills:* matters.

FROM

THE REPENTANCE OF ROBERT GREENE, MASTER OF ARTS

(1592)

THE LIFE AND DEATH OF ROBERT GREENE, MASTER OF ARTS

I need not make long discourse of my parents, who for their gravity and honest life were well known and esteemed amongst their neighbors; namely, in the city of Norwich, where I was bred and born. But as out of one selfsame clod of clay there sprouts both stinking weeds and delightful flowers; so from honest parents often grow most dishonest children; for my father had care to have me in my nonage brought up at school, that I might through the study of good letters grow to be a friend to myself, a profitable member to the commonwealth, and a comfort to him in his age. But as early pricks the tree that will prove a thorn; so even in my first years I began to follow the filthiness of mine own desires, and neither to listen to the wholesome advertisements of my parents, nor be ruled by the careful correction of my master. For being at the University of Cambridge, I light amongst wags as lewd as myself, with whom I consumed the flower of my youth, who drew me to travel into Italy and Spain, in which places I saw and practiced such villainy as is abominable to declare. Thus by their counsel I sought to furnish myself with coin, which I procured by cunning sleights from my father and my friends, and my mother pampered me so long, and secretly helped me to the oil of angels,[46] that I grew thereby prone to all mischief; so that being then conversant with notable braggarts, boon companions, and ordinary spendthrifts, that practiced sundry superficial studies, I became as a scion grafted into the same stock, whereby I did absolutely participate of their nature and qualities.

At my return into England I ruffled out in my silks, in the habit of malcontent, and seemed so discontent that no place would please me to abide in, nor no vocation cause me to stay myself in; but after I had by degrees proceeded Master of Arts, I left the University and away to London, where (after I had continued some short time, and driven myself out of credit with sundry of my friends) I became an author of plays, and a penner of love pamphlets, so that I soon grew famous in that quality, that who for that trade grown so ordinary about London as Robin Greene? Young yet in years, though old in wickedness, I began to resolve that there was nothing bad that was profitable; whereupon I grew so rooted in all mischief that

[46] *oil of angels:* slang for "money."

I had as great a delight in wickedness as sundry hath in godliness; and as much felicity I took in villainy as others had in honesty.

Thus was the liberty I got in my youth the cause of my licentious living in my age, and being the first step to hell, I find it now the first let [47] from heaven.

But I would wish all my native countrymen that read this my repentance: first to fear God in their whole life, which I never did; secondly, to obey their parents and to listen unto the wholesome counsel of their elders; so shall their days be multiplied upon them here on earth, and inherit the crown of glory in the kingdom of heaven. I exhort them also to leave the company of lewd and ill livers; for conversing with such copesmates[48] draws them into sundry dangerous inconveniences; nor let them haunt the company of harlots, whose throats are as smooth as oil, but their feet lead the steps unto death and destruction; for they like sirens with their sweet enchanting notes soothed me up in all kind of ungodliness.

Oh, take heed of harlots (I wish you, the unbridled youth of England), for they are the basilisks [49] that kill with their eyes, they are the sirens that allure with their sweet looks; and they lead their favorers unto their destruction, as a sheep is led unto the slaughter.

From whoredom I grew to drunkenness, from drunkenness to swearing and blaspheming the name of God; hereof grew quarrels, frays, and continual controversies which are now as worms in my conscience gnawing me incessantly. And did I not through hearty repentance take hold of God's mercies, even these detestable sins would drench me down into the damnable pit of destruction; for *Stipendium peccati mors*.[50]

Oh know, good countrymen, that the horrible sins and intolerable blasphemy I have used against the majesty of God is a block in my conscience, and that so heavy that there were no way with me but desperation, if the hope of Christ's death and passion did not help to ease me of so intolerable and heavy a burthen.

I have long with the deaf adder [51] stopped mine ears against the voice of God's ministers, yea, my heart was hardened with Pharaoh against all the motions that the spirit of God did at any time work in my mind, to turn me from my detestable kind of living.

Yet let me confess a truth, that even once, and yet but once, I felt a fear and horror in my conscience, and then the terror of God's judgments did manifestly teach me that my life was bad, that by sin I deserved damnation, and that such was the greatness of my sin that I deserved no redemption. And this inward motion I received in Saint Andrew's church in the city of Norwich, at a lecture or sermon then preached by a godly learned man,

---

[47] *let:* bar.

[48] *copesmates:* companions.

[49] *basilisks:* small imaginary serpents, which could kill by a glance. Pliny, *Natural History,* VIII, xxxiii.

[50] *Stipendium . . . mors:* "The wages of sin is death."

[51] *deaf adder:* Psalm 58:4–5: "they [the wicked] are like the deaf adder that stoppeth her ear; which will not harken to the voice of charmers, charming never so wisely."

whose doctrine, and the manner of whose teaching, I liked wonderful well; yea (in my conscience) such was his singleness of heart and zeal in his doctrine that he might have converted the most monster of the world.

Well, at that time, whosoever was worst, I knew myself as bad as he; for being new come from Italy (where I learned all the villainies under the heavens), I was drowned in pride, whoredom was my daily exercise, and gluttony with drunkenness was my only delight.

At this sermon the terror of God's judgments did manifestly teach me that my exercises were damnable, and that I should be wiped out of the book of life if I did not speedily repent my looseness of life and reform my misdemeanors.

At this sermon the said learned man (who doubtless was the child of God) did beat down sin in such pithy and persuasive manner that I began to call unto mind the danger of my soul, and the prejudice that at length would befall me for those gross sins which with greediness I daily committed; insomuch as sighing I said in myself, "Lord, have mercy upon me, and send me grace to amend and become a new man."

But this good motion lasted not long in me; for no sooner had I met with my copesmates, but seeing me in such a solemn humor they demanded the cause of my sadness; to whom when I had discovered that I sorrowed for my wickedness of life, and that the preacher's words had taken a deep impression in my conscience, they fell upon me in jesting manner, calling me puritan and precisian,[52] and wished I might have a pulpit, with such other scoffing terms, that by their foolish persuasion the good and wholesome lesson I had learned went quite out of my remembrance; so that I fell again with the dog to my old vomit, and put my wicked life in practice, and that so throughly [53] as ever I did before.

Thus although God sent his holy spirit to call me, and though I heard him, yet I regarded it no longer than the present time, when suddenly forsaking it, I went forward obstinately in my miss.[54] Nevertheless, soon after, I married a gentleman's daughter of good account, with whom I lived for a while; but forasmuch as she would persuade me from my willful wickedness, after I had a child by her, I cast her off, having spent up the marriage money which I obtained by her.

Then left I her at six or seven,[55] who went into Lincolnshire, and I to London; where in short space I fell into favor with such as were of honorable and good calling. But here note that though I knew how to get a friend, yet I had not the gift or reason how to keep a friend; for he that was my dearest friend, I would be sure so to behave myself towards him that he should ever after profess to be my utter enemy, or else vow never after to come in my company.

Thus my misdemeanors (too many to be recited) caused the most part of those so much to despise me that in the end I became friendless, except

[52] *precisian:* a Puritan.

[53] *throughly:* thoroughly.

[54] *miss:* mistake.

[55] *at six or seven:* at loose ends.

it were in a few alehouses, who commonly for my inordinate expenses would make much of me, until I were on the score far more than ever I meant to pay by twenty nobles thick.[56] After I had wholly betaken me to the penning of plays (which was my continual exercise) I was so far from calling upon God that I seldom thought on God, but took such delight in swearing and blaspheming the name of God that none could think otherwise of me than that I was the child of perdition.

These vanities [57] and other trifling pamphlets I penned of love and vain fantasies was my chiefest stay of living, and for those my vain discourses I was beloved of the more vainer sort of people, who being my continual companions, came still to my lodging, and there would continue quaffing, carousing, and surfeiting with me all the day long.

But I thank God that he put it in my head to lay open the most horrible cozenages of the common cony-catchers, cozeners, and cross-biters, which I have indifferently [58] handled in those my several discourses already imprinted. And my trust is that those discourses will do great good, and be very beneficial to the commonwealth of England.

But oh, my dear wife, whose company and sight I have refrained these six years: I ask God and thee forgiveness for so greatly wronging thee, of whom I seldom or never thought until now. Pardon me, I pray thee, wheresoever thou art, and God forgive me all my offenses.

And now to you all that live and revel in such wickedness as I have done, to you I write, and in God's name wish you to look to yourselves, and to reform yourselves for the safeguard of your own souls; dissemble not with God, but seek grace at his hands; he hath promised it, and he will perform it.

God doth sundry times defer his punishment unto those that run a wicked race; but *Quod defertur non aufertur* (that which is deferred is not quittanced),[59] a day of reckoning will come, when the Lord will say: "Come, give account of thy stewardship." What God determineth, man cannot prevent; he that binds two sins together cannot go unpunished in the one; so long the pot goeth to the pit that at last it comes broken home.

Therefore, all my good friends, hope not in money, nor in friends, in favors, in kindred; they are all uncertain, and they are furthest off when men think them most nigh. Oh were I now to begin the flower of my youth, were I now in the prime of my years, how far would I be from my former follies! What a reformed course of life would I take! But it is too late; only now the comfortable mercies of the Lord is left me to hope in.

It is bootless for me to make any long discourse to such as are graceless as I have been. All wholesome warnings are odious unto them, for they with the spider suck poison out of the most precious flowers, and to such as God hath in his secret counsel elected, few words will suffice. But how-

---

[56] *by twenty nobles thick:* by a margin of twenty nobles ("noble" was the old name for angel or half-sovereign, worth ten shillings).

[57] *these vanities:* I.e., plays.

[58] *indifferently:* judicially.

[59] *quittanced:* remitted.

soever my life hath been, let my repentant end be a general example to all the youth in England to obey their parents, to fly whoredom, drunkenness, swearing, blaspheming, contempt of the Word, and such grievous and gross sins, lest they bring their parents' heads with sorrow to their graves, and lest (with me) they be a blemish to their kindred, and to their posterity forever.

Thus may you see how God hath secret to himself the times of calling; and when he will have them into his vineyard, some he calls in the morning, some at noon, and some in the evening, and yet hath the last his wages as well as the first. For as his judgments are inscrutable, so are his mercies incomprehensible. And therefore let all men learn these two lessons: not to despair, because God may work in them through his spirit at the last hour; nor to presume, lest God give them over for their presumption, and deny them repentance, and so they die impenitent; which *finalis impenitentia* is a manifest sin against the Holy Ghost.

To this doth that golden sentence of St. Augustine allude, which he speaketh of the thief hanging on the cross. "There was," saith he, "one thief saved and no more, therefore presume not; and there was one saved, and therefore despair not."

* * *

THE MANNER OF THE DEATH AND LAST END OF ROBERT GREENE, MASTER OF ARTS

After that he had penned the former discourse, then lying sore sick of a surfeit which he had taken with drinking, he continued most patient and penitent; yea, he did with tears forsake the world, renounced swearing, and desired forgiveness of God and the world for all his offenses; so that during all the time of his sickness, which was about a month's space, he was never heard to swear, rave, or blaspheme the name of God, as he was accustomed to do before that time—which greatly comforted his well-willers, to see how mightily the grace of God did work in him.

He confessed himself that he was never heartsick, but said that all his pain was in his belly. And, although he continually scoured, yet still his belly swelled, and never left swelling upward until it swelled him at the heart and in his face.

During the whole time of his sickness, he continually called upon God and recited these sentences following: "Oh Lord, forgive my manifold offenses. Oh Lord, have mercy upon me. Oh Lord, forgive me my secret sins, and in thy mercy, Lord, pardon them all. Thy mercy, Lord, is above thy works." And with such-like godly sentences he passed the time, even till he gave up the ghost.

And this is to be noted, that his sickness did not so greatly weaken him, but that he walked to his chair and back again the night before he departed; and then, being feeble, laying him down on his bed about nine of the clock at night, a friend of his told him that his wife had sent him commendations, and that she was in good health; whereat he greatly rejoiced, confessed that he had mightily wronged her, and wished that he might see her before he departed; whereupon, feeling his time was but short, he took pen and ink and wrote her a letter to this effect:

Sweet wife, as ever there was any good will or friendship between thee and me, see this bearer (my host) satisfied of his debt; I owe him ten pound, and but for him I had perished in the streets. Forget and forgive my wrongs done unto thee, and Almighty God have mercy on my soul. Farewell till we meet in heaven, for on earth thou shalt never see me more. This 2 of September, 1592.

Written by thy dying husband,
ROBERT GREENE.

MAESIA'S SONG[60]

SWEET are the thoughts that savor of content;
  The quiet mind is richer than a crown;
Sweet are the nights in careless slumber spent;
  The poor estate scorns Fortune's angry frown.
Such sweet content, such minds, such sleep, such bliss,
Beggars enjoy, when princes oft do miss.

The homely house that harbors quiet rest;
  The cottage that affords no pride nor care;
The mean[61] that 'grees with country music best;
  The sweet consort[62] of mirth and music's fare;
Obscured life sets down a type of bliss:
A mind content both crown and kingdom is.

[60] From *Farewell to Folly* (1591).

[61] *mean:* the middle part in music, here metaphorical.

[62] *consort:* harmony.

SEPHESTIA'S SONG TO HER CHILD[63]

Weep not, my wanton, smile upon my knee,
When thou art old there's grief enough for thee.
Mother's wag, pretty boy,
Father's sorrow, father's joy,
When thy father first did see
Such a boy by him and me,
He was glad, I was woe;
Fortune changed made him so,
When he left his pretty boy,
Last his sorrow, first his joy.

Weep not, my wanton, smile upon my knee,
When thou art old there's grief enough for thee.
Streaming tears that never stint,
Like pearl-drops from a flint,
Fell by course from his eyes,
That one another's place supplies.
Thus he grieved in every part;
Tears of blood fell from his heart,
When he left his pretty boy,
Father's sorrow, father's joy.

Weep not, my wanton, smile upon my knee,
When thou art old there's grief enough for thee.
The wanton smiled, father wept,
Mother cried, baby leapt;
More he crowed, more we cried,
Nature could not sorrow hide.
He must go, he must kiss
Child and mother, baby bliss,
For he left his pretty boy,
Father's sorrow, father's joy.
Weep not, my wanton, smile upon my knee,
When thou art old there's grief enough for thee.

THE SHEPHERD'S WIFE'S SONG[64]

Ah, what is love? It is a pretty thing,
As sweet unto a shepherd as a king;
And sweeter too,

63 From *Menaphon* (1589).

64 From *Greene's Mourning Garment* (1590).

For kings have cares that wait upon a crown,
And cares can make the sweetest love to frown.
Ah then, ah then,
If country loves such sweet desires do gain,
What lady would not love a shepherd swain?

His flocks once folded, he comes home at night
As merry as a king in his delight;
And merrier too,
For kings bethink them what the state require,
Where shepherds careless carol by the fire.
Ah then, ah then,
If country loves such sweet desires do gain,
What lady would not love a shepherd swain?

He kisseth first, then sits as blithe to eat
His cream and curds as doth the king his meat;
And blither too,
For kings have often fears when they do sup,
Where shepherds dread no poison in their cup.
Ah then, ah then,
If country loves, &c.

To bed he goes, as wanton then, I ween,
As is a king in dalliance with a queen;
More wanton too,
For kings have many griefs affects to move,
Where shepherds have no greater grief than love.
Ah then, ah then,
If country loves, &c.

Upon his couch of straw he sleeps as sound
As doth the king upon his bed of down;
More sounder too,
For cares cause kings full oft their sleep to spill,
Where weary shepherds lie and snort their fill.
Ah then, ah then,
If country loves, &c.

Thus with his wife he spends the year, as blithe
As doth the king at every tide or sithe;
And blither too,
For kings have wars and broils to take in hand,
When shepherds laugh and love upon the land.
Ah then, ah then,
If country loves, &c.

Gabriel Harvey[1]

1550?–1630

FOUR LETTERS AND CERTAIN SONNETS

(1592)

FROM

THE SECOND LETTER

I LITTLE delight in the rehearsal of such paltry; but who like Elderton[2] for balleting, Greene for pamphleting, both for good fellowship and bad conditions? Railing was the hippocras[3] of the drunken rhymester and quipping[4] the marchpane of the mad libeler. They 'scape fair that go scot-free in such saucy reckonings. I have known some, read of many, and heard of more, that wantonly quipped other and soundly nipped themselves. The hottest blood of choler may be cooled; and, as the fiercest fury of wildfire, so the fiercest wildfire of fury consumeth itself. Howbeit a common mischief would be prevented; and it generally concerneth all, and particularly behooveth everyone to look about him when he heareth the bells ringing backward and seeth the fire running forward and beholdeth even Death in person shooting his peremptory bolts. You understand me without a gloss, and here is matter enough for a new civil war, or shall I say for a new Troyan siege, if this poor letter should fortune to come in print. I deal directly and will plainly tell you my fancy, if Titius[5] continue to upbraid Caius with everything and nothing. I neither name Martin Marprelate nor shame Pap-with-a-Hatchet[6] nor mention any other but Elderton and Greene, two notorious mates and the very ringleaders of the rhyming and scribbling

---

1 For introduction and bibliography, see pp. 414–416.

2 *Elderton:* William Elderton, notorious as a drinker and writer of broadside ballads, who had recently died.

3 *hippocras:* a flavored wine.

4 *quipping:* the reference is to Greene's *A Quip for an Upstart Courtier.*

5 *Titius:* a vain and presumptuous poetaster in Horace's *Epistle* III.

6 *Martin . . . hatchet:* Martin was the pseudonym of the authors of Puritan tracts attacking the bishops; *Pappe with an Hatchet* (1589) was one of the replies, written by John Lyly; it contained an attack on Harvey. See Lyly's *Works,* ed. Bond, III, 391.

crew. But Titius, or rather Zoilus [7] in his spiteful vein, will so long flurt at Homer, and Thersites [8] in his peevish mode so long fling at Agamemnon that they will become extremely odious and intolerable to all good learning and civil government; and in attempting to pull down or disgrace other without order, must needs finally overthrow themselves without relief. Orators have challenged a special liberty and poets claimed an absolute license; but no liberty without bounds, nor any license without limitation. Invectives by favor have been too bold, and satires by usurpation too presumptuous; I overpass Archilochus,[9] Aristophanes, Lucian,[10] Julian,[11] Aretine,[12] and that whole venomous and viperous brood of old and new railers, even Tully and Horace otherwhiles overreached; and I must needs say, Mother Hubbard,[13] in heat of choler, forgetting the pure sanguine of her sweet *Faerie Queene,* willfully overshot her malcontented self, as elsewhere I have specified at large, with the good leave of unspotted friendship. Examples in some ages do exceeding much hurt. Sallust [14] and Clodius [15] learned of Tully to frame artificial declamations and pathetical invectives against Tully himself and other worthy members of that most flourishing state. If Mother Hubbard in the vein of Chaucer happen to tell one canicular [16] tale, father Elderton and his son Greene, in the vein of Skelton or Scogan, will counterfeit an hundred dogged fables, libels, calumnies, slanders, lies for the whetstone, and whatnot, and most currishly snarl and bite where they should most kindly fawn and lick. Every private excess is dangerous, but such public enormities, incredibly pernicious and insupportable. And who can tell what huge outrages might amount of such quarrelous and tumultuous causes? Honor is precious, worship of value, fame invaluable. They perilously threaten the commonwealth that go about to violate the inviolable parts thereof. Many will sooner lose their lives than the least jot of their reputation. Lord, what mortal feuds, what furious combats, what cruel bloodshed, what horrible slaughterdom have been committed for the point of honor and some few courtly ceremonies! Though meaner persons do not so highly overprize their credit, yet who taketh not discourtesy unkindly, or slander displeasingly? For mine own part, I am to make an use of my adversary's abuse and will endeavor to reform any default whereof I may justly or probably be impeached. Some emulation hath already done me good, both for supply of great imperfections and for increase of small perfections. I have (and who hath not?) found it better to be tickled and

[7] *Zoilus:* a grammarian who attacked Homer for his fabulous and incredible stories.

[8] *Thersites:* the deformed railer in the *Iliad.*

[9] *Archilochus:* Ionian satirist (*ca.* 720–676 B.C.).

[10] *Lucian:* Greek writer born *ca.* 120, who wrote dialogues attacking the gods.

[11] *Julian:* the Apostate, Roman emperor (361–333) who wrote satires.

[12] *Aretine:* Pietro Aretino (1492–1557), famous Italian satirist, "scourge of princes."

[13] *Mother Hubbard:* Spenser's satire, *Mother Hubberds Tale* (1591).

[14] *Sallust:* the historian, enemy of Cicero.

[15] *Clodius:* P. Clodius Pulcher, profligate enemy of Cicero.

[16] *canicular:* canine. Spenser's *Mother Hubberds Tale* takes place in the dog-days.

stinged of a busy enemy than to be coyed and lulled of an idle friend. Plutarch is gravely wise, and Machiavel subtly politic; but in either of them, what sounder or finer piece of cunning than to reap commodity by him that seeketh my displeasure, and to play upon the advantage of his detection of my infirmities? Other caviling or mote-spying malice confoundeth itself, and I continue my accustomed simplicity to answer vanity with silence, though peradventure not without danger of inviting a new injury by entertaining an old. Patience hath trained me to pocket up more heinous indignities and even to digest an age of iron. They that can do little must be contented to suffer much. My betters need not take it grievously to be taunted or reproached in that book where St. Peter and Christ himself are Lucianically and scoffingly alleged, the one for begging, the other for granting a foolish boon, pretended ever since the fatal destiny of the gentle craft. Some men will have their swing and their bugs-words,[17] though it be against all God-forbids; and what Caesar's might or Cato's integrity or what saint's devotion can stop such mouths? Yet neither themselves the better nor other the worse, that depend not on their allowance, but rely on their own justification and desire to confute their impudency not with words but with deeds. Howbeit I am not to prejudice my brother alive [18] or to smother the wrong offered to my brother deceased, or to tolerate the least defamation of my good father, whom no ill-willer could ever touch with any dishonesty or discredit in any sort. Nothing more dear or inestimable than a man's good name; and albeit I contemn such pelting injuries vainly devised against myself, yet I am not to neglect so intolerable a wrong so notoriously published against them. There is law for desperatest outlaws and order for most disorderly fellows. They that cannot govern themselves must be ruled by other, and pay for their folly. Whiles I was thus, or to like effect, resolving with myself and discoursing with some special friends, not only writing unto you,[19] I was suddenly certified that the king of the paper stage, so the gentleman termed Greene, had played his last part, and was gone to Tarlton; [20] whereof I protest I was nothing glad, as was expected, but unfeignedly sorry, as well because I could have wished he had taken his leave with a more charitable farewell, as also because I was deprived of that remedy in law that I intended against him in the behalf of my father, whose honest reputation I was in many duties to tender. Yet to some conceited wit that could take delight to discover knaveries or were a fit person to augment the history of cony-catchers, Oh Lord, what a pregnant occasion were here presented to display lewd vanity in his lively colors and to decipher the very mysteries of that base art! Petty cozeners are not worth the naming; he, they say, was the monarch of cross-biters [21] and the very em-

[17] *bugs-words:* swaggering language.

[18] *brother alive:* Richard, the astrologer and divine. John, M.D. (died 1592), was also an astrologer.

[19] *writing unto you:* The letter is addressed to Christopher Bird of Walden.

[20] *Tarlton:* famous clown and jester, died 1588.

[21] *cross-biters:* framers and blackmailers.

peror of shifters.[22] I was altogether unacquainted with the man and never once saluted him by name; but who in London hath not heard of his dissolute and licentious living, his fond disguising of a Master of Art with ruffianly hair, unseemly apparel, and more unseemly company; his vainglorious and Thrasonical [23] braving; his piperly extemporizing and Tarltonizing; his apish counterfeiting of every ridiculous and absurd toy; his fine cozening of jugglers and finer juggling with cozeners; his villainous cogging and foisting; [24] his monstrous swearing and horrible forswearing; his impious profaning of sacred texts; his other scandalous and blasphemous raving; his riotous and outrageous surfeiting; his continual shifting of lodgings; his plausible mustering and banqueting of roisterly acquaintance at his first coming; his beggarly departing in every hostess's debt; his infamous resorting to the Bankside, Shoreditch, Southwark, and other filthy haunts; his obscure lurking in basest corners; his pawning of his sword, cloak, and whatnot when money came short; his impudent pamphleting, fantastical interluding,[25] and desperate libeling when other cozening shifts failed; his employing of Ball (surnamed "Cutting" Ball) till he was intercepted [26] at Tyburn,[27] to levy a crew of his trustiest companions to guard him, in danger of arrests; his keeping of the foresaid Ball's sister, a sorry ragged quean,[28] of whom he had his base son, Infortunatus [29] Greene; his forsaking of his own wife, too honest for such a husband—particulars are infinite—his contemning of superiors, deriding of other, and defying of all good order?

Compare base fellows and noble men together, and what, in a manner, wanted he of the ruffianly and variable nature of Catiline or Antony but the honorable fortunes of Catiline and Antony? They that have seen much more than I have heard (for so I am credibly informed) can relate strange and almost incredible comedies of his monstrous disposition, wherewith I am not to infect the air or defile this paper. There be enough, and enough such histories, both dead and living, though youth be not corrupted or age accloyed with his legendary.[30] Truly I have been ashamed to hear some ascertained reports of his most woeful and rascal estate: how the wretched fellow (or shall I say the prince of beggars?) laid all to gage [31] for some few shillings, and was attended by lice, and would pitifully beg a penny pot of malmsey, and could not get any of his old acquaintance to comfort or visit him in his extremity but Mistress Appleby and the mother of Infortunatus. Alas, even his fellow writer,[32] a proper young man, if advised

[22] *shifters:* thieves.

[23] *Thrasonical:* bragging, from Thraso, the braggart soldier in Terence's *Eunuchus.*

[24] *cogging and foisting:* cheating at dice.

[25] *interluding:* writing plays.

[26] *intercepted:* hanged.

[27] *Tyburn:* the place for public executions, near the present Marble Arch.

[28] *quean:* whore.

[29] *Infortunatus:* His real name was Fortunatus.

[30] *accloyed . . . legendary:* nauseated by the stories about him.

[31] *laid all to gage:* pawned everything.

[32] *fellow writer:* Nashe, who was not in London during Greene's last days. Harvey's tone toward him becomes much sharper in the next letter, after he has seen *Pierce Penniless.*

in time, that was a principal guest at that fatal banquet of pickle herring (I spare his name, and in some respects wish him well), came never more at him, but either would not or haply could not perform the duty of an affectionate and faithful friend. The poor cordwainer's wife was his only nurse, and the mother of Infortunatus his sole companion, but when Mistress Appleby came, as much to expostulate injuries with her as to visit him. God help good fellows when they cannot help themselves! Slender relief in the predicament of privations and feigned habits. Miserable man, that must perish or be succored by counterfeit or impotent supplies. I once bemoaned the decayed and blasted estate of M. Gascoigne, who wanted not some commendable parts of conceit and endeavor; but unhappy M. Gascoigne, how lordly happy in comparison of most unhappy M. Greene! He never envied me so much as I pitied him from my heart; especially when his hostess Isam, with tears in her eyes and sighs from a deeper fountain (for she loved him dearly) told me of his lamentable begging of a penny pot of malmsey; and sir-reverence how lousy he and the mother of Infortunatus were (I would her surgeon found her no worse than lousy); and how he was fain, poor soul, to borrow her husband's shirt whiles his own was a-washing; and how his doublet and hose and sword were sold for three shillings; and beside, the charges of his winding sheet, which was four shillings; and the charges of his burial yesterday in the New Church yard near Bedlam, which was six shillings and fourpence; how deeply he was indebted to her poor husband, as appeared by his own bond of ten pounds which the good woman kindly showed me and beseeched me to read the writing beneath, which was a letter to his abandoned wife in the behalf of his gentle host—not so short as persuasible in the beginning, and pitiful in the ending:

> Doll, I charge thee by the love of our youth and by my soul's rest, that thou wilt see this man paid; for if he and his wife had not succored me I had died in the streets.
>
> ROBERT GREENE.

Oh what notable matter were here for a green head or Lucianical conceit that would take pleasure in the pain of such sorry distressed creatures! Whose afflicted case, to every charitable or compassionate mind cannot but seem most commiserable, if not for their own cause, yet for God's sake, who deserveth infinitely of them whom he acquitteth, not according to judgment but according to mercy. I rather hope of the dead as I wish to the living, that grace might finally abound where wickedness did overflow, and that Christ in his divine goodness should miraculously forgive the man that in his devilish badness blasphemously reviled God. The dead bite not, and I am none of those that bite the dead. When I begin to conflict with ghosts, then look for my confutation of his fine Quip or quaint dispute—whom his sweet hostess, for a tender farewell, crowned with a garland of bays, to show that a tenth Muse honored him more being dead than all the nine honored him alive. I know not whether Skelton,[33] Elderton, or some like-flourishing poet were so interred; it was his own request, and his nurse's devotion; and haply some of his favorites may imitate the example. One that wished him a better lodging than in a poor journeyman's house and a better grave than in that churchyard in Bedlam hath performed a little piece of greater duty to a laureate poet:

Here lies the man whom Mistress Isam crowned with bays—
She, she that joyed to hear her Nightingale's sweet lays.

* * *

FROM

THE THIRD LETTER

That best and his only physician knoweth what spiritual physic I commended unto him when I beheld in his meager and ghastly countenance, that I cannot rehearse without some fit of compassion. We must in order follow him, that should in nature have gone before him, and I know not by what destiny he followed him first that foled[34] him last. How he departed, his ghostly mother Isam can truliest and will favorabliest report; how he lived, London remembereth. O, what a lively picture of vanity! But O, what a deadly image of misery! And O, what a terrible caveat for such and such! I am not to extenuate or prejudice his wit, which could not anyway be great, though someway not the least of our vulgar writers, and many ways very ungracious; but who ever esteemed him either wise, or learned, or honest, or anyway credible? How many gentlemen and other say of him, "Let the paltry fellow go. Lord, what a lewd companion was he! What an egregious makeshift!" Where should cony-catchers have gotten such a secretary? How shall cozenage do for a new register, or fantasticality for a new author? They wrong him much with their epitaphs and other solemn devices that entitle him not at the least "The Second Toy of London, the Stale of Paul's, the Ape of Euphues, the Vice of the Stage, the Mocker of the Simple World, the Flouter of his Friends, the Foe of Himself," and so forth. What durst he not utter with his tongue, or divulge with his pen, or countenance with his face? Or whom cared he for but a careless crew of his own associates? Peruse his famous books, and instead of *Omne tulit punctum qui miscuit utile dulci,*[35] that forsooth was his professed posy,[36] lo, a wild head full of mad brain and a thousand crotchets, a scholar, a discourser, a courtier, a ruffian, a gamester, a lover, a soldier, a traveler, a

---

[33] *Skelton:* see above, pp. 15–26.

[34] *foled:* foiled.

[35] *Omne . . . dulci:* Horace, *Ars poetica,* 343: "He gets the vote who mingles the useful and the pleasant."

[36] *posy:* motto.

merchant, a broker,[37] an artificer,[38] a botcher,[39] a pettifogger,[40] a player, a cozener, a railer, a beggar, an omnigatherum,[41] a gay nothing; a storehouse of bald and baggage stuff, unworth the answering or reading; a trivial and triobolar [42] author for knaves and fools, an image of idleness, an epitome of fantasticality, a mirror of vanity, *Vanitas vanitatum et omnia vanitas*.[43] Alas, that any should say, as I have heard divers affirm, "His wit was nothing but a mint of knavery, himself a deviser of juggling feats, a forger of covetous practices, an inventor of monstrous oaths, a derider of all religions, a contemner of God and man, a desperate Lucianist, an abominable Aretinist, an arch-atheist, and he arch-deserved to be well hanged seven years ago." Twenty and twenty such familiar speeches I overpass and bury the whole legendary [44] of his life and death in the sepulcher of eternal silence. I will not condemn or censure his works, which I never did so much as superficially overrun, but as some few of them occursively presented themselves in stationers' shops and some other houses of my acquaintance. But I pray God they have not done more harm by corruption of manners than good by quickening of wit, and I would some buyers had either more reason to discern or less appetite to desire such novels.[45] The world is full enough of fooleries, though the humor be not feasted with such luxurious and riotous pamphlets.

* * *

Flourishing M. Greene is most woefully faded, and whilst I am bemoaning his over-piteous decay and discoursing the usual success of such rank wits, lo, all on the sudden, his sworn brother, M. Pierce [46] Penniless (still more paltry, but what remedy? We are already over shoes and must now go through), lo, his inwardest companion, that tasted of the fatal herring, cruelly pinched with want, vexed with discredit, tormented with other men's felicity and overwhelmed with his own misery, in a raving and frantic mood, most desperately exhibiteth his supplication to the devil. A strange title, an odd wit, and a mad whoreson, I warrant him. Doubtless it will prove some dainty device, quaintly contrived, by way of humble supplication to the high and mighty prince of darkness; not dunsically [47] botched up, but rightfully conveyed according to the style and tenor of Tarlton's precedent, his famous play [48] of the Seven Deadly Sins, which most deadly but most lively play I might have seen in London, and was very gently invited thereunto at Oxford by Tarlton himself, of whom I mer-

[37] *broker:* pander.

[38] *artificer:* trickster.

[39] *botcher:* a patcher of worthless trifles.

[40] *pettifogger:* one who picks petty quarrels.

[41] *omnigatherum:* a catch-all.

[42] *triobolar:* worthless.

[43] *Vanitas . . . vanitas:* "Vanity of vanities and nothing but vanity."

[44] *legendary:* legend.

[45] *novels:* novelties.

[46] *Pierce:* Nashe.

[47] *dunsically:* from Duns Scotus, the scholastic philosopher, whence also the word "dunce."

[48] *play:* written in 1585; it was a very popular comedy.

rily demanding which of the seven was his own deadly sin he bluntly answered after this manner, "By God, the sin of other gentlemen—Lechery!"

* * *

[AGAINST MALCONTENT WRITERS]

Right magnanimity never droopeth; sweet music requickeneth the heaviest spirits of dumpish melancholy; fine poetry abhorreth the loathsome and ugly shape of forlorn pensiveness; what gentle mind detesteth not cursed and damnable desperation? All abject dolefulness is woefully base and basely woeful. The die, the ball, the sponge, the sieve, the wheel [49] of fortune, Fortune herself—a trifle, a jest, a toy in philosophy and divine resolution. Be a musician and poet unto thyself, that art both, and a ringleader of both unto other! Be a man; be a gentleman; be a philosopher; be a divine; be thy resolute self! Not the slave of fortune, that for every flea-biting crieth out "Alas!" and for a few hungry meals, like a Greek parasite, misuseth the tragedy of Hecuba; [50] but the friend of virtue, that is richest in poverty, freest in bondage, bravest in jeopardy, cheerfulest in calamity. Be rather wise and unfortunate, with the silver swan, than fortunate and unwise, with the golden ass. Remember thine own marginal emblem: *Fortuna favet fatuis.*[51] Oh, solace thy miraculous self and cheer the Muses in cheering thy dainty soul, sweetly drunken with their delicious Helicon and the restorative nectar of the gods. What can I say more? That cordial liquor and that heavenly restorative be thy sovereign comfort, and scorn the baseness of every crazed or fainting thought that may argue a degenerate mind. And so much briefly touching thy dear self, whom I hope never to find so pathetically distressed or so tragically disguised again.

Now a word or two concerning him who in charity kisseth thy hand and in pity wisheth thee better luck. May it please gentle Pierce, in the divine fury of his ravished spirit, to be graciously good unto his poor friends, who would be somewhat loath to be silly sheep for the wolf or other sheep-biter. I dare undertake, the abused author [52] of the Astrological Discourse (every page thereof under correction of inspired and supernatural conceits, discovereth more art and judgment than the whole supplication of the parturient mountain) notwithstanding the notorious diabolical discourse of the said Pierce, a man better acquainted with the devils of hell than with the stars of heaven, shall unfeignedly pray for him, and only pray him to report the known truth of his approved learning and living without favor.

---

[49] *die . . . wheel:* all symbols of luck or bad luck.

[50] *tragedy of Hecuba:* The story of the Queen of Troy was a favorite sad tale. See *Hamlet,* II, ii, 523 ff.

[51] *Fortuna . . . fatuis:* "Fortune favors fools."

[52] *abused author:* Harvey's brother Richard. He is abused by Nashe in *Pierce Penilesse;* see below, p. 446.

Otherwise it were not greatly amiss, a little to consider that he, which in the ruff of his freshest jollity was fain to cry M. Churchyard [53] amercy in print, may be orderly driven to cry more peccavi's than one. I would think the Counter, M. Churchyard, his hostess Penia, and such other sensible lessons might sufficiently have taught him that Penniless is not Lawless, and that a poet's or painter's license is a poor security to privilege debt or defamation. I would wish the burned child not to forget the hot element, and would advise overweening youths to remember themselves and the good ancient oracle of sage Apollo. There is a certain thing called modesty, if they could light upon it, and, by my young master's leave, some pretty smack of discretion would relish well.

* * *

I will not cry "Absurd, absurd!" as he madly exclaimeth "Monstrous, monstrous!" But who in that university can deny but M. Harvey read the public philosophy lecture with special good liking and (many will say) with singular commendation, when this mighty lashing gentleman, now well-read in the late exploits of Untruss, and for Tarlton's amplifications [54] A per se A,[55] was not so much as *idoneus auditor civilis scientiae?* [56] What he is improved since, excepting his good old *Flores Poetarum,*[57] and Tarlton's surmounting rhetoric, with a little Euphuism, and Greeneness enough, which were all prettily stale before he put hand to pen, I report me to the favorablest opinion of those who know his prefaces, rhymes, and the very tympany [58] of his Tarltonizing wit, his Supplication to the Devil (Oh that is the devil and all!). I am so far from doting upon mine own or my brother's writings, in any matter of moment, that I use to censure them with a more curious judgment than I examine anything else; wherein my ear is so loath to flatter me and my conceit so afraid to cozen me that my mind ever remaineth unsatisfied, and nothing hitherto could fulfill my desire—insatiably covetous to do better. But as those perfunctory discourses are (which were more hastily than speedily published, without my privity), let the best of them go for waste paper and serve the basest shops, if the worst of them import not more public or private use than his gayest flower that may thank Greene or Tarlton for his garland. Were my brother not my brother, but some familiar acquaintance, I might in truth and should in reason make other comparisons, with applause enough; for what indifferency seeth not the difference, or what so silly as he could make Pierce, with voice or pen? (Notwithstanding those miracles of the white raven in

[53] *M. Churchyard:* Thomas Churchyard (1520–1604).

[54] *exploits of Untruss . . . Tarlton's amplifications:* a reference to Nashe's *Pierce Penilesse:* see below, p. 449.

[55] *A per se A:* From the alphabet in a hornbook or primer with a pun on "per se": "Percy": "Pierce."

[56] *idoneus . . . scientiae:* "a proper student of polite learning."

[57] *Flores Poetarum:* anthology of phrases and figures from the Latin poets.

[58] *tympany:* bombast.

the clouds.) But the University, the City, the whole realm, all good learning and civil government be their judge, and my mouth especially in this Martinish and Counter-Martinish age: wherein the spirit of contradiction reigneth and everyone superaboundeth in his own humor, even to the annihilating of any other, without rhyme or reason.

Thomas Nashe[1]

1567–1601

FROM

PIERCE PENNILESS, HIS SUPPLICATION TO THE DEVIL

(1592)

[AN INVECTIVE AGAINST ENEMIES OF POETRY]

WITH the enemies of poetry I care not if I have a bout, and those are they that term our best writers but babbling ballad-makers, holding them fantastical fools, that have wit but cannot tell how to use it. I myself have been so censured among some dull-headed divines,[2] who deem it no more cunning to write an exquisite poem than to preach pure Calvin or distill the juice of a commentary in a quarter sermon.[3] Prove it when you will, you slow-spirited Saturnists,[4] that have nothing but the pilferies of your pen to polish an exhortation withal; no eloquence but tautologies to tie the ears of your auditory unto you; no invention but "here it is to be noted, I stole this note out of Beza [5] or Marlorat"; [6] no wit to move, no passion to urge, but only an ordinary form of preaching, blown up by use of often hearing and speaking; and you shall find there goes more exquisite pains and purity of wit to the writing of one such rare poem as *Rosamund* [7] than to a hundred of your dunstical sermons.

Should we (as you) borrow all out of others, and gather nothing of ourselves, our names should be baffuld [8] on every bookseller's stall, and not a chandler's mustard-pot but would wipe his mouth with our waste paper.

---

[1] For introduction and bibliography, see pp. 414–416.

[2] *dull-headed divines:* specifically, the Reverend Richard Harvey, brother of Gabriel, in an epistle prefixed to some copies of *The Lamb of God* (1590).

[3] *quarter sermon:* quarterly sermon.

[4] *Saturnists:* dull, morose persons.

[5] *Beza:* Theodore Beza (1519–1605), successor of Calvin at Geneva; most eminent Protestant divine in Europe.

[6] *Marlorat:* Augustine Marlorat (1506–1563), another of the Geneva reformers.

[7] *Rosamund:* See below, p. 619.

[8] *baffuld:* treated with scorn.

"New herrings, new!" we must cry, every time we make ourselves public, or else we shall be christened with a hundred new titles of idiotism. Nor is poetry an art whereof there is no use in a man's whole life but to describe discontented thoughts and youthful desires; for there is no study but it doth illustrate and beautify. How admirably shine those divines above the common mediocrity, that have tasted the sweet springs of Parnassus!

Silver-tongued Smith,[9] whose well-tuned style hath made thy death the general tears of the Muses, quaintly couldst thou devise heavenly ditties to Apollo's lute, and teach stately verse to trip it as smoothly as if Ovid and thou had but one soul. Hence alone did it proceed that thou wert such a plausible pulpit man, that before thou enteredst into the rough ways of theology thou refinedst, preparedst, and purifiedst thy mind with sweet poetry. If a simple man's censure may be admitted to speak in such an open theater of opinions, I never saw abundant reading better mixed with delight, or sentences which no man can challenge of profane affectation sounding more melodious to the ear or piercing more deep to the heart.

To them that demand what fruits the poets of our time bring forth, or wherein they are able to prove themselves necessary to the state, thus I answer: first and foremost, they have cleansed our language from barbarism and made the vulgar sort here in London (which is the fountain whose rivers flow round about England) to aspire to a richer purity of speech than is communicated with the commonality of any nation under heaven. The virtuous by their praises they encourage to be more virtuous; to vicious men they are as infernal hags to haunt their ghosts with eternal infamy after death. The soldier, in hope to have his high deeds celebrated by their pens, despiseth a whole army of perils, and acteth wonders exceeding all human conjecture. Those that care neither for God nor the devil, by their quills are kept in awe. *Multi famam,* saith one, *pauci conscientiam verentur.*[10]

Let God see what he will, they would be loath to have the shame of the world. What age will not praise immortal Sir Philip Sidney, whom noble Salustius [11] (that thrice singular French poet) hath famoused; together with Sir Nicholas Bacon, Lord Keeper, and merry Sir Thomas More, for the chief pillars of our English speech. Not so much but Chaucer's host, Bailly in Southwark, and his wife of Bath he keeps such a stir with, in his *Canterbury Tales,* shall be talked of whilst the Bath is used, or there be ever a bad house in Southwark. Gentles, it is not your lay chronographers, that write of nothing but of mayors and sheriffs and the dear year and the great frost, that can endow your names with never-dated glory; for they want the wings of choice words to fly to heaven, which we have; they cannot sweeten a discourse, or wrest admiration from men reading, as we can, reporting the meanest accident. Poetry is the honey of all flowers, the quintessence of

---

[9] *Smith:* Henry Smith (1550–1591), a very popular preacher. He published some verse in Latin.

[10] *Multi . . . verentur:* "Many respect fame; only a few, conscience," Pliny, *Epistles,* III, 20.

[11] *Salustius:* Guillaume de Saluste du Bartas (1544–1590).

all sciences, the marrow of wit, and the very phrase of angels. How much better is it, then, to have an elegant lawyer to plead one's cause, than a stutting townsman that loseth himself in his tale and doth nothing but make legs; [12] so much it is better for a nobleman or gentleman to have his honor's story related, and his deeds emblazoned, by a poet, than a citizen.

Alas, poor Latinless authors, they are so simple they know not what they do; they no sooner spy a new ballad, and his name to it that compiled it, but they put him in for one of the learned men of our time. I marvel how the masterless men, that set up their bills in Paul's [13] for services, and such as paste up their papers on every post, for arithmetic and writing schools, 'scape eternity amongst them. I believe both they and the knight marshal's men, that nail up mandates at the court gate for annoying the palace with filth or making water, if they set their names to the writing, will shortly make up the number of the learned men of our time, and be as famous as the rest. For my part, I do challenge no praise of learning to myself, yet have I worn a gown in the University, and so hath *caret tempus non habet moribus;* [14] but this I dare presume, that if any Maecenas bind me to him by his bounty or extend some sound liberality to me worth the speaking of, I will do him as much honor as any poet of my beardless years shall in England. Not that I am so confident what I can do, but that I attribute so much to my thankful mind above others, which I am persuaded would enable me to work miracles.

On the contrary side, if I be evil intreated, or sent away with a flea in mine ear, let him look that I will rail on him soundly; not for an hour or a day, whiles the injury is fresh in my memory; but in some elaborate polished poem, which I will leave to the world when I am dead, to be a living image to all ages of his beggarly parsimony and ignoble illiberality; and let him not (whatsoever he be) measure the weight of my words by this book, where I write *quicquid in buccam venerit,*[15] as fast as my hand can trot; but I have terms (if I be vexed) laid in steep in *aqua fortis* [16] and gunpowder, that shall rattle through the skies and make an earthquake in a peasant's ears. Put case (since I am not yet out of the theme of wrath) that some tired jade belonging to the press, whom I never wronged in my life, hath named me expressly in print [17] (as I will not do him) and accuse me of want of learning, upbraiding me for reviving in an epistle of mine, the reverent memory of Sir Thomas More, Sir John Cheke, Doctor Watson, Doctor Haddon, Doctor Carr, Master Ascham, as if they were no meat but

---

[12] *make legs:* bow and scrape.

[13] *bills in Paul's:* Advertisements for jobs were commonly posted on the west door of the cathedral.

[14] *caret . . . moribus:* (bad Latin) I.e., "even unlearned persons have worn a University gown."

[15] *quicquid . . . venerit:* "whatever occurs to me."

[16] *in steep in aqua fortis:* soaking in nitric acid.

[17] R. Harvey in *The Lamb of God.* Nashe has a marginal note at this point which reads: "I would tell you in what book it is, but I am afraid it would make his book sell in his latter days, which hitherto hath lain dead and been a great loss to the printer."

for his mastership's mouth, or none but some such as the son of a ropemaker were worthy to mention them. To show how I can rail, thus would I begin to rail on him, "Thou that hadst thy hood turned over thy ears when thou wert a bachelor, for abusing of Aristotle and setting him upon the school gates painted with ass's ears on his head, is it any discredit for me, thou great babound,[18] thou pigmy braggart, thou pamphleter of nothing but paeans,[19] to be censured by thee, that hast scorned the prince of philosophers? Thou that in thy dialogues sold'st honey for a halfpenny, and the choicest writers extant for cues[20] apiece, that camest to the logic schools when thou wert a freshman and writ'st phrases, off with thy gown and untruss, for I mean to lash thee mightily. Thou hast a brother,[21] hast thou not, student in almanacs, go to, I'll stand to it, fathered one of thy bastards (a book, I mean) which being of thy begetting was set forth under his name?"

* * *

[OF SLOTH, AND THE VALUE OF PLAYS]

Setting jesting aside, I hold it a great disputable question which is a more evil man, of him that is an idle glutton at home or a retchless[22] unthrift abroad. The glutton at home doth nothing but engender diseases, pamper his flesh unto lust, and is good for none but his own gut; the unthrift abroad exerciseth his body at dancing school, fence school, tennis, and all such recreations; the vintners, the victualers, the dicing houses, and who not get by him. Suppose he lose a little now and then at play; it teacheth him wit. And how should a man know to eschew vices, if his own experience did not acquaint him with their inconveniences? *Omne ignotum pro magnifico est:*[23] that villainy we have made no assays in, we admire. Besides, my vagrant reveler haunts plays and sharpens his wits with frequenting the company of poets; he emboldens his blushing face by courting fair women on the sudden, and looks into all estates by conversing with them in public places. Now tell me whether of these two, the heavy-headed gluttonous house-dove, or this lively wanton young gallant, is like to prove the wiser man and better member in the commonwealth. If my youth might not be thought partial, the fine qualified gentleman, although unstayed, should carry it clean away from the lazy clownish drone.

Sloth in nobility, courtiers, scholars, or any men is the chiefest cause that brings them in contempt. For as industry and unfatigable toil raiseth mean

---

[18] *babound:* baboon.

[19] *paeans:* a reference to R. Harvey's *Ephemeron, sive Paean* (1583).

[20] *cues:* quadrans, ⅛ of a penny.

[21] *brother:* John Harvey, who published almanacs for 1583 and 1589.

[22] *retchless:* reckless.

[23] *Omne . . . est:* Tacitus, *Agricola,* 30. Nashe translates.

persons from obscure houses to high thrones of authority, so sloth and sluggish security causeth proud lords to tumble from the towers of their starry descents and be trod underfoot of every inferior Besonian.[24] Is it the lofty treading of a galliard or fine grace in telling of a love tale amongst ladies, can make a man reverenced of the multitude? No; they care not for the false glistering of gay garments or the insinuating courtesy of a carpet peer; but they delight to see him shine in armor and oppose himself to honorable danger, to participate a voluntary penury with his soldiers and relieve part of their wants out of his own purse. That is the course he that will be popular must take, which if he neglect and sit dallying at home, nor will be awaked by any indignities out of his love dream, but suffer every upstart groom to defy him, set him at naught and shake him by the beard unrevenged, let him straight take orders and be a churchman, and then his patience may pass for a virtue; but otherwise he shall be suspected of cowardice and not cared for of any. The only enemy to sloth is contention and emulation, as to propose one man to myself that is the only mirror of our age and strive to outgo him in virtue. But this strife must be so tempered that we fall not from the eagerness of praise to the envying of their persons, for then we leave running to the goal of glory to spurn at a stone that lies in our way; and so did Atalanta in the midst of her course stoop to take up the golden apple that her enemy scattered in her way, and was outrun by Hippomenes.[25] The contrary to this contention and emulation is security, peace, quiet, tranquillity—when we have no adversary to pry into our actions, no malicious eye whose pursuing our private behavior might make us more vigilant over our imperfections than otherwise we would be.

That state or kingdom that is in league with all the world, and hath no foreign sword to vex it, is not half so strong or confirmed to endure as that which lives every hour in fear of invasion. There is a certain waste of the people for whom there is no use but war; and these men must have some employment still to cut them off; *Nam si foras hostem non habent, domi invenient.*[26] If they have no service abroad, they will make mutinies at home. Or if the affairs of the state be such as cannot exhale all these corrupt excrements, it is very expedient they have some light toys to busy their heads withal, cast before them as bones to gnaw upon, which may keep them from having leisure to intermeddle with higher matters.

To this effect, the policy of plays is very necessary, howsoever some shallow-brained censurers (not the deepest searchers into the secrets of government) mightily oppugn them. For whereas the afternoon being idlest time of the day, wherein men that are their own masters (as gentlemen of the court, the Inns of the Court, and the number of captains and soldiers about London) do wholly bestow themselves upon pleasure, and that pleas-

[24] *Besonian:* beggar, rogue.

[25] *Atalanta . . . Hippomenes:* The story is told by Ovid, *Metamorphoses,* X, 662–680.

[26] *Nam . . . invenient:* Adapted from Livy, Book XXX, xliv, 9. Nashe translates.

ure they divide (how virtuously, it skills not) either into gaming, following of harlots, drinking, or seeing a play; is it not then better (since of four extremes all the world cannot keep them but they will choose one) that they should betake them to the least, which is plays? Nay, what if I prove plays to be no extreme, but a rare exercise of virtue? First, for the subject of them, (for the most part) it is borrowed out of our English chronicles, wherein our forefathers' valiant acts (that have lain long buried in rusty brass and worm-eaten books) are revived, and they themselves raised from the grave of oblivion, and brought to plead their aged honors in open presence; than which, what can be a sharper reproof to these degenerate effeminate days of ours?

How would it have joyed brave Talbot,[27] the terror of the French, to think that after he had lain two hundred years in his tomb, he should triumph again on the stage, and have his bones new embalmed with the tears of ten thousand spectators at least (at several times) who in the tragedian that represents his person imagine they behold him fresh bleeding.

I will defend it against any collian[28] or clubfisted usurer of them all, there is no immortality can be given a man on earth like unto plays. What talk I to them of immortality, that are the only underminers of honor, and do envy any man that is not sprung up by base brokery like themselves. They care not if all the ancient houses were rooted out, so that like the burgomasters of the Low Countries they might share the government amongst them as states, and be quartermasters of our monarchy. All arts to them are vanity; and if you tell them what a glorious thing it is to have Henry the Fifth represented on the stage leading the French king prisoner, and forcing both him and the Dolphin to swear fealty, "Aye, but," will they say, "what do we get by it?" Respecting neither the right of fame that is due to true nobility deceased, nor what hopes of eternity are to be proposed to adventurous minds, to encourage them forward, but only their execrable lucre and filthy unquenchable avarice.

They know when they are dead they shall not be brought upon the stage for any goodness, but in a merriment of the usurer and the devil, or buying arms of the herald, who gives them the lion without tongue, tail, or talons, because his master whom he must serve is a townsman and a man of peace, and must not keep any quarreling beasts to annoy his honest neighbors.

In plays, all cozenages, all cunning drifts over-gilded with outward holiness, all stratagems of war, all the cankerworms that breed on the rust of peace, are most lively anatomized; they show the ill success of treason, the fall of hasty climbers, the wretched end of usurpers, the misery of civil dissension, and how just God is evermore in punishing of murther. And to prove every one of these allegations could I propound the circumstances of

---

[27] *Talbot:* in the play "Harey the VI" produced by Strange's men for Henslowe on March 3, 1592. What relation this play had to the Shakespearean *I Henry VI* is uncertain, but Nashe's reference would fit I, iv, 39–43, and II, iii, 14–24.

[28] *collian:* rascal (the usual form is "cullion").

this play and that play, if I meant to handle this theme otherwise than *obiter*.[29] What should I say more? They are sour pills of reprehension wrapped up in sweet words. Whereas some petitioners of the counsel against them object, they corrupt the youth of the city and withdraw prentices from their work; they heartily wish they might be troubled with none of their youth nor their prentices; for some of them (I mean the ruder handicrafts' servants) never come abroad but they are in danger of undoing; and as for corrupting them when they come, that's false; for no play they have encourageth any man to tumults or rebellion, but lays before such the halter and the gallows; or praiseth or approveth pride, lust, whoredom, prodigality, or drunkenness, but beats them down utterly. As for the hindrance of trades and traders of the city by them, that is an article foisted in by the vintners, alewives, and victualers, who surmise if there were no plays they should have all the company that resort to them lie boozing and beer-bathing in their houses every afternoon. Nor so, nor so, good brother bottle-ale, for there are other places besides where money can bestow itself; the sign of the smock will wipe your mouth clean; and yet I have heard ye have made her a tenant to your taphouses. But what shall he do that hath spent himself? Where shall he haunt? Faith, when dice, lust, and drunkenness, and all, have dealt upon him, if there be never a play for him to go to for his penny, he sits melancholy in his chamber, devising upon felony or treason, and how he may best exalt himself by mischief.

In Augustus' time (who was the patron of all witty sports) there happened a great fray in Rome about a player, insomuch as all the city was in an uproar; whereupon, the emperor (after the broil was somewhat overblown) called the player before him, and asked what was the reason that a man of his quality durst presume to make such a brawl about nothing. He smilingly replied, "It is good for thee, Oh Caesar, that the people's heads are troubled with brawls and quarrels about us and our light matters; for otherwise they would look into thee and thy matters." Read Lipsius[30] or any profane or Christian politician, and you shall find him of this opinion. Our players are not as the players beyond sea, a sort of squirting bawdy comedians, that have whores and common courtesans to play women's parts, and forbear no immodest speech or unchaste action that may procure laughter; but our scene is more stately furnished than ever it was in the time of Roscius, our representations honorable and full of gallant resolution, not consisting like theirs of pantaloon, a whore, and a zany,[31] but of emperors, kings, and princes; whose true tragedies (*Sophocleo cothurno*)[32] they do vaunt.

Not Roscius nor Aesope,[33] those admired tragedians that have lived ever

---

[29] *obiter:* by the way.

[30] *Lipsius:* Justus Lipsius (1547–1606), Belgian scholar and historian.

[31] *pantaloon, zany:* type parts in the *commedia dell' arte.*

[32] *Sophocleo cothurno:* "with Sophoclean dignity."

[33] *Roscius, Aesope:* These two Roman actors flourished about 70 B.C.

since before Christ was born, could ever perform more in action than famous Ned Allen.[34] I must accuse our poets of sloth and partiality that they will not boast in large impressions what worthy men (above all nations) England affords. Other countries cannot have a fiddler break a string but they will put it in print, and the old Romans in the writings they published thought scorn to use any but domestical examples of their own home-bred actors, scholars, and champions, and them they would extol to the third and fourth generation; cobblers, tinkers, fencers, none escaped them, but they mingled them all in one gallimaufry of glory.

Here I have used a like method, not of tying myself to mine own country, but by insisting in the experience of our time; and if I ever write anything in Latin (as I hope one day I shall), not a man of any desert here amongst us, but I will have up. Tarlton,[35] Ned Allen, Knell, Bentley,[36] shall be made known to France, Spain, and Italy; and not a part that they surmounted in, more than other, but I will there note and set down, with the manner of their habits and attire.[37]

FROM

STRANGE NEWS OF THE INTERCEPTING CERTAIN LETTERS

(1592) [38]

[CONCERNING SPENSER]

As touching the liberty of orators and poets, I will confer with thee somewhat gravely, although thou beest a goosecap and hast no judgment. A liberty they have, thou sayest, "but no liberty without bounds, no license without limitation." Jesu, what mister wonders [39] dost thou tell us! Everything hath an end, and a pudding hath two. "That liberty, poets of late in their invectives have exceeded"; they have borne their sword up where it is not lawful for a poynado, that is but the page of prowess, to intermeddle.

Thou bringest in Mother Hubbard for an instance. Go no further, but here confess thyself a flat nodgecomb [40] before all this congregation, for thou hast dealt by thy friend as homely as thou didst by thy father. Who publicly accused or of late brought Mother Hubbard into question, that thou shouldst by rehearsal rekindle against him the sparks of displeasure

[34] *Ned Allen:* Edward Alleyn (1566–1626), partner and son-in-law of Henslowe, the manager. He retired from the stage about 1603–4. He founded Dulwich College.

[35] *Tarlton:* Richard Tarlton (d. 1588), the most popular Elizabethan comedian.

[36] *Knell, Bentley:* actors older than Alleyn, and famous in the period before 1588. Both were Queen's men.

[37] Nashe never fulfilled this resolution.

[38] See Harvey's *Four Letters,* p. 436.

[39] *mister wonders:* kind of wonders.

[40] *nodgecomb:* ninny.

that were quenched? Forgot he "the pure sanguine of his *Faerie Queene,*" sayest thou? A pure sanguine sot art thou, that in vainglory to have Spenser known for thy friend, and that thou hast some interest in him, censurest him worse than his deadliest enemy would do. If any man were undeservedly touched in it, thou hast revived his disgrace that was so touched in it by renaming it when it was worn out of all men's mouths and minds. Besides, whereas before I thought it a made matter of some malicious moralizers against him, and no substance of slander in truth, now, when thou, that proclaimest thyself the only familiar of his bosom and therefore shouldst know his secrets, gives it out in print that he overshot himself therein, it cannot choose but be suspected to be so indeed.

Immortal Spenser, no frailty hath thy fame but the imputation of this idiot's friendship! Upon an unspotted Pegasus should thy gorgeous-attired *Faerie Queene* ride triumphant through all Report's dominions, but that this mud-born bubble, this boil on the brow of the University, this bladder of pride new blown challengeth some interest in her prosperity. Of pitch who hath any use at all, shall be abused by it in the end.

High grass that flourisheth for a season on the housetop, fadeth before the harvest calls for it and may well make a fair show, but hath no sweetness in it. Such is this Ass *in presenti,*[41] this gross painted image of pride, who would fain counterfeit a good wit, but scornful pity, his best patron, knows it becomes him as ill as an unwieldy elephant to imitate a whelp in his wantonness.

* * *

[HARVEY'S INKHORN TERMS]

The flowers of your *Four Letters* it may be I have overlooked more narrowly and done my best devoir to assemble them together into pathetical posy, which I will here present to Master Orator Edge for a New Year's gift, leaving them to his wordy discretion to be censured, whether they be current in Inkhornism or no:

"Conscious mind; canicular tales; egregious an argument (whenas egregious is never used in English but in the extreme ill part); ingenuity; jovial mind; valorous authors; inkhorn adventures; inkhorn pads; putative opinions; putative artists; energetical persuasions; rascality; materiality; artificiality; fantasticality; divine entelechy; loud mentery; deceitful perfidy; addicted to theory; the world's great incendiary; sirenized furies; sovereignty immense; abundant cautels; cautelous and adventurous; cordial liquor; Catilinaries and Philippics; perfunctory discourses; David's sweetness Olympic; the Idee high and deep abyss of excellence; the only unicorn of the Muses; the Aretinish mountain of huge exaggerations; the

41 *Ass in presenti:* a pun based on a familiar rule in Lilly's Latin grammar: *As in praesenti, perfectum format in avi* ("Forms ending in 'as' in the present tense end in 'avi' in the perfect tense").

gracious law of amnesty; amicable terms; amicable end; effectuate; addoulce his melody; Magi; polymechany; extensively employed; precious trainment; novelettes; notoriety; negotiations; mechanician."

Nor are these all, for every third line hath some of this over-racked absonism.[42] Nor do I altogether scum off all these as the new-engendered foam of the English, but allow some of them for a need to fill up a verse—as "trainment," and one or two words more which the liberty of prose might well have spared. In a verse, when a word of three syllables cannot thrust in but sidelings, to joint him even we are oftentimes fain to borrow some lesser quarry of elocution from the Latin, always retaining this for a principle: that a leak of indesinence,[43] as a leak in a ship, must needly be stopped with what matter soever.

Chaucer's authority, I am certain, shall be alleged against me[44] for a many of these balductums.[45] Had Chaucer lived to this age, I am verily persuaded he would have discarded the one half of the harsher sort of them. They were the ooze which overflowing barbarism, withdrawn to her Scottish northern channel, had left behind her. Art, like young grass in the spring of Chaucer's flourishing, was glad to peep up through any slime of corruption, to be beholden to she cared not whom for apparel, traveling in those cold countries. There is no reason that she, a banished queen into this barren soil, having monarchized it so long amongst the Greeks and Romans, should, although war's fury had humbled her to some extremity, still be constrained, when she hath recovered her state, to wear the robes of adversity, jet it in her old rags, when she is wedded to new prosperity. *Utere moribus praeteritis,* saith Caius Caesar in Aulus Gellius, *loquere verbis praesentibus.*[46]

Thou art mine enemy, Gabriel, and that which is more, a contemptible underfoot enemy, or else I would teach thy old Truantship[47] the true use of words, as also how more inclinable verse is than prose to dance after the horrisonant[48] pipe of inveterate antiquity. It is no matter, since thou hast brought godly instruction out of love with thee; use thy own destruction, reign sole emperor of Inkhornism! I wish unto thee all superabundant increase of the singular gifts of absurdity and vainglory; from this time forth for ever, ever, ever, evermore mayest thou be canonized as the nonpareil of impious epistlers, the short shredder-out of sandy sentences without lime, as Quintilian termed Seneca all lime and no sand, all matter and no circumstance; the factor for the fairies and night-urchins in supplanting and setting aside the true children of the English, and suborning inkhorn changelings in their stead; the gallimauferyer of all styles in one standish, as imitating everyone and having no separate form of writing of thy own;

---

[42] *absonism:* solecism in language.

[43] *indesinence:* lack of proper ending.

[44] *Chaucer's . . . me:* Nashe's "certainty" is ill-founded. The inkhornisms are not Chaucerian.

[45] *balductums:* trash, nonsense.

[46] *Utere . . . praesentibus:* "Follow ancient manners, but use modern language."

[47] *Truantship:* In *Foure Letters* Harvey refers to himself as an old truant.

[48] *horrisonant:* discordant.

and, to conclude, the only feather-driver of phrases and putter-of-a-good-word-to-it-when-thou-hast-once-got-it that is betwixt this and the Alps. So be it, world without end. Chroniclers, hear my prayers; good Master Stowe, be not unmindful of him.

[NASHE ON HIMSELF AS A WRITER]

But something even now, Gabriel, thou wert girding against my "prefaces and rhymes, and the tympany of my Tarltonizing wit." Well, these be your words, "prefaces and rhymes." Let me study a little—"prefaces and rhymes" —*Minime vero, si ais nego.*[49] I never printed rhyme in my life, but those verses in the beginning of *Pierce Penniless,* though you have set forth

The stories quaint of many a doughty fly,
That read a lecture to the vent'rous elf.[50]

And so forth, as followeth in chambling row. Prefaces two,[51] or a pair of epistles, I will receive into the protection of my parentage, out of both which, suck out one solecism or misshapen English word if thou canst for thy guts.

Wherein have I borrowed from Greene or Tarlton, that I should thank them for all I have? Is my style like Greene's or my jests like Tarlton's? Do I talk of any counterfeit birds, or herbs, or stones, or rake up any new-found poetry from under the walls of Troy?[52] If I do, trip me with it; but I do not; therefore I'll be so saucy as trip you with the grand lie. 'Ware stumbling of whetstones in the dark, there, my masters!

This will I proudly boast (yet am I nothing akindred to the three brothers), that the vein which I have, be it a median vein or a madman, is of my own begetting, and calls no man father in England but myself, neither Euphues, nor Tarlton, nor Greene.

Not Tarlton nor Greene but have been contented to let my simple judgment overrule them in some matters of wit. *Euphues* I read when I was a little ape in Cambridge, and then I thought it was *ipse ille;*[53] it may be excellent good still, for aught I know, for I looked not on it this ten year; but to imitate it I abhor, otherwise than it imitates Plutarch, Ovid, and the choicest Latin authors.

If you be advised, I took "shortest vowels and longest mutes"[54] in the beginning of my book, as suspicious of being accessary to the making of a

[49] *Minime . . . nego:* "No, not at all; if you say it, I deny it."

[50] *The stories . . . elf:* a quotation from a sonnet by Harvey in *Foure Letters.*

[51] *Prefaces two:* introductory epistles to Greene's *Menaphon* (1589) and to the first edition of Sidney's *Astrophel and Stella* (1591).

[52] *rake up any . . . Troy:* Nashe elsewhere speaks with scorn of the trite subject of the siege of Troy.

[53] *ipse ille:* "the very thing."

[54] *"shortest . . . mutes":* a quotation from a sonnet against Greene in the first of *Foure Letters.* In the beginning of *Strange Newes* Nashe had said the poem was by Harvey even though it is represented as written by one Christopher Bird of Saffron Walden.

sonnet whereto Master Christopher Bird's name is set; there I said that you mute [55] forth many such phrases in the course of your book, which I would point at as I passed by. Here I am as good as my word, for I note that thou, being afraid of beraying [56] thyself with writing, wouldst fain be a mute, when it is too late to repent. Again thou reviest on us and sayest that mutes are coursed and vowels hunted. Thou art no mute, yet shalt thou be hunted and coursed to the full. I will never leave thee as long as I am able to lift a pen.

Whether I seek to be counted a terrible bull-beggar [57] or no, I'll bait thee worse than a bull, so that thou shalt desire somebody on thy knees to help thee with letters of commendation to Bull the Hangman, that he may dispatch thee out of the way before more affliction come upon thee. All the invective and satirical spirits shall then be thy familiars, as the furies in hell are the familiars of sinful ghosts, to follow them and torment them without intermission; thou shalt be double-girt with girds, and scoffed at till those that stand by do nothing but cough with laughing.

Thou sayest I profess the art of railing; thou shalt not say so in vain, for, if there be any art or depth in it more than Aretine or Agrippa [58] have discovered or dived into, look that I will sound it and search it to the uttermost, but e'er I have done with thee I'll leave thee the miserablest creature that the sun ever saw.

There is no kind of peaceable pleasure in poetry, but I can draw equally in the same yoke with the haughtiest of those foul-mouthed backbiters that say I can do nothing but rail. I have written in all sorts of humors privately, I am persuaded, more than any young man of my age in England.

FROM

SUMMER'S LAST WILL AND TESTAMENT [59]

SPRING, the sweet spring, is the year's pleasant king,
Then blooms each thing, then maids dance in a ring,
Cold doth not sting, the pretty birds do sing:
  Cuckoo, jug-jug, pu-we, to-witta-woo! [60]

The palm and may make country houses gay,
Lambs frisk and play, the shepherds pipe all day,

---

[55] *mute:* void excrement.

[56] *beraying:* befouling.

[57] *bull-beggar:* bogey, bugbear.

[58] *Agrippa:* Henricus Cornelius Agrippa (1486–1535), German physician and writer who attacked modern versions of Christianity. His *De incertitudine et vanitate scientiarum* was a favorite book of Nashe's.

[59] *Summer's Last Will and Testament* was performed before the Archbishop of Canterbury in his palace at Croydon, October, 1592.

[60] *Cuckoo . . . to-witta-woo:* the calling of the cuckoo, nightingale, lapwing, and owl respectively. For the owl, see Shakespeare's song "When icicles do hang," *Love's Labour's Lost,* V, ii, 902.

And we hear aye birds tune this merry lay:
  Cuckoo, jug-jug, pu-we, to-witta-woo!

The fields breathe sweet, the daisies kiss our feet,
Young lovers meet, old wives a-sunning sit,
In every street these tunes our ears do greet:
  Cuckoo, jug-jug, pu-we, to-witta-woo!
    Spring, the sweet spring!

A LITANY IN TIME OF PLAGUE

Adieu, farewell, earth's bliss;
This world uncertain is;
Fond are life's lustful joys;
Death proves them all but toys;
None from his darts can fly;
I am sick, I must die.
  Lord, have mercy on us!

Rich men, trust not in wealth,
Gold cannot buy you health;
Physic himself must fade.
All things to end are made,
The plague full swift goes by;
I am sick, I must die.
  Lord, have mercy on us!

Beauty is but a flower
Which wrinkles will devour;
Brightness falls from the air;
Queens have died young and fair;
Dust hath closed Helen's eye.
I am sick, I must die.
  Lord, have mercy on us!

Strength stoops unto the grave,
Worms feed on Hector brave;
Swords may not fight with fate,
Earth still holds ope her gate.
"Come, come!" the bells do cry.
I am sick, I must die.
  Lord, have mercy on us.

Wit with his wantonness
Tasteth death's bitterness;
Hell's executioner
Hath no ears for to hear
What vain art can reply.
I am sick, I must die.
  Lord, have mercy on us.

Haste, therefore, each degree,
To welcome destiny;
Heaven is our heritage,
Earth but a player's stage;
Mount we unto the sky.
I am sick, I must die.
  Lord, have mercy on us.

Richard Hakluyt and the Voyagers

THE Renaissance awakened Europe to the glory and beauty of the past civilization of Greece and Rome. It also opened new worlds which heretofore had been but Utopian dreams. The imagination had dwelt on Cathay, the Golden Age, Paradise, and The Fountain of Youth, but a more practical and mercenary turn of mind saw far countries as a source of gold and other wealth. Romanticism and mercantilism combined to establish, in the sixteenth century, our modern interest in travel and geography.

England absorbed these aspects of the Renaissance late, but her progress was rapid, her success in many ways phenomenal. Before her, Portugal and Spain had led in the race for new lands and bullion. Englishmen, however, were truly insular in the first part of the sixteenth century. They were coastwise sailors. In 1497, at the end of the previous century, John Cabot, a citizen of Venice, set out from Bristol under a patent from Henry VII and reached the coast of Labrador, but Spaniards and French were soon to cap his exploit. In 1513 Balboa saw the Pacific; in 1520 the Portuguese navigator Magellan sailed around South America and reached the Philippines, where he died. The French, too, under Verrazano, Jacques Cartier, and others, made important voyages to America.

For fifty years after John Cabot's voyage, the English made little progress as explorers. Fearful of conflict with Spain, which held the western routes, and with Portugal, which dominated the eastern, by the Cape of Good Hope, English navigators turned north. In May, 1553, Sir Hugh Willoughby and Richard Chancellor, representing the newly formed society of Merchant Adventurers, set out for Northern Asia.

But Martin Frobisher's voyages to the northwest, and Hawkins' and Drake's in the Spanish Indies, drew attention from the Northeast Passage. The solid revival of the Northwest project, however, is the work of Sir Humphrey Gilbert, half-brother of Ralegh, who had previously plotted a Northeast project with Jenkinson. Gilbert's *A Discourse of a discoverie for a new passage to Cataia,* published in 1576, was the real beginning of the exploits of Frobisher and John Davis, each of whom made his voyages from 1576 to 1587.

In the meantime in 1580 Drake returned treasure-laden after a three years' voyage of circumnavigation, piracy, and discovery. The "Master Thief of the Unknown" entertained the Queen at dinner on his ship, the *Golden Hind,* at Deptford, and from her hands received his knighthood. Drake was the terror of the seas, feared by Spanish and Portuguese. He was known to them as *El Draco Ingles* (with a pun on "Drake" and "dragon"); yet his real importance in history is not as a freebooter but as the founder of the great tradition of the British navy. The victory over the Armada in 1588 was really his victory.

Drake was a fighter, not a colonizer. It was Sir Humphrey Gilbert who first thought seriously of colonization. He wished to found a colony near Newfoundland, but in his second voyage Gilbert went down with his ship soon after he had shouted to his companions in another vessel, "We are as near to Heaven by sea as by land."

Ralegh, who was originally in command of a ship in Gilbert's last voyage, but did not sail with the fleet, took up Gilbert's work. In 1584 he sent two small ships to America under the command of Philip Amadas and Arthur Barlow. They reached Virginia, were received graciously by the Indians, and brought home reports which seemed promising even to the Queen herself, by whom the colony was named. In 1585 Ralegh got together seven ships. It was rumored that Sir Philip Sidney would command the fleet, but the Queen would not allow Sidney to accept the post. Sir Richard Grenville, Ralegh's cousin, was given the command, but Grenville, though a great fighting officer, was a poor colonial organizer, and the colony failed.

One last effort of Ralegh to colonize closes the history of Elizabethan voyages. In 1595 he led an expedition up the Orinoco and published the account of his trip in an excellent piece of English prose: *The Discoverie of the Large, Rich and Bewtiful Empire of Guiana.* Twenty-three years later, Ralegh, after one of the most puzzling careers of any Elizabethan, died on the scaffold. His death, according to his namesake, Professor Walter Raleigh, "marks the end of the heroic age; with him the poets and architects who had prophesied and planned pass away, and the accountants and builders begin their long and tedious trek of erecting the fabric of the Empire."

For its knowledge of the sea dogs and the rise of English sea power the world is indebted to a self-effacing, industrious clergyman, "Richard Hakluyt, Preacher" (1553–1616). He was born, probably in London, in 1553, educated at Westminster School and Christ Church, Oxford, where he received his B.A. in 1574 and his M.A. three years later.

As a boy he visited his older cousin Richard, in the Middle Temple, and became so interested in the maps and globes he saw there that he dedicated the rest of his life to the study of English exploration. At Oxford he read all the extant travels in Greek, Latin, Italian, English, Spanish, and Portuguese. In 1582 he published his first book, *Divers Voyages touching The Discoverie of America,* dedicated to Sir Philip Sidney. A year later he considered taking part in Gilbert's second voyage, but instead for five years took the post of chaplain to Sir Edward Stafford, ambassador to Paris. During this time he worked tirelessly bringing together all the accounts of the English voyages he could in any way secure. In 1589 he published the first folio editions of *The Principall Navigations, Traffiques, Voiages, and Discoveries of the English Nation,* and enlarged it to a three-volume folio edition in 1598–1600. It is this work that Froude called "the prose epic of the modern English nation."

Hakluyt was a conscientious editor of enormous industry. He was faithful to his sources and was judicious in cutting and revising ornately written accounts of voyages which came into his hands. To seek out the only living survivor of a Labrador expedition of 1536, he once traveled two hundred miles. He searched English and Continental libraries and talked with English and foreign sailors on their returns from voyages. He knew every map-maker, traveler, merchant-venturer, explorer, imperialist of his time; and even the great men of the court

—Sidney, Walsingham, Howard—passed on what they knew to him. He never sailed himself, but he knew more than any sailor.

He was a quiet, pious man, but above all (as Professor Raleigh says) he was a "zealot for the map and flag." He received ecclesiastical preferment, finally becoming archdeacon of Westminster in 1603. At his death in 1616 his manuscripts passed to the Reverend Samuel Purchas, who published further accounts of the voyages based on Hakluyt's collections.

Throughout the *Principall Navigations* one can see constant strains of British character and the qualities which make the great collection so representative of the Elizabethan spirit. The desire to see new worlds is interwoven with the lust for gold and with the hope of conquest. Along with the expressed missionary idea of adding new nations to Protestantism is the mounting hatred of Spain. The dogged energy and zeal of English navigators and seamen, which drew praise even from their enemies, is graphically depicted. Fighters like Drake, Hawkins, and Grenville, dreamers such as Ralegh, empire visionaries like Gilbert, and gentlemen-adventurers like Essex crowd Hakluyt's pages.

How thoroughly Hakluyt's work expresses the spirit of the Elizabethan age will be apparent to anyone who notes in the literature and life of the period the effect of widening horizons on imagination and ideas. Spenser justified the plausibility of his imagined fairyland by pointing to the voyages of discovery:

Who euer heard of th' Indian Peru?
Or who in venturous vessell measured
The *Amazons* huge river now found trew?
Or fruitfullest *Virginia* who did ever vew?

Yet all these were, when no man did them know;
Yet have from wisest ages hidden beene:
And later times things more unknowne shall show.
Why then should witlesse man so much misweene
That nothing is, but that which he hath seene?

The energy of the voyagers is the energy of Elizabethan life; their heroic pattern and their illimitable world were shared by Marlowe and Shakespeare.

* * *

A selection from Ralegh's *Discoverie of . . . Guiana* is printed, pp. 502–510. A map of the routes taken by the voyagers is printed on pp. 508–509.

Bibliography: Richard Hakluyt, *The Principal Navigations, Voyages, Traffiques, and Discoveries of the English Nation,* 12 vols., Glasgow, 1903–1905 (Hakluyt Society, Extra Series. Volume 12 reprints Professor Walter Raleigh's *The English Voyages of the Sixteenth Century* [1904]); C. R. Beazley, ed., *Voyages and Travels mainly during the Sixteenth and Seventeenth Centuries,* 2 vols., Westminster, 1903 (reprinted from Arber's English Garner); G. B. Parks, *Richard Hakluyt and the English Voyages,* New York (American Geographical Society, Special Publication, No. 10), 1930; Alexander Brown, *The Genesis of the United States,* 2 vols., Boston, 1890; R. R. Cawley, *The Voyages and Elizabethan Drama,* Boston, 1938 (The Modern Language Association of America, Monograph Series, VIII); *Unpathed Waters: Studies in the Influence of the Voyagers on Elizabethan Literature,* Princeton University Press, 1940; S. C. Chew, *The Crescent and the Rose,* New York, 1937; Henry Stevens of Vermont, *Thomas Harriot and his Associates,* privately printed, 1900; E. Lynam (ed.), *Richard Hakluyt and his Successors,* London, 1946.

FROM

THE PRINCIPALL NAVIGATIONS, TRAFFIQUES, VOIAGES, AND DISCOVERIES OF THE ENGLISH NATION

A report of the voyage and success thereof, attempted in the year of our Lord 1583 by Sir Humphrey Gilbert,[29] knight, with other gentlemen assisting him in that action, intended to discover and to plant Christian inhabitants in place convenient upon those large and ample countries extended northward from the Cape of Florida, lying under very temperate climes, esteemed fertile and rich in minerals, yet not in actual possession of any Christian prince, written by M. Edward Hayes, gentleman, and principal actor in the same voyage, who alone continued unto the end and by God's special assistance returned home with his retinue safe and entire.

. . . Orders thus determined, and promises mutually given to be observed, every man withdrew himself unto his charge, the anchors being already weighed, and our ships under sail, having a soft gale of wind, we began our voyage upon Tuesday, the eleventh day of June, in the year of our Lord 1583, having in our fleet at our departure from Causet Bay [30] these

[29] *Sir Humphrey Gilbert:* (1539–1583) stepbrother of Sir Walter Ralegh, headed an unsuccessful expedition to America in 1578 and a second expedition, described in this selection, in 1583.

[30] *Causet Bay:* (also in this account called Causon Bay) Cawsand Bay near Plymouth.

ships, whose names and burthens, with the names of the captains and masters of them, I have also inserted, as follows:

1 The *Delight,* alias the *George,* of burthen 120 tons, was admiral: in which went the general, and William Winter, captain in her and part-owner, and Richard Clarke, master.

2 The bark *Ralegh* set forth by M. Walter Ralegh, of the burthen of 200 tons, was then vice-admiral: in which went M. Butler, captain, and Robert Davis of Bristol, master.

3 The *Golden Hind,* of burthen 40 tons, was then rear-admiral: in which went Edward Hayes, captain and owner, and William Cox of Limehouse, master.

4 The *Swallow,* of burthen 40 tons: in her was captain Maurice Browne.

5 The *Squirrel,* of burthen 10 tons: in which went captain William Andrews, and one Cade, master.

We were in number in all about 260 men, among which we had of every faculty good choice, as shipwrights, masons, carpenters, smiths, and suchlike, requisite to such an action; also mineral men and refiners. Besides, for solace of our people and allurement of the savages, we were provided of music in good variety; not omitting the least toys, as morris dancers, hobbyhorse,[31] and May-like conceits to delight the savage people whom we intended to win by all fair means possible. And to that end we were indifferently furnished of all petty haberdashery [32] wares to barter with those simple people.

In this manner we set forward, departing (as has been said) out of Causon Bay the eleventh day of June, being Tuesday. The weather and wind were fair and good all day, but a great storm of thunder and wind fell the same night.

Thursday following, when we hailed one another in the evening (according to the order before specified) they signified unto us out of the vice-admiral, that both the captain and very many of the men were fallen sick. And about midnight the vice-admiral forsook us, notwithstanding we had the wind east, fair and good. But it was after credibly reported that they were infected with a contagious sickness and arrived greatly distressed at Plymouth: the reason I could never understand. Sure I am no cost was spared by their owner, Master Ralegh, in setting them forth. Therefore, I leave it unto God.

By this time we were in 48 degrees of latitude, not a little grieved with the loss of the most puissant ship in our fleet, after whose departure the *Golden Hind* succeeded in the place of vice-admiral and removed her flag from the mizzen unto the foretop.

From Saturday, the 15th of June, until the 28th, which was upon a Friday, we never had fair day without fog or rain, and winds bad, much to

[31] *morris . . . hobbyhorse:* English folk dancers.

[32] *haberdashery:* small articles pertaining to dress: ribbons, tape, threads, and other small wares.

the west-northwest, whereby we were driven southward unto 41 degrees scarce.

About this time of the year the winds are commonly west towards the Newfoundland, keeping ordinarily within two points of west to the south or to the north, whereby the course thither falls out to be long and tedious after June, while in March, April, and May, it had been performed out of England in 22 days and less. We had wind always so scant from west-northwest, and from west-southwest again, that our traverse was great, running south unto 41 degrees almost, and afterwards north into 51 degrees.

Also we were encumbered with much fog and mists in manner palpable, in which we could not keep so well together but were dissevered, losing the company of the *Swallow* and the *Squirrel* upon the 20th day of July, when we met again at several places upon the Newfoundland coast the third of August, as shall be declared in place convenient.

Saturday, the 27th of July, we might descry not far from us as it were mountains of ice driven upon the sea, being then in 50 degrees, which were carried southward to the weather of us; whereby may be conjectured that some current doth set that way from the north.

Before we come to Newfoundland about 50 leagues on this side, we pass the banks, which are high grounds rising within the sea and under water, yet deep enough and without danger, being commonly not less than 25 and 30 fathom water upon them. The same (as it were some vein of mountains within the sea) do run along, and from the Newfoundland, beginning northward about 52 or 53 degrees of latitude, and to extend into the south infinitely. The breadth of this bank is somewhere more, and somewhere less, but we found the same about 10 leagues over, having sounded both on this side thereof, and the other toward Newfoundland, but found no ground with almost 200 fathom of line, both before and after we had passed the bank. The Portugals, and French chiefly, have a notable trade of fishing upon this bank, where are sometimes a hundred or more sails of ships, who commonly begin the fishing in April, and have ended by July. That fish is large, always wet, having no land near to dry, and is called corre fish.

During the time of fishing, a man shall know without sounding when he is upon the bank, by the incredible multitude of seafowl hovering over the same, to prey upon the offals and garbish [33] of fish thrown out by fishermen and floating upon the sea.

Upon Tuesday, the 11th of June, we forsook the coast of England. So again Tuesday, the 30th of July (seven weeks after) we got sight of land, being immediately embayed in the Grand Bay, or some other great bay. The certainty whereof we could not judge, so great haze and fog did hang upon the coast, as neither we might discern the land well, nor take the sun's height. But by our best computation we were then in the 51 degrees of latitude.

---

[33] *garbish:* garbage.

Forsaking this bay and uncomfortable coast (nothing appearing unto us but hideous rocks and mountains, bare of trees and void of any herbs) we followed the coast to the south, with weather fair and clear.

We had sight of an island named Penguin, of a fowl there breeding in abundance, almost incredible, which cannot fly, their wings not able to carry their body, being very large (not much less than a goose) and exceeding fat, which the Frenchmen use to take without difficulty upon that island, and to barrel them up with salt. But for lingering of time we had made us there the like provision.

Trending this coast, we came to the island called Baccalaos, being not past two leagues from the main. To the south thereof lieth Cape S. Francis, 5 leagues distant from Baccalaos, between which goeth in a great bay, by the vulgar sort called the Bay of Conception. Here we met with the *Swallow* again, whom we had lost in the fog, and all her men altered into other apparel, whereof it seemed their store was so amended, that for joy and congratulation of our meeting, they spared not to cast up into the air and overboard, their caps and hats in good plenty. The captain although himself was very honest and religious, yet was he not appointed of men to his humor and desert, who for the most part were such as had been by us surprised upon the narrow seas of England, being pirates and had taken at that instant certain Frenchmen laden, one bark with wines, and another with salt. Both which we rescued and took the man-of-war with all her men, which was the same ship now called the *Swallow,* following still their kind so oft, as (being separated from the general) they found opportunity to rob and spoil. And because God's justice did follow the same company, even to destruction, and to the overthrow also of the captain (though not consenting to their misdemeanor) I will not conceal anything that maketh to the manifestation and approbation of his judgments, for examples of others, persuaded that God more sharply took revenge upon them, and hath tolerated longer as great outrage in others, by how much these went under protection of his cause and religion, which was then pretended.

Therefore, upon further inquiry it was known how this company met with a bark returning home after the fishing with his freight, and because the men in the *Swallow* were very near exhausted of victuals and chiefly of apparel, doubtful withal where or when to find and meet with their admiral, they besought the captain they might go aboard this Newlander, only to borrow what might be spared, the rather because the same was bound homeward. Leave given, not without charge to deal favorably, they came aboard the fisherman, whom they rifled of tackle, sails, cables, victuals and the men of their apparel, not sparing by torture (winding cords about their heads) to draw out what else they thought good. This done with expedition (like men skillful in such mischief) as they took their cockboat to go aboard their own ship, it was overwhelmed in the sea and certain of these men there drowned. The rest were preserved even by those silly souls whom they had before spoiled, who saved and delivered them aboard the *Swallow*. What became afterward of the poor Newlander, perhaps destitute of sails and furniture [34] sufficient to carry them home (whither they had not less to run than 700 leagues) God alone knows, who took vengeance not long after of the rest that escaped at this instant, to reveal the fact, and justify to the world God's judgment inflicted upon them, as shall be declared in place convenient.

Thus after we had met with the *Swallow,* we held on our course southward, until we came against the harbor called S. John, about 5 leagues from the former Cape of S. Francis, where before the entrance into the harbor, we found also the frigate or *Squirrel* lying at anchor, whom the English merchants (that were and always be admirals by turns interchangeably over the fleets of fishermen within the same harbor) would not permit to enter into the harbor. Glad of so happy meeting both of the *Swallow* and the frigate in one day (being Saturday, the 3rd of August) we made ready our fights [35] and prepared to enter the harbor, any resistance to the contrary notwithstanding, there being within of all nations, to the number of 36 sails. But first the general dispatched a boat to give them knowledge of his coming for no ill intent, having commission from her Majesty for his voyage he had in hand. And immediately we followed with a slack gale, and in the very entrance (which is but narrow, not above 2 butts length) the admiral fell upon a rock on the larboard side by great oversight, in that the weather was fair, the rock much above water fast by the shore, where neither went any sea gate. But we found such readiness in the English merchants to help us in that danger, that without delay there were brought a number of boats, which towed off the ship and cleared her of danger.

Having taken place convenient in the road, we let fall anchors, the captains and masters repairing aboard our admiral, whither also came immediately the masters and owners of the fishing fleet of Englishmen to understand the general's intent and cause of our arrival there. They were all satisfied when the general had showed his commission and purpose to take possession of those lands to the behalf of the Crown of England and the advancement of Christian religion in those paganish regions. Requiring but their lawful aid for repairing of his fleet and supply of some necessaries, so far as conveniently might be afforded him, both out of that and other harbors adjoining. In lieu whereof, he made offer to gratify them, with any favor and privilege, which upon their better advice they should demand, the like being not to be obtained hereafter for greater price. So craving expedition of his demand, minding to proceed further south without long detention in those parts, he dismissed them, after promise given of their best endeavor to satisfy speedily his so reasonable request. The merchants with their masters departed, and they caused forthwith to be discharged all the great ordnance of their fleet in token of our welcome.

It was further determined that every ship of our fleet should deliver unto the merchants and masters of that harbor a note of all their wants, which

[34] *furniture:* equipment, rigging, stores, and tackle.

[35] *fights:* screens used during a naval engagement to protect and conceal the crew.

done, the ships, English as well as strangers, were taxed at an easy rate to make supply. And besides, commissioners were appointed, part of our own company and part of theirs, to go into other harbors adjoining (for our English merchants command all there) to levy our provision. Whereunto, the Portugals, above other nations, did most willingly and liberally contribute. Insomuch as we were presented, above our allowance, with wines, marmalades, most fine rusk or biscuit, sweet oils, and sundry delicacies. Also we wanted not of fresh salmons, trout, lobsters, and other fresh fish brought daily unto us. Moreover, as the manner is in their fishing, every week to choose their admiral anew, or rather they succeed in orderly course, and have weekly their admiral's feast solemnized, even so, the general, captains, and masters of our fleet were continually invited and feasted. To grow short, in our abundance at home, the entertainment had been delightful, but after our wants and tedious passage through the ocean, it seemed more acceptable and of greater contentation,[36] by how much the same was unexpected in that desolate corner of the world, where at other times of the year, wild beasts and birds have only the fruition of all those countries, which now seemed a place very populous and much frequented.

The next morning being Sunday and the 4th of August, the general and his company were brought on land by English merchants, who showed unto us their accustomed walks unto a place they call the Garden. But nothing appeared more than nature itself without art, who confusedly had brought forth roses abundantly, wild, but odoriferous, and to sense very comfortable. Also the like plenty of raspberries, which do grow in every place.

Monday following, the general had his tent set up, who being accompanied with his own followers, summoned the merchants and masters, both English and strangers to be present at his taking possession of those countries. Before whom openly was read and interpreted unto the strangers his commission, by virtue whereof, he took possession in the same harbor of S. John, and 200 leagues every way, invested the Queen's Majesty with the title and dignity thereof, had delivered unto him (after the custom of England) a rod and a turf of the same soil, entering possession also for him, his heirs and assigns forever. And signified unto all men, that from that time forward, they should take the same land as a territory appertaining to the Queen of England, and himself authorized under her Majesty to possess and enjoy it. And to ordain laws for the government thereof, agreeable (so near as conveniently might be) unto the laws of England, under which all people coming thither hereafter, either to inhabit, or by way of traffic, should be subjected and governed. And especially at the same time for a beginning, he proposed and delivered three laws to be in force immediately. That is to say, the first for religion, which in public exercise should be according to the Church of England. The second for maintenance of her Majesty's right and possession of those territories, against which if anything were attempted prejudicial, the party or parties offending should

[36] *contentation:* satisfaction.

be adjudged and executed as in case of high treason, according to the laws of England. The third, if any person should utter words sounding to the dishonor of her Majesty, he should lose his ears and have his ships and goods confiscate.

These contents published, obedience was promised by general voice and consent of the multitude as well of Englishmen as strangers, praying for continuance of this possession and government begun. After this, the assembly was dismissed. And afterward were erected not far from that place the Arms of England engraven in lead, and fixed upon a pillar of wood. Yet further and actually to establish this possession taken in the right of her Majesty, and to the behoof of Sir Humphrey Gilbert, knight, his heirs and assigns forever, the general granted in fee-farm [37] divers parcels of land lying by the waterside, both in this harbor of S. John, and elsewhere, which was to the owners a great commodity, being thereby assured (by their proper inheritance) of grounds convenient to dress and to dry their fish, whereof many times before they did fail, being prevented by them that came first into the harbor. For which grounds they did covenant to pay a certain rent and service unto Sir Humphrey Gilbert, his heirs or assigns forever, and yearly to maintain possession of the same, by themselves or their assigns.

Now remained only to take in provision granted, according as every ship was taxed, which did fish upon the coast adjoining. In the meanwhile, the general appointed men unto their charge, some to repair and trim the ships; others to attend in gathering together our supply and provisions; others to search the commodities and singularities of the country, to be found by sea or land, and to make relation unto the general what either themselves could know by their own travel and experience, or by good intelligence of Englishmen or strangers, who had longest frequented the same coast. Also some observed the elevation of the Pole and drew plots of the country exactly graded. And by that I could gather by [38] each man's several relation, I have drawn a brief description of the Newfoundland, with the commodities by sea or land already made, and such also as are in possibility and great likelihood to be made. Nevertheless, the cards and plots that were drawing, with the due gradation of the harbors, bays, and capes, did perish with the admiral. Wherefore, in the description following, I must omit the particulars of such things.

A Brief Relation of the Newfoundland Land, and the Commodities thereof.

That which we do call the Newfoundland, and the Frenchmen Baccalaos, is an island, or rather (after the opinion of some) it consists of sundry is-

[37] *fee-farm:* that kind of tenure in which the land is held in fee simple (absolute ownership) but subject to a perpetual fixed rent, without any other services.

[38] *And by . . . by:* and by that which I could gather from.

lands and broken lands, situated in the north regions of America, upon the gulf and entrance of the great river called S. Lawrence in Canada. Into the which, navigation may be made both on the south and north side of this island. The land lieth south and north, containing in length between three and 400 miles, accounting from Cape Race (which is in 46 degrees, 25 minutes) unto the Grand Bay in 52 degrees of septentrional latitude. The island round about has very many good bays and harbors, safe roads for ships, the like not to be found in any part of the known world.

The common opinion that is had of intemperature and extreme cold that should be in this country, as of some part it may be verified, namely, the north, where I grant it is more cold than in countries of Europe, which are under the same elevation. Even so it cannot stand with reason and nature of the clime, that the south parts should be so intemperate as the bruit hath gone. For as the same do lie under the climates of Briton, Anjou, Poictou in France, between 46 and 49 degrees, so can they not so much differ from the temperature of those countries, unless upon the outcoast lying open unto the ocean and sharp winds, it must indeed be subject to more cold than further within the land, where the mountains are interposed, as walls and bulwarks, to defend and to resist the asperity and rigor of the sea and weather. Some hold opinion that the Newfoundland might be more subject to cold, by how much it lieth high and near unto the middle region. I grant that not in Newfoundland alone, but in Germany, Italy, and Africa, even under the Equinoctial Line, the mountains are extremely cold and seldom uncovered of snow. In their culm [39] and highest tops, which comes to pass by the same reason that they extended toward the middle region, yet in the countries lying beneath them, it is found quite contrary. Even so all hills having their descents, the valleys also and low grounds must be likewise hot or temperate, as the clime doth give in Newfoundland, though I am of opinion that the sun's reflection is much cooled and cannot be so forcible in Newfoundland, nor generally throughout America, as in Europe or Africa. By how much the sun in his diurnal course from east to west passeth over (for the most part) dry land and sandy countries, before he arriveth at the west of Europe or Africa, whereby his motion increaseth heat, with little or no qualification by moist vapors. Where, on the contrary he passeth from Europe and Africa unto America over the ocean, from whence it draweth and carrieth with him abundance of moist vapors, which do qualify and enfeeble greatly the sun's reverberation upon this country, chiefly of Newfoundland, being so much to the northward. Nevertheless, as I said before, the cold cannot be so intolerable under the latitude of 46, 47, and 48 (especiall[y] within land) that it should be uninhabitable, as some do suppose, seeing also there are very many people more to the north by a great deal. And in these south parts there are certain beasts, ounces or leopards, and birds in like manner, which in the summer we have seen, not heard of in countries of extreme and vehement coldness. Besides, as in the months of

[39] *culm:* summit.

June, July, August, and September, the heat is somewhat more than in England at those seasons, so men remaining upon the south parts near unto Cape Race, until after Hollandtide,[40] have not found the cold so extreme, nor much differing from the temperature of England. Those which have arrived there after November and December have found the snow exceeding deep, whereat no marvel, considering the ground upon the coast is rough and uneven, and the snow is driven into the places most declining as the like is to be seen with us. The like depth of snow happily shall not be found within land upon the plainer countries, which also are defended by the mountains, breaking off the violence of winds and weather. But admitting extraordinary cold in those south parts, above that with us here, it cannot be so great as in Sweedland,[41] much less in Moscovia or Russia. Yet are the same countries very populous, and the rigor of cold is dispensed with by the commodity of stoves, warm clothing, meats, and drinks, all of which need not be wanting in Newfoundland, if we had intent there to inhabit.

In the south parts we found no inhabitants, which by all likelihood have abandoned those coasts, the same being so much frequented by Christians. But in the north are savages altogether harmless. Touching the commodities of this country, serving either for sustenance of inhabitants, or for maintenance of traffic, there are and may be made divers. So that it seemed nature hath recompensed that only defect and incommodity of some sharp cold, by many benefits, viz., with incredible quantity and no less variety of kinds of fish in the sea and fresh waters, as trout, salmons, and other fish to us unknown; also cod, which alone draws many nations thither, and is become the most famous fishing of the world; abundance of whales, for which also is a very great trade in the bays of Placentia and the Grand Bay, where is made train oils[42] of the whale; herring, the largest that have been heard of, and exceeding the Malstrond herring of Norway, but hitherto was never benefit taken of the herring fishing. There are sundry other fish very delicate, namely the bonito,[43] lobsters, turbot, with others infinite not sought after. Oysters having pearl but not orient in color. I took it by reason they were not gathered in season.

Concerning the inland commodities, as well to be drawn from this land, as from the exceeding large countries adjoining, there is nothing which our east and northerly countries of Europe do yield, but the like also may be made in them as plentifully by time and industry. Namely, rosin, pitch, tar, soap ashes, deal-board,[44] masts for ships, hides, furs, flax, hemp, corn, cables, cordage, linen cloth, metals, and many more. All which the countries will afford, and the soil is apt to yield.

---

[40] *Hollandtide:* Allhallowtide, that is, the season of All Saints, November 1.

[41] *Sweedland:* Sweden.

[42] *train oils:* oils obtained by boiling from the blubber of whales.

[43] *bonito:* the striped tunny of the mackerel family.

[44] *deal-board:* twin board of fir or pine.

The trees for the most in those south parts are fir trees, pine, and cypress, all yielding gum and turpentine.

Cherry trees bearing fruit no bigger than a small pea. Also pear trees, but fruitless. Other trees of some sorts to us unknown.

The soil along the coast is not deep of earth, bringing forth abundantly peason [45] small, yet good feeding for cattle. Roses passing sweet, like unto our musk roses in form, raspases,[46] a berry which we call hurts, good and wholesome to eat. The grass and herbs do fatten sheep in very short space, proved by English merchants which have carried sheep thither for fresh victual and had them raised exceeding fat in less than three weeks. Peason which our countrymen have sown in the time of May, have come up fair, and been gathered in the beginning of August, of which our general had a present acceptable for the rareness, being the first fruits coming up by art and industry in that desolate and dishabited land.

Lakes or pools of fresh water, both on the tops of the mountains and in the valleys. In which are said to be muskles [47] not unlike to have pearls, which I had put in trial, if by mischance falling unto me, I had not been let from that and other good experiments I was minded to make.

Fowl both of water and land in great plenty and diversity. All kind of green fowl. Others as big as bustards,[48] yet not the same. A great white fowl called by some a gaunt.[49]

Upon the land divers sorts of hawks, as falcons and others by report. Partridges most plentiful, larger than ours, gray and white of color, and rough-footed like doves, which our men after one flight did kill with cudgels, they were so fat and unable to fly. Birds, some like blackbirds, linnets, canary birds, and other very small. Beasts of sundry kinds, red deer, buffles [50] or a beast, as it seemed by the track and foot, very large in manner of an ox. Bears, ounces or leopards, some greater and some lesser, wolves, foxes, which to the northward a little further are black, whose fur is esteemed in some countries of Europe very rich. Otters, beavers, martens. And in the opinion of most men that saw it, the general had brought unto him a sable alive, which he sent unto his brother Sir John Gilbert, knight of Devonshire, but it was never delivered, as I after understood. We could not observe the hundredth part of creatures in those unhabited lands, but these mentioned may induce us to glorify the magnificent God, who hath superabundantly replenished the earth with creatures serving for the use of man, though man hath not used a fifth part of the same, which the more doth aggravate the fault and foolish sloth in many of our nation, choosing rather to live indirectly and very miserably to live and die within this realm pestered with inhabitants, than to adventure as becometh men, to obtain an habitation in those remote lands, in which nature very prodigally doth minister unto men's endeavors, and for art to work upon.

---

[45] *peason:* dialect plural of "pease," the original singular of "pea."

[46] *raspases:* raspasis, raspberry.

[47] *muskles:* mussels.

[48] *Others . . . bustards:* perhaps the Canada goose. The bustard was a very large bird.

[49] *gaunt:* gannet.

[50] *buffles:* buffaloes.

For besides these already recounted and infinite more, the mountains generally make show of mineral substance. Iron very common, lead, and somewhere copper. I will not aver of richer metals, although by the circumstances following, more than hope may be conceived thereof.

For amongst other charges given to inquire out the singularities of this country, the general was most curious in the search of metals, commanding the mineral man and refiner especially to be diligent. The same was a Saxon born, honest and religious, named Daniel, who after search brought at first some sort of ore, seeming rather to be iron than other metal. The next time he found ore, which with no small show of contentment he delivered unto the general, using protestation, that if silver were the thing which might satisfy the general and his followers, there it was, advising him to seek no further, the peril whereof he undertook upon his life (as dear unto him as the Crown of England unto her Majesty, that I may use his own words) if it fell not out accordingly.

Myself, at this instant more likely to die than to live, by mischance could not follow this confident opinion of our refiner to my own satisfaction, but afterward demanding our general's opinion therein, and to have some part of the ore, he replied: "Content yourself, I have seen enough, and were it but to satisfy my private humor, I would proceed no further. The promise unto my friends, and necessity to bring also the south countries within compass of my patent near expired, as we have already done these north parts, do only persuade me further. And touching the ore, I have sent it aboard, whereof I would have no speech to be made so long as we remain within harbor. Here being both Portugals, Biscains, and Frenchmen not far off, from whom must be kept any bruit or muttering of such matter. When we are at sea proof shall be made. If it be to our desire, we may return the sooner hither again." Whose answer I judged reasonable, and contenting me well, wherewith I will conclude this narration and description of the Newfoundland, and proceed to the rest of our voyage, which ended tragically.

While the better sort of us were seriously occupied in repairing our wants, and contriving of matters for the commodity of our voyage, others of another sort and disposition were plotting mischief. Some casting to steal away our shipping by night, watching opportunity by the general's and captain's lying on the shore, whose conspiracies discovered, they were prevented. Others drew together in company and carried away, out of the harbors adjoining, a ship laden with fish, setting the poor men on shore. A great many more of our people stole into the woods to hide themselves, attending time and means to return home by such shipping as daily departed from the coast. Some were sick of fluxes,[51] and many dead, and in brief, by one means or other our company was diminished, and many by the general licensed to return home. Insomuch as after we had reviewed our people, resolved to see an end of our voyage, we grew scant of men to fur-

[51] *fluxes:* probably dysentery.

nish all our shipping and it seemed good therefore unto the general to leave the *Swallow* with such provision as might be spared for transporting home the sick people.

The captain of the *Delight* or admiral returned to England, in whose stead was appointed Captain Maurice Browne, before captain of the *Swallow,* who also brought with him into the *Delight* all his men of the *Swallow,* which before have been noted for outrage perpetrated and committed upon fishermen there met at sea.

The general made choice to go in his frigate, the *Squirrel* (whereof the captain also was amongst them that returned to Engand), the same frigate being most convenient to discover upon the coast and to search into every harbor and creek, which a great ship could not do. Therefore, the frigate was prepared with her nettings and fights, and overcharged with bases and such small ordnance, more to give a show, than with judgment to foresee unto the safety of her and the men, which afterward was an occasion also of their overthrow.

Now having made ready our shipping, that is to say, the *Delight,* the *Golden Hind,* and the *Squirrel,* and put aboard our provision, which was wines, bread or rusk, fish wet and dry, sweet oils, besides many other, as marmalades, figs, lemons barreled, and suchlike. Also we had other necessary provisions for trimming our ships, nets, and lines to fish withal, boats or pinnaces [52] fit for discovery. In brief, we were supplied of our wants commodiously, as if we had been in a country or some city populous and plentiful of all things.

We departed from this harbor of S. John's upon Tuesday, the 20th of August, which we found by exact observation to be in 47 degrees, 40 minutes. And the next day by night we were at Cape Race, 25 leagues from the same harbor.

This cape lieth south-southwest from S. John's. It is a low land, being off from the cape about half a league. Within the sea riseth up a rock against the point of the cape, which thereby is easily known. It is in latitude 46 degrees, 25 minutes.

Under this cape we were becalmed a small time, during which we laid out hooks and lines to take cod and drew in less than two hours, fish so large and in such abundance, that many days after we fed upon no other provision.

From hence we shaped our course unto the island of Sablon, if conveniently it would so fall out, also directly to Cape Breton.

Sablon lies to the seaward of Cape Breton about 25 leagues, whither we were determined to go upon intelligence we had of a Portugal (during our abode in S. John's) who was himself present, when the Portugals (above thirty years past) did put into the same island both neat [53] and swine to breed, which were since exceedingly multiplied. This seemed unto us very happy tidings, to have in an island lying so near to the main, which we

[52] *pinnaces:* small boats.

[53] *neat:* cattle.

intended to plant upon, such store of cattle, whereby we might at all times conveniently be relieved of victual, and served of store for breed.

In this course we trended along the coast, which from Cape Race stretches into the northwest, making a bay which some called Trepassa. Then it goeth out again toward the west, and maketh a point, which with Cape Race lieth in manner east and west. But this point inclineth to the north. To the west of which goeth in the Bay of Placentia. We sent men on land to take view of the soil along this coast, whereof they made good report, and some of them had will to be planted there. They saw pease growing in great abundance everywhere.

The distance between Cape Race and Cape Breton is 87 leagues. In which navigation we spent eight days, having many times the wind indifferent good. Yet could we never attain sight of any land all that time, seeing we were hindered by the current. At last we fell into such flats and dangers, that hardly any of us escaped, where, nevertheless, we lost our admiral with all the men and provision, not knowing certainly the place. Yet, for inducing men of skill to make conjecture, by our course and way we held from Cape Race thither (that thereby the flats and dangers may be inserted in sea-cards, for warning to others that may follow the same course hereafter) I have set down the best reckonings that were kept by expert men, William Cox, master of the *Hind,* and John Paul, his mate, both of Limehouse.

* * *

Monday [54] in the afternoon we passed in the sight of Cape Race, having made as much way in little more than two days and nights back again, as before we had done in eight days from Cape Race unto the place where our ship perished. Which hindrance thitherward, and speed back again, is to be imputed unto the swift current, as well as to the winds, which we had more large in our return.

This Monday the general came aboard the *Hind* to have the surgeon of the *Hind* dress his foot, which he hurt by treading upon a nail. At what time we comforted each other with hope of hard success to be all past, and of the good to come. So agreeing to carry out lights always by night, that we might keep together, he departed into his frigate, being by no means to be entreated to tarry in the *Hind,* which had been more for his security. Immediately after followed a sharp storm, which we overpassed for that time. Praised be God.

The weather fair, the general came aboard the *Hind* again to make merry together with the captain, master, and company, which was the last meeting and continued there from morning until night. During which time there passed sundry discourses, touching on affairs past and to come, lamenting greatly the loss of his great ship, more of his men, but most of all of his books and notes and what else I know not, for which he was out of measure grieved, the same doubtless being some matter of more impor-

---

[54] *Monday:* I.e., September 2, 1583.

tance than his books, which I could not draw from him. Yet by circumstance, I gathered the same to be the ore which Daniel the Saxon had brought with him to Newfoundland. Whatsoever it was, the remembrance touched him so deep, as not able to contain himself, he beat his boy in great rage, even at the same time, so long after the miscarrying of the great ship, because upon a fair day, when we were becalmed upon the coast of Newfoundland, near unto Cape Race, he sent his boy aboard the admiral, to fetch certain things. Amongst which, this being chief, was yet forgotten and left behind. After which time he could never conveniently send again aboard the great ship; much less he doubted her ruin so near at hand.

Herein my opinion was better confirmed diversely, and by sundry conjectures, which maketh me have the greater hope of this rich mine. For whereas the general had never before good conceit of these north parts of the world, now his mind was wholly fixed upon the Newfoundland. And as before he refused not to grant assignments liberally to them that required the same into these north parts, now he became contrarily affected, refusing to make any so large grants, especially of S. John's, which certain English merchants made suit for, offering to employ their money and travail upon the same, yet neither by their own suit, nor of others of his own company, whom he seemed willing to pleasure, it could be obtained.

Also laying down his determination in the spring following, for disposing of his voyage then to be reattempted, he assigned the captain and master of the *Golden Hind* unto the south discovery, and reserved unto himself the north, affirming that this voyage had won his heart from the south, and that he was now become a northern man altogether.

Last, being demanded what means he had at his arrival in England to compass the charges of so great preparation as he intended to make the next spring, having determined upon two fleets, one for the south and another for the north, "Leave that to me," he replied, "I will ask a penny of no man. I will bring good tidings unto her Majesty, who will be so gracious, to lend me 10,000 pounds," willing us therefore to be of good cheer. For he did thank God, he said, with all his heart for that he had seen, the same being enough for us all, and that we needed not to seek any further. And these last words he would often repeat, with demonstration of great fervency of mind, being himself very confident and settled in belief of inestimable good by this voyage, which the greater number of his followers nevertheless mistrusted altogether, not being made partakers of those secrets, which the general kept unto himself. Yet all of them that are living may be witnesses of his words and protestations, which sparingly I have delivered.

Leaving the issue of this good hope unto God, who knoweth the truth only, and can at his good pleasure bring the same to light, I will hasten to the end of this tragedy, which must be knit up in the person of our general. And as it was God's ordinance upon him, even so the vehement persuasion and entreaty of his friends could nothing avail, to divert him from a willful resolution of going through in his frigate, which was overcharged upon their decks with fights, nettings, and small artillery, too cumbersome for so small a boat that was to pass through the Ocean Sea at that season of the year, when by course we might expect much storm of foul weather, whereof indeed we had enough.

But when he was entreated by the captain, master, and other of his well-willers of the *Hind,* not to venture in the frigate, this was his answer, "I will not forsake my little company going homeward with whom I have passed so many storms and perils." And in very truth, he was urged to be so over-hard, by hard reports given of him that he was afraid of the sea, although this was rather rashness than advised resolution to prefer the wind of a vain report to the weight of his own life.

Seeing he would not bend to reason, he had provision out of the *Hind,* such as was wanting aboard his frigate. And so we committed him to God's protection and set him aboard his pinnace, we being more than 300 leagues onward of our way home.

By that time we had brought the islands of Azores south of us, yet we then keeping much to the north, until we had got into the height and elevation of England, we met with very foul weather and terrible seas, breaking short and high, pyramid-wise. The reason whereof seemed to proceed either of hilly grounds high and low within the sea (as we see hills and dales upon the land) upon which the seas do mount and fall, or else, the cause proceedeth of diversity of winds, shifting often in sundry points, all which having power to move the great ocean, which again is not presently settled, so many seas do encounter together, as there had been diversity of winds. Howsoever it comes to pass, men which all their lifetime had occupied the sea, never saw more outrageous seas. We had also upon our mainyard, an apparition of a little fire by night, which seamen do call Castor and Pollux.[55] But we had only one, which they take an evil sign of more tempest; the same is usual in storms.

Monday, the ninth of September, in the afternoon, the frigate was near cast away, oppressed by waves, yet at that time recovered, and giving forth signs of joy, the general sitting abaft with a book in his hand, cried out unto us in the *Hind* (so oft as we did approach within hearing), "We are as near to heaven by sea as by land," reiterating the same speech, well beseeming a soldier, resolute in Jesus Christ, as I can testify he was.

The same Monday night, about twelve of the clock, or not long after, the frigate being ahead of us in the *Golden Hind,* suddenly her lights were out, whereof as it were in a moment, we lost the sight, and withal our watch cried the general was cast away, which was too true. For in that moment the frigate was devoured and swallowed up of the sea. Yet still we looked out all that night, and ever after, until we arrived upon the coast of England, omitting no small sail at sea, unto which we gave not the tokens between us agreed upon, to have perfect knowledge of each other, if we should at any time be separated.

---

[55] *a little fire . . . Pollux:* also known as "corposant" and "St. Elmo's fire."

In great torment of weather, and peril of drowning, it pleased God to send safe home the *Golden Hind,* which arrived in Falmouth, the 22nd day of September, being Sunday, not without as great danger escaped in a flaw, coming from the southeast with such thick mist, that we could not discern land, to put in right with the haven.

* * *

FROM

A brief and true report of the new-found land of Virginia:[56] of the commodities there found, and to be raised, as well merchantable as others. Written by Thomas Hariot,[57] servant to Sir Walter Ralegh, a member of the colony and there employed in discovering a full twelvemonth.

OF THE NATURE AND MANNERS OF THE PEOPLE

It resteth I speak a word or two of the natural inhabitants, their natures and manners, leaving large discourse thereof until time more convenient hereafter. Now only so far forth, as that you may know how they in respect of troubling our inhabiting and planting, are not to be feared, but that they shall have cause both to fear and love us, that shall inhabit with them.

They are a people clothed with loose mantles made of deerskins, and aprons of the same round about their middles, all else naked, of such a difference of stature only as we in England, having no edge tools or weapons of iron or steel to offend us withal, neither know they how to make any. Those weapons that they have, are only bows made of witch hazel and arrows of reeds, flat-edged truncheons also of wood about a yard long, neither have they anything to defend themselves but targets made of barks, and some armors made of sticks wickered together with thread.

Their towns are but small, and near the seacoast but few, some containing but ten or twelve houses, some twenty; the greatest that we have seen has been but of thirty houses. If they be walled, it is only done with barks

56 *Virginia:* This was "The third voyage made by a ship sent in the year 1586, to the reliefe of the Colony planted in Virginia, at the sole charges of Sir Walter Ralegh" (*The Principal Navigations,* Hakluyt Society ed., VIII, 346). The expedition was under the leadership of Sir Richard Grenville.

57 *Thomas Hariot:* (1560–1621) mathematician and astronomer, mathematical tutor to Ralegh, and a surveyor on the 1586 voyage. His *Briefe and True Report . . . of Virginia* was first issued in 1588; in 1590, together with White's drawings of the natives, it was published by De Bry in Latin, German, English, and French. Hakluyt included it in *The Principall Navigations,* 1600.

of trees made fast to stakes, or else with poles only fixed upright and close one by another.

Their houses are made of small poles, made fast at the tops in round form after the manner as is used in many arbories in our gardens of England, in most towns covered with barks, and in some with artificial mats made of long rushes, from the tops of the houses down to the ground. The length of them is commonly double to the breadth; in some places they are but twelve and sixteen yards long, and in some other we have seen of four-and-twenty.

In some places of the country, one only town belongs to the government of a *Wiroans* or Chief Lord, in other some two or three, in some six, eight, and more. The greatest Wiroans that yet we had dealing with had but eighteen towns in his government and able to make not above seven or eight hundred fighting men at the most. The language of every government is different from any other, and the further they are distant, the greater is the difference.

Their manner of wars amongst themselves is either by sudden surprising one another most commonly about the dawning of the day, or moonlight, or else by ambushes, or some subtle devices. Set battles are very rare, except it fall out where there are many trees, where either party may have some hope of defense, after the delivery of every arrow, in leaping behind some or other.

If there fall out any wars between us and them, what their fight is likely to be, we having advantages against them so many manner of ways, as by our discipline, our strange weapons and devices else, especially ordnance great and small, it may easily be imagined, by the experience we have had in some places, the turning up of their heels against us in running away was their best defense.

In respect of us they are a people poor, and for want of skill and judgment in the knowledge and use of our things, do esteem our trifles before things of greater value. Notwithstanding, in their proper manner (considering the want of such means as we have), they seem very ingenious. For although they have no such tools, nor any such crafts, sciences, and arts as we, yet in those things they do, they show excellency of wit.[58] And by how much they upon due consideration shall find our manner of knowledges and crafts to exceed theirs in perfection, and speed for doing or execution, by so much the more is it probable that they should desire our friendship and love, and have the greater respect for pleasing and obeying us. Whereby may be hoped, if means of good government be used, that they may in short time be brought to civility and the embracing of true religion.

Some religion they have already, which although it be far from the truth, yet being as it is, there is hope it may be the easier and sooner reformed.

They believe that there are many gods, which they call *Mantoac,* but of different sorts and degrees, one only chief and great god, which hath been

---

[58] *wit:* here, intelligence.

from all eternity. Who, as they affirm, when he purposed to make the world, made first other gods of a principal order to be as means and instruments to be used in the creation and government to follow, and after the sun, moon, and stars as petty gods, and the instruments of the other order more principal. First, they say, were made waters, out of which by the gods was made all diversity of creatures that are visible or invisible.

For mankind, they say a woman was made first which, by the working of one of the gods, conceived and brought forth children. And in such sort, they say, they had their beginning. But how many years or ages have passed since, they say they can make no relation, having no letters nor other such means as we to keep records of the particularities of times past, but only tradition from father to son.

They think that all the gods are of human shape, and therefore, they represent them by images in the forms of men, which they call *Kewasowok,* one alone is called *Kewas.* These they place in houses appropriate or temples, which they call *Machicomuck,* where they worship, pray, sing, and make many times offering unto them. In some Machicomuck, we have seen but one Kewas, in some two, and in other some three. The common sort think them to be also gods.

They believe also the immortality of the soul that, after this life as soon as the soul is departed from the body, according to the works it hath done, it is either carried to heaven, the habitat of gods, there to enjoy perpetual bliss and happiness, or else to a great pit or hole, which they think to be in the furthest parts of their part of the world toward the sunset, there to burn continually. The place they call *Popogusso.*

For the confirmation of this opinion, they told me two stories of two men that had been lately dead and revived again. The one happened, but a few years before our coming into the country, of a wicked man, which having been dead and buried, the next day the earth of the grave being seen to move, was taken up again, who made declaration where his soul had been. That is to say, very near entering into Popogusso, had not one of the gods saved him, and gave him leave to return again and teach his friends what they should do to avoid that terrible place of torment. The other happened in the same year we were there, but in a town that was sixty miles from us, and it was told me for strange news, that one being dead, buried, and taken up again as the first, showed that although his body had lain dead in the grave, yet his soul was alive and had traveled far in a long broad way, on both sides whereof grew most delicate and pleasant trees, bearing more rare and excellent fruits, than ever he had seen before or was able to express, and at length came to most brave and fair houses, near which he met his father that had been dead before, who gave him great charge to go back again and show his friends what good they were to do to enjoy the pleasures of that place, which when he had done he should after come again.

What subtlety soever be in the Wiroances and priests, this opinion worked so much in many of the common and simple sort of people, that it maketh them have great respect to their governors, and also great care what they do, to avoid torment after death, and to enjoy bliss, although notwithstanding there is punishment ordained for malefactors, as stealers, whoremongers, and other sort of wicked-doers, some punished with death, some with forfeitures, some with beating, according to the greatness of the facts.

And this is the sum of their religion, which I learned by having special familiarity with some of their priests. Wherein they were not so sure grounded, nor gave such credit to their traditions and stories, but through conversing with us they were brought into great doubts of their own, and no small admiration of ours, with earnest desire in many, to learn more than we had means for want of perfect utterance in their language to express.

Most things they saw with us, as mathematical instruments, sea compasses, the virtue of the lodestone in drawing iron, a perspective glass whereby was showed many strange sights, burning glasses, wild fireworks, guns, hooks, writing and reading, spring-clocks that seem to go of themselves, and many other things that we had were so strange unto them, and so far exceeded their capacities to comprehend the reason and means how they should be made and done, that they thought they were rather the works of gods than of men, or at the leastwise, they had been given and taught us by the gods. Which made many of them have such opinion of us, as that if they knew not the truth of God and religion already, it was rather to be had from us whom God so specially loved, than from a people that were so simple as they found themselves to be in comparison of us. Whereupon greater credit was given unto that we spoke of, concerning such matters.

Many times and in every town where I came, according as I was able, I made declaration of the contents of the Bible, that therein was set forth the true and only God, and his mighty works, that therein was contained the true doctrine of salvation through Christ, with many particulars of miracles and chief points of religion, as I was able then to utter, and thought fit for the time. And although I told them the book materially and of itself was not of any such virtue, as I thought they did conceive, but only the doctrine therein contained, yet would many be glad to touch it, to embrace it, to kiss it, to hold it to their breasts and heads, and stroke over all their body with it, to show their hungry desire of that knowledge which was spoken of.

The Wiroans with whom we dwelt, called Wingina, and many of his people would be glad many times to be with us at our prayers, and many times call upon us both in his own town, as also in others whither he sometimes accompanied us, to pray and sing psalms, hoping thereby to be partaker of the same effects which we by that means also expected.

Twice this Wiroans was so grievously sick that he was like to die, and as he lay languishing, doubting of any help by his own priests, and thinking he was in such danger for offending us and thereby our God, sent for some of us to pray and be a means to our God that it would please him either that he might live, or after death dwell with him in bliss, so likewise were the requests of many others in the like case.

On a time also when their corn began to wither by reason of a drought which happened extraordinarily, fearing that it had come to pass by reason that in something they had displeased us, many would come to us and desire us to pray to our God of England, that he would preserve their corn, promising that when it was ripe we also should be partakers of the fruit.

There could at no time happen any strange sickness, losses, hurts, or any other cross unto them, but that they would impute to us the cause or means thereof, for offending or not pleasing us. One other rare and strange accident, leaving others, will I mention before I end, which moved the whole country that either knew or heard of us, to have us in wonderful admiration.

There was no town where we had any subtle device practiced against us, we leaving it unpunished or not revenged (because we sought by all means possible to win them by gentleness) but that within a few days after our departure from every such town, the people began to die very fast and many in short space, in some towns about twenty, in some forty, and in one sixscore, which in truth was very many in respect of their numbers. This happened in no place that we could learn, but where we had been, where they used some practice against us and after such time. The disease also was so strange, that they neither knew what it was, nor how to cure it, the like by report of the oldest men in the country never happened before, time out of mind, a thing specially observed by us, as also by the natural inhabitants themselves. Insomuch that when some of the inhabitants which were our friends, and especially the Wiroans Wingina, had observed such effects in four or five towns to follow their wicked practices, they were persuaded that it was the work of our God through our means, and that we by him might kill and slay whom we would without weapons, and not come near them. And thereupon when it had happened that they had understanding that any of their enemies had abused us in our journeys, hearing that we had wrought no revenge with our weapons, and fearing upon some cause the matter should so rest, did come and entreat us that we would be a means to our God that they as others had dealt ill with us might in like sort die, alleging how much it would be for our credit and profit, as also theirs, and hoping furthermore that we would do so much at their requests in respect of the friendship we professed them.

Whose entreaties although we showed that they were ungodly, affirming that our God would not subject himself to any such prayers and requests of men, that indeed all things have been and were to be done according to his good pleasure as he had ordained, that we to show ourselves his true servants ought rather to make petition for the contrary, that they with them might live together with us, be made partakers of his truth, and serve him in righteousness, but notwithstanding in such sort, that we refer that, as all other things, to be done according to his divine will and pleasure, and as by his wisdom he had ordained to be best.

Yet because the effect fell out so suddenly and shortly after according to their desires, they thought nevertheless it came to pass by our means and that we in using such speeches unto them, did but dissemble the matter, and therefore came unto us to give us thanks in their manner, that although we satisfied them not in promise, yet in deeds and effect we had fulfilled their desires.

This marvelous accident in all the country wrought so strange opinions of us that some people could not tell whether to think us gods or men, and the rather because that all the space of their sickness, there was no man of ours known to die, or that was specially sick. They noted also that we had no women amongst us, neither that we did care for any of theirs.

Some, therefore, were of opinion that we were not born of women, and therefore not mortal, but that we were men of an old generation many years past, then risen again to immortality.

Some would likewise seem to prophesy that there were more of our generation yet to come to kill theirs and take their places as some thought the purpose was, by that which was already done. Those that were immediately to come after us they imagined to be in the air, yet invisible and without bodies, and that they by our entreaty and for the love of us did make the people to die in that sort as they did, by shooting invisible bullets into them.

To confirm this opinion, their physicians (to excuse their ignorance in curing the disease) would not be ashamed to say, but earnestly make the simple people believe that the strings of blood that they sucked out of the sick bodies, were the strings wherewithal the invisible bullets were tied and cast. Some also thought that we shot them ourselves out of our pieces, from the place where we dwelt, and killed the people in any town that had offended us, as we listed, how far distant from us soever it were. And other some said that it was the special work of God for our sakes, as we ourselves have cause in some sort to think no less, whatsoever some do, or may imagine to the contrary, specially some astrologers, knowing of the eclipse of the sun which we saw the same year before in our voyage thitherward, which unto them appeared very terrible. And also of a comet which began to appear but a few days before the beginning of the said sickness. But to exclude them from being the special causes of so special an accident, there are further reasons than I think fit at this present to be alleged. These their opinions I have set down the more at large, that it may appear unto you that there is good hope they may be brought through discreet dealing and government to the embracing of the truth, and consequently to honor, obey, fear, and love us.

And although some of our company towards the end of the year showed themselves too fierce in slaying some of the people in some towns, upon causes that on our part might easily enough have been borne withal, yet notwithstanding, because it was on their part justly deserved, the alteration of their opinions generally and for the most part concerning us is the less to be doubted. And whatsoever else they may be, by carefulness of ourselves need nothing at all to be feared.

An extract of a Spanish letter written from Pueblo de los Angeles in Nueva Espanna in October, 1597, touching the discovery of the rich isles of California, being distant eight days' sailing from the main.

We have seen a letter written the eighth of October, 1597, out of a town called Pueblo de los Angeles situate eighteen leagues from Mexico, making mention of the Islands of California situate two or three hundred leagues from the mainland of Nueva Espanna, in Mar del Sur: as that thither have been sent before that time some people to conquer them, which with loss of some twenty men were forced back. After that they had well visited and found those islands or countries to be very rich of gold and silver mines and of very fair oriental pearls, which were caught in good quantity upon one fathom and a half, passing in beauty the pearls of the Island Margarita, the report thereof caused the Viceroy of Mexico to send a citizen of Mexico with two hundred men to conquer the same. Therein also was affirmed that within eight days they could sail thither from the main.

The course which Sir Francis Drake held from the haven of Guatulco[59] in the South Sea on the back side of Nueva Espanna to the northwest of California as far as forty-three degrees, and his return back along the said coast to thirty-eight degrees, where finding a fair and goodly haven, he landed; and staying there many weeks, and discovering many excellent things in the country and great show of rich mineral matter and being offered the dominion of the country by the lord of the same, he took possession thereof in the behalf of her Majesty, and named it Nova Albion.

We kept our course from the Isle of Cano, which lieth in eight degrees of northerly latitude, and within two leagues of the main of Nicaragua, where we calked and trimmed our ship, along the coast of Nueva Espanna, until we came to the haven and town of Guatulco, which, as we were informed, had but seventeen Spaniards dwelling in it, and we found it to stand in fifteen degrees and fifty minutes.

As soon as we were entered this haven we landed, and went presently to

[59] *Guatulco:* Acapulco.

the town and to the town house, where we found a judge sitting in judgment, he being associate with three other officers, upon three negroes that had conspired the burning of the town, both which judges and prisoners we took, and brought them a-shipboard and caused the chief judge to write his letter to the town, to command all the townsmen to avoid, that we might safely water there. Which being done, and they departed, we ransacked the town and in one house we found a pot of the quantity of a bushel full of royals [60] of plate, which we brought to our ship.

And here one Thomas Moone, one of our company, took a Spanish gentleman as he was flying out of the town, and searching him, he found a chain of gold about him and other jewels, which we took and so let him go.

At this place our general among other Spaniards, set ashore his Portugal pilot, which he took at the Island of Cape Verde, out of a ship of Saint Marie port of Portugal, and having set them ashore, we departed thence.

Our general at this place and time thinking himself both in respect of his private injuries received from the Spaniards, as also of their contempts and indignities offered to our country and prince in general, sufficiently satisfied, and revenged, and supposing that her Majesty at his return would rest contented with this service, purposed to continue no longer upon the Spanish coasts, but began to consider and to consult of the best way for his country.

He thought it not good to return by the straits, for two special causes: the one, lest the Spaniards should there wait and attend for him in great number and strength, whose hands he, being left but one ship, could not possibly escape. The other cause was the dangerous situation of the mouth of the straits of the south side, with continual storms raining and blustering, as he found by experience, besides the shoals and sands upon the coast. Wherefore he thought it not a good course to adventure that way. He resolved therefore to avoid these hazards, to go forward to the islands of the Malucas, and there hence to sail the course of the Portugals by the Cape of Bona Sperança.

Upon this resolution, he began to think of his best way for the Malucas, and finding himself, where he now was, becalmed, he saw that of necessity he must be enforced to take a Spanish course, namely to sail somewhat northerly to get a wind. We therefore set sail and sailed 800 leagues at the least for a good wind, and thus much we sailed from the 16th of April (after our old style) till the third of June.

The fifth day of June, being in forty-three degrees towards the Arctic pole, being speedily come out of the extreme heat, we found the air so cold, that our men being pinched with the same, complained of the extremity thereof, and the further we went, the more the cold increased upon us, whereupon we thought it best for that time to seek land, and did so, finding it not mountainous, but low plainland, and we drew back again without

---

[60] *royals:* gold coins.

landing, till we came within thirty-eight degrees towards the line. In which height it pleased God to send us into a fair and good bay, with a good wind to enter the same.

In this bay we anchored the seventeenth of June, and the people of the country, having their houses close by the water's side, showed themselves unto us, and sent a present to our general.

When they came unto us, they greatly wondered at the things which we brought, but our general, according to his natural and accustomed humanity, courteously entreated them, and liberally bestowed on them necessary things to cover their nakedness, whereupon they supposed us to be gods, and would not be persuaded to the contrary. The presents which they sent unto our general were feathers and cawls [61] of net work.

Their houses are digged round about with earth, and have from the uttermost brims of the circle clefts of wood set upon them, joining close together at the top like a spire steeple, which by reason of that closeness are very warm.

Their bed is the ground with rushes strawed on it, and lying about the house, they have the fire in the midst. The men go naked, the women take bulrushes and kemb [62] them after the manner of hemp, and thereof make their loose garments, which being knit about their middles, hang down about their hips, having also about their shoulders a skin of deer, with the hair upon it. These women are very obedient and serviceable to their husbands.

After they were departed from us, they came and visited us the second time, and brought with them feathers and bags of tobacco for presents. And when they came to the top of the hill, at the bottom whereof we had pitched our tents, they stayed themselves, where one appointed for speaker wearied himself with making a long oration, which done, they left their bows upon the hill and came down with their presents.

In the meantime the women remaining on the hill, tormented themselves lamentably, tearing their flesh from their cheeks, whereby we perceived that they were about a sacrifice. In the meantime our general, with his company, went to prayer, and to reading of the Scriptures, at which exercise they were attentive and seemed greatly to be affected with it. But when they were come unto us they restored again unto us those things which before we had bestowed upon them.

The news of our being there being spread through the country, the people that inhabited round about came down, and amongst them the king himself, a man of a goodly stature, and comely personage, with many other tall and warlike men, before whose coming were sent two ambassadors to our general, to signify that their king was coming, in doing of which mes-

[61] *cawls:* Hakluyt prints "cals," which may be netted baskets, or "cauls," netted caps or headdresses.

[62] *kemb:* comb.

sage, their speech was continued about half an hour. This ended, they by signs requested our general to send something by their hand to their king, as a token that his coming might be in peace. Wherein our general having satisfied them, they returned with glad tidings to their king, who marched to us with a princely majesty, the people crying continually after their manner, and as they drew near unto us, so did they strive to behave themselves in their actions with comeliness.

In the forefront was a man of a goodly personage, who bare the scepter or mace before the king, whereupon hanged two crowns, a less and a bigger, with three chains of a marvelous length. The crowns were made of knitwork wrought artificially with feathers of divers colors. The chains were made of a bony substance, and few be the persons among them that are admitted to wear them, and of that number also the persons are stinted, as some ten, some twelve, etc. Next unto him which bare the scepter, was the king himself, with his guard about his person, clad with cony[63] skins and other skins. After them followed the naked common sort of people, every one having his face painted, some with white, some with black, and other colors, and having in their hands one thing or other for a present, not so much as their children, but they also brought their presents.

In the meantime, our general gathered his men together, and marched within his fenced place, making against their approaching a very warlike show. They being trooped together in their order, and a general salutation being made, there was presently a general silence. Then he that bare the scepter before the king, being informed by another, whom they assigned to that office, with a manly and lofty voice, proclaimed that which the other spake to him in secret, continuing half an hour, which ended, and a general amen, as it were, given, the king, with the whole number of men and women (the children excepted) came down without any weapon, who descending to the foot of the hill, set themselves in order.

In coming towards our bulwarks and tents, the scepter-bearer began a song, observing his measures in a dance, and that with a stately countenance, whom the king with his guard, and every degree of persons following, did in like manner sing and dance, saving only the women, which danced and kept silence. The general permitted them to enter within our bulwark, where they continued their song and dance a reasonable time. When they had satisfied themselves, they made signs to our general to sit down, to whom the king, and divers others made several orations, or rather supplication, that he would take their province and kingdom into his hand, and become their king, making signs that they would resign unto him their right and title of the whole land, and become his subjects. In which to persuade us the better, the king and the rest with one consent and with great reverence, joyfully singing a song, did set the crown upon his head, enriched his neck with all their chains and offered unto him many other

---

[63] *cony:* rabbit.

things, honoring him by the name of *Hioh,* adding thereunto, as it seemed, a sign of triumph, which thing our general thought not meet to reject, because he knew not what honor and profit it might be to our country. Wherefore in the name, and to the use of her Majesty, he took the scepter, crown, and dignity of the said country in his hands, wishing that the riches and treasure thereof might so conveniently be transported to the enriching of her kingdom at home, as it aboundeth in the same.

The common sort of the people leaving the king and his guard with our general, scattered themselves together with their sacrifices among our people, taking a diligent view of every person; and such as pleased their fancy (which were the youngest) they, enclosing them about, offered their sacrifices unto them with lamentable weeping, scratching, and tearing the flesh from their faces with their nails, whereof issued abundance of blood. But we used signs to them of disliking this, and stayed their hands from force, and directed them upwards to the living God, whom only they ought to worship. They showed unto us their wounds, and craved help of them at our hands, whereupon we gave them lotions, plasters, and ointments agreeing to the state of their griefs, beseeching God to cure their diseases. Every third day they brought their sacrifices unto us, until they understood our meaning, that we had no pleasure in them. Yet they could not be long absent from us, but daily frequented our company to the hour of our departure, which departure seemed so grievous unto them, that their joy was turned into sorrow. They entreated us, that being absent we would remember them, and by stealth provided a sacrifice, which we disliked.

Our necessary business being ended, our general with his company traveled up into the country to their villages, where we found herds of deer by a thousand in a company, being most large and fat of body.

We found the whole country to be a warren of a strange kind of conies, their bodies in bigness as be the Barbary conies, their heads as the heads of ours, the feet of a want,[64] and the tail of a rat, being of great length; under her chin on either side a bag into the which she gathered her meat when she hath filled her belly abroad. The people eat their bodies and make great account of their skins, for their king's coat was made of them.

Our general called this country, Nova Albion, and that for two causes: the one in respect of the white banks and cliffs, which lie towards the sea, and the other, because it might have some affinity with our country in name, which sometime was so called.

There is no part of earth here to be taken up, wherein there is not some special likelihood of gold or silver.

At our departure hence our general set up a monument of our being there, as also of her Majesty's right and title to the same, namely, a plate nailed upon a fair great post, whereupon was engraven her Majesty's name, the day and year of our arrival there, with the free giving up of the province and people into her Majesty's hands, together with her Highness' picture

---

[64] *want:* mole.

and arms, in a piece of sixpence of current English money under the plate, whereunder was also written the name of our general.

It seemeth that the Spaniards hitherto had never been in this part of the country, neither did ever discover the land by many degrees to the southwards of this place.

Sir Walter Ralegh

1552–1618

SIR WALTER RALEGH was born in Devonshire about 1552, went to Oxford but left in 1572 without a degree, fought in wars on the Continent, and in 1575 was living in the Middle Temple, with perhaps more interest in literature than in law. By some display of his brilliant personality (not by covering a puddle with his cloak) he attracted the attention of the Queen, and for ten years (1582–1592) he was a court favorite, receiving offices, grants, monopolies, jockeying for position with jealous and powerful rivals, flattering the Queen, and planning the exploration and colonization of a new world. He dressed gorgeously, and he was a wit; but of greater significance was his abiding vision of an imperial England, his constant hatred of Spain, and his eager speculative curiosity in matters of science, agriculture, and philosophy.

His poetry is the poetry of the courtier; he did not deign to print it, and it is with difficulty that an editor decides upon the authenticity and text of any verse attributed to him. But in a still more important sense it is courtly poetry: it shows a keen bitterness about life which comes from trying to maintain one's foothold on the slippery slopes of royal favor. We are reminded of Wyatt half a century earlier. Ralegh was a philosopher, too; in 1594 he was investigated for atheism, and a parson quoted him as saying, "I have been a scholar some time in Oxford; I have answered under a bachelor of art and had talk with divers; yet hitherunto in this point (to wit, what the reasonable soul of man is) have I not by any been resolved."

Yet with his skepticism, his disillusionment, Ralegh was still a romantic. He forms, with Sidney, Spenser, and Marlowe, the quadrumvirate of Elizabethan romanticism. His long poem to the Queen, *Cynthia,* which Spenser praised so highly, is lost, except for a rough draft of some appended stanzas. His romanticism is most evident in his prose—in the narrative of his cousin Sir Richard Grenville's last fight in the *Revenge* (see pp. 492–502, below) and in *The History of the World.*

He fell from power in 1592, for marrying (some said after seducing) Elizabeth Throckmorton, one of the Queen's maids of honor. And under King James he was kept in prison on a trumped-up charge of treason; there, from 1603 to 1618, he performed scientific experiments and wrote history, and he was released only once, to make his ill-fated last voyage to Guiana in 1617. He was a passionate man, like Hotspur and Hamlet, and of course he had enemies. Yet by 1618 popular sympathy was so much in his favor that, as Trevelyan said, "the ghost of Ralegh pursued the House of Stuart to the scaffold."

Had he not earned a name as the founder of Virginia, the eloquent and grave historian, "a seafaring man, a soldier and a courtier," as he described himself on the scaffold, he would still be the poet Spenser praised, "the sommers Nightingale" who

> . . . tooke in hond
> My pipe, before that aemuled of many,
> And plaid theron; (for well that skill he cond)
> Himselfe as skilfull in that art as any.

Bibliography: *The Poems of Sir Walter Ralegh*, ed. A. M. C. Latham, London, 1929, revised edition 1950; Tucker Brooke, "Sir Walter Ralegh as Poet and Philosopher," *ELH*, V (1938), 93–112; Ernest A. Strathmann, *Sir Walter Ralegh, A Study in Elizabethan Skepticism*, New York, 1951; E. Edwards, *Life of Sir Walter Ralegh*, 1868; W. Stebbing, *Sir Walter Raleigh*, 1899; E. Thompson, *Sir Walter Ralegh*, New Haven, 1935; H. R. Williamson, *Sir Walter Raleigh*, New York, 1951.

A Report of the Truth of the Fight About the Isles of Azores This Last Summer [1] Betwixt the *Revenge,*[2] One of Her Majesty's Ships, and an Armada [3] of the King of Spain

BECAUSE the rumors are diversely spread, as well in England as in the Low Countries and elsewhere, of this late encounter between her Majesty's ships and the Armada of Spain; and that the Spaniards according to their usual manner fill the world with their vainglorious vaunts, making great appearance of victories, when on the contrary themselves are most commonly and shamefully beaten and dishonored; thereby hoping to possess the ignorant multitude by anticipating and forerunning false reports; it is agreeable with all good reason, for manifestation of the truth, to overcome falsehood and untruth, that the beginning, continuance, and success of this late honorable encounter of Sir Richard Grenville [4] and other her Majesty's captains, with the Armada of Spain, should be truly set down and published without partiality or false imaginations. And it is no marvel that the Spaniard should seek by false and slanderous pamphlets, advisoes, and letters, to cover their own loss and to derogate from others their due honors, especially in this fight being performed far off; seeing they were not ashamed in the year 1588, when they purposed the invasion of this land, to publish in sundry languages, in print, great victories in words, which they pleaded to have obtained against this realm; and spread the same in a most false sort over all parts of France, Italy, and elsewhere. When shortly after it was happily manifested in very deed to all nations how their navy, which they termed invincible, consisting of 140 sail [5] of ships, not only of their own kingdom but strengthened with the greatest argosies, Portugal carracks,[6] Florentines,

---

[1] *this last summer:* 1591.

[2] *Revenge:* a ship of 500 tons and 250 men. It had been Drake's ship in the fight with the Armada, 1588.

[3] *Armada:* here, a fleet of armed ships. Ralegh also uses the term for a single warship.

[4] *Sir Richard Grenville* (*ca.* 1541–1591), Ralegh's first cousin, had commanded Ralegh's first expedition to colonize Roanoke Island in 1585. Ralegh's prose account is the chief source for Tennyson's famous ballad *The Revenge: A Ballad of the Fleet,* first published in 1878.

[5] *140 sail:* Ralegh wrote "240"; the correction is Hakluyt's.

[6] *carracks:* large ships.

and huge hulks of other countries, were by thirty of her Majesty's own ships of war, and a few of our own merchants, by the wise, valiant, and most advantageous conduction of the Lord Charles Howard, high admiral of England, beaten and shuffled together; even from the Lizard in Cornwall, first to Portland, where they shamefully left Don Pedro de Valdes with his mighty ship; from Portland to Calais, where they lost Hugo de Moncado, with the gallias [7] of which he was captain; and from Calais driven with squibs [8] from their anchors, were chased out of the sight of England, round about Scotland and Ireland. Where for the sympathy of their barbarous religion, hoping to find succor and assistance, a great part of them were crushed against the rocks, and those others that landed, being very many in number, were notwithstanding broken, slain, and taken, and so sent from village to village, coupled in halters, to be shipped into England. Where her Majesty of her princely and invincible disposition disdaining to put them to death, and scorning either to retain or entertain them, they were all sent back again to their countries, to witness and recount the worthy achievements of their invincible and dreadful navy. Of which the number of soldiers, the fearful burthen of their ships, the commanders' names of every squadron, with all other their magazines of provisions, were put in print, as an army and navy unresistable and disdaining prevention.[9] With all which so great and terrible an ostentation they did not in all their sailing round about England so much as sink or take one ship, bark, pinnace,[10] or cockboat[11] of ours, or ever burned so much as one sheepcote of this land. Whenas on the contrary Sir Francis Drake, with only eight hundred soldiers, not long before landed in their Indies and forced Santiago, Santo Domingo, Cartagena, and the forts of Florida. And after that Sir John Norris marched from Peniche in Portugal, with a handful of soldiers, to the gates of Lisbon, being above forty English miles. Where the earl of Essex himself and other valiant gentlemen braved the city of Lisbon, encamped at the very gates; from whence after many days' abode, finding neither promised party nor provision to batter,[12] they made retreat by land in despite of all their garrisons both of horse and foot.

In this sort I have a little digressed from my first purpose, only by the necessary comparison of theirs and our actions; the one covetous of honor without vaunt of ostentation; the other so greedy to purchase the opinion of their own affairs and by false rumors to resist the blasts of their own dishonors as they will not only not blush to spread all manner of untruths, but even for the least advantage, be it but for the taking of one poor adventurer of the English, will celebrate the victory with bonfires in every town, always spending more in faggots than the purchase was worth they obtained. Whenas we never yet thought it worth the consumption of two

---

[7] *gallias:* galleys.

[8] *squibs:* exploding shot.

[9] *disdaining prevention:* scorning resistance.

[10] *pinnace:* a small two-masted ship.

[11] *cockboat:* dory or lifeboat.

[12] *batter:* seize upon, strike.

billets when we have taken eight or ten of their Indian ships at one time and twenty of the Brazil fleet. Such is the difference between true valor and ostentation, and between honorable actions and frivolous vainglorious vaunts. But now to return to my first purpose.

The Lord Thomas Howard, with six of her Majesty's ships, six victualers of London, the bark *Ralegh,* and two or three pinnaces, riding at anchor near unto Flores, one of the westerly islands of the Azores, the last of August in the afternoon, had intelligence by one Captain Middleton of the approach of the Spanish Armada. Which Middleton being in a very good sailer had kept them company three days before, of good purpose, both to discover their forces the more, as also to give advice to my Lord Thomas of their approach. He had no sooner delivered the news but the fleet was in sight.

Many of our ships' companies were on shore in the island, some providing ballast for their ships, others filling of water and refreshing themselves from the land with such things as they could either for money or by force recover. By reason whereof our ships being all pestered and roomaging,[13] everything out of order, very light for want of ballast. And that which was most to our disadvantage, the one-half part of the men of every ship sick and utterly unserviceable. For in the *Revenge* there were ninety diseased; in the *Bonaventure* not so many in health as could handle her mainsail. For had not twenty men been taken out of a bark of Sir George Cary's, his being commanded to be sunk, and those appointed to her, she had hardly ever recovered England. The rest for the most part were in little better state. The names of her Majesty's ships were these as followeth: the *Defiance,* which was admiral, the *Revenge,* vice-admiral, the *Bonaventure* commanded by Captain Cross, the *Lion* by George Fenner, the *Foresight* by Mr. Thomas Vavasour, and the *Crane* by Duffield. The *Foresight* and the *Crane* being but small ships; only the other were of the middle size; the rest, besides the bark *Ralegh* commanded by Captain Thin, were victualers and of small force or none.

The Spanish fleet having shrouded their approach by reason of the island, were now so soon at hand as our ships had scarce time to weigh their anchors, but some of them were driven to let slip their cables and set sail. Sir Richard Grenville was the last weighed, to recover the men that were upon the island, which otherwise had been lost. The Lord Thomas with the rest very hardly recovered the wind, which Sir Richard Grenville not being able to do was persuaded by the master and others to cut his mainsail and cast about, and to trust to the sailing of his ship; for the squadron of Seville were on his weather bow. But Sir Richard utterly refused to turn from the enemy, alleging that he would rather choose to die than to dishonor himself, his country, and her Majesty's ship, persuading his company that he would pass through the two squadrons in despite of them, and en-

---

13 *pestered and roomaging:* busied with various occupations, and the cargo not arranged.

force those of Seville to give him way. Which he performed upon divers of the foremost, who, as the mariners term it, sprang their luff,[14] and fell under the lee of the *Revenge*. But the other course had been the better, and might right well have been answered [15] in so great an impossibility of prevailing. Notwithstanding, out of the greatness of his mind he could not be persuaded.

In the meanwhile as he attended those which were nearest him, the great *San Philip* being in the wind of him and coming towards him becalmed his sails in such sort as the ship could neither make way nor feel the helm, so huge and high cargoed was the Spanish ship, being of a thousand and five hundred tons. Who after laid the *Revenge* aboard.[16] When he was thus bereft of his sails, the ships that were under his lee, luffing up, also laid him aboard; of which the next was the admiral of the Biscaines, a very mighty and puissant ship commanded by Brittandona. The said *Philip* carried three tier of ordnance on a side, and eleven pieces in every tier. She shot eight forthright out of her chase,[17] besides those of her stern ports.

After the *Revenge* was entangled with this *Philip,* four other boarded her; two on her larboard and two on her starboard. The fight thus beginning at three of the clock in the afternoon continued very terrible all that evening. But the great *San Philip* having received the lower tier of the *Revenge,* discharged with crossbar-shot,[18] shifted herself with all diligence from her sides, utterly misliking her first entertainment. Some say that the ship foundered, but we cannot report it for truth unless we were assured.

The Spanish ships were filled with companies of soldiers, in some two hundred besides the mariners, in some five, in others eight hundred. In ours there were none at all, beside the mariners, but the servants of the commanders and some few voluntary gentlemen only. After many interchanged volleys of great ordnance and small shot, the Spaniards deliberated to enter the *Revenge,* and made divers attempts, hoping to force her by the multitudes of their armed soldiers and musketeers, but were still repulsed again and again, and at all times beaten back into their own ships or into the seas.

In the beginning of the fight the *George Noble* of London, having received some shot through her by the armadas, fell under the lee of the *Revenge* and asked Sir Richard what he would command him, being but one of the victualers and of small force. Sir Richard bid him save himself and leave him to his fortune.

After the fight had thus without intermission continued while the day lasted and some hours of the night, many of our men were slain and hurt, and one of the great galleons of the armada and the admiral of the hulks [19]

[14] *sprang their luff:* headed into the wind too far.

[15] *answered:* justified.

[16] *laid* [*the R.*] *aboard:* came alongside.

[17] *chase:* bow.

[18] *crossbar-shot:* a ball with projecting bars.

[19] *admiral of the hulks:* chief of the supply ships.

both sunk, and in many other of the Spanish ships great slaughter was made. Some write that Sir Richard was very dangerously hurt almost in the beginning of the fight and lay speechless for a time ere he recovered. But two of the *Revenge's* own company, brought home in a ship of lime from the islands, examined by some of the lords and others, affirmed that he was never so wounded as that he forsook the upper deck, till an hour before midnight; and then being shot into the body with a musket, as he was a-dressing was again shot into the head, and withal his chirurgeon wounded to death. This agreeth also with an examination taken by Sir Francis Godolphin of four other mariners of the same ship being returned, which examination the said Sir Francis sent unto Master William Killigrew of her Majesty's privy chamber.

But to return to the fight, the Spanish ships which attempted to board the *Revenge,* as they were wounded and beaten off, so always others came in their places, she having never less than two mighty galleons by her sides and aboard her. So that ere the morning, from three of the clock the day before, there had fifteen several armadas assailed her; and all so ill approved their entertainment as they were by the break of day far more willing to hearken to a composition than hastily to make any more assaults or entries. But as the day increased, so our men decreased; and as the light grew more and more, by so much more grew our discomforts. For none appeared in sight but enemies, saving one small ship called the *Pilgrim,* commanded by Jacob Whiddon, who hovered all night to see the success, but in the morning bearing with the *Revenge,* was hunted like a hare amongst many ravenous hounds, but escaped.

All the powder of the *Revenge* to the last barrel was now spent, all her pikes broken, forty of her best men slain, and the most part of the rest hurt. In the beginning of the fight she had but one hundred free from sickness, and fourscore and ten sick, laid in hold upon the ballast. A small troop to man such a ship, and a weak garrison to resist so mighty an army. By those hundred all was sustained, the volleys, boardings, and enterings of fifteen ships of war, besides those which beat her at large. On the contrary, the Spanish were always supplied with soldiers brought from every squadron; all manner of arms and powder at will. Unto ours there remained no comfort at all, no hope, no supply either of ships, men, or weapons; the masts all beaten overboard, all her tackle cut asunder, her upper work altogether razed, and in effect evened she was with the water, but the very foundation or bottom of a ship, nothing being left overhead either for flight or defense.

Sir Richard, finding himself in this distress and unable any longer to make resistance, having endured in this fifteen hours' fight the assault of fifteen several armadas all by turns aboard him, and by estimation eight hundred shot of great artillery, besides many assaults and entries; and that himself and the ship must needs be possessed by the enemy, who were now all cast in a ring round about him, the *Revenge* not able to move one way or other but as she was moved with the waves and billow of the sea; commanded the master gunner, whom he knew to be a most resolute man, to split and sink the ship; that thereby nothing might remain of glory or victory to the Spaniards, seeing in so many hours' fight and with so great a navy they were not able to take her, having had fifteen hours' time, above ten thousand [20] men, and fifty-and-three sail of men-of-war to perform it withal; and persuaded the company, or as many as he could induce, to yield themselves unto God and to the mercy of none else, but as they had like valiant resolute men repulsed so many enemies they should not now shorten the honor of their nation by prolonging their own lives for a few hours or a few days.

The master gunner readily condescended, and divers others; but the captain and the master were of another opinion, and besought Sir Richard to have care of them; alleging that the Spaniard would be as ready to entertain a composition as they were willing to offer the same; and that there being divers sufficient and valiant men yet living, and whose wounds were not mortal, they might do their country and prince acceptable service hereafter. And that whereas Sir Richard had alleged that the Spaniards should never glory to have taken one ship of her Majesty, seeing that they had so long and so notably defended themselves, they answered that the ship had six foot water in hold, three shot under water which were so weakly stopped as with the first working of the sea she must needs sink, and was besides so crushed and bruised as she could never be removed out of the place.

And as the matter was thus in dispute, and Sir Richard refusing to hearken to any of those reasons, the master of the *Revenge* (while the captain won unto him the greater party) was convoyed aboard the general, Don Alfonso Baçan. Who finding none over-hasty to enter the *Revenge* again, doubting lest Sir Richard would have blown them up and himself, and perceiving by the report of the master of the *Revenge* his dangerous disposition, yielded that all their lives should be saved, the company sent for England, and the better sort to pay such reasonable ransom as their estate would bear, and in the mean season to be free from galley or imprisonment. To this he so much the rather condescended as well, as I have said, for fear of further loss and mischief to themselves, as also for the desire he had to recover Sir Richard Grenville; whom for his notable valor he seemed greatly to honor and admire.

When this answer was returned, and that safety of life was promised, the common sort being now at the end of their peril, the most drew back from Sir Richard and the master gunner, being no hard matter to dissuade men from death to life. The master gunner, finding himself and Sir Richard thus prevented and mastered by the greater number, would have slain himself with a sword, had he not been by force withheld and locked into his cabin. Then the general sent many boats aboard the *Revenge,* and divers of our men fearing Sir Richard's disposition stole away aboard the general and other ships. Sir Richard, thus overmatched, was sent unto by Alfonso Baçan to remove out of the *Revenge,* the ship being marvelous unsavory,

---

[20] *above ten thousand:* Hakluyt's correction of Ralegh's "15,000."

filled with blood and bodies of dead and wounded men like a slaughter-house. Sir Richard answered that he might do with his body what he list, for he esteemed it not, and as he was carried out of the ship he swounded, and reviving again desired the company to pray for him. The general used Sir Richard with all humanity, and left nothing unattempted that tended to his recovery, highly commending his valor and worthiness, and greatly bewailing the danger wherein he was, being unto them a rare spectacle and a resolution seldom approved, to see one ship turn toward so many enemies, to endure the charge and boarding of so many huge armadas, and to resist and repel the assaults and entries of so many soldiers. All which and more is confirmed by a Spanish captain of the same armada, and a present actor in the fight, who being severed from the rest in a storm was by the *Lion* of London, a small ship, taken, and is now prisoner in London.

The general commander of the armada was Don Alfonso Baçan, brother to the Marques of Santa Cruz. The admiral of the Biscaine squadron was Brittandona. Of the squadron of Seville, the Marques of Arumburch. The hulks and flyboats were commanded by Luis Coutinho. There were slain and drowned in this fight well near one thousand [21] of the enemies, and two special commanders, Don Luis de Sant John, and Don George de Prunaria de Mallaga, as the Spanish captain confesseth, besides divers others of special account whereof as yet report is not made.

The admiral of the hulks and the *Ascension* of Seville were both sunk by the side of the *Revenge;* one other recovered the road of St. Michael and sunk also there; a fourth ran herself with the shore to save her men. Sir Richard died, as it is said, the second or third day aboard the general, and was by them greatly bewailed. What became of his body, whether it were buried in the sea or on the land, we know not; the comfort that remaineth to his friends is that he hath ended his life honorably in respect of the reputation won to his nation and country, and of the same to his posterity, and that being dead he hath not outlived his own honor.

For the rest of her Majesty's ships that entered not so far into the fight as the *Revenge,* the reasons and causes were these. There were of them but six in all, whereof two but small ships; the *Revenge* engaged past recovery; the island of Flores was on the one side, fifty-three sail of the Spanish, divided into squadrons, on the other, all as full filled with soldiers as they could contain; almost the one-half of our men sick and not able to serve; the ships grown foul, unroomaged, and scarcely able to bear any sail for want of ballast, having been six months at the sea before. If all the rest had entered, all had been lost. For the very hugeness of the Spanish fleet, if no other violence had been offered, would have crushed them between them into shivers. Of which the dishonor and loss to the Queen had been far greater than the spoil or harm that the enemy could anyway have received. Notwithstanding, it is very true that the Lord Thomas would have entered between the squadrons, but the rest would not condescend; and the master

---

21 *one thousand:* Hakluyt's correction of Ralegh's "2,000."

of his own ship offered to leap into the sea rather than to conduct that her Majesty's ship and the rest to be a prey to the enemy, where there was no hope nor possibility either of defense or victory. Which also in my opinion had ill sorted or answered the discretion and trust of a general, to commit himself and his charge to an assured destruction, without hope or any likelihood of prevailing; thereby to diminish the strength of her Majesty's navy, and to enrich the pride and glory of the enemy. The *Foresight* of the Queen's, commanded by Master Thomas Vavasour, performed a very great fight, and stayed two hours as near the *Revenge* as the weather would permit him, not forsaking the fight till he was like to be encompassed by the squadrons and with great difficulty cleared himself. The rest gave divers volleys of shot and entered as far as the place permitted, and their own necessities to keep the weather gage of [22] the enemy, until they were parted by night.

A few days after the fight was ended and the English prisoners dispersed into the Spanish and Indies ships there arose so great a storm from the west and northwest that all the fleet was dispersed, as well the Indian fleet which were then come unto them as the rest of the armada that attended their arrival, of which fourteen sail, together with the *Revenge,* and in her two hundred Spaniards, were cast away upon the isle of St. Michael. So it pleased them to honor the burial of that renowned ship the *Revenge,* not suffering her to perish alone, for the great honor she achieved in her lifetime. On the rest of the islands there were cast away in this storm fifteen or sixteen more of the ships of war; and of a hundred and odd sail of the Indies fleet, expected this year in Spain, what in this tempest, and what before in the bay of Mexico, and about the Bermudas, there were seventy and odd consumed and lost, with those taken by our ships of London, besides one very rich Indian ship which set herself on fire, being boarded by the *Pilgrim,* and five other taken by Master Wats his ships of London, between the Havana and Cape S. Antonio. The fourth of this month of November we received letters from the Terceira [23] affirming that there are three thousand bodies of men remaining in that island, saved out of the perished ships; and that by the Spaniards' own confession there are ten thousand cast away in this storm, besides those that are perished between the islands and the main. Thus it hath pleased God to fight for us and to defend the justice of our cause against the ambitious and bloody pretenses of the Spaniard, who seeking to devour all nations are themselves devoured. A manifest testimony how injust and displeasing their attempts are in the sight of God, who hath pleased to witness by the success of their affairs his mislike of their bloody and injurious designs purposed and practised against all Christian princes, over whom they seek unlawful and ungodly rule and empery.

One day or two before this wrack happened to the Spanish fleet, whenas some of our prisoners desired to be set on shore upon the islands, hoping

---

[22] *the weather gage of:* to the windward of.

[23] *Terceira:* one of the Azores.

to be from thence transported into England, which liberty was formerly by the general promised, one Maurice Fitz-John, son of old John of Desmond, a notable traitor, cousin-german [24] to the late earl of Desmond,[25] was sent to the English from ship to ship to persuade them to serve the King of Spain. The arguments he used to induce them were these: the increase of pay, which he promised to be trebled; advancement to the better sort; and the exercise of the true Catholic religion and safety of their souls to all. For the first, even the beggarly and unnatural behavior of those English and Irish rebels that served the King in that present action was sufficient to answer that first argument of rich pay. For so poor and beggarly they were as for want of apparel they stripped their poor countrymen prisoners out of their ragged garments worn to nothing by six months' service, and spared not to despoil them even of their bloody shirts from their wounded bodies, and the very shoes from their feet; a notable testimony of their rich entertainment and great wages. The second reason was hope of advancement if they served well and would continue faithful to the King. But what man can be so blockishly ignorant ever to expect place or honor from a foreign king, having no argument or persuasion than his own disloyalty; to be unnatural to his own country that bred him, to his parents that begat him, and rebellious to his true prince to whose obedience he is bound by oath, by nature, and by religion? No, they are only assured to be employed in all desperate enterprises, to be held in scorn and disdain ever among those whom they serve. And that ever traitor was either trusted or advanced I could never yet read, neither can I at this time remember any example. And no man could have less becomed the place of an orator for such a purpose than this Maurice of Desmond. For the earl his cousin being one of the greatest subjects in that kingdom of Ireland, having almost whole countries in his possession, so many goodly manors, castles, and lordships, the Count Palatine of Kerry, five hundred gentlemen of his own name and family to follow him, besides others—all which he possessed in peace for three or four hundred years—was in less than three years after his adhering to the Spaniards and rebellion beaten from all his holds, not so many as ten gentlemen of his name left living, himself taken and beheaded by a soldier of his own nation, and his land given by a parliament to her Majesty and possessed by the English; his other cousin, Sir John of Desmond, taken by Master John Zouch and his body hanged over the gates of his native city to be devoured by ravens; the third brother of Sir James hanged, drawn, and quartered in the same place. If he had withal vaunted of his success of his own house, no doubt the argument would have moved much and wrought great effect; which because he for that present forgot, I thought it good to remember in his behalf. For matter of religion, it would require a particular volume if I should set down how irreligiously they cover their greedy and ambitious pretenses with that veil of piety. But sure I am that

[24] *cousin-german:* first cousin.

[25] *earl of Desmond:* the most troublesome of Irish rebels under Elizabeth, executed in 1585.

there is no kingdom or commonwealth in all Europe but, if they be reformed,[26] they then invade it for religion sake; if it be, as they term, Catholic, they pretend title; as if the kings of Castile were the natural heirs of all the world; and so between both no kingdom is unsought. Where they dare not with their own forces to invade, they basely entertain the traitors and vagabonds of all nations; seeking by those and by their renegade Jesuits to win parts, and have by that mean ruined many noble houses and others in this land, and have extinguished both their lives and families. What good, honor, or fortune ever man yet by them achieved is yet unheard of or unwritten. And if our English papists do but look into Portugal, against whom they have no pretense of religion, how the nobility are put to death, imprisoned, their rich men made a prey, and all sorts of people captived, they shall find that the obedience even of the Turk is easy and a liberty in respect of the slavery and tyranny of Spain. What they have done in Sicily, in Naples, Milan, and in the Low Countries; who hath there been spared for religion at all? And it cometh to my remembrance of a certain burgher of Antwerp, whose house being entered by a company of Spanish soldiers, when they first sacked the city, he besought them to spare him and his goods, being a good Catholic, and one of their own party and faction. The Spaniards answered that they knew him to be of a good conscience for himself, but his money, plate, jewels, and goods were all heretical and therefore good prize. So they abused and tormented the foolish Fleming, who hoped that an Agnus Dei had been a sufficient target against all force of that holy and charitable nation. Neither have they at any time, as they protest, invaded the kingdoms of the Indies and Peru and elsewhere but only led thereunto rather to reduce the people to Christianity than for either gold or empery. Whenas in one only island, called Hispaniola, they have wasted thirty hundred thousand of the natural people, besides many millions else in other places of the Indies; a poor and harmless people, created of God, and might have been won to his knowledge, as many of them were, and almost as many as ever were persuaded thereunto. The story whereof is at large written by a bishop of their own nation called Bartholomew de las Casas, and translated into English and many other languages, entitled *The Spanish Cruelties.*[27] Who would therefore repose trust in such a nation of ravenous strangers, and especially in those Spaniards which more greedily thirst after English blood than after the lives of any other people of Europe, for the many overthrows and dishonors they have received at our hands, whose weakness we have discovered to the world, and whose forces at home, abroad, in Europe, in India, by sea and land, we have even with handfuls of men and ships overthrown and dishonored. Let not therefore any Englishman, of what religion soever, have other opinion of the Spaniards but that those whom he seeketh to win of our nation he esteemeth base and traitorous, unworthy persons, or unconstant fools; and that he

[26] *reformed:* Protestant.

[27] *The Spanish Cruelties:* The English version was published in 1583 under the title *The Spanish Colony.*

useth his pretense of religion for no other purpose but to bewitch us from the obedience of our natural prince, thereby hoping in time to bring us to slavery and subjection, and then none shall be unto them so odious and disdained as the traitors themselves, who have sold their country to a stranger, and forsaken their faith and obedience contrary to nature and religion; and contrary to that human and general honor, not only of Christians, but of heathen and irreligious nations, who have always sustained what labor soever, and embraced even death itself, for their country, prince, or commonwealth.

To conclude, it hath ever to this day pleased God to prosper and defend her Majesty, to break the purposes of malicious enemies, of forsworn traitors, and of unjust practises and invasions. She hath ever been honored of the worthiest kings, served by faithful subjects, and shall by the favor of God resist, repel, and confound all whatsoever attempts against her sacred person or kingdom. In the meantime let the Spaniard and traitor vaunt of their success; and we her true and obedient vassals guided by the shining light of her virtues shall always love her, serve her, and obey her to the end of our lives.

The discovery of the large, rich, and beautiful empire of Guiana, with relation of the great and golden city of Manoa, which the Spaniards call El Dorado, and the provinces of Emeria, Aromaia, Amapaia, and other countries, with their rivers adjoining. Performed in the year 1595 by Sir Walter Ralegh, Knight, Captain of Her Majesty's Guard, Lord Warden of the Stannaries,[28] and Her Highness' Lieutenant-General of the County of Cornwall.

To the Right Honorable my singular good lord and kinsman Charles Howard,[29] Knight of the Garter, Baron and Councilor, and of the Admirals of England the most renowned, and to the Right Honorable Sir Robert Cecil, Knight, Councilor in her Highness' Privy Councils.

For your Honors' many honorable and friendly parts, I have hitherto only returned promises, and now for answer of both your adventures, I have sent you a bundle of papers, which I have divided between your

[28] *Stannaries:* the mines of Cornwall and Devon, over which Ralegh was appointed warden by Queen Elizabeth in 1585.

[29] *Charles Howard:* (1536–1624), Earl of Nottingham, lord admiral of England in 1585, and commander-in-chief against the Spanish Armada.

lordship and Sir Robert Cecil in these two respects chiefly: first for that it is reason, that wasteful factors, when they have consumed such stocks as they had in trust, do yield some color for the same in their account; secondly, for that I am assured, that whatsoever shall be done, or written by me, shall need a double protection and defense. The trial that I had of both your loves, when I was left of all, but of malice and revenge, makes me still presume, that you will be pleased (knowing what little power I had to perform aught, and the great advantage of forewarned enemies) to answer that out of knowledge, which others shall but object out of malice. In my more happy times as I did especially honor you both, so I found that your loves sought me out in the darkest shadow of adversity, and the same affection which accompanied my better fortune, soared not away from me in my many miseries, all which though I cannot requite, yet I shall ever acknowledge. And the great debt which I have no power to pay, I can do no more for a time but confess to be due. It is true that as my errors were great, so they have yielded very grievous effects, and if aught might have been deserved in former times to have counterpoised any part of offenses, the fruit thereof, as it seemeth, was long before fallen from the tree, and the dead stock only remained. I did therefore even in the winter of my life undertake these travels, fitter for bodies less blasted with misfortunes, for men of greater ability, and for minds of better encouragement, that thereby, if it were possible, I might recover but the moderation of excess and the least taste of the greatest plenty formerly possessed. If I had known other way to win, if I had imagined how greater adventures might have regained, if I could conceive what farther means I might yet use, but even to appease so powerful displeasure, I would not doubt but for one year more to hold fast my soul in my teeth, till it were performed. Of that little remain I had, I have wasted in effect all herein. I have undergone many constructions. I have been accompanied with many sorrows, with labor, hunger, heat, sickness, and peril. It appears, notwithstanding, that I made no other bravado of going to the sea, than was meant, and that I was never hidden in Cornwall, or elsewhere, as was supposed. They have grossly belied me, that forejudged that I would rather become a servant to the Spanish King, than return, and the rest were much mistaken, who would have persuaded that I was too easeful and sensual to undertake a journey of so great travel. But, if what I have done receive the gracious construction of a painful pilgrimage, and purchase the least remission, I shall think all too little, and that there were wanting to the rest many miseries. But if both the times past, the present, and what may be in the future do all by one grain of gall continue in eternal distaste, I do not then know whether I should bewail myself, either for my too much travel and expense, or condemn myself for doing less than that, which can deserve nothing. From myself I have deserved no thanks, for I am returned a beggar, and withered; but that I might have bettered my poor estate, it shall appear by the following discourse if I had not only respected her Majesty's future honor and riches. It became not the former fortune in which I once lived to go journeys of picory;[30] it had sorted ill with the offices of honor which by her Majesty's grace I hold this day in England to run from cape to cape and from place to place for the pillage of ordinary prizes. Many years since, I had knowledge by relation, of that mighty rich and beautiful empire of Guiana, and of that great and golden city, which the Spaniards call El Dorado, and the naturals,[31] Manoa, which city was conquered, re-edified,[32] and enlarged by a younger son of Guainacapa, Emperor of Peru, at such time as Francisco Pizarro and others conquered the said empire from his two elder brethren, Guascar and Atabalipa, both then contending for the same, the one being favored by the Orejones of Cuzco, the other by the people of Caxamalca. I sent my servant, Jacob Whiddon, the year before to get knowledge of the passages, and I had some light from Captain Parker, sometime my servant, and now attending on your lordship, that such a place there was to the southward of the great Bay of Charuas, or Guanipa; but I found that it was six hundred miles farther off than they supposed and many other impediments to them unknown and unheard. After I had displanted Don Antonio de Berreo, who was upon the same enterprise, leaving my ships at Trinidad, at the Port called Curiapan, I wandered four hundred miles into the said country by land and river. The particulars I will leave to the following discourse. The country hath more quantity of gold by manifold, than the best parts of the Indies or Peru. All the most of the kings of the borders are already become her Majesty's vassals, and seem to desire nothing more than her Majesty's protection and the return of the English nation. It hath another ground and assurance of riches and glory than the voyages of the West Indies, an easier way to invade the best parts thereof than by the common course. The King of Spain is not so impoverished, by taking three or four port towns in America, as we suppose, neither are the riches of Peru or Nueva Espanna so left by the seaside, as it can be easily washed away with a great flood, or spring tide, or left dry upon the sands on a low ebb. The port towns are few and poor in respect of the rest within the land, and are of little defense, and are only rich, when the fleets are to receive the treasure for Spain. And we might think the Spaniards very simple, having so many horses and slaves, if they could not upon two days' warning carry all the gold they have into the land, and far enough from the reach of our footmen, especially the Indies being (as they are for the most part) so mountainous, so full of woods, rivers, and marshes. In the port towns of the Province of Venezuela, as Cumana, Coro, and S. Iago, whereof Coro and S. Iago were taken by Captain Preston, and Cumana and S. Joseph by us, we found not the value of one rail of plate in either: but the cities of Barquasimeta, Valencia, S. Sebastian, Cororo, S. Lucia, Laguna, Maracaiba, and Truxillo are not so easily invaded. Neither does the burning of those on

[30] *picory:* marauding, looting.
[31] *naturals:* natives.
[32] *re-edified:* rebuilt.

the coast impoverish the King of Spain any one ducat; and if we sack the river of Hacha, S. Marta, and Cartagena, which are the ports of Nuevo Reyno, and Popayan, there are besides within the land, which are indeed rich and populous, the towns and cities of Merida, Lagrita, S. Christophor, the great cities of Pamplon, S. Fe de Bogota, Tunxa, and Mozo where the esmeralds[33] are found, the towns and cities of Marequita, Velez, la Villa de Leva, Palma, Unda, Angustura, the great city of Timana, Tocaima, S. Aguila, Pasto, Juago, the great city of Popayan itself, Los Remedios, and the rest. If we take the ports and villages within the Bay of Uraba, in the kingdom or rivers of Darien and Caribana, the cities and towns of S. Juan de Roydas, of Cassaris, of Antiocha, Caramanta, Cali, and Anserma have gold enough to pay the King's part, and are not easily invaded by the way of the ocean, or if Nombre de Dios and Panama be taken in the Province of Castilla del Oro, and the villages upon the rivers of Cenu and Chagre; Peru hath besides those and besides the magnificent cities of Quito and Lima so many islands, ports, cities, and mines, as if I should name them with the rest, it would seem incredible to the reader, all of which, because I have written a particular treatise of the West Indies, I will omit in repetition at this time, seeing that in the said treatise I have anatomized the rest of the sea towns as well of Nicaragua, Yucatan, Nueva Espanna, and the islands, as those of the inland and by what means they may be best invaded, as far as any mean judgment can comprehend. But I hope it shall appear that there is a way found to answer every man's longing, a better Indies for her Majesty than the King of Spain hath any. Which, if it shall please her Highness to undertake, I shall most willingly end the rest of my days in following the same. If it be left to the spoils and sackage of common persons, if the love and service of so many nations be despised, so great riches and so mighty an empire refused, I hope her Majesty will yet take my humble desire and my labor therein in gracious part, which, if it had not been in respect of her Highness' future honor and riches, could have laid hands on and ransomed many of the kings and Casiqui of the country, and have had a reasonable proportion of gold for their redemption. However, I have chosen to bear the burden of poverty than reproach and rather to endure a second travel and the chances thereof, than to have defaced an enterprise of so great assurance, until I knew whether it pleased God to put a disposition in her princely and royal heart either to follow or foreslow the same. I will therefore leave it to his ordinance that hath only power in all things, and do humbly pray that your honors will excuse such errors, as without the defense of art, overrun in every part of the following discourse, in which I have neither studied phrase, form, nor fashion, that you will be pleased to esteem me as your own (though over-dearly bought) and I shall ever remain ready to do you all honor and service.

W. R.

---

[33] *esmeralds:* emeralds.

To the Reader

Because there have been divers opinions conceived of the gold ore brought from Guiana, and for that an alderman of London and an officer of her Majesty's mint hath given out that the same is of no price, I have thought good by the addition of these lines to give answer as well to the said malicious slander, as to other objections. It is true that while we abode at the island of Trinidad, I was informed by an Indian that not far from the port, where we anchored, there were found certain mineral stones which they esteemed to be gold and were thereunto persuaded the rather for that they had seen both English and Frenchmen gather and embark some quantities thereof. Upon this likelihood I sent forty men and gave order that each one should bring a stone of that mine to make trial of its goodness, which being performed, I assured them at their return, that the same was marcasite, and of no riches or value. Notwithstanding, divers trusting more to their own sense, than to my opinion, kept of the said marcasite, and have tried thereof since my return in divers places. In Guiana itself I never saw marcasite, but all the rocks, mountains, all stones in the plains, woods and by the rivers' side are in effect through-shining and seem marvelous rich, which being tried to be no marcasite, are the true signs of rich minerals, but are no other than *el madre del oro,* as the Spaniards term them, which is the mother of gold, or as it is said by others, the scum of gold. Of divers sorts of these, many of my company brought also into England, every one taking the fairest for the best, which is not general. For mine own part I did not countermand any man's desire or opinion, and I could have afforded them little if I should have denied them the pleasure of their own fancies therein. But I was resolved that gold must be found either in grains separate from the stone, as it is in most of the rivers in Guiana, or else in a kind of hard stone, which we call the white spar, of which I saw divers hills and in sundry places, but had neither time nor men, nor instruments fit for labor. Nearer unto one of the rivers I found of the said white spar or flint a very great ledge or bank, which I endeavored to break by all means I could, because there appeared on the outside some small grains of gold, but finding no mean to work the same upon the upper part, seeking the sides and circuit of the said rock, I found a cliff in the same from whence with daggers, and with the head of an ax, we got out some small quantity thereof, of which kind of white stone, wherein gold engendered, we saw divers hills, and rocks in every part of Guiana wherein we traveled. Of this there have been many trials, and in London it was first said [34] by M. Westwood, a refiner dwelling in Wood Street, and it held after the rate of 12,000 or 13,000 pounds a ton. Another sort was afterward tried by M. Bulmar and M. Dimock, assay master, and it held after the rate of 23,000 pounds a ton. There was some of it again tried by M. Palmer, comptroller of the mint, and M. Dimock in Goldsmiths' Hall and it held after

34 *said:* assayed.

26,900 pounds a ton. There was also at the same time, and by the same persons a trial made of the dust of the said mine which held 8 pounds 6 ounces weight of gold in the hundred. There was likewise at the same time a trial of an image of copper made in Guiana, which held a third-part of gold, besides divers trials made in the country, and by others in London. But because there came ill with the good and besides the said alderman was not presented with the best, it hath pleased him, therefore, to scandal all the rest and to deface the enterprise as much as in him lieth. It hath also been concluded by divers, that if there had been any such ore in Guiana, and the same discovered, that I would have brought home a greater quantity thereof. First, I was not bound to satisfy any man of the quantity, but such only as adventured, if any store had been returned thereof. But it is very true that had all their mountains been of massive gold, it was impossible for us to have made any longer stay to have wrought the same and whosoever hath seen with what strength of stone the best gold ore is environed, he will not think it easy to be had out in heaps, and especially by us, who had neither men, instruments, nor time, as it is said before, to perform the same. There were on this discovery no less than one hundred persons who can all witness that when we passed any branch of the river to view the land within, and stayed from our boats but six hours, we were driven to wade to the eyes, at our return, and if we attempted the same, the day following it was impossible either to ford it, or to swim it, both by reason of the swiftness and also for that the borders were so pestered with fast woods, as neither boat nor man could find place, either to land or to embark. For, in June, July, August, and September, it is impossible to navigate any of those rivers, for such is the fury of the current, and there are so many trees and woods overflown, as if any boat but touch upon any tree or stake, it is impossible to save any one person therein, and ere we departed the land it ran with such swiftness, as we drove down most commonly against the wind, little less than one hundred miles a day. Besides our vessels were no other than wherries, one little barge, a small cockboat, and a bad galiota,[35] which we framed in haste for that purpose at Trinidad, and those little boats had nine or ten men apiece, with all their victuals and arms. It is further true, that we were about four hundred miles from our ships, and had been a month from them, which also we left weakly manned in an open road, and had promised our return in fifteen days. Others have devised that the same ore was had from Barbary, and that we carried it with us into Guiana. Surely, the singularity of that device I do not well comprehend. For mine own part, I am not so much in love with these long voyages, as to devise, thereby, to cozen myself, to lie hard, to fare worse, to be subjected to perils, to diseases, to ill savors, to be parched and withered, and withal to sustain the care and labor of such an enterprise, except the same had more comfort than the fetching of marcasite in Guiana,

[35] *galiota* (Spanish *"galeota,"* English "galliot"), a small boat propelled by sails and oars.

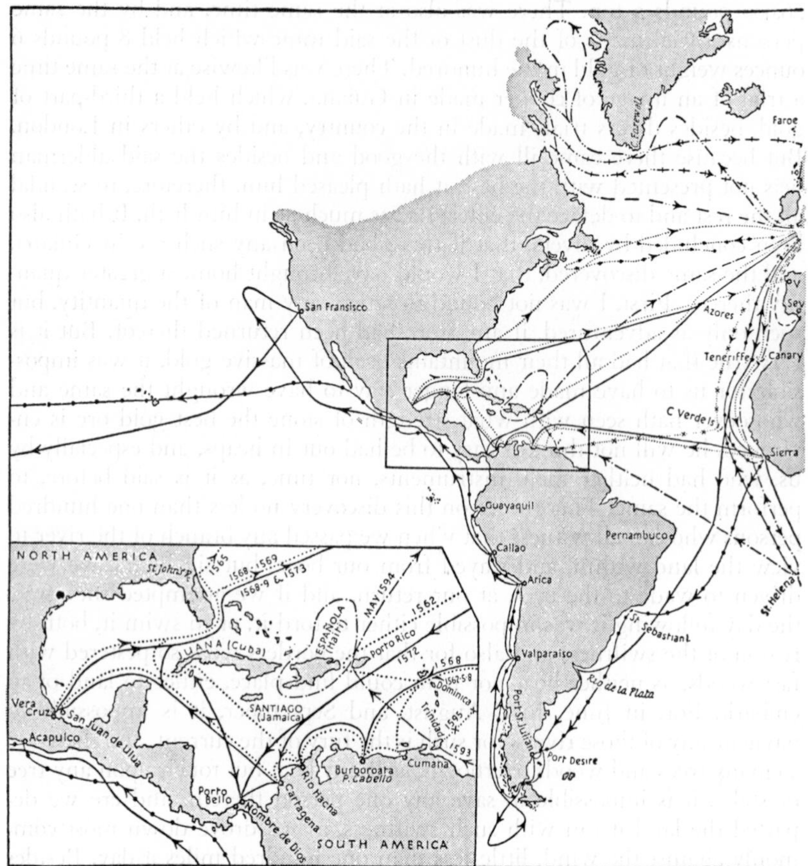

Elizabethan Voyages

or buying of gold ore in Barbary. But I hope the better sort will judge me by themselves and that the way of deceit is not the way of honor or good opinion. I have herein consumed much time and many crowns and I had no other respect or desire than to serve her Majesty and my country thereby. If the Spanish nation had been of like belief to these detractors, we should little have feared or doubted their attempts, wherewith we now are daily threatened. But if we now consider the actions both of Charles V, who had the maidenhead of Peru, and the abundant treasures of Atabalipa, together with the affairs of the Spanish King now living, what territories he hath purchased, what he hath added to the acts of his predecessors, how many kingdoms he hath endangered, how many armies, garrisons, and navies he hath and doth maintain, the great losses which he hath repaired, as in '88 above one hundred sail of great ships with their artillery, and that no year is less unfortunate but that many vessels, treasures, and people are devoured, and yet notwithstanding he beginneth again like a storm to threaten

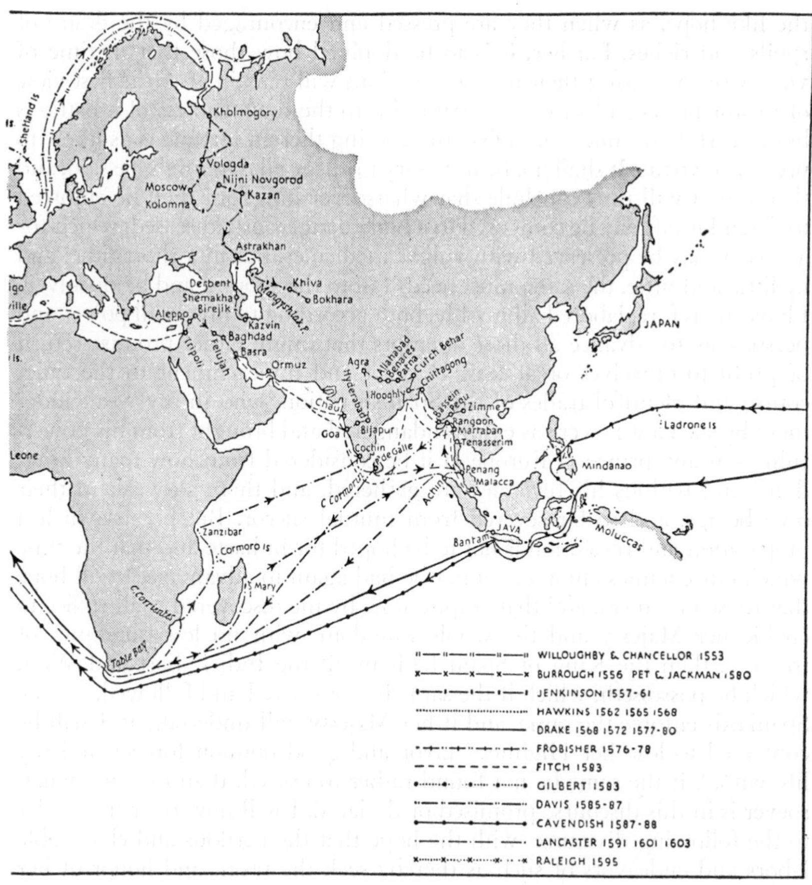

Courtesy J. B. Black, The Reign of Elizabeth

shipwreck to us all—we shall find that these abilities rise not from the trades of sacks and Seville oranges,[36] nor from aught else than either Spain, Portugal, or any of his other provinces produce. It is his Indian gold that endangered and disturbed all the nations of Europe. It purchased intelligence, creepeth into councils, and setteth bound loyalty at liberty in the greatest monarchies of Europe. If the Spanish King can keep us from foreign enterprises and from the impeachment of his trades, either by offer of invasion, or by besieging us in Britain, Ireland, or elsewhere, he hath then brought the work of our peril in great forwardness. Those princes which abound in treasure have great advantages over the rest, if they once constrain them to a defensive war, where they are driven once a year or oftener to cast lots for their own garments, and from such shall all trades and intercourse be taken away, to the general loss and impoverishment of the kingdom and commonweal so reduced. Besides, when our men are constrained to fight, it hath not

[36] *sacks and Seville oranges:* wines and bitter oranges.

the like hope, as when they are pressed and encouraged by the desire of spoils and riches. Farther, it is to be doubted how those that in time of victory seem to affect their neighbor nations will remain after the first view of misfortunes or ill success; to trust also to the doubtfulness of a battle is but a fearful and uncertain adventure, seeing therein fortune is as likely to prevail, as virtue. It shall not be necessary to allege all that might be said, and therefore, I will thus conclude that whatsoever kingdom shall be enforced to defend itself may be compared to a body dangerously diseased, which for a season may be preserved with vulgar medicines, but in a short time, and by little and little, the same must needs fall to the ground and be dissolved. I have, therefore, labored all my life, both according to my small power and persuasion, to advance all those attempts that might either promise return of profit to ourselves or at least be a let and impeachment to the quiet course and plentiful trades of the Spanish nation, who in my weak judgment by such a war were as easily endangered and brought from his powerfulness as any prince of Europe, if it be considered from how many kingdoms and nations his revenues are gathered, and those so weak in their own beings, and so far severed from mutual succor. But because such a preparation and resolution is not to be hoped for in haste and that the time which our enemies embrace cannot be had again to advantage, I will hope that these provinces, and that empire now by me discovered shall suffice to enable her Majesty and the whole kingdom, with no less quantities of treasure, than the King of Spain hath in all the Indies, East and West, which he possesseth, which if the same be considered and followed, ere the Spaniards enforce the same, and if her Majesty will undertake it, I will be contented to lose her Highness' favor and good opinion forever and my life withal, if the same be not found rather to exceed, than to equal whatsoever is in this discourse promised or declared. I will now refer the reader to the following discourse, with the hope that the perilous and chargeable labors and endeavors of such as thereby seek the profit and honor of her Majesty, and the English nation, shall by men of quality and virtue receive such construction, and good acceptance, as themselves would look to be rewarded withal in the like.

W. R.

FROM

THE HISTORY OF THE WORLD

BUT for myself, I shall never be persuaded that God hath shut up all light of learning within the lantern of Aristotle's brains; or that it was ever said unto him, as unto Esdras, *Accendam in corde tuo lucernam intellectus;*[37] that God hath given invention but to the heathen, and that they only have invaded nature, and found the strength and bottom thereof; the same nature having consumed all her store, and left nothing of price to after-ages. That these and these be the causes of these and these effects, time hath taught us, and not reason; and so hath experience, without art. The cheese-wife knoweth it as well as the philosopher that sour runnet[38] doth coagulate her milk into a curd. But if we ask a reason of this cause, why the sourness doth it, whereby it doth it, and the manner how, I think that there is nothing to be found in vulgar philosophy to satisfy this and many other like vulgar questions. But man, to cover his ignorance in the least things, who cannot give a true reason for the grass under his feet, why it should be green rather than red or of any other color; that could never yet discover the way and reason of nature's working in those which are far less noble creatures than himself, who is far more noble than the heavens themselves; "Man," saith Solomon, "that can hardly discern the things that are upon the earth, and with great labor find out the things that are before us";[39] that hath so short a time in the world as he no sooner begins to learn than to die; that hath in his memory but borrowed knowledge; in his understanding, nothing truly; that is ignorant of the essence of his own soul, and which the wisest of the naturalists (if Aristotle be he) could never so much as define but by the action and effect, telling us what it works (which all men know as well as he), but not what it is, which neither he nor any else doth know but God that created it ("For though I were perfect, yet I know not my soul," saith Job)[40]—man, I say, that is but an idiot in the next cause of his own life, and in the cause of all the actions of his life, will, notwithstanding, examine the art of God in creating the world; of God, who, saith Job, "is so excellent as we know him not";[41] and examine the beginning of the work which had end before mankind had a beginning of being. He will disable God's power to make a world without matter to make it of. He will rather give the motes of the air for a cause; cast the work on neces-

[37] *Accendam . . . intellectus:* "I shall light a candle of understanding in thine heart" II. Esdras 14:25.

[38] *runnet:* rennet, used to curdle milk.

[39] Ecclesiastes 8:17.

[40] Job 9:21.

[41] Job 36:26.

sity or chance; bestow the honor thereof on Nature; make two powers, the one to be the author of the matter, the other of the form; and lastly, for want of a workman, have it eternal. Which latter opinion Aristotle, to make himself the author of a new doctrine, brought into the world and his sectators have maintained it.

* * *

If the phrase be weak and the style not everywhere like itself, the first shows their legitimation and true parent; the second will excuse itself upon the variety of matter. For Virgil, who wrote his eclogues *gracili avena,*[42] used stronger pipes when he sounded the wars of Aeneas. It may also be laid to my charge that I use divers Hebrew words in my first book and elsewhere, in which language others may think (and I myself acknowledge it) that I am altogether ignorant; but it is true that some of them I find in Montanus, others, in Latin character, in S. Senensis, and of the rest I have borrowed the interpretation of some of my learned friends. But say I had been beholding to neither, yet were it not to be wondered at, having had eleven years' leisure to attain the knowledge of that or any other tongue.

Howsoever, I know that it will be said by many, that I might have been more pleasing to the reader if I had written the story of mine own times, having been permitted to draw water as near the well-head as another. To this I answer that whosoever in writing a modern history shall follow truth too near the heels, it may haply strike out his teeth. There is no mistress or guide that hath led her followers and servants into greater miseries. He that goes after her too far off loseth her sight and loseth himself; and he that walks after her at a middle distance, I know not whether I should call that kind of course temper or baseness.

It is true that I never travailed after men's opinions when I might have made the best use of them; and I have now too few days remaining to imitate those that, either out of extreme ambition or extreme cowardice or both, do yet, when death hath them on his shoulders, flatter the world between the bed and the grave. It is enough for me, being in that state I am, to write of the eldest times; wherein also why may it not be said that in speaking of the past I point at the present, and tax the vices of those that are yet living in their persons that are long since dead, and have it laid to my charge. But this I cannot help, though innocent. And certainly if there be any that, finding themselves spotted like the tigers of old time, shall find fault with me for painting them over anew, they shall therein accuse themselves justly and me falsely.

---

[42] *gracili avena:* with slender pipe, in simple style.

[GUESSWORK AND CERTAINTY IN GEOGRAPHY AND HISTORY]

I neither do reprehend the boldness of Torniellus in conjecturing, nor the modesty of Scaliger and Sethus Calvisius [43] in forbearing to set down as warrantable such things as depend only upon likelihood. For things whereof the perfect knowledge is taken away from us by antiquity must be described in history; as geographers in their maps describe those countries whereof as yet there is made no true discovery—that is, either by leaving some part blank, or by inserting The Land of Pigmies, Rocks of Lodestone, with headlands, bays, great rivers and other particularities agreeable to common report though many times controlled by following experience and found contrary to truth. Yet indeed the ignorance growing from distance of place allows not such liberty to a describer as that which ariseth from the remedyless oblivion of consuming time. For it is true that the poet saith:

neque fervidis
pars inclusa caloribus
mundi, nec Boreae finitium latus,
durataeque sole nives,
mercatorem abigunt: horrida callidi
vincunt aequora navitiae.

Nor southern heat nor northern snow
That freezing to the ground doth grow
The subject regions can fence
And keep the greedy merchant thence.
The subtle shipmen way will find,
Storm never so the seas with wind.

Therefore the fictions, or let them be called conjectures, painted in maps do serve only to mislead such discoverers as rashly believe them, drawing upon the publishers either some angry curses or well-deserved scorn; but to keep their own credit, they cannot serve always.

To which purpose I remember a pretty jest of Don Pedro de Sarmiento, a worthy Spanish gentleman who had been employed by his king in planting a colony upon the Straits of Magellan. For when I asked him, being then my prisoner, some question about an island in those straits which methought might have done either benefit or displeasure to his enterprise, he told me merrily that it was to be called Painter's Wife's Island—saying that whilst the fellow drew that map, his wife, sitting by, desired him to

[43] *Calvisius:* Seth Kallwitz (1556–1615), writer on music.

put in one country for her, that she, in imagination, might have an island of her own.

But in filling up the blanks of old histories, we need not be so scrupulous. For it is not to be feared that time should run backward and, by restoring the things themselves to knowledge, make our conjectures appear ridiculous. What if some good copy of an ancient author could be found, showing, if we have it not already, the perfect truth of these uncertainties? Would it have been more shame to have believed, in the meanwhile, Annius or Torniellus than to have believed nothing? Here I will not say that the credit which we give to Annius may chance otherwhiles to be given to one of those authors whose names he pretendeth. Let it suffice that in regard of authority, I had rather trust Scaliger or Torniellus than Annius; yet [rather] him than them, if his assertion be more probable and more agreeable to approved histories than their conjecture (as in this point it seems to me), it having moreover gotten some credit by the approbation of many, and those not meanly learned.

[LEGENDS OF BEASTS GUARDING TREASURE]

Tostatus also gathereth a fantastical opinion out of Rabanus,[44] who makes Ophir to be a country whose mountains of gold are kept by griffins, which mountains Solinus affirmeth to be in Scythia Asiatica, in these words: *Nam cum auro et gemmis affluant, griphes tenent universa, alites ferocissimae, Arimaspi cum his dimicant,* etc. "For whereas these countries abound in gold and rich stone, the griffins defend the one and the other (a kind of fowl the fiercest of all other), with which griffins a nation of people called Arimaspi make war."

These Arimaspi are said to have been men with one eye only, like unto the Cyclops of Sicily, of which Cyclops Herodotus and Aristeus make mention, and so doth Lucan in his third book, and Valerius Flaccus, and D. Siculus in the story of Alexander Macedon. But, for mine own opinion, I believe none of them. And for these Arimaspi, I take it that this name signifying "One-eyed" was first given them by reason that they used to wear a vizard of defence with one sight in the middle to serve both eyes, and not that they had by nature any such defect. But Solinus borroweth these things out of Pliny, who speaks of such a nation in the extreme north, at a place called Gisolitron, or the Cave of the Northeast Wind. For the rest, as all fables were commonly grounded upon some true stories or other things done, so might these tales of the griffins receive this moral: that if those men which fight against so many dangerous passages for gold, or other riches of this world, had their perfect senses and were

[44] *Rabanus:* Hrabanus Maurus Magnentius (776–856), theological writer.

not deprived of half of their eyesight, at least of the eye of right reason and understanding, they would content themselves with a quiet and moderate estate, and not subject themselves to famine, corrupt air, violent heat and cold, and to all sorts of miserable diseases.

And though this fable be fained in this place, yet if such a tale were told of some other places of the world where wild beasts or serpents defend mountains of gold, it might be avowed. For there are in many places of the world, especially in America, many high and impassable mountains which are very rich and full of gold, inhabited only with tigers, lions and other ravenous and cruel beasts, into which if any man ascend, except his strength be very great, he shall be sure to find the same war which the Arimaspi make against the griffins. Not that the one or other had any sense of gold, or seek to defend that metal, but being disquieted or made afraid, of themselves or their young ones, they grow enraged and adventurous. In like sort it may be said that the alligators (which the Egyptians call the crocodiles) defend those pearls which lie in the lakes of the inland, for many times the poor Indians are eaten up by them when they dive for the pearl. And though the alligators know not the pearl, yet they find favor in the flesh and blood of the Indians, whom they devour.

[OF THE LAST REFUGES OF THE DEVIL TO MAINTAIN HIS KINGDOM]

Now the Devil, because he cannot play upon the open stage of this world as in those days, and being still as industrious as ever, finds it more for his advantage to creep into the minds of men, and, inhabiting in the temples of their hearts, works them to a more effectual adoration of himself than ever. For whereas he first taught them to sacrifice to monsters, to dead stones cut into faces of beasts, birds and other mixed natures, he now sets before them the high and shining idol of glory, the all-commanding image of bright gold. He tells them that Truth is the goddess of dangers and oppressions; that chastity is the enemy of nature; and, lastly, that as all virtue, in general, is without taste, so pleasure satisfieth and delighteth every sense. For true wisdom, saith he, is exercised in nothing else than in the obtaining of power to oppress and of riches to maintain plentifully our worldly delights. And if this arch-politician find in his pupils any remorse, any fear or feeling of God's future judgment, he persuades them that God hath so great need of men's souls that he will accept them at any time and upon any conditions (interrupting by his vigilant endeavors all offer of timeful return towards God by laying those great blocks of rugged poverty and despised contempt in the narrow passage leading to his divine presence). But as the mind of man hath two ports, the one always frequented by the entrance of manifold vanities, the other desolate and overgrown with grass, by which enter our charitable thoughts and divine contemplations; so hath that of death a double and twofold opening, worldly misery passing by the one, worldly prosperity by the other. At the entrance of the one we find our sufferings and patience to attend us, all which have gone before us to prepare our joys; at the other our cruelties, covetousness, licentiousness, injustice and oppressions, the harbingers of most fearful and terrible sorrow, staying for us. And as the Devil, our most industrious enemy, was ever most diligent, so is he now more laborious than ever, the long day of mankind drawing fast towards an evening and the world's tragedy and time near at an end.

[THE CONCLUSION OF THE HISTORY]

Now these great kings and conquering nations have been the subject of those ancient histories which have been preserved and yet remain among us, and withal of so many tragical poets, as in the persons of powerful princes and other mighty men have complained against infidelity, time, destiny, and most of all against the variable success of worldly things and instability of fortune. To these undertakings the greatest lords of the world have been stirred up rather by the desire of fame, which ploweth up the air and soweth in the wind, than by the affection of bearing rule, which draweth after it so much vexation and so many cares. And that this is true, the good advice of Cineas to Pyrrhus[45] proves. And certainly, as fame hath often been dangerous to the living, so is it to the dead of no use at all, because separate from knowledge. Which, were it otherwise, and the extreme ill bargain of buying this lasting discourse understood by them which are dissolved; they themselves would then rather have wished to have stolen out of the world without noise than to be put in mind that they have purchased the report of their actions in the world by rapine, oppression and cruelty, by giving in spoil the innocent and laboring soul to the idle and insolent, and by having emptied the cities of the world of their ancient inhabitants and filled them again with so many and so variable sorts of sorrows.

Since the fall of the Roman Empire (omitting that of the Germans, which had neither greatness nor continuance) there hath been no state fearful in the East but that of the Turk; nor in the West any prince that hath spread his wings far over his nest but the Spaniard, who, since the time that Ferdinand expelled the Moors out of Granada, have made many attempts to make themselves masters of all Europe. And it is true that, by the treasures of both Indies and by the many kingdoms which they possess in Europe, they are at this day the most powerful. But as the Turk is

[45] Plutarch tells how Cineas tried to persuade Pyrrhus that the pleasures anticipated from conquest are available without the toil and peril of war.

now counterpoised by the Persian, so instead of so many millions as have been spent by the English, French and Netherlands in a defensive war, and in diversions against them, it is easy to demonstrate that with the charge of two hundred thousand pound continued but for two years or three at the most, they may not only be persuaded to live in peace, but all their swelling and overflowing streams may be brought back into their natural channels and old banks. These two nations, I say, are at this day the most eminent and to be regarded—the one seeking to root out the Christian religion altogether, the other, the truth and sincere profession thereof; the one, to join all Europe to Asia, the other, the rest of all Europe to Spain.

For the rest, if we seek a reason of the succession and continuance of this boundless ambition in mortal men, we may add to that which hath been already said, that the kings and princes of the world have always laid before them the actions, but not the ends, of those great ones which preceded them. They are always transported with the glory of the one, but they never mind the misery of the other till they find the experience in themselves. They neglect the advice of God while they enjoy life, or hope it; but they follow the counsel of Death upon his first approach. It is he that puts into man all the wisdom of the world, without speaking a word, which God, with all the words of his law, promises, or threats, doth not infuse. Death, which hateth and destroyeth man, is believed; God, which hath made him and loves him, is always deferred. "I have considered," saith Solomon, "all the works that are under the sun, and, behold, all is vanity and vexation of spirit,"[46] but who believes it till Death tells it us? It was Death which, opening the conscience of Charles the Fifth, made him enjoin his son Philip to restore Navarre; and King Francis the First of France to command that justice should be done upon the murderers of the Protestants in Merindol and Cabrières, which till then he neglected. It is therefore Death alone that can suddenly make man to know himself. He tells the proud and insolent that they are but abjects, and humbles them at the instant; makes them cry, complain, and repent, yea, even to hate their forepast happiness. He takes the account of the rich, and proves him a beggar, a naked beggar, which hath interest in nothing but in the gravel that fills his mouth. He holds a glass before the eyes of the most beautiful, and makes them see therein their deformity and rottenness, and they acknowledge it.

O eloquent, just, and mighty Death! whom none could advise, thou hast persuaded; what none hath dared, thou hast done; and whom all the world hath flattered, thou only hast cast out of the world and despised; thou has drawn together all the far-stretched greatness, all the pride, cruelty, and ambition of man, and covered it all over with these two narrow words, *Hic jacet!*

---

[46] Ecclesiastes 1:14.

Methought I saw the grave where Laura lay,[1]
Within that temple where the vestal flame
Was wont to burn; and passing by that way
To see that buried dust of living fame,
Whose tomb fair love and fairer virtue kept,
All suddenly I saw the Fairy Queen;
At whose approach the soul of Petrarch wept,
And from thenceforth those graces were not seen,
For they this Queen attended; in whose stead
Oblivion laid him down on Laura's hearse.
Hereat the hardest stones were seen to bleed,
And groans of buried ghosts the heavens did pierce;
Where Homer's sprite did tremble all for grief,
And cursed th' access of that celestial thief.

THE NYMPH'S REPLY[2] TO THE SHEPHERD

If all the world and love were young,
And truth in every shepherd's tongue,
These pretty pleasures might me move
To live with thee and be thy love.

Time drives the flocks from field to fold
When rivers rage and rocks grow cold,
And Philomel [3] becometh dumb;
The rest complains of cares to come.

The flowers do fade, and wanton fields
To wayward winter reckoning yields;
A honey tongue, a heart of gall,
Is fancy's spring, but sorrow's fall.

Thy gowns, thy shoes, thy beds of roses,
Thy cap, thy kirtle, and thy posies
Soon break, soon wither, soon forgotten,—
In folly ripe, in reason rotten.

---

[1] A commendatory sonnet prefixed to Spenser's *Faerie Queene* (1590). Ralegh was a patron of Spenser; he brought him to court and encouraged the publication of his great work. *Laura:* the lady celebrated in Petrarch's sonnets.

[2] *Nymph's reply:* an answer to Marlowe's poem on p. 393. Donne, Herrick, and another, anonymous, poet, in *England's Helicon* (1600), also wrote imitations of Marlowe's poem.

[3] *Philomel:* the nightingale.

Thy belt of straw and ivy buds,
Thy coral clasps and amber studs,
All these in me no means can move
To come to thee and be thy love.

But could youth last and love still breed,
Had joys no date [4] nor age no need,
Then these delights my mind might move
To live with thee and be thy love.

WHAT is our life? a play of passion; [5]
Our mirth, the music of division; [6]
Our mothers' wombs the tiring-houses [7] be
Where we are dressed for this short comedy.
Heaven the judicious sharp spectator is,
That sits and marks still [8] who doth act amiss;
Our graves that hide us from the searching sun
Are like drawn curtains when the play is done.
Thus march we playing to our latest rest;
Only we die in earnest—that's no jest.

LIKE to a hermit poor in place obscure
I mean to spend my days of endless doubt,
To wail such woes as time cannot recure,
Where none but love shall ever find me out.
My food shall be of care and sorrow made,
My drink naught else but tears fall'n from mine eyes;
And for my light in such obscured shade
The flames shall serve which from my heart arise.
A gown of gray my body shall attire,
My staff of broken hope whereon I'll stay;
Of late repentance linked with long desire
The couch is framed whereon my limbs I'll lay;
And at my gate despair shall linger still
To let in death when love and fortune will.

---

[4] *date:* ending.

[5] Set to music by Orlando Gibbons, in *The First Set of Madrigals and Motets* (1612).

[6] *music of division:* the more rapid accompaniment to, or variation on, a theme.

[7] *tiring-houses:* dressing rooms.

[8] *still:* constantly.

NATURE, that washed her hands in milk,[9]
And had forgot to dry them,
Instead of earth took snow and silk,
At love's request to try them,
If she a mistress could compose
To please love's fancy out of those.

Her eyes he would should be of light,
A violet breath, and lips of jelly;
Her hair not black, nor overbright,
And of the softest down her belly;
As for her inside he'd have it
Only of wantonness and wit.

At love's entreaty such a one
Nature made, but with her beauty
She hath framed a heart of stone;
So as love, by ill destiny,
Must die for her whom nature gave him,
Because her darling would not save him.

But time (which nature doth despise,
And rudely gives her love the lie,
Makes hope a fool, and sorrow wise)
His hands do neither wash nor dry;
But being made of steel and rust,
Turns snow and silk and milk to dust.

The light, the belly, lips, and breath,
He dims, discolors, and destroys;
With those he feeds but fills not death,
Which sometimes were the food of joys.
Yea, time doth dull each lively wit,
And dries all wantonness with it.

Oh, cruel time! which takes in trust
Our youth, our joys, and all we have,
And pays us but with age and dust;
Who in the dark and silent grave
When we have wandered all our ways
Shuts up the story of our days.

---

9 This poem survived in several MSS, but was not published until 1902. In the year of Ralegh's death, however, the following expanded version of the last stanza was published with the heading "By Sir W. R. which he writ the night before his execution."

Even such is time, which takes in trust
Our youth, our joys, and all we have,
And pays us but with age and dust,
Within the dark and silent grave;
When we have wavered all our ways,
Shuts up the story of our days,
And from which earth, and grave, and dust,
The Lord will raise me up, I trust.

See V. B. Heltzel, *Huntington Library Bulletin,* No. 10 (1936), 185–188.

THE LIE[10]

Go, soul, the body's guest,
Upon a thankless errand;
Fear not to touch the best;
The truth shall be thy warrant.
Go, since I needs must die,
And give the world the lie.

Say to the court, it glows
And shines like rotten wood;
Say to the church, it shows
What's good, and doth no good.
If church and court reply,
Then give them both the lie.

Tell potentates, they live
Acting by others' action;
Not loved unless they give,
Not strong but by a faction.
If potentates reply,
Give potentates the lie.

Tell men of high condition,
That manage the estate,
Their purpose is ambition,
Their practise only hate.
And if they once reply,
Then give them all the lie.

Tell them that brave it most,
They beg for more by spending,
Who, in their greatest cost,
Seek nothing but commending.
And if they make reply,
Then give them all the lie.

Tell zeal it wants devotion;
Tell love it is but lust;
Tell time it is but motion;
Tell flesh it is but dust.
And wish them not reply,
For thou must give the lie.

---

[10] This poem provoked many answers.

Tell age it daily wasteth;
Tell honor how it alters;
Tell beauty how she blasteth;
Tell favor how it falters.
And as they shall reply,
Give every one the lie.

Tell wit how much it wrangles
In tickle [11] points of niceness;
Tell wisdom she entangles
Herself in overwiseness.
And when they do reply,
Straight give them both the lie.

Tell physic of her boldness;
Tell skill it is pretension;
Tell charity of coldness;
Tell law it is contention.
And as they do reply,
So give them still the lie.

Tell fortune of her blindness;
Tell nature of decay;
Tell friendship of unkindness;
Tell justice of delay.
And if they will reply,
Then give them all the lie.

Tell arts they have no soundness,
But vary by esteeming;
Tell schools they want profoundness,
And stand too much on seeming.
If arts and schools reply,
Give arts and schools the lie.

Tell faith it's fled the city;
Tell how the country erreth;
Tell manhood shakes off pity;
Tell virtue least preferreth.
And if they do reply,
Spare not to give the lie.

So when thou hast, as I
Commanded thee, done blabbing—
Although to give the lie
Deserves no less than stabbing—
Stab at thee he that will,
No stab the soul can kill.

[11] *tickle:* delicate.

THE PASSIONATE MAN'S PILGRIMAGE[12]

Give me my scallop-shell[13] of quiet,
My staff of faith to walk upon,
My scrip of joy, immortal diet,
My bottle of salvation,
My gown of glory, hope's true gage,[14]
And thus I'll take my pilgrimage.

Blood must be my body's balmer,
No other balm will there be given,
Whilst my soul like a white palmer
Travels to the land of heaven,
Over the silver mountains,
Where spring the nectar fountains;
And there I'll kiss
The bowl of bliss,
And drink my eternal fill
On every milken hill.
My soul will be a-dry before,
But after it will ne'er thirst more;
And by the happy blissful way
More peaceful pilgrims I shall see
That have shook off their gowns of clay
And go appareled fresh like me.
I'll bring them first
To slake their thirst,
And then to taste those nectar suckets,[15]
At the clear wells
Where sweetness dwells,
Drawn up by saints in crystal buckets.

And when our bottles and all we
Are filled with immortality,
Then the holy paths we'll travel,
Strewed with rubies thick as gravel,
Ceilings of diamonds, sapphire floors,
High walls of coral, and pearl bowers,
From thence to heaven's bribeless hall
Where no corrupted voices brawl,
No conscience molten into gold,

---

[12] First printed in Anthony Scoloker's *Diaphantus* (1604).

[13] *scallop-shell:* symbol of a pilgrim.

[14] *gage:* pledge, pawn, forfeit.

[15] *suckets:* sweetmeats.

Nor forged accusers bought and sold,
No cause deferred, nor vain-spent journey,
For there Christ is the king's attorney,
Who pleads for all, without degrees,
And he hath angels,[16] but no fees.
When the grand twelve million jury
Of our sins and sinful fury,
'Gainst our souls black verdicts give,
Christ pleads his death, and then we live.
Be thou my speaker, taintless pleader,
Unblotted [17] lawyer, true proceeder;
Thou movest salvation even for alms,
Not with a bribed lawyer's palms.
And this is my eternal plea
To him that made heaven, earth, and sea,
Seeing my flesh must die so soon,
And want a head to dine next noon,
Just at the stroke when my veins start and spread,
Set on my soul an everlasting head.
Then am I ready, like a palmer fit,
To tread those blest paths which before I writ.

Farewell, false love, the oracle of lies,[18]
A mortal foe and enemy to rest;
An envious boy, from whom all cares arise,
A bastard vile, a beast with rage possessed;
A way of error, a temple full of treason,
In all effects contrary unto reason.

A poisoned serpent covered all with flowers,
Mother of sighs and murtherer of repose,
A sea of sorrows from whence are drawn such showers
As moisture lends to every grief that grows;
A school of guile, a net of deep deceit,
A gilded hook that holds a poisoned bait.

---

16 *angels:* a pun on the coin of that name, worth about 10 shillings.

17 *unblotted:* unsullied.

18 Set to music by William Byrd in *Psalmes, Sonets and Songs* (1588). Aside from a prefatory sonnet to Gascoigne's *Steel Glass* (1576), this is the earliest of Ralegh's poems to appear in print.

A fortress foiled [19] which reason did defend,
A siren song, a fever of the mind,
A maze wherein affection finds no end,
A raging cloud that runs before the wind,
A substance like the shadow of the sun,
A goal of grief for which the wisest run.

A quenchless fire, a nurse of trembling fear,
A path that leads to peril and mishap;
A true retreat of sorrow and despair,
An idle boy that sleeps in pleasure's lap,
A deep distrust of that which certain seems,
A hope of that which reason doubtful deems.

Sith then thy trains [20] my younger years betrayed,
And for my faith ingratitude I find,
And sith repentance hath my wrongs bewrayed [21]
Whose course was ever contrary to kind—
False love, desire, and beauty frail, adieu!
Dead is the root whence all these fancies grew.

[19] *foiled:* overthrown.
[20] *Sith:* since; *trains:* tricks, stratagems.
[21] *bewrayed:* revealed.

The Sonnet Cycles

BETWEEN the time when Wyatt and Surrey showed the possibilities offered by the sonnet in English and the penultimate decade of the sixteenth century, little was done with the form. Gascoigne, in his *Certain Notes of Instruction* (1575), defined the sonnet, and most poets made use of it for dedications and occasional poems, but it was only in the eighties that the great vogue of the cycle of sonnets, addressed by the poet to a mistress real or imaginary, began. Petrarch, with his sonnets to Laura, was the ultimate model, but the English poets found themes and ideas in lesser Italians and in the many French imitators of the Italians.

The sonnet is a highly artificial form; the sonnet cycle, with its conventional themes (the lover's woes, the mistress' beauty, Cupid's behavior, sleep, eternal fame, etc.), its conceits drawn from natural science, navigation, law, medicine, war, etc., is just as artificial. But dependence upon a French or Italian source, or the adoption of familiar and well-understood conventions, does not mean deadness or sterility. An Elizabethan poet was interested primarily in the poem itself, not in the relationship between that poem and the poet's personal or private life, nor in the claim to "originality" which certain Romantic doctrines substitute for excellence.

A few actual ladies are represented by the poetical names: Sidney's Stella was Penelope Devereux, Lady Rich, and she was also apparently Constable's Diana; Drayton's Idea was probably Ann Goodere, the daughter of the poet's patron; and Daniel's Delia may have been the Countess of Pembroke, the patroness herself. But even this circumstance does not warrant the reading of any cycle as strict autobiography. Dr. Giles Fletcher gave a playful warning that his Licia might be "learning's image, or some heavenly wonder which the precisest may not mislike. . . . It may be my conceit, and pretend nothing."

About two dozen sonnet cycles from this period survive. Their poets include Sidney, Spenser, Shakespeare, Constable, Daniel, Drayton, Lodge, and Drummond, as well as poets whose names we do not know. The sonnets illustrate all varieties of quality and all varieties of taste. The rise and fall of the vogue of the sonnet cycle is a typical chapter in literary history. It begins with the violent enthusiasm with which Nashe introduced the first surreptitious edition of *Astrophel and Stella* in 1591: "Wherefore, break off your dance, you fairies and elves! and from the fields, with the torn carcasses of your timbrels! for your kingdom is expired. Put out your rushlights, you poets and rhymers! and bequeath your crazed quatorzains to the chandlers! for lo, here he cometh that hath broken your legs." And the end is coming when Sir John Davies pens his "gulling" sonnets and the virile voice of Donne expresses a reaction against Petrarchism.

BIBLIOGRAPHY: Sidney Lee, *Elizabethan Sonnets,* Westminster, 1904; Janet G. Scott, *Les Sonnets Elisabéthains,* Paris, 1929; S. Daniel, *Poems and A Defence of Rhyme,* ed. A. C. Sprague, Harvard, 1930; Ruth Hughey, "The Harington MS at Arundel Castle," *4 Library XV* (1935), 388–444; L. C. John, *The Elizabethan Sonnet Sequences,* Columbia, 1938.

HENRY CONSTABLE

DIANA (1592)

DECADE V, Sonnets viii and ix[1]

Dear to my soul, then leave me not forsaken!
Fly not, my heart within thy bosom sleepeth.
Even from myself and sense I have betaken
Me unto thee for whom my spirit weepeth,
And on the shore of that salt teary sea,
Couched in a bed of unseen seeming pleasure,
Where in imaginary thoughts thy fair self lay;
But being waked, robbed of my life's best treasure,
I call the heavens, air, earth, and seas to hear
My love, my truth, and black disdained estate;
Beating the rocks with bellowings of despair,
Which still with plaints my words reverberate;
Sighing, "Alas, what shall become of me?"
Whilst echo cries, "What shall become of me?"

Whilst echo cries, "What shall become of me?"[2]
And desolate, my desolations pity,
Thou in thy beauty's carrack[3] sit'st to see
My tragic downfall, and my funeral ditty.
No timbrel,[4] but my heart thou play'st upon,
Whose strings are stretched unto the highest key;
The diapason, love; love is the unison;[5]

---

[1] The 1594 edition of *Diana* is divided into eight "decades," or groups of ten sonnets each.

[2] An example of "linking" sonnets by repeating the last line of one as the first line of the next.

[3] *carrack:* a large armed merchant ship, of the type used by the Spaniards to transport treasure from the New World.

[4] *timbrel:* tamborine.

[5] *diapason, unison:* the harmony of all the notes and the single line of melody. "Diapason" could refer to a chord struck on a lute as well as to the more familiar organ effect.

In love my life and labors waste away.
Only regardless to the world thou leav'st me,
Whilst slain hopes, turning from the feast of sorrow
Unto despair, their king which ne'er deceives me,
Captives my heart, whose black night hates the morrow;
And he in ruth of my distressed cry
Plants me a weeping star within my eye.

DECADE VI, Sonnet II [6]

To live in hell and heaven to behold;
To welcome life and die a living death;
To sweat with heat, and yet be freezing cold;
To grasp at stars and lie the earth beneath;
To tread a maze that never shall have end;
To burn in sighs and starve [7] in daily tears;
To climb a hill and never to descend;
Giants to kill, and quake at childish fears;
To pine for food, and watch th' Hesperian tree; [8]
To thirst for drink, and nectar still to draw;
To live accursed, whom men hold blest to be,
And weep those wrongs which never creature saw:
If this be love, if love in these be founded,
My heart is love, for these in it are grounded.

FROM

TODD MS

III, IV [9]

Miracle of the world, I never will deny
That former poets praise the beauty of their days,

[6] Based on Desportes, *Diane,* I, xxix. Compare Daniel's Sonnet IX, p. 646, below.

[7] *starve:* to die gradually, not necessarily of hunger.

[8] *Hesperian tree:* a tree which bore the golden apples finally secured by Hercules.

[9] Printed in Park's *Harleian Miscellany,* IX, 498–499.

The MS is now Dyce MS 44 at the South Kensington Museum. In this MS the sonnets are divided into three parts, each part having three arguments and each argument seven sonnets. Part I, of the "variable affections of love," treats the beginning of his love (first 7), the praise of his mistress (second 7), and "several accidents happening in the time of his love" (third 7). This sonnet is No. 4 of the third 7. It is labeled "To his mistress upon occasion of a Petrarch he gave her, showing the reason why the Italian commentators dissent so much in the exposition thereof." The theme resembles that of Shakespeare's Sonnet CVI.

But all those beauties were but figures of thy praise
And all those poets did of thee but prophesy.
Thy coming to the world hath taught us to descry
What Petrarch's Laura meant, for truth the lip bewrays.
Lo, why th' Italians, yet which never saw thy rays,
To find out Petrach's sense such forged glosses try:
The beauties which he in a veil enclosed beheld
But revelations were within his secret heart,
By which in parables thy coming he foretold.
His songs were hymns of thee, which only now before
Thy image should be sung; for thou that goddess art
Which only we without idolatry adore.

FROM

HARLEIAN MS 7553

TO ST. PETER AND ST. PAUL[10]

He that for fear his Master did deny,
And at a maiden's voice amazed stood,
The mightiest monarch of the earth withstood,
And on his Master's cross rejoiced to die.
He whose blind zeal did rage with cruelty
And helped to shed the first of martyrs' blood,
By light from heaven his blindness understood,
And with the chief apostle slain doth lie.
Oh three times happy two! Oh golden pair!
Who with your blood did lay the church's ground
Within the fatal town which twins did found,
And settled there the Hebrew fisher's chair
Where first the Latin shepherd raised his throne,
And since, the world and church were ruled by one.

[10] Constable was a Catholic. His religious sonnets were not published in Elizabethan times, but survive in Harleian MS 7553 in the British Museum and were printed by Park in *Heliconia,* Vol. II.

THOMAS LODGE

PHILLIS (1593)

XIII[11]

Love guards the roses of thy lips
And flies about them like a bee;
If I approach he forward skips,
And if I kiss he stingeth me.
Love in thine eyes doth build his bower,
And sleeps within their pretty shine;
And if I look the boy will lour,
And from their orbs shoot shafts divine.
Love works thy heart within his fire,
And in my tears doth firm the same;
And if I tempt it will retire,
And of my plaints doth make a game.
Love, let me cull her choicest flowers,
And pity me, and calm her eye,
Make soft her heart, dissolve her lours,
Then will I praise thy deity.
But if thou do not, Love, I'll truly serve her
In spite of thee, and by firm faith deserve her.

XXXI[12]

Devoid of reason, thrall to foolish ire,
I walk and chase a savage fairy still,
Now near the flood, straight on the mounting hill.
Now midst the woods of youth and vain desire.
For leash I bear a cord of careful grief;
For brach[13] I lead an overforward mind;
My hounds are thoughts, and rage despairing blind,
Pain, cruelty, and care without relief.
But they, perceiving that my swift pursuit
My flying fairy cannot overtake,
With open mouths their prey on me do make,
Like hungry hounds that lately lost their suit,
And full of fury on their master feed,
To hasten on my hapless death with speed.

---

[11] This poem has one more quatrain than the regular sonnet, and all but the last two lines are tetrameter. Of the 40 poems in *Phillis* only 27 are sonnets.

[12] Based on Ronsard, *Amours*, I, cxx.

[13] *brach:* a hound hunting by scent.

XXXIV[14]

I WOULD in rich and golden-colored rain,
With tempting showers in pleasant sort descend
Into fair Phillis' lap, my lovely friend,
When sleep her sense with slumber doth restrain.
I would be changed to a milk-white bull,
When midst the gladsome fields she should appear,
By pleasant fineness to surprise my dear
Whilst from their stalks she pleasant flowers did pull.
I were content to weary out my pain
To be Narcissus, so she were a spring,
To drown in her those woes my heart do wring.
And more: I wish transformed to remain,
That whilst I thus in pleasure's lap did lie,
I might refresh desire, which else would die.

DR. GILES FLETCHER

LICIA (1593?)

XXV[15]

SEVEN are the lights that wander in the skies,
And at these seven I wonder in my love:
So see the moon, how pale she doth arise,
Standing amazed as though she durst not move;
So is my sweet much paler than the snow,
Constant her looks, those looks that cannot change.
Mercury the next, a god sweet-tongued we know,
But her sweet voice doth wonders speak more strange.
The rising sun doth boast him of his pride,
And yet my love is far more fair than he.
The warlike Mars can wieldless[16] weapons guide,
But yet that god is far more weak than she.
The lovely Venus seemeth to be fair,
But at her best, my love is far more bright.
Saturn for age with groans doth dim the air,
Whereas my love with smiles doth give it light.
Gaze at her brows, where heaven ingrafted is;
Then sigh, and swear, there is no heaven but this.

[14] Based on Ronsard, *Amours,* I, xx.

[15] This and the following sonnet are based on Angerianus, *Erotopaegnion* (contemporary Neo-Latin source).

[16] *wieldless:* that cannot be wielded.

XXVIII

In time the strong and stately turrets fall,
In time the rose and silver lilies die,
In time the monarchs captive are, and thrall,
In time the sea and rivers are made dry;
The hardest flint in time doth melt asunder;
Still-living fame in time doth fade away;
The mountains proud we see in time come under;
And earth, for age, we see in time decay.
The sun in time forgets for to retire
From out the east where he was wont to rise;
The basest thoughts we see in time aspire,
And greedy minds in time do wealth despise.
Thus all, sweet fair, in time must have an end,
Except thy beauty, virtues, and thy friend.

XLVII [17]

Like Memnon's rock,[18] touched with the rising sun,
Which yields a sound and echoes forth a voice,
But when it's drowned in western seas, is done,
And drowsy-like leaves off to make a noise;
So I, my love, enlightened with your shine,
A poet's skill within my soul I shroud—
Not rude, like that which finer wits decline,
But such as Muses to the best allowed.
But when your figure and your shape is gone,
I speechless am, like as I was before;
Or if I write, my verse is filled with moan
And blurred with tears by falling in such store.
Then muse not, Licia, if my muse be slack,
For when I wrote I did thy beauty lack.

---

[17] Based on Gruterus (Dutch humanist, 1560–1627), *Harmosyne*.

[18] *Memnon's rock*: a colossal statue near Thebes which according to tradition gave forth a musical note when struck by the rays of the rising sun.

B. BARNES

PARTHENOPHIL (1593)

LXIII [19]

Jove for Europa's love took shape of bull,
And for Calisto played Diana's part,
And in a golden shower he filled full
The lap of Danae, with celestial art.
Would I were changed but to my mistress' gloves,
That those white lovely fingers I might hide;
That I might kiss those hands which mine heart loves!
Or else that chain of pearl (her neck's vain pride)
Made proud with her neck's veins, that I might fold
About that lovely neck, and her paps tickle!
Or her to compass, like a belt of gold!
Or that sweet wine, which down her throat doth trickle,
To kiss her lips and lie next at her heart,
Run through her veins, and pass by pleasure's part!

LXVI

Ah, sweet Content! where is thy mild abode?
Is it with shepherds and light-hearted swains
Which sing upon the downs and pipe abroad,
Tending their flocks and cattle on the plains?
Ah, sweet Content! where dost thou safely rest?
In heaven with angels which the praises sing
Of Him that made, and rules at His behest,
The minds and hearts of every living thing?
Ah, sweet Content! where doth thine harbor hold?
Is it in churches, with religious men
Which please the gods with prayers manifold,
And in their studies meditate it then?
Whether thou dost in heaven or earth appear,
Be where thou wilt, thou wilt not harbor here.

---

[19] This sonnet is attacked by Marston; see p. 658. Similar examples of bad taste are to be found in R. Belleau, *Qu'il se voudrait transformé en tout ce que touche sa Maistresse,* in de Baïf's *Meline,* I, 40, and in Watson's *Hecatompathia,* XXVIII.

W. PERCY

COELIA (1594)

XIX

It shall be said I died for Coelia;
Then quick, thou grisly man of Erebus,
Transport me hence unto Proserpina,
To be adjudged as willful amorous,
To be hung up within the liquid air,
For all the sighs which I in vain have wasted;
To be through Lethe's waters cleansed fair,
For those dark clouds which have my looks o'ercasted;
To be condemned to everlasting fire,
Because at Cupid's fire I willful brent me;
And to be clad for deadly dumps in mire.
Among so many plagues which shall torment me
One solace I shall find, when I am over,—
It will be known I died a constant lover.

ANONYMOUS

ZEPHERIA (1594)

CANZON 26

When we, in kind embracements, had agreed
To keep a royal banquet on our lips,
How soon have we another feast decreed,
And how, at parting, have we mourned by fits!
Eftsoons in absence have we wailed much more
Till those void hours of intermission
Were spent, that we might revel as before.
How have we bribed time for expedition!
And when remitted to our former love plays,
How have we, overweening in delight,
Accused the father sexton of the days
That then with eagle's wings he took his flight.
But now, old man, fly on as swift as thought,
Sith eyes from love, and hope from heart, is wrought.

R. LYNCHE

DIELLA (1596)

IV

WHAT sugared terms, what all-persuading art,
What sweet mellifluous words, what wounding looks
Love used for his admittance to my heart!
Such eloquence was never read in books.
He promised pleasure, rest, and endless joy,
Fruition of the fairest she alive.
His pleasure, pain; rest, trouble; joy, annoy,
Have I since found, which me of bliss deprive.
The Trojan horse thus have I now let in,
Wherein enclosed these armed men were placed—
Bright eyes, fair cheeks, sweet lips, and milk-white skin;
These foes my life have overthrown and razed.
Fair outward shows prove inwardly the worst,
Love looketh fair, but lovers are accurst.

W. SMITH

CHLORIS (1596)

COLIN, my dear and most entire beloved,[20]
My muse audacious stoops her pitch to thee,
Desiring that thy patience be not moved
By these rude lines, written here you see;
Fain would my muse, whom cruel love hath wronged,
Shroud her love labors under thy protection,
And I myself with ardent zeal have longed
That thou mightst know to thee my true affection.
Therefore, good Colin, graciously accept
A few sad sonnets which my muse hath framed;
Though they but newly from the shell are crept,
Suffer them not by envy to be blamed.
But underneath the shadow of thy wings
Give warmth to these young-hatched orphan things.

[20] This and two other dedicatory sonnets are addressed "To the most excellent and learned Shepherd Colin Clout" (Spenser).

B. GRIFFIN

FIDESSA (1596)

XV[21]

CARE-CHARMER sleep, sweet ease in restless misery,
The captive's liberty, and his freedom's song,
Balm of the bruised heart, man's chief felicity,
Brother of quiet death, when life is too, too long!
A comedy it is, and now an history—
What is not sleep unto the feeble mind!
It easeth him that toils and him that's sorry,
It makes the deaf to hear, to see the blind.
Ungentle sleep, thou helpest all but me,
For when I sleep my soul is vexed most.
It is Fidessa that doth master thee;
If she approach, alas, thy power is lost.
But here she is. See, how he runs amain!
I fear at night he will not come again.

XXIII[22]

FLY to her heart; hover about her heart.
With dainty kisses mollify her heart.
Pierce with thy arrows her obdurate heart.
With sweet allurements ever move her heart.
At midday and at midnight touch her heart.
Be lurking closely, nestle about her heart.
With power (thou art a god!) command her heart.
Kindle thy coals of love about her heart.
Yea, even into thyself transform her heart.
Ah, she must love! Be sure thou have her heart.
And I must die, if thou have not her heart.
Thy bed, if thou rest well, must be her heart.
He hath the best part, sure, that hath her heart;
What have I not, if I have but her heart!

[21] Compare Sidney's *Astrophel and Stella,* XXXIX and Daniel's *Delia,* XLV.

[22] An example of the form called "like-loose."

XXXV

I HAVE not spent the April of my time,
The sweet of youth, in plotting in the air,
But do at first adventure seek to climb,
Whilst flowers of blooming years are green and fair.
I am no leaving of all-withering age,
I have not suffered many winter lours;
I feel no storm unless my love do rage,
And then in grief I spend both days and hours.
This yet doth comfort, that my flower lasted
Until it did approach my sun too near,
And then, alas, untimely was it blasted,
So soon as once thy beauty did appear.
But after all, my comfort rests in this,
That for thy sake my youth decayed is.

H. LOK

SONNETS OF THE CHRISTIAN PASSIONS (1597)[23]

WORDS may well want, both ink and paper fail,
Wits may grow dull, and will may weary grow,
And world's affairs may make my pen more slow,
But yet my heart and courage shall not quail.
Though cares and troubles do my peace assail
And drive me to delay thy praise awhile,
Yet all the world shall not from thoughts exile
Thy mercies, Lord, by which my plaints prevail.
And though the world with face should grateful smile
And me her peddler's pack of pleasures show,
No hearty love on her I would bestow,
Because I know she seeks me to beguile;
Ne will defile my happy peace of mind
For all the solace I in earth may find.

[23] Lok wrote three hundred religious sonnets, and there are collections by Breton and Drummond.

William Shakespeare

(1564–1616)

IF IT were possible to forget for a moment that Shakespeare was the author of the plays, and to consider him only as a nondramatic poet, his relationship to his predecessors and contemporaries would seem very close indeed. Happily, too, for our purpose, his nondramatic poetry all belongs to the early period of his career, so that in it he is purely Elizabethan. He was born in Stratford in 1564; he was twelve years younger than Spenser and Ralegh, ten years younger than Sidney, two years younger than Daniel, one year younger than Drayton, and the same age as Marlowe.

His nondramatic poems include three groups: the narrative poems, *Venus and Adonis* and *The Rape of Lucrece;* the sonnets; and the lyrics or songs included in the plays. In all the groups is to be found something very directly and very intimately from the man himself, just as in all of them we can see the influence of his age.

In 1598 Francis Meres referred to Shakespeare's "sugared sonnets among his private friends." The private friends kept them private (except for two sonnets) until in 1609 the publisher Thomas Thorpe brought them out with the famous and mystifying dedication: TO. THE. ONLIE. BEGETTER. OF. THESE. INSVING. SONNETS. Mr. W. H. ALL. HAPPINESSE. AND. THAT. ETERNITIE. PROMISED. BY. OVR. EVER-LIVING. POET. WISHETH. THE. WELL-WISHING. ADVENTVRER. IN. SETTING. FORTH. T. T.

The only things clear in this dedication are that the ever-living poet is Shakespeare and that T. T. is the publisher Thorpe. Who "Mr. W. H." is, man knoweth not. If the "begetter" means the inspirer, then he is the friend referred to in the series; if begetter means "procurer," then he may be any person who delivered the manuscript to Thorpe. The leading candidate for the friend is Henry Wriothesley (pronounced Rizley), Earl of Southampton, the patron of *Venus* and *Lucrece;* the runner-up is William Herbert, Earl of Pembroke, patron of the first Folio of Shakespeare's plays (1623). From this point on the darkness thickens. For the identification of the Dark Lady, or of the Rival Poet, we have only the most inadequate and tantalizing of clues. The amount of conjecture that has been published on the subject is staggering; as Sir Edmund Chambers says, "More folly has been written about the sonnets than about any other Shakespearean topic."

The sonnets are written in the form, developed by Surrey, of three quatrains and a couplet. They utilize many of the conventions of the Petrarchan mode, but they are less directly derivative than most English sonnets of the nineties. The imagery is drawn from the most varied sources: medicine, law, business, science, the stage, military life, music, navigation, astronomy. The feeling for nature is vivid and strong. In eloquence and music they are unsurpassed among all the Elizabethans, and only Sidney approaches them. Finally, the profound sense of time and of death, the terrible realization of the outer limits of human moral possibilities reveal the mind of only the man who could create *Hamlet* and *Lear*.

Much of the same creative ability and poetic skill that distinguishes Shakespeare as a dramatist is evident in the songs in his plays. Shakespeare was not an innovator in the kinds of songs he employed or in the effects he sought for. Compared to his contemporaries and especially to his successors, such as Jonson and Beaumont and Fletcher, he introduced songs sparingly. But, according to Mr. Richmond Noble (*Shakespeare's Use of Song,* p. 12) ". . . he it was who made the play with song occurring in it a consistent art-form; it was he who first grasped all the possibilities afforded by song for forwarding the action and who made it a vital part in his dramatic scheme."

Shakespeare wrote all the conventional forms, serenades, greenwood and nature songs, drinking songs, dirges, and mad songs; occasionally (as in *Othello* and *II Henry IV*) he altered popular ballads. He attained greatest success in songs in the comedies. In their ease, their artful artlessness, their technical skill, and their functional value (placing a scene or character, opening or closing a scene, creating a mood, being an integral part of the action), the songs surpass those of Shakespeare's contemporaries. There is little of the extraneousness about them which characterizes so much of the song in Elizabethan drama. The contemporary music for all except two or three songs has been lost, but Shakespeare's lyrics have attracted both good and bad composers from the seventeenth century to the present.

BIBLIOGRAPHY: E. K. Chambers, *William Shakespeare, A Study of Facts and Problems,* Oxford, 1930; H. Granville-Barker and G. B. Harrison, *A Companion to Shakespeare Studies,* New York, 1934, especially Chapter IV, "Shakespeare the Poet," by George Rylands; *The Sonnets,* ed. H. E. Rollins, *New Variorum Shakespeare,* Philadelphia, 1944; *Shakespeare's Sonnets,* ed. Tucker Brooke, New York, 1936; *The Sonnets of Shakespeare,* ed. T. G. Tucker, Cambridge, 1924; E. Hubler, *The Sense of Shakespeare's Sonnets,* Princeton, 1952; Hallett Smith, *Elizabethan Poetry* (1952), 171–193; T. W Baldwin, *On the Literary Genetics of Shakespeare's Poems and Sonnets,* Urbana, 1950.

SONNETS

II[1]

When forty winters shall besiege thy brow
And dig deep trenches in thy beauty's field,
Thy youth's proud livery,[2] so gazed on now,
Will be a tottered weed,[3] of small worth held:
Then being asked where all thy beauty lies,
Where all the treasure of thy lusty days,
To say, within thine own deep-sunken eyes,
Were an all-eating shame and thriftless praise.
How much more praise deserved thy beauty's use,[4]
If thou couldst answer, "This fair child of mine
Shall sum my count and make my old excuse,"[5]
Proving his beauty by succession thine!
This were to be new made when thou art old,
And see thy blood warm when thou feel'st it cold.

V

Those hours that with gentle work did frame
The lovely gaze[6] where every eye doth dwell,
Will play the tyrants to the very same
And that unfair[7] which fairly doth excel:
For never-resting time leads summer on
To hideous winter and confounds him there;
Sap checked with frost and lusty leaves quite gone,
Beauty o'ersnowed and bareness everywhere:
Then, were not summer's distillation left,
A liquid prisoner pent in walls of glass,[8]
Beauty's effect with beauty were bereft,
Nor it,[9] nor no remembrance what it was:
But flowers distilled, though they with winter meet,
Leese[10] but their show; their substance still lives sweet.

[1] The first seventeen sonnets are addressed to a young man, urging him to perpetuate his beauty by marrying and having children. More seventeenth-century manuscript copies of Sonnet II are extant than of any other of Shakespeare's.

[2] *livery:* dress.

[3] *tottered weed:* tattered clothing.

[4] *use:* interest or profit.

[5] *Shall . . . excuse:* shall make the last item in my account books and present an excuse for me who am old.

[6] *gaze:* sight.

[7] *unfair:* make ugly.

[8] *summer's . . . glass:* Cf. Sidney's *Arcadia,* III, 5: "Have you ever seen a pure Rosewater kept in a crystal glass; how fine it looks, how sweet it smells, while that beautiful glass imprisons it?"

[9] *it:* would it remain.

[10] *leese:* lose.

XII

WHEN I do count the clock that tells the time,
And see the brave [11] day sunk in hideous night;
When I behold the violet past prime,
And sable curls, all silvered o'er with white;
When lofty trees I see barren of leaves,
Which erst [12] from heat did canopy the herd,
And summer's green all girded up in sheaves,
Borne on the bier with white and bristly beard,
Then of thy beauty do I question make,[13]
That thou among the wastes of time must go,
Since sweets and beauties do themselves forsake
And die as fast as they see others grow;
And nothing 'gainst time's scythe can make defense
Save breed, to brave [14] him when he takes thee hence.

XV

WHEN I consider every thing that grows
Holds in perfection but a little moment,
That this huge stage presenteth naught but shows
Whereon the stars in secret influence [15] comment;
When I perceive that men as plants increase,
Cheered and checked e'en by the selfsame sky,
Vaunt in their youthful sap, at height decrease,
And wear their brave state out of memory;
Then the conceit of this inconstant [16] stay
Sets you most rich in youth before my sight,
Where wasteful time debateth with decay,
To change your day of youth to sullied night;
And all in war with time for love of you,
As he takes from you, I engraft you new.[17]

---

[11] *brave:* beautiful.
[12] *erst:* formerly.
[13] *question make:* consider, contemplate.
[14] *brave:* defy.
[15] *secret influence:* the power of the stars over earthly events, according to astrology.
[16] *conceit:* thought; *inconstant:* transitory.
[17] *engraft you new:* Shakespeare's first use in the sonnets of the conventional promise of immortality through the poet's verses.

XVIII [18]

SHALL I compare thee to a summer's day?
Thou art more lovely and more temperate:
Rough winds do shake the darling buds of May,
And summer's lease hath all too short a date:
Sometime too hot the eye of heaven shines,
And often is his gold complexion dimmed;
And every fair from fair sometime declines,
By chance or nature's changing course untrimmed; [19]
But thy eternal summer shall not fade,
Nor lose possession of that fair thou ow'st; [20]
Nor shall death brag thou wander'st in his shade,
When in eternal lines to time thou grow'st:
So long as men can breathe, or eyes can see,
So long lives this, and this gives life to thee.

XX [21]

A WOMAN's face with nature's own hand painted
Hast thou, the master-mistress of my passion; [22]
A woman's gentle heart, but not acquainted
With shifting change, as is false women's fashion;
An eye more bright than theirs, less false in rolling,
Gilding the object whereupon it gazeth;
A man in hue, all hues [23] in his controlling,
Which steals men's eyes and women's souls amazeth;
And for a woman wert thou first created;
Till nature, as she wrought thee, fell a-doting,
And by addition me of thee defeated,[24]
By adding one thing to my purpose nothing.
But since she prick'd thee out for women's pleasure,
Mine be thy love, and thy love's use their treasure.

---

[18] It is not absolutely certain that the sonnets after XVII are all addressed to a man, but the opinion of most scholars is that the rest of the sonnets through CXXVI are addressed to the same person as the first group. They drop the theme of marriage and "breed" at this point and celebrate various phases of a love and friendship between the two men.

[19] *untrimmed:* stripped of gay apparel.

[20] *ow'st:* ownest.

[21] The only sonnet of the series in which there are only feminine (two-syllable) rhymes.

[22] *passion:* poem.

[23] *all hues:* Because the quarto prints "all *Hews*" some editors have suspected a pun and have constructed a mythical Will Hughes to fit the Mr. W. H. of the dedication.

[24] *defeated:* deprived.

XXI

So is it not with me as with that Muse [25]
Stirred by a painted beauty [26] to his verse,
Who heaven itself for ornament doth use
And every fair with his fair doth rehearse,[27]
Making a couplement of proud compare,
With sun and moon, with earth and sea's rich gems,
With April's first-born flowers, and all things rare
That heaven's air in this huge rondure [28] hems.
Oh! let me, true in love, but truly write,
And then believe me, my love is as fair
As any mother's child, though not so bright
As those gold candles fixed in heaven's air:
Let them say more that like of hearsay well;
I will not praise that purpose not to sell.

XXIII

As an unperfect actor on the stage,
Who with his fear is put besides [29] his part,
Or some fierce thing replete with too much rage,
Whose strength's abundance weakens his own heart;
So I, for fear of trust,[30] forget to say
The perfect ceremony of love's rite,
And in mine own love's strength seem to decay,
O'ercharged with burthen of my own love's might.
Oh, let my books [31] be then the eloquence
And dumb presagers [32] of my speaking breast;
Who plead for love, and look for recompense,
More than the tongue that more hath more expressed.[33]
Oh, learn to read what silent love hath writ:
To hear with eyes belongs to love's fine wit.

---

[25] *Muse:* poet.

[26] *painted beauty:* a lady, made up with cosmetics, in contrast to the naturally beautiful male.

[27] *rehearse:* relate.

[28] *rondure:* circle.

[29] *is put besides:* forgets.

[30] *for fear of trust:* lacking self-confidence.

[31] *books:* possibly *Venus and Adonis* and *The Rape of Lucrece.*

[32] *presagers:* indicators (referring to actors in a dumb show, carrying on the image of line 1).

[33] *More . . . expressed:* more than the tongue of another who has expressed more fully the ardors of love.

XXVI

Lord of my love, to whom in vassalage
Thy merit hath my duty strongly knit,
To thee I send this written ambassage,[34]
To witness duty, not to show my wit:
Duty so great, which wit so poor as mine
May make seem bare, in wanting words to show it,
But that I hope some good conceit of thine
In thy soul's thought, all naked, will bestow [35] it;
Till whatsoever star that guides my moving,
Points on me graciously with fair aspect,
And puts apparel on my tottered loving,
To show me worthy of thy sweet respect:
Then may I dare to boast how I do love thee;
Till then not show my head where thou mayst prove me.

XXVII [36]

Weary with toil, I haste me to my bed,
The dear repose for limbs with travel tired;
But then begins a journey in my head,
To work my mind, when body's work's expired:
For then my thoughts, from far where I abide,
Intend a zealous pilgrimage to thee,
And keep my drooping eyelids open wide,
Looking on darkness which the blind do see:
Save that my soul's imaginary [37] sight
Presents thy shadow [38] to my sightless view,
Which, like a jewel hung in ghastly night,
Makes black night beauteous and her old face new.
Lo, thus, by day my limbs, by night my mind,
For thee and for myself no quiet find.

---

[34] *ambassage:* message. Perhaps in this case, a parcel of sonnets. This sonnet closely parallels the dedication to *Lucrece*. See above, p. 243.

[35] *bestow:* dignify.

[36] Sonnets XXVII–XXXII reflect a journey of the poet; if these are autobiographical they may refer to a tour in the provinces by Shakespeare's company of actors.

[37] *imaginary:* imaginative.

[38] *shadow:* image.

XXIX

WHEN, in disgrace with fortune and men's eyes,
I all alone beweep my outcast state,
And trouble deaf heaven with my bootless [39] cries,
And look upon myself, and curse my fate,
Wishing me like to one more rich in hope,
Featured like him, like him with friends possessed,
Desiring this man's art and that man's scope,
With what I most enjoy contented least;
Yet in these thoughts myself almost despising,
Haply I think on thee—and then my state,
Like to the lark at break of day arising
From sullen earth, sings hymns at heaven's gate;
For thy sweet love remembered such wealth brings
That then I scorn to change my state with kings.

XXX [40]

WHEN to the sessions [41] of sweet silent thought
I summon up remembrance of things past,
I sigh the lack of many a thing I sought,
And with old woes new wail [42] my dear time's waste:
Then can I drown an eye, unused to flow,
For precious friends hid in death's dateless [43] night,
And weep afresh love's long since canceled woe,
And moan the expense [44] of many a vanished sight:
Then can I grieve at grievances foregone,[45]
And heavily from woe to woe tell [46] o'er
The sad account of fore-bemoaned moan,
Which I new pay as if not paid before.
But if the while I think on thee, dear friend,
All losses are restored and sorrows end.

[39] *bootless:* futile.

[40] A companion sonnet to XXIX, with "memory" as the link.

[41] *sessions:* sittings of court.

[42] *new wail:* bewail anew.

[43] *dateless:* endless.

[44] *expense:* loss.

[45] *grievances foregone:* old subjects for grief.

[46] *tell:* count.

XXXIII[47]

Full many a glorious morning have I seen
Flatter the mountain-tops with sovereign eye,
Kissing with golden face the meadows green,
Gilding pale streams with heavenly alchemy;
Anon permit the basest clouds to ride
With ugly rack[48] on his celestial face,
And from the forlorn world his visage hide,
Stealing unseen to west with this disgrace:[49]
Even so my sun one early morn did shine
With all-triumphant splendor on my brow;
But, out, alack! he was but one hour mine,
The region cloud[50] hath mask'd him from me now.
Yet him for this my love no whit disdaineth;
Suns of the world may stain when heaven's sun staineth.

XXXVIII

How can my Muse want subject to invent
While thou dost breathe, that pour'st into my verse
Thine own sweet argument,[51] too excellent
For every vulgar paper to rehearse?
Oh, give thyself the thanks, if aught in me
Worthy perusal stand against[52] thy sight;
For who's so dumb that cannot write to thee,
When thou thyself dost give invention light?[53]
Be thou the tenth Muse, ten times more in worth
Than those old nine which rhymers invocate;
And he that calls on thee, let him bring forth
Eternal numbers to outlive long date.[54]
If my slight Muse do please these curious[55] days,
The pain be mine, but thine shall be the praise.

---

[47] The first of a group of sonnets which have to do with unfaithfulness on the part of the poet's friend. See Sonnet XLI.

[48] *rack:* high cloud.

[49] *disgrace:* blemish.

[50] *region cloud:* clouds of upper air.

[51] *argument:* subject matter.

[52] *against:* in.

[53] *give invention light:* hold the poet's candle.

[54] *numbers:* verses; *date:* time.

[55] *curious:* fastidious.

XLI

THOSE pretty wrongs that liberty commits,
When I am sometime absent from thy heart,
Thy beauty and thy years full well befits,
For still [56] temptation follows where thou art.
Gentle thou art, and therefore to be won,
Beauteous thou art, therefore to be assailed;
And when a woman woos, what woman's son
Will sourly leave her till she have prevailed?
Ay me! but yet thou mightst my seat [57] forbear,
And chide thy beauty and thy straying youth,
Who lead thee in their riot even there
Where thou art forced to break a twofold truth,
Hers, by thy beauty tempting her to thee,
Thine, by thy beauty being false to me.

L

How heavy [58] do I journey on the way,
When what I seek, my weary travel's end,
Doth teach that ease and that repose to say,
"Thus far the miles are measured from thy friend!"
The beast that bears me, tired with my woe,
Plods dully on, to bear that weight [59] in me,
As if by some instinct the wretch did know
His rider loved not speed, being made from thee: [60]
The bloody spur cannot provoke him on
That sometimes anger thrusts into his hide;
Which heavily he answers with a groan,
More sharp to me than spurring to his side;
For that same groan doth put this in my mind:
My grief lies onward, and my joy behind.

---

[56] *still:* always.

[57] *seat:* Cf. *Othello,* II, i, 307: "I do suspect the lusty Moor hath leap'd into my seat."

[58] *heavy:* sadly.

[59] *to bear that weight:* explains "dully."

[60] *being made from thee:* if directed away from thee.

LIV

Oh how much more doth beauty beauteous seem
By that sweet ornament which truth doth give!
The rose looks fair, but fairer we it deem
For that sweet odor which doth in it live.
The canker-blooms [61] have full as deep a dye
As the perfumed tincture [62] of the roses,
Hang on such thorns, and play as wantonly
When summer's breath their masked buds discloses:
But, for their virtue only is their show,
They live unwooed, and unrespected [63] fade;
Die to themselves.[64] Sweet roses do not so;
Of their sweet deaths are sweetest odors made:
And so of you, beauteous and lovely youth,
When that shall fade, my verse distills [65] your truth.

LV

Not marble, nor the gilded monuments
Of princes, shall outlive this powerful rhyme;
But you shall shine more bright in these contents [66]
Than unswept stone, besmeared with sluttish time.[67]
When wasteful war shall statues overturn,
And broils root out the work of masonry,
Nor Mars his [68] sword nor war's quick fire shall burn
The living record of your memory.
'Gainst death and all-oblivious enmity
Shall you pace forth; your praise shall still find room
Even in the eyes of all posterity
That wear this world out to the ending doom.[69]
So, till the judgment that [70] yourself arise,
You live in this, and dwell in lovers' eyes.

---

[61] *canker-blooms:* dog roses, wild and without scent.

[62] *tincture:* color.

[63] *unrespected:* unregarded.

[64] *to themselves:* alone.

[65] *that:* beauty and youth; *distills:* preserves the essence of.

[66] *contents:* (accent second syllable) what is contained in these verses.

[67] *Than . . . time:* than in a stone tomb or effigy, which unclean time defaces and covers with dust.

[68] *Nor Mars his:* neither Mars'.

[69] *That . . . doom:* who outlast this world and live till Judgment Day.

[70] *that:* when.

LIX[71]

If there be nothing new, but that which is
Hath been before, how are our brains beguiled,
Which, laboring for invention, bear amiss
The second burthen of a former child!
Oh, that record[72] could with a backward look,
Even of five hundred courses of the sun,
Show me your image in some antique book,
Since mind at first in character[73] was done.
That I might see what the old world could say
To this composed wonder[74] of your frame;
Whether we are mended[75] or whe'r better they,
Or whether revolution be the same.[76]
Oh, sure I am, the wits of former days
To subjects worse have given admiring praise.

LX

Like as the waves make towards the pebbled shore,
So do our minutes hasten to their end;
Each changing place with that which goes before,
In sequent toil all forwards do contend.[77]
Nativity, once in the main of light,[78]
Crawls to maturity, wherewith being crowned,
Crooked eclipses 'gainst his glory fight,
And time that gave doth now his gift confound.
Time doth transfix the flourish[79] set on youth
And delves the parallels[80] in beauty's brow,
Feeds on the rarities of nature's truth,
And nothing stands but for his scythe to mow.
And yet to times in hope[81] my verse shall stand,
Praising thy worth, despite his cruel hand.

---

[71] This sonnet and LX are based on a passage in Ovid (*Metamorphoses,* XV, 176 ff.) expounding a philosophy of flux and cyclical change.

[72] *record:* (accent second syllable) memory.

[73] *in character:* in letters.

[74] *composed wonder:* wonderful composition.

[75] *mended:* improved.

[76] *Or . . . same:* or whether the new cycle exactly corresponds to the old.

[77] *In . . . contend:* toiling and following each other, the waves struggle to press forward.

[78] *main of light:* the sea of light at sunrise.

[79] *transfix the flourish:* remove the embellishment.

[80] *delves the parallels:* digs the parallel furrows (cf. Sonnet II).

[81] *times in hope:* future times.

LXIII

Against [82] my love shall be, as I am now,
With time's injurious hand crushed and o'erworn;
When hours have drained his blood and filled his brow
With lines and wrinkles; when his youthful morn
Hath traveled on to age's steepy [83] night,
And all those beauties whereof now he's king
Are vanishing or vanished out of sight,
Stealing away the treasure of his spring;
For such a time do I now fortify
Against confounding [84] age's cruel knife,
That he shall never cut from memory
My sweet love's beauty, though [85] my lover's life:
His beauty shall in these black lines be seen,
And they shall live, and he in them still green.

LXIV [86]

When I have seen by time's fell [87] hand defaced
The rich-proud cost of outworn buried age; [88]
When sometime lofty towers I see down-razed,
And brass eternal slave to mortal rage;
When I have seen the hungry ocean gain
Advantage on the kingdom of the shore,
And the firm soil win of [89] the watery main,
Increasing store with loss, and loss with store;
When I have seen such interchange of state,
Or state [90] itself confounded to decay,—
Ruin hath taught me thus to ruminate,
That time will come and take my love away.
This thought is as a death, which [91] cannot choose
But weep to have that which it fears to lose.

---

[82] *Against:* in anticipation of the time when.

[83] *steepy:* steep; youth and age are pictured as two sides of a hill, age the steeper, and because it is closer to death, the darker (hence "night").

[84] *confounding:* destroying.

[85] *though:* Supply "he takes."

[86] This, like the other sonnets on time and change, shows the influence of the fifteenth book of Ovid's *Metamorphoses.*

[87] *fell:* fierce, cruel.

[88] *rich-proud . . . age:* costly tombs and monuments.

[89] *win of:* take from.

[90] *state:* in line 9 *state* means "condition"; in line 10 it means "magnificence" or "greatness."

[91] *which:* this thought which.

LXVI [92]

TIRED with all these, for restful death I cry:
As, to behold desert [93] a beggar born,
And needy nothing trimmed in jollity,[94]
And purest faith unhappily forsworn,
And gilded honor shamefully misplaced,[95]
And maiden virtue rudely strumpeted,
And right perfection wrongfully disgraced,
And strength by limping sway [96] disabled,
And art made tongue-tied by authority,[97]
And folly, doctor-like, controlling skill,
And simple truth miscalled simplicity,[98]
And captive good attending captain ill: [99]
Tired with all these, from these would I be gone,
Save that, to die,[100] I leave my love alone.

LXXI [101]

No longer mourn for me when I am dead
Than you shall hear the surly sullen bell [102]
Give warning to the world that I am fled
From this vile world, with vilest worms to dwell:
Nay, if you read this line, remember not
The hand that writ it; for I love you so,
That I in your sweet thoughts would be forgot,
If thinking on me then should make you woe.
Oh, if, I say, you look upon this verse
When I perhaps compounded am with clay,
Do not so much as my poor name rehearse,
But let your love even with my life decay;
Lest the wise world should look into your moan,
And mock you with me after I am gone.

---

[92] This sonnet introduces a group of eight sonnets "on the moral infection of the world and its effect upon the friend" (Brooke). See XCIV and XCV, below.

[93] *desert:* deserving, worth.

[94] *needy nothing trimmed in jollity:* the undeserving gorgeously dressed.

[95] *misplaced:* bestowed amiss.

[96] *limping sway:* incompetent authority.

[97] *art . . . authority:* possibly a reference to censorship in the theater.

[98] *simplicity:* simple-mindedness.

[99] *captive . . . ill:* Evil as a conqueror leading Good as a prisoner in triumphal procession.

[100] *to die:* by dying.

[101] This and LXXIII are two of a group of five sonnets on the contemplation of the poet's death.

[102] *bell:* The bell was tolled to announce the death of a member of the parish—one stroke for each year of his life.

LXXIII [103]

THAT time of year thou mayst in me behold
When yellow leaves, or none, or few, do hang
Upon those boughs which shake against the cold,
Bare ruined choirs, where late the sweet birds sang.
In me thou see'st the twilight of such day
As after sunset fadeth in the west;
Which by and by black night doth take away,
Death's second self, that seals up all in rest.
In me thou see'st the glowing of such fire,
That on the ashes of his youth doth lie,
As the death-bed whereon it must expire,
Consumed with that which it was nourished by.[104]
This thou perceivest, which makes thy love more strong,
To love that well which thou must leave ere long.

LXXVI

WHY is my verse so barren of new pride,[105]
So far from variation or quick change?
Why with the time do I not glance aside
To new-found methods and to compounds strange?
Why write I still all one, ever the same,
And keep invention in a noted weed,[106]
That every word doth almost tell my name,
Showing their birth and where [107] they did proceed?
Oh, know, sweet love, I always write of you,
And you and love are still my argument;
So all my best is dressing old words new,
Spending again what is already spent:
For as the sun is daily new and old,
So is my love still telling what is told.

---

[103] The three striking images in this sonnet and the adaptation of the quatrain structure to them have earned this sonnet praise as "the finest example of the Shakespearian mode" (Alden).

[104] *Consumed . . . by:* choked by the ashes which once nourished its flame.

[105] *new pride:* ostentatious novelty. For an interesting discussion of the verbal simplicity of Shakespeare's style, see Brooke's edition, pp. 4–8. For other poets' comments on their own style, see Sidney, Sonnet LXXIV, p. 259, and Drayton, Sonnet, *To the Reader,* p. 742.

[106] *invention in a noted weed:* composition in a well-known dress or style.

[107] *where:* whence.

LXXX[108]

Oh how I faint when I of you do write,
Knowing a better spirit doth use your name,
And in the praise thereof spends all his might,
To make me tongue-tied, speaking of your fame!
But since your worth wide as the ocean is,
The humble as the proudest sail doth bear,
My saucy bark, inferior far to his,
On your broad main doth willfully appear.
Your shallowest help will hold me up afloat,
Whilst he upon your soundless deep doth ride;
Or, being wrecked, I am a worthless boat,
He of tall building and of goodly pride:
Then if he thrive and I be cast away,
The worst was this: my love was my decay.

LXXXVI

Was it the proud full sail of his great verse,
Bound for the prize of all too precious you,
That did my ripe thoughts in my brain inhearse,[109]
Making their tomb the womb wherein they grew?
Was it his spirit, by spirits taught to write
Above a mortal pitch, that struck me dead?
No, neither he, nor his compeers by night[110]
Giving him aid, my verse astonished.[111]
He, nor that affable familiar ghost
Which nightly gulls him with intelligence,[112]
As victors, of my silence cannot boast;
I was not sick of any fear from thence:
But when your countenance filled up his line,
Then lacked I matter; that enfeebled mine.

[108] This and LXXXVI are two of a group of eight sonnets dealing with an unnamed Rival Poet, who also dedicates his verses to the friend. There is no certainty whatever as to the identity of this rival, but Drayton and Chapman have been the two most popular guesses.

[109] *inhearse:* put into a coffin.

[110] *compeers by night:* the spirits of line 5; but those who see Chapman as the rival poet have interpreted this as a reference to his group.

[111] *astonished:* dismayed.

[112] *gulls him with intelligence:* cheats him with [false] news.

XCIV [113]

THEY that have power to hurt and will do none,
That do not do the thing they most do show,
Who, moving others, are themselves as stone,
Unmoved, cold, and to temptation slow;
They rightly do inherit heaven's graces
And husband nature's riches from expense; [114]
They are the lords and owners of their faces,
Others but stewards of their excellence.
The summer's flower is to the summer sweet,
Though to itself it only live and die,
But if that flower with base infection meet,
The basest weed outbraves his dignity:
For sweetest things turn sourest by their deeds;
Lilies that fester smell far worse than weeds.[115]

XCV [116]

How sweet and lovely dost thou make the shame
Which, like a canker in the fragrant rose,
Doth spot the beauty of thy budding name!
Oh, in what sweets dost thou thy sins inclose!
That tongue that tells the story of thy days,
Making lascivious comments on thy sport,
Cannot dispraise but in a kind of praise;
Naming thy name blesses an ill report.[117]
Oh, what a mansion have those vices got
Which for their habitation chose out thee,
Where beauty's veil doth cover every blot
And all things turns [118] to fair that eyes can see!
Take heed, dear heart, of this large privilege; [119]
The hardest knife ill used doth lose his edge.

---

[113] In Brooke's rearrangement this sonnet and XCV belong to the group about "The Corrupting World." See LXVI and note. Compare this sonnet with *Hamlet,* III, ii, 59–79.

[114] *husband . . . expense:* do not squander nature's gifts in passion.

[115] This line occurs in the apocryphal Shakespearean play *Edward III* (II, i, 451), licensed December 1, 1595.

[116] Linked to Sonnet XCIV by the image of diseased flowers.

[117] *Naming . . . report:* The naming of your name is as the sign of the cross to negative the evil that is said of you.

[118] *all things turns:* turns all things.

[119] *privilege:* license.

XCVIII

From you have I been absent in the spring,
When proud-pied [120] April, dressed in all his trim,
Hath put a spirit of youth in everything,
That heavy Saturn [121] laughed and leaped with him.
Yet nor the lays of birds, nor the sweet smell
Of different flowers in odor and in hue,
Could make me any summer's story tell,
Or from their proud lap pluck them where they grew;
Nor did I wonder at [122] the lily's white,
Nor praise the deep vermilion in the rose;
They were but sweet, but figures of delight,
Drawn after you, you pattern of all those.
Yet seemed it winter still, and, you away,
As with your shadow I with these did play.

CIV

To me, fair friend, you never can be old,
For as you were when first your eye I eyed
Such seems your beauty still. Three winters cold
Have from the forests shook three summers' pride,
Three beauteous springs to yellow autumn turned
In process [123] of the seasons have I seen,
Three April perfumes in three hot Junes burned,
Since first I saw you fresh, which yet are green.
Ah, yet doth beauty, like a dial-hand,[124]
Steal from his figure, and no pace perceived;
So your sweet hue, which methinks still doth stand,
Hath motion, and mine eye may be deceived:
For fear of which, hear this, thou age unbred: [125]
Ere you were born was beauty's summer dead.

[120] *proud-pied:* magnificent in many colors.

[121] *heavy Saturn:* god of melancholy.

[122] *wonder at:* admire.

[123] *process:* procession.

[124] *dial-hand:* hand of a watch.

[125] *age unbred:* unborn generation.

CVI [126]

When in the chronicle of wasted [127] time
I see descriptions of the fairest wights,
And beauty making beautiful old rhyme
In praise of ladies dead and lovely knights,
Then, in the blazon [128] of sweet beauty's best,
Of hand, of foot, of lip, of eye, of brow,
I see their antique pen would have expressed
Even such a beauty as you master now.
So all their praises are but prophecies
Of this our time, all you prefiguring;
And, for [129] they looked but with divining eyes,
They had not skill enough your worth to sing:
For we,[130] which now behold these present days,
Have eyes to wonder, but lack tongues to praise.

CVII [131]

Not mine own fears, nor the prophetic soul
Of the wide world dreaming on things to come,
Can yet the lease of my true love control,[132]
Supposed as forfeit to a confined doom.[133]
The mortal moon [134] hath her eclipse endured,
And the sad augurs mock their own presage; [135]
Incertainties now crown themselves assured,
And peace [136] proclaims olives of endless age.
Now with the drops of this most balmy time
My love looks fresh, and death to me subscribes,[137]
Since, spite of him, I'll live in this poor rhyme,
While he insults o'er dull and speechless tribes:
And thou in this shalt find thy monument,
When tyrants' crest and tombs of brass are spent.

---

[126] Cf. Constable's sonnet, "Miracle of the world," p. 528.

[127] *wasted:* past.

[128] *blazon:* exhibition, as of arms in heraldry.

[129] *for:* because.

[130] *For we:* for even we.

[131] This is the only sonnet of Shakespeare's which clearly refers to contemporary events. Lines 5 and 6 probably refer to Queen Elizabeth's successfully passing her "climacteric" year, her 63rd, in September, 1596.

[132] *the lease . . . control:* put an end to my love.

[133] *Supposed . . . doom:* which I have thought doomed to early forfeiture.

[134] *mortal moon:* Elizabeth, known as Cynthia to Elizabethan poets.

[135] *sad augurs . . . presage:* the astrologers and almanac-makers who had predicted calamity in this year now ridicule their own predictions.

[136] *peace:* Henri IV made an agreement with Elizabeth.

[137] *subscribes:* submits.

CX [138]

Alas, 'tis true I have gone here and there
And made myself a motley [139] to the view,
Gored [140] mine own thoughts, sold cheap what is most dear
Made old offenses of affections new; [141]
Most true it is that I have looked on truth
Askance and strangely; but, by all above,
These blenches [142] gave my heart another youth,
And worse essays [143] proved thee my best of love.
Now all is done, have what shall have no end:
Mine appetite I never more will grind [144]
On newer proof, to try an older friend,
A god in love, to whom I am confined.
Then give me welcome, next my heaven the best,
Even to thy pure and most most loving breast.

CXVI

Let me not to the marriage of true minds
Admit impediments.[145] Love is not love
Which alters when it alteration finds,
Or bends with the remover to remove: [146]
Oh, no! it is an ever-fixed mark,
That looks on tempests and is never shaken;
It is the star to every wandering bark,
Whose worth's unknown, although his height [147] be taken.
Love's not Time's fool, though rosy lips and cheeks
Within his [148] bending sickle's compass come;
Love alters not with his brief hours and weeks,
But bears it out even to the edge of doom.[149]
If this be error and upon me proved,
I never writ, nor no man ever loved.

---

[138] This sonnet is the second in a group which deal with the poet's absence from the friend and an unfaithfulness to him. The first three lines are usually supposed to refer to Shakespeare's career as an actor.

[139] *motley:* a clown, from his varicolored costume.

[140] *gored:* wounded.

[141] *Made . . . new:* offended by changing old friends for new.

[142] *blenches:* offenses.

[143] *worse essays:* trials of what is worse.

[144] *grind:* whet.

[145] *impediments:* From the marriage service: "If any of you know cause or just impediment why these persons should not be joined together . . ."

[146] *remover to remove:* the inconstant to prove unfaithful.

[147] *worth's . . . height:* Riches contained in the star are not known, though the star's altitude may be known and used for practical navigation.

[148] *his:* Time's; so also in line 11.

[149] *edge of doom:* the brink of the Last Judgment.

CXXVIII [150]

How oft, when thou, my music, music play'st,
Upon that blessed wood whose motion sounds
With thy sweet fingers, when thou gently sway'st
The wiry concord that mine ear confounds,
Do I envy those jacks [151] that nimble leap
To kiss the tender inward of thy hand,
Whilst my poor lips, which should that harvest reap,
At the wood's boldness by thee blushing stand!
To be so tickled, they would change their state
And situation with those dancing chips,
O'er whom thy fingers walk with gentle gait,
Making dead wood more blest than living lips.
Since saucy jacks so happy are in this,
Give them thy fingers, me thy lips to kiss.

CXXIX [152]

TH' EXPENSE of spirit in a waste of shame
Is lust in action; and till action, lust
Is perjured, murderous, bloody, full of blame,
Savage, extreme, rude, cruel, not to trust; [153]
Enjoyed no sooner but despised straight;
Past reason hunted; and no sooner had,
Past reason hated, as a swallowed bait,
On purpose laid to make the taker mad:
Mad in pursuit, and in possession so;
Had, having, and in quest to have, extreme;
A bliss in proof,[154] and proved, a very woe;
Before, a joy proposed; behind, a dream.
All this the world well knows; yet none knows well
To shun the heaven that leads men to this hell.

---

150 This is the second sonnet of the second large sequence of the series, devoted to a Dark Lady, who, if she existed in real life, has never been certainly identified. Professor Brooke characterizes her: "She was a harlot, but also a woman of quality; in social rank very likely—for she played the spinet and had a taste for courtly verse—and certainly in personality." He suggests that she was the model for Cressida and Cleopatra.

151 *jacks:* in the virginal, or spinet, pieces of wood attached to the keys and holding quills which pluck the strings. The jacks leaped nimbly, as the sonnet says, but it is rather the keys than the jacks which would "kiss the tender inward" of the player's hand.

152 Compare Sonnet CXLVI.

153 *Th' expense . . . trust:* The word order slightly obscures the meaning. Lust, when put into action, spills spirit (life, vitality) in a desert of shame; before it is put into action, lust is perjured, murderous, etc.

154 *in proof:* during the experience.

CXXX [155]

My mistress' eyes are nothing like the sun;
Coral is far more red than her lips' red;
If snow be white, why then her breasts are dun;
If hairs be wires, black wires grow on her head.
I have seen roses damasked,[156] red and white,
But no such roses see I in her cheeks;
And in some perfumes is there more delight
Than in the breath that from my mistress reeks.
I love to hear her speak, yet well I know
That music hath a far more pleasing sound;
I grant I never saw a goddess go; [157]
My mistress, when she walks, treads on the ground.
And yet, by heaven, I think my love as rare
As any she belied with false compare.

CXXXV [158]

Whoever hath her wish, thou hast thy *Will,*
And *Will* to boot, and *Will* in overplus,
More than enough am I that vex thee still,
To thy sweet will making addition thus.
Wilt thou, whose will is large and spacious,
Not once vouchsafe to hide my will in thine?
Shall will in others seem right gracious,
And in my will no fair acceptance shine?
The sea, all water, yet receives rain still,
And in abundance addeth to his store;
So thou, being rich in *Will,* add to thy *Will*
One ill of mine, to make thy large *Will* more.
Let no unkind "No!" fair beseechers kill;
Think all but one, and me in that one *Will.*

---

[155] An anti-Petrarchan sonnet. All of the details denied by the poet to his mistress are commonly attributed by other Elizabethan sonneteers to their ladies.

[156] *damasked:* mingled red and white.

[157] *go:* walk.

[158] This punning sonnet seems to mean that the Dark Lady had another person named Will besides the poet. Some suggest that this was her husband, some that it is the poet's friend of the first series. The common noun "will" has several meanings, which are played on here: (1) volition (line 4); (2) carnal desire (lines 5–8).

CXXXVIII [159]

WHEN my love swears that she is made of truth,
I do believe her, though I know she lies,
That she might think me some untutored youth,
Unlearned in the world's false subtleties.
Thus vainly thinking that she thinks me young,
Although she knows my days are past the best,
Simply [160] I credit her false-speaking tongue:
On both sides thus is simple truth suppressed.
But wherefore says she not she is unjust? [161]
And wherefore say not I that I am old?
Oh, love's best habit [162] is in seeming trust,
And age in love loves not to have years told.
Therefore I lie with her and she with me,
And in our faults by lies we flattered be.

CXLIII

Lo, as a careful housewife runs to catch
One of her feathered creatures [163] broke away,
Sets down her babe, and makes all swift dispatch
In pursuit of the thing she would have stay;
Whilst her neglected child holds her in chase,
Cries to catch her whose busy care is bent
To follow that which flies before her face,
Not prizing [164] her poor infant's discontent:
So runn'st thou after that which flies from thee,
Whilst I thy babe chase thee afar behind;
But if thou catch thy hope, turn back to me,
And play the mother's part, kiss me, be kind:
So will I pray that thou mayst have thy *Will,*[165]
If thou turn back and my loud crying still.

---

[159] This sonnet was the first poem in *The Passionate Pilgrime* (1599) in a slightly different version. Shakespeare was accordingly thirty-five or younger when he wrote it. (Cf. line 6.)

[160] *simply:* like a simpleton.

[161] *unjust:* faithless.

[162] *habit:* deportment.

[163] *feathered creatures:* possibly a quibble on the feathers worn by gallants.

[164] *prizing:* being concerned about.

[165] *Will:* See Sonnet CXXXV and note.

CXLIV [166]

Two loves I have of comfort and despair,
Which like two spirits do suggest me still: [167]
The better angel is a man right fair,
The worser spirit a woman, colored ill.
To win me soon to hell, my female evil
Tempteth my better angel from my side,
And would corrupt my saint to be a devil,
Wooing his purity with her foul pride.
And whether that my angel be turned fiend
Suspect I may, yet not directly tell;
But being both from me, both to each [168] friend,
I guess one angel in another's hell.
Yet this shall I ne'er know, but live in doubt,
Till my bad angel fire [169] my good one out.

CXLVI [170]

Poor soul, the center of my sinful earth,
Lord of [171] these rebel powers that thee array,
Why dost thou pine within and suffer dearth,
Painting thy outward walls so costly gay?
Why so large cost, having so short a lease,
Dost thou upon thy fading mansion spend?
Shall worms, inheritors of this excess,
Eat up thy charge? Is this thy body's end?
Then, soul, live thou upon thy servant's loss,
And let that pine to aggravate [172] thy store;
Buy terms [173] divine in selling hours of dross;
Within be fed, without be rich no more.
So shalt thou feed on death, that feeds on men,
And death once dead, there's no more dying then.

---

[166] First printed in *The Passionate Pilgrime* (1599). It is similar in phrasing to Drayton's *Idea,* Sonnet XX, of the same year. This, with two other sonnets, CXXXIII and CXXXIV, brings together the Dark Lady and the friend. Sonnets XXXIII and XLI may refer to the same situation.

[167] *suggest:* tempt; *still:* constantly.

[168] *from me:* away from me; *to each:* to each other.

[169] *fire:* drive out with fire.

[170] As a repentance sonnet, compare with Sidney's "Leave me, O love," p. 269.

[171] *Lord of:* Herford's conjecture, to take the place of the repeated last three words of line 1 in the Quarto.

[172] *aggravate:* increase.

[173] *terms:* long periods.

CXLVII

My love is as a fever, longing still[174]
For that which longer nurseth the disease;
Feeding on that which doth preserve the ill,
Th' uncertain sickly appetite to please.
My reason, the physician to my love,
Angry that his prescriptions are not kept,
Hath left me, and I desperate now approve[175]
Desire is death, which physic did except.[176]
Past cure I am, now reason is past care,[177]
And frantic-mad with evermore unrest;
My thoughts and my discourse as madmen's are,
At random from the truth vainly expressed;
For I have sworn thee fair, and thought thee bright,
Who art as black as hell, as dark as night.

CLI

Love is too young to know what conscience is;
Yet who knows not conscience is born of love?
Then, gentle cheater, urge not my amiss,
Lest guilty of my faults thy sweet self prove:
For, thou betraying me, I do betray
My nobler part to my gross body's treason;
My soul doth tell my body that he may
Triumph in love; flesh stays no farther reason,
But, rising at thy name, doth point out thee
As his triumphant prize. Proud of this pride,
He is contented thy poor drudge to be,
To stand in thy affairs, fall by thy side.
No want of conscience hold it that I call
Her "love" for whose dear love I rise and fall.

---

[174] *longing still:* constantly craving.

[175] *approve:* prove that.

[176] *Desire . . . except:* Desire, which refused the physic of reason, is death.

[177] *past care:* indifferent, and no longer in medical charge.

Lyrics

SECOND only to the drama, lyric poetry is one of the finest products of the Elizabethan age. Everyone wrote lyrics, from the Queen herself to the lowliest ballad-writer, but the tradition was essentially a courtly one. Ability to write verse and to sing was the accomplishment of the gentleman, following Castiglione's pattern that the true courtier should be not only a man of action but a practiser of the arts of poetry and music as well. The early literary influences were Italian also. From the small Petrarchan stream which first flowed in English through the work of Wyatt and Surrey came the development of the more or less formal lyric poetry of the sonnet cycles.

Though the sonnet was the most widely used and highly developed lyric form, Elizabethan lyric poetry is remarkable for its variety of song measures and for its range of themes. Sir E. K. Chambers finds Elizabethan poetry "characteristically light-hearted," but although the carefree spirit and love predominate, the serious themes of fortune, death, and the questioning of life are found in the songs of almost every lyricist. In skill of execution the lyric reached a perfection parallel to its sister art, music, and a great body of Elizabethan poetry cannot be considered apart from its musical settings.

For convenience it is customary to consider the lyrics outside the sonnets in three groups: miscellaneous lyrics (anonymous lyrics and lyrics of minor writers), lyrics in the song books, and songs in the plays. The lyrics in the prose romances are usually studied with the miscellaneous lyrics.

Although the courtier's code forbade a gentleman to publish his own verses, manuscript copies in circulation somehow found their way into the hands of enterprising printers who published them. Mainly through the efforts of printers like Richard Tottel and his followers, the Elizabethans came to know their lyric poets in miscellanies, or anthologies, perhaps a development from the custom of keeping commonplace books. In the last quarter of the century some ten miscellanies were issued, from *The Paradise of Dainty Devices* in 1576 to Davison's *Poetical Rhapsody* (1602).

In the miscellanies and in the manuscript collections that have been preserved is a wealth of lyric poetry in many forms. The courtly traditions of love provide many themes. "Would you have a love song, or a song of good life?" the Clown in *Twelfth Night* asked Sir Toby Belch. Sir Toby's preference for "A love song, a love song" would, perhaps, have been any Elizabethan's choice. But after Spenser's *Shepheardes Calender* (1579), a turning point in the serious development of artistic English poetry, pastoral lyrics abound, skillful in their stories of the loves of Phillis and Coridon and others of the pastoral crew.

The lyric is fundamentally by definition a song, and in no period of English literature are poetry and music so closely allied.

> If music and sweet poetry agree,
> As they must needs (the sister and the brother)

wrote Richard Barnfield; the Elizabethan song books are splendid examples of the agreement. Though the first English song books were directly inspired by the Italian madrigal collections, the madrigal in the hands of English composers soon became a highly developed form even surpassing its models. William Byrd, perhaps the greatest Elizabethan composer, published in 1588 his *Psalmes, Sonets, and Songs of sadnes and pietie,* and in the same year Nicholas Yonge issued *Musica Transalpina,* a collection of Italian madrigals. These collections, in which the works of over twenty-five composers have been preserved, started a vogue which lasted until the early decades of the next century. The madrigal was in reality a complicated art form, an unaccompanied song of from three to six voices, polyphonic in structure. It was usually sung by groups, sitting around a table. Each voice part was printed in a small quarto volume. No one voice carried the melody, as was usual in part songs, but all parts were of equal interest, and often one or more melodic themes were here intricately interwoven in the voices. Similar complication occurred in the words. From a poem usually of a single stanza of from six to ten lines, phrases were repeated and altered. To illustrate these descriptions, Dr. Fellowes' example from Thomas Morley's *Canzonets* (1593) will serve. The simple lyric follows:

What ails my darling thus to sit alone so weary?
Say why is my dear now not merry?
Oh cease, alas, to grieve thee,
And here a kiss take to relieve thee.
Up now! arise!—how can my love lie sleeping?
And see yon lusty leaping.

The actual words sung by the three voices illustrate the rearrangement of the first two lines which the composer made.

Cantus. What ails my darling, say what ails my darling, what ails my sweet pretty darling, what ails my sweet, what ails mine own sweet darling? What ails my darling dear thus sitting all alone, sitting all alone, all alone so weary? Say, why is my dear now not merry?

Altus. What ails my darling, say what ails my darling, what ails my darling dear, what ails mine only sweet, mine only sweet darling? What ails my darling, what ails my darling dear, sitting all alone, sitting all alone so weary? Say what grieves my dear that she is not merry?

Bassus. What ails my darling, say what ails my darling, what ails my darling, say what ails my dainty dainty darling, what ails mine own sweet darling? What ails my dainty darling, my dainty darling so to sit alone, so to sit alone so weary, and is not merry?

(*English Madrigal Composers,* p. xx.)

Another type of song which attained great popularity was the solo song, lute song, or air, for the most part a characteristically English form. John Dowland, one of the most celebrated composers and lutenists of his time, published the earliest English book of airs in 1597. Like the madrigal, the air continued in popularity into the early decades of the seventeenth century. Over twenty composers are represented in at least thirty books of airs up to 1622.

The air was a solo song for which there was accompaniment on the lute, viola da gamba or other viols. The song could be performed as a solo with instrumental accompaniment, or voices could be used to sing or reinforce the instrumental parts. The lutenists selected words from the great store of lyric poetry at hand, and because of the homophonic nature of music could make one setting to serve a poem of several stanzas. Only rarely do the composers acknowledge the authorship of the poems. Thomas Campion (who is treated separately below) is the only composer known to have written his own words. To the books of airs English literature owes the preservation of many of its finest lyrics.

Song in English drama has had a continuous tradition from the medieval miracle plays to the present, but in Elizabethan drama at its height, songs had an importance never equaled since, with the possible exception of Restoration drama. Only a part of the texts and very little of the music of dramatic songs have been preserved, for frequently a song in a play is indicated but not printed. Possibly, as in the case of music for the plays, poets other than the playwright were engaged to write the songs. Many dramatic songs, especially in the early plays, were set to well-known ballad and dance tunes. The songs were often extraneous, that is, they did not forward the action or serve as some integral part of the atmosphere of the play, but in the hands of Shakespeare and a few of his fellow dramatists, such as Fletcher, the songs are skillfully woven into the texture of the play. In many cases the singer had no part in the action, but was called in for a song or two. The number of songs in the plays varies from one to ten or a dozen, but throughout tragedy and comedy alike songs were scattered.

The taste for lyric poetry and song was widespread in an age where everybody sang, and where vocal music, both sacred and secular, reached such a high peak of development.

BIBLIOGRAPHY: Norman Ault, *Elizabethan Lyrics,* New York, 1925; M. W. Black, *Elizabethan and Seventeenth-Century Lyrics,* New York, 1938; E. H. Fellowes, *English Madrigal Verse,* 2nd ed., Oxford, 1929; E. B. Reed, *Songs from the British Drama,* New Haven, 1925; *English Lyrical Poetry,* New Haven, 1912.

Professor Hyder E. Rollins has edited the following miscellanies for the Harvard University Press. *Tottel's Miscellany,* 1557 (2 vols., 1928); *The Paradise of Dainty Devices,* 1576 (1927); *A Gorgeous Gallery of Gallant Inventions,* 1578 (1926); *A Handful of Pleasant Delights,* 1584 (1924); *The Phoenix Nest,* 1593 (1931); *The Arbor of Amorous Devices,* 1597 (1936); *England's Helicon,* 1600 (2 vols., 1935); *A Poetical Rhapsody,* 1602 (2 vols., 1931–1932).

Canon E. H. Fellowes has edited the madrigalists in *The English Madrigal School,* 36 vols., London, 1913–1924, and the lutenist composers in *The English School of Lutenist Song Writers,* London, 1920———. William Chappell, *Popular Music of The Olden Time,* 2 vols., London [1855], and a revised edition by H. E. Wooldridge, 1893; J. M. Gibbon, *Melody and the Lyric,* London, 1930.

W. J. Lawrence, *The Elizabethan Playhouse and Other Studies,* London, 1912; J. R. Moore, "The Songs of the Public Theaters in the Time of Shakespeare," *JEGP,* XXVIII (1929), 162–202; Bruce Pattison, *Music and Poetry in the English Renaissance,* London, 1947; G. Bontoux, *La Chanson en Angleterre au temps d'Elisabeth,* Paris, 1938.

MINOR LYRICS

ELIZABETH[1]

1533–1603

When I was fair and young, and favor graced me,[2]
Of many was I sought, their mistress for to be;
But I did scorn them all, and answered them therefore,
Go, go, go, seek some otherwhere,
Importune me no more!

How many weeping eyes I made to pine with woe,
How many sighing hearts, I have no skill to show;
Yet I the prouder grew, and answered them therefore,
Go, go, go, seek some otherwhere,
Importune me no more!

Then spake fair Venus' son, that proud victorious boy,
And said: Fine dame, since that you be so coy,
I will so pluck your plumes that you shall say no more,
Go, go, go, seek some otherwhere,
Importune me no more!

When he had spake these words, such change grew in my breast
That neither night nor day since that, I could take any rest.
Then lo! I did repent that I had said before,
Go, go, go, seek some otherwhere,
Importune me no more!

[1] *Elizabeth:* The Queen is accredited with the following verses, but the attribution is not certain. The author of *The Arte of English Poesie* (ed. G. D. Willcock and Alice Walker, Cambridge, 1936, p. 63) after discussing Elizabethan poets, writes: "But last in recitall and first in degree is the Queene our souveraigne lady, whose learned, delicate, noble Muse, easily surmounteth all the rest that have written before her time or since, for sence, sweetness and subtillitie, be it in ode, Elegie, Epigram, or any other kinds of poeme Heroick or Lyricke, wherein it shall please her Maiestie to employ her penne, euen by as much oddes as her owne excellent estate and degree exceedeth all the rest of her most humble vassals."

[2] From Bodley MS Rawlinson Poet. 85.

The doubt of future foes exiles my present joy,[3]
And wit me warns to shun such snares as threaten mine annoy.
For falsehood now doth flow and subject faith doth ebb,
Which would not be if reason ruled or wisdom weaved the web.
But clouds of toys untried do cloak aspiring minds,
Which turn to rain of late repent by course of changed winds.
The top of hope supposed, the root of ruth will be,
And fruitless all their graffed guiles, as shortly ye shall see.
The dazzled eyes with pride, which great ambition blinds,
Shall be unseeled [4] by worthy wights whose foresight falsehood finds.
The daughter of debate that eke discord doth sow
Shall reap no gain where former rule hath taught still peace to grow.
No foreign banished wight shall anchor in this port;
Our realm it brooks no stranger's force, let them elsewhere resort.
Our rusty sword with rest shall first his edge employ
To poll the tops that seek such change and gape for joy.

THOMAS, LORD VAUX

1510–1556

THE AGED LOVER RENOUNCETH LOVE [5]

I loathe that I did love,
In youth that I thought sweet,
As time requires for my behove,
Methinks they are not meet.

My lusts they do me leave,
My fancies all be fled,
And tract of time begins to weave
Gray hairs upon my head.

For age with stealing steps
Hath clawed me with his crutch,
And lusty life away she leaps
As there had been none such.

My Muse doth not delight
Me as she did before;
My hand and pen are not in plight,
As they have been of yore.

For reason me denies
This youthly idle rhyme;
And day by day to me she cries,
"Leave off these toys in time."

[3] Appears in George Puttenham's *Arte of English Poesie* (1589; ed. Willcock and Walker, p. 248) as an example of "Expolitis."

[4] *unseeled:* The figure is from falconry. To seel is to close the eyes of the hawk by drawing threads through the lids.

[5] The poem, printed in *Tottel's Miscellany* (1557; ed. Rollins, pp. 165–166), was so popular that it was licensed for publication as a broadside ballad. Tunes named from the first line (see Chappell, *Popular Music,* I, 216) were used for several other lyrics. It is cleverly "misquoted" in *Hamlet,* V, i, 69 ff.

The wrinkles in my brow,
  The furrows in my face,
Say, limping age will lodge him now
  Where youth must give him place.

The harbinger of death,
  To me I see him ride,
The cough, the cold, the gasping breath
  Doth bid me to provide

A pickaxe and a spade,
  And eke a shrouding sheet,
A house of clay for to be made
  For such a guest most meet.

Methinks I hear the clark
  That knolls the carefull knell,
And bids me leave my woeful wark,
  Ere nature me compel.

My keepers knit the knot
  That youth did laugh to scorn,
Of me that clean shall be forgot
  As I had not been born.

Thus must I youth give up,
  Whose badge I long did wear;
To them I yield the wanton cup
  That better may it bear.

Lo, here the bared skull,
  By whose bald sign I know
That stooping age away shall pull
  Which youthful years did sow.

For beauty with her band
  These crooked cares hath wrought,
And shipped me into the land
  From whence I first was brought.

And ye that bide behind,
  Have ye none other trust:
As ye of clay were cast by kind,
  So shall ye waste to dust.

RICHARD EDWARDS

1523?–1566

AMANTIUM IRAE AMORIS REDINTEGRATIO EST [6]

In going to my naked bed, as one that would have slept,
I heard a wife sing to her child, that long before had wept;
She sighed sore, and sang full sweet to bring the babe to rest,
That would not rest but cried still, in sucking at her breast.

[6] From *The Paradise of Dainty Devices* (1576; ed. Rollins, pp. 42–43), an anthology made by the printer Henry Disle, from a commonplace book left by Richard Edwards, poet, playwright, musician, and master of the Children of the Chapel Royal. There is a musical setting in the "Mulliner MS" B. M. Additional 30513.

She was full weary of her watch,[7] and grieved with her child,
She rocked it and rated [8] it, until on her it smiled.
Then did she say, "Now have I found this proverb true to prove,
The falling out of faithful friends, renewing is of love." [9]

Then took I paper, pen, and ink, this proverb for to write,
In register for to remain of such a worthy wight.[10]
As she proceeded thus in song unto her little brat [11]
Much matter uttered she of weight, in place whereas she sat;
And proved plain there was no beast, nor creature bearing life,
Could well be known to live in love, without discord and strife.
Then kissed she her little babe, and sware, by God above,
"The falling out of faithful friends, renewing is of love."

She said that neither king, ne prince, ne lord could live aright,
Until their puissance they did prove, their manhood, and their might;
When manhood shall be matched so, that fear can take no place,
Then weary works makes warriors each other to embrace,
And leave their force that failed them, which did consume the rout
That might before have lived their time and nature out.
Then did she sing, as one that thought no man could her reprove,
"The falling out of faithful friends, renewing is of love."

She said she saw no fish, ne fowl, nor beast within her haunt
That met a stranger in their kind, but could give it a taunt.
Since flesh might not endure, but rest must wrath succeed,
And force the fight to fall to play, in pasture where they feed,
So noble nature can well end the works she hath begun,
And bridle well that will not cease her tragedy in some.
Thus in her song she oft rehearsed, as did her well behove,
"The falling out of faithful friends, renewing is of love."

"I marvel much, pardy," quoth she, "for to behold the rout,
To see man, woman, boy, and beast, to toss the world about;
Some kneel, some crouch, some beck, some check, and some can smoothly smile,
And some embrace others in arms, and there think many a wile;
Some stand aloof at cap and knee, some humble, and some stout,
Yet are they never friends indeed until they once fall out!"
Thus ended she her song, and said, before she did remove,
"The falling out of faithful friends, renewing is of love."

[7] *watch:* vigil.
[8] *rated:* scolded.
[9] The refrain here follows the reading of editions from 1578 on; the first edition reads "is the renewing of love."
[10] *wight:* person, being.
[11] *brat:* simply child.

BARNABE GOOGE[12]

1540–1594

OUT OF SIGHT, OUT OF MIND

The oftener seen, the more I lust,
  The more I lust, the more I smart,
The more I smart, the more I trust,
  The more I trust, the heavier heart;
The heavy heart breeds mine unrest,
Thy absence, therefore, like I best.

The rarer seen, the less in mind,
  The less in mind, the lesser pain,
The lesser pain, less grief I find,
  The lesser grief, the greater gain,
The greater gain, the merrier I,
Therefore I wish thy sight to fly.

The further off, the more I joy,
  The more I joy, the happier life,
The happier life, less hurts annoy,
  The lesser hurts, pleasure most rife:
Such pleasures rife shall I obtain
When distance doth depart us twain.

EDWARD DE VERE, EARL OF OXFORD[13]

1550–1604

If women could be fair and yet not fond,
Or that their love were firm, not fickle, still,
I would not marvel that they make men bond,
By service long to purchase their good will.
  But when I see how frail those creatures are,
  I muse that men forget themselves so far.

[12] Barnabe Googe was a translator and minor poet whose eclogues are among the early examples of pastoral poetry in English. "Out of Sight" is from his *Eglogs, Epytaphes and Sonettes* (1563).

[13] Edward de Vere, seventeenth Earl of Oxford, was a favorite courtier of Queen Elizabeth's; his work may be regarded as good specimens of Elizabethan courtly poetry. "If women could be fair," from Bodley MS Rawlinson Poet. 85, was set (with several verbal variants) for five voices by William Byrd in *Psalmes, Sonets, and Songs* (1588).

To mark the choice they make and how they change,
How oft from Phoebus they do fly to Pan,
Unsettled still, like haggards wild they range,
These gentle birds that fly from man to man;
  Who would not scorn, and shake them from the fist,
  And let them fly, fair fools, which way they list?

Yet for disport we fawn and flatter both,
To pass the time when nothing else can please;
And train them to our lure with subtle oath
Till, weary of their wiles, ourselves we ease;
  And then we say, when we their fancy try,
  To play with fools, oh, what a fool was I!

What cunning can express [14]
The favor of her face
To whom in this distress
I do appeal for grace?
  A thousand Cupids fly
  About her gentle eye.

From whence each throws a dart
That kindleth soft sweet fire
Within my sighing heart,
Possessed by desire.
  No sweeter life I try
  Than in her love to die.

The lily in the field
That glories in his white,
For pureness now must yield
And render up his right.
  Heaven pictured in her face
  Doth promise joy and grace.

Fair Cynthia's silver light
That beats on running streams
Compares not with her white,
Whose hairs are all sunbeams.
  Her virtues so do shine
  As day unto mine eyne.

With this there is a red
Exceeds the damask rose,
Which in her cheeks is spread,
Whence every favor grows.
  In sky there is no star
  That she surmounts not far.

When Phoebus from the bed
Of Thetis doth arise,
The morning blushing red
In fair carnation wise,
  He shows it in her face
  As queen of every grace.

This pleasant lily-white,
This taint of roseate red,
This Cynthia's silver light,
This sweet fair Dea spread,
  These sunbeams in mine eye,
  These beauties make me die!

[14] From the *Phoenix Nest* (1593; ed. Rollins, pp. 62–63).

NICHOLAS BRETON[15]

1545?–1626?

Say that I should say I love ye,
  Would you say 'tis but a saying?
But if love in prayers move ye,
  Will you not be moved with praying?

Think I think that love should know ye,
  Will you think 'tis but a thinking?
But if love the thought do show ye,
  Will ye lose your eyes with winking?

Write that I do write you blessed,
  Will you write 'tis but a writing?
But if truth and love confess it,
  Will ye doubt the true inditing?

No: I say, and think, and write it,—
  Write, and think, and say your pleasure.
Love and truth and I indite it,
  You are blessed out of measure.

PHILLIDA AND CORIDON[16]

In the merry month of May,
In a morn by break of day
Forth I walked by the wood-side,
Whereas May was in his pride.
There I spied, all alone,
Phillida and Coridon.
Much ado there was, God wot,
He would love and she would not.
She said, "Never man was true";
He said, "None was false to you."
He said he had loved her long.
She said, "Love should have no wrong."
Coridon would kiss her then;

[15] Nicholas Breton, one of the most facile and popular versifiers of his time, suffered from hasty production, but his pastorals rank high. "Say that I should say" and "Phillida and Coridon" were printed in *England's Helicon* (1600; ed. Rollins, pp. 192–193).

[16] Set as a three-man's song and sung at an entertainment for the Queen given by the Earl of Hertford in 1591. Elizabeth applauded the song and asked that it be sung again. The song is also set in Michael East's *Madrigales* (1604).

She said maids must kiss no men
Till they did for good and all.
Then she made the shepherd call
All the heavens to witness truth,
Never loved a truer youth.
Thus, with many a pretty oath,
Yea and nay, and faith and troth,
Such as silly shepherds use
When they will not love abuse,
Love which had been long deluded
Was with kisses sweet concluded.
And Phillida with garlands gay
Was made the lady of the May.

PASTORAL[17]

Who can live in heart so glad
As the merry country lad?
Who upon a fair green balk
May at pleasure sit and walk,
And amid the azure skies
See the morning sun arise,
While he hears in every spring
How the birds do chirp and sing;
Or before the hounds in cry
See the hare go stealing by;
Or along the shallow brook,
Angling with a baited hook,
See the fishes leap and play
In a blessed sunny day;
Or to hear the partridge call
Till she have her covey all;
Or to see the subtle fox,
How the villain plies the box;[18]
After feeding on his prey,
How he closely sneaks away
Through the hedge and down the
furrow
Till he gets into his burrow;
Then the bee to gather honey;
And the little black-haired coney,
On a bank for sunny place,
With her forefeet wash her face—
Are not these, with thousands mo
Than the courts of kings do know,
The true pleasing spirit's sights
That may breed true love's de-
lights?
But withal this happiness,
To behold that shepherdess
To whose eyes all shepherds yield,
All the fairest of the field,
Fair Aglaia, in whose face
Lives the shepherd's highest grace;
In whose worthy wonder praise
See what her true shepherd says:
She is neither proud nor fine,
But in spirit more divine.
She can neither lour nor leer,
But a sweeter smiling cheer.
She had never painted face,
But a sweeter smiling grace.
She can never love dissemble,
Truth doth so her thoughts as-
semble,
That where wisdom guides her will

[17] From *The Passionate Shepherd* (1604).

[18] *plies the box:* plays a trick, runs along the box hedge.

She is kind and constant still.
All in sum, she is that creature,
Of that truest comfort's nature,
That doth show (but in exceedings)
How their praises had their breedings.
Let then poets feign their pleasure
In their fictions of love's treasure;
Proud high spirits seek their graces
In their idol painted faces;
My love's spirit's lowliness,
In affection's humbleness,
Under heaven no happiness
Seeks but in this shepherdess.
For whose sake I say and swear
By the passions that I bear,
Had I got a kingly grace,
I would leave my kingly place,
And in heart be truly glad
To become a country lad,
Hard to lie, and go full bare,
And to feed on hungry fare,
So I might but live to be
Where I might but sit to see
Once a day, or all day long,
The sweet subject of my song;
In Aglaia's only eyes
All my worldly paradise.

SIR EDWARD DYER[19]

1540?–1607

My mind to me a kingdom is;
  Such present joys therein I find
That it excels all other bliss
  That earth affords or grows by kind.
Though much I want which most would have,
Yet still my mind forbids to crave.

No princely pomp, no wealthy store,
  No force to win the victory,
No wily wit to salve a sore,
  No shape to feed a loving eye;
To none of these I yield as thrall.
For why[20] my mind doth serve for all.

I see how plenty suffers oft,
  And hasty climbers soon do fall;
I see that those which are aloft
  Mishap doth threaten most of all;
They get with toil, they keep with fear.
Such cares my mind could never bear.

Content I live, this is my stay;
  I seek no more than may suffice;
I press to bear no haughty sway;
  Look, what I lack my mind supplies;
Lo, thus I triumph like a king,

[19] Sir Edward Dyer, friend of Fulke Greville and Sir Philip Sidney, is best known for his lyric "My mind to me," etc. (See R. M. Sargent, *At The Court of Queen Elizabeth,* 1935, pp. 213–218.) The lyric, which combines stoic and Senecan philosophizing, was one of the most popular in the sixteenth and seventeenth centuries and exists in manuscript and broadside-ballad versions. Six stanzas were set in 1588 by William Byrd in his *Psalmes, Sonets, and Songs,* apparently the first printed version. The present text is based on Bodley MS Rawlinson Poet. 85.

[20] *For why:* because.

Content with that my mind doth bring.

Some have too much, yet still do crave;
I little have, and seek no more.
They are but poor, though much they have,
And I am rich with little store.
They poor, I rich; they beg, I give;
They lack, I leave; they pine, I live.

I laugh not at another's loss;
I grudge not at another's gain;
No worldly waves my mind can toss;
My state at one doth still remain.
I fear no foe, I fawn no friend;
I loathe not life, nor dread my end.

Some weigh their pleasure by their lust,
Their wisdom by their rage of will;
Their treasure is their only trust;
A cloaked craft their store of skill.
But all the pleasure that I find
Is to maintain a quiet mind.

My wealth is health and perfect ease;
My conscience clear my choice defense;
I neither seek by bribes to please,
Nor by deceit to breed offense.
Thus do I live; thus will I die.
Would all did so as well as I!

ROBERT SOUTHWELL[21]

1561?–1595

UPON THE IMAGE OF DEATH

Before my face the picture hangs
That daily should put me in mind
Of these cold names and bitter pangs
That shortly I am like to find;
But yet, alas, full little I
Do think hereon that I must die.

I often look upon a face
Most ugly, grisly, bare, and thin;
I often view the hollow place
Where eyes and nose had sometimes been;
I see the bones across that lie,
Yet little think that I must die.

I read the label underneath,
That telleth me whereto I must;
I see the sentence eke that saith
Remember, man, that thou art dust!
But yet, alas, but seldom I
Do think indeed that I must die.

Continually at my bed's head
A hearse[22] doth hang, which doth me tell
That I ere morning may be dead,
Though now I feel myself full well;

[21] Robert Southwell, a Jesuit priest and poet, was arrested in 1592 and later hanged. See P. Janelle, *Robert Southwell, The Writer,* Clermont-Ferrand, 1935.

[22] *hearse:* a canopy of black to place over the coffin.

But yet, alas, for all this, I
Have little mind that I must die.

The gown which I do use to wear,
The knife wherewith I cut my meat,
And eke that old and ancient chair
Which is my only usual seat,—
All those do tell me I must die,
And yet my life amend not I.

My ancestors are turned to clay,
And many of my mates are gone;
My youngers daily drop away,
And can I think to 'scape alone?
No, no, I know that I must die,
And yet my life amend not I.

Not Solomon for all his wit,
Nor Samson, though he were so strong,
No king nor person ever yet
Could 'scape but death laid him along;
Wherefore I know that I must die,
And yet my life amend not I.

Though all the East did quake to hear
Of Alexander's dreadful name,
And all the West did likewise fear
To hear of Julius Caesar's fame,
Yet both by death in dust now lie;
Who then can 'scape but he must die?

If none can 'scape death's dreadful dart,
If rich and poor his beck obey,
If strong, if wise, if all do smart,
Then I to 'scape shall have no way.
Oh, grant me grace, Oh God, that I
My life may mend, sith I must die.

THE BURNING BABE

As I in hoary winter's night stood shivering in the snow,
Surprised I was with sudden heat which made my heart to glow;
And lifting up a fearful eye to view what fire was near,
A pretty babe all burning bright did in the air appear;
Who, scorched with excessive heat, such floods of tears did shed
As though his floods should quench his flames which with his tears were fed.
"Alas," quoth he, "but newly born in fiery heats I fry,
Yet none approach to warm their hearts or feel my fire but I!
My faultless breast the furnace is, the fuel wounding thorns,
Love is the fire, and sighs the smoke, the ashes shame and scorns;
The fuel justice layeth on, and mercy blows the coals,
The metal in this furnace wrought are men's defiled souls,
For which, as now on fire I am to work them to their good,
So will I melt into a bath to wash them in my blood."
With this he vanished out of sight and swiftly shrunk away,
And straight I called unto mind that it was Christmas day.

CHIDIOCK TICHBORNE

1558?–1586

TICHBORNE'S ELEGY, WRITTEN WITH HIS OWN HAND IN THE TOWER BEFORE HIS EXECUTION [1586][23]

My prime of youth is but a frost of cares,
My feast of joy is but a dish of pain,
My crop of corn is but a field of tares,
And all my good is but vain hope of gain;
The day is past, and yet I saw no sun,
And now I live, and now my life is done.

My tale was heard and yet it was not told,
My fruit is fallen and yet my leaves are green,
My youth is spent and yet I am not old,
I saw the world and yet I was not seen;
My thread is cut and yet it is not spun,
And now I live, and now my life is done.

I sought my death and found it in my womb,
I looked for life and saw it was a shade,
I trod the earth and knew it was my tomb,
And now I die, and now I was but made;
My glass is full, and now my glass is run,
And now I live, and now my life is done.

[23] From *Verses of Prayse and Joye written upon Her Maiesties Preseruation* (1586) (i.e., from the Babington Plot). Tichborne, one of the seven conspirators who were executed, may not have written this popular poem himself. It was set to music in John Mundy's *Songs and Psalmes* (1594), Michael East's *Madrigales* (1604), and Richard Alison's *An Howres Recreation in Musicke* (1606).

RICHARD BARNFIELD [24]

1574–1627

TO HIS FRIEND MASTER R. L.,[25] IN PRAISE OF MUSIC AND POETRY

If music and sweet poetry agree,
As they must needs (the sister and the brother),
Then must the love be great 'twixt thee and me,
Because thou lov'st the one, and I the other.
Dowland [26] to thee is dear, whose heavenly touch
Upon the lute doth ravish human sense;
Spenser to me, whose deep conceit is such
As, passing all conceit, needs no defense.
Thou lov'st to hear the sweet melodious sound
That Phoebus' lute (the queen of music) makes;
And I in deep delight am chiefly drowned
Whenas himself to singing he betakes.
One god is god of both (as poets feign),
One knight [27] loves both, and both in thee remain.

As it fell upon a day [28]
In the merry month of May,
Sitting in a pleasant shade
Which a grove of myrtles made,
Beasts did leap and birds did sing,
Trees did grow and plants did spring;
Everything did banish moan,
Save the nightingale alone.
She, poor bird, as all forlorn,
Leaned her breast up-till [29] a thorn
And there sung the doleful'st ditty,
That to hear it was great pity.

[24] In the *Passionate Pilgrime* (1599) three poems (the two printed in this selection and "The unknown shepherd's complaint") by Barnfield were printed as Shakespeare's. For discussion see *Shakespeare's Poems* (ed. Rollins), pp. 542, 556. They had been printed in 1598, however, as Barnfield's in *Poems in Divers Humors,* published with Barnfield's *The Encomion of Lady Pecunia,* from which these texts are taken.

[25] *Master R. L.:* probably not Richard Linche, the poet, as Grosart suggests, but a musician.

[26] *Dowland:* John Dowland (1563–1626), famous lutenist and composer of airs.

[27] *One knight:* probably Sir George Carey to whom Dowland dedicated his *First Booke of Songes or Ayres* (1597). Spenser dedicated *Muiopotmos* (1590) to Sir George's wife.

[28] The version in *England's Helicon* (1600; ed. Rollins, pp. 57–58) replaces lines 27–56 by a couplet.

[29] *up-till:* against.

"Fie, fie, fie," now would she cry,
"Teru, teru," by and by;
That to hear her so complain,
Scarce I could from tears refrain;
For her griefs so lively shown
Made me think upon mine own.
Ah, thought I, thou mourn'st in vain;
None takes pity on thy pain;
Senseless trees, they cannot hear thee;
Ruthless bears, they will not cheer thee.
King Pandion,[30] he is dead,
All thy friends are lapped in lead.
All thy fellow birds do sing,
Careless of thy sorrowing.
Whilst as fickle fortune smiled,
Thou and I were both beguiled.
Every one that flatters thee
Is no friend in misery:
Words are easy, like the wind,
Faithful friends are hard to find;
Every man will be thy friend
Whilst thou hast wherewith to spend,
But if store of crowns be scant,
No man will supply thy want.
If that one be prodigal,
Bountiful they will him call;
And with such-like flattering
Pity but he were a king.
If he be addict to vice,
Quickly him they will entice;
If to women he be bent,
They have at commandement;
But if fortune once do frown,
Then farewell his great renown;
They that fawned on him before
Use his company no more.
He that is thy friend indeed
He will help thee in thy need:
If thou sorrow, he will weep;
If thou wake, he cannot sleep;
Thus of every grief, in heart,
He with thee doth bear a part.
These are certain signs to know
Faithful friend from flatt'ring foe.

ANONYMOUS LYRICS

A PROPER SONG, ENTITLED: FAIN WOULD I HAVE A PRETTY THING TO GIVE UNTO MY LADY[1]

To the tune of *Lusty Gallant*

FAIN would I have a pretty thing
 To give unto my lady;
I name no thing, nor I mean no thing,
 But as pretty a thing as may be.

Twenty journeys would I make,
 And twenty ways would hie me,
To make adventure for her sake,
 To set some matter by me.

[30] *King Pandion:* King of Athens, father of Philomela and Procne.

[1] The ballad was included in *A Handful of Pleasant Delights* (1584) but was written as early as 1566. The tune, *Lusty Gallant,* is in Chappell's *Popular Music,* I, 91–92.

But I would fain have a pretty thing, &c.,
I name no thing, nor I mean no thing, &c.

Some do long for pretty knacks,
And some for strange devices;
God send me that my lady lacks,
I care not what the price is.
Thus fain, &c.

Some go here, and some go there,
Where gazes be not geason;[2]
And I go gaping everywhere,
But still come out of season.
Yet fain, &c.

I walk the town and tread the street,
In every corner seeking
The pretty thing I cannot meet,
That's for my lady's liking.
Fain, &c.

The mercers pull me going by,
The silky-wives say, What lack ye?
The thing you have not, then say I,
Ye foolish fools, go pack ye.
But fain, &c.

It is not all the silk in Cheap,[3]
Nor all the golden treasure,
Nor twenty bushels on a heap,
Can do my lady pleasure.
But fain, &c.

The gravers of the golden shows
With jewels do beset me;
The seamsters in the shops that sews,
They do nothing but let me.
But fain, &c.

But were it in the wit of man
By any means to make it,
I could for money buy it than,[4]
And say, Fair lady, take it.
Thus fain, &c.

---

[2] *geason:* rare.
[3] *Cheap:* Cheapside, famous in Elizabethan times as a street of fine shops.
[4] *than:* then.

Oh lady, what a luck is this,
  That my good willing misseth
To find what pretty thing it is
  That my good lady wisheth.

Thus fain would I have had this pretty thing
  To give unto my lady;
I said no harm, nor I meant no harm,
  But as pretty a thing as may be.

A NEW COURTLY SONNET, OF THE LADY GREENSLEEVES[5]

To the new tune of *Greensleeves*

Greensleeves was all my joy,
  Greensleeves was my delight;
Greensleeves was my heart of gold,
  And who but Lady Greensleeves?

Alas, my love, ye do me wrong
  To cast me off discourteously;
And I have loved you so long,
  Delighting in your company.

Greensleeves was all my joy,
  Greensleeves was my delight;
Greensleeves was my heart of gold,
  And who but Lady Greensleeves?

I have been ready at your hand
  To grant whatever you would crave;
I have both waged life and land,
  Your love and good will for to have.

Greensleeves was all my joy, &c.

I bought thee kerchiefs to thy head,
  That were wrought fine and gallantly;
I kept thee both at board and bed,
  Which cost my purse well-favoredly.[6]

Greensleeves was all my joy, &c.

[5] Appeared in *A Handful of Pleasant Delights* (1584), though written as early as 1580. Shakespeare mentions the tune in *The Merry Wives of Windsor,* II, i, 64 and V, v, 22, and the music is in Chappell's *Popular Music,* I, 227–233.

[6] *well-favoredly:* handsomely.

I bought thee petticoats of the best,
  The cloth so fine as fine might be;
I gave thee jewels for thy chest,
  And all this cost I spent on thee.

Greensleeves was all my joy, &c.

Thy smock of silk both fair and white,
  With gold embroidered gorgeously;
Thy petticoat of sendal [7] right,
  And thus I bought thee gladly.

Greensleeves was all my joy, &c.

Thy girdle of gold so red,
  With pearls bedecked sumptuously,
The like no other lasses had,
  And yet thou wouldst not love me.

Greensleeves was all my joy, &c.

Thy purse and eke thy gay gilt knives,
  Thy pin case, gallant to the eye,
No better wore the burgess' wives,
  And yet thou wouldst not love me.

Greensleeves was all my joy, &c.

Thy crimson stockings all of silk,
  With gold all wrought above the knee,
Thy pumps as white as was the milk,
  And yet thou wouldst not love me.

Greensleeves was all my joy, &c.

Thy gown was of the grossy [8] green,
  Thy sleeves of satin hanging by,
Which made thee be our harvest queen,
  And yet thou wouldst not love me.

Greensleeves was all my joy, &c.

Thy garters fringed with the gold,
  And silver aglets [9] hanging by,
Which made thee blithe for to behold,
  And yet thou wouldst not love me.

Greensleeves was all my joy, &c.

---

[7] *sendal:* thin silk fabric.

[8] *grossy:* thickish, luxuriant; or more likely a misprint for grassy.

[9] *aglets:* pendants or metal spangles attached to lace or fringe.

My gayest gelding I thee gave,
  To ride wherever liked thee;
No lady ever was so brave,
  And yet thou wouldst not love me.

Greensleeves was all my joy, &c.

My men were clothed all in green,
  And they did ever wait on thee;
All this was gallant to be seen,
  And yet thou wouldst not love me.

Greensleeves was all my joy, &c.

They set thee up, they took thee down,
  They served thee with humility;
Thy foot might not once touch the ground,
  And yet thou wouldst not love me.

Greensleeves was all my joy, &c.

For every morning when thou rose
  I sent thee dainties orderly,
To cheer thy stomach from all woes,
  And yet thou wouldst not love me.

Greensleeves was all my joy, &c.

Thou couldst desire no earthly thing,
  But still thou hadst it readily;
Thy music still to play and sing,
  And yet thou wouldst not love me.

Greensleeves was all my joy, &c.

And who did pay for all this gear
  That thou didst spend when pleased thee?
Even I that am rejected here,
  And thou disdain'st to love me.

Greensleeves was all my joy, &c.

Well, I will pray to God on high
  That thou my constancy mayest see;
And that yet once before I die
  Thou wilt vouchsafe to love me.

Greensleeves was all my joy, &c.

Greensleeves, now farewell, adieu,
  God I pray to prosper thee;
For I am still thy lover true,
  Come once again and love me.

Greensleeves was all my joy, &c.

AS YOU CAME FROM THE HOLY LAND OF WALSINGHAM[10]

As you came from the holy land
  Of Walsingham,
Met you not with my true love,
  By the way as you came?

"How should I know your true love
  That have met many a one
As I came from the holy land,
  That have come, that have gone?"

She is neither white nor brown,
  But as the heavens fair;
There is none hath her form so divine,
  On the earth, in the air.

"Such a one did I meet, good sir,
  With angel-like face,
Who like a nymph, like a queen did appear
  In her gait, in her grace."

She hath left me here alone,
  All alone unknown,
Who sometime loved me as her life,
  And called me her own.

"What is the cause she hath left thee alone,
  And a new way doth take,
That sometime did thee love as herself,
  And her joy did thee make?"

I have loved her all my youth,
  But now am old as you see;
Love liketh not the falling fruit,
  Nor the withered tree.

For love is a careless child,
  And forgets promise past;
He is blind, he is deaf, when he list,
  And in faith never fast.

---

10 Text from Deloney's *Garland of Good Will* [n.d.]. Another version, with several verbal variants, is in Bodley MS Rawlinson Poet. 85 (reprinted in Ault, *Elizabethan Lyrics*, pp. 278–279). The poem is frequently ascribed to Ralegh. *Walsingham:* seat of the shrine of Our Lady of Walsingham from the thirteenth century.

His desire is fickle found,
  And a trustless joy;
He is won with a world of despair,
  And is lost with a toy.

Such is the love of womenkind,
  Or the word, love, abused,
Under which many childish desires
  And conceits are excused.

But love, it is a durable fire
  In the mind ever burning,
Never sick, never dead, never cold,
  From itself never turning.

PHILLIDA'S LOVE-CALL TO HER CORYDON, AND HIS REPLYING [11]

Phil. CORYDON, arise my Corydon,
  Titan shineth clear.
Cor. Who is it that calleth Corydon?
  Who is it that I hear?
Phil. Phillida, thy true love, calleth thee.
  Arise then, arise then,
    Arise and keep thy flock with me.
Cor. Phillida, my true love, is it she?
  I come then, I come then,
    I come and keep my flock with thee.

Phil. Here are cherries ripe, my Corydon,
  Eat them for my sake.
Cor. Here's my oaten pipe, my lovely one,
  Sport for thee to make.
Phil. Here are threads, my true love, fine as silk,
  To knit thee, to knit thee
    A pair of stockings white as milk.
Cor. Here are reeds, my true love, fine and neat,
  To make thee, to make thee
    A bonnet to withstand the heat.

[11] Text from *England's Helicon* (1600), signed "Ignoto" (ed. Rollins, pp. 69–71). In Bodley MS Rawlinson Poet. 148, f. 88^{v}, there is another version with many variants and some music.

Phil. I will gather flowers, my Corydon,
To set in thy cap.
Cor. I will gather pears, my lovely one,
To put in thy lap.
Phil. I will buy my true love garters gay
For Sundays, for Sundays,
To wear about his legs so tall.
Cor. I will buy my true love yellow say [12]
For Sundays, for Sundays,
To wear about her middle small.

Phil. When my Corydon sits on a hill,
Making melody,—
Cor. When my lovely one goes to her wheel,
Singing cheerily,—
Phil. Sure methinks my true love doth excel
For sweetness, for sweetness,
Our Pan, that old Arcadian knight.
Cor. And methinks my true love bears the bell
For clearness, for clearness,
Beyond the nymphs that be so bright.

Phil. Had my Corydon, my Corydon,
Been, alack, my [13] swain,—
Cor. Had my lovely one, my lovely one,
Been in Ida plain,—
Phil. Cynthia Endymion had refused,
Preferring, preferring
My Corydon to play withal;
Cor. The queen of love had been excused.
Bequeathing, bequeathing
My Phillida the golden ball.

Phil. Yonder comes my mother, Corydon,
Whither shall I fly?
Cor. Under yonder beech, my lovely one,
While she passeth by.
Phil. Say to her thy true love was not here.
Remember, remember,
Tomorrow is another day.
Cor. Doubt me not, my true love. Do not fear.
Farewell then, farewell then,
Heaven keep our loves alway.

[12] *say:* fine cloth.

[13] *my:* Bullen, to improve the sense, suggested "her," i.e., Cynthia's.

CRABBED AGE AND YOUTH [14]

CRABBED age and youth cannot live together:
Youth is full of pleasance,[15] age is full of care;
Youth like summer morn, age like winter weather;
Youth like summer brave, age like winter bare.
Youth is full of sport, age's breath is short;
  Youth is nimble, age is lame;
Youth is hot and bold, age is weak and cold;
  Youth is wild, and age is tame.
Age, I do abhor thee, youth, I do adore thee;
  Oh! my love, my love is young:
Age, I do defy thee: Oh! sweet shepherd, hie thee,
  For methinks thou stay'st too long.

PHILLIDA FLOUTS ME [16]

OH, WHAT a plague is love!
  How shall I bear it?
She will unconstant prove,
  I greatly fear it.
She so molests my mind
  That my wit faileth;
She wavers with the wind,
  As the ship saileth.
Please her best I may,
She looks another way:
Alack and well-a-day!
    Phillida flouts me.

At the fair yesterday
  She would not see me,
But turned another way
  When she came nigh me.
Dick had her in to dine;
  He might intreat [17] her.
Will had her to the wine;
  I could not get her.
With Daniel did she dance;
At me she looked askance.
Oh thrice unhappy chance!
    Phillida flouts me.

---

14 The text is from *The Passionate Pilgrime* (1599). Most critics do not accept this poem as Shakespeare's though many consider it "worthy of him." (See H. E. Rollins, ed. *Shakespeare's Poems*, pp. 546–549.)

15 *pleasance:* gaiety.

16 Several versions exist, some as broadside ballads popular in the seventeenth century. The text here is that of the Shirburn MS; the stanzas given are those in *Wit Restored* (1658), in slightly different order. Though the poem was written before 1603, M. W. Black comments (*Elizabethan and Seventeenth-Century Lyrics*, p. 534), "[It] might almost be said to strike the keynote of Cavalier song."

17 *intreat:* persuade.

Fair maid, be not so coy,
  Never disdain me;
I am my mother's boy;
  Sweet, entertain me.
She'll give me, when she dies,
  All things befitting:
Her poultry and her bees,
  With her goose sitting,
A pair of mattress beds,
A barrel full of shreds,—
And yet, for all my goods,
    Phillida flouts me.

She hath a clout[18] of mine,
  Wrought with good coventry,
Which she keeps for a sign
  Of my fidelity;
But, in faith, if she flinch,
  She shall not wear it:
To Tib, my t' other wench,
  I mean to bear it.
Yet it will kill my heart
So quickly to depart.
Death, kill me with thy dart!
    Phillida flouts me.

Thou shalt eat curds and cream,
  All the year lasting;
And drink the crystal stream,
  Pleasant in tasting;
Whig[19] and whey whilst thou burst,
  And bramble berries,
Pie lid and pasty crust,
  Pears, plums, and cherries.
Thy garments shall be thin,
Made of a wether's skin—
Yet all's not worth a pin.
    Phillida flouts me.

Maiden, look what you do
  And in time take me;
I can have other two,
  If you forsake me:
For Doll, the dairymaid,
  Laughed on me lately,
And wanton Winifred
  Favors me greatly.
One threw milk on my clothes,
T'other plays with my nose;
What loving signs be those!
    Phillida flouts me.

I cannot work and sleep,
  Both, at all season:
Love wounds my heart so deep,
  Without all reason.
I do consume, alas,
  With care and sorrow.
E'en like a sort of beasts
  Pinned[20] in a meadow.
I shall be dead, I fear,
Within this thousand year,
And all for very care:
    Phillida flouts me.

[18] *clout:* kerchief.
[19] *whig:* buttermilk.
[20] *pinned:* enclosed.

ODE [21]

ABSENCE, hear thou my protestation
Against thy strength,
Distance and length:
Do what thou canst for alteration,
For hearts of truest mettle
Absence doth join, and time doth settle.

Who loves a mistress of such quality,
He soon hath found
Affection's ground
Beyond time, place, and all mortality.
To hearts that cannot vary
Absence is present, time doth tarry.

My senses want their outward motions
Which now within
Reason doth win,
Redoubled in her secret notions;
Like rich men that take pleasure
In hiding more than handling treasure.

By absence this good means I gain,
That I can catch her,
Where none can watch her,
In some close corner of my brain;
There I embrace and kiss her,
And so I both enjoy and miss her.

MADRIGAL [22]

MY love in her attire doth show her wit,
It doth so well become her;
For every season she hath dressings fit,
For winter, spring, and summer.
No beauty she doth miss
When all her robes are on;
But beauty's self she is
When all her robes are gone.

---

[21] From Francis Davison's *Poetical Rhapsody* (1602). The poem has often been attributed to Donne, but Grierson (*The Poems of John Donne,* II [1912], cl ff.) claims the poem for John Hoskins.

[22] Also from Davison's *Poetical Rhapsody* (1602).

LYRICS FROM SONG BOOKS

FROM

WILLIAM BYRD'S *PSALMS, SONNETS, AND SONGS OF SADNESS AND PIETY* (1588) [1]

XII

THOUGH Amaryllis dance in green
    Like fairy queen;
    And sing full clear
Corinna can, with smiling, cheer.
Yet since their eyes make heart so sore,
Heigh ho, heigh ho, 'chill [2] love no more.

My sheep are lost for want of food,
    And I so wood,[3]
    That all the day
I sit and watch a herdmaid gay,
Who laughs to see me sigh so sore,
Heigh ho, heigh ho, 'chill love no more.

Her loving looks, her beauty bright
    Is such delight,
    That all in vain
I love to like and lose my gain,
For her that thanks me not therefor,
Heigh ho, heigh ho, 'chill love no more.

Ah wanton eyes, my friendly foes,
    And cause of woes,
    Your sweet desire
Breeds flames of ice and freeze in fire.
Ye scorn to see me weep so sore,
Heigh ho, heigh ho, 'chill love no more.

Love ye who list, I force him not,
    Sith, God it wot,
    The more I wail,
The less my sighs and tears prevail.

---

[1] In this collection for five voices "Though Amaryllis" is included in "The Sonets and Pastorales." Of the setting Fellowes comments (*English Madrigal Composers,* 1921, p. 163), "This is one of the best specimens of Byrd's lighter vein."

[2] *'chill:* the rustic dialect form for "I will," (i)ch (w)ill.

[3] *wood:* frantic.

What shall I do but say therefore,
Heigh ho, heigh ho, 'chill love no more.

XXXII [4]

Lulla, la lulla, lulla lullaby.
My sweet little baby, what meanest thou to cry?
Be still, my blessed babe, though cause thou hast to mourn,
Whose blood most innocent to shed the cruel king hath sworn.
And lo, alas, behold what slaughter he doth make,
Shedding the blood of infants all, sweet Savior, for thy sake.
A King is born, they say, which King this king would kill.
Oh woe, and woeful heavy day, when wretches have their will!

Lulla, la lulla, lulla lullaby.
My sweet little baby, what meanest thou to cry?
Three kings this King of kings to see are come from far,
To each unknown, with offerings great, by guiding of a star.
And shepherds heard the song which angels bright did sing,
Giving all glory unto God for coming of this King,
Which must be made away, King Herod would him kill.
Oh woe, and woeful heavy day, when wretches have their will!

Lulla, la lulla, lulla lullaby.
My sweet little baby, what meanest thou to cry?
Lo, my little babe, be still, lament no more;
From fury thou shalt step aside, help have we still [5] in store.
We heavenly warning have some other soil to seek,
From death must fly the Lord of life, as lamb both mild and meek.
Thus must my babe obey the king that would him kill.
Oh woe, and woeful heavy day, when wretches have their will!

Lulla, la lulla, lulla lullaby.
My sweet little baby, what meanest thou to cry?
But thou shalt live and reign as Sibyls [6] have foresaid,
As all the prophets prophesy, whose mother, yet a maid
And perfect virgin pure, with her breasts shall upbreed
Both God and man, that all hath made, the Son of heavenly seed,
Whom caitiffs none can 'tray,[7] whom tyrants none can kill.
Oh joy, and joyful happy day, when wretches want their will!

---

[4] Included in the "songs of sadnes and pietie."

[5] *still:* always.

[6] *Sibyls:* prophetesses.

[7] *whom caitiffs none can 'tray:* whom no villains can betray.

FROM

THOMAS MORLEY'S *CANZONETS* (1593)

VIII

Blow, shepherds, blow your pipes with gladsome glee resounding.
See where the fair Eliza comes with love and grace abounding.
Run, nymphs, apace, go meet her,
With flowers and garlands greet her.
All hail, Eliza fair, the country's pride and goddess!
Long may'st thou live the shepherds' Queen and lovely mistress!

XX

Arise, get up, my dear love, rise, make haste, begone thee!
Lo, where the bride, fair Daphne bright, still stays on thee!
Hark! Oh hark! Yon merry wanton maidens squealing!
Spice cake, sops in wine, spice cakes, are a-dealing!
Run then, run apace,
Get a bride lace
And a gilt rosemary branch while yet there is catching,
And then hold fast for fear of old snatching.
Alas, my love, why weep ye?
Oh fear not that, dear love, the next day keep we.
List, hark yon minstrels! How fine they firk[8] it!
And see how the maids jerk it!
With Kate and Will,
Tom and Jill,
Hey ho brave,
Now a skip,
There a trip,
Finely set aloft,
On a fine wedding day,
All for fair Daphne's wedding day!

[8] *firk*: dance.

FROM

THOMAS MORLEY'S *MADRIGALS TO FOUR VOICES . . . THE FIRST BOOK* (1594)

I

April is in my mistress' face,
And July[9] in her eyes hath place,
Within her bosom is September,
But in her heart a cold December.

FROM

JOHN DOWLAND'S[10] *THE FIRST BOOK OF SONGS OR AIRS* (1597)

XI

Come away, come, sweet love! The golden morning breaks;
All the earth, all the air of love and pleasure speaks.
Teach thine arms then to embrace,
And sweet rosy lips to kiss,
And mix our souls in mutual bliss;
Eyes were made for beauty's grace,
Viewing, rueing love-long pain,
Procured by beauty's rude disdain.

Come away, come, sweet love! The golden morning wastes,
While the sun from his sphere his fiery arrows casts
Making all the shadows fly,
Playing, staying in the grove
To entertain the stealth of love.
Thither, sweet love, let us hie,
Flying, dying in desire,
Winged with sweet hopes and heavenly fire.

Come away, come, sweet love! Do not in vain adorn
Beauty's grace, that should rise like to the naked morn.
Lilies on the riverside
And fair Cyprian flowers new-blown

[9] *July* is pronounced Jūlȳ.

[10] John Dowland: See above, p. 578, n. 26. "Come away" is also included in *England's Helicon* (1600; ed. Rollins, pp. 158–159).

Desire no beauties but their own,
Ornament is nurse of pride;
Pleasure measure love's delight.
Haste then, sweet love, our wished flight!

XIII

Sleep, wayward thoughts, and rest you with my love.
  Let not my Love be with my love displeased.
Touch not, proud hands, lest you her anger move,
  But pine you with my longings long diseased.[11]
Thus while she sleeps I sorrow for her sake,
So sleeps my Love, and yet my love doth wake.

But Oh the fury of my restless fear;
  The hidden anguish of my flesh desires;
The glories and the beauties, that appear
  Between her brows near Cupid's closed fires.
Thus while she sleeps moves sighing for her sake.
So sleeps my Love, and yet my love doth wake.

My love doth rage, and yet my Love doth rest.
  Fear in my love, and yet my Love secure.
Peace in my Love, and yet my love oppressed,
  Impatient yet of perfect temperature.[12]
Sleep, dainty Love, while I sigh for thy sake.
So sleeps my Love, and yet my love doth wake.

FROM

JOHN DOWLAND'S *THIRD AND LAST BOOK OF SONGS OR AIRS* (1603)

XV

Weep you no more, sad fountains;
  What need you flow so fast?
Look how the snowy mountains
  Heaven's sun doth gently waste.

---

[11] *diseased:* ill at ease, i.e., dis-eased.

[12] *temperature:* constitutional bent of mind, disposition.

But my sun's heavenly eyes
  View not your weeping,
  That now lie sleeping
Softly, now softly lies
    Sleeping.

Sleep is a reconciling,
  A rest that peace begets.
Doth not the sun rise smiling
  When fair at even he sets?
Rest you then, rest, sad eyes,
  Melt not in weeping
  While she lies sleeping
Softly, now softly lies
    Sleeping.

FROM

ROBERT JONES'S *THE FIRST BOOK OF SONGS AND AIRS* (1600)

I

  A WOMAN'S looks
  Are barbed hooks,
  That catch by art
  The strongest heart,
When yet they spend no breath.
  But let them speak,
  And sighing break
  Forth into tears,
  Their words are spears
That wound our souls to death.

  The rarest wit
  Is made forget,
  And like a child
  Is oft beguiled
With Love's sweet-seeming bait.
  Love with his rod
  So like a god
  Commands the mind
  We cannot find.
Fair shows hide foul deceit.

  Time, that all things
  In order brings,
  Hath taught me now
  To be more slow
In giving faith to speech,
  Since women's words
  No truth affords,
  And when they kiss
  They think by this
Us men to overreach.

FROM

TOBIAS HUME'S *MUSICAL HUMORS. THE FIRST PART OF AIRS* (1605)

I

The soldier's song

I SING the praise of honored wars,
The glory of well-gotten scars,
The bravery of glittering shields,
Of lusty hearts and famous fields;
For that is music worth the ear of Jove,
A sight for kings, and still the soldier's love.

Look! Oh, methinks I see
The grace of chivalry;
The colors are displayed,
The captains bright arrayed.
See now the battle's ranged,
Bullets now thick are changed.
Hark! shots and wounds abound,
The drums alarum sound.
The captains cry: Za-za!
The trumpets sound ta-ra!
Oh, this is music worth the ear of Jove,
A sight for kings, and still the soldier's love.

III

TOBACCO, tobacco, sing sweetly for tobacco!
Tobacco is like love, Oh love it;
For you see, I will prove it.
Love maketh lean the fat men's tumor,
So doth tobacco.
Love still dries up the wanton humor,
So doth tobacco.
Love makes men sail from shore to shore,
So doth tobacco.
'Tis fond love often makes men poor,
So doth tobacco.
Love makes men scorn all coward fears,
So doth tobacco.

Love often sets men by the ears,
So doth tobacco.
Tobacco, tobacco, sing sweetly for tobacco!
Tobacco is like love, Oh love it;
For you see I have proved it.

FROM

ORLANDO GIBBONS'S *FIRST SET OF MADRIGALS AND MOTETS* (1612)

I

THE silver swan, who living had no note,
When death approached, unlocked her silent throat;
Leaning her breast against the reedy shore,
Thus sung her first and last, and sung no more:
"Farewell, all joys; Oh death, come close mine eyes;
More geese than swans now live, more fools than wise."

SONGS FROM PLAYS

FROM

GAMMER GURTON'S NEEDLE (1575)

BACK and side go bare, go bare,
Both foot and hand go cold;
But, belly, God send thee good ale enough,
Whether it be new or old.

I cannot eat but little meat,
My stomach is not good;
But sure I think that I can drink
With him that wears a hood.
Though I go bare, take ye no care,
I am nothing a-cold;
I stuff my skin so full within
Of jolly good ale and old.

Back and side go bare, go bare,
  Both foot and hand go cold;
But, belly, God send thee good ale enough,
  Whether it be new or old.

I love no roast but a nut-brown toast,[1]
  And a crab [2] laid in the fire;
A little bread shall do me stead,
  Much bread I not desire.
No frost nor snow, no wind, I trow,
  Can hurt me if I would,
I am so wrapped, and throughly lapped
  Of jolly good ale and old.

Back and side go bare, &c.

And Tib my wife, that as her life
  Loveth well good ale to seek,
Full oft drinks she, till ye may see
  The tears run down her cheeks.
Then doth she troll [3] to me the bowl,
  Even as a maltworm should,
And saith, "Sweetheart, I took my part
  Of this jolly good ale and old."

Back and side go bare, &c.

Now let them drink, till they nod and wink,
  Even as good fellows should do;
They shall not miss to have the bliss
  Good ale doth bring men to;
And all poor souls that have scoured bowls
  Or have them lustily trolled,
God save the lives of them and their wives,
  Whether they be young or old.

Back and side go bare, go bare,
  Both foot and hand go cold;
But, belly, God send thee good ale enough,
  Whether it be new or old.

---

1 *nut-brown toast:* Browned bread was often dipped in beverages.

2 *crab:* crab apple.

3 *troll:* pass around.

FROM

MISOGONUS (*ca.* 1560?)

A song to the tune of *Heart's Ease*[4]

Sing care away with sport and play,
  Pastime is all our pleasure;
If well we fare for naught we care,
  In mirth consist our treasure.

Let snudges[5] lurk and drudges work,
  We do defy their slavery;
He is but a fool that goes to school,
  All we delight in bravery.

What doth avail far hence to sail
  And lead our life in toiling;
Or to what end should we here spend
  Our days in irksome moiling?

It is the best to live at rest,
  And take 't as God doth send it,
To haunt each wake and mirth to make,
  And with good fellows spend it.

Nothing is worse than a full purse
  To niggards and to pinchers;
They always spare and live in care,
  There's no man loves such flinchers.

The merry man with cup and can
  Lives longer than doth twenty;
The miser's wealth doth hurt his health,
  Examples we have plenty.

'Tis a beastly thing to lie musing
  With pensiveness and sorrow,
For who can tell that he shall well
  Live here until the morrow?

[4] *to the tune of Heart's Ease:* Many of the songs in Elizabethan drama were written to popular ballad tunes or dance tunes, although the names of the melodies are not always indicated as here.

[5] *snudges:* sneaking fellows.

We will therefore for evermore,
  While this our life is lasting,
Eat, drink, and sleep, and lemans [6] keep;
  It's popery to use fasting.

In cards and dice our comfort lies,
  In sporting and in dancing,
Our minds to please and live at ease,
  And sometimes to use prancing.

With Bess and Nell we love to dwell,
  In kissing and in haking; [7]
But whoop ho holly, with trolly lolly,
  To them we'll now be walking.

FROM

JOHN PHILLIPS'S *COMEDY OF PATIENT AND MEEK GRISSELL* (*ca.* 1566)

Lulla by baby, lulla by baby,
Thy nurse will tend thee, as duly as may be.

Be still, my sweet sweeting, no longer do cry,
    Sing lulla by baby, lulla by baby.
Let dolors be fleeting, I fancy thee, I,
    To rock and to lull thee, I will not delay me.
  Lulla by baby, &c.

What creature now living would hasten thy woe?
    Sing lulla by, lulla by, lulla by baby.
See for thy relieving, the time I bestow,
    To dance, and to prance thee, as prett'ly as may be.
  Lulla by baby, &c.

The gods be thy shield and comfort in need,
    Sing lulla by, lulla by, lulla by baby;
They give thee good fortune and well for to speed,
    And this to desire, I will not delay me.
  Lulla by baby, &c.

[6] *lemans:* lovers.   [7] *haking:* idling.

FROM

JOHN PICKERING'S *NEW INTERLUDE OF VICE, CONTAINING THE HISTORY OF HORESTES* (1567)

Haltersick entereth and singeth this song to the tune of "Have over the water to Floride" or "Selengers round." [8]

FAREWELL, adieu, that courtly life,
To war we tend to go;
It is good sport to see the strife
Of soldiers in a row.
  How merrily they forward march
  These enemies to slay,
  With hey, trim, and trixie too,
  Their banners they display.

Now shall we have the golden cheats,[9]
When others want the same;
And soldiers have full many feats
Their enemies to tame;
  With cocking [10] here, and booming there,
  They break their foe's array;
  And lusty lads amid the fields
  Their ensigns do display.

The drum and flute play lustily,
The trumpet blows amain,
And venturous knights courageously
Do march before their train
  With spears in rest, so lively dressed
  In armor bright and gay;
  With hey, trim, and trixie too,
  Their banners they display.

---

[8] *Selengers round:* I.e., "Sellenger's round," a popular dance and ballad tune. See Chappell's *Popular Music,* I, 69–71.

[9] *cheats:* booty.

[10] *cocking:* fighting.

FROM

COMMON CONDITIONS (*ca.* 1576)

Lustily, lustily, lustily let us sail forth,
The wind trim doth serve us, it blows at the north.

All things we have ready, and nothing we want,
To furnish our ship that rideth hereby:
Victuals and weapons, they be nothing scant,
Like worthy mariners ourselves we will try.
Lustily, lustily, &c.

Her flags be new trimmed set flaunting aloft,
Our ship for swift swimming, oh, she doth excel;
We fear no enemies, we have escaped them oft;
Of all ships that swimmeth, she beareth the bell.[11]
Lustily, lustily, &c.

And here is a master excelleth in skill,
And our master's mate, he is not to seek;[12]
And here is a boatswain will do his good will,
And here is a shipboy, we never had his leek.[13]
Lustily, lustily, &c.

If fortune then fail not, and our next viage[14] prove,
We will return merrily, and make good cheer,
And hold all together as friends linked in love;
The cans shall be filled with wine, ale, and beer.
Lustily, lustily, &c.

FROM

GEORGE PEELE'S[15] *ARRAIGNMENT OF PARIS* (1584)

Oenone. Fair and fair and twice so fair,
As fair as any may be;
The fairest shepherd on our green,
A love for any lady.

[11] *beareth the bell:* is in the foremost rank, is the best.

[12] *not to seek:* is not lacking.

[13] *leek:* like.

[14] *viage:* voyage.

[15] George Peele (*ca.* 1558–*ca.* 1597), one of the "University Wits." *The Arraignment of Paris* was (according to its title page) "presented before the Queen's Majesty by the Children of her Chapel," probably in 1581.

Paris. Fair and fair and twice so fair,
As fair as any may be;
Thy love is fair for thee alone,
And for no other lady.

Oenone. My love is fair, my love is gay,
As fresh as been the flowers in May,
And of my love my roundelay,
My merry, merry, merry roundelay
Concludes with Cupid's curse:[16]
They that do change old love for new,
Pray gods they change for worse.

Ambo simul. They that do change, &c.
Oenone. Fair and fair, &c.
Paris. Fair and fair, &c. Thy love is fair, &c.
Oenone. My love can pipe, my love can sing,
My love can many a pretty thing,
And of his lovely praises ring
My merry, merry roundelays.
Amen to Cupid's curse:
They that do change, &c.
Paris. They that do change, &c.
Ambo. Fair and fair, &c.

FROM

GEORGE PEELE'S *POLYHYMNIA* (1590)[17]

His golden locks time hath to silver turned;
Oh, time too swift, oh, swiftness never ceasing!
His youth 'gainst time and age hath ever spurned,
But spurned in vain; youth waneth by increasing.
Beauty, strength, youth, are flowers but fading seen;
Duty, faith, love, are roots, and ever green.

His helmet now shall make a hive for bees,
And lover's sonnets turned to holy psalms,
A man-at-arms must now serve on his knees,
And feed on prayers, which are age his alms;

---

[16] *Cupid's curse:* a reference to a "sonnet" in the passage preceding the song.

[17] *Polyhymnia,* a description in blank verse of a tournament held before Elizabeth on the occasion of her birthday, 1590. The selection describes Sir Henry Lee (1530–1610), the Queen's champion who, too old to take part, had asked the Earl of Cumberland to succeed him. See E. K. Chambers, *Sir Henry Lee,* 1936.

But though from court to cottage he depart,
His saint is sure of his unspotted heart.

And when he saddest sits in homely cell,
He'll teach his swains this carol for a song:
Blest be the hearts that wish my sovereign well,
Cursed be the souls that think her any wrong!
Goddess, allow this aged man his right,
To be your beadsman now, that was your knight.

FROM

GEORGE PEELE'S *HUNTING OF CUPID* (*ca.* 1591) [18]

What thing is love? for (well I wot) love is a thing.
It is a prick, it is a sting,
It is a pretty, pretty thing;
It is a fire, it is a coal,
Whose flame creeps in at every hole;
And as my wit doth best devise,
Love's dwelling is in ladies' eyes,
From whence do glance love's piercing darts
That make such holes into our hearts;
And all the world herein accord
Love is a great and mighty lord;
And when he list [19] to mount so high,
With Venus he in heaven doth lie,
And evermore hath been a god
Since Mars and she played even and odd.

[18] *Hunting of Cupid:* The play is lost except for a few fragments. The song is in part (lines 1–7 with variations) found in John Bartlet's *Booke of Ayres* (1606).

[19] *list:* wishes.

FROM

JOHN WEBSTER'S[20] *WHITE DEVIL* (1612)

CALL for the robin redbreast and the wren,
Since o'er shady groves they hover,
And with leaves and flowers do cover
The friendless bodies of unburied men.
Call unto his funeral dole
The ant, the field mouse, and the mole,
To rear him hillocks that shall keep him warm,
And, when gay tombs are robbed, sustain no harm;
But keep the wolf far thence, that's foe to men,
For with his nails he'll dig them up again.

[20] John Webster (*ca.* 1580–1634?). Lines 9–10 are parodied in T. S. Eliot's *The Waste Land* (ll. 74–75).

Richard Hooker

1554–1600

THE GREATEST philosopher of the Church of England, Hooker is also one of the masters of English prose. He was born in Exeter and educated at Oxford under the patronage of Bishop Jewel, Bishop of Salisbury, the author of the *Apology for the Church of England* (1562). After Jewel's death he was befriended by Edwin Sandys, Bishop of London (later Archbishop of York) and became tutor to the younger Edwin Sandys. He became a fellow of Corpus Christi College in 1577, and two years later Public Lecturer in Hebrew to the University. He took orders, and in 1581 was invited to preach at Paul's Cross in London. According to Izaak Walton, Hooker's biographer, the mildness of Hooker's temperament was evident at the university: "God and Nature blessed him with so blessed a bashfulness that in his younger days his pupils might easily look him out of countenance."

In 1584 Hooker was appointed to a benefice, and in 1585 he was made Master of the Temple. Here he came into conflict with Walter Travers, an afternoon lecturer at the Temple and one of the foremost Puritan spokesmen. The controversy between the two clergymen was a display, for the lawyers of the Temple, of the conservative English, and the radical Calvinist, doctrines in religion and church government. As someone expressed it, when Hooker was preaching and Travers lecturing at the Temple, "the forenoon sermon spake Canterbury and the afternoon Geneva." This conflict, in which Hooker conducted himself with calm moderation, was the background for Hooker's great appeal to the Reformers for reasonableness in the preface to *The Laws of Ecclesiastical Polity*. In that Preface, says Walton, "There was such bowels of love, and such a commixture of that love with reason, as was never exceeded but in Holy Writ."

Hooker's marriage to Joan Churchman, of which Walton gives an entertaining but erroneous account, provided him with a father-in-law, John Churchman, who was important in the higher councils of the Merchant Taylors' Company; at John Churchman's house in Watling Street Hooker's great book was planned and much of it written. In 1591 Hooker resigned the Mastership of the Temple, and in 1595 he became a country parson at Bishopsbourne near Canterbury.

His book, *The Laws of Ecclesiastical Polity,* began to appear in 1593. The book had to be financed by the generosity and courage of Hooker's friend Edwin Sandys, for the printers were unwilling to take the risk, the author was unable to do so, and the Church which Hooker was defending had other uses for its funds. Only the first five books were published during Hooker's lifetime.

Book I of *Ecclesiastical Polity* deals with laws in general and their various kinds, picturing a universe operating under natural and divine law and founded upon reason; Book II deals with the nature, authority and adequacy of scripture; Book III concerns the scriptural bases for worship and government; Book IV defends the rites and ceremonies of the English church; Book V, longer than the first four together, is a commentary on the *Book of Common Prayer*. Books VI, VII and VIII deal with various embodiments of authority—elders, bishops, kings and popes.

In a field of controversy where the prevailing style was bitter invective, slander, and personal abuse, Hooker was a model of sweet reasonableness and temperance. Even in comparison with such a grand controversialist as Milton, Hooker seems the more humane, the more civilized, the more enlightened. In him the *via media* found its embodiment and supreme expression.

BIBLIOGRAPHY: Izaak Walton, "Mr. Richard Hooker," in *Lives,* many editions; C. J. Sisson, *The Judicious Marriage of Mr. Hooker,* Cambridge, 1940, corrects Walton in many respects; E. N. S. Thompson, "Richard Hooker among the Controversialists" *P.Q.* XX (1941), 454–464; D. C. Boughner. "Notes on Hooker's Prose" *RES* XV (1939), 194–200; Peter Munz, *The Place of Hooker in the History of Thought,* London, 1952. F. J. Shirley, *Richard Hooker and Contemporary Political Ideas,* London, 1949.

FROM

THE LAWS OF ECCLESIASTICAL POLITY

The Preface

AMONGST ourselves, there was in King Edward's days some question moved by reason of a few men's scrupulosity touching certain things. And beyond seas, of them which fled in the days of Queen Mary, some contenting themselves abroad with the use of their own service book at home authorized before their departure out of the realm, others liking better the common prayer book of the Church of Geneva translated, those smaller contentions before begun were by this mean somewhat increased. Under the happy reign of Her Majesty which now is, the greatest matter a while contended for was the wearing of the cap and surplice, till there came Admonitions Directed Unto the High Court of Parliament, by men who, concealing their names, thought it glory enough to discover their minds and affections, which were now universally bent even against all the orders and laws wherein this Church is found unconformable to the platform of Geneva. Concerning the defender of which admonitions, all that I mean to say is this: "There will come a time when three words uttered with charity and meekness shall receive a far more blessed reward than three thousand volumes written with disdainful sharpness of wit." But the manner of men's writing must not alienate our hearts from the truth if it appear they have the truth, as the followers of the same defender do think he hath, and in that persuasion they follow him no otherwise than himself doth Calvin, Beza and others, with the like persuasion that they in this cause had the truth. We being as fully persuaded otherwise, it resteth that some kind of trial be used to find out which part is in error.

The first mean whereby Nature teacheth men to judge good from evil, as well in laws as in other things, is the force of their own discretion. Hereunto therefore Saint Paul referreth oftentimes his own speech to be considered by them that heard him, "I speak as to them which have understanding; judge ye what I say."[1] Again, afterward, "Judge in yourselves, is it comely that a woman pray uncovered?"[2] The exercise of this kind of judgment our Savior requireth in the Jews.[3] In them of Berea[4]

[1] I. Corinthians 10:15.

[2] I. Corinthians 11:13.

[3] Luke 12:57.

[4] The inhabitants of the Macedonian city of Berea who "received the word with all readiness of mind" when Paul preached to them. Acts 14:10–11.

the Scripture commendeth it. Finally, whatsoever we do, if our own secret judgment consent not unto it as fit and good to be done, the doing of it, to us, is sin, although the thing itself be allowable. Saint Paul's rule therefore generally is, "Let every man in his own mind be fully persuaded of that thing which he either alloweth or doth."[5] Some things are so familiar and plain that truth from falsehood and good from evil is most easily discerned in them, even by men of no deep capacity. And of that nature, for the most part are things absolutely unto all men's salvation necessary, either to be held or denied, either to be done or avoided. For which cause Saint Augustine acknowledgeth that they are not only set down, but also plainly set down in scripture, so that he which heareth or readeth may, without any great difficulty, understand. Other things also there are belonging, though in a lower degree of importance, unto the offices of Christian men, which, because they are more obscure, more intricate and hard to be judged of, therefore God hath appointed some to spend their whole time principally in the study of things divine, to the end that in these more doubtful cases their understanding might be a light to direct others. "If the understanding power or faculty of the soul be," saith the Grand Physician,[6] "like unto the bodily sight, not of equal sharpness in all, what can be more convenient than that, even as the dark-sighted man is directed by the clear about things visible, so likewise in matters of deeper discourse the wise in heart do show the simple where his way lieth?" In the doubtful cases of law, what man is there who seeth not how requisite it is that professors of skill in that faculty be our directors? So is it in all other kinds of knowledge. And even in this kind likewise the Lord hath himself appointed that "the Priest's lips should preserve knowledge, and that other men should seek the truth at his mouth, because he is the messenger of the Lord of Hosts."[7] Gregory Nazianzen,[8] offended at the people's too great presumption in controlling the judgment of them to whom in such cases they should rather have submitted their own, seeketh by earnest entreaty to stay them within their bounds: "Presume not, ye that are sheep, to make yourselves guides of them that should guide you; neither seek ye to overskip the fold which they about you have pitched. It sufficeth for your part, if ye can well frame yourselves to be ordered. Take not upon you to judge your judges, nor to make them subject to your laws who should be a law to you. For God is not a God of sedition and confusion but of order and of peace." But ye will say that if the guides of the people be blind, the common sort of men must not close up their own eyes and be led by the conduct of such; if the priest be partial in the law, the flock must not therefore depart from the ways of sincere truth, and in simplicity yield to be followers of him for his place' sake and office over them. Which thing, though in itself most true, is in your defense notwithstanding weak;

[5] Romans 14:5.
[6] Galen.
[7] Malachi 2:7.
[8] St. Gregory of Nazianzus, d. 389 A.D. Bishop of Constantinople.

because the matter wherein ye think that ye see and imagine that your ways are sincere is of far deeper consideration than any one amongst five hundred of you conceiveth. Let the vulgar sort amongst you know that there is not the least branch of the cause wherein they are so resolute but to the trial of it a great deal more appertaineth than their concept doth reach unto. I write not this in disgrace of the simplest that way given, but I would gladly they knew the nature of that cause wherein they think themselves thoroughly instructed and are not; by means whereof they daily run themselves, without feeling their own hazard, upon the dint of the Apostle's sentence against evil speakers as touching things wherein they are ignorant.[9] If it be granted a thing unlawful for private men, not called into public consultation, to dispute which is the best state of civil polity, with a desire of bringing in some other kind than that under which they already live, for of such disputes I take it his meaning was,—if it be a thing confessed that of such questions they cannot determine without rashness, inasmuch as a great part of them consisteth in special circumstances, and for one kind as many reasons may be brought as for another, —is there any reason in the world why they should better judge what kind of regiment ecclesiastical is the fittest? For in the civil state more insight and, in those affairs, more experience a great deal needs be granted them, than in this they can possibly have. When they which write in defence of your discipline and commend it unto the highest [10] not in the least cunning manner, are forced notwithstanding to acknowledge that with whom the truth is they know not, they are not certain—what certainty or knowledge can the multitude have thereof? Weigh what doth move the common sort so much to favor this innovation and it shall soon appear unto you that the force of particular reasons which for your several opinions are alleged is a thing whereof the multitude never did nor could consider as to be therewith wholly carried; but certain general inducements are used to make saleable your cause in gross; and when once men have cast a fancy towards it, any slight declaration of specialties will serve to lead forward men's inclinable and prepared minds. The method of winning the people's affection unto a general liking of "the Cause," for so ye term it, hath been this: First, in the hearing of the multitude, the faults, especially of higher callings, are ripped up with marvellous exceeding severity and sharpness of reproof, which being oftentimes done, begetteth a great good opinion of integrity, zeal and holiness to such constant reprovers of sin as by likelihood would never be so much offended at that which is evil, unless themselves were singularly good. The next thing hereunto is to impute all faults and corruptions wherewith the world aboundeth unto the kind of ecclesiastical government established. Wherein, as by reproving faults, they purchased unto themselves with the multitude a name to

[9] II. Peter 2:12.

[10] i.e. Queen Elizabeth. The *Humble Petition of the Commonalty,* 1588, said "we are very babes and children, not knowing our right hand from our left in matters that concern the Kingdom of Heaven."

be virtuous; so by finding out this kind of cause they obtain to be judged wise above others, whereas in truth unto the form even of Jewish government, which the Lord himself, they all confess, did establish, with like show of reason they might impute those faults which the prophets condemn in the governors of that commonwealth as to the English kind of regiment ecclesiastical, (whereof also God himself though in other sort is author) the stains and blemishes found in our state, which springing from the root of human frailty and corruption, not only are, but have always been more or less,—yea, and for anything we know to the contrary will be till the world's end,—complained of, what form of government soever take place. Having gotten thus much sway in the hearts of men, a third step is to propose their own form of church government as the only sovereign remedy of all evils, and to adorn it with all the glorious titles that may be. And the nature, as of men that have sick bodies, so likewise of the people in the crazedness of their minds possessed with dislike and discontentment at things present, is to imagine that any thing the virtue whereof they hear commended would help them, but that most which they least have tried. The fourth degree of inducement is by fashioning the very notions and conceits of men's minds in such sort that when they read the scriptures they may think that everything soundeth towards the advancement of that discipline and to the utter disgrace of the contrary. Pythagoras, by bringing up his scholars in the speculative knowledge of numbers, made their conceits therein so strong that when they came to the contemplation of things natural they imagined that in every particular thing they even beheld, as it were with their eyes, how the elements of number gave essence and being to the works of nature. A thing in reason impossible, which notwithstanding through their misfashioned preconceit appeared unto them no less certain than if nature had written it in the very foreheads of all the creatures of God.

Book I, Chapter 10

That which hitherto we have set down is, I hope, sufficient to show their brutishness which imagine that religion and virtue are only as men will accompt of[11] them, that we might make as much accompt, if we would, of the contrary, without any harm unto ourselves, and that in nature they are as indifferent one as the other. We see then how nature itself teacheth laws and statutes to live by. The laws which have been hitherto mentioned do bind men absolutely, even as they are men, although they have never any settled fellowship, never any solemn agreement amongst themselves what to do or not to do. But forasmuch as we are not by ourselves sufficient to furnish ourselves with competent store of things needful for such a life as our nature doth desire, a life fit for the dignity of man, therefore to supply those defects and imperfections which are in us living single

[11] *accompt* of: value.

and solely, by ourselves, we are naturally induced to seek communion and fellowship with others. This was the cause of men's uniting themselves at the first in politic societies, which societies could not be without government, nor government without a distinct kind of law from that which hath been already declared. Two foundations there are which bear up public societies, the one a natural inclination whereby all men desire a sociable life and fellowship, the other an order expressly or secretly agreed upon, touching the manner of their union in living together. The latter is that which we call the law of a commonweal, the very soul of a politic body, the parts whereof are by law animated, held together and set on work in such actions as the common good requireth. Laws politic, ordained for external order and regiment amongst men, are never framed as they should be, unless presuming the will of man to be inwardly obstinate, rebellious, and averse from all obedience unto the sacred laws of his nature,—in a word, unless presuming man to be in regard of his depraved mind little better than a wild beast,—they do accordingly provide notwithstanding so to frame his outward actions that they be no hindrance unto the common good for which societies are instituted; unless they do this, they are not perfect. It resteth therefore that we consider how nature findeth out such laws of government as serve to direct even nature depraved to a right end. All men desire to lead in this world an happy life. That life is led most happily, wherein all virtue is exercised without impediment or let. The Apostle [12] in exhorting men to contentment, although they have in this world no more than very bare food and raiment, giveth us thereby to understand that those are even the lowest of things necessary; that if we should be stripped of all those things without which we might possibly be, yet these must be left, that destitution in these is such an impediment, as till it be removed, suffereth not the mind of man to admit any other care. For this cause first God assigned Adam maintenance of life and then appointed him a law to observe. For this cause after men began to grow to a number, the first thing we read they gave themselves unto was the tilling of the earth and the feeding of cattle. Having by this mean whereon to live, the principal actions of their life afterward are noted by the exercise of their religion. True it is that the Kingdom of God must be the first thing in our purposes and desires. But inasmuch as righteous life presupposeth life, inasmuch as to live virtuously it is impossible except we live, therefore the first impediment which naturally we endeavor to remove is penury and want of things without which we cannot live. Unto life many implements are necessary; moe,[13] if we seek, as all men naturally do, such a life as hath in it joy, comfort, delight and pleasure. To this end we see how quickly sundry arts mechanical were found out in the very prime of the world. As things of greatest necessity are always first provided for, so things of greatest dignity are most accompted of by all such as judge rightly. Although therefore riches be a thing which every man wisheth, yet

[12] I. Timothy 6:8.

[13] *moe:* more.

no man of judgment can esteem it better to be rich than wise, virtuous and religious. If we be both or either of these, it is not because we are so born. For into the world we come as empty of the one as of the other, as naked in mind as we are in body. Both which necessities of man had at the first no other helps and supplies than only domestical, such as that which the prophet implieth, saying, "Can a mother forget her child?",[14] such as that which the Apostle mentioneth, saying, "He that careth not for his own is worse than an infidel"; [15] such as that concerning Abraham, "Abraham will command his sons and his household after him that they keep the way of the Lord." [16] But neither that which we learn of ourselves, nor that which others teach us, can prevail where wickedness and malice have taken deep root. If therefore when there was but as yet one only family in the world, no means of instruction human or divine could prevent effusion of blood, how could it be chosen but that when families were multiplied and increased upon earth, after separation each providing for itself, envy, strife, contention and violence must grow amongst them? For hath not nature furnished man with wit and valor, as it were with armor, which may be used as well unto extreme evil as good? Yea, were they not used by the rest of the world unto evil, unto the contrary only by Seth, Enoch, and those few the rest in that line? [17] We all make complaint of the iniquity of our times; not unjustly, for the days are evil. But compare them with those times wherein there were no civil societies, with those times wherein there was as yet no manner of public regiment established, with those times wherein there were not above eight persons righteous living upon the face of the earth, and we have surely good cause to think that God hath blessed us exceedingly and hath made us behold most happy days. To take away all such mutual grievances, injuries and wrongs, there was no way but only by growing into composition and agreement amongst themselves by ordaining some kind of government public and by yielding themselves subject thereunto, that unto whom they granted authority to rule and govern, by them the peace, tranquility and happy estate of the rest might be procured . . .

Book I, Chapter 12

. . . The first principles of the law of nature are easy: hard it were to find men ignorant of them; but concerning the duty which Nature's law doth require at the hands of men in a number of things particular, so far hath the natural understanding even of sundry whole nations been darkened, that they have not discerned—no, not gross iniquity,—to be sin. Again, being so prone as we are to fawn upon ourselves, and to be ignorant as much as may be of our own deformities, without the feeling sense whereof we are most wretched, even so much the more because not knowing them

[14] Isaiah 49:17.

[15] I. Timothy 5:8.

[16] Genesis 18:19.

[17] Genesis 4:25–26.

we cannot as much as desire to have them taken away, how should our festered sores be cured but that God hath delivered a law as sharp as the two-edged sword, piercing the very closest and most unsearchable corners of the heart which the law of nature can hardly, human laws by no means possible, reach unto? Hereby we know even secret concupiscence to be sin, and are made fearful to offend, though it be but in a wandering cogitation . . .

Book I, Chapter 14

Although the scripture of God therefore be stored with infinite variety of matter in all kinds, although it abound with all sorts of laws, yet the principal intent of scripture is to deliver the laws of duties supernatural. Oftentimes it hath been in very solemn manner disputed whether all things necessary unto salvation be necessarily set down in the holy scriptures or no. If we define that necessary unto salvation whereby the way to salvation is in any sort made more plain, apparent and easy to be known, then is there no part of true philosophy, no art of accompt, no kind of science rightly so called, but the scripture must contain it. If only those things be necessary, as surely none else are, without the knowledge and practice whereof it is not the will and pleasure of God to make any ordinary grant of salvation, it may be, notwithstanding, and oftentimes hath been, demanded, how the books of holy scripture contain in them all necessary things, when of things necessary the very chiefest is to know what books we are bound to esteem holy, which point is confessed impossible for the scripture itself to teach. Whereunto we may answer with truth that there is not in the world any art or science, which proposing unto itself an end, as every one doth some end or other, hath been therefore thought defective if it have not delivered simply whatsoever is needful to the same end; but all kinds of knowledge have their certain bounds and limits: each of them presupposeth many necessary things learned in other sciences and known beforehand. He that should take upon him to teach men how to be eloquent in pleading causes must needs deliver unto them whatsoever precepts are requisite unto that end; otherwise he doth not the thing which he taketh upon him. Seeing then no man can plead eloquently unless he be able first to speak, it followeth that ability of speech is in this case a thing most necessary. Notwithstanding every man would think it ridiculous that he which undertaketh by writing to instruct an orator should therefore deliver all the precepts of grammar, because his profession is to deliver precepts necessary unto eloquent speech, yet so that they which are to receive them be taught beforehand so much of that which is thereunto necessary as comprehendeth the skill of speaking. In like sort, albeit scripture do profess to contain in it all things which are necessary unto salvation, yet the meaning cannot be simply of all things that are necessary, but all things that are necessary in some certain kind or form, as: all things that are necessary and either could not at all or could not easily be known by the light of natural discourse; all things which are necessary to be known that we may be saved, but known with presupposal of knowledge concerning certain principles whereof it receiveth us already presuaded and then instructeth us in all the residue that are necessary. In the number of these principles one is the sacred authority of scripture. Being therefore persuaded by other means that these scriptures are the oracles of God, themselves do then teach us the rest and lay before us all the duties which God requireth at our hands as necessary unto salvation. Further, there hath been some doubt likewise whether "containing in scripture" do import express setting down in plain terms, or else "comprehending" in such sort that by reason we may from thence conclude all things which are necessary. Against the former of these two constructions, instance hath sundry ways been given. For our belief in the Trinity, the co-eternity of the Son of God with his Father, the proceeding of the Spirit from the Father and the Son, the duty of baptising infants,—these with such other principal points, the necessity whereof is by none denied, are notwithstanding in scripture nowhere to be found by express literal mention, only deduced they are out of scripture by collection. This kind of comprehension in scripture being therefore received, still there is doubt how far we are to proceed by collection before the full and complete measure of things necessary be made up. For let us not think that as long as the world doth endure, the wit of man shall be able to sound the bottom of that which may be concluded out of the scripture, especially if things contained by collection do so far extend as to draw in whatsoever may be at any time out of the scripture but probably and conjecturally surmised. But let necessary collection be made requisite, and we may boldly deny that of all those things which at this day are with so great necessity urged upon this church under the name of Reformed Church discipline, there is any one which their books hitherto have made manifest to be contained in the scripture. Let them, if they can, allege but one properly belonging to their cause, and not common to them and us, and show the deduction thereof out of scripture to be necessary. It hath been already showed how all things necessary unto salvation, in such sort as before we have maintained, must needs be possible for men to know, and that many things are in such sort necessary, the knowledge whereof is by the light of nature impossible to be attained. Whereupon it followeth that either all flesh is excluded from possibility of salvation, which to think were most barbarous, or else that God hath by supernatural means revealed the way of life so far as doth suffice. For this cause God hath so many times and ways spoken to the sons of men. Neither hath he by speech only, but by writing also, instructed and taught his church. The cause of writing hath been to the end that things by him revealed unto the world might have the longer continuance, and the greater certainty of assurance, by how much that which standeth on record hath in both those respects preeminence above that which passeth from hand to hand and hath no pens but the tongues, no books but the ears, of men to record it. The several books of scripture having had each some several occasion and particular purpose which caused them to be written, the contents thereof are according to the exigence of that special end whereunto they are intended. Hereupon it groweth that every book of holy scripture doth take out of all kinds of truth, natural, historical, foreign, supernatural, so much as the matter handled requireth. Now forasmuch as there hath been reason alleged sufficient to conclude that all things necessary unto salvation must be made known, and that God himself hath therefore revealed his will, because otherwise men could not have known so much as is necessary, his surceasing to speak to the world since the publishing of the Gospel of Jesus Christ and the delivery of the same in writing is unto us a manifest token that the way of salvation is now sufficiently opened and that we need no other means for our full instruction than God hath already furnished us withal. . . .

Samuel Daniel

1562–1619

SAMUEL DANIEL was born in 1562 in Somerset, the son and brother of musicians. He attended Magdalen College, Oxford, but left without a degree. After his literary debut as a translator, he traveled in Italy, and soon after his return became a follower of Mary, Countess of Pembroke, sister to Sidney and patroness of poets. He expresses in *Musophilus* his debtorship to Fulke Greville also. In 1591 the first, unauthorized edition of *Astrophel and Stella* inaugurated the great English sonnet vogue of the nineties, and among the sonnets appended to Sidney's cycle were twenty-eight by Daniel. In the next year the poet issued his own collection called *Delia,* and dedicated them to the Countess of Pembroke. She was intended to see herself in the heroine of the sonnets, but of course she knew the conventions of Petrarch and the French poets too well to take the protestations of love quite literally. Daniel used principally the English sonnet form invented by Surrey, and this choice may have influenced Shakespeare after him.

The Complaint of Rosamund is contemporaneous with *Delia.* It belongs to the type of poem made popular by *The Mirror for Magistrates,* which had included not only the tragic tales of the falls of princes, but a few examples of unfortunate women, such as Elstred and Jane Shore. The verse form and the general tone may have been in Shakespeare's mind when he composed *The Rape of Lucrece.*

Daniel's work after 1592 shows increasingly the influence of the Pembroke circle. He composed classical tragedies (*Cleopatra,* 1594; *Philotas,* 1604) in the manner of the French neoclassicist Robert Garnier; he composed six epistles in verse to various noblemen and ladies; and he wrote in *Musophilus* (first published in 1599) a verse dialogue in defense of learning. His English patriotism is apparent in his versified history of the civil wars between the houses of York and Lancaster and a prose history of England. In 1603 he wrote *A Defense of Rhyme* in answer to Thomas Campion's *Observations in the Art of English Poesie.* After the accession of King James he was occasionally employed as a writer of court masques.

Daniel died in 1619, having led for some years a retired life in the country. He was apparently a conservative and restrained individual, reflective and moral, earnest in his love of beauty, civilization, and learning. He revised his poems again and again, eliminating feminine rhymes, making his references more accurate, and curbing the Elizabethan wantonness of fancy which occasionally appeared in his early versions. He has been called by Professor Sprague "something of a neo-classicist before his time." His contemporaries noticed his reticence; Spenser says of him in *Colin Clouts Come Home Againe:*

Yet doth his trembling Muse but lowly flie,
As daring not too rashly mount on hight,
And doth her tender plumes as yet but trie
In love's soft laies and looser thoughts delight.
Then rouze thy feathers quickly, Daniell,
And to what course thou please thyself advance:
But most, me seemes, thy accent will excell
In tragick plaints and passionate mischance.

Ben Jonson called him a "verser" and "no poet," but as "well-languaged Daniel" he has won the respect of such later poets as Wordsworth and Coleridge and A. E. Housman.

Bibliography: *Poems and A Defense of Rhyme,* ed. A. C. Sprague, Harvard, 1930; G. K. Brady, *Samuel Daniel,* Urbana, 1923; M. H. Shackford, "Samuel Daniel's Poetical Epistles," *SP,* XLV (1948) 180–195; Hallett Smith, *Elizabethan Poetry* (1952), 104–108, 157–161.

THE COMPLAINT OF ROSAMUND[1]

Out from the horror of infernal deeps
My poor afflicted ghost comes here to plain it,[2]
Attended with my shame that never sleeps,
The spot wherewith my kind [3] and youth did stain it;
My body found a grave where to contain it,
A sheet could hide my face, but not my sin,
For fame finds never tomb t' inclose it in.

And which is worse, my soul is now denied
Her transport to the sweet Elysian rest,
The joyful bliss for ghosts repurified,
The ever-springing gardens of the blest;
Charon denies me waftage with the rest,
And says my soul can never pass the river,
Till lovers' sighs on earth shall it deliver.

So shall I never pass, for how should I
Procure this sacrifice amongst the living?
Time hath long since worn out the memory
Both of my life and life's unjust depriving;
Sorrow for me is dead for aye reviving.
Rosamund hath little left her but her name,
And that disgraced, for time hath wronged the same.

No muse suggests the pity of my case;
Each pen doth overpass my just complaint,
Whilst others are preferred, though far more base;
Shore's wife [4] is graced, and passes for a saint;
Her legend justifies her foul attaint.
Her well-told tale did such compassion find
That she is passed, and I am left behind.

Which seen with grief, my miserable ghost
(Whilom [5] invested in so fair a veil,
Which whilst it lived was honored of the most,
And being dead, gives matter to bewail)

---

[1] *Rosamund:* mistress of King Henry II (*reg.* 1154–1189).

[2] *plain it:* complain.

[3] *kind:* nature (here, "sex").

[4] *Shore's wife:* Jane Shore, mistress of Edward IV (*reg.* 1461–1483).

[5] *Whilom:* once.

Comes to solicit thee, since others fail,
To take this task and in thy woeful song
To form my case and register my wrong.

Although I know thy just lamenting muse,
Toiled in th' affliction of thine own distress,
In others' cares hath little time to use,
And therefore mayst esteem of mine the less;
Yet as thy hopes attend happy redress,
The joys depending on a woman's grace,
So move thy mind a woeful woman's case.

Delia may hap to deign to read our story,
And offer up her sigh among the rest,
Whose merit would suffice for both our glory,
Whereby thou mightst be graced and I be blest;
That indulgence would profit me the best,
Such power she hath by whom thy youth is led,
To joy the living and to bless the dead.

So I, through beauty made the woeful'st wight,
By beauty might have comfort after death,
That dying fairest, by the fairest might
Find life above on earth, and rest beneath.
She that can bless us with one happy breath,
Give comfort to thy muse to do her best,
That thereby thou mayst joy and I might rest.

Thus said, forthwith moved with a tender care
And pity, which myself could never find,
What she desired my muse deigned to declare,
And therefore willed her boldly tell her mind;
And I, more willing, took this charge assigned
Because her griefs were worthy to be known,
And telling hers, might hap forget mine own.

Then write, quoth she, the ruin of my youth,
Report the downfall of my slippery state;
Of all my life reveal the simple truth,
To teach to others what I learnt too late.
Exemplify my frailty, tell how fate
Keeps in eternal dark our fortunes hidden,
And ere they come, to know them 'tis forbidden.

For whilst the sunshine of my fortune lasted,
I joyed the happiest warmth, the sweetest heat
That ever yet imperious beauty tasted;
I had what glory ever flesh could get,

But this fair morning had a shameful set.
Disgrace darked honor, sin did cloud my brow,
As note the sequel, and I'll tell thee how.

The blood I stained was good and of the best,
My birth had honor and my beauty fame;
Nature and fortune joined to make me blest,
Had I had grace t' have known to use the same.
My education showed from whence I came,
And all concurred to make me happy first,
That so great hope might make me more accursed.

Happy lived I whilst parents' eye did guide
The indiscretion of my feeble ways,
And country home kept me from being eyed,
Where best unknown I spent my sweetest days;
Till that my friends mine honor sought to raise
To higher place, which greater credit yields,
Deeming such beauty was unfit for fields.

From country then to court I was preferred,
From calm to storms, from shore into the deeps;
There where I perished, where my youth first erred;
There where I lost the flower which honor keeps;
There where the worser thrives, the better weeps.
Ah me, poor wench, on this unhappy shelf
I grounded me and cast away myself.

For thither comed [6] (when years had armed my youth
With rarest proof of beauty ever seen,
When my reviving eye had learnt the truth
That it had power to make the winter green,
And flower affections whereas none had been),
Soon could I teach my brow to tyrannize,
And make the world do homage to mine eyes.

For age, I saw (though years with cold conceit
Congealed their thoughts against a warm desire)
Yet sigh their want, and look at such a bait;
I saw how youth was wax before the fire;
I saw by stealth, I framed my look a liar,
Yet well perceived how fortune made me then
The envy of my sex, and wonder unto men.

Look how a comet at the first appearing
Draws all men's eyes with wonder to behold it;
Or as the saddest tale at sudden hearing

[6] *comed:* come (dial.).

Makes silent listening unto him that told it;
So did my speech when rubies did unfold it,
So did the blazing of my blush appear
T' amaze the world, that holds such sights so dear.

Ah, beauty! siren! fair enchanting good!
Sweet silent rhetoric of persuading eyes!
Dumb eloquence,[7] whose power doth move the blood
More than the words or wisdom of the wise!
Still harmony, whose diapason lies
Within a brow, the key which passions move
To ravish sense and play a world in love!

What might I then not do whose power was such?
What cannot women do that know their power?
What woman knows it not (I fear too much)
How bliss or bale lies in their laugh or lour,
Whilst they enjoy their happy blooming flower,
Whilst nature decks her with her proper fair
Which cheers the world, joys each sight, sweetens th' air?[8]

Such one was I, my beauty was mine own,
No borrowed blush which bankrupt beauties seek;
That new-found shame, a sin to us unknown,
Th' adulterate beauty of a falsed cheek,
Vile stain to honor and to women eke,
Seeing that time our fading must detect,
Thus with defect to cover our defect.

Impiety of times, chastity's abater,
Falsehood, wherein thyself thyself deniest,
Treason to counterfeit the seal of nature,
The stamp of heaven, impressed by the highest,
Disgrace unto the world, to whom thou liest,
Idol unto thyself, shame to the wise,
And all that honor thee idolatrize.

Far was that sin from us whose age was pure,
When simple beauty was accounted best,
The time when women had no other lure
But modesty, pure cheeks, a virtuous breast,—
This was the pomp wherewith my youth was blest;

---

[7] *Ah . . . eloquence:* Sir John Davies ridiculed this conceit in his 45th epigram:

"Dacus with some good color and pretense
Terms his love's beauty 'silent eloquence';
For she doth lay more colors on her face
Than ever Tully used, his speech to grace."

[8] *Whilst nature . . . air:* Daniel revised this couplet in 1599 to read:

"Whilst nature decks them in their best attires
Of youth and beauty, which the world admires."

These were the weapons which mine honor won
In all the conflicts that my eyes begun;

Which were not small—I wrought on no mean object;
A crown was at my feet, scepters obeyed me;
Whom fortune made my king, love made my subject;
Who did command the land most humbly prayed me;
Henry the second, that so highly weighed me,
Found well, by proof, the privilege of beauty,
That it had power to countermand all duty.

For after all his victories in France,
Triumphing in the honor of his deeds,
Unmatched by sword, was vanquished by a glance,
And hotter wars within his bosom breeds—
Wars whom whole legions of desires feeds,
Against all which my chastity opposes;
The field of honor virtue never loses.

No armor might be found that could defend
Transpiercing rays of crystal-pointed eyes;
No stratagem, no reason could amend,
No, not his age; [9] yet old men should be wise.
But shows deceive, outward appearance lies;
Let none for seeming so think saints of others,
For all are men, and all have sucked their mothers.

Who would have thought a monarch would have ever
Obeyed his handmaid of so mean a state?
Vulture ambition feeding on his liver,
Age having worn his pleasures out of date;
But hap comes never or it comes too late,
For such a dainty which his youth found not
Unto his feeble age did chance allot.

Ah Fortune, never absolutely good,
For that some cross still counterchecks our luck;
As here behold th' incompatible blood:
Of age and youth was that whereon we stuck,
Whose loathing we from Nature's breasts do suck
As opposite to what our blood requires,
For equal age doth equal like desires.

But mighty men in highest honor sitting
Naught but applause and pleasure can behold;
Soothed in their liking, careless what is fitting,
May not be suffered once to think they are old,

[9] *his age:* historically, Henry was forty-one.

Not trusting what they see, but what is told.
Miserable fortune to forget so far
The state of flesh, and what our frailties are.

Yet must I needs excuse so great defect,
For drinking of the Lethe of mine eyes.
He's forced forget himself and all respect
Of majesty whereon his state relies,
And now of loves and pleasures must devise,
For thus revived again, he serves and su'th
And seeks all means to undermine my youth.

Which never by assault he could recover,
So well encamped in strength of chaste desires;
My clean-armed thoughts repelled an unchaste lover;
The Crown that could command what it requires
I lesser prized than chastity's attires,
The unstained veil which innocents adorns,
The ungathered rose, defended with the thorns.

And safe mine honor stood, till that in truth
One of my sex, of place and nature bad,
Was set in ambush to entrap my youth,
One in the habit of like frailty clad,
One who the livery of like weakness had,
A seeming matron, yet a sinful monster,
As by her words the chaster sort may conster.[10]

She set upon me with the smoothest speech
That court and age could cunningly devise;
The one authentic made her fit to teach,
The other learned her how to subtilize.
Both were enough to circumvent the wise,
A document that well might teach the sage
That there's no trust in youth, nor hope in age.

"Daughter," saith she, "behold thy happy chance,
That hast the lot cast down into thy lap,
Whereby thou mayst thy honor great advance,
Whilst thou, unhappy, wilt not see thy hap;
Such fond respect thy youth doth so enwrap,
T' oppose thyself against thine own good fortune
That points thee out and seems thee to importune.

"Dost thou not see how that thy king, thy Jove,
Lightens forth glory on thy dark estate,
And showers down gold and treasure from above,

[10] *conster:* understand.

Whilst thou dost shut thy lap against thy fate?
Fie, fondling, fie! Thou wilt repent too late
The error of thy youth, that canst not see
What is the fortune that doth follow thee

"Thou must not think thy flower can always flourish,
And that thy beauty will be still admired;
But that those rays which all these flames do nourish,
Canceled with time, will have their date expired,
And men will scorn what now is so desired.
Our frailty's doom is written in the flowers,
Which flourish now and fade ere many hours.

"Read in my face the ruins of my youth,
The wreck of years upon my aged brow;
I have been fair, I must confess the truth,
And stood upon such nice respects as thou.
I lost my time, and I repent it now;
But were I to begin my youth again,
I would redeem the time I spent in vain.

"But thou hast years and privilege to use them;
Thy privilege doth bear beauty's great seal;
Besides, the law of nature doth excuse them,
To whom thy youth may have a just appeal.
Esteem not fame more than thou dost thy weal,—
Fame, whereof the world seems to make such choice,
Is but an echo, and an idle voice.

"Then why should this respect of honor bound us
In th' imaginary lists of reputation?
Titles which cold severity hath found us,
Breath of the vulgar, foe to recreation,
Melancholy's opinion, custom's relation,
Pleasure's plague, beauty's scourge, hell to the fair
To leave the sweet for castles in the air.

"Pleasure is felt, opinion but conceived,
Honor a thing without us, not our own,
Whereof we see how many are bereaved
Which should have reaped the glory they had sown,
And many have it, yet unworthy known.
So breathes his blasts this many-headed beast,
Whereof the wisest have esteemed least.

"The subtle city women, better learned,
Esteem them chaste enough that best seem so;
Who, though they sport, it shall not be discerned—

Their face bewrays [11] not what their bodies do.
'Tis wary walking that doth safeliest go.
With show of virtue, as the cunning knows,
Babes are beguiled with sweets, and men with shows.

"Then use thy talent; youth shall be thy warrant,
And let not honor from thy sports detract.
Thou must not fondly think thyself transparent,
That those who see thy face can judge the fact;
Let her have shame that cannot closely act,
And seem the chaste, which is the chiefest art,
For what we seem each sees; none knows our heart.

"The mighty, who can with such sins dispense,
Instead of shame do honors great bestow;
A worthy author doth redeem th' offense
And makes the scarlet sin as white as snow.
The majesty that doth descend so low
Is not defiled, but pure remains therein,
And being sacred, sanctifies the sin.

"What, dost thou stand on this, that he is old?
Thy beauty hath the more to work upon.
Thy pleasure's want shall be supplied with gold;
Cold age dotes most when the heat of youth is gone.
Enticing words prevail with such a one;
Alluring shows most deep impression strikes,
For age is prone to credit what it likes."

. . . .[12]

I saw the sin wherein my foot was ent'ring,
I saw how that dishonor did attend it,
I saw the shame whereon my flesh was vent'ring,
Yet had I not the power for to defend it.
So weak is sense, when error hath condemned it;
We see what's good, and thereto we consent,
But yet we choose the worst, and soon repent.

And now I come to tell the worst of illness,
Now draws the date of mine affliction near,
Now when the dark had wrapped up all in stillness
And dreadful black had dispossessed the clear;
Comed was the night, mother of sleep and fear,
Who with her sable mantle friendly covers
The sweet-stolen sports of joyful meeting lovers.

---

[11] *bewrays:* reveals.

[12] Here 119 lines are omitted. In them Rosamund debates with herself.

When lo, I joyed my lover, not my love,
And felt the hand of lust most undesired,
Enforced th' unproved bitter-sweet to prove,
Which yields no mutual pleasure when 'tis hired.
Love's not constrained, nor yet of due required;
Judge they who are unfortunately wed
What 'tis to come unto a loathed bed.

But soon his age received his short contenting
And sleep sealed up his languishing desires.
When he turns to his rest, I to repenting;
Into myself my waking thought retires.
My nakedness had proved my senses liars.
Now opened were mine eyes to look therein,
For first we taste the fruit, then see our sin.

Now did I find myself unparadised
From those pure fields of my so clean beginning.
Now I perceived how ill I was advised;
My flesh gan loathe the new-felt touch of sinning.
Shame leaves us by degrees, not at first winning,
For nature checks a new offense with loathing,
But use of sin doth make it seem as nothing.[13]

And use of sin did work in me a boldness,
And love in him incorporates such zeal
That jealousy, increased with age's coldness,
Fearing to lose the joy of all his weal,
Or doubting time his stealth might else reveal,
He's driven to devise some subtle way
How he might safeliest keep so rich a prey.

A stately palace he forthwith did build,
Whose intricate innumerable ways
With such confused errors [14] so beguiled
Th' unguided enterers with uncertain strays,
And doubtful turnings kept them in delays,
With bootless labor leading them about,
Able to find no way, nor in, nor out.

Within the closed bosom of which frame
That served a center to that goodly round
Were lodgings, with a garden to the same,
With sweetest flowers that ever adorned the ground,
And all the pleasures that delight hath found

[13] *nothing:* the *o* was long in Elizabethan pronunciation.

[14] *errors:* wandering ways.

To entertain the sense of wanton eyes,
Fuel of love, from whence lust's flames arise.

Here I, enclosed from all the world asunder,
The Minotaur [15] of shame, kept for disgrace,
The monster of fortune and the world's wonder,
Lived cloistered in so desolate a case.
None but the king might come into the place,
With certain maids that did attend my need,
And he himself came guided by a threed.[16]

Oh Jealousy, daughter of Envy and Love,
Most wayward issue of a gentle sire,
Fostered with fears, thy father's joys t' improve,
Mirth-marring monster, born a subtle liar,
Hateful unto thyself, flying thine own desire,
Feeding upon suspect that doth renew thee,
Happy were lovers if they never knew thee!

Thou hast a thousand gates thou enterest by,
Conducting trembling passions to our heart;
Hundred-eyed Argus, ever-waking spy,
Pale hag, infernal fury, pleasure's smart,
Envious observer, prying in every part,
Suspicious, fearful, gazing still [17] about thee,
Oh would to God that love could be without thee!

Thou didst deprive, through false suggesting fear,
Him of content and me of liberty,
(The only good that women hold so dear)
And turnst my freedom to captivity,
First made a prisoner ere an enemy,
Enjoined the ransom of my body's shame,
Which though I paid could not redeem the same.

What greater torment ever could have been,
Than to enforce the fair to live retired?
For what is beauty if it be not seen?
Or what is 't to be seen if not admired,
And though admired, unless in love desired?
Never were cheeks of roses, locks of amber,
Ordained to live imprisoned in a chamber.

Nature created beauty for the view,
Like as the fire for heat, the sun for light;
The fair do hold this privilege as due

[15] *Minotaur:* a legendary monster in Crete, who like Rosamund was kept in a labyrinth.

[16] *threed:* thread.

[17] *still:* constantly.

By ancient charter, to live most in sight,
And she that is debarred it, hath not right.
In vain our friends in this use their dehorting,[18]
For beauty will be where is most resorting.

Witness the fairest streets that Thames doth visit,
The wondrous concourse of the glitt'ring fair;
For what rare woman decked with beauty is it
That thither covets not to make repair?
The solitary country may not stay her;
Here is the center of all beauties best,
Excepting Delia, left t' adorn the west.[19]

Here doth the curious with judicial eyes
Contemplate beauty gloriously attired;
And herein all our chiefest glory lies,
To live where we are praised and most desired.
Oh, how we joy to see ourselves admired,
Whilst niggardly our favors we discover;
We love to be beloved, yet scorn the lover.

Yet would to God my foot had never moved
From country safety, from the fields of rest,
To know the danger to be highly loved,
And live in pomp to brave among the best;
Happy for me, better had I been blest,
If I unluckily had never strayed,
But lived at home a happy country maid,

Whose unaffected innocency thinks
No guileful fraud, as doth the courtly liver;
She's decked with truth; the river where she drinks
Doth serve her for her glass, her counsel-giver;
She loves sincerely, and is loved ever;
Her days are peace, and so she ends her breath—
True life, that knows not what's to die till death.

So should I never have been regist'red
In the black book of the unfortunate,
Nor had my name enrolled with maids misled,
Which bought their pleasures at so high a rate;
Nor had I taught, through my unhappy fate,
This lesson, which myself learnt with expense,
How most it hurts that most delights the sense.

---

[18] *dehorting:* dissuading. In 1599 Daniel removed the feminine ending on this couplet.

[19] *west:* presumably Wilton, the seat of the Countess of Pembroke.

Shame follows sin, disgrace is duly given,
Impiety will out, never so closely done;
No walls can hide us from the eye of heaven,
For shame must end what wickedness begun;
Forth breaks reproach when we least think thereon,
And this is ever proper unto courts,
That nothing can be done but fame reports.

Fame doth explore what lies most secret hidden,
Ent'ring the closet of the palace dweller,
Abroad revealing what is most forbidden;
Of truth and falsehood both an equal teller,
'Tis not a guard can serve for to expel her.
The sword of justice cannot cut her wings,
Nor stop her mouth from utt'ring secret things.

And this our stealth she could not long conceal
From her whom such a forfeit most concerned,
The wronged queen, who could so closely deal
That she the whole of all our practise learned,
And watched a time when least it was discerned,
In absence of the king, to wreak her wrong
With such revenge as she desired long.

The labyrinth she entered by that threed
That served a conduct to my absent lord,
Left there by chance, reserved for such a deed,
Where she surprised me whom she so abhorred.
Enraged with madness, scarce she speaks a word,
But flies with eager fury to my face,
Off'ring me most unwomanly disgrace.

Look how a tigress that hath lost her whelp
Runs fiercely ranging through the woods astray,
And seeing herself deprived of hope or help,
Furiously assaults what's in her way,
To satisfy her wrath, not for a prey;
So fell she on me in outrageous wise,
As could disdain and jealousy devise.

And after all her vile reproaches used,
She forced me take the poison she had brought
To end the life that had her so abused,
And free her fears and ease her jealous thought.
No cruelty her wrath could leave unwrought,
No spiteful act that to revenge is common,
No beast being fiercer than a jealous woman.

Those hands that beauty's ministers had been
Must now give death, that me adorned of late;
That mouth that newly gave consent to sin,
Must now receive destruction in thereat.
That body which my lusts did violate
Must sacrifice itself t' appease the wrong.
So short is pleasure; glory lasts not long.

The poison soon dispersed through all my veins
Had dispossessed my living senses quite,
When naught-respecting death, the last of pains,
Placed his pale colors, th' ensign of his might,
Upon his new-got spoil before his right;
Thence chased my soul, setting my day ere noon,
When I least thought my joys could end so soon.

. . . .[20]

Then were my funerals not long deferred,
But done with all the rites pomp could devise,
At Godstow,[21] where my body was interred,
And richly tombed in honorable wise,
Where yet as now scarce any note descries
Unto these times the memory of me,
Marble and brass so little lasting be.

For those walls which the credulous-devout
And apt-believing ignorant did found
With willing zeal that never called in doubt
That time their works should ever so confound,
Lie like confused heaps as underground,
And what their ignorance esteemed so holy
The wiser ages do account as folly.

And were it not thy favorable lines
Reedified the wreck of my decays,
And that thy accents willingly assigns
Some farther date, and give me longer days,
Few in this age had known my beauty's praise.
But thus renewed, my fame redeems some time,
Till other ages shall neglect thy rhyme.

Then, when confusion in her course shall bring
Sad desolation on the times to come,
When mirthless Thames shall have no swan to sing,

---

[20] 91 lines about the King's grief are omitted.

[21] *Godstow:* a nunnery near Oxford.

All music silent, and the Muses dumb,
And yet even then it must be known to some
That once they flourished, though not cherished so,
And Thames had swans as well as ever Po.

But here an end, I may no longer stay thee,
I must return t' attend at Stygian flood;
Yet ere I go, this one word more I pray thee,
Tell Delia now her sigh may do me good,
And will her note the frailty of our blood;
And if I pass unto those happy banks,
Then she must have her praise, thy pen her thanks.

So vanished she, and left me to return
To prosecute the tenor of my woes,
Eternal matter for my muse to mourn;
But yet the world hath heard too much of those,
My youth such errors must no more disclose.
I'll hide the rest, and grieve for what hath been;
Who made me known must make me live unseen.

MUSOPHILUS[22]

Do not profane the work of doing well,
Seduced man, that canst not look so high
From out that mist of earth, as thou canst tell
The ways of right which virtue doth descry,
That overlooks the base, contemptible,
And low-laid follies of mortality;
Nor mete out truth and right-deserving praise
By that wrong measure of confusion,
The vulgar foot that never takes his ways
By reason, but by imitation,
Rolling on with the rest, and never weighs
The course which he should go, but what is gone.
Well were it with mankind if what the most
Did like were best; but ignorance will live
By others' square, as by example lost,
And man to man must th' hand of error give
That none can fall alone, at their own cost,
And all because men judge not, but believe.

[22] *Musophilus* is a dialogue between a character of that name (meaning "lover of the muses") and Philocosmus ("lover of the world") on the use and value of learning and the arts. One long speech of Musophilus and a part of another are given.

For what poor bounds have they whom but th' earth bounds?
What is their end whereto their care attains,
When the thing got relieves not, but confounds,
Having but travail to succeed their pains?
What joy hath he of living, that propounds
Affliction but his end, and grief his gains?
Gathering, encroaching, wresting, joining to,
Destroying, building, decking, furnishing,
Repairing, altering, and so much ado
To his soul's toil and body's travailing,—
And all this doth he, little knowing who
Fortune ordains to have th' inheriting.
And his fair house raised high in envy's eye,
Whose pillars reared, perhaps, on blood and wrong,
The spoils and pillage of iniquity,
Who can assure it to continue long?
If rage spared not the walls of piety,
Shall the profanest piles of sin keep strong?
How many proud aspiring palaces
Have we known made the prey of wrath and pride,
Leveled with th' earth, left to forgetfulness
Whilst titlers their pretended rights decide,
Or civil tumults, or an orderless
Order, pretending change of some strong side?
Then where is that proud title of thy name?
Written in ice of melting vanity.
Where is thine heir left to possess the same?
Perhaps not so well as in beggary.
Something may rise to be beyond the shame
Of vile and unregarded poverty,
Which I confess, although I often strive
To clothe in the best habit of my skill,
In all the fairest colors I can give,
Yet for all that methinks she looks but ill;
I cannot brook that face, which dead-alive
Shows a quick body but a buried will.
Yet oft we see the bars of this restraint
Holds goodness in, which loose wealth would let fly,
And fruitless riches, barrener than want,
Brings forth small worth from idle liberty,
Which when disorders shall again make scant,
It must refetch her state from poverty.
But yet in all this interchange of all,
Virtue, we see, with her fair grace stands fast;
For what high races hath there come to fall
With low disgrace, quite vanished and past,

Since Chaucer lived, who yet lives, and yet shall,
Though (which I grieve to say) but in his last.
Yet what a time hath he wrested from time
And won upon the mighty waste of days,
Unto th' immortal honor of our clime
That by his means came first adorned with bays;
Unto the sacred relics of whose rhyme
We yet are bound in zeal to offer praise.
And could our lines, begotten in this age,
Obtain but such a blessed hand of years,
And scape the fury of that threat'ning rage
Which in confused clouds ghastly appears,
Who would not strain his travails to engage
When such true glory should succeed his cares?
But whereas he came planted in the spring,
And had the sun before him of respect,
We, set in th' autumn, in the withering
And sullen season of a cold defect,
Must taste those sour distastes the times do bring
Upon the fullness of a cloyed neglect;
Although the stronger constitutions shall
Wear out th' infection of distempered days,
And come with glory to outlive this fall,
Recov'ring of another spring of praise,
Cleared from th' oppressing humors wherewithal
The idle multitude surcharge their lays.
Whenas, perhaps, the words thou scornest now
May live, the speaking picture of the mind,
The extract of the soul that labored how
To leave the image of herself behind,
Wherein posterity, that love to know,
The just proportion of our spirits may find.
For these lines are the veins, the arteries,
And undecaying life-strings of those hearts
That still shall pant, and still shall exercise
The motion, spirit and nature both imparts;
And shall with those alive so sympathize
As, nourished with their powers, enjoy their parts.
Oh blessed letters, that combine in one
All ages past, and make one live with all,
By you we do confer with who are gone,
And the dead-living unto council call;
By you th' unborn shall have communion
Of what we feel and what doth us befall.
Soul of the world, knowledge, without thee
What hath the earth that truly glorious is?

Why should our pride make such a stir to be,
To be forgot? What good is like to this,
To do worthy the writing, and to write
Worthy the reading, and the world's delight?
And let th' unnatural and wayward race,
Born of one womb with us, but to our shame.
That never read t' observe, but to disgrace,
Raise all the tempest of their power to blame;
That puff of folly never can deface
The work a happy genius took to frame.
Yet why should civil learning seek to wound
And mangle her own members with despite?
Prodigious wits that study to confound
The life of wit, to seem to know aright,
As if themselves had fortunately found
Some stand from off the earth beyond our sight,
Whence, overlooking all as from above,
Their grace is not to work, but to reprove—
But how came they placed in so high degree,
Above the reach and compass of the rest?
Who hath admitted them only to be
Free denizens of skill, to judge the best?
From whom the world as yet could never see
The warrant of their wit soundly expressed.
T' acquaint our times with that perfection
Of high conceit, which only they possess,
That we might have things exquisitely done,
Measured with all their strict observances,
Such would, I know, scorn a translation,
Or bring but others' labors to the press;
Yet, oft these monster-breeding mountains will
Bring forth small mice of great expected skill.
Presumption, ever fullest of defects,
Fails in the doing to perform her part;
And I have known proud words and poor effects
Of such indeed as do condemn this art;
But let them rest, it ever hath been known,
They others' virtues scorn that doubt their own.
And for the divers disagreeing chords
Of inter-jangling ignorance that fill
The dainty ears and leave no room for words,
The worthier minds neglect, or pardon will;
Knowing the best he hath, he frankly 'fords,
And scorns to be a niggard of his skill.
And that the rather, since this short-lived race,
Being fatally the sons but of one day,

That now with all their power ply it apace,
To hold out with the greatest might they may
Against confusion, that hath all in chase,
To make of all a universal prey.
For now great nature hath laid down at last
That mighty birth wherewith so long she went,
And overwent the times of ages past
Here to lie in, upon our soft content,
Where, fruitful, she hath multiplied so fast
That all she hath on these times seemed t' have spent.
All that which might have many ages graced
Is born in one, to make one cloyed with all,
Where plenty hath impressed a deep distaste
Of best and worst, and all in general,
That goodness seems goodness to have defaced,
And virtue hath to virtue given the fall.
For emulation, that proud nurse of wit,
Scorning to stay below or come behind,
Labors upon that narrow top to sit
Of sole perfection in the highest kind;
Envy and wonder, looking after it,
Thrust likewise on the selfsame bliss to find,
And so, long striving till they can no more,
Do stuff the place, or others' hopes shut out,
Who, doubting to overtake those gone before,
Give up their care and cast no more about;
And so in scorn leave all as fore-possessed,
And will be none where they may not be best.
Ev'n like some empty creek that long hath lain
Left or neglected of the river by,
Whose searching sides, pleased with a wand'ring vein,
Finding some little way that close did lie,
Steal in at first, then other streams again
Second the first, then more than all supply,
Till all the mighty main hath borne, at last,
The glory of his chiefest power that way,
Plying this new-found pleasant room so fast,
Till all be full, and all be at a stay;
And then about and back again doth cast,
Leaving that, full, to fall another way:
So fares this humorous [23] world, that evermore
Rapt with the current of a present course,
Runs into that which lay contemned before,
Then, glutted, leaves the same and falls t' a worse.

---

[23] *humorous:* giddy.

Now zeal holds all, no life but to adore,
Then cold in spirit, and faith is of no force;
Straight, all that holy was unhallowed lies,
The scattered carcasses of ruined vows;
Then truth is false, and now hath blindness eyes,
Then zeal trusts all, now scarcely what it knows,
That evermore, too foolish or too wise,
It fatal is to be seduced with shows.
Sacred religion, mother of form and fear,
How gorgeously sometimes dost thou sit decked!
What pompous vestures do we make thee wear!
What stately piles we prodigal erect!
How sweet perfumed thou art, how shining clear!
How solemnly observed, with what respect!
Another time, all plain and quite threadbare,
Thou must have all within and naught without,
Sit poorly without light, disrobed, no care
Of outward grace to amuse the poor devout,
Powerless, unfollowed, scarcely men can spare
The necessary rites to set thee out.
Either truth, goodness, virtue, are not still[24]
The selfsame which they are, and always one,
But alter to the project of our will;
Or we our actions make them wait upon,
Putting them in the livery of our skill,
And cast them off again when we have done.
You mighty lords that with respected grace
Do at the stern of fair example stand,
And all the body of this populace
Guide with the only turning of your hand,
Keep a right course, bear up from all disgrace,
Observe the point of glory to our land,
Hold up disgraced knowledge from the ground,
Keep virtue in request, give worth her due,
Let not neglect with barbarous means confound
So fair a good to bring in night anew.
Be not, oh, be not accessory found
Unto her death, that must give life to you.
Where will you have your virtuous name safe laid?
In gorgeous tombs, in sacred cells secure?
Do you not see those prostrate heaps betrayed
Your fathers' bones, and could not keep them sure?
And will you trust deceitful stones fair laid,
And think they will be to your honor truer?

[24] *still:* always.

No, no, unsparing time will proudly send
A warrant unto wrath, that with one frown
Will all these mockeries of vain glory rend,
And make them as before, ungraced, unknown,
Poor idle honors that can ill defend
Your memories that cannot keep their own.
And whereto serve that wondrous trophy [25] now,
That on the goodly plain near Wilton stands?
That huge dumb heap that cannot tell us how,
Nor what, nor whence it is, nor with whose hands,
Nor for whose glory, it was set to show
How much our pride mocks that of other lands.
Whereon, when as the gazing passenger
Hath greedy looked with admiration,
And fain would know his birth, and what he were,
How there erected, and how long agone,
Inquires, and asks his fellow traveler
What he hath heard, and his opinion,
And he knows nothing; then he turns again
And looks, and sighs, and then admires afresh,
And in himself with sorrow doth complain
The misery of dark forgetfulness,
Angry with time that nothing should remain
Our greatest wonder's wonder to express.
Then ignorance, with fabulous discourse,
Robbing fair art and cunning of their right,
Tells how those stones were by the devil's force
From Afric brought to Ireland in a night,
And thence to Britainy by magic course,
From giants' hands redeemed by Merlin's sleight,
And then near Ambri [26] placed, in memory
Of all those noble Britons murthered [27] there
By Hengist [28] and his Saxon treachery,
Coming to parle in peace at unaware.
With this old legend then credulity
Holds her content, and closes up her care.
But is antiquity so great a liar?
Or do her younger sons her age abuse,
Seeing after-comers still so apt t' admire
The grave authority that she doth use,
That reverence and respect dares not require

[25] *wondrous trophy:* Stonehenge, on Salisbury Plain.

[26] *Ambri:* Mt. Ambrius, near Salisbury. See Geoffrey of Monmouth, *Historia Regum Britanniae,* Chaps. IX–XII.

[27] For the story see Nennius, *Historia Britonum,* sec. 46.

[28] *Hengist:* Jutish chief (d. 488), cofounder of the Kingdom of Kent.

Proof of her deeds, or once her words refuse?
Yet wrong they did us to presume so far
Upon our easy credit and delight;
For, once found false, they straight became to mar
Our faith and their own reputation quite,
That now her truths hardly believed are,
And though sh' avouch the right, she scarce hath right.
And as for thee, thou huge and mighty frame
That stands corrupted so with time's despite,
And giv'st false evidence against their fame
That set thee there to testify their right,
And art become a traitor to their name
That trusted thee with all the best they might,
Thou shalt stand still belied and slandered,
The only gazing-stock of ignorance,
And by thy guile the wise, admonished,
Shall never more desire such heaps t' advance,
Nor trust their living glory with the dead
That cannot speak; but leave their fame to chance,
Considering in how small a room do lie,
And yet lie safe, as fresh as if alive,
All those great worthies of antiquity
Which long forelived thee and shall long survive,
Who stronger tombs found for eternity
Than could the powers of all the earth contrive;
Where they remain these trifles to upbraid,
Out of the reach of spoil and way of rage,
Though time with all his power of years hath laid
Long battery, backed with undermining age;
Yet they make head only with their own aid,
And war with his all-conquering forces wage,
Pleading the heavens' prescription to be free,
And t' have a grant t' endure as long as he.

. . . .

Power above powers, Oh heavenly eloquence,[29]
That with the strong rein of commanding words
Dost manage, guide, and master th' eminence
Of men's affections more than all their swords,—
Shall we not offer to thy excellence
The richest treasure that our wit affords?
Thou that canst do much more with one poor pen
Than all the powers of princes can effect,
And draw, divert, dispose, and fashion men

---

[29] The peroration of Musophilus.

Better than force or rigor can direct,—
Should we this ornament of glory then,
As th' unmaterial fruits of shades, neglect?
Or should we, careless, come behind the rest
In power of words, that go before in worth?
Whenas our accents, equal to the best,
Is able greater wonders to bring forth;
When all that ever hotter spirits expressed,
Comes bettered by the patience of the north.
And who, in time, knows whither we may vent
The treasure of our tongue, to what strange shores
This gain of our best glory shall be sent
T' enrich unknowing nations with our stores?
What worlds in th' yet unformed occident
May come refined with th' accents that are ours?
Or who can tell for what great work in hand
The greatness of our style is now ordained?
What powers it shall bring in, what spirits command,
What thoughts let out, what humors keep restrained,
What mischief it may powerfully withstand,
And what fair ends may thereby be attained?
And as for Poesy, mother of this force,
That breeds, brings forth, and nourishes this might,
Teaching it in a loose yet measured course
With comely motions how to go upright;
And fostering it with bountiful discourse,
Adorns it thus in fashions of delight,
What should I say, since it is well approved
The speech of heaven, with whom they have commerce
That only seem out of themselves removed
And do with more than human skills converse?
Those numbers wherewith heaven and earth are moved
Show, weakness speaks in prose, but power in verse.
Wherein thou likewise seemest to allow
That th' acts of worthy men should be preserved;
As in the holiest tombs we can bestow
Upon their glory that have well deserved,
Wherein thou dost no other virtue show
Than what most barbarous countries have observed;
When all the happiest nations hitherto
Did with no lesser glory speak than do.
Now to what else thy malice shall object,
For schools and arts, and their necessity—
When from my Lord, whose judgment must direct
And form and fashion my ability,
I shall have got more strength, thou shalt expect

Out of my better leisure my reply.
And if herein the curious sort shall deem
My will was carried far beyond my force,
And that it is a thing doth ill beseem
The function of a poem to discourse,
Thy learned judgment which I most esteem,
Worthy Fulke Greville,[30] must defend this course;
By whose mild grace and gentle hand, at first
My infant muse was brought in open sight
From out the darkness wherein it was nursed
And made to be partaker of the light,—
Which peradventure never else had durst
T' appear in place, but had been smothered quite;
And now herein encouraged by thy praise
Is made so bold and vent'rous to attempt
Beyond example, and to try those ways
That malice from our forces thinks exempt,
To see if we our wronged lines could raise
Above the reach of lightness and contempt.

ULYSSES AND THE SIREN[31]

Siren: Come, worthy Greek, Ulysses, come,
Possess these shores with me;
The winds and seas are troublesome,
And here we may be free.
Here may we sit and view their toil
That travail in the deep,
And joy the day in mirth the while,
And spend the night in sleep.

Ulysses: Fair nymph, if fame or honor were
To be attained with ease,
Then would I come and rest me there,
And leave such toils as these.
But here it dwells, and here must I
With danger seek it forth;
To spend the time luxuriously
Becomes not men of worth.

---

[30] *Fulke Greville:* (1554–1628) the friend and biographer of Sidney, himself a philosopher and poet.

[31] A. E. Housman (*The Name and Nature of Poetry*) said of the first stanza, "Diction and movement alike, it is perfect. It is made out of the most ordinary words, yet it is pure from the least alloy of prose; and however much nearer heaven the art of poetry may have mounted, it has never flown on a surer or lighter wing."

Siren: Ulysses, Oh be not deceived
With that unreal name;
This honor is a thing conceived,
And rests on others' fame.
Begotten only to molest
Our peace, and to beguile
The best thing of our life, our rest,
And give us up to toil.

Ulysses: Delicious nymph, suppose there were
Nor honor nor report,
Yet manliness would scorn to wear
The time in idle sport.
For toil doth give a better touch,
To make us feel our joy;
And ease finds tediousness, as much
As labor yields annoy.

Siren: Then pleasure likewise seems the shore
Whereto tends all your toil,
Which you forgo to make it more,
And perish oft the while.
Who may disport them diversly,
Find never tedious day,
And ease may have variety
As well as action may.

Ulysses: But natures of the noblest frame
These toils and dangers please,
And they take comfort in the same
As much as you in ease,
And with the thoughts of actions past
Are recreated still;
When pleasure leaves a touch at last
To show that it was ill.

Siren: That doth opinion only cause
That's out of custom bred,
Which makes us many other laws
Than ever nature did.
No widows wail for our delights,
Our sports are without blood;
The world, we see, by warlike wights
Receives more hurt than good.

Ulysses: But yet the state of things require
These motions of unrest,
And these great spirits of high desire

Seem born to turn them best,
To purge the mischiefs that increase
And all good order mar;
For oft we see a wicked peace
To be well changed for war.

Siren: Well, well, Ulysses, then I see
I shall not have thee here,
And therefore I will come to thee,
And take my fortunes there.
I must be won that cannot win,
Yet lost were I not won;
For beauty hath created been
T' undo, or be undone.

A PASTORAL[32]

OH happy golden age,
Not for that rivers ran
With streams of milk, and honey dropped from trees;
Not that the earth did gauge
Unto the husbandman
Her voluntary fruits, free without fees;
Not for no cold did freeze,
Nor any cloud beguile
Th' eternal flowering spring
Wherein lived everything
And whereon the heavens perpetually did smile;
Not for no ship had brought
From foreign shores or wars[33] or wares ill sought.

But only for that name,
That idle name of wind,
That idol of deceit, that empty sound
Called Honor, which became
The tyrant of the mind
And so torments our nature without ground,
Was not yet vainly found,
Nor yet sad griefs imparts
Amidst the sweet delights
Of joyful amorous wights;
Nor were his hard laws known to free-born hearts,

[32] This is a translation of a chorus in Act I, scene ii of Tasso's *Aminta*, in the verse form of the original.

[33] *or wars:* either wars.

But golden laws like these
Which nature wrote: *That's lawful which doth please.*

Then amongst flowers and springs,
Making delightful sport,
Sat lovers without conflict, without flame,
And nymphs and shepherds sing,
Mixing in wanton sort
Whisperings with songs, then kisses with the same
Which from affection came;
The naked virgin then
Her roses fresh reveals
Which now her veil conceals;
The tender apples in her bosom seen;
And oft in rivers clear
The lovers with their loves consorting were.

Honor, thou first didst close
The spring of all delight,
Denying water to the amorous thirst,
Thou taught'st fair eyes to lose
The glory of their light,
Restrained from men, and on themselves reversed.
Thou in a lawn didst first
Those golden hairs encase
Late spread unto the wind;
Thou mad'st loose grace unkind,
Gav'st bridle to their words, art to their pace.
Oh Honor, is it thou
That mak'st that stealth which love doth free allow?

It is thy work that brings
Our griefs and torments thus;
But thou, fierce lord of nature and of love,
The qualifier of kings,
What dost thou here with us
That are below thy power, shut from above?
Go, and from us remove;
Trouble the mighty's sleep!
Let us, neglected, base,
Live still without thy grace,
And th' use of th' ancient happy ages keep.
Let's love; this life of ours
Can make no truce with time, that all devours.

Let's love! The sun doth set and rise again,
But whenas our short light
Comes once to set, it makes eternal night.

DELIA[34]

(1592)

III

If it so hap this offspring of my care,
These fatal anthems, sad and mournful songs
Come to their view who like afflicted are,
Let them yet sigh their own and moan my wrongs;
But untouched hearts, with unaffected eye,
Approach not to behold so great distress.
Clearsighted you soon note what is awry,
Whilst blinded ones mine errors never guess.
You blinded souls whom youth and error lead,
You outcast eaglets, dazzled with your sun,
Ah, you and none but you my sorrows read;
You best can judge the wrongs that she hath done.
That she hath done, the motive of my pain,
Who, whilst I love, doth kill me with disdain.

IV

These plaintive verse,[35] the posts of my desire,
Which haste for succor to her slow regard,
Bear not report of any slender fire,
Forging a grief to win a fame's reward.
Nor are my passions limned[36] for outward hue,
For that no colors can depaint my sorrows;
Delia herself and all the world may view
Best in my face how cares hath tilled deep furrows.
No bays I seek to deck my mourning brow,
Oh clear-eyed rector of the holy hill;[37]
My humble accents crave the olive bough
Of her mild pity and relenting will.
These lines I use t' unburthen mine own heart;
My love affects no fame, nor 'steems of art.

---

[34] The texts are based on the edition of A. C. Sprague, who usually adopts the reading of the first authorized edition, 1592. Daniel revised *Delia* four times, and his later revisions remove some of the Elizabethan flavor of the poems. The numbering of the sonnets follows Sprague, not Lee.

[35] *verse:* the plural, as in Old and Middle English.

[36] *limned:* drawn, painted.

[37] *rector:* ruler (i.e., Apollo); *holy hill:* Mt. Parnassus.

VI

Fair is my love, and cruel as she's fair:
Her brow shades frowns, although her eyes are sunny,
Her smiles are lightning, though her pride despair,
And her disdains are gall, her favors honey.
A modest maid, decked with a blush of honor,
Whose feet do tread green paths of youth and love;
The wonder of all eyes that look upon her,
Sacred on earth, designed a saint above.
Chastity and Beauty, which were deadly foes,
Live reconciled friends within her brow;
And had she pity to conjoin with those,
Then who had heard the plaints I utter now?
Oh had she not been fair and thus unkind,
My muse had slept, and none had known my mind.

IX [38]

If this be love, to draw a weary breath,
Paint on floods till the shore cry to the air,
With downward looks still reading on the earth
The sad memorials of my love's despair;
If this be love, to war against my soul,
Lie down to wail, rise up to sigh and grieve me,
The never-resting stone of care to roll,
Still to complain my griefs, and none relieve me;
If this be love, to clothe me with dark thoughts,
Haunting untrodden paths to wail apart,
My pleasures, horror; music, tragic notes,
Tears in my eyes and sorrow at my heart;
If this be love, to live a living death—
Oh then love I, and draw this weary breath.

[38] Based on Desportes, *Diane,* I, xxix. This was Sonnet 22 in the "Poems and Sonnets of Sundry Other Noblemen and Gentlemen" appended to the surreptitious Newman edition of Sidney's *Astrophel and Stella* in 1591.

XXXI[39]

Look, Delia, how we 'steem the half-blown rose,
The image of thy blush and summer's honor,
Whilst in her tender green she doth inclose
That pure sweet beauty time bestows upon her.
No sooner spreads her glory in the air
But straight her full-blown pride is in declining.
She then is scorned that late adorned the fair;
So clouds thy beauty after fairest shining.
No April can revive thy withered flowers,
Whose blooming grace adorns thy glory now;
Swift speedy time, feathered with flying hours,
Dissolves the beauty of the fairest brow.
Oh let not then such riches waste in vain,
But love whilst that thou mayst be loved again.

XXXIII[40]

When men shall find thy flower, thy glory pass,
And thou, with careful brow sitting alone,
Received hast this message from thy glass,
That tells thee truth, and says that all is gone,
Fresh shalt thou see in me the wounds thou madest,
Though spent thy flame, in me the heat remaining,
I that have loved thee thus before thou fadest,
My faith shall wax, when thou art in thy waning.
The world shall find this miracle in me,
That fire can burn when all the matter's spent;
Then what my faith hath been thyself shall see,
And that thou wast unkind thou mayst repent.
Thou mayst repent that thou hast scorned my tears,
When winter snows upon thy golden[41] hairs.

---

[39] Based on Tasso, *Gerusalemme Liberata,* XVI, 14–15. Spenser made two versions of the same source, in *Faerie Queene,* II, xii, xxiv–xxv and *Amoretti,* LXX (see p. 337).

[40] Imitated from Tasso, *Rime Amorose,* 57.

[41] *golden:* changed to *sable* in later editions.

XLV[42]

CARE-CHARMER sleep, son of the sable night,
Brother to death, in silent darkness born,
Relieve my languish and restore the light;
With dark forgetting of my cares, return.
And let the day be time enough to mourn
The shipwreck of my ill-adventured youth;
Let waking eyes suffice to wail their scorn
Without the torment of the night's untruth.
Cease, dreams, th' imagery of our day desires,
To model forth the passions of the morrow;
Never let rising sun approve you liars,
To add more grief to aggravate my sorrow.
Still let me sleep, embracing clouds in vain,
And never wake to feel the day's disdain.

XLVI

LET others sing of knights and paladins
In aged accents and untimely[43] words,
Paint shadows in imaginary lines
Which well the reach of their high wits records;
But I must sing of thee and those fair eyes.
Authentic shall my verse in time to come,
When yet th' unborn shall say, "Lo where she lies,
Whose beauty made him speak that else was dumb."
These are the arks, the trophies I erect,
That fortify thy name against old age;
And these thy sacred virtues must protect
Against the dark and time's consuming rage.
Though th' error of my youth they shall discover,
Suffice, they show I lived and was thy lover.

---

[42] Based on Desportes, *Hippolyte,* lxxv. [43] *untimely:* obsolete.

XLVIII

None other fame mine unambitious muse
Affected ever but t' eternize thee;
All other honors do my hopes refuse,
Which meaner prized and momentary be.
For God forbid I should my papers blot
With mercenary lines, with servile pen,
Praising virtues in them that have them not,
Basely attending on the hopes of men.
No, no, my verse respects nor Thames nor theaters,
Nor seeks it to be known unto the great;
But Avon, rich [44] in fame though poor in waters,
Shall have my song, where Delia hath her seat.
Avon shall be my Thames and she my song;
I'll sound her name the river all along.

[44] *Avon:* not the famous river that flows through Stratford, but a river of the same name in Wiltshire; *rich:* later changed to "poor," and line 14 altered to read, "No other prouder brooks shall hear my wrong."

Joseph Hall • John Marston

1574–1656 1575–1634

JOSEPH HALL, who proclaimed himself the first English satirist, overlooking Wyatt and Gascoigne and Lodge, to go no further back, was a recent Cambridge graduate of the age of twenty-three when his first three books *Virgidemiarum* appeared in 1597. He professed himself a follower of Spenser (Colin) and he reflected his master's archaisms and the literary opinions expressed in *The Teares of the Muses.* He used the heroic couplet and began the development of a style suitable to formal satire in English. His first venture was popular enough so that he produced three more books in the same year, the first three books called "toothless" satires and the last three "biting" satires. (To this distinction a later antagonist of Hall's, John Milton, applied the scornful words, "That such a poem should be toothless, I still affirm it to be a bull, taking away the essence of what it calls itself. For if it bite neither the persons nor the vices, how is it a satire? And if it bites either, how is it toothless? So that toothless satires are as if he had said toothless teeth.") Hall affirms that in his first satire he has tried to imitate the sour and crabbed face of Juvenal's, but that otherwise he is independent of models, Ariosto and one base French satire being the only modern examples he knows of. His subjects cover literature, morals, and social customs, and his style, though lacking in the epigrammatic quality of the masters of a century later, received the praise of Warton and of Pope.

John Marston, of Brasenose College, Oxford, and the Middle Temple, was twenty-two when he published *The Metamorphosis of Pigmalions Image and Certaine Satyres* in 1598 and a collection called *The Scourge of Villanie* later in the same year. He used the pen-name "W. Kinsayder," and he immediately came into conflict with Hall. The *Reactio* printed in the *Scourge* ridicules Hall's literary judgments and his pretensions as a poet. Marston's inspiration as a satirist comes from a strong cynicism and melancholy; he was a dramatist who early portrayed the malcontent type, of which Shakespeare's Hamlet is the most famous representative. But there are signs that Marston himself was more like Jaques than like Hamlet; his revulsion against sensuality may be a battle against part of his own nature, and his *Pigmalions Image* is as pornographic as anything he attacks. His style is often rough and harsh (as the Elizabethans thought the classical satire of Juvenal and Persius was) and sometimes a highly compressed syntax makes the meaning obscure. But Marston is never without vigor, and his plays as well as his poems show a strong mind and personality. He was no unworthy antagonist of Ben Jonson in "the war of the theaters."

The satires of Marston and Hall aroused public attention so intense that there are several replies to them, and references in the *Parnassus* plays performed at Cambridge show the interest of contemporary undergraduates in the quarrel.

On June 1, 1599, however, the Archbishop of Canterbury and the Bishop of London directed the Stationers' Company to burn Hall's and Marston's satires along with other books.

Hall and Marston both became divines, the former rising to be Bishop of Exeter and later of Norwich. Hall wrote a prose satire in Latin, *Mundus alter et idem* (1605), and some "characters" in 1608, which have resemblances to his verse satire. He died in 1656 after suffering hardship under the Puritans. Marston retired from a literary life in London to study philosophy at Oxford, received holy orders in 1609, and lived a retired country parson's life until his death in 1634.

BIBLIOGRAPHY: HALL: *Poems*, ed. A. Davenport, Liverpool, 1945; K. Schulze, *Die Satiren Halls*, Berlin, 1910; P. A. Smith, "Hall, our English Seneca" *PMLA*, LXIII (1948), 1191–1204; A. Stein, "Hall's Imitation of Juvenal" *MLR*, XLIII (1948), 315–322; Hallett Smith, *Elizabethan Poetry* (1952), 227–238; J. B. Leishman, ed., *The Three Parnassus Plays*, London, 1949.

MARSTON: A. Stein, "The Second English Satirist," *MLR*, XXXVIII (1943), 273–8; Theodore Spencer, "John Marston," *Criterion*, XIII (1934), 581–599; S. Schoenbaum, "The Precarious Balance of John Marston," *PMLA*, LXVII (1952), 1069–1078; biographical articles by R. E. Brettle in *RES*, III (1927), 398, and *MLR*, XXII (1927), 7–14 and 317–319.

JOSEPH HALL
VIRGIDEMIARUM[1]

Six Books

Satires

BOOK I

Prologue

I first adventure,[2] with foolhardy might,
To tread the steps of perilous despite.
I first adventure; follow me who list,
And be the second English satirist.
Envy waits on my back, Truth on my side;
Envy will be my page, and Truth my guide.
Envy the margent [3] holds, and Truth the line.
Truth doth approve, but Envy doth repine.
For in this smoothing age who durst indite
Hath made his pen an hired parasite
To claw the back of him that beastly lives,
And prank base men in proud superlatives.
Whence damned vice is shrouded quite from shame,
And crowned with virtue's meed, immortal name!
Infamy dispossessed of native due,
Ordained of old on looser life to sue;
The world's eye bleared with those shameless lies,
Masked in the show of meal-mouthed poesies.
Go, daring Muse, on with thy thankless task,
And do the ugly face of vice unmask.
And if thou canst not thine high flight remit
So as it mought [4] a lowly satire fit,
Let lowly satires rise aloft to thee.
Truth be thy speed, and truth thy patron be.

---

[1] *Virgidemiarum:* (six books) of whipping-rods or blows made with them.

[2] *first adventure:* Hall had been preceded by Gascoigne and Lodge in the Elizabethan period.

[3] *margent:* margin.

[4] *mought:* might.

BOOK I

Satire III

WITH some pot-fury, ravished from their wit,
They sit and muse on some no-vulgar writ.
As frozen dunghills in a winter's morn
That void of vapor seemed all beforn,[5]
Soon as the sun sends out his piercing beams
Exhale out filthy smoke and stinking steams,
So doth the base and the fore-barren brain
Soon as the raging wine begins to reign.
One higher pitched doth set his soaring thought
On crowned kings [6] that Fortune hath low brought;
Or some upreared, high-aspiring swain,
As it might be the Turkish Tamberlaine.[7]
Then weeneth he his base drink-drowned sprite
Rapt to the threefold loft of heaven height,
When he conceives upon his feigned stage
The stalking steps of his great personage,
Graced with huff-cap terms and thundering threats,
That his poor hearers' hair quite upright sets.
Such soon as some brave-minded hungry youth
Sees fitly frame to his wide-strained mouth
He vaunts his voice upon an hired stage,
With high-set steps and princely carriage;
Now swooping in side-robes of royalty
That erst did scrub in lousy brokery; [8]
There if he can with terms Italianate,
Big-sounding sentences, and words of state,
Fair patch me up his pure iambic verse,
He ravishes the gazing scaffolders.[9]
Then certes was the famous Corduban [10]
Never but half so high tragedian.
Now, lest such frightful shows of Fortune's fall
And bloody tyrant's rage should chance appal
The dead-struck audience, 'midst the silent rout
Comes leaping in a self-misformed lout,
And laughs, and grins, and frames his mimic face,
And jostles straight into the prince's place.

---

5 *beforn:* before.

6 *crowned kings:* a reference to the *Mirror for Magistrates.*

7 *Turkish Tamberlaine:* Marlowe's two-part play. Tamburlaine was Scythian, not Turkish.

8 *brokery:* secondhand goods.

9 *scaffolders:* spectators who sat on the stage.

10 *Corduban:* Seneca, who was born at Cordova.

Then doth the theater echo all aloud
With gladsome noise of that applauding crowd.
A goodly hotchpotch! when vile russetings [11]
Are match with monarchs and with mighty kings.
A goodly grace to sober tragic Muse
When each base clown his clumsy fist doth bruise,[12]
And show his teeth in double rotten row,
For laughter at his self-resembled show.
Meanwhile our poets in high parliament
Sit watching every word and gesturement,
Like curious censors of some doughty gear,
Whispering their verdict in their fellow's ear.
Woe to the word whose margent in their scroll
Is noted with a black condemning coal!
But if each period might the synod please,
Ho!— Bring the ivy boughs and bands of bays.
Now when they part and leave the naked stage
'Gins the bare hearer, in a guilty rage,
To curse and ban, and blame his lickerous [13] eye
That thus hath lavished his late halfpenny.[14]
Shame that the Muses should be bought and sold
For every peasant's brass, on each scaffold!

BOOK I

Satire IV

Too popular is tragic poesy,
Straining his tiptoes for a farthing fee,
And doth beside on rhymeless numbers tread;
Unbid iambics flow from careless head.
Some braver brain in high heroic rhymes
Compileth worm-eat stories of old times;
And he like some imperious Maronist [15]
Conjures the muses that they him assist.
Then strives he to bombast his feeble lines
With far-fetched phrase—
And maketh up his hard-betaken tale
With strange enchantments, fetched from darksome vale,
Of some Melissa,[16] that by tragic doom

[11] *russetings:* peasants, rustics (who wear russet clothes).

[12] *bruise:* from knocking on the benches to applaud.

[13] *lickerous:* eager.

[14] *halfpenny:* the price of general admission to the pit.

[15] *Maronist:* an imitator of Virgil.

[16] *Melissa:* character in *Orlando Furioso* of Ariosto.

To Tuscan's soil transporteth Merlin's tomb.
Painters and poets, hold your ancient right;
Write what you will, and write not what you might;
(Their limits be their list, their reason, will.)
But if some painter in presuming skill
Should paint the stars in center of the earth,
Could ye forbear some smiles and taunting mirth?
But let no rebel satire dare traduce
Th' eternal legends of thy fairy muse,
Renowned Spenser! whom no earthly wight
Dares once to emulate, much less dares despite.
Salust of France, and Tuscan Ariost,[17]
Yield up the laurel garland ye have lost;
And let all others willow wear with me,
Or let their undeserving temples bared be.

BOOK V

Satire III

ΚΟΙΝΑ ΦΙΛΩΝ[18]

THE satire should be like the porcupine,
That shoots sharp quills out in each angry line,
And wounds the blushing cheek and fiery eye
Of him that hears, and readeth guiltily.
Ye antique satires, how I bless your days
That brooked your bolder style, their own dispraise,
And well near wish, yet joy my wish is vain,
I had been then, or they were now again!
For now our ears been of more brittle mold
Than those dull earthen ears that were of old;
Sith theirs, like anvils, bore the hammer's head,
Our glass can never touch unshivered.
But from the ashes of my quiet style
Henceforth may rise some raging rough Lucile[19]
That may with Aeschylus both find and leese[20]
The snaky tresses of th' Eumenides.[21]
Meanwhile, sufficeth me, the world may say
That I these vices loathed another day,

---

[17] *Salust of France:* Guillaume de Salluste du Bartas, French poet (1544–1590); *Ariost:* Lodovico Ariosto, Italian poet (1474–1533).

[18] ΚΟΙΝΑ ΦΙΛΩΝ: friends own their goods in common.

[19] *Lucile:* Lucilius, the father of Roman satire.

[20] *leese:* loose.

[21] *Eumenides:* the Furies. Aeschylus wrote a tragedy called *Eumenides.*

Which I have done with as devout a cheer
As he that rounds Paul's pillars in the ear[22]
Or bends his ham down in the naked quire.
'Twas ever said, Frontine, and ever seen
That golden clerks but wooden lawyers been.
Could ever wise man wish, in good estate
The use of all things indiscriminate?
Who wots not yet how well this did beseem
The learned master[23] of the academe?
Plato is dead, and dead is his device,
Which some thought witty, none thought ever wise;
Yet certes Maecha is a Platonist
To all, they say, save whoso do not list,
Because her husband, a far-trafficked man
Is a professed Peripatetian.[24]
And so our grandsires were in ages past
That let their lands lie all so widely waste
That nothing was in pale or hedge ypent[25]
Within some province or whole shire's extent.
As nature made the earth, so did it lie,
Save for the furrows of their husbandry;
Whenas the neighbor lands so couched lain
That all bore show of one fair champian,[26]
Some headless cross they digged on their lea
Or rolled some marked mere-stone[27] in the way.
Poor simple men! for what mought that avail
That my field might not fill my neighbor's pail
More than a pilled stick[28] can stand in stead
To bar Cynedo from his neighbor's bed,
More than the threadbare client's poverty
Debars the attorney of his wonted fee?
If they were thriftless, mought not we amend,
And with more care our dangered fields defend?
Each man can guard what thing he deemeth dear,
As fearful merchants do their female heir,
Which, were it not for promise of their wealth,
Need not be stalled up for fear of stealth,

---

22 *rounds Paul's Pillars in the ear:* whispers to the pillars in St. Paul's cathedral (while saying his prayers).

23 *learned master:* Plato. The reference is to Book IV of the *Republic,* in which communism, even to ownership of women and children, is prescribed for the guardians of the state.

24 *Peripatetian:* A Peripatetic philosopher; here, one who travels.

25 *ypent:* shut up.

26 *champian:* champaign, field.

27 *mere-stone:* boundary stone.

28 *pilled stick:* stick stripped of bark.

Would rather stick upon the bellman's cries,
Though proffered for a branded Indian's price.[29]
Then raise we muddy bulwarks on our banks,
Beset around with treble quickset [30] ranks,
Or if those walls be overweak a ward,[31]
The squared brick may be a better guard.
Go to, my thrifty yeoman, and uprear
A brazen wall to shend [32] thy land from fear;
Do so, and I shall praise thee all the while,
So be thou stake not up the common style,
So be thou hedge in naught but what's thine own,
So be thou pay what tithes thy neighbors done,[33]
So be thou let not lie in fallowed plain
That which was wont yield usury of grain.
But when I see thy pitched stakes do stand
On thy encroached piece of common land,
Whiles thou discommonest [34] thy neighbor's kine
And warn'st that none feed on thy field save thine,
Brag no more, Scrobius, of thy mudded banks,
Nor thy deep ditches, nor three quickset ranks.
Oh happy days of old Deucalion,[35]
When one was landlord of the world alone!
But now, whose choler would not rise? to yield
A peasant half-stakes of his new-mown field,
Whiles yet he may not for the treble price
Buy out the remnant of his royalties? [36]
Go on and thrive, my petty tyrant's pride,
Scorn thou to live, if others live beside;
And trace [37] proud Castile that aspires to be
In his old age a young fifth monarchy,[38]
Or the red hat [39] that cries the luckless main,
For wealthy Thames to change his lowly Rhene.

---

29 *stick . . . price:* trust to the night watchman for protection, though the heiress were worth only the price of an Indian slave.

30 *quickset:* hedge of growing shrubs.

31 *ward:* protection.

32 *shend:* shut out.

33 *done:* do.

34 *discommonest:* deprive of common pasture.

35 *Deucalion:* the Noah of Greek mythology.

36 *royalties:* rights in the land.

37 *trace:* follow.

38 *fifth monarchy:* world of the future. The four monarchies were Assyria, Persia, Macedon, and Rome.

39 *red hat:* symbol of a Catholic cardinal. Schulze suggests that the reference is to William Allen (1532–1594) who at Rheims and Douai trained young Englishmen and sent them home to work for the Catholic cause.

JOHN MARSTON

THE SCOURGE OF VILLAINY

Satire VIII

Inamorato, Curio

Curio, aye me! thy mistress' monkey's dead;
Alas, alas, her pleasure's buried!
Go, woman's slave, perform his exequies,
Condole his death in mournful elegies.
Tut, rather Paeans sing, hermaphrodite;
For that sad death gives life to thy delight.
Sweet-faced Corinna, deign the riband tie
Of thy cork-shoe,[1] or else thy slave will die;
Some puling sonnet tolls his passing bell,
Some sighing elegy must ring his knell,
Unless bright sunshine of thy grace revive
His wambling [2] stomach, certes he will dive
Into the whirlpool of devouring death,
And to some mermaid sacrifice his breath.
Then Oh, Oh then, to thy eternal shame,
And to the honor of sweet Curio's name,
This epitaph, upon the marble stone,
Must fair be graved of that true-loving one:
Here lieth he, he lieth here,
That bounced [3] and pity cried,
The door not oped, fell sick, alas,
Alas, fell sick and died.
What Myrmidon, or hard Dolopian,[4]
What savage-minded rude Cyclopian,[5]
But such a sweet pathetic Paphian [6]
Would force to laughter? Ho, Amphitrion,[7]
Thou art no cuckold. What, though Jove dallied,
During thy wars in fair Alcmena's bed,
Yet Hercules, true born, that imbecility
Of corrupt nature, all apparently
Appears in him. Oh foul indignity!

---

1 *cork-shoe:* there is a suggestion of wantonness here, since courtesans first wore cork-soled shoes.

2 *wambling:* turning, queasy.

3 *bounced:* knocked.

4 *Myrmidon:* warrior subjects of Achilles who followed him to Troy; *Dolopian:* powerful Thessalian warriors at Troy.

5 *Cyclopian:* gigantic, lawless race of shepherds in Sicily.

6 *Paphian:* worshiper of Aphrodite, who landed at Paphos after her birth among the waves.

7 *Amphitrion:* husband of Alcmena, the mother of Hercules.

I heard him vow himself a slave to Omphale,[8]
Puling, "Ay me!" Oh valor's obloquy!
He that the inmost nooks of hell did know,
Whose ne'er-crazed [9] prowess all did overthrow,
Lies streaking [10] brawny limbs in weakening bed,
Perfumed, smooth-kembed, new-glazed, fair surphuled.[11]
Oh that the boundless power of the soul
Should be subjected to such base control!
Big-limbed Alcides, doff thy honor's crown;
Go spin, huge slave, lest Omphale should frown.
By my best hopes, I blush with grief and shame
To broach the peasant baseness of our name.
  Oh, now my ruder hand begins to quake
To think what lofty cedars I must shake;
But if the canker fret, the barks of oaks,
Like humbler shrubs, shall equal bear the strokes
Of my respectless rude satiric hand.
Unless the Destine's adamantine band
Should tie my teeth, I cannot choose but bite,
To view Mavortius metamorphosed quite,
To puling sighs, and into "Ay me's" state,
With voice distinct, all fine articulate,
Lisping, "Fair saint, my woe compassionate;
By heaven, thine eye is my soul-guiding fate!"
  The god of wounds had wont on Cyprian [12] couch
To streak himself, and with incensing touch
To faint his force only when wrath had end;
But now, 'mong furious garboils,[13] he doth spend
His feebled valor in tilt and tourneying
With wet-turned kisses, melting, dallying.
A pox upon't that Bacchis' [14] name should be
The watchword given to the soldiery!
Go, troop to field, mount thy obscured fame,
Cry out, "St. George!"; invoke thy mistress' name;
Thy mistress and St. George, alarum cry!
Weak force, weak aid, that sprouts from luxury.[15]
  Thou tedious workmanship of lust-stung Jove,
Down from thy skies, enjoy our females' love!
Some fifty more Beotian [16] girls will sue

[8] *Omphale:* Lydian mistress of Hercules, who made him wear women's clothes and spin wool.

[9] *crazed:* broken, cracked, impaired.

[10] *streaking:* stretching.

[11] *kembed:* combed; *glazed:* painted; *surphuled:* painted with cosmetic.

[12] *Cyprian:* lewd, from Cyprus, where Venus was worshiped.

[13] *garboils:* tumult, commotion.

[14] *Bacchis:* a whore.

[15] *luxury:* lust.

[16] *Beotian:* referring to the fifty daughters of Thespis of Beotia, with whom Hercules lay in one night.

To have thy love, so that thy back be true.
Oh now methinks I hear swart Martius cry,
Swooping along in war's feigned maskery,
By Lais' starry front [17] he'll forthwith die
In cluttered [18] blood, his mistress' livery,
Her fancy's colors waves upon his head.
Oh well-fenced Albion, mainly manly sped
When those that are soldadoes [19] in thy state
Do bear the badge of base, effeminate,
Even on their plumy crests—brutes sensual,
Having no spark of intellectual!
Alack, what hope, when some rank nasty wench
Is subject of their vows and confidence?
Publius hates vainly to idolatrize,
And laughs that papists honor images;
And yet (Oh madness!) these mine eyes did see
Him melt in moving plaints, obsequiously
Imploring favor; twining his kind arms,
Using enchantments, exorcisms, charms,
The oil of sonnets, wanton blandishment,
The force of tears, and seeming languishment
Unto the picture of a painted lass!
I saw him court his mistress' looking glass,
Worship a busk-point—which, in secrecy
I fear was conscious of strange villainy;
I saw him crouch, devote his livelihood,
Swear, protest, vow peasant servitude
Unto a painted puppet; to her eyes
I heard him swear his sighs to sacrifice.
But if he get her itch-allaying pin,
Oh sacred relic! straight he must begin
To rave outright; then thus: "Celestial bliss!
Can heaven grant so rich a grace as this?
Touch it not, by the Lord, sir, 'tis divine!
It once beheld her radiant eyes' bright shine!
Her hair embraced it; Oh thrice-happy prick,
That there was throned and in her hair didst stick!"
Kiss, bless, adore it, Publius—never lin; [20]
Some sacred virtue lurketh in the pin.
Oh frantic, fond, pathetic passion!
Is't possible such sensual action
Should clip the wings of contemplation?

---

[17] *Lais:* famous Greek courtesan; *front:* forehead.

[18] *cluttered:* clotted.

[19] *soldadoes:* soldiers (Span.).

[20] *lin:* cease, leave off.

Or can it be the spirit's function,
The soul, not subject to dimension,
Should be made slave to reprehension
Of crafty nature's paint? Fie! can our soul
Be underling to such a vile control?
  Saturio wished himself his mistress' busk,[21]
That he might sweetly lie and softly lusk [22]
Between her paps; then must he have an eye
At either end, that freely might descry
Both hills and dales. But out on Phrigio,
That wished he were his mistress' dog, to go
And lick her milk-white fist! Oh pretty grace!
That pretty Phrigio begs but Pretty's place.
Parthenophil, thy wish I will omit;
So beastly 'tis, I may not utter it.
But Punicus, of all I'll bear with thee,
That fain wouldst by thy mistress' smug monkey.
Here's one would be a flea (jest comical!)
Another, his sweet lady's verdingal [23]
To clip her tender breech; another he
Her silver-handled fan would gladly be;
Here's one would be his mistress' necklace, fain
To clip her fair and kiss her azure vein.
Fond fools, well wished! And pity but should be,
For beastly shape to brutish souls agree.
  If Laura's painted lip do deign a kiss
To her enamored slave, "Oh heaven's bliss!"
Straight he exclaims, "not to be matched with this!"
Blaspheming dolt! go, threescore sonnets write
Upon a picture's kiss, Oh raving sprite!
  I am not sapless, old, or rheumatic,
No Hipponax,[24] misshapen stigmatic,
That I should thus inveigh 'gainst amorous sprite
Of him whose soul doth turn hermaphrodite;
But I do sadly grieve and inly vex
To view the base dishonor of our sex.
  Tush! guiltless doves—when gods, to force foul rapes
Will turn themselves to any brutish shapes:
Base bastard powers, whom the world doth see
Transformed to swine for sensual luxury!
The son of Saturn [25] is become a bull

[21] *busk:* a "stay" for a corset.
[22] *lusk:* to lie at ease.
[23] *verdingal:* farthingale, hoop skirt.
[24] *Hipponax:* Greek satirist, famous for his ugliness and severity.
[25] *son of Saturn:* Jove came to Europa in the shape of a bull.

To crop the beauties of some female trull.
Now, when he hath his first wife, Metis,[26] sped,
And fairly choked lest foul gods should be bred
Of that fond mule; Themis,[27] his second wife,
Hath turned away, that his unbridled life
Might have more scope; yet, last, his sister's love
Must satiate the lustful thoughts of Jove.
Now doth the lecher in a cuckoo's shape
Commit a monstrous and incestuous rape.
Thrice sacred gods! and Oh thrice blessed skies
Whose orbs include such virtuous deities!
  What should I say? Lust hath confounded all;
The bright gloss of our intellectual
Is foully soiled. The wanton wallowing
In fond delights, and amorous dallying
Hath dusked the fairest splendor of our soul;
Nothing now left but carcass, loathsome, foul,
For sure, if that some sprite remained still,
Could it be subject to lewd Lais' will?
  Reason, by prudence in her function,
Had wont to tutor all our action,
Aiding, with precepts of philosophy,
Our feebled nature's imbecility;
But now affection, will, concupiscence,
Have got o'er reason chief preeminence.
'Tis so; else how could such vile baseness taint
As force it be made slave to nature's paint?
Methinks the spirit's Pegase,[28] fantasy,
Should hoist the soul from such base slavery;
But now I see, and can right plainly show
From whence such abject thoughts and actions grow.
  Our adverse body, being earthy, cold,
Heavy, dull mortal, would not long enfold
A stranger inmate, that was backward still
To all his dungy, brutish, sensual will;
Now hereupon our intellectual,
Compact of fire all celestial,
Invisible, immortal, and divine,
Grew straight to scorn his landlord's muddy slime;
And therefore now is closely slunk away,
Leaving his smoky house of mortal clay,
Adorned with all his beauty's lineaments

---

[26] *Metis:* Jove swallowed his first wife lest she bear a child wiser and more powerful than he.

[27] *Themis:* goddess of law and order.

[28] *Pegase:* Pegasus, the winged horse of Bellerophon.

And brightest gems of shining ornaments,
His parts divine, sacred, spiritual,
Attending on him; leaving the sensual
Base hangers-on lusking at home in slime,
Such as wont to stop Port Esquiline.[29]
Now doth the body, led with senseless will,
The which, in reason's absence, ruleth still,
Rave, talk idly, as 't were some deity,
Adoring female painted puppetry;
Playing at put-pin, doting on some glass
Which, breathed but on, his falsed gloss doth pass;
Toying with babies,[30] and with fond pastime,
Some children's sport, deflowering of chaste time;
Employing all his wits in vain expense,
Abusing all his organons of sense.
  Return, return, sacred Synderesis![31]
Inspire our trunks! Let not such mud as this
Pollute us still. Awake our lethargy;
Raise us from out our brainsick foolery!

[29] *Port Esquiline:* a privy.
[30] *babies:* dolls.
[31] *Synderesis:* the elevating and sustaining power of the soul.

George Chapman

1559?–1634

A CYNICAL critic once said that if Keats had not looked into Chapman's Homer, the reputation of the Elizabethan translator would today be very small. Yet such a remark is far from the truth, for Chapman's monumental translation is one of the important poetic products of Elizabethan England, and Keats' reverence for it is a tie which binds him to Chapman, Marlowe, and the vigor of Elizabethan poetic art.

Chapman was a learned poet, second only to Jonson and Marlowe; yet there is no evidence that he took a university degree. He is supposed, however, to have attended both Oxford and Cambridge. Considerable speculation has been made on Chapman as the "rival poet" of Shakespeare's sonnets, but no conclusive evidence has been presented. After a lifetime of work for patrons and the stage, Chapman died in poverty.

Chapman has been studied mainly as a playwright and translator, and perhaps his poetry outside the translations deserves its comparative neglect by scholars. His first poetry, *The Shadow of Night* (1594) and *Ovid's Banquet of Sense* (1595) are to one critic, "prize obscurities." His completion of Marlowe's *Hero and Leander* by four sestiads in 1598 shows him to be at the time a much lesser Marlowe. In the same year he published his *Seven Books of the Iliads* (Books I–II, VII–XI), his first work as a translator of Homer, which he dedicated to the Earl of Essex, "the most Honoured now living instance of Achillean virtues." Over ten years later Chapman published revisions and additions to his work, first translating twelve books, and then in *The Iliads of Homer Prince of Poets* (1611), the whole *Iliad*. In 1615 the *Odyssey* was published separately, and a year later *The Whole Works of Homer*.

The Troy story itself the Elizabethans knew, not from Homer, but from a long cycle of non-Homeric literature beginning with Latin versions of the supposed eyewitness accounts of Dictys and Dares, who were the chief sources and the unquestioned authorities in the Middle Ages. From these early annals sprang metrical romances in French and in English and a Latin prose redaction by the thirteenth-century Sicilian writer, Guido delle Colonne, which in turn furnished Chaucer and Lydgate with material. The first book printed in English was Caxton's *Recuyell of the Historyes of Troye* (1464), actually a translation from a French prose compilation based on Guido.

Homer was studied in the English universities but evidently did not attract translators or adapters. In fact, before Chapman, only two English translations of Homer were published in the sixteenth century, Arthur Hall's *Ten Books of Homer's Iliades* (1581) from a French source, and Peter Colse's *Penelope's Complaint* (1596).

Perhaps the reason for the neglect of the Homeric story of Troy may be found in the tradition that the legendary founder of the British race was Brut, great-grandson of Aeneas, who built Troynovant or New Troy (later known as London). Dictys and Dares and the medieval sources of the Troy story presented the Trojan, not Greek point of view; Homer was of course Greek in sympathy.

Chapman's Homer is vigorous, robust, often very free and considerably amplified from the original. Coleridge found the *Iliad* "as truly an original poem as the *Faery Queen*." Swinburne labeled the translation "romantic, laborious, Elizabethan," then followed his epithets with praise. It is clear that Chapman's Homer, with all its faults as an exact translation, combines in an extensive work of high artistic order the energy, the feeling for beauty, the learning, and the belief in English as a literary language which are characteristics of the best literature of Elizabethan England.

Bibliography: *The Poems of George Chapman,* ed. Phyllis B. Bartlett, New York, 1941; F. L. Schoell, *Etudes sur l'Humanisme continental en Angleterre,* Paris, 1926; J. Robertson, "Early Life of Chapman" *MLR,* XL (1945), 157–165; M. Eccles, "Chapman's Early Years" *SP,* XLIII (1946), 176–193; C. J. Sisson and R. Butman, "George Chapman, 1612–22: Some New Facts," *MLR,* XLVI (1951), 185–90; J. Jacquot, *George Chapman,* Paris, 1951; H. C. Fay, "Chapman's Materials," *RES,* n.s. II (1951), 121–128.

FROM

THE ILIADS OF HOMER PRINCE OF POETS

(1611)

FROM

THE EPISTLE DEDICATORY[1]

To the High-Born Prince of Men, Henry; Thrice Royal Inheritor to the United Kingdoms of Great Britain, etc.

Since perfect happiness, by princes sought,
Is not with birth born, nor exchequers bought;
Nor follows in great trains; nor is possessed
With any outward state; but makes him blest
That governs inward; and beholdeth there
All his affections stand about him bare;
That by his power can send to Tower and death
All traitorous passions, marshaling beneath
His justice his mere will; and in his mind
Holds such a scepter, as can keep confined
His whole life's actions in the royal bounds
Of virtue and religion; and their grounds
Takes in to sow his honors, his delights,
And complete empire; you should learn these rights
(Great prince of men) by princely precedents;
Which here, in all kinds, my true zeal presents
To furnish your youth's groundwork, and first state;
And let you see one Godlike man create
All sorts of worthiest men; to be contrived
In your worth only; giving him revived,
For whose life Alexander would have given
One of his kingdoms; who (as sent from heaven,
And thinking well, that so divine a creature
Would never more enrich the race of nature)

[1] Coleridge (*Notes on Chapman's Homer*) remarked: "The dedication to the Iliad is a noble copy of verses, especially those lines beginning, 'Oh! 'tis wondrous much . . .'" [ll. 29–61.]

Kept as his crown his works, and thought them still
His angels, in all power to rule his will;
And would affirm that Homer's poesy
Did more advance his Asian victory,
Than all his armies. Oh! 'tis wondrous much
(Though nothing prized) that the right virtuous touch
Of a well-written soul to virtue moves.
Nor have we souls to purpose, if their loves
Of fitting objects be not so inflamed.
How much, then, were this kingdom's main soul maimed,
To want this great inflamer of all powers
That move in human souls? All realms but yours
Are honored with him, and hold blest that state
That have his works to read and contemplate:
In which, humanity to her height is raised,
Which all the world (yet, none enough) hath praised.
Seas, earth, and heaven, he did in verse comprise,
Outsung the Muses, and did equalize
Their king Apollo; being so far from cause
Of princes' light thoughts, that their gravest laws
May find stuff to be fashioned by his lines.
Through all the pomp of kingdoms still he shines,
And graceth all his gracers. Then let lie
Your lutes, and viols, and more loftily
Make the heroics of your Homer sung;
To drums and trumpets set his angel's tongue,
And, with the princely sport of hawks you use,
Behold the kingly flight of his high Muse,
And see how, like the phoenix,[2] she renews
Her age and starry feathers in your sun;
Thousands of years attending, every one
Blowing the holy fire, and throwing in
Their seasons, kingdoms, nations, that have been
Subverted in them; laws, religions, all
Offered to change and greedy funeral;
Yet still your Homer lasting, living, reigning,
And proves, how firm truth builds in poets' feigning.

[2] *phoenix:* a unique bird which died and rose from its own ashes. It is illustrated on the Queen's left in the frontispiece.

FROM

THE FIRST BOOK

[*Nestor's Speech to Achilles and Agamemnon*]

Up to both sweet-spoken Nestor stood,
The cunning Pylian orator; whose tongue poured forth a flood
Of more than honey-sweet discourse; two ages were increased
Of divers-languaged men, all born in his time and deceased,
In sacred Pylos, where he reigned, amongst the third-aged men,
He (well-seen in the world) advised, and thus expressed it then:
"Oh Gods, our Greek earth will be drowned in just tears; rapeful Troy,
Her king, and all his sons, will make as just a mock, and joy,
Of these disjunctions; if of you, that all our host excel
In counsel, and in skill of fight, they hear this. Come, repel
These young men's passions. Y' are not both (put both your years in one)
So old as I: I lived long since, and was companion
With men superior to you both, who yet would ever hear
My counsels with respect. Mine eyes yet never witness were,
Nor ever will be, of such men as then delighted them;
Perithous, Exadius, and godlike Polypheme,
Caeneus, and Dryas, prince of men, Aegean Theseus,
A man like heaven's immortals formed; all, all most vigorous,
Of all men that even those days bred; most vigorous men, and fought
With beasts most vigorous, mountain beasts (for men in strength were naught
Matched with their forces), fought with them, and bravely fought them down.
Yet even with these men I conversed, being called to the renown
Of their societies, by their suits, from Pylos far, to fight
In th' Asian kingdom; and I fought to a degree of might
That helped even their mights; against such, as no man now would dare
To meet in conflict; yet even these, my counsels still would hear,
And with obedience crown my words. Give you such palm to them;
'Tis better than to wreak your wrath. Atrides! give not stream
To all thy power, nor force his prize; but yield her still his own,
As all men else do. Nor do thou encounter with thy crown,
(Great son of Peleus) since no king that ever Jove allowed
Grace of scepter equals him. Suppose thy nerves endowed
With strength superior, and thy birth, a very goddess gave;
Yet he of force is mightier, since what his own nerves have
Is amplified with just command of many other. King of men,

Command thou then thyself, and I with my prayers will obtain
Grace of Achilles, to subdue his fury; whose parts are
Worth our entreaty, being chief check to all our ill in war."

FROM

THE THIRD BOOK

The Argument

Paris, betwixt the hosts, to single fight,
Of all the Greeks dares the most hardy knight.
King Menelaus doth accept his brave,
Conditioning that he again should have
Fair Helena, and all she brought to Troy,
If he subdued; else Paris should enjoy
Her and her wealth in peace. Conquest doth grant
Her dear wreath to the Grecian combatant;
But Venus to her champion's life doth yield
Safe rescue, and conveys him from the field
Into his chamber, and for Helen sends,
Whom much her lover's foul disgrace offends.
Yet Venus still for him makes good her charms,
And ends the second combat in his arms.

Another Argument

Gamma the single fight doth sing
'Twixt Paris and the Spartan king.

When every least commander's will best soldiers had obeyed,
And both the hosts were ranged for fight, the Trojans would have frayed
The Greeks with noises, crying out, in coming rudely on,
At all parts like the cranes that fill, with harsh confusion
Of brutish clanges, all the air, and in ridiculous war
(Eschewing the unsuffered storms, shot from the winter's star)
Visit the ocean, and confer the Pygmei soldiers'[3] death.
The Greeks charged silent, and like men bestowed their thrifty breath
In strength of far-resounding blows, still entertaining care
Of either's rescue, when their strength did their engagements dare.
And as, upon a hill's steep tops, the south wind pours a cloud,

[3] *Pygmei soldiers:* The fable of the battle of the cranes and pygmies is first mentioned here.

To shepherds thankless, but by thieves, that love the night, allowed,
A darkness letting down that blinds a stone's cast off men's eyes,
Such darkness from the Greeks' swift feet (made all of dust) did rise.
But, ere stern conflict mixed both strengths, fair Paris stepped before
The Trojan host; athwart his back a panther's hide he wore,
A crooked bow, and sword, and shook two brazen-headed darts;
With which well-armed, his tongue provoked the best of Grecian hearts
To stand with him in single fight. Whom when the man wronged most
Of all the Greeks so gloriously saw stalk before the host;
As when a lion is rejoiced (with hunger half forlorn)
That finds some sweet prey, as a hart, whose grace lies in his horn,
Or sylvan goat, which he devours, though never so pursued
With dogs and men; so Sparta's king exulted, when he viewed
The fair-faced Paris so exposed to his so thirsted wreak,
Whereof his good cause made him sure. The Grecian front did break,
And forth he rushed, at all parts armed, leaped from his chariot,
And royally prepared for charge. Which seen, cold terror shot
The heart of Paris, who retired as headlong from the king
As in him he had shunned his death. And as a hilly spring
Presents a serpent to a man, full underneath his feet,
Her blue neck, swollen with poison, raised, and her sting out, to greet
His heedless entry, suddenly his walk he altereth,
Starts back amazed, is shook with fear, and looks as pale as death;
So Menelaus Paris scared; so that divine-faced foe
Shrunk in his beauties. Which beheld by Hector, he let go
This bitter check at him: "Accursed, made but in beauty's scorn,
Impostor, woman's man! Oh heaven, that thou hadst ne'er been born,
Or, being so manless, never lived to bear man's noblest state,
The nuptial honor! Which I wish, because it were a fate
Much better for thee than this shame. This spectacle doth make
A man a monster. Hark! how loud the Greeks laugh, who did take
Thy fair form for a continent of parts as fair. A rape
Thou mad'st of nature, like their queen. No soul, an empty shape,
Takes up thy being; yet how spite to every shade of good
Fills it with ill! For as thou art, thou couldst collect a brood
Of others like thee, and far hence fetch ill enough to us,
Even to thy father; all these friends make those foes mock them thus
In thee, for whose ridiculous sake so seriously they lay
All Greece, and fate, upon their necks. Oh wretch! Not dare to stay
Weak Menelaus? But 'twas well; for in him thou hadst tried
What strength lost beauty can infuse, and with the more grief died
To feel thou robb'dst a worthier man, to wrong a soldier's right.
Your harp's sweet touch, curled locks, fine shape, and gifts so exquisite,
Given thee by Venus, would have done your fine dames little good,

When blood and dust had ruffled them, and had as little stood
Thyself in stead; but what thy care of all these in thee flies
We should inflict on thee ourselves. Infectious cowardice
In thee hath terrified our host; for which thou well deserv'st
A coat of tombstone, not of steel in which, for form, thou serv'st."
  To this thus Paris spake (for form, that might inhabit heaven),
"Hector, because thy sharp reproof is out of justice given,
I take it well; but though thy heart, inured to these affrights,
Cuts through them as an ax through oak, that more used more excites
The workman's faculty, whose art can make the edge go far,
Yet I, less practised than thyself in these extremes of war,
May well be pardoned, though less bold; in these your worth exceeds,
In others mine. Nor is my mind of less force to the deeds
Required in war, because my form more flows in gifts of peace.
Reproach not, therefore, the kind gifts of golden Cyprides.[4]
All heaven's gifts have their worthy price; as little to be scorned
As to be won with strength, wealth, state; with which to be adorned
Some men would change state, wealth, or strength. But, if your martial heart
Wish me to make my challenge good, and hold it such a part
Of shame to give it over thus, cause all the rest to rest,
And, 'twixt both hosts, let Sparta's king and me perform our best
For Helen and the wealth she brought; and he that overcomes
Or proves superior any way, in all your equal dooms,
Let him enjoy her utmost wealth, keep her, or take her home,
The rest strike leagues of endless date, and hearty friends become;
You dwelling safe in gleby[5] Troy, and Greeks retire their force
T' Achaia, that breeds fairest dames, and Argos, fairest horse."

FROM

THE SIXTH BOOK

[*Hector to Andromache*]

"Be well assured, wife, all these things in my kind cares are weighed.
But what a shame and fear it is to think how Troy would scorn
(Both in her husbands and her wives, whom long-trained gowns adorn)
That I should cowardly fly off! The spirit I first did breathe
Did never teach me that; much less, since the contempt of death
Was settled in me, and my mind knew what a worthy was,
Whose office is to lead in fight and give no danger pass

[4] *Cyprides:* Venus.

[5] *gleby:* rich, fertile.

Without improvement. In this fire must Hector's trial shine;
Here must his country, father, friends, be in him, made divine.
And such a stormy day shall come, in mind and soul I know,
When sacred Troy shall shed her towers, for tears of overthrow;[6]
When Priam, all his birth and power, shall in those tears be drowned.
But neither Troy's posterity, so much my soul doth wound,
Priam nor Hecuba herself, nor all my brothers' woes
(Who though so many, and so good, must all be food for foes),
As thy sad state; when some rude Greek shall lead thee weeping hence;
These free days clouded, and a night of captive violence
Loading thy temples: out of which thine eyes must never see,
But spin the Greek wives' webs of task, and their fetch-water be,
To Argos, from Messeides, or clear Hyperia's spring;
Which (howsoever thou abhorr'st) Fate's such a shrewish thing
She will be mistress; whose cursed hands, when they shall crush out
cries
From thy oppressions (being behold by other enemies)
Thus they will nourish thy extremes: 'This dame was Hector's wife,
A man, that at the wars of Troy, did breathe the worthiest life
Of all their army.' This again, will rub thy fruitful wounds,
To miss the man, that to thy bands could give such narrow bounds.
But that day shall not wound mine eyes; the solid heap of night
Shall interpose, and stop mine ears against thy plaints, and plight."
This said, he reached to take his son; who (of his arms afraid,
And then the horse-hair plume, with which he was so overlaid,
Nodded so horribly) he clinged back to his nurse, and cried.
Laughter affected his great sire, who doffed and laid aside
His fearful helm, that on the earth, cast round about it, light;
Then took and kissed his loving son, and (balancing his weight
In dancing him) these loving vows to living Jove he used,
And all the other bench of Gods: "Oh you that have infused

---

[6] *and my mind . . . overthrow:* These lines amplify Homer's original considerably. Arnold commented (in *On Translating Homer,* ed. Rouse, p. 58): "You see how ingeniously Homer's plain thought is *tormented*. . . ." Cf. lines 1–24 with the following prose translation of Lang, Leaf, and Myers:

"Then great Hector of the glancing helm answered her: 'Surely I take thought for all these things, my wife; but I have very sore shame of the Trojans and Trojan dames with trailing robes, if like a coward I shrink away from battle. Moreover, mine own soul forbiddeth me, seeing I have learnt ever to be valiant and fight in the forefront of the Trojans, winning my father's great glory and mine own. Yea, of a surety I know this in heart and soul; the day shall come for holy Ilios to be laid low, and Priam and the folk of Priam of the good ashen spear. Yet doth the anguish of the Trojans hereafter not so much trouble me, neither Hekabe's own, neither king Priam's, neither my brethren's, the many and brave that shall fall in the dust before their foemen, as doth thine anguish in the day when some mail-clad Achaian shall lead thee weeping and rob thee of the light of freedom. So shalt thou abide in Argos and ply the loom at another woman's bidding, and bear water from fount Messeis or Hypereia, being grievously entreated, and sore constraint shall be laid upon thee.'"

Soul to this infant, now set down, this blessing on his star:
Let his renown be clear as mine; equal his strength in war;
And make his reign so strong in Troy, that years to come may yield
His facts this fame, when, rich in spoils, he leaves the conquered field
Sown with his slaughters: 'These high deeds exceed his father's worth.'
And let this echoed praise supply the comforts to come forth
Of his kind mother, with my life." This said, the heroic sire
Gave him his mother; whose fair eyes, fresh streams of love's salt fire
Billowed on her soft cheeks, to hear the last of Hector's speech,
In which his vows comprised the sum of all he did beseech
In her wished comfort. So she took, into her odorous breast,
Her husband's gift; who (moved to see her heart so much oppressed)
He dried her tears, and thus desired: "Afflict me not (dear wife)
With these vain griefs. He doth not live, that can disjoin my life
And this firm bosom, but my fate; and Fate, whose wings can fly?
Noble, ignoble, Fate controls. Once born, the best must die.
Go home and set thy housewifery on these extremes of thought;
And drive war from them with thy maids; keep them from doing
naught.
These will be nothing; leave the cares of war to men and me,
In whom (of all the Ilion race) they take their highest degree."

FROM

THE EIGHTEENTH BOOK

[*Achilles' Shield*]

THIS said, he [7] left her there, and forth did to his bellows go,
Apposed [8] them to the fire again, commanding them to blow.
Through twenty holes made to his hearth at once blew twenty pair
That fired his coals, sometimes with soft, sometimes with vehement
air,
As he willed and his work required. Amids the flame he cast
Tin, silver, precious gold, and brass; and in the stock he placed
A mighty anvil; his right hand a weighty hammer held,
His left his tongs. And first he forged a strong and spacious shield,
Adorned with twenty several hues; about whose verge he beat
A ring, threefold and radiant, and on the back he set
A silver handle. Fivefold were the equal lines he drew

[7] *he:* Vulcan, who at the request of Thetis, mother of Achilles, has agreed to make a shield for Achilles.

[8] *Apposed:* applied.

About the whole circumference, in which his hand did shew
(Directed with a knowing mind) a rare variety:
For in it he presented earth; in it the sea and sky;
In it the never-wearied sun, the moon exactly round,
And all those stars with which the brows of ample heaven are crowned,
Orion, all the Pleiades, and those seven Atlas got,
The close-beamed Hyades, the Bear, surnamed the Chariot,
That turns about heaven's axletree, holds ope a constant eye
Upon Orion; and, of all the cressets [9] in the sky,
His golden forehead never bows to th' ocean empery.
  Two cities in the spacious shield he built, with goodly state
Of divers-languaged men. The one did nuptials celebrate,
Observing at them solemn feasts, the brides from forth their bowers
With torches ushered through the streets, a world of paramours
Excited by them; youths and maids in lovely circles danced,
To whom the merry pipe and harp the spritely sounds advanced,
The matrons standing in the doors admiring. Otherwhere
A solemn court of law was kept, where throngs of people were.
The case in question was a fine imposed on one that slew
The friend of him that followed it, and for the fine did sue,
Which th' other pleaded he had paid. The adverse part denied,
And openly affirmed he had no penny satisfied.
Both put it to arbiterment; the people cried 'twas best
For both parts; and th' assistants too, gave their dooms like the rest.
The heralds made the people peace; the seniors then did hear
The voiceful heralds' scepters; sat within a sacred sphere
On polished stones, and gave by turns their sentence; in the court
Two talents gold were cast for him, that judged in justest sort.
  The other city other wars employed as busily:
Two armies glittering in arms of one confederacy
Besieged it; and a parley had with those within the town.
Two ways they stood resolved,—to see the city overthrown,
Or that the citizens should heap in two parts all their wealth
And give them half. They neither liked, but armed themselves by
    stealth,
Left all their old men, wives, and boys behind to man their walls,
And stole out to their enemy's town. The queen of martials [10]
And Mars himself conducted them,—both which being forged of gold
Must needs have golden furniture, and men might so behold
They were presented deities; the people Vulcan forged
Of meaner metal. When they came where that was to be urged

[9] *cressets:* literally iron baskets to hold pitched rope, coal, or wood to be burned for light; here figuratively for stars.

[10] *queen of martials:* Athena.

For which they went, within a vale close to a flood whose stream
Used to give all their cattle drink, they there enambushed them;
And sent two scouts out to descry when th' enemy's herds and sheep
Were setting out. They straight came forth, with two that used to keep
Their passage always, both which piped and went on merrily,
Nor dreamed of ambuscadoes there. The ambush then let fly,
Slew all their white-fleeced sheep, and neat,[11] and by them laid their
guard.
When those in siege before the town so strange an uproar heard
Behind, amongst their flocks and herds—being then in council set—
They then start up, took horse, and soon their subtle enemy met,
Fought with them on the river's shore, where both gave mutual blows
With well-piled [12] darts. Amongst them all perverse Contention rose,
Amongst them Tumult was enraged, amongst them ruinous Fate
Had her red finger; some they took in an unhurt estate,
Some hurt, yet living; some quite slain, and those they tugged to them
By both the feet, stripped off and took their weeds, with all the stream
Of blood upon them that their steels had manfully let out;
They fared as men alive indeed drew dead indeed about.
To these the fiery artisan did add a new-eared [13] field,
Larged [14] and thrice plowed, the soil being soft and of a wealthy yield;
And many men at plow he made, that drave earth here and there,
And turned up stitches orderly,—at whose end when they were
A fellow ever gave their hands full cups of luscious wine,
Which emptied, for another stitch the earth they undermine,
And long till th' utmost bound be reached of all the ample close.
The soil turned up behind the plow all black like earth arose,
Though forged of nothing else but gold; and lay in show as light
As if it had been plowed indeed, miraculous to sight.
There grew by this a field of corn, high, ripe, where reapers
wrought,
And let thick handfuls fall to earth, for which some other brought
Bands and made sheaves. Three binders stood and took the handfuls
reaped
From boys that gathered quickly up, and by them armfuls heaped.
Amongst these, at a furrow's end, the king stood pleased at heart,
Said no word, but his scepter showed. And from him much apart
His harvest-bailiffs underneath an oak a feast prepared,
And having killed a mighty ox, stood there to see him shared,
Which women for their harvest-folks (then come to sup) had dressed,
And many white wheat-cakes bestowed, to make it up a feast.
He set near this a vine of gold that cracked beneath the weight

[11] *neat:* cattle.
[12] *well-piled:* well-pointed.
[13] *new-eared:* newly plowed.
[14] *Larged:* spacious.

Of bunches black with being ripe, to keep which at the height
A silver rail ran all along, and round about it flowed
An azure moat, and to this guard a quickset [15] was bestowed,
Of tin,—one only path to all, by which the pressmen came
In time of vintage. Youths, and maids that bore not yet the flame
Of manly Hymen, baskets bore of grapes and mellow fruit.
A lad that sweetly touched a harp to which his voice did suit
Centered the circles of that youth, all whose skill could not do
The wantons' pleasure to their minds, that danced, sung, whistled too.
A herd of oxen then he carved, with high raised heads, forged all
Of gold and tin for color mixed, and bellowing from their stall
Rushed to their pastures at a flood, that echoed all their throats,
Exceeding swift and full of reeds; and all in yellow coats
Four herdsmen followed; after whom nine mastiffs went. In head
Of all the herd, upon a bull that deadly bellowed
Two horrid lions ramped and seized and tugged off, bellowing still.
Both men and dogs came; yet they tore the hide, and lapped their fill
Of black blood, and the entrails ate. In vain the men assayed
To set their dogs on; none durst pinch, but cur-like stood and bayed
In both the faces of their kings, and all their onsets fled.
Then in a passing pleasant vale the famous artsman fed
Upon a goodly pasture-ground rich flocks of white-fleeced sheep,
Built stables, cottages, and cotes, that did the shepherds keep
From wind and weather. Next to these he cut a dancing-place
All full of turnings, that was like the admirable maze
For fair-haired Ariadne made by cunning Daedalus;
And in it youths and virgins danced, all young and beauteous,
And glued in another's palms. Weeds that the wind did toss
The virgins wore; the youths, woven coats that cast a faint dim gloss
Like that of oil. Fresh garlands, too, the virgins' temples crowned.
The youths gilt swords wore at their thighs, with silver baldrics bound.
Sometimes all wound close in a ring, to which as fast they spun
As any wheel a turner makes, being tried how it will run,
While he is set; and out again as full of speed they wound,
Not one left fast, or breaking hands. A multitude stood round,
Delighted with their nimble sport; to end which, two begun
Mids all a song, and turning sung the sport's conclusion.
All this he circled in the shield, with pouring round about
In all his rage the ocean, that it might never out.
This shield thus done, he forged for him such curets, as outshined
The blaze of fire: a helmet then (through which no steel could find
Forced passage) he composed, whose hue, a hundred colors took,
And in the crest, a plume of gold, that each breath stirred, he stuck.

---

[15] *quickset:* hedge.

FROM

HOMER'S ODYSSEY

(1615?)

FROM

THE TWELFTH BOOK

[*Ulysses and the Sirens*]

I FIRST informed them that we were to fly
The heavenly-singing Sirens' harmony,
And flower-adorned meadow; and that I
Had charge to hear their song, but fettered fast
In bands, unfavored, to the erected mast,
From whence if I should pray or use command
To be enlarged, they should with much more band
Contain my strugglings. This I simply told
To each particular, nor would withhold
What most enjoined mine own affection's stay,
That theirs the rather might be taught to obey.
In mean time flew our ships, and straight we fetched
The Sirens' isle; a spleenless wind so stretched
Her wings to waft us, and so urged our keel.
But having reached this isle, we could not feel
The least gasp of it, it was stricken dead,
And all the sea in prostrate slumber spread;
The Sirens' devil charmed all. Up then flew
My friends to work, struck sail, together drew,
And under hatches stowed them, sat, and plied
The polished oars, and did in curls divide
The white-head waters. My part then came on.
A mighty waxen cake I set upon,
Chopped it in fragments with my sword, and wrought
With strong hand every piece, till all were soft.
The great power of the sun, in such a beam
As then flew burning from his diadem,
To liquefaction helped us. Orderly
I stopped their ears; and they as fair did ply
My feet and hands with cords, and to the mast
With other halsers made me soundly fast.
Then took they seat, and forth our passage strook;
The foamy sea beneath their labor shook.
Rowed on, in reach of an erected voice,

The Sirens soon took note, without our noise,
Tuned those sweet accents that made charms so strong,
And these learned numbers made the Sirens' song:
"Come here, thou worthy of a world of praise,
That dost so high the Grecian glory raise,
Ulysses! Stay thy ship, and that song hear
That none passed ever but it bent his ear,
But left him ravished, and instructed more
By us than any ever heard before.
For we know all things whatsoever were
In wide Troy labored; whatsoever there
The Grecians and the Trojans both sustained
By those high issues that the gods ordained.
And whatsoever all the earth can show
To inform a knowledge of desert, we know."
This they gave accent in the sweetest strain
That ever opened an enamored vein.
When my constrained heart needs would have mine ear
Yet more delighted, force way forth, and hear.
To which end I commanded with all sign
Stern looks could make (for not a joint of mine
Had power to stir) my friends to rise, and give
My limbs free way. They freely strived to drive
Their ship still on. When, far from will to loose,
Eurylochus and Perimedes rose
To wrap me surer, and oppressed me more
With many a halser than had use before.
When, rowing on without the reach of sound,
My friends unstopped their ears, and me unbound,
And that isle quite we quitted.

FROM

PETRARCH'S SEVEN PENITENTIAL PSALMS

(1612)

To Young Imaginaries in Knowledge [16]

Never for common signs dispraise or praise;
Nor art, nor want of art, for what he says

[16] The poem is based upon passages in Epictetus, *Discourses,* IV, v, vii, and viii. For calling their attention to the poem and providing them with proof sheets of her text and notes, the editors are indebted to Dr. Phyllis Bartlett.

Ascribe to any. Men may both ways make
In form and speech, a man's quick doom mistake.
All then that stand in any rank of art
Certain decrees have, how they shall impart
That which is in them; which decrees, because
They are within men, making there the laws
To all their actions, hardly show without,
And, till their ensigns are displayed, make doubt
To go against or with them, nor will they
So well in words as in their deeds display.
Decrees are not degrees.[17] If thou shalt give
Titles of learning to such men as live
Like rude plebeians, since they have degrees,
Thou shalt do like plebeians. He that sees
A man held learn'd do rudely rather may
Take, for that deed, his learned name away
Than give 't him for his name. True learning's act
And special object is so to compact
The will and every active power in man
That, more than men illiterate, he can
Keep all his actions in the narrow way
To God and goodness, and there force their stay
As in charmed circles. Terms, tongues, reading—all
That can within a man, called learned, fall,
Whose life is led yet like an ignorant man's,
Are but as tools to gouty artisans
That cannot use them; or like children's arts
That out of habit and by roots of hearts [18]
Construe and parse their lessons, yet discern
Naught of the matter whose good words they learn;
Or like our chemic Magi [19] that can call
All terms of art out, but no gold at all;
And so are learn'd like them, of whom none knows
His art's clear truth, but are mere cinifloes.[20]
  But sacred learning, men so much profane
That when they see a learn'd-accounted man
Lives like a brute man, they will never take
His learn'd name from him, for opinions' sake,
But on the false ground brutishly conclude
That learning profits not. You beastly rude!
Know, it more profits, being exact and true,
Than all earth's highways choked with herds of you.
  But must degrees and terms, and time in schools

[17] *degrees:* academic degrees.

[18] *by roots of hearts:* learning by heart, mere memory work.

[19] *chemic Magi:* alchemists.

[20] *cinifloes:* "superficial servants of the arts" (Bartlett).

Needs make men learn'd, in life being worse than fools?
What other art lives in so happy air
That only for his habit and his hair
His false professors' worth you will commend?
Are there not precepts, matter, and an end
To every science? Which, not kept nor shown
By understanding, understanding known
By fact, the end by things to th' end directed,
What hap or hope have they to be protected?
Yet find such greatest friends, and such profess
Most learning and will press for most access
Into her presence and her priviest state
When they have hardly knocked yet at her gate.
External circumscription never serves
To prove us men: blood, flesh, nor bones nor nerves,
But that which all these useth and doth guide—
God's image in a soul eternified,
Which he that shows not in such acts as tend
To that eterness,[21] making that their end,
In this world nothing knows, nor after can,
But is more any creature than a man.
This rather were the way, if thou wouldst be
A true proficient in philosophy:
Dissemble what thou studiest, till alone
By thy impartial contention
Thou prov'st thee fit to do as to profess.
And if thou still profess it not, what less
Is thy philosophy, if in thy deeds
Rather than signs and shadows, it proceeds?
Show with what temper thou dost drink and eat;
How far from wrong thy deeds are, anger's heat;
How thou sustain'st and abstain'st; how far gone
In appetite and aversation;[22]
To what account thou dost affections call,
Both natural and adventitial;[23]
That thou art faithful, pious, humble, kind,
Enemy to envy, of a cheerful mind,
Constant and dauntless. All this when men see
Done with the learned'st, then let censure thee.[24]
But if so dull and blind of soul they are,
Not to acknowledge heavenly Mulciber[25]
To be a famous artist by his deeds,

---

21 *eterness:* eternity.
22 *aversation:* aversion.
23 *adventitial:* adventitious, accidental.
24 *then let censure thee:* elliptical for "then let them censure thee."
25 *Mulciber:* Vulcan.

But they must see him in his working weeds,
What ill is it, if thou art never known
To men so poor of apprehension?
Are they within thee, or so much with thee
As thou thyself art? Can their dull eyes see
Thy thoughts at work? Or how like one that's sworn
To thy destruction, all thy powers are borne
T' entrap thyself, whom thou dost hardlier please
Than thou canst them? Arm, then, thy mind with these:
I have decrees set down 'twixt me and God;
I know his precepts, I will bear his load.
But what men throw upon me, I reject;
No man shall let[26] the freedom I elect.
I have an owner that will challenge me,
Strong to defend, enough to satisfy;
The rod of Mercury will charm all these
And make them neither strange nor hard to please.
And these decrees in houses constitute
Friendship and love; in fields cause store of fruit;
In cities, riches and in temples, zeal;
And all the world would make one commonweal.
Shun braggart glory; seek no place, no name;
No shows, no company, no laughing game,
No fashion, nor no champion of thy praise,
As children sweetmeats love, and holidays.
Be knowing shamefastness[27] thy grace and guard,
As others are with doors, walls, porters, barred.
Live close awhile; so fruits grow, so their seed
Must in the earth a little time lie hid;
Spring by degrees, and so be ripe at last.
But if the ear be to the blade's top passed
Before the joint amidst the blade be knit,
The corn is lank, and no sun ripens it.
Like which art thou, young novice; flourishing
Before thy time, winter shall burn thy spring.
The husbandman dislikes his field's fair birth
When timeless[28] heat beats on unready earth,
Grieves lest his fruits with air should be too bold,
And not endure the likely-coming cold.
Comfort the root, then, first; then let appear
The blade's joint, knit; and then produce the ear.
So nature's self thou shalt constrain and be
Blessed with a worthy crop in spite of thee.

---

[26] *let:* hinder.
[27] *knowing shamefastness:* wise modesty.
[28] *timeless:* untimely.

Thomas Dekker

1570?–1641?

THOMAS DEKKER was born and brought up in London. Six of his prose pamphlets concern the city, and Londoners and London life furnish much of the background of his plays. Scattered bits of documentary evidence and Dekker's own works reveal a professional writer, a playwright whose hand was in over forty plays, and a prolific pamphleteer. Henslowe's *Diary* records in 1597/8 and in 1598/9 notes of payment to release Dekker from prison for debt, and it is also thought that the dramatist spent three years (1613–1616) in King's Bench prison. Yet Dekker's plays and his prose do not reflect any bitterness arising from a precarious, hand-to-mouth existence. Dekker was, for the most part, a genial observer of life about him. He was also adept, whenever he wished to be, in the use of pleasant irony, and he could be as serious as a preacher in calling London to recognize its sins. Although he paraded the foibles of the gallant, he did not aim to correct them. He exposed thieves and rogues of the city, but he did not set up any puritan program of reform. The geniality of many of his dramatic characters is mirrored in his own actions. In a quarrel over the stage with Ben Jonson, Dekker answered Jonson's blunt attack on him in *The Poetaster* with vigor and good humor in his own *Satiro-mastix.*

Interest in Dekker has been principally centered in his plays, especially those he wrote alone. He did collaborate in numerous plays with other dramatists of his time, Jonson, Massinger, Middleton, Webster, and Ford. In two of his own plays, *The Shoemaker's Holiday* (1600), and *The Honest Whore* (I, 1604; II, 1630), Dekker displays in turn his ability to romanticize London middle-class life and to create characters with deep human traits.

Dekker's prose pamphlets have a range of subject wider than those of Greene or Nashe. He knew and wrote vividly about London life, its gallants, its citizens, its sins, and its plagues. He published two works exposing the current methods of cheating and thieving, and also a mock-almanac and some devotional prose.

His prose work actually began in 1603 with the publication of *The Wonderfull Yeare,* a tract on the death of Elizabeth and the plague. The bulk of his pamphlets was written before 1610 and includes *The Belman of London,* an account of sharpers and rogues, of which three editions were published in 1608, and *The Guls Horne-booke* (1609). As documents revealing the social life of Elizabethan and Jacobean times, they are invaluable, but they are also examples of the best of Elizabethan journalistic prose, which has a distinctive directness, dignity, and simplicity. One of the strong influences on Dekker's style was the Bible. The following passage from the introduction to *The Seven Deadly Sinnes of London* (1606) shows both this influence and Dekker's love for London.

"O London, thou art great in glory, and envied for thy greatness. Thy towers, thy temples, and thy pinnacles stand upon thy head like borders of fine gold; thy waters like fringes of silver hang at the hems of thy garments. Thou art the goodliest of thy neighbors, but the proudest; the wealthiest but the most wanton. Thou hast all things in thee to make thee fairest, and all things in thee to make thee foulest, for thou art attired like a bride, drawing all that look upon thee to be in love with thee, but there is much harlot in thine eyes."

BIBLIOGRAPHY: *The Non-Dramatic Works of Thomas Dekker,* ed. A. B. Grosart, 5 vols., London, 1884–1886; F. P. Wilson, ed., *The Plague Pamphlets of Thomas Dekker,* Oxford, 1925; H. F. B. Brett-Smith, *The Seven Deadly Sins of London,* Oxford, 1922; R. B. McKerrow, ed., *The Gull's Horn book,* London, 1904; Mary L. Hunt, *Thomas Dekker,* New York, 1911; K. L. Gregg, *Thomas Dekker: A Study in Economic and Social Backgrounds,* University of Washington Publications: Language and Literature, II, no. 2, Seattle, 1924.

FROM

THE SHOEMAKER'S HOLIDAY

(1600)

COLD's the wind, and wet's the rain,
Saint Hugh [1] be our good speed;
Ill is the weather that bringeth no gain,
Nor helps good hearts in need.

Troll the bowl, the jolly nut-brown bowl,
And here, kind mate, to thee;
Let's sing a dirge for Saint Hugh's soul,
And down it merrily.

Down-a-down, hey, down-a-down,
Hey derry derry down-a-down,
Close with the tenor, boy;
Ho! well done, to me let come,
Ring compass, gentle joy.

Troll the bowl, the nut-brown bowl,
And here, kind, &c. (*As often as there be men to drink.*)

(*At last, when all have drunk, this verse.*)

Cold's the wind, and wet's the rain,
Saint Hugh be our good speed;
Ill is the weather that bringeth no gain,
Nor helps good hearts in need.

FROM

THE PLEASANT COMEDY OF PATIENT GRISILL [2]

(1603)

GOLDEN slumbers kiss your eyes,
Smiles awake you when you rise;
Sleep, pretty wantons, do not cry,

[1] *Saint Hugh:* patron saint of shoemakers.

[2] Dekker's authorship of the songs in *Patient Grisill* is in doubt. See *TLS,* October 25, 1941, p. 531.

And I will sing a lullaby,
Rock them, rock them, lullaby.

Care is heavy, therefore sleep you,
You are care, and care must keep you;
Sleep, pretty wantons, do not cry,
And I will sing a lullaby,
Rock them, rock them, lullaby.

FROM

THE SUN'S DARLING[3]

(1656)

Cast away care, he that loves sorrow
Lengthens not a day, nor can buy tomorrow;
  Money is trash, and he that will spend it,
  Let him drink merrily, fortune will send it.
Merrily, merrily, merrily, oh, ho!
Play it off stiffly, we may not part so.

Wine is a charm, it heats the blood too,
Cowards it will arm, if the wine be good too;
  Quickens the wit, and makes the back able,
  Scorns to submit to the watch or constable.
Merrily, &c.

Pots fly about, give us more liquor,
Brothers of a rout, our brains will flow quicker;
  Empty the cask, score up, we care not;
  Fill all the pots again, drink on, and spare not.
Merrily, &c.

[3] *The Sun's Darling:* a masque by Dekker and John Ford performed in 1624, published in 1656.

FROM

THE GULL'S HORNBOOK

(1609)

CHAPTER VI

How a gallant should behave himself in a playhouse

THE theater is your poets' Royal Exchange,[1] upon which their muses (that are now turned to merchants) meeting, barter away that light commodity of words for a lighter ware than words, plaudities, and the breath of the great beast; which, like the threatenings of two cowards, vanish all into air. Players and their factors,[2] who put away the stuff, and make the best of it they possibly can (as indeed 'tis their parts so to do), your gallant, your courtier, and your captain had wont to be the soundest paymasters; and I think are still the surest chapmen; [3] and these, by means that their heads are well stocked, deal upon this comical freight by the gross; when your groundling and gallery-commoner [4] buys his sport by the penny and, like a haggler, is glad to utter [5] it again by retailing.

Sithence then the place is so free in entertainment, allowing a stool as well to the farmer's son as to your Templer; [6] that your stinkard [7] has the selfsame liberty to be there in his tobacco fumes, which your sweet courtier hath; and that your carman [8] and tinker claim as strong a voice in their suffrage, and sit to give judgment on the play's life and death, as well as the proudest momus [9] among the tribe of critic; it is fit that he, whom the most tailors' bills do make room for, when he comes, should not be basely (like a viol) cased up in a corner.

Whether therefore the gatherers of the public or private playhouse stand to receive the afternoon's rent, let our gallant, having paid it, presently advance himself up to the throne of the stage. I mean not into the lord's room, which is now but the stage's suburbs; no, those boxes, by the iniquity of

1 *Royal Exchange:* the most important center of Elizabethan finance, founded by Sir Thomas Gresham and opened by Queen Elizabeth in 1566.

2 *factors:* managers.

3 *chapmen:* merchants.

4 *groundling, gallery-commoner:* occupants of the pit and gallery.

5 *utter:* sell, vend.

6 *Templer:* lawyer.

7 *stinkard:* one who stinks, a term of abuse.

8 *carman:* cartman.

9 *momus:* mocker, fool.

custom, conspiracy of waiting women and gentleman ushers,[10] that there sweat together, and the covetousness of sharers,[11] are contemptibly thrust into the rear, and much new satin is there damned by being smothered to death in darkness. But on the very rushes where the comedy is to dance, yea, and under the state of[12] Cambises[13] himself, must our feathered estridge,[14] like a piece of ordnance, be planted, valiantly (because impudently) beating down the mews and hisses of the opposed rascality.

For do but cast up a reckoning, what large comings-in are pursed up by sitting on the stage. First a conspicuous eminence is gotten; by which means the best and most essential parts of a gallant (good clothes, a proportionable leg, white hand, the Persian lock,[15] and a tolerable beard) are perfectly revealed.

By sitting on the stage you have a signed patent to engross the whole commodity of censure,[16] may lawfully presume to be a girder[17] and stand at the helm to steer the passage of scenes; yet no man shall once offer to hinder you from obtaining the title of an insolent, overweening coxcomb.

By sitting on the stage, you may, without traveling for it, at the very next door ask whose play it is; and, by that quest of inquiry, the law warrants you to avoid much mistaking; if you know not the author, you may rail against him and peradventure so behave yourself that you may enforce the author to know you.

By sitting on the stage, if you be a knight you may happily get you a mistress; if a mere Fleet-street gentleman, a wife; but assure yourself, by continual residence, you are the first and principal man in election to begin the number of We Three.[18]

By spreading your body on the stage, and by being a justice in examining of plays, you shall put yourself into such true scenical authority that some poet shall not dare to present his muse rudely upon your eyes, without having first unmasked her, rifled her, and discovered all her bare and most mystical parts before you at a tavern, when you most knightly shall, for his pains, pay for both their suppers.

By sitting on the stage, you may, with small cost, purchase the dear acquaintance of the boys;[19] have a good stool for sixpence; at any time know what particular part any of the infants present; get your match lighted, examine the play-suits' lace, and perhaps win wagers upon laying 'tis cop-

---

[10] *gentleman ushers:* gentlemen acting as ushers to a person of superior rank.

[11] *sharers:* members of a company of players who paid the expenses and received the profits, and employed the "journeymen" members of the company.

[12] *under the state of:* like, in the person of, or under the canopied throne of.

[13] *Cambises: King Cambyses,* a tragedy by Thomas Preston, 1570, was noted for its bombast. Cf. Shakespeare, *I Henry IV,* II, iv, 425.

[14] *estridge:* ostrich.

[15] *the Persian lock:* evidently a long curl or lovelock.

[16] *signed patent . . . censure:* an exclusive right or license for a monopoly on all faultfinding.

[17] *girder:* one who swears and cavils.

[18] *We Three:* a reference to the old joke of handing a person a picture of two fools, inscribed "We Three Loggerheads Be."

[19] *boys:* boy actors.

per, etc. And to conclude, whether you be a fool or a justice of peace, a cuckold or a captain, a lord mayor's son or a dawcock,[20] a knave or an undersheriff; of what stamp soever you be, current or counterfeit, the stage, like time, will bring you to most perfect light and lay you open; neither are you to be hunted from thence, though the scarecrows in the yard hoot at you, hiss at you, spit at you, yea, throw dirt even in your teeth; 'tis most gentlemanlike patience to endure all this and to laugh at the silly animals; but if the rabble, with a full throat, cry, "Away with the fool," you were worse than a madman to tarry by it; for the gentleman and the fool should never sit on the stage together.

Marry, let this observation go hand in hand with the rest; or rather, like a country servingman, some five yards before them. Present not yourself on the stage (especially at a new play) until the quaking prologue hath (by rubbing) got color into his cheeks, and is ready to give the trumpets their cue that he's upon point to enter; for then it is time, as though you were one of the properties or that you dropped out of the hangings, to creep from behind the arras, with your tripos or three-footed stool in one hand and a teston [21] mounted between a forefinger and a thumb in the other; for if you should bestow your person upon the vulgar when the belly of the house is but half full, your apparel is quite eaten up, the fashion lost, and the proportion of your body in more danger to be devoured than if it were served up in the counter amongst the poultry; avoid that as you would the bastome.[22] It shall crown you with rich commendation to laugh aloud in the midst of the most serious and saddest scene of the terriblest tragedy; and to let that clapper, your tongue, be tossed so high that all the house may ring of it. Your lords use it; your knights are apes to the lords, and do so too; your Inn-a-Court-man is zany to the knights, and (marry, very scurvily) comes likewise limping after it; be thou a beagle to them all, and never lin [23] snuffing, till you have scented them; for by talking and laughing (like a plowman in a morris) [24] you heap Pelion upon Ossa,[25] glory upon glory; as first, all the eyes in the galleries will leave walking after the players and only follow you; the simplest dolt in the house snatches up your name, and when he meets you in the streets, or that you fall into his hands in the middle of a watch, his word shall be taken for you; he'll cry "He's such a gallant," and you pass. Secondly, you publish your temperance to the world, in that you seem not to resort thither to taste vain pleasures with a hungry appetite; but only as a gentleman to spend a foolish hour or two, because you can do nothing else; thirdly, you mightily disrelish the audience and disgrace the author; marry, you take up (though it be at the worst hand) a strong opinion of your own judgment, and enforce the poet

[20] *dawcock:* jackdaw, i.e., foolish prattler.
[21] *teston:* sixpence.
[22] *bastome:* (more often "baston") cudgel.
[23] *lin:* cease.
[24] *morris:* morris dance.
[25] *Pelion upon Ossa:* Pelion and Ossa were two mountains in Thessaly which the Titans piled together and then heaped on Olympus in an attempt to overthrow the gods.

to take pity of your weakness and, by some dedicated sonnet, to bring you into a better paradise only to stop your mouth.

If you can, either for love or money, provide yourself a lodging by the water side; for, above the convenience it brings to shun shoulder-clapping and to ship away your cockatrice [26] betimes in the morning, it adds a kind of state unto you to be carried from thence to the stairs of your playhouse; hate a sculler (remember that) worse than to be acquainted with one o' the scullery. No, your oars are your only sea-crabs, board them, and take heed you never go twice together with one pair; often shifting is a great credit to gentlemen; and that dividing of your fare will make the poor watersnakes be ready to pull you in pieces to enjoy your custom; no matter whether upon landing you have money or no; you may swim in twenty of their boats over the river upon ticket; marry, when silver comes in, remember to pay treble their fare, and it will make your flounder-catchers to send more thanks after you when you do not draw than when you do; for they know it will be their own another day.

Before the play begins, fall to cards; you may win or lose (as fencers do in a prize) and beat one another by confederacy, yet share the money when you meet at supper; notwithstanding, to gull the ragamuffins that stand aloof gaping at you, throw the cards (having first torn four or five of them) round about the stage, just upon the third sound,[27] as though you had lost; it skills not if the four knaves lie on their backs, and outface the audience; there's none such fools as dare take exceptions at them, because, ere the play go off, better knaves than they will fall into the company.

Now, sir, if the writer be a fellow that hath either epigrammed you, or hath had a flirt at your mistress, or hath brought either your feather, or your red beard, or your little legs, etc., on the stage, you shall disgrace him worse than by tossing him in a blanket or giving him the bastinado [28] in a tavern, if, in the middle of his play (be it pastoral or comedy, moral or tragedy), you rise with a screwed and discontented face from your stool to be gone; no matter whether the scenes be good or no; the better they are the worse do you distaste them; and, being on your feet, sneak not away like a coward, but salute all your gentle acquaintance that are spread either on the rushes or on stools about you, and draw what troop you can from the stage after you. The mimics are beholden to you for allowing them elbowroom; their poet cries, perhaps, "A pox go with you," but care not for that, there's no music without frets.

Marry, if either the company or indisposition of the weather bind you to sit it out, my counsel is then that you turn plain ape, take up a rush, and tickle the earnest ears of your fellow gallants, to make other fools fall a-laughing; mew at passionate speeches, blare at merry, find fault with the music, whew at the children's action, whistle at the songs; and above

[26] *cockatrice:* originally a fabulous serpent said to kill by a glance. Here it means "prostitute."

[27] *third sound:* of the trumpets announcing the beginning of the performance.

[28] *bastinado:* cudgeling.

all, curse the sharers, that whereas the same day you had bestowed forty shillings on an embroidered felt and feather (Scotch-fashion) for your mistress in the court or your punk [29] in the city, within two hours after you encounter with the very same block on the stage, when the haberdasher swore to you the impression was extant but that morning.

To conclude, hoard up the finest playscraps you can get, upon which your lean wit may most savorly feed, for want of other stuff, when the Arcadian and Euphuized gentlewomen have their tongues sharpened to set upon you; that quality (next to your shuttlecock) is the only furniture to a courtier that's but a new beginner, and is but in his A B C [30] of compliment. The next places that are filled, after the playhouses be emptied, are (or ought to be) taverns. Into a tavern then let us next march, where the brains of one hogshead must be beaten out to make up another.

CHAPTER VII

How a gallant should behave himself in a tavern

Whosoever desires to be a man of good reckoning in the city, and (like your French lord) to have as many tables furnished as lackeys (who, when they keep least, keep none), whether he be a young quat [31] of the first year's revenue or some austere and sullen-faced steward who (in despite of a great beard, a satin suit, and a chain of gold wrapped in cipers) [32] proclaims himself to any (but to those to whom his lord owes money) for a rank coxcomb, or whether he be a country gentleman that brings his wife up to learn the fashion, see the tombs at Westminster, the lions in the Tower, or to take physic; or else is some young farmer, who many times makes his wife in the country believe he hath suits in law, because he will come up to his lechery; be he of what stamp he will that hath money in his purse, and a good conscience to spend it, my counsel is that he take his continual diet at a tavern, which (out of question) is the only *rendezvous* of boon company; and the drawers [33] the most nimble, the most bold, and most sudden proclaimers of your largest bounty.

Having therefore thrust yourself into a case most in fashion (how coarse soever the stuff be, 'tis no matter so it hold fashion), your office is (if you mean to do your judgment right) to inquire out those taverns which are best customed, whose masters are oftenest drunk (for that confirms their taste, and that they choose wholesome wines), and such as stand furthest from the counters; where, landing yourself and your followers, your first complement shall be to grow most inwardly acquainted with the drawers, to learn their names, as Jack, and Will, and Tom, to dive into their inclina-

---

[29] *punk:* prostitute.

[30] *A B C:* primer.

[31] *quat:* a pimple; here "a youngster."

[32] *cipers:* cypress.

[33] *drawers:* tapsters.

tions, as whether this fellow useth to the fencing school, this to the dancing school; whether that young conjurer (in hogsheads) at midnight keeps a gelding now and then to visit his cockatrice, or whether he love dogs, or be addicted to any other eminent and citizen-like quality; and protest yourself to be extremely in love, and that you spend much money in a year, upon any one of those exercises which you perceive is followed by them. The use which you shall make of this familiarity is this: if you want money five or six days together, you may still pay the reckoning with this most gentleman-like language, "Boy, fetch me money from the bar," and keep yourself most providently from a hungry melancholy in your chamber. Besides, you shall be sure, if there be but one faucet that can betray neat [34] wine to the bar, to have that arraigned before you sooner than a better and worthier person.

The first question you are to make (after the discharging of your pocket of tobacco and pipes, and the household stuff thereto belonging) shall be for an inventory of the kitchen; for it were more than most tailor-like, and to be suspected you were in league with some kitchenwench, to descend yourself, to offend your stomach with the sight of the larder, and happily to grease your accoutrements. Having therefore received this bill, you shall (like a captain putting up dead pays) [35] have many salads stand on your table, as it were for blanks to the other more serviceable dishes; and according to the time of the year, vary your fare, as capon is a stirring meat sometime, oysters are a swelling meat sometimes, trout a tickling meat sometimes, green goose and woodcock a delicate meat sometimes, especially in a tavern, where you shall sit in as great state as a church-warden amongst his poor parishioners at Pentecost or Christmas.

For your drink, let not your physician confine you to any one particular liquor; for as it is requisite that a gentleman should not always be plodding in one art, but rather be a general scholar (that is, to have a lick at all sorts of learning, and away), so 'tis not fitting a man should trouble his head with sucking at one grape, but that he may be able (now there is a general peace) to drink any stranger drunk in his own element of drink, or more properly in his own moist language.

Your discourse at the table must be such as that which you utter at your ordinary; [36] your behavior the same, but somewhat more careless; for where your expense is great, let your modesty be less; and though you should be mad in a tavern, the largeness of the items will bear with your incivility; you may, without prick to your conscience, set the want of your wit against the superfluity and sauciness of their reckonings.

If you desire not to be haunted with fiddlers (who by the statute have as much liberty as rogues to travel into any place, having the passport of the house about them) bring then no women along with you; but if you

---

[34] *neat:* pure, unadulterated.

[35] *like . . . pays:* The original edition reads "deer pays"; Nott emended it to "dead": the captain collects pay for dead soldiers.

[36] *ordinary:* a public eating place.

love the company of all the drawers, never sup without your cockatrice; for, having her there, you shall be sure of most officious attendance. Inquire what gallants sup in the next room, and if they be any of your acquaintance do not you (after the city fashion) send them in a pottle of wine, and your name, sweetened in two pitiful papers of sugar, with some filthy apology crammed into the mouth of a drawer; but rather keep a boy in fee, who underhand shall proclaim you in every room, what a gallant fellow you are, how much you spend yearly in taverns, what a great gamester, what custom you bring to the house, in what witty discourse you maintain a table, what gentlewomen or citizens' wives you can with a wet finger [37] have at any time to sup with you, and suchlike. By which encomiastics of his, they that know you not shall admire you and think themselves to be brought into a paradise but to be meanly in your acquaintance; and if any of your endeared friends be in the house, and beat the same ivy bush [38] that yourself does, you may join companies and be drunk together most publicly.

But in such a deluge of drink, take heed that no man counterfeit himself drunk, to free his purse from the danger of the shot; [39] 'tis a usual thing now among gentlemen; it had wont be the quality of cockneys. I would advise you to leave so much brains in your head as to prevent this. When the terrible reckoning (like an indictment) bids you hold up your hand, and that you must answer it at the bar, you must not abate one penny in any particular, no, though they reckon cheese to you when you have neither eaten any, nor could ever abide it, raw or toasted; but cast your eye only upon the totalis, and no further; for to traverse the bill would betray you to be acquainted with the rates of the market, nay more, it would make the vintners believe you were *pater familias,* and kept a house; which, I assure you, is not now in fashion.

If you fall to dice after supper, let the drawers be as familiar with you as your barber, and venture their silver amongst you; no matter where they had it; you are to cherish the unthriftiness of such young tame pigeons, if you be a right gentleman; for when two are yoked together by the purse strings, and draw the chariot of Madam Prodigality, when one faints in the way and slips his horns let the other rejoice and laugh at him.

At your departure forth the house, to kiss mine hostess over the bar, or to accept of the courtesy of the cellar when 'tis offered you by the drawers (and you must know that kindness never creeps upon them but when they see you almost cleft to the shoulders), or to bid any of the vintners good night, is as commendable as for a barber after trimming to lave your face with sweet water.

To conclude, count it an honor either to invite or be invited to any rifling; [40] for commonly, though you find much satin there, yet you shall

---

[37] *wet finger:* at the snap of the fingers.

[38] *ivy bush:* the sign of a tavern that sold wine.

[39] *shot:* reckoning.

[40] *rifling:* raffling or dicing.

likewise find many citizens' sons, and heirs, and younger brothers there, who smell out such feasts more greedily than tailors hunt upon Sundays after weddings. And let any hook draw you either to a fencer's supper or to a player's that acts such a part for a wager; for by this means you shall get experience, by being guilty to their abominable shaving.

CHAPTER VIII

How a gallant is to behave himself passing through the city, at all hours of the night, and how to pass by any watch

After the sound of pottle-pots is out of your ears, and that the spirit of wine and tobacco walks in your brain, the tavern door being shut upon your back, cast about to pass through the widest and goodliest streets in the city. And if your means cannot reach to the keeping of a boy, hire one of the drawers, to be as a lanthorne unto your feet, and to light you home; and still as you approach near any nightwalker that is up as late as yourself, curse and swear (like one that speaks High Dutch) [41] in a lofty voice, because your men have used you so like a rascal in not waiting upon you, and vow the next morning to pull their blue cases [42] over their ears, though, if your chamber were well searched, you give only sixpence a week to some old woman to make your bed, and that she is all the serving-creatures you give wages to. If you smell a watch (and that you may easily do, for commonly they eat onions to keep them in sleeping, which they account a medicine against cold) or if you come within danger of their brown bills, let him that is your candlestick and holds up your torch from dropping (for to march after a link [43] is shoemaker-like), let *Ignis Fatuus,*[44] I say, being within the reach of the constable's staff, ask aloud, "Sir Giles," or "Sir Abram, will you turn this way, or down that street?" It skills not though there be none dubbed in your bunch; the watch will wink at you, only for the love they bear to arms and knighthood; marry, if the sentinel and his court of guard stand strictly upon his martial law and cry "Stand," commanding you to give the word, and to show reason why your ghost walks so late, do it in some jest (for that will show you have a desperate wit, and perhaps make him and his halberdiers afraid to lay foul hands upon you) or, if you read a *mittimus* [45] in the constable's book, counterfeit to be a Frenchman, a Dutchman, or any other nation whose country is in peace with your own; and you may pass the pikes; for being not able to understand you, they cannot by the customs of the city take your examination, and so by consequence they have nothing to say to you.

[41] *High Dutch:* a language that one does not understand, gibberish.

[42] *blue cases:* blue clothes. Servants ordinarily wore blue.

[43] *link:* torch made of tow and pitch.

[44] *Ignis Fatuus:* "Will-o'-the-wisp," that is, the boy carrying the torch.

[45] *mittimus:* a warrant.

If the night be old, and that your lodging be some place into which no artillery of words can make a breach, retire, and rather assault the doors of your punk, or (not to speak broken English) your sweet mistress, upon whose white bosom you may languishingly consume the rest of darkness that is left, in ravishing (though not restorative) pleasures, without expenses, only by virtue of four or five oaths (when the siege breaks up, and at your marching away with bag and baggage) that the last night you were at dice, and lost so much in gold, so much in silver; and seem to vex most that two such Elizabeth twenty-shilling pieces, or four such spur-ryals[46] (sent you with a cheese and a baked meat from your mother) rid away amongst the rest. By which tragical yet politic speech you may not only have your night-work done gratis, but also you may take diet there the next day and depart with credit, only upon the bare word of a gentleman to make her restitution.

All the way as you pass (especially being approached near some of the gates) talk of none but lords, and such ladies with whom you have played at primero,[47] or danced in the presence the very same day. It is a chance to lock up the lips of an inquisitive bellman; and being arrived at your lodging door, which I would counsel you to choose in some rich citizen's house, salute at parting no man but by the name of Sir (as though you had supped with knights), albeit you had none in your company but your Perinado,[48] or your ingle.[49]

Happily it will be blown abroad that you and your shoal of gallants swum through such an ocean of wine, that you danced so much money out at heels, and that in wild fowl there flew away thus much; and I assure you, to have the bill of your reckoning lost of purpose, so that it may be published, will make you to be held in dear estimation; only the danger is, if you owe money, and that your revealing gets your creditors by the ears; for then look to have a peal of ordnance thundering at your chamber door the next morning. But if either your tailor, mercer, haberdasher, silkman, cutter, linen draper, or sempster stand like a guard of Switzers about your lodging, watching your uprising, or, if they miss of that, your downlying in one of the counters, you have no means to avoid the galling of their small-shot than by sending out a light-horseman to call your apothecary to your aid, who, encountering this desperate band of your creditors, only with two or three glasses in his hand, as though that day you purged, is able to drive them all to their holes like so many foxes; for the name of taking physic is a sufficient *quietus est* to any endangered gentleman, and gives an acquittance (for the time) to them all, though the twelve companies stand with their hoods to attend your coming forth and their officers with them.

I could now fetch you about noon (the hour which I prescribed you be-

---

[46] *spur-ryals:* gold coins, worth fifteen shillings.

[47] *primero:* a gambling card game.

[48] *Perinado:* hermaphrodite.

[49] *ingle:* catamite.

fore to rise at) out of your chamber, and carry you with me into Paul's Churchyard; where planting yourself in a stationer's shop, many instructions are to be given you, what books to call for, how to censure of new books, how to mew at the old, how to look in your tables and inquire for such and such Greek, French, Italian, or Spanish authors, whose names you have there, but whom your mother for pity would not give you so much wit as to understand. From thence you should blow yourself into the tobacco-ordinary, where you are likewise to spend your judgment (like a quack-salver)[50] upon that mystical wonder, to be able to discourse whether your cane or your pudding be sweetest, and which pipe has the best bore, and which burns black, which breaks in the burning, etc. Or, if you itch to step into the barber's, a whole dictionary cannot afford more words to set down notes what dialogues you are to maintain whilst you are doctor of the chair there. After your shaving, I could breathe you in a fence-school, and out of that cudgel you into a dancing school, in both which I could weary you, by showing you more tricks than are in five galleries or fifteen prizes. And, to close up the stomach of this feast, I could make cockneys, whose fathers have left them well, acknowledge themselves infinitely beholden to me, for teaching them by familiar demonstration how to spend their patrimony and to get themselves names when their fathers are dead and rotten. But lest too many dishes should cast into a surfeit, I will now take away; yet so that, if I perceive you relish this well, the rest shall be (in time) prepared for you. Farewell.

FROM

THE WONDERFUL YEAR[51]

(1603)

[THE SICKNESS AND DEATH OF QUEEN ELIZABETH]

Vertumnus,[52] being attired in his accustomed habit of changeable silk, had newly passed through the first and principal court-gate of heaven; to whom, for a farewell, and to show how dutiful he was in his office, Janus, that bears two faces under one hood, made a very mannerly low leg and, because he was the only porter at that gate, presented unto this king of the months all the New Year's gifts, which were more in number and

[50] *quack-salver:* quack doctor.

[51] *The Wonderful Year* (1603), after the description of the sickness and death of Queen Elizabeth, gives a vivid picture of London in the plague of 1603. Several of its details Defoe borrowed in his *Journal of the Plague Year* (1722).

[52] *Vertumnus:* Roman (Italian) god of the seasons.

more worth than those that are given to the Great Turk or the emperor of Persia. On went Vertumnus in his lusty progress, Priapus, Flora, the Driads and Hamadriads with all the wooden rabble of those that dressed orchards and gardens perfuming all the ways that he went, with the sweet odors that breathed from flowers, herbs, and trees, which now began to peep out of prison; by virtue of which excellent airs, the sky got a most clear complexion, looked smug and smooth, and had not so much as a wart sticking on her face. The sun likewise was freshly and very richly appareled in cloth of gold like a bridegroom, and instead of gilded rosemary,[53] the horns of the Ram, being the sign of that celestial bride-house where he lay, to be married to the spring, were not like your common horns parcel-gilt,[54] but double double-gilt with the liquid gold that melted from his beams; for joy whereof the lark sung at his window every morning, the nightingale every night. The cuckoo, like a single sole fiddler that reels from tavern to tavern, plied it all the day long. Lambs frisked up and down in the valleys; kids and goats leapt to and fro on the mountains; shepherds sat piping, country wenches singing; lovers made sonnets for their lasses, whilst they made garlands for their lovers. And as the country was frolic, so was the city merry. Olive trees, which grow nowhere but in the garden of peace, stood, as common as beech does at midsummer, at every man's door; branches of palm were in every man's hand. Streets were full of people, people full of joy; every house seemed to have a Lord of Misrule in it, in every house there was so much jollity. No screech-owl frighted the silly countryman at midnight, nor any drum the citizen at noonday, but all was more calm than a still water, all hushed, as if the spheres had been playing in consort.[55] In conclusion, heaven looked like a palace, and the great hall of earth like a paradise.

But Oh, the short-lived felicity of man! Oh world, of what slight and thin stuff is thy happiness! Just in the midst of this jocund holiday, a storm rises in the west. Westward, from the top of a Rich-mount,[56] descended a hideous tempest, that shook cedars, terrified the tallest pines, and cleft in sunder even the hardest hearts of oak. And if such great trees were shaken, what think you became of the tender eglantine and humble hawthorn? They could not, doubtless, but droop; they could not choose but die with the terror. The element, taking the Destinies' part, who indeed set abroach this mischief, scowled on the earth, and, filling her high forehead full of black wrinkles, tumbling long up and down, like a great-bellied wife, her sighs being whirlwinds and her groans thunder, at length she fell in labor and was delivered of a pale, meager, weak child named Sickness, whom Death, with a pestilence, would needs take upon him to nurse, and did so. This starveling, being come to his full growth, had an office given him for noth-

---

[53] *Rosemary* was strewn about the floor and worn in posies at weddings. It was also used as a prophylactic against the plague.

[54] *parcel-gilt:* partly gilt.

[55] *consort:* harmony.

[56] *Rich-mount:* I.e., Richmond, where Elizabeth went on January 21, 1602/3, and died two months later, March 24.

ing (and that's a wonder in this age); Death made him his herald, attired him like a courtier, and, in his name, charged him to go into the privy chamber of the English queen to summon her to appear in the Star Chamber of Heaven.

The summons made her start, but, having an invincible spirit, did not amaze her; yet whom would not the certain news of parting from a kingdom amaze? But she knew where to find a richer, and therefore lightly regarded the loss of this, and thereupon made ready for that heavenly coronation, being (which was most strange) most dutiful to obey, that had so many years so powerfully commanded. She obeyed Death's messenger and yielded her body to the hands of Death himself. She died, resigning her scepter to posterity and her soul to immortality.

The report of her death, like a thunderclap, was able to kill thousands; it took away hearts from millions; for, having brought up, even under her wing, a nation that was almost begotten and born under her, that never shouted any other *Ave* than for her name, never saw the face of any prince but herself, never understood what that strange outlandish word "change" signified—how was it possible but that her sickness should throw abroad an universal fear, and her death an astonishment? She was the courtier's treasure, therefore he had cause to mourn; the lawyer's sword of justice, he might well faint; the merchant's patroness, he had reason to look pale; the citizen's mother, he might best lament; the shepherd's goddess, and should not he droop? Only the soldier, who had walked a long time upon wooden legs and was not able to give arms, though he were a gentleman, had bristled up the quills of his stiff porcupine mustachio, and swore by no beggars that now was the hour come for him to bestir his stumps; usurers and brokers, that are the devil's ingles and dwell in the Long Lane [57] of hell, quaked like aspen leaves at his oaths; those that before were the only cutthroats in London now stood in fear of no other death, but my *Signor Soldado* was deceived; the tragedy went not forward.

Never did the English nation behold so much black worn as there was at her funeral. It was then but put on to try if it were fit, for the great day of mourning was set down in the book of heaven, to be held afterwards. That was but the dumb-show; the tragical act hath been playing ever since. Her hearse, as it was borne, seemed to be an island swimming in water, for round about it there rained showers of tears; about her deathbed, none, for her departure was so sudden and so strange that men knew not how to weep, because they had never been taught to shed tears of that making. They that durst not speak their sorrows whispered them; they that durst not whisper, sent them forth in sighs. Oh, what an earthquake is the alteration of a state! Look from the chamber of presence to the farmer's cottage: and you shall find nothing but distraction; the whole kingdom seems a wilderness, and the people in it are transformed to wild men.

---

[57] *Long Lane:* in Aldersgate; described by Stow (*Survey,* ed. Kingsford, II, 28) as "now lately builded on both sides with tenements for brokers, tiplers, and suchlike."

Michael Drayton

1563–1631

OF two Elizabethan poets who came from Warwickshire one stands as the genius of his age—Shakespeare. The other, Michael Drayton, is nevertheless a more representative Elizabethan poet. Drayton makes use of and, in some cases, perfects the poetic forms and fashions of his time. The range of his subject matter and his skill and versatility in versification are at once remarkable and typical in his age. But his voluminous work, popular in his own day, is known to most readers today mainly from a few bright gems which anthologists have culled from it. The man himself rarely emerges sharply from his poetry, although he does make a few clear pronouncements about his art. Yet Drayton's intense patriotism, like Spenser's (but brought to earth), and his solidity and confident skill are always apparent. As a poet, he has more strength than Daniel, with whom he is so often compared.

Of Drayton's early life little is known. He was brought up in the family of Sir Henry Goodere at Polesworth Hall. He testifies in his verse letter to Henry Reynolds of his own early interest in reading. There is no evidence that he was a university man. With the exception of some hack work for the theater, his livelihood was largely the generosity of a series of patrons.

Drayton published his first work, *The Harmonie of the Church*, in 1591—some metrical paraphrases of passages of Scripture. His last poems were published in 1637, six years after his death. His poetry, which is essentially Elizabethan throughout, extends through a literary period often foreign to his nature and spirit, but Drayton was (whether he wished it or not) responsive to almost every literary trend. Consequently some of his last poems belong really to Jacobean and Caroline verse. His most exquisite single accomplishment, *Nymphidia,* is a mixture of Chaucerian and Elizabethan elements, all refined by a concise verse technique characteristic of Caroline poets. Drayton published pastorals, sonnets (see p. 742), Ovidian mythology (*Endimion and Phoebe,* 1595) and Ovidian love-epistles (*England's Heroicall Epistles,* 1597), odes, and lyrics. But his most ambitious project was a long poem about the English countryside; its title page conveys some idea of its scope: *POLY-OLBION, or a Chorographicall Description of Tracts, Riuers, Mountaines, Forests, and other Parts of this renowned Isle of Great Britaine, with intermixture of the most Remarquable Stories, Antiquities, Wonders, Rarityes, Pleasures, and Commodities of the same: Digested in a Poem by Michael Drayton, Esq.* The first part appeared in 1612, and the poet was kept busy until 1622 on what he called his "strange Herculean task." The last years of his life produced two volumes of poetry, the most notable pieces in them being his *Epistle to Henry Reynolds on Poets and Poetry* and his *Nymphidia.*

Drayton died in 1631 and was buried in Westminster Abbey. Some literary historians call him, rather than Milton, the last of the Elizabethans. He tried his hand at every popular poetic form in his day and in many attained a high degree of success. He was workmanlike; he was constantly revising his verse. All his poetry breathes competence, clarity, and charm, and in it there is a delightful play of fancy, but little of "the higher faculty of the imagination." Mr. Cyril Brett has aptly remarked that the task of criticizing Drayton "at first seems that of criticizing many poets, not one."

BIBLIOGRAPHY: *The Works of Michael Drayton,* ed. J. W. Hebel, 5 vols., Oxford, 1931–1941; *Minor Poems,* ed. C. Brett, 1907; O. Elton, *Michael Drayton: a Critical Study,* London, 1905; R. Noyes, *Drayton's Literary Vogue Since 1631,* Bloomington [Indiana], 1935; B. H. Newdigate, *Michael Drayton and his Circle,* Oxford, 1941. I. A. Shapiro, "Drayton at Polesworth" *N & Q,* CXCIV (1949), 496; M. Praz, "Michael Drayton," *English Studies,* XXVIII (1947), 97–107; D. Taylor, "Drayton and the Countess of Bedford," *SP,* XLIX (1952), 214–228.

FROM

IDEA, THE SHEPHERD'S GARLAND[1]

(1593)

The Eighth Eclogue

Far in the country of Arden
There wonned a knight hight Cassemen,
   As bold as Isenbras;[2]
Fell was he and eager bent
In battle and in tournament,
   As was the good Sir Thopas.[3]
He had, as antique stories tell,
A daughter cleped Dowsabell,
   A maiden fair and free;
And for she was her father's heir,
Full well she was yconned the lere[4]
   Of mickle courtesy.
The silk well couth she[5] twist and twine,
And make the fine marchpine,[6]
   And with the needle work;
And she couth help the priest to say
His matins on a holyday,
   And sing a psalm in kirk.
She ware a frock of frolic green
Might well beseem a maiden queen,
   Which seemly was to see;
A hood to that so neat and fine,
In color like the columbine,
   Ywrought full featously.[7]

---

[1] A pastoral poem in nine eclogues, in which the inspiration from Spenser's *Shepheardes Calender* is more apparent than in any other Elizabethan poem (see *RES,* XIII [1937], 272–281 for influence of language). In the eighth eclogue Gorbo laments the passing of the golden age; Motto comforts him with the pastoral lyric here given:

A pretie Tale, which when I was a boy
My toothles Grandame oft hath tolde to me.

[2] *Isenbras:* variant spelling of Isumbras, hero of medieval metrical romance, *Sir Isumbras.*

[3] *Sir Thopas:* the hero of a tale told by Chaucer in *The Canterbury Tales.*

[4] *yconned the lere:* made to learn the lore.

[5] *couth she:* she knew how to, etc.

[6] *marchpine:* marchpane, marzipan, confection made of pounded almonds and sugar.

[7] *featously:* neatly, carefully.

Her feature all as fresh above
As is the grass that grows by Dove,
  As lithe as lass of Kent;
Her skin as soft as Lemster [8] wool,
As white as snow on Peakish hull, [9]
  Or swan that swims in Trent.
This maiden in a morn betime
Went forth when May was in her prime
  To get sweet cetywall,[10]
The honeysuckle, the harlock,[11]
The lily, and the ladysmock,
  To deck her summer hall.
Thus as she wandered here and there,
Ypicking of the bloomed breer,
  She chanced to espy
A shepherd sitting on a bank;
Like chanticleer he crowed crank,[12]
  And piped with merry glee.
He leared [13] his sheep as he him list,
When he would whistle in his fist,
  To feed about him round,
Whilst he full many a carol sung,
Until the fields and meadows rung,
  And that the woods did sound.
In favor this same shepherd's swain
Was like the bedlam Tamburlaine,
  Which held proud kings in awe.
But meek he was as lamb mought be,
Ylike that gentle Abel he,
  Whom his lewd brother slaw.
This shepherd ware a sheep-gray cloak,
Which was of the finest loke [14]
  That could be cut with shear;
His mittens were of bauzens' [15] skin,
His cockers were of cordiwin,[16]
  His hood of meniveere; [17]
His awl and lingel [18] in a thong,

---

[8] *Lemster:* Leominster.

[9] *Peakish hull:* Drayton may be using the form "hull" for "hill" and may allude to the Peak, high tableland in the north of Derbyshire, which is described in the twenty-sixth song of the *Poly-Olbion,* ll. 359–494.

[10] *cetywall:* setwall, the plant valerian.

[11] *harlock:* an unidentified flower.

[12] *crank:* lustily.

[13] *leared:* guided.

[14] *loke:* lock of wool.

[15] *bauzens':* badgers'.

[16] *cockers:* casings for the leg; *cordiwin:* cordwain, cordovan.

[17] *meniveere:* miniver, a grayish fur.

[18] *lingel:* waxed thread.

His tar-box [19] on his broad belt hung,
His breech of cointrie blue.[20]
Full crisp and curled were his locks,
His brows as white as Albion rocks,
So like a lover true.
And piping still he spent the day,
So merry as the popinjay;
Which liked Dowsabell,
That would she aught or would she naught,
This lad would never from her thought,
She in love-longing fell.
At length she tucked up her frock,
White as the lily was her smock,
She drew the shepherd nigh.
But then the shepherd piped a good [21]
That all his sheep forsook their food
To hear his melody.
"Thy sheep," quoth she, "cannot be lean,
That have a jolly shepherd's swain
The which can pipe so well."
"Yea but," saith he, "their shepherd may,
If piping thus he pine away
In love of Dowsabell."
"Of love, fond boy, take thou no keep,"
Quoth she, "look well unto thy sheep
Lest they should hap to stray."
Quoth he, "So had I done full well,
Had I not seen fair Dowsabell
Come forth to gather May."
With that she gan to vail [22] her head;
Her cheeks were like the roses red,
But not a word she said.
With that the shepherd gan to frown;
He threw his pretty pipes adown,
And on the ground him laid.
Saith she, "I may not stay till night
And leave my summer hall undight,[23]
And all for long of thee."
"My cote," [24] saith he, "nor yet my fold,
Shall neither sheep nor shepherd hold,

19 *tar-box:* a box used by shepherds to hold tar as a salve for sheep.

20 *cointrie blue:* Coventry blue, a thread made in Coventry, frequently used for embroidery, was conventional pastoral wear.

21 *a good:* so well.

22 *vail:* lower.

23 *undight:* unadorned.

24 *cote:* small cottage.

Except thou favor me."
Saith she, "Yet liefer I were dead,
Than I should lose my maidenhead,
And all for love of men."
Saith he, "Yet are you too unkind,
If in your heart you cannot find
To love us now and then;
And I to thee will be as kind
As Colin [25] was to Rosalind,
Of courtesy the flower."
"Then will I be as true," quoth she,
"As ever maiden yet might be
Unto her paramour."
With that she bent her snow-white knee;
Down by the shepherd kneeled she,
And him she sweetly kissed.
With that the shepherd whooped for joy;
Quoth he, "There's never shepherd's boy
That ever was so blist."

FROM

ENGLAND'S HEROICAL EPISTLES [26]

(1599)

HENRY HOWARD, EARL OF SURREY, TO THE LADY GERALDINE [27]

The Argument

The Earl of Surrey, that renowned lord,
Th' old English glory bravely that restored,
That prince and poet (a name more divine),
Falling in love with beauteous Geraldine
Of the Geraldi, which derive their name
From Florence, whither, to advance her fame,
He travels, and in public jousts maintained

[25] *Colin:* Spenser; see *The Shepheardes Calender,* p. 312, above.

[26] *England's Heroical Epistles:* Starting with letters exchanged between nine pairs of famous lovers in the first edition, 1597, Drayton added letters from three more pairs of lovers in the editions of 1598 and 1599. During Drayton's lifetime alone, the poem was reprinted thirteen times.

[27] On Surrey and Geraldine, see p. 66, above. Surrey's travels in Italy were first popularized in Nashe's *Unfortunate Traveller* (1594).

Her beauty peerless, which by arms he gained;
But staying long, fair Italy to see,
To let her know him constant still to be,
From Tuscany this letter to her writes,
Which her rescription instantly invites.

From learned Florence, long time rich in fame,
From whence thy race, thy noble grandsires, came
To famous England, that kind nurse of mine,
Thy Surrey sends to heavenly Geraldine;
Yet let not Tuscan think I do it wrong,
That I from thence write in my native tongue,
That in these harsh-tuned cadences I sing,
Sitting so near the Muses' sacred spring;
But rather think itself adorned thereby,
That England reads the praise of Italy.
Though to the Tuscans I the smoothness grant,
Our dialect no majesty doth want
To set thy praises in as high a key
As France, or Spain, or Germany, or they.
What day I quit the foreland of fair Kent,
And that my ship her course for Flanders bent,
Yet think I with how many a heavy look
My leave of England and of thee I took,
And did entreat the tide, if it might be,
But to convey me one sigh back to thee.
Up to the deck a billow lightly skips,
Taking my sigh, and down again it slips;
Into the gulf itself it headlong throws,
And as a post to England-ward it goes.
As I sat wondering how the rough seas stirred,
I might far off perceive a little bird,
Which, as she fain from shore to shore would fly,
Had lost herself in the broad vasty sky,
Her feeble wing beginning to deceive her,
The seas of life still gaping to bereave her;
Unto the ship she makes, which she discovers,
And there, poor fool, a while for refuge hovers.
And when at length her flagging pinion fails,
Panting she hangs upon the rattling sails,
And being forced to loose her hold with pain,
Yet beaten off, she straight lights on again,
And tossed with flaws,[28] with storms, with wind, with weather,
Yet still departing thence, still turneth thither;

[28] *flaws:* sudden gusts of wind.

Now with the poop, now with the prow doth bear,
Now on this side, now that, now here, now there.
Methinks these storms should be my sad depart,
The silly helpless bird is my poor heart,
The ship to which for succor it repairs,
That is yourself, regardless of my cares.
Of every surge doth fall, or waves doth rise,
To some one thing I sit and moralize.
  When for thy love I left the Belgic shore,
Divine Erasmus and our famous More,[29]
Whose happy presence gave me such delight
As made a minute of a winter's night,
With whom a while I stayed at Rotterdam,
Now so renowned by Erasmus' name;
Yet every hour did seem a world of time
Till I had seen that soul-reviving clime,[30]
And thought the foggy Netherlands unfit,
A watery soil to clog a fiery wit.
And as that wealthy Germany I passed,
Coming unto the Emperor's court at last,
Great learn'd Agrippa,[31] so profound in art,
Who the infernal secrets doth impart,
When of thy health I did desire to know,
Me in a glass my Geraldine did show,
Sick in thy bed and, for thou couldst not sleep,
By [32] a wax taper set the light to keep;
I do remember thou didst read that ode
Sent back whilst I in Thanet made abode,
Where when thou cam'st unto that word of love,
Even in thine eyes I saw how passion strove;
That snowy lawn which covered thy bed,
Methought looked white, to see thy cheek so red,
Thy rosy cheek, oft changing in my sight,
Yet still was red, to see the lawn so white;
The little taper which should give thee light,
Methought waxed dim to see thine eye so bright;
Thine eye again supplied the taper's turn,
And with his beams more brightly made it burn;
The shrugging air about thy temples hurls
And wrapped thy breath in little clouded curls,
And as it did ascend, it straight did seize it,

[29] *Erasmus, More:* See introduction to Roger Ascham, pp. 77–78, above.
[30] *soul-reviving clime:* Florence.
[31] *Agrippa:* Cornelius Agrippa (1486–1535), scholar and writer on occult sciences.
[32] *By:* near-by.

And as it sunk, it presently did raise it.
Canst thou by sickness banish beauty so?
Which if put from thee knows not where to go,
To make her shift and for her succor seek
To every riveled [33] face, each bankrupt cheek.
If health preserved, thou beauty still dost cherish,
If that neglected, beauty soon doth perish.
Care draws on care, woe comforts woe again,
Sorrow breeds sorrow, one grief brings forth twain;
If live or die, as thou dost so do I,
If live, I live, and if thou die, I die:
One heart, one love, one joy, one grief, one troth,
One good, one ill, one life, one death to both.
  If Howard's blood thou hold'st as but too vile,
Or not esteem'st of Norfolk's princely style,
If Scotland's coat no mark of fame can lend,
That lion placed in our bright silver bend,[34]
(Which as a trophy beautifies our shield
Since Scottish blood discolored Flodden field,[35]
When the proud Cheviot our brave ensign bare
As a rich jewel in a lady's hair,
And did fair Bramston's neighboring valleys choke
With clouds of cannons, fire-disgorged smoke),
Or Surrey's earldom insufficient be
And not a dower so well contenting thee,
Yet am I one of great Apollo's heirs,
The sacred Muses challenge me for theirs.
By princes my immortal lines are sung,
My flowing verses graced with ev'ry tongue;
The little children, when they learn to go,
By painful mothers daded [36] to and fro,
Are taught my sugared numbers to rehearse,
And have their sweet lips seasoned with my verse.
  When heav'n would strive to do the best it can,
And put an angel's spirit into a man,
The utmost power it hath it then doth spend
When to the world a poet it doth intend;
That little diff'rence 'twixt the gods and us,
By them confirmed, distinguished only thus:
Whom they, in birth, ordain to happy days,
The gods commit their glory to our praise;

---

[33] *riveled:* shriveled.

[34] *That lion . . . bend:* Drayton explains this line concerning the "blazon of the Howards Honourable Armour" in detail in his "Annotations" to the poem.

[35] *Flodden field:* The English, led by Surrey's father, defeated the Scotch here in 1513.

[36] *daded:* led and supported, as with a child learning to walk.

T' eternal life when they dissolve their breath,
We likewise share a second power by death.
  When time shall turn those amber locks to gray,
My verse again shall gild and make them gay,
And trick them up in knotted curls anew,
And to thy autumn give a summer's hue;
That sacred power that in my ink remains
Shall put fresh blood into thy withered veins,
And on thy red decayed, thy whiteness dead,
Shall set a white more white, a red more red;
When thy dim sight thy glass cannot descry,
Nor thy crazed mirror can discern thine eye,
My verse, to tell th' one what the other was,
Shall represent them both, thine eye and glass,
Where both thy mirror and thine eye shall see
What once thou saw'st in that, that saw in thee,
And to them both shall tell the simple truth,
What that in pureness was, what thou in youth.
  If Florence once should lose her old renown,
As famous Athens, now a fisher town,
My lines for thee a Florence shall erect
Which great Apollo ever shall protect,
And with the numbers from my pen that falls
Bring marble mines to re-erect those walls.
Nor beauteous Stanhope, whom all tongues report
To be the glory of the English court,
Shall by our nation be so much admired,
If ever Surrey truly were inspired.
And famous Wyatt, who in numbers sings
To that enchanting Thracian harper's strings,
To whom Phoebus, the poets' god, did drink
A bowl of nectar filled up to the brink,
And sweet-tongued Bryan,[37] whom the Muses kept
And in his cradle rocked him whilst he slept,
In sacred verses most divinely penned,
Upon thy praises ever shall attend.
  What time I came into this famous town
And made the cause of my arrival known,
Great Medici a list for triumphs built;
Within the which, upon a tree of gilt,
Which was with sundry rare devices set,
I did erect thy lovely counterfeit
To answer those Italian dames' desire,

[37] *Bryan:* Sir Francis Bryan (d. 1550), friend and fellow poet of Wyatt's to whom Wyatt addressed a poem in *Tottel's Miscellany.*

Which daily came thy beauty to admire;
By which my lion, in his gaping jaws,
Held up my lance, and in his dreadful paws
Reacheth my gauntlet unto him that dare
A beauty with my Geraldine's compare.
Which, when each manly valiant arm assays,
After so many brave triumphant days
The glorious prize upon my lance I bare,
By herald's voice proclaimed to be thy share.
The shivered staves, here for thy beauty broke,
With fierce encounters passed at ev'ry shock,
When stormy courses answered cuff for cuff,
Denting proud beavers with the counter-buff,
Upon an altar, burnt with holy flame,
I sacrificed as incense to thy fame;
Where, as the phoenix [38] from her spiced fume
Renews herself in that she doth consume,
So from these sacred ashes live we both,
Ev'n as that one Arabian wonder doth.
  When to my chamber I myself retire,
Burnt with the sparks that kindled all this fire,
Thinking of England, which my hope contains,
The happy isle where Geraldine remains,
Of Hunsdon, where those sweet celestial eyne
At first did pierce this tender breast of mine,
Of Hampton Court and Windsor, where abound
All pleasures that in paradise were found;
Near that fair castle is a little grove,
With hanging rocks all covered from above,
Which on the bank of goodly Thames doth stand,
Clipped by the water from the other land,
Whose bushy top doth bid the sun forbear
And checks his proud beams that would enter there;
Whose leaves still mutt'ring as the air doth breathe,
With the sweet bubbling of the stream beneath,
Doth rock the senses, whilst the small birds sing,
Lulled asleep with gentle murmuring;
Where light-foot fairies sport at prison-base
(No doubt there is some power frequents the place),
There the soft poplar and smooth beech do bear
Our names together carved ev'rywhere,
And Gordian knots do curiously entwine

---

[38] *phoenix:* a mythical bird, which lived for five or six hundred years in the Arabian desert, then burned itself, but emerged from its own ashes with renewed youth to live on for another cycle of years. See also line 224.

The names of Henry and of Geraldine.
Oh, let this grove in happy times to come
Be called the lovers' blest Elysium;
Whither my mistress wonted to resort,
In summer's heat in those sweet shades to sport;
A thousand sundry names I have it given,
And called it Wonder-hider, Cover-heaven,
The roof where beauty her rich court doth keep,
Under whose compass all the stars do sleep.
There is one tree which now I call to mind,
Doth bear these verses carved in his rind:
When Geraldine shall sit in thy fair shade,
Fan her sweet tresses with perfumed air,
Let thy large boughs a canopy be made
To keep the sun from gazing on my fair;
And when thy spreading branched arms be sunk,
And thou no sap nor pith shalt more retain,
Ev'n from the dust of thy unwieldy trunk
I will renew thee, phoenix-like, again,
And from thy dry decayed root will bring
A new-born stem, another Aeson's spring.[39]
I find no cause, nor judge I reason why
My country should give place to Lombardy;
As goodly flowers on Thamesis do grow
As beautify the banks of wanton Po;
As many nymphs as haunt rich Arno's strand,
By silver Severn tripping hand in hand;
Our shade's as sweet, though not to us so dear,
Because the sun hath greater power there;
This distant place doth give me greater woe,
Far off, my sighs the farther have to go.
Ah absence! why shouldst thou seem so long?
Or wherefore shouldst thou offer time such wrong,
Summer so soon to steal on winter's cold,
Or winter's blasts so soon make summer old?
Love did us both with one self arrow strike,
Our wound's both one, our cure should be the like,
Except thou hast found out some mean by art,
Some powerful med'cine to withdraw the dart;
But mine is fixed, and absence being proved,
It sticks too fast, it cannot be removed.
Adieu, adieu, from Florence when I go
By my next letters Geraldine shall know,

[39] *Aeson's spring:* Aeson, father of Jason, was restored to youth by Medea after the return of the Argonauts. (Ovid, *Metamorphoses,* VII, 162 ff.)

Which if good fortune shall by course direct,
From Venice by some messenger expect;
Till when, I leave thee to thy heart's desire:
By him that lives thy virtues to admire.

ODES

To the Virginian Voyage [40]

You brave heroic minds
Worthy your country's name,
That honor still pursue,
Go, and subdue,
Whilst loit'ring hinds
Lurk here at home, with shame.

Britons, you stay too long;
Quickly aboard bestow you,
And with a merry gale
Swell your stretched sail,
With vows as strong
As the winds that blow you.

Your course securely steer,
West and by south forth keep,
Rocks, lee shores, nor shoals,
When Aeolus scowls,
You need not fear,
So absolute the deep.

And cheerfully at sea,
Success you still entice,
To get the pearl and gold,
And ours to hold,
Virginia,
Earth's only paradise,

Where nature hath in store
Fowl, venison, and fish,
And the fruitful'st soil
Without your toil
Three harvests more,
All greater than your wish.

And the ambitious vine
Crowns with his purple mass,
The cedar reaching high
To kiss the sky,
The cypress, pine,
And useful sassafras.

To whose the golden age
Still nature's laws doth give,
No other cares that tend,
But them to defend
From winter's age,
That long there doth not live.

Whenas the luscious smell
Of that delicious land,
Above the seas that flows,
The clear wind throws,
Your hearts to swell
Approaching the dear strand,

In kenning of the shore,
Thanks to God first given,
Oh you, the happi'st men,
Be frolic then,
Let cannons roar,
Frighting the wide heaven.

[40] First published in *Poems Lyrick and Pastorall* (1606). J. Q. Adams has shown (*MLN*, XXV [1918], 405) that "The ode is for the most a metrical version of certain prose passages in Hakluyt's First Voyage to Virginia as printed in his *Principall Navigations. . . .*" [ed. Hakluyt Society, III, 297 ff.] The patent for the voyage was sealed on April 6, 1606, and the expedition of 3 ships and 140 men left the Thames in December.

And in regions far
Such heroes bring ye forth
As those from whom we came,
And plant our name
Under that star
Not known unto our north.

And as there plenty grows
Of laurel everywhere,
Apollo's sacred tree,
You it may see
A poet's brows
To crown, that may sing there.

Thy voyages attend,
Industrious Hakluyt,[41]
Whose reading shall enflame
Men to seek fame,
And much commend
To after times thy wit.

To the Cambro-Britons [42] and Their Harp, His Ballad of Agincourt [43]

Fair stood the wind for France,
When we our sails advance,
Nor now to prove our chance,
Longer will tarry;
But putting to the main
At Kaux, the mouth of Seine,
With all his martial train,
Landed King Harry.[44]

And taking many a fort,
Furnished in warlike sort,
Marcheth towards Agincourt,
In happy hour;
Skirmishing day by day
With those that stopped his way,
Where the French gen'ral lay
With all his power.

Which in his height of pride,
King Henry to deride,
His ransom to provide
To the King sending;
Which he neglects the while
As from a nation vile,
Yet with an angry smile
Their fall portending.

And turning to his men,
Quoth our brave Henry then:
Though they to one be ten,
Be not amazed.
Yet have we well begun,
Battles so bravely won
Have ever to the sun
By fame been raised.

And for myself, quoth he,
This my full rest shall be,
England ne'er mourn for me,
Nor more esteem me;
Victor I will remain,
Or on this earth lie slain,
Never shall she sustain
Loss to redeem me.

Poitiers and Crecy tell,
When most their pride did swell,
Under our swords they fell;
No less our skill is
Than when our grandsire great,
Claiming the regal seat
By many a warlike feat,
Lopped the French lilies.

---

[41] *Hakluyt:* See pp. 460–489, above.

[42] *Cambro-Britons:* probably Humphrey Lloyd (d. 1568), writer on Cambria, and John Williams, goldsmith to James I and a friend of Drayton's, who are addressed in the *Poly-Olbion*. See *Works,* IV (1933), vii, and V (1941). 148, 230.

[43] *Agincourt:* The battle, fought in 1415, is also the subject of the fourth act of Shakespeare's *Henry V*. Holinshed's *Chronicle* is Drayton's main source together with earlier ballads.

[44] *King Harry:* Henry V (*reg.* 1413–1422).

The Duke of York so dread
The eager vaward [45] led;
With the main Henry sped
  Amongst his henchmen.
Excester [46] had the rear,
A braver man not there,
Oh Lord, how hot they were
  On the false Frenchmen!

They now to fight are gone,
Armor on armor shone,
Drum now to drum did groan,
  To hear was wonder,
That with cries they make
The very earth did shake,
Trumpet to trumpet spake,
  Thunder to thunder.

Well it thine age became,
Oh noble Erpingham,[47]
Which didst the signal aim
  To our hid forces;
When from a meadow by,
Like a storm suddenly,
The English archery
  Stuck the French horses.

With Spanish yew so strong,
Arrows a cloth-yard long,
That like to serpents stung,
  Piercing the weather;
None from his fellow starts,
But playing manly parts,
And like true English hearts,
  Stuck close together.

When down their bows they threw,
And forth their bilboes [48] drew,
And on the French they flew,
  Not one was tardy;
Arms were from shoulders sent,
Scalps to the teeth were rent,
Down the French peasants went;
  Our men were hardy.

This while our noble King,
His broad sword brandishing,
Down the French host did ding,
  As to o'erwhelm it;
And many a deep wound lent,
His arms with blood besprent,
And many a cruel dent
  Bruised his helmet.

Gloster,[49] that Duke so good,
Next of the royal blood,
For famous England stood
  With his brave brother;
Clarence, in steel so bright,
Though but a maiden knight,
Yet in that furious fight,
  Scarce such another.

Warwick in blood did wade,
Oxford the foe invade,
And cruel slaughter made,
  Still as they ran up;
Suffolk his ax did ply,
Beaumont and Willoughby
Bare them right doughtily,
  Ferrers and Fanhope.

Upon Saint Crispin's day [50]
Fought was this noble fray,
Which fame did not delay
  To England to carry;
Oh, when shall English men
With such acts fill a pen,
Or England breed again
  Such a King Harry?

---

[45] *vaward:* vanward.

[46] *Excester:* Exeter.

[47] *Erpingham:* Sir Thomas Erpingham, "an old knight . . . a man of great experience in the warre, with a warder in his hand" (according to Holinshed), had the honor of beginning the battle.

[48] *bilboes:* swords, rapiers (from Bilboa in Spain).

[49] *Gloster:* Humphrey, Duke of Gloucester, brother to Henry V. Drayton errs in making him senior to Thomas, Duke of Clarence.

[50] *Saint Crispin's day:* October 25, 1415.

To His Rival

Her loved I most,
By thee that's lost,
Though she were won with leisure;
She was my gain,
But to my pain,
Thou spoil'st me of my treasure.

The ship full fraught
With gold, far sought,
Though ne'er so wisely helmed
May suffer wrack
In sailing back,
By tempest overwhelmed.

But she, good sir,
Did not prefer
You, for that I was ranging;
But for that she
Found faith in me
And she loved to be changing.

Therefore boast not
Your happy lot,
Be silent now you have her;
The time I knew
She slighted you,
When I was in her favor.

None stands so fast,
But may be cast
By Fortune, and disgraced:
Once I did wear
Her garter there,
Where you her glove have placed.

I had the vow
That thou hast now,
And glances to discover
Her love to me;
And she to thee
Reads but old lessons over.

She hath no smile
That can beguile,
But as my thought I know it;
Yea, to a hair,
Both when and where,
And how she will bestow it.

What now is thine
Was only mine,
And first to me was given;
Thou laugh'st at me,
I laugh at thee,
And thus we two are even.

But I'll not mourn,
But stay my turn,
The wind may come about, sir;
And once again
May bring me in,
And help to bear you out, sir.

FROM

POLY-OLBION

(1612)

THE THIRTEENTH SONG

The Argument

This song our shire of Warwick sounds;
Revives old Arden's ancient bounds.

Through many shapes the Muse here roves;
Now sporting in those shady groves,
The tunes of birds oft stays to hear;
Then, finding herds of lusty deer,
She huntress-like the hart pursues;
And like a hermit walks, to choose
The simples everywhere that grow;
Comes Anker's glory next to show,
Tells Guy of Warwick's famous deeds;
To th' vale of Red-horse then proceeds,
To play her part the rest among;
There shutteth up her thirteenth song.

Upon the Midlands now th' industrious muse doth fall,
That shire which we the heart of England well may call,
As she herself extends (the midst which is decreed)
Betwixt St. Michael's Mount and Berwick-bord'ring Tweed,
Brave Warwick, that abroad so long advanced her bear,[51]
By her illustrious earls renowned everywhere,
Above her neighboring shires which always bore her head.
  My native country then, which so brave spirits hast bred,
If there be virtue yet remaining in thy earth,
Or any good of thine thou breath'dst into my birth,
Accept it as thine own whilst now I sing of thee,
Of all thy later brood th' unworthiest though I be.
  Muse, first of Arden tell, whose footsteps yet are found
In her rough woodlands, more than any other ground
That mighty Arden held even in her height of pride,
Her one hand touching Trent, the other Severn's side.
  The very sound of these the wood nymphs doth awake,
When thus of her own self the ancient forest spake:
  My many goodly sites when first I came to show,
Here opened I the way to mine own overthrow;
For when the world found out the fitness of my soil,
The gripple [52] wretch began immediately to spoil
My tall and goodly woods, and did my grounds inclose,
By which in little time my bounds I came to lose.
  When Britain first her fields with villages had filled,
Her people waxing still and wanting where to build,
They oft dislodged the hart and set their houses where
He in the broom and brakes had long time made his lair.
Of all the forests here within this mighty isle,
If those old Britons then me sovereign did instyle,

[51] *bear:* Selden's annotation is: "The ancient Coat of that Earldome."

[52] *gripple:* greedy.

I needs must be the great'st, for greatness 'tis alone
That gives our kind the place, else were there many a one
For pleasantness of shade that far doth me excel.
But of our forests' kind the quality to tell,
We equally partake with woodland as with plain,
Alike with hill and dale, and every day maintain
The sundry kinds of beasts upon our copious wastes
That men for profit breed, as well as those of chase.
  Here Arden of herself ceased any more to show,
And with her sylvan joys the muse along doth go.
  When Phoebus lifts his head out of the winter's wave,
No sooner doth the earth her flowery bosom brave,
At such time as the year brings on the pleasant spring,
But Hunts-up [53] to the morn the feathered sylvans sing,
And in the lower grove, as on the rising knoll,
Upon the highest spray of every mounting pole,
Those quiristers are perched with many a speckled breast.
Then from her burnished gate the goodly glitt'ring east
Gilds every lofty top, which late the humorous night
Bespangled had with pearl to please the morning's sight;
On which the mirthful choirs with their clear open throats
Unto the joyful morn so strain their warbling notes
That hills and valleys ring, and even the echoing air
Seems all composed of sounds, about them everywhere.
The throstle, with shrill sharps, as purposely he song
T' awake the lustless sun, or chiding that so long
He was in coming forth that should the thickets thrill;
The woosell [54] near at hand, that hath a golden bill,
As nature him had marked of purpose t' let us see
That from all other birds his tunes should different be;
For with their vocal sounds they sing to pleasant May.
Upon his dulcet pipe the merle [55] doth only play;
When in the lower brake the nightingale hard by
In such lamenting strains the joyful hours doth ply,
As though the other birds she to her tunes would draw;
And but that nature, by her all-constraining law,
Each bird to her own kind this season doth invite,
They else, alone to hear that charmer of the night
(The more to use their ears) their voices sure would spare,
That moduleth her tunes so admirably rare,
As man to set in parts [56] at first had learned of her.

---

[53] *Hunts-up:* an early morning song.

[54] *woosell:* ouzel. See Shakespeare's song from *Midsummer Night's Dream,* III, i, 128.

[55] *merle:* European blackbird (Latin: *merula*). Marginal note: "Of all Birds, only the Blackbird whistleth."

[56] *to set in parts:* to compose part songs.

To Philomel the next, the linnet we prefer,
And by that warbling bird the wood lark place we then,
The red sparrow, the nope,[57] the redbreast, and the wren,
The yellowpate, which though she hurt the blooming tree,
Yet scarce hath any bird a finer pipe than she;
And of these chanting fowls the goldfinch not behind,
That hath so many sorts descending from her kind.
The tydie [58] for her notes as delicate as they,
The laughing hecco,[59] then the counterfeiting jay,
The softer with the shrill (some hid among the leaves,
Some in the taller trees, some in the lower greaves),[60]
Thus sing away the morn, until the mounting sun
Through thick exhaled fogs his golden head hath run,
And through the twisted tops of our close covert creeps
To kiss the gentle shade, this while that sweetly sleeps.
And near to these our thicks,[61] the wild and frightful herds,
Not hearing other noise but this of chattering birds,
Feed fairly on the lands; both sorts of seasoned deer,—
Here walk the stately red, the freckled fallow there;
The bucks and lusty stags amongst the rascals [62] strewed,
As sometime gallant spirits amongst the multitude.

. . . .[63]

To forests that belongs, but yet this is not all:
With solitude what sorts that here's not wondrous rife?
Whereas the hermit leads a sweet retired life,
From villages replete with ragg'd and sweating clowns,
And from the loathsome airs of smoky citied towns.
Suppose 'twixt noon and night the sun his halfway wrought,
The shadows to be large by his descending brought,
Who with a fervent eye looks through the twiring [64] glades
And his dispersed rays commixeth with the shades,
Exhaling the milch dew, which there had tarried long
And on the ranker grass till past the noon-stead hong,
Whenas the hermit comes out of his homely cell,
Where from all rude resort he happily doth dwell;
Who in the strength of youth a man-at-arms hath been,
Or one who of this world the vileness having seen,
Retires him from it quite, and with a constant mind
Man's beastliness so loathes, that, flying human kind,

---

[57] *nope:* bullfinch (Warwickshire dialect).

[58] *tydie:* tidy, the golden-crested wren (?) or blue titmouse (?).

[59] *hecco:* woodpecker.

[60] *greaves:* branches.

[61] *thicks:* thickets.

[62] *rascals:* lean deer.

[63] 69 lines omitted here describe the hunting of the hart.

[64] *twiring:* winking, peeping, perhaps of the light in the glades.

The black and darksome nights, the bright and gladsome days
Indifferent are to him, his hope on God that stays.
Each little village yields his short and homely fare;
To gather wind-fall'n sticks his great'st and only care,
Which every aged tree still yieldeth to his fire.
  This man that is alone a king in his desire,
By no proud ignorant lord is basely overawed,
Nor his false praise affects who, grossly being clawed,
Stands like an itchy moyle;[65] nor of a pin he weighs
What fools abused kings and humorous ladies raise.
His free and noble thought ne'er envies at the grace
That oftentimes is given unto a bawd most base,
Nor stirs it him to think on the impostor vile
Who seeming what he's not, doth sensually beguile
The sottish purblind world; but absolutely free,
His happy time he spends the works of God to see
In those so sundry herbs which there in plenty grow,
Whose sundry strange effects he only seeks to know.
And in a little maund, being made of osiers[66] small,
Which serveth him to do full many a thing withal,
He very choicely sorts his simples got abroad.

. . . . . .[67]

  But from our hermit here the muse we must enforce,
And zealously proceed in our intended course:
How Arden of her rills and riverets doth dispose;
By Alcester how Alne to Arrow eas'ly flows,
And mildly being mixed, to Avon hold their way;
And likewise toward the north, how lovely tripping Rhea
T' attend the lustier Tame is from her fountain sent;
So little Cole and Blythe go on with him to Trent;
His Tamworth at the last he in his way doth win,
There playing him awhile till Anker should come in,
Which trifleth 'twixt her banks, observing state, so slow
As though into his arms she scorned herself to throw;
Yet Arden willed her Tame to serve her on his knee,
For by that nymph alone they both should honored be.
The forest so much fall'n from what she was before,
That to her former height fate could her not restore,
Though oft in her behalf the genius of the land
Importuned the heavens with an auspicious hand.

---

[65] *moyle:* Drayton's spelling of the obsolete "moil," meaning a cow without horns.

[66] *maund:* hand basket; *osiers:* pliable twigs.

[67] 44 lines, describing the various herbs, plants, and simples, are omitted here.

Yet granted at the last, the aged nymph to grace,
They by a lady's [68] birth would more renown that place
Than if her woods their heads above the hills should seat;
And for that purpose first made Coventry so great
(A poor thatched village then, or scarcely none at all,
That could not once have dreamed of her now stately wall),
And thither wisely brought that goodly virgin band,
Th' eleven thousand maids,[69] chaste Ursula's command,
Whom then the Briton kings gave her full power to press,
For matches to their friends in Brittany the less.
At whose departure thence, each by her just bequest
Some special virtue gave, ordaining it to rest
With one of their own sex, that there her birth should have,
Till fullness of the time which fate did choicely save
Until the Saxons' reign, when Coventry at length
From her small mean regard recovered state and strength,
By Leofric, her lord, yet in base bondage held,
The people from her marts by tollage who expelled;
Whose duchess,[70] which desired this tribute to release,
Their freedom often begged. The duke, to make her cease,
Told her that if she would his loss so far enforce,
His will was she should ride stark nak'd upon a horse
By daylight through the street; which certainly he thought
In her heroic breast so deeply would have wrought,
That in her former suit she would have left to deal.
But that most princely dame, as one devoured with zeal,
Went on, and by that mean the city clearly freed.

. . . .[71]

But whilst about this tale smooth Anker trifling stays,
Unto the lustier Tame as loath to come her ways,
The flood entreats her thus: Dear brook, why dost thou wrong
Our mutual love so much, and tediously prolong
Our mirthful marriage hour, for which I still prepare?
Haste to my broader banks, my joy and only care.
For as of all my floods thou art the first in fame,
When frankly thou shalt yield thine honor to my name,
I will protect thy state; then do not wrong thy kind.
What pleasure hath the world that here thou mayst not find? [72]

---

[68] *lady's:* Anne Goodere's.

[69] *eleven thousand maids:* St. Ursula's virgins.

[70] *duchess:* Godiva.

[71] Here are omitted 20 lines on the names Godiva, Goodere, Ankor, Arden, Anne, etc.

[72] The remaining 116 lines of the song describe the rest of the landscape of the shire and end with a eulogy of the Vale of Redhorse.

NYMPHIDIA, THE COURT OF FAIRY

Old Chaucer doth of Thopas tell,
Mad Rabelais of Pantagruel,
A latter third of Dowsabell,
With such poor trifles playing;
Others the like have labored at
Some of this thing, and some of that,
And many of they know not what,
But that they must be saying.

Another sort there be that will
Be talking of the Fairies still,
Nor ever can they have their fill,
As they were wedded to them;
No tales of them their thirst can slake,
So much delight therein they take,
And some strange thing they fain would make,
Knew they the way to do them.

Then since no Muse hath been so bold,
Or of the later, or the old,
Those elvish secrets to unfold
Which lie from others' reading,
My active Muse to light shall bring
The court of that proud Fairy King,
And tell there of the reveling;
Jove prosper my proceeding.

And thou, Nymphidia,[73] gentle fay,
Which meeting me upon the way
These secrets didst to me bewray,
Which I now am in telling;
My pretty light fantastic maid,
I here invoke thee to my aid,
That I may speak what thou hast said,
In numbers smoothly swelling.

---

[73] *Nymphidia:* from a Greek adjective meaning *bridal.*

This palace standeth in the air,
By necromancy placed there,
That it no tempests needs to fear,
Which way soe'er it blow it.
And somewhat southward toward the noon,
Whence lies a way up to the moon,
And thence the Fairy can as soon
Pass to the earth below it.

The walls of spiders' legs are made,
Well mortised and finely laid;
He was the master of his trade
It curiously that builded;
The windows of the eyes of cats,
And for the roof, instead of slats,
Is covered with the skins of bats,
With moonshine that are gilded.

Hence Oberon him sport to make
(Their rest when weary mortals take,
And none but only fairies wake)
Descendeth for his pleasure.
And Mab his merry queen by night
Bestrides young folks that lie upright,
In elder times the Mare that hight,
Which plagues them out of measure.

Hence shadows, seeming idle shapes
Of little frisking elves and apes
To earth do make their wanton 'scapes,
As hope of pastime hastes them,
Which maids think on the hearth they see
When fires well-near consumed be,
There dancing heys by two and three,
Just as their fancy casts them.

These make our girls their sluttery rue,
By pinching them both black and blue,
And put a penny in their shoe
The house for cleanly sweeping;
And in their courses make that round,
In meadows and in marshes found,
Of them so called the Fairy ground,
Of which they have the keeping.

These when a child haps to be got
Which after proves an idiot,
When folk perceive it thriveth not,
The fault therein to smother
Some silly doting brainless calf
That understands things by the half
Say that the fairy left this aufe [74]
And took away the other.

But listen and I shall you tell
A chance in Fairy that befell,
Which certainly may please some well
In love and arms delighting;
Of Oberon that jealous grew
Of one of his own Fairy crew,
Too well, he feared, his queen that knew,
His love but ill requiting.

Pigwiggen was this Fairy knight,
One wondrous gracious in the sight
Of fair Queen Mab, which day and night
He amorously observed;
Which made King Oberon suspect
His service took too good effect,
His sauciness and often checked
And could have wished him starved.

Pigwiggen gladly would commend
Some token to Queen Mab to send,
If sea, or land, could aught him lend
Were worthy of her wearing;
At length this lover doth devise
A bracelet made of emmet's [75] eyes,
A thing he thought that she would prize,
No whit her state impairing,

And to the queen a letter writes,
Which he most curiously endites,
Conjuring her by all the rites
Of love, she would be pleased
To meet him, her true servant, where
They might without suspect or fear
Themselves to one another clear
And have their poor hearts eased.

[74] *aufe:* an elf's child.

[75] *emmets':* ants'.

"At midnight the appointed hour,
And for the queen a fitting bower"
Quoth he, "is that fair cowslip flower
On Hipcut Hill that groweth;
In all your train there's not a fay
That ever went to gather May
But she hath made it in her way,
The tallest there that groweth."

When by Tom Thumb, a Fairy page,
He sent it and doth him engage
By promise of a mighty wage
It secretly to carry;
Which done, the queen her maids doth call
And bids them to be ready all;
She would go see her summer hall,
She could no longer tarry.

Her chariot ready straight is made,
Each thing therein is fitting laid,
That she by nothing might be stayed,
For naught must her be letting;
Four nimble gnats the horses were,
Their harnesses of gossamer,
Fly Cranion [76] her charioteer
Upon the coach-box getting.

Her chariot of a snail's fine shell
Which for the colors did excel,
The fair Queen Mab becoming well
So lively was the limning;
The seat, the soft wool of the bee;
The cover, gallantly to see,
The wing of a pied butterfly,
I trow 'twas simple trimming.

The wheels composed of crickets' bones
And daintily made for the nonce,
For fear of rattling on the stones
With thistledown they shod it;
For all her maidens much did fear
If Oberon had chanced to hear
That Mab his queen should have been there
He would not have abode it.

[76] *Cranion:* daddy long-legs.

She mounts her chariot with a trice,
Nor would she stay for no advice
Until her maids that were so nice
To wait on her were fitted,
But ran herself away alone,
Which when they heard, there was not one
But hasted after to be gone
As she had been diswitted.

Hop, and Mop, and Drop so clear,
Pip, and Trip, and Skip that were
To Mab their sovereign ever dear,
Her special maids of honor;
Fib and Tib, and Pink and Pin,
Tick and Quick, and Jill and Jin,
Tit and Nit, and Wap and Win,
The train that wait upon her.

Upon a grasshopper they got,
And what with amble and with trot,
For hedge nor ditch they spared not
But after her they hie them.
A cobweb over them they throw
To shield the wind if it should blow;
Themselves they wisely could bestow
Lest any should espy them.

But let us leave Queen Mab a while,
Through many a gate, o'er many a stile,
That now had gotten by this wile,
Her dear Pigwiggen kissing,
And tell how Oberon doth fare,
Who grew as mad as any hare
When he had sought each place with care
And found his queen was missing.

By grisly Pluto he doth swear,
He rent his clothes and tore his hair,
And as he runneth here and there
An acorn cup he greeteth,
Which soon he taketh by the stalk,
About his head he lets it walk,
Nor doth he any creature balk,[77]
But lays on all he meeteth.

[77] *balk:* avoid in passing.

The Tuscan poet[78] doth advance
The frantic paladin of France,
And those more ancient do enhance
Alcides[79] in his fury,
And others Ajax Telamon;[80]
But to this time there hath been none
So bedlam as our Oberon,
Of which I dare assure you.

And first encountering with a wasp,
He in his arms the fly doth clasp
As though his breath he forth would grasp,
Him for Pigwiggen taking;
"Where is my wife, thou rogue?" quoth he,
"Pigwiggen, she is come to thee;
Restore her, or thou diest by me!"
Whereat, the poor wasp quaking

Cries, "Oberon, great Fairy King,
Content thee, I am no such thing;
I am a wasp, behold my sting!"
At which the Fairy started;
When soon away the wasp doth go;
Poor wretch was never frighted so,
He thought his wings were much too slow,
O'erjoyed they so were parted.

He next upon a glow-worm light,
(You must suppose it now was night)
Which, for her hinder part was bright,
He took to be a devil,
And furiously her doth assail
For carrying fire in her tail;
He thrashed her rough coat with his flail;
The mad king feared no evil.

"Oh," quoth the glow-worm, "hold thy hand,
Thou puissant king of Fairyland,
Thy mighty strokes who may withstand;
Hold, or of life despair I!"
Together then herself doth roll,
And tumbling down into a hole
She seemed as black as any coal
Which vexed away the Fairy.

---

[78] *Tuscan poet:* Ariosto, in his *Orlando Furioso.*
[79] *Alcides:* Hercules, hero of tragedies by Sophocles and Seneca.
[80] *Ajax Telamon:* hero of a tragedy by Sophocles.

From thence he ran into a hive;
Amongst the bees he letteth drive,
And down their combs begins to rive,
All likely to have spoiled;
Which with their wax his face besmeared
And with their honey daubed his beard;
It would have made a man afeared
To see how he was moiled.[81]

A new adventure him betides;
He met an ant, which he bestrides
And post thereon away he rides
Which with his haste doth stumble
And came full over on her snout;
Her heels so threw the dirt about
For she by no means could get out
But over him doth tumble,

And being in this piteous case
And all beslurried,[82] head and face,
On runs he in this wild goose chase,
As here and there he rambles,
Half blind, against a molehill hit
And for a mountain taking it
For all he was out of his wit,
Yet to the top he scrambles.

And being gotten to the top
Yet there himself he could not stop
But down on th'other side doth chop,
And to the foot came rumbling,
So that the grubs therein that bred,
Hearing such turmoil overhead,
Thought surely they had all been dead,
So fearful was the jumbling.

And falling down into a lake
Which him up to the neck doth take,
His fury somewhat it doth slake;
He calleth for a ferry;
Where you may some recovery note:
What was his club he made his boat,
And in his oaken cup doth float
As safe as in a wherry.

[81] *moiled:* bedaubed.

[82] *beslurried:* dirtied.

Men talk of the adventures strange
Of Don Quixote, and of their change,
Through which he armed oft did range,
Of Sancho Panza's travel;
But should a man tell every thing
Done by this frantic Fairy King
And them in lofty numbers sing,
It well his wits might gravel.

Scarce set on shore but therewithal
He meeteth Puck, which most men call
Hobgoblin, and on him doth fall
With words from frenzy spoken.
"Ho, Ho!" quoth Hob, "God save thy grace,
Who dressed thee in this piteous case?
He thus that spoiled my sovereign's face,
I would his neck were broken."

This Puck seems but a dreaming dolt,
Still walking like a ragged colt,
And oft out of a bush doth bolt
Of purpose to deceive us,
And leading us makes us to stray
Long winter's nights out of the way,
And when we stick in mire and clay,
Hob doth with laughter leave us.

"Dear Puck," quoth he, "my wife is gone;
As e'er thou lov'st King Oberon,
Let everything but this alone,
With vengeance and pursue her;
Bring her to me, alive or dead,
Or that vile thief Pigwiggen's head;
That villain hath defiled my bed;
He to this folly drew her."

Quoth Puck, "My liege, I'll never lin,
But I will thorough thick and thin,
Until at length I bring her in;
My dearest lord, ne'er doubt it;
Thorough brake, thorough brier,
Thorough muck, thorough mire,
Thorough water, thorough fire,
And thus goes Puck about it."

This thing Nymphidia overheard,
That on this mad king had a guard,
Not doubting of a great reward
For first this business broaching;
And through the air away doth go
Swift as an arrow from the bow,
To let her sovereign Mab to know
What peril was approaching.

The Queen, bound with love's powerful'st charm,
Sat with Pigwiggen arm in arm;
Her merry maids that thought no harm
About the room were skipping;
A humble-bee, their minstrel, played
Upon his hautboy; every maid
Fit for this revels was arrayed,
The hornpipe neatly tripping.

In comes Nymphidia and doth cry,
"My sovereign, for your safety, fly,
For there is danger but too nigh,
I posted to forewarn you;
The King hath sent Hobgoblin out
To seek you all the fields about,
And of your safety you may doubt,
If he but once discern you!"

When like an uproar in a town
Before them everything went down,
Some tore a ruff and some a gown,
'Gainst one another justling;
They flew about like chaff i'the wind;
For haste some left their masks behind;
Some could not stay their gloves to find;
There never was such bustling.

Forth ran they by a secret way
Into a brake that near them lay;
Yet much they doubted there to stay,
Lest Hob should hap to find them;
He had a sharp and piercing sight,
All one to him the day and night,
And therefore were resolved by flight
To leave this place behind them.

At length one chanced to find a nut
In th'end of which a hole was cut,
Which lay upon a hazel root,
There scattered by a squirrel
Which out the kernel gotten had,
When quoth this fay, "Dear Queen, be glad;
Let Oberon be ne'er so mad,
I'll set you safe from peril.

"Come all into this nut," quoth she,
"Come closely in; be ruled by me;
Each one may here a choser be;
For room ye need not wrastle,
Nor need ye be together heapt";
So one by one therein they crept
And lying down, they soundly slept,
As safe as in a castle.

Nymphidia that this while doth watch,
Perceived if Puck the queen should catch,
That he would be her over-match,
Of which she well bethought her;
Found it must be some powerful charm,
The Queen against him that must arm
Or surely he would do her harm,
For throughly he had sought her.

And listening if she aught could hear
That her might hinder or might fear,
But finding still the coast was clear,
Nor creature had descried her;
Each circumstance and having scanned,
She came thereby to understand
Puck would be with them out of hand,
When to her charms she hied her.

And first her fern seed doth bestow,
The kernel of the mistletoe,
And here and there, as Puck should go,
With terror to affright him,
She night-shade strews to work him ill,
Therewith her vervain and her dill,
That hindreth witches of their will,
Of purpose to despite him.

Then sprinkles she the juice of rue,
That groweth underneath the yew,
With nine drops of the midnight dew
From lunary distilling;
The moldwarp's brain mixed therewithal,
And with the same the pismire's gall,
For she in nothing short would fall,
The Fairy was so willing.

Then thrice under a briar doth creep,
Which at both ends was rooted deep,
And over it three times she leap,
Her magic much availing;
Then on Proserpina doth call,
And so upon her spell doth fall
Which here to you repeat I shall,
Not in one tittle failing:

By the croaking of the frog,
By the howling of the dog,
By the crying of the hog,
Against the storm arising;
By the evening curfew bell,
By the doleful dying knell,
Oh, let this my direful spell,
Hob, hinder thy surprising.

By the mandrake's dreadful groans,
By the lubrican's [83] sad moans,
By the noise of dead men's bones
In charnel houses rattling;
By the hissing of the snake,
The rustling of the fire-drake,
I charge thee thou this place forsake,
Nor of Queen Mab be prattling.

By the whirlwind's hollow sound,
By the thunder's dreadful stound,
Yells of spirits underground,
I charge thee not to fear us;
By the screech-owl's dismal note,
By the black night-raven's throat,
I charge thee, Hob, to tear thy coat
With thorns if thou come near us.

[83] *lubrican:* leprechaun.

Her spell thus spoke, she stepped aside
And in a chink herself doth hide
To see thereof what would betide,
For she doth only mind him;
When presently she Puck espies,
And well she marked his gloating eyes
How under every leaf he pries
In seeking still to find them.

But once the circle got within,
The charms to work do straight begin,
And he was caught as in a gin;
For as he thus was busy,
A pain he in his headpiece feels,
Against a stubbed tree he reels
And up went poor Hobgoblin's heels,
Alas, his brain was dizzy.

At length upon his feet he gets;
Hobgoblin fumes, Hobgoblin frets,
And, as again he forward sets
And through the bushes scrambles,
A stump doth trip him in his pace,
Down comes poor Hob upon his face
And lamentably tore his case
Amongst the briars and brambles.

"A plague upon Queen Mab," quoth he,
And all her maids, wheree'er they be!
I think the devil guided me
To see her so provoked."
Where, stumbling at a piece of wood,
He fell into a ditch of mud,
Where to the very chin he stood
In danger to be choked.

Now, worse than e'er he was before,
Poor Puck doth yell, poor Puck doth roar;
That waked Queen Mab, who doubted sore
Some treason hath been wrought her,
Until Nymphidia told the queen
What she had done, what she had seen,
Who then had well-near cracked her spleen
With very extreme laughter.

But leave we Hob to clamber out,
Queen Mab and all her Fairy rout,
And come again to have a bout
With Oberon yet madding;
And with Pigwiggen now distraught,
Who was much troubled in his thought,
That he so long the queen had sought
And through the fields was gadding.

And as he runs he still doth cry,
"King Oberon, I thee defy
And dare thee here in arms to try
For my dear Lady's honor,
For that she is a queen right good,
In whose defense I'll shed my blood,
And that thou in this jealous mood
Hast layed this slander on her."

And quickly arms him for the field,
A little cockle-shell his shield,
Which he could very bravely wield
Yet could it not be pierced;
His spear, a bent[84] both stiff and strong
And well-near of two inches long;
The pile[85] was of a horse-fly's tongue,
Whose sharpness naught reversed.

And puts him on a coat of mail,
Which was of a fish's scale,
That when his foe should him assail,
No point should be prevailing;
His rapier was a hornet's sting;
It was a very dangerous thing,
For, if he chanced to hurt the King,
It would be long in healing.

His helmet was a beetle's head,
Most horrible and full of dread,
That able was to strike one dead,
Yet did it well become him;
And, for a plume, a horse's hair,
Which, being tossed with the air
Had force to strike his foe with fear
And turn his weapon from him.

[84] *bent:* blade of grass.

[85] *pile:* point.

Himself he on an earwig set,
Yet scarce he on his back could get,
So oft and high he did corvet
Ere he himself could settle;
He made him turn and stop and bound,
To gallop, and to trot the round;
He scarce could stand on any ground
He was so full of mettle.

When soon he met with Thomalin,
One that a valiant knight had been,
And to King Oberon of kin.
Quoth he, "Thou manly Fairy,
Tell Oberon I come prepared,
Then bid him stand upon his guard;
This hand his baseness shall reward,
Let him be ne'er so wary.

"Say to him thus, that I defy
His slanders and his infamy,
And, as a mortal enemy
Do publicly proclaim him;
Withal, that if I had mine own,
He should not wear the Fairy crown,
But with a vengeance should come down,
Nor we a king should name him."

This Thomalin could not abide,
To hear his sovereign vilified,
But to the Fairy court him hied;
Full furiously he posted
With everything Pigwiggen said,
How title to the crown he laid
And in what arms he was arrayed,
As how himself he boasted.

'Twixt head and foot, from point to point
He told th'arming of each joint,
In every piece, how neat and quaint,
For Thomalin could do it;
How fair he sat, how sure he rid,
As of the courser he bestrid,
How managed and how well he did;
The king, which listened to it,

Quoth he, "Go, Thomalin, with speed,
Provide me arms, provide my steed
And everything that I shall need;
By thee I will be guided;
To straight account call thou thy wit,
See there be wanting not a whit
In everything see thou me fit,
Just as my foe's provided."

Soon flew this news through Fairyland,
Which gave Queen Mab to understand
The combat that was then in hand
Betwixt those men so mighty;
Which greatly she began to rue,
Perceiving that all Fairy knew
The first occasion from her grew
Of these affairs so weighty.

Wherefore, attended with her maids,
Through fogs and mists and damps she wades
To Proserpine, the Queen of Shades
To treat that it would please her
The cause into her hands to take
For ancient love and friendship's sake,
And soon thereof an end to make,
Which of much care would ease her.

A while there let we Mab alone,
And come we to King Oberon,
Who, armed to meet his foe, is gone
For proud Pigwiggen crying;
Who sought the Fairy king as fast,
And had so well his journies cast,
That he arrived at the last,
His puissant foe espying.

Stout Thomalin came with the king;
Tom Thumb doth on Pigwiggen bring,
That perfect were in everything
To single fights belonging;
And therefore they themselves engage
To see them exercise their rage
With fair and comely equipage,
Not one the other wronging.

So like in arms these champions were
As they had been a very pair,
So that a man would almost swear
That either had been either;
Their furious steeds began to neigh
That they were heard a mighty way;
Their staves upon their rests they lay;
Yet, e'er they flew together,

Their seconds minister an oath
Which was indifferent to them both
That on their knightly faith and troth
No magic them supplied,
And sought them that they had no charms
Wherewith to work each other's harms,
But came with simple open arms
To have their causes tried.

Together furiously they ran,
That to the ground came horse and man;
The blood out of their helmets span,
So sharp were their encounters.
And though they to the earth were thrown,
Yet quickly they regained their own;
Such nimbleness was never shown,
They were two gallant mounters.

When in a second course again
They forward came with might and main,
Yet which had better of the twain
The seconds could not judge yet;
Their shields were into pieces cleft,
Their helmets from their heads were reft,
And to defend them nothing left
These champions would not budge yet.

Away from them their staves they threw;
Their cruel swords they quickly drew,
And freshly they the fight renew,
That every stroke redoubled;
Which made Proserpina take heed
And make to them the greater speed,
For fear lest they too much should bleed,
Which wondrously her troubled.

When to th'infernal Styx she goes,
She takes the fogs from thence that rose,
And in a bag doth them enclose;
When well she had them blended,
She hies her then to Lethe spring,
A bottle and thereof doth bring
Wherewith she meant to work the thing
Which only she intended.

Now Proserpine with Mab is gone
Unto the place where Oberon
And proud Pigwiggen, one to one,
Both to be slain were likely;
And there themselves they closely hide
Because they would not be espied,
For Proserpine meant to decide
The matter very quickly,

And suddenly unties the poke
Which out of it sent such a smoke
As ready was them all to choke,
So grievous was the pother;
So that the knights each other lost
And stood as still as any post,
Tom Thumb nor Thomalin could boast
Themselves of any other.

But when the mist gan somewhat cease,
Proserpina commandeth peace,
And that a while they should release
Each other of their peril;
"Which here," quoth she, "I do proclaim
To all, in dreadful Pluto's name,
That, as ye will eschew his blame,
You let me hear the quarrel.

"But here yourselves you must engage
Somewhat to cool your spleenish rage;
Your grievous thirst and to assuage
That first you drink this liquor,
Which shall your understanding clear,
As plainly shall to you appear,
Those things from me that you shall hear,
Conceiving much the quicker."

This Lethe water, you must know,
The memory destroyeth so
That of our weal or of our woe
It all remembrance blotted;
Of it nor can you ever think;
For they no sooner took this drink
But naught into their brains could sink
Of what had them besotted.

King Oberon forgotten had
That he for jealousy ran mad,
But of his queen was wondrous glad
And asked how they came thither;
Pigwiggen likewise doth forget
That he Queen Mab had ever met,
Or that they were so hard beset
When they were found together.

Nor neither of them both had thought
That e'er they had each other sought,
Much less that they a combat fought,
But such a dream were loathing;
Tom Thumb had got a little sup,
And Thomalin scarce kissed the cup,
Yet had their brains so sure locked up,
That they remembered nothing.

Queen Mab and her light maids the while
Among themselves do closely smile
To see the king caught with this wile,
With one another jesting;
And to the Fairy court they went
With mickle joy and merriment,
Which thing was done with good intent,
And thus I left them feasting.

TO MY MOST DEARLY LOVED HENRY REYNOLDS,[86] ESQUIRE, OF POETS AND POESIE

My dearly loved friend, how oft have we
In winter evenings, meaning to be free,
To some well-chosen place used to retire;
And there, with moderate meat and wine and fire
Have passed the hours contentedly with chat,
Now talked of this, and then discoursed of that;
Spoke our own verses 'twixt ourselves, if not
Other men's lines which we by chance had got,
Or some stage pieces famous long before,
Of which your happy memory had store.
And I remember you much pleased were
Of those who lived long ago to hear
As well as of those of these latter times
Who have enriched our language with their rhymes,
And in succession, how still up they grew,
Which is the subject that I now pursue.
For, from my cradle, you must know that I
Was still inclined to noble poesy,
And when that once *Pueriles*[87] I had read,
And newly had my Cato construed,
In my small self I greatly marvelled then,
Amongst all other, what strange kind of men
These poets were; and, pleased with the name,
To my mild tutor merrily I came,
For I was then a proper goodly page,
Much like a pigmy, scarce ten years of age;
Clasping my slender arms about his thigh,
"Oh my dear master, cannot you," quoth I,
"Make me a poet? Do it, if you can,
And you shall see, I'll quickly be a man."
Who me thus answered smiling, "Boy," quoth he,
"If you'll not play the wag, but I may see
You ply your learning, I will shortly read
Some poets to you." Phoebus be my speed,
To't hard went I, when shortly he began,
And first read to me honest Mantuan,[88]

[86] Poet and critic, author of *Mythomystes* (1632).

[87] *Pueriles:* moral sayings in Latin, taught to beginners.

[88] *Mantuan: Baptista Spagnuoli* (1448–1516) whose Latin eclogues were read in school. Cf. *Love's Labour's Lost* IV, ii, 98–102.

Then Virgil's eclogues; being entered thus,
Methought I straight had mounted Pegasus
And in his full career could make him stop,
And bound upon Parnassus' bi-cleft top.
I scorned your ballad then, though it were done
And had for finis—William Elderton.[89]
But soft, in sporting with this childish jest,
I from my subject have too long digressed;
Then to the matter that we took in hand;
Jove and Apollo for the muses stand.
  That noble Chaucer, in those former times
Then first enriched our English with his rhymes,
And was the first of ours that ever brake
Into the Muses' treasure, and first spake
In weighty numbers, delving in the mine
Of perfect knowledge, which he could refine
And coin for current, and as much as then
The English language could express to men
He made it do, and by his wondrous skill
Gave us much light from his abundant quill.
  And honest Gower, who, in respect of him,
Had only sipped at Aganippe's brim,
And though in years this last was him before,
Yet fell he far short of the other's store.
  When after those, four ages, very near,
They with the muses which conversed, were
That princely Surrey, early in the time
Of the eighth Henry, who was then the prime
Of England's noble youth; with him there came
Wyatt, with reverence whom we still do name
Amongst our poets. Bryan [90] had a share
With the two former, which accompted are
That time's best makers, and the authors were
Of those small poems which the title bear
Of *Songs and Sonnets,* wherein oft they hit
On many dainty passages of wit.
  Gascoigne and Churchyard after them again
In the beginning of Eliza's reign
Accompted were great meterers many a day,
But not inspired with brave fire; had they
Lived but a little longer, they had seen
Their works before them to have buried been.
  Grave moral Spenser, after these, came on,

[89] *Elderton:* the most famous Elizabethan ballad-maker.

[90] *Bryan:* Sir Francis Bryan, courtier, translator and poet.

Than whom I am persuaded there was none
Since the blind bard his *Iliads* up did make,
Fitter a task like that to undertake:
To set down boldly, bravely to invent,
In all high knowledge, surely excellent.
 The noble Sidney with this last arose,
That Heroë for numbers and for prose,
That throughly paced our language as to show
The plenteous English hand in hand might go
With Greek and Latin, and did first reduce
Our tongue from Lyly's writing, then in use—
Talking of stones, stars, plants, of fishes, flies,
Playing with words and idle similes;
As th'English apes and very zanies be
Of everything that they do hear and see,
So, imitating his ridiculous tricks,
They spake and writ all like mere lunatics.
 Then Warner,[91] though his lines were not so trimmed,
Nor yet his poem so exactly limbed
And neatly jointed, but the critic may
Easily reprove him, yet thus let me say:
For my old friend, some passages there be
In him, which I protest have taken me
With almost wonder, so fine, clear and new
As yet they have been equalled by few.
 Neat Marlowe, bathed in the Thespian springs,
Had in him those brave translunary things
That the first poets had; his raptures were
All air and fire, which made his verses clear,
For that fine madness still he did retain
Which rightly should possess a poet's brain.
 And surely Nashe, though he a proser were,
A branch of laurel yet deserves to bear;
Sharply satiric was he, and that way
He went, since that his being, to this day
Few have attempted, and I surely think
Those words shall hardly be set down with ink
Shall scorch and blast, so as his could, where he
Would inflict vengeance; and be it said of thee,
Shakespeare, thou hadst as smooth a comic vein,
Fitting the sock, and in thy natural brain
As strong conception and as clear a rage
As any one that trafficked with the stage.
 Amongst these Samuel Daniel, whom if I

[91] *Warner:* William Warner (1558?–1609), author of *Albion's England* (1586).

May speak of, but to censure do deny,
Only have heard some wise men him rehearse
To be too much historian in verse;
His rhymes were smooth, his meters well did close,
But yet his manner better fitted prose.
Next these, learn'd Jonson in this list I bring,
Who had drunk deep of the Pierian spring,
Whose knowledge did him worthily prefer,
And long was lord here of the theater,
Who in opinion made our learn'd'st to stick
Whether in poems rightly dramatic
Strong Seneca or Plautus, he or they,
Should bear the buskin or the sock away.
Others again here lived in my days
That have of us deserved no less praise
For their translations than the daintiest wit
That on Parnassus thinks he high'st doth sit,
And for a chair may 'mongst the muses call
As the most curious maker of them all;
As reverent Chapman, who hath brought to us
Musaeus, Homer and Hesiodus
Out of the Greek, and by his skill hath reared
Them to that height and to our tongue endeared
That, were those poets at this day alive
To see their books thus with us to survive,
They would think, having neglected them so long,
They had been written in the English tongue.
  And Sylvester,[92] who from the French more weak
Made Bartas of his six days' labor speak
In natural English, who, had he there stayed
He had done well, and never have bewrayed
His own invention to have been so poor
Who still wrote less in striving to write more.
  Then dainty Sandys,[93] that hath to English done
Smooth, sliding Ovid, and hath made him run
With so much sweetness and unusual grace
As though the neatness of the English pace
Should tell the jetting Latin that it came
But slowly after, as though stiff and lame.
  So Scotland sent us hither, for our own
That man whose name I ever would have known
To stand by mine, that most ingenious knight,

[92] *Sylvester:* Joshua Sylvester (1563–1618), translator of DuBartas.

[93] *Sandys:* George Sandys, translator of Ovid (1621).

My Alexander,[94] to whom in his right
I want extremely, yet in speaking thus
I do but show the love that was 'twixt us,
And not his numbers which were brave and high,
So like his mind was his clear poesy,
And my dear Drummond,[95] to whom much I owe
For his much love, and proud I was to know
His poesy, for which two worthy men
I Menstry still shall love, and Hawthornden.
Then the two Beaumonts [96] and my Browne [97] arose,
My dear companions whom I freely chose
My bosom friends and in their several ways
Rightly born poets, and in these last days
Men of much note and no less nobler parts,
Such as have freely told to me their hearts
As I have mine to them. But if you shall
Say in your knowledge that these be not all
Have writ in numbers, be informed that I
Only myself to these few men do tie
Whose works oft printed, set on every post,
To public censure subject have been most;
For such whose poems, be they ne'er so rare,
In private chambers that encloistered are
And by transcription daintily must go,
As though the world unworthy were to know
Their rich composures,[98] let those men that keep
These wondrous relics in their judgment deep
And cry them up, let such pieces be
Spoke of by those that shall come after me;
I pass not for them, nor do mean to run
In quest of these that them applause have won
Upon our stages in these latter days
That are so many. Let them have their bays
That do deserve it; let those wits that haunt
Those public circuits, let them freely chaunt
Their fine composures and their praise pursue,
And so, my dear friend, for this time adieu.

[94] *Alexander:* Sir William Alexander of Menstry, Earl of Sterling (1567?–1640).

[95] *Drummond:* William Drummond of Hawthornden (1585–1649).

[96] *Beaumonts:* Sir John (1583–1627) and Francis the playwright (1584–1616).

[97] *Browne:* William (1591–1643?), pastoral poet.

[98] These lines are sometimes thought to refer to the poetry of Donne.

IDEA

TO THE READER OF THESE SONNETS[1]

INTO these loves who but for passion looks,
At this first sight here let him lay them by,
And seek elsewhere, in turning other books
Which better may his labor satisfy.
No farfetched sigh shall ever wound my breast,
Love from mine eye a tear shall never wring,
Nor in *Ah me's* my whining sonnets dressed;
A libertine, fantastically I sing.
My verse is the true image of my mind,
Ever in motion, still desiring change;
And as thus to variety inclined,
So in all humors sportively I range;
My muse is rightly of the English strain,
That cannot long one fashion entertain.

I[2]

LIKE an adventurous seafarer am I,
Who hath some long and dangerous voyage been,
And called to tell of his discovery,
How far he sailed, what countries he had seen;
Proceeding from the port whence he put forth,
Shows by his compass how his course he steered,
When east, when west, when south, and when by north,
As how the pole to every place was reared,
What capes he doubled, of what continent,
The gulfs and straits that strangely he had passed,
Where most becalmed, where with foul weather spent,
And on what rocks in peril to be cast—
Thus, in my love, time calls me to relate
My tedious travels and oft-varying fate.

[1] First found in 1599 ed. Our text of all Drayton's sonnets is taken from the collection of 1619.

[2] First included in 1619.

VI[3]

How many paltry, foolish, painted things,
That now in coaches trouble every street,
Shall be forgotten, whom no poet sings,
Ere they be well wrapped in their winding sheet!
Where I to thee eternity shall give,
When nothing else remaineth of these days,
And queens hereafter shall be glad to live
Upon the alms of thy superfluous praise.
Virgins and matrons reading these my rhymes
Shall be so much delighted with thy story
That they shall grieve they lived not in these times,
To have seen thee, their sex's only glory.
So shalt thou fly above the vulgar throng,
Still to survive in my immortal song.

VIII[4]

There's nothing grieves me but that age should haste
That in my days I may not see thee old;
That where those two clear, sparkling eyes are placed
Only two loopholes then I might behold.
That lovely arched, ivory, polished brow
Defaced with wrinkles that I might but see—
Thy dainty hair, so curled and crisped now
Like grizzled moss upon some aged tree;
Thy cheek, now flush with roses, sunk and lean;
Thy lips, with age as any wafer thin;
Thy pearly teeth out of thy head so clean,
That when thou feedst, thy nose shall touch thy chin.
These lines that now thou scornst, which should delight thee,
Then would I make thee read, but to despite thee.

---

[3] First included in 1619.

[4] First included in 1619.

IX[5]

As other men, so I myself do muse
Why in this sort I wrest invention so,
And why these giddy metaphors I use,
Leaving the path the greater part do go.
I will resolve you. I am lunatic,
And ever this in madmen you shall find:
What they last thought of, when the brain grew sick,
In most distraction they keep that in mind.
Thus talking idly in this bedlam fit,
Reason and I, you must conceive, are twain;
'Tis nine years now since first I lost my wit,
Bear with me, then, though troubled be my brain.
With diet and correction, men distraught
(Not too far past) may to their wits be brought.

XX[6]

An evil spirit, your beauty, haunts me still,
Wherewith, alas, I have been long possessed,
Which ceaseth not to tempt me to each ill,
Nor gives me once but one poor minute's rest;
In me it speaks, whether I sleep or wake,
And when by means to drive it out I try,
With greater torments then it me doth take,
And tortures me in most extremity;
Before my face it lays down my despairs,
And hastes me on unto a sudden death,
Now tempting me to drown myself in tears,
And then in sighing to give up my breath.
Thus am I still provoked to every evil
By this good wicked spirit, sweet angel devil.

[5] First included in 1602.

[6] First included in 1599.

XXXVII [7]

Dear, why should you command me to my rest,
When now the night doth summon all to sleep?
Methinks this time becometh lovers best;
Night was ordained together friends to keep.
How happy are all other living things,
Which though the day disjoin by several flight,
The quiet evening yet together brings,
And each returns unto his love at night!
Oh thou that art so courteous else to all,
Why shouldst thou, Night, abuse me only thus,
That every creature to his kind dost call,
And yet 'tis thou dost only sever us?
Well could I wish it would be ever day,
If when night comes you bid me go away.

XLIV [8]

Whilst thus my pen strives to eternize thee,
Age rules my lines with wrinkles in my face,
Where, in the map of all my misery,
Is modeled out the world of my disgrace;
Whilst in despite of tyrannizing times,
Medea-like I make thee young again,
Proudly thou scorn'st my world-outwearing rhymes,
And murther'st virtue with thy coy disdain.
And though in youth my youth untimely perish
To keep thee from oblivion and the grave,
Ensuing ages yet my rhymes shall cherish,
Where I, entombed, my better part shall save;
And though this earthly body fade and die,
My name shall mount upon eternity.

[7] First included in 1602.

[8] First included in 1599.

LXI[9]

SINCE there's no help, come let us kiss and part;
Nay, I have done, you get no more of me,
And I am glad, yea glad with all my heart
That thus so cleanly I myself can free;
Shake hands forever, cancel all our vows,
And when we meet at any time again,
Be it not seen in either of our brows
That we one jot of former love retain.
Now at the last gasp of love's latest breath,
When, his pulse failing, passion speechless lies,
When faith is kneeling by his bed of death,
And innocence is closing up his eyes,
Now if thou wouldst, when all have given him over,
From death to life thou mightst him yet recover.

[9] First included in 1619. Rossetti called this sonnet "almost the best in the language, if not quite."

Thomas Campion

1567–1620

THOMAS CAMPION, one of the most sensitive lyric poets of the Elizabethan or, indeed, any age, was a man of many talents. He wrote music as well as poetry, and was by turns a law student and a physician. As a young law student he began writing verse. Five of his poems appeared unsigned in Newman's surreptitious edition of Sidney's *Astrophel and Stella* in 1591. Ten years later he published, in collaboration with Philip Rossiter, *A Book of Airs* which contains his first work as a composer. He continued to publish his airs until 1617.

In 1602 he published a prose treatise, *Observations in the Art of English Poesie,* dealing with the question of rhyme and quantity in English verse. This knotty problem had bothered Sidney and Spenser as well as a host of minor poets and theorists; there are some horrible examples extant of Elizabethan attempts to write English quantitative verse according to classical rules. Campion saw that English has both quantity and accent, and that any completely satisfactory system of versification will have to take account of both. Because of his marvellously sensitive ear, and his devotion to classical models, Campion was able to succeed in demonstrating his theories by successful examples. In the whole period his only peer is Ben Jonson.

Because in his controversial pamphlet Campion had been scornful of rhyme, he was answered by Daniel, whose English loyalty would brook no attack on the practise of his countrymen. But as a matter of fact the issue was irrelevant. Campion, when he felt like it, could rhyme as smoothly as any. And in the control of his line length, the skillful modulation of vowel sounds, and the manipulation of a subtle but vivid imagery, he far surpassed those whom he looked down on as mere "rhymers."

BIBLIOGRAPHY: *Campion's Works,* ed. Percival Vivian, Oxford, 1909; T. MacDonagh, *Thomas Campion and the Art of English Poetry,* Dublin, 1913; M. W. Kastendieck, *England's Musical Poet: Thomas Campion,* New York, 1938; Campion's settings are reprinted in E. H. Fellowes, ed., *The English School of Lutenist Song-Writers* (Second Series), London, 1926. R. W. Beringer, "Campion's Share in *A Book of Airs,*" *PMLA,* LVIII (1943), 938–948; R. W. Short, "Metrical Theory and Practise of Campion," *PMLA,* LIX (1944), 1003–1018; H. M. Schueller, "Renaissance Forerunners of the Neoclassic Lyric," *MLN,* LXII (1947), 310–316; C. W. Peltz, "Thomas Campion, an Elizabethan Neoclassicist," *MLQ,* XI (1950), 3–6; Hallett Smith, *Elizabethan Poetry* (1952), 257–289.

FROM

RICHARD ALISON'S

AN HOUR'S RECREATION IN MUSIC

(1606)

WHAT if a day, or a month, or a year [1]
Crown thy delights with a thousand sweet contentings?
Cannot a chance of a night or an hour
Cross thy desires with as many sad tormentings?
    Fortune, honor, beauty, youth
    Are but blossoms dying;
    Wanton pleasure, doting love
    Are but shadows flying.
    All our joys are but toys,
    Idle thoughts deceiving;
    None have power of an hour
    In their lives' bereaving.

Earth's but a point to the world, and a man
Is but a point to the world's compared centure;
Shall then the point of a point be so vain
As to triumph in a sely point's adventure?
    All is hazard that we have,
    There is nothing biding;
    Days of pleasure are like streams
    Through fair meadows gliding.
    Weal and woe, time doth go,
    Time is never turning;
    Secret fates guide our states,
    Both in mirth and mourning.

---

[1] Though the authorship is in dispute, most scholars believe these verses to be Campion's. It became one of the most popular lyrics of the time and was circulated in longer versions as a broadside ballad. (See *The Shirburn Ballads,* ed. Clark, p. 238, *The Roxburghe Ballads,* ed. Chappell, I, 348.)

FROM

A BOOK OF AIRS

(1601)

I[2]

My sweetest Lesbia, let us live and love,
And though the sager sort our deeds reprove,
Let us not weigh them. Heaven's great lamps do dive
Into their west, and straight again revive,
But soon as once set is our little light,
Then must we sleep one ever-during night.

If all would lead their lives in love like me,
Then bloody swords and armor should not be;
No drum nor trumpet peaceful sleeps should move,
Unless alarm came from the camp of love.
But fools do live, and waste their little light,
And seek with pain their ever-during night.

When timely death my life and fortune ends,
Let not my hearse be vexed with mourning friends,
But let all lovers, rich in triumph, come
And with sweet pastimes grace my happy tomb;
And Lesbia, close up thou my little light,
And crown with love my ever-during night.

VI

When to her lute Corinna sings,
Her voice revives the leaden strings,
And doth in highest notes appear
As any challenged echo clear;
But when she doth of mourning speak,
Ev'n with her sighs the strings do break.

And as her lute doth live or die,
Led by her passion, so must I:
For when of pleasure she doth sing,
My thoughts enjoy a sudden spring,
But if she doth of sorrow speak,
Ev'n from my heart the strings do break.

[2] Imitated and partly translated from Catullus, V, "Vivamus, mea Lesbia, atque amemus."

X

Follow your saint, follow with accents sweet;
Haste you, sad notes, fall at her flying feet.
There, wrapped in cloud of sorrow, pity move,
And tell the ravisher of my soul I perish for her love.
But if she scorns my never-ceasing pain,
Then burst with sighing in her sight and ne'er return again.

All that I sung still to her praise did tend,
Still she was first, still she my songs did end.
Yet she my love and music both doth fly,
The music that her echo is and beauty's sympathy.
Then let my notes pursue her scornful flight:
It shall suffice that they were breathed and died for her delight.

XII

Thou art not fair for all thy red and white,
For all those rosy ornaments in thee;
Thou art not sweet, though made of mere delight,
Nor fair nor sweet, unless you pity me.
I will not soothe thy fancies; thou shalt prove
That beauty is no beauty without love.

Yet love not me, nor seek thou to allure
My thoughts with beauty, were it more divine;
Thy smiles and kisses I cannot endure,
I'll not be wrapped up in those arms of thine.
Now show it, if thou be a woman right,—
Embrace, and kiss, and love me in despite.

XVIII

The man of life upright,
Whose guiltless heart is free
From all dishonest deeds,
Or thought of vanity;

The man whose silent days
In harmless joys are spent,
Whom hopes cannot delude,
Nor sorrow discontent;

That man needs neither towers
Nor armor for defense,
Nor secret vaults to fly
From thunder's violence.

He only can behold
With unaffrighted eyes
The horrors of the deep
And terrors of the skies.

Thus, scorning all the cares
That fate or fortune brings,
He makes the heaven his book,
His wisdom heavenly things,

Good thoughts his only friends,
His wealth a well-spent age,
The earth his sober inn
And quiet pilgrimage.

XX

When thou must home to shades of underground,
And there arrived, a new admired guest,
The beauteous spirits do engirt thee round,
White Iope, blithe Helen, and the rest,
To hear the stories of thy finished love
From that smooth tongue whose music hell can move,

Then wilt thou speak of banqueting delights,
Of masques and revels which sweet youth did make,
Of tourneys and great challenges of knights,
And all these triumphs for thy beauty's sake;
When thou hast told these honors done to thee,
Then tell, Oh tell, how thou didst murther me.

FROM

OBSERVATIONS IN THE ART OF ENGLISH POESY

(1602)

Rose-cheeked Laura, come,[3]
Sing thou smoothly with thy beauty's
Silent music, either other
 Sweetly gracing.

Lovely forms do flow
From concent[4] divinely framed;
Heav'n is music, and thy beauty's
 Birth is heavenly.

These dull notes we sing
Discords need for helps to grace them;
Only beauty purely loving
 Knows no discord,

But still moves delight,
Like clear springs renewed by flowing,
Ever perfect, ever in themselves
 Eternal.

FROM

TWO BOOKS OF AIRS

(*ca.* 1613)

Book I, *VII*

To music bent is my retired mind,
And fain would I some song of pleasure sing,
But in vain joys no comfort now I find;
From heavenly thoughts all true delight doth spring.

[3] An illustration given by Campion of the principles of quantitative versification in his *Observations.*

[4] *concent:* playing or singing together in harmony.

Thy power, Oh God, thy mercies, to record,
Will sweeten every note and every word.

All earthly pomp or beauty to express,
Is but to carve in snow, on waves to write.
Celestial things, though men conceive them less,
Yet fullest are they in themselves of light;
Such beams they yield as know no means to die,
Such heat they cast as lifts the spirit high.

XX

Jack and Joan they think no ill,
But loving live, and merry still;
Do their weekdays' work, and pray
Devoutly on the holyday;
Skip and trip it on the green,
And help to choose the summer queen;
Lash out,[5] at a country feast,
Their silver penny with the best.

Well can they judge of nappy ale,
And tell at large a winter tale;
Climb up to the apple loft
And turn the crabs [6] till they be soft.
Tib is all the father's joy,
And little Tom the mother's boy.
All their pleasure is content;
And care, to pay their yearly rent.
Joan can call by name her cows
And deck her windows with green boughs;
She can wreaths and tutties [7] make,
And trim with plums a bridal cake.
Jack knows what brings gain or loss,
And his long flail can stoutly toss,
Makes the hedge, which others break,
And ever thinks what he doth speak.

Now, you courtly dames and knights,
That study only strange delights,
Though you scorn the home-spun gray

---

[5] *lash out:* squander, spend lavishly.
[6] *crabs:* crab apples.
[7] *tutties:* nosegays.

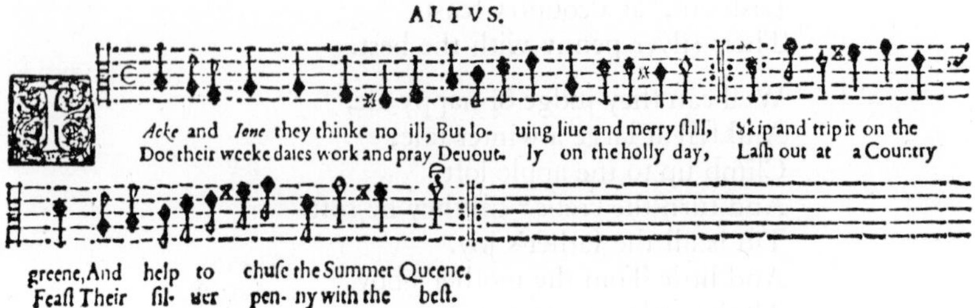

Courtesy Huntington Library

Music from Campion's Two Books of Airs

And revel in your rich array,
Though your tongues dissemble deep
And can your heads from danger keep,
Yet, for all your pomp and train,
Securer lives the silly swain.

Book II, VII

Give beauty all her right,
She's not to one form tied;
Each shape yields fair delight,
Where her perfections bide.

Helen, I grant, might pleasing be,
And Ros'mond [8] was as sweet as she.

Some the quick eye commends;
Some swelling lips and red;
Pale looks have many friends,
Through sacred sweetness bred.
Meadows have flowers that pleasure move,
Though roses are the flowers of love.

Free beauty is not bound
To one unmoved clime;
She visits every ground,
And favors every time.
Let the old loves with mine compare,
My sovereign is as sweet and fair.

FROM

THE THIRD AND FOURTH BOOK OF AIRS

(*ca.* 1617)

Book III, *XXVII*

Never love unless you can
Bear with all the faults of man;
Men sometimes will jealous be,
Though but little cause they see,
And hang the head, as discontent,
And speak what straight they will repent.

Men that but one saint adore
Make a show of love to more;
Beauty must be scorned in none,
Though but truly served in one;
For what is courtship but disguise?
True hearts may have dissembling eyes.

Men when their affairs require
Must a while themselves retire,
Sometimes hunt, and sometimes hawk,

---

[8] *Ros'mond:* mistress of Henry II (*reg.* 1154–1189), subject of Daniel's *Complaint of Rosamund;* see p. 619.

And not ever sit and talk.
If these and such like you can bear,
Then like, and love, and never fear.

Book IV, *VII*

There is a garden in her face,
Where roses and white lilies grow,
A heavenly paradise is that place,
Wherein all pleasant fruits do flow.
There cherries grow, which none may buy
Till "Cherry ripe!"[9] themselves do cry.

Those cherries fairly do enclose
Of orient pearl a double row;
Which when her lovely laughter shows,
They look like rosebuds filled with snow.
Yet them nor peer nor prince can buy,
Till "Cherry ripe!" themselves do cry.

Her eyes like angels watch them still;
Her brows like bended bows do stand,
Threatening with piercing frowns to kill
All that attempt with eye or hand
Those sacred cherries to come nigh,
Till "Cherry ripe!" themselves do cry.

XXIV

Fain would I wed a fair young man that night and day could please me,
When my mind or body grieved that had the power to ease me.
Maids are full of longing thoughts that breed a bloodless sickness,
And that, oft I hear men say, is only cured by quickness.
Oft I have been wooed and praised, but never could be moved;
Many for a day or so I have most dearly loved,
But this foolish mind of mine straight loathes the thing resolved;
If to love be sin in me, that sin is soon absolved.
Sure I think I shall at last fly to some holy order;
When I once am settled there, then can I fly no farther.
Yet I would not die a maid, because I had a mother,
As I was by one brought forth, I would bring forth another.

---

[9] *"Cherry ripe!"*: a familiar cry of London street vendors.

Ben Jonson

1573–1637

Although he was a great and dominating figure of the age, Jonson was really hostile to most of the prevailing literary ideals and practices of Elizabethan England. He opposed a stout and stubborn classicism of form and realism of subject matter to the romantic, exuberant, individualistic art of such writers as Shakespeare, Spenser and Ralegh. Though he failed, in his own time, to win fellow writers or the public to his cause, he lived long enough and had enough disciples so that he became one of the polar figures of seventeenth century poetry. If in the theater Jonson occupies a place reserved for him alone as the rival of Shakespeare, in nondramatic poetry he has no peer in his time except Donne.

Jonson was the posthumous son of a minister; his stepfather was a bricklayer and for a time the young Jonson was one also. He had the good fortune to attend Westminster School and acquire the foundations of his impressive classical learning from William Camden, but he had to proceed to his stepfather's craft and then to the army instead of to Oxford or Cambridge. After returning from the wars in the Low Countries, where by his own account he distinguished himself by winning a spectacular combat in the sight of both armies, he drifted into the theater and almost immediately into trouble. He was imprisoned in 1597 for his share in a supposedly seditious play called *The Isle of Dogs.* In 1598 he fought and killed a fellow actor, Gabriel Spencer, in a duel. He was found guilty of murder but escaped hanging by pleading the old technicality of "benefit of clergy." While in prison he was converted to Catholicism, but he returned to the Church of England in 1610.

In 1598 Jonson's first important comedy, *Every Man In His Humour,* was produced by the Chamberlain's men, with William Shakespeare in the cast. It marked the beginning of Jonson's literary crusade against theatrical sensationalism, romantic plots, violation of the classical unities and in favor of decorum, "deeds and language such as men do use," and the ancient doctrine of comedy as a corrective. Jonson had a contempt for the public which sat very oddly on a practising playwright; from the defiant "By God, 'tis good, and if you like't, you may" in 1600 to the "come leave the loathèd stage" almost thirty years later, his attitude was consistent.

Jonson's career was turbulent; as one of his biographers has wittily said, his devotion to classic calm kept him involved in a series of violent brawls. But he finally became Poet Laureate; for ten years he could escape the stage by writing masques for the royal entertainments at court; and he had the satisfaction of seeing all the promising younger poets look up to him as Father

Ben, supreme arbiter and model in all that had to do with wit and the writer's art.

Much of the flavor of Jonson's personality and of his talk is preserved for us in the conversations recorded by the Scottish poet William Drummond of Hawthornden, whom Jonson visited on a walking trip in 1619. It is here that we learn that "Shakespeare wanted art," that "Donne, for not keeping of accent, deserved hanging" but was "the first poet in the world in some things." Jonson also told Drummond that he wrote all his poems in prose first, as Camden had taught him, and that of all the compliments that could be paid him, he liked most to be called honest.

For all of Jonson's theories, he was able to see the greatness of his polar opposite, Shakespeare, and his tribute to him in the first folio is as fine a piece of criticism as the language affords. Perhaps the vision of old Thomas Fuller, in his life of Shakespeare in the *Worthies,* has some basis in fact:

"Many were the wit-combats between him and Ben Jonson, which two I behold like a Spanish great gallion and an English man-of-war: Master Jonson, like the former, was built far higher in learning, solid but slow in his performances; Shakespeare, with the English man-of-war, lesser in bulk but lighter in sailing, could turn with all tides, tack about and take advantage of all winds by the quickness of his wit and invention."

BIBLIOGRAPHY: *Ben Jonson,* ed. Herford and Simpson, 11 volumes, Oxford, 1925–1952; Marchette Chute, *Ben Jonson of Westminster,* New York, 1953; G. E. Bentley, *Shakespeare and Jonson, Their Seventeenth Century Reputations Compared,* Chicago, 1945; *The Swan of Avon and the Bricklayer of Westminster,* Princeton, 1948; W. M. Evans, *Ben Jonson and Elizabethan Music,* Lancaster, Pa., 1929; R. S. Walker, "Jonson's Lyric Poetry," *Criterion* XIII (1933–34), 430–48; P. Simpson, "The Art of Ben Jonson," *Essays and Studies* XXX (1944), 35–49; L. J. Potts, "Ben Jonson and the Seventeenth Century" *Essays and Studies,* new series vol. II (1949), 7–24; Douglas Bush, *English Literature of the Earlier Seventeenth Century,* Oxford, 1945, pp. 104–111.

EPIGRAMS

TO WILLIAM CAMDEN [1]

CAMDEN, most reverend head, to whom I owe
All that I am in arts, all that I know,
(How nothing's that?) to whom my country owes
The great renown and name wherewith she goes.
Than thee the age sees not that thing more grave,
More high, more holy, that she more would crave.
What name, what skill, what faith hast thou in things!
What sight in searching the most antique springs!

[1] *Camden:* William Camden, the great antiquarian and author of *Brittania,* had been Jonson's teacher at Westminster School.

What weight and what authority in thy speech!
Man scarce can make that doubt, but thou canst teach.
Pardon free truth, and let thy modesty,
Which conquers all, be once overcome by thee.
Many of thine this better could, than I,
But, for their powers, accept my piety.

TO JOHN DONNE

Donne, the delight of Phoebus and each Muse,
Who, to thy one, all other brains refuse;
Whose every work, of thy most early wit,
Came forth example and remains so yet,
Longer a-knowing than most wits do live.
And which no affection praise enough can give.
To it thy language, letters, arts, best life,
Which might with half mankind maintain a strife.
All which I meant to praise, and yet I would
But leave, because I cannot as I should.

ON MY FIRST SON

Farewell, thou child of my right hand, and joy;
My sin was too much hope of thee, loved boy;
Seven years thou wert lent to me, and I thee pay,
Exacted by thy fate, on the just day.
Oh, could I lose all father, now! For why
Will man lament the state he should envy?
To have so soon scaped world's, and flesh's rage,
And, if no other misery, yet age?
Rest in soft peace, and, asked, say here doth lie
Ben Jonson his best piece of poetry,
For whose sake, henceforth, all his vows be such,
As what he loves may never like too much.

INVITING A FRIEND TO SUPPER

Tonight, grave sir, both my poor house, and I
Do equally desire your company;
Not that we think us worthy such a guest,
But that your worth will dignify our feast
With those that come, whose grace may make that seem
Something, which else could hope for no esteem.
It is the fair acceptance, sir, creates
The entertainment perfect, not the cates.

Yet shall you have, to rectify your palate,
An olive, capers, or some better salad
Ushering the mutton; with a short-legg'd hen,
If we can get her, full of eggs, and then
Lemons, and wine for sauce; to these, a cony
Is not to be despaired of, for our money;
And, though fowl now be scarce, yet there are clerks,
The sky not falling, think we may have larks.[2]
I'll tell you of more, and lie, so you will come:
Of partridge, pheasant, woodcock, of which some
May yet be there, and godwit,[3] if we can;
Knat,[4] rail,[5] and ruff[6] too. Howsoe'r, my man
Shall read a piece of Virgil, Tacitus,
Livy, or of some better book to us,
Of which we'll speak our minds, amidst our meat;
And I'll profess no verses to repeat.
To this, if aught appear which I not know of,
That will the pastry, not my paper, show of.
Digestive cheese and fruit there sure will be;
But that which most doth take my Muse and me,
Is a pure cup of rich Canary wine,
Which is the Mermaid's[7] now, but shall be mine;
Of which had Horace, or Anacreon tasted,
Their lives, as do their lines, till now had lasted.
Tobacco,[8] nectar, or the Thespian spring,
Are all but Luther's beer[9] to this I sing.
Of this we will sup free, but moderately,
And we will have no Pooley, or Parrot[10] by,
Nor shall our cups make any guilty men;
But, at our parting we will be as when
We innocently met. No simple word
That shall be uttered at our mirthful board,
Shall make us sad next morning or affright
The liberty that we'll enjoy tonight.

---

[2] A joking reference to the old proverb, "When the sky falls, we shall have larks."

[3] *godwit:* a marsh bird, considered a delicacy.

[4] *knat:* a kind of sandpiper.

[5] *rail:* the land-rail or corn-crake.

[6] *ruff:* another kind of sandpiper.

[7] *Mermaid's:* the famous tavern's.

[8] *Tobacco:* often thought of as liquid in the period: a common phrase is to "drink tobacco."

[9] *Luther's beer:* German beer, regarded as inferior by the English.

[10] *Pooley . . . Parrot:* two notorious informers, government spies. Pooley was present when Marlowe was killed.

EPITAPH ON SALOMON PAVY, A CHILD OF QUEEN ELIZABETH'S CHAPEL

Weep with me, all you that read
This little story,
And know, for whom a tear you shed,
Death's self is sorry.
'Twas a child, that so did thrive
In grace and feature,
As Heaven and Nature seemed to strive
Which owned the creature.
Years he numbered scarce thirteen
When Fates turned cruel,
Yet three filled zodiacs[11] had he been
The stage's jewel,
And did act, what now we moan,
Old men so duly,
As, sooth, the Parcae thought him one,
He played so truly.
So, by error, to his fate
They all consented;
But viewing him since (alas, too late)
They have repented.
And have sought, to give new birth,
In baths to steep him;
But, being so much too good for earth,
Heaven vows to keep him.

EPITAPH ON ELIZABETH, L. H.

Wouldst thou hear, what man can say
In a little? Reader, stay.
Underneath this stone doth lie
As much beauty, as could die,
Which in life did harbor give
To more virtue, than doth live.
If at all she had a fault,
Leave it buried in this vault.
One name was Elizabeth,
Th'other let it sleep with death;
Fitter where it died to tell,
Than that it lived at all. Farewell.

[11] *three filled zodiacs:* three years. Salomon acted on the London stage 1600–1602, and had parts in Jonson's *Cynthia's Revels* and *Poetaster*.

ODES

TO PENSHURST[12]

Thou art not, Penshurst, built to envious show
Of touch[13] or marble, nor canst boast a row
Of polished pillars or a roof of gold;
Thou hast no lantern whereof tales are told,
Or stair, or courts, but stand'st an ancient pile,
And these grudged at, art reverenced the while.
Thou joy'st in better marks, of soil, of air,
Of wood, of water; therein thou art fair.
Thou hast thy walks for health as well as sport:
Thy Mount, to which the dryads do resort,
Where Pan and Bacchus their high feasts have made
Beneath the broad beech and the chestnut shade;
That taller tree, which of a nut was set
At his great birth where all the Muses met.[14]
There in the writhed bark, are cut the names
Of many a sylvan, taken with his flames.
And thence the ruddy satyrs oft provoke
The lighter fauns to reach thy Lady's Oak.[15]
Thy copse, too, named of Gamage,[16] thou hast there,
That never fails to serve thee seasoned deer,
When thou wouldst feast or exercise thy friends.
The lower land, that to the river bends,
Thy sheep, thy bullocks, kine, and calves do feed;
The middle grounds thy mares and horses breed.
Each bank doth yield thee conies; and the tops
Fertile of wood, Ashour, and Sidney's copse,[17]
To crown thy open table doth provide
The purpled pheasant with the speckled side:
The painted partridge lies in every field,
And, for thy mess, is willing to be killed.
And if the high-swollen Medway fail thy dish,
Thou hast thy ponds that pay thee tribute fish,
Fat, aged carps, that run into thy net,
And pikes, now weary their own kind to eat,

[12] *Penshurst:* the family estate of the Sidneys, in Kent.

[13] *touch:* a kind of black marble.

[14] The reference is to Sir Philip Sidney.

[15] *Lady's Oak:* an oak tree so named in Penshurst Park.

[16] *Gamage:* Lady Gamage used to feed the deer there. She married Lord Sidney in 1584.

[17] Copses at Penshurst still bear these names.

As loath the second draught or cast to stay,
Officiously[18] at first themselves betray.
Bright eels, that emulate them and leap on land,
Before the fisher, or into his hand.
Then hath thy orchard fruit, thy garden flowers,
Fresh as the air, and new as are the hours.
The early cherry, with the later plum,
Fig, grape, and quince, each in his time doth come;
The blushing apricot, and woolly peach
Hang on thy walls, that every child may reach.
And though thy walls be of the country stone,
They are reared with no man's ruin, no man's groan;
There's none that dwell about them wish them down,
But all come in, the farmer and the clown
And no one empty-handed, to salute
Thy lord and lady, though they have no suit.[19]
Some bring a capon, some a rural cake,
Some nuts, some apples; some that think they make
The better cheeses, bring 'em, or else send
By their ripe daughters, whom they would commend
This way to husbands, and whose baskets bear
An emblem of themselves in plum or pear.
But what can this, more than express their love,
Add to thy free provisions, far above
The need of such, whose liberal board doth flow,
With all that hospitality doth know?
Where comes no guest but is allowed to eat,
Without his fear, and of thy lord's own meat;
Where the same beer and bread and self-same wine,
That is his Lordship's, shall be also mine.
And I not fain to sit (as some, this day,
At great men's tables) and yet dine away.
Here no man tells my cups, nor, standing by,
A waiter doth my gluttony envy,
But gives me what I call and lets me eat;
He knows, below, he shall find plenty of meat.
Thy tables hoard not up for the next day,
Nor, when I take my lodging, need I pray
For fire, or lights, or livery;[20] all is there;
As if thou, then, wert mine, or I reigned here.
There's nothing I can wish, for which I stay.
That found King James, when hunting late, this way,
With his brave son, the Prince, they saw thy fires

[18] *officiously:* dutifully.
[19] *suit:* plea, request.
[20] *livery:* provision.

Shine bright on every hearth as the desires
Of thy penates had been set on flame,
To entertain them, or the country came,
With all their zeal, to warm their welcome here.
What (great, I will not say, but) sudden cheer
Did'st thou, then, make 'em! and what praise was heaped
On thy good lady, then, who therein reaped
The just reward of her high housewifery;
To have her linen, plate, and all things nigh,
When she was far, and not a room but drest,
As if it had expected such a guest!
These, Penshurst, are thy praise, and yet not all.
Thy lady's noble, fruitful, chaste withal.
His children thy great lord may call his own—
A fortune, in this age, but rarely known.
They are, and have been, taught religion; thence
Their gentler spirits have sucked innocence.
Each morn and even they are taught to pray,
With the whole household, and may, every day,
Read, in their virtuous parents' noble parts,
The mysteries of manners, arms, and arts.
Now, Penshurst, they that will proportion thee
With other edifices, when they see
Those proud, ambitious heaps, and nothing else,
May say, their lords have built, but thy lord dwells.

To the memory of my beloved,

The AUTHOR

Mr. William Shakespeare:

And

what he hath left us.[21]

To draw no envy, Shakespeare, on thy name,
Am I thus ample to thy book and fame,
While I confess thy writings to be such,
As neither man nor muse can praise too much;
'Tis true, and all men's suffrage. But these ways
Were not the paths I meant unto thy praise;
For silliest Ignorance on these may light,
Which, when it sounds at best, but echoes right;

[21] From the first folio edition of Shakespeare's *Works*, 1623.

Or blind Affection, which doth ne'er advance
The truth, but gropes, and urgeth all by chance;
Or crafty Malice might pretend this praise,
And think to ruin where it seemed to raise.
These are, as some infamous bawd or whore,
Should praise a matron; what could hurt her more?
But thou art proof against them, and indeed
Above th'ill fortune of them, or the need.
I therefore will begin. Soul of the Age!
The applause, delight, the wonder of our stage!
My Shakespeare, rise; I will not lodge thee by
Chaucer, or Spenser, or bid Beaumont lie
A little further to make thee a room;[22]
Thou art a monument without a tomb,
And art alive still, while thy book doth live,
And we have wits to read, and praise to give.
That I not mix thee so, my brain excuses;
I mean with great, but disproportioned Muses:
For, if I thought my judgment were of years,
I should commit thee surely with thy peers,
And tell how far thou didst our Lyly out-shine,
Or sporting Kyd, or Marlowe's mighty line.
And though thou hadst small Latin and less Greek,
From thence to honor thee I would not seek
For names; but call forth thund'ring Aeschylus,
Euripides, and Sophocles to us
Paccuvius, Accius, him of Cordova dead,[23]
To life again, to hear thy buskin tread,
And shake a stage; or when thy socks were on,
Leave thee alone, for the comparison
Of all that insolent Greece or haughty Rome
Sent forth, or since did from their ashes come.
Triumph, my Britain, thou hast one to show
To whom all scenes of Europe homage owe.
He was not of an age, but for all time!
And all the Muses still were in their prime
When, like Apollo, he came forth to warm
Our ears, or like a Mercury to charm.
Nature herself was proud of his designs,
And joyed to wear the dressing of his lines,
Which were so richly spun, and woven so fit,
As, since, she will vouchsafe no other wit.

[22] A reference to William Basse's *Elegy on Shakespeare.*

[23] Pacuvius and Accius are mentioned together in Horace, Epodes II, i, 56. *Him of Cordova dead* is Seneca.

The merry Greek, tart Aristophanes,
Neat Terence, witty Plautus, now not please,
But antiquated, and deserted lie
As they were not of Nature's family.
Yet must I not give Nature all; thy art,
My gentle Shakespeare, must enjoy a part.
For though the poet's matter nature be,
His art doth give the fashion. And, that he
Who casts to write a living line must sweat,
(Such as thine are) and strike the second heat
Upon the Muses' anvil, turn the same,
(And himself with it) that he thinks to frame,
Or for the laurel, he may gain a scorn,
For a good poet's made, as well as born.
And such wert thou. Look how the father's face
Lives in his issue, even so the race
Of Shakespeare's mind and manners brightly shines
In his well turned and true-filed lines:
In each of which, he seems to shake a lance,
As brandished at the eyes of Ignorance.
Sweet Swan of Avon! What a sight it were
To see thee in our waters yet appear,
And make those flights upon the banks of Thames,
That so did take Eliza, and our James!
But stay, I see thee in the hemisphere
Advanced and made a constellation there!
Shine forth, thou star of poets, and with rage
Or influence, chide or cheer the drooping stage,
Which, since thy flight from hence, hath mourned like night,
And despairs day, but for thy volume's light.

TO CELIA

Come my Celia, let us prove,
While we may, the sports of love;
Time will not be ours forever;
He at length our good will sever.
Spend not then his gifts in vain.
Suns that set may rise again;
But if once we lose this light,
'Tis with us perpetual night.
Why should we defer our joys?
Fame and rumor are but toys.
Cannot we delude the eyes
Of a few poor household spies,

Or his easier ears beguile,
So removed by our wile?
'Tis no sin love's fruit to steal;
But the sweet theft to reveal,
To be taken, to be seen,
These have crimes accounted been.

TO CELIA

Drink to me only with thine eyes,
And I will pledge with mine;
Or leave a kiss but in the cup,
And I'll not look for wine.
The thirst that from the soul doth rise,
Doth ask a drink divine:
But might I of Jove's nectar sup,
I would not change for thine.

I sent thee late a rosy wreath,
Not so much honoring thee,
As giving it a hope, that there
It could not withered be.
But thou thereon did'st only breathe,
And sent'st it back to me;
Since when it grows, and smells, I swear,
Not of itself, but thee.

A WITCH'S CHARM

The owl is abroad, the bat and the toad,
And so is the cat-a-mountain;
The ant and the mole sit both in a hole
And frog peeps out o' the fountain;
The dogs, they do bay, and the timbrels play,
The spindle is now a-turning;
The moon, it is red, and the stars are fled,
But all the sky is a-burning.
The ditch is made, and our nails the spade,
With pictures full of wax and of wool;
Their livers I stick with needles quick;
There lacks but the blood to make up the flood.
Quickly, dame, then! Bring your part in!

Spur, spur, upon little Martin;[24]
Merrily, merrily, make him sail,
A worm in his mouth and a thorn in's tail,
Fire above and fire below,
With a whip i' your hand to make him go!
O, now, she's come;
Let all be dumb.

A HYMN TO GOD THE FATHER

Hear me, O God!
A broken heart,
Is my best part;
Use still thy rod,
That I may prove
Therein thy love.

If thou hadst not
Been stern to me,
But left me free,
I had forgot
Myself and thee.

For sin's so sweet,
As minds ill bent
Rarely repent,
Until they meet
Their punishment.

Who more can crave
Than thou hast done?
That gav'st a Son,
To free a slave,
First made of naught;
With all since bought.

Sin, Death, and Hell,
His glorious Name
Quite overcame,

[24] "Their little Martin is he that calls them to their conventicles, which is done in a human voice; but coming forth, they find him in the shape of a great buck goat, upon whom they ride to their meetings"—Jonson's note.

Yet I rebel,
And slight the same.

HAVE you seen but a bright lily grow,[25]
Before rude hands have touched it?
Have you marked but the fall o'the snow
Before the soil hath smutched it?
Have you felt the wool o' the beaver?
Or swan's down ever?
Or have smelt o'the bud o'the brier?
Or the nard i' the fire?
Or have tasted the bag o'the bee?
Oh so white! Oh so soft! Oh so sweet is she!

IN DEFENSE OF THEIR INCONSTANCY

HANG up those dull and envious fools,
That talk abroad of woman's change,
We were not bred to sit on stools,
Our proper virtue is to range;
Take that away, you take our lives,
We are no women then, but wives.

Such as in valor would excel,
Do change, though man, and often fight,
Which we in love must do as well,
If ever we will love aright.
The frequent varying of the deed,
Is that which doth perfection breed.

Nor is't inconstancy to change
For what is better, or to make,
By searching, what before was strange,
Familiar, for the use's sake;

[25] This lyric Jonson used in various ways, as the second stanza of a song in *The Devil is an Ass,* as the last stanza of a poem to Charis in *Underwood,* and as the first stanza of a poem that remained in manuscript. It was also popular as a song and was parodied by Suckling in *The Sad One.*

The good from bad is not descried,
But as 'tis often vext and tried.

And this profession of a store
In love, doth not alone help forth
Our pleasure, but preserves us more
From being forsaken, than doth worth;
For were the worthiest woman curst
To love one man, he'd leave her first.

It was a beauty that I saw,
So pure, so perfect, as the frame
Of all the universe was lame
To that one figure, could I draw
Or give least line of it a law.
A skein of silk without a knot,
A fair march made without a halt,
A curious form without a fault,
A printed book without a blot:
All beauty, and without a spot.

ODE: TO HIMSELF[26]

Come leave the loathèd stage
And the more loathsome age,
Where pride and impudence, in faction knit,
Usurp the chair of wit,
Indicting and arraigning every day
Something they call a play.
Let their fastidious, vain
Commission of the brain
Run on, and rage, sweat, censure, and condemn;
They were not made for thee, less thou for them.
Say that thou pour'st them wheat
And they will acorns eat;
'Twere simple fury, still, thy self to waste
On such as have no taste.

[26] Jonson first wrote this in 1629, angry at the failure of his play *The New Inn*.

To offer them a surfeit of pure bread
Whose appetites are dead?
No, give them grains their fill,
Husks, draff to drink, and swill.
If they love lees and leave the lusty wine,
Envy them not, their palate's with the swine.
No doubt some mouldy tale
Like *Pericles,*[27] and stale
As the shrieve's crusts, and nasty as his fish-
scraps, out of every dish,
Thrown forth, and raked into the common tub,[28]
May keep up the play-club;
There, sweepings do as well
As the best-ordered meal.
For, who the relish of these guests will fit,
Needs set them but the alms-basket of wit.

And much good do't you then,
Brave plush- and velvet-men;
Can feed on orts,[29] and, safe in your stage-clothes,
Dare quit, upon your oaths,
The stagers and the stage-wrights too, your peers,
Of larding your large ears
With their foul comic socks,
Wrought upon twenty blocks,
Which, if they are torn, and turned, and patched enough,
The gamesters share your guilt, and you their stuff.

Leave things so prostitute
And take the Alcaic [30] lute,
Or thine owne Horace' or Anacreon's lyre;
Warm thee by Pindar's fire:
And though thy nerves [31] be shrunk and blood be cold
Ere years have made thee old,
Strike that disdainful heat
Throughout, to their defeat;
As curious fools, and envious of thy strain,
May, blushing, swear no palsy's in thy brain.
But when they hear thee sing
The glories of thy king,

---

[27] Shakespeare's *Pericles* had been printed in 1609.

[28] The reference is to the gathering of scraps for the poor, collected from the tables after a sheriff's feast.

[29] *orts:* scraps, leavings.

[30] *Alcaic:* so called from Alcaeus, imitated by Horace.

[31] *nerves:* sinews.

His zeal to God, and his just awe o'er men;
They may, blood-shaken, then,
Feel such a flesh-quake to possess their powers
As they shall cry, like ours
In sound of peace or wars,
No harp ere hit the stars,
In tuning forth the acts of his sweet reign,
And raising Charles his chariot 'bove his Wain.[32]

AN EXECRATION UPON VULCAN[33]

And why to me this, thou lame lord of fire,
What had I done that might call on thine ire?
Or urge thy greedy flame, thus to devour
So many my years' labors in an hour?
I ne'er attempted, Vulcan, 'gainst thy life;
Nor made least line of love to thy loose wife;[34]
Or in remembrance of thy affront and scorn,
With clowns, and tradesmen, kept thee closed in horn.[35]
'Twas Jupiter that hurl'd thee headlong down,
And Mars, that gave thee a Lantern for a crown.
Was it because thou wert of old denied
By Jove to have Minerva for thy bride,
That since thou tak'st all envious care and pain,
To ruin any issue of the brain?
Had I wrote treason there, or heresy,
Imposture, witchcraft, charms, or blasphemy,
I had deserved, then, thy consuming looks,
Perhaps, to have been burned with my books.
But, on thy malice, tell me, didst thou spy
Any, least loose or scurrile paper, lie
Concealed, or kept there, that was fit to be,
By thy own vote, a sacrifice to thee?
Did I there wound the honor of the crown?
Or tax the glories of the church and gown?
Itch to defame the state? or brand the times?
And my self most, in some self-boasting rhymes?
If none of these, then why this fire? Or find

[32] *Wain:* The Big Dipper was called Charles's Wain.

[33] Written in 1623, after a fire had destroyed Jonson's writing desk.

[34] *loose wife:* Venus.

[35] The labored jest in these lines refers to Vulcan's horns (as a cuckold, when his wife Venus lay with Mars) and the old lantern (spelled *lanthorn*) in which the flame was enclosed in translucent horn.

A cause before, or leave me one behind.
Had I compiled from Amadis de Gaul,
Th'Esplandians, Arthurs, Palmerins, and all
The learned library of Don Quixote;[36]
And so some goodlier monster had begot;
Or spun out riddles, and weaved fifty tomes
Of logogryphs,[37] and curious palindromes,[38]
Or pomped for[39] those hard trifles, anagrams,
Or eteostichs,[40] or those finer flammes[41]
Of eggs, and halberds, cradles, and a hearse,
A pair of scissors, and a comb in verse;[42]
Acrostics and *telestichs,*[43] on jump names,[44]
Thou then hadst had some color for thy flames,
On such my serious follies. But, thou'lt say,
There were some pieces of as base allay,
And as false stamp there: parcels of a play,
Fitter to see the fire-light than the day,
Adulterate monies such as might not go;
Thou should'st have stayed till public fame said so.
She is the judge, thou executioner;
Or if thou needs would'st trench upon her power,
Thou mightst have yet enjoyed thy cruelty
With some more thrift and more variety;
Thou mightst have had me perish, piece by piece,
To light tobacco, or save roasted geese,
Singe capons, or poor pigs, dropping their eyes;
Condemned me to the ovens with the pies;
And so, have kept me dying a whole age,
Not ravished all hence in a minute's rage.
But that's a mark whereof thy rites do boast,
To make consumption, ever, where thou go'st;
Had I foreknown of this thy least desire
T'have held a triumph, or a feast of fire,
Especially in paper; that, that steam
Had tickled your large nostril; many a ream
To redeem mine, I had sent in. "Enough!"
Thou should'st have cry'd, and all been proper stuff.

---

[36] *Amadis . . . Quixote:* various romances.

[37] *logogryphs:* riddles.

[38] *palindromes:* phrases which read the same backward as forward.

[39] *pomped for:* boasted of.

[40] *eteostichs:* chronograms, sentences in which key letters give the date in Roman numerals.

[41] *flammes:* conceits.

[42] Verses so printed as to imitate these shapes on the page.

[43] An acrostic spells a word or name by using the first letter of each line of verse; a telestich does the same thing using the last letter.

[44] *jump names:* exact names.

The Talmud and the Alcoran had come,
With pieces of the Legend,[45] the whole sum
Of errant Knighthood, with their dames, and dwarfs,
Their charmed boats, and their enchanted wharfs;
The Tristrams, Lanc'lots, Turpins, and the Peers,
All the mad Rolands, and sweet Olivers;[46]
To Merlin's marvels and his Cabal's loss,
With the chimera of the Rosy-Crosse,[47]
Their seals, their characters, hermetic rings,
Their jem of riches and bright stone, that brings
Invisibility and strength and tongues;
The Art of Kindling the True Coal, by Lungs;[48]
With Nicholas Pasquil's, *Meddle With your Match,*[49]
And the strong lines that so the time do catch:
Or Captain Pamphlet's horse and foot, that sally
Upon th'Exchange, still, out of Pope's Head Alley;[50]
The weekly Corrants, with Paul's seal;[51] and all
Th'admir'd discourses of the prophet Ball:[52]
These, had'st thou pleased either to dine, or sup,
Had made a meal for Vulcan to lick up.
But in my desk, what was there to accite[53]
So ravenous and vast an appetite?
I dare not say a body, but some parts
There were of search and mast'ry in the arts.
All the old Venusine, in poetry,
And lighted by the Stagirite, could spy,[54]
Was there made English; with a grammar too,
To teach some that their nurses could not do,
The purity of language; and among
The rest, my journey into Scotland sung,
With all th'adventures; three books not afraid
To speak the fate of the Sicilian Maid
To our own ladies;[55] and in story there

[45] *Legend:* The Legenda Aurea, a collection of saints' lives.

[46] *Tristrams . . . Olivers:* heroes of romance.

[47] *Merlin's . . . Crosse:* books of magic and esoteric lore.

[48] *The Art . . . Lungs:* a pretended book by an alchemist's apprentice, Lungs, on how to keep a fire going. The true coal had to be of beech and the apprentice had to blow, not use bellows.

[49] *Nicholas . . . Match:* a crack at Nicholas Breton, who issued many pamphlets with *Pasquil* in the title.

[50] *Captain . . . Alley:* a Captain Gainsford, who issued newsletters from Pope's Head Alley. Jonson satirized him in *The Staple of News.*

[51] *Corrants . . . seal:* corantos or newsletters sold in St. Paul's churchyard.

[52] *prophet Ball:* a tailor notorious for his false prophecies.

[53] *accite:* provoke.

[54] *Venusine . . . spy:* a translation of Horace's *Art of Poetry* with illustrations from Aristotle's *Poetics.*

[55] *three books . . . ladies:* John Barclay's *Argenis,* which Jonson had translated at the invitation of the king.

Of our fifth Henry, eight of his nine year;
Wherein was oil, beside the succor spent,
Which noble Carew, Cotton, Selden lent;[56]
And twice-twelve-years' stored up humanity,
With humble gleanings in divinity,
After the Fathers, and those wiser guides
Whom faction had not drawn to study sides.
How in these ruins, Vulcan, thou dost lurk,
All soot and embers, odious as thy work!
I now begin to doubt, if ever Grace,
Or Goddess, could be patient of thy face.
Thou woo Minerva? or to wit aspire?
'Cause thou canst halt, with us, in arts, and fire!
Son of the wind! for so thy mother gone
With lust conceived thee; father thou hadst none;[57]
When thou wert born, and that thou look'st at best
She durst not kiss, but flung thee from her breast,
And so did Jove, who ne'er meant thee his cup;
No mar'el the clowns of Lemnos took thee up,[58]
For none but smiths would have made thee a God.
Some alchemist there may be yet, or odd
Squire of the squibs,[59] against the pageant day,
May to thy name a Vulcanal say;
And for it lose his eyes with gun powder,
As th'other may his brains with quicksilver.
Well fare the wise-men yet, on the Bankside,
My friends, the watermen! They could provide
Against thy fury, when to serve their needs,
They made a Vulcan of a sheaf of reeds,
Whom they durst handle in their holiday coats,
And safely trust to dress, not burn, their boats.
But, Oh those reeds! Thy mere[60] disdain of them
Made thee beget that cruel stratagem,
Which some are pleased to style but thy mad prank
Against the Globe, the glory of the Bank.[61]
Which, though it were the fort of the whole parish,

---

[56] *oil . . . lent:* the industry and learning of the three great antiquarians of the age, Richard Carew, Sir Robert Cotton and John Selden.

[57] According to classical authorities Vulcan was the son of Juno but had no father.

[58] Cf. Milton: "from morn/To noon he fell, from noon to dewy eve,/A summer's day, and with the setting sun/Dropt from the zenith, like a falling star/On Lemnos the Aegean isle."—*Paradise Lost* I, 742 ff.

[59] *Squire . . . squibs:* a reference to John Squire's Lord Mayor's show for 1620.

[60] *mere:* complete.

[61] The burning of the Globe playhouse on June 29, 1613, was caused by some wadding from cannon ("chambers") shot off during a performance of Shakespeare's *Henry VIII.*

Flanked with a ditch, and forced out of a marish,
I saw with two poor chambers taken in
And razed, e'er thought could urge, This might have been!
See the world's ruins! Nothing but the piles
Left! And wit since to cover it with tiles.
The Brethren,[62] they straight noised it out for news,
'Twas verily some relic of the stews,
And this a sparkle of that fire let loose
That was raked up in the Winchestrian goose
Bred on the Bank, in time of Popery,
When Venus there maintained the mystery.
But others fell with that conceit by the ears,
And cried, it was a threat'ning to the bears
And that accursed ground, the Paris Garden;[63]
Nay, sighed a sister, 'twas the nun, Kate Arden,[64]
Kindled the fire! But then did one return,
No fool would his own harvest spoil or burn!
If that were so, thou rather would'st advance
The place that was thy wife's inheritance.
O no, cried all, Fortune,[65] for being a whore,
Scaped not his justice any jot the more:
He burnt that idol of the Revels too:
Nay, let Whitehall[66] with Revels have to do,
Though but in dances, it shall know his power;
There was a Judgment shown too in an hour.
He is true Vulcan still! He did not spare
Troy, though it were so much his Venus' care.
Fool, wilt thou let that in example come?
Did not she save from thence, to build a Rome?
And what hast thou done in these petty spites,
More than advanced the houses, and their rites?
I will not argue thee, from those, of guilt,
For they were burnt but to be better built.
'Tis true, that in thy wish they were destroyed
Which thou hast only vented, not enjoyed.
So wouldst thou have run upon the Rolls by stealth,[67]
And didst invade part of the Commonwealth,

[62] *Brethren . . . mystery:* the Puritans claimed the fire resulted from the burning sores of venereal disease ("Winchestrian goose") which lay smoldering on the Bankside ever since pre-Reformation times when stews or whorehouses were licensed there.

[63] *bears . . . Paris Garden:* Paris Garden was a landing-place on the south side of the Thames. The Bear Garden, used for baiting bears, was near it.

[64] *Kate Arden:* one of "Venus' nuns."

[65] *Fortune:* the Fortune theater, Cripplegate, burned in 1621.

[66] *Whitehall:* the old banqueting house in Whitehall burned in 1618.

[67] The Six Clerks' Office was burned in 1621.

In those records, which, were all chronicle(r)s gone,
Will be remembered by Six Clerks to one.
But say, all six good men, what answer ye?
Lies there no writ out of the chancery
Against this Vulcan? No injunction?
No order? no decree? Though we be gone
At common law, methinks in his despite
A court of equity should do us right,
But to confine him to the brew-houses,
The glass-house, dye-vats, and their furnaces;
To live in sea-coal and go forth in smoke;
Or, lest that vapor might the City choke,
Condemn him to the brick kilns, or some Hill-
foot (out in Sussex) to an iron mill;
Or in small fagots have him blaze about
Vile taverns, and the drunkards piss him out;
Or in the bellman's lantern, like a spy,
Burn to a snuff, and then stink out, and die.
I could invent a sentence, yet were worse;
But I'll conclude all in a civil curse:
Pox on your flameship, Vulcan, if it be
To all as fatal as 't hath been to me,
And to Paul's steeple,[68] which was unto us
'Bove all your fireworks had at Ephesus,
Or Alexandria;[69] and though a divine
Loss, remains yet, as unrepaired as mine.
Would you had kept your forge at Aetna still,
And there made swords, bills, glaves, and arms your fill;
Maintained the trade at Bilbo,[70] or else-where,
Struck in at Milan with the cutler there;
Or stayed but where the friar[71] and you first met,
Who from the devil's arse did guns beget;
Or fixed in the Low Countries, where you might
On both sides do your mischiefs with delight;
Blow up and ruin, mine and countermine,
Make your petards and grenades, all your fine
Engines of murder, and receive the praise
Of massacring mankind so many ways.
We ask your absence here; we all love peace

[68] The steeple of the old Gothic St. Paul's was struck by lightning and burned in 1561.

[69] *Ephesus . . . Alexandria:* The temple at Ephesus was burned by Herostratus in 356 B.C.; the library at Alexandria was burned by the caliph Omar in 640 A.D.

[70] *Bilbo:* Bilbao, in Spain, famous for its swordblades.

[71] *friar:* Roger Bacon, reputed inventor of gunpowder.

And pray the fruits thereof, and the increase;
So doth the king, and most of the king's men
That have good places; therefore once again
Pox on thee, Vulcan, thy Pandora's pox,[72]
And all the evils that flew out of her box
Light on thee! Or, if those plagues will not do,
Thy wife's pox on thee, and Bess Broughton's,[73] too.

A SONG

Oh do not wanton with those eyes,
Lest I be sick with seeing;
Nor cast them down, but let them rise,
Lest shame destroy their being.
Oh be not angry with those fires,
For then their threats will kill me;
Nor look too kind on my desires,
For then my hopes will spill me.
Oh do not steep them in thy tears,
For so will sorrow slay me;
Nor spread them as distract with fears,
Mine own enough betray me.

OVER THE DOOR AT THE ENTRANCE INTO THE APOLLO[74]

Welcome all, who lead or follow,
To the Oracle of Apollo.
Here he speaks out of his pottle,[75]
Or the tripos, his tower-bottle:[76]
All his answers are divine,
Truth itself doth flow in wine.
"Hang up all the poor hop-drinkers,"

---

72 *thy Pandora's pox:* Pandora was made out of earth by Vulcan; her box contained all of the evils from which mankind has suffered, so Jonson includes "the pox" (syphilis) as one of these

73 *Bess Broughton:* a famous courtesan, whose life is recorded by Aubrey.

74 *Apollo:* a room in the tavern of The Devil and St. Dunstan near Temple Bar, where Jonson presided over convivial meetings of his younger disciples, poets and wits. Over the door there was a bust of Apollo (which is still extant) and these verses.

75 *pottle:* two quart tankard.

76 *tower-bottle:* a bottle shaped like a tower.

Cries old Sym,[77] the king of skinkers.[78]
He the half of life abuses,
That sits watering with the Muses.
Those dull girls, no good can mean us;
Wine it is the milk of Venus
And the poets' horse accounted;
Ply it, and you all are mounted.
'Tis the true Phoebian liquor,
Clears the brains, makes wit the quicker,
Pays all debts, cures all diseases,
And at once three senses pleases.
Welcome all who lead or follow
To the oracle of Apollo.

Slow, slow, fresh fount, keep time with my salt tears;
Yet slower, yet, Oh faintly, gentle springs!
List to the heavy part the music bears,
Woe weeps out her division, when she sings.
Droop herbs and flowers;
Fall grief in showers;
Our beauties are not ours. Oh, I could still
Like melting snow upon some craggy hill,
Drop, drop, drop, drop,
Since nature's pride is now a withered daffodil.

Queen and huntress, chaste and fair,
Now the sun is laid to sleep,
Seated in thy silver chair,
State in wonted manner keep;
Hesperus intreats thy light,
Goddess excellently bright.

Earth, let not thy envious shade
Dare itself to interpose;
Cynthia's shining orb was made

[77] *Sym:* Simon Wadlow, the keeper of the tavern.

[78] *skinkers:* tapsters.

Heaven to clear, when day did close.
Bless us then with wished sight,
Goddess excellently bright.

Lay thy bow of pearl apart,
And thy crystal-shining quiver;
Give unto the flying hart
Space to breathe, how short soever.
Thou that mak'st a day of night,
Goddess excellently bright.

Still to be neat, still to be drest,
As you were going to a feast;
Still to be powdered, still perfumed;
Lady, it is to be presumed,
Though art's hid causes are not found,
All is not sweet, all is not sound.

Give me a look, give me a face
That makes simplicity a grace;
Robes loosely flowing, hair as free;
Such sweet neglect more taketh me
Than all th'adulteries of art.
They strike mine eyes, but not my heart.

The fairy beam upon you,
The stars to-glister on you,
A moon of light
In the noon of night,
Till the firedrake hath o'ergone you.
The wheel of fortune guide you,
The boy with the bow beside you
Run aye in the way
Till the bird of day
And the luckier lot betide you.

If I freely may discover
What would please me in my lover:
I would have her fair and witty,
Savoring more of court than city;
A little proud, but full of pity.
Light and humorous in her toying,
Oft building hopes and soon destroying,
Long but sweet in the enjoying,
Neither too easy, nor too hard;
All extremes I would have barred.

She should be allowed her passions,
So they were but used as fashions;
Sometimes froward, and then frowning,
Sometimes sickish, and then swowning,
Every fit with change still crowning.
Purely jealous I would have her,
Then only constant when I crave her.
'Tis a virtue should not save her.
Thus, nor her delicates would cloy me,
Neither her peevishness annoy me.

VENUS' RUNAWAY

First Grace:

Beauties, have ye seen this toy
Called love, a little boy,
Almost naked, wanton, blind,
Cruel now, and then as kind?
If he be amongst ye, say;
He is Venus' runaway.

Second Grace:

She that will but now discover
Where the winged wag doth hover,
Shall tonight receive a kiss,
How or where herself would wish;
But who brings him to his mother
Shall have that kiss and another.

Third Grace:

H'hath of marks about him plenty;
You shall know him, among twenty.

All his body is a fire,
And his breath a flame entire,
That being shot, like lightning, in,
Wounds the heart, but not the skin.

First Grace:

At his sight, the sun hath turned,
Neptune in the waters burned;
Hell hath felt a greater heat,
Love himself forsook his seat.
From the center to the sky,
Are his trophies reared high.

Second Grace:

Wings he hath, which though ye clip,
He will leap from lip to lip,
Over liver, lights, and heart,
But not stay in any part;
And, if chance his arrow misses,
He will shoot himself, in kisses.

Third Grace:

He doth bear a golden bow
And a quiver, hanging low,
Full of arrows, that out-brave
Dian's shafts, where, if he have
Any head more sharp than other,
With that first he strikes his mother.

First Grace:

Still the fairest are his fuel.
When his days are to be cruel,
Lovers' hearts are all his food
And his baths their warmest blood.
Nought but wounds his hand doth season,
And he hates none like to Reason.

Second Grace:

Trust him not. His words, though sweet,
Seldom with his heart do meet.
All his practice is deceit,
Every gift it is a bait.
Not a kiss but poison bears,
And most treason in his tears.

Third Grace:

Idle minutes are his reign;
Then the straggler makes his gain
By presenting maids with toys,
And would have ye think 'em joys.
'Tis the ambition of the elf,
T'have all childish, as himself.

First Grace:

If by these ye please to know him,
Beauties, be not nice, but show him.

Second Grace:

Though he had a will to hide him,
Now, we hope, ye'll not abide him,

Third Grace:

Since ye hear his falser play
And that he is Venus' runaway.

John Donne

1572–1631

REBEL and atheist too, with respect to the prevailing traditions of Elizabethan poetry, John Donne sprang from the most conservative part of Elizabethan society. Both his parents were Catholics; his maternal grandfather was John Heywood the epigrammatist. Donne matriculated from Hart Hall, Oxford, at the age of twelve; Catholics often sent their sons to the university early so they could get an education before they were 16, the age at which they could continue in residence only if they took the oath of supremacy. Donne is said to have attended Cambridge also. In 1591 he was at one of the inns of court in London; in 1597, perhaps after having already travelled on the continent, he was a member of Essex's Cadiz expedition, and he also went on the expedition to the Azores. Soon after his return he became secretary to Sir Thomas Egerton, Keeper of the Great Seal and Lord High Chancellor. By 1601 he had served as a member of parliament and had fallen in love with Anne More, niece of Lady Egerton and daughter of Sir George More, Chancellor of the Garter and Lieutenant of the Tower of London. At the end of 1601 Donne and Anne More were secretly married, and Donne's career was ruined. He was discharged and imprisoned, and he had to go through an expensive and protracted lawsuit to recover his wife. For some years they lived on the charity of relatives and friends, while Donne studied and hoped in vain for some opportunity for a career which would utilize his great intellect and learning and enable him to support his growing family.

For at least ten years Donne had been struggling with the problem of the true and right religion, whether the Catholicism in which he had been brought up, the Protestantism of the Church of England or the reformed Puritan doctrine of Geneva. By 1607 he must have settled upon the Church of England, for in that year Thomas Morton, Dean of Gloucester, urged him to take Orders, but he refused. By early 1609 a dozen of his Holy Sonnets had been written; in the next year he published the *Pseudo-Martyr,* written at the command of King James to refute the Catholic objections to the oath of supremacy. In the same year occurred the death of Elizabeth Drury, the fifteen-year old daughter of Sir Robert Drury; it was to give Donne the occasion to celebrate her virtues and their implications in his two most ambitious poems. These celebrated the first and second anniversaries of her death, but more significantly they displayed the passionate, curious and virile mind of John Donne deep in the great philosophical and religious problems of his day. These two Anniversaries are the only poems Donne himself published. In 1612 Donne travelled with Sir Robert Drury on the continent. A year later he applied for the post of ambassador to Venice, and in 1614 was again in Parliament, as member for Taunton; but it was becoming clear that in the opinion of King James and others Donne's abilities had to find their expression in the church or nowhere. In January 1615 he was ordained, and six years later he became Dean of St. Paul's. He was one of the greatest of preachers in the golden age of English pulpit oratory, and his sermons and meditations are classics of English prose as his love-songs and holy sonnets are immortal verse.

It used to be said that there were two Donnes—Jack Donne, the wild young man about town, and the solemn Dr. John Donne, who had his picture painted in his shroud to remind him of his mortality. But the sensitive reader will observe a kind of gravity or solemnity in the background of many of the gay, reckless early songs and an earthly passion in the most sombre lines of his holy sonnets or sermons.

Donne has traditionally been considered the greatest of the "metaphysical" poets. This term, popularized by Dr. Johnson, can easily be misunderstood. Viewed as one of the kinds of rebellion against Elizabethan styles and conventions, metaphysical poetry may be said to be at once more intellectual, more personally passionate, and more concerned to work out, in the form of conceits or ingenious comparisons, the fusion of thought and feeling. The figures of speech are taken seriously; metaphor is pushed into the foreground of the poem and becomes a principle of organization. At the same time, Donne's poetry makes use of a dramatic rhetoric and of speech rhythms, developing a style which had been foreshadowed in Wyatt and occasionally in Sidney but breaking out into such violent prosodic effects that Ben Jonson could say that "Donne, for not keeping of accent, deserved hanging."

Nevertheless, Jonson thought, Donne is the first poet in the world for some things. Wit and paradox, irony and ambiguity, energy and distinctiveness—these are the qualities in which Donne's poems establish themselves as supreme. When such qualities are valued, Donne is valued.

BIBLIOGRAPHY: *Complete Poetry and Selected Prose*, ed. John Hayward, Bloomsbury, 1929; *Complete Poetry and Selected Prose*, ed. Charles M. Coffin, New York, 1952; *The Poems of John Donne*, ed. H. J. C. Grierson, Oxford, 1912; J. B. Leishman, *The Monarch of Wit*, London, 1951; *The Metaphysical Poets*, Oxford, 1934; *John Donne: The Divine Poems*, ed. Helen Gardner, Oxford, 1952; E. M. Simpson, *A Study of the Prose Works of John Donne*, Oxford, 1924 and 1948; Joan Bennett, *Four Metaphysical Poets*, Cambridge 1934 and 1953; Helen C. White, *The Metaphysical Poets*, New York, 1936; Charles M. Coffin, *John Donne and the New Philosophy*, New York, 1937; L. Unger, *Donne's Poetry and Modern Criticism*, Chicago, 1950; Rosemond Tuve, *Elizabethan and Metaphysical Imagery*, Chicago, 1947; *The Sermons of John Donne*, ed. G. M. Potter and E. M. Simpson, Berkeley and Los Angeles, 1953—; Marjorie Nicolson, *The Breaking of the Circle*, Evanston, 1950; V. Harris, *All Coherence Gone*, Chicago, 1949; Margaret Wiley, *The Subtle Knot*, London, 1952; G. Williamson, "Textual Difficulties in the Interpretation of Donne's Poetry," *MP* XXXVIII (1940) 37–72; L. L. Martz, "John Donne in Meditation," *ELH* XIV (1947) 247–273; Clay Hunt, *Donne's Poetry*, New Haven, 1954.

THE GOOD-MORROW

I WONDER, by my troth, what thou and I
Did, till we loved! Were we not weaned till then,
But sucked on country pleasures, childishly?
Or snorted we in the seven sleepers' den? [1]
T'was so; But this, all pleasures fancies be.
If ever any beauty I did see,
Which I desired, and got, t'was but a dream of thee.

And now good morrow to our waking souls,
Which watch not one another out of fear;
For love all love of other sights controls,[2]
And makes one little room an everywhere.
Let sea-discoverers to new worlds have gone,
Let maps to other, worlds on worlds have shown,
Let us possess one world; each hath one, and is one.

My face in thine eye, thine in mine appears,
And true plain hearts do in the faces rest;
Where can we find two better hemispheres
Without sharp North, without declining West?
Whatever dies was not mixed equally;
If our two loves be one, or thou and I
Love so alike that none do slacken, none can die.

SONG

Go and catch a falling star,
  Get with child a mandrake root,[3]
Tell me where all past years are,
  Or who cleft the Devil's foot,
Teach me to hear mermaids singing,
  Or to keep off envy's stinging,
      And find
      What wind
Serves to advance an honest mind.

---

[1] Seven Christian youths fled from persecution about 150 A.D. and found refuge in a cave, where they slept for two centuries.

[2] *controls:* Destroys, eliminates.

[3] The forked root of the mandrake was often thought to resemble a human body; there were many legends and superstitions about it.

If thou beest born to strange sights,
  Things invisible to see,
Ride ten thousand days and nights,
  Till age snow white hairs on thee,
Thou, when thou return'st, wilt tell me
All strange wonders that befell thee,
        And swear
        Nowhere
Lives a woman true, and fair.

If thou findst one, let me know,
  Such a pilgrimage were sweet;
Yet do not, I would not go,
  Though at next door we might meet;
Though she were true when you met her,
And last till you write your letter,
        Yet she
        Will be
False, ere I come, to two, or three.

THE UNDERTAKING

I HAVE done one braver thing
  Than all the Worthies[4] did,
And yet a braver thence doth spring,
  Which is, to keep that hid.

It were but madness now t'impart
  The skill of specular stone,[5]
When he which can have learned the art
  To cut it, can find none.

So, if I now should utter this,
  Others (because no more
Such stuff to work upon, there is,)
  Would love but as before.

But he who loveliness within
  Hath found, all outward loathes,
For he who color loves, and skin,
  Loves but their oldest clothes.

[4] *Worthies:* the traditional heroes.

[5] *specular stone:* a legendary kind of stone which would reflect, like a mirror.

If, as I have, you also do
  Virtue, attired in woman, see,
And dare love that, and say so too,
  And forget the He and She;

And if this love, though placed so,
  From profane men you hide,
Which will no faith on this bestow,
  Or, if they do, deride;

Then you have done a braver thing
  Than all the Worthies did;
And a braver thence will spring,
  Which is, to keep that hid.

THE SUN RISING

Busy old fool, unruly sun,
  Why dost thou thus,
Through windows and through curtains call on us?
Must to thy motions lovers' seasons run?
  Saucy pedantic wretch, go chide
  Late school boys and sour prentices,
 To tell court huntsmen that the King will ride,
 Call country ants to harvest offices;
Love, all alike, no season knows nor clime,
Nor hours, days, months, which are the rags of time.

  Thy beams, so reverend and strong
  Why shouldst thou think?
I could eclipse and cloud them with a wink,
But that I would not lose her sight so long;
  If her eyes have not blinded thine,
  Look, and tomorrow late, tell me,
 Whether both the Indias of spice and mine [6]
 Be where thou leftst them, or lie here with me.
Ask for those kings whom thou saw'st yesterday,
And thou shalt hear, All here in one bed lay.

  She is all states, and all princes, I,
  Nothing else is.
Princes do but play us; compared to this,

[6] *both the Indias:* the East Indies, source of spices, and the West Indies, of gold and silver.

All honor's mimic, all wealth alchemy.
    Thou, sun, art half as happy as we,
    In that the world's contracted thus;
  Thine age asks ease, and since thy duties be
  To warm the world, that's one in warming us.
Shine here to us, and thou art every where;
This bed thy center is, these walls, thy sphere.

THE INDIFFERENT

I CAN love both fair and brown,
Her whom abundance melts, and her whom want betrays,
Her who loves loneness best, and her who masks and plays,
Her whom the country formed, and whom the town,
Her who believes, and her who tries,
Her who still weeps with spongy eyes,
And her who is dry cork, and never cries;
I can love her, and her, and you, and you,
I can love any, so she be not true.

Will no other vice content you?
Will it not serve your turn to do as did your mothers?
Or have you all old vices spent, and now would find out others?
Or doth a fear that men are true torment you?
Oh we are not, be not you so;
Let me, and do you, twenty know.
Rob me, but bind me not, and let me go.
Must I, who came to travail thorough [7] you
Grow your fixed subject, because you are true?

Venus heard me sigh this song,
And by love's sweetest part, variety, she swore,
She heard not this till now; and that it should be so no more.
She went, examined, and returned ere long,
And said, alas, Some two or three
Poor heretics in love there be,
Which think to 'stablish dangerous constancy.
But I have told them, Since you will be true,
You shall be true to them who are false to you.

[7] *thorough:* through.

THE CANONIZATION

For God's sake hold your tongue, and let me love,
Or chide my palsy, or my gout,
My five gray hairs, or ruined fortune, flout,
With wealth your state, your mind with arts improve,
Take you a course,[8] get you a place,
Observe His Honor, or His Grace,
Or the King's real, or his stamped face [9]
Contemplate,—what you will, approve,
So you will let me love.

Alas, alas, who's injured by my love?
What merchant's ships have my sighs drowned?
Who says my tears have overflowed his ground?
When did my colds a forward spring remove?
When did the heats which my veins fill
Add one more to the plaguy bill? [10]
Soldiers find wars, and lawyers find out still
Litigious men, which quarrels move,
Though she and I do love.

Call us what you will, we are made such by love;
Call her one, me another fly,
We're tapers too, and at our own cost die,
And we in us find the eagle and the dove.
The phoenix riddle hath more wit
By us,—we two being one, are it.
So, to one neutral thing both sexes fit.
We die and rise the same, and prove
Mysterious by this love.

We can die by it, if not live by love,
And if unfit for tombs and hearse
Our legend be, it will be fit for verse;
And if no piece of chronicle we prove,
We'll build in sonnets pretty rooms;
As well a well-wrought urn becomes
The greatest ashes, as half-acre tombs,
And by these hymns, all shall approve
Us canonized for love:

[8] of action.
[9] on coins.
[10] *plaguy bill:* a list of persons dead of the plague.

And thus invoke us: You whom reverend love
  Made one another's hermitage;
You, to whom love was peace, that now is rage;
  Who did the whole world's soul contract, and drove
    Into the glasses of your eyes
    (So made such mirrors, and such spies,
That they did all to you epitomize,)
  Countries, towns, courts: Beg from above
  A pattern of your love!

SONG

Sweetest love, I do not go,
  For weariness of thee,
Nor in hope the world can show
  A fitter love for me;
    But since that I
Must die at last, 'tis best,
To use my self in jest
  Thus by fained deaths to die;

Yesternight the sun went hence,
  And yet is here today,
He hath no desire nor sense,
  Nor half so short a way:
    Then fear not me
But believe that I shall make
Speedier journeys, since I take
  More wings and spurs than he.

O how feeble is man's power,
  That if good fortune fall,
Cannot add another hour,
  Nor a lost hour recall!
    But come bad chance,
And we join to it our strength
And we teach it art and length,
  It self o'er us t' advance.

When thou sigh'st, thou sigh'st not wind,
  But sigh'st my soul away,[11]

[11] The soul was supposed to leave the body in a sigh.

When thou weep'st, unkindly kind,
  My life's blood doth decay.
    It cannot be
That thou lov'st me, as thou say'st,
If in thine my life thou waste,
  That art the best of me.

Let not thy divining heart
  Forethink me any ill,
Destiny may take thy part,
  And may thy fears fulfill;
    But think that we
Are but turn'd aside to sleep;
They who one another keep
  Alive, ne'er parted be.

LOVE'S GROWTH

I SCARCE believe my love to be so pure
  As I had thought it was,
  Because it doth endure
Vicissitude and season, as the grass;
Methinks I lied all winter, when I swore
My love was infinite, if spring make it more.
But if this medicine, love, which cures all sorrow
With more, not only be no quintessence,
But mixed of all stuffs, paining soul or sense,
And of the sun his working vigor borrow,
Love's not so pure and abstract as they use
To say, which have no mistress but their Muse;
But as all else, being elemented too,
Love sometimes would contemplate, sometimes do.

And yet no greater, but more eminent,
  Love by the spring is grown;
  As, in the firmament,
Stars by the Sun are not enlarged, but shown,
Gentle love deeds, as blossoms on a bough,
From love's awakened root do bud out now.
If, as in water stirred more circles be
Produced by one, love such additions take,
Those like so many spheres, but one heaven make,
For they are all concentric unto thee.

And though each spring do add to love new heat,
As princes do in times of action get
New taxes, and remit them not in peace,
No winter shall abate the spring's increase.

LOVE'S ALCHEMY

Some that have deeper digged love's mine than I,
Say where his centric happiness doth lie;
  I have loved, and got, and told,
But should I love, get, tell, till I were old,
I should not find that hidden mystery;
  Oh, 'tis imposture all:
And as no chemic [12] yet the elixir got,
  But glorifies his pregnant pot,
  If by the way to him befall
Some odoriferous thing, or medicinal;
 So lovers dream a rich and long delight,
 But get a winter-seeming summer's night.

Our ease, our thrift, our honor, and our day,
Shall we for this vain bubble's shadow pay?
  Ends love in this, that my man
Can be as happy as I can if he can
Endure the short scorn of a bridegroom's play?
  That loving wretch that swears,
'Tis not the bodies marry, but the minds,
  Which he in her angelic finds,
  Would swear as justly that he hears,
In that day's rude hoarse minstrelsy, the spheres.
 Hope not for mind in women; at their best
 Sweetness and wit they are, but mummy, possest.

THE FLEA

Mark but this flea, and mark in this,
How little that which thou deniest me is;
It sucked me first, and now sucks thee,
And in this flea our two bloods mingled be;
Thou know'st that this cannot be said

[12] *chemic:* alchemist.

A sin, nor shame, nor loss of maidenhead,
  Yet this enjoys before it woo,
  And pampered swells with one blood made of two,
  And this, alas, is more than we would do.

Oh stay, three lives in one flea spare,
Where we almost, yea more than married, are.
This flea is you and I, and this
Our marriage bed and marriage temple is;
Though parents grudge, and you, w'are met,
And cloystered in these living walls of jet,
  Though use make you apt to kill me
  Let not to that, self-murder added be,
  And sacrilege, three sins in killing three.

Cruel and sudden, hast thou since
Purpled thy nail, in blood of innocence?
Wherein could this flea guilty be,
Except in that drop which it sucked from thee?
Yet thou triumph'st, and say'st that thou
Find'st not thy self nor me the weaker now;
  'Tis true, then learn how false fears be;
  Just so much honor, when thou yield'st to me,
  Will waste, as this flea's death took life from thee.

THE APPARITION

When by thy scorn, Oh murderess, I am dead,
And that thou thinkst thee free
From all solicitation from me,
Then shall my ghost come to thy bed,
And thee, fained vestal, in worse arms shall see;
Then thy sick taper will begin to wink,
And he whose thou art then, being tired before,
Will, if thou stir, or pinch to wake him, think
    Thou call'st for more,
And in false sleep will from thee shrink,
And then, poor aspen wretch, neglected thou
Bathed in a cold quicksilver sweat wilt lie
    A verier ghost than I;
What I will say, I will not tell thee now,
Lest that preserve thee; and since my love is spent,
I had rather thou shouldst painfully repent,
Than by my threatenings rest still innocent.

THE BROKEN HEART

He is stark mad, whoever says
  That he hath been in love an hour;
Yet not that love so soon decays,
  But that it can ten in less space devour;
Who will believe me, if I swear
That I have had the plague a year?
  Who would not laugh at me, if I should say,
  I saw a flask of powder burn a day?

Ah, what a trifle is a heart,
  If once into love's hands it come!
All other griefs allow a part
  To other griefs, and ask themselves but some;
They come to us; but us Love draws,
He swallows us, and never chaws.
  By him, as by chain'd shot, whole ranks do die,
  He is the tyrant pike, our hearts the fry.

If 'twere not so, what did become
  Of my heart, when I first saw thee?
I brought a heart into the room,
  But from the room I carried none with me:
If it had gone to thee, I know
Mine would have taught thine heart to show
  More pity unto me; but Love, alas,
  At one first blow did shiver it as glass.

Yet nothing can to nothing fall,
  Nor any place be empty quite,
Therefore I think my breast hath all
  Those pieces still, though they be not unite;
And now as broken glasses show
A hundred lesser faces, so
  My rags of heart can like, wish, and adore,
  But after one such love can love no more.

A VALEDICTION: FORBIDDING MOURNING

As virtuous men pass mildly away,
And whisper to their souls to go,
Whilst some of their sad friends do say
The breath goes now, and some say, No;

So let us melt, and make no noise,
No tear-floods, nor sigh-tempests move,
'Twere profanation of our joys
To tell the laiety our love.

Moving of th'earth brings harms and fears,
Men reckon what it did and meant;
But trepidation of the spheres,
Though greater far, is innocent.[13]

Dull sublunary lovers' love
(Whose soul is sense) cannot admit
Absence, because it doth remove
Those things which elemented it.

But we by a love so much refined
That our selves know not what it is,
Inter-assured of the mind,
Care less, eyes, lips, and hands to miss.

Our two souls therefore, which are one,
Though I must go, endure not yet
A breach, but an expansion,
Like gold to airy thinness beat.

If they be two, they are two so
As stiff twin compasses are two;
Thy soul, the fixt foot, makes no show
To move, but doth, if th'other do.

And though it in the center sit,
Yet when the other far doth roam,

[13] Earthquakes are supposed to have sinister meaning for human beings, but the greater celestial motions are considered harmless.

It leans and harkens after it,
  And grows erect, as that comes home.

Such wilt thou be to me, who must
  Like th'other foot, obliquely run;
Thy firmness draws my circle just,
  And makes me end where I begun.

THE ECSTASY

WHERE, like a pillow on a bed,
  A pregnant bank swelled up to rest
The violet's reclining head,
  Sat we two, one another's best.
Our hands were firmly cemented
  With a fast balm, which thence did spring.
Our eye-beams twisted, and did thread
  Our eyes upon one double string;
So t'intergraft our hands, as yet
  Was all the means to make us one;
And pictures in our eyes to get
  Was all our propagation.
As 'twixt two equal armies, Fate
  Suspends uncertain victory,
Our souls, (which to advance their state,
  Were gone out) hung 'twixt her and me.
And whilst our souls negotiate there,
  We like sepulchral statues lay;
All day the same our postures were,
  And we said nothing all the day.
If any, so by love refined,
  That he soul's language understood,
And by good love were grown all mind,
  Within convenient distance stood,
He (though he knew not which soul spake,
  Because both meant, both spake the same)
Might thence a new concoction [14] take,
  And part far purer than he came.
This ecstasy doth unperplex,
  We said, and tell us what we love;
We see by this it was not sex;
  We see we saw not what did move;
But as all several souls contain

[14] *concoction:* distillation, purification.

Mixture of things, they know not what,
Love these mixt souls, doth mix again,
And makes both one, each this and that.
A single violet transplant,
The strength, the colour, and the size,
(All which before was poor, and scant,)
Redoubles still, and multiplies.
When love, with one another so
Interinanimates two souls,
That abler soul, which thence doth flow,
Defects of loneliness controls.
We then, who are this new soul, know,
Of what we are composed, and made,
For, th'atomies of which we grow,
Are souls, whom no change can invade.
But Oh alas, so long, so far
Our bodies why do we forbear?
They are ours, though they are not we; we are
The intelligences, they the spheres.[15]
We owe them thanks because they thus,
Did us to us at first convey,
Yielded their senses' force to us,
Nor are dross to us, but allay.[16]
On man heaven's influence works not so
But that it first imprints the air,
So soul into the soul may flow,
Though it to body first repaire.
As our blood labors to beget
Spirits as like souls as it can,
Because such fingers need to knit
That subtle knot which makes us man:
So must pure lovers' souls descend
T'affections, and to faculties
Which sense may reach and apprehend;
Else a great Prince in prison lies.
To our bodies turn we then, that so
Weak men on love revealed may look;
Love's mysteries in souls do grow,
But yet the body is his book.
And if some lover, such as we,
Have heard this dialogue of one,
Let him still mark us; he shall see
Small change when we are to bodies gone.

[15] In the old astronomy each planet or star was moved in its sphere by an angel or "intelligence."

[16] *allay:* alloy.

LOVE'S DEITY

I LONG to talk with some old lover's ghost,
Who died before the god of love was born;
I cannot think that he who then loved most
Sunk so low as to love one which did scorn.
But since this god produced a destiny,
And that vice-nature, custom, lets it be,
I must love her, that loves not me.

Sure, they which made him god, meant not so much,
Nor he, in his young godhead practised it.
But when an even flame two hearts did touch,
His office was indulgently to fit
Actives to passives. Correspondency
Only his subject was; it cannot be
Love, till I love her, that loves me.

But every modern god will now extend
His vast prerogative as far as Jove.
To rage, to lust, to write to, to commend,
All is the purlieu of the god of love.
Oh were we wakened by this tyranny
To ungod this child again, it could not be
I should love her, who loves not me!

Rebel and atheist too, why murmur I,
As though I felt the worst that love could do?
Love might make me leave loving, or might try
A deeper plague, to make her love me too,
Which, since she loves before, I am loath to see;
Falsehood is worse than hate; and that must be,
If she whom I love, should love me.

THE FUNERAL

WHOEVER comes to shroud me, do not harm
Nor question much
That subtle wreath of hair which crowns my arm;
The mystery, the sign you must not touch,
For 'tis my outward soul,

Viceroy to that, which then to heaven being gone,
    Will leave this to control,
And keep these limbs, her provinces, from dissolution.

For if the sinewy thread my brain lets fall
    Through every part
Can tie those parts and make me one of all;
These hairs, which upward grew, and strength and art
    Have from a better brain,
Can better do it; except she meant that I
    By this should know my pain,
As prisoners then are manacled, when they are condemned to die.

What e'er she meant by it, bury it with me,
    For since I am
Love's martyr, it might breed idolatry,
If into others' hands these relics came;
    As 'twas humility
To afford to it all that a soul can do,
    So 'tis some bravery,
That since you would save none of me, I bury some of you.

THE RELIC

When my grave is broke up again
Some second guest to entertain,
(For graves have learned that woman-head
To be to more than one a bed)
    And he that digs it, spies
A bracelet of bright hair about the bone,
    Will he not let us alone,
And think that there a loving couple lies,
Who thought that this device might be some way
To make their souls, at the last busy day,
Meet at this grave, and make a little stay?

If this fall in a time, or land,
Where mis-devotion doth command,
Then he that digs us up, will bring
Us to the Bishop and the King,
    So make us relics; then
Thou shalt be a Mary Magdalen, and I
    A something else thereby;

All women shall adore us, and some men;
And since at such time, miracles are sought,
I would have that age by this paper taught
What miracles we harmless lovers wrought.

First, we lov'd well and faithfully,
Yet knew not what we lov'd, nor why,
Difference of sex no more we knew,
Than our guardian angels do;
Coming and going, we
Perchance might kiss, but not between those meals;
Our hands ne'r touched the seals,
Which nature, injured by late law, sets free:
These miracles we did; but now, alas,
All measure and all language I should pass,
Should I tell what a miracle she was.

NEGATIVE LOVE

I NEVER stooped so low, as they
Which on an eye, cheek, lip, can prey;
Seldom to them, which soar no higher
Than virtue or the mind to admire;
For sense and understanding may
Know what gives fuel to their fire.
My love, though silly, is more brave,
For may I miss when e'er I crave,
If I know yet what I would have.

If that be simply perfectest
Which can by no way be expressed
But negatives, my love is so.
To all which all love, I say No.
If any who deciphers best
What we know not, our selves, can know,
Let him teach me that nothing. This
As yet my ease and comfort is:
Though I speed not, I cannot miss.

FAREWELL TO LOVE

WHILST yet to prove,[17]
I thought there was some deity in love,
So did I reverence, and gave
Worship; as atheists at their dying hour
Call what they cannot name an unknown power,
As ignorantly did I crave:
Thus when
Things not yet known are coveted by men,
Our desires give them fashion, and so
As they wax lesser, fall, as they size, grow.

But, from late fair
His highness sitting in a golden chair,[18]
Is not less cared for after three days
By children, than the thing which lovers so
Blindly admire, and with such worship woo;
Being had, enjoying it decays:
And thence,
What before pleas'd them all, takes but one sense,
And that so lamely, as it leaves behind
A kind of sorrowing dullness to the mind.

Ah cannot we,
As well as cocks and lions jocund be,
After such pleasures? Unless wise
Nature decreed (since each such act, they say,
Diminisheth the length of life a day)
This, as she would man should despise
The sport,
Because that other curse of being short,
And only for a minute made to be,
Eagers desire to raise posterity.[19]

Since so, my mind
Shall not desire what no man else can find,
I'll no more dote and run
To pursue things which had indamaged me.

---

[17] *whilst . . . prove:* while still inexperienced.

[18] A figure of gilt gingerbread, bought at a fair.

[19] Sharpens desire for offspring. Donne is referring to the Aristotelian idea that the sexual impulse is a part of man's longing for immortality through descendants.

And when I come where moving beauties be,
  As men do when the summer's sun
    Grows great,
Though I admire their greatness, shun their heat;
  Each place can afford shadows. If all fail,
'Tis but applying worm-seed to the tail.

A LECTURE UPON THE SHADOW

Stand still, and I will read to thee
A lecture, love, in Love's philosophy.
    These three hours that we have spent,
    Walking here, two shadows went
Along with us, which we ourselves produced;
But now the sun is just above our head,
    We do those shadows tread,
    And to brave clearness all things are reduced.
  So whilst our infant loves did grow,
  Disguises did, and shadows, flow
  From us, and our cares; but now 'tis not so.

That love hath not attained the high'st degree,
Which is still diligent lest others see.

Except our loves at this noon stay,
We shall new shadows make the other way.
    As the first were made to blind
    Others, these which come behind
Will work upon ourselves and blind our eyes.
If our loves faint and westwardly decline,
    To me thou, falsely, thine,
    And I to thee mine actions shall disguise.
  The morning shadows wear away,
  But these grow longer all the day,
  But oh, love's day is short, if love decay.

Love is a growing, or full constant light,
And his first minute, after noon, is night.

ELEGY V. HIS PICTURE

Here, take my picture; though I bid farewell,
Thine, in my heart, where my soul dwells, shall dwell.

'Tis like me now, but I dead, 'twill be more
When we are shadows both, than 'twas before.
When weather-beaten I come back, my hand,
Perhaps with rude oars torn, or sunbeams tanned,
My face and breast of haircloth, and my head
With care's rash sudden storms being o'erspread,
My body a sack of bones, broken within,
And powder's blue stains scattered on my skin;
If rival fools tax thee to have loved a man
So foul and course as, Oh, I may seem then,
This shall say what I was; and thou shalt say,
Do his hurts reach me? doth my worth decay?
Or do they reach his judging mind, that he
Should now love less, what he did love to see?
That which in him was fair and delicate
Was but the milk, which in love's childish state
Did nurse it; who now is grown strong enough
To feed on that, which to disused tastes seems tough.

ELEGY IX. THE AUTUMNAL

No spring, nor summer beauty hath such grace,
  As I have seen in one autumnal face.
Young beauties force our love, and that's a rape;
  This doth but counsel, yet you cannot 'scape.
If t'were a shame to love, here t'were no shame,
  Affection here takes Reverence's name.
Were her first years the golden age, that's true;
  But now she's gold oft tried, and ever new.
That was her torrid and inflaming time,
  This is her tolerable tropic clime.
Fair eyes, who asks more heat than comes from hence,
  He in fever wishes pestilence.
Call not these wrinkles graves; if graves they were,
  They were Love's graves, for else he is no where.
Yet lies not Love dead here, but here doth sit
  Vowed to this trench, like an anachorit.[20]
And here, till hers, which must be his death, come,
  He doth not dig a grave, but build a tomb.
Here dwells he, though he sojourn everywhere
  In progress, yet his standing house is here.
Here, where still evening is, not noon, nor night;

[20] *anachorit:* anchorite, hermit.

Where no voluptuousness, yet all delight.
In all her words, unto all hearers fit,
You may at revels, you at council sit.
This is love's timber, youth his under-wood;
There be, as wine in June, enrages blood,
Which then comes seasonablest, when our taste
And appetite to other things, is past.
Xerxes' strange Lydian love, the platane tree,[21]
Was lov'd for age, none being so large as she,
Or else because, being young, nature did bless
Her youth with age's glory, barrenness.
If we love things long sought, age is a thing
Which we are fifty years in compassing.
If transitory things, which soon decay,
Age must be loveliest at the latest day.
But name not winter-faces, whose skin's slack,
Lank as an unthrift's purse, but a soul's sack;
Whose eyes seek light within, for all here's shade;
Whose mouths are holes, rather worn out, than made,
Whose every tooth to a several place is gone,
To vex their souls at resurrection;
Name not these living death's-heads unto me,
For these, not ancient, but antique be.
I hate extremes; yet I had rather stay
With tombs than cradles to wear out a day.
Since such love's natural lation[22] is, may still
My love descend and journey down the hill,
Not panting after growing beauties, so
I shall ebb out with them who homeward go.

ELEGY XVI. ON HIS MISTRESS

By our first strange and fatal interview,
By all desires which thereof did ensue,
By our long starving hopes, by that remorse
Which my words' masculine persuasive force
Begot in thee, and by the memory
Of hurts which spies and rivals threatened me,
I calmly beg; but by thy father's wrath,
By all pains which want and divorcement hath,

[21] Herodotus tells how Xerxes fell in love with a plane-tree, hung it with gold and appointed a guardian for it.

[22] *lation:* Local motion.

I conjure thee, and all the oaths which I
And thou have sworn to seal joint constancy,
Here I unswear, and overswear them thus,
Thou shalt not love by ways so dangerous.
Temper, Oh fair love, love's impetuous rage,
By my true mistress still, not my feigned page;
I'll go, and, by thy kind leave, leave behind
Thee, only worthy to nurse in my mind,
Thirst to come back; Oh, if thou die before,
My soul from other lands to thee shall soar.
Thy else almighty beauty cannot move
Rage from the seas, nor thy love teach them love,
Nor tame wild Boreas' harshness; thou hast read
How roughly he in pieces shivered
Fair Orithea, whom he swore he loved.[23]
Fall ill or good, 'tis madness to have proved
Dangers unurged; feed on this flattery,
That absent lovers one in th'other be.
Dissemble nothing, not a boy, nor change
Thy body's habit, nor mind's; be not strange
To thy self only; all will spy in thy face
A blushing womanly discovering grace;
Richly clothed apes are called apes, and as soon,
Eclipsed as bright, we call the moon the moon.
Men of France, changeable chamelions,
Spittals of diseases, shops of fashions,
Love's fuellers, and the rightest company
Of players which upon the world's stage be,
Will quickly know thee, and no less, alas!
Th'indifferent Italian, as we pass
His warm land, well content to think thee page,
Will hunt thee with such lust and hideous rage,
As Lot's fair guests were vext.[24] But none of these
Nor spongy hydroptic Dutch shall thee displease,
If thou stay here. Oh stay here, for, for thee
England is only a worthy gallery,
To walk in expectation, till from thence
Our greatest King call thee to his presence.
When I am gone, dream me some happiness,
Nor let thy looks our long hid love confess,
Nor praise, nor dispraise me, nor bless nor curse
Openly love's force, nor, in bed, fright thy nurse

[23] The roughness of Boreas, the north wind, to his bride Oreithyia is described in Ovid, *Metamorphoses VI*, 682 ff., though the god does not shiver her in pieces.

[24] Genesis 19:1–10.

With midnight's startings, crying out, "Oh, Oh
Nurse, Oh my love is slain! I saw him go
O'er the white Alps alone! I saw him, I,
Assail'd, fight, taken, stabbed, bleed, fall, and die!"
Augur me better chance, except dread Jove
Think it enough for me to have had thy love.

ELEGY XIX. TO HIS MISTRESS GOING TO BED

Come, Madam, come, all rest my powers defy,
Until I labor, I in labor lie.
The foe oft-times having the foe in sight,
Is tired with standing though he never fight.
Off with that girdle, like heaven's zone glistering,
But a far fairer world incompassing.
Unpin that spangled breastplate which you wear
That th' eyes of busy fools may be stopped there.
Unlace yourself, for that harmonious chime,
Tells me from you, that now it is bedtime.
Off with that happy busk, which I envy,
That still can be, and still can stand so nigh.
Your gown going off, such beauteous state reveals,
As when from flowery meads the hills' shadow steals.
Off with that wiry coronet and show
The hairy diadem which on you doth grow;
Now off with those shoes, and then safely tread
In this love's hallowed temple, this soft bed.
In such white robes, heaven's angels used to be
Received by men; thou, angel, bringest with thee
A heaven like Mahomet's Paradise; and though
Ill spirits walk in white, we easily know,
By this these angels from an evil sprite:
Those set our hairs, but these our flesh upright.
License my roving hands, and let them go.
Before, behind, between, above, below.
O my America! my new-found-land,
My kingdom, safeliest when with one man manned,
My mine of precious stones, my empiry,[25]
How blest am I in this discovering thee!
To enter in these bonds, is to be free;
Then where my hand is set, my seal shall be.

[25] *empiry:* empire.

Full nakedness! All joys are due to thee,
As souls unbodied, bodies unclothed must be,
To taste whole joys. Gems which you women use
Are like Atlanta's balls, cast in men's views,
That when a fool's eye lighteth on a gem,
His earthly soul may covet theirs, not them.
Like pictures, or like books' gay coverings made
For laymen, are all women thus arrayed;
Themselves are mystic books, which only we
(Whom their imputed grace will dignify)
Must see revealed. Then since that I may know,
As liberally, as to a midwife, show
Thyself; cast all, yea, this white linen hence,
[Here] is no penance, much less innocence.[26]
To teach thee, I am naked first; why then
What needst thou have more covering than a man?

SATIRE III. RELIGION

Kind pity chokes my spleen; brave scorn forbids
Those tears to issue which swell my eyelids;
I must not laugh, nor weep sins, and be wise,
Can railing then cure these worn maladies?
Is not our mistress, fair Religion,
As worthy of all our souls' devotion,
As virtue was to the first blinded age?
Are not heaven's joys as valiant to assuage
Lusts, as earth's honor was to them? Alas,
As we do them in means, shall they surpass
Us in the end, and shall thy father's spirit
Meet blind philosophers in heaven, whose merit
Of strict life may be imputed faith, and hear
Thee, whom he taught so easy ways and near
To follow, damned? Oh if thou dar'st, fear this;
This fear great courage and high valour is.
Dar'st thou aid mutinous Dutch, and dar'st thou lay
Thee in ships, wooden sepulchers, a prey
To leaders' rage, to storms, to shot, to dearth?
Dar'st thou dive seas and dungeons of the earth?
Hast thou courageous fire to thaw the ice
Of frozen north discoveries? and thrice
Colder than salamanders, like divine

---

[26] Penance and innocence are both symbolized by wearing white robes.

Children in the oven, fires of Spain, and the line,
Whose countries limbecks to our bodies be,
Canst thou for gain bear? And must every he
Which cries not, "Goddess!" to thy Mistress, draw,
Or eat thy poisonous words? Courage of straw!
Oh desperate coward, wilt thou seem bold, and
To thy foes and his (who made thee to stand
Sentinel in his world's garrison) thus yield,
And for the forbidden wars, leave th'appointed field?
Know thy foes: The foul Devil (whom thou
Strivest to please,) for hate, not love, would allow
Thee fain his whole realm to be quit; and as
The world's all parts wither away and pass,
So the world's self, thy other loved foe, is
In her decrepit wane, and thou, loving this,
Dost love a withered and worn strumpet; last,
Flesh (itself's death) and joys which flesh can taste,
Thou lovest; and thy fair goodly soul, which doth
Give this flesh power to taste joy, thou dost loathe.
Seek true religion. Oh where? Mirreus,
Thinking her unhoused here, and fled from us,
Seeks her at Rome—there, because he doth know
That she was there a thousand years ago.
He loves her rags so, as we here obey
The statecloth where the Prince sat yesterday.
Crantz to such brave loves will not be inthralled,
But loves her only, who at Geneva is called
Religion,—plain, simple, sullen, young,
Contemptuous, yet unhandsome, as among
Lecherous humors, there is one that judges
No wenches wholesome but course country drudges.
Graius stays still at home here, and because
Some preachers, vile ambitious bawds, and laws
Still new, like fashions, bid him think that she
Which dwells with us, is only perfect, he
Embraceth her whom his Godfathers will
Tender to him, being tender, as wards still
Take such wives as their guardians offer, or
Pay values. Careless Phrygius doth abhor
All, because all cannot be good, as one
Knowing some women whores, dares marry none.
Graccus loves all as one, and thinks that so
As women do in divers countries go
In divers habits, yet are still one kind,
So doth, so is religion; and this blind-

ness too much light breeds; but unmoved thou
Of force must one, and forced but one allow;
And the right; ask thy father which is she,
Let him ask his; though truth and falsehood be
Near twins, yet truth a little elder is;
Be busy to seek her, believe me this:
He's not of none, nor worst, that seeks the best.
To adore, or scorn an image, or protest,
May all be bad; doubt wisely. In strange way
To stand inquiring right, is not to stray;
To sleep, or run wrong, is. On a huge hill,
Cragged, and steep, Truth stands, and he that will
Reach her, about must, and about must go,
And what the hill's suddenness resists, win so;
Yet strive so, that before age, death's twilight,
Thy soul rest, for none can work in that night.
To will implies delay, therefore now do.
Hard deeds, the bodies pains; hard knowledge too
The mind's endeavours reach, and mysteries
Are like the sun, dazzling, yet plain to all eyes.
Keep the truth which thou hast found; men do not stand
In so ill case here, that God hath with his hand
Signed kings' blank-charters to kill whom they hate.
Nor are they vicars, but hangmen to fate.
Fool and wretch, wilt thou let thy soul be tied
To man's laws, by which she shall not be tried
At the last day? Oh, will it then boot thee
To say a Philip, or a Gregory,
A Harry, or a Martin taught thee this?
Is not this excuse for mere contraries
Equally strong? Cannot both sides say so?
That thou mayest rightly obey power, her bounds know;
Those past, her nature and name is changed; to be
Then humble to her is idolatry.
As streams are, power is; those blest flowers that dwell
At the rough stream's calm head, thrive and do well,
But having left their roots, and themselves given
To the stream's tyrannous rage, alas, are driven
Through mills, and rocks, and woods, and at last, almost
Consumed in going, in the sea are lost.
So perish souls, which more choose men's unjust
Power from God claimed, than God himself to trust.

LETTERS TO SEVERAL PERSONAGES

THE CALM

Our storm is past, and that storm's tyrannous rage,
A stupid calm, but nothing it, doth 'suage.
The fable is inverted, and far more
A block afflicts, now, than a stork before.[27]
Storms chafe, and soon wear out themselves, or us;
In calms, Heaven laughs to see us languish thus.
As steady as I can wish that my thoughts were,
Smooth as thy mistress' glass, or what shines there,
The sea is now. And, as the isles which we
Seek, when we can move, our ships rooted be.
As water did in storms, now pitch runs out;
As lead, when a fired church becomes one spout.
And all our beauty, and our trim, decays,
Like courts removing, or like ended plays.
The fighting place now seamen's rags supply,
And all the tackling is a frippery.[28]
No use of lanterns, and in one place lay
Feathers and dust, today and yesterday.
Earth's hollowness, which the world's lungs are,
Have no more wind than the upper vault of air.
We can nor lost friends, nor sought foes recover,
But meteorlike, save that we move not, hover.
Only the calenture [29] together draws
Dear friends, which meet dead in great fishes' jaws;
And on the hatches as on altars lies
Each one, his own priest, and own sacrifice.
Who live, that miracle do multiply
Where walkers in hot ovens, do not die.[30]
If in despite of these, we swim, that hath
No more refreshing, than our brimstone bath,
But from the sea, into the ship we turn,
Like parboil'd wretches, on the coals to burn.
Like Bajazet encag'd, the shepherd's scoff,[31]

---

[27] In Aesop's fable, the frogs asked Jupiter for a king. He gave them a log of wood, which they scorned, so he gave them a stork, which ate them.

[28] *frippery:* a second-hand clothes shop.

[29] *calenture:* a tropical disease, in the delirium of which sailors sometimes took the sea for green fields and jumped overboard.

[30] Daniel 3:12–30.

[31] The famous scene in Marlowe's *Tamburlaine,* Part I, Act IV, scene ii. Bajazeth, the Turkish emperor, is exhibited in a cage and scoffed at by his conqueror, the shepherd Tamburlaine.

Or like slack sinew'd Samson, his hair off,
Languish our ships. Now, as a myriad
Of ants durst th' Emperor's loved snake invade,[32]
The crawling galleys, sea-jails, finny chips,
Might brave our pinnaces, now bed-rid ships.
Whether a rotten state, and hope of gain,
Or to disuse me from the queasy pain
Of being beloved, and loving, or the thirst
Of honor, or fair death, out pushed me first,
I lose my end; for here as well as I
A desperate may live, and a coward die.
Stag, dog, and all which from, or towards flies,
Is paid with life, or prey, or doing dies.
Fate grudges us all, and doth subtly lay
A scourge, gainst which we all forget to pray;
He that at sea prays for more wind, as well
Under the poles may beg cold, heat in hell.
What are we then? How little more alas
Is man now, than before he was? He was
Nothing; for us, we are for nothing fit;
Chance, or ourselves still disproportion it.
We have no power, no will, no sense; I lie,
I should not then thus feel this misery.

TO SIR HENRY WOTTON

Sir, more than kisses, letters mingle souls;
For thus friends absent speak. This ease controls
The tediousness of my life; but for these
I could ideate nothing which could please,
But I should wither in one day, and pass
To a bottle of hay, that am a lock of grass.
Life is a voyage, and in our life's ways
Countries, courts, towns are rocks, or remoraes;[33]
They break or stop all ships, yet our state's such,
That though than pitch they stain worse, we must touch.
If in the furnace of the even line,
Or under th'adverse icy poles thou pine,
Thou know'st two temperate regions girded in
Dwell there: But Oh, what refuge canst thou win
Parched in the Court, and in the country frozen?

[32] An incident in Suetonius' *Life of Tiberius.*

[33] *remoraes:* fish supposed to be able to stop a ship by attaching themselves to it with a suction disc.

Shall cities, built of both extremes, be chosen?
Can dung and garlic be a perfume? or can
A scorpion and torpedo cure a man? [34]
Cities are worst of all three; of all three
(O knotty riddle) each is worst equally.
Cities are sepulchers; they who dwell there
Are carcasses, as if no such there were.
And courts are theaters, where some men play
Princes, some slaves, all to one end, and of one clay.
The Country is a desert, where no good,
Gained (as habits, not born), is understood.
There men become beasts, and prone to more evils;
In cities, blocks; [35] and in a lewd court, devils.
As in the first chaos confusedly
Each element's qualities were in th' other three;
So pride, lust, covetize, being several
To these three places, yet all are in all,
And mingled thus, their issue incestuous.
Falsehood is denizened. Virtue is barbarous.
Let no man say there, "Virtue's flinty wall
Shall lock vice in me; I'll do none, but know all."
Men are sponges, which to pour out, receive;
Who know false play, rather than lose, deceive.
For in best understandings sin began,
Angels sinned first, then devils, and then man.
Only perchance beasts sin not; wretched we
Are beasts in all but white integrity.
I think if men which in these places live
Durst look for themselves, and themselves retrieve,
They would like strangers greet themselves, seeing then
Utopian youth, grown old, Italian.
Be thou thine own home, and in thy self dwell;
In anywhere, continuance maketh hell.
And seeing the snail, which everywhere doth roam,
Carrying his own house still, still is at home,
Follow (for he is easy paced) this snail,
Be thine own palace, or the world's thy jail.
And in the world's sea, do not like cork sleep
Upon the water's face; nor in the deep
Sink like a lead without a line: but as
Fishes glide, leaving no print where they pass,
Nor making sound, so closely thy course go,

[34] Can something desirable be made of two undesirable extremes? Scorpions and torpedoes (electric catfish) were both considered poisonous, but in opposite ways.

[35] *blocks:* stupid persons, blockheads.

Let men dispute, whether thou breathe, or no.
Only in this one thing, be no Galenist:[36] To make
Court's hot ambitions wholesome, do not take
A dram of country's dullness; do not add
Correctives, but as chemics, purge the bad.
But, Sir, I advise not you, I rather do
Say o'er those lessons, which I learned of you:
Whom, free from German schisms, and lightness
Of France, and fair Italy's faithlessness,
Having from these sucked all they had of worth,
And brought home that faith which you carried forth,
I throughly love. But if my self, I have won
To know my rules, I have, and you have

DONNE.

FROM

THE FIRST ANNIVERSARY

How witty's ruin! how importunate
Upon mankind! it labored to frustrate
Even God's purpose; and made woman, sent
For man's relief, cause of his languishment.
They were to good ends, and they are so still,
But accessory, and principal in ill;
For the first marriage was our funeral:
One woman at one blow then killed us all,
And singly, one by one, they kill us now.
We do delightfully ourselves allow
To that consumption, and, profusely blind,
We kill ourselves to propagate our kind.[37]
And yet we do not that, we are not men;
There is not now that mankind which was then,
Whenas the sun and man did seem to strive
(Joint tenants of the world) who should survive;
When stag, and raven, and the long-lived tree,
Compared with man, died in minority;
When, if a slow paced star had stolen away

Shortness of life.

[36] Physicians of the school of Galen believed in balancing the body's humours; those of the school of Paracelsus ("chemics") believed in driving out (purging) the bad with its opposite.

[37] Donne here refers to the old notion that the sexual act shortens life by a day. See his *Farewell to Love*.

From the observer's making, he might stay
Two or three hundred years to see't again,
And then make up his observation plain;
When, as the age was long, the size was great;
Man's growth confessed and recompensed the meat;
So spacious and large, that every soul
Did a fair kingdom and large realm control;
And when the very stature, thus erect,
Did that soul a good way towards heaven direct.
Where is this mankind now? Who lives to age
Fit to be made Methusalem his page?
Alas, we scarce live long enough to try
Whether a true-made clock run right or lie.
Old grandsires talk of yesterday with sorrow,
And for our children we reserve tomorrow.
So short is life that every peasant strives,
In a torn house, or field, to have three lives.
And as in lasting, so in length is man
Contracted to an inch, who was a span; *Smallness of stature.*
For had a man at first in forests strayed,
Or shipwrecked in the sea, one would have laid
A wager, that an elephant, or whale,
That met him, would not hastily assail
A thing so equal to him; now alas,
The fairies, and the pigmies well may pass
As credible; mankind decays so soon,
We are scarce our fathers' shadows cast at noon;
Only death adds t'our length, nor are we grown
In stature to be men till we are none.
But this were light, did our less volume hold
All the old text, or had we changed to gold
Their silver, or disposed into less glass
Spirits of virtue which then scattered was.
But 'tis not so: w'are not retired, but damped;
And as our bodies, so our minds are cramped;
'Tis shrinking, not close weaving that hath thus
In mind and body both bedwarfed us.
We seem ambitious God's whole work to undo;
Of nothing he made us, and we strive too,
To bring our selves to nothing back; and we
Do what we can, to do't so soon as He.
With new diseases on our selves we war,
And with new physic, a worse engine far.
Thus man, this world's vice-emperor, in whom
All faculties, all graces are at home,

And if in other creatures they appear,
They're but man's ministers, and legates there,
To work on their rebellions, and reduce
Them to civility and to man's use:
This man, whom God did woo, and loath t'attend
Till man came up, did down to man descend,
This man, so great, that all that is, is his,
Oh what a trifle, and poor thing he is!
If man were any thing, he's nothing now:
Help, or at least some time to waste, allow
T'his other wants, yet when he did depart
With her whom we lament, he lost his heart.
She, of whom th'ancients seem'd to prophesy,
When they called virtues by the name of *she;*
She in whom virtue was so much refined,
That for allay unto so pure a mind
She took the weaker sex; she that could drive
The poisonous tincture and the stain of Eve
Out of her thoughts and deeds and purify
All by a true religious alchemy;
She, she is dead; she's dead; when thou knowest this,
Thou knowest how poor a trifling thing man is.
And learn'st thus much by our Anatomy,
The heart being perished, no part can be free.
And that except thou feed (not banquet) on
The supernatural food, religion,
Thy better growth grows withered, and scant;
Be more than man, or thou'rt less than an ant.
Then, as mankind, so is the world's whole frame
Quite out of joint, almost created lame:
For, before God had made up all the rest,
Corruption entered, and depraved the best;
It seized the angels, and then first of all
The world did in her cradle take a fall,
And turned her brains, and took a general maim,
Wronging each joint of th'universal frame.
The noblest part, man, felt it first; and then
Both beasts and plants, curst in the curse of man.
So did the world from the first hour decay,
Decay of nature in other parts.
That evening was beginning of the day,
And now the springs and summers which we see,
Like sons of women after fifty be.
And new philosophy calls all in doubt,
The element of fire is quite put out;
The sun is lost, and th'earth, and no man's wit

Can well direct him where to look for it.
And freely men confess that this world's spent,
When in the planets, and the firmament
They seek so many new; then see that this
Is crumbled out again to his atomies.
'Tis all in pieces, all coherence gone;
All just supply, and all relation:
Prince, subject, father, son, are things forgot,
For every man alone thinks he hath got
To be a phoenix, and that then can be
None of that kind, of which he is, but he.

FROM

OF THE PROGRESS OF THE SOUL: THE SECOND ANNIVERSARY

The entrance.

Nothing could make me sooner to confess
That this world had an everlastingness,
Than to consider that a year is run
Since both this lower world's, and the sun's sun,
The lustre and the vigor of this all,
Did set; 'twere blasphemy to say, did fall.
But as a ship which hath struck sail, doth run
By force of that force which before, it won;
Or as sometimes in a beheaded man,
Though at those two red seas which freely ran,
One from the trunk, another from the head,
His soul be sailed to her eternal bed,
His eyes will twinkle and his tongue will roll,
As though he beckoned and called back his soul,
He grasps his hands, and he pulls up his feet
And seems to reach and to step forth to meet
His soul; when all these motions which we saw,
Are but as ice, which crackles at a thaw;
Or as a lute, which in moist weather rings
Her knell alone, by cracking of her strings;
So struggles this dead world, now she is gone,
For there is motion in corruption.
As some days are at the creation named,
Before the sun, the which framed days, was framed,
So after this sun's set, some show appears

And orderly vicissitude of years.
Yet a new Deluge, and of Lethe flood,
Hath drown'd us all. All have forgot all good,
Forgetting her, the main reserve of all.
Yet in this deluge, gross and general,
Thou seest me strive for life; my life shall be,
To be hereafter praised, for praising thee;
Immortal Maid, who though thou wouldst refuse
The name of mother, be unto my Muse
A father, since her chast ambition is,
Yearly to bring forth such a child as this.
These hymns may work on future wits, and so
May great-grand children of thy praises grow.
And so, though not revive, embalm and spice
The world, which else would putrefy with vice.
For thus man may extend thy progeny,
Until men do but vanish and not die.
These hymns, thy issue, may increase so long,
As till God's great *Venite* change the song.
Thirst for that time, Oh my insatiate soul,
And serve thy thirst, with God's safe-sealing bowl.
Be thirsty still, and drink still till thou go
To th'only health, to be hydroptic so.
Forget this rotten world, and unto thee
Let thine own times as an old story be.
Be not concerned; study not why, nor when;
Do not so much as not believe a man.
For though to err be worst, to try truths forth
Is far more business than this world is worth.
The world is but a carcass; thou art fed
By it, but as a worm that carcass bred;
And why shouldst thou, poor worm, consider more,
When this world will grow better than before,
Than those thy fellow worms do think upon
That carcass's last resurrection.
Forget this world, and scarce think of it so
As of old clothes cast off a year ago.
To be thus stupid is alacrity;
Men thus lethargic have best memory.
Look upward; that's towards her, whose happy state
We now lament not, but congratulate.
She to whom all this world was but a stage,
Where all sat harkening how her youthful age
Should be employed, because in all she did,
Some figure of the golden times was hid.

A just disestimation of the world.

Who could not lack whate'er this world could give,
Because she was the form that made it live;
Nor could complain, that this world was unfit
To be stayed in, then when she was in it;
She that first tried indifferent desires
By virtue, and virtue by religious fires,
She to whose person Paradise adhered,
As courts to princes, she whose eyes ensphered
Starlight enough, t'have made the south control
(Had she been there) the star-full northern pole,
She, she is gone; she is gone; when thou knowest this,
What fragmentary rubbish this world is
Thou knowest, and that it is not worth a thought;
He honors it too much that thinks it nought.
Think then, my soul, that death is but a groom,
Which brings a taper to the outward room
Whence thou spiest first a little glimmering light,
And after brings it nearer to thy sight,
For such approaches doth heaven make in death.
Think thy self labouring now with broken breath,
And think those broken and soft notes to be
Division,[38] and thy happiest harmony.
Think thee laid on thy death-bed, loose and slack
And think that, but unbinding of a pack,
To take one precious thing, thy soul from thence.
Think thyself parched with fever's violence,
Anger thine ague more, by calling it
Thy physic; chide the slackness of the fit.
Think that thou hear'st thy knell, and think no more,
But that, as bells call'd thee to church before,
So this, to the triumphant church, calls thee.
Think Satan's sergeants round about thee be,
And think that but for legacies they thrust;
Give one thy pride, t'another give thy lust;
Give them those sins which they gave thee before,
And trust th'immaculate blood to wash thy score.
Think thy friends weeping round, and think that they
Weep but because they go not yet thy way.
Think that they close thine eyes, and think in this,
That they confess much in the world amiss
Who dare not trust a dead man's eye with that,
Which they from God and angels cover not.
Think that they shroud thee up, and think from thence

Contemplation of our state in our death-bed.

[38] *division:* a florid run or variation on a theme.

They reinvest thee in white innocence.
Think that thy body rots, and (if so low,
Thy soul exalted so, thy thoughts can go,)
Think thee a Prince, who of themselves create
Worms which insensibly devour their state.
Think that they bury thee, and think that right
Lays thee to sleep but a Saint Lucy's night.[39]
Think these things cheerfully; and if thou be
Drowsy or slack, remember then that she,
She whose complexion [40] was so even made,
That which of her ingredients should invade
The other three, no fear, no art could guess;
So far were all removed from more or less.
But as in mithridate [41] or just perfumes,
Where all good things being met, no one presumes
To govern, or to triumph on the rest,
Only because all were, no part was best.
And as, though all do know, that quantities
Are made of lines, and lines from points arise,
None can these lines or quantities unjoint,
And say this is a line, or this a point,
So though the elements and humors were
In her, one could not say, this governs there.
Whose even constitution might have won
Any disease to venture on the sun
Rather than her, and make a spirit fear,
That he to disuniting, subject were.
To whose proportions if we would compare
Cubes, th'are unstable; circles angular;
She who was such a chain as fate employs
To bring mankind all fortunes it enjoys;
So fast, so even wrought, as one would think,
No accident could threaten any link;
She, she embraced a sickness, gave it meat,
The purest blood and breath, that e'er it eat;
And hath taught us that though a good man hath
Title to heaven, and plead it by his faith,
And though he may pretend a conquest, since
Heaven was content to suffer violence,
Yea, though he plead a long possession too,
(For they're in heaven on earth who heaven's works do)

---

39 *St. Lucy's night:* the longest night in the year.

40 *complexion:* balance of humours.

41 *mithridate:* the universal antidote, named after the Persian king who gradually accustomed himself to poisons. The ideal remedy would in Galenic theory have to be a perfectly balanced one.

Incommodities of the Soul in the Body.

Though he had right and power and place, before,
Yet Death must usher and unlock the door.
Think further on thyself, my soul, and think
How thou at first wast made but in a sink;
Think that it argued some infirmity,
That those two souls, which then thou found'st in me,
Thou fedst upon, and drewst into thee, both
My second soul of sense, and first of growth.[42]
Think but how poor thou wast, how obnoxious;
Whom a small lump of flesh could poison thus.
This curded milk, this poor unlittered whelp
My body, could, beyond escape or help,
Infect thee with original sin, and thou
Couldst neither then refuse, nor leave it now.
Think that no stubborn sullen anchorit,
Which, fixt to a pillar or a grave, doth sit
Bedded and bathed in all his ordures, dwells
So foully as our souls in their first-built cells.
Think in how poor a prison thou didst lie
After, enabled but to suck and cry.
Think, when 'twas grown to most, 'twas a poor inn,
A province packed up in two yards of skin,
And that usurped or threatened with the rage
Of sickness, or their true mother, age.
But think that Death hath now enfranchised thee,
Thou hast thy expansion now, and liberty;
Think that a rusty piece, discharged, is flown
In pieces, and the bullet is his own,
And freely flies. This to thy soul allow:
Think thy shell broke, think thy soul hatched but now.

Her liberty by death.

And think this slow-paced soul, which late did cleave
To a body, and went but by the body's leave,
Twenty, perchance, or thirty mile a day,
Dispatches in a minute all the way
'Twixt heaven and earth; she stays not in the air,
To look what meteors there themselves prepare;[43]
She carries no desire to know, nor sense,
Whether the air's middle region be intense;
For th' element of fire she doth not know,
Whether she past by such a place or no;
She baits not at the moon, nor cares to try

---

[42] Plato thought there were three separate souls: of growth, of sense, and of intelligence. Aristotle, Aquinas, and Donne consider them merged into one soul.

[43] Meteors were supposedly caused by the effect of cold upper air upon exhalations from the earth.

Whether in that new world, men live and die.
Venus retards her not, to inquire, how she
Can, (being one star) Hesper, and Vesper be.
He that charmed Argus' eyes, sweet Mercury,
Works not on her, who now is grown all eye;
Who, if she meet the body of the sun,
Goes through, not staying till his course be run;
Who finds in Mars his camp no corps of guard;
Nor is by Jove, nor by his father barred;
But ere she can consider how she went,
At once is at and through the firmament.
And as these stars were but so many beads
Strung on one string, speed undistinguished leads
Her through those spheres, as through the beads a string,
Whose quick succession makes it still one thing;
As doth the pith, which, lest our bodies slack,
Strings fast the little bones of neck, and back;
So by the soul doth death string heaven and earth;
For when our soul enjoys this her third birth,
(Creation gave her one, a second, grace,)
Heaven is as near and present to her face
As colors are, and objects, in a room
Where darkness was before when tapers come.
This must, my soul, thy long-short progress be.
To advance these thoughts, remember then, that she,
She, whose fair body no such prison was,
But that a soul might well be pleased to pass
An age in her; she whose rich beauty lent
Mintage to other beauties, for they went
But for so much as they were like to her;
She, in whose body (if we dare prefer
This low world, to so high a mark as she,)
The western treasure, eastern spicery,
Europe, and Africa, and the unknown rest
Were easily found, or what in them was best;
And when we've made this large discovery
Of all, in her some one part then will be
Twenty such parts, whose plenty and riches is
Enough to make twenty such worlds as this;
She, whom had they known who did first betroth
The tutelar angels, and assigned one, both
To nations, cities, and to companies,
To functions, offices, and dignities,
And to each several man, to him, and him,
They would have given her one for every limb;
She, of whose soul, if we may say 'twas gold,

Her body was th' electrum,[44] and did hold
Many degrees of that; we understood
Her by her sight; her pure and eloquent blood
Spoke in her cheeks, and so distinctly wrought,
That one might almost say her body thought.
She, she, thus richly and largely housed, is gone,
And chides us slow-paced snails who crawl upon
Our prison's prison, earth, nor think us well
Longer than whilst we bear our brittle shell.
But 'twere but little to have changed our room,
If, as we were in this our living tomb
Oppressed with ignorance, we still were so.
Poor soul, in this thy flesh what dost thou know?
Thou know'st thy self so little, as thou know'st not,
How thou didst die, nor how thou wast begot.
Thou neither know'st how thou at first cam'st in,
Now how thou took'st the poison of man's sin.
Nor dost thou, (though thou know'st, that thou art so)
By what way thou art made immortal, know.
Thou art too narrow, wretch, to comprehend
Even thy self,—yea though thou wouldst but bend
To know thy body. Have not all souls thought
For many ages, that our body's wrought
Of air, and fire, and other elements?
And now they think of new ingredients,
And one soul thinks one, and another way
Another thinks, and 'tis an even lay.
Know'st thou but how the stone doth enter in
The bladder's cave, and never break the skin?
Know'st thou how blood, which to the heart doth flow,
Doth from one ventricle to th'other go?
And for the putrid stuff which thou dost spit,
Know'st thou how thy lungs have attracted it?
There are no passages, so that there is
(For ought thou know'st) piercing of substances.
And of those many opinions which men raise
Of nails and hairs, dost thou know which to praise?
What hope have we to know our selves, when we
Know not the least things which for our use be?
We see in authors too stiff to recant,
A hundred controversies of an ant;
And yet one watches, starves, freezes and sweats,
To know but catechisms and alphabets
Of unconcerning things, matters of fact;
How others on our stage their parts did act;

[44] *electrum:* a mixture of gold and silver.

What Caesar did, yea, and what Cicero said.
Why grass is green, or why our blood is red,
Are mysteries which none have reached unto.
In this low form, poor soul, what wilt thou do?
When wilt thou shake off this pedantery,
Of being taught by sense and fantasy?
Thou look'st through spectacles; small things seem great
Below; but up unto the watch-tower get,
And see all things despoiled of fallacies.
Thou shalt not peep through lattices of eyes,
Nor hear through labyrinths of ears, nor learn
By circuit, or collections to discern.[45]
In heaven thou straight know'st all concerning it,
And what concerns it not shalt straight forget.
There thou (but in no other school) may'st be
Perchance, as learned and as full, as she,
She who all libraries had throughly read
At home in her own thoughts, and practised
So much good as would make as many more.
She whose example they must all implore,
Who would or do, or think well, and confess
That all the virtuous actions they express,
Are but a new and worse edition
Of her some one thought or one action.
She who in th'art of knowing heaven, was grown
Here upon earth, to such perfection
That she hath, ever since to heaven she came,
In a far fairer print, but read the same.
She, she not satisfied with all this weight,
(For so much knowledge, as would over-freight
Another, did but ballast her) is gone
As well t'enjoy, as get perfection.
And calls us after her, in that she took,
Taking her self, our best and worthiest book.

GOODFRIDAY, 1613. RIDING WESTWARD

Let man's soul be a sphere, and then, in this,
The intelligence that moves, devotion is,
And as the other spheres, by being grown

[45] Angels, and the soul after death, learn directly and immediately, not by the human rational processes of "circuit" and "collections."

Subject to foreign motions, lose their own,
And being by others hurried every day,
Scarce in a year their natural form obey,
Pleasure or business, so, our souls admit
For their first mover, and are whirled by it.
Hence is't, that I am carried towards the west
This day, when my soul's form bends towards the east.
There I should see a sun, by rising, set,
And by that setting endless day beget:
But that Christ on this cross did rise and fall,
Sin had eternally benighted all.
Yet dare I almost be glad I do not see
That spectacle, of too much weight for me.
Who sees God's face, that is self-life, must die;
What a death were it then to see God die?
It made his own lieutenant, Nature, shrink;
It made his footstool crack, and the sun wink.
Could I behold those hands which span the poles,
And tune all spheres at once, pierced with those holes?
Could I behold that endless height which is
Zenith to us, and to our antipodes,
Humbled below us? Or that blood which is
The seat of all our souls, if not of His,
Make dirt of dust, or that flesh which was worn
By God, for his apparel, ragg'd and torn?
If on these things I durst not look, durst I
Upon his miserable mother cast mine eye,
Who was God's partner here, and furnished thus
Half of that sacrifice which ransomed us?
Though these things, as I ride, be from mine eye,
They are present yet unto my memory,
For that looks towards them; and thou look'st towards me,
O Saviour, as thou hang'st upon the tree.
I turn my back to thee but to receive
Corrections, till thy mercies bid thee leave.
O think me worth thine anger; punish me;
Burn off my rusts and my deformity;
Restore thine image so much, by thy grace,
That thou may'st know me, and I'll turn my face.

HOLY SONNETS

I AM a little world made cunningly
Of elements and an angelic sprite,
But black sin hath betrayed to endless night
My world's both parts, and Oh! both parts must die.
You which beyond that heaven which was most high
Have found new spheres, and of new lands can write,
Pour new seas in mine eyes, that so I might
Drown my world with my weeping earnestly,
Or wash it if it must be drowned no more:
But Oh, it must be burnt! Alas, the fire
Of lust and envy have burnt it heretofore,
And made it fouler. Let their flames retire,
And burn me, O Lord, with a fiery zeal
Of thee and thy house, which doth in eating heal.

At the round earth's imagined corners, blow
Your trumpets, angels, and arise, arise
From death, you numberless infinities
Of souls, and to your scattered bodies go,
All whom the flood did, and fire shall o'erthrow,
All whom war, dearth, age, agues, tyrannies,
Despair, law, chance, hath slain, and you whose eyes
Shall behold God, and never taste death's woe.
But let them sleep, Lord, and me mourn a space,
For, if above all these, my sins abound,
'Tis late to ask abundance of thy grace,
When we are there; here on this lowly ground,
Teach me how to repent; for that's as good
As if thou hadst sealed my pardon with thy blood.

If poisonous minerals, and if that tree
Whose fruit threw death on else immortal us,
If lecherous goats, if serpents envious
Cannot be damned, alas, why should I be?
Why should intent or reason, born in me,
Make sins, else equal, in me more heinous?
And mercy being easy and glorious
To God, in his stern wrath why threatens he?
But who am I, that dare dispute with thee,
O God? Oh! of thine only worthy blood,
And my tears, make a heavenly Lethean flood,
And drown in it my sins' black memory.
That thou remember them, some claim as debt;
I think it mercy if thou wilt forget.

Death, be not proud, though some have called thee
Mighty and dreadful, for thou art not so;
For those whom thou think'st thou dost overthrow
Die not, poor Death, nor yet canst thou kill me.
From rest and sleep, which but thy pictures be,
Much pleasure; then from thee much more must flow,
And soonest our best men with thee do go,
Rest of their bones, and soul's delivery.
Thou art slave to fate, chance, kings, and desperate men,
And dost with poison, war, and sickness dwell,
And poppy or charms can make us sleep as well
And better than thy stroke; why swell'st thou then?
One short sleep past, we wake eternally
And death shall be no more; Death, thou shalt die.

Batter my heart, three-personed God; for you
As yet but knock, breathe, shine, and seek to mend;
That I may rise and stand, o'erthrow me, and bend
Your force to break, blow, burn and make me new.
I, like an usurpt town, to another due,
Labour to admit you, but Oh, to no end;
Reason, your viceroy in me, me should defend,
But is captived, and proves weak or untrue.
Yet dearly I love you, and would be loved fain,
But am betrothed unto your enemy.
Divorce me, untie or break that knot again;
Take me to you, imprison me, for I,
Except you enthrall me, never shall be free,
Nor ever chaste, except you ravish me.

A HYMN TO GOD THE FATHER

Wilt thou forgive that sin where I begun,
  Which is my sin, though it were done before?
Wilt thou forgive those sins through which I run,
  And do them still, though still I do deplore?
    When thou hast done, thou hast not done,
      For I have more.

Wilt thou forgive that sin by which I won
  Others to sin and made my sin their door?
Wilt thou forgive that sin which I did shun
  A year or two, but wallowed in a score?
    When thou hast done, thou hast not done,
      For I have more.

I have a sin of fear, that when I have spun
  My last thread, I shall perish on the shore;
Swear by thy self, that at my death thy sun
  Shall shine as it shines now and heretofore;
    And, having done that, thou hast done,
      I have no more.

HYMN TO GOD MY GOD, IN MY SICKNESS

Since I am coming to that holy room
  Where, with thy choir of saints forevermore,
I shall be made thy music; as I come
  I tune the instrument here at the door,
  And what I must do then, think now before.

Whilst my physicians by their love are grown
  Cosmographers, and I their map, who lie
Flat on this bed, that by them may be shown
  That this is my southwest discovery
  Per fretum febris, by these straits to die,

I joy, that in these straits, I see my west;
  For, though their currents yield return to none,
What shall my west hurt me? As west and east
  In all flat maps (and I am one) are one,
  So death doth touch the resurrection.

Is the Pacific Sea my home? Or are
  The eastern riches? Is Jerusalem?
Anyan, and Magellan, and Gibraltar,
  All straits, and none but straits, are ways to them,
  Whether where Japhet dwelt, or Cham, or Sen.

We think that Paradise and Calvary,
  Christ's cross, and Adam's tree, stood in one place;
Look Lord, and find both Adams met in me;
  As the first Adam's sweat surrounds my face,
  May the last Adam's blood my soul embrace.

So, in his purple wrapped, receive me, Lord;
  By these his thorns give me his other crown;
And, as to others' souls I preached thy word,
  By this my text, my sermon to mine own;
  Therefore that he may raise the Lord throws down.

SERMONS

Preached at the Funeral of Sir William Cokayne, Knight, Alderman of London. Dec. 12th, 1626

. . . HOW imperfect is all our knowledge! What one thing do we know perfectly? Whether we consider arts or sciences, the servant knows but according to the proportion of his master's knowledge in that art, and the scholar knows but according to the proportion of his master's knowledge in that science. Young men mend not their sight by using old men's spectacles; and yet we look upon nature but with Aristotle's spectacles, and upon the body of man but with Galen's and upon the frame of the world but with Ptolemy's spectacles. Almost all knowledge is rather like a child that is embalmed to make mummy, than that is nursed to make a man; rather conserved in the stature of the first age, than grown to be greater. And if there be any addition to knowledge, it is rather a new knowledge than a greater knowledge; rather a singularity in a desire of proposing something that was not known at all before than an improving, an advancing, a multiplying of former inceptions; and by that means, no knowledge comes to be perfect. One philosopher thinks he is dived to the bottom, when he says he knows nothing but this, that he knows nothing; and yet another thinks, that he hath expressed more knowledge than he, in saying that he knows not so much as that, that he knows nothing. St. Paul found that to be all knowledge, to know Christ; and Mahomet thinks himself wise therefore, because he knows not, acknowledges not Christ, as St. Paul does. Though a man knew not that every sin casts another shovel of brimstone upon him in Hell, yet if he knew that every riotous feast cuts off a year and every wanton night seven years of his seventy in this world, it were some degree towards perfection in knowledge. He that purchases a manor will think to have an exact survey of the land, but who thinks of taking so exact a survey of his conscience, how that money was got that purchased that manor? We call that a man's means, which he hath; but that is truly his means, what way he came by it. And yet how few are there, when a state comes to any great proportion, that know that,—that know what they have, what they are worth? We have seen great wills dilated into glorious uses and into pious uses, and then too narrow an estate to reach to it. And we have seen wills where the testator thinks he hath bequeathed all, and he hath not known half of his own worth. When thou knowest a wife, a son, a servant, a friend no better, but that that wife betrays thy bed, and that son thine estate, and that servant thy credit, and that friend thy secret, what canst thou say thou knowest? But we must not insist upon this consideration of knowledge; for, though knowledge be of a spiritual nature, yet it is but as a terrestrial spirit, conversant upon earth. Spiritual things, of a more rarified nature than knowledge, even faith itself, and all that grows from that in us, falls within this rule which we have in hand, that even in spiritual things, nothing is perfect . . .

I need not call in new philosophy,[1] that denies a settledness, an acquiescence in the very body of the earth, but makes the earth to move in that place where we thought the sun had moved; I need not that help, that the earth itself is in motion, to prove this, that nothing upon earth is permanent. The assertion will stand of itself, till some man assign me some instance, something that a man may rely upon, and find permanent. Consider the greatest bodies upon earth, the monarchies—objects which one would think Destiny might stand and stare at, but not shake. Consider the smallest bodies upon earth, the hairs of our head,—objects which one would think Destiny would not observe or could not discern. And yet, Destiny, (to speak to a natural man) and God, (to speak to a Christian) is no more troubled to make a monarchy ruinous, than to make a hair gray. Nay, nothing needs be done to either, by God or Destiny; a monarchy will ruin, as a hair will grow gray, of itself. In the elements themselves, of which all sub-elementary things are composed, there is no acquiescence, but a vicissitudinary transmutation into one another; air condensed becomes water, a more solid body, and air rarified becomes fire, a body more disputable and inapparent. It is so in the conditions of men, too; a merchant condensed, kneaded and packed up in a great estate, becomes a Lord; and a merchant rarified, blown up by a perfidious factor, or by a riotous son, evaporates into air, into nothing, and is not seen. And if there were anything permanent and durable in this world, yet we got nothing by it, because howsoever that might last in itself, yet we could not last to enjoy it. If our goods were not amongst moveables, yet we ourselves are; if they could stay with us, yet we cannot stay with them, which is another consideration in this part.

The world is a great volume, and man the index of that book. Even in the body of man, you may turn to the whole world. This body is an illustration of all nature, God's recapitulation of all that he had said before in his *Fiat lux,* and *Fiat firmamentum,*[2] and in all the rest, said or done, in all the six days. Propose this body to thy consideration in the highest exaltation thereof, as it is the Temple of the Holy Ghost,—nay, not in a metaphor or comparison of a temple, or any other similitudinary thing, but as it was really and truly the very body of God, in the person of Christ, and yet this body must wither, must decay, must languish, must perish. When Goliath [3] had armed and fortified this body, and Jezebel [4] had painted and perfumed this body, and Dives [5] had pampered and larded this body, as God said to *Ezekiel,* when he brought him to the dry bones, *"Fili hominis,* Son of Man doest thou think these bones can live?" [6] They said in their hearts

[1] *new philosophy:* science.
[2] Genesis 1:3, 6.
[3] I. Samuel 17.
[4] I. Kings 21; II. Kings 9.
[5] Luke 16:19.
[6] Ezekiel 37:3.

to all the world, Can these bodies die? And they are dead. Jezebel's dust is not amber, nor *Goliath's* dust *Terra sigillata,* medicinal; nor does the serpent, whose meat they are both, find any better relish in Dives' dust than in Lazarus'. But as in our former part, where our foundation was, that in nothing, no spiritual thing, there was any perfectness, which we illustrated in the weaknesses of knowledge, and faith, and hope, and charity, yet we concluded that for all those defects, God accepted those their religious services; so in this part, where our foundation is, that nothing in temporal things is permanent, as we have illustrated that, by the decay of that which is God's noblest piece in nature, the body of man; so we shall also conclude that, with this goodness of God, that for all this dissolution, and putrefaction, he affords this body a resurrection.

St. Paul's. "The First of the Prebend of Cheswick's Five Psalms." May 8, 1625

THE applause of the people is vanity; popularity is vanity. At how dear a rate doth that man buy the people's affections, that pays his own head for their hats! How cheaply doth he sell his prince's favor, that hath nothing for it, but the people's breath! And what age doth not see some examples of so ill merchants of their own honors and lives too! How many men, upon confidence of that flattering gale of wind, the breath and applause of the people, have taken in their anchors, (that is, departed from their true and safe hold, the right of the law and the favor of the prince) and as soon as they hoisted their sails, (that is, entered into any by-action) have found the wind in their teeth, that is, those people whom they trusted in, armed against them! And as it is in civil and secular, so it is in ecclesiastical and spiritual things too. How many men, by a popular hunting after the applause of the people in their manner of preaching, and humoring them in their distempers, have made themselves incapable of preferment in the church where they took their orders, and preached themselves into a necessity of running away into foreign parts, that are receptacles of seditious and schismatical separatists, and have been put there to learn some trade and become artificers for their sustentation? The same people that welcomed Christ from the Mount of Olives into Jerusalem upon Sunday, with their "Hosannas to the Son of David," upon Friday mocked him in Jerusalem, with their "Hail King of the Jews," and blew him out of Jerusalem to Golgotha, with the pestilent breath, with the tempestuous whirlwind of their "Crucifiges."[7] And of them who have called the Master Beelzebub, what shall any servant look for? *Surely men of low degree are vanity.*[8]

And then, under the same oath and asseveration, *Surely,* as surely as the other, *men of high degree are a lie.* Doth David mean these men, whom he calls a *lie,* to be any less than those whom he called *vanity?* Less than

[7] *Crucifige:* crucify him.

[8] Psalms 62:9.

vanity, than emptiness, than nothing, nothing can be; and low and high are to this purpose, and in this consideration, (compared with God, or considered without God) equally nothing. He that hath the largest patrimony and space of earth, in the earth, must hear me say that all that was nothing. And if he ask, "But what was this whole kingdom, what all Europe, what all the world?" It was all, not so much as another nothing, but all one and the same nothing as thy dunghill was.

St. Paul's. Christmas Day in the Evening. 1624

THE air is not so full of motes, of atoms, as the church is of mercies. And as we can suck in no part of air, but we take in those motes, those atoms; so here in the congregation we cannot suck in a word from the preacher, we cannot speak, we cannot sigh a prayer to God, but that that whole breath and air is made of mercy. But we call not upon you from this text to consider God's ordinary mercy, that which he exhibits to all in the ministry of his church; nor his miraculous mercy, his extraordinary deliverances of states and churches; but we call upon particular consciences, by occasion of this text, to call to mind God's occasional mercies to them—such mercies as a regenerate man will call mercies, though a natural man would call them accidents, or occurrences, or contingencies. A man wakes at midnight full of unclean thoughts, and he hears a passing-bell; this is an occasional mercy, if he call that his own knell, and consider how unfit he was to be called out of the world then, how unready to receive that voice, "Fool, this night they shall fetch away thy soul." The adulterer, whose eye waits for the twilight, goes forth and casts his eyes upon forbidden houses, and would enter, and sees a LORD HAVE MERCY UPON US upon the door; this is an occasional mercy, if this bring him to know that they who lie sick of the plague within pass through a furnace, but by God's grace, to heaven; and he, without, carries his own furnace to hell, his lustful loins to everlasting perdition. What an occasional mercy had Balaam, when his ass catechized him! [9] What an occasional mercy had one thief, when the other catechized him so, *Art not thou afraid being under the same condemnation?* [10] What an occasional mercy had all they that saw that, when the Devil himself fought for the name of Jesus, and wounded the sons of Sceva for exorcising in the name of Jesus, with that indignation, with that increpation,[11] "Jesus we know, and Paul we know, but who are ye?" [12] If I should declare what God hath done (done occasionally) for my soul, where he instructed me for fear of falling, where he raised me when I was fallen, perchance you would rather fix your thoughts upon my illness, and wonder at that, than at God's goodness and glorify him in that; rather wonder at my sins, than at his mercies; rather consider how ill a man I was, than how good a God he is. If I should inquire upon what occasion God elected me and writ my

[9] Numbers 22:21–35.

[10] Luke 23:40.

[11] *increpation:* reproof, rebuke.

[12] Acts 19:14–15.

name in the book of life, I should sooner be afraid that it were not so, than find a reason why it should be so. God made sun and moon to distinguish seasons, and day, and night, and we cannot have the fruits of the earth but in their seasons. But God hath made no decree to distinguish the seasons of his mercies. In paradise, the fruits were ripe the first minute; and in heaven it is always autumn: his mercies are ever in their maturity. We ask *panem quotidianum,* our daily bread, and God never says, "You should have come yesterday." He never says "You must again tomorrow"; but today if you will hear his voice, today he will hear you. If some king of the earth have so large an extent of dominion, in north and south, as that he hath winter and summer together in his dominions; so large an extent east and west, as that he hath day and night together in his dominions; much more hath God mercy and judgment together. He brought light out of darkness, not out of a lesser light; he can bring thy summer out of winter, though thou have no spring. Though in the ways of fortune, or understanding, or conscience, thou have been benighted till now, wintered and frozen, clouded and eclipsed, damped and benumbed, smothered and stupified till now, now God comes to thee, not as in the dawning of the day, not as in the bud of the spring, but as the sun at noon to illustrate all shadows, as the sheaves in harvest to fill all penuries. All occasions invite his mercies, and all times are his seasons.

MEDITATION[13]

PERCHANCE he for whom this bell tolls may be so ill as that he knows not it tolls for him; and perchance I may think myself so much better than I am, as that they who are about me and see my state, may have caused it to toll for me, and I know not that. The church is catholic, universal; so are all her actions; all that she does, belongs to all. When she baptizes a child, that action concerns me, for that child is thereby connected to that Head which is my Head too, and engraffed into that body, whereof I am a member. And when she buries a man, that action concerns me. All mankind is of one author, and is one volume; when one man dies, one chapter is not torn out of the book, but translated into a better language, and every chapter must be so translated. God employs several translators; some pieces are translated by age, some by sickness, some by war, some by justice; but God's hand is in every translation; and his hand shall bind up all our scattered leaves again for that library where every book shall lie open to one another. As therefore the bell that rings to a sermon calls not upon the preacher only, but upon the congregation to come, so this bell calls us all; but how much more he, who am brought so near the door by this sickness.

[13] One of the *Devotions Upon Emergent Occasions* written by Donne during a serious illness in 1623. The theme of this Meditation (XVII) is "The bell rings out, and tells me in him, that I am dead."

There was a contention as far as a suit, (in which both piety and dignity, religion and estimation, were mingled) which of the religious orders should ring to prayers first in the morning; and it was determined, that they should ring first that rose earliest. If we understand aright the dignity of this bell that tolls for our evening prayer, we would be glad to make it ours by rising early, in that application, that it might be ours as well as his whose indeed it is. The bell doth toll for him that thinks it doth; and though it intermit again, yet from that minute that that occasion wrought upon him, he is united to God. Who casts not up his eye to the sun when it rises? But who takes off his eye from a comet when that breaks out? Who bends not his ear to any bell which upon any occasion rings? But who can remove it from that bell which is passing a piece of himself out of this world? No man is an island, entire of itself; every man is a piece of the continent, a part of the main; if a clod be washed away by the sea, Europe is the less, as well as if a promontory were, as well as if a manor of thy friend's or of thine own were. Any man's death diminishes me, because I am involved in mankind; and therefore never send to know for whom the bell tolls; it tolls for thee. Neither can we call this a begging of misery or a borrowing of misery, as though we were not miserable enough of ourselves, but must fetch in more from the next house, in taking upon us the misery of our neighbors. Truly it were an excusable covetousness if we did; for affliction is a treasure, and scarce any man hath enough of it. No man hath affliction enough that is not matured and ripened by it, and made fit for God by that affliction. If a man carry treasure in bullion, or in a wedge of gold, and have none coined into current monies, his treasure will not defray him as he travels. Tribulation is treasure in the nature of it, but it is not current money in the use of it, except we get nearer and nearer our home, heaven, by it. Another man may be sick too, and sick to death, and this affliction may lie in his bowels, as gold in a mine, and be of no use to him; but this bell, that tells me of his affliction, digs out and applies that gold to me, if by this consideration of another's danger, I take mine own into contemplation, and so secure myself by making my recourse to my God, who is our only security.

LETTERS

To Sir Henry Wotton(?) [1600(?)]

SIR,

Only in obedience I send you some of my paradoxes; I love you and myself and them too well to send them willingly, for they carry with them a confession of their lightness and your trouble and my shame. But indeed they were made rather to deceive Time than her daughter Truth, although they have been written in an age when any thing is strong enough to overthrow her. If they make you to find better reasons against them they do their office, for they are but swaggerers, quiet enough if you resist them. If perchance they be prettily gilt, that is their best, for they are not hatched;[14] they are rather alarums to Truth, to arm her, than enemies; and they have only this advantage to escape from being called ill things, that they are no things. Therefore take heed of allowing any of them lest you make another. Yet, Sir, though I know their low price, except I receive by your next letter an assurance upon the religion of your friendship that no copy shall be taken, for any respect, of these or any other my compositions sent to you, I shall sin against my conscience if I send you any more. I speak that in plainness which becomes (methinks) our honesties; and therefore call not this distrustful but a free spirit. I mean to acquaint you with all mine; and to my satires there belongs some fear and to some elegies and these, perhaps, shame. Against both which affections although I be tough enough, yet I have a riddling disposition to be ashamed of fear and afraid of shame. Therefore I am desirous to hide them without any over-reckoning of them or their maker. But they are not worth thus much words in their dispraise. I will step to a better subject, your last letter, to which I need not tell I made no answer but I had need excuse it. All your letter I embrace and believe it when it speaks of yourself and when of me too, if the good words which you speak of me be meant of my intentions to goodness; for else, alas, no man is more beggarly in actual virtue than I. I am sorry you should (with any great earnestness) desire anything of P. Aretinus,[15] not that he could infect, but that it seems you are already infected with the common opinion of him. Believe me, he is much less than his fame and was too well paid by the Roman church in that coin which he coveted most, where his books were by the Council of Trent forbidden; which if they had been permitted to have been worn by all, long ere this had been worn out. His divinity was but a syrup to enwrap his profane books to get them passage, yet in these books which have divine titles there is least harm as in his letters most good; his others have no other singularity in them but that they are forbidden. The psalms (which you ask) if I cannot shortly procure you one to possess, I can and will at any time borrow for you. In the meantime Sir have the honor of forgiving two faults together: my not writing last time and my abrupt ending now.

To A Lord, Upon Presenting of Some of His Work to Him [1624]

MY LORD,

To make myself believe that our life is something, I use in my thoughts to compare it to something, if it be like anything that is something. It is like a sentence, so much as may be uttered in a breathing; and such a difference as is in styles, is in our lives, contracted and dilated. And as in some

[14] *hatched:* inlaid with precious metals.

[15] *Aretinus:* Pietro Aretino (1492–1556) "the Scourge of Princes," Italian satirist.

styles there are open parentheses, sentences within sentences; so there are lives within our lives. I am in such a parenthesis now, in a convalescence, when I thought myself very near my period. God brought me into a low valley, and from thence showed me high Jerusalem, upon so high a hill as that he thought it fit to bid me stay and gather more breath. This I do, by meditating, by expostulating, by praying; for, since I am barred of my ordinary diet, which is reading, I make these my exercises, which is another part of physic. And these meditations and expostulations and prayers, I am bold to send to your Lordship; that as this which I live now is a kind of second life, I may deliver myself over to your Lordship in this life, with the same affection and devotion as made me yours in all my former life; and as long as any image of this world sticks in my soul, shall ever remain your Lordship's, &c.

THE TRUE CHARACTER OF A DUNCE[16]

HE HATH a soul drowned in a lump of flesh, or is a piece of earth that Prometheus put not half his proportion of fire into. A thing that hath neither edge of desire, nor feeling of affection in it; the most dangerous creature for confirming an atheist, who would swear his soul were nothing but the bare temperature of his body. He sleeps as he goes, and his thoughts seldom reach an inch further than his eyes. The most part of the faculties of his soul lie fallow, or are like the restive jades that no spur can drive forwards towards the pursuit of any worthy designs. One of the most unprofitable of God's creatures, being, as he is, a thing put clean besides the right use, made fit for the cart and the flail, and by mischance entangled among books and papers. A man cannot tell possibly what he is now good for, save to move up and down and fill room, or to serve as *animatum instrumentum* for others to work withal in base employments, or to be foil for better wits, or to serve (as they say monsters do) to set out the variety of nature and ornament of the universe. He is mere nothing of himself, neither eats, nor drinks, nor goes, nor spits, but by imitation, for all which he hath set-forms and fashions, which he never varies, but sticks to with the like plodding constancy that a mill-horse follows his trace. But the Muses and the Graces are his hard mistresses, though he daily invocate them; though he sacrifice hecatombs, they still look asquint. You shall note him oft (besides his dull eye, and lowering head, and a certain clammy benumbed pace) by a fair displayed beard, a night cap, and a gown whose very wrinkles proclaim him the true genius of formality. But of all others, his discourse and compositions best speak him; both of them are much of one stuff and fashion. He speaks just what his books or last company said

[16] One of the Characters printed in the 1622 edition of the popular anthology called *Overbury's Wife*.

unto him, without varying one whit, and very seldom understands himself. You may know by his discourse where he was last: for what he heard or read yesterday, he now dischargeth his memory or note-book of, not his understanding, for it never came there. What he hath, he flings abroad at all adventures without accommodating it to time, place, persons, or occasions. He commonly loseth himself in his tale, and flutters up and down windless without recovery, and whatsoever next presents itself, his heavy conceit seizeth upon, and goeth along with, however heterogeneal to his matter in hand. His jests are either old flayed proverbs, or lean, starved-hackney apothegms, or poor verbal quips, outworn by serving-men, tapsters, and milkmaids, even laid aside by balladers. He assents to all men that bring any shadow of reason, and you may make him when he speaks most dogmatically, even with one breath, to aver poor contradictions. His compositions differ only *terminorum positione* from dreams—nothing but rude heaps of immaterial, incoherent, drossy, rubbish stuff, promiscuously thrust up together, enough to infuse dullness and barrenness of conceit into him that is so prodigal of his ears as to give the hearing. Enough to make a man's memory ache with suffering such dirty stuff cast into it. As unwelcome to any true conceit as sluttish morsels or wallowish potions to a nice stomach, which while he empties himself of, it sticks in his teeth, nor can he be delivered without sweat, and sighs, and hems, and coughs, enough to shake his granddam's teeth out of her head. He spits, and scratches, and spawls,[17] and turns like sick men from one elbow to another, and deserves as much pity during his torture, as men in fits of tertian fevers or self-lashing penitentiaries.[18] In a word, rip him quite asunder and examine every shred of him; you shall find him to be just nothing but the subject of nothing, the object of contempt. Yet such as he is, you must take him, for there is no hope he should ever become better.

PARADOXES AND PROBLEMS

Paradox VI. That It Is Possible to Find Some Virtue in Some Women

I AM not of that seared [19] impudence that I dare defend women or pronounce them good; yet we see physicians allow some virtue in every poison. Alas, why should we except women, since certainty, they are good for physic at least, so as some wine is good for a fever. And though they be the occasioners of many sins, they are also the punishers and revengers of the same sins. For I have seldom seen one which consumes his substance and body upon them, escape diseases or beggary; and this is their justice.

[17] *spawls:* spits.

[18] *penitentiaries:* penitents.

[19] *seared:* insensitive, unfeeling.

And if *suum cuique dare*[20] be the fulfilling of all civil justice, they are most just; for they deny that which is theirs to no man.

Tanquam non liceat nulla puella negat.

And who may doubt of great wisdom in them, that doth but observe with how much labor and cunning our justicers and other dispensers of the laws study to embrace them, and how zealously our preachers dehort men from them, only by urging their subtleties and policies and wisdom which are in them? Or who can deny them a good measure of fortitude, if he consider how valiant men they have overthrown, and being themselves overthrown, how much and how patiently they bear? And though they be most intemperate, I care not, for I undertook to furnish them with *some* virtue, not with *all*. Necessity, which makes even bad things good, prevails also for them, for we must say of them, as of some sharp pinching laws: If men were free from infirmities, they were needless. These or none must serve for reasons, and it is my great happiness that examples prove not rules, for to confirm this opinion, the world yields not one example.

[20] *suum cuique dare:* to give everyone his own.

Sir Francis Bacon, Viscount St. Alban

1561–1626

BACON was the son of Sir Nicholas Bacon, Lord Keeper of the Great Seal, and his second wife, the learned lady Anne Cooke; he was the nephew of the great Burleigh. At Cambridge he disliked the traditional Aristotelian curriculum; after three years there he proceeded to Gray's Inn to study law. In his struggles for advancement at court he was again and again frustrated, and when he did find an energetic patron and supporter it was the ill-fated Earl of Essex, in whose prosecution Bacon was ironically to have a part. Some diplomatic service, some hard work in parliamentary committees, much time spent in flattering court favorites and suing for government appointments—these were the preoccupations of the most brilliant philosophical mind of the age. In 1607 Bacon's ambitions began to be fulfilled: he became Solicitor General in that year, Attorney General in 1613, Lord Keeper in 1617, Lord Chancellor in 1618. He was raised to the peerage as Baron Verulam in 1618 and was made Viscount St. Alban in 1621. But almost immediately after the last honor was conferred, Bacon's enemies in Parliament brought charges of bribery against him and he was deprived of office. He had done nothing that was not commonplace among judges of the time, but conformity to custom is not always a valid excuse. Bacon himself said, according to his secretary, "I was the justest judge that was in England these fifty years. But it was the justest censure in Parliament that was these two hundred years."

Bacon is not so genial and attractive an essayist as his great French predecessor, Montaigne. His volume of ten essays in 1597 (supplemented by *Meditationes Sacrae* and *Colors of Good and Evil*) grew to thirty-eight in 1612 and fifty-eight in 1625. Bacon revised, expanded, and modified his earlier essays; he was moving from the sage apothegm to philosophical discourse.

Bacon's great contribution to thought was his attack upon the heavy medieval structure which dominated the learning of his time. He showed how a knowledge of nature might be procured if men would only rid themselves of musty, outworn habits of thinking. But even more important than his method were his propaganda for learning and his insistence upon the connection between understanding and physical reality. As Metz says, "Bacon has established a vital connexion between theory and practice, knowledge and life, and has done so not, like his less-gifted later followers, by degrading knowledge, but by assigning to it a mission of the highest order. In this, Bacon's thought and feeling are entirely modern, and there is no vestige of medievalism left." He was regarded as the spirit presiding over the investigations of Boyle and others in the middle of the seventeenth century. However antiquated his attitudes, his systems, and his ambitions may now seem, Bacon's prestige and influence made a climate in which research could flourish.

Bacon's style is worth study; he was a conscious craftsman in prose and he tried to make his language the vehicle for clarity and precision of thought. As a contemporary said of him, "he did rather drive at a masculine and clear expression than at any fineness or affectation of phrases."

BIBLIOGRAPHY: *The Works,* ed. J. Spedding, R. L. Ellis, and D. D. Heath, London, 1857–1859; F. H. Anderson, *The Philosophy of Francis Bacon,* Chicago, 1948; K. R. Wallace, *Francis Bacon on Communication and Rhetoric,* Chapel Hill, 1943; A. N. Whitehead, *Science and the Modern World,* New York, 1925; Basil Willey, *The Seventeenth Century Background,* London, 1934; R. F. Jones, *Ancients and Moderns,* St. Louis, 1936; R. S. Crane, "The Relation of Bacon's *Essays* to His Program for the Advancement of Learning," and M. W. Croll, "Attic Prose: Lipsius, Montaigne, Bacon," both in *Schelling Anniversary Papers,* New York, 1923; G. Bullough, "Bacon and the Defence of Learning," and R. Metz, "Bacon's Part in the Intellectual Movement of His Time," both in *Seventeenth Century Studies Presented to Sir Herbert Grierson,* Oxford, 1938.

FROM

ESSAYS OR COUNSELS, CIVIL AND MORAL

To the Right Honorable, My Very Good Lord, the Duke of Buckingham, His Grace Lord High Admiral of England

Excellent Lord,

Solomon says, "A good name is as a precious ointment," and I assure myself, such will your grace's name be with posterity; for your fortune and merit, both, have been eminent, and you have planted things that are like to last. I do now publish my *Essays,* which, of all my other works, have been most current, for that, as it seems, they come home to men's business and bosoms. I have enlarged them both in number and weight, so that they are indeed a new work. I thought it therefore agreeable to my affection and obligation to your grace to prefix your name before them, both in English and in Latin. For I do conceive that the Latin volume of them, being in the universal language, may last as long as books last. My *Instauration* I dedicated to the King; my *History of Henry the Seventh,* which I have now also translated into Latin, and my *Portions of Natural History* to the Prince; and these I dedicate to your Grace, being of the best fruits that by the good increase which God gives to my pen and labors I could yield. God lead your Grace by the hand.

Your Grace's most obliged and faithful servant,
Francis St. Alban

OF DISCOURSE

(1597)

Some in their discourse desire rather commendation of wit in being able to hold all arguments, than of judgment in discerning what is true, as if it were a praise to know what might be said, and not what should be thought.

Some have certain commonplaces and themes wherein they are good, and want variety: which kind of poverty is for the most part tedious, and now and then [1] ridiculous.

[1] *now and then:* "when it is once perceived" (1625 edition).

The honorablest part of talk is to guide[2] the occasion, and again to moderate and pass to somewhat else.[3]

It is good to vary and mix[4] speech of the present occasion with argument, tales with reasons, asking of questions with telling of opinions, and jest with earnest.[5]

But some things are privileged from jest,[6] namely Religion, matters of state, great persons, and man's present business of importance, and any case that deserveth pity.[7]

He that questioneth much shall learn much, and content much, specially if he apply his questions to the skill of the person of whom he asketh, for he shall give them occasion to please themselves in speaking, and himself shall continually gather knowledge.[8]

If you dissemble sometimes your knowledge of that you are thought to know, you shall be thought another time to know that, you know not.

Speech of a man's self is not good often,[9] and there is but one case wherein a man may commend himself with good grace, and that is in commending virtue in another, especially if it be such a virtue as whereunto himself pretendeth.[10]

Discretion of speech is more than eloquence, and to speak agreebly to him with whom we deal is more than to speak in good words or in good order.

A good continued speech without a good speech of interlocution showeth slowness; and a good reply or second speech without a good set[11] speech

---

[2] *guide:* "give" (1625 edition).

[3] 1625 edition adds: "for then a man leads the dance."

[4] *to vary and mix:* "in discourse and speech of conversation, to vary and intermingle" (1625 edition).

[5] 1625 edition adds: "for it is a dull thing to tire, and, as we say now, to jade anything too far."

[6] *But some . . . jest:* "As for jest, there be certain things which ought to be privileged from it:" (1625 edition).

[7] 1625 edition adds: "Yet there be some that think their wits have been asleep, except they dart out somewhat that is piquant and to the quick. That is a vein which would be bridled: *Parce puer stimulis, et fortius utere Loris* [Spare the whip, boy, and hold the reins tighter]. And generally, men ought to find the difference between saltness and bitterness. Certainly, he that hath a satirical vein, as he maketh others afraid of his wit, so he had need be afraid of others' memory."

[8] 1625 edition adds: "But let his questions not be troublesome, for that is fit for a poser. And let him be sure to leave other men their turns to speak. Nay, if there be any that would reign and take up all the time, let him find means to take them off and bring others on, as musicians use to do with those that dance too long galliards."

[9] *Speech . . . often:* "Speech of a man's self ought to be seldom and well-chosen. I knew one, was wont to say, in scorn, 'He must needs be a wise man, he speaks so much of himself'" (1625 edition).

[10] 1625 edition adds: "Speech of touch toward others should be sparingly used, for discourse ought to be as a field, without coming home to any man. I knew two noblemen of the west part of England, whereof the one was given to scoff, but kept ever royal cheer in his house. The other would ask of those that had been at the other's table, 'Tell truly, was there never a flout or dry blow given?' To which the guest would answer [that] such and such a thing passed. The lord would say, 'I thought he would mar a good dinner!'"

[11] *set:* "settled" (1625 edition).

showeth shallowness and weakness; as we see in beasts, that those that are weakest in the course are yet nimblest in the turn.[12]

To use too many circumstances ere one come to the matter is wearisome; to use none at all is blunt.

OF TRUTH

What is truth? said jesting Pilate; and would not stay for an answer. Certainly there be that delight in giddiness, and count it a bondage to fix a belief; affecting free-will in thinking, as well as in acting. And though the sects of philosophers of that kind be gone, yet there remain certain discoursing wits, which are of the same veins, though there be not so much blood in them as was in those of the ancients. But it is not only the difficulty and labor which men take in finding out of truth; nor again, that when it is found, it imposeth upon men's thoughts, that doth bring lies in favor; but a natural though corrupt love of the lie itself. One of the later school of the Grecians examineth the matter, and is at a stand to think what should be in it, that men should love lies; where neither they make for pleasure, as with poets; nor for advantage, as with the merchant, but for the lie's sake. But I cannot tell: this same truth is a naked and open daylight, that doth not show the masks and mummeries and triumphs of the world half so stately and daintily as candle-lights. Truth may perhaps come to the price of a pearl, that showeth best by day, but it will not rise to the price of a diamond or carbuncle,[13] that showeth best in varied lights. A mixture of a lie doth ever add pleasure. Doth any man doubt that if there were taken out of men's minds vain opinions, flattering hopes, false valuations, imaginations as one would, and the like, but it would leave the minds of a number of men poor shrunken things, full of melancholy and indisposition, and unpleasing to themselves? One of the fathers, in great severity, called poesy *vinum daemonum,* because it filleth the imagination, and yet it is but with the shadow of a lie. But it is not the lie that passeth through the mind, but the lie that sinketh in, and settleth in it, that doth the hurt, such as we spake of before. But howsoever these things are thus in men's depraved judgments and affections, yet truth, which only doth judge itself, teacheth that the inquiry of truth, which is the love-making, or wooing of it, the knowledge of truth, which is the presence of it, and the belief of truth, which is the enjoying of it, is the sovereign good of human nature. The first creature of God, in the works of the days, was the light of the sense; the last was the light of reason; and His sabbath work ever since is the illumination of His Spirit. First, He breathed light upon the face of the matter, or chaos; then He breathed light into the face of man; and still He breatheth and inspireth

[12] 1625 edition adds: "as it is betwixt the greyhound and the hare."

[13] *carbuncle:* ruby.

light into the face of His chosen. The poet[14] that beautified the sect that was otherwise inferior to the rest saith yet excellently well: "It is a pleasure to stand upon the shore, and to see ships tossed upon the sea: a pleasure to stand in the window of a castle, and to see a battle, and the adventures thereof below: but no pleasure is comparable to the standing upon the vantage ground of truth" (a hill not to be commanded, and where the air is always clear and serene), "and to see the errors, and wanderings, and mists, and tempests, in the vale below": so always that this prospect be with pity, and not with swelling or pride. Certainly, it is heaven upon earth to have a man's mind move in charity, rest in providence, and turn upon the poles of truth.

To pass from theological and philosophical truth to the truth of civil business; it will be acknowledged even by those that practise it not, that clear and round dealing is the honor of man's nature, and that mixture of falsehood is like alloy in coin of gold and silver, which may make the metal work the better, but it embaseth it. For these winding and crooked courses are the goings of the serpent; which goeth basely upon the belly, and not upon the feet. There is no vice that doth so cover a man with shame as to be found false and perfidious; and therefore Montaigne saith prettily, when he inquired the reason why the word of the lie should be such a disgrace, and such an odious charge, saith he, "If it be well weighed, to say that a man lieth, is as much as to say that he is brave towards God and a coward towards men." For a lie faces God, and shrinks from man. Surely the wickedness of falsehood and breach of faith cannot possibly be so highly expressed, as in that it shall be the last peal to call the judgments of God upon the generations of men, it being foretold that when Christ cometh, he shall not "find faith upon the earth."

OF MARRIAGE AND SINGLE LIFE

He that hath wife and children hath given hostages to fortune; for they are impediments to great enterprises, either of virtue or mischief. Certainly the best works, and of greatest merit for the public, have proceeded from the unmarried or childless men, which both in affection and means have married and endowed the public. Yet it were great reason that those that have children should have greatest care of future times, unto which they know they must transmit their dearest pledges. Some there are who, though they lead a single life, yet their thoughts do end with themselves, and account future times impertinences. Nay, there are some other that account wife and children but as bills of charges. Nay more, there are some foolish rich covetous men that take a pride in having no children, because they may be thought so much the richer. For perhaps they have heard some

[14] *poet:* Lucretius; his sect was the Epicureans.

talk, "Such an one is a great rich man," and another except to it, "Yea, but he hath a great charge of children"; as if it were an abatement to his riches. But the most ordinary cause of a single life is liberty, especially in certain self-pleasing and humorous minds, which are so sensible of every restraint, as they will go near to think their girdles and garters to be bonds and shackles. Unmarried men are best friends, best masters, best servants, but not always best subjects, for they are light to run away, and almost all fugitives are of that condition. A single life doth well with churchmen, for charity will hardly water the ground where it must first fill a pool. It is indifferent for judges and magistrates, for if they be facile and corrupt, you shall have a servant five times worse than a wife. For soldiers, I find the generals commonly in their hortatives put men in mind of their wives and children; and I think the despising of marriage amongst the Turks maketh the vulgar soldier more base. Certainly wife and children are a kind of discipline of humanity; and single men, though they be many times more charitable, because their means are less exhaust, yet, on the other side, they are more cruel and hard-hearted (good to make severe inquisitors), because their tenderness is not so oft called upon. Grave natures, led by custom, and therefore constant, are commonly loving husbands, as was said of Ulysses, *Vetulam suam praetulit immortallati.*[15] Chaste women are often proud and froward, as presuming upon the merit of their chastity. It is one of the best bonds, both of chastity and obedience, in the wife if she think her husband wise, which she will never do if she find him jealous. Wives are young men's mistresses, companions for middle age, and old men's nurses, so as a man may have a quarrel to marry when he will. But yet he was reputed one of the wise men that made answer to the question when a man should marry: "A young man not yet, an elder man not at all." It is often seen that bad husbands have very good wives; whether it be that it raiseth the price of their husbands' kindness when it comes, or that the wives take a pride in their patience. But this never fails, if the bad husbands were of their own choosing, against their friends' consent; for then they will be sure to make good their own folly.

OF LOVE

The stage is more beholding to love than the life of man. For as to the stage, love is ever matter of comedies, and now and then of tragedies; but in life it doth much mischief, sometimes like a siren, sometimes like a fury. You may observe, that amongst all the great and worthy persons whereof the memory remaineth, either ancient or recent, there is not one that hath

[15] *Vetulam . . . immortallati:* "He preferred his chaste wife to immortality."

been transported to the mad degree of love; which shows that great spirits and great business do keep out this weak passion. You must except, nevertheless, Marcus Antonius, the half partner of the empire of Rome, and Appius Claudius, the decemvir and lawgiver; whereof the former was indeed a voluptuous man, and inordinate; but the latter was an austere and wise man. And therefore it seems (though rarely) that love can find entrance, not only into an open heart, but also into a heart well fortified, if watch be not well kept. It is a poor saying of Epicurus, *Satis magnum alter alteri theatrum sumus:* [16] as if man, made for the contemplation of heaven and all noble objects, should do nothing but kneel before a little idol, and make himself a subject, though not of the mouth, as beasts are, yet of the eye, which was given him for higher purposes. It is a strange thing to note the excess of this passion, and how it braves the nature and value of things by this, that the speaking in a perpetual hyperbole is comely in nothing but in love. Neither is it merely in the phrase. For whereas it hath been well said that the arch-flatterer, with whom all the petty flatterers have intelligence, is a man's self, certainly the lover is more. For there was never proud man thought so absurdly well of himself as the lover doth of the person loved; and therefore it was well said, "That it is impossible to love and to be wise." Neither doth this weakness appear to others only, and not to the party loved, but to the loved most of all, except the love be reciproque. For it is a true rule, that love is ever rewarded, either with the reciproque, or with an inward and secret contempt; by how much the more men ought to beware of this passion, which loseth not only other things, but itself. As for the other losses, the poet's relation doth well figure them, "That he that preferred Helena,[17] quitted the gifts of Juno and Pallas." For whosoever esteemeth too much of amorous affection, quitteth both riches and wisdom. This passion hath his floods in the very times of weakness, which are great prosperity and great adversity, though this latter hath been less observed. Both which times kindle love, and make it more fervent, and therefore show it to be the child of folly. They do best who, if they cannot but admit love, yet make it keep quarter, and sever it wholly from their serious affairs and actions of life. For if it check once with business, it troubleth men's fortunes, and maketh men that they can nowise be true to their own ends. I know not how, but martial men are given to love. I think it is but as they are given to wine, for perils commonly ask to be paid in pleasures. There is in man's nature a secret inclination and motion towards love of others, which if it be not spent upon some one or a few, doth naturally spread itself towards many, and maketh men become humane and charitable, as it is seen sometimes in friars. Nuptial love maketh mankind, friendly love perfecteth it, but wanton love corrupteth and embaseth it.

[16] *Satis . . . sumus:* "Each of us is a large enough theater to somebody else."

[17] *he . . . Helena:* Paris, who chose beauty rather than wisdom or power.

OF GREAT PLACE

Men in great place are thrice servants—servants of the sovereign or state, servants of fame, and servants of business. So as they have no freedom, neither in their persons, nor in their actions, nor in their times. It is a strange desire to seek power and to lose liberty; or to seek power over others, and to lose power over a man's self. The rising unto place is laborious, and by pains men come to greater pains; and it is sometimes base, and by indignities men come to dignities. The standing is slippery, and the regress is either a downfall, or at least an eclipse, which is a melancholy thing. *Cum non sis qui fueris, non esse cur velis vivere.*[18] Nay, retire men cannot when they would, neither will they when it were reason; but are impatient of privateness even in age and sickness, which require the shadow; like old townsmen, that will be still sitting at their street-door, though thereby they offer age to scorn. Certainly great persons had need to borrow other men's opinions to think themselves happy; for if they judge by their own feeling, they cannot find it; but if they think with themselves what other men think of them, and that other men would fain be as they are, then they are happy as it were by report, when perhaps, they find the contrary within. For they are the first that find their own griefs, though they be the last that find their own faults. Certainly men in great fortunes are strangers to themselves, and while they are in the puzzle of business they have no time to tend their health either of body or mind. *Illi mors gravis incubat, qui notus nimis omnibus, ignotus moritur sibi.*[19] In place there is licence to do good and evil; whereof the latter is a curse: for in evil the best condition is not to will, the second not to can. But power to do good is the true and lawful end of aspiring; for good thoughts, though God accept them, yet towards men are little better than good dreams, except they be put in act; and that cannot be without power and place, as the vantage and commanding ground. Merit and good works is the end of man's motion, and conscience of the same is the accomplishment of man's rest: for if a man can be partaker of God's theater, he shall likewise be partaker of God's rest. *Et conversus Deus, ut aspiceret opera, quae fecerunt manus suae, vidit quod omnia essent bona nimis,*[20] and then the Sabbath.

In the discharge of thy place set before thee the best examples; for imitation is a globe of precepts. And after a time set before thee thine own example; and examine thyself strictly whether thou didst not best at first. Neglect not also the examples of those that have carried themselves ill

---

[18] *Cum . . . vivera:* "Since you are not what you were, you should not wish to live longer."

[19] *Illi . . . sibi:* "Death lies heavily upon the man who dies famous but unknown to himself."

[20] *Et . . . nimis:* Genesis 1:31 (Vulgate).

in the same place; not to set off thyself by taxing their memory, but to direct thyself what to avoid. Reform, therefore, without bravery or scandal of former times and persons; but yet set it down to thyself, as well to create good precedents as to follow them. Reduce things to the first institution, and observe wherein and how they have degenerate; but yet ask counsel of both times—of the ancient time what is best, and of the latter time what is fittest. Seek to make thy course regular, that men may know beforehand what they may expect; but be not too positive and peremptory; and express thyself well when thou digressest from thy rule. Preserve the right of thy place, but stir not questions of jurisdiction; and rather assume thy right in silence, and *de facto,* than voice it with claims and challenges. Preserve likewise the rights of inferior places; and think it more honor to direct in chief than to be busy in all. Embrace and invite helps and advices touching the execution of thy place; and do not drive away such as bring thee information as meddlers, but accept of them in good part. The vices of authority are chiefly four: delays, corruption, roughness, and facility. For delays, give easy access, keep times appointed, go through with that which is in hand, and interlace not business but of necessity. For corruption, do not only bind thine own hands or thy servants' hands from taking, but bind the hands of suitors also from offering. For integrity used doth the one, but integrity professed, and with a manifest detestation of bribery, doth the other. And avoid not only the fault, but the suspicion. Whosoever is found variable, and changeth manifestly without manifest cause, giveth suspicion of corruption. Therefore, always when thou changest thine opinion or course, profess it plainly, and declare it, together with the reasons that move thee to change, and do not think to steal it. A servant or a favorite, if he be inward, and no other apparent cause of esteem, is commonly thought but a by-way to close corruption. For roughness, it is a needless cause of discontent: severity breedeth fear, but roughness breedeth hate. Even reproofs from authority ought to be grave, and not taunting. As for facility, it is worse than bribery; for bribes come but now and then; but if importunity or idle respects lead a man, he shall never be without. As Solomon saith, "To respect persons is not good; for such a man will transgress for a piece of bread."

It is most true that was anciently spoken: "A place showeth the man." And it showeth some to the better and some to the worse. *Omnium consensu capax imperii, nisi imperasset,*[21] saith Tacitus of Galba; but of Vespasian he saith, *Solus imperantium Vespasianus mutatus in melius:*[22] though the one was meant of sufficiency, the other of manners and affection. It is an assured sign of a worthy and generous spirit, whom honor amends; for honor is, or should be, the place of virtue; and as in nature things move violently to their place, and calmly in their place, so virtue

[21] *Omnium . . . imperasset:* "Everyone would have thought him capable of ruling, if he had not ruled."

[22] *Solus . . . melius:* "Of all the emperors, Vespasian alone improved."

in ambition is violent, in authority settled and calm. All rising to great place is by a winding stair; and if there be factions, it is good to side a man's self whilst he is in the rising, and to balance himself when he is placed. Use the memory of thy predecessor fairly and tenderly; for if thou dost not, it is a debt will sure be paid when thou art gone. If thou have colleagues, respect them; and rather call them when they look not for it, than exclude them when they have reason to look to be called. Be not too sensible or too remembering of thy place in conversation and private answers to suitors, but let it rather be said, "When he sits in place he is another man."

OF STUDIES

Studies serve for delight, for ornament, and for ability. Their chief use for delight is in privateness and retiring; for ornament, is in discourse; and for ability, is in the judgment and disposition of business. For expert men can execute, and perhaps judge of particulars, one by one; but the general counsels, and the plots and marshalling of affairs come best from those that are learned. To spend too much time in studies is sloth; to use them too much for ornament is affectation; to make judgment wholly by their rules is the humor of a scholar. They perfect nature, and are perfected by experience: for natural abilities are like natural plants, that need pruning by study; and studies themselves do give forth directions too much at large, except they be bounded in by experience. Crafty men contemn studies, simple men admire them, and wise men use them; for they teach not their own use; but that is a wisdom without them and above them, won by observation. Read not to contradict and confute, nor to believe and take for granted, nor to find talk and discourse, but to weigh and consider. Some books are to be tasted, others to be swallowed, and some few to be chewed and digested; that is, some books are to be read only in parts; others to be read, but not curiously; and some few to be read wholly, and with diligence and attention. Some books also may be read by deputy, and extracts made of them by others; but that would be only in the less important arguments and the meaner sort of books; else distilled books are, like common distilled waters, flashy things. Reading maketh a full man, conference a ready man, and writing an exact man. And, therefore, if a man write little, he had need have a great memory; if he confer little, he had need have a present wit; and if he read little, he had need have much cunning, to seem to know that he doth not. Histories make men wise; poets, witty; the mathematics, subtile; natural philosophy, deep; moral, grave; logic and rhetoric, able to contend. *Abeunt studia in mores.*[23] Nay, there is no stond or impediment in the wit but may be wrought out by fit studies, like as diseases of the body may have appropriate exercises.

[23] *Abeunt . . . mores:* "Studies develop manners."

Bowling is good for the stone and reins, shooting for the lungs and breast, gentle walking for the stomach, riding for the head, and the like. So if a man's wit be wandering, let him study the mathematics; for in demonstrations, if his wit be called away never so little, he must begin again. If his wit be not apt to distinguish or find differences, let him study the schoolmen; for they are *Cymini sectores.*[24] If he be not apt to beat over matters, and to call up one thing to prove and illustrate another, let him study the lawyers' cases. So every defect of the mind may have a special receipt.

FROM

NOVUM ORGANUM

XXXVIII

The idols and false notions which are now in possession of the human understanding, and have taken deep root therein, not only so beset men's minds that truth can hardly find entrance, but even after entrance obtained, they will again in the very instauration of the sciences meet and trouble us, unless men being forewarned of the danger fortify themselves as far as may be against their assaults.

XXXIX

There are four classes of idols which beset men's minds. To these for distinction's sake I have assigned names,—calling the first class *Idols of the Tribe;* the second, *Idols of the Cave;* the third, *Idols of the Market-place;* the fourth, *Idols of the Theater.*

XL

The formation of ideas and axioms by true induction is no doubt the proper remedy to be applied for the keeping off and clearing away of idols. To point them out, however, is of great use, for the doctrine of idols is to the interpretation of nature what the doctrine of the refutation of sophisms is to common logic.

XLI

The Idols of the Tribe have their foundation in human nature itself, and in the tribe or race of men. For it is a false assertion that the sense of man is the measure of things. On the contrary, all perceptions, as well of the

[24] *sectores:* hairsplitters.

sense as of the mind, are according to the measure of the individual and not according to the measure of the universe. And the human understanding is like a false mirror, which, receiving rays irregularly, distorts and discolors the nature of things by mingling its own nature with it.

XLII

The Idols of the Cave are the idols of the individual man. For everyone (besides the errors common to human nature in general) has a cave or den of his own, which refracts and discolors the light of nature; owing either to his own proper and peculiar nature or to his education and conversation with others; or to the reading of books, and the authority of those whom he esteems and admires; or to the differences of impressions, accordingly as they take place in a mind preoccupied and predisposed or in a mind indifferent and settled; or the like. So that the spirit of man (according as it is meted out to different individuals) is in fact a thing variable and full of perturbation, and governed as it were by chance. Whence it was well observed by Heraclitus that men look for sciences in their own lesser worlds, and not in the greater or common world.

XLIII

There are also idols formed by the intercourse and association of men with each other, which I call Idols of the Market-place, on account of the commerce and consort of men there. For it is by discourse that men associate; and words are imposed according to the apprehension of the vulgar. And therefore the ill and unfit choice of words wonderfully obstructs the understanding. Nor do the definitions or explanations wherewith in some things learned men are wont to guard and defend themselves, by any means set the matter right. But words plainly force and overrule the understanding, and throw all into confusion, and lead men away into numberless empty controversies and idle fancies.

XLIV

Lastly, there are idols which have immigrated into men's minds from the various dogmas of philosophies, and also from wrong laws of demonstration. These I call Idols of the Theater; because in my judgment all the received systems are but so many stage-plays, representing worlds of their own creation after an unreal and scenic fashion. Nor is it only of the systems now in vogue, or only of the ancient sects and philosophies, that I speak: for many more plays of the same kind may yet be composed and in like artificial manner set forth; seeing that errors the most widely different have nevertheless causes for the most part alike. Neither again do I mean this only of entire systems, but also of many principles and axioms in science, which by tradition, credulity, and negligence have come to be received.

But of these several kinds of idols I must speak more largely and exactly, that the understanding may be duly cautioned.

XLV

The human understanding is of its own nature prone to suppose the existence of more order and regularity in the world than it finds. And though there be many things in nature which are singular and unmatched, yet it devises for them parallels and conjugates and relatives which do not exist. Hence the fiction that all celestial bodies move in perfect circles; spirals and dragons being (except in name) utterly rejected. Hence too the element of fire with its orb is brought in, to make up the square with the other three which the sense perceives. Hence also the ratio of density of the so-called elements is arbitrarily fixed at ten to one. And so on of other dreams. And these fancies affect not dogmas only, but simple notions also.

XLVI

The human understanding when it has once adopted an opinion (either as being the received opinion or as being agreeable to itself) draws all things else to support and agree with it. And though there be a greater number and weight of instances to be found on the other side, yet these it either neglects and despises, or else by some distinction sets aside and rejects; in order that by this great and pernicious predetermination the authority of its former conclusions may remain inviolate. And therefore it was a good answer that was made by one who when they showed him hanging in a temple a picture of those who had paid their vows as having escaped shipwreck, and would have him say whether he did not now acknowledge the power of the gods,—"Aye," asked he again, "but where are they painted that were drowned after their vows?" And such is the way of all superstition, whether in astrology, dreams, omens, divine judgments, or the like; wherein men, having a delight in such vanities, mark the events where they are fulfilled, but where they fail, though this happen much oftener, neglect and pass them by. But with far more subtlety does this mischief insinuate itself into philosophy and the sciences; in which the first conclusion colors and brings into conformity with itself all that come after, though far sounder and better. Besides, independently of that delight and vanity which I have described, it is the peculiar and perpetual error of the human intellect to be more moved and excited by affirmatives than by negatives; whereas it ought properly to hold itself indifferently disposed towards both alike. Indeed in the establishment of any true axiom, the negative instance is the more forcible of the two.

XLVII

The human understanding is moved by those things most which strike and enter the mind simultaneously and suddenly, and so fill the imagination; and then it feigns and supposes all other things to be somehow, though it cannot see how, similar to those few things by which it is surrounded. But for that going to and fro to remote and heterogeneous instances, by which axioms are tried as in the fire, the intellect is altogether slow and unfit, unless it be forced thereto by severe laws and overruling authority.

XLVIII

The human understanding is unquiet; it cannot stop or rest, and still presses onward, but in vain. Therefore it is that we cannot conceive of any end or limit to the world; but always as of necessity it occurs to us that there is something beyond. Neither again can it be conceived how eternity has flowed down to the present day: for that distinction which is commonly received of infinity in time past and in time to come can by no means hold; for it would thence follow that one infinity is greater than another, and that infinity is wasting away and tending to become finite. The like subtlety arises touching the infinite divisibility of lines, from the same inability of thought to stop. But this inability interferes more mischievously in the discovery of causes: for although the most general principles in nature ought to be held merely positive, as they are discovered, and cannot with truth be referred to a cause; nevertheless the human understanding being unable to rest still seeks something prior in the order of nature. And then it is that in struggling towards that which is further off it falls back upon that which is more nigh at hand,—namely, on final causes; which have relation clearly to the nature of man rather than to the nature of the universe, and from this source have strangely defiled philosophy. But he is no less an unskilled and shallow philosopher who seeks causes of that which is most general, than he who in things subordinate and subaltern omits to do so.

XLIX

The human understanding is no dry light, but receives an infusion from the will and affections; whence proceed sciences which may be called "sciences as one would." For what a man had rather were true he more readily believes. Therefore he rejects difficult things from impatience of research; sober things, because they narrow hope; the deeper things of nature, from superstition; the light of experience, from arrogance and pride, lest his mind should seem to be occupied with things mean and transitory; things not commonly believed, out of deference to the opinion of the vulgar. Numberless in short are the ways, and sometimes imperceptible, in which the affections color and infect the understanding.

L

But by far the greatest hindrance and aberration of the human understanding proceeds from the dullness, incompetency, and deceptions of the senses; in that things which strike the sense outweigh things which do not immediately strike it, though they be more important. Hence it is that speculation commonly ceases where sight ceases, insomuch that of things invisible there is little or no observation. Hence all the working of the spirits inclosed in tangible bodies lies hid and unobserved of men. So also all the more subtle changes of form in the parts of coarser substances (which they commonly call alteration, though it is in truth local motion through exceedingly small spaces) is in like manner unobserved. And yet unless these two things just mentioned be searched out and brought to light, nothing great can be achieved in nature, as far as the production of works is concerned. So again the essential nature of our common air, and of all bodies less dense than air (which are very many), is almost unknown. For the sense by itself is a thing infirm and erring; neither can instruments for enlarging or sharpening the senses do much: but all the truer kind of interpretation of nature is effected by instances and experiments fit and apposite; wherein the sense decides touching the experiment only, and the experiment touching the point in nature and the thing itself.

LI

The human understanding is of its own nature prone to abstractions and gives a substance and reality to things which are fleeting. But to resolve nature into abstractions is less to our purpose than to dissect her into parts; as did the school of Democritus, which went further into nature than the rest. Matter rather than forms should be the object of our attention, its configurations and changes of configuration, and simple action, and law of action or motion; for forms are figments of the human mind, unless you will call those laws of action forms.

LII

Such then are the idols which I call Idols of the Tribe; and which take their rise either from the homogeneity of the substance of the human spirit, or from its preoccupation, or from its narrowness, or from its restless motion, or from an infusion of the affections, or from the incompetency of the senses, or from the mode of impression.

LIII

The Idols of the Cave take their rise in the peculiar constitution, mental or bodily, of each individual; and also in education, habit, and accident. Of this kind there is a great number and variety; but I will instance those the pointing out of which contains the most important caution, and which have most effect in disturbing the clearness of the understanding.

LIV

Men become attached to certain particular sciences and speculations, either because they fancy themselves the authors and inventors thereof, or because they have bestowed the greatest pains upon them and become most habituated to them. But men of this kind, if they betake themselves to philosophy and contemplations of a general character, distort and color them in obedience to their former fancies; a thing especially to be noticed in Aristotle, who made his natural philosophy a mere bondservant to his logic, thereby rendering it contentious and well nigh useless. The race of chemists again out of a few experiments of the furnace have built up a fantastic philosophy, framed with reference to a few things; and Gilbert also, after he had employed himself most laboriously in the study and observation of the lodestone, proceeded at once to construct an entire system in accordance with his favorite subject.

LV

There is one principal and as it were radical distinction between different minds, in respect of philosophy and the sciences; which is this: that some minds are stronger and apter to mark the differences of things, others to mark their resemblances. The steady and acute mind can fix its contemplations and dwell and fasten on the subtlest distinctions; the lofty and discursive mind recognizes and puts together the finest and most general resemblances. Both kinds however easily err in excess, by catching the one at gradations, the other at shadows.

LVI

There are found some minds given to an extreme admiration of antiquity, others to an extreme love and appetite for novelty; but few so duly tempered that they can hold the mean, neither carping at what has been well laid down by the ancients, nor despising what is well introduced by the moderns. This however turns to the great injury of the sciences and philosophy: since these affectations of antiquity and novelty are the humors of partisans rather than judgments; and truth is to be sought for not in the felicity of any age, which is an unstable thing, but in the light of nature and experience, which is eternal. These factions therefore must be abjured, and care must be taken that the intellect be not hurried by them into assent.

LVII

Contemplations of nature and of bodies in their simple form break up and distract the understanding, while contemplations of nature and bodies in their composition and configuration overpower and dissolve the understanding: a distinction well seen in the school of Leucippus and Democritus as compared with the other philosophies. For that school is so busied with the particles that it hardly attends to the structure; while the others are so lost in admiration of the structure that they do not penetrate to the simplicity of nature. These kinds of contemplation should therefore be alternated and taken by turns; that so the understanding may be rendered at once penetrating and comprehensive, and the inconveniences above mentioned, with the idols which proceed from them, may be avoided.

LVIII

Let such then be our provision and contemplative prudence for keeping off and dislodging the Idols of the Cave, which grow for the most part either out of the predominance of a favorite subject, or out of an excessive tendency to compare or to distinguish, or out of partiality for particular ages, or out of the largeness or minuteness of the objects contemplated. And generally let every student of nature take this as a rule,—that whatever his mind seizes and dwells upon with peculiar satisfaction is to be held in suspicion, and that so much the more care is to be taken in dealing with such questions to keep the understanding even and clear.

LIX

But the Idols of the Market-place are the most troublesome of all: idols which have crept into the understanding through the alliances of words and names. For men believe that their reason governs words; but it is also true that words react on the understanding; and this it is that has rendered philosophy and the sciences sophistical and inactive. Now words, being commonly framed and applied according to the capacity of the vulgar, follow those lines of division which are most obvious to the vulgar understanding. And whenever an understanding of greater acuteness or a more diligent observation would alter those lines to suit the true divisions of nature, words stand in the way and resist the change. Whence it comes to pass that the high and formal discussions of learned men end oftentimes in disputes about words and names; with which (according to the use and wisdom of the mathematicians) it would be more prudent to begin, and so by means of definitions reduce them to order. Yet even definitions cannot cure this evil in dealing with natural and material things; since the definitions themselves consist of words, and those words beget others: so that it is necessary to recur to individual instances, and those in due series and order; as I shall say presently when I come to the method and scheme for the formation of notions and axioms.

LX

The idols imposed by words on the understanding are of two kinds. They are either names of things which do not exist (for as there are things left unnamed through lack of observation, so likewise are there names which result from fantastic suppositions and to which nothing in reality corresponds), or they are names of things which exist, but yet confused and ill-defined, and hastily and irregularly derived from realities. Of the former kind are Fortune, the Prime Mover, Planetary Orbits, Elements of Fire, and like fictions which owe their origin to false and idle theories. And this class of idols is more easily expelled, because to get rid of them it is only necessary that all theories should be steadily rejected and dismissed as obsolete.

But the other class, which springs out of a faulty and unskillful abstraction, is intricate and deeply rooted. Let us take for example such a word as humid, and see how far the several things which the word is used to signify agree with each other; and we shall find the word humid to be nothing else than a mark loosely and confusedly applied to denote a variety of actions which will not bear to be reduced to any constant meaning. For it both signifies that which easily spreads itself round any other body; and that which in itself is indeterminate and cannot solidize; and that which readily yields in every direction; and that which easily divides and scatters itself; and that which easily unites and collects itself; and that which readily flows and is put in motion; and that which readily clings to another body and wets it; and that which is easily reduced to a liquid, or being solid easily melts. Accordingly when you come to apply the word,—if you take it in one sense, flame is humid; if in another, air is not humid; if in another, fine dust is humid; if in another, glass is humid. So that it is easy to see that the notion is taken by abstraction only from water and common and ordinary liquids, without any due verification.

There are however in words certain degrees of distortion and error. One of the least faulty kinds is that of names of substances, especially of lowest species and well-deduced (for the notion of chalk and of mud is good, of earth bad); a more faulty kind is that of actions, as to generate, to corrupt, to alter; the most faulty is of qualities (except such as are the immediate objects of the sense) as heavy, light, rare, dense, and the like. Yet in all these cases some notions are of necessity a little better than others, in proportion to the greater variety of subjects that fall within the range of the human sense.

LXI

But the Idols of the Theater are not innate, nor do they steal into the understanding secretly, but are plainly impressed and received into the mind from the play-books of philosophical systems and the perverted rules of demonstration. To attempt refutations in this case would be merely inconsistent with what I have already said: for since we agree neither upon principles nor upon demonstrations there is no place for argument. And this is so far well, inasmuch as it leaves the honor of the ancients untouched. For they are no wise disparaged—the question between them and me being only as to the way. For as the saying is, the lame man who keeps the right road outstrips the runner who takes a wrong one. Nay it is obvious that when a man runs the wrong way, the more active and swift he is the further he will go astray.

But the course I propose for the discovery of science is such as leaves but little to the acuteness and strength of wits, but places all wits and understandings nearly on a level. For as in the drawing of a straight line or a perfect circle, much depends on the steadiness and practice of the hand, if it be done by aim of hand only, but if with the aid of rule or compass, little or nothing; so is it exactly with my plan. But though particular confutations would be of no avail, yet touching the sects and general divisions of such systems I must say something; something also touching the external signs which show that they are unsound; and finally something touching the causes of such great infelicity and of such lasting and general agreement in error; that so the access to truth may be made less difficult, and the human understanding may the more willingly submit to its purgation and dismiss its idols.

LXII

Idols of the Theater, or of Systems, are many, and there can be and perhaps will be yet many more. For were it not that now for many ages men's minds have been busied with religion and theology; and were it not that civil governments, especially monarchies, have been averse to such novelties, even in matters speculative; so that men labor therein to the peril and harming of their fortunes,—not only unrewarded, but exposed also to contempt and envy: doubtless there would have arisen many other philosophical sects like to those which in great variety flourished once among the Greeks. For as on the phenomena of the heavens many hypotheses may be constructed, so likewise (and more also) many various dogmas may be set up and established on the phenomena of philosophy. And in the plays of this philosophical theater you may observe the same thing which is found in the theater of the poets, that stories invented for the stage are more compact and elegant, and more as one would wish them to be, than true stories out of history.

In general however there is taken for the material of philosophy either a great deal out of a few things, or a very little out of many things; so that on both sides philosophy is based on too narrow a foundation of experiment and natural history, and decides on the authority of too few cases. For the rational school of philosophers snatches from experience a variety of common instances, neither duly ascertained nor diligently examined and weighed, and leaves all the rest to meditation and agitation of wit.

There is also another class of philosophers, who having bestowed much diligent and careful labor on a few experiments, have thence made bold to educe and construct systems; wresting all other facts in a strange fashion to conformity therewith.

And there is yet a third class, consisting of those who out of faith and veneration mix their philosophy with theology and traditions; among whom the vanity of some has gone so far aside as to seek the origin of science among spirits and genii. So that this parent stock of errors—this false philosophy—is of three kinds; the sophistical, the empirical, and the superstitious.

XCV

Those who have handled sciences have been either men of experiment or men of dogmas. The men of experiment are like the ant; they only collect and use: the reasoners resemble spiders, who make cobwebs out of their own substance. But the bee takes a middle course, it gathers its material from the flowers of the garden and of the field, but transforms and digests it by a power of its own. Not unlike this is the true business of philosophy: for it neither relies solely or chiefly on the powers of the mind, nor does it take the matter which it gathers from natural history and mechanical experiments and lay it up in the memory whole, as it finds it; but lays it up in the understanding altered and digested. Therefore from a closer and purer league between these two faculties, the experimental and the rational, (such as has never yet been made) much may be hoped.

XCVI

We have as yet no natural philosophy that is pure; all is tainted and corrupted: in Aristotle's school by logic; in Plato's by natural theology; in the second school of Platonists, such as Proclus and others, by mathematics, which ought only to give definiteness to natural philosophy, not to generate or give it birth. From a natural philosophy pure and unmixed, better things are to be expected.

XCVII

No one has yet been found so firm of mind and purpose as resolutely to compel himself to sweep away all theories and common notions, and to apply the understanding, thus made fair and even, to a fresh examination of particulars. Thus it happens that human knowledge, as we have it, is a mere medley and ill-digested mass, made up of much credulity and much accident, and also of the childish notions which we at first imbibed. Now if anyone of ripe age, unimpaired senses, and well-purged mind, apply himself anew to experience and particulars, better hopes may be entertained of that man. In which point I promise to myself a like fortune to that of Alexander the Great; and let no man tax me with vanity till he have heard the end; for the thing which I mean tends to the putting off of all vanity. For of Alexander and his deeds Aeschines spake thus: "Assuredly we do not live the life of mortal men; but to this end were we born, that in after ages wonders might be told of us;" as if what Alexander had done seemed to him miraculous. But in the next age Titus Livius took a better and a deeper view of the matter, saying in effect, that Alexander "had done no more than take courage to despise vain apprehensions." And a like judgment I suppose may be passed on myself in future ages: that I did no great things, but simply made less account of things that were accounted great. In the meanwhile, as I have already said, there is no hope except in a new birth of science; that is, in raising it regularly up from experience and building it afresh; which no one (I think) will say has yet been done or thought of.

CXXII

It may be thought also a strange and a harsh thing that we should at once and with one blow set aside all sciences and all authors; and that too without calling in any of the ancients to our aid and support, but relying on our own strength.

And I know that if I had chosen to deal less sincerely, I might easily have found authority for my suggestions by referring them either to the old times before the Greeks (when natural science was perhaps more flourishing, though it made less noise, not having yet passed into the pipes and trumpets of the Greeks), or even, in part at least, to some of the Greeks themselves; and so gained for them both support and honor; as men of no family devise for themselves by the good help of genealogies the nobility of a descent from some ancient stock. But for my part, relying on the evidence and truth of things, I reject all forms of fiction and imposture; nor do I think that it matters any more to the business in hand, whether the discoveries that shall now be made were long ago known to the ancients, and have their settings and their risings according to the vicissitude of things and course of ages, than it matters to mankind whether the new world be that island of Atlantis with which the ancients were acquainted, or now discovered for the first time. For new discoveries must be sought from the light of nature, not fetched back out of the darkness of antiquity.

And as for the universality of the censure, certainly if the matter be truly considered, such a censure is not only more probable but more modest too, than a partial one would be. For if the errors had not been rooted in primary notions, there must have been some true discoveries to correct the false. But the errors being fundamental, and not so much of false judgment as of inattention and oversight, it is no wonder that men have not obtained what they have not tried for, nor reached a mark which they never set up, nor finished a course which they never entered on or kept.

And as for the presumption implied in it; certainly if a man undertakes by steadiness of hand and power of eye to describe a straighter line or more perfect circle than anyone else, he challenges a comparison of abilities; but if he only says that he with the help of a rule or a pair of compasses can draw a straighter line or a more perfect circle than anyone else can by eye and hand alone, he makes no great boast. And this remark, be it observed, applies not merely to this first and inceptive attempt of mine, but to all that shall take the work in hand hereafter. For my way of discovering sciences goes far to level men's wits, and leaves but little to individual excellence; because it performs everything by the surest rules and demonstrations. And therefore I attribute my part in all this, as I have often said, rather to good luck than to ability, and account it a birth of time rather than of wit. For certainly chance has something to do with men's thoughts, as well as with their works and deeds.

Robert Burton

1577–1640

ROBERT BURTON was an Oxford don, a scholar and a recluse who held several church livings but devoted himself to the writing and revision of his strange, elaborate masterpiece, *The Anatomy of Melancholy,* first published in 1621. It is a huge, conglomerate work, the culmination of a tradition of medical and psychological treatises on melancholy. Burton sprinkles his text with classical (and some modern) quotations and references to authority. He is appallingly learned, often amusing, frequently eloquent, and always more than ample to his subject. His book is an inexhaustible storehouse of quaint lore, odd information, and curious stories. Yet it is a serious monument of psychological, moral, and scientific philosophizing. Burton is not systematic in any of the three fields, and Douglas Bush remarks of him that "sitting between Bacon and Hobbes, he appears as a kind of gargoyle between the two spires of the cathedral of English scientific thought."

"I write of melancholy, by being busy to avoid melancholy," he says in his preface (signed "Democritus Junior"), and he explains how he prepared himself for his long task: "I have confusedly tumbled over divers authors in our libraries, with small profit for want of art, order, memory, judgment." He looks at the world from a scholar's detached point of view, not to scoff or laugh at everything, he says, "but with a mixed passion."

He divides his book elaborately into Partitions, Sections, Members, and Subsections; he spares the reader nothing. The Third Partition (the last) covers Love and Love Melancholy, with many minor subdivisions, and Religious Melancholy. We select from the Love Melancholy portion a Member on the subject of Charity. It is a part of the main theme of his book, "that all the world is melancholy or mad, dotes, and every member of it."

BIBLIOGRAPHY: *Robert Burton and the Anatomy of Melancholy: Papers by Sir William Osler, Professor Edward Bensly, and Others,* ed. F. Madan, Oxford, 1926; Bergen Evans, *The Psychiatry of Robert Burton,* New York, 1944; W. R. Mueller, *The Anatomy of Robert Burton's England,* Berkeley, 1952; *The Anatomy of Melancholy by Robert Burton now for the first time with the Latin completely given in translation;* ed. F. Dell and P. Jordan-Smith, New York, 1929.

FROM

THE ANATOMY OF MELANCHOLY

PARTITION 3, SECTION I, MEMBER 3

Charity composed of all three Kinds, Pleasant, Profitable, Honest

BESIDES this love that comes from profit, pleasant, honest (for one good turn asks another in equity), that which proceeds from the law of nature, or from discipline and philosophy, there is yet another love compounded of all these three, which is charity, and includes piety, dilection, benevolence, friendship, even all those virtuous habits; for love is the circle equant of all other affections, of which Aristotle dilates at large in his Ethics, and is commanded by God, which no man can well perform, but he that is a Christian, and a true regenerate man; this is, "To love God above all, and our neighbor as ourself;" for this love is *lychnus accendens et accensus,* a communicating light, apt to illuminate itself as well as others. All other objects are fair, and very beautiful, I confess; kindred, alliance, friendship, the love that we owe to our country, nature, wealth, pleasure, honor, and such moral respects, &c., of which read copious Aristotle in his morals; a man is beloved of a man, in that he is a man; but all these are far more eminent and great, when they shall proceed from a sanctified spirit, that hath a true touch of religion, and a reference to God. Nature binds all creatures to love their young ones; a hen to preserve her brood will run upon a lion, a hind will fight with a bull, a sow with a bear, a silly sheep with a fox. So the same nature urgeth a man to love his parents, (*dii me pater omnes oderint, ni te magis quam oculos amem meos!*) and this love cannot be dissolved, as Tully holds, "without detestable offence:" but much more God's commandment, which enjoins a filial love, and an obedience in this kind. "The love of brethren is great, and like an arch of stones, where if one be displaced, all comes down," no love so forcible and strong, honest, to the combination of which, nature, fortune, virtue, happily concur; yet this love comes short of it. *Dulce et decorum pro patriâ mori,* it cannot be expressed, what a deal of charity that one name of country contains. *Amor laudis et patria pro stipendio est;* the Decii did *se devovere,* Horatii, Curii, Scaevola, Regulus Codrus, sacrifice themselves for their country's peace and good.

"Una dies Fabios ad bellum miserat omnes,
Ad bellum missos perdidit una dies."

"One day the Fabii stoutly warred,
One day the Fabii were destroyed."

Fifty thousand Englishmen lost their lives willingly near Battle Abbey, in defence of their country. P. Æmilius, 1. 6. speaks of six senators of Calais that came with halters in their hands to the king of England, to die for the rest. This love makes so many writers take such pains, so many historiographers, physicians, &c., or at least, as they pretend, for common safety, and their country's benefit. *Sanctum nomen amicitiae, sociorum communio sacra;* friendship is a holy name, and a sacred communion of friends. "As the sun is in the firmament, so is friendship in the world," a most divine and heavenly band. As nuptial love makes, this perfects mankind, and is to be preferred (if you will stand to the judgment of Cornelius Nepos) before affinity or consanguinity, *plus in amicitiâ valet similitudo morum quam affinitas,* &c. the cords of love bind faster than any other wreath whatsoever. Take this away, and take all pleasure, joy, comfort, happiness, and true content out of the world; 'tis the greatest tie, the surest indenture, strongest band, and, as our modern Maro decides it, is much to be preferred before the rest.

"Hard is the doubt, and difficult to deem,
When all three kinds of love together meet;
And do dispart the heart with power extreme,
Whether shall weigh the balance down; to wit,
The dear affection unto kindred sweet,
Or raging fire of love to women kind,
Or zeal of friends, combin'd by virtues meet;
But of them all the band of virtuous mind,
Methinks the gentle heart should most assured bind.

"For natural affection soon doth cease,
And quenched is with Cupid's greater flame;
But faithful friendship doth them both suppress,
And them with mastering discipline doth tame,
Through thoughts aspiring to eternal fame.
For as the soul doth rule the earthly mass,
And all the service of the body frame,
So love of soul doth love of body pass,
No less than perfect gold surmounts the meanest brass."

A faithful friend is better than gold, a medicine of misery, an only possession; yet this love of friends, nuptial, heroical, profitable, pleasant, honest, all three loves put together, are little worth, if they proceed not from a true Christian illuminated soul, if it be not done *in ordine ad Deum,* for God's sake. "Though I had the gift of prophecy, spake with tongues of men and angels, though I feed the poor with all my goods, give my body to be burned, and have not this love, it profiteth me nothing," I Cor. xiii. 1, 3. 'tis *splendidum peccatum,* without charity. This is an all-apprehending love, a deifying love, a refined, pure, divine love, the quintessence of all love, the true philosopher's stone, *Non potest enim,* as Austin infers, *veraciter amicus esse hominis, nisi fuerit ipsius primitus veritatis,* He is no true friend that loves not God's truth. And therefore this is true love indeed, the cause of all good to mortal men that reconciles all creatures, and glues them together in perpetual amity and firm league; and can no more abide bitterness, hate, malice, than fair and foul weather, light and darkness, sterility and plenty may be together; as the sun in the firmament (I say), so is love in the world; and for this cause, 'tis love without an addition, love, love of God, and love of men. "The love of God begets the love of man; and by this love of our neighbor, the love of God is nourished and increased." By this happy union of love, "all well governed families and cities are combined, the heavens annexed, and divine souls complicated, the world itself composed, and all that is in it conjoined in God, and reduced to one. This love causeth true and absolute virtues, the life, spirit, and root of every virtuous action, it finisheth prosperity, easeth adversity, corrects all natural incumbrances, inconveniences, sustained by faith and hope, which with this our love make an indissoluble twist, a Gordian knot, an equilateral triangle, and yet the greatest of them is love," 1 Cor. xiii. 13, "which inflames our souls with a divine heat, and being so inflamed, purged, and so purgeth, elevates to God, makes an atonement, and reconciles us unto him." That other love infects the soul of man, this cleanseth; that depresses, this rears; that causeth cares and troubles, this quietness of mind; this informs, that deforms our life; that leads to repentance, this to heaven. For if once we be truly linked and touched with this charity, we shall love God above all, our neighbor as ourself, as we are enjoined, Mark xii. 31. Matt. xix. 19. perform those duties and exercises, even all the operations of a good Christian.

"This love suffereth long, it is bountiful, envieth not, boasteth not itself, is not puffed up, it deceiveth not, it seeketh not his own things, is not provoked to anger, it thinketh not evil, it rejoiceth not in iniquity, but in truth. It suffereth all things, believeth all things, hopeth all things," 1 Cor. xiii. 4, 5, 6, 7; "it covereth all trespasses," Prov. x. 12; "a multitude of sins," 1 Pet. iv. 8, as our Saviour told the woman in the Gospel, that washed his feet, "many sins were forgiven her, for she loved much," Luke vii. 47; "it will defend the fatherless and the widow," Isa. i. 17; "will seek no revenge, or be mindful of wrong," Levit. xix. 18; "will bring home his brother's ox if he go astray, as it is commanded," Deut. xxii. 1; "will resist evil, give to him that asketh, and not turn from him that borroweth, bless them that curse him, love his enemy," Matt. v; "bear his brother's burthen," Gal. vi. 7. He that so loves will be hospitable, and distribute to the necessities of the saints; he will, if it be possible, have peace with all men, "feed his enemy if he be hungry, if he be athirst give him drink;" he will perform those seven works of mercy, "he will make himself equal to them of the lower sort, rejoice with them that rejoice, weep with them that weep," Rom. xii; he will speak truth to his neighbor, be courteous and tender-hearted, "forgiving others for Christ's sake, as God forgave him," Eph. iv. 32; "he will be like minded," Phil. ii. 2. "Of one judgment; be humble, meek, long-suffering," Colos. iii. "Forbear, forget and forgive," xii. 13. 23. and what he doth shall be heartily done to God, and not to men. "Be pitiful and courteous," 1 Pet. iii. "Seek peace and follow it." He will love his brother, not in word and tongue, but in deed and truth, John iii. 18. "and he that loves God, Christ will love him that is begotten of him," John v. 1, &c. Thus should we willingly do, if we had a true touch of this charity, of this divine love, if we could perform this which we are enjoined, forget and forgive, and compose ourselves to those Christian laws of love.

"io felix hominum genus,
Si vestros animos amor
Quo coelum regitur regat"

"Angelical souls, how blessed, how happy should we be, so loving, how might we triumph over the devil, and have another heaven upon earth!"

But this we cannot do; and which is the cause of all our woes, miseries, discontent, melancholy, want of this charity. We do *invicem angariare,* contemn, consult, vex, torture, molest, and hold one another's noses to the grindstone hard, provoke, rail, scoff, calumniate, challenge, hate, abuse (hard-hearted, implacable, malicious, peevish, inexorable as we are), to satisfy our lust or private spleen, for toys, trifles, and impertinent occasions, spend ourselves, goods, friends, fortunes, to be revenged on our adversary, to ruin him and his. 'Tis all our study, practice, and business how to plot mischief, mine, countermine, defend and offend, ward ourselves, injure others, hurt all; as if we were born to do mischief, and that with such eagerness and bitterness, with such rancour, malice, rage, and fury, we prosecute our intended designs, that neither affinity or consanguinity, love or fear of God or men can contain us: no satisfaction, no composition will be accepted, no offices will serve, no submission; though he shall upon his knees, as Sarpedon did to Glaucus in Homer, acknowledging his error, yield himself with tears in his eyes, beg his pardon, we will not relent, forgive, or forget, till we have confounded him and his, "made dice of his bones," as they say, see him rot in prison, banish his friends, followers, *et omne invisum genus,* rooted him out and all his posterity. Monsters of men as we are, dogs, wolves, tigers, fiends, incarnate devils, we do not only contend, oppress, and tyrannise ourselves, but as so many firebrands, we set on, and animate others: our whole life is a perpetual combat, a conflict, a set battle, a snarling fit. *Eris dea* is settled in our tents, *Omnia de lite,* opposing wit to wit, wealth to wealth, strength to strength, fortunes to fortunes, friends to friends, as at a sea-fight, we turn our broadsides, or two millstones with continual attrition, we fire ourselves, or break another's backs and both are ruined and consumed in the end. Miserable wretches, to fat and enrich ourselves, we care not how we get it, *Quocunque modo rem;* how many thousands we undo, whom we oppress, by whose ruin and downfall we arise, whom we injure, fatherless children, widows, common societies, to satisfy our own private lust. Though we have myriads, abundance of wealth and treasure (pitiless, merciless, remorseless, and uncharitable in the highest degree), and our poor brother in need, sickness, in great extremity, and now ready to be starved for want of food, we had rather, as the fox told the ape, his tail should sweep the ground still, than cover his buttocks; rather spend it idly, consume it with dogs, hawks, hounds, unnecessary buildings, in riotous apparel, ingurgitate, or let it be lost, than he should have part of it; rather take from him that little which he hath, than relieve him.

Like the dog in the manger, we neither use it ourselves, let others make use of or enjoy it; part with nothing while we live: for want of disposing our household, and setting things in order, set all the world together by the ears after our death. Poor Lazarus lies howling at his gates for a few crumbs, he only seeks chippings, offals; let him roar and howl, famish, and eat his own flesh, he respects him not. A poor decayed kinsman of his sets upon him by the way in all his jollity, and runs begging bareheaded by him, conjuring by those former bonds of friendship, alliance, consanguinity, &c., uncle, cousin, brother, father,

——"Per ego has lachrymas, dextramque tuam te,
Si quidquam de te merui, fuit ant tibi quidquam
Dulce meum, misere mei."

"Show some pity for Christ's sake, pity a sick man, an old man," &c., he cares not, ride on: pretend sickness, inevitable loss of limbs, goods, plead suretyship, or shipwreck, fires, common calamities, show thy wants and imperfections.

"Et si per sanctum juratus dicat Osyrim,
Credite, non ludo, crudeles tollite claudum."

"Swear, protest, take God and all his angels to witness, *quaere peregrinum,* thou art a counterfeit crank, a cheater, he is not touched with it, *pauper ubique jacet,* ride on, he takes no notice of it." Put up a supplication to him in the name of a thousand orphans, a hospital, a spittel, a prison, as he goes by, they cry out to him for aid, ride on, *surdo narras,* he cares not, let them eat stones, devour themselves with vermin, rot in their own dung, he cares not. Show him a decayed haven, a bridge, a school, a fortification, &c., or some public work, ride on; good your worship, your honor, for God's sake, your country's sake, ride on. But show him a roll wherein his name shall be registered in golden letters, and commended to all posterity, his arms set up, with his devices to be seen, then peradventure he will stay and contribute; or if thou canst thunder upon him, as Papists do, with satisfactory and meritorious works, or persuade him by this means he shall save his soul out of hell, and free it from purgatory (if he be of any religion), then in all likelihood he will listen and stay; or that he have no children, no near kinsman, heir, he cares for, at least, or cannot well tell otherwise how or where to bestow his possessions (for carry them with him he cannot), it may be then he will build some school or hospital in his life, or be induced to give liberally to pious uses after his death. For I dare boldly say, vain-glory, that opinion of merit, and this enforced necessity, when they know not otherwise how to leave, or what better to do with them, is the main cause of most of our good works. I will not urge this to derogate from any man's charitable devotion, or bounty in this kind to censure any good work; no doubt there be many sanctified, heroical and worthy-minded men, that in true zeal, and for virtue's sake (divine spirits), that out of commiseration and pity extend their liberality, and as much as in them lies do good to all men, clothe the naked, feed the hungry, comfort the sick and needy, relieve all, forget and forgive injuries, as true charity requires; yet most part there is *simulatum quid,* a deal of hypocrisy in this kind, much default and defect. Cosmo de Medici, that rich citizen of Florence, ingenuously confessed to a near friend of his, that would know of him why he built so many public and magnificent palaces, and bestowed so liberally on scholars, not that he loved learning more than others, "but to eternise his own name, to be immortal by the benefit of scholars; for when his friends were dead, walls decayed, and all inscriptions gone, books would remain to the world's end." The lanthorn in Athens was built by Zenocles, the theatre by Pericles, the famous port Pyraeum by Musicles, Pallas Palladium by Phidias, the Pantheon by Callicratidas; but these brave monuments are decayed all, and ruined long since, their builders' names alone flourish by meditation of writers. And as he said of that Marian oak, now cut down and dead, *nullius Agricolae manu culta stirps tam diluturna quam quae poetae versu siminari potest,* no plant can grow so long as that which is *ingenio sata,* set and manured by those ever-living wits. Allong Backuth, that weeping oak, under which Deborah, Rebecca's nurse, died, and was buried, may not survive the memory of such everlasting monuments. Vain glory and emulation (as to most men) was the cause efficient, and to be a trumpeter of his own fame, Cosmo's sole intent so to do good, that all the world might take notice of it. Such for the most part is the charity of our times, such our benefactors, Mecaenases and patrons. Show me amongst so many myriads, a truly devout, a right, honest, upright, meek, humble, a patient, innocuous, innocent, a merciful, a loving, a charitable man! *Probus quis nobiscum vivit?* Show me a Caleb or a Joshua! *Dic mihi Musa virum*—show a virtuous woman, a constant wife, a good neighbor, a trusty servant, an obedient child, a true friend, &c. Crows in Africa are not so scant. He that shall examine this iron age wherein we live, where love is cold, *et jam terras Astrea reliquit,* justice fled with her assistants, virtue expelled,

> *——"y Justitiae soror,*
> *Incorrupta fides, nudaque veritas,"—*

all goodness gone, where vice abounds, the devil is loose, and see one man vilify and insult over his brother, as if he were an innocent, or a block, oppress, tyrannise, prey upon, torture him, vex, gall, torment and crucify him, starve him, where is charity? He that shall see men swear and forswear, lie and bear false witness, to advantage themselves, prejudice others, hazard goods, lives, fortunes, credit, all, to be revenged on their enemies, men so unspeakable in their lusts, unnatural in malice, such bloody designments, Italian blaspheming, Spanish renouncing, &c, may well ask where is charity? He that shall observe so many lawsuits, such endless contention, such plotting, undermining, so much money spent with such eagerness and fury, every man for himself, his own ends, the devil for all: so many distressed souls, such lamentable complaints, so many factions, conspiracies, seditions, oppressions, abuses, injuries, such grudging, repining, discontent, so much emulation, envy, so many brawls, quarrels, monomachies, &c., may well require what is become of charity? when we see and read of such cruel wars, tumults, uproars, bloody battles, so many men slain, so many cities ruinated, &c. (for what else is the subject of all our stories almost, but bills, bows, and guns!) so many murders and massacres, &c., where is charity? Or see men wholly devote to God, churchmen, professed divines, holy men, "to make the trumpet of the gospel the trumpet of war," a company of hell-born Jesuits, and fiery-spirited friars, *facem praeferre* to all seditions: as so many firebrands set all the world by the ears (I say nothing of their contentions and railing books, whole ages spent in writing one against another, and that with such virulency and bitterness, *Bionaeis sermonibus et sale nigro*), and by their bloody inquisitions, that in thirty years, Bale saith, consumed 39 princes, 148 earls, 235 barons, 14,755 commons; worse than those ten persecutions, may justly doubt where is charity? *Obsecro vos quales hi demum Christiani!* Are these Christians? I beseech you tell me: he that shall observe and see these things, may say to them as Cato to Caesar, *credo quae de inferis dicuntur falsa existimas,* "sure I think thou art of opinion there is neither heaven nor hell." Let them pretend religion, zeal, make what shows they will, give alms, peace-makers, frequent sermons, if we may guess at the tree by the fruit they are no better than hypocrites, epicures, atheists, with the "fool in their hearts they say there is no God." 'Tis no marvel then if being so uncharitable, hard-hearted as we are, we have so frequent and so many discontents, such melancholy fits, so many bitter pangs, mutual discords, all in a combustion, often complaints, so common grievances, general mischiefs, *si tantae in terris tragaediae, quibus labefactatur et miserè laceratur humanum genus,* so many pestilences, wars, uproars, losses, deluges, fires, inundations, God's vengeance and all the plagues of Egypt, come upon us, since we are so currish one towards another, so respectless of God, and our neighbors, and by our crying sins pull these miseries upon our own heads. Nay more, 'tis justly to be feared, which Josephus once said of his countrymen Jews, "if the Romans had not come when they did to sack their city, surely it had been swallowed up with some earthquake, deluge, or fired from heaven as Sodom and Gomorrah: their desperate malice, wickedness and peevishness was such." 'Tis to be suspected, if we continue these wretched ways, we may look for the like heavy visitations to come upon us. If we had any sense or feeling of these things, surely we should not go on as we do, in such irregular courses, practise all manner of impieties; our whole carriage would not be so averse from God. If a man would but consider, when he is in the midst and full career of such prodigious and uncharitable actions, how displeasing they are in God's sight, how noxious to himself, as Solomon told Joab, 1 Kings, ii. "The Lord shall bring this blood upon their heads." Prov. i. 27, "sudden desolation and destruction shall come like a whirlwind upon them: affliction, anguish, the reward of his hand shall be given him," Isa. iii. 11, &c., "they shall fall into the pit they have digged for others," and when they are scraping, tyrannising, getting, wallowing in their wealth, "this night, O fool, I will take away thy soul," what a severe account they must make; and how "gracious on the other side a charitable man is in God's eyes," *haurit sibi gratiam*. Matt. v. 7, "Blessed are the merciful, for they shall obtain mercy: he that lendeth to the poor, gives to God," and how it shall be restored to them again; "how by their patience and long-suffering they shall heap coals on their enemies' heads," Rom. xii. "and he that followeth after righteousness and mercy, shall find righteousness and glory;" surely they would check their desires, curb in their unnatural, inordinate affections, agree amongst themselves, abstain from doing evil, amend their lives, and learn to do well. "Behold how comely and good a thing it is for brethren to live together in union: it is like the precious ointment, &c. How odious to contend one with the other!" *Miseri quid luctatiunculis hisce volumus? ecce mors supra caput est, et supremum illud tribunal, ubi et dicta et facta nostra examinanda sunt: Sapiamus!* "Why do we contend and vex one another? behold death is over our heads, and we must shortly give an account of all our uncharitable words and actions: think upon it: and be wise."

Robert Herrick

1591–1674

THE most gifted of the followers of Ben Jonson, Herrick is also one of the most intimate, familiar, and attractive of all the English lyric poets. His models are classical—Horace and Ovid and Catullus, notably; but his content is local, provincial, and English. He gives us a delightful picture of country life and its pleasures, with a certain nostalgia—as if he were portraying the Elizabethan world, before civil strife over matters of church and state had distracted men's minds and embittered their attitudes. As a matter of fact he does depict a past world; it is the timeless Arcadia of the poets and painters. But Herrick makes Arcadia more immediate and credible with his farmyard details, the name of his maid and his dog, and his all but irrepressible humor.

He was born in London, the son of a goldsmith; he was apprenticed to an uncle, also a goldsmith, but finally, at the age of twenty-two, went to Cambridge, where he received the degrees of B.A. in 1617 and M.A. in 1620. For some time he lived in London, but from 1629 to 1647 he was vicar of Dean Prior in the diocese of Exeter—"this dull Devonshire," as he calls it. He was evicted by the Puritans, returned to London, lived there fifteen years, and finally was restored to Dean Prior in 1662.

Herrick's praise of youth and love gave him "access," as he says, "to sing of cleanly wantonness." His Julias and Corinnas are imaginary and wholly delightful. His song to all of them, "To the Virgins, to Make Much of Time," has been called by one authority the most popular poem written in the seventeenth century. He writes to Corinna the finest May-morning song in the language, slyly mingling religious observances and imagery with the pagan intention and environment of the day's activities. And "The Night-Piece, to Julia," presumably in origin an exercise on a metrical scheme by Ben Jonson, becomes one of the most delicate, subtle, and lovely masterpieces of indirect statement ever achieved in poetry.

Herrick needs little introduction or recommendation; the delights of his poetry are apparent. But though he is not as thorny and obscure as a metaphysical poet, he achieves many subtle effects. It would be a mistake to read him too simply.

BIBLIOGRAPHY: *The Poetical Works*, ed. F. W. Moorman, Oxford, 1915; F. W. Moorman, *Robert Herrick*, London, 1910; P. Aiken, *The Influence of the Latin Elegists on English Lyric Poetry, 1600–1650*, Orono, Maine, 1932; F. Delattre, *Robert Herrick*, Paris, 1911.

FROM

HESPERIDES

(1648)

THE ARGUMENT OF HIS BOOK

I SING of brooks, of blossoms, birds, and bowers:
Of April, May, of June, and July flowers.
I sing of May-poles, hock-carts,[1] wassails, wakes,[2]
Of bridegrooms, brides, and of their bridal cakes.
I write of youth, of love, and have access
By these, to sing of cleanly wantonness.

I sing of dews, of rains, and piece by piece
Of balm, of oil, of spice, and ambergris.
I sing of time's trans-shifting; and I write
How roses first came red, and lilies white.
I write of groves, of twilights, and I sing
The court of Mab, and of the Fairy King.
I write of hell; I sing (and ever shall)
Of heaven, and hope to have it after all.

HIS ANSWER TO A QUESTION

SOME would know
Why I so
Long still do tarry,
And ask why
Here that I
Live, and not marry?
Thus I those
Do oppose:
What man would be here
Slave to thrall,
If at all
He could live free here?

---

1 *hock-cart:* the ceremonial last cart of the harvest.

2 *wakes:* popular festivals, originally connected with the church.

UPON THE LOSS OF HIS MISTRESSES

I HAVE lost, and lately, these
Many dainty mistresses:
Stately Julia, prime of all;
Sappho next, a principal;
Smooth Anthea, for a skin
White, and heaven-like crystalline;
Sweet Electra, and the choice
Myrrha, for the lute, and voice.
Next, Corinna, for her wit,
And for the graceful use of it;
With Perilla—all are gone;
Only Herrick's left alone,
For to number sorrow by
Their departures hence, and die.

DISCONTENTS IN DEVON

MORE discontents I never had
Since I was born, than here;
Where I have been, and still am, sad,
In this dull Devonshire;
Yet justly too I must confess,
I ne'er invented such
Ennobled numbers for the press
Than where I loathed so much.

DELIGHT IN DISORDER

A SWEET disorder in the dress
Kindles in clothes a wantonness;
A lawn about the shoulders thrown
Into a fine distraction;
An erring lace, which here and there
Enthralls the crimson stomacher;
A cuff neglectful, and thereby
Ribbons to flow confusedly;

A winning wave (deserving note)
In the tempestuous petticoat;
A careless shoe-string, in whose tie
I see a wild civility:
Do more bewitch me, than when art
Is too precise in every part.

CORINNA'S GOING A-MAYING

Get up, get up, for shame, the blooming morn
Upon her wings presents the god unshorn.[3]
See how Aurora throws her fair
Fresh-quilted colors through the air!
Get up, sweet slug-a-bed, and see
The dew bespangling herb and tree.
Each flower has wept, and bowed toward the East,
Above an hour since; yet you not dressed,
Nay! not so much as out of bed?
When all the birds have matins said,
And sung their thankful hymns, 'tis sin,
Nay, profanation to keep in;
Whenas a thousand virgins on this day
Spring, sooner than the lark, to fetch in May.

Rise, and put on your foliage, and be seen
To come forth, like the spring-time, fresh and green
And sweet as Flora. Take no care
For jewels for your gown, or hair;
Fear not, the leaves will strew
Gems in abundance upon you;
Besides, the childhood of the day has kept,
Against you come, some orient pearls unwept;
Come, and receive them while the light
Hangs on the dew-locks of the night:
And Titan on the eastern hill
Retires himself, or else stands still
Till you come forth. Wash, dress, be brief in praying:
Few beads are best, when once we go a-maying.

Come, my Corinna, come; and, coming, mark
How each field turns a street, each street a park

[3] *the god unshorn:* Apollo, the sun god.

Made green, and trimmed with trees; see how
Devotion gives each house a bough,
Or branch; each porch, each door, ere this,
An ark, a tabernacle is,
Made up of white-thorn neatly interwove;
As if here were those cooler shades of love.
Can such delights be in the street,
And open fields, and we not see't?
Come, we'll abroad; and let's obey
The proclamation made for May:
And sin no more, as we have done, by staying;
But, my Corinna, come, let's go a-maying.

There's not a budding boy or girl this day
But is got up, and gone to bring in May.
A deal of youth, ere this, is come
Back, and with white-thorn laden home.
Some have dispatched their cakes and cream,
Before that we have left to dream;
And some have wept, and wooed, and plighted troth,
And chose their priest, ere we can cast off sloth.
Many a green-gown [4] has been given;
Many a kiss, both odd and even:
Many a glance too has been sent
From out the eye, love's firmament;
Many a jest told of the keys betraying
This night, and locks picked, yet we're not a-maying.

Come, let us go, while we are in our prime,
And take the harmless folly of the time.
We shall grow old apace and die
Before we know our liberty.
Our life is short, and our days run
As fast away as does the sun;
And as a vapor, or a drop of rain,
Once lost, can ne'er be found again:
So when or you or I are made
A fable, song, or fleeting shade,
All love, all liking, all delight
Lies drowned with us in endless night.
Then while time serves, and we are but decaying,
Come, my Corinna, come, let's go a-maying.

---

[4] *green-gown:* i.e., a grass-stained dress.

TO LIVE MERRILY, AND TO TRUST TO GOOD VERSES

Now is the time for mirth,
Nor cheek or tongue be dumb;
For with the flow'ry earth
The golden pomp is come.

The golden pomp is come;
For now each tree does wear,
Made of her pap and gum,
Rich beads of amber here.

Now reigns the rose, and now
Th' Arabian dew besmears
My uncontrollèd brow
And my retorted [5] hairs.

Homer, this health to thee,
In sack of such a kind
That it would make thee see
Though thou wert ne'er so blind.

Next, Virgil I'll call forth
To pledge this second health
In wine, whose each cup's worth
An Indian commonwealth.

A goblet next I'll drink
To Ovid, and suppose,
Made he the pledge, he'd think
The world had all one nose.[6]

Then this immensive cup
Of aromatic wine,
Catullus, I quaff up
To that terse muse of thine.

Wild I am now with heat;
O Bacchus! cool thy rays!
Or frantic, I shall eat
Thy thyrse, and bite the bays.

[5] *retorted:* twisted or bent backward.

[6] *nose:* a punning reference to Ovid's name *Naso.*

Round, round the roof does run;
And being ravished thus,
Come, I will drink a tun
To my Propertius.

Now, to Tibullus, next,
This flood I drink to thee;
But stay, I see a text
That this presents to me.

Behold, Tibullus lies
Here burnt, whose small return
Of ashes scarce suffice
To fill a little urn.

Trust to good verses then;
They only will aspire,
When pyramids, as men,
Are lost i' th' funeral fire.

And when all bodies meet,
In Lethe to be drowned,
Then only numbers sweet
With endless life are crowned.

TO THE VIRGINS, TO MAKE MUCH OF TIME

Gather ye rosebuds while ye may,
Old Time is still a-flying;
And this same flower that smiles today,
Tomorrow will be dying.

The glorious lamp of heaven, the sun,
The higher he's a-getting,
The sooner will his race be run,
And nearer he's to setting.

That age is best which is the first,
When youth and blood are warmer;
But being spent, the worse, and worst
Times still succeed the former.

Then be not coy, but use your time;
And while ye may, go marry:
For having lost but once your prime,
You may for ever tarry.

TO MUSIC, TO BECALM HIS FEVER

CHARM me asleep, and melt me so
With thy delicious numbers,
That being ravished, hence I go
Away in easy slumbers.
Ease my sick head,
And make my bed,
Thou power that canst sever
From me this ill,
And quickly still,
Though thou not kill
My fever.

Thou sweetly canst convert the same
From a consuming fire
Into a gentle-licking flame,
And make it thus expire.
Then make me weep
My pains asleep,
And give me such reposes
That I, poor I,
May think thereby
I live and die
'Mongst roses.

Fall on me like a silent dew,
Or like those maiden showers
Which by the peep of day do strew
A baptism o'er the flowers.
Melt, melt my pains
With thy soft strains,
That having ease me given,
With full delight
I leave this light
And take my flight
For heaven.

THE HOCK-CART, OR HARVEST HOME:

To the Right Honorable Mildmay, Earl of Westmoreland

Come, sons of summer, by whose toil
We are the lords of wine and oil;
By whose tough labors and rough hands
We rip up first, then reap our lands.
Crowned with the ears of corn, now come,
And to the pipe sing harvest home.
Come forth, my lord, and see the cart
Dressed up with all the country art.
See here a maukin,[7] there a sheet
As spotless pure as it is sweet;
The horses, mares, and frisking fillies,
Clad all in linen, white as lilies;
The harvest swains and wenches bound
For joy to see the hock-cart crowned.
About the cart hear how the rout
Of rural younglings raise the shout,
Pressing before, some coming after:
Those with a shout, and these with laughter.
Some bless the cart; some kiss the sheaves;
Some prank them up with oaken leaves;
Some cross the fill-horse; [8] some with great
Devotion stroke the home-borne wheat;
While other rustics, less attent
To prayers than to merriment,
Run after with their breeches rent.
Well on, brave boys, to your lord's hearth,
Glitt'ring with fire, where for your mirth
Ye shall see first the large and chief
Foundation of your feast, fat beef,
With upper stories, mutton, veal,
And bacon, which makes full the meal;
With several dishes standing by,
As here a custard, there a pie,
And here all-tempting frumenty.[9]
And for to make the merry cheer,

[7] *maukin:* a coarse cloth.
[8] *fill-horse:* the lead horse.
[9] *frumenty:* a dish made of hulled wheat boiled in milk and seasoned.

If smirking wine be wanting here,
There's that which drowns all care, stout beer,
Which freely drink to your lord's health;
Then to the plow, the commonwealth,
Next to your flails, your fans, your fats;[10]
Then to the maids with wheaten hats;
To the rough sickle and crook'd scythe,
Drink, frolic boys, till all be blithe.
Feed and grow fat, and as ye eat
Be mindful that the lab'ring neat,[11]
As you, may have their fill of meat.[12]
And know, besides, ye must revoke
The patient ox unto his yoke,
And all go back unto the plow
And harrow, though they're hanged up now.
And, you must know, your lord's word's true:
Feed him you must, whose food fills you,
And that this pleasure is like rain,
Not sent ye for to drown your pain
But for to make it spring again.

TO ANTHEA, WHO MAY COMMAND HIM ANYTHING

Bid me to live, and I will live
Thy protestant to be:
Or bid me love, and I will give
A loving heart to thee.

A heart as soft, a heart as kind,
A heart as sound and free
As in the whole world thou canst find,
That heart I'll give to thee.

Bid that heart stay, and it will stay,
To honor thy decree;
Or bid it languish quite away,
And't shall do so for thee.

Bid me to weep, and I will weep,
While I have eyes to see;

---

[10] *fats:* vats.
[11] *neat:* cattle.
[12] *meat:* food.

And having none, yet I will keep
A heart to weep for thee.

Bid me despair, and I'll despair,
Under that cypress tree;
Or bid me die, and I will dare
E'en death, to die for thee.

Thou art my life, my love, my heart,
The very eyes of me;
And hast command of every part,
To live and die for thee.

TO DAFFODILS

Fair daffodils, we weep to see
You haste away so soon;
As yet the early-rising sun
Has not attained his noon.
Stay, stay,
Until the hasting day
Has run
But to the even-song;
And, having prayed together, we
Will go with you along.

We have short time to stay, as you;
We have as short a spring;
As quick a growth to meet decay,
As you, or any thing.
We die,
As your hours do, and dry
Away
Like to the summer's rain;
Or as the pearls of morning's dew,
Ne'er to be found again.

HIS PRAYER TO BEN JONSON

When I a verse shall make,
Know I have prayed thee,

For old religion's sake,
Saint Ben, to aid me.

Make the way smooth for me,
When I, thy Herrick,
Honoring thee, on my knee
Offer my lyric.

Candles I'll give to thee,
And a new altar;
And thou, Saint Ben, shalt be
Writ in my psalter.

THE NIGHT-PIECE, TO JULIA[13]

HER eyes the glow-worm lend thee;
The shooting stars attend thee;
And the elves also,
Whose little eyes glow
Like the sparks of fire, befriend thee.

No will-o'-the-wisp mis-light thee;
Nor snake or slow-worm bite thee;
But on, on thy way,
Not making a stay,
Since ghost there's none to affright thee.

Let not the dark thee cumber;
What though the moon does slumber?
The stars of the night
Will lend thee their light,
Like tapers clear without number.

Then, Julia, let me woo thee,
Thus, thus to come unto me;
And when I shall meet
Thy silv'ry feet,
My soul I'll pour into thee.

---

13 Compare Jonson's "A Witch's Charm" above, p. 767.

HIS PRAYER FOR ABSOLUTION

For those my unbaptizèd rhymes,
Writ in my wild unhallowed times;
For every sentence, clause, and word,
That's not inlaid with Thee, my Lord,
Forgive me, God, and blot each line
Out of my book that is not Thine.
But if, 'mongst all, Thou find'st here one
Worthy Thy benediction,
That one of all the rest shall be
The glory of my work and me.

A THANKSGIVING TO GOD FOR HIS HOUSE

Lord, Thou hast given me a cell
    Wherein to dwell,
A little house, whose humble roof
    Is weather-proof;
Under the spars of which I lie
    Both soft and dry;
Where Thou, my chamber for to ward,
    Hast set a guard
Of harmless thoughts, to watch and keep
    Me while I sleep.
Low is my porch, as is my fate,
    Both void of state;
And yet the threshold of my door
    Is worn by the poor,
Who thither come and freely get
    Good words, or meat.
Like as my parlor, so my hall
    And kitchen's small;
A little buttery, and therein
    A little bin,
Which keeps my little loaf of bread
    Unchipped, unflead; [14]
Some brittle sticks of thorn or brier

[14] *unflead:* unbroken.

Make me a fire,
Close by whose living coal I sit,
And glow like it.
Lord, I confess too when I dine,
The pulse [15] is Thine,
And all those other bits that be
There placed by Thee;
The worts, the purslane,[16] and the mess
Of watercress,
Which of Thy kindness Thou hast sent;
And my content
Makes those, and my belovèd beet
To be more sweet.
'Tis Thou that crown'st my glittering hearth
With guiltless mirth,
And giv'st me wassail bowls to drink,
Spiced to the brink.
Lord, 'tis Thy plenty-dropping hand
That soils [17] my land,
And giv'st me, for my bushel sown,
Twice ten for one;
Thou mak'st my teeming hen to lay
Her egg each day;
Besides my healthful ewes to bear
Me twins each year;
The while the conduits of my kine
Run cream for wine.
All these, and better, Thou dost send
Me, to this end,
That I should render for my part
A thankful heart;
Which, fired with incense, I resign
As wholly Thine;
But the acceptance, that must be,
My Christ, by Thee.

ANOTHER GRACE FOR A CHILD

HERE a little child I stand,
Heaving up my either hand;

[15] *pulse:* peas, beans, lentils.
[16] *worts, purslane:* cabbages, salad greens.
[17] *soils:* fertilizes.

Cold as paddocks[18] though they be,
Here I lift them up to Thee,
For a benison to fall
On our meat and on us all. Amen.

To his book's end this last line he'd have placed:
Jocund his Muse was, but his life was chaste.

[18] *paddocks:* toads.

George Herbert

1593–1633

HERBERT was the son of Donne's friend Magdalen Herbert, and the brother of Edward, Lord Herbert of Cherbury and Sir Henry Herbert, Master of the Revels. He was related to the Earls of Pembroke, and the story goes that when King James, impressed by the clever Latinity of a letter from Cambridge thanking him for the gift of a copy of his Latin works, asked the Earl of Pembroke if he knew the author, one George Herbert, the Earl replied that indeed he knew him as a kinsman, but "he loved him more for his learning and virtue than for that he was of his name and family." We owe the story to Izaac Walton, who wrote Herbert's life as well as Donne's, but who never knew Herbert personally and in his narrative stresses rather too much the saintly side of his subject's character.

Herbert was no doubt always destined for the ministry, and certainly his brilliant and devoted mother wished that calling for him; but his success as Public Orator of Cambridge University, a courtierlike position which could and sometimes did lead to a career as Secretary of State, encouraged secular ambitions in him. He came from a background of aristocracy, wealth, and cultivation; he loved society and he loved fine clothes. He might have been another Sir Philip Sidney.

Indeed, Sidney's influence upon Herbert was great, as a poet as well as a chivalric symbol; the translation of the Psalms and the *Astrophel and Stella* both left their imprint upon Herbert's style. The influence of Donne is also obvious, though once it has been recognized, the differences between the two poets are perhaps more interesting than the similarities.

Herbert served as Public Orator from 1620 until the death of King James in 1625 discouraged his hopes of court preferment; in 1626 he was ordained a deacon, and after a period of struggle and indecision, motivated in part at least by his sense of unworthiness, he was ordained priest in 1630 and presented to the rectory of Bemerton near Salisbury. There for the three remaining years of his life, he devoted himself to the ministry, to meditation, and to poetry. He had written sacred poems ever since his undergraduate days at Cambridge, but the bulk of the poems posthumously published as *The Temple* were probably written in the Bemerton period.

Herbert is a poet of great clarity, vividness, and intensity. It has been said of him that his characteristic lyric is a love poem to God, but it is also true that he is a most sensitive portrayer of moods—restlessness, despair, anguish, joy, delight, gratitude, all of them deeply felt parts of the great experience, Love. And since, for Herbert, divine poems are sacrifices and tributes, his own will be found to be scrupulously shaped and turned, their language purified and their form designed as art. As Bacon said, in the dedication of his translation of some psalms, "in respect of Divinitie, and Poesie, met, (whereof the one is the Matter, the other the Stile of this little Writing) I could not make better choice" than George Herbert.

BIBLIOGRAPHY: *The Works of George Herbert,* ed. F. E. Hutchinson, Oxford, 1941; F. E. Hutchinson, "George Herbert" in *Seventeenth Century Studies Presented to Sir Herbert Grierson,* Oxford, 1938; Rosemond Tuve, *A Reading of George Herbert,* London, 1952; Louis L. Martz, *The Poetry of Meditation,* New Haven, 1954; Joan Bennett, *Four Metahysical Poets,* Cambridge, 1934; Helen C. White, *The Metaphysical Poets,* New York, 1936; J. B. Leishman, *The Metaphysical Poets,* Oxford, 1934; Aldous Huxley, *Texts and Pretexts,* London, 1932.

THE ALTAR[1]

A broken ALTAR, Lord, thy servant rears,
Made of a heart, and cemented with tears;
Whose parts are as thy hand did frame
No workman's tool hath touched the same.[2]
A HEART alone
Is such a stone
As nothing but
Thy power doth cut.
Wherefore each part
Of my hard heart
Meets in this frame
To praise thy name;
That, if I chance to hold my peace
These stones to praise thee may not cease.[3]
Oh let thy blessed SACRIFICE be mine
And sanctify this ALTAR to be thine.

THE SACRIFICE[4]

OH ALL ye who pass by [5] whose eyes and mind
To worldly things are sharp, but to me blind,
To me, who took eyes that I might you find;
Was ever grief like mine?

The princes of my people make a head
Against their Maker; they do wish me dead
Who cannot wish, except I give them bread;
Was ever grief like mine?

[1] One of Herbert's two "shaped verses," placed at the beginning of the central section of Herbert's *Temple,* called "The Church." Poems of this type were composed by the Elizabethans, but their subjects were usually amorous. Sylvester included "shaped verses" in the dedicatory poems to his translation of DuBartas' *Divine Weeks and Works* (1605).

[2] *No . . . same:* See Exodus 20:25.

[3] *These stones . . . cease:* See Luke 19:40.

[4] A Good Friday poem, based on the traditional *Improperia* or Reproaches supposedly spoken by Christ from the Cross.

[5] *all ye who pass by:* Lamentations 1:12.

Without me each one who doth now me brave
Had to this day been an Egyptian slave.[6]
They use that power against me which I gave.
Was ever grief like mine?

Mine own Apostle who the bag did bear,[7]
Though he had all I had, did not forbear
To sell me also and to put me there;
Was ever grief like mine?

For thirty pence he did my death devise
Who at three hundred did the ointment prize,
Not half so sweet as my sweet sacrifice;
Was ever grief like mine?

Therefore my soul melts, and my heart's dear treasure
Drops blood, the only beads my words to measure;
Oh let this cup pass, if it be thy pleasure;[8]
Was ever grief like mine?

These drops being tempered with a sinner's tears
A balsam are for both the hemispheres,
Curing all wounds but mine,—all but my fears;
Was ever grief like mine?

Yet my disciples sleep; I cannot gain
One hour of watching, but their drowsy brain
Comforts not me and doth my doctrine stain;
Was ever grief like mine?

Arise, arise, they come! Look how they run!
Alas! What haste they make to be undone!
How with their lanterns they do seek the sun!
Was ever grief like mine?

With clubs and staves they seek me as a thief
Who am the Way and Truth, the true relief,
Most true to those who are my greatest grief;
Was ever grief like mine?

Judas, dost thou betray me with a kiss?
Canst thou find hell about my lips and miss
Of life, just at the gates of life and bliss?
Was ever grief like mine?

---

[6] *Without me . . . slave:* Moses is often regarded, in Christian literature and iconography, as a type of Christ. See I Corinthians 10:1–4 and lines 122 and 138 below.

[7] *Mine own Apostle . . . bear:* Judas.

[8] *Oh let . . . pleasure:* Mark 14:36; Luke 22:42.

See, they lay hold on me, not with the hands
Of faith, but fury; yet at their commands
I suffer binding who have loosed their bands;
Was ever grief like mine?

All my disciples fly; fear puts a bar
Betwixt my friends and me. They leave the star
That brought the wise men of the East from far.
Was ever grief like mine?

Then from one ruler to another, bound
They lead me, urging that it was not sound
What I taught: comments would the text confound.
Was ever grief like mine?

The priest and rulers all false witness seek
'Gainst him who seeks not life but is the meek
And ready Paschal Lamb of this great week:
Was ever grief like mine?

Then they accuse me of great blasphemy
That I did thrust into the Deity
Who never thought that any robbery;[9]
Was ever grief like mine?

Some said that I the Temple to the floor
In three days razed and raised as before;
Why, he that built the world can do much more;
Was ever grief like mine?

Then they condemn me all with that same breath
Which I do give them daily, unto death.
Thus Adam my first breathing rendereth;[10]
Was ever grief like mine?

They bind and lead me unto Herod; he
Sends me to Pilate. This makes them agree;
But yet their friendship is my enmity;
Was ever grief like mine?

Herod and all his hands do set me light[11]
Who teach all hands to war, fingers to fight,

---

9 *Who . . . robbery:* Philippians 2:6.

10 *Thus Adam . . . rendereth:* I Corinthians 15:45.

11 *set me light:* despise me, view me with contempt.

And only am the Lord of Hosts and Might;
Was ever grief like mine?

Herod in judgment sits, while I do stand;
Examines me with a censorious hand;
I him obey, who all things else command;
Was ever grief like mine?

The Jews accuse me with despitefulness
And, vying malice with my gentleness,
Pick quarrels with their only happiness;
Was ever grief like mine?

I answer nothing, but with patience prove
If stony hearts will melt with gentle love.
But who does hawk at[12] eagles with a dove?
Was ever grief like mine?

My silence rather doth augment their cry;
My dove doth back into my bosom fly
Because the raging waters still are high;
Was ever grief like mine?

Hark, how they cried aloud still, "Crucify!
It is not fit he live a day!" they cry,
Who cannot live less than eternally;
Was ever grief like mine?

Pilate, a stranger, holdeth off; but they,
Mine own dear people, cry "Away, away!"[13]
With noises confused frighting the day;
Was ever grief like mine?

Yet still they shout and cry and stop their ears,
Putting my life among their sins and fears
And therefore wish my blood on them and theirs;
Was ever grief like mine?

See how spite cankers things. These words aright
Used, and wished, are the whole world's light;
But honey is their gall, brightness their night;
Was ever grief like mine?

[12] *Hawk at:* hunt.

[13] *"Away, away!":* John 19:15.

They chose a murderer, and all agree
In him to do themselves a courtesy,
For it was their own case who killed me;
Was ever grief like mine?

And a seditious murderer he was,
But I, the Prince of Peace—peace that doth pass
All understanding, more than heaven doth glass; [14]
Was ever grief like mine?

Why, Caesar is their only king, not I; [15]
He clave the stony rock when they were dry,
But surely not their hearts, as I well try;
Was ever grief like mine?

Ah, how they scourge me! yet my tenderness
Doubles each lash; and yet their bitterness
Winds up my grief to a mysteriousness.
Was ever grief like mine?

They buffet him and box him as they list
Who grasps the earth and heaven with his fist
And never yet, whom he would punish, missed;
Was ever grief like mine?

Behold, they spit on me in scornful wise
Who by my spittle gave the blind man eyes,
Leaving his blindness to my enemies;
Was ever grief like mine?

My face they cover, though it be divine.
As Moses' face was veiled, so is mine,
Lest on their double-dark souls either shine;
Was ever grief like mine?

Servants and abjects [16] flout me; they are witty:
"Now prophesy who strikes thee!" [17] is their ditty;
So they in me deny themselves all pity;
Was ever grief like mine?

And now I am delivered unto death
Which each one calls for so, with utmost breath,

---

[14] *glass:* reflect, mirror.
[15] *Caesar . . . I:* See John 19:15.
[16] *abjects:* degraded persons.
[17] *prophesy . . . thee:* Luke 22:64.

That he before me well nigh suffereth;
Was ever grief like mine?

Weep not, dear friends, since I for both have wept
When all my tears were blood, the while you slept;
Your tears for your own fortunes should be kept;
Was ever grief like mine?

Then with a scarlet robe they me array,
Which shows my blood to be the only way
And cordial left to repair man's decay.
Was ever grief like mine?

Then on my head a crown of thorns I wear,
For these are all the grapes Sion doth bear,
Though I my vine planted and watered there; [18]
Was ever grief like mine?

So sits the earth's great curse in Adam's fall
Upon my head; [19] so I remove it all
From th'earth unto my brows and bear the thrall;
Was ever grief like mine?

Then with the reed they gave to me before
They strike my head, the rock from whence all store
Of heavenly blessings issue evermore;
Was ever grief like mine?

They bow their knees to me and cry, "Hail, King!"
Whatever scoffs and scornfulness can bring,
I am the floor, the sink, where they it fling;
Was ever grief like mine?

Yet, since man's scepters are as frail as reeds,
And thorny all their crowns, bloody their weeds,
I who am Truth, turn into truth their deeds;
Was ever grief like mine?

The soldiers also spit upon that face
Which angels did desire to have the grace
And prophets, once to see, but found no place;
Was ever grief like mine?

---

[18] *these are all the grapes . . . there:* See Isaiah 5:1–7.

[19] *So sits . . . head:* I.e., thorns, part of Adam's curse (Genesis 3:18) now form Christ's crown.

Thus trimmed, forth they bring me to the rout
Who "Crucify him!" cry, with one strong shout.
God holds his peace at man, and man cries out;
Was ever grief like mine?

They lead me in once more, and putting then
Mine own clothes on, they lead me out again.
Whom devils fly, thus is he tossed of men;
Was ever grief like mine?

And now, weary of sport, glad to engross[20]
All spite in one, counting my life their loss,
They carry me to my most bitter cross;
Was ever grief like mine?

My cross I bear myself until I faint;
Then Simon bears it for me by constraint—
The decreed burden of each mortal saint;
Was ever grief like mine?

Oh all ye who pass by behold and see![21]
Man stole the fruit, but I must climb the tree,—
The Tree of Life to all but only me;
Was ever grief like mine?

Lo, here I hang, charged with a world of sin,
The greater world o' th' two, for that came in
By words, but this by sorrow I must win;
Was ever grief like mine?

Such sorrow as, if sinful man could feel,
Or feel his part, he would not cease to kneel
Till all were melted, though he were all steel;
Was ever grief like mine?

But *Oh my God, my God!* why leavest thou me,
The Son in whom thou dost delight to be?
My God, my God ——[22]
Never was grief like mine.

Shame tears my soul, my body many a wound;
Sharp nails pierce this, but sharper that confound;

---

[20] *engross:* gather up, concentrate.
[21] *all ye . . . see:* Lamentations 1:12.
[22] *My God, my God:* Matthew 27:46; Mark 15:34.

Reproaches, which are free, while I am bound.
Was ever grief like mine?

Now heal thyself, physician; now come down.
Alas! I did so, when I left my crown
And Father's smile for you, to feel his frown;
Was ever grief like mine?

In healing not my self, there doth consist
All that salvation which ye now resist;
Your safety in my sickness doth subsist;
Was ever grief like mine?

Betwixt two thieves I spent my utmost breath,
As he that for some robbery suffereth;
Alas, what have I stolen from you? Death.
Was ever grief like mine?

A King my title is, prefixed on high,
Yet by my subjects am condemned to die
A servile death in servile company;
Was ever grief like mine?

They give me vinegar mingled with gall
But more with malice; yet when they did call,
With manna, angels' food, I fed them all.
Was ever grief like mine?

They part my garments and by lot dispose
My coat, the type of love, which once cured those
Who sought for help, never malicious foes;
Was ever grief like mine?

Nay, after death their spite shall further go,
For they will pierce my side, I full well know,
That, as sin came, so sacraments might flow;
Was ever grief like mine?

But now I die; now all is finished:
My woe, man's weal; and now I bow my head.
Only let others say, when I am dead,
Never was grief like mine.

JORDAN (I)[23]

Who says that fictions only and false hair
Become a verse? Is there in truth no beauty?
Is all good structure in a winding stair?
May no lines pass, except they do their duty
    Not to a true, but painted chair?

Is it no verse, except enchanted groves
And sudden arbors[24] shadow coarse-spun lines?
Must purling streams refresh a lover's loves?
Must all be veiled while he that reads, divines,
    Catching the sense at two removes?

Shepherds are honest people, let them sing;
Riddle who list, for me, and pull for prime,[25]
I envy no man's nightingale or spring;
Nor let them punish me with loss of rhyme,
    Who plainly say, My God, my King.

VANITY (I)

    The fleet astronomer can bore
And thread the spheres with his quick-piercing mind;
He views their stations, walks from door to door,
    Surveys as if he had designed
To make a purchase there; he sees their dances,
    And knoweth long before
Both their full-eyed aspects[26] and secret glances.[27]

    The nimble diver with his side
Cuts through the working waves, that he may fetch

---

[23] The significance of the title is not clear, but Hutchinson quotes a suggestive passage from Lodge, who, formerly a secular poet, now calls himself "cleansed from the leprosy of my lewd lines, and being washed in the Jordan of grace, employ my labor to the comfort of the faithful."

[24] *sudden arbors:* arbors that appear unexpectedly. Gardens were designed to contain surprises.

[25] *pull for prime:* draw in the attempt to get a card of each suit, in the game of primero.

[26] *full-eyed aspects:* relative positions in the sky as seen by an observer on earth.

[27] *secret glances:* more subtle relationships, as when one or another heavenly body is not visible to the observer.

His dearly-earned pearl which God did hide
On purpose from the venturous wretch,
That He might save his life, and also hers
Who with excessive pride
Her own destruction and his danger wears.

The subtle chemic [28] can divest
And strip the creature naked, till he find
The callow [29] principles within their nest:
There he imparts to them his mind,
Admitted to their bed-chamber [30] before
They appear trim and dressed
To ordinary suitors at the door.

What hath not man sought out and found,
But his dear God? Who yet His glorious law
Embosoms in us, mellowing the ground
With showers and frosts, with love and awe,
So that we need not say, "Where's this command?"
Poor man, thou searchest round
To find out death, but missest life at hand!

THE PEARL

Matt. 13:45

I KNOW the ways of learning; both the head
And pipes that feed the press and make it run; [31]
What Reason hath from Nature borrowed,
Or of itself, like a good housewife, spun
In laws and policy; what the stars conspire,
What willing Nature speaks, what forced by fire; [32]
Both th' old discoveries and the new-found seas,
The stock and surplus,[33] cause and history,—
All these stand open, or I have the keys;
Yet I love Thee.

28 *chemic:* chemist.

29 *callow:* naked, unfeathered; hence "within their nest."

30 *Admitted to their bed-chamber:* The research chemist is compared to the courtier who is admitted to the royal bedchamber before the king is dressed.

31 *the press:* a figure combining the olive press, perhaps from Zechariah 4:12, and the printing press.

32 *forced by fire:* as in chemical experiments.

33 *stock and surplus:* inherited knowledge and what we add to it.

I know the ways of honor, what maintains
The quick returns of courtesy and wit;
In vies of favours whether [34] party gains;
When glory swells the heart, and moldeth it
To all expressions both of hand and eye,
Which on the world a true-love knot may tie,
And bear the bundle, wheresoe'er it goes;
How many drams of spirit there must be
To sell my life unto my friends or foes;
Yet I love Thee.

I know the ways of pleasure, the sweet strains,
The lullings and the relishes of it;
The propositions of hot blood and brains;
What mirth and music mean; what love and wit
Have done these twenty hundred years and more;
I know the projects of unbridled store.[35]
My stuff is flesh, not brass; my senses live,
And grumble oft that they have more in me
Then he that curbs them, being but one to five:
Yet I love Thee.

I know all these, and have them in my hand:
Therefore not seeled,[36] but with open eyes
I fly to Thee, and fully understand
Both the main sale and the commodities; [37]
And at what rate and price I have Thy love,
With all the circumstances that may move:
Yet through the labyrinths, not my groveling wit
But Thy silk-twist let down from heav'n to me
Did both conduct and teach me how by it
To climb to Thee.

SIN'S ROUND

Sorry I am, my God, sorry I am
That my offences course it in a ring.
My thoughts are working like a busy flame,
Until their cockatrice [38] they hatch and bring:

[34] *whether:* which.

[35] *unbridled store:* boundless plenty.

[36] *seeled:* sewn up, as the eyelids of falcons were sewn together during training.

[37] *commodities:* discounts.

[38] *cockatrice:* a fabulous creature hatched by a serpent from the egg of the cock.

And when they once have perfected their draughts,
My words take fire from my inflamed thoughts.

My words take fire from my inflamed thoughts,
Which spit it forth like the Sicilian hill;[39]
They vent the wares, and pass them with their faults,
And by their breathing ventilate[40] the ill;
But words suffice not; where are lewd intentions,
My hands do join to finish the inventions.

My hands do join to finish the inventions,
And so my sins ascend three stories high,
As Babel grew before there were dissensions.[41]
Yet ill deeds loiter not; for they supply
New thoughts of sinning; wherefore, to my shame,
Sorry I am; my God, sorry I am.

PEACE

Sweet Peace, where dost thou dwell? I humbly crave,
Let me once know.
I sought thee in a secret cave,
And asked if Peace were there.
A hollow wind did seem to answer, "No;
Go seek elsewhere."

I did, and going, did a rainbow note;
Surely, thought I,
This is the lace of Peace's coat;
I will search out the matter.
But while I looked, the clouds immediately
Did break and scatter.

Then went I to a garden, and did spy
A gallant flower,
The crown-imperial.[42] "Sure," said I,
"Peace at the root must dwell."
But when I digged, I saw a worm devour
What showed so well.

[39] *Sicilian hill:* Mount Etna.

[40] *ventilate:* increase the flame by blowing; the cockatrice's breath was supposed to be poisonous.

[41] *As Babel . . . dissensions:* Genesis 11:1–9.

[42] *crown-imperial:* a spring-blooming herb bearing at the top of the stalk a cluster of bell-shaped flowers.

At length I met a reverend good old man,
Whom when for Peace
I did demand, he thus began:
"There was a Prince of old
At Salem [43] dwelt, who lived with good increase
Of flock and fold.

"He sweetly lived; yet sweetness did not save
His life from foes.
But after death out of his grave
There sprang twelve stalks of wheat;
Which many wondering at, got some of those
To plant and set.

"It prospered strangely, and did soon disperse
Through all the earth;
For they that taste it do rehearse
That virtue lies therein;
A secret virtue, bringing peace and mirth
By flight of sin.

"Take of this grain, which in my garden grows,
And grows for you;
Make bread of it; and that repose
And peace, which every where
With so much earnestness you do pursue,
Is only there."

CONFESSION

Oh what a cunning guest
Is this same Grief! within my heart I made
Closets, and in them many a chest;
And like a master in my trade,
In those chests, boxes; in each box a till.
Yet Grief knows all, and enters when he will.

No screw, no piercer [44] can
Into a piece of timber work and wind
As God's afflictions into man.

[43] *a Prince . . . Salem:* Melchisedec, King of Salem, was regarded as a type of Christ. See Genesis 14:18 and Hebrews 7:2.

[44] *piercer:* auger, bit.

When He a torture hath designed;
They are too subtle for the subtlest hearts,
And fall like rheums upon the tenderest parts.[45]

We are the earth, and they,
Like moles within us, heave and cast about;
And till they foot [46] and clutch their prey,
They never cool, much less give out.
No smith can make such locks but they have keys;
Closets are halls to them, and hearts highways.

Only an open breast
Doth shut them out so that they cannot enter,
Or if they enter, cannot rest,
But quickly seek some new adventure:
Smooth open hearts no fastening have; but fiction [47]
Doth give a hold and handle to affliction.

Wherefore my faults and sins,
Lord, I acknowledge; take thy plagues away:
For since confession pardon wins,
I challenge here the brightest day,
The clearest diamond; let them do their best,
They shall be thick and cloudy to [48] my breast.

THE COLLAR[49]

I STRUCK the board and cried, "No more;
I will abroad!"
What, shall I ever sigh and pine?
My lines and life are free,—free as the road,
Loose as the wind, as large as store.
Shall I be still in suit? [50]
Have I no harvest but a thorn
To let me blood, and not restore
What I have lost with cordial fruit?
Sure there was wine
Before my sighs did dry it; there was corn

[45] *fall . . . parts:* It was proverbial that rheums (colds) seized upon the weakest parts of the body.

[46] *foot:* seize with claws.

[47] *fiction:* deceit, pretense.

[48] *to:* compared to.

[49] *Collar:* restraint, from the common figure "to slip the collar," meaning to escape from control or discipline.

[50] *still in suit:* always begging, like a suitor at court.

Before my tears did drown it;
Is the year only lost to me?
Have I no bays to crown it,
No flowers, no garlands gay? all blasted,
All wasted?
Not so, my heart; but there is fruit,
And thou hast hands.
Recover all thy sigh-blown age
On double pleasures; leave thy cold dispute
Of what is fit and not; forsake thy cage,
Thy rope of sands
Which petty thoughts have made; and made to thee
Good cable, to enforce and draw,
And be thy law,
While thou didst wink[51] and wouldst not see.
Away! take heed;
I will abroad.
Call in thy death's-head there, tie up thy fears;
He that forbears
To suit and serve his need
Deserves his load.
But as I raved and grew more fierce and wild
At every word,
Methought I heard one calling, "Child,"
And I replied, "My Lord."

THE PULLEY[52]

WHEN God at first made man,
Having a glass of blessings standing by,
"Let us," said He, "pour on him all we can;
Let the world's riches, which dispersed lie,
Contract into a span."

So strength first made a way;
Then beauty flowed, then wisdom, honor, pleasure;
When almost all was out, God made a stay,
Perceiving that, alone of all his treasure,
Rest in the bottom lay.

[51] *wink:* close the eyes (longer than momentarily).

[52] *Pulley:* here visualized as a device by which force exerted in one direction produces work in the opposite direction.

"For if I should," said He,
"Bestow this jewel also on my creature,
He would adore my gifts in stead of me,
And rest in Nature, not the God of Nature:
So both should losers be.

"Yet let him keep the rest,
But keep them with repining restlessness;
Let him be rich and weary, that at least,
If goodness lead him not, yet weariness
May toss him to my breast."

THE FLOWER

How fresh, oh Lord, how sweet and clean
Are thy returns! even as the flowers in spring,
To which, besides their own demesne,
The late-past frosts' tributes of pleasure bring;[53]
Grief melts away
Like snow in May,
As if there were no such cold thing.

Who would have thought my shriveled heart
Could have recovered greenness? It was gone
Quite under ground; as flowers depart
To see their mother-root, when they have blown,
Where they together
All the hard weather,
Dead to the world, keep house unknown.

These are thy wonders, Lord of power,
Killing and quickening, bringing down to hell
And up to heaven in an hour;
Making a chiming of a passing-bell.[54]
We say amiss
This or that is;[55]
Thy word is all, if we could spell.

---

[53] *the flowers . . . bring:* The flowers bring to Spring, their liege lord, not only the tribute of their own beauty, but also the tribute of pleasure, overdue, from the late-past frosts.

[54] *Making . . . passing-bell:* The passing-bell, signifying death, is a single bell tolled continuously in a monotone at regular intervals; a chiming is the sound of many bells swung just enough to make the clappers strike with a quick succession of strokes, signifying joy.

[55] *is:* is in itself, unchangeably.

Oh that I once past changing were,
Fast in thy Paradise, where no flower can wither;
Many a spring I shoot up fair,
Offering at[56] heaven, growing and groaning thither;
Nor doth my flower
Want a spring shower,
My sins and I joining together.

But while I grow in a straight line,
Still upwards bent, as if heaven were mine own,
Thy anger comes, and I decline:
What frost to that? what pole is not the zone
Where all things burn,
When thou dost turn,
And the least frown of thine is shown?[57]

And now in age I bud again,
After so many deaths I live and write;
I once more smell the dew and rain,
And relish versing. Oh, my only light,
It cannot be
That I am he
On whom thy tempests fell all night.

These are thy wonders, Lord of love,
To make us see we are but flowers that glide;[58]
Which when we once can find and prove,
Thou hast a garden for us where to bide;
Who would be more,
Swelling through store,
Forfeit their Paradise by their pride.

THE FORERUNNERS

The harbingers[59] are come. See, see their mark;
White is their color, and behold my head.
But must they have my brain? must they dispark[60]
Those sparkling notions which therein were bred?

[56] *offering at:* aiming at.

[57] *what pole . . . shown:* God's anger or frown is so cold that polar frost is equatorial heat by comparison.

[58] *glide:* slip away easily.

[59] *harbingers:* servants sent ahead of a royal procession to reserve accommodations by chalking the doors of houses (see line 35); here, of course, white hairs.

[60] *dispark:* disimpark, turn out of a park, usually spoken of deer.

Must dullness turn me to a clod?
Yet have they left me, "Thou art still my God." [61]

Good men ye be to leave me my best room,
Ev'n all my heart, and what is lodged there;
I pass not,[62] I, what of the rest become,
So "Thou art still my God" be out of fear.
He will be pleased with that ditty;
And if I please Him, I write fine and witty.

Farewell, sweet phrases, lovely metaphors.
But will ye leave me thus? when ye before
Of stews and brothels only knew the doors,
Then did I wash you with my tears, and more,
Brought you to church well-drest and clad:
My God must have my best, ev'n all I had.

Lovely enchanting language, sugar-cane,
Honey of roses, whither wilt thou fly?
Hath some fond lover 'ticed thee to thy bane?
And wilt thou leave the Church, and love a sty?
Fie! thou wilt soil they broidered coat,
And hurt thyself and him that sings the note.

Let foolish lovers, if they will love dung,
With canvas, not with arras, clothe their shame;
Let Folly speak in her own native tongue.
True Beauty dwells on high; ours is a flame
But borrowed thence to light us thither.
Beauty and beauteous words should go together.

Yet if you go, I pass not; take your way.
For "Thou art still my God" is all that ye
Perhaps with more embellishment can say.
Go, birds of spring; let winter have his fee;
Let a bleak paleness chalk the door,
So all within be livelier than before.

---

[61] *Thou . . . God:* Psalms 31:14.

[62] *pass not:* reck not, care not. See line 31.

LOVE (III)[63]

Love bade me welcome; yet my soul drew back,
Guilty of dust and sin.
But quick-eyed Love, observing me grow slack
From my first entrance in,
Drew nearer to me, sweetly questioning
If I lacked any thing.

"A guest," I answered, "worthy to be here";
Love said, "You shall be he."
"I, the unkind, ungrateful? Ah, my dear,
I cannot look on Thee."
Love took my hand, and smiling did reply,
"Who made the eyes but I?"

"Truth, Lord; but I have marred them; let my shame
Go where it doth deserve."
"And know you not," says Love, "Who bore the blame?"
"My dear, then I will serve."
"You must sit down," says Love, "and taste my meat."
So I did sit and eat.

---

63 The final poem in "The Church," the central section of Herbert's volume *The Temple.*

Sir Thomas Browne

1605–1682

BROWNE was a physician of Norwich, born in London and educated at Winchester, Oxford, and schools of medicine on the continent. His interest in science was genuine and lively; he compiled in his *Pseudodoxia Epidemica,* or *Vulgar Errors* (1646), a treatise on alleged scientific facts, some of them as old as Pliny or older, which could be disproved by observation and experiment. But Browne was even more a philospher and a poet of meditation than a scientist. His remarkable prose style, resonant and involved, with its quaint Latinity and its lovely cadences, ornamented his curious speculations on the most abstruse subjects, such as burial customs in *Hydriotaphia: Urn Burial* or the quincunx and the number five in *The Garden of Cyrus* (both 1658).

His most important book, the famous *Religio Medici,* was written in 1635, when the author was a young man. He reveals in this book much of his own character and personality; it has the same kind of interest as the essays of Montaigne. But it is also a fundamental book for the age in which Browne lived; questions of religious observance, of salvation, of the conflict between reason and faith—all these receive the attention of a humane, sensitive, individualistic, but tolerant man. At thirty he has the benign humor, the patient, detached interest of a man of seventy:

"Methinks I have outlived myself, and begin to be weary of the sun; I have shaken hands with delight; in my warm blood and canicular days, I perceive I do anticipate the vices of age; the world to me is but a dream or mock-show, and we all therein but pantalones and antics, to my severer contemplation."

Many of his contemplations were less severe, and even when the subject is a somber one, Browne's curious and speculative mind is sometimes almost playful. He can be appreciated both as one of the great stylists in English prose and as a significant thinker about the mysteries of God and man.

BIBLIOGRAPHY: *The Works of Sir Thomas Browne,* ed. G. Keynes, London, 1928–1931; W. P. Dunn, *Sir Thomas Browne, A Study in Religious Philosophy,* Menasha, Wis., 1926; D. Bischoff, *Sir Thomas Browne als Stilkünstler,* Heidelberg, 1943; Robert Sencourt, *Outflying Philosophy,* Hildesheim, 1924; O. Leroy, *Le Chevalier Thomas Browne,* Paris, 1931; E. S. Merton, *Science and Imagination in Sir Thomas Browne,* New York, 1949; Basil Willey, *The Seventeenth Century Background,* London, 1934.

RELIGIO MEDICI

THE FIRST PART

FOR my religion, though there be several circumstances that might persuade the world I have none at all, as the general scandal of my profession, the natural course of my studies, the indifferency of my behavior and discourse in matters of religion, neither violently defending one, nor with that common ardor and contention opposing another; yet, in despite hereof, I dare without usurpation assume the honorable style of a Christian. Not that I merely owe this title to the font, my education, or the clime wherein I was born, as being bred up either to confirm those principles my parents instilled into my unwary understanding, or by a general consent proceed in the religion of my country; but having in my riper years and confirmed judgment seen and examined all, I find myself obliged by the principles of grace and the law of mine own reason, to embrace no other name but this. Neither doth herein my zeal so far make me forget the general charity I owe unto humanity, as rather to hate than pity Turks, infidels, and (what is worse) Jews; rather contenting myself to enjoy that happy style, than maligning those who refuse so glorious a title.

SECTION 2

But, because the name of a Christian is become too general to express our faith, there being a geography of religions as well as lands, and every clime distinguished not only by their laws and limits, but circumscribed by their doctrines and rules of faith; to be particular, I am of that reformed new-cast religion, wherein I dislike nothing but the name; of the same belief our Savior taught, the apostles disseminated, the fathers authorized, and the martyrs confirmed; but by the sinister ends of princes, the ambition and avarice of prelates, and the fatal corruption of times, so decayed, impaired, and fallen from its native beauty, that it required the careful and charitable hands of these times to restore it to its primitive integrity. Now the accidental occasion whereupon, the slender means whereby, the low and abject condition of the person by whom so good a work was set on foot, which in our adversaries beget contempt and scorn, fills me with wonder, and is the very same objection the insolent pagans first cast at Christ and his disciples.

SECTION 3

Yet have I not so shaken hands with those desperate resolutions, who had rather venture at large their decayed bottom, than bring her in to be new trimmed in the dock; who had rather promiscuously retain all than abridge any, and obstinately be what they are, than what they have been, as to stand in diameter and swords point with them. We have reformed from them, not against them; for, omitting those improperations [1] and terms of scurrility between us, which only difference our affections, and not our cause, there is between us one common name and appellation, one faith and necessary body of principles common to us both; and therefore I am not scrupulous to converse and live with them, to enter their churches in defect of ours, and either pray with them, or for them. I could never perceive any rational consequence from those many texts which prohibit the children of Israel to pollute themselves with the temples of the heathens; we being all Christians, and not divided by such detested impieties as might profane our prayers, or the place wherein we make them; or that a resolved conscience may not adore her creator any where, especially in places devoted to his service; where, if their devotions offend him, mine may please him; if theirs profane it, mine may hallow it. Holy-water and crucifix (dangerous to the common people) deceive not my judgment, nor abuse my devotion at all. I am, I confess, naturally inclined to that which misguided zeal terms superstition. My common conversation I do acknowledge austere, my behavior full of rigor, sometimes not without morosity; yet at my devotion I love to use the civility of my knee, my hat, and hand, with all those outward and sensible motions which may express or promote my invisible devotion. I should violate my own arm rather than a church, nor willingly deface the name of saint or martyr. At the sight of a cross or crucifix I can dispense with my hat, but scarce with the thought or memory of my Savior. I cannot laugh at, but rather pity, the fruitless journeys of pilgrims, or condemn the miserable condition of friars; for, though misplaced in circumstances, there is something in it of devotion. I could never hear the Ave-Mary bell without an elevation; or think it a sufficient warrant, because they erred in one circumstance, for me to err in all, that is, in silence and dumb contempt. While, therefore, they directed their devotion to her, I offered mine to God, and rectified the errors of their prayers by rightly ordering mine own. At a solemn procession I have wept abundantly, while my consorts, blind with opposition and prejudice, have fallen into an excess of scorn and laughter. There are, questionless, both in Greek, Roman, and African churches, solemnities and ceremonies whereof the wiser zeals do make a Christian use, and stand condemned by us, not as evil in themselves, but as allurements and baits of superstition to those vulgar heads that look asquint on the face of Truth, and those unstable judgments that cannot consist in the narrow point and center of virtue without a reel or stagger to the circumference.

---

[1] *improperations:* taunts, insults.

SECTION 4

As there were many reformers, so likewise many reformations; every country proceeding in a particular way and method, according as their national interest, together with their constitution and clime, inclined them; some angrily, and with extremity; others calmly, and with mediocrity, not rending, but easily dividing the community, and leaving an honest possibility of a reconciliation; which though peaceable spirits do desire, and may conceive that revolution of time and the mercies of God may effect, yet that judgment that shall consider the present antipathies between the two extremes, their contrarieties in condition, affection, and opinion, may with the same hopes expect an union in the poles of heaven.

SECTION 5

But, to difference myself nearer and draw into a lesser circle, there is no church whose every part so squares unto my conscience; whose articles, constitutions, and customs seem so consonant unto reason, as it were framed to my particular devotion, as this whereof I hold my belief, the Church of England; to whose faith I am a sworn subject, and therefore in a double obligation subscribe unto her articles, and endeavor to observe her constitutions. Whatsoever is beyond, as points indifferent, I observe according to the rules of my private reason, or the humor and fashion of my devotion; neither believing this, because Luther affirmed it, or disproving that, because Calvin hath disavouched it. I condemn not all things in the Council of Trent, nor approve all in the Synod of Dort. In brief, where the scripture is silent, the church is my text; where that speaks, it is but my comment; where there is a joint silence of both, I borrow not the rules of my religion from Rome or Geneva, but the dictates of my own reason. It is an unjust scandal of our adversaries, and a gross error in ourselves, to compute the nativity of our religion from Henry the Eighth, who, though he rejected the Pope, refused not the faith of Rome, and effected no more than what his own predecessors desired and assayed in ages past, and was conceived the State of Venice would have attempted in our days. It is as uncharitable a point in us to fall upon those popular scurrilities and opprobrious scoffs of the Bishop of Rome, to whom, as a temporal Prince, we owe the duty of good language. I confess there is cause of passion between us: by his sentence I stand excommunicated; heretic is the best language he affords me; yet can no ear witness I ever returned him the name of antichrist, man of sin, or whore of Babylon. It is the method of charity to suffer without reaction: those usual satires and invectives of the pulpit may perchance produce a good effect on the vulgar, whose ears are opener to rhetoric than logic; yet do they in no wise confirm the faith of wiser believers, who know that a good cause needs not to be patroned by passion, but can sustain itself upon a temperate dispute.

SECTION 6

I could never divide myself from any man upon the difference of an opinion, or be angry with his judgment for not agreeing with me in that from which perhaps within a few days I should dissent myself. I have no genius to disputes in religion, and have often thought it wisdom to decline them, especially upon a disadvantage, or when the cause of truth might suffer in the weakness of my patronage. Where we desire to be informed, it is good to contest with men above ourselves; but to confirm and establish our opinions, it is best to argue with judgments below our own, that the frequent spoils and victories over their reasons may settle in ourselves an esteem and confirmed opinion of our own. Every man is not a proper champion for truth, nor fit to take up the gauntlet in the cause of verity. Many, from the ignorance of these maxims and an inconsiderate zeal unto truth, have too rashly charged the troops of error, and remain as trophies unto the enemies of truth. A man may be in as just possession of truth as of a city, and yet be forced to surrender; it is therefore far better to enjoy her with peace, than to hazard her on a battle. If, therefore, there rise any doubts in my way, I do forget them, or at least defer them till my better settled judgment and more manly reason be able to resolve them; for I perceive every man's own reason is his best Oedipus,[2] and will, upon a reasonable truce, find a way to loose those bonds wherewith the subtleties of error have enchained our more flexible and tender judgments. In philosophy, where truth seems double-faced, there is no man more paradoxical than myself; but in divinity I love to keep the road; and, though not in an implicit, yet an humble faith, follow the great wheel of the church, by which I move, not reserving any proper poles or motion from the epicycle of my own brain. By this means I leave no gap for heresies, schisms, or errors, of which at present I hope I shall not injure truth to say I have no taint or tincture. I must confess my greener studies have been polluted with two or three; not any begotten in the latter centuries, but old and obsolete, such as could never have been revived, but by such extravagant and irregular heads as mine. For indeed heresies perish not with their authors, but, like the river Arethuse,[3] though they lose their currents in one place, they rise up again in another. One general council is not able to extirpate one single heresy: it may be cancelled for the present; but revolution of time, and the like aspects from heaven, will restore it, when it will flourish till it be condemned again. For as though there were a metempsychosis, and the soul of one man passed into another, opinions do find, after certain revolutions, men and minds like those that first begat them. To see ourselves again, we need not look for Plato's year:[4] every man is

[2] *Oedipus:* riddle solver.

[3] That loseth itself in Greece and riseth again in Sicily.—Browne's note.

[4] A revolution of certain thousand years, when all things should return unto their former estate, and he be teaching again in his school as when he delivered this opinion.—Browne's note.

not only himself; there hath been many Diogenes, and as many Timons, though but few of that name; men are lived over again, the world is now as it was in ages past; there was none then, but there hath been some one since that parallels him, and is, as it were, his revived self.

SECTION 7

Now the first of mine was that of the Arabians, that the souls of men perished with their bodies, but should yet be raised again at the last day. Not that I did absolutely conceive a mortality of the soul; but if that were, which faith, not philosophy, hath yet thoroughly disproved, and that both entered the grave together, yet I held the same conceit thereof that we all do of the body, that it should rise again. Surely it is but the merits of our unworthy natures, if we sleep in darkness until the last alarm. A serious reflex upon my own unworthiness did make me backward from challenging this prerogative of my soul; so that I might enjoy my Savior at the last, I could with patience be nothing almost unto eternity.

The second was that of Origen, that God would not persist in his vengeance forever, but after a definite time of his wrath, he would release the damned souls from torture, which error I fell into upon a serious contemplation of the great attribute of God, his mercy; and did a little cherish it in myself, because I found therein no malice, and a ready weight to sway me from the other extreme of despair, whereunto melancholy and contemplative natures are too easily disposed.

A third there is, which I did never positively maintain or practice, but have often wished it had been consonant to truth, and not offensive to my religion, and that is, the prayer for the dead; whereunto I was inclined from some charitable inducements, whereby I could scarce contain my prayers for a friend at the ringing of a bell, or behold his corpse without an orison for his soul. It was a good way, methought, to be remembered by posterity, and far more noble than an history.

These opinions I never maintained with pertinacity, or endeavored to inveigle any man's belief unto mine, nor so much as ever revealed or disputed them with my dearest friends; by which means I neither propagated them in others, nor confirmed them in myself; but suffering them to flame upon their own substance, without addition of new fuel, they went out insensibly of themselves. Therefore these opinions, though condemned by lawful councils, were not heresies in me, but bare errors and single lapses of my understanding, without a joint depravity of my will. Those have not only depraved understandings, but diseased affections, which cannot enjoy a singularity without an heresy, or be the author of an opinion without they be of a sect also. This was the villainy of the first schism of Lucifer, who was not content to err alone, but drew into his faction many legions of spirits; and upon this experience he tempted only Eve, as well understanding the communicable nature of sin, and that to deceive but one, was tacitly and upon consequence to delude them both.

SECTION 8

That heresies should arise, we have the prophesy of Christ; but that old ones should be abolished, we hold no prediction. That there must be heresies, is true, not only in our church, but also in any other. Even in doctrines heretical, there will be super-heresies; and Arians not only divided from their church, but also among themselves. For heads that are disposed unto schism and complexionally propense to innovation are naturally indisposed for a community, nor will be ever confined unto the order or economy of one body; and therefore, when they separate from others, they knit but loosely among themselves, nor contented with a general breach or dichotomy with their church do subdivide and mince themselves almost into atoms. It is true that men of singular parts and humors have not been free from singular opinions and conceits in all ages; retaining something, not only beside the opinion of his own church or any other, but also any particular author; which, notwithstanding, a sober judgment may do without offence or heresy; for there is yet, after all the decrees of councils and the niceties of the schools, many things untouched, unimagined, wherein the liberty of an honest reason may play and expatiate with security, and far without the circle of an heresy.

SECTION 9

As for those wingy mysteries in divinity and airy subtleties in religion which have unhinged the brains of better heads, they never stretched the *Pia Mater* of mine. Methinks there be not impossibilities enough in religion for an active faith; the deepest mysteries ours contains have not only been illustrated, but maintained, by syllogism and the rule of reason. I love to lose myself in a mystery, to pursue my reason to an *O altitudo!* It is my solitary recreation to pose my apprehension with those involved enigmas and riddles of the Trinity, with incarnation and resurrection. I can answer all the objections of Satan and my rebellious reason with that odd resolution I learned of Tertullian, *Certum est quia impossibile est.* I desire to exercise my faith in the difficultest point; for to credit ordinary and visible objects is not faith, but persuasion. Some believe the better for seeing Christ's sepulcher, and, when they have seen the Red Sea, doubt not of the miracle. Now, contrarily, I bless myself and am thankful that I lived not in the days of miracles, that I never saw Christ nor his disciples. I would not have been one of those Israelites that passed the Red Sea, nor one of Christ's patients on whom he wrought his wonders; then had my faith been thrust upon me, nor should I enjoy that greater blessing pronounced to all that believe and saw not. It is an easy and necessary belief, to credit what our eye and sense hath examined. I believe he was dead, and buried, and rose again; and desire to see him in his glory, rather than to contemplate him in his cenotaph or sepulcher. Nor is this much to believe; as we have reason, we owe this faith unto history. They only had the advantage of a bold and noble faith who lived before his coming, who upon obscure prophesies and mystical types could raise a belief and expect apparent impossibilities.

SECTION 10

It is true, there is an edge in all firm belief, and with an easy metaphor we may say, the sword of faith; but in these obscurities I rather use it in the adjunct the apostle gives it, a buckler; under which I conceive a wary combatant may lie invulnerable. Since I was of understanding to know we knew nothing, my reason hath been more pliable to the will of faith; I am now content to understand a mystery without a rigid definition, in an easy and Platonic description. That allegorical description of Hermes [5] pleaseth me beyond all the metaphysical definitions of divines. Where I cannot satisfy my reason, I love to humor my fancy: I had as lief you tell me that *anima est angelus hominis, est Corpus Dei,* as *Entelechia;—Lux est umbra Dei,* as *actus perspicui.*[6] Where there is an obscurity too deep for our reason, it is good to sit down with a description, periphrasis, or adumbration; for by acquainting our reason how unable it is to display the visible and obvious effects of nature, it becomes more humble and submissive unto the subtleties of faith; and thus I teach my haggard and unreclaimed reason to stoop unto the lure of faith. I believe there was already a tree whose fruit our unhappy parents tasted, though, in the same chapter when God forbids it, it is positively said, the plants of the field were not yet grown, for God had not caused it to rain upon the earth. I believe that the serpent, (if we shall literally understand it) from his proper form and figure, made his motion on his belly before the curse. I find the trial of the pucellage and virginity of women, which God ordained the Jews, is very fallible. Experience and history informs me, that not only many particular women, but likewise whole nations, have escaped the curse of childbirth, which God seems to pronounce upon the whole sex. Yet do I believe that all this is true, which indeed my reason would persuade me to be false; and this I think is no vulgar part of faith, to believe a thing not only above, but contrary to, reason and against the arguments of our proper senses.

SECTION 17

This is the ordinary and open way of his providence, which art and industry have in a good part discovered, whose effects we may foretell without an oracle. To foreshow these, is not prophesy, but prognostication.

[5] A sphere of which the center is everywhere, the circumference nowhere.—Browne's note, translated.

[6] *anima . . . perspicui:* famous scholastic definitions: "The soul is man's angel or spirit, is the Body of God—the entelechy." "Light is the shadow of God—the act of seeing."

There is another way, full of meanders and labyrinths, whereof the devil and spirits have no exact ephemerides;[7] and that is a more particular and obscure method of his providence, directing the operations of individuals and single essences. This we call *fortune,* that serpentine and crooked line, whereby he draws those actions his wisdom intends, in a more unknown and secret way. This cryptic and involved method of his providence have I ever admired; nor can I relate the history of my life, the occurrences of my days, the escapes of dangers, and hits of chance, with a *bezo las manos*[8] to fortune, or a bare *gramercy* to my good stars. Abraham might have thought the ram in the thicket came thither by accident; human reason would have said that mere chance conveyed Moses in the Ark to the sight of Pharaoh's Daughter. What a labyrinth is there in the story of Joseph, able to convert a stoic! Surely there are in every man's life certain rubs, doublings, and wrenches, which pass a while under the effects of chance, but at the last, well examined, prove the mere hand of God. It was not dumb chance, that, to discover the *Fougade* or powder plot, contrived a miscarriage in the letter. I like the victory of '88 the better for that one occurrence which our enemies imputed to our dishonor and the partiality of fortune, to wit, the tempests and contrariety of winds. King Philip did not detract from the nation, when he said, *he sent his Armado to fight with men, and not to combat with the winds.* Where there is a manifest disproportion between the powers and forces of two several agents, upon a maxim of reason we may promise the victory to the superior; but when unexpected accidents slip in, and unthought of occurrences intervene, these must proceed from a power that owes no obedience to those axioms; where, as in the writing upon the wall, we may behold the hand, but see not the spring that moves it. The success of that petty province of Holland (of which the Grand Seigneur[9] proudly said, *if they should trouble him as they did the Spaniard, he would send his men with shovels and pick-axes, and throw it into the sea*) I cannot altogether ascribe to the ingenuity and industry of the people, but the mercy of God, that hath disposed them to such a thriving genius; and to the will of his providence, that disposeth her favor to each country in their pre-ordinate season. All cannot be happy at once; for, because the glory of one state depends upon the ruin of another, there is a revolution and vicissitude of their greatness, and must obey the swing of that wheel, not moved by intelligences, but by the hand of God, whereby all estates arise to their zenith and vertical points according to their predestinated periods. For the lives, not only of men, but of commonwealths, and the whole world, run not upon an helix that still enlargeth, but on a circle, where, arriving to their meridian, they decline in obscurity, and fall under the horizon again.

---

[7] *ephemerides:* calendar.

[8] *bezo las manos:* salute; "I kiss the hands" (Sp.).

[9] *Grand Seigneur:* the Great Turk, Ottoman Emperor.

SECTION 18

These must not therefore be named the effects of fortune, but in a relative way, and as we term the works of nature. It was the ignorance of man's reason that begat this very name, and by a careless term miscalled the providence of God; for there is no liberty for causes to operate in a loose and straggling way; nor any effect whatsoever, but hath its warrant from some universal or superior cause. It is not a ridiculous devotion to say a prayer before a game at tables; for even in sortileges and matters of greatest uncertainty, there is a settled and pre-ordered course of effects. It is we that are blind, not Fortune. Because our eye is too dim to discover the mystery of her effects, we foolishly paint her blind, and hoodwink the providence of the Almighty. I cannot justify that contemptible proverb, *That fools only are fortunate,* that insolent paradox *That a wise man is out of the reach of fortune,* much less those opprobrious epithets of poets, *whore, bawd,* and *strumpet.* It is, I confess, the common fate of men of singular gifts of mind to be destitute of those of fortune, which doth not any way deject the spirit of wiser judgments, who thoroughly understand the justice of this proceeding; and being enriched with higher donatives, cast a more careless eye on these vulgar parts of felicity. It is a most unjust ambition to desire to engross the mercies of the Almighty, not to be content with the goods of mind, without a possession of those of body or fortune; and it is an error worse than heresy, to adore these complemental and circumstantial pieces of felicity, and undervalue those perfections and essential points of happiness wherein we resemble our maker. To wiser desires it is satisfaction enough to deserve, though not to enjoy, the favors of fortune; let providence provide for fools. It is not partiality, but equity in God, who deals with us but as our natural parents: those that are able of body and mind he leaves to their deserts; to those of weaker merits he imparts a larger portion, and pieces out the defect of one by the excess of the other. Thus have we no just quarrel with nature for leaving us naked; or to envy the horns, hoofs, skins and furs of other creatures, being provided with reason, that can supply them all. We need not labor with so many arguments to confute judicial astrology; for, if there be a truth therein, it doth not injure divinity. If to be born under Mercury disposeth us to be witty, under Jupiter to be wealthy, I do not owe a knee unto these, but unto that merciful hand that hath ordered my indifferent and uncertain nativity unto such benevolous aspects. Those that hold that all things are governed by fortune, had not erred, had they not persisted there. The Romans, that erected a temple to Fortune, acknowledged therein, though in a blinder way, somewhat of divinity; for, in a wise supputation, all things begin and end in the Almighty. There is a nearer way to heaven than Homer's chain; an easy logic may conjoin heaven and earth in one argument, and with less than a *sorites* [10] resolve all things into God. For though

[10] *sorites:* a series of arguments.

we christen effects by their most sensible and nearest causes, yet is God the true and infallible cause of all; whose concourse, though it be general, yet does it subdivide itself into the particular actions of everything, and is that spirit, by which each singular essence not only subsists, but performs in operation.

SECTION 21

I confess I have perused them all, and can discover nothing that may startle a discreet belief; yet are there heads carried off with the wind and breath of such motives. I remember a doctor in physic, of Italy, who could not perfectly believe the immortality of the soul, because Galen seemed to make a doubt thereof. With another I was familiarly acquainted in France, a divine, and a man of singular parts, that on the same point was so plunged and gravelled with three lines of Seneca, that all our antidotes, drawn from both scripture and philosophy, could not expel the poison of his error. There are a set of heads, that can credit the relations of mariners, yet question the testimonies of St. Paul; and peremptorily maintain the traditions of Aelian or Pliny, yet in histories of scripture raise queries and objections, believing no more than they can parallel in human authors. I confess there are in scripture stories that do exceed the fables of poets, and to a captious reader sound like Gargantua or Bevis. Search all the legends of times past, and the fabulous conceits of these present, and it will be hard to find one that deserves to carry the buckler unto Samson; yet is all this of an easy possibility, if we conceive a divine concourse, or an influence but from the little finger of the Almighty. It is impossible that either in the discourse of man, or in the infallible voice of God, to the weakness of our apprehensions, there should not appear irregularities, contradictions and antinomies: myself could show a catalogue of doubts, never yet imagined nor questioned, as I know, which are not resolved at the first hearing; not fantastic queries or objections of air; for I cannot hear of atoms in Divinity. I can read the history of the pigeon that was sent out of the Ark, and returned no more, yet not question how she found out her mate that was left behind; that Lazarus was raised from the dead, yet not demand where in the interim his soul awaited, or raise a law-case, whether his heir might lawfully detain his inheritance bequeathed unto him by his death, and he, though restored to life, have no plea or title unto his former possessions. Whether Eve was framed out of the left side of Adam, I dispute not; because I stand not yet assured which is the right side of a man, or whether there be any such distinction in nature; that she was edified out of the rib of Adam I believe, yet raise no question who shall arise with that rib at the resurrection. Whether Adam was an hermaphrodite, as the rabbins contend upon the letter of the text, because it is contrary to reason, there should be an hermaphrodite before there was a woman, or a composition of two natures before there was a second composed. Likewise, whether the world was created in autumn, summer, or the spring, because it was created in them all; for whatsoever sign the sun possesseth, those four seasons are actually existent. It is the nature of this luminary to distinguish the several seasons of the year, all which it makes at one time in the whole earth, and successive in any part thereof. There are a bundle of curiosities, not only in philosophy but in divinity, proposed and discussed by men of most supposed abilities, which indeed are not worthy our vacant hours, much less our serious studies: pieces only fit to be placed in Pantagruel's library, or bound up with Tartaretus *De modo Cacandi.*[11]

SECTION 34

These are certainly the magisterial and masterpieces of the Creator, the flower, or (as we may say) the best part of nothing, actually existing, what we are but in hopes and probability. We are only that amphibious piece between a corporal and spiritual essence, that middle form that links those two together, and makes good the method of God and nature, that jumps not from extremes, but unites the incompatible distances by some middle and participating natures. That we are the breath and similitude of God, it is indisputable, and upon record of Holy Scripture; but to call ourselves a microcosm, or little world, I thought it only a pleasant trope of rhetoric, till my near judgment and second thoughts told me there was a real truth therein. For first we are a rude mass, and in the rank of creatures which only are, and have a dull kind of being, not yet privileged with life, or preferred to sense or reason; next we live the life of plants, the life of animals, the life of men, and at last the life of spirits, running on in one mysterious nature those five kinds of existences, which comprehend the creatures, not only of the world, but of the universe. Thus is man that great and true *amphibium,* whose nature is disposed to live, not only like other creatures in divers elements, but in divided and distinguished worlds. For though there be but one to sense, there are two to reason, the one visible, the other invisible; whereof Moses seems to have left description and of the other so obscurely, that some parts thereof are yet in controversy. And truly, for the first chapters of Genesis, I must confess a great deal of obscurity; though divines have to the power of human reason endeavored to make all go in a literal meaning, yet those allegorical interpretations are also probable, and perhaps the mystical method of Moses bred up in the hieroglyphical schools of the Egyptians.

SECTION 39

Some divines count Adam thirty years old at his creation, because they suppose him created in the perfect age and stature of man. And surely we are all out of the computation of our age, and every man is some months elder than he bethinks him, for we live, move, have a being, and are sub-

[11] In Rabelais, a French author.—Browne's note.

ject to the actions of the elements and the malice of diseases in that other world, the truest microcosm, the womb of our mother. For besides that general and common existence we are conceived to hold in our chaos, and whilst we sleep within the bosom of our causes, we enjoy a being and life in three distinct worlds, wherein we receive most manifest graduations. In that obscure world and womb of our mother, our time is short, computed by the moon, yet longer than the days of many creatures that behold the sun; ourselves being not yet without life, sense and reason; though for the manifestation of its actions, it awaits the opportunity of objects, and seems to live there but in its root and soul of vegetation. Entering afterwards upon the scene of the world, we arise up and become another creature, performing the reasonable actions of man, and obscurely manifesting that part of divinity in us; but not in complement and perfection, till we have once more cast our secondine, that is, this slough of flesh, and are delivered into the last world, that is, that ineffable place of Paul, that proper *ubi* of spirits. The smattering I have of the philosopher's stone (which is something more than the perfect exaltation of gold) hath taught me a great deal of divinity, and instructed my belief, how that immortal spirit and incorruptible substance of my soul may lie obscure, and sleep a while within this house of flesh. Those strange and mystical transmigrations that I have observed in silk-worms, turned my philosophy into divinity. There is in these works of nature, which seem to puzzle reason, something divine, and hath more in it than the eye of a common spectator doth discover.

SECTION 40

I am naturally bashful; nor hath conversation, age, or travel, been able to effront or enharden me; yet I have one part of modesty which I have seldom discovered in another, that is, (to speak truly) I am not so much afraid of death, as ashamed thereof. It is the very disgrace and ignominy of our natures, that in a moment can so disfigure us, that our nearest friends, wife and children stand afraid and start at us. The birds and beasts of the field, that before in a natural fear obeyed us, forgetting all allegiance, begin to prey upon us. This very conceit hath in a tempest disposed and left me willing to be swallowed up in the abyss of waters, wherein I had perished unseen, unpitied, without wondering eyes, tears of pity, lectures of mortality, and none had said, *Quantum mutatus ab illo!* [12] Not that I am ashamed of the anatomy of my parts, or can accuse nature for playing the bungler in any part of me, or my own vicious life for contracting any shameful disease upon me whereby I might not call myself as wholesome a morsel for the worms as any.

SECTION 41

Some, upon the courage of a fruitful issue, wherein, as in the truest chronicle, they seem to outlive themselves, can with greater patience away with

[12] *Quantum . . . illo:* "How much changed from that!"

death. This conceit and counterfeit subsisting in our progenies seems to me a mere fallacy, unworthy the desires of a man that can but conceive a thought of the next world; who, in a nobler ambition, should desire to live in his substance in heaven, rather than his name and shadow in the earth. And therefore at my death I mean to take a total adieu of the world, not caring for a monument, history, or epitaph, not so much as the bare memory of my name to be found anywhere but in the universal register of God. I am not yet so cynical as to approve the Testament of Diogenes;[13] nor do I altogether allow that rodomontado of Lucan,

——*Caelo tegitur, qui non habet urnam.*

He that unburied lies wants not his hearse,
For unto him a tomb's the universe.

but commend in my calmer judgment those ingenuous intentions that desire to sleep by the urns of their fathers, and strive to go the neatest way unto corruption. I do not envy the temper of crows and daws, nor the numerous and weary days of our fathers before the flood. If there be any truth in astrology, I may outlive a Jubilee:[14] as yet I have not seen one revolution of Saturn,[15] nor hath my pulse beat thirty years; and yet, excepting one, have seen the ashes and left under ground all the kings of Europe; have been contemporary to three emperors, four grand signiors, and as many Popes. Methinks I have outlived myself, and begin to be weary of the sun; I have shaken hands with delight; in my warm blood and canicular days, I perceive I do anticipate the vices of age; the world to me is but a dream or mock-show, and we all therein but Pantalones[16] and antics, to my severer contemplation.

SECTION 52

I thank God, and with joy I mention it, I was never afraid of hell, nor never grew pale at the description of that place. I have so fixed my contemplations on heaven, that I have almost forgot the idea of hell, and am afraid rather to lose the joys of the one, than endure the misery of the other: to be deprived of them is a perfect hell, and needs, methinks, no addition to complete our afflictions. That terrible term has never detained me from sin, nor do I owe any good action to the name thereof. I fear God, yet am not afraid of him; his mercies make me ashamed of my sins, before his judgments afraid thereof. These are the forced and secondary method of his wisdom, which he uses but as the last remedy, and upon provocation; a course rather to deter the wicked, than incite the virtuous to his worship. I can hardly think there was ever any scared into heaven; they

[13] Who willed his friend not to bury him, but hang him up with a staff in his hand to fright away the crows.—Browne's note.

[14] The Jewish computation for 50 years.—Browne's note.

[15] The Planet of Saturn makes his revolution once in 30 years.—Browne's note.

[16] A French word for antics.—Browne's note.

go the fairest way to heaven that would serve God without a hell; other mercenaries, that crouch into him in fear of hell, though they term themselves the servants, are indeed but the slaves of the Almighty.

SECTION 58

The number of those who pretend unto salvation, and those infinite swarms who think to pass through the eye of this needle, have much amazed me. That name and compellation of *little flock*, does not comfort, but deject, my devotion; especially when I reflect upon mine own unworthiness, wherein, according to my humble apprehensions, I am below them all. I believe there shall never be an anarchy in heaven; but, as there are hierarchies among the angels, so shall there be degrees of priority among the Saints. Yet is it (I protest) beyond my ambition to aspire unto the first ranks; my desires only are, and I shall be happy therein, to be but the last man, and bring up the rear in heaven.

SECTION 59

Again, I am confident and fully persuaded, yet dare not take my oath, of my salvation. I am as it were sure, and do believe without all doubt, that there is such a city as Constantinople; yet for me to take my oath thereon were a kind of perjury, because I hold no infallible warrant from my own sense to confirm me in the certainty thereof. And truly, though many pretend an absolute certainty of their salvation, yet, when an humble soul shall contemplate her own unworthiness, she shall meet with many doubts, and suddenly find how little we stand in need of the precept of St. Paul, *Work out your salvation with fear and trembling.* That which is the cause of my election, I hold to be the cause of my salvation, which was the mercy and *beneplacit*[17] of God, before I was, or the foundation of the world. *Before Abraham was, I am,* is the saying of Christ; yet is it true in some sense, if I say it of myself; for I was not only before myself, but Adam, that is, in the idea of God, and the decree of that synod held from all eternity. And in this sense, I say, the world was before the creation, and at an end before it had a beginning; and thus was I dead before I was alive. Though my grave be England, my dying place was Paradise, and Eve miscarried of me before she conceived of Cain.

THE SECOND PART

Now for that other virtue of charity, without which faith is a mere notion, and of no existence, I have ever endeavored to nourish the merciful disposition and humane inclination I borrowed from my parents, and regulate it to the written and prescribed laws of charity. And if I hold the true anatomy of myself, I am delineated and naturally framed to such a piece

[17] *beneplacit:* pleasure.

of virtue; for I am of a constitution so general, that it consorts and sympathizes with all things. I have no antipathy, or rather idiosyncrasy, in diet, humor, air, anything. I wonder not at the French for their dishes of frogs, snails and toadstools, nor at the Jews for locusts and grasshoppers; but being among them, make them my common viands, and I find they agree with my stomach as well as theirs. I could digest a salad gathered in a church yard as well as in a garden. I cannot start at the presence of a serpent, scorpion, lizard, or salamander; at the sight of a toad or viper, I find in me no desire to take up a stone to destroy them. I feel not in myself those common antipathies that I can discover in others; those national repugnances do not touch me, nor do I behold with prejudice the French, Italian, Spaniard, or Dutch; but where I find their actions in balance with my countrymen's, I honor, love and embrace them in the same degree. I was born in the eighth climate, but seem for to be framed and constellated unto all. I am no plant that will not prosper out of a garden. All places, all airs, make unto me one country; I am in England everywhere, and under any meridian. I have been shipwrecked, yet am not enemy with the sea or winds; I can study, play, or sleep in a tempest. In brief, I am averse from nothing; my conscience would give me the lie if I should say I absolutely detest or hate any essence but the devil; or so at least abhor anything, but that we might come to composition. If there be any among those common objects of hatred I do condemn and laugh at, it is that great enemy of reason, virtue and religion, the multitude: that numerous piece of monstrosity, which, taken asunder, seem men and the reasonable creatures of God, but confused together, make but one great beast, and a monstrosity more prodigious than hydra. It is no breach of charity to call these fools; it is the style all holy writers have afforded them, set down by Solomon in canonical scripture, and a point of our faith to believe so. Neither in the name of multitude do I only include the base and minor sort of people; there is a rabble even among the gentry, a sort of plebeian heads, whose fancy moves with the same wheel as these; men in the same level with mechanics, though their fortunes do somewhat gild their infirmities, and their purses compound for their follies. But as, in casting account, three or four men together come short in account of one man placed by himself below them; so neither are a troop of these ignorant *doradoes* [18] of that true esteem and value, as many a forlorn person, whose condition does place him below their feet. Let us speak like politicians: there is a nobility without heraldry, a natural dignity, whereby one man is ranked with another, another filed before him, according to the quality of his desert, and preeminence of his good parts. Though the corruption of these times and the bias of present practice wheel another way, thus it was in the first and primitive commonwealths, and is yet in the integrity and cradle of well-ordered polities, till corruption gets ground,

---

[18] *doradoes:* rich men.

—ruder desires laboring after that which wiser considerations condemn, everyone having a liberty to amass and heap up riches, and they a license or faculty to do or purchase anything.

SECTION 5

There is, I think, no man that apprehends his own miseries less than myself, and no man that so nearly apprehends another's. I could lose an arm without a tear, and with few groans, methinks, be quartered into pieces; yet can I weep most seriously at a play, and receive with true passion the counterfeit grief of those known and professed impostures. It is a barbarous part of inhumanity to add unto any afflicted party's misery, or endeavor to multiply in any man a passion whose single nature is already above his patience. This was the greatest affliction of Job, and those oblique expostulations of his friends a deeper injury than the downright blows of the devil. It is not the tears of our own eyes only, but of our friends also, that do exhaust the current of our sorrows; which, falling into many streams, runs more peaceably, and is contented with a narrower channel. It is an act within the power of charity to translate a passion out of one breast into another, and to divide a sorrow almost out of itself; for an affliction, like a dimension, may be so divided, as, if not individable, at least to become insensible. Now with my friend I desire not to share or participate, but to engross, his sorrows; that, by making them mine own, I may more easily discuss them; for in mine own reason, and within myself, I can command that which I cannot entreat without myself, and with the circle of another. I have often thought those noble pairs and examples of friendship not so truly histories of what had been, as fictions of what should be; but I now perceive nothing in them but possibilities, nor anything in the heroic examples of Damon and Pythias, Achilles and Patroclus, which methinks upon some grounds I could not perform within the narrow compass of myself. That a man should lay down his life for his friend, seems strange to vulgar affections, and such as confine themselves within that worldly principle, *Charity begins at home*. For mine own part I could never remember the relations that I held unto myself, nor the respect that I owe unto my own nature, in the cause of God, my country and my friends. Next to these three, I do embrace myself. I confess I do not observe that order that the schools ordain our affections, to love our parents, wives, children, and then our friends; for, excepting the injunctions of religion, I do not find in myself such a necessary and indissoluble sympathy to all those of my blood. I hope I do not break the fifth commandment, if I conceive I may love my friend before the nearest of my blood, even those to whom I owe the principles of life. I never yet cast a true affection on a woman, but I have loved my friend as I do virtue, my soul, my God. From hence I think I do conceive how God loves man, what happiness there is in the love of God. Omitting all other, there are three most mystical unions: two natures in one person; three persons in one nature; one soul in two bodies; for though indeed they be really divided, yet are they so united, as they seem but one, and make rather a duality than two distinct souls.

SECTION 8

I thank God, among those millions of vices I do inherit and hold from Adam, I have escaped one, and that a mortal enemy to charity, the first and father-sin, not only of man, but of the devil, pride: a vice whose name is comprehended in a monosyllable, but in its nature not circumscribed with a world. I have escaped it in a condition that can hardly avoid it. Those petty acquisitions and reputed perfections that advance and elevate the conceits of other men, add no feathers unto mine. I have seen a grammarian tower and plume himself over a single line in Horace, and show more pride in the construction of one ode, than the author in the composure of the whole book. For my own part, besides the jargon and patois of several provinces, I understand no less than six languages; yet I protest I have no higher conceit of myself, than had our fathers before the confusion of Babel, when there was but one language in the world, and none to boast himself either linguist or critic. I have not only seen several countries, beheld the nature of their climes, the chorography of their provinces, topography of their cities, but understood their several laws, customs and policies; yet cannot all this persuade the dullness of my spirit unto such an opinion of myself, as I behold in nimbler and conceited heads, that never looked a degree beyond their nests. I know the names and somewhat more, of all the constellations in my horizon; yet I have seen a prating mariner, that could only name the pointers and the North Star, out-talk me, and conceit himself a whole sphere above me. I know most of the plants of my country, and of those about me; yet I think I do not know so many as when I did but know a hundred, and had scarcely ever simpled further than Cheapside. For, indeed, heads of capacity, and such as are not full with a handful or easy measure of knowledge, think they know nothing till they know all; which being impossible, they fall upon the opinion of Socrates, and only know they know not anything. I cannot think that Homer pined away upon the riddle of the fishermen; or that Aristotle, who understood the uncertainty of knowledge, and confessed so often the reason of man too weak for the works of nature, did ever drown himself upon the flux and reflux of Euripus.[19] We do but learn today what our better advanced judgments will unteach tomorrow; and Aristotle does but instruct us, as Plato did him; that is, to confute himself. I have run through all sorts, yet find no rest in any: though our first studies and junior endeavors may style us peripatetics, stoics, or academics; yet I perceive the wisest heads prove, at last, almost all sceptics, and stand like Janus in the field of knowledge. I have therefore one common and authentic philosophy I learned in the schools, whereby I discourse and

[19] *Euripus:* any place in the sea where the tide is violent.

satisfy the reason of other men; another more reserved, and drawn from experience, whereby I content mine own. Solomon, that complained of ignorance in the height of knowledge, has not only humbled my conceits, but discouraged my endeavors. There is yet another conceit that has sometimes made me shut my books, which tells me it is a vanity to waste our days in the blind pursuit of knowledge; it is but attending a little longer, and we shall enjoy that by instinct and infusion, which we endeavor at here by labor and inquisition. It is better to sit down in a modest ignorance, and rest contented with the natural blessing of our own reasons, than buy the uncertain knowledge of this life with sweat and vexation, which death gives every fool gratis, and is an accessary of our glorification.

SECTION 9

I was never yet once, and commend their resolutions who never marry twice. Not that I disallow of second marriage; as neither, all cases of polygamy, which, considering some times, and the unequal number of both sexes, may be also necessary. The whole world was made for man, but the twelfth part of man for woman; man is the whole world and the breath of God; woman the rib and crooked piece of man. I could be content that we might procreate like trees, without conjunction, or that there were any way to perpetuate the world without this trivial and vulgar way of coition: it is the foolishest act a wise man commits in all his life; nor is there anything that will more deject his cooled imagination, when he shall consider what an odd and unworthy piece of folly he has committed.[20] I speak not in prejudice, nor am averse from that sweet sex, but naturally amorous of all that is beautiful. I can look a whole day with delight upon a handsome picture, though it be but of an horse. It is my temper, and I like it the better, to affect all harmony; and sure there is music even in the beauty, and the silent note which Cupid strikes, far sweeter than the sound of an instrument. For there is a music wherever there is a harmony, order, or proportion, and thus far we may maintain the music of the spheres; for those well-ordered motions and regular paces, though they give no sound unto the ear, yet to the understanding they strike a note most full of harmony. Whosoever is harmonically composed delights in harmony, which makes me much distrust the symmetry of those heads which declaim against all church music. For myself, not only from my obedience, but my particular genius, I do embrace it, for even that vulgar and tavern music, which makes one man merry, another mad, strikes in me a deep fit of devotion and profound contemplation of the first composer. There is something in it of divinity more than the ear discovers: it is an hieroglyphical and shadowed lesson of the whole world, and creatures of God; such a melody to the ear, as the whole world, well under-

[20] *it is the foolishest . . . committed:* Despite this view, Browne married in 1641 and had twelve children.

stood, would afford the understanding. In brief, it is a sensible fit of that harmony which intellectually sounds in the ears of God. I will not say, with Plato, the soul is an harmony, but harmonical, and has its nearest sympathy unto music. Thus some, whose temper of body agrees and humors the constitution of their souls, are born poets, though indeed, all are naturally inclined unto rhythm. This made Tacitus, in the very first line of his story, fall upon a verse; and Cicero, the worst of poets, but declaiming for a poet, falls in the very first sentence upon a perfect hexameter. I feel not in me those sordid and unchristian desires of my profession; I do not secretly implore and wish for plagues, rejoice at famines, revolve ephemerides and almanacs in expectation of malignant aspects, fatal conjunctions, and eclipses. I rejoice not at unwholesome springs, nor unseasonable winters. My prayer goes with the husbandman's; I desire everything in its proper season, that neither men nor the times be put out of temper. Let me be sick myself, if sometimes the malady of my patient be not a disease unto me. I desire rather to cure his infirmities than my own necessities. Where I do him no good, I think it is scarce honest gain; though I confess it is but the worthy salary of our well-intended endeavors. I am not only ashamed, but heartily sorry, that, besides death, there are diseases incurable, yet not for my own sake, or that they be beyond my art, but for the general cause and sake of humanity, whose common cause I apprehend as mine own. And to speak more generally, those three noble professions which all civil commonwealths do honor are raised upon the fall of Adam, and are not any way exempt from their infirmities; these are not only diseases incurable in physic, but cases indissolvable in laws, vices incorrigible in divinity. If general councils may err, I do not see why particular courts should be infallible. Their perfectest rules are raised upon the erroneous reasons of man, and the laws of one do but condemn the rules of another; as Aristotle oft-times the opinions of his predecessors, because, though agreeable to reason, yet were not consonant to his own rules, and the logic of his proper principles. Again to speak nothing of the sin against the Holy Ghost, whose cure not only, but whose nature is unknown, I can cure the gout or stone in some, sooner than Divinity, pride or avarice in others. I can cure vices by physic when they remain incurable by Divinity, and shall obey my pills when they condemn their precepts. I boast nothing, but plainly say, we all labor against our own cure; for death is the cure of all diseases. There is no *Catholicon* or universal remedy I know, but this, which, though nauseous to queasy stomachs, yet to prepared appetites is nectar, and a pleasant potion of immortality.

SECTION II

Now for my life, it is a miracle of thirty years, which to relate, were not a history, but a piece of poetry, and would sound to common ears like a fable. For the world, I count it not an inn, but an hospital; and a place not to live, but to die in. The world that I regard is myself; it is the microcosm of my own frame that I cast mine eye on; for the other, I use it but like my globe, and turn it round sometimes for my recreation. Men that look upon my outside, perusing only my condition and fortunes, do err in my altitude; for I am above Atlas his shoulders. The earth is a point not only in respect of the heavens above us, but of that heavenly and celestial part within us. That mass of flesh that circumscribes me, limits not my mind. That surface that tells the heavens it has an end, cannot persuade me I have any. I take my circle to be above three hundred and sixty; though the number of the Ark do measure my body, it comprehends not my mind. While I study to find how I am a microcosm, or little world, I find myself something more than the great. There is surely a piece of divinity in us, something that was before the elements, and owes no homage unto the sun. Nature tells me I am the image of God, as well as scripture. He that understands not thus much, has not his introduction or first lesson, and is yet to begin the alphabet of man. Let me not injure the felicity of others, if I say I am as happy as any: *Ruat caelum, fiat voluntas tua,* salveth all; so that whatsoever happens, it is but what our daily prayers desire. In brief, I am content; and what should Providence add more? Surely this is it we call happiness, and this do I enjoy; with this I am happy in a dream, and as content to enjoy a happiness in a fancy, as others in a more apparent truth and reality. There is surely a nearer apprehension of any thing that delights us in our dreams, than in our waked senses: without this I were unhappy; for my awaked judgment discontents me, ever whispering unto me, that I am from my friend; but my friendly dreams in the night requite me, and make me think I am within his arms. I thank God for my happy dreams, as I do for my good rest; for there is a satisfaction in them unto reasonable desires, and such as can be content with a fit of happiness: and surely it is not a melancholy conceit to think we are all asleep in this world, and that the conceits of this life are as mere dreams to those of the next; as the phantasms of the night, to the conceits of the day. There is an equal delusion in both, and the one doth but seem to be the emblem or picture of the other: we are somewhat more than ourselves in our sleeps, and the slumber of the body seems to be but the waking of the soul. It is the ligation of sense, but the liberty of reason; and our waking conceptions do not match the fancies of our sleeps. At my nativity my ascendant was the watery sign of Scorpius; I was born in the planetary hour of Saturn, and I think I have a piece of that leaden planet in me. I am no way facetious, nor disposed for the mirth and galliardize[21] of company; yet in one dream I can compose a whole comedy, behold the action, apprehend the jests, and laugh myself awake at the conceits thereof. Were my memory as faithful as my reason is then fruitful, I would never study but in my dreams; and this time also would I choose for my devotions, but our grosser memories

[21] *galliardize:* gaiety, revelry.

have then so little hold of our abstracted understandings, that they forget the story and can only relate to our awaked souls a confused and broken tale of that that has passed. Aristotle, who has written a singular tract *Of Sleep,* hath not, methinks, thoroughly defined it; nor yet Galen, though he seem to have corrected it; for those *Noctambuloes* and night-walkers, though in their sleep, do yet enjoy the action of their senses. We must therefore say that there is something in us that is not in the jurisdiction of Morpheus; and that those abstracted and ecstatic souls do walk about in their own corpse, as spirits with the bodies they assume, wherein they seem to hear, see and feel, though indeed the organs are destitute of sense, and their natures of those faculties that should inform them. Thus it is observed, that men sometimes, upon the hour of their departure, do speak and reason above themselves; for then the soul, beginning to be freed from the ligaments of the body, begins to reason like herself, and to discourse in a strain above mortality.

SECTION 13

The method I should use in distributive justice, I often observe in commutative; and keep a geometrical proportion in both, whereby becoming equable to others, I become unjust to myself, and supererogate in that common principle, *Do unto others as thou wouldst be done unto thyself.* I was not born unto riches, neither is it, I think, my star to be wealthy; or, if it were, the freedom of my mind, and frankness of my disposition, were able to contradict and cross my fates. For to me, avarice seems not so much a vice, as a deplorable piece of madness; to conceive ourselves urinals, or be persuaded that we are dead, is not so ridiculous, not so many degrees beyond the power of hellebore, as this. The opinions of theory, and positions of men, are not so void of reason as their practised conclusions. Some have held that snow is black, that the earth moves, that the soul is air, fire, water; but all this is philosophy, and there is no delirium, if we do not speculate the folly and indisputable dotage of avarice to that subterraneous idol and god of the earth. I do confess I am an atheist; I cannot persuade myself to honor that the world adores; whatsoever virtue its prepared substance may have within my body, it has no influence nor operation without. I would not entertain a base design, or an action that should call me villain, for the Indies; and for this only do I love and honor my own soul, and have methinks two arms too few to embrace myself. Aristotle is too severe, that will not allow us to be truly liberal without wealth and the bountiful hand of fortune. If this be true, I must confess I am charitable only in my liberal intentions, and bountiful well-wishes; but if the example of the mite be not only an act of wonder, but an example of the noblest charity, surely poor men may also build hospitals, and the rich alone have not erected cathedrals. I have a private method which others observe not; I take the opportunity of myself to do good; I borrow occasion of charity from mine own necessities, and supply the wants of others, when I am in most need myself. For it is an honest stratagem to take advantage of ourselves, and so to husband the acts of virtue, that, where they are defective in one circumstance, they may repay their want and multiply their goodness in another. I have not Peru in my desires, but a competence, and ability to perform those good works to which he hath inclined my nature. He is rich who hath enough to be charitable, and it is hard to be so poor that a noble mind may not find a way to this piece of goodness. *He that giveth to the poor, lendeth to the Lord:* there is more rhetoric in that one sentence, than in a library of sermons; and indeed, if those sentences were understood by the reader, with the same emphasis as they are delivered by the author, we needed not those volumes of instructions, but might be honest by an epitome. Upon this motive only I cannot behold a beggar without relieving his necessities with my purse, or his soul with my prayers; these scenical and accidental differences between us, cannot make me forget that common and untouched part of us both. There is under these *centoes* [22] and miserable outsides, these mutilate and semi-bodies, a soul of the same alloy with our own, whose genealogy is God as well as ours, and in as fair a way to salvation as ourselves. Statists that labor to contrive a commonwealth without poverty, take away the object of charity, not understanding only the commonwealth of a Christian, but forgetting the prophecy [23] of Christ.

[22] *centoes:* rags, patches.

[23] The poor ye shall have always with you.—Browne's note.

Sir John Suckling · Richard Lovelace

1609–1642 1618–1657

SUCKLING and Lovelace are usually considered the two typical Cavalier poets, expressing in gay or mournful songs the attitudes of the royalist gentlemen who lived a carefree life until the Rebellion caught up with them. Suckling was a Norfolk gentleman who was educated at Cambridge and Gray's Inn, traveled on the continent between 1628 and 1630, and served under Gustavus Adolphus. He had a command in the first Bishops' War at home in 1639, but instead of military fame he won notoriety for dressing his troops in elegant finery. He was a gambler and a man-about-town, and is credited with inventing the game of cribbage. He wrote plays in the fashionable style. In 1641 he was involved in a royalist plot and had to escape to France; he died there, according to Aubrey, by suicide. His poems, published after his death, were popular in the Restoration period, when he was praised as "natural, easy Suckling."

Lovelace was a Kentish courtier-gentleman who sacrificed his fortune in the King's cause. He was educated at the Charterhouse and Oxford, and spent the years 1643–1646 abroad. He was twice imprisoned, in 1642 and 1648. His *Lucasta* appeared in 1649. An appealing seriousness and dignity distinguishes him from the more frivolous Suckling.

BIBLIOGRAPHY: *The Works of Sir John Suckling*, ed. A. H. Thompson, 1910; F. O. Henderson, "Traditions of *Précieux* and *Libertin* in Suckling's Poetry," *ELH*, IV (1937), 274–298; *Poems of Richard Lovelace*, ed. C. H. Wilkinson, Oxford, 1925 and 1930; C. H. Hartmann, *The Cavalier Spirit and Its Influence on the Life and Work of Richard Lovelace*, London, 1925.

Sir John Suckling

1609–1642

A SONG TO A LUTE[1]

Hast thou seen the down in the air
When wanton blasts have tossed it?
  Or the ship on the sea,
When ruder waves have crossed it?
Hast thou marked the crocodile's weeping,
Or the fox's sleeping?
Or hast viewed the peacock in his pride,
  Or the dove by his bride,
When he courts for his lechery?
O, so fickle, O, so vain, O, so false, so false is she!

SONG

Why so pale and wan, fond lover?
  Prithee, why so pale?
Will, when looking well can't move her,
  Looking ill prevail?
  Prithee, why so pale?

Why so dull and mute, young sinner?
  Prithee, why so mute?
Will, when speaking well can't win her,
  Saying nothing do't?
  Prithee, why so mute?

Quit, quit, for shame; this will not move,
  This cannot take her.
If of herself she will not love,
  Nothing can make her:
  The devil take her!

[1] See Jonson's lyric "Have you seen but a bright lily grow," p. 769.

SONG

No, no, fair heretic, it needs must be
But an ill love in me,
And worse for thee,
For were it in my power
To love thee now this hour
More than I did the last,
'Twould then so fall
I might not love at all.
Love that can flow, and can admit increase,
Admits as well an ebb, and may grow less.

True love is still the same; the torrid zones
And those more frigid ones
It must not know:
For love grown cold or hot
Is lust or friendship, not
The thing we have;
For that's a flame would die,
Held down or up too high.
Then think I love more than I can express,
And would love more, could I but love thee less.

SONNET II

Of thee, kind boy, I ask no red and white,
To make up my delight;
No odd becoming graces,
Black eyes, or little known-not-whats in faces;
Make me but mad enough, give me good store
Of love for her I court;
I ask no more,
'Tis love in love that makes the sport.

There's no such thing as that we beauty call,
It is mere cozenage all;
For though some, long ago,
Liked certain colors mingled so and so,
That doth not tie me now from choosing new;

If I a fancy take
  To black and blue,
That fancy doth it beauty make.

'Tis not the meat, but 'tis the appetite
  Makes eating a delight;
  And if I like one dish
More than another, that a pheasant is;
What in our watches, that in us is found,
So to the height and nick
  We up be wound,
No matter by what hand or trick.

SONNET III

Oh! for some honest lover's ghost,[2]
  Some kind unbodied post
  Sent from the shades below!
  I strangely long to know
Whether the nobler chaplets wear,
Those that their mistress' scorn did bear,
  Or those that were used kindly.

For whatsoe'er they tell us here
  To make those sufferings dear,
  'Twill there, I fear, be found
  That to the being crowned
To have loved alone will not suffice,
Unless we also have been wise
  And have our loves enjoyed.

What posture can we think him in,
  That here unloved again
  Departs, and is thither gone
  Where each sits by his own?
Or how can that Elysium be,
Where I my mistress still must see
  Circled in other's arms?

For there the judges all are just,
  And Sophonisba [3] must

[2] See Donne's "Love's Deity" above, p. 799.

[3] *Sophonisba:* Carthaginian princess, given in marriage by her father to the rival of the man she loved.

Be his whom she held dear,
Not his who loved her here;
The sweet Philoclea,[4] since she died,
Lies by her Pyrocles his side,
Not by Amphialus.

Some bays, perchance, or myrtle bough,
For difference crowns the brow
Of those kind souls that were
The noble martyrs here;
And if that be the only odds
(As who can tell?), ye kinder gods,
Give me the woman here.

THE CONSTANT LOVER

Out upon it! I have loved
Three whole days together;
And am like to love three more,
If it prove fair weather.

Time shall moult away his wings,
Ere he shall discover
In the whole wide world again
Such a constant lover.

But the spite on't is, no praise
Is due at all to me:
Love with me had made no stays
Had it any been but she.

Had it any been but she,
And that very face,
There had been at least ere this
A dozen dozen in her place.

THE SIEGE

'Tis now, since I sat down before
That foolish fort, a heart,

[4] *Philoclea:* heroine in Sidney's *Arcadia* who loves and finally marries Pyrocles, not her suitor Amphialus.

(Time strangely spent) a year and more,
  And still I did my part:

Made my approaches, from her hand
  Unto her lip did rise,
And did already understand
  The language of her eyes;

Proceeded on with no less art—
  My tongue was engineer;
I thought to undermine the heart
  By whispering in the ear.

When this did nothing, I brought down
  Great cannon-oaths, and shot
A thousand thousand to the town;
  And still it yielded not.

I then resolved to starve the place
  By cutting off all kisses,
Praising and gazing on her face
  And all such little blisses.

To draw her out, and from her strength,
  I drew all batteries in,
And brought myself to lie at length
  As if no siege had been.

When I had done what man could do
  And thought the place mine own,
The enemy lay quiet too,
  And smiled at all was done.

I sent to know from whence and where
  These hopes and this relief;
A spy informed, Honor was there,
  And did command in chief.

"March, march," quoth I; "the word straight give;
  Let's lose no time, but leave her;
That giant upon air will live,
  And hold it out for ever.

"To such a place our camp remove
  As will no siege abide;

I hate a fool that starves her love,
  Only to feed her pride."

A BALLAD UPON A WEDDING[5]

I TELL thee, Dick, where I have been,
Where I the rarest things have seen,
  Oh, things without compare!
Such sights again cannot be found
In any place on English ground,
  Be it at wake[6] or fair.

At Charing Cross, hard by the way
Where we (thou know'st) do sell our hay,
  There is a house with stairs;
And there I did see coming down
Such folk as are not in our town,
  Vorty,[7] at least, in pairs.

Amongst the rest, one pestilent fine
(His beard no bigger, though, than thine)
  Walked on before the rest.
Our landlord looks like nothing to him;
The King (God bless him!), 'twould undo him
  Should he go still so dressed.

At course-a-park,[8] without all doubt,
He should have been the first taken out
  By all the maids i' the town,
Though lusty Roger there had been,
Or little George upon the Green,
  Or Vincent of the Crown.

But wot you what? the youth was going
To make an end of all his wooing;
  The parson for him stayed.
Yet by his leave, for all his haste,
He did not so much wish all past,
  Perchance, as did the maid.

---

[5] Written for an aristocratic wedding in 1641. The feigned rustic simplicity is for comic effect.

[6] *wake:* any popular festival.

[7] *Vorty:* forty (rustic).

[8] *course-a-park:* a country game.

The maid—and thereby hangs a tale;
For such a maid no Whitsun-ale [9]
Could ever yet produce;
No grape, that's kindly ripe, could be
So round, so plump, so soft as she,
Nor half so full of juice.

Her finger was so small the ring
Would not stay on, which they did bring;
It was too wide a peck:
And to say truth (for out it must),
It looked like the great collar (just)
About our young colt's neck.

Her feet beneath her petticoat,
Like little mice stole in and out,
As if they feared the light;
But oh, she dances such a way,
No sun upon an Easter day
Is half so fine a sight!

He would have kissed her once or twice,
But she would not, she was so nice,
She would not do't in sight;
And then she looked as who should say,
"I will do what I list today,
And you shall do't at night."

Her cheeks so rare a white was on,
No daisy makes comparison
(Who sees them is undone),
For streaks of red were mingled there,
Such as are on a Catherine pear
(The side that's next the sun).

Her lips were red, and one was thin
Compared to that was next her chin
(Some bee had stung it newly);
But, Dick, her eyes so guard her face
I durst no more upon them gaze
Than on the sun in July.

Her mouth so small, when she does speak,
Thou'dst swear her teeth her words did break,

[9] *Whitsun-ale:* a country festival at Whitsuntide.

That they might passage get;
But she so handled still the matter,
They came as good as ours, or better,
And are not spent a whit.

If wishing should be any sin,
The parson himself had guilty been
(She looked that day so purely);
And did the youth so oft the feat
At night, as some did in conceit,
It would have spoiled him, surely.

Passion o' me, how I run on!
There's that that would be thought upon,
I trow, besides the bride.
The business of the kitchen's great,
For it is fit that man should eat,
Nor was it there denied.

Just in the nick the cook knocked thrice,
And all the waiters in a trice
His summons did obey;
Each serving-man, with dish in hand,
Marched boldly up, like our trained band,
Presented, and away.

When all the meat was on the table,
What man of knife or teeth was able
To stay to be entreated?
And this the very reason was—
Before the parson could say grace,
The company was seated.

Now hats fly off, and youths carouse;
Healths first go round, and then the house;
The bride's came thick and thick:
And when 'twas named another's health,
Perhaps he made it hers by stealth;
And who could help it, Dick?

O' the sudden up they rise and dance;
Then sit again and sigh and glance;
Then dance again and kiss;
Thus several ways the time did pass,
Whilst every woman wished her place,
And every man wished his!

By this time all were stol'n aside
To counsel and undress the bride,
  But that he must not know;
But yet 'twas thought he guessed her mind,
And did not mean to stay behind
  Above an hour or so.

When in he came, Dick, there she lay
Like new-fall'n snow melting away
  ('Twas time, I trow, to part);
Kisses were now the only stay,
Which soon she gave, as who would say,
  "God be with ye, with all my heart."

But just as heavens would have to cross it,
In came the bridesmaids with the posset.
  The bridegroom eat in spite,
For had he left the women to't,
It would have cost two hours to do't,
  Which were too much that night.

At length the candle's out, and now
All that they had not done, they do.
  What that is, who can tell?
But I believe it was no more
Than thou and I have done before
  With Bridget and with Nell.

Richard Lovelace

1618–1657

SONG
TO LUCASTA. GOING BEYOND THE SEAS

If to be absent were to be
        Away from thee;
    Or that when I am gone,
    You or I were alone,
  Then, my Lucasta, might I crave
Pity from blustering wind or swallowing wave.

But I'll not sigh one blast or gale
        To swell my sail,
    Or pay a tear to 'suage
    The foaming blow-god's rage;
  For whether he will let me pass
Or no, I'm still as happy as I was.

Though seas and land be 'twixt us both,
        Our faith and troth,
    Like separated souls,
    All time and space controls;
  Above the highest sphere we meet,
Unseen, unknown, and greet as angels greet.

So then we do anticipate
        Our after-fate,
    And are alive i' the skies,
    If thus our lips and eyes
  Can speak like spirits unconfined
In Heaven, their earthy bodies left behind.

SONG
TO LUCASTA. GOING TO THE WARS

Tell me not, sweet, I am unkind,
That from the nunnery
Of thy chaste breast and quiet mind
To war and arms I fly.

True, a new mistress now I chase,
The first foe in the field;
And with a stronger faith embrace
A sword, a horse, a shield.

Yet this inconstancy is such
As you too shall adore;
I could not love thee, dear, so much,
Loved I not honor more.

GRATIANA DANCING AND SINGING

See! with what constant motion,
Even and glorious as the sun,
Gratiana steers that noble frame,
Soft as her breast, sweet as her voice,
That gave each winding law and poise,
And swifter than the wings of fame.

She beat the happy pavement
By such a star made firmament,
Which now no more the roof envies,
But swells up high with Atlas even,
Bearing the brighter, nobler heaven
And in her all the deities.

Each step trod out a lover's thought
And the ambitious hopes he brought,
Chained to her brave feet with such arts,
Such sweet command and gentle awe,

As when she ceased, we sighing saw
  The floor lay paved with broken hearts.

So did she move; so did she sing
Like the harmonious spheres that bring
  Unto their rounds their music's aid;
Which she performed such a way
As all th' enamored world will say
  The Graces danced, and Apollo played.

ODE
THE GRASSHOPPER

To My Noble Friend, Mr. Charles Cotton

O thou that swing'st upon the waving hair
Of some well-filled oaten beard,
Drunk ev'ry night with a delicious tear
Dropped thee from heav'n, where now th'art reared;

The joys of earth and air are thine entire,
That with thy feet and wings dost hop and fly;
And, when thy poppy works, thou dost retire
To thy carved acorn-bed to lie.

Up with the day, the sun thou welcom'st then,
Sport'st in the gilt plats of his beams,
And all these merry days mak'st merry men,
Thyself, and melancholy streams.

But ah, the sickle! Golden ears are cropped;
Ceres and Bacchus bid good night;
Sharp frosty fingers all your flowers have topped,
And what scythes spared, winds shave off quite.

Poor verdant fool! and now green ice! thy joys
Large and as lasting as thy perch of grass,
Bid us lay in 'gainst winter rain, and poise
Their floods with an o'erflowing glass.

Thou best of men and friends! we will create
A genuine summer in each other's breast,

And spite of this cold time and frozen fate,
Thaw us a warm seat to our rest.

Our sacred hearths shall burn eternally
As vestal flames; the North Wind, he
Shall strike his frost-stretched wings, dissolve, and fly
This Ætna in epitome.

Dropping December shall come weeping in,
Bewail th' usurping of his reign;
But when in show'rs of old Greek [1] we begin,
Shall cry he hath his crown again.

Night as clear Hesper shall our tapers whip
From the light casements where we play,
And the dark hag from her black mantle strip,
And stick there everlasting day.

Thus richer than untempted kings are we,
That asking nothing, nothing need:
Though lord of all that seas embrace, yet he
That wants himself is poor indeed.

SONG

TO ALTHEA. FROM PRISON

When Love with unconfinèd wings
Hovers within my gates,
And my divine Althea brings
To whisper at the grates;
When I lie tangled in her hair
And fettered to her eye,
The birds that wanton in the air
Know no such liberty.

When flowing cups run swiftly round,
With no allaying Thames,
Our careless heads with roses bound,
Our hearts with loyal flames;
When thirsty grief in wine we steep,
When healths and draughts go free,

---

[1] *Greek:* wine.

Fishes that tipple in the deep
Know no such liberty.

When, like committed[2] linnets, I
With shriller throat shall sing
The sweetness, mercy, majesty,
And glories of my King;
When I shall voice aloud how good
He is, how great should be,
Enlargèd winds that curl the flood
Know no such liberty.

Stone walls do not a prison make,
Nor iron bars a cage:
Minds innocent and quiet take
That for an hermitage.
If I have freedom in my love,
And in my soul am free,
Angels alone, that soar above,
Enjoy such liberty.

SONG

THE SCRUTINY

Why should you swear I am forsworn,
Since thine I vowed to be?
Lady, it is already morn,
And 'twas last night I swore to thee
That fond impossibility.

Have I not loved thee much and long,
A tedious twelve hours' space?
I must all other beauties wrong,
And rob thee of a new embrace,
Could I still dote upon thy face.

Not but all joy in thy brown hair
By others may be found;
But I must search the black and fair,
Like skilful mineralists that sound
For treasure in unplowed-up ground.

---

[2] *committed:* caged.

Then, if when I have loved my round,
Thou prov'st the pleasant she,
With spoils of meaner beauties crowned
I laden will return to thee,
Even sated with variety.

Seventeenth-Century Lyrics

GEORGE WITHER

1588–1667

FROM

FAIR VIRTUE, THE MISTRESS OF PHILARETE (1622)

Shall I, wasting in despair,
Die because a woman's fair?
Or make pale my cheeks with care
'Cause another's rosy are?
Be she fairer than the day,
Or the flowery meads in May,
  If she be not so to me,
  What care I how fair she be?

Shall my heart be grieved or pined
'Cause I see a woman kind?
Or a well-disposed nature
Joined with a lovely feature?
Be she meeker, kinder than
Turtledove or pelican,[1]
  If she be not so to me,
  What care I how kind she be?

Shall a woman's virtues move
Me to perish for her love?
Or, her well-deserving known,
Make me quite forget mine own?
Be she with that goodness blest
Which may gain her name of best,
  If she be not such to me,
  What care I how good she be?

---

[1] *pelican:* The pelican was supposed to feed her young with her own blood; hence the bird is a common Renaissance symbol of loving-kindness.

'Cause her fortune seems too high,
Shall I play the fool and die?
Those that bear a noble mind,
Where they want of riches find,
Think what with them they would do
That without them dare to woo;
And unless that mind I see,
What care I how great she be?

Great, or good, or kind, or fair,
I will ne'er the more despair;
If she love me, this believe,
I will die ere she shall grieve
If she slight me when I woo,
I can scorn and let her go;
For if she be not for me,
What care I for whom she be?

JAMES SHIRLEY

1596–1666

The glories of our blood and state
Are shadows, not substantial things;
There is no armor against fate;
Death lays his icy hand on kings:
Sceptre and crown
Must tumble down,
And in the dust be equal made
With the poor crooked scythe and spade.

Some men with swords may reap the field,
And plant fresh laurels where they kill;
But their strong nerves at last must yield;
They tame but one another still:
Early or late,
They stoop to fate,
And must give up their murmuring breath,
When they, pale captives, creep to death.

The garlands wither on your brow,
Then boast no more your mighty deeds;
Upon death's purple altar now,
See where the victor-victim bleeds:

Your heads must come
To the cold tomb;
Only the actions of the just
Smell sweet and blossom in their dust.

SIR HENRY WOTTON

1568–1639

ON HIS MISTRESS, THE QUEEN OF BOHEMIA [2]

You meaner beauties of the night,
That poorly satisfy our eyes
More by your number than your light;
You common people of the skies,
What are you when the sun shall rise?

You curious chanters of the wood,
That warble forth Dame Nature's lays,
Thinking your voices understood
By your weak accents; what's your praise
When Philomel her voice shall raise?

You violets, that first appear,
By your purple mantles known,
Like the proud virgins of the year,
As if the spring were all your own;
What are you when the rose is blown?

So when my Mistress shall be seen
In form and beauty of her mind,
By virtue first, then choice, a Queen,
Tell me, if she were not designed
The eclipse and glory of her kind?

---

[2] *Queen of Bohemia:* Elizabeth, daughter of James I, married to Frederick, Elector Palatine and King of Bohemia.

WILLIAM BROWNE OF TAVISTOCK

1591–1643(?)

ON THE DEATH OF MARIE, COUNTESS OF PEMBROKE (1621)

Underneath this marble hearse
Lies the subject of all verse:
Sidney's sister, Pembroke's mother;
Death, ere thou hast slain another,
Fair, and learn'd, and good as she,
Time shall throw a dart at thee.

RICHARD CORBET, BISHOP OF OXFORD AND NORWICH

1582–1635

A PROPER NEW BALLAD, INTITLED THE FAIRIES' FAREWELL, OR GOD A MERCY WILL

To be sung or whistled, to the tune of *Meadow Brow* by the learned, by the unlearned to the tune of *Fortune.*

Farewell, rewards and fairies,
Good housewives now may say,
For now foul sluts in dairies
Do fare as well as they.
And though they sweep their hearths no less
Than maids were wont to do,
Yet who of late for cleanliness
Finds sixpence in her shoe?

Lament, lament, old abbeys,
The fairies lost command;
They did but change priests' babies,
But some have changed your land,
And all your children sprung from thence
Are now grown Puritans;

Who live as changelings ever since,
For love of your demesnes.

At morning and at evening both
You merry were and glad,
So little care of sleep or sloth
These pretty ladies had;
When Tom came home from labor,
Or Ciss to milking rose,
Then merrily went their tabor,
And nimbly went their toes.

Witness those rings and roundelays
Of theirs, which yet remain,
Were footed in Queen Mary's days
On many a grassy plain;
But since of late Elizabeth,
And later James, came in,
They never danced on any heath
As when the time hath been.

By which we note the fairies
Were of the old profession;
Their songs were Ave Maries,
Their dances were processions;
But now, alas, they all are dead,
Or gone beyond the seas,
Or further from religion fled,
Or else they take their ease.

A tell-tale in their company
They never could endure,
And whoso kept not secretly
Their mirth was punished sure;
It was a just and Christian deed
To pinch such black and blue;
Oh, how the commonwealth doth need
Such justices as you!

Now they have left our quarters,
A register they have,
Who can preserve their charters,
A man both wise and grave;
A hundred of their merry pranks
By one that I could name

Are kept in store; con twenty thanks
To William for the same.

To William Chourne of Staffordshire[3]
Give land and praises due,
Who every meal can mend your cheer
With tales both old and true;
To William all give audience,
And pray ye for his noddle,
For all the fairies' evidence
Were lost, if that were addle.

SIR WILLIAM DAVENANT

1606–1668

The lark now leaves his wat'ry nest,
And climbing shakes his dewy wings;
He takes this window for the east,
And to implore your light he sings:
Awake, awake! the morn will never rise
Till she can dress her beauty at your eyes.

The merchant bows unto the seaman's star,
The plowman from the sun his season takes;
But still the lover wonders what they are
Who look for day before his mistress wakes.
Awake, awake, break through your veils of lawn;
Then draw your curtains, and begin the dawn.

HENRY KING

1592–1669

THE EXEQUY[4]

Accept, thou shrine of my dead saint,
Instead of dirges, this complaint;
And for sweet flowers to crown thy hearse,
Receive a strew of weeping verse
From thy grieved friend, whom thou might'st see
Quite melted into tears for thee.

[3] *William Chourne of Staffordshire:* Corbet's father-in-law.

[4] In memory of the poet's wife.

Dear loss! since thy untimely fate
My task hath been to meditate
On thee, on thee; thou art the book,
The library whereon I look,
Though almost blind. For thee, loved clay,
I languish out, not live, the day,
Using no other exercise
But what I practise with mine eyes;
By which wet glasses I find out
How laxily time creeps about
To one that mourns; this, only this,
My exercise and business is.
So I compute the weary hours
With sighs dissolvèd into showers.

Nor wonder if my time go thus
Backward and most preposterous;
Thou hast benighted me; thy set
This eve of blackness did beget,
Who wast my day, though overcast
Before thou hadst thy noontide passed;
And I remember must in tears,
Thou scarce hadst seen so many years
As day tells hours. By thy clear sun
My love and fortune first did run;
But thou wilt never more appear
Folded within my hemisphere,
Since both thy light and motion
Like a fled star is fall'n and gone;
And 'twixt me and my soul's dear wish
An earth now interposed is,
Which such a strange eclipse doth make
As ne'er was read in almanac.

I could allow thee for a time
To darken me and my sad clime;
Were it a month, a year, or ten,
I would thy exile live till then,
And all that space my mirth adjourn,
So thou wouldst promise to return,
And putting off thy ashy shroud,
At length disperse this sorrow's cloud.

But woe is me! the longest date
Too narrow is to calculate

These empty hopes; never shall I
Be so much blest as to descry
A glimpse of thee, till that day come
Which shall the earth to cinders doom,
And a fierce fever must calcine
The body of this world like thine,
My little world. That fit of fire
Once off, our bodies shall aspire
To our souls' bliss; then we shall rise
And view ourselves with clearer eyes
In that calm region where no night
Can hide us from each other's sight.

Meantime, thou hast her, earth; much good
May my harm do thee. Since it stood
With Heaven's will I might not call
Her longer mine, I give thee all
My short-lived right and interest
In her whom living I loved best;
With a most free and bounteous grief,
I give thee what I could not keep.
Be kind to her, and prithee look
Thou write into thy doomsday book
Each parcel of this rarity
Which in thy casket shrined doth lie.
See that thou make thy reck'ning straight,
And yield her back again by weight;
For thou must audit on thy trust
Each grain and atom of this dust,
As thou wilt answer Him that lent,
Not gave thee, my dear monument.

So close the ground, and 'bout her shade
Black curtains draw; my bride is laid.
Sleep on, my love, in thy cold bed,
Never to be disquieted!
My last good-night! Thou wilt not wake
Till I thy fate shall overtake;
Till age, or grief, or sickness must
Marry my body to that dust
It so much loves, and fill the room
My heart keeps empty in thy tomb.
Stay for me there, I will not fail
To meet thee in that hollow vale.
And think not much of my delay;

I am already on the way,
And follow thee with all the speed
Desire can make, or sorrows breed.
Each minute is a short degree,
And ev'ry hour a step towards thee.
At night when I betake to rest,
Next morn I rise nearer my west
Of life, almost by eight hours' sail,
Than when sleep breathed his drowsy gale.

Thus from the sun my bottom steers,
And my day's compass downward bears;
Nor labor I to stem the tide
Through which to thee I swiftly glide.

'Tis true, with shame and grief I yield,
Thou like the van first took'st the field,
And gotten hath the victory
In thus adventuring to die
Before me, whose more years might crave
A just precedence in the grave.
But hark! my pulse like a soft drum
Beats my approach, tells thee I come;
And slow howe'er my marches be,
I shall at last sit down by thee.

The thought of this bids me go on,
And wait my dissolution
With hope and comfort. Dear, forgive
The crime, I am content to live
Divided, with but half a heart,
Till we shall meet and never part.

SIR JOHN DENHAM

1615–1669

FROM

COOPER'S HILL

My eye, descending from the hill, surveys
Where Thames amongst the wanton valleys strays.
Thames, the most loved of all the ocean's sons,
By his old sire, to his embraces runs,

Hasting to pay his tribute to the sea,
Like mortal life to meet eternity.
Though with those streams he no resemblance hold,
Whose foam is amber and their gravel gold;
His genuine, and less guilty wealth to explore,
Search not his bottom, but survey his shore,
O'er which he kindly spreads his spacious wing,
And hatches plenty for the ensuing spring.

Not then destroys it with too fond a stay,
Like mothers which their infants overlay;
Nor with a sudden and impetuous wave,
Like profuse kings, resumes the wealth he gave.
No unexpected inundations spoil
The mower's hopes, nor mock the plowman's toil;
But God-like his unwearied bounty flows;
First loves to do, then loves the good he does.
Nor are his blessings to his banks confined,
But free and common as the sea or wind;
When he to boast, or to disperse his stores,
Full of the tributes of his grateful shores,
Visits the world, and in his flying towers
Brings home to us, and makes the Indies ours;
Finds wealth where 'tis, bestows it where it wants,
Cities in deserts, woods in cities plants,
So that to us no thing, no place is strange,
While his fair bosom is the world's exchange.
O could I flow like thee, and make thy stream
My great example, as it is my theme!
Though deep, yet clear, though gentle, yet not dull,
Strong without rage, without o'er-flowing full.

Jeremy Taylor

1613–1667

"WHEN the name of Jeremy Taylor is no longer remembered with reverence," wrote Hazlitt, "genius will have become a mockery, and virtue an empty shade." He was a writer of great eloquence and a gifted preacher. Born the son of a Cambridge barber, he had a distinguished career at Cambridge University and at Oxford also. He was a protégé of Archbishop Laud and for a time a chaplain to the King. In 1645 he was captured by Parliamentary troops; after his release he remained in seclusion at Golden Grove, the seat of the Earl of Carbery in Wales, for about ten years. At the Restoration he was made a Bishop in Ireland.

Taylor was a favorite, not only of Hazlitt, but also of others of the romantic period. The praises heaped on him by them seem somewhat extravagant now, but one sensitive modern critic has pointed out that he is a writer "with one gift, and only one, of the highest quality." As Logan Pearsall Smith puts it: "It is, then, this gift of splendid metaphor, of flashing before our eyes pictures which are of the highest poetic beauty, and clothed with a soft radiance of words, which is Jeremy Taylor's special gift and supreme endowment. It is this and almost this alone which makes him a great writer and explains the otherwise almost fantastic comparison of his genius to that of Shakespeare. For lacking as he lacked most of the other qualities of Shakespeare's greatness, Jeremy Taylor nevertheless, as Coleridge pointed out, almost rivals Shakespeare in that supremest gift of the poet, the power of embodying his thought in images of beauty and splendor."

Taylor's masterpiece, *Holy Dying,* is a work in the long tradition of writings on the *ars moriendi,* the art of dying well. It is a fitting companion for the meditations of Sir Thomas Browne and Dr. Donne.

BIBLIOGRAPHY: *The Golden Grove,* ed. Logan Pearsall Smith, Oxford, 1930; W. J. Brown, *Jeremy Taylor,* London, 1925; W. F. Mitchell, *English Pulpit Oratory from Andrewes to Tillotson,* London, 1932.

FROM

THE RULE AND EXERCISES OF HOLY DYING

CHAPTER I, SECTION IV

Consideration of the miseries of man's life

AS our life is very short, so it is very miserable; and therefore it is well it is short. God, in pity to mankind, lest his burden should be insupportable and his nature an intolerable load, hath reduced our state of misery to an abbreviature; and the greater our misery is, the less while it is like to last; the sorrows of a man's spirit being like ponderous weights, which by the greatness of their burden make a swifter motion, and descend into the grave to rest and ease our wearied limbs; for then only we shall sleep quietly, when those fetters are knocked off, which not only bound our souls in prison, but also ate the flesh till the very bones opened the secret garments of their cartilages, discovering their nakedness and sorrow.

Here is no place to sit down in, but you must rise as soon as you are set, for we have gnats in our chambers, and worms in our garden, and spiders and flies in the palaces of the greatest kings. How few men in the world are prosperous! What an infinite number of slaves and beggars, of persecuted and oppressed people, fill all corners of the earth with groans, and heaven itself with weeping prayers and sad remembrances! How many provinces and kingdoms are afflicted by a violent war, or made desolate by popular diseases! Some whole countries are remarked with fatal evils, or periodical sicknesses. Grand Cairo in Egypt feels the plague every three years returning like a quartan ague, and destroying many thousands of persons. All the inhabitants of Arabia the desert are in continual fear of being buried in huge heaps of sand, and therefore dwell in tents and ambulatory houses, or retire to unfruitful mountains, to prolong an uneasy and wilder life. And all the countries round about the Adriatic Sea feel such violent convulsions by tempests and intolerable earthquakes, that sometimes whole cities find a tomb, and every man sinks with his own house made ready to become his monument, and his bed is crushed into the disorders of a grave. Was not all the world drowned at one deluge and breach of the divine anger; and shall not all the world again be destroyed by fire? Are there not many thousands that die every night, and that groan and weep sadly every day? But what shall we think of that great evil which for the sins of men God hath suffered to possess the greatest part of mankind? Most of the men that are now alive, or that have been living for many ages, are Jews, Heathens, or Turks; and God was pleased to suffer a base epileptic person, a villain and a vicious, to set up a religion which hath filled all the nearer parts of Asia, and much of Africa, and some part of Europe; so that the greatest number of men and women born in so many kingdoms and provinces are infallibly made Mahometans, strangers and enemies to Christ by whom alone we can be saved. This consideration is extremely sad, when we remember how universal and how great an evil it is, that so many millions of sons and daughters are born to enter into the possession of devils to eternal ages. These evils are miseries of great parts of mankind, and we cannot easily consider more particularly the evils which happen to us, being the inseparable affections or incidents to the whole nature of man.

We find that all the women in the world are either born for barrenness, or the pains of childbirth, and yet this is one of our greatest blessings; but such indeed are the blessings of this world, we cannot be well with nor without many things. Perfumes make our heads ache, roses prick our fingers, and in our very blood, where our life dwells, is the scene under which nature acts many sharp fevers and heavy sicknesses. It were too sad if I should tell how many persons are afflicted with evil spirits, with spectres and illusions of the night; and that huge multitudes of men and women live upon man's flesh; nay, worse yet, upon the sins of men, upon the sins of their sons and of their daughters, and they pay their souls down for the bread they eat, buying this day's meal with the price of the last night's sin.

Or if you please in charity to visit a hospital, which is indeed a map of the whole world, there you shall see the effects of Adam's sin, and the ruins of human nature; bodies laid up in heaps like the bones of a destroyed town, *homines precarii spiritus et male haerentis,* men whose souls seem to be borrowed, and are kept there by art and the force of medicine, whose miseries are so great that few people have charity or humanity enough to visit them, fewer have the heart to dress them, and we pity them in civility or with a transient prayer, but we do not feel their sorrows by the mercies of a religious pity; and therefore as we leave their sorrows in many degrees unrelieved and uneased, so we contract by our unmercifulness a guilt by which ourselves become liable to the same calamities. Those many that need pity, and those infinities of people that refuse to pity, are miserable upon a several charge, but yet they almost make up all mankind.

All wicked men are in love with that which entangles them in huge varieties of troubles; they are slaves to the worst of masters, to sin and to the devil, to a passion, and to an imperious woman. Good men are for ever prosecuted, and God chastises every son whom he receives, and whatsoever is easy is trifling and worth nothing, and whatsoever is excellent is not to be obtained without labor and sorrow; and the conditions and states of men that are free from great cares are such as have in them nothing rich and orderly, and those that have are stuck full of thorns and trouble. Kings are full of care; and learned men in all ages have been observed to be very poor, *et honestas miserias accusant,* "they complain of their honest miseries."

But these evils are notorious and confessed; even they also whose felicity men stare at and admire, besides their splendor and the sharpness of their light, will with their appendant sorrows wring a tear from the most resolved eye; for not only the winter quarter is full of storms and cold and darkness, but the beauteous spring hath blasts and sharp frosts, the fruitful teeming summer is melted with heat, and burnt with the kisses of the sun her friend, and choked with dust, and the rich autumn is full of sickness; and we are weary of that which we enjoy, because sorrow is its biggest portion: and when we remember that upon the fairest face is placed one of the worst sinks of the body, the nose, we may use it not only as a mortification to the pride of beauty, but as an allay to the fairest outside of condition which any of the sons and daughters of Adam do possess. For look upon kings and conquerors: I will not tell that many of them fall into the condition of servants, and their subjects rule over them, and stand upon the ruins of their families, and that to such persons the sorrow is bigger than usually happens in smaller fortunes; but let us suppose them still conquerors, and see what a goodly purchase they get by all their pains, and amazing fears, and continual dangers. They carry their arms beyond Ister, and pass the Euphrates, and bind the Germans with the bounds of the river Rhine: I speak in the style of the Roman greatness; for nowadays the biggest fortune swells not beyond the limits of a petty province or two, and a hill confines the progress of their prosperity, or a river checks it; but whatsoever tempts the pride and vanity of ambitious persons is not so big as the smallest star which we see scattered in disorder and unregarded upon the pavement and floor of heaven. And if we would suppose the pismires had but our understandings, they also would have the method of a man's greatness and divide their little molehills into provinces and exarchates; and if they also grew as vicious and as miserable, one of their princes would lead an army out and kill his neighbor ants, that he might reign over the next handful of a turf. But then if we consider at what price and with what felicity all this is purchased, the sting of the painted snake will quickly appear, and the fairest of their fortunes will properly enter into this account of human infelicities.

We may guess at it by the constitution of Augustus's fortune, who struggled for his power first with the Roman citizens, then with Brutus and Cassius and all the fortune of the republic; then with his colleague Mark Antony; then with his kindred and nearest relatives; and after he was wearied with slaughter of the Romans, before he could sit down and rest in his imperial chair, he was forced to carry armies into Macedonia, Galatia, beyond Euphrates, Rhine, and Danubius; and when he dwelt at home in greatness and within the circles of a mighty power, he hardly escaped the sword of the Egnatii, of Lepidus, Caepio, and Murena; and after he had entirely reduced the felicity and grandeur into his own family, his daughter, his only child, conspired with many of the young nobility, and being joined with adulterous complications, as with an impious sacrament, they affrighted and destroyed the fortune of the old man, and wrought him more sorrow than all the troubles that were hatched in the baths and beds of Egypt between Antony and Cleopatra. This was the greatest fortune that the world had then or ever since, and therefore we cannot expect it to be better in a less prosperity.

The prosperity of this world is so infinitely soured with the overflowing of evils, that he is counted the most happy who hath the fewest; all conditions being evil and miserable, they are only distinguished by the number of calamities. The collector of the Roman and foreign examples, when he had reckoned two-and-twenty instances of great fortunes, every one of which had been allayed with great variety of evils; in all his reading or experience, he could tell but of two who had been famed for an entire prosperity, Quintus Metellus, and Gyges the king of Lydia; and yet concerning the one of them he tells that his felicity was so inconsiderable (and yet it was the bigger of the two) that the oracle said that Aglaus Sophidius the poor Arcadian shepherd was more happy than he, that is, he had fewer troubles; for so indeed we are to reckon the pleasures of this life; the limit of our joy is the absence of some degrees of sorrow, and he that hath the least of this, is the most prosperous person. But then we must look for prosperity not in palaces or courts of princes, not in the tents of conquerors, or in the gaieties of fortunate and prevailing sinners; but something rather in the cottages of honest, innocent, and contented persons, whose mind is no bigger than their fortune, nor their virtue less than their security. As for others, whose fortune looks bigger, and allures fools to follow it like the wandering fires of the night, till they run into rivers or are broken upon rocks with staring and running after them, they are all in the condition of Marius, than whose condition nothing was more constant, and nothing more mutable; if we reckon them amongst the happy, they are the most happy men; if we reckon them amongst the miserable, they are the most miserable. For just as is a man's condition, great or little, so is the state of his misery; all have their share; but kings and princes, great generals and consuls, rich men and mighty, as they have the biggest business and the biggest charge, and are answerable to God for the greatest accounts, so they have the biggest trouble; that the uneasiness of their appendage may divide the good and evil of the world, making the poor man's fortune as eligible as the greatest; and also restraining the vanity of man's spirit, which a great fortune is apt to swell from a vapor to a bubble; but God in mercy hath mingled wormwood with their wine, and so restrained the drunkenness and follies of prosperity.

Man never hath one day to himself of entire peace from the things of the world, but either something troubles him, or nothing satisfies him, or his very fulness swells him and makes him breathe short upon his bed. Men's joys are troublesome, and besides that the fear of losing them takes away the present pleasure, and a man hath need of another felicity to preserve this, they are also wavering and full of trepidation, not only from their inconstant nature, but from their weak foundation: they arise from vanity, and they dwell upon ice, and they converse with the wind, and they have the wings of a bird, and are serious but as the resolutions of a child, commenced by chance, and managed by folly, and proceed by inadvertency, and end in vanity and forgetfulness. So that as Livius Drusus said of himself, he never had any play-days or days of quiet when he was a boy, for he was troublesome and busy, a restless and unquiet man; the same may every man observe to be true of himself; he is always restless and uneasy, he dwells upon the waters, and leans upon thorns, and lays his head upon a sharp stone.

Richard Crashaw

1612–1649

RICHARD CRASHAW was the son of a Puritan zealot, William Crashaw, a preacher at the Temple and a fierce opponent of the Roman Catholic Church, to which his poet son was to become a convert. William Crashaw died when his son was fourteen, and the boy was taken under the protection of two lawyers, Sir Henry Yelverton and Sir Randolph Carew. He was sent to school at the Charterhouse in 1629 and won an exhibition to Peterhouse, Cambridge, in 1631. At both school and university his environment was royalist and High Church. He was graduated B.A. in 1634 and became a fellow of Peterhouse soon after. This college was famous among all those at Cambridge for what its critics called its "Popish superstitious practices."

Crashaw was a frequent visitor to the nearby community of Little Gidding, where his friend Nicholas Ferrar led his family in a religious life of remarkable piety. By 1639 Crashaw was in orders and was curate of Little St. Mary's, Cambridge, a Peterhouse living adjoining the college. There he maintained an ascetic discipline and spent many nights "watching," in a holy devotion similar to that practiced at Little Gidding.

Among Crashaw's friends at Cambridge were the poets Abraham Cowley and Joseph Beaumont, the latter of whom introduced to Cambridge the lore of the Spanish mystic St. Teresa (1515–1582). Crashaw had written religious verse ever since his school days, but the new stream of the Counter Reformation and the influence of the Jesuit poet Strada and especially of Giambattista Marino (1569–1625) determined the direction of his poetic development.

In 1642 Crashaw with other Cambridge fellows subcribed to the support of the King; in 1643 Cromwell seized Cambridge, and in 1644 Crashaw left Cambridge for the continent. In 1645 he was received into the Roman Catholic Church and went to Paris to the court of Queen Henrietta Maria. He suffered hardship during this period and later, but for a time he enjoyed the patronage of Susan Villiers, Countess of Denbigh, and indeed of the Queen, who wrote to the Pope in Crashaw's behalf when he went to Rome in 1646. The poet died in 1649 at Loreto.

Crashaw is the best representative in English of the baroque style in literary art. His poetry represents a remarkable equivalent of the famous baroque sculpture of Bernini, the "Ecstasy of St. Teresa" in Santa Maria della Vittoria in Rome. The characteristics of baroque art—a swelling, flamboyant movement which presses against the boundaries of the space, and, if we consider baroque to be the art of the Counter Reformation, a transfer of the stimuli of earthly passions to sacred subjects so that "the five senses are made portals to heaven" —these are the salient traits of Crashaw's verse.

Bibliography: *Crashaw's Poetical Works,* ed. L. C. Martin, Oxford, 1927; Mario Praz, *Secentismo e Marinismo in Inghilterra,* Firenze, 1925; Ruth Wallerstein, *Richard Crashaw: A Study in Style and Poetic Development,* Madison, 1935; Austin Warren, *Richard Crashaw, A Study in Baroque Sensibility,* University, La., 1939; Helen C. White, *The Metaphysical Poets,* New York, 1936; Joan Bennett, *Four Metaphysical Poets,* Cambridge, 1934; R. M. Adams, "Taste and Bad Taste in Metaphysical Poetry: Richard Crashaw and Dylan Thomas," *Hudson Review,* VIII (1955), 61–77. R. Wellek, "The Concept of Baroque in Literary Scholarship," *Journal of Aesthetics,* V (1946), 77–109.

WISHES

Whoe'er she be,
That not impossible she
That shall command my heart and me;

Where'er she lie,
Locked up from mortal eye,
In shady leaves of destiny,

Till that ripe birth
Of studied fate stand forth,
And teach her fair steps to our earth;

Till that divine
Idea take a shrine
Of crystal flesh through which to shine;

Meet you her, my wishes,
Bespeak her to my blisses,
And be ye called my absent kisses.

I wish her beauty,
That owes not all his duty
To gaudy tire,[1] or glist'ring shoe-tie;

Something more than
Taffeta or tissue can,
Or rampant feather, or rich fan;

More than the spoil
Of shop, or silkworm's toil,
Or a bought blush, or a set smile;

A face that's best
By its own beauty dressed,
And can alone command the rest;

---

[1] *tire:* attire, dress.

A face made up
Out of no other shop
Than what nature's white hand sets ope;

A cheek where youth
And blood, with pen of truth
Write what the reader sweetly ru'th;

A cheek where grows
More than a morning rose,
Which to no box his being owes;

Lips where all day
A lover's kiss may play,
Yet carry nothing thence away;

Looks that oppress
Their richest tires, but dress
And clothe their simplest nakedness.

Eyes that displace
The neighbor diamond, and out-face
That sunshine by their own sweet grace;

Tresses that wear
Jewels but to declare
How much themselves more precious are;

Whose native ray
Can tame the wanton day
Of gems, that in their bright shades play—

Each ruby there,
Or pearl that dare appear,
Be its own blush, be its own tear;

A well-tamed heart,
For whose more noble smart
Love may be long choosing a dart;

Eyes that bestow
Full quivers on love's bow,
Yet pay less arrows than they owe;

Smiles that can warm
The blood, yet teach a charm,
That chastity shall take no harm;

Blushes that bin
The burnish of no sin,
Nor flames of aught too hot within;

Joys that confess
Virtue their mistress,
And have no other head to dress;

Fears, fond and flight,
As the coy bride's, when night
First does the longing lover right;

Tears, quickly fled
And vain, as those are shed
For a dying maidenhead;

Days that need borrow
No part of their good morrow
From a fore-spent night of sorrow;

Days that, in spite
Of darkness, by the light
Of a clear mind are day all night;

Nights sweet as they
Made short by lovers' play,
Yet long by the absence of the day;

Life that dares send
A challenge to his end,
And, when it comes, say, "Welcome, friend!"

Sidneian showers
Of sweet discourse,[2] whose powers
Can crown old winter's head with flowers;

Soft silken hours,
Open suns, shady bowers;
'Bove all, nothing within that lowers;

---

[2] *Sidneian . . . discourse:* the courtly conversations in Sidney's *Arcadia.*

Whate'er delight
Can make day's forehead bright,
Or give down to the wings of night.

In her whole frame
Have nature all the name,
Art and ornament the shame.

Her flattery,
Picture and poesy:
Her counsel her own virtue be.

I wish her store
Of worth may leave her poor
Of wishes, and I wish—no more.

Now if time knows
That her whose radiant brows
Weave them a garland of my vows;

Her whose just bays
My future hopes can raise,
A trophy to her present praise;

Her that dares be
What these lines wish to see:
I seek no further—it is she.

'Tis she, and here
Lo! I unclothe and clear
My wishes' cloudy character.

May she enjoy it
Whose merit dare apply it,
But modesty dares still deny it.

Such worth as this is
Shall fix my flying wishes,
And determine them to kisses.

Let her full glory,
My fancies, fly before ye!
Be ye my fictions, but her story.

ON MARRIAGE

I WOULD be married, but I'd have no wife:
I would be married to a single life.

EPITHALAMIUM

COME, virgin tapers of pure wax,
  Made in the hive of Love, all white
As snow, and yet as cold, where lacks
  Hymen's holy heat and light;
    Where blooming kisses
      Their beds yet keep
    And steep their blisses
      In rosy sleep;
Where sister buds yet wanting brothers
Kiss their own lips in lieu of others;
Help me to mourn a matchless maidenhead
          That now is dead.

A fine, thin negative thing it was,
  A nothing with a dainty name
Which pruned her plumes in Self-Love's glass
  Made up of fancy and fond fame;
    Within the shade
      Of its own wing
    It sat and played
      A self-crowned king;
A froward flower whose peevish pride
Within itself itself did hide,
Flying all fingers, and even thinking much
          Of its own touch.

This bird indeed the phoenix was
  Late chased by Love's revengeful arrows,
Whose wars now left the wonted pass
  As spared the little lives of sparrows
    To hunt this fool
      Whose froward pride
    Love's noble school
      And courts denied,

And froze the fruit of fair desire
Which flourisheth in mutual fire
'Gainst Nature, who 'mong all the webs she spun
Ne'er wove a nun.

She, of Cupid's shafts afraid
Left her own balm-breathing East,
And in a western bosom made
A softer and a sweeter nest;
There did she rest
In the sweet shade
Of a soft breast
Whose beauties made
Thames oft stand still and lend a glass
While in her own she saw Heaven's face
And sent him full of her fair name's report
To Thetis' court.

And now poor Love was at a stand:
The crystal castle which she kept
Was proof against the proudest hand;
There in safest hold she slept;
His shafts' expense
Left there no smart,
But bounding thence
Broached his own heart;
At length a fort he did devise
Built in noble Brampston's[3] eyes,
And aiming thence, this matchless maidenhead
Was soon found dead.

Yet Love in death did wait upon her
Granting leave she should expire
In her fumes and have the honor
T'exhale in flames of his own fire,
Her funeral pile
The marriage bed;
In a sighed smile
She vanished.
So rich a dress of death ne'er famed
The cradles where her kindred flamed;
So sweet her mother-phoenixes of the East
Ne'er spiced their nest.

[3] *Brampston:* probably Sir John Bramston the younger (1611–1700), who married Alice Abdy in 1635.

With many pretty, peevish trials
  Of angry yielding, faint denyings,
Melting Noes and mild denials,
  Dying lives and short-lived dyings,
    With doubtful eyes,
      Half smiles, half tears;
    With trembling joys
      And jocund fears,
Twixt the pretty twilight strife
Of dying maid and dawning wife,
Twixt rain and sunshine, this sweet maidenhead
        Alas is dead.

Happy he whose wakeful joys
  Kept the prize of this rich loss;
Happy she whose watery eyes
  Kiss no worse a weeping cross;
    Thrice happy he
      Partakes her store,
    Thrice happy she
      Hath still the more.
Think not sweet bride, that faint shower slakes
The fires he from thy fair eyes takes;
Thy drops are salt, and while they think to tame
        Sharpen his flame.

Blest bridegroom, ere the rain be laid,
  Use good weather while it proves;
Those drops that wash away the maid
  Shall water your warm-planted loves;
    Fair youth, make haste
      Ere it be dry:
    The sweet brine taste
      From her moist eye;
Thy lips will find such dew as this is
Best season for a lover's kisses;
And those thy morning stars will better please
        Bathed in those seas.

Nor may thy vine, fair oak, embrace thee
  With ivy arms and empty wishes,
But with full bosom interlace thee
  And reach her clusters to thy kisses;
    Safe may she rest
      Her laden boughs

On thy firm breast
And fill thy vows
Up to the brim, till she make even
Their full tops with the fair-eyed heaven,
And heaven to gild those glorious heroes' birth
Stoop and kiss earth.

Long may this happy heaven-tied band
Exercise its most holy art,
Keeping her heart within his hand,
Keeping his hand upon her heart;
But from her eyes
Feel he no charms;
Find she no joy
But in his arms;
May each maintain a well-fledged nest
Of winged loves in either's breast;
Be each of them a mutual sacrifice
Of either's eyes.

May their whole life a sweet song prove
Set to two well-composed parts
By music's noblest master, Love,
Played on the strings of both their hearts;
Whose mutual sound
May ever meet
In a just round,
Not short though sweet;
Long may heaven listen to the song
And think it short though it be long;
Oh, prove't a well-set song indeed, which shows
Sweet'st in the close!

THE FLAMING HEART

Upon the book and picture of the seraphical Saint Teresa, as she is usually expressed with a seraphim beside her.

O HEART! the equal poise of love's both parts,
Big alike with wounds and darts,
Live in these conquering leaves; live all the same,
And walk through all tongues one triumphant flame;
Live here, great heart, and love and die and kill,

And bleed and wound, and yield and conquer still.
Let this immortal life, where'er it comes,
Walk in a crowd of loves and martyrdoms.
Let mystic deaths wait on 't, and wise souls be
The love-slain witnesses of this life of thee:
O sweet incendiary! show here thy art,
Upon this carcass of a hard cold heart;
Let all thy scattered shafts of light, that play
Among the leaves of thy large books of day,
Combined against this breast, at once break in
And take away from me myself and sin!
This gracious robbery shall thy bounty be,
And my best fortunes such fair spoils of me.
O thou undaunted daughter of desires!
By all thy dower of lights and fires;
By all the eagle in thee, all the dove;
By all thy lives and deaths of love;
By thy large draughts of intellectual day,
And by thy thirsts of love more large than they;
By all thy brim-filled bowls of fierce desire,
By thy last morning's draught of liquid fire;
By the full kingdom of that final kiss
That seized thy parting soul, and sealed thee His;
By all the heav'ns thou hast in Him,
Fair sister of the seraphim,
By all of Him we have in thee,
Leave nothing of myself in me!
Let me so read thy life that I
Unto all life of mine may die!

A HYMN TO THE NAME AND HONOR OF THE ADMIRABLE SAINT TERESA

Foundress of the Reformation of the Discalced Carmelites, both men and women. A woman for angelical height of speculation, for masculine courage of performance, more than a woman; who yet a child outran maturity, and durst plot a martyrdom.

Love, thou art absolute sole lord
Of life and death. To prove the word,
We'll now appeal to none of all
Those thy old soldiers, great and tall,

Ripe men of martyrdom, that could reach down
With strong arms their triumphant crown;
Such as could with lusty breath
Speak loud into the face of death
Their great Lord's glorious name; to none
Of those whose spacious bosoms spread a throne
For Love at large to fill. Spare blood and sweat,
And see Him take a private seat,
Making His mansion in the mild
And milky soul of a soft child.
  Scarce has she learnt to lisp the name
Of martyr, yet she thinks it shame
Life should so long play with that breath
Which spent can buy so brave a death.
She never undertook to know
What death with love should have to do;
Nor has she e'er yet understood
Why to show love she should shed blood;
Yet though she cannot tell you why,
She can love and she can die.
  Scarce has she blood enough to make
A guilty sword blush for her sake;
Yet has she a heart dares hope to prove
How much less strong is death than love.
  Be love but there, let poor six years
Be posed with the maturest fears
Man trembles at, you straight shall find
Love knows no nonage, nor the mind.
'Tis love, not years or limbs, that can
Make the martyr or the man.
  Love touched her heart, and lo it beats
High, and burns with such brave heats,
Such thirsts to die, as dares drink up
A thousand cold deaths in one cup.
Good reason, for she breathes all fire;
Her weak breast heaves with strong desire
Of what she may with fruitless wishes
Seek for amongst her mother's kisses.
  Since 'tis not to be had at home,
She'll travel to a martyrdom.
No home for hers confesses she
But where she may a martyr be.
  She'll to the Moors and trade with them
For this unvalued diadem.
She'll offer them her dearest breath,

With Christ's name in 't, in change for death.
She'll bargain with them, and will give
Them God, teach them how to live
In Him; or, if they this deny,
For Him she'll teach them how to die.
So shall she leave amongst them sown
Her Lord's blood, or at least her own.
 Farewell then, all the world, adieu!
Teresa is no more for you.
Farewell, all pleasures, sports, and joys,
Never till now esteemed toys;
Farewell, whatever dear may be,
Mother's arms, or father's knee;
Farewell house and farewell home,
She's for the Moors and martyrdom!
 Sweet, not so fast! lo, thy fair Spouse
Whom thou seek'st with so swift vows
Calls thee back, and bids thee come
T' embrace a milder martyrdom.
 Blest powers forbid thy tender life
Should bleed upon a barbarous knife;
Or some base hand have power to rase
Thy breast's chaste cabinet, and uncase
A soul kept there so sweet; oh no,
Wise Heav'n will never have it so.
Thou art Love's victim, and must die
A death more mystical and high;
Into Love's arms thou shalt let fall
A still surviving funeral.
His is the dart must make the death
Whose stroke shall taste thy hallowed breath;
A dart thrice dipped in that rich flame
Which writes thy Spouse's radiant name
Upon the roof of heaven, where aye
It shines, and with a sovereign ray
Beats bright upon the burning faces
Of souls which in that name's sweet graces
Find everlasting smiles. So rare,
So spiritual, pure, and fair
Must be th' immortal instrument
Upon whose choice point shall be sent
A life so loved; and that there be
Fit executioners for thee,
The fair'st and first-born sons of fire,

Blest seraphim, shall leave their choir
And turn Love's soldiers, upon thee
To exercise their archery.
  Oh, how oft shalt thou complain
Of a sweet and subtle pain,
Of intolerable joys,
Of a death, in which who dies
Loves his death and dies again,
And would for ever so be slain,
And lives and dies, and knows not why
To live, but that he thus may never leave to die!
  How kindly will thy gentle heart
Kiss the sweetly killing dart!
And close in his embraces keep
Those delicious wounds, that weep
Balsam to heal themselves with. Thus
When these thy deaths, so numerous,
Shall all at last die into one,
And melt thy soul's sweet mansion;
Like a soft lump of incense, hasted
By too hot a fire, and wasted
Into perfuming clouds, so fast
Shalt thou exhale to heaven at last
In a resolving sigh; and then,
Oh, what? Ask not the tongues of men;
Angels cannot tell; suffice,
Thyself shall feel thine own full joys
And hold them fast for ever. There,
So soon as thou shalt first appear,
The moon of maiden stars, thy white
Mistress, attended by such bright
Souls as thy shining self, shall come
And in her first ranks make thee room;
Where 'mongst her snowy family
Immortal welcomes wait for thee.
Oh, what delight when revealed life shall stand
And teach thy lips heaven with his hand,
On which thou now mayst to thy wishes
Heap up thy consecrated kisses.
What joys shall seize thy soul when she,
Bending her blessed eyes on thee,
Those second smiles of heaven, shall dart
Her mild rays through thy melting heart!
  Angels, thy old friends, there shall greet thee,

Glad at their own home now to meet thee.
  All thy good works which went before
And waited for thee at the door
Shall own thee there, and all in one
Weave a constellation
Of crowns, with which the King, thy Spouse,
Shall build up thy triumphant brows.
  All thy old woes shall now smile on thee,
And thy pains sit bright upon thee;
All thy sorrows here shall shine,
All thy sufferings be divine;
Tears shall take comfort and turn gems,
And wrongs repent to diadems.
Even thy deaths shall live, and new
Dress the soul that erst they slew;
Thy wounds shall blush to such bright scars
As keep account of the Lamb's wars.
  Those rare works where thou shalt leave writ
Love's noble history, with wit
Taught thee by none but Him, while here
They feed our souls, shall clothe thine there.
Each heavenly word by whose hid flame
Our hard hearts shall strike fire, the same
Shall flourish on thy brows, and be
Both fire to us and flame to thee,
Whose light shall live bright in thy face
By glory, in our hearts by grace.
  Thou shalt look round about and see
Thousands of crowned souls throng to be
Themselves thy crown; sons of thy vows,
The virgin-births with which thy sovereign Spouse
Made fruitful thy fair soul, go now
And with them all about thee, bow
To Him. "Put on," He'll say, "put on,
My rosy love, that, thy rich zone
Sparkling with the sacred flames
Of thousand souls whose happy names
Heav'n keeps upon thy score. Thy bright
Life brought them first to kiss the light
That kindled them to stars." And so
Thou with the Lamb, thy Lord, shalt go,
And whereso'er He sets His white
Steps, walk with Him those ways of light
Which who in death would live to see
Must learn in life to die like thee.

SAINT MARY MAGDALENE; OR, THE WEEPER

Lo! where a wounded heart with bleeding eyes conspire,
Is she a flaming fountain, or a weeping fire?

Hail, sister springs!
Parents of silver-footed rills!
Ever-bubbling things!
Thawing crystal! snowy hills,
Still spending, never spent! I mean
Thy fair eyes, sweet Magdalene!

Heavens thy fair eyes be,
Heavens of ever-falling stars;
'Tis seed-time still with thee,
And stars thou sow'st whose harvest dares
Promise the earth to countershine
Whatever makes heav'n's forehead fine.

But we're deceivèd all.
Stars indeed they are, too true,
For they but seem to fall,
As heaven's other spangles do.
It is not for our earth and us
To shine in things so precious.

Upwards thou dost weep;
Heaven's bosom drinks the gentle stream;
Where the milky rivers creep,
Thine floats above and is the cream.
Waters above th' heavens, what they be
We are taught best by thy tears and thee.

Every morn from hence
A brisk cherub something sips,
Whose sacred influence
Adds sweetness to his sweetest lips;
Then to his music, and his song
Tastes of this breakfast all day long.

Not in the evening's eyes,
When they red with weeping are
For the sun that dies,
Sits sorrow with a face so fair;
Nowhere but here did ever meet
Sweetness so sad, sadness so sweet.

When sorrow would be seen
In her brightest majesty,
For she is a queen,
Then is she dressed by none but thee;
Then, and only then, she wears
Her proudest pearls; I mean thy tears.

The dew no more will weep,
The primrose's pale cheek to deck;
The dew no more will sleep
Nuzzled in the lily's neck;
Much rather would it be thy tear,
And leave them both to tremble here.

There's no need at all
That the balsam-sweating bough
So coyly should let fall
His med'cinable tears, for now
Nature hath learnt to extract a dew
More sovereign and sweet from you.

Yet let the poor drops weep,
Weeping is the ease of woe;
Softly let them creep,
Sad that they are vanquished so;
They, though to others no relief,
Balsam may be for their own grief.

Such the maiden gem
By the purpling vine put on,
Peeps from her parent stem
And blushes at the bridegroom sun;
This wat'ry blossom of thy eyne,
Ripe, will make the richer wine.

When some new bright guest
Takes up among the stars a room,
And heaven will make a feast,

    Angels with crystal vials come
And draw from these full eyes of thine
Their Master's water, their own wine.

      Golden though he be,
    Golden Tagus murmurs though;
    Were his way by thee,
    Content and quiet he would go;
So much more rich would he esteem
Thy silver, than his golden stream.

      Well does the May that lies
    Smiling in thy cheeks confess
    The April in thine eyes;
    Mutual sweetness they express:
No April e'er lent kinder showers,
Nor May returned more faithful flowers.

      O cheeks! beds of chaste loves
    By your own showers seasonably dashed;
    Eyes! nests of milky doves
    In your own wells decently washed;
O wit of Love! that thus could place
Fountain and garden in one face.

      O sweet contest, of woes
   With loves, of tears with smiles disputing!
    O fair and friendly foes,
    Each other kissing and confuting!
While rain and sunshine, cheeks and eyes;
Close in kind contrarieties.

      But can these fair floods be
    Friends with the bosom fires that fill thee?
    Can so great flames agree
    Eternal tears should thus distil thee?
O floods, O fires, O suns, O showers!
Mixed and made friends by Love's sweet powers.

      'Twas his well-pointed dart
    That digged these wells and dressed this vine;
    And taught the wounded heart
    The way into these weeping eyne.
Vain loves, avaunt! bold hands, forbear!
The Lamb hath dipped His white foot here.

And now where'er He strays
Among the Galilean mountains,
Or more unwelcome ways,
He's followed by two faithful fountains,
Two walking baths, two weeping motions,
Portable and compendious oceans.

O thou, thy Lord's fair store!
In thy so rich and rare expenses,
Even when He showed most poor,
He might provoke the wealth of princes;
What prince's wanton'st pride e'er could
Wash with silver, wipe with gold?

Who is that King, but He
Who call'st His crown to be called thine,
That thus can boast to be
Waited on by a wand'ring mine,
A voluntary mint, that strows
Warm silver showers where'er He goes!

O precious prodigal!
Fair spendthrift of thyself! thy measure,
Merciless love, is all,
Even to the last pearl in thy treasure;
All places, times, and objects be
Thy tears' sweet opportunity.

Does the day-star rise?
Still thy tears do fall and fall.
Does day close his eyes?
Still the fountain weeps for all.
Let night or day do what they will,
Thou hast thy task, thou weepest still.

Does thy song lull the air?
Thy falling tears keep faithful time.
Does thy sweet-breathed prayer
Up in clouds of incense climb?
Still at each sigh, that is, each stop,
A bead, that is, a tear, does drop.

At these thy weeping gates,
Watching their wat'ry motion,
Each winged moment waits,

Takes his tear and gets him gone;
By thine eye's tinct ennobled thus,
Time lays him up; he's precious.

Not "So long she lived"
Shall thy tomb report of thee,
But "So long she grieved";
Thus must we date thy memory.
Others by moments, months, and years,
Measure their ages, thou by tears.

So do perfumes expire;
So sigh tormented sweets, oppressed
With proud unpitying fire;
Such tears the suff'ring rose that's vexed
With ungentle flames does shed,
Sweating in a too warm bed.

Say, ye bright brothers,
The fugitive sons of those fair eyes,
Your fruitful mothers,
What make you here? What hopes can 'tice
You to be born? What cause can borrow
You from those nests of noble sorrow?

Whither away so fast?
For sure the sordid earth
Your sweetness cannot taste,
Nor does the dust deserve your birth.
Sweet, whither haste you then? O say
Why you trip so fast away!

"We go not to seek
The darlings of Aurora's bed,
The rose's modest cheek,
Nor the violet's humble head;
Though the field's eyes, too, weepers be
Because they want such tears as we.

"Much less mean we to trace
The fortune of inferior gems,
Preferred to some proud face,
Or perched upon feared diadems:
Crowned heads are toys. We go to meet
A worthy object, our Lord's feet."

CHARITAS NIMIA; OR, THE DEAR BARGAIN

Lord, what is man? why should he cost Thee
So dear? what had his ruin lost Thee?
Lord, what is man, that Thou hast over-bought
So much a thing of naught?

Love is too kind, I see, and can
Make but a simple merchant-man.
'Twas for such sorry merchandise
Bold painters have put out his eyes.

Alas, sweet Lord! what were't to Thee
If there were no such worms as we?
Heaven ne'er the less still heaven would be,
Should mankind dwell.
In the deep hell.
What have his woes to do with Thee?

Let him go weep
O'er his own wounds;
Seraphims will not sleep,
Nor spheres let fall their faithful rounds.

Still would the youthful spirit sing,
And still Thy spacious palace ring;
Still would those beauteous ministers of light
Burn all as bright,
And bow their flaming heads before Thee;
Still thrones and dominations would adore Thee.
Still would those ever-wakeful sons of fire
Keep warm Thy praise
Both nights and days,
And teach Thy loved name to their noble lyre.

Let froward dust then do its kind,
And give itself for sport to the proud wind.
Why should a piece of peevish clay plead shares

In the eternity of Thy old cares?
Why shouldst Thou bow Thy awful breast to see
What mine own madnesses have done with me?

Should not the king still keep his throne
Because some desperate fool's undone?
Or will the world's illustrious eyes
Weep for every worm that dies?

    Will the gallant sun
    E'er the less glorious run?
Will he hang down his golden head,
Or e'er the sooner seek his western bed,
    Because some foolish fly
    Grows wanton, and will die?

If I were lost in misery,
What was it to Thy heaven and Thee?
    What was it to Thy precious blood
If my foul heart called for a flood?

What if my faithless soul and I
    Would needs fall in
    With guilt and sin;
What did the Lamb that He should die?
What did the Lamb that He should need,
When the wolf sins, Himself to bleed?

    If my base lust
Bargained with death and well-beseeming dust,
    Why should the white
    Lamb's bosom write
    The purple name
    Of my sin's shame?
Why should His unstained breast make good
My blushes with His own heart-blood?

O my Saviour, make me see
How dearly Thou has paid for me;
That, lost again, my life may prove,
As then in death, so now in love.

TO THE NOBLEST AND BEST OF LADIES THE COUNTESS OF DENBIGH

Persuading her to resolution in religion, and to render herself without further delay into the communion of the Catholic Church

WHAT heaven-entreated heart is this,
Stands trembling at the gate of bliss,
Holds fast the door, yet dares not venture
Fairly to open it, and enter;
Whose definition is a doubt
'Twixt life and death, 'twixt in and out?
Say, lingering fair, why comes the birth
Of your brave soul so slowly forth?
Plead your pretenses, Oh, you strong
In weakness, why you choose so long
In labor of yourself to lie,
Not daring quite to live nor die.
Ah, linger not, loved soul! A slow
And late consent was a long no;
Who grants at last, long time tried
And did his best to have denied.
What magic bolts, what mystic bars
Maintain the will in these strange wars!
What fatal, yet fantastic, bands
Keep the free heart from its own hands!
So when the year takes cold we see
Poor waters their own prisoners be;
Fettered and locked up fast they lie
In a sad self-captivity.
The astonished nymphs their flood's strange fate deplore,
To see themselves their own severer shore.
Thou that alone canst thaw this cold,
And fetch the heart from its stronghold,
Almighty Love! end this long war,
And of a meteor make a star.
Oh, fix this fair indefinite,
And 'mongst thy shafts of sovereign light
Choose out that sure decisive dart
Which has the key of this close heart,
Knows all the corners of 't, and can control

The self-shut cabinet of an unsearched soul.
Oh, let it be at last Love's hour;
Raise this tall trophy of thy power;
Come once the conquering way, not to confute
But kill this rebel-word, "irresolute,"
That so, in spite of all this peevish strength
Of weakness, she may write, "Resolved at length."
Unfold at length, unfold, fair flower,
And use the season of Love's shower;
Meet His well-meaning wounds, wise heart!
And haste to drink the wholesome dart,
That healing shaft, which Heaven till now
Hath in Love's quiver hid for you
Oh dart of Love! arrow of light!
Oh happy you, if it hit right!
It must not fall in vain, it must
Not mark the dry regardless dust.
Fair one, it is your fate, and brings
Eternal worlds upon its wings.
Meet it with wide-spread arms, and see
Its seat your soul's just center be.
Disband dull fears, give faith the day;
To save your life, kill your delay;
It is Love's siege, and sure to be
Your triumph, though His victory.
'Tis cowardice that keeps this field,
And want of courage not to yield.
Yield then, Oh yield, that Love may win
The fort at last, and let life in;
Yield quickly, lest perhaps you prove
Death's prey before the prize of Love.
This fort of your fair self, if 't be not won,
He is repulsed indeed, but you're undone.

Andrew Marvell

1621–1678

THE finest of the metaphysical poets after Donne, and sometimes quite his equal, Andrew Marvell was a friend and respected colleague of John Milton. He was born in Yorkshire and grew up at Hull, where his father was headmaster of the Grammar School. He won a scholarship to Cambridge and wrote poetry there. In 1639 he proceeded B.A. and not long afterward went to the continent, where he spent four years in travel. In 1650 he entered the service of Lord Fairfax, the recently retired Parliamentary general, as a tutor to his daughter Mary at Nunappleton (or Appleton) House, which he celebrated in a long poem. His two years at Nunappleton may have been his happiest and most creative period. He was recommended by Milton, then Latin Secretary, for a government post, but official delays brought him again into tutoring; this time his pupil was the ward of Oliver Cromwell. In 1657 he became associated with Milton in the Latin Secretaryship and two years later was elected a Member of Parliament for Hull; he served in this capacity until his death. He was eminent as a defender of tolerance in religion and politics, and his whole public life seems to bear out Milton's statement that he was a man "of singular desert for the state to make use of."

Most of Marvell's poetry belongs to the period 1645–1660; after the Restoration he made a reputation as a satirist. He is remarkable for the easy way he absorbs philosophical speculation or scientific curiosity into his verse, and for his happy identification of the poet's moods with gentle states of nature. Meditation and song are never very far apart in Marvell's verse, and he becomes almost a symbolist poet when he treats his favorite image, greenness. The tone of "To His Coy Mistress" is remarkably virile and unaffected in comparison with that of most of the love poetry of the time. In this and a few other poems, indeed, Marvell transcends his age and becomes one of the permanent English poets.

BIBLIOGRAPHY: *The Poems and Letters of Andrew Marvell,* ed. H. M. Margoliouth, Oxford, 1927; Pierre Legouis, *André Marvell,* Paris, 1928; Ruth Wallerstein, *Seventeenth Century Poetic,* Madison, 1950; V. Sackville-West, *Andrew Marvell,* London, 1929; M. C. Bradbrook and M. G. Lloyd Thomas, *Andrew Marvell,* Cambridge, 1940; Douglas Bush, *English Literature in the Earlier Seventeenth Century,* Oxford, 1945, pp. 158–164; *Andrew Marvell, 1621–1678, Tercentenary Tributes,* Oxford, 1922.

ON A DROP OF DEW

SEE how the orient dew,
Shed from the bosom of the morn
Into the blowing roses,
Yet careless of its mansion new,
For the clear region where 'twas born
Round in itself encloses,
And in its little globe's extent
Frames as it can its native element; [1]
How it the purple flow'r does slight,
Scarce touching where it lies,
But gazing back upon the skies,
Shines with a mournful light
Like its own tear,
Because so long divided from the sphere.
Restless it rolls and unsecure,
Trembling lest it grow impure,
Till the warm sun pity its pain,
And to the skies exhale it back again.
So the soul, that drop, that ray
Of the clear fountain of eternal day,
Could it within the human flower be seen,
Remembr'ring still its former height,
Shuns the sweet leaves and blossoms green;
And recollecting its own light,
Does, in its pure and circling thoughts express
The greater heaven in an heaven less.
In how coy a figure wound,
Every way it turns away;
So the world excluding round,
Yet receiving in the day;
Dark beneath but bright above,
Here disdaining, there in love;
How loose and easy hence to go,
How girt and ready to ascend;
Moving but on a point below,
It all about does upwards bend.
Such did the manna's [2] sacred dew distil,
White and entire, though congealed and chill;

---

[1] *element:* heaven, where dew supposedly originated.

[2] *manna's:* See Exodus 16:13–21.

Congealed on earth, but does, dissolving, run
Into the glories of th' almighty sun.

BERMUDAS

WHERE the remote Bermudas ride,
In the ocean's bosom unespied,
From a small boat, that rowed along,
The listening winds received this song:
"What should we do but sing His praise,
That led us through the watery maze,
Unto an isle so long unknown,
And yet far kinder than our own?
Where He the huge sea-monsters wracks,
That lift the deep upon their backs;
He lands us on a grassy stage,
Safe from the storms and prelates' rage.
He gave us this eternal spring,
Which here enamels every thing,
And sends the fowls to us in care,
On daily visits through the air;
He hangs in shades the orange bright,
Like golden lamps in a green night,
And does in the pomegranates close
Jewels more rich than Ormus [3] shows;
He makes the figs our mouths to meet,
And throws the melons at our feet;
But apples [4] plants of such a price,
No tree could ever bear them twice;
With cedars chosen by His hand,
From Lebanon, He stores the land,
And makes the hollow seas, that roar,
Proclaim the ambergris on shore;
He cast (of which we rather boast)
The Gospel's pearl upon our coast,
And in these rocks for us did frame
A temple where to sound His name.
Oh! let our voice His praise exalt,
Till it arrive at Heaven's vault,

---

[3] *Ormus:* Hormuz, on the Persian Gulf. Compare *Paradise Lost,* II, 1–2: "High on a throne of royal state, which far / Outshone the wealth of Ormus and of Ind."

[4] *apples:* pineapples.

Which thence perhaps, rebounding, may
Echo beyond the Mexique Bay."
Thus sung they in the English boat,
An holy and a cheerful note;
And all the way, to guide their chime,
With falling oars they kept the time.

A DIALOGUE BETWEEN THE SOUL AND BODY

Soul. Oh, who shall from this dungeon raise
A soul enslaved so many ways?
With bolts of bones, that fettered stands
In feet, and manacled in hands;
Here blinded with an eye, and there
Deaf with the drumming of an ear;
A soul hung up, as 'twere, in chains
Of nerves, and arteries, and veins;
Tortured, besides each other part,
In a vain head and double heart?

Body. Oh, who shall me deliver whole
From bonds of this tyrannic soul?
Which, stretched upright, impales me so
That mine own precipice I go;
And warms and moves this needless[5] frame,
(A fever could but do the same,)
And, wanting where its spite to try,
Has made me live to let me die
A body that could never rest
Since this ill spirit it possessed.

Soul. What magic could me thus confine
Within another's grief to pine?
Where, whatsoever it complain,
I feel, that cannot feel, the pain;
And all my care itself employs,
That to preserve which me destroys;
Constrained not only to endure
Diseases, but, what's worse, the cure;
And, ready oft the port to gain,
Am shipwrecked into health again.

[5] *needless:* having no want.

Body. But Physic yet could never reach
The maladies thou me dost teach;
Whom first the cramp of hope does tear,
And then the palsy shakes of fear;
The pestilence of love does heat,
Or hatred's hidden ulcer eat;
Joy's cheerful madness does perplex,
Or sorrow's other madness vex;
Which knowledge forces me to know,
And memory will not forego;
What but a soul could have the wit
To build me up for sin so fit?
So architects do square and hew
Green trees that in the forest grew.

THE NYMPH COMPLAINING FOR THE DEATH OF HER FAWN

THE wanton troopers riding by
Have shot my fawn, and it will die.
Ungentle men! they cannot thrive
Who killed thee. Thou ne'er didst alive
Them any harm, alas! nor could
Thy death yet do them any good.
I'm sure I never wished them ill;
Nor do I for all this, nor will:
But, if my simple prayers may yet
Prevail with Heaven to forget
Thy murder, I will join my tears,
Rather than fail. But, Oh my fears!
It cannot die so. Heaven's king
Keeps register of everything,
And nothing may we use in vain;
Even beasts must be with justice slain,
Else men are made their deodands.[6]
Though they should wash their guilty hands
In this warm life-blood which doth part
From thine, and wound me to the heart,
Yet could they not be clean; their stain
Is dyed in such a purple grain.

[6] *deodands:* Moving things which cause someone's death are in old English law forfeit to the lord of the manor, who gives them to charity (hence *deodand:* gift to God).

There is not such another in
The world, to offer for their sin.
  Unconstant Sylvio, when yet
I had not found him counterfeit,
One morning (I remember well),
Tied in this silver chain and bell,
Gave it to me: nay, and I know
What he said then, I'm sure I do:
Said he, "Look how your huntsman here
Hath taught a fawn to hunt his deer."
But Sylvio soon had me beguiled;
This waxed tame, while he grew wild,
And quite regardless of my smart,
Left me his fawn, but took his heart.
  Thenceforth I set myself to play
My solitary time away
With this; and, very well content,
Could so mine idle life have spent;
For it was full of sport, and light
Of foot and heart, and did invite
Me to its game: it seemed to bless
Itself in me; how could I less
Than love it? O, I cannot be
Unkind to a beast that loveth me.
  Had it lived long, I do not know
Whether it too might have done so
As Sylvio did; his gifts might be
Perhaps as false, or more, than he;
But I am sure, for aught that I
Could in so short a time espy,
Thy love was far more better then
The love of false and cruel men.
  With sweetest milk and sugar first
I it at my own fingers nursed;
And as it grew, so every day
It waxed more white and sweet than they.
It had so sweet a breath! And oft
I blushed to see its foot more soft
And white, shall I say than my hand?
Nay, any lady's of the land.
  It is a wondrous thing how fleet
'Twas on those little silver feet;
With what a pretty skipping grace
It oft would challenge me the race;
And, when't had left me far away,

'Twould stay, and run again, and stay;
For it was nimbler much than hinds,
And trod as if on the four winds.
  I have a garden of my own,
But so with roses overgrown,
And lilies, that you would it guess
To be a little wilderness;
And all the spring-time of the year
It only lovèd to be there.
Among the beds of lilies I
Have sought it oft, where it should lie,
Yet could not, till itself would rise,
Find it, although before mine eyes;
For, in the flaxen lilies' shade,
It like a bank of lilies laid.
Upon the roses it would feed,
Until its lips e'en seem to bleed.
And then to me 'twould boldly trip,
And print those roses on my lip.
But all its chief delight was still
On roses thus itself to fill,
And its pure virgin limbs to fold
In whitest sheets of lilies cold:
Had it lived long, it would have been
Lilies without, roses within.
  Oh help! Oh help! I see it faint
And die as calmly as a saint!
See how it weeps! the tears do come
Sad, slowly, dropping like a gum.
So weeps the wounded balsam; so
The holy frankincense doth flow;
The brotherless Heliades [7]
Melt in such amber tears as these.
  I in a golden vial will
Keep these two crystal tears, and fill
It till it do o'erflow with mine,
Then place it in Diana's shrine.
  Now my sweet fawn is vanished to
Whither the swans and turtles [8] go;
In fair Elysium to endure,
With milk-like lambs, and ermines pure.

---

[7] *Heliades:* the daughters of the sun, Helios, who so lamented the death of their brother Phaeton that they were changed into poplars and their tears into amber.

[8] *turtles:* turtledoves.

Oh do not run too fast: for I
Will but bespeak thy grave, and die.
  First, my unhappy statue shall
Be cut in marble; and withal,
Let it be weeping too; but there
The engraver sure his art may spare;
For I so truly thee bemoan,
That I shall weep, though I be stone,
Until my tears, still dropping, wear
My breast, themselves engraving there;
There at my feet shalt thou be laid,
Of purest alabaster made;
For I would have thine image be
White as I can, though not as thee.

TO HIS COY MISTRESS

HAD we but world enough, and time,
This coyness, lady, were no crime.
We would sit down, and think which way
To walk, and pass our long love's day.
Thou by the Indian Ganges' side
Shouldst rubies find: I by the tide
Of Humber would complain. I would
Love you ten years before the flood,
And you should, if you please, refuse
Till the conversion of the Jews;
My vegetable love should grow
Vaster than empires and more slow;
An hundred years should go to praise
Thine eyes, and on thy forehead gaze;
Two hundred to adore each breast,
But thirty thousand to the rest;
An age at least to every part,
And the last age should show your heart.
For, lady, you deserve this state,
Nor would I love at lower rate.
  But at my back I always hear
Time's wingèd chariot hurrying near,
And yonder all before us lie
Deserts of vast eternity.
Thy beauty shall no more be found,
Nor, in thy marble vault, shall sound

My echoing song; then worms shall try
That long-preserved virginity,
And your quaint honour turn to dust,
And into ashes all my lust:
The grave's a fine and private place,
But none, I think, do there embrace.
Now therefore, while the youthful hue
Sits on thy skin like morning dew,
And while thy willing soul transpires
At every pore with instant fires,
Now let us sport us while we may,
And now, like amorous birds of prey,
Rather at once our time devour,
Than languish in his slow-chapt power.[9]
Let us roll all our strength and all
Our sweetness up into one ball,
And tear our pleasures with rough strife,
Thorough the iron gates of life;
Thus, though we cannot make our sun
Stand still, yet we will make him run.

THE GALLERY

Clora, come view my soul, and tell
Whether I have contrived it well:
Now all its several lodgings lie,
Composed into one gallery,
And the great arras-hangings, made
Of various facings, by are laid,
That, for all furniture, you'll find
Only your picture in my mind.

Here thou art painted in the dress
Of an inhuman murderess;
Examining [10] upon our hearts
Thy fertile shop of cruel arts,
Engines more keen than ever yet
Adornèd tyrant's cabinet,
Of which the most tormenting are,
Black eyes, red lips, and curlèd hair.

---

[9] *his slow-chapt power:* the power of his slowly devouring jaws.

[10] *examining:* testing.

But, on the other side, thou'rt drawn,
Like to Aurora in the dawn;
When in the east she slumbering lies,
And stretches out her milky thighs,
While all the morning choir does sing
And manna falls and roses spring,
And, at thy feet, the wooing doves
Sit perfecting their harmless loves.

Like an enchantress here thou show'st,
Vexing thy restless lover's ghost;
And, by a light obscure, dost rave
Over his entrails, in the cave,
Divining thence, with horrid care,
How long thou shalt continue fair;
And (when informed) them throw'st away
To be the greedy vulture's prey.

But, against that, thou sitt'st afloat,
Like Venus in her pearly boat;
The halcyons, calming all that's nigh,
Betwixt the air and water fly;
Or, if some rolling wave appears,
A mass of ambergris it bears,
Nor blows more wind than what may well
Convoy the perfume to the smell.

These pictures, and a thousand more,
Of thee, my gallery do store,
In all the forms thou canst invent,
Either to please me, or torment;
For thou alone, to people me,
Art grown a numerous colony,
And a collection choicer far
Than or Whitehall's, or Mantua's [11] were.

But of these pictures, and the rest,
That at the entrance likes me best,
Where the same posture and the look
Remains with which I first was took;
A tender shepherdess, whose hair
Hangs loosely playing in the air,
Transplanting flowers from the green hill
To crown her head and bosom fill.

---

[11] *Whitehall's, or Mantua's:* King Charles I bought the art collection of the Duke of Mantua and added it to his gallery at Whitehall.

THE FAIR SINGER

To make a final conquest of all me,
Love did compose so sweet an enemy,
In whom both beauties to my death agree,
Joining themselves in fatal harmony,
That, while she with her eyes my heart does bind,
She with her voice might captivate my mind.

I could have fled from one but singly fair;
My disentangled soul itself might save,
Breaking the curlèd trammels of her hair;
But how should I avoid to be her slave,
Whose subtle art invisibly can wreathe
My fetters of the very air I breathe?

It had been easy fighting in some plain,
Where victory might hang in equal choice,
But all resistance against her is vain,
Who has the advantage both of eyes and voice;
And all my forces needs must be undone,
She having gainèd both the wind and sun.

THE DEFINITION OF LOVE

My Love is of a birth as rare
  As 'tis, for object, strange and high;
It was begotten by Despair
  Upon Impossibility.

Magnanimous Despair alone
  Could show me so divine a thing,
Where feeble Hope could ne'er have flown,
  But vainly flapped its tinsel wing.

And yet I quickly might arrive
  Where my extended soul is fixed,
But Fate does iron wedges drive,
  And always crowds itself betwixt.

For Fate with jealous eye does see
  Two perfect loves, nor lets them close;
Their union would her ruin be,
  And her tyrannic power depose.

And therefore her decrees of steel
  Us as the distant poles have placed,
(Though Love's whole world on us doth wheel),
  Not by themselves to be embraced,

Unless the giddy heaven fall,
  And earth some new convulsion tear,
And, us to join, the world should all
  Be cramped into a planisphere.

As lines, so loves oblique, may well
  Themselves in every angle greet:
But ours, so truly parallel,
  Though infinite, can never meet.

Therefore the love which us doth bind,
  But Fate so enviously debars,
Is the conjunction of the mind,
  And opposition of the stars.

THE MOWER, AGAINST GARDENS

Luxurious [12] man, to bring his vice in use,
  Did after him the world seduce,
And from the fields the flowers and plants allure,
  Where Nature was most plain and pure.
He first enclosed within the gardens square
  A dead and standing pool of air,
And a more luscious earth for them did knead,
  Which stupefied them while it fed.
The pink grew then as double as his mind;
  The nutriment did change the kind.
With strange perfumes he did the roses taint;
  And flowers themselves were taught to paint.
The tulip white did for complexion seek,
  And learned to interline its cheek;

[12] *luxurious:* voluptuous, lecherous.

Its onion root they then so high did hold,
  That one was for a meadow sold:[13]
Another world was searched through oceans new,
  To find the marvel of Peru;[14]
And yet these rarities might be allowed
  To man, that sovereign thing and proud,
Had he not dealt between the bark and tree,
  Forbidden mixtures there to see.
No plant now knew the stock from which it came;
  He grafts upon the wild the tame,
That the uncertain and adulterate fruit
  Might put the palate in dispute.
His green seraglio has its eunuchs too,
  Lest any tyrant him outdo;
And in the cherry he does Nature vex,
  To procreate without a sex.
'Tis all enforced, the fountain and the grot,
  While the sweet fields do lie forgot,
Where willing Nature does to all dispense
  A wild and fragrant innocence;
And fauns and fairies do the meadows till
  More by their presence than their skill.
Their statues polished by some ancient hand,
  May to adorn the gardens stand;
But, howsoe'er the figures do excel,
  The Gods themselves with us do dwell.

THE MOWER TO GLOW-WORMS

Ye living lamps, by whose dear light
The nightingale does sit so late,
And studying all the summer night,
Her matchless songs does meditate;

Ye country comets, that portend
No war nor prince's funeral,
Shining unto no higher end
Than to presage the grass's fall;

---

[13] *one . . . sold:* The tulip craze, with fantastic prices for a single bulb, reached its height in Holland in 1634–1637.

[14] *marvel of Peru:* a plant, *Mirabilia Peruviana.*

Ye glow-worms, whose officious flame
To wandering mowers shows the way,
That in the night have lost their aim,
And after foolish fires do stray;

Your courteous lights in vain you waste,
Since Juliana here is come,
For she my mind hath so displaced,
That I shall never find my home.

THE MOWER'S SONG

My mind was once the true survey
Of all these meadows fresh and gay,
And in the greenness of the grass
Did see its hopes as in a glass,
When Juliana came, and she
What I do to the grass does to my thoughts and me.

But these, while I with sorrow pine,
Grew more luxuriant still and fine,
That not one blade of grass you spied
But had a flower on either side,
When Juliana came, and she
What I do to the grass does to my thoughts and me.

Unthankful meadows, could you so
A fellowship so true forego
And in your gaudy May-games meet
While I lay trodden under feet?
When Juliana came, and she
What I do to the grass does to my thoughts and me.

But what you in compassion ought
Shall now in my revenge be wrought;
And flowers and grass and I and all
Will in one common ruin fall,
For Juliana comes, and she
What I do to the grass does to my thoughts and me.

And thus, ye meadows, which have been
Companions of my thoughts more green,
Shall now the heraldry become

With which I shall adorn my tomb,
For Juliana comes, and she
What I do to the grass does to my thoughts and me.

THE GARDEN

How vainly men themselves amaze
To win the palm, the oak, or bays;[15]
And their uncessant labors see
Crowned from some single herb or tree,
Whose short and narrow-vergèd shade
Does prudently their toils upbraid;
While all the flowers and trees do close,
To weave the garlands of repose!

Fair Quiet, have I found thee here,
And Innocence, thy sister dear?
Mistaken long, I sought you then
In busy companies of men.
Your sacred plants, if here below,
Only among the plants will grow;
Society is all but rude
To this delicious solitude.

No white nor red was ever seen
So amorous as this lovely green.
Fond lovers, cruel as their flame,
Cut in these trees their mistress' name:
Little, alas! they know or heed,
How far these beauties hers exceed!
Fair trees! wheres'e'er your bark I wound,
No name shall but your own be found.

When we have run our passion's heat,
Love hither makes his best retreat.
The gods, that mortal beauty chase,
Still in a tree did end their race;
Apollo hunted Daphne so,
Only that she might laurel grow;
And Pan did after Syrinx speed,
Not as a nymph, but for a reed.

[15] *palm . . . oak . . . bays:* symbols of distinction in war or athletics, civic affairs, and poetry.

What wondrous life is this I lead!
Ripe apples drop about my head;
The luscious clusters of the vine
Upon my mouth do crush their wine;
The nectarine and curious peach
Into my hands themselves do reach;
Stumbling on melons, as I pass,
Ensnared with flowers, I fall on grass.

Meanwhile the mind, from pleasure less,
Withdraws into its happiness;
The mind, that ocean where each kind
Does straight its own resemblance find; [16]
Yet it creates, transcending these,
Far other worlds, and other seas,
Annihilating all that's made
To a green thought in a green shade.

Here at the fountain's sliding foot,
Or at some fruit-tree's mossy root,
Casting the body's vest aside,
My soul into the boughs does glide:
There, like a bird, it sits and sings,
Then whets and combs its silver wings,
And, till prepared for longer flight,
Waves in its plumes the various light.

Such was that happy garden-state,
While man there walked without a mate;
After a place so pure and sweet,
What other help could yet be meet?
But 'twas beyond a mortal's share
To wander solitary there:
Two paradises 'twere in one,
To live in paradise alone.

How well the skilful gardener drew,
Of flowers and herbs, this dial new;
Where, from above, the milder sun
Does through a fragrant zodiac run,
And, as it works, the industrious bee
Computes its time as well as we!

---

[16] *that ocean . . . find:* a reference to the old superstition that every land animal had its corresponding marine type.

How could such sweet and wholesome hours
Be reckoned but with herbs and flowers?

UPON APPLETON HOUSE

To My Lord Fairfax

Within this sober frame expect
Work of no foreign architect
That unto caves the quarries drew,
And forests did to pastures hew;
Who, of his great design in pain,
Did for a model vault his brain;
Whose columns should so high be raised,
To arch the brows which on them gazed.

Why should, of all things, man, unruled,
Such unproportioned dwellings build?
The beasts are by their dens expressed,
And birds contrive an equal nest;
The low-roofed tortoises do dwell
In cases fit of tortoise-shell;
No creature loves an empty space;
Their bodies measure out their place.

But he, superfluously spread,
Demands more room alive than dead;
And in his hollow palace goes
Where winds, as he, themselves may lose.
What need of all this marble crust
To impark the wanton mote of dust,
That thinks by breadth the world to unite,
Though the first builders failed in height?

But all things are composèd here,
Like nature, orderly, and near;
In which we the dimensions find
Of that more sober age and mind,
When larger-sizèd men did stoop
To enter at a narrow loop,
As practising, in doors so strait,
To strain themselves through Heaven's gate.

And surely, when the after-age
Shall hither come in pilgrimage,
These sacred places to adore,
By Vere [17] and Fairfax trod before,
Men will dispute how their extent
Within such dwarfish confines went;
And some will smile at this, as well
As Romulus his bee-like cell.[18]

Humility alone designs
Those short but admirable lines
By which, ungirt and unconstrained,
Things greater are in less contained.
Let others vainly strive t' immure
The circle in the quadrature!
These holy mathematics can
In every figure equal man.

Yet thus the laden house does sweat,
And scarce endures the master great;
But, where he comes, the swelling hall
Stirs, and the square grows spherical;
More by his magnitude distressed,
Than he is by its straitness pressed:
And too officiously it slights
That in itself, which him delights.

So honor better lowness bears,
Than that unwonted greatness wears;
Height with a certain grace does bend,
But low things clownishly ascend.
And yet what needs there here excuse,
Where everything does answer use?
Where neatness nothing can condemn,
Nor pride invent what to contemn?

. . . .

When in the east the morning ray
Hangs out the colors of the day,
The bee through these known alleys hums,
Beating the dian [19] with its drums.
Then flowers their drowsy eyelids raise,

---

[17] *Vere:* Sir Horace Vere, Fairfax's father-in-law and former commanding officer.

[18] *Romulus . . . cell:* a thatched cottage preserved at Rome as the house of Romulus; it is here compared to a beehive.

[19] *dian:* reveille.

Their silken ensigns each displays,
And dries its pan yet dank with dew,
And fills its flask with odors new.

These, as their governor goes by,
In fragrant volleys they let fly,
And to salute their governess
Again as great a charge they press:
None for the virgin nymph; for she
Seems, with the flowers, a flower to be.
And think so still! though not compare
With breath so sweet, or cheek so fair!

Well shot, ye firemen! Oh how sweet
And round your equal fires do meet;
Whose shrill report no ear can tell,
But echoes to the eye and smell!
See how the flowers, as at parade,
Under their colors stand displayed;
Each regiment in order grows,
That of the tulip, pink, and rose.

But when the vigilant patrol
Of stars walks round about the pole,
Their leaves that to the stalks are curled
Seem to their staves the ensigns furled.
Then in some flower's belovèd hut,
Each bee, as sentinel, is shut,
And sleeps so too, but, if once stirred,
She runs you through, nor asks the word.

Oh thou, that dear and happy isle,
The garden of the world erewhile,
Thou Paradise of the four seas,
Which Heaven planted us to please,
But, to exclude the world, did guard
With watery, if not flaming sword,—
What luckless apple did we taste,
To make us mortal, and thee waste?

Unhappy! shall we never more
That sweet militia restore,
When gardens only had their towers
And all the garrisons were flowers;
When roses only arms might bear,

And men did rosy garlands wear?
Tulips, in several colors barred,
Were then the Switzers of our guard;[20]

The gardener had the soldier's place,
And his more gentle forts did trace;
The nursery of all things green
Was then the only magazine;
The winter quarters were the stoves,
Where he the tender plants removes.
But war all this doth overgrow:
We ordnance plant, and powder sow.

And yet there walks one on the sod,
Who, had it pleasèd him and God,
Might once have made our gardens spring
Fresh as his own, and flourishing.
But he preferred to the Cinque Ports[21]
These five imaginary forts,
And, in those half-dry trenches, spanned
Power which the ocean might command.

For he did, with his utmost skill,
Ambition weed, but conscious till;
Conscience, that heaven-nursèd plant,
Which most our earthly gardens want.
A prickling leaf it bears, and such
As that which shrinks at every touch,
But flowers eternal, and divine,
That in the crowns of Saints do shine.

. . . . . .

How safe, methinks, and strong behind
These trees, have I encamped my mind;
Where beauty, aiming at the heart,
Bends in some tree its useless dart,
And where the world no certain shot
Can make, or me it toucheth not,
But I on it securely play,
And gall its horsemen all the day.

---

[20] *Tulips . . . guard:* The Swiss guards at the Vatican still wear the uniform of black, red, and yellow stripes.

[21] *Cinque Ports:* originally five coastal towns in England with certain special privileges and important places to defend in wartime; occasionally used symbolically for the five senses.

Bind me, ye woodbines, in your twines;
Curl me about, ye gadding vines;
And oh, so close your circles lace,
That I may never leave this place!
But, lest your fetters prove too weak,
Ere I your silken bondage break,
Do you, O brambles, chain me too,
And, courteous briars, nail me through!

Here in the morning tie my chain,
Where the two woods have made a lane,
While, like a guard on either side,
The trees before their lord divide;
This, like a long and equal thread,
Betwixt two labyrinths does lead.
But, where the floods did lately drown,
There at the evening stake me down.

For now the waves are fallen and dried,
And now the meadows fresher dyed,
Whose grass, with moisture color dashed,
Seems as green silks but newly washed.
No serpent new, nor crocodile,
Remains behind our little Nile;
Unless itself you will mistake,
Among these meads the only snake.

See in what wanton harmless folds
It everywhere the meadow holds,
And its yet muddy back doth lick,
Till as a crystal mirror slick,
Where all things gaze themselves, and doubt
If they be in it, or without;
And for his shade which therein shines,
Narcissus-like, the sun too pines.

Oh what a pleasure 'tis to hedge
My temples here with heavy sedge;
Abandoning my lazy side,
Stretched as a bank unto the tide;
Or to suspend my sliding foot
On the osier's underminèd root,
And in its branches tough to hang,
While at my lines the fishes twang!

But now away my hooks, my quills,[22]
And angles, idle utensils!
The young Maria walks to-night:
Hide, trifling youth, thy pleasures slight;
'Twere shame that such judicious eyes
Should with such toys a man surprise;
She that already is the law
Of all her sex, her age's awe.

See how loose Nature, in respect
To her, itself doth recollect,
And every thing so whisht [23] and fine,
Starts forthwith to its bonne mine.[24]
The sun himself of her aware,
Seems to descend with greater care,
And, lest she see him go to bed,
In blushing clouds conceals his head.

So when the shadows laid asleep,
From underneath these banks do creep,
And on the river, as it flows,
With ebon shuts [25] begin to close,
The modest halcyon comes in sight,
Flying betwixt the day and night;
And such a horror calm and dumb,
Admiring Nature does benumb;

The viscous air, wheres'er she fly,
Follows and sucks her azure dye;
The jellying stream compacts below,
If it might fix her shadow so;
The stupid fishes hang, as plain
As flies in crystal overta'en.
And men the silent scene assist,
Charmed with the sapphire-wingèd mist.

Maria such, and so doth hush
The world, and through the evening rush.
No new-born comet such a train
Draws through the sky, nor star new slain.
For straight those giddy rockets fail,
Which from the putrid earth exhale;

---

[22] *quills:* floats.
[23] *whisht:* quiet, still.
[24] *bonne mine:* best appearance.
[25] *shuts:* shutters.

But by her flames, in Heaven tried,
Nature is wholly vitrified.

'Tis she that to these gardens gave
That wondrous beauty which they have;
She straightness on the woods bestows;
To her the meadow sweetness owes;
Nothing could make the river be
So crystal pure, but only she,
She yet more pure, sweet, straight, and fair
Than gardens, woods, meads, rivers are.

Therefore what first she on them spent,
They gratefully again present;
The meadow carpets where to tread,
The garden flowers to crown her head,
And for a glass the limpid brook,
Where she may all her beauties look;
But, since she would not have them seen,
The wood about her draws a screen.

For she to higher beauties raised,
Disdains to be for lesser praised.
She counts her beauty to converse
In all the languages as hers;
Nor yet in those herself employs,
But for the wisdom, not the noise;
Nor yet that wisdom would affect,
But as 'tis Heaven's dialect.
. . . .

Meantime, ye fields, springs, bushes, flowers,
Where yet she leads her studious hours,
(Till Fate her worthily translates,
And find a Fairfax for our Thwaites)
Employ the means you have by her,
And in your kind yourselves prefer;
That, as all virgins she precedes,
So you all woods, streams, gardens, meads.

For you, Thessalian Tempe's seat
Shall now be scorned as obsolete;
Aranjuez, as less, disdained;
The Bel-Retiro,[26] as constrained;

[26] *Aranjuez, Bel-Retiro:* famous royal gardens near Madrid.

But name not the Idalian grove,
For 'twas the seat of wanton love;
Much less the dead's Elysian fields;
Yet nor to them your beauty yields.

'Tis not, what once it was, the world,
But a rude heap together hurled;
All negligently overthrown,
Gulfs, deserts, precipices, stone;
Your lesser world contains the same,
But in more decent order tame;
You, Heaven's center, Nature's lap,
And Paradise's only map.

But now the salmon-fishers moist
Their leathern boats begin to hoist;
And, like Antipodes in shoes,
Have shod their heads in their canoes.
How tortoise-like, but not so slow,
These rational amphibii go!
Let's in; for the dark hemisphere
Does now like one of them appear.

Izaak Walton

1593–1683

THE masterpiece of English pastoral was written during the troubled days of the Commonwealth. Walton's *The Compleat Angler,* partly autobiography, partly handbook on fishing, is primarily a celebration of the virtues of *otium,* which is the essence of pastoral. The contented mind, the inner calm that can be attained by an appreciation of country life and country pleasures, the renunciation of modern nervous hurry and rush, ambition and intrigue—this is what interests Walton more than the technique of catching fish. The fisherman's life encourages contemplation, and for this reason it is good.

Walton's writing was the expression of simple piety. Besides the classic *Compleat Angler* he composed five biographies, of which his lives of Hooker, Donne, and Herbert are still of great interest. He treated his subjects in the older manner of respectful veneration, not in the modern critical or suspicious or supercilious way. To him the life of a good man was a narrative to show the reader how a good life might be led—it was as simple as that. Yet Walton was not without humor and a sense of irony. His style is simple and lucid; he avoids ornate rhetoric, but he is capable of delicate nuances of feeling and of meaning.

BIBLIOGRAPHY: *The Compleat Walton,* ed. G. Keynes, London, 1929; Stapleton Martin, *Izaak Walton and His Friends,* London, 1904; John Butt, "Izaak Walton's Methods in Biography," *ESEA,* XIX (1934), 67–84.

FROM

THE COMPLEAT ANGLER

THE THIRD DAY (*continued*). ON THE NATURE AND BREEDING OF THE TROUT, AND HOW TO FISH FOR HIM

CHAPTER IV

Piscator, Venator, Milk-Woman, Maudlin, Hostess

PISCATOR. The Trout is a fish highly valued, both in this and foreign nations. He may be justly said, as the old poet said of wine, and we English say of venison, to be a generous fish: a fish that is so like the buck, that he also has his seasons; for it is observed, that he comes in and goes out of season with the stag and buck. Gesner says, his name is of a German offspring; and says he is a fish that feeds clean and purely, in the swiftest streams, and on the hardest gravel; and that he may justly contend with all fresh water fish, as the Mullet may with all sea fish, for precedency and daintiness of taste; and that being in right season, the most dainty palates have allowed precedency to him.

And before I go farther in my discourse, let me tell you, that you are to observe, that as there be some barren does that are good in summer, so there be some barren Trouts that are good in winter; but there are not many that are so; for usually they be in their perfection in the month of May, and decline with the buck. Now you are to take notice, that in several countries, as in Germany, and in other parts, compared to ours, fish do differ much in their bigness, and shape, and other ways; and so do Trouts. It is well known that in the Lake Leman, the Lake of Geneva, there are Trouts taken of three cubits long; as is affirmed by Gesner, a writer of good credit: and Mercator says, the Trouts that are taken in the Lake of Geneva are a great part of the merchandise of that famous city. And you are further to know, that there be certain waters that breed Trouts remarkable, both for their number and smallness. I know a little brook in Kent, that breeds them to a number incredible, and you may take them twenty or forty in an hour, but none greater than about the size of a Gudgeon. There are also, in divers rivers, especially that relate to, or be near to the sea, as Winchester, or the Thames about Windsor, a little Trout called a Samlet, or Skegger Trout, in both which places I have caught twenty or forty at a standing, that will bite as fast and as freely as Minnows:

these be by some taken to be young Salmons; but in those waters they never grow to be bigger than a Herring.

There is also in Kent, near to Canterbury, a Trout called there a Fordidge Trout, a Trout that bears the name of the town where it is usually caught, that is accounted the rarest of fish; many of them near the bigness of a Salmon, but known by their different colour; and in their best season they cut very white: and none of these have been known to be caught with an angle, unless it were one that was caught by Sir George Hastings, an excellent angler, and now with God: and he hath told me, he thought that Trout bit not for hunger but wantonness; and it is the rather to be believed, because both he, then, and many others before him, have been curious to search into their bellies, what the food was by which they lived; and have found out nothing by which they might satisfy their curiosity.

Concerning which you are to take notice, that it is reported by good authors, that grasshoppers and some fish have no mouths, but are nourished and take breath by the porousness of their gills, man knows not how: and this may be believed, if we consider that when the raven hath hatched her eggs, she takes no further care, but leaves her young ones to the care of the God of nature, who is said, in the Psalms, 'to feed the young ravens that call upon him.' And they be kept alive and fed by a dew; or worms that breed in their nests; or some other ways that we mortals know not. And this may be believed of the Fordidge Trout, which, as it is said of the stork, that he knows his season, so he knows his times, I think almost his day of coming into that river out of the sea; where he lives, and, it is like, feeds, nine months of the year, and fasts three in the river of Fordidge. And you are to note, that those townsmen are very punctual in observing the time of beginning to fish for them; and boast much, that their river affords a Trout that exceeds all others. And just so does Sussex boast of several fish; as, namely, a Shelsey Cockle, a Chichester Lobster, an Arundel Mullet, and an Amerly Trout.

And, now, for some confirmation of the Fordidge Trout: you are to know that this Trout is thought to eat nothing in the fresh water; and it may be the better believed, because it is well known, that swallows, and bats, and wagtails, which are called half-year birds, and not seen to fly in England for six months in a year, but about Michaelmas leave us for a hotter climate, yet some of them that have been left behind their fellows, have been found, many thousands at a time, in hollow trees, or clay caves, where they have been observed to live, and sleep out the whole winter, without meat. And so Albertus observes, That there is one kind of frog that hath her mouth naturally shut up about the end of August, and that she lives so all the winter: and though it be strange to some, yet it is known to too many among us to be doubted.

And so much for these Fordidge Trouts, which never afford an angler sport, but either live their time of being in the fresh water, by their meat formerly gotten in the sea, not unlike the swallow or frog, or, by the virtue of the fresh water only; or, as the birds of Paradise and the chameleon are said to live, by the sun and the air.

There is also in Northumberland a Trout called a Bull-trout, of a much greater length and bigness than any in these southern parts; and there are, in many rivers that relate to the sea, Salmon-trouts, as much different from others, both in shape and in their spots, as we see sheep in some countries differ one from another in their shape and bigness, and in the fineness of the wool: and, certainly, as some pastures breed larger sheep; so do some rivers, by reason of the ground over which they run, breed larger Trouts.

Now the next thing that I will commend to your consideration is, that the Trout is of a more sudden growth than other fish. Concerning which, you are also to take notice, that he lives not so long as the Perch, and divers other fishes do, as Sir Francis Bacon hath observed in his History of Life and Death.

And next you are to take notice, that he is not like the Crocodile, which if he lives never so long, yet always thrives till his death: but 'tis not so with the Trout; for after he is come to his full growth, he declines in his body, and keeps his bigness, or thrives only in his head till his death. And you are to know, that he will, about, especially before, the time of his spawning, get, almost miraculously, through weirs and flood-gates, against the stream; even through such high and swift places as is almost incredible. Next, that the Trout usually spawns about October or November, but in some rivers a little sooner or later; which is the more observable, because most other fish spawn in the spring or summer, when the sun hath warmed both the earth and water, and made it fit for generation. And you are to note, that he continues many months out of season; for it may be observed of the Trout, that he is like the buck or the ox, that will not be fat in many months, though he go in the very same pastures that horses do, which will be fat in one month: and so you may observe, That most other fishes recover strength, and grow sooner fat and in season than the Trout doth.

And next you are to note, That till the sun gets to such a height as to warm the earth and the water, the Trout is sick, and lean, and lousy, and unwholesome; for you shall, in winter, find him to have a big head, and, then, to be lank and thin and lean; at which time many of them have sticking on them sugs, or trout-lice; which is a kind of a worm, in shape like a clove, or pin with a big head, and sticks close to him, and sucks his moisture; those, I think, the Trout breeds himself: and never thrives till he free himself from them, which is when warm weather comes; and, then, as he grows stronger, he gets from the dead still water into the sharp streams and the gravel, and, there, rubs off these worms or lice; and then, as he grows stronger, so he gets him into swifter and swifter streams, and there lies at the watch for any fly or minnow that comes near to him; and he especially loves the May-fly, which is bred of the cod-worm, or cadis; and these make the Trout bold and lusty, and he is usually fatter and better meat at the end of that month than at any time of the year.

Now you are to know that it is observed, that usually the best Trouts are either red or yellow; though some, as the Fordidge Trout, be white and yet good; but that is not usual: and it is a note observable, that the female Trout hath usually a less head, and a deeper body than the male Trout, and is usually the better meat. And note, that a hog back and a little head, to either Trout, Salmon or any other fish, is a sign that that fish is in season.

But yet you are to note, that as you see some willows or palm-trees bud and blossom sooner than others do, so some Trouts be, in rivers, sooner in season: and as some hollies, or oaks, are longer before they cast their leaves, so are some Trouts, in rivers, longer before they go out of season.

And you are to note, that there are several kinds of Trouts: but these several kinds are not considered but by very few men; for they go under the general name of Trouts; just as pigeons do, in most places; though it is certain, there are tame and wild pigeons; and of the tame, there be helmits and runts, and carriers and cropers, and indeed too many to name. Nay, the Royal Society have found and published lately, that there be thirty and three kinds of spiders; and yet all, for aught I know, go under that one general name of spider. And it is so with many kinds of fish, and of Trouts especially; which differ in their bigness, and shape, and spots, and colour. The great Kentish hens may be an instance, compared to other hens: and, doubtless, there is a kind of small Trout, which will never thrive to be big; that breeds very many more than others do, that be of a larger size: which you may rather believe, if you consider that the little wren and titmouse will have twenty young ones at a time, when, usually, the noble hawk, or the musical thrassel or blackbird, exceed not four or five.

And now you shall see me try my skill to catch a Trout; and at my next walking, either this evening or tomorrow morning, I will give you direction how you yourself shall fish for him.

Venator. Trust me, master, I see now it is a harder matter to catch a Trout than a Chub; for I have put on patience, and followed you these two hours, and not seen a fish stir, neither at your minnow nor your worm.

Piscator. Well, scholar, you must endure worse luck sometime, or you will never make a good angler. But what say you now? there is a Trout now, and a good one too, if I can but hold him; and two or three turns more will tire him. Now you see he lies still, and the sleight is to land him: reach me that landing-net. So. Sir, now he is mine own: what say you now, is not this worth all my labour and your patience?

Venator. On my word, master, this is a gallant Trout; what shall we do with him?

Piscator. Marry, e'en eat him to supper: we'll go to my hostess from whence we came; she told me, as I was going out of door, that my brother Peter, a good angler and a cheerful companion, had sent word he would lodge there tonight, and bring a friend with him. My hostess has two beds, and I know you and I may have the best: we'll rejoice with my brother Peter and his friend, tell tales, or sing ballads, or make a catch, or find some harmless sport to content us, and pass away a little time without offence to God or man.

Venator. A match, good master, let's go to that house, for the linen looks white, and smells of lavender, and I long to lie in a pair of sheets that smell so. Let's be going, good master, for I am hungry again with fishing.

Piscator. Nay, stay a little, good scholar. I caught my last Trout with a worm; now I will put on a minnow, and try a quarter of an hour about yonder trees for another; and, so, walk towards our lodging. Look you, scholar, thereabout we shall have a bite presently, or not at all. Have with you, Sir: o' my word I have hold of him. Oh! it is a great logger-headed Chub; come, hang him upon that willow twig, and let's be going. But turn out of the way a little, good scholar! toward yonder high honeysuckle hedge; there we'll sit and sing, whilst this shower falls so gently upon the teeming earth, and gives yet a sweeter smell to the lovely flowers that adorn these verdant meadows.

Look! under that broad beech-tree I sat down, when I was last this way a-fishing; and the birds in the adjoining grove seemed to have a friendly contention with an echo, whose dead voice seemed to live in a hollow tree near to the brow of that primrose-hill. There I sat viewing the silver streams glide silently towards their centre, the tempestuous sea; yet sometimes opposed by rugged roots and pebble-stones, which broke their waves, and turned them into foam; and sometimes I beguiled time by viewing the harmless lambs; some leaping securely in the cool shade, whilst others sported themselves in the cheerful sun; and saw others craving comfort from the swollen udders of their bleating dams. As I thus sat, these and other sights had so fully possest my soul with content, that I thought, as the poet has happily exprest it,

> I was for that time lifted above earth;
> And possest joys not promis'd in my birth.

As I left this place, and entered into the next field, a second pleasure entertained me; 'twas a handsome milk-maid, that had not yet attained so much age and wisdom as to load her mind with any fears of many things that will never be, as too many men too often do; but she cast away all care, and sung like a nightingale. Her voice was good, and the ditty fitted for it; it was that smooth song which was made by Kit Marlow, now at least fifty years ago; and the milk-maid's mother sung an answer to it, which was made by Sir Walter Raleigh, in his younger days. They were old-fashioned poetry, but choicedly good; I think much better than the strong lines that are now in fashion in this critical age. Look yonder! on my word, yonder, they both be a-milking again. I will give her the Chub, and persuade them to sing those two songs to us.

God speed you, good woman! I have been a-fishing; and am going to Bleak Hall to my bed; and having caught more fish than will sup myself and my friend, I will bestow this upon you and your daughter, for I use to sell none.

Milk-Woman. Marry! God requite you, Sir, and we'll eat it cheerfully. And if you come this way a-fishing two months hence, a grace of God! I'll give you a syllabub of new verjuice, in a new-made haycock, for it. And my Maudlin shall sing you one of her best ballads; for she and I both love all anglers, they be such honest, civil, quiet men. In the meantime will you drink a draught of red cow's milk? you shall have it freely.

Piscator. No, I thank you; but, I pray, do us a courtesy that shall stand you and your daughter in nothing, and yet we will think ourselves still something in your debt: it is but to sing us a song that was sung by your daughter when I last passed over this meadow, about eight or nine days since.

Milk-Woman. What song was it, I pray? Was it, 'Come, Shepherds, deck your herds'? or, 'As at noon Dulcina rested'? or, 'Phillida flouts me'? or, 'Chevy Chace'? or, 'Johnny Armstrong'? or, 'Troy Town'?

Piscator. No, it is none of those; it is a song that your daughter sung the first part, and you sung the answer to it.

Milk-Woman. O, I know it now. I learned the first part in my golden age, when I was about the age of my poor daughter; and the latter part, which indeed fits me best now, but two or three years ago, when the cares of the world began to take hold of me: but you shall, God willing, hear them both; and sung as well as we can, for we both love anglers. Come, Maudlin, sing the first part to the gentlemen, with a merry heart; and I'll sing the second when you have done.

THE MILK-MAID'S SONG

Come, live with me, and be my love,
And we will all the pleasures prove,
That valleys, groves, or hills, or fields,
Or woods, and steepy mountains yields;

Where we will sit upon the rocks,
And see the shepherds feed our flocks,
By shallow rivers, to whose falls
Melodious birds sing madrigals.

And I will make thee beds of roses;
And, then, a thousand fragrant posies;
A cap of flowers, and a kirtle,
Embroidered all with leaves of myrtle;

A gown made of the finest wool,
Which from our pretty lambs we pull;

Slippers, lin'd choicely for the cold,
With buckles of the purest gold;

A belt of straw and ivy-buds,
With coral clasps, and amber studs.
And if these pleasures may thee move,
Come, live with me, and be my love.

Thy silver dishes, for thy meat,
As precious as the Gods do eat,
Shall, on an ivory table, be
Prepared each day for thee and me.

The shepherd swains shall dance and sing
For thy delight, each May morning.
If these delights thy mind may move,
Then live with me, and be my love.

Venator. Trust me, master, it is a choice song, and sweetly sung by honest Maudlin. I now see it was not without cause that our good queen Elizabeth did so often wish herself a milk-maid all the month of May, because they are not troubled with fears and cares, but sing sweetly all the day, and sleep securely all the night; and without doubt, honest, innocent, pretty Maudlin does so. I'll bestow Sir Thomas Overbury's milk-maid's wish upon her, 'that she may die in the Spring; and, being dead, may have good store of flowers stuck round about her winding-sheet.'

THE MILK-MAID'S MOTHER'S ANSWER

If all the world and love were young,
And truth in every shepherd's tongue,
These pretty pleasures might me move
To live with thee, and be thy love.

But Time drives flocks from field to fold;
When rivers rage, and rocks grow cold;
Then Philomel becometh dumb;
And age complains of cares to come.

The flowers do fade, and wanton fields
To wayward winter reckoning yields.
A honey tongue, a heart of gall,
Is fancy's spring, but sorrow's fall.

Thy gowns, thy shoes, thy beds of roses,
Thy cap, thy kirtle, and thy posies,
Soon break, soon wither, soon forgotten;
In folly ripe, in reason rotten.

Thy belt of straw, and ivy buds,
Thy coral clasps, and amber studs,
All these in me no means can move
To come to thee, and be thy love.

What should we talk of dainties, then
Of better meat than's fit for men?
These are but vain: that's only good
Which God hath blessed, and sent for food.

But could youth last, and love still breed;
Had joys no date, nor age no need;
Then those delights my mind might move
To live with thee, and be thy love.

Mother. Well! I have done my song. But stay, honest anglers; for I will make Maudlin sing you one short song more. Maudlin! sing that song that you sung last night, when young Coridon the shepherd played so purely on his oaten pipe to you and your cousin Betty.

Maudlin. I will, mother.

I married a wife of late,
The more's my unhappy fate:
I married her for love,
As my fancy did me move,
And not for a worldly estate:

But oh! the green sickness
Soon changed her likeness;
And all her beauty did fail.
But 'tis not so
With those that go
Thro' frost and snow,
As all men know,
And carry the milking-pail.

Piscator. Well sung, good woman; I thank you. I'll give you another dish of fish one of these days; and then beg another song of you. Come, scholar! let Maudlin alone: do not you offer to spoil her voice. Look! yonder comes mine hostess, to call us to supper. How now! is my brother Peter come?

Hostess. Yes, and a friend with him. They are both glad to hear that you are in these parts; and long to see you; and long to be at supper, for they be very hungry.

Henry Vaughan

1622–1695

A WELSH physician who called himself "Silurist" after the ancient inhabitants of his part of Wales, Henry Vaughan, with his twin brother Thomas, was educated at Oxford; they suffered for their loyalty to the royalist side in the Civil War. Vaughan's first book of poems, in 1646, showed him to be initially a follower of Jonson and Randolph as well as of Donne and Herbert. His religious interests gradually predominated, however, and his commitment to the metaphysical tradition was complete by 1655, when he published the second installment of *Silex Scintillans* ("shimmering flint"—a heart of stone from which fire is struck by divine action) in 1655. In his preface to that book Vaughan wrote that the age was given to "a constant, sensual volutation or wallowing in impure thoughts and scurrilous conceits, which both defile their authors, and as many more as they are communicated to." He was not referring only to others: "and here, because I would prevent a just censure by my free confession, I must remember, that I myself have for many years together languished of this very sickness; and it is no long time since I have recovered." His conversion from profane to sacred poetry he describes as follows: "The first that with any effectual success attempted a diversion of this foul and overflowing stream was the blessed man Mr. George Herbert, whose holy life and verse gained many pious converts (of whom I am the least) and gave the first check to a most flourishing and admired wit of his time."

The tribute to Herbert is deserved; he may be tracked everywhere in the snow of the sacred poetry of the mid-century. But Vaughan's conversion (if that is the proper term for a process so gradual) owed something also to the political and ecclesiastical upheavals of the Revolution; in his book of prose devotions called *The Mount of Olives* (1652) he writes:

"We could not have lived in an age of more instruction, had we been left to our own choice. We have seen such vicissitiudes and examples of human frailty as the former world, had they happened in those ages, would have judged prodigies. We have seen princes brought to their graves by a new way, and the highest order of human honors trampled upon by the lowest. We have seen Judgment beginning at God's Church, and (what hath been never heard of since it was redeemed and established by his blessed Son) we have seen His ministers cast out of the sanctuary and barbarous persons, without light or perfection, usurping holy offices. 'A day, an hour, a minute,' saith Casaubon, 'is sufficient to overturn and extirpate the most settled governments, which seem to have been founded and rooted in adamant.' Suddenly do the high things of this world come to an end, and their delectable things pass away, for when they seem to be in their flowers and full strength, they perish to astonishment. And sure the ruin of the most goodly pieces seems to tell that the dissolution of the whole is not far off."

Vaughan's mysticism, his direct perception of the other world as a world of light, and his sense of the unity of all things give his poetry a distinctive character. He has reminded many readers of Wordsworth, not only because he has a similar nostalgia for childhood and innocence, but also because, as Joan Bennett remarks, "both believe in the creation as the expression of a single mind; they turn to nature not only to envy and admire, but to discover." He will remind other readers, because of his acute sensitiveness to physical details in nature and his Welsh tendency to lushness of sound effects, of such later poets as Gerard Manley Hopkins and Dylan Thomas.

BIBLIOGRAPHY: *The Works of Henry Vaughan,* ed. L. C. Martin, Oxford, 1914; Elizabeth Holmes, *Henry Vaughan and the Hermetic Philosophy,* Oxford, 1932; Joan Bennett, *Four Metaphysical Poets,* Cambridge, 1934; J. B. Leishman, *The Metaphysical Poets,* Oxford, 1934; Edmund Blunden, *On the Poems of Henry Vaughan,* London, 1927; Helen C. White, *The Metaphysical Poets,* New York, 1936; S. L. Bethell, "The Poetry of Henry Vaughan, Silurist" in *The Cultural Revolution of the Seventeenth Century,* London, n.d.; E. L. Marilla, "Henry Vaughan and the Civil War," *JEGP,* XLI (1942), 514–526, and "The Religious Conversion of Vaughan," *RES,* XXI (1945), 15–22; Richard H. Walters, "Henry Vaughan and the Alchemists," *RES,* XXIII (1947), 107–122; Ralph M. Wardle, "Thomas Vaughan's Influence on Henry Vaughan," *PMLA,* LI (1936), 936–952; F. E. Hutchinson, *Henry Vaughan,* Oxford, 1947; L. C. Martin, "Henry Vaughan and the Theme of Infancy" in *Seventeenth Century Studies Presented to Sir Herbert Grierson,* Oxford, 1938.

A RHAPSODY[1]

Occasionally written upon a meeting with some of his friends at the Globe Tavern, in a chamber painted overhead with a cloudy sky and some few dispersed stars, and on the sides with landscapes, hills, shepherds and sheep.

Darkness and stars i' the midday! They invite
Our active fancies to believe it night;
For taverns need no sun, but for a sign,
Where rich tobacco and quick tapers shine,
And royal, witty sack, the poet's soul,
With brighter suns than he doth gild the bowl,
As though the pot and poet did agree,
Sack should to both illuminator be.
That artificial cloud with its curled brow
Tells us 'tis late, and that blue space below
Is fired with many stars; mark how they break
In silent glances o'er the hills and speak
The evening to the plains, where, shot from far,
They meet in dumb salutes, as one great star.
  The room, methinks, grows darker, and the air
Contracts a sadder color, and less fair;
Or is't the drawer's skill,—hath he no arts
To blind us so we can't know pints from quarts?
No, no, 'tis night; look where the jolly clown
Musters his bleating herd and quits the down.
Hark how his rude pipe frets the quiet air
Whilst every hill proclaims Lycoris fair.
Rich, happy man, that canst thus watch and sleep,
Free from all cares but thy wench, pipe, and sheep.
  But see, the moon is up; view where she stands
Sentinel o'er the door, drawn by the hands
Of some base painter, that for gain hath made
Her face the landmark to the tippling trade.
This cup to her, that to Endymion give;
'Twas wit at first, and wine, that made them live.
Choke may the painter! and his box disclose
No other colors than his fiery nose;

[1] From Vaughan's *Poems* of 1646, written in the tradition of Ben Jonson and Thomas Randolph.

And may we no more of his pencil see
Than two churchwardens and mortality.
  Should we go now a-wandering, we should meet
With catchpoles, whores, and carts in every street;
Now, when each narrow lane, each nook and cave,
Signposts and shop-doors, pimp for every knave;
When riotous, sinful plush and tell-tale spurs
Walk Fleet Street and the Strand; when the soft stirs
Of bawdy ruffled silks turn night to day,
And the loud whip and coach scolds all the way;
When lust of all sorts, and each itchy blood [2]
From the Tower-wharf to Cymbeline and Lud [3]
Hunts for a mate, and the tired footman reels
'Twixt chairmen, torches, and the hackney wheels—
  Come, take the other dish; it is to him
That made his horse a senator,[4] each brim
Looks big as mine; the gallant, jolly beast
Of all the herd, you'll say, was not the least.
  Now crown the second bowl, rich as his worth
I'll drink it to: He that, like fire broke forth
Into the senate's face, crossed Rubicon
And the state's pillars, with their laws thereon,
And made the dull gray beards and furred gowns fly
Into Brindisium to consult and lie.
  This to brave Sulla! Why should it be said
We drink more to the living than the dead?
Flatterers and fools do use it; let us laugh
At our own honest mirth, for they that quaff
To honor others do like those that sent
Their gold and plate to strangers to be spent.
  Drink deep! This cup be pregnant, and the wine
Spirit of wit, to make us all divine,
That, big with sack and mirth, we may retire
Possessors of more souls and nobler fire;
And, by the influence of this painted sky
And labored forms, to higher matters fly;
So, if a nap shall take us, we shall all,
After full cups, have dreams poetical.
    Let's laugh now, and the pressed grape drink,
    Till the drowsy day-star wink;

[2] *blood:* rake, roisterer.

[3] *Cymbeline and Lud:* i.e., to Ludgate, which displayed statues of the legendary King Lud and his sons.

[4] *him . . . senator:* the Roman emperor Caligula; this allusion and the following ones to Julius Caesar and to Sulla reflect the poet's contempt for the Senate (i.e., the English Parliament).

And in our merry, mad mirth, run
Faster and further than the sun;
And let none his cup forsake
Till that star again doth wake;
So we men below shall move
Equally with the gods above.

VANITY OF SPIRIT[5]

Quite spent with thoughts, I left my cell and lay
Where a shrill spring tuned to the early day.
  I begged here long, and groaned to know
  Who gave the clouds so brave a bow,
  Who bent the spheres, and circled in
  Corruption with this glorious ring;
  What is His name, and how I might
  Descry some part of His great light.
I summoned nature, pierced through all her store,[6]
Broke up some seals which none had touched before;
  Her womb, her bosom, and her head
  Where all her secrets lay abed,
  I rifled quite; and having passed
  Through all her creatures, came at last
  To search myself, where I did find
  Traces and sounds of a strange kind.
Here of this mighty spring I found some drills,
With echoes beaten from the eternal hills;
  Weak beams and fires flashed to my sight,
  Like a young east, or moonshine night,
  Which showed me in a nook cast by
  A piece of much antiquity,
  With hieroglyphics quite dismembered,
  And broken letters scarce remembered.
I took them up and, much joyed, went about
To unite those pieces, hoping to find out
  The mystery; but this ne'er done,
  That little light I had was gone:
  It grieved me much. At last, said I,
  Since in these veils my eclipsed eye
  May not approach Thee (for at night
  Who can have commerce with the light?),
  I'll disapparel, and to buy
  But on half glance, most gladly die.

[5] From *Silex Scintillans* (1650).

[6] *store:* plenty (as in Herbert's poems).

THE RETREAT[7]

Happy those early days, when I
Shined in my angel infancy;
Before I understood this place
Appointed for my second race,
Or taught my soul to fancy aught
But a white, celestial thought;
When yet I had not walked above
A mile or two from my first Love,
And looking back, at that short space,
Could see a glimpse of His bright face;
When on some gilded cloud or flower
My gazing soul would dwell an hour,
And in those weaker glories spy
Some shadows of eternity;
Before I taught my tongue to wound
My conscience with a sinful sound,
Or had the black art to dispense
A several sin to every sense,
But felt through all this fleshly dress
Bright shoots of everlastingness.
  Oh, how I long to travel back,
And tread again that ancient track!
That I might once more reach that plain
Where first I left my glorious train;
From whence the enlightened spirit sees
That shady city of palm trees.
But, ah! my soul with too much stay
Is drunk, and staggers in the way.
Some men a forward motion love;
But I by backward steps would move,
And when this dust falls to the urn,
In that state I came, return.

THE MORNING WATCH

Oh joys! Infinite sweetness! With what flowers
And shoots of glory my soul breaks and buds!

---

[7] Vaughan's ideas about childhood resemble those of Wordsworth in the "Ode: Intimations of Immortality," but it has not been shown that Wordsworth knew Vaughan's poem.

All the long hours
Of night, and rest
Through the still shrouds
Of sleep, and clouds,
This dew fell on my breast.
Oh how it bloods [8]
And spirits all my earth! Hark! In what rings
And hymning circulations the quick world
Awakes and sings;
The rising winds
And falling springs,
Birds, beasts,—all things
Adore Him in their kinds.
Thus all is hurled
In sacred hymns and order: the great chime
And symphony of nature. Prayer is
The world in tune,
A spirit-voice
And vocal joys
Whose echo is heaven's bliss.
Oh let me climb
When I lie down! The pious soul by night
Is like a clouded star whose beams, though said
To shed their light
Under some cloud
Yet are above
And shine and move
Beyond that misty shroud;
So, in my bed,
That curtained grave, though sleep, like ashes, hide
My lamp and life, both shall in Thee abide.

PEACE

My soul, there is a country
Far beyond the stars,
Where stands a winged sentry
All skilful in the wars.
There, above noise and danger,
Sweet Peace sits crowned with smiles,
And one born in a manger
Commands the beauteous files.

[8] *bloods:* arouses, excites.

He is thy gracious friend,
  And (Oh my soul, awake!)
Did in pure love descend
  To die here for thy sake.
If thou canst get but thither,
  There grows the flower of peace,
The rose that cannot wither,
  Thy fortress and thy ease.
Leave, then, thy foolish ranges [9]
  For none can thee secure
But one who never changes,
  Thy God, thy life, thy cure.

AND DO THEY SO?

Romans 8:19

Etenim res creatae exerto capite observantes expectant revelationem Filiorum Dei.[10]

AND do they so? Have they a sense
  Of aught but influence? [11]
Can they their heads lift, and expect,
  And groan too? Why the elect
Can do no more; my volumes said
  They were all dull and dead;
They judged them senseless, and their state
  Wholly inanimate.
  Go, go, seal up thy looks,
    And burn thy books.

I would I were a stone, or tree,
  Or flower, by pedigree,
Or some poor highway herb, or spring
  To flow, or bird to sing!
Then should I, tied to one sure state,
  All day expect my date; [12]
But I am sadly loose, and stray
  A giddy blast each way;
  O let me thus range,
    Thou canst not change!

[9] *ranges:* wanderings.

[10] *Etenim . . . Dei:* "For created things wait with eager longing for the revealing of the sons of God." The Latin is Beza's.

[11] *influence:* the effect of environment.

[12] *date:* final destiny.

Sometime I sit with Thee and tarry
  An hour or so, then vary;
Thy other creatures in this scene
  Thee only aim and mean;
Some rise to seek Thee, and with heads
  Erect, peep from their beds;
Others, whose birth is in the tomb,
  And cannot quit the womb,
  Sigh there, and groan for Thee,
    Their liberty.

Oh let me not do less! Shall they
  Watch, while I sleep or play?
Shall I Thy mercies still abuse
  With fancies, friends, or news?
Oh brook it not! Thy blood is mine,
  And my soul should be Thine;
Oh brook it not! why wilt Thou stop,
  After whole showers, one drop?
  Sure Thou wilt joy to see
    Thy sheep with Thee.

THE DAWNING

Ah! what time wilt Thou come? when shall that cry,
"The Bridegroom's coming,"[13] fill the sky?
Shall it in the evening run,
When our words and works are done?
Or will Thy all-surprising light
    Break at midnight,
When either sleep or some dark pleasure
Possesseth mad man without measure?
Or shall these early fragrant hours
    Unlock Thy bowers,
And with their blush of light descry
Thy locks crowned with eternity?
Indeed, it is the only time
That with Thy glory doth best chime;
All now are stirring, every field
    Full hymns doth yield,
The whole creation shakes off night,
And for Thy shadow looks the light;

---

[13] *"The Bridegroom's coming"*: Matthew 25:6.

Stars now vanish without number,
Sleepy planets set and slumber,
The pursy [14] clouds disband and scatter,
All except some sudden matter;
Not one beam triumphs, but from afar
That morning star.
Oh, at what time soever, Thou,
Unknown to us, the heavens wilt bow,
And with Thy angels in the van
Descend to judge poor careless man,
Grant I may not like puddle lie
In a corrupt security,
Where, if a traveler water crave,
He finds it dead and in a grave;
But as this restless vocal spring
All day and night doth run and sing,
And though here born, yet is acquainted
Elsewhere, and flowing keeps untainted,
So let me all my busy age
In Thy free services engage;
And though while here of force I must
Have commerce sometimes with poor dust,
And in my flesh, though vile and low,
As this doth in her channel flow,
Yet let my course, my aim, my love,
And chief acquaintance be above;
So when that day and hour shall come
In which Thyself will be the sun,
Thou'lt find me dressed and on my way,
Watching the break of Thy great day.

THE WORLD

I SAW eternity the other night
Like a great ring of pure and endless light,
All calm as it was bright;
And round beneath it, time, in hours, days, years,
Driven by the spheres,
Like a vast shadow moved, in which the world
And all her train were hurled.
The doting lover in his quaintest strain
Did there complain;

[14] *pursy:* swollen, heavy.

Near him, his lute, his fancy, and his flights,
  Wit's sour delights,
With gloves and knots [15] the silly snares of pleasure,
  Yet his dear treasure,
All scattered lay, while he his eyes did pour
  Upon a flower.

The darksome statesman, hung with weights and woe,
Like a thick midnight fog, moved there so slow
  He did not stay nor go;
Condemning thoughts, like mad eclipses, scowl
  Upon his soul,
And crowds of crying witnesses without
  Pursued him with one shout.
Yet digged the mole, and lest his ways be found,
  Worked under ground,
Where he did clutch his prey. But one did see
  That policy:
Churches and altars fed him; perjuries
  Were gnats and flies;
It rained about him blood and tears; but he
  Drank them as free.

The fearful miser on a heap of rust
Sat pining all his life there, did scarce trust
  His own hands with the dust;
Yet would not place one piece above, but lives
  In fear of thieves.
Thousands there were as frantic as himself,
  And hugged each one his pelf:
And downright epicure placed heaven in sense,
  And scorned pretense;
While others, slipped into a wide excess,
  Said little less;
The weaker sort, slight trivial wares enslave,
  Who think them brave;
And poor, despised Truth sat counting by
  Their victory.

Yet some, who all this while did weep and sing,
And sing and weep, soared up into the ring;
  But most would use no wing.
"Oh fools!" said I, "thus to prefer dark night
  Before true light!

---

15 *knots:* bunches of ribbon, or perhaps bouquets of flowers.

To live in grots and caves, and hate the day
  Because it shows the way,
The way which from this dead and dark abode
  Leads up to God;
A way where you might tread the sun and be
  More bright than he!"
But, as I did their madness so discuss,
  One whispered thus:
"This ring the Bridegroom did for none provide,
  But for His bride."

I WALKED THE OTHER DAY, TO SPEND MY HOUR

I walked the other day, to spend my hour,
    Into a field,
Where I sometimes had seen the soil to yield
    A gallant flower;
But winter now had ruffled all the bower
    And curious store
  I knew there heretofore.

Yet I, whose search loved not to peep and peer
    I' the face of things,
Thought with myself, there might be other springs
    Besides this here,
Which, like cold friends, sees us but once a year;
    And so the flower
  Might have some other bower.

Then taking up what I could nearest spy,
    I digged about
That place where I had seen him to grow out;
    And by and by
I saw the warm recluse alone to lie,
    Where, fresh and green,
  He lived of us unseen.

Many a question intricate and rare
    Did I there strow; [16]
But all I could extort was, that he now
    Did there repair

[16] *strow:* strew, scatter.

Such losses as befall him in this air,
And would ere long
Come forth most fair and young.

This past, I threw the clothes quite o'er his head;
And, stung with fear
Of my own frailty, dropped down many a tear
Upon his bed;
Then, sighing, whispered, "Happy are the dead!
What peace doth now
Rock him asleep below!"

And yet, how few believe such doctrine springs
From a poor root,
Which all the winter sleeps here under foot,
And hath no wings
To raise it to the truth and light of things,
But is still trod
By every wandering clod.

Oh Thou! whose spirit did at first inflame
And warm the dead,
And by a sacred incubation fed
With life this frame,
Which once had neither being, form, nor name,
Grant I may so
Thy steps track here below,

That in these masques and shadows I may see
Thy sacred way;
And by those hid ascents climb to that day
Which breaks from Thee,
Who art in all things, though invisibly;
Show me Thy peace,
Thy mercy, love, and ease.

And from this care, where dreams and sorrows reign,
Lead me above,
Where light, joy, leisure, and true comforts move
Without all pain;
There, hid in Thee, show me his life again,
At whose dumb urn
Thus all the year I mourn!

THEY are all gone into the world of light,[17]
And I alone sit lingering here.
Their very memory is fair and bright
And my sad thoughts doth clear.

It glows and glitters in my cloudy breast,
Like stars upon some gloomy grove,
Or those faint beams in which this hill is dressed
After the sun's remove.

I see them walking in an air of glory,
Whose light doth trample on my days;
My days, which are at best but dull and hoary,
Mere glimmering and decays.

Oh holy hope, and high humility,
High as the heavens above!
These are your walks, and you have showed them me
To kindle my cold love.

Dear, beauteous death! the jewel of the just,
Shining nowhere but in the dark;
What mysteries do lie beyond thy dust,
Could man outlook that mark!

He that hath found some fledged [18] bird's nest may know
At first sight if the bird be flown;
But what fair well or grove he sings in now,
That is to him unknown.

And yet, as angels in some brighter dreams
Call to the soul when man doth sleep,
So some strange thoughts transcend our wonted themes,
And into glory peep.

If a star were confined into a tomb,
Her captive flames must needs burn there;
But when the hand that locked her up gives room,
She'll shine through all the sphere.

Oh Father of eternal life, and all
Created glories under Thee!

---

[17] From the 1655 edition of *Silex Scintillans.* This famous poem is one of a series of elegies which Vaughan left untitled.

[18] *fledged:* feathered, fully plumed.

Resume Thy spirit from this world of thrall
Into true liberty!

Either disperse these mists, which blot and fill
My perspective [19] still as they pass;
Or else remove me hence unto that hill
Where I shall need no glass.

THE NIGHT

THROUGH that pure virgin shrine,
That sacred veil drawn o'er Thy glorious noon,
That men might look and live, as glowworms shine,
And face the moon,
Wise Nicodemus saw such light
As made him know his God by night.

Most blest believer he,
Who in that land of darkness and blind eyes
Thy long-expected healing wings could see,
When Thou didst rise!
And, what can never more be done,
Did at midnight speak with the Sun!

Oh who will tell me where
He found Thee at that dead and silent hour?
What hallowed solitary ground did bear
So rare a flower,
Within whose sacred leaves did lie
The fulness of the Deity?

No mercy-seat of gold,
No dead and dusty cherub, nor carved stone,
But His own living works did my Lord hold
And lodge alone;
Where trees and herbs did watch and peep
And wonder, while the Jews did sleep.

Dear night! this world's defeat,
The stop to busy fools, care's check and curb,
The day of spirits, my soul's calm retreat
Which none disturb!

[19] *perspective:* telescope or other optical instrument.

Christ's progress and His prayer time;
The hours to which high Heaven doth chime;

God's silent, searching flight;
When my Lord's head is filled with dew, and all
His locks are wet with the clear drops of night;
His still, soft call;
His knocking time; the soul's dumb watch,
When spirits their fair kindred catch.

Were all my loud, evil days
Calm and unhaunted as is thy dark tent,
Whose peace but by some angel's wing or voice
Is seldom rent,
Then I in heaven all the long year
Would keep, and never wander here.

But living where the sun
Doth all things wake, and where all mix and tire
Themselves and others, I consent and run
To every mire,
And by this world's ill-guiding light,
Err more than I can do by night.

There is in God—some say—
A deep but dazzling darkness, as men here
Say it is late and dusky, because they
See not all clear.
Oh for that night, where I in Him
Might live invisible and dim!

QUICKNESS

False life, a foil and no more, when
Wilt thou be gone?
Thou foul deception of all men
That would not have the true come on.

Thou art a moon-like toil, a blind
Self-posing state,
A dark contest of waves and wind,
A mere tempestuous debate.

Life is a fixed, discerning light,
A knowing joy;
No chance or fit, but ever bright
And calm and full, yet doth not cloy.

'Tis such a blissful thing that still
Doth vivify
And shine and smile and hath the skill
To please without eternity.

Thou art a toilsome mole, or less;
A moving mist;
But life is what none can express:
A quickness which my God hath kissed.

Thomas Hobbes

1588–1679

THE greatest philosopher of the generation after Bacon, Hobbes was pre-eminent in political philosophy, psychology, and metaphysics. He lived to be ninety-one, and it was not until he was almost forty that the reading of Euclid opened his eyes to the possibilities inherent in logical thinking. But he had already been in the employ of Bacon, and he was to contribute as much, or more, to the philosophy of science as his master had done.

He spent many years as a tutor and companion in the household of the Cavendish family; he traveled in Europe and conversed with Galileo and other advanced thinkers. In 1640 Hobbes went to Paris as a pioneer royalist exile; he remained there eleven years and was for a while mathematical tutor to the future King Charles II. Devout and godly Englishmen were worried, for Hobbes' materialistic views were well known and he was regarded as hardly distinguishable from an atheist.

In his great work, *Leviathan* (1651), Hobbes erects an elaborate defense for the authority and power of the state, but unlike the Stuarts whom he served, Hobbes did not believe in Divine Right. In fact, he professed not to believe in natural right either, but in submission to authority as the price we pay for peace, order, and security. But even these are not the prime goals of man, Hobbes thinks. "The felicity of this life consisteth not in the repose of a mind satisfied. For there is no such *finis ultimus* [utmost aim] nor *summum bonum* [greatest good] as is spoken of in the books of the old moral philosophers. . . . I put for a general inclination of all mankind a perpetual and restless desire of power after power, that ceaseth only in death."

If the fundamental basis of politics is the struggle for power, the fundamental principle in science is motion. Likewise there is a fundamental principle of psychology by which all human feelings, perceptions, and actions can be regarded as modes of motion.

Hobbes terrified his own time; he undermined traditional common notions and the respectable Aristotelian ways of thinking taught in the universities. He was a nominalist, a materialist; according to him man was merely a bundle of appetites and desires. These positions may have seemed frightening because they suggested the future of thought.

BIBLIOGRAPHY: *Leviathan,* many editions; Sir Leslie Stephen, *Hobbes,* London, 1904; Basil Willey, *The Seventeenth Century Background,* London, 1934; A. E. Taylor, "An Apology for Mr. Hobbes" in *Seventeenth Century Studies Presented to Sir Herbert Grierson,* Oxford, 1938; C. D. Thorpe, *The Aesthetic Theory of Thomas Hobbes,* Ann Arbor, 1940; Marjorie Nicolson, "Milton and Hobbes," *SP,* XXIII (1926), 405–433.

FROM

LEVIATHAN

CHAPTER IV. OF SPEECH

THE invention of printing, though ingenious, compared with the invention of letters is no great matter. But who was the first that found the use of letters, is not known. He that first brought them into Greece, men say was Cadmus, the son of Agenor, king of Phoenicia. A profitable invention for continuing the memory of time past, and the conjunction of mankind dispersed into so many and distant regions of the earth; and withal difficult, as proceeding from a watchful observation of the divers motions of the tongue, palate, lips, and other organs of speech; whereby to make as many differences of characters, to remember them. But the most noble and profitable invention of all other, was that of speech, consisting of names or appellations, and their connection; whereby men register their thoughts, recall them when they are past, and also declare them one to another for mutual utility and conversation; without which there had been amongst men neither commonwealth, nor society, nor contract, nor peace, no more than amongst lions, bears, and wolves. The first author of speech was God himself, that instructed Adam how to name such creatures as He presented to his sight; for the Scripture goeth no further in this matter. But this was sufficient to direct him to add more names, as the experience and use of the creatures should give him occasion; and to join them in such manner, by degrees, as to make himself understood; and so, by succession of time, so much language might be gotten as he had found use for; though not so copious as an orator or philosopher has need of; for I do not find anything in the Scripture out of which, directly or by consequence, can be gathered that Adam was taught the names of all figures, numbers, measures, colors, sounds, fancies, relations; much less the names of words and speech, as general, special, affirmative, negative, interrogative, optative, infinitive, all which are useful; and least of all, of entity, intentionality, quiddity, and other insignificant words of the school.

But all this language gotten and augmented by Adam and his posterity was again lost at the Tower of Babel, when, by the hand of God, every man was stricken, for his rebellion, with an oblivion of his former language. And being hereby forced to disperse themselves into several parts of the world, it must needs be that the diversity of tongues that now is, proceeded by degrees from them, in such manner as need, the mother of all inventions, taught them; and in tract of time grew everywhere more copious.

The general use of speech is to transfer our mental discourse into verbal, or the train of our thoughts into a train of words; and that for two commodities, whereof one is the registering of the consequences of our thoughts; which, being apt to slip out of our memory and put us to a new labor, may again be recalled by such words as they were marked by. So that the first use of names is to serve for marks, or notes of remembrance. Another is, when many use the same words, to signify, by their connection and order, one to another, what they conceive, or think of each matter; and also what they desire, fear, or have any other passion for. And for this use they are called signs. Special uses of speech are these: first, to register what by cogitation we find to be the cause of anything, present or past, and what we find things present or past may produce or effect; which, in sum, is acquiring of arts. Secondly, to show to others that knowledge which we have attained; which is, to counsel and teach one another. Thirdly, to make known to others our wills and purposes, that we may have the mutual help of one another. Fourthly to please and delight ourselves and others, by playing with our words, for pleasure or ornament, innocently.

To these uses, there are also four correspondent abuses. First, when men register their thoughts wrong by the inconstancy of the signification of their words; by which they register for their conception, that which they never conceived, and so deceive themselves. Secondly, when they use words metaphorically; that is, in other sense that that they are ordained for, and thereby deceive others. Thirdly, by words, when they declare that to be their will which is not. Fourthly, when they use them to grieve one another; for seeing nature hath armed living creatures, some with teeth, some with horns, and some with hands, to grieve an enemy, it is but an abuse of speech, to grieve him with the tongue, unless it be one whom we are obliged to govern; and then it is not to grieve, but to correct and amend. . . .

Seeing then that truth consisteth in the right ordering of names in our affirmations, a man that seeketh precise truth had need to remember what every name he uses stands for, and to place it accordingly, or else he will find himself entangled in words, as a bird in lime twigs, the more he struggles the more belimed. And therefore in geometry, which is the only science that it hath pleased God hitherto to bestow on mankind, men begin at settling the significations of their words; which settling of significations they call definitions, and place them in the beginning of their reckoning.

By this it appears how necessary it is for any man that aspires to true knowledge, to examine the definitions of former authors; and either to correct them, where they are negligently set down, or to make them himself. For the errors of definitions multiply themselves according as the reckoning proceeds, and lead men into absurdities, which at last they see, but cannot avoid without reckoning anew from the beginning, in which lies the foundation of their errors. From whence it happens that they which trust to books do as they that cast up many little sums into a greater, without considering whether those little sums were rightly cast up or not; and at last finding the error visible, and not mistrusting their first grounds, know not which way to clear themselves, but spend time in fluttering over their books; as birds that entering by the chimney, and finding themselves enclosed in a chamber, flutter at the false light of a glass window, for want of wit to consider which way they came in. So that in the right definition of names lies the first use of speech, which is the acquisition of science; and in wrong, or no definitions, lies the first abuse, from which proceed all false and senseless tenets; which make those men that take their instruction from an authority of books, and not from their own meditation, to be as much below the condition of ignorant men as men endued with true science are above it. For between true science and erroneous doctrines, ignorance is in the middle. Natural sense and imagination are not subject to absurdity. Nature itself cannot err; and as men abound in copiousness of language, so they become more wise, or more mad, than ordinary. Nor is it possible without letters for any man to become either excellently wise, or, unless his memory be hurt by disease or ill constitution of organs, excellently foolish. For words are wise men's counters, they do but reckon by them; but they are the money of fools, that value them by the authority of an Aristotle, a Cicero, or a Thomas, or any other doctor whatsoever, if but a man. . . .

CHAPTER V. OF REASON AND SCIENCE

When a man reasoneth, he does nothing else but conceive a sum total, from addition of parcels; or conceive a remainder, from subtraction of one sum from another; which, if it be done by words, is conceiving of the consequence of the names of all the parts, to the names of the whole; or from the names of the whole and one part, to the name of the other part. And though in some things, as in numbers, besides adding and subtracting, men name other operations, as multiplying and dividing, yet they are the same; for multiplication is but adding together of things equal; and division, but subtracting of one thing as often as we can. These operations are not incident to numbers only, but to all manner of things that can be added together and taken one out of another. For as arithmeticians teach to add and subtract in numbers; so the geometricians teach the same in lines, figures, solid and superficial, angles, proportions, times, degrees of swiftness, force, power, and the like; the logicians teach the same in consequences of words; adding together two names to make an affirmation, and two affirmations to make a syllogism, and many syllogisms to make a demonstration; and from the sum or conclusion of a syllogism, they subtract one proposition to find the other. Writers of politics add together pactions [1] to find men's duties; and lawyers, laws and facts, to find what is right and wrong in the actions of private men. In sum, in what matter soever there is place for addition and subtraction, there also is place for reason; and where these have no place, there reason has nothing at all to do.

Out of all which we may define, that is to say determine, what that is which is meant by this word reason, when we reckon it amongst the faculties of the mind. For reason, in this sense, is nothing but reckoning, that is adding and subtracting, of the consequences of general names agreed upon for the marking and signifying of our thoughts. I say marking them when we reckon by ourselves, and signfying when we demonstrate or approve our reckonings to other men.

And, as in arithmetic, unpracticed men must, and professors themselves may often, err, and cast up false; so also in any other subject of reasoning, the ablest, most attentive, and most practiced men may deceive themselves, and infer false conclusions; not but that reason itself is always right reason, as well as arithmetic is a certain and infallible art; but no one man's reason, nor the reason of any one number of men, makes the certainty; no more than an account is therefore well cast up because a great many men have unanimously approved it. And therefore, as when there is a controversy in an account, the parties must by their own accord set up, for right reason, the reason of some arbitrator or judge, to whose sentence they will both stand, or their controversy must either come to blows or be undecided, for want of a right reason constituted by nature; so it is also in all debates of what kind soever. And when men that think themselves wiser than all others, clamor and demand right reason for judge, yet seek no more but that things should be determined by no other men's reason but their own, it is as intolerable in the society of men, as it is in play after trump is turned, to use for trump on every occasion that suit whereof they have most in their hand. For they do nothing else that will have every of their passions, as it comes to bear sway in them, to be taken for right reason, and that in their own controversies; betraying their want of right reason by the claim they lay to it.

The use and end of reason is not the finding of the sum and truth of one, or a few consequences, remote from the first definitions, and settled significations of names; but to begin at these, and proceed from one consequence to another. For there can be no certainty of the last conclusion, without a certainty of all those affirmations and negations on which it was grounded and inferred. As when a master of a family, in taking an account, casteth up the sums of all the bills of expense into one sum, and not regarding how each bill is summed up by those that give them in account, nor what it is he pays for; he advantages himself no more than if he allowed the account in gross, trusting to every of the accountants' skill and honesty; so also in reasoning of all other things, he that takes up conclusions on the trust of authors, and doth not fetch them from the first items in every

[1] *pactions:* agreements.

reckoning, which are the significations of names settled by definitions, loses his labor, and does not know anything, but only believeth.

When a man reckons without the use of words, which may be done in particular things, as when upon the sight of any one thing, we conjecture, what was likely to have preceded, or is likely to follow upon it; if that which he thought likely to follow, follows not, or that which he thought likely to have preceded it, hath not preceded it, this is called error; to which even the most prudent men are subject. But when we reason in words of general signification, and fall upon a general inference which is false, though it be commonly called error, it is indeed an absurdity, or senseless speech. For error is but a deception, in presuming that somewhat is past or to come; of which, though it was not past, or not to come, yet there was no impossibility discoverable. But when we make a general assertion, unless it be a true one, the possibility of it is inconceivable. And words whereby we conceive nothing but the sound, are those we call absurd, insignificant, and nonsense. And therefore if a man should talk to me of a round quadrangle, or, accidents of bread in cheese, or immaterial substances, or of a free subject, a free will, or any free, but free from being hindered by opposition; I should not say he were in an error, but that his words were without meaning, that is to say, absurd.

I have said before, in the second chapter, that a man did excel all other animals in this faculty, that when he conceived anything whatsoever, he was apt to inquire the consequences of it, and what effects he could do with it. And now I add this other degree of the same excellence, that he can by words reduce the consequences he finds to general rules, called theorems, or aphorisms; that is, he can reason, or reckon, not only in number, but in all other things whereof one may be added unto, or subtracted from another.

But this privilege is allayed by another; and that is, by the privilege of absurdity, to which no living creature is subject but man only. And of men, those are of all most subject to it that profess philosophy. For it is most true that Cicero saith of them somewhere, that there can be nothing so absurd but may be found in the books of philosophers. And the reason is manifest. For there is not one of them that begins his ratiocination from the definitions, or explications of the names they are to use; which is a method that hath been used only in geometry, whose conclusions have thereby been made indisputable.

(i) The first cause of absurd conclusions I ascribe to the want of method, in that they begin not their ratiocination from definitions; that is, from settled significations of their words; as if they could cast account without knowing the value of the numeral words, one, two, and three.

And whereas all bodies enter into account upon divers considerations, which I have mentioned in the precedent chapter; these considerations being diversely named, divers absurdities proceed from the confusion, and unfit connection of their names into assertions. And therefore:

(ii) The second cause of absurd assertions, I ascribe to the giving of names of bodies to accidents, or of accidents to bodies; as they do that say, faith is 'infused,' or 'inspired'; when nothing can be poured, or breathed into anything, but body; and that, extension is body; that phantasms are spirits, etc.

(iii) The third I ascribe to the giving of the names of the accidents of bodies without us, to the accidents of our own bodies; as they do that say the color is in the body, the sound is in the air, etc.

(iv) The fourth, to the giving of the names of bodies to names or speeches; as they do that say that there be things universal; that a living creature is genus, or a general thing, etc.

(v) The fifth, to the giving of the names of accidents to names and speeches; as they do that say the nature of a thing is its definition, a man's command is his will, and the like.

(vi) The sixth, to the use of metaphors, tropes, and other rhetorical figures, instead of words proper. For though it be lawful to say, for example, in common speech, "the way goeth, or leadeth hither, or thither"; "the proverb says this or that," whereas ways cannot go, nor proverbs speak; yet in reckoning, and seeking of truth, such speeches are not to be admitted.

(vii) The seventh, to names that signify nothing, but are taken up and learned by rote from the schools, as 'hypostatical,' 'transubstantiate,' 'consubstantiate,' 'eternal-now,' and the like canting of schoolmen.

To him that can avoid these things it is not easy to fall into any absurdity, unless it be by the length of an account; wherein he may perhaps forget what went before. For all men by nature reason alike, and well, when they have good principles. For who is so stupid, as both to mistake in geometry, and also to persist in it when another detects his error to him?

By this it appears that reason is not, as sense and memory, born with us; nor gotten by experience only, as prudence is, but attained by industry; first in apt imposing of names; and secondly by getting a good and orderly method in proceeding from the elements, which are names, to assertions made by connection of one of them to another; and so to syllogisms, which are the connections of one assertion to another, till we come to a knowledge of all the consequences of names appertaining to the subject in hand; and that is it, men call science. And whereas sense and memory are but knowledge of fact, which is a thing past and irrevocable, science is the knowledge of consequences, and dependence of one fact upon another; by which, out of that we can presently do, we know how to do something else when we will, or the like another time; because when we see how anything comes about, upon what causes, and by what manner; when the like causes come into our power, we see how to make it produce the like effects.

Children therefore are not endued with reason at all, till they have attained the use of speech; but are called reasonable creatures, for the possibility apparent of having the use of reason in time to come. And the most part of men, though they have the use of reasoning a little way, as in numbering to some degree, yet it serves them to little use in common life; in which they govern themselves, some better, some worse, according to their differences of experience, quickness of memory, and inclinations to several ends; but especially according to good or evil fortune, and the errors of one another. For as for science, or certain rules of their actions, they are so far from it, they know not what it is. Geometry they have thought conjuring; but for other sciences, they who have not been taught the beginnings and some progress in them, that they may see how they be acquired and generated, are in this point like children, that having no thought of generation, are made believe by the women that their brothers and sisters are not born, but found in the garden.

But yet they that have no science, are in better and nobler condition, with their natural prudence, than men that by misreasoning, or by trusting them that reason wrong, fall upon false and absurd general rules. For ignorance of causes, and of rules, does not set men so far out of their way, as relying on false rules, and taking for causes of what they aspire to, those that are not so, but rather causes of the contrary.

To conclude, the light of human minds is perspicuous words, but by exact definitions first snuffed and purged from ambiguity; reason is the pace; increase of science, the way; and the benefit of mankind, the end. And, on the contrary, metaphors, and senseless and ambiguous words, are like *ignes fatui;* and reasoning upon them is wandering amongst innumerable absurdities; and their end, contention and sedition, for contempt.

As much experience is prudence, so is much science *sapience.* For though we usually have one name of wisdom for them both, yet the Latins did always distinguish between *prudentia* and *sapientia,* ascribing the former to experience, the latter to science. But to make their difference appear more clearly, let us suppose one man endued with an excellent natural use and dexterity in handling his arms; and another to have added to that dexterity, an acquired science, of where he can offend, or be offended by his adversary, in every possible posture or guard. The ability of the former would be to the ability of the latter, as prudence to sapience; both useful, but the latter infallible. But they that trusting only to the authority of books, follow the blind blindly, are like him that, trusting to the false rules of a master of fence, ventures presumptuously upon an adversary that either kills or disgraces him.

The signs of science are some, certain and infallible; some, uncertain. Certain, when he that pretendeth the science of anything, can teach the same—that is to say, demonstrate the truth thereof perspicuously to another; uncertain, when only some particular events answer to his pretence, and upon many occasions prove so as he says they must. Signs of prudence are all uncertain; because to observe by experience, and remember all circumstances that may alter the success, is impossible. But in any business whereof a man has not infallible science to proceed by, to forsake his own natural judgment, and be guided by general sentences read in authors and subject to many exceptions, is a sign of folly, and generally scorned by the name of pedantry. And even of those men themselves that in councils of the commonwealth love to show their reading of politics and history, very few do it in their domestic affairs, where their particular interest is concerned; having prudence enough for their private affairs, but in public they study more the reputation of their own wit than the success of another's business.

CHAPTER XIII. OF THE NATURAL CONDITION OF MANKIND AS CONCERNING THEIR FELICITY, AND MISERY

Nature hath made men so equal in the faculties of the body and mind as that, though there be found one man sometimes manifestly stronger in body or of quicker mind than another, yet when all is reckoned together, the difference between man and man is not so considerable, as that one man can thereupon claim to himself any benefit, to which another may not pretend as well as he. For as to the strength of body, the weakest has strength enough to kill the strongest, either by secret machination, or by confederacy with others that are in the same danger with himself.

And as to the faculties of the mind—setting aside the arts grounded upon words, and especially that skill of proceeding upon general and infallible rules, called science; which very few have, and but in few things; as being not a native faculty, born with us; nor attained, as prudence, while we look after somewhat else—I find yet a greater equality amongst men, than that of strength. For prudence is but experience, which equal time equally bestows on all men, in those things they equally apply themselves unto. That which may perhaps make such equality incredible, is but a vain conceit of one's own wisdom, which almost all men think they have in a greater degree than the vulgar—that is, all men but themselves and a few others, whom by fame, or for concurring with themselves, they approve. For such is the nature of men, that howsoever they may acknowledge many others to be more witty, or more eloquent, or more learned, yet they will hardly believe there be many so wise as themselves; for they see their own wit at hand, and other men's at a distance. But this proveth rather that men are in that point equal, than unequal. For there is not ordinarily a greater sign of the equal distribution of anything, than that every man is contented with his share.

From this equality of ability, ariseth equality of hope in the attaining of our ends. And therefore if any two men desire the same thing, which nevertheless they cannot both enjoy, they become enemies; and in the way to their end, which is principally their own conservation, and sometimes their delectation only, endeavor to destroy or subdue one another. And from hence it comes to pass that where an invader hath no more to fear than another man's single power; if one plant, sow, build, or possess a convenient seat, others may probably be expected to come prepared with forces united, to dispossess and deprive him, not only of the fruit of his labor, but also of his life or liberty. And the invader again is in the like danger of another.

And from this diffidence of one another, there is no way for any man to secure himself so reasonable as anticipation; that is, by force or wiles to master the persons of all men he can, so long, till he see no other power great enough to endanger him, and this is no more than his own conservation requireth, and is generally allowed. Also because there be some, that taking pleasure in contemplating their own power in the acts of conquest, which they pursue farther than their security requires; if others that otherwise would be glad to be at ease within modest bounds, should not by invasion increase their power, they would not be able long time, by standing only on their defense, to subsist. And by consequence, such augmentation of dominion over men being necessary to a man's conservation, it ought to be allowed him.

Again, men have no pleasure, but on the contrary a great deal of grief, in keeping company, where there is no power able to overawe them all. For every man looketh that his companion should value him at the same rate he sets upon himself; and upon all signs of contempt, or undervaluing, naturally endeavors, as far as he dares (which amongst them that have no common power to keep them in quiet, is far enough to make them destroy each other), to extort a greater value from his contemners by damage, and from others by the example.

So that in the nature of man, we find three principal causes of quarrel. First, competition; second, diffidence; thirdly, glory.

The first maketh men invade for gain; the second, for safety; and the third, for reputation. The first use violence to make themselves masters of other men's persons, wives, children, and cattle; the second, to defend them; the third, for trifles, as a word, a smile, a different opinion, and any other sign of undervalue, either direct in their persons, or by reflection in their kindred, their friends, their nation, their profession, or their name.

Hereby it is manifest that during the time men live without a common power to keep them all in awe, they are in that condition which is called war; and such a war as is of every man against every man. For war consisteth not in battle only, or the act of fighting, but in a tract of time wherein the will to contend by battle is sufficiently known, and therefore the notion of time is to be considered in the nature of war, as it is in the nature of weather. For as the nature of foul weather lieth not in a shower or two of rain, but in an inclination thereto of many days together; so the nature of war consisteth not in actual fighting, but in the known disposition thereto, during all the time there is no assurance to the contrary. All other time is peace.

Whatsoever therefore is consequent to a time of war, where every man is enemy to every man; the same is consequent to the time wherein men live without other security than what their own strength and their own invention shall furnish them withal. In such condition there is no place for industry, because the fruit thereof is uncertain, and consequently no culture of the earth; no navigation, nor use of the commodities that may be imported by sea; no commodious building; no instruments of moving, and removing, such things as require much force; no knowledge of the face of the earth; no account of times; no arts; no letters; no society; and which is worst of all, continual fear, and danger of violent death; and the life of man, solitary, poor, nasty, brutish, and short.

It may seem strange to some man that has not well weighed these things, that nature should thus dissociate, and render men apt to invade and destroy one another; and he may therefore, not trusting to this inference, made from the passions, desire perhaps to have the same confirmed by experience. Let him therefore consider with himself, when taking a journey, he arms himself and seeks to go well accompanied; when going to sleep, he locks his doors; when even in his house he locks his chests; and this when he knows there be laws, and public officers, armed, to revenge all injuries shall be done him; what opinion he has of his fellow-subjects, when he rides armed; of his fellow-citizens, when he locks his doors; and of his children, and servants, when he locks his chests. Does he not there as much accuse mankind by his actions, as I do my words? But neither of us accuse man's nature in it. The desires and other passions of man, are in themselves no sin. No more are the actions that proceed from those passions, till they know a law that forbids them, which till laws be made they cannot know; nor can any law be made, till they have agreed upon the person that shall make it.

It may peradventure be thought, there was never such a time nor condition of war as this; and I believe it was never generally so, over all the world; but there are many places where they live so now. For the savage people in many places of America, except the government of small families, the concord whereof dependeth on natural lust, have no government at all and live at this day in that brutish manner, as I said before. Howsoever, it may be perceived what manner of life there would be, where there were no common power to fear; by the manner of life which men that have formerly lived under a peaceful government, use to degenerate into in a civil war.

But though there had never been any time wherein particular men were in a condition of war one against another; yet in all times, kings and persons of sovereign authority, because of their independency, are in continual jealousies, and in the state and posture of gladiators; having their weapons pointing, and their eyes fixed on one another; that is, their forts, garrisons, and guns upon the frontiers of their kingdoms; and continual spies upon their neighbors; which is a posture of war. But because they uphold thereby the industry of their subjects, there does not follow from it that misery which accompanies the liberty of particular men.

To this war of every man against every man, this also is consequent: that nothing can be unjust. The notions of right and wrong, justice and injustice, have there no place. Where there is no common power, there is no law; where no law, no injustice. Force and fraud are in war the two cardinal virtues. Justice and injustice are none of the faculties neither of the body nor mind. If they were, they might be in a man that were alone in the world, as well as his senses and passions. They are qualities that relate to men in society, not in solitude. It is consequent also to the same conditions, that there be no propriety, no dominion, no mine and thine distinct; but only that to be every man's, that he can get; and for so long as he can keep it. And thus much for the ill condition which man by mere nature is actually placed in; though with a possibility to come out of it, consisting partly in the passions, partly in his reason.

The passions that incline men to peace are fear of death, desire of such things as are necessary to commodious living, and a hope by their industry to obtain them. And reason suggesteth convenient articles of peace, upon which men may be drawn to agreement. These articles are they which otherwise are called the Laws of Nature whereof I shall speak more particularly in the two following chapters.

Abraham Cowley

1618–1667

A POET who absorbed much from the Elizabethans, and from Jonson and Donne, Cowley yet seems curiously modern. His qualities are grace and elegance, precision and naturalness of diction. He was born in London, educated at Westminster and Cambridge, and ejected from his fellowship when Cromwell took the university. He fled to Oxford and then to France, where he was for a time secretary to the exiled Queen. He aided his friend Crashaw. In 1654 he returned to England and was imprisoned; he studied medicine and took his M.D. at Oxford in 1657.

His first precocious volume of verse was published in 1633. Cowley's literary ambitions began early and extended far. He wrote plays, essays, a religious epic (unfinished), love poems in the metaphysical manner, and with most success the ode, both the ordinary English ode and the more carefully designed and elaborate form based on Pindar. He also paraphrased some of the light, worldly poems of Anacreon.

Cowley's reputation has swung from one extreme to the other; highly regarded in his own time, he was pilloried in Dr. Johnson's famous Life of Cowley, which expresses the eighteenth century's revulsion at metaphysical poetry. Now he is again respected, and his personal stamp, his charm, and his lucid, untroubled humor make him one of the most congenial of seventeenth-century writers.

Bibliography: *The English Works of Abraham Cowley,* ed. A. R. Waller, Cambridge, 1905–1906; A. H. Nethercot, *Abraham Cowley, The Muses' Hannibal,* London, 1931; J. Loiseau, *Abraham Cowley: Sa Vie, Son Oeuvre,* Paris, 1931; *Abraham Cowley's Reputation in England,* Paris, 1931; Ruth Wallerstein, "Cowley as a Man of Letters," *Transactions of the Wisconsin Academy,* XXVII (1932); T. S. Eliot, "A Note on Two Odes of Cowley" in *Seventeenth Century Studies Presented to Sir Herbert Grierson,* Oxford, 1938.

THE SPRING

Though you be absent here, I needs must say
The trees as beauteous are, and flowers as gay
As ever they were wont to be;
Nay, the birds' rural music, too,
Is as melodious and free
As if they sung to pleasure you;
I saw a rosebud ope this morn—I'll swear
The blushing morning opened not more fair.

How could it be so fair, and you away?
How could the trees be beauteous, flowers so gay?
Could they remember but last year,
How you did them, they you, delight,
The sprouting leaves which saw you here
And called their fellows to the sight
Would, looking round for the same sight in vain,
Creep back into their silent barks again.

Where'er you walked, trees were as reverend made
As when, of old, gods dwelt in every shade.
Is't possible they should not know
What loss of honor they sustain
That thus they smile and flourish now
And still their former pride retain?
Dull creatures! 'Tis not without cause that she
Who fled the god of wit was made a tree.

In ancient times sure they much wiser were,
When they rejoiced the Thracian verse to hear;
In vain did nature bid them stay;
When Orpheus had his song begun,
They called their wandering roots away
And bade them silent to him run.
How would those learned trees have followed you?
You would have drawn them and their poet too.

But who can blame them now? for, since you're gone
They're here the only fair, and shine alone.
You did their natural rights invade;

Wherever you did walk or sit
The thickest boughs could make no shade
Although the sun had granted it;
The fairest flowers could please no more, near you,
Than painted flowers, set next to them, could do.

Whene'er, then, you come hither, that shall be
The time which this to others is, to me.
The little joys which here are now
The name of punishments do bear,
When by their sight they let us know
How we deprived of greater are.
'Tis you the best of seasons with you bring;
This is for beasts, and that for men, the spring.

THE CHANGE

Love in her sunny eyes does basking play,
Love walks the pleasant mazes of her hair,
Love does on both her lips forever stray
And sows and reaps a thousand kisses there.
In all her outward parts Love's always seen,
But oh, he never went within.

Within, Love's foes, his greatest foes, abide:
Malice, Inconstancy, and Pride.
So the earth's face trees, herbs and flowers do dress
With other beauties numberless,
But at the center, Darkness is, and Hell;
There wicked spirits, and there the damnéd dwell.

With me, alas, quite contrary it fares;
Darkness and Death lies in my weeping eyes;
Despair and Paleness in my face appears,
And Grief and Fear, Love's greatest enemies.
But, like the Persian tyrant, Love within
Keeps his proud court and ne'er is seen.

Oh, take my heart, and by that means you'll prove
Within, too, stored enough of Love;
Give me but yours, I'll by that change so thrive
That Love in all my parts shall live.
So powerful is this change, it render can
My outside, woman, and your inside, man.

TO MR. HOBBES

Vast bodies of philosophy
I oft have seen and read,
But all are bodies dead
Or bodies by art fashionèd;
I never yet the living soul could see
But in thy books and thee.
'Tis only God can know
Whether the fair idea thou dost show
Agree entirely with His own or no.
This I dare boldly tell:
'Tis so like truth 'twill serve our turn as well.
Just, as in nature, thy proportions be,
As full of concord their variety,
As firm the parts upon their center rest,
And all so solid are that they, at least
As much as nature, emptiness detest.

Long did the mighty Stagirite [1] retain
The universal intellectual reign,
Saw his own country's short-liv'd leopard [2] slain;
The stronger Roman eagle did outfly,
Oftener renewed his age, and saw that die.
Mecca itself, in spite of Mahomet [3] possessed,
And chased by a wild deluge from the east,
His monarchy new planted in the west.
But as in time each great imperial race
Degenerates and gives some new one place,
So did this noble empire waste,
Sunk by degrees from glories past,
And in the schoolmen's hands it perished quite at last.
Then naught but words it grew,
And those all barbarous, too.
It perished, and it vanished there,
The life and soul breathed out, became but empty air.

---

1 *Stagirite:* Aristotle.

2 The Grecian empire, which in the Visions of Daniel is represented by a leopard with four wings upon the back and four heads.—Cowley's note.

3 Because his law, being adapted to the barbarous humour of those people he had first to deal withal, and aiming only at greatness of empire by the sword, forbids all the studies of learning, which nevertheless flourished admirably under the Saracen monarchy and continued so, till it was extinguished with that empire by the inundation of the Turks and other nations.—Cowley's note.

The fields which answered well the ancients' plow,
Spent and worn out, return no harvest now,
In barren age wild and unglorious lie,
    And boast of past fertility,
The poor relief of present poverty.
    Food and fruit we now must want,
    Unless new lands we plant.
We break up tombs with sacrilegious hands,
    Old rubbish we remove;
To walk in ruins, like vain ghosts, we love,
    And with fond divining wands
    We search among the dead
    For treasures burièd
    Whilst still the liberal earth does hold
So many virgin mines of undiscovered gold.

The Baltic, Euxine, and the Caspian,
And slender-limbed Mediterranean
Seem narrow creeks to thee, and only fit
For the poor wretched fisher-boats of wit.
Thy nobler vessel the vast ocean tries
    And nothing sees but seas and skies
    Till unknown regions it descries,
Thou great Columbus of the golden lands of new philosophies.
    Thy task was harder much than his,
    For thy learn'd America is
    Not only found out first by thee
And rudely left to future industry,
    But thy eloquence and thy wit
Has planted, peopled, built and civilized it.

    I little thought before
    (Nor being my own self so poor
    Could comprehend so vast a store)
    That all the wardrobe of rich eloquence
    Could have afforded half enough
    Of bright, of new and lasting stuff
To clothe the mighty limbs of thy gigantic scene.
Thy solid reason like the shield from heaven
    To the Trojan hero[4] given,
Too strong to take a mark from any mortal dart,
Yet shines with gold and gems in every part,
And wonders on it grav'd by the learn'd hand of art,

---

[4] *Trojan hero:* Aeneas, whose shield is described in *Aeneid,* VIII.

A shield that gives delight
Even to the enemies' sight
Then when they're sure to lose the combat by't.

Nor can the snow which now cold age does shed
Upon thy reverend head
Quench or allay the noble fires within,
But all which thou hast been
And all that youth can be, thou'rt yet,
So fully still dost thou
Enjoy the manhood and the bloom of wit,
And all the natural heat, but not the fever too.
So contraries on Aetna's top conspire,
Here hoary frosts, and by them breaks out fire.
A secure peace the faithful neighbors keep;
Th'emboldened snow next to the flame does sleep.
And if we weigh, like thee,
Nature and causes, we shall see
That thus it needs must be:
To things immortal time can do no wrong,
And that which never is to die forever must be young.

OF WIT

Tell me, oh tell, what kind of thing is wit,
Thou who master art of it.
For the first matter loves variety less;
Less women love't, either in love or dress.
A thousand different shapes it bears,
Comely in thousand shapes appears.
Yonder we saw it plain, and here 'tis now,
Like spirits in a place, we know not how.

London, that vents of false ware so much store,
In no ware deceives us more,
For men, led by the color and the shape,
Like Zeuxis'[5] birds, fly to the painted grape;
Some things do through our judgment pass
As through a multiplying glass;
And sometimes, if the object be too far,
We take a falling meteor for a star.

[5] *Zeuxis:* celebrated Greek painter who flourished about 400 B.C. The story that he painted grapes so realistically that birds pecked at them comes from Pliny.

Hence 'tis a wit, that greatest word of fame,
  Grows such a common name;
And wits by our creation they become
Just so as tit'lar bishops made at Rome.
  'Tis not a tale, 'tis not a jest
  Admired with laughter at a feast,
Nor florid talk which can that title gain;
The proofs of wit forever must remain.

'Tis not to force some lifeless verses meet
  With their five gouty feet;
All everywhere, like man's, must be the soul,
And reason the inferior powers control.
  Such were the numbers which could call
  The stone into the Theban wall;
Such miracles are ceased, and now we see
No towns or houses raised by poetry.

Yet 'tis not to adorn and gild each part:
  That shows more cost than art.
Jewels at nose and lips but ill appear;
Rather than all things wit, let none be there.
  Several lights will not be seen
  If there be nothing else between.
Men doubt, because they stand so thick i' th' sky,
If those be stars which paint the galaxy.

'Tis not when two like words make up one noise:
  Jests for Dutch men and English boys;
In which who finds out wit, the same may see
In an'grams and acrostics, poetry.
  Much less can that have any place
  At which a virgin hides her face;
Such dross the fire must purge away; 'tis just
The author blush there where the reader must.

'Tis not such lines as almost crack the stage
  When Bajazet begins to rage,
Nor a tall metaphor in the bombast way,
Nor the dry chips of short-lunged Seneca;
  Nor upon all things to obtrude
  And force some odd similitude.
What is it, then, which, like the Power Divine,
We only can by negatives define?

In a true piece of wit all things must be,
Yet all things there agree.
As in the ark, joined without force or strife,
All creatures dwelt, all creatures had that life;
Or as the primitive forms of all
(If we compare great things with small)
Which without discord or confusion lie
In that strange mirror of the Deity.

But love, that molds one man up out of two
Makes me forget and injure you.
I took you for myself, sure, when I thought
That you in any thing were to be taught.
Correct my error with thy pen,
And if any ask me then
What thing right wit and height of genius is,
I'll only show your lines and say " 'Tis this."

DRINKING[6]

The thirsty earth soaks up the rain,
And drinks, and gapes for drink again.
The plants suck in the earth, and are
With constant drinking fresh and fair.
The sea itself, which one would think
Should have but little need of drink,
Drinks ten thousand rivers up,
So filled that they o'erflow the cup.
The busy sun—and one would guess
By his drunken, fiery face no less—
Drinks up the sea, and when he's done,
The moon and stars drink up the sun.
They drink and dance by their own light;
They drink and revel all the night.
Nothing in nature's sober found,
But an eternal health goes round.
Fill up the bowl then, fill it high,
Fill all the glasses there, for why
Should every creature drink but I?
Why, man of morals, tell me why?

---

[6] The history of this lyric, from Anacreon to Shelley, is pleasantly told in Gilbert Highet's *A Clerk of Oxenford* (New York, 1954; pp. 156–164).

Characters

A CHARACTER is a brief, pointed description of a human type. It may be either satiric or sympathetic; it may probe deeply or describe the surface appearance. But it should give a feeling of finality, as if the type is permanently fixed and everywhere recognizable. Theophrastus, who apparently invented the character about the beginning of the third century B.C. in Athens, began by defining a trait or quality and then illustrating it by a description, as in his character of "The Surly Man":

"Surliness is a lack of amenity in speech. The Surly Man is the sort of person who, when asked 'Who is that?' answers 'Don't come bothering me!' He does not reply when spoken to. When he is selling something he does not say to purchasers, 'I want so much,' but 'How much d'you offer?' He tells those who send him presents on a feast day that there is something behind it. He will not accept the excuses of a passer-by who has accidentally pushed him or brushed against him or trodden on his foot. If one of his friends asks him to contribute to a subscription, he answers, 'I shall give nothing,' and then comes in presently with his contribution, muttering, 'Good money wasted!' When he stumbles on a stone in the street he curses it. He will not wait long for anyone. He refuses to sing, recite poems or dance. He is even likely not to pray to the gods."

Characters have been written in all periods of English literary history, from Chaucer to Wordsworth (the "Character of the Happy Warrior" is traditional in its inspiration), but the seventeenth century is the period when the character flourished most bountifully, both in prose and in verse. Ben Jonson's humour types in his comedies have a relationship to the character, for although those stage figures like Bobadill and Cob and Zeal-of-the-Land-Busy have names and are in one sense individuals, yet the most important thing about them is that they are representative types. The genre is a most congenial one to the moralist; accordingly, it is no surprise to find that Joseph Hall, the self-proclaimed first English satirist, published in 1608 some prose *Characters of Virtues and Vices*. Six years later a volume including a poem called "The Wife" by Sir Thomas Overbury, whose murder was the prime scandal of the Jacobean court, contained a collection of *Characters or Witty Descriptions of the Properties of Sundry Persons*. Overbury himself wrote a few of them, but the dramatist John Webster and other writers contributed the remainder. Among the many seventeenth-century writers who produced characters, the most gifted is probably the specialist John Earle, whose *Microcosmography, or A Piece of the World Discovered in Essays and Characters* was published in 1628. Earle's seventy-eight characters form a varied and lively gallery of seventeenth-century (and perhaps more permanent) types, ranging from "A Young Raw Preacher" to "A Handsome Hostess," and from "A Contemplative Man" to "A Drunkard."

BIBLIOGRAPHY: Richard Aldington, *A Book of Characters,* London, n.d.; Gwendolen Murphy, *A Cabinet of Characters,* London, 1925; *The Overburian Characters,* ed. W. J. Paylor, Oxford, 1936.

Sir Thomas Overbury

1581–1613

A GOOD WOMAN

A GOOD woman is a comfort, like a man. She lacks of him nothing but heat. Thence is her sweetness of disposition, which meets his stoutness more pleasingly; so wool meets iron easier than iron, and turns resisting into embracing. Her greatest learning is religion, and her thoughts are on her own sex, or on men, without casting the difference. Dishonesty never comes nearer than her ears, and then wonder stops it out, and saves virtue the labour. She leaves the neat youth, telling his luscious tales, and puts back the serving-man's putting forward, with a frown; yet her kindness is free enough to be seen, for it hath no guilt about it; and her mirth is clear, that you may look through it, into virtue, but not beyond. She hath not behavior at a certain, but makes it to her occasion. She hath so much knowledge as to love it, and if she have it not at home, she will fetch it, for this sometimes in a pleasant discontent she dares chide her sex, though she use it never the worse. She is much within, and frames outward things to her mind, not her mind to them. She wears good clothes, but never better; for she finds no degree beyond decency. She hath a content of her own, and so seeks not a husband, but finds him. She is indeed most, but not much of description, for she is direct and one, and hath not the variety of ill. Now she is given fresh and alive to a husband, and she doth nothing more than love him, for she hath taken him to that purpose. So his good becomes the business of her actions, and she doth herself kindness upon him. After his, her chiefest virtue is a good husband. For she is he.

A COURTIER

To all men's thinking is a man, and to most men the finest; all things else are defined by the understanding, but this by the senses; but his surest mark is, that he is to be found only about princes. He smells and putteth away much of his judgment about the situation of his clothes. He knows no man that is not generally known. His wit, like the marigold, openeth with the sun, and therefore he riseth not before ten of the clock. He puts more confidence in his words than meaning, and more in his pronunciation than his words. Occasion is his Cupid, and he hath but one receipt of making love. He follows nothing but inconstancy, admires nothing but beauty, honours nothing but fortune, loves nothing. The sustenance of his discourse is news, and his censure like a shot depends upon the charging. He is not, if he be out of court, but fish-like breathes destruction, if out of his own element. Neither his motion, or aspect are regular, but he moves by the upper spheres, and is the reflection of higher substances.

If you find him not here, you shall in Paul's, with a pick-tooth in his hat, a cape-cloak, and a long stocking.

A WISE MAN

Is the truth of the true definition of man, that is, a reasonable creature. His disposition alters, he alters not. He hides himself with the attire of the vulgar; and in indifferent things is content to be governed by them. He looks according to nature, so goes his behavior. His mind enjoys a continual smoothness; so cometh it that his consideration is always at home. He endures the faults of all men silently, except his friends, and to them he is the mirror of their actions; by this means, his peace cometh not from fortune, but himself. He is cunning in men, not to surprise, but keep his own, and beats off their ill affected humors no otherwise than if they were flies. He chooseth not friends by the subsidy-book, and is not luxurious after acquaintance. He maintains the strength of his body, not by delicates, but temperance, and his mind, by giving it pre-eminence over his body. He understands things, not by their form, but qualities; and his comparisons intend not to excuse but to provoke him higher. He is not subject to casualties; for fortune hath nothing to do with the mind, except those drowned in the body; but he hath divided his soul from the case of his soul, whose weakness he assists no otherwise than commiseratively, not that it is his, but that it is. He is thus, and will be thus, and lives subject neither to time nor his frailties, the servant of virtue, and by virtue, the friend of the highest.

A FAIR AND HAPPY MILKMAID

Is a country wench, that is so far from making herself beautiful by art, that one look of hers is able to put all face-physic out of countenance. She knows a fair look is but a dumb orator to commend virtue, therefore minds it not. All her excellencies stand in her so silently, as if they had stolen upon her without her knowledge. The lining of her apparel (which is herself) is far better than the outsides of tissue: for though she be not arrayed in the spoil of the silk-worm, she is decked in innocency, a far better wearing. She doth not, with lying long abed, spoil both her complexion and conditions; nature hath taught her, too immoderate sleep is rust to the soul; she rises therefore with chanticleer, her dame's cock, and at night makes the lamb her curfew. In milking a cow, and straining the teats through her fingers it seems that so sweet a milk-press makes the milk the whiter or sweeter; for never came almond glove or aromatic ointment on her palm to taint it. The golden ears of corn fall and kiss her feet when she reaps them, as if they wished to be bound and led prisoners by the same hand that felled them. Her breath is her own, which scents all the year long of June, like a new made haycock. She makes her hand hard with labour, and her heart soft with pity: and when winter evenings fall early (sitting at her merry wheel), she sings a defiance to the giddy wheel of fortune. She doth all things with so sweet a grace, it seems ignorance will not suffer her to do ill, being her mind is to do well. She bestows her year's wages at the next fair; and in choosing her garments, counts no bravery in the world, like decency. The garden and the bee-hive are all her physic and chirurgery, and she lives the longer for it. She dares go alone, and unfold sheep in the night, and fears no manner of ill, because she means none. Yet to say truth, she is never alone, for she is still accompanied with old songs, honest thoughts, and prayers, but short ones; yet they have their efficacy, in that they are not palled with ensuing idle cogitations. Lastly, her dreams are so chaste that she dare tell them, only a Friday's dream is all her superstition; that she conceals for fear of anger. Thus lives she, and all her care is that she may die in the spring-time, to have store of flowers stuck upon her winding sheet.

WHAT A CHARACTER IS

If I must speak the schoolmaster's language, I will confess that character comes from this infinite mood *χαράξω* that signifyeth to engrave, or make a deep impression. And for that cause, a letter (as A. B.) is called a character.

Those elements which we learn first, leaving a strong seal in our memories.

Character is also taken from an Egyptian hieroglyphic, for an impress, or short emblem; in little comprehending much.

To square out a character by our English level, it is a picture (real or personal) quaintly drawn, in various colours, all of them heightened by one shadowing.

It is a quick and soft touch of many strings, all shutting up in one musical close; it is wit's descant on any plain song.

John Earle

1601–1665

A PLAIN COUNTRY FELLOW

IS ONE that manures his ground well, but lets himself lie fallow and untilled. He has reason enough to do his business, and not enough to be idle or melancholy. He seems to have the punishment of Nebuchadnezzar, for his conversation is among beasts, and his talons none of the shortest, only he eats not grass, because he loves not salads. His hand guides the plough, and the plough his thoughts, and his ditch and landmark is the very mound of his meditations. He expostulates with his oxen very understandingly, and speaks gee and ree, better than English. His mind is not much distracted with objects, but if a good fat cow come in his way, he stands dumb and astonished, and though his haste be never so great, will fix here half an hour's contemplation. His habitation is some poor thatched roof, distinguished from his barn by the loop-holes that let out smoke, which the rain had long since washed through, but for the double ceiling of bacon on the inside, which has hung there from his grandsire's time, and is yet to make rashers for posterity. His dinner is his other work, for he sweats at it as much as at his labour; he is a terrible fastener on a piece of beef, and you may hope to stave the guard off sooner. His religion is a part of his copyhold, which he takes from his landlord, and refers it wholly to his discretion. Yet if he give him leave he is a good Christian to his power, (that is) comes to church in his best clothes, and sits there with his neighbours, where he is capable of only two prayers, for rain, and fair weather. He apprehends God's blessings only in a good year, or a fat pasture, and never praises him but on good ground. Sunday he esteems a day to make merry in, and thinks a bagpipe as essential to it as evening prayer, where he walks very solemnly after service with his hands coupled behind him, and censures the dancing of his parish. His compliment with his neighbour is a good thump on the back, and his salutation some blunt curse. He thinks nothing to be vices but pride and ill-husbandry, from which he will gravely dissuade the youth, and has some thrifty hobnail proverbs to clout his discourse. He is a niggard all the week, except only market-day, where, if his corn sell well, he thinks he may be drunk with a good conscience. His feet never stink so unbecomingly as when he trots after a lawyer in Westminster-hall, and even cleaves the ground with hard scraping in beseeching his worship to take his money. He is sensible of no calamity but the burning of a stack of corn or overflowing of a meadow, and thinks Noah's flood the greatest plague that ever was, not because it drowned the world, but spoiled the grass. For death he is never troubled, and if he get in but his harvest before, let it come when it will, he cares not.

A CONTEMPLATIVE MAN

Is a scholar in this great university the world; and the same his book and study. He cloisters not his meditations in the narrow darkness of a room, but sends them abroad with his eyes, and his brain travels with his feet. He looks upon man from a high tower, and sees him trulier at this distance in his infirmities and poorness. He scorns to mix himself in men's actions, as he would to act upon a stage, but sits aloft on the scaffold a censuring spectator. He will not lose his time by being busy, or make so poor a use of the world as to hug and embrace it. Nature admits him as a partaker of her sports, and asks his approbation as it were of her own works and variety. He comes not in company, because he would not be solitary, but finds discourse enough with himself, and his own thoughts are his excellent playfellows. He looks not upon a thing as a yawning stranger at novelties, but his search is more mysterious and inward, and he spells heaven out of earth. He knits his observations together and makes a ladder of them all to climb to God. He is free from vice, because he has no occasion to employ it, and is above those ends that make man wicked. He has learnt all can here be taught him, and comes now to heaven to see more.

A DRUNKARD

Is one that will be a man to-morrow morning, but is now what you will make him, for he is in the power of the next man, and is a friend the better. One that hath let go himself from the hold and stay of reason, and lies open to the mercy of all temptations. No lust but finds him disarmed and fenceless, and with the least assault enters. If any mischief escape him, it was not his fault, for he was laid as fair for it as he could. Every man sees him, as Ham saw his father in the first of this sin, an uncovered man, and, though his garment be on, uncovered; the secretest part of his soul lying in the nakedest manner visible: all his passions come out now, all his vanities, and those shamefuller humours which discretion clothes. His body becomes at last like a miry way, where the spirits are beclogged and cannot pass: all his members are out of office, and his heels do but trip up one another. He is a blind man with eyes, and a cripple with legs on. All the use he has of this vessel himself, is to hold thus much; for his drinking is but a scooping in of so many quarts, which are filled out into his body, and that filled out again into the room, which is commonly as drunk as he. Tobacco serves to air him after a washing, and is his only breath and breathing while. He is the greatest enemy to himself, and the next to his friend, and then most in the act of his kindness, for his kindness is but trying a mastery, who shall sink down first: and men come from him as from a battle, wounded and bound up. Nothing takes a man off more from his credit and business, and makes him more recklessly careless what becomes of all. Indeed he dares not enter on a serious thought, or if he do, it is such melancholy that it sends him to be drunk again.

Edmund Waller

1606–1687

WALLER was a wealthy country gentleman of wit and culture and a member of Parliament who came to be regarded by his contemporaries as a very important poet. He spent some years abroad as an exile but was pardoned by Parliament and allowed to return home. He celebrated Cromwell in 1655 and Charles II in 1660; when the King asked Waller to explain why the Cromwell poem was better, the answer was "Sir, we poets never succeed so well in writing truth as in writing fiction."

Waller's contributions to the development of a smooth, flowing style, especially in the heroic couplet, impressed the Augustan age rather more than they do modern literary historians. But the reader who wishes to share temporarily the outlook of men of the seventeenth century cannot neglect Waller, and his verse still seems pleasant and accomplished.

Bibliography: *Poems,* ed. G. Thorn-Drury, London, 1905; Ruth Wallerstein, "The Rhetoric and Metre of the Heroic Couplet," *PMLA,* L (1935), 166–209; G. Williamson, "The Rhetorical Pattern of Neoclassical Wit," *MP,* XXXIII (1935–1936), 55–81.

GO, LOVELY ROSE

Go, lovely rose,
Tell her that wastes her time and me
That now she knows,
When I resemble her to thee,
How sweet and fair she seems to be.

Tell her that's young,
And shuns to have her graces spied,
That hadst thou sprung
In deserts, where no men abide,
Thou must have uncommended died.

Small is the worth
Of beauty from the light retired;
Bid her come forth,
Suffer herself to be desired,
And not blush so to be admired.

Then die, that she
The common fate of all things rare
May read in thee;
How small a part of time they share,
That are so wondrous sweet and fair.

FROM

THE BATTLE OF THE SUMMER ISLANDS[1]

CANTO I

What fruits they have, and how heaven smiles
Upon those late-discovered isles.

Aid me, Bellona,[2] while the dreadful fight
Betwixt a nation and two whales I write.
Seas stained with gore I sing, adventurous toil,

[1] *Summer Islands:* Bermuda.

[2] *Bellona:* goddess of war, here invoked jocularly as a muse.

And how these monsters did disarm an isle.
  Bermudas, walled with rocks, who does not know?
That happy island where huge lemons grow,
And orange trees, which golden fruit do bear,
The Hesperian garden boasts of none so fair;
Where shining pearl, coral, and many a pound,
On the rich shore, of ambergris is found.
The lofty cedar, which to heaven aspires,
The prince of trees, is fuel for their fires;
The smoke by which their loaded spits do turn,
For incense might on sacred altars burn;
Their private roofs on odorous timber borne,
Such as might palaces for kings adorn.
The sweet palmettos a new Bacchus yield,
With leaves as ample as the broadest shield,
Under the shadow of whose friendly boughs
They sit, carousing where their liquor grows.
Figs there unplanted through the fields do grow,
Such as fierce Cato did the Romans show,
With the rare fruit inviting them to spoil
Carthage, the mistress of so rich a soil.
The naked rocks are not unfruitful there,
But, at some constant seasons, every year
Their barren tops with luscious food abound,
And with the eggs of various fowls are crowned.
Tobacco is the worst of things which they
To English landlords, as their tribute, pay.
Such is the mold that the blest tenant feeds
On precious fruits, and pays his rent in weeds.
With candied plantains, and the juicy pine,
On choicest melons, and sweet grapes, they dine,
And with potatoes fat their wanton swine.
Nature these cates with such a lavish hand
Pours out among them, that our coarser land
Tastes of that bounty, and does cloth return,
Which not for warmth but ornament is worn;
For the kind spring, which but salutes us here,
Inhabits there, and courts them all the year.
Ripe fruits and blossoms on the same trees live;
At once they promise what at once they give.
So sweet the air, so moderate the clime,
None sickly lives, or dies before his time.
Heaven sure has kept this spot of earth uncursed
To show how all things were created first.
The tardy plants in our cold orchards placed

Reserve their fruit for the next age's taste.
There a small grain in some few months will be
A firm, a lofty, and a spacious tree.
The Palma Christi and the fair pawpaw,
Now but a seed, preventing nature's law,
In half the circle of the hasty year
Project a shade, and lovely fruit do wear.
And as their trees, in our dull region set,
But faintly grow, and no perfection get,
So in this northern tract our hoarser throats
Utter unripe and ill-constrainèd notes,
Where the supporter of the poets' style,
Phoebus, on them eternally does smile.
Oh! how I long my careless limbs to lay
Under the plantain's shade, and all the day
With amorous airs my fancy entertain,
Invoke the Muses, and improve my vein!
No passion there in my free breast should move,
None but the sweet and best of passions, love.
There while I sing, if gentle love be by,
That tunes my lute, and winds the strings so high,
With the sweet sound of Sacharissa's[3] name
I'll make the listening savages grow tame.—
But while I do these pleasing dreams indite,
I am diverted from the promised fight.[4]

AT PENSHURST

Had Sacharissa lived when mortals made
Choice of their deities, this sacred shade
Had held an altar to her power, that gave
The peace and glory which these alleys have;
Embroidered so with flowers where she stood,
That it became a garden of a wood.
Her presence has such more than human grace
That it can civilize the rudest place;
And beauty too, and order, can impart,
Where nature ne'er intended it, nor art.
The plants acknowledge this, and her admire
No less than those of old did Orpheus' lyre;
If she sit down, with tops all towards her bowed,

---

[3] *Sacharissa:* Dorothy Sidney, daughter of the Earl of Leicester.

[4] The remaining two cantos describe the fight in mock-heroic style.

They round about her into arbors crowd;
Or if she walk, in even ranks they stand,
Like some well marshalled and obsequious band.
Amphion so made stones and timber leap
Into fair figures from a confused heap;
And in the symmetry of her parts is found
A power like that of harmony in sound.
  Ye lofty beeches, tell this matchless dame
That if together ye fed all one flame,
It could not equalize the hundredth part
Of what her eyes have kindled in my heart!
Go, boy, and carve this passion on the bark
Of yonder tree, which stands the sacred mark
Of noble Sidney's birth; when such benign,
Such more than mortal-making stars did shine,
That there they cannot but for ever prove
The monument and pledge of humble love;
His humble love whose hopes shall ne'er rise higher
Than for a pardon that he dares admire.

TO A LADY SINGING A SONG OF HIS OWN COMPOSING

Chloris! yourself you so excel,
When you vouchsafe to breathe my thought,
That, like a spirit, with this spell
Of my own teaching, I am taught.

That eagle's fate and mine are one,
Which, on the shaft that made him die,
Espied a feather of his own,
Wherewith he wont to soar so high.

Had Echo, with so sweet a grace,
Narcissus' loud complaints returned,
Not for reflection of his face,
But of his voice, the boy had burned.

Dorothy Osborne (Lady Temple)

1627–1695

THE youngest child in the large family of Sir Peter Osborne of Chicksands, Bedfordshire, Dorothy Osborne had many relatives distinguished for intellectual and political or social achievements. But Sir Peter's large fortune was largely sacrificed during the Civil War; as Lieutenant-Governor of the island of Guernsey he was responsible for holding it for the King. With the population of the island against him, he stoutly held little Castle Cornet for the Crown, while supplies failed to arrive and Lady Osborne sold her plate and borrowed money to supply him. He finally withdrew to St. Malo, not daring to come home, and it was on the way to visit him in 1648 that his daughter Dorothy met William Temple, the future author, diplomat, and patron of Jonathan Swift. She was twenty-one, he was twenty. Their prospects of marriage were not bright, for on both sides the relatives of the young people thought they could do better. Dorothy's brother Henry, who had little use for romantic attachments, was a particular barrier. But finally at Christmas, 1654, Dorothy Osborne and William Temple were married.

Dorothy's letters are remarkable for the personality they reveal. A woman of sense, of charm, with an observant eye for absurdities of character and a bold, faithful unswerving heart, she confesses to attacks of "the spleen," and she asks, with feminine concern, whether it is true that her appearance is too stately.

Her correspondence was not printed in full until 1888, but many a man far removed from the age of William Temple has fallen in love with the girl who wrote those inimitable letters to him.

BIBLIOGRAPHY: *The Letters of Dorothy Osborne,* ed. G. C. Moore Smith, Oxford, 1928; *Letters,* ed. E. Parry, Everyman edition, London, n.d.; Lord David Cecil, *Two Quiet Lives,* London, 1948.

FROM

LETTERS TO WILLIAM TEMPLE

[Thursday–Saturday, June 2–4, 1653]

Sir,

I have been reckoning up how many faults you lay to my charge in your last letter, and I find I am severe, unjust, unmerciful and unkind; oh me how should one do to mend all these? 'Tis work for an age and 'tis to be feared I shall be so old before I am good that 'twill not be considerable to anybody but myself whether I am so or not. I say nothing of the pretty humor you fancied me in, in your dream, because 'twas but a dream. Sure if it had been anything else, I should have remembered that my Lord L.[1] loves to have his chamber and his bed to himself. But seriously, now, I wonder at your patience; how could you hear me talk so senselessly, though 'twere but in your sleep, and not be ready to beat me? What nice, mistaken points of honor I pretended to and yet could allow him a room in the same bed with me! Well, dreams are pleasant things to people whose humors are so, but to have the spleen and dream upon't is a punishment I would not wish my greatest enemy. I seldom dream or remember them unless they have been so sad as to put me into such disorder as I can hardly recover when I am awake, and some of those I am confident I shall never forget.

You ask me how I pass my time here. I can give you a perfect account not only of what I do for the present but what I am likely to do this seven year if I stay here so long. I rise in the morning reasonably early, and before I am ready [2] I go round the house till I am weary of that, and then into the garden till it grows too hot for me. About ten o'clock I think of making me ready, and when that's done I go into my father's chamber, from thence to dinner, where my cousin Molle [3] and I sit in great state, in a room and at a table that would hold a great many more. After dinner we sit and talk till Mr. B.[4] comes in question and then I am gone. The heat of the day is spent in reading or working and then about six or seven o'clock I walk out into a common that lies hard by the house where a great many young wenches keep sheep and cows and sit in the shade singing of ballads.

---

[1] *Lord L.:* probably Philip, Lord Lisle, born 1619, second son of the Earl of Leicester.

[2] *ready:* dressed.

[3] *Molle:* Henry Molle, Fellow of King's College, Cambridge, at this time a man of fifty-five.

[4] *Mr. B.:* a suitor for Dorothy's hand named Bennet, who was favored by Cousin Molle.

I go to them and compare their voices and beauties to some ancient shepherdesses that I have read of and find a vast difference there, but trust me, I think these are as innocent as those could be. I talk to them, and find they want nothing to make them the happiest people in the world but the knowledge that they are so. Most commonly when we are in the midst of our discourse, one looks about her and spies her cows going into the corn and then away they all run as if they had wings at their heels. I, that am not so nimble, stay behind, and when I see them driving home their cattle I think 'tis time for me to retire too. When I have supped, I go into the garden and so to the side of a small river that runs by it, where I sit down and wish you with me. (You had best say this is not kind neither!) In earnest, 'tis a pleasant place and would be much more so to me if I had your company. I sit there sometimes till I am lost with thinking, and were it not for some cruel thoughts of the crossness of our fortunes that will not let me sleep there, I should forget there were such a thing to be done as going to bed. Since I writ this my company is increased by two, my brother Harry and a fair niece, the eldest of my brother Peyton's [5] daughters. She is so much a woman that I am almost ashamed to say I am her aunt, and so pretty that if I had any design to gain a servant [6] I should not like her company. But I have none, and therefore shall endeavor to keep her here as long as I can persuade her father to spare her, for she will easily consent to it, having so much of my humor (though it be the worst thing in her) as to like a melancholy place and little company.

My brother John is not come down again nor am I certain when he will be here. He went from London into Gloucestershire to my sister who was very ill, and his youngest girl of which he was very fond is since dead, but I believe by that time his wife has a little recovered her sickness and the loss of her child, he will be coming this way. My father is reasonably well but keeps his chamber still and will hardly, I am afraid, ever be so perfectly recovered as to come abroad again. I am sorry for poor Walker,[7] but you need not doubt of what he has of yours in his hands, for it seems he does not use to do his work himself (I speak seriously); he keeps a Frenchman that sets all his seals and rings. If what you say of my Lady Leppington [8] be of your own knowledge I shall believe you, but otherwise I can assure you I have heard from people who pretend to know her very well that her kindness to Compton was very moderate, and that she never liked him so well as when he died and gave her his estate. But they might be deceived, and 'tis not so strange as that you should imagine a coldness and an indif-

---

5 *Peyton:* her brother-in-law, Sir Thomas Peyton.

6 *servant:* a suitor or lover.

7 *Walker:* Dorothy has spoken in an earlier letter of the Frenchman who sets her seals and rings, in the employ of one Walker, near the Exchange. Temple must have written of some misfortune befalling Walker.

8 *Lady Leppington:* the widow of Lord Leppington, heir of Henry Carey, Earl of Monmouth. The Compton referred to later in the sentence was Colonel Henry Compton, killed in a duel in May, 1652.

ference in my letter where I so little meant it; but I am not displeased you should desire my kindness enough to apprehend the loss of it when it is safest. Only I would not have you apprehend it so far as to believe it possible. That were an injury to all the assurances I have given you and if you love me you cannot think me unworthy. I should think myself so if I found you indifferent to me, that I have had so long and so particular a friendship for. But sure, this is more than I need to say. You are enough in my heart to know all my thoughts, and if so, you know better than I can tell you how much I am Yours

[Saturday, June 25, 1653]

SIR,

You amaze me with your story of Tom Cheek.[9] I am certain he could not have it where you imagine, and 'tis a miracle to me that he remembers there is such a one in the world as his cousin D. O. I am sure he has not seen her this six years, and I think but once in his life. If he has spread his opinion in that family, I shall quickly hear on't, for my cousin Molle is now gone to Kimolten to my Lord Manchester and from thence he goes to Moor Park to my cousin Franklin's, and in one or both he will be sure to meet with it. The matter is not great, for though I confess I do naturally hate the noise and talk of the world, and should be best pleased never to be known in't on any occasion whatsoever, yet since it can never be wholly avoided one must satisfy one's self by doing nothing that one need care who knows. I do not think it a propos to tell anybody that you and I are very good friends, and it were better, sure, if nobody knew it but we ourselves, but if, in spite of all our caution it be discovered, 'tis no treason nor anything else that's ill; and if anybody should tell me that I had a greater kindness and esteem for you than for anyone besides, I do not think I should deny it.

However, you do oblige me in not owning any such thing, for, as you say, I have no reason to take it ill that you endeavor to preserve me a liberty, though I am never likely to make use on't. Besides that, I agree with you, too, that certainly 'tis much better you should owe my kindness to nothing but your own merit and my inclination than that there should lie any other necessity upon me of making good my word to you.

For God's sake do not complain that you do not see me; I believe I do not suffer less in't than you, but 'tis not to be helped. If I had a picture that were fit for you, you should have it. I have but one that's anything like, and that's a great one, but I will send it some time or other to Cooper or Hoskins [10] and have a little one drawn by it, if I cannot be in town to sit my self.

---

[9] *Cheek:* Thomas Cheke, a cousin of Dorothy's, had started a story that she and Temple were virtually engaged, which Temple denied.

[10] *Cooper or Hoskins:* the chief miniaturists of the time.

You undo me by but dreaming how happy we might have been, when I consider how far we are from it in reality. Alas, how can you talk of defying fortune? Nobody lives without it, and therefore why should you imagine you could? I know not how my brother comes to be so well informed as you say, but I am certain he knows the utmost of the injuries you have received from her; [11] 'tis not possible she should have used you worse than he says.

We have had another debate, but much more calmly. 'Twas just upon his going up to town, and perhaps he thought it not fit to part in anger. Not to wrong him, he never said to me (whate'er he thought) a word in prejudice of you in your own person, and I never heard him accuse anything but your fortune and my indiscretion; and whereas I did expect that (at least in compliment to me) he should have said we had been a couple of fools well met, he says by my troth he does not blame you, but bids me not deceive myself to think you have any great passion for me.

If you have done with the first part of Cyrus [12] I should be glad Mr. Hollingsworth had it, because I mentioned some such thing in my last to my Lady, but there is no haste of restoring the other unless she should send to me for it which I believe she will not. I have a third tome here against you have done with the second, and to encourage you let me assure you that the more you read of them you will like them still better. Oh me, whilst I think on't let me ask you one question seriously, and pray resolve me truly: do I look so stately as people apprehend? I vow to you I made nothing on't when Sir Emperor [13] said so, because I had no great opinion of his judgment, but Mr. Freeman [14] makes me mistrust myself extremely (not that I am sorry I did appear so to him, since it kept me from the displeasure of refusing an offer which I do not perhaps deserve), but that it is a scurvy quality in itself, and I am afraid I have it in great measure if I showed any of it to him, for whom I have so much of respect and esteem. If it be so, you must needs know it, for though my kindness will not let me look so upon you, you can see what I do to other people; and besides there was a time when we ourselves were indifferent to one another. Did I do so then or have I learn't it since? For God's sake tell me, that I may try to mend it. I could wish, too, that you would lay your commands on me to forbear fruit; here is enough to kill a thousand such as I am, and so excellently good that nothing but your power can secure me. Therefore forbid me, that I may live to be Your

[11] *injuries . . . her:* i.e., Temple's injuries from fortune, his financial difficulties.

[12] *Cyrus: Artamène, ou le Grand Cyrus,* by Mlle. de Scudéry. It appeared in ten tomes or parts, and ran to fifteen thousand pages.

[13] *Sir Emperor:* Sir Justinian Isham, a suitor whom Dorothy described as "the vainest impertinent self-conceited coxcomb that ever I saw."

[14] *Mr. Freeman:* William Freeman, a neighbor. He remained a friend of Dorothy's for thirty years.

[Saturday, July 16, 1653]

Sir,

I received your last sooner by a day than I expected; it was not the less welcome but the carrier was who brought me none. I admired at myself to remember how I have been transported with the sight of that pitiful fellow, and now that I knew he had no letter for me, how coldly I looked upon him. Nan tells me he had the curiosity to ask your boy questions; I should never have suspected it, and yet he had the wit to do a thing last week few such people would have done. My brother, coming from London, met him going up and called to him and asked what letters he had of mine; the fellow said None, I did not use to send by him. My brother said I told him he had and bid him call for them; he said there was some mistake in't for he had none, and so they parted for a while. But my brother not satisfied with this, rides after him and in some anger threatened the poor fellow, who would not be frightened out of his letter but looked very simply and said now he remembered himself, he had carried a letter for me about a fortnight or three weeks agone to my Lady D. R.[15] but he was sure he had none now. My brother smiled at his innocence and left him, and I was hugely pleased to hear how he had been defeated. You will have time enough to think of a new address; he goes no more till after harvest, and you will receive this by your old friend Collins; but because my brother is with him every week as soon as he comes, and takes up all the letters, if you please let yours be made up in some other form than usual and directed to Mr. Ed Gibson at Ch.[16] in some odd hand, and be at the charge, pray, of buying a twopenny seal a-purpose for these letters.

Would you could make your words good that my eyes can dispel all melancholy clouded humors; I would look in the glass all day long but [17] I could clear up my own. Alas, they are so far from that, they would teach one to be sad that knew nothing on't, for in other people's opinions as well as my own they have the most of it in them that eyes can have. My mother, I remember, used to say that I needed not tears to persuade my trouble, and that I had looks so far beyond them that, were all the friends I had in the world dead, more could not be expressed than such a sadness in my eyes; this indeed I think is natural to them, or at least long custom has made it so. 'Tis most true that our friendship has been brought up hardly enough, and possibly it thrives the better for't. 'Tis observed that surfeits kill more than fasting does, but ours is in no danger of that. My brother would persuade me there is no such thing in the world as a constant friendship. People, he says, that marry with great passion for one another, as they think, come afterwards to lose it they know not how, besides the multitude of such as are false and mean it. I cannot be of his opinion, though I confess there are too many examples on't. I have

---

[15] *Lady D. R.:* Lady Diana Rich.

[16] *Ed. Gibson at Ch.:* the Reverend Edward Gibson, vicar of Hawnes, apparently at this time living at Chicksands, the Osborne home.

[17] *but:* provided.

always believed there might be a friendship perfect, like that you describe, and methinks I find something like it in myself; but sure 'tis not to be taught, it must come naturally to those that have it, and those that have it not can ne'er be made to understand it. You needed not have feared that I should take occasion, from your not answering my last, not to write this week. You are as much pleased, you say, with writing to me as I can be to receive your letters—why should you not think the same of me? In earnest, you may, and if you love me you will. But then how much more satisfied should I be if there were no need of these, and we might talk all that we write and more. Shall we ever be so happy? Last night I was in the garden till eleven o'clock. It was the sweetest night that e'er I saw, the garden looked so well and the jasmine smelt beyond all perfumes, and yet I was not pleased. The place had all the charms it used to have when I was most satisfied with it, and had you been there I should have liked it much more than ever I did, but that not being, it was no more to me than the next field, and only served me for a place to rêve [18] in without disturbance.

What a sad story you tell me of the little Marquise! [19] Poor woman; yet she's happy she's dead, for such her life could not be very pleasing to her. When we were both girls I had a great acquaintance there; they lived by us at Chelsea, and as long as his son lived, Sir Theodore did me the honor to call me daughter. But whilst I was first in France he died, and with him my converse with the family, for though my mother had occasion to be often there yet I went very seldom with her. They were still so passionate for their son that I never failed of setting them all a-crying and then I was no company for them. But this poor lady had a greater loss of my Lord Hastings who died just when they should have been married, and sure she could not think she had recovered it at all by marrying this buffle-headed marquis. And yet one knows not neither what she might think; I remember I saw her with him in the park a little while after they were married and she kissed him the kindliest that could be in the midst of all the company. I shall never wish to see a worse sight than 'twas, nor to be anything longer than I am your faithful

[18] *rêve:* dream.

[19] *the little Marquise:* Elizabeth de Mayerne, Marquise de Cugnac. She was the daughter of the famous physician Sir Theodore de Mayerne, and she had been about to marry Lord Hastings when he died in 1649. See the Hastings elegies, pp. 1076–1090.

The Hastings Elegies

1649

AN interesting comparison of some of the leading poets of the mid-century was offered by the publication of a volume called *Lachrymae Musarum* in 1649. It contained ninety-seven elegies for a young nobleman, Henry Hastings, son and heir apparent of Ferdinando Hastings, sixth Earl of Huntingdon, and his countess, Lucy. The subject of all this poetical mourning was in his twentieth year and engaged to be married to Elizabeth de Mayerne when he died of the smallpox in July, 1649. Nothing is known of him aside from these poems, but he must have been a young man of some promise, even if not quite so much as his elegists proclaimed.

Among the contributors were Sir Aston Cokaine, a Derbyshire squire who was to achieve a minor reputation as a poet and playwright, and his young cousin, Charles Cotton, who was Hastings' own age and was to become known as a poet of burlesque and a friend and collaborator of Izaac Walton's. Thomas Pestell, Sr., a country parson, left enough verse of some quality (mostly in manuscript) to justify publication of a scholarly edition, in 1940. Robert Herrick was already well known, his *Hesperides* and *Noble Numbers* having been published in the previous year. Sir John Denham, famous as the author of the topographical poem *Cooper's Hill,* was an important precursor of the neoclassic style in verse. Andrew Marvell continued the metaphysical tradition. But that tradition is sometimes said to have reached its ignominious end in the notorious elegy by the youthful John Dryden, with its famous conceits on the smallpox. The funeral elegy was an important form in the seventeenth century, and volumes such as *Lachrymae Musarum* and *Iusta Edouardo King* (which contained Milton's *Lycidas*) offer much to the student of form and style in poetry. The selections here given are of course uneven in quality; they represent varieties of taste and ability in the period.

SIR ASTON COKAINE
1608–1684

Know all to whom these few sad lines shall come,
This melancholy epicedium,[1]
The young Lord Hastings' death occasioned it,
Amidst a storm of lamentations writ;
Tempests of sighs and groans, and flowing eyes,
Whose yielding balls dissolve to delugies;
And mournful numbers that with dreadful sound
Wait this bemoaned body to the ground,
Are all and the last duties we can pay
The noble spirit that is fled away.
'Tis gone, alas! 'tis gone, though it did leave
A body rich in all nature could give;
Superior in beauty to the youth
That won the Spartan Queen [2] to forfeit truth,
Break wedlock's strictest bonds and be his wife,
Environed with tumults all her life.
His years were in the balmy spring of age,
Adorned with blossoms ripe for marriage,
And but mature; his sweet conditions known
To be so good, they could be none but's own.
Our English nation was enamored more
Of his full worths than Rome was heretofore
Of great Vespatian's Jew-subduing heir,[3]
The love and the delight of mankind here.
After a large survey of histories,
Our critics (curious in honor, wise
In paralleling generous souls) will find
This youthful lord did bear as brave a mind.
His few but well-spent years had mastered all
The liberal arts, and his sweet tongue could fall
Into the ancient dialects, dispense
Sacred Judea's amplest eloquence,
The Latin idiom elegantly true,
And Greek as rich as Athens ever knew.
The Italian and the French do both confess

[1] *epicedium:* dirge.
[2] *youth, Spartan queen:* Paris and Helen.
[3] *heir:* Titus, called "the delight of mankind."

Him perfect in their modern languages.
At his nativity, what angry star
Malignant influences flung so far?
What *Caput Algols*[4] and what dire aspects
Occasioned so tragical effects?
As soon as Death this fatal blow had given,
I fancy mighty Clarence[5] sighed in heaven,
And, till this glorious soul arrived there,
Recovered not from his amaze and fear.
Had this befallen in ancient credulous times,
He had been deified by poets' rhymes;
That age, enamored on his graces, soon
Majestic fanes in adoration
Would have raised to his memory, and there
On golden altars, year succeeding year,
Burnt holy incense and Sabaean gums,
That curls of vapor from those hecatombs
Should reach his soul in heaven. But we must pay
No such oblations in our purer way;
A nobler service we him owe than that,
His fair example ever t'emulate.
With the advantage of our double years,
Let's imitate him, and, through all affairs
And all encounters of our lives, intend
To live like him, and make so good an end.
To aim at brave things is an evident sign
In spirits, that to honor they incline;
And, though they do come short in the contest,
'Tis full of glory to have done one's best.
You mournful parents, whom the fates compel
To bear the loss of this great miracle,
This wonder of our times, amidst a sigh,
Surrounded with your thickest calamity,
Reflect on joy; think what an happiness
(Though human nature here conceits it less)
It was to have a son of so much worth;
He was too good to grace the wretched earth.
As silver Trent through our north counties glides,
Adorned with swans and crowned with flowery sides,
And, rushing into mightier Humber's waves,
Augments the regal Estuarium's braves,
So he, after a life of eighteen years,
Well managed, as example to our peers,

[4] *Caput Algols:* Medusa's head in the constellation Perseus.

[5] *Clarence:* According to the title page of *Lachrymae Musarum,* Hastings was heir-general of Clarence, brother of King Edward IV.

In's early youth, encountering sullen Fate,
O'ercome, became a trophy to his state.
Didst thou sleep, Hymen? or art lately grown
T'affect the subterranean region?
Enamored on bleared Libertina's eyes,
Hoarse howling dirges and the baleful cries
Of inauspicious voices, and above
Thy starlike torch, with horrid tombs in love?
Thou art; or surely hadst opposed this high
Affront of Death against thy deity;
Nor wronged an excellent virgin, who had given
Her heart to him, who hath his soul to heaven;
Whose beauties thou hast clouded and whose eyes
Drowned in tears of these sad exequies.
Those famed heroes of the golden age,
Those demigods, whose virtues did assuage
And calm the furies of the wildest minds
That were grown savage, even against their kinds,
Might from their constellations have looked down
And by this young lord seen themselves outgone.
Farewell, admired spirit, that art free
From this strict portion of mortality.
Ashby,[6] proud of the honor to enshrine
The beauteous body, whence the soul divine
Did lately part, be careful of thy trust,
That no profane hand wrong that hallowed dust.
The costly marble needs no friend t'engrave
Upon it any doleful epitaph;
No good man's tongue that office will decline
While years succeeding reach the end of time.

CHARLES COTTON

1630–1687

Amongst the mourners that attend his hearse
With flowing eyes, and with each tear a verse
T'embalm his fame and his dear merit save
Uninjured from the oblivion of the grave,
A sacrificer I am come to be
Of this poor offering to his memory.
Oh could our pious meditations thrive

[6] *Ashby:* Formerly the seat of the Earls of Huntingdon, Ashby Castle was destroyed by order of Parliament in 1645.

So well to keep his better part alive!
So that, instead of him, we could but find
Those fair examples of his lettered mind;
Virtuous emulation then might be
Our hopes of good men, though not such as he.
But in his hopeful progress since he's crossed,
Pale virtue droops, now her best pattern's lost.
'Twas hard, neither divine nor human parts,
The strength of goodness, learning, and of arts,
Full crowds of friends, nor all the prayers of them,
Now that he was the pillar of his stem,
Affection's mark, secure of all men's hate,
Could rescue him from the sad stroke of fate.
Why was not th'air dressed in prodigious forms,
To groan in thunder, and to weep in storms?
And, as at some men's fall, why did not his
In nature work a metamorphosis?
No, he was gentle, and his soul was sent
A silent victim to the firmament.
Weep, ladies, weep; lament great Hastings' fall;
His house is buried in his funeral;
Bathe him in tears, till there appear no trace
Of those sad blushes in his lovely face;
Let there be in't of guilt no seeming sense,
Nor other color than of innocence.
For he was wise and good, though he was young,
Well suited to the stock from which he sprung,
And what in youth is ignorance and vice
In him proved piety of an excellent price.
Farewell, dear Lord, and since thy body must
In time return to its first matter, dust,
Rest in thy melancholy tomb in peace, for who
Would longer live, that could but now die so?

THOMAS PESTELL, SR.

1584–1659

For the Right Honorable Lucy, Countess of Huntingdon, 1649.

HER SOLILOQUY, OR HER MEDITATION

'Tis mystic union, man and wife,
Yet scarce distinct from single life,
Till like the sun, a son arise,

And set them both before their eyes:
No sweeter, braver, fairer sight
Than thus to stand in their own light.
And such a son I joyed (Ay me!
Was ever such a son as he?)
And felt what fervent spirits of love
Orbs of maternal bowels move.
I would not shun those outward snares
Of shape, of shining eyes and hairs,
Which still, the more they catch or wound,
More pleasing still their power I found.
And it is lawful, godly too,
To love what God's own fingers do,
Whose angels still are sweetly faced,
Himself with perfect beauty graced.
But eager virtue from the clay
In words and actions making way
To sense, in all that heard or saw
Became a fierce almighty law
And stooped all hearts that were not stone
Or drowned in malice, or in moan
Like mine. So overgone with woe,
My very reason bids it go,
Nor lies it in the power of wit
By reason to recover it.

THE RATIONAL REPLY

By reason to recover it,
Sans forlorn hope, or wings of wit,
Who serves you his main battle brings.
Hark how the feathered tempest sings,
Your clouds of grief transpiercing quite,
Or hurrying to disordered flight.
Then, sorrow vanquished, on his hearse
Rears trophies of victorious verse.
First, let us ask Impatience why
At gentle Death's approach we cry.
Sweet favorite of heaven, that flies
With Cupid's face but Hermes' eyes,
Whose rods and snakes and seeming harms
Our souls in slumber wisely charms.
For that poor spark called life, the brand,
The rush we carry in our hand,
Which dropping and defiling spends:
Death gives delight that never ends.

Oh mad mistake! Sea tossed, a calm,
And wounded, we reject a balm;
Rabid for want of rest, we keep
A bawling and refuse to sleep;
Dead-weary tired, yet scorn to stay;
And cripples, hurl our crutch away.
But these are general; for your pain
Here's water of a special vein,
Wherein no relish you shall feel
Of sulphury wit, but Reason's steel.
What could you wish your son? A pair
Of dove-like eyes; as Joseph fair;
Straight as young mountain-pines, whose arms
The sun with early kisses warms;
Gilds, blazons so each leaf and limb
That paint is dirt, and metal dim.
He was all this, and all that we
Can fetch from beauty's pedigree.
The case so bright, what radiance threw
The jewel that it did indue!
The Queen that held the throne in state
Of Grace, there dressed and re-create;
Till like a lark from earthly cage
Enlarged and fired with strong new rage
She mounts and sings in heaven. And what?
May we not fall some drops thereat?
Good reason, if the tears you shed
From joyful brain's expansion spread,
Call it not grief; foul envy 'tis
To whine at saints enshrined in bliss.
Reflect on all the whole world's frame;
It climbs and twines to whence it came:
So beams that shine and streams that flow
Back to their sun and ocean go.
So vernal flowers, which at their birth
Thrust up pure crowns from impure earth,
Grow by degrees full ripe, and then
Must hide them in their roots again.
    He parted in perfection's time,
In golden number, and in prime
Of life, of love, and white report
For virtue; past the ranker sort
Of flash-green youths; no vicious stain
Envenoming his blood or brain;
From duels, drink, dice, cares, age, laws,

Faces of dames, and eagle's claws
Exempt, he laughs at us that still
Bleat round the bottom of the hill.
    Last, think of your clear open way
To heaven, obstructed by his stay,
While more than mermaid, face and words
All ear-wax melts and breaks all cords.
Did not his look, his voice and deed
With full commerce of pleasure feed
Your sense and soul? which now takes wing,
Checks not at aught, nor spies fair thing
Worth stooping at. Oh, let it fly
To quarries there above the sky.

ROBERT HERRICK

1591–1674

THE NEW CHARON,

Upon the death of Henry Lord Hastings

The Musical part being set by M. Henry Lawes.
The Speakers, Charon and Eucosmeia.

Euc. Charon, O Charon, draw thy boat to th' shore,
    And to thy many take in one soul more.
Cha. Who calls? Who calls? *Euc.* One overwhelmed with ruth;
    Have pity either on my tears or youth,
    And take me in who am in deep distress;
    But first cast off thy wonted churlishness.
Cha. I will be gentle as that air which yields
    A breath of balm along th'Elysian fields.
    Speak, what art thou? *Euc.* One, once that had a lover
    Than which, thyself ne'er wafted sweeter over.
    He was—— *Cha.* Say what. *Euc.* Ay me, my woes are deep.
Cha. Prithee relate, while I give ear and weep.
Euc. He was an Hastings, and that one name has
    In it all good that is and ever was.
    He was my life, my love, my joy, but died
    Some hours before I should have been his bride.
Chorus: Thus, thus the Gods celestial still decree
        For human joy, contingent misery.
Euc. The hallowed tapers all prepared were,

And Hymen called to bless the rites. *Cha.* Stop there!
Euc. Great are my woes. *Cha.* And great must that grief be
That makes grim Charon thus to pity thee.
But now come in. *Euc.* More let me yet relate.
Cha. I cannot stay; more souls for waftage wait
And I must hence. *Euc.* Yet let me thus much know,
Departing hence, where good and bad souls go.
Cha. Those souls which ne'er were drenched in pleasure's stream,
The fields of Pluto are reserved for them;
Where, dressed with garlands, there they walk the ground,
Whose blessed youth with endless flowers is crowned.
But such as have been drowned in this wild sea,
For those is kept the Gulf of Hecate,
Where with their own contagion they are fed
And there do punish and are punishèd.
This known, the rest of thy sad story tell
When on the flood that nine times circles Hell
Chorus: We sail along, to visit mortals never,
But there to live, where love shall last forever.

SIR JOHN DENHAM

1615–1669

Reader, preserve thy peace; those busy eyes
Will weep at their own sad discoveries,
When every line they add improves thy loss
Till, having viewed the whole, they sum a cross
Such as derides thy passion's best relief
And scorns the succors of thy easy grief.
Yet, lest thy ignorance betray thy name
Of man, and pious, read and mourn; the shame
Of an exemption from just sense doth show
Irrational beyond excessive woe.
Since reason then can privilege a tear,
Manhood, uncensured, pay that tribute here
Upon this noble urn. Here, here remains
Dust far more precious than in India's veins;
Within these cold embraces ravished lies
That which completes the age's tyrannies,
Who, weak to such another, ill appear,
For what destroys our hope secures our fear.
What sin unexpiated in this land
Of groans hath guided so severe a hand?

The late great victim that your altars knew,[7]
You angry gods, might have excused this new
Oblation, and have spared one lofty light
Of virtue to inform our steps aright,
By whose example good, condemned we
Might have run on to kinder destiny.
But as the leader of the herd fell first,
A sacrifice to quench the raging thirst
Of inflamed vengeance for past crimes, so none
But this white fatted youngling could atone,
By his untimely fate, that impious smoke
That sullied earth and did Heaven's pity choke.
Let it suffice for us that we have lost,
In him, more than the widowed world can boast
In any lump of her remaining clay.
Fair as the gray-eyed morn he was; the day,
Youthful and climbing upwards still, imparts
No haste like that of his increasing parts;
Like the meridian-beam, his virtue's light
Was seen, as full of comfort, and as bright.
Ah that that noon had been fixed as clear! But he
That only wanted immortality
To make him perfect, now submits to night,
In the black bottom of whose sable spite
He leaves a cloud of flesh behind and flies,
Refined, all ray and glory, to the skies.
Great Saint, shine there in an eternal sphere
And tell those powers to whom thou now draw'st near
That, by our trembling sense, in Hastings dead,
Their anger, and our ugly faults, are read,
The short lines of whose life did to our eyes
Their love and majesty epitomize.
Tell them whose stern decrees impose our laws,
The feasted grave may close her hollow jaws.
Though sin search nature, to provide her here
A second entertainment half so dear,
She'll never meet a plenty like this hearse
Till Time present her with the universe.

[7] *victim that your altars knew:* King Charles I was executed on January 30, 1649. See also line 27.

ANDREW MARVELL
1621–1678

Go, intercept some fountain in the vein [8]
Whose virgin-source yet never steeped the plain.
Hastings is dead, and we must find a store
Of tears untouched and never wept before.
Go, stand betwixt the morning and the flowers,
And, ere they fall, arrest the early showers.
Hastings is dead, and we, disconsolate,
With early tears must mourn his early fate.
Alas, his virtues did his death presage;
Needs must he die that doth outrun his age.
The phlegmatic and slow prolongs his day
And on Time's wheel sticks like a remora.
What man is he that hath not Heaven beguiled
And is not thence mistaken for a child,
While those of growth more sudden and more bold
Are hurried hence, as if already old?
For there above they number not as here,
But weigh to man the geometric year.
  Had he but at this measure still increased
And on the Tree of Life once made a feast
As that of Knowledge, what loves had he given
To earth, and then what jealousies to Heaven!
But 'tis a maxim of that state, that none
Lest he become like them, taste more than one.
Therefore the democratic stars did rise
And all that worth from hence did ostracize.
  Yet as some prince that for state jealousy
Secures his nearest and most loved ally,
His thought with richest triumphs entertains,
And in the choicest pleasures charms his pains,
So he, not banished hence, but there confined,
There better recreates his active mind.
  Before the crystal palace where he dwells,
The armèd angels hold their carrousels,
And underneath, he views the tournaments
Of all these sublunary elements.
But most he doth th'eternal book behold
On which the happy names do stand enrolled,

[8] *the vein:* bedrock.

And gladly there can all his kindred claim,
But most rejoices at his mother's name.
The gods themselves cannot their joy conceal,
But draw their veils, and their pure beams reveal;
Only they drooping Hymeanaeus note,
Who, for sad purple, tears his saffron coat
And trails his torches through the starry hall
Reversèd, at his darling's funeral.
And Aesculapius, who, ashamed and stern,
Himself at once condemneth, and Mayern;[9]
Like some sad chemist, who, prepared to reap
The golden harvest, sees his glasses leap.
For how immortal must their race have stood,
Had Mayern once been mixed with Hastings blood!
How sweet and verdant would these laurels be
Had they been planted on that balsam-tree!
But what could he, good man, although he bruised
All herbs, and them a thousand ways infused?
All he had tried, but all in vain, he saw,
And wept, as we, without redress or law.
For man, alas, is but the Heavens' sport;
And Art indeed is long, but life is short.

JOHN DRYDEN

1631–1700

Must noble Hastings immaturely die,
The honor of his ancient family?
Beauty and learning thus together meet
To bring a winding- for a wedding-sheet?
Must virtue prove death's harbinger? Must she,
With him expiring, feel mortality?
Is Death (Sin's wages) Grace's now? Shall Art
Make us more learned, only to depart?
If merit be disease, if virtue death;
To be good, not to be; who'd then bequeath
Himself to discipline? Who'd not esteem
Labor a crime; study, self-murder deem?
Our noble youth now have pretence to be
Dunces securely, ignorant healthfully.

[9] *Mayern:* Sir Theodore de Mayerne (1573–1655), physician to the late King and father of Elizabeth de Mayerne, Hastings' fiancée.

Rare linguist, whose worth speaks itself, whose praise,
Though not his own, all tongues besides do raise;
Than whom, great Alexander may seem less,
Who conquered men, but not their languages.
In his mouth nations speak; his tongue might be
Interpreter to Greece, France, Italy.
His native soil was the four parts o' th' earth;
All Europe was too narrow for his birth.
A young apostle, and (with reverence may
I speak it) inspired with gift of tongues, as they.
Nature gave him, a child, what men in vain
Oft strive, by art though furthered, to obtain.
His body was an orb; his sublime soul
Did move on virtue's and on learning's pole,
Whose regular motions better to our view
Than Archimedes' sphere the heavens did shew.
Graces and virtues, languages and arts,
Beauty and learning, filled up all the parts.
Heav'n's gifts, which do, like falling stars, appear
Scattered in others; all, as in their sphere
Were fixed and conglobulate in's soul; and thence
Shone through his body with sweet influence;
Letting their glories so on each limb fall,
The whole frame rendered was celestial.
Come, learned Ptolemy,[10] and trial make
If thou this hero's altitude canst take;
But that transcends thy skill; thrice happy all
Could we but prove thus astronomical.
Lived Tycho[11] now, struck with this ray, which shone
More bright i' th' morn than others beam at noon,
He'd take his astrolabe and seek out here
What new star 'twas did gild our hemisphere.
Replenished then with such rare gifts as these,
Where was room left for such a foul disease?
The nation's sin hath drawn that veil which shrouds
Our dayspring in so sad benighting clouds.
Heaven would no longer trust its pledge, but thus
Recalled it, rapt its Ganymede from us.
Was there no milder way but the smallpox,
The very filth'ness of Pandora's box?
So many spots, like naeves,[12] our Venus soil?

[10] *Ptolemy:* Alexandrian astronomer and geographer, second century A.D.

[11] *Tycho:* Tycho Brahe (1546–1601), Danish astronomer.

[12] *naeves:* spots, blemishes.

One jewel set off with so many a foil?
Blisters with pride swelled, which through's flesh did sprout
Like rose-buds stuck i'th' lily-skin about.
Each little pimple had a tear in it
To wail the fault its rising did commit;
Who rebel-like, with their own lord at strife
Thus made an insurrection 'gainst his life.
Or were these gems sent to adorn his skin,
The cabinet of a richer soul within?
No comet need foretell his change drew on
Whose corpse might seem a constellation.
Oh had he died of old, how great a strife
Had been, who from his death should draw their life?
Who should, by one rich draught, become whate'er
Seneca, Cato, Numa, Caesar, were:
Learn'd, virtuous, pious, great, and have by this
An universal metempsychosis.
Must all these ag'd sires in one funeral
Expire? All die in one so young, so small?
Who, had he lived his life out, his great fame
Had swol'n 'bove any Greek or Roman name.
But hasty winter, with one blast, hath brought
The hopes of autumn, summer, spring, to naught.
Thus fades the oak i'th' sprig, i'th' blade the corn;
Thus, without young, this phoenix dies, newborn.
Must then old three-legg'd graybeards with their gout,
Catarrhs, rheums, aches, live three ages out;
Time's offal, only fit for th' hospital,
Or t' hang an antiquary's room withal?
Must drunkards, lechers, spent with sinning, live
With such helps as broths, possets, physic give?
None live, but such as should die? Shall we meet
With none but ghostly fathers in the street?
Grief makes me rail; sorrow will force its way,
And showers of tears tempestuous sighs best lay.
The tongue may fail, but overflowing eyes
Will weep out lasting streams of elegies.
But thou, O virgin-widow, left alone
Now thy belov'd, heaven-ravished spouse is gone,
(Whose skillful sire in vain strove to apply
Med'cines, when thy balm was no remedy)
With greater than Platonic love, O wed
His soul, though not his body, to thy bed.
Let that make thee a mother; bring thou forth

Th'ideas of his virtue, knowledge, worth;
Transcribe th'original in new copies; give
Hastings o'th' better part; so shall he live
In's nobler half, and the great grandsire be
Of an heroic divine progeny,
An issue which t'eternity shall last,
Yet but th'irradiations which he cast.
Erect no mausoleums, for his best
Monument is his spouse's marble breast.

GENERAL BIBLIOGRAPHY

THE ELIZABETHAN AGE

POLITICAL, ECONOMIC AND SOCIAL HISTORY: A. L. Rowse, *The England of Elizabeth,* London, 1950; J. B. Black, *The Reign of Elizabeth,* Oxford, 1936; A. F. Pollard, *The History of England, 1547–1603;* J. E. Neale, *Queen Elizabeth,* London, 1934; J. A. Froude, *History of England from the Fall of Wolsey to the Defeat of the Spanish Armada,* London, 1870–72; E. P. Cheyney, *A History of England from the Defeat of the Armada to the Death of Elizabeth,* New York, 1926; Conyers Read, *Mr. Secretary Walsingham,* Oxford, 1925; R. H. Tawney, *Religion and the Rise of Capitalism,* London, 1926; R. H. Tawney and E. Power, *Tudor Economic Documents,* London, 1924; W. H. Dunham and S. Pargellis, eds., *Complaint and Reform in England,* New York, 1938. H. D. Traill, *Social England,* London, 1897 and 1901–04; *Shakespeare's England,* Oxford, 1916.

CHURCH HISTORY: W. H. Frere, *The English Church in the Reigns of Elizabeth and James,* London, 1911; R. W. Dixon, *History of the Church of England,* Oxford, 1878–1902; J. H. Pollen, *The English Catholics in the Reign of Elizabeth,* London, 1920; A. F. Scott Pearson, *Thomas Cartwright and Elizabethan Puritanism,* Cambridge, 1925; W. Haller, *The Rise of Puritanism,* New York, 1938.

INTELLECTUAL HISTORY: H. O. Taylor, *Thought and Expression in the Sixteenth Century,* New York, 1920; Preserved Smith, *A History of Modern Culture,* New York, 1930–34; Hardin Craig, *The Enchanted Glass,* New York, 1936; E. M. W. Tillyard, *The Elizabethan World Picture,* London, 1943, and *The English Renaissance, Fact or Fiction?* Baltimore, 1952; Theodore Spencer, *Shakespeare and the Nature of Man,* New York, 1942; L. B. Wright, *Middle-Class Culture in Elizabethan England,* Chapel Hill, 1935; F. R. Johnson, *Astronomical Thought in Renaissance England,* Baltimore, 1937; P. Kocher, *Science and Religion in Elizabethan England,* San Marino, 1953.

THE FINE ARTS: Bruce Pattison, *Music and Poetry of the English Renaissance,* London, 1948; E. Walker, *A History of Music in England,* Oxford, 1907; E. H. Fellowes, *The English Madrigal Composers,* Oxford, 1921; P. C. Buck, *Tudor Church Music,* London, 1923–30; M. C. Boyd, *Elizabethan Music and Music Criticism,* Philadelphia, 1940; W. Chappell, *Popular Music of the Olden Time,* London, 1855; R. Blomfield, *History of Renaissance Architecture in England,* London, 1897; J. A. Gotch and W. T. Brown, *Architecture of the Renaissance in England,* London, 1891–94; T. Garner and A. Stratton, *The Domestic Architecture of England during the Tudor Period,* London, 1911 and 1929; R. Blomfield, *The Formal Garden in England,* London, 1901; C. H. C. Baker and W. G. Constable, *English Painting of the Sixteenth and Seventeenth Centuries,* New York, 1930; S. Colvin, *Early Engraving and Engravers in*

England, 1545–1695, London, 1905; F. B. Williams, Jr., *Elizabethan England*, Boston, 1939.

WRITING, PRINTING AND PUBLISHING: P. Sheavyn, *The Literary Profession in the Elizabethan Age*, Manchester, 1909; D. N. Smith, "Authors and Patrons" in *Shakespeare's England* II, Oxford, 1916; R. B. McKerrow, *An Introduction to Bibliography for Literary Students*, Oxford, 1928; A. W. Pollard, *Shakespeare's Fight with the Pirates*, London, 1917; W. W. Greg, *English Literary Autographs*, Oxford, 1925–32, and (ed.) *Records of the Court of the Stationers' Company*, London, 1930; Percy Simpson, *Proofreading in the Sixteenth, Seventeenth and Eighteenth Centuries*, London, 1935.

GENERAL BIBLIOGRAPHIES: F. W. Bateson, ed., *Cambridge Bibliography of English Literature*, Vol. I, Cambridge, 1940; Conyers Read, ed., *Bibliography of British History, Tudor Period*, Oxford, 1933; A. W. Pollard and G. R. Redgrave, ed., *A Short-Title Catalogue of books . . . 1475–1640*, London, 1927; E. Arber, ed., *A Transcript of the Registers of the Company of Stationers*, London, 1875–94.

HISTORY AND CRITICISM OF LITERATURE: V. de Sola Pinto, *The English Renaissance*, New York, 1938; Thomas Warton, *The History of English Poetry*, ed. Hazlitt, vol. IV, London, 1871; George Saintsbury, *A History of Elizabethan Literature*, London, 1887; W. J. Courthope, *A History of English Poetry*, vols. II and III, London, 1903; F. E. Schelling, *English Literature during the Lifetime of Shakespeare*, New York, 1910; J. M. Berdan, *Early Tudor Poetry*, New York, 1920; Louis B. Wright, *Middle-Class Culture in Elizabethan England*, Chapel Hill, 1935; Douglas Bush, *Mythology and the Renaissance Tradition in English Poetry*, Minneapolis, 1932; Sidney Lee, *The French Renaissance in England*, New York, 1910; E. C. Dunn, *The Literature of Shakespeare's England*, New York, 1936; H. J. C. Grierson, *Cross-Currents in English Literature of the XVII Century*, London, 1929; Edmund Gosse, *Seventeenth Century Studies*, London, 1883; Geoffrey Tillotson, *Essays in Criticism and Research*, Cambridge, 1942; E. A. Baker, *The History of the English Novel*, vol. II, London, 1929; F. P. Wilson, *Elizabethan and Jacobean*, Oxford, 1945; Hallett Smith, *Elizabethan Poetry*, Harvard, 1952; C. S. Lewis, *English Literature in the Sixteenth Century*, Oxford, 1954.

GEOGRAPHY AND EXPLORATON: E. G. R. Taylor, *Tudor Geography 1485–1583*, London, 1930, and *Late Tudor and Early Stuart Geography, 1583–1650*, London, 1934; A. L. Rowse, *Sir Richard Grenville of the Revenge*, London, 1937; J. A. Williamson, *The Age of Drake*, London, 1938, 2nd ed. 1946, and *Hawkins of Plymouth*, London, 1949.

THE SEVENTEENTH CENTURY

SOCIAL AND POLITICAL HISTORY: Godfrey Davies, *Bibliography of British History, Stuart Period, 1603–1714*, Oxford, 1928, and *The Early Stuarts, 1603–1660*, Oxford, 1937; G. N. Clark, *The Seventeenth Century*, Oxford, 1929; S. R. Gardiner, *History of England from the Accession of James I to the Outbreak of the Civil War*, London, 1884, and *History of the Great Civil War*, London, 1893, and *History of the Common-*

wealth and Protectorate, London, 1903; C. Firth, *Last Years of the Protectorate,* London, 1909; C. V. Wedgwood, *The King's Peace,* New York, 1955.

Literary, Intellectual and Religious History: Basil Willey, *The Seventeenth Century Background,* London, 1934; Douglas Bush, *English Literature in the Earlier Seventeenth Century,* Oxford, 1945; H. J. C. Grierson, *Cross Currents in English Literature of the Seventeenth Century,* London, 1929; C. V. Wedgwood, *Seventeenth Century English Literature,* Oxford, 1950; F. P. Wilson, *Elizabethan and Jacobean,* Oxford, 1945; R. Tuve, *Elizabethan and Metaphysical Imagery,* Chicago, 1947; Helen C. White, *English Devotional Literature, 1600–1640,* Madison, 1931, and *The Metaphysical Poets,* New York, 1936; J. B. Leishman, *The Metaphysical Poets,* Oxford, 1934; Theodore Spencer and Mark Van Doren, *Studies in Metaphysical Poetry,* New York, 1939; Joan Bennett, *Four Metaphysical Poets,* Cambridge, 1934; K. B. Murdock, *The Sun at Noon,* New York, 1939; William Haller, *The Rise of Puritanism,* New York, 1938, and *Liberty and Reformation,* New York, 1954; Louis L. Martz, *The Poetry of Meditation,* New Haven, 1954.

1550–1559

ENGLISH LITERATURE	ENGLISH DRAMA	FOREIGN LITERATURE	HISTORY, RELIGION, POLITICS, SCIENCE
Spenser b. 1552?		Ronsard, *Odes* and *Amours* 1550, 1554	Edward VI r. 1547–53
Ralegh b. 1552?			
Hakluyt b. 1552	*Jacke Jugeler* 1553–58		Mary Tudor r. 1553–58
	Wealth and Health 1558		
	Gammer Gurton's Needle c. 1552–63		Elizabeth r. 1558–1603
Wm. Baldwin, *Mirror for Magistrates* (suppressed first edition) 1555	*Ralph Roister Doister* 1550–53		
			Latimer and Ridley burned 1555
Kyd b. 1557?			
Tottel's Miscellany 1557			
Thomas Lodge b. 1558?			
George Peele b. 1558?			
George Chapman b. 1559			Act of Uniformity 1559

1560–1569

ENGLISH LITERATURE	ENGLISH DRAMA	FOREIGN LITERATURE	HISTORY, RELIGION, POLITICS, SCIENCE
Bacon b. 1561	*Misogonus* c. 1560		Thirty-nine Articles 1560
Hoby tr. *Courtier* 1561			Calvinism victorious in Scotland 1560

1560–1569 (*Cont.*)

S. Daniel b. 1562	Sackville and Norton, *Gorboduc* 1562	Lope de Vega b. 1562	Sternhold and Hopkins *Psalms* 1562
M. Drayton b. 1563			
Foxe, *Actes and Monuments* 1563			
Shakespeare b. 1564			Galileo b. 1564
Marlowe b. 1564			
		Cinthio, *Hecatommithi* 1565	
Painter, *Palace of Pleasure* 1566	Gascoigne, *Jocasta* 1566 Gascoigne, *Supposes* 1566		
Th. Nashe b. 1567			Mary of Scotland in England
Th. Campion b. 1567			
R. Ascham d. 1568			

1570–1579

Ascham, *Schoolmaster* pub. 1570			
T. Dekker b. 1570?			Kepler b. 1571
T. Middleton b. 1570?		Camoens, *Lusiad* 1572	Battle of Lepanto 1571
Gascoigne, *100 Sundry Flowers* 1573		Tasso, *Aminta* 1573	Massacre of St. Bartholomew 1572

1570–1579 (*Cont.*)

Joseph Hall b. 1574	Leicester's company founded 1574		Revolt of Netherlands; beginning of Dutch wars 1572
Gascoigne, *Posies* 1575	Entertainment at Kenilworth 1575		
Gascoigne, *Steel Glass* 1576	Theater built 1576		Frobisher's Voyages 1576–77
Gascoigne d. 1577	Curtain c. 1577		Drake's circumnavigation 1577–80
Holinshed, *Chronicles* 1577		Du Bartas, *La Semaine* 1578	
Lyly, *Euphues: Anatomy of Wit* 1578			William Harvey b. 1578
Proctor, *Gorgeous Gallery of Gallant Inventions* 1578			
Spenser, *Shepherds' Calendar* 1579	Fletcher b. 1579		
Gosson, *School of Abuse* 1579			
Lodge, *Reply to Gosson* 1579			
North tr. Plutarch's *Lives* 1579			

1580–1589

Spenser and Harvey, *Three Letters* 1580	Webster b. 1580?	Montaigne, *Essais* 1580 Belleforest, *Histoires Tragiques* 1580	

Lyly, *Euphues and his England* 1580			
Hakluyt, *Divers Voyages* 1582		Tasso, *Gerusalemme Liberata* 1581	
Watson, *Hecatompathia* 1582			
	Queen's company founded 1583 Massinger b. 1583 Lyly, *Campaspe* 1584 *Sapho and Phao* 1584 Peele, *Arraignment of Paris* 1584		
Sidney d. 1586	Ford b. 1586		
Greene, *Pandosto* 1588	*Famous Victories of Henry V* 1586		Mary Queen of Scots executed 1587
Greene, *Menaphon* 1589 (preface by Nashe)	Kyd, *Spanish Tragedy* c. 1587		Spanish Armada 1588
Hakluyt, *Principal Navigations* 1589	Marlowe, *Tamburlaine* c. 1587–88		Marprelate Controversy 1588
Lodge, *Glancus and Scilla* 1589	Greene, *Friar Bacon* 1589–92		

1590–1599

Lodge, *Rosalynde* 1590	Marlowe, *Jew of Malta* c. 1590	Du Bartas d. 1590	
Sidney, *Arcadia* pub. 1590	Kyd, *Hamlet* c. 1590		

1590–1599 (*Cont.*)

Spenser, *The Faerie Queene* I–III 1590	Shakespeare, II and III *Henry VI* 1591		
Greene, *Cony-Catching Pamphlets* 1591	Shakespeare, *Love's Labour's Lost* 1590–97		
Lyly, *Endimion* 1591			
Robert Herrick b. 1591			
William Browne b. 1591			
Ralegh, *Fight about the Azores* 1591	Marlowe, *Dr. Faustus* 1588–92		
Sidney, *Astrophel* (first authorized edition) 1591	Shakespeare, I *Henry VI* 1592		Hooker, *Laws of Ecclesiastical Polity* I–V 1594–97
Spenser, *Complaints* 1591 *Daphnaida* 1591	Shakespeare, *Richard III* 1592–97 Shakespeare, *Two Gentlemen of Verona* 1590–98		
Constable, *Diana* 1592, 1594	Rose Theatre opened c. 1592	Montaigne d. 1592	
Daniel, *Delia* 1592	Kyd, *Spanish Tragedy* pub. 1592		
Greene-Nashe-Harvey Quarrel 1592–93			
Phoenix Nest 1593			
Drayton, *Idea, The Shepherd's Garland* 1593	Marlowe d. 1593	Amyot d. 1593	
Lodge, *Phillis* 1593			

Shakespeare, *Venus and Adonis* 1593			
Drayton, *Idea's Mirror* (sonnets) 1594	Swan Theatre built 1594–1600		
Nashe, *Unfortunate Traveller* 1594			
Shakespeare, *Lucrece* 1594			
Spenser, *Amoretti* 1595	Kyd d. 1595	Tasso d. 1595	Ralegh's Guiana voyage 1595
Colin Clout's Come Home Again 1595	Shakespeare, *Romeo and Juliet* 1591–97 Shakespeare, *Richard II* 1594–95 Shakespeare, *Midsummer Night's Dream* 1594–98		Drake d. 1595
Ralegh, *Discovery of Guiana* 1596	Blackfriars Theater opened 1596		Descartes b. 1596
Spenser, *The Faerie Queene* IV–VI 1596 *Prothalamion* 1596 *Foure Hymnes* 1596	Shirley b. 1596 Shakespeare, *Merchant of Venice* 1594–96	Bodin d. 1596	Expedition to Cadiz 1596
	Peele d. 1597		
Hall *Virgidemiae, I–III* 1597	Shakespeare, *Henry IV* 1596–98		
Bacon, *Essays* (ten) 1597			
Drayton, *England's Heroical Epistles* 1597			

1590–1599 (*Cont.*)

Chapman, *Seven Books of the Iliads* 1598			Edict of Nantes 1598 Burleigh d. 1598
Hakluyt, *Principal Navigations* 1598	*Parnassus* plays at Cambridge 1598–1602		
Marlowe, *Hero and Leander* 1598	Shakespeare, *Much Ado about Nothing* 1598–1600		
Marston, *Scourg of Villainy* 1598			
Spenser d. 1599	Globe Theatre opened 1599		Essex in Ireland 1599
Daniel, *Musophilus* 1599	Shakespeare, *Henry V* 1599 *Julius Caesar* 1598–99 *As You Like It* 1598–1600		

1600–1603

England's Parnassus 1600	Fortune Theatre opened 1600	Calderon b. 1600	East India Company founded 1600
England's Helicon 1600	Shakespeare, *Merry Wives of Windsor* 1598–1602		Execution of Essex 1601
Thomas Deloney d. 1600?	*Twelfth Night* 1600–02		

Thomas Nashe d. 1601	Jonson, *Poetaster* 1601		
Sir Thomas North d. 1601?	Shakespeare, *Hamlet* 1599–1601		
Daniel, *Works* 1601	Shakespeare, *Troilus and Cressida* 1601–03 *All's Well* c. 1601–03		
	Heywood, *Woman Killed with Kindness* 1603 Jonson, *Sejanus* 1603		Death of Elizabeth 1603 James I r. 1603–25

INDEX OF FIRST LINES OF POETRY

INDEX OF AUTHORS AND TITLES